THE KAYE BOOK OF CRICKET RECORDS

The KAYE book of CRICKET RECORDS

by

BILL FRINDALL

KAYE & WARD
LONDON

First published by

KAYE & WARD LIMITED

194-200 BISHOPSGATE, LONDON, E.C.2

1968

SBN 7182 0758 0

PRINTED IN ENGLAND BY C. TINLING AND COMPANY LIMITED

LIVERPOOL, LONDON AND PRESCOT

PREFACE

ALTHOUGH the attendance figures for paying spectators at county matches have fallen by 75% compared with 1947, the level of general interest in cricket has probably never been higher in Britain. Public opinion polls conducted in 1966 revealed remarkably high numbers of people playing week-end cricket, reading the cricket press, following sound and vision broadcasts of matches, and even dialling the G.P.O's. Test Match score service. With these new devotees has grown a greater interest in the game's history and records. Many have turned to the subject of cricket statistics for their hobby and as a way of keeping alive their interest in the game during the winter months. It is for these enthusiasts that this book is primarily intended.

Seven home seasons have passed since the last comprehensive work on this subject was published (Roy Webber's revised 'Playfair Book of Cricket Records') and both this, and the abridged, pocket version published shortly after the author's sudden death in 1962, have long been unobtainable except as collector's items from secondhand sources. If the external demand for providing an up-to-date volume based in content and format on Webber's admirable work was obvious, the pressure from within was even stronger. I have been infatuated with all aspects of cricket since my early boyhood when I was taught how to score before I had held a bat; a fact obvious to anyone sufficiently fleet of sight to have witnessed one of my brief visits to the crease. One eminent statistician warned me that he would not have attempted this revision in less than five years but, although I was born on the first day of the timeless Test of Kingsmead, I could not agree with him. Memory returned these lines of that incurable romantic and optimist, Robert Browning:

That low man goes on adding one to one,
His hundred's soon hit:
This high man, aiming at a million,
Misses an unit.

I hope that I have not missed too many units!

No work of this range can be entirely free from error or omission and such are the inaccuracies of many original records and scores that perfectionist statisticians are forever doomed to misery and thoughts of suicide. Although every effort has been made to minimise such defects, with thoughts of further editions in mind, I should be very pleased to hear about any that have been overlooked.

All the records are complete to the end of the 1967 English season with the Indian tour of East Africa also taken into account. The Test Match records are complete to the start of the Australia v. India series on 23rd December, 1967.

I have followed the customary procedure of including as official Tests all matches featuring South Africa since her withdrawal from the Commonwealth and her consequent automatic expulsion from the then Imperial Cricket Conference in 1961.

Roy Webber revised W. G. Grace's figures by eliminating all the apparently minor matches and thus removed two centuries and the 'Double' of 1873 from his career records in the process. There are strong arguments to show that these 'minor' matches were first-class according to the standards of the day and were certainly considered so by contemporary statisticians. Perhaps the books were 'cooked' in one or two instances to allow his aggregates to exceed certain targets but this cannot be proved. Should we take it upon ourselves to rewrite the records of a career which began 102 years ago and which have been accepted by the majority of statisticians for six decades? I feel that like the veracity of Shakespeare's authorship, Grace's figures cannot at this point in time be challenged and torn apart. A note of Webber's revised figures will be found in the career records section.

Recent publications have included in their wicket partnership records instances where three partners have contributed, one of the originals having retired hurt. There are only two batsmen at the wicket at a time and if one retires hurt that partnership ends in technically an 'unfinished' state and another begins with a new partner, but for the same wicket of the innings. A good example of this occurred in the 1959-60 series between England and the West Indies. The third wicket added 243 runs in the West Indies first innings at Sabina Park, Jamaica, but this total was composed of two century partnerships within that one wicket. McMorris retired hurt after he and Sobers had put on 133, and then Nurse helped the latter add a further 110. The school of thought which accepts this as a partnership of 243 could produce an opening stand to which all the members of the team had contributed with nine retiring hurt!

Throughout the text * denotes a not-out innings or an unfinished partnership.

In the Test Match records, the exact ground is shown by an indicator number for those seven centres where two or more different grounds have staged Tests. Here is the key to those indicators:—

Bombay[1]	Gymkhana
Bombay	Brabourne Stadium
Brisbane[1]	Exhibition Ground
Brisbane[2]	Woolloongabba
Durban[1]	Lord's
Durban[2]	Kingsmead
Johannesburg[1]	Old Wanderers
Johannesburg[2]	Ellis Park
Johannesburg[3]	Wanderers
Lahore[1]	Lawrence Gardens
Lahore[2]	Lahore Stadium
Madras[1]	Chepauk
Madras[2]	Corporation (Nehru) Stadium
Melbourne	Melbourne Cricket Ground
Melbourne[1]	East Melbourne †

Cheam, Surrey. BILL FRINDALL
January, 1968.

† Since the text of this book went to press, new evidence has been found to show that the 1878-79 Test positively did *not* take place at the East Melbourne ground. Thus all Test Matches played in Melbourne have been at the Melbourne Cricket ground.

ACKNOWLEDGEMENTS

CARRYING out this labour of love has been made all the more pleasurable by the kind and enthusiastic efforts of friends who have helped me in a variety of ways and in time far more precious than mine.

Michael Fordham, who shares John Wisden's birthdate but not the year, was Roy Webber's helper and friend for eleven years and is now a B.B.C. Scorer and the 'Playfair Cricket Monthly's' senior statistician. Besides lending me his own amendments, and answering innumerable queries, he allowed me to ransack his personal library.

Major Rowland Bowen, Editor and Publisher of 'The Cricket Quarterly', allowed a complete stranger to plague him with questions and offered many corrections and new items, the direct result of his own painstaking research.

Geoffrey Saulez and Barry McCaully gave valuable assistance in checking the career records in the Test Match and first-class sections respectively.

Mr A. H. Wagg provided many otherwise inaccessible facts and figures, answered a host of questions and lent me a valuable book.

Mr B. J. Wakley provided some new information on the fastest innings in Tests from his copies of the famous 'Fergie's' scoresheets.

Gordon Ross, Editor of the 'Playfair Cricket Monthly', very generously allowed this revision of the 'Playfair Book of Cricket Records'.

To all these generous friends my very grateful thanks.

But above all, this volume could not have been compiled without the patience and long-suffering devotion of my wife, Maureen, who for the past four months has coped alone with the demands of three boisterous children, whilst I have deserted her for a world of books, figures and the typewriter.

Lastly, I want to add my tribute to the late Roy Webber whom I heard, read, and admired but unfortunately never had the pleasure of meeting. He explored the field of statistics and scoring for cricket commentaries far more comprehensively than anyone before him and made life that much easier for those lucky enough to follow.

BILL FRINDALL

To the memory of
Jack Price
Roy Webber
and
Arthur Wrigley

CONTENTS

TEST MATCH RECORDS—1876–77 TO 1967

RESULTS AND SCORES

RESULTS SUMMARY

THE GROUNDS

PLAYERS' RECORDS—BOWLING

FIRST CLASS CRICKET RECORDS

MATCH RECORDS OF TOURING TEAMS

OFFICES, HONOURS AND AWARDS

MISCELLANEOUS RECORDS

Page

NON-FIRST-CLASS COMPETITION RECORDS

Test Match Records

1876-77 to 1967

KEY TO TEST MATCH GROUNDS

(Where more than one ground has been used at a Centre)

Bombay[1]	Gymkhana
Bombay	Brabourne Stadium
Brisbane[1]	Exhibition Ground
Brisbane[2]	Woolloongabba
Durban[1]	Lord's
Durban[2]	Kingsmead
Johannesburg[1]	Old Wanderers
Johannesburg[2]	Ellis Park
Johannesburg[3]	Wanderers
Lahore[1]	Lawrence Gardens
Lahore[2]	Lahore Stadium
Madras[1]	Chepauk
Madras[2]	Corporation (Nehru) Stadium
Melbourne	Melbourne Cricket Ground
Melbourne[1]	East Melbourne

RESULTS AND SCORES OF ALL TEST MATCHES

ENGLAND v. AUSTRALIA

Venue and Result	*England* *1st inns*	*England* *2nd inns*	*Australia* *1st inns*	*Australia* *2nd inns*
1876-77 *in Australia*				
Melbourne—Australia 45 runs	196	108	245	104
Melbourne—England 4 wkts	261	122-6	122	259
1878-79 *in Australia*				
Melbourne[1]—Australia 10 wkts	113	160	256	19-0
1880 *in England*				
Oval—England 5 wkts	420	57-5	149	327
1881-82 *in Australia*				
Melbourne—Drawn	294	308	320	127-3
Sydney—Australia 5 wkts	133	232	197	169-5
Sydney—Australia 6 wkts	188	134	260	66-4
Melbourne—Drawn	309	234-2	300	—
1882 *in England*				
Oval—Australia 7 runs	101	77	63	122
1882-83 *in Australia*				
Melbourne—Australia 9 wkts	177	169	291	58-1
Melbourne—England Inns & 27 runs	294	—	114	153
Sydney—England 69 runs	247	123	218	83
Sydney—Australia 4 wkts	263	197	262	199-6
1884 *in England*				
Manchester—Drawn	95	180-9	182	—
Lord's—England Inns & 5 runs	379	—	229	145
Oval—Drawn	346	85-2	551	—
1884-85 *in Australia*				
Adelaide—England 8 wkts	369	67-2	243	191
Melbourne—England 10 wkts	401	7-0	279	126
Sydney—Australia 6 runs	133	207	181	165
Sydney—Australia 8 wkts	269	77	309	38-2
Melbourne—England Inns & 98 runs	386	—	163	125
1886 *in England*				
Manchester—England 4 wkts	223	107-6	205	123
Lord's—England Inns & 106 runs	353	—	121	126
Oval—England Inns & 217 runs	434	—	68	149
1886-87 *in Australia*				
Sydney—England 13 runs	45	184	119	97
Sydney—England 71 runs	151	154	84	150

Venue and Result	England 1st inns	England 2nd inns	Australia 1st inns	Australia 2nd inns
1887-88 *in Australia*				
Sydney—England 126 runs	113	137	42	82
1888 *in England*				
Lord's—Australia 61 runs	53	62	116	60
Oval—England Inns & 137 runs ...	317	—	80	100
Manchester—England Inns & 21 runs	172	—	81	70
1890 *in England*				
Lord's—England 7 wkts	173	137-3	132	176
Oval—England 2 wkts	100	95-8	92	102
Manchester—Abandoned	—	—	—	—
1891-92 *in Australia*				
Melbourne—Australia 54 runs	264	158	240	236
Sydney—Australia 72 runs	307	157	145	391
Adelaide—England Inns & 230 runs ...	499	—	100	169
1893 *in England*				
Lord's—Drawn	334	234-8d	269	—
Oval—England Inns & 43 runs... ...	483	—	91	349
Manchester—Drawn	243	118-4	204	236
1894-95 *in Australia*				
Sydney—England 10 runs	325	437	586	166
Melbourne—England 94 runs	75	475	123	333
Adelaide—Australia 382 runs	124	143	238	411
Sydney—Australia Inns & 147 runs ...	65	72	284	—
Melbourne—England 6 wkts	385	298-4	414	267
1896 *in England*				
Lord's—England 6 wkts	292	111-4	53	347
Manchester—Australia 3 wkts	231	305	412	125-7
Oval—England 66 runs	145	84	119	44
1897-98 *in Australia*				
Sydney—England 9 wkts	551	96-1	237	408
Melbourne—Australia Inns & 55 runs	315	150	520	—
Adelaide—Australia Inns & 13 runs ...	278	282	573	—
Melbourne—Australia 8 wkts	174	263	323	115-2
Sydney—Australia 6 wkts	335	178	239	276-4
1899 *in England*				
Nottingham—Drawn	193	155-7	252	230-8d
Lord's—Australia 10 wkts	206	240	421	28-0
Leeds—Drawn	220	19-0	172	224
Manchester—Drawn	372	94-3	196	346-7d
Oval—Drawn	576	—	352	254-5
1901-02 *in Australia*				
Sydney—England Inns & 124 runs ...	464	—	168	172
Melbourne—Australia 229 runs... ...	61	175	112	353
Adelaide—Australia 4 wkts	388	247	321	315-6
Sydney—Australia 7 wkts	317	99	299	121-3
Melbourne—Australia 32 runs	189	178	144	255

Venue and Result	England 1st inns	England 2nd inns	Australia 1st inns	Australia 2nd inns
1902 *in England*				
Birmingham—Drawn	376-9d	—	36	46-2
Lord's—Drawn	102-2	—	—	—
Sheffield—Australia 143 runs	145	195	194	289
Manchester—Australia 3 runs	262	120	299	86
Oval—England 1 wkt	183	263-9	324	121
1903-04 *in Australia*				
Sydney—England 5 wkts	577	194-5	285	485
Melbourne—England 185 runs	315	103	122	111
Adelaide—Australia 216 runs	245	278	388	351
Sydney—England 157 runs	249	210	131	171
Melbourne—Australia 218 runs... ...	61	101	247	133
1905 *in England*				
Nottingham—England 213 runs ...	196	426-5d	221	188
Lord's—Drawn	282	151-5	181	—
Leeds—Drawn	301	295-5d	195	224-7
Manchester—England Inns & 80 runs	446	—	197	169
Oval—Drawn	430	261-6d	363	124-4
1907-08 *in Australia*				
Sydney—Australia 2 wkts	273	300	300	275-8
Melbourne—England 1 wkt	382	282-9	266	397
Adelaide—Australia 245 runs	363	183	285	506
Melbourne—Australia 308 runs... ...	105	186	214	385
Sydney—Australia 49 runs	281	229	137	422
1909 *in England*				
Birmingham—England 10 wkts ...	121	105-0	74	151
Lord's—Australia 9 wkts	269	121	350	41-1
Leeds—Australia 126 runs	182	87	188	207
Manchester—Drawn	119	108-3	147	279-9d
Oval—Drawn	352	104-3	325	339-5d
1911-12 *in Australia*				
Sydney—Australia 146 runs	318	291	447	308
Melbourne—England 8 wkts	265	219-2	184	299
Adelaide—England 7 wkts	501	112-3	133	476
Melbourne—England Inns & 225 runs	589	—	191	173
Sydney—England 70 runs	324	214	176	292
1912 *in England*				
Lord's—Drawn	310-7d	—	282-7	—
Manchester—Drawn	203	—	14-0	—
Oval—England 244 runs	245	175	111	65
1920-21 *in Australia*				
Sydney—Australia 377 runs	190	281	267	581
Melbourne—Australia Inns & 91 runs	251	157	499	—
Adelaide—Australia 119 runs	447	370	354	582
Melbourne—Australia 8 wkts	284	315	389	211-2
Sydney—Australia 9 wkts	204	280	392	93-1

Venue and Result	England 1st inns	England 2nd inns	Australia 1st inns	Australia 2nd inns
1921 in England				
Nottingham—Australia 10 wkts... ...	112	147	232	30-0
Lord's—Australia 8 wkts	187	283	342	131-2
Leeds—Australia 219 runs	259	202	407	273-7d
Manchester—Drawn	362-4d	44-1	175	—
Oval—Drawn	403-8d	244-2	389	—
1924-25 in Australia				
Sydney—Australia 193 runs	298	411	450	452
Melbourne—Australia 81 runs	479	290	600	250
Adelaide—Australia 11 runs	365	363	489	250
Melbourne—England Inns & 29 runs ...	548	—	269	250
Sydney—Australia 307 runs	167	146	295	325
1926 in England				
Nottingham—Drawn	32-0	—	—	—
Lord's—Drawn	475-3d	—	383	194-5
Leeds—Drawn	294	254-3	494	—
Manchester—Drawn	305-5	—	335	—
Oval—England 289 runs	280	436	302	125
1928-29 in Australia				
Brisbane[1]—England 675 runs	521	342-8d	122	66
Sydney—England 8 wkts	636	16-2	253	397
Melbourne—England 3 wkts	417	332-7	397	351
Adelaide—England 12 runs	334	383	369	336
Melbourne—Australia 5 wkts	519	257	491	287-5
1930 in England				
Nottingham—England 93 runs	270	302	144	335
Lord's—Australia 7 wkts	425	375	729-6d	72-3
Leeds—Drawn	391	95-3	566	—
Manchester—Drawn	251-8	—	345	—
Oval—Australia Inns & 39 runs ...	405	251	695	—
1932-33 in Australia				
Sydney—England 10 wkts	524	1-0	360	164
Melbourne—Australia 111 runs... ...	169	139	228	191
Adelaide—England 338 runs	341	412	222	193
Brisbane[2]—England 6 wkts	356	162-4	340	175
Sydney—England 8 wkts	454	168-2	435	182
1934 in England				
Nottingham—Australia 238 runs ...	268	141	374	273-8d
Lord's—England Inns & 38 runs ...	440	—	284	118
Manchester—Drawn	627-9d	123-0d	491	66-1
Leeds—Drawn	200	229-6	584	—
Oval—Australia 562 runs	321	145	701	327
1936-37 in Australia				
Brisbane[2]—England 322 runs	358	256	234	58
Sydney—England Inns & 22 runs ...	426-6d	—	80	324
Melbourne—Australia 365 runs... ...	76-9d	323	200-9d	564
Adelaide—Australia 148 runs	330	243	288	433
Melbourne—Australia Inns & 200 runs	239	165	604	—

Venue and Result	England 1st inns	England 2nd inns	Australia 1st inns	Australia 2nd inns
1938 *in England*				
Nottingham—Drawn	658-8d	—	411	427-6
Lord's—Drawn	494	242-8d	422	204-6
Manchester—Abandoned	—	—	—	—
Leeds—Australia 5 wkts	223	123	242	107-5
Oval—England Inns & 579 runs ...	903-7d	—	201	123
1946-47 *in Australia*				
Brisbane²—Australia Inns & 332 runs ...	141	172	645	—
Sydney—Australia Inns & 33 runs ...	255	371	659-8d	—
Melbourne—Drawn	351	310-7	365	536
Adelaide—Drawn	460	340-8d	487	215-1
Sydney—Australia 5 wkts	280	186	253	214-5
1948 *in England*				
Nottingham—Australia 8 wkts	165	441	509	98-2
Lord's—Australia 409 runs	215	186	350	460-7d
Manchester—Drawn	363	174-3d	221	92-1
Leeds—Australia 7 wkts	496	365-8d	458	404-3
Oval—Australia Inns & 149 runs ...	52	188	389	—
1950-51 *in Australia*				
Brisbane²—Australia 70 runs	68-7d	122	228	32-7d
Melbourne—Australia 28 runs	197	150	194	181
Sydney—Australia Inns & 13 runs ...	290	123	426	—
Adelaide—Australia 274 runs	272	228	371	403-8d
Melbourne—England 8 wkts	320	95-2	217	197
1953 *in England*				
Nottingham—Drawn	144	120-1	249	123
Lord's—Drawn	372	282-7	346	368
Manchester—Drawn	276	—	318	35-8
Leeds—Drawn	167	275	266	147-4
Oval—England 8 wkts	306	132-2	275	162
1954-55 *in Australia*				
Brisbane²—Australia Inns & 154 runs ...	190	257	601-8d	—
Sydney—England 38 runs	154	296	228	184
Melbourne—England 128 runs	191	279	231	111
Adelaide—England 5 wkts	341	97-5	323	111
Sydney—Drawn	371-7d	—	221	118-6
1956 *in England*				
Nottingham—Drawn	217-8d	188-3d	148	120-3
Lord's—Australia 185 runs	171	186	285	257
Leeds—England Inns & 42 runs ...	325	—	143	140
Manchester—England Inns & 170 runs	459	—	84	205
Oval—Drawn	247	182-3d	202	27-5
1958-59 *in Australia*				
Brisbane²—Australia 8 wkts	134	198	186	147-2
Melbourne—Australia 8 wkts	259	87	308	42-2
Sydney—Drawn	219	287-7d	357	54-2
Adelaide—Australia 10 wkts	240	270	476	36-0
Melbourne—Australia 9 wkts	205	214	351	69-1

Venue and Result	England 1st inns	England 2nd inns	Australia 1st inns	Australia 2nd inns
1961 *in England*				
Birmingham—Drawn	195	401-4	516-9d	—
Lord's—Australia 5 wkts	206	202	340	71-5
Leeds—England 8 wkts	299	62-2	237	120
Manchester—Australia 54 runs	367	201	190	432
Oval—Drawn	256	370-8	494	—
1962-63 *in Australia*				
Brisbane[2]—Drawn	389	278-6	404	362-4d
Melbourne—England 7 wkts	331	237-3	316	248
Sydney—Australia 8 wkts	279	104	319	67-2
Adelaide—Drawn	331	223-4	393	293
Sydney—Drawn	321	268-8d	349	152-4
1964 *in England*				
Nottingham—Drawn	216-8d	193-9d	168	40-2
Lord's—Drawn	246	—	176	168-4
Leeds—Australia 7 wkts	268	229	389	111-3
Manchester—Drawn	611	—	656-8d	4-0
Oval—Drawn	182	381-4	379	—
1965-66 *in Australia*				
Brisbane[2]—Drawn	280	186-3	443-6d	—
Melbourne—Drawn	558	5-0	358	426
Sydney—England Inns & 93 runs ...	488	—	221	174
Adelaide—Australia Inns & 9 runs ...	241	266	516	—
Melbourne—Drawn	485-9d	69-3	543-8d	—

ENGLAND v. SOUTH AFRICA

Venue and Result	England 1st inns	England 2nd inns	South Africa 1st inns	South Africa 2nd inns
1888-89 *in South Africa*				
Port Elizabeth—England 8 wkts ...	148	67-2	84	129
Cape Town—England Inns & 202 runs	292	—	47	43
1891-92 *in South Africa*				
Cape Town—England Inns & 189 runs	369	—	97	83
1895-96 *in South Africa*				
Port Elizabeth—England 288 runs ...	185	226	93	30
Johannesburg[1]—England Inns & 197 runs	482	—	151	134
Cape Town—England Inns & 33 runs	265	—	115	117

Venue and Result	England 1st inns	England 2nd inns	South Africa 1st inns	South Africa 2nd inns
1898-99 *in South Africa*				
Johannesburg[1]—England 32 runs ...	145	237	251	99
Cape Town—England 210 runs ...	92	330	177	35
1905-06 *in South Africa*				
Johannesburg[1]—South Africa 1 wkt ...	184	190	91	287-9
Johannesburg[1]—South Africa 9 wkts ...	148	160	277	33-1
Johannesburg[1]—South Africa 243 runs...	295	196	385	349-5d
Cape Town—England 4 wkts	198	160-6	218	138
Cape Town—South Africa Inns & 16 runs	187	130	333	—
1907 *in England*				
Lord's—Drawn	428	—	140	185-3
Leeds—England 53 runs	76	162	110	75
Oval—Drawn	295	138	178	159-5
1909-10 *in South Africa*				
Johannesburg[1]—South Africa 19 runs ...	310	224	208	345
Durban[1]—South Africa 95 runs ...	199	252	199	347
Johannesburg[1]—England 3 wkts ...	322	221-7	305	237
Cape Town—South Africa 4 wkts ...	203	178	207	175-6
Cape Town—England 9 wkts	417	16-1	103	327
1912 *in England*				
Lord's—England Inns & 62 runs ...	337	—	58	217
Leeds—England 174 runs ...	242	238	147	159
Oval—England 10 wkts	176	14-0	95	93
1913-14 *in South Africa*				
Durban[1]—England Inns & 157 runs ...	450	—	182	111
Johannesburg[1]—England Inns & 12 runs	403	—	160	231
Johannesburg[1]—England 91 runs ...	238	308	151	304
Durban[1]—Drawn	163	154-5	170	305-9d
Port Elizabeth—England 10 wkts ...	411	11-0	193	228
1922-23 *in South Africa*				
Johannesburg[1]—South Africa 168 runs...	182	218	148	420
Cape Town—England 1 wkt	183	173-9	113	242
Durban[2]—Drawn	428	11-1	368	—
Johannesburg[1]—Drawn	244	376-6d	295	247-4
Durban[2]—England 109 runs	281	241	179	234
1924 *in England*				
Birmingham—England Inns & 18 runs	438	—	30	390
Lord's—England Inns & 18 runs ...	531-2d	—	273	240
Leeds—England 9 wkts	396	60-1	132	323
Manchester—Drawn	—	—	116-4	—
Oval—Drawn	421-8	—	342	—

Venue and Result	England 1st inns	England 2nd inns	South Africa 1st inns	South Africa 2nd inns
1927-28 in South Africa				
Johannesburg[1]—England 10 wkts ...	313	57-0	196	170
Cape Town—England 87 runs ...	133	428	250	224
Durban[2]—Drawn	430	132-2	246	464-8d
Johannesburg[1]—South Africa 4 wkts ...	265	215	328	156-6
Durban[2]—South Africa 8 wkts ...	282	118	332-7d	69-2
1929 in England				
Birmingham—Drawn	245	308-4d	250	171-1
Lord's—Drawn	302	312-8d	322	90-5
Leeds—England 5 wkts	328	186-5	236	275
Manchester—England Inns & 32 runs	427-7d	—	130	265
Oval—Drawn	258	264-1	492-8d	—
1930-31 in South Africa				
Johannesburg[1]—South Africa 28 runs ...	193	211	126	306
Cape Town—Drawn	350	252	513-8d	—
Durban[2]—Drawn	223-1d	—	177	145-8
Johannesburg[1]—Drawn	442	169-9d	295	280-7
Durban[2]—Drawn	230	72-4	252	219-7d
1935 in England				
Nottingham—Drawn	384-7d	—	220	17-1
Lord's—South Africa 157 runs	198	151	228	278-7d
Leeds—Drawn	216	294-7d	171	194-5
Manchester—Drawn	357	231-6d	318	169-2
Oval—Drawn	534-6d	—	476	287-6
1938-39 in South Africa				
Johannesburg[1]—Drawn	422	291-4d	390	108-1
Cape Town—Drawn	559-9d	—	286	201-2
Durban[2]—England Inns & 13 runs ...	469-4d	—	103	353
Johannesburg[1]—Drawn	215	203-4	349-8d	—
Durban[2]—Drawn	316	654-5	530	481
1947 in England				
Nottingham—Drawn	208	551	533	166-1
Lord's—England 10 wkts	554-8d	26-0	327	252
Manchester—England 7 wkts	478	130-3	339	267
Leeds—England 10 wkts...	317-7d	47-0	175	184
Oval—Drawn	427	325-6d	302	423-7
1948-49 in South Africa				
Durban[2]—England 2 wkts	253	128-8	161	219
Johannesburg[2]—Drawn	608	—	315	270-2
Cape Town—Drawn	308	276-3d	356	142-4
Johannesburg[2]—Drawn	379	253-7d	257-9d	194-4
Port Elizabeth—England 3 wkts ...	395	174-7	379	187-3d

Venue and Result	England 1st inns	England 2nd inns	South Africa 1st inns	South Africa 2nd inns
1951 *in England*				
Nottingham—South Africa 71 runs ...	419-9d	114	483-9d	121
Lord's—England 10 wkts	311	16-0	115	211
Manchester—England 9 wkts	211	142-1	158	191
Leeds—Drawn	505	—	538	87-0
Oval—England 4 wkts	194	164-6	202	154
1955 *in England*				
Nottingham—England Inns & 5 runs ...	334	—	181	148
Lord's—England 71 runs	133	353	304	111
Manchester—South Africa 3 wkts ...	284	381	521-8d	145-7
Leeds—South Africa 224 runs	191	256	171	500
Oval—England 92 runs	151	204	112	151
1956-57 *in South Africa*				
Johannesburg[3]—England 131 runs ...	268	150	215	72
Cape Town—England 312 runs ...	369	220-6d	205	72
Durban[2]—Drawn	218	254	283	142-6
Johannesburg[3]—South Africa 17 runs ...	251	214	340	142
Port Elizabeth—South Africa 58 runs ...	110	130	164	134
1960 *in England*				
Birmingham—England 100 runs ...	292	203	186	209
Lord's—England Inns & 73 runs ...	362-8d	—	152	137
Nottingham—England 8 wkts	287	49-2	88	247
Manchester—Drawn	260	153-7d	229	46-0
Oval—Drawn	155	479-7d	419	97-4
1964-65 *in South Africa*				
Durban[2]—England Inns & 104 runs ...	485-5d	—	155	226
Johannesburg[3]—Drawn	531	—	317	336-6
Cape Town—Drawn	442	15-0	501-7d	346
Johannesburg[3]—Drawn	384	153-6	390-6d	307-3d
Port Elizabeth—Drawn	435	29-1	502	178-4d
1965 *in England*				
Lord's—Drawn	338	145-7	280	248
Nottingham—South Africa 94 runs ...	240	224	269	289
Oval—Drawn	202	308-4	208	392

ENGLAND v. WEST INDIES

Venue and Result	England 1st inns	England 2nd inns	West Indies 1st inns	West Indies 2nd inns
1928 *in England*				
Lord's—England Inns & 58 runs ...	401	—	177	166
Manchester—England Inns & 30 runs	351	—	206	115
Oval—England Inns & 71 runs... ...	438	—	238	129

Venue and Result	England 1st inns	England 2nd inns	West Indies 1st inns	West Indies 2nd inns
1929-30 in West Indies				
Bridgetown—Drawn	467	167-3	369	384
Port of Spain—England 167 runs ...	208	425-8d	254	212
Georgetown—West Indies 289 runs ...	145	327	471	290
Kingston—Drawn	849	272-9d	286	408-5
1933 in England				
Lord's—England Inns & 27 runs ...	296	—	97	172
Manchester—Drawn	374	—	375	225
Oval—England Inns & 17 runs... ...	312	—	100	195
1934-35 in West Indies				
Bridgetown—England 4 wkts	81-7d	75-6	102	51-6d
Port of Spain—West Indies 217 runs ...	258	107	302	280-6d
Georgetown—Drawn	226	160-6d	184	104-5
Kingston—West Indies Inns & 161 runs	271	103	535-7d	—
1939 in England				
Lord's—England 8 wkts	404-5d	100-2	277	225
Manchester—Drawn	164-7d	128-6d	133	43-4
Oval—Drawn	352	366-3	498	—
1947-48 in West Indies				
Bridgetown—Drawn	253	86-4	296	351-9d
Port of Spain—Drawn	362	275	497	72-3
Georgetown—West Indies 7 wkts ...	111	263	297-8d	78-3
Kingston—West Indies 10 wkts ...	227	336	490	76-0
1950 in England				
Manchester—England 202 runs... ...	312	288	215	183
Lord's—West Indies 326 runs	151	274	326	425-6d
Nottingham—West Indies 10 wkts ...	223	436	558	103-0
Oval—West Indies Inns & 56 runs ...	344	103	503	—
1953-54 in West Indies				
Kingston—West Indies 140 runs ...	170	316	417	209-6d
Bridgetown—West Indies 181 runs ...	181	313	383	292-2d
Georgetown—England 9 wkts	435	75-1	251	256
Port of Spain—Drawn	537	98-3	681-8d	212-4d
Kingston—England 9 wkts	414	72-1	139	346
1957 in England				
Birmingham—Drawn	186	583-4d	474	72-7
Lord's—England Inns & 36 runs ...	424	—	127	261
Nottingham—Drawn	619-6d	64-1	372	367
Leeds—England Inns & 5 runs ...	279	—	142	132
Oval—England Inns & 237 runs ...	412	—	89	86

Venue and Result	England 1st inns	England 2nd inns	West Indies 1st inns	West Indies 2nd inns
1959-60 in West Indies				
Bridgetown—Drawn	482	71-0	563-8d	—
Port of Spain—England 256 runs ...	382	230-9d	112	244
Kingston—Drawn	277	305	353	175-6
Georgetown—Drawn	295	334-8	402-8d	—
Port of Spain—Drawn	393	350-7d	338-8d	209-5
1963 in England				
Manchester—West Indies 10 wkts ...	205	296	501-6d	1-0
Lord's—Drawn	297	228-9	301	229
Birmingham—England 217 runs ...	216	278-9d	186	91
Leeds—West Indies 221 runs	174	231	397	229
Oval—West Indies 8 wkts	275	223	246	255-2
1966 in England				
Manchester—West Indies Inns & 40 runs	167	277	484	—
Lord's—Drawn	355	197-4	269	369-5d
Nottingham—West Indies 139 runs ...	325	253	235	482-5d
Leeds—West Indies Inns & 55 runs ...	240	205	500-9d	—
Oval—England Inns & 34 runs... ...	527	—	268	225

ENGLAND v. NEW ZEALAND

Venue and Result	England 1st inns	England 2nd inns	New Zealand 1st inns	New Zealand 2nd inns
1929-30 in New Zealand				
Christchurch—England 8 wkts ...	181	66-2	112	131
Wellington—Drawn	320	107-4	440	164-4d
Auckland—Drawn	330-4d	—	96-1	—
Auckland—Drawn	540	22-3	387	—
1931 in England				
Lord's—Drawn	454	146-5	224	469-9d
Oval—England Inns & 26 runs... ...	416-4d	—	193	197
Manchester—Drawn	224-3	—	—	—
1932-33 in New Zealand				
Christchurch—Drawn	560-8d	—	223	35-0
Auckland—Drawn	548-7d	—	158	16-0
1937 in England				
Lord's—Drawn	424	226-4d	295	175-8
Manchester—England 130 runs... ...	358-9d	187	281	134
Oval—Drawn	254-7d	31-1	249	187
1946-47 in New Zealand				
Christchurch—Drawn	265-7d	—	345-9d	—
1949 in England				
Leeds—Drawn	372	267-4d	341	195-2
Lord's—Drawn	313-9d	306-5	484	—
Manchester—Drawn	440-9d	—	293	348-7
Oval—Drawn	482	—	345	308-9d
1950-51 in New Zealand				
Christchurch—Drawn	550	—	417-8d	46-3
Wellington—England 6 wkts	227	91-4	125	189

Venue and Result	England 1st inns	England 2nd inns	New Zealand 1st inns	New Zealand 2nd inns
1954-55 *in New Zealand*				
Dunedin—England 8 wkts	209-8d	49-2	125	132
Auckland—England Inns & 20 runs ...	246	—	200	26
1958 *in England*				
Birmingham—England 205 runs ...	221	215-6d	94	137
Lord's—England Inns & 148 runs ...	269	—	47	74
Leeds—England Inns & 71 runs ...	267-2d	—	67	129
Manchester—England Inns & 13 runs	365-9d	—	267	85
Oval—Drawn	219-9d	—	161	91-3
1958-59 *in New Zealand*				
Christchurch—England Inns & 99 runs	374	—	142	133
Auckland—Drawn	311-7	—	181	—
1962-63 *in New Zealand*				
Auckland—England Inns & 215 runs ...	562-7d	—	258	89
Wellington—England Inns & 47 runs ...	428-8d	—	194	187
Christchurch—England 7 wkts	253	173-3	266	159
1965 *in England*				
Birmingham—England 9 wkts	435	96-1	116	413
Lord's—England 7 wkts	307	218-3	175	347
Leeds—England Inns & 187 runs ...	546-4d	—	193	166
1965-66 *in New Zealand*				
Christchurch—Drawn	342	201-5d	347	48-8
Dunedin—Drawn	254-8d	—	192	147-9
Auckland—Drawn	222	159-4	296	129

ENGLAND v. INDIA

Venue and Result	England 1st inns	England 2nd inns	India 1st inns	India 2nd inns
1932 *in England*				
Lord's—England 158 runs	259	275-8d	189	187
1933-34 *in India*				
Bombay[1]—England 9 wkts	438	40-1	219	258
Calcutta—Drawn...	403	7-2	247	237
Madras[1]—England 202 runs	335	261-7d	145	249
1936 *in England*				
Lord's—England 9 wkts	134	108-1	147	93
Manchester—Drawn	571-8d	—	203	390-5
Oval—England 9 wkts	471-8d	64-1	222	312
1946 *in England*				
Lord's—England 10 wkts	428	48-0	200	275
Manchester—Drawn	294	153-5d	170	152-9
Oval—Drawn	95-3	—	331	—

Venue and Result	England 1st inns	England 2nd inns	India 1st inns	India 2nd inns
1951-52 in India				
New Delhi—Drawn	203	368-6	418-6d	—
Bombay—Drawn	456	55-2	485-9d	208
Calcutta—Drawn...	342	252-5d	344	103-0
Kanpur—England 8 wkts	203	76-2	121	157
Madras[1]—India Inns & 8 runs	266	183	457-9d	—
1952 in England				
Leeds—England 7 wkts	334	128-3	293	165
Lord's—England 8 wkts	537	79-2	235	378
Manchester—England Inns & 207 runs	347-9d	—	58	82
Oval—Drawn	326-6d	—	98	—
1959 in England				
Nottingham—England Inns & 59 runs	422	—	206	157
Lord's—England 8 wkts	226	108-2	168	165
Leeds—England Inns & 173 runs ...	483-8d	—	161	149
Manchester—England 171 runs... ...	490	265-8d	208	376
Oval—England Inns & 27 runs... ...	361	—	140	194
1961-62 in India				
Bombay—Drawn	500-8d	184-5d	390	180-5
Kanpur—Drawn	244	497-5	467-8d	—
New Delhi—Drawn	256-3	—	466	—
Calcutta—India 187 runs	212	233	380	252
Madras[2]—India 128 runs	281	209	428	190
1963-64 in India				
Madras[2]—Drawn...	317	241-5	457-7d	152-9d
Bombay—Drawn	233	206-3	300	249-8d
Calcutta—Drawn...	267	145-2	241	300-7d
New Delhi—Drawn	451	—	344	463-4
Kanpur—Drawn	559-8d	—	266	347-3
1967 in England				
Leeds—England 6 wkts	550-4d	126-4	164	510
Lord's—England Inns & 124 runs ...	386	—	152	110
Birmingham—England 132 runs ...	298	203	92	277

ENGLAND v. PAKISTAN

Venue and Result	England 1st inns	England 2nd inns	Pakistan 1st inns	Pakistan 2nd inns
1954 in England				
Lord's—Drawn	117-9d	—	87	121-3
Nottingham—England Inns & 129 runs	558-6d	—	157	272
Manchester—Drawn	359-8d	—	90	25-4
Oval—Pakistan 24 runs	130	143	133	164

Venue and Result	*England* 1st inns	*England* 2nd inns	*Pakistan* 1st inns	*Pakistan* 2nd inns
1961-62 *in Pakistan*				
Lahore[2]—England 5 wkts	380	209-5	387-9d	200
Dacca—Drawn	439	38-0	393-7d	216
Karachi—Drawn...	507	—	253	404-8
1962 *in England*				
Birmingham—England Inns & 24 runs	544-5d	—	246	274
Lord's—England 9 wkts	370	86-1	100	355
Leeds—England Inns & 117 runs ...	428	—	131	180
Nottingham—Drawn	428-5d	—	219	216-6
Oval—England 10 wkts	480-5d	27-0	183	323
1967 *in England*				
Lord's—Drawn	369	241-9d	354	88-3
Nottingham—England 10 wkts	252-8d	3-0	140	114
Oval—England 8 wkts	440	34-2	216	255

AUSTRALIA v. SOUTH AFRICA

Venue and Result	*Australia* 1st inns	*Australia* 2nd inns	*South Africa* 1st inns	*South Africa* 2nd inns
1902-03 *in South Africa*				
Johannesburg[1]—Drawn	296	372-7d	454	101-4
Johannesburg[1]—Australia 159 runs ...	175	309	240	85
Cape Town—Australia 10 wkts ...	252	59-0	85	225
1910-11 *in Australia*				
Sydney—Australia Inns & 114 runs ...	528	—	174	240
Melbourne—Australia 89 runs	348	327	506	80
Adelaide—South Africa 38 runs ...	465	339	482	360
Melbourne—Australia 530 runs... ...	328	578	205	171
Sydney—Australia 7 wkts	364	198-3	160	401
1912 *in England*				
Manchester—Australia Inns & 88 runs	448	—	265	95
Lord's—Australia 10 wkts	390	48-0	263	173
Nottingham—Drawn	219	—	329	—
1921-22 *in South Africa*				
Durban[1]—Drawn	299	324-7d	232	184-7
Johannesburg[1]—Drawn	450	7-0	243	472-8d
Cape Town—Australia 10 wkts ...	396	1-0	180	216
1931-32 *in Australia*				
Brisbane[2]—Australia Inns & 163 runs ...	450	—	170	117
Sydney—Australia Inns & 155 runs ...	469	—	153	161
Melbourne—Australia 169 runs... ...	198	554	358	225
Adelaide—Australia 10 wkts	513	73-0	308	274
Melbourne—Australia Inns & 72 runs	153	—	36	45

Venue and Result	Australia 1st inns	Australia 2nd inns	South Africa 1st inns	South Africa 2nd inns
1935-36 *in South Africa*				
Durban[2]—Australia 9 wkts	429	102-1	248	282
Johannesburg[1]—Drawn	250	274-2	157	491
Cape Town—Australia Inns & 78 runs	362-8d	—	102	182
Johannesburg[1]—Australia Inns & 184 runs	439	—	157	98
Durban[2]—Australia Inns & 6 runs ...	455	—	222	227
1949-50 *in South Africa*				
Johannesburg[2]—Australia Inns & 85 runs	413	—	137	191
Cape Town—Australia 8 wkts	526-7d	87-2	278	333
Durban[2]—Australia 5 wkts	75	336-5	311	99
Johannesburg[2]—Drawn	465-8d	259-2	352	—
Port Elizabeth—Australia Inns & 259 runs	549-7d	—	158	132
1952-53 *in Australia*				
Brisbane[2]—Australia 96 runs	280	277	221	240
Melbourne—South Africa 82 runs ...	243	290	227	388
Sydney—Australia Inns & 38 runs ...	443	—	173	232
Adelaide—Drawn	530	233-3d	387	177-6
Melbourne—South Africa 6 wkts ...	520	209	435	297-4
1957-58 *in South Africa*				
Johannesburg[3]—Drawn	368	162-3	470-9d	201
Cape Town—Australia Inns & 141 runs	449	—	209	99
Durban[2]—Drawn	163	292-7	384	—
Johannesburg[3]—Australia 10 wkts ...	401	1-0	203	198
Port Elizabeth—Australia 8 wkts ...	291	68-2	214	144
1963-64 *in Australia*				
Brisbane[2]—Drawn	435	144-1d	346	13-1
Melbourne—Australia 8 wkts	447	136-2	274	306
Sydney—Drawn	260	450-9d	302	326-5
Adelaide—South Africa 10 wkts ...	345	331	595	82-0
Sydney—Drawn	311	270	411	76-0
1966-67 *in South Africa*				
Johannesburg[3]—South Africa 233 runs	325	261	199	620
Cape Town—Australia 6 wkts	542	180-4	353	367
Durban[2]—South Africa 8 wkts ...	147	334	300	185-2
Johannesburg[3]—Drawn	143	148-8	332-9d	—
Port Elizabeth—South Africa 7 wkts ...	173	278	276	179-3

AUSTRALIA v. WEST INDIES

Venue and Result	Australia 1st inns	Australia 2nd inns	West Indies 1st inns	West Indies 2nd inns
1930-31 *in Australia*				
Adelaide—Australia 10 wkts	376	172-0	296	249
Sydney—Australia Inns & 172 runs ...	369	—	107	90
Brisbane[1]—Australia Inns & 217 runs ...	558	—	193	148
Melbourne—Australia Inns & 122 runs	328-8d	—	99	107
Sydney—West Indies 30 runs	224	220	350-6d	124-5d

Venue and Result	Australia 1st inns	Australia 2nd inns	West Indies 1st inns	West Indies 2nd inns
1951-52 *in Australia*				
Brisbane[2]—Australia 3 wkts	226	236-7	216	245
Sydney—Australia 7 wkts	517	137-3	362	290
Adelaide—West Indies 6 wkts	82	255	105	233-4
Melbourne—Australia 1 wkt	216	260-9	272	203
Sydney—Australia 202 runs	116	377	78	213
1954-55 *in West Indies*				
Kingston—Australia 9 wkts	515-9d	20-1	259	275
Port of Spain—Drawn	600-9d	—	382	273-4
Georgetown—Australia 8 wkts	257	133-2	182	207
Bridgetown—Drawn	668	249	510	234-6
Kingston—Australia Inns & 82 runs ...	758-8d	—	357	319
1960-61 *in Australia*				
Brisbane[2]—Tied	505	232	453	284
Melbourne—Australia 7 wkts	348	70-3	181	233
Sydney—West Indies 222 runs	202	241	339	326
Adelaide—Drawn	366	273-9	393	432-6d
Melbourne—Australia 2 wkts	356	258-8	292	321
1964-65 *in West Indies*				
Kingston—West Indies 179 runs ...	217	216	239	373
Port of Spain—Drawn	516	—	429	386
Georgetown—West Indies 212 runs ...	179	144	355	180
Bridgetown—Drawn	650-6d	175-4d	573	242-5
Port of Spain—Australia 10 wkts ...	294	63-0	224	131

AUSTRALIA v. NEW ZEALAND

Venue and Result	Australia 1st inns	Australia 2nd inns	New Zealand 1st inns	New Zealand 2nd inns
1945-46 *in New Zealand*				
Wellington—Australia Inns & 103 runs	199-8d	—	42	54

AUSTRALIA v. INDIA

Venue and Result	Australia 1st inns	Australia 2nd inns	India 1st inns	India 2nd inns
1947-48 *in Australia*				
Brisbane[2]—Australia Inns & 226 runs ...	382-8d	—	58	98
Sydney—Drawn	107	—	188	61-7
Melbourne—Australia 233 runs... ...	394	255-4d	291-9d	125
Adelaide—Australia Inns & 16 runs ...	674	—	381	277
Melbourne—Australia Inns & 177 runs	575-8d	—	331	67
1956-57 *in India*				
Madras[2]—Australia Inns & 5 runs ...	319	—	161	153
Bombay—Drawn	523-7d	—	251	250-5
Calcutta—Australia 94 runs	177	189-9d	136	136

Venue and Result	Australia 1st inns	Australia 2nd inns	India 1st inns	India 2nd inns
1959-60 *in India*				
New Delhi—Australia Inns & 127 runs	468	—	135	206
Kanpur—India 119 runs	219	105	152	291
Bombay—Drawn	387-8d	34-1	289	226-5d
Madras[2]—Australia Inns & 55 runs ...	342	—	149	138
Calcutta—Drawn...	331	121-2	194	339
1964-65 *in India*				
Madras[2]—Australia 139 runs	211	397	276	193
Bombay—India 2 wkts	320	274	341	256-8
Calcutta—Drawn...	174	143-1	235	—

AUSTRALIA v. PAKISTAN

Venue and Result	Australia 1st inns	Australia 2nd inns	Pakistan 1st inns	Pakistan 2nd inns
1956-57 *in Pakistan*				
Karachi—Pakistan 9 wkts	80	187	199	69-1
1959-60 *in Pakistan*				
Dacca—Australia 8 wkts...	225	112-2	200	134
Lahore[2]—Australia 7 wkts	391-9d	122-3	146	366
Karachi—Drawn	257	83-2	287	194-8d
1964-65 *in Pakistan*				
Karachi—Drawn	352	227-2	414	279-8d
1964-65 *in Australia*				
Melbourne—Drawn	448	88-2	287	326

SOUTH AFRICA v. NEW ZEALAND

Venue and Result	South Africa 1st inns	South Africa 2nd inns	New Zealand 1st inns	New Zealand 2nd inns
1931-32 *in New Zealand*				
Christchurch–South Africa Inns & 12 runs	451	—	293	146
Wellington—South Africa 8 wkts ...	410	150-2	364	193
1952-53 *in New Zealand*				
Wellington—South Africa Inns & 180 runs	524-8d	—	172	172
Auckland—Drawn	377	200-5d	245	31-2
1953-54 *in South Africa*				
Durban[2]—South Africa Inns & 58 runs	437-9d	—	230	149
Johannesburg[2]—South Africa 132 runs	271	148	187	100
Cape Town—Drawn	326	159-3	505	—
Johannesburg[2]—South Africa 9 wkts ...	243	25-1	79	188
Port Elizabeth—South Africa 5 wkts ...	237	215-5	226	222

Venue and Result	*South Africa* 1*st inns*	2*nd inns*	*New Zealand* 1*st inns*	2*nd inns*
1961-62 *in South Africa*				
Durban[2]—South Africa 30 runs ...	292	149	245	166
Johannesburg[3]—Drawn	322	178-6d	223	165-4
Cape Town—New Zealand 72 runs ...	190	335	385	212-9d
Johannesburg[3]—Sth Africa Inns & 51 runs	464	—	164	249
Port Elizabeth—New Zealand 40 runs	190	273	275	228
1963-64 *in New Zealand*				
Wellington—Drawn	302	218-2d	253	138-6
Dunedin—Drawn	223	42-3	149	138
Auckland—Drawn	371	200-5d	263	191-8

WEST INDIES v. NEW ZEALAND

Venue and Result	*West Indies* 1*st inns*	2*nd inns*	*New Zealand* 1*st inns*	2*nd inns*
1951-52 *in New Zealand*				
Christchurch—West Indies 5 wkts ...	287	142-5	236	189
Auckland—Drawn	546-6d	—	160	17-1
1955-56 *in New Zealand*				
Dunedin—West Indies Inns & 71 runs	353	—	74	208
Christchurch—West Indies Inns & 64 runs	386	—	158	164
Wellington—West Indies 9 wkts ...	404	13-1	208	208
Auckland—New Zealand 190 runs ...	145	77	255	157-9d

WEST INDIES v. INDIA

Venue and Result	*West Indies* 1*st inns*	2*nd inns*	*India* 1*st inns*	2*nd inns*
1948-49 *in India*				
New Delhi—Drawn	631	—	454	220-6
Bombay—Drawn	629-6d	—	273	333-3
Calcutta—Drawn...	366	336-9d	272	325-3
Madras[1]—West Indies Inns & 193 runs	582	—	245	144
Bombay—Drawn	286	267	193	355-8
1952-53 *in West Indies*				
Port of Spain—Drawn	438	142-0	417	294
Bridgetown—West Indies 142 runs ...	296	228	253	129
Port of Spain—Drawn	315	192-2	279	362-7d
Georgetown—Drawn	364	—	262	190-5
Kingston—Drawn	576	92-4	312	444
1958-59 *in India*				
Bombay—Drawn	227	323-4d	152	289-5
Kanpur—West Indies 203 runs ...	222	443-7d	222	240
Calcutta—West Indies Inns & 336 runs	614-5d	—	124	154
Madras[2]—West Indies 295 runs ...	500	168-5d	222	151
New Delhi—Drawn	644-8d	—	415	275

Venue and Result	West Indies 1st inns	2nd inns	India 1st inns	2nd inns
1961-62 in West Indies				
Port of Spain—West Indies 10 wkts ...	289	15-0	203	98
Kingston—West Indies Inns & 18 runs	631-8d	—	395	218
Bridgetown—West Indies Inns & 30 runs	475	—	258	187
Port of Spain—West Indies 7 wkts ...	444-9d	176-3	197	422
Kingston—West Indies 123 runs ...	253	283	178	235
1966-67 in India				
Bombay—West Indies 6 wkts	421	192-4	296	316
Calcutta—West Indies Inns & 45 runs...	390	—	167	178
Madras[1]—Drawn	406	270-7	404	323

WEST INDIES v. PAKISTAN

Venue and Result	West Indies 1st inns	2nd inns	Pakistan 1st inns	2nd inns
1957-58 in West Indies				
Bridgetown—Drawn	579-9d	28-0	106	657-8d
Port of Spain—West Indies 120 runs ...	325	312	282	235
Kingston—West Indies Inns & 174 runs	790-3d	—	328	288
Georgetown—West Indies 8 wkts ...	410	317-2	408	318
Port of Spain—Pakistan Inns & 1 run ...	268	227	496	—
1958-59 in Pakistan				
Karachi—Pakistan 10 wkts	146	245	304	88-0
Dacca—Pakistan 41 runs	76	172	145	144
Lahore[1]—West Indies Inns & 156 runs	469	—	209	104

NEW ZEALAND v. INDIA

Venue and Result	New Zealand 1st inns	2nd inns	India 1st inns	2nd inns
1955-56 in India				
Hyderabad—Drawn	326	212-2	498-4d	—
Bombay—India Inns & 27 runs ...	258	136	421-8d	—
New Delhi—Drawn	450-2d	112-1	531-7d	—
Calcutta—Drawn...	336	74-6	132	438-7d
Madras[2]—India Inns & 109 runs ...	209	219	537-3d	—
1964-65 in India				
Madras[2]—Drawn...	315	62-0	397	199-2d
Calcutta—Drawn...	462-9d	191-9d	380	92-3
Bombay—Drawn	297	80-8	88	463-5d
New Delhi—India 7 wkts	262	272	465-8d	73-3

NEW ZEALAND v. PAKISTAN

Venue and Result	New Zealand *1st inns*	*2nd inns*	Pakistan *1st inns*	*2nd inns*
1955-56 *in Pakistan*				
Karachi—Pakistan Inns & 1 run	164	124	289	—
Lahore[1]—Pakistan 4 wkts	348	328	561	117-6
Dacca—Drawn	70	69-6	195-6d	—
1964-65 *in New Zealand*				
Wellington—Drawn	266	179-7d	187	140-7
Auckland—Drawn	214	166-7	226	207
Christchurch—Drawn	202	223-5	206	309-8d
1964-65 *in Pakistan*				
Rawalpindi—Pakistan Inns & 64 runs	175	79	318	—
Lahore[2]—Drawn	482-6d	—	385-7d	194-8d
Karachi—Pakistan 8 wkts	285	223	307-8d	202-2

INDIA v. PAKISTAN

Venue and Result	India *1st inns*	*2nd inns*	Pakistan *1st inns*	*2nd inns*
1952-53 *in India*				
New Delhi—India Inns & 70 runs ...	372	—	150	152
Lucknow—Pakistan Inns & 43 runs ...	106	182	331	—
Bombay—India 10 wkts	387-4d	45-0	186	242
Madras[1]—Drawn	175-6	—	344	—
Calcutta—Drawn...	397	28-0	257	236-7d
1954-55 *in Pakistan*				
Dacca—Drawn	148	147-2	257	158
Bahawalpur—Drawn	235	209-5	312-9d	—
Lahore[1]—Drawn	251	74-2	328	136-5d
Peshawar—Drawn	245	23-1	188	182
Karachi—Drawn	145	69-2	162	241-5d
1960-61 *in India*				
Bombay—Drawn	449-9d	—	350	166-4
Kanpur—Drawn	404	—	335	140-3
Calcutta—Drawn...	180	127-4	301	146-3d
Madras[2]—Drawn...	539-9d	—	448-8d	59-0
New Delhi—Drawn	463	16-0	286	250

RESULTS SUMMARY

RESULTS SUMMARY OF ALL TEST MATCHES, 1876-77 to 1967

		Tests	*Won by*							*Tie*	*Draw*
			E	*A*	*SA*	*WI*	*NZ*	*I*	*P*		
England	v. Australia	198	65	79	–	–	–	–	–	–	54
	v. South Africa	102	46	–	18	–	–	–	–	–	38
	v. West Indies	50	17	–	–	16	–	–	–	–	17
	v. New Zealand	37	17	–	–	–	0	–	–	–	20
	v. India	37	18	–	–	–	–	3	–	–	16
	v. Pakistan	15	8	–	–	–	–	–	1	–	6
Australia	v. South Africa	49	–	29	7	–	–	–	–	–	13
	v. West Indies	25	–	14	–	5	–	–	–	1	5
	v. New Zealand	1	–	1	–	–	0	–	–	–	–
	v. India	16	–	9	–	–	–	2	–	–	5
	v. Pakistan	6	–	2	–	–	–	–	1	–	3
South Africa	v. New Zealand	17	–	–	9	–	2	–	–	–	6
West Indies	v. New Zealand	6	–	–	–	4	1	–	–	–	1
	v. India	23	–	–	–	12	–	0	–	–	11
	v. Pakistan	8	–	–	–	4	–	–	3	–	1
New Zealand	v. India	9	–	–	–	–	0	3	–	–	6
	v. Pakistan	9	–	–	–	–	0	–	4	–	5
India	v. Pakistan	15	–	–	–	–	–	2	1	–	12
		623	171	134	34	41	3	10	10	1	219

	Tests	*Won*	*Lost*	*Drawn*	*Tied*	*Toss Won*
England	439	171	117	151	–	223
Australia	295	134	80	80	1	142
South Africa ...	168	34	77	57	–	76
West Indies ...	112	41	35	35	1	61
New Zealand ...	79	3	38	38	–	43
India	100	10	40	50	–	49
Pakistan	53	10	16	27	–	29

ENGLAND v. AUSTRALIA—IN ENGLAND

Year	*Totals*				*Nottingham*			*Lord's*			*Manchester*			*Leeds*			*Oval*			*Birmingham*			*Sheffield*		
	Pl.	*E.*	*A.*	*D.*	*E.*	*A.*	*D.*	*E.*	*A.*	*D.*	*E.*	*A.*	*D.*	*E.*	*A.*	*D.*	*E.*	*A.*	*D.*	*E.*	*A.*	*D.*	*E.*	*A.*	*D.*
1880	1	1	–	–	–	–	–	–	–	–	–	–	–	–	–	–	1	–	–	–	–	–	–	–	–
1882	1	–	1	–	–	–	–	–	–	–	–	–	–	–	–	–	–	1	–	–	–	–	–	–	–
1884	3	1	–	2	–	–	–	1	–	–	–	–	1	–	–	–	–	–	1	–	–	–	–	–	–
1886	3	3	–	–	–	–	–	1	–	–	1	–	–	–	–	–	1	–	–	–	–	–	–	–	–
1888	3	2	1	–	–	–	–	–	1	–	1	–	–	–	–	–	1	–	–	–	–	–	–	–	–
1890	2	2	–	–	–	–	–	1	–	–	–	–	–	–	–	–	1	–	–	–	–	–	–	–	–
1893	3	1	–	2	–	–	–	–	–	1	–	–	1	–	–	–	1	–	–	–	–	–	–	–	–
1896	3	2	1	–	–	–	–	1	–	–	–	1	–	–	–	–	1	–	–	–	–	–	–	–	–
1899	5	–	1	4	–	–	1	–	1	–	–	–	1	–	–	1	–	–	1	–	–	–	–	–	–
1902	5	1	2	2	–	–	–	–	–	1	–	1	–	–	–	–	1	–	–	–	–	1	–	1	–
1905	5	2	–	3	1	–	–	–	–	1	1	–	–	–	–	1	–	–	1	–	–	–	–	–	–
1909	5	1	2	2	–	–	–	–	1	–	–	–	1	–	1	–	–	–	1	1	–	–	–	–	–
1912	3	1	–	2	–	–	–	–	–	1	–	–	1	–	–	–	1	–	–	–	–	–	–	–	–
1921	5	–	3	2	–	1	–	–	1	–	–	–	1	–	1	–	–	–	1	–	–	–	–	–	–
1926	5	1	–	4	–	–	1	–	–	1	–	–	1	–	–	1	1	–	–	–	–	–	–	–	–
1930	5	1	2	2	1	–	–	–	1	–	–	–	1	–	–	1	–	1	–	–	–	–	–	–	–
1934	5	1	2	2	–	1	–	1	–	–	–	–	1	–	–	1	–	1	–	–	–	–	–	–	–
1938	4	1	1	2	–	–	1	–	–	1	–	–	–	–	1	–	1	–	–	–	–	–	–	–	–
1948	5	–	4	1	–	1	–	–	1	–	–	–	1	–	1	–	–	1	–	–	–	–	–	–	–
1953	5	1	–	4	–	–	1	–	–	1	–	–	1	–	–	1	1	–	–	–	–	–	–	–	–
1956	5	2	1	2	–	–	1	–	1	–	1	–	–	1	–	–	–	–	1	–	–	–	–	–	–
1961	5	1	2	2	–	–	–	–	1	–	–	1	–	1	–	–	–	–	1	–	–	1	–	–	–
1964	5	–	1	4	–	–	1	–	–	1	–	–	1	–	1	–	–	–	1	–	–	–	–	–	–
	91	25	24	42	2	3	6	5	8	8	4	3	12	2	5	6	11	4	8	1	–	2	–	1	–

ENGLAND v. AUSTRALIA—IN AUSTRALIA

Year	*Tests*				*Melbourne*			*Sydney*			*Brisbane*			*Adelaide*		
	Pl.	*E.*	*A.*	*D.*	*E.*	*A.*	*D.*	*E.*	*A.*	*D.*	*E.*	*A.*	*D.*	*E.*	*A.*	*D.*
1876-77 ...	2	1	1	–	1	1	–	–	–	–	–	–	–	–	–	–
1878-79 ...	1	–	1	–	–	1	–	–	–	–	–	–	–	–	–	–
1881-82 ...	4	–	2	2	–	–	2	–	2	–	–	–	–	–	–	–
1882-83 ...	4	2	2	–	1	1	–	1	1	–	–	–	–	–	–	–
1884-85 ...	5	3	2	–	2	–	–	–	2	–	–	–	–	1	–	–
1886-87 ...	2	2	–	–	–	–	–	2	–	–	–	–	–	–	–	–
1887-88 ...	1	1	–	–	–	–	–	1	–	–	–	–	–	–	–	–
1891-92 ...	3	1	2	–	–	1	–	–	1	–	–	–	–	1	–	–
1894-95 ...	5	3	2	–	2	–	–	1	1	–	–	–	–	–	1	–
1897-98 ...	5	1	4	–	–	2	–	1	1	–	–	–	–	–	1	–
1901-02 ...	5	1	4	–	–	2	–	1	1	–	–	–	–	–	1	–
1903-04 ...	5	3	2	–	1	1	–	2	–	–	–	–	–	–	1	–
1907-08 ...	5	1	4	–	1	1	–	–	2	–	–	–	–	–	1	–
1911-12 ...	5	4	1	–	2	–	–	1	1	–	–	–	–	1	–	–
1920-21 ...	5	–	5	–	–	2	–	–	2	–	–	–	–	–	1	–
1924-25 ...	5	1	4	–	1	1	–	–	2	–	–	–	–	–	1	–
1928-29 ...	5	4	1	–	1	1	–	1	–	–	1	–	–	1	–	–
1932-33 ...	5	4	1	–	–	1	–	2	–	–	1	–	–	1	–	–
1936-37 ...	5	2	3	–	–	2	–	1	–	–	1	–	–	–	1	–
1946-47 ...	5	–	3	2	–	–	1	–	2	–	–	1	–	–	–	1
1950-51 ...	5	1	4	–	1	1	–	–	1	–	–	1	–	–	1	–
1954-55 ...	5	3	1	1	1	–	–	1	–	1	–	1	–	1	–	–
1958-59 ...	5	–	4	1	–	2	–	–	–	1	–	1	–	–	1	–
1962-63 ...	5	1	1	3	1	–	–	–	1	1	–	–	1	–	–	1
1965-66 ...	5	1	1	3	–	–	2	1	–	–	–	–	1	–	1	–
	107	40	55	12	15	20	5	16	20	3	3	4	2	6	11	2
Totals	198	65	79	54												

ENGLAND v. SOUTH AFRICA—IN ENGLAND

	Tests Pl. E. S. D.	Nottingham E. S. D.	Lord's E. S. D.	Manchester E. S. D.	Leeds E. S. D.	Oval E. S. D.	Birmingham E. S. D.
1907	3 1 – 2	– – –	– – 1	– – –	1 – –	– – 1	– – –
1912	3 3 – –	– – –	1 – –	– – –	1 – –	1 – –	– – –
1924	5 3 – 2	– – –	1 – –	– – 1	1 – –	– – 1	1 – –
1929	5 2 – 3	– – –	– – 1	1 – –	1 – –	– – 1	– – 1
1935	5 – 1 4	– – 1	– 1 –	– – 1	– – 1	– – 1	– – –
1947	5 3 – 2	– – 1	1 – –	1 – –	1 – –	– – 1	– – –
1951	5 3 1 1	– 1 –	1 – –	1 – –	– – 1	1 – –	– – –
1955	5 3 2 –	1 – –	1 – –	– 1 –	– 1 –	1 – –	– – –
1960	5 3 – 2	1 – –	1 – –	– – 1	– – –	– – 1	1 – –
1965	3 – 1 2	– 1 –	– – 1	– – –	– – –	– – 1	– – –
	44 21 5 18	2 2 2	6 1 3	3 1 3	5 1 2	3 – 7	2 – 1

ENGLAND v. SOUTH AFRICA—IN SOUTH AFRICA

	Tests Pl. E. S. D.	Port Elizabeth E. S. D.	Cape Town E. S. D.	Johannesburg E. S. D.	Durban E. S. D.
1888-89	2 2 – –	1 —	1 – –	– – –	– – –
1891-92	1 1 – –	– – –	1 – –	– – –	– – –
1895-96	3 3 – –	1 – –	1 – –	1 – –	– – –
1898-99	2 2 – –	– – –	1 – –	1 – –	– – –
1905-06	5 1 4 –	– – –	1 1 –	– 3 –	– – –
1909-10	5 2 3 –	– – –	1 1 –	1 1 –	– 1 –
1913-14	5 4 – 1	1 – –	– – –	2 – –	1 – 1
1922-23	5 2 1 2	– – –	1 – –	– 1 1	1 – 1
1927-28	5 2 2 1	– – –	1 – –	1 1 –	– 1 1
1930-31	5 – 1 4	– – –	– – 1	– 1 1	– – 2
1938-39	5 1 – 4	– – –	– – 1	– – 2	1 – 1
1948-49	5 2 – 3	1 – –	– – 1	– – 2	1 – –
1956-57	5 2 2 1	– 1 –	1 – –	1 1 –	– – 1
1964-65	5 1 – 4	– – 1	– – 1	– – 2	1 – –
	58 25 13 20	4 1 1	9 2 4	7 8 8	5 2 7
Totals ...	102 46 18 38				

ENGLAND v. WEST INDIES—IN ENGLAND

	Tests Pl. E. W. D.	Lord's E. W. D.	Manchester E. W. D.	Oval E. W. D.	Nottingham E. W. D.	Birmingham E. W. D.	Leeds E. W. D.
1928	3 3 – –	1 – –	1 – –	1 – –	– – –	– – –	– – –
1933	3 2 – 1	1 – –	– – 1	1 – –	– – –	– – –	– – –
1939	3 1 – 2	1 – –	– – 1	– – 1	– – –	– – –	– – –
1950	4 1 3 –	– 1 –	1 – –	– 1 –	– 1 –	– – –	– – –
1957	5 3 – 2	1 – –	– – –	1 – –	– – 1	– – 1	1 – –
1963	5 1 3 1	– – 1	– 1 –	– 1 –	– – –	1 – –	– 1 –
1966	5 1 3 1	– – 1	– 1 –	1 – –	– 1 –	– – –	– 1 –
	28 12 9 7	4 1 2	2 2 2	4 2 1	– 2 1	1 – 1	1 2 –

ENGLAND v. WEST INDIES—IN WEST INDIES

	Tests Pl.	E.	W.	D.		Bridge-town E.	W.	D.	Port of Spain E.	W.	D.	George-town E.	W.	D.	Kingston E.	W.	D.
1929-30	4	1	1	2	... ...	–	–	1	1	–	–	–	1	–	–	–	1
1934-35	4	1	2	1	... ...	1	–	–	–	1	–	–	–	1	–	1	–
1947-48	4	–	2	2	... ...	–	–	1	–	–	1	–	1	–	–	1	–
1953-54	5	2	2	1	... ...	–	1	–	–	–	1	1	–	–	1	1	–
1959-60	5	1	–	4	... ...	–	–	1	1	–	1	–	–	1	–	–	1
	22	5	7	10		1	1	3	2	1	3	1	2	2	1	3	2
Totals	50	17	16	17													

ENGLAND v. NEW ZEALAND—IN ENGLAND

	Tests Pl.	E.	N.	D.		Lord's E.	N.	D.	Oval E.	N.	D.	Man-chester E.	N.	D.	Leeds E.	N.	D.	Birming-ham E.	N.	D.
1931 ...	3	1	–	2	...	–	–	1	1	–	–	–	–	1	–	–	–	–	–	–
1937 ...	3	1	–	2	...	–	–	1	–	–	1	1	–	–	–	–	–	–	–	–
1949 ...	4	–	–	4	...	–	–	1	–	–	1	–	–	1	–	–	1	–	–	–
1958 ...	5	4	–	1	...	1	–	–	–	–	1	1	–	–	1	–	–	1	–	–
1965 ...	3	3	–	–	...	1	–	–	–	–	–	–	–	–	1	–	–	1	–	–
	18	9	–	9		2	–	3	1	–	3	2	–	2	2	–	1	2	–	–

ENGLAND v. NEW ZEALAND—IN NEW ZEALAND

	Tests Pl.	E.	N.	D.		Christ-church E.	N.	D.	Welling-ton E.	N.	D.	Auckland E.	N.	D.	Dunedin E.	N.	D.
1929-30	4	1	–	3	... ...	1	–	–	–	–	1	–	–	2	–	–	–
1932-33	2	–	–	2	... ...	–	–	1	–	–	–	–	–	1	–	–	–
1946-47	1	–	–	1	... ...	–	–	1	–	–	–	–	–	–	–	–	–
1950-51	2	1	–	1	... ...	–	–	1	1	–	–	–	–	–	–	–	–
1954-55	2	2	–	–	... ...	–	–	–	–	–	–	1	–	–	1	–	–
1958-59	2	1	–	1	... ...	1	–	–	–	–	–	–	–	1	–	–	–
1962-63	3	3	–	–	... ...	1	–	–	1	–	–	1	–	–	–	–	–
1965-66	3	–	–	3	... ...	–	–	1	–	–	–	–	–	1	–	–	1
	19	8	–	11		3	–	4	2	–	1	2	–	5	1	–	1
Totals	37	17	–	20													

ENGLAND v. INDIA—IN ENGLAND

	Tests Pl.	E.	I.	D.	Lord's E.	I.	D.	Man-chester E.	I.	D.	Oval E.	I.	D.	Leeds E.	I.	D.	Notting-ham E.	I.	D.	Birming-ham E.	I.	D.
1932 ...	1	1	–	–	1	–	–	–	–	–	–	–	–	–	–	–	–	–	–	–	–	–
1936 ...	3	2	–	1	1	–	–	–	–	1	1	–	–	–	–	–	–	–	–	–	–	–
1946 ...	3	1	–	2	1	–	–	–	–	1	–	–	1	–	–	–	–	–	–	–	–	–
1952 ...	4	3	–	1	1	–	–	1	–	–	–	–	1	1	–	–	–	–	–	–	–	–
1959 ...	5	5	–	–	1	–	–	1	–	–	1	–	–	1	–	–	1	–	–	–	–	–
1967 ...	3	3	–	–	1	–	–	–	–	–	–	–	–	1	–	–	–	–	–	1	–	–
	19	15	–	4	6	–	–	2	–	2	2	–	2	3	–	–	1	–	–	1	–	–

ENDLAND v. INDIA—IN INDIA

	Tests Pl.	E.	I.	D.		Bombay E. I. D.	Calcutta E. I. D.	Madras E. I. D.	New Delhi E. I. D.	Kanpur E. I. D.
1933-34	3	2	–	1	...	1 – –	– – 1	1 – –	– – –	– – –
1951-52	5	1	1	3	...	– – 1	– – 1	– 1 –	– – 1	1 – –
1961-62	5	–	2	3	...	– – 1	– 1 –	– 1 –	– – 1	– – 1
1963-64	5	–	–	5	...	– – 1	– – 1	– – 1	– – 1	– – 1
	18	3	3	12		1 – 3	– 1 3	1 2 1	– – 3	1 – 2
Total	37	18	3	16						

ENGLAND v. PAKISTAN—IN ENGLAND

	Tests Pl.	E.	P.	D.	Lord's E. P. D.	Nottingham E. P. D.	Manchester E. P. D.	Oval E. P. D.	Birmingham E. P. D.	Leeds E. P. D.
1954 ...	4	1	1	2	– – 1	1 – –	– – 1	– 1 –	– – –	– – –
1962 ...	5	4	–	1	1 – –	– – 1	– – –	1 – –	1 – –	1 – –
1967 ...	3	2	–	1	– – 1	1 – –	– – –	1 – –	– – –	– – –
	12	7	1	4	1 – 2	2 – 1	– – 1	2 1 –	1 – –	1 – –

ENGLAND v. PAKISTAN—IN PAKISTAN

	Tests Pl.	E.	P.	D.		Lahore E. P. D.	Dacca E. P. D.	Karachi E. P. D.
1961-62	3	1	–	2	... ...	1 – –	– – 1	– – 1
Total	15	8	1	6				

AUSTRALIA v. SOUTH AFRICA—IN AUSTRALIA

	Tests Pl.	A.	S.	D.		Sydney A. S. D.	Melbourne A. S. D.	Adelaide A. S. D.	Brisbane A. S. D.
1910-11	5	4	1	–	... ...	2 – –	2 – –	– 1 –	– – –
1931-32	5	5	–	–	... ...	1 – –	2 – –	1 – –	1 – –
1952-53	5	2	2	1	... ...	1 – –	– 2 –	– – 1	1 – –
1963-64	5	1	1	3	... ...	– – 2	1 – –	– 1 –	– – 1
	20	12	4	4		4 – 2	5 2 –	1 2 1	2 – 1

AUSTRALIA v. SOUTH AFRICA—IN SOUTH AFRICA

	Tests Pl.	A.	S.	D.		Johannesburg A. S. D.	Cape Town A. S. D.	Durban A. S. D.	Port Elizabeth A. S. D.
1902-03	3	2	–	1	... ...	1 – 1	1 – –	– – –	– – –
1921-22	3	1	–	2	... ...	– – 1	1 – –	– – 1	– – –
1935-36	5	4	–	1	... ...	1 – 1	1 – –	2 – –	– – –
1949-50	5	4	–	1	... ...	1 – 1	1 – –	1 – –	1 – –
1957-58	5	3	–	2	... ...	1 – 1	1 – –	– – 1	1 – –
1966-67	5	1	3	1	... ...	– 1 1	1 – –	– 1 –	– 1 –
	26	15	3	8		4 1 6	6 – –	3 1 2	2 1 –

AUSTRALIA v. SOUTH AFRICA—IN ENGLAND

	Tests Pl.	A.	S.	D.	Manchester A. S. D.	Lord's A. S. D.	Nottingham A. S. D.
1912 ...	3	2	–	1	1 – –	1 – –	– – 1
Totals	49	29	7	13			

AUSTRALIA v. WEST INDIES—IN AUSTRALIA

	Tests Pl.	A.	W.	D.	T.	Adelaide A. W. D.	Sydney A. W. D.	Brisbane A. W. D. T.	Melbourne A. W. D.
1930-31	5	4	1	–	–	1 – –	1 1 –	1 – – –	1 – –
1951-52	5	4	1	–	–	– 1 –	2 – –	1 – – –	1 – –
1960-61	5	2	1	1	1	– – 1	– 1 –	– – – 1	2 – –
	15	10	3	1	1	1 1 1	3 2 –	2 – – 1	4 – –

AUSTRALIA v. WEST INDIES—IN WEST INDIES

	Tests Pl.	A.	W.	D.	T.	Kingston A. W. D.	Port of Spain A. W. D.	Bridgetown A. W. D.	Georgetown A. W. D.
1954-55	5	3	–	2	–	2 – –	– – 1	– – 1	1 – –
1964-65	5	1	2	2	–	– 1 –	1 – 1	– – 1	– 1 –
	10	4	2	4	–	2 1 –	1 – 2	– – 2	1 1 –
Totals	25	14	5	5	1				

AUSTRALIA v. NEW ZEALAND—IN NEW ZEALAND

	Test Pl.	A.	N.	D.	Wellington A. N. D.
1945-46	1	1	–	–	1 – –

AUSTRALIA v. INDIA—IN AUSTRALIA

	Tests Pl.	A.	I.	D.	Brisbane A. I. D.	Sydney A. I. D.	Melbourne A. I. D.	Adelaide A. I. D.
1947-48	5	4	–	1	1 – –	– – 1	2 – –	1 – –

AUSTRALIA v. INDIA—IN INDIA

	Tests Pl.	A.	I.	D.	Madras A. I. D.	Bombay A. I. D.	Calcutta A. I. D.	New Delhi A. I. D.	Kanpur A. I. D.
1956-57	3	2	–	1	1 – –	– – 1	1 – –	– – –	– – –
1959-60	5	2	1	2	1 – –	– – 1	– – 1	1 – –	– 1 –
1964-65	3	1	1	1	1 – –	– 1 –	– – 1	– – –	– – –
	11	5	2	4	3 – –	– 1 2	1 – 2	1 – –	– 1 –
Totals	16	9	2	5					

AUSTRALIA v. PAKISTAN—IN AUSTRALIA

	Test Pl.	A.	P.	D.	Melbourne A. P. D.
1964-65	1	–	–	1	– – 1

AUSTRALIA v. PAKISTAN—IN PAKISTAN

	Tests Pl.	A.	P.	D.	Karachi A. P. D.	Dacca A. P. D.	Lahore A. P. D.
1956-57	1	–	1	–	– 1 –	– – –	– – –
1959-60	3	2	–	1	– – 1	1 – –	1 – –
1964-65	1	–	–	1	– – 1	– – –	– – –
	5	2	1	2	– 1 2	1 – –	1 – –
Totals	6	2	1	3			

SOUTH AFRICA v. NEW ZEALAND—IN SOUTH AFRICA

	Tests Pl.	S.	N.	D.	Durban S. N. D.	Johannesburg S. N. D.	Cape Town S. N. D.	Port Elizabeth S. N. D.
1953-54	5	4	–	1	1 – –	2 – –	– – 1	1 – –
1961-62	5	2	2	1	1 – –	1 – 1	– 1 –	– 1 –
	10	6	2	2	2 – –	3 – 1	– 1 1	1 1 –

SOUTH AFRICA v. NEW ZEALAND—IN NEW ZEALAND

	Tests Pl.	S.	N.	D.	Christchurch S. N. D.	Wellington S. N. D.	Auckland S. N. D.	Dunedin S. N. D.
1931-32	2	2	–	–	1 – –	1 – –	– – –	– – –
1952-53	2	1	–	1	– – –	1 – –	– – 1	– – –
1963-64	3	–	–	3	– – –	– – 1	– – 1	– – 1
	7	3	–	4	1 – –	2 – 1	– – 2	– – 1
Totals	17	9	2	6				

WEST INDIES v. NEW ZEALAND—IN NEW ZEALAND

	Tests Pl.	W.	N.	D.	Christchurch W. N. D.	Auckland W. N. D.	Dunedin W. N. D.	Wellington W. N. D.
1951-52	2	1	–	1	1 – –	– – 1	– – –	– – –
1955-56	4	3	1	–	1 – –	– 1 –	1 – –	1 – –
	6	4	1	1	2 – –	– 1 1	1 – –	1 – –

WEST INDIES v. INDIA—IN WEST INDIES

	Tests Pl.	W.	I.	D.	Port of Spain W. I. D.	Bridgetown W. I. D.	Georgetown W. I. D.	Kingston W. I. D.
1952-53	5	1	–	4	– – 2	1 – –	– – 1	– – 1
1961-62	5	5	–	–	2 – –	1 – –	– – –	2 – –
	10	6	–	4	2 – 2	2 – –	– – 1	2 – 1

WEST INDIES v. INDIA—IN INDIA

	Tests Pl.	W.	I.	D.	New Delhi W. I. D.	Bombay W. I. D.	Calcutta W. I. D.	Madras W. I. D.	Kanpur W. I. D.
1948-49	5	1	–	4	– – 1	– – 2	– – 1	1 – –	– – –
1958-59	5	3	–	2	– – 1	– – 1	1 – –	1 – –	1 – –
1966-67	3	2	–	1	– – –	1 – –	1 – –	– – 1	– – –
	13	6	–	7	– – 2	1 – 3	2 – 1	2 – 1	1 – –
	23	12	–	11					

WEST INDIES v. PAKISTAN—IN WEST INDIES

	Tests Pl.	W.	P.	D.	Bridgetown W. P. D.	Port of Spain W. P. D.	Kingston W. P. D.	Georgetown W. P. D.
1957-58	5	3	1	1	– – 1	1 1 –	1 – –	1 – –

WEST INDIES v. PAKISTAN—IN PAKISTAN

	Tests Pl.	W.	P.	D.	Karachi W. P. D.	Dacca W. P. D.	Lahore W. P. D.
1958-59	3	1	2	–	– 1 –	– 1 –	1 – –
Totals	8	4	3	1			

NEW ZEALAND v. INDIA—IN INDIA

	Tests Pl.	N.	I.	D.	Hyderabad N. I. D.	Bombay N. I. D.	New Delhi N. I. D.	Calcutta N. I. D.	Madras N. I. D.
1955-56	5	–	2	3	– – 1	– 1 –	– – 1	– – 1	– 1 –
1964-65	4	–	1	3	– – –	– – 1	– 1 –	– – 1	– – 1
	9	–	3	6	– – 1	– 1 1	– 1 1	– – 2	– 1 1

NEW ZEALAND v. PAKISTAN—IN NEW ZEALAND

	Tests Pl.	N.	P.	D.	Wellington N. P. D.	Auckland N. P. D.	Christchurch N. P. D.
1964-65	3	–	–	3	– – 1	– – 1	– – 1

NEW ZEALAND v. PAKISTAN—IN PAKISTAN

	Tests Pl.	N.	P.	D.			Karachi N. P. D.	Lahore N. P. D.	Dacca N. P. D.	Rawal-pindi N. P. D.
1955-56	3	–	2	1	...	... ...	– 1 –	– 1 –	– – 1	– – –
1964-65	3	–	2	1	...	... ...	– 1 –	– – 1	– – –	– 1 –
	6	–	4	2			– 2 –	– 1 1	– – 1	– 1 –
Totals	9	–	4	5						

INDIA v. PAKISTAN—IN INDIA

	Tests Pl.	I.	P.	D.	New Delhi I. P. D.	Lucknow I. P. D.	Bombay I. P. D.	Madras I. P. D.	Calcutta I. P. D.	Kanpur I. P. D.
1952-53	5	2	1	2	1 – –	– 1 –	1 – –	– – 1	– – 1	– – –
1960-61	5	–	–	5	– – 1	– – –	– – 1	– – 1	– – 1	– – 1
	10	2	1	7	1 – 1	– 1 –	1 – 1	– – 2	– – 2	– – 1

INDIA v. PAKISTAN—IN PAKISTAN

	Tests Pl.	I.	P.	D.		Dacca I. P. D.	Bahawal-pur I. P. D.	Lahore I. P. D.	Pesha-war I. P. D.	Karachi I. P. D.
1954-55	5	–	–	5	...	– – 1	– – 1	– – 1	– – 1	– – 1
Totals	15	2	1	12						

THE GROUNDS

A GUIDE TO THE TEST MATCH GROUNDS

Official Test Matches have been played in seven countries and at 36 centres—if one counts the two London grounds as separate centres. There simplicity ends, for at no fewer than seven of these centres more than one ground has been used. At Johannesburg official Tests have been played on three different grounds: the Old Wanderers, Ellis Park, and the New Wanderers (formerly Kent Park).

Where any of these seven centres is referred to in the Test Match Records section of this volume, the exact ground is denoted by an indicator number (e.g. Johannesburg²) which refers to the Key given in the following tables, and which is summarised in the Preface and repeated at intervals throughout the text of the Test Match section.

Test Match Centre	*No. of Tests*	*Year of First Test*	*Grounds*
ENGLAND			
Birmingham ...	12	1902	Edgbaston
Leeds	31	1899	Headingley
Lord's, London ...	53	1884	Lord's Cricket Ground
Manchester ...	42†	1884	Old Trafford
Nottingham ...	25	1899	Trent Bridge
Oval, London ...	51	1880	Kennington Oval
Sheffield	1	1902	Bramall Lane
AUSTRALIA			
Adelaide	27	1884	Adelaide Oval
Brisbane	16	1928	[1]Exhibition Ground (1928 to 1930-31) [2]Woolloongabba (1931-32 to date)
Melbourne ...	54	1877	Melbourne Cricket Ground [1]East Melbourne (1879 Test only)
Sydney	51	1882	Sydney Cricket Ground (No. 1)
SOUTH AFRICA			
Cape Town ...	23	1889	Newlands
Durban	22	1910	[1]Lord's (1910 to 1921-22) [2]Kingsmead (1922-23 to date)
Johannesburg ...	38	1896	[1]Old Wanderers (1896 to 1946-47) [2]Ellis Park (1947-48 to 1955-56) [3]New Wanderers (1956-57 to date)
Port Elizabeth ...	11	1889	St George's (Crusader Park)
WEST INDIES			
Bridgetown ...	10	1930	Kensington Oval
Georgetown ...	9	1930	Bourda
Kingston	13	1930	Sabina Park
Port of Spain ...	15	1930	Queen's Park (St. Clair) Oval
NEW ZEALAND			
Auckland	12	1930	Eden Park
Christchurch ...	11	1930	Lancaster Park
Dunedin	4	1955	Carisbrook
Wellington ...	9	1930	Basin Reserve
INDIA			
Bombay	15	1933	[1]Gymkhana (1933-34 only) Brabourne Stadium (1948-49 to date)
Calcutta	14	1934	Eden Gardens
Hyderabad ...	1	1955	Fateh Maidan
Kanpur (Cawnpore)	6	1952	Green Park
Lucknow	1	1952	University Ground
Madras	14	1934	[1]Chepauk (1933-34 to 1952-53, and 1966-67) [2]Corporation (Nehru) Stadium (1955-56 to 1964-65)
New Delhi ...	10	1948	Feroz Shah Kotla

† A further two matches, making a scheduled total of 44 matches in Manchester, were abandoned without a ball bowled in 1890 and 1938 respectively.

Test Match Centre		*No. of Tests*	*Year of First Test*	*Grounds*
PAKISTAN				
Bahawalpur	...	1	1955	Dring Stadium
Dacca ...	...	5	1955	Dacca Stadium
Karachi ...	...	8	1955	National Stadium
Lahore ...	...	6	1955	[1]Lawrence Gardens (Bagh-e-Jinnah) (1954-55 to 1958-59) [2]Lahore Stadium (1959-60 to date)
Peshawar ...	...	1	1955	Gymkhana
Rawalpindi	...	1	1965	Club

RECORD SCORES FOR EACH TEST MATCH CENTRE

	Highest			*Lowest*		
Birmingham	583-4d	England v. W. Indies	1957	30	S. Africa v. England	1924
Leeds	584	Australia v. England	1934	67	N. Zealand v. England	1958
Lord's	729-6d	Australia v. England	1930	47	N. Zealand v. England	1958
Manchester	656-8d	Australia v. England	1964	58	India v. England	1952
Nottingham	658-8d	England v. Australia	1938	88	S. Africa v. England	1960
Oval	903-7d	England v. Australia	1938	44	Australia v. England	1896
Sheffield	289	Australia v. England	1902	145	England v. Australia	1902
Adelaide	674	Australia v. India	1947-48	82	Australia v. W. Indies	1951-52
Brisbane	645	Australia v. England	1946-47	58	Australia v. England	1936-37
				58	India v. Australia	1947-48
Melbourne	604	Australia v. England	1936-37	36	S. Africa v. Australia	1931-32
Sydney	659-8d	Australia v. England	1946-47	42	Australia v. England	1887-88
Cape Town	559-9d	England v. S. Africa	1938-39	35	S. Africa v. England	1898-99
Durban	654-5	England v. S. Africa	1938-39	75	Australia v. S. Africa	1949-50
Johannesburg	620	S. Africa v. Australia	1966-67	72	S. Africa v. England	1956-57
Port Elizabeth	549-7d	Australia v. S. Africa	1949-50	30	S. Africa v. England	1895-96
Bridgetown	668	Australia v. W. Indies	1954-55	102	W. Indies v. England	1934-35
Georgetown	471	W. Indies v. England	1929-30	111	England v. W. Indies	1947-48
Kingston	849	England v. W. Indies	1929-30	103	England v. W. Indies	1934-35
Port of Spain	681-8d	W. Indies v. England	1953-54	98	India v. W. Indies	1961-62
Auckland	562-7d	England v. N. Zealand	1962-63	26	N. Zealand v. England	1954-55
Christchurch	560-8d	England v. N. Zealand	1932-33	112	N. Zealand v. England	1929-30
Dunedin	353	W. Indies v. N. Zealand	1955-56	74	N. Zealand v. W. Indies	1955-56
Wellington	524-8d	S. Africa v. N. Zealand	1952-53	42	N. Zealand v. Australia	1945-46
Bombay	629-6d	W. Indies v. India	1948-49	136	N. Zealand v. India	1955-56
Calcutta	614-5d	W. Indies v. India	1958-59	124	India v. W. Indies	1958-59
Hyderabad	498-4d	India v. N. Zealand	1955-56	326	N. Zealand v. India	1955-56
Kanpur	559-8d	England v. India	1963-64	105	Australia v. India	1959-60
Lucknow	331	Pakistan v. India	1952-53	106	India v. Pakistan	1952-53
Madras	582	W. Indies v. India	1948-49	138	India v. Australia	1959-60
New Delhi	644-8d	W. Indies v. India	1958-59	135	India v. Australia	1959-60
Bahawalpur	312-9d	Pakistan v. India	1954-55	235	India v. Pakistan	1954-55
Dacca	439	England v. Pakistan	1961-62	70	N. Zealand v. Pakistan	1955-56
Karachi	507	England v. Pakistan	1961-62	80	Australia v. Pakistan	1956-57
Lahore	561	Pakistan v. N. Zealand	1955-56	104	Pakistan v. W. Indies	1958-59
Peshawar	245	India v. Pakistan	1954-55	182	Pakistan v. India	1954-55
Rawalpindi	318	Pakistan v. N. Zealand	1964-65	79	N. Zealand v. Pakistan	1964-65

HIGHEST INDIVIDUAL SCORE FOR EACH TEST MATCH CENTRE

Birmingham	285*	P. B. H. May: England v. West Indies	1957
Leeds	334	D. G. Bradman: Australia v. England	1930
Lord's	254	D. G. Bradman: Australia v. England	1930
Manchester	311	R. B. Simpson: Australia v. England	1964
Nottingham	278	D. C. S. Compton: England v. Pakistan	1954
Oval	364	L. Hutton: England v. Australia	1938
Sheffield	119	C. Hill: Australia v. England	1902
Adelaide	299*	D. G. Bradman: Australia v. South Africa	1931-32
Brisbane	226	D. G. Bradman: Australia v. South Africa	1931-32
Melbourne	307	R. M. Cowper: Australia v. England	1965-66
Sydney	287	R. E. Foster: England v. Australia	1903-04
Cape Town	209	R. G. Pollock: South Africa v. Australia	1966-67
Durban	243	E. Paynter: England v. South Africa	1938-39
Johannesburg	231	A. D. Nourse, Jnr.: South Africa v. Australia	1935-36
Port Elizabeth	167	A. L. Hassett: Australia v. South Africa	1949-50
Bridgetown	337	Hanif Mohammad: Pakistan v. West Indies	1957-58
Georgetown	209	C. A. Roach: West Indies v. England	1929-30
Kingston	365*	G. St. A. Sobers: West Indies v. Pakistan	1957-58
Port of Spain	207	E. D. Weekes: West Indies v. India	1952-53
Auckland	336*	W. R. Hammond: England v. New Zealand	1932-33
Christchurch	227	W. R. Hammond: England v. New Zealand	1932-33
Dunedin	123	E. D. Weekes: West Indies v. New Zealand	1955-56
Wellington	255*	D. J. McGlew: South Africa v. New Zealand	1952-53
Bombay	223	V. M. Mankad: India v. New Zealand	1955-56
Calcutta	256	R. B. Kanhai: West Indies v. India	1958-59
Hyderabad	223	P. R. Umrigar: India v. New Zealand	1955-56
Kanpur	198	G. St. A. Sobers: West Indies v. India	1958-59
Lucknow	124*	Nazar Mohammad: Pakistan v. India	1952-53
Madras	231	V. M. Mankad: India v. New Zealand	1955-56
New Delhi	230*	B. Sutcliffe: New Zealand v. India	1955-56
Bahawalpur	142	Hanif Mohammad: Pakistan v. India	1954-55
Dacca	165	G. Pullar: England v. Pakistan	1961-62
Karachi	205	E. R. Dexter: England v. Pakistan	1961-62
Lahore	217	R. B. Kanhai: West Indies v. Pakistan	1958-59
Peshawar	108	P. R. Umrigar: India v. Pakistan	1954-55
Rawalpindi	76	B. R. Taylor: New Zealand v. Pakistan	1964-65

BEST INNINGS BOWLING ANALYSIS FOR EACH TEST MATCH CENTRE

Birmingham	7-17	W. Rhodes: England v. Australia	1902
Leeds	8-59	C. Blythe: England v. South Africa	1907
Lord's	8-43	H. Verity: England v. Australia	1934
Manchester	10-53	J. C. Laker: England v. Australia	1956
Nottingham	8-107	B. J. T. Bosanquet: England v. Australia	1905
Oval	8-29	S. F. Barnes: England v. South Africa	1912
Sheffield	6-49	S. F. Barnes: England v. Australia	1902

Best Innings Bowling Analysis for each Test Match Centre—*Cont.*

Adelaide ...	8-43	A. E. Trott: Australia v. England	1894-95
Brisbane ...	7-60	K. R. Miller: Australia v. England ...	1946-47
Melbourne ...	9-121	A. A. Mailey: Australia v. England ...	1920-21
Sydney ...	8-35	G. A. Lohmann: England v. Australia ...	1886-87
Cape Town ...	8-11	J. Briggs: England v. South Africa ...	1888-89
Durban ...	8-69	H. J. Tayfield: South Africa v. England ...	1956-57
Johannesburg	9-28	G. A. Lohmann: England v. South Africa	1895-96
Port Elizabeth	8-7	G. A. Lohmann: England v. South Africa	1895-96
Bridgetown ...	8-38	L. R. Gibbs: West Indies v. India	1961-62
Georgetown ...	7-44	I. W. Johnson: Australia v. West Indies ...	1954-55
Kingston ...	7-34	T. E. Bailey: England v. West Indies ...	1953-54
Port of Spain	7-70	W. Voce: England v. West Indies	1929-30
Auckland ...	7-53	D. Atkinson: West Indies v. New Zealand	1955-56
Christchurch	7-75	F. S. Trueman: England v. New Zealand	1962-63
Dunedin ...	6-23	S. Ramadhin: West Indies v. New Zealand	1955-56
Wellington ...	7-76	F. E. Woolley: England v. New Zealand ...	1929-30
Bombay ...	7-157	B. S. Chandrasekhar: India v. West Indies	1966-67
Calcutta ...	7-49	Ghulam Ahmed: India v. Australia ...	1956-57
Hyderabad ...	7-128	S. P. Gupte: India v. Pakistan	1955-56
Kanpur ...	9-69	J. S. Patel: India v. Australia	1959-60
Lucknow ...	7-42	Fazal Mahmood: Pakistan v. India ...	1952-53
Madras ...	8-55	V. M. Mankad: India v. England	1951-52
New Delhi ...	8-52	V. M. Mankad: India v. Pakistan	1952-53
Bahawalpur ...	6-74	P. R. Umrigar: India v. Pakistan	1954-55
Dacca ...	6-21	Khan Mohammad: Pakistan v. New Zealand	1955-56
Karachi ...	7-80	Fazal Mahmood: Pakistan v. Australia ...	1956-57
Lahore ...	7-75	L. F. Kline: Australia v. Pakistan	1959-60
Peshawar ...	5-63	S. P. Gupte: India v. Pakistan	1954-55
Rawalpindi ...	4-5	Pervez Sajjad: Pakistan v. New Zealand ...	1964-65

TEAM RECORDS

HIGHEST INNINGS TOTALS

903-7d	England v. Australia (Oval)	1938
849	England v. West Indies (Kingston)	1929-30
790-3d	West Indies v. Pakistan (Kingston)	1957-58
758-8d	Australia v. West Indies (Kingston)	1954-55
729-6d	Australia v. England (Lord's)	1930
701	Australia v. England (Oval)	1934
695	Australia v. England (Oval)	1930
681-8d	West Indies v. England (Port of Spain)	1953-54
674	Australia v. India (Adelaide)	1947-48
668	Australia v. West Indies (Bridgetown)	1954-55
659-8d	Australia v. England (Sydney)	1946-47
658-8d	England v. Australia (Nottingham)	1938
657-8d	Pakistan v. West Indies (Bridgetown)	1957-58
656-8d	Australia v. England (Manchester)	1964

Highest Innings Totals—*Cont.*

654-5	England v. South Africa (Durban[2])	1938-39
650-6d	Australia v. West Indies (Bridgetown)	1964-65
645	Australia v. England (Brisbane[2])	1946-47
644-8d	West Indies v. India (New Delhi)	1958-59
636	England v. Australia (Sydney)	1928-29
631-8d	West Indies v. India (Kingston)	1961-62
631	West Indies v. India (New Delhi)	1948-49
629-6d	West Indies v. India (Bombay)	1948-49
627-9d	England v. Australia (Manchester)	1934
620	South Africa v. Australia (Johannesburg[3])	1966-67
619-6d	England v. West Indies (Nottingham)	1957
614-5d	West Indies v. India (Calcutta)	1958-59
611	England v. Australia (Manchester)	1964
608	England v. South Africa (Johannesburg[2])	1948-49
604	Australia v. England (Melbourne)	1936-37
601-8d	Australia v. England (Brisbane[2])	1954-55
600-9d	Australia v. West Indies (Port of Spain)	1954-55
600	Australia v. England (Melbourne)	1924-25
595	South Africa v. Australia (Adelaide)	1963-64
589	England v. Australia (Melbourne)	1911-12
586	Australia v. England (Sydney)	1894-95
584	Australia v. England (Leeds)	1934
583-4d	England v. West Indies (Birmingham)	1957
582	Australia v. England (Adelaide)	1920-21
582	West Indies v. India (Madras[1])	1948-49
581	Australia v. England (Sydney)	1920-21
579-9d	West Indies v. Pakistan (Bridgetown)	1957-58
578	Australia v. South Africa (Melbourne)	1910-11
577	England v. Australia (Sydney)	1903-04
576	England v. Australia (Oval)	1899
576	West Indies v. India (Kingston)	1952-53
575-8d	Australia v. India (Melbourne)	1947-48
573	Australia v. England (Adelaide)	1897-98
573	West Indies v. Australia (Bridgetown)	1964-65
571-8d	England v. India (Manchester)	1936
566	Australia v. England (Leeds)	1930
564	Australia v. England (Melbourne)	1936-37
563-8d	West Indies v. England (Bridgetown)	1959-60
562-7d	England v. New Zealand (Auckland)	1962-63
561	Pakistan v. New Zealand (Lahore[1])	1955-56
560-8d	England v. New Zealand (Christchurch)	1932-33
559-8d	England v. India (Kanpur)	1963-64
559-9d	England v. South Africa (Cape Town)	1938-39
558-6d	England v. Pakistan (Nottingham)	1954
558	Australia v. West Indies (Brisbane[1])	1930-31
558	West Indies v. England (Nottingham)	1950
558	England v. Australia (Melbourne)	1965-66
554-8d	England v. South Africa (Lord's)	1947
554	Australia v. South Africa (Melbourne)	1931-32
551	Australia v. England (Oval)	1884
551	England v. Australia (Sydney)	1897-98
551	England v. South Africa (Nottingham)	1947
550-4d	England v. India (Leeds)	1967
550	England v. New Zealand (Christchurch)	1950-51

Highest Innings Totals—*Cont.*

Note: The highest innings totals by New Zealand and India are:—

505	New Zealand v. South Africa (Cape Town)	1953-54
539-9d	India v. Pakistan (Madras[2])	1960-61

HIGHEST SECOND INNINGS TOTALS
(First innings in brackets)

657-8d	(106)	Pakistan v. West Indies (Bridgetown)	1957-58
654-5	(316)	England v. South Africa (Durban[2])	1938-39
620	(199)	South Africa v. Australia (Johannesburg[3]) ...	1966-67
583-4d	(186)	England v. West Indies (Birmingham)	1957
582	(354)	Australia v. England (Adelaide)	1920-21
581	(267)	Australia v. England (Sydney)	1920-21
578	(328)	Australia v. South Africa (Melbourne)	1910-11
564	(200-9d)	Australia v. England (Melbourne)	1936-37
554	(198)	Australia v. South Africa (Melbourne)	1931-32
551	(208)	England v. South Africa (Nottingham)	1947

LOWEST INNINGS TOTALS

26	New Zealand v. England (Auckland)	1954-55
30	South Africa v. England (Port Elizabeth)	1895-96
30	South Africa v. England (Birmingham)	1924
35	South Africa v. England (Cape Town)	1898-99
36	Australia v. England (Birmingham)	1902
36	South Africa v. Australia (Melbourne)	1931-32
42	Australia v. England (Sydney)	1887-88
42	New Zealand v. Australia (Wellington)	1945-46
43	South Africa v. England (Cape Town)	1888-89
44	Australia v. England (Oval)	1896
45	England v. Australia (Sydney)	1886-87
45	South Africa v. Australia (Melbourne)	1931-32
47	South Africa v. England (Cape Town)	1888-89
47	New Zealand v. England (Lord's)	1958
52	England v. Australia (Oval)	1948
53	England v. Australia (Lord's)	1888
53	Australia v. England (Lord's)	1896
54	New Zealand v. Australia (Wellington)	1945-46
58	South Africa v. England (Lord's)	1912
58	Australia v. England (Brisbane[2])	1936-37
58	India v. Australia (Brisbane[2])	1947-48
58	India v. England (Manchester)	1952
60	Australia v. England (Lord's)	1888

The lowest innings totals by the other countries are:

87	Pakistan v. England (Lord's)	1954
76	West Indies v. Pakistan (Dacca)	1958-59

The following innings closed at a low total:

32-7d	Australia v. England (Brisbane[2])	1950-51
35-8	Australia v. England (Manchester)	1953
48-8	New Zealand v. England (Christchurch)	1965-66
51-6d	West Indies v. England (Bridgetown)	1934-35

Lowest Innings Totals—*Cont.*

On the following occasions a country was dismissed for totals of less than 100 *in both innings of the match*:

42 & 82	Australia v. England (Sydney)	1887-88
53 & 62	England v. Australia (Lord's)	1888
81 & 70	Australia v. England (Manchester)	1888
47 & 43	South Africa v. England (Cape Town)	1888-89
97 & 83	South Africa v. England (Cape Town)	1891-92
65 & 72	England v. Australia (Sydney)	1894-95
93 & 30	South Africa v. England (Port Elizabeth)	1895-96
95 & 93	South Africa v. England (Oval)	1912
36 & 45	South Africa v. Australia (Melbourne)	1931-32
42 & 54	New Zealand v. Australia (Wellington)	1945-46
58 & 98	India v. Australia (Brisbane[2])	1947-48
58 & 82	India v. England (Manchester)	1952
89 & 86	West Indies v. England (Oval)	1957
47 & 74	New Zealand v. England (Lord's)	1958

HIGHEST FOURTH INNINGS TOTALS

TO WIN

		Venue	*Series*
404-3	Australia v. England	Leeds	1948
336-5	Australia v. South Africa	Durban[2]	1949-50
332-7	England v. Australia	Melbourne	1928-29
317-2	West Indies v. Pakistan	Georgetown	1957-58
315-6	Australia v. England	Adelaide	1901-02

TO DRAW

		Venue	*Series*	*Runs set in 4th innings*
654-5	England v. South Africa	Durban[2]	1938-39	696
423-7	South Africa v. England	Oval	1947	451
408-5	West Indies v. England	Kingston	1929-30	836
355-8	India v. West Indies	Bombay	1948-49	361
326-5	South Africa v. Australia	Sydney	1963-64	409
325-3	India v. West Indies	Calcutta	1948-49	431
310-7	England v. Australia	Melbourne	1946-47	551
308-4	England v. South Africa	Oval	1965	399

TO LOSE

		Venue	*Series*	*Losing Margin*
411	England v. Australia	Sydney	1924-25	193
376	India v. England	Manchester	1959	171
370	England v. Australia	Adelaide	1920-21	119
363	England v. Australia	Adelaide	1924-25	11
339	Australia v. South Africa	Adelaide	1910-11	38
336	Australia v. England	Adelaide	1928-29	12
335	Australia v. England	Nottingham	1930	93
335	South Africa v. New Zealand	Cape Town	1961-62	72
333	Australia v. England	Melbourne	1894-95	94
327	England v. West Indies	Georgetown	1929-30	289
323	England v. Australia	Melbourne	1936-37	365
316	England v. West Indies	Kingston	1953-54	140
313	England v. West Indies	Bridgetown	1953-54	181
304	South Africa v. England	Johannesburg[1]	1913-14	91

HIGHEST MATCH AGGREGATES

Aggregate Scores		*Year*	*Days Played*
1981 for 35 wkts	South Africa v. England (Durban[2])	1938-39	10*
1815 for 34 wkts	West Indies v. England (Kingston)	1929-30	9†
1753 for 40 wkts	Australia v. England (Adelaide)	1920-21	6
1723 for 31 wkts	England v. Australia (Leeds)	1948	5
1661 for 36 wkts	West Indies v. Australia (Bridgetown)	1954-55	6
1646 for 40 wkts	Australia v. South Africa (Adelaide)	1910-11	6
1640 for 25 wkts	West Indies v. Australia (Bridgetown)	1964-65	6
1619 for 40 wkts	Australia v. England (Melbourne)	1924-25	7
1611 for 40 wkts	Australia v. England (Sydney)	1924-25	7
1601 for 29 wkts	England v. Australia (Lord's)	1930	4
1562 for 37 wkts	Australia v. England (Melbourne)	1946-47	6
1554 for 35 wkts	Australia v. England (Melbourne)	1928-29	8
1541 for 35 wkts	Australia v. England (Sydney)	1903-04	6
1528 for 24 wkts	West Indies v. England (Port of Spain)	1953-54	6
1514 for 40 wkts	Australia v. England (Sydney)	1894-95	6
1502 for 29 wkts	Australia v. England (Adelaide)	1946-47	6

*No play on one day †No play on two days

LOWEST MATCH AGGREGATES

(*Completed Matches*)

Aggregate Scores		*Year*
234 for 29 wkts ...	Australia v. South Africa (Melbourne) ...	1931-32
291 for 40 wkts ...	England v. Australia (Lord's)	1888
295 for 28 wkts ...	New Zealand v. Australia (Wellington) ...	1945-46
309 for 29 wkts ...	West Indies v. England (Bridgetown)... ...	1934-35
323 for 30 wkts ...	England v. Australia (Manchester)	1888
363 for 40 wkts ...	England v. Australia (Oval)	1882
374 for 40 wkts ...	Australia v. England (Sydney)	1887-88
378 for 30 wkts ...	England v. South Africa (Oval)	1912
382 for 30 wkts ...	South Africa v. England (Cape Town) ...	1888-89
389 for 38 wkts ...	England v. Australia (Oval)	1890
390 for 30 wkts ...	England v. New Zealand (Lord's)	1958
392 for 40 wkts ...	England v. Australia (Oval)	1896

LARGEST MARGINS OF VICTORY

		Year
Inns and 579 runs	England v. Australia (Oval)	1938
Inns and 336 runs	West Indies v. India (Calcutta)	1958-59
Inns and 332 runs	Australia v. England (Brisbane[2])	1946-47
Inns and 259 runs	Australia v. South Africa (Port Elizabeth) ...	1949-50
Inns and 237 runs	England v. West Indies (Oval)	1957
Inns and 230 runs	England v. Australia (Adelaide)	1891-92
Inns and 226 runs	Australia v. India (Brisbane[2])	1947-48
Inns and 225 runs	England v. Australia (Melbourne)	1911-12
Inns and 217 runs	England v. Australia (Oval)	1886
Inns and 217 runs	Australia v. West Indies (Brisbane[1])	1930-31
Inns and 215 runs	England v. New Zealand (Auckland) ...	1962-63
Inns and 207 runs	England v. India (Manchester)	1952
Inns and 202 runs	England v. South Africa (Cape Town) ...	1888-89
Inns and 200 runs	Australia v. England (Melbourne)	1936-37

Largest Margins of Victory—*Cont.*

			Year
675 runs	...	England v. Australia (Brisbane[1])	1928-29
562 runs	...	Australia v. England (Oval)	1934
530 runs	...	Australia v. South Africa (Melbourne) ...	1910-11
409 runs	...	Australia v. England (Lord's)	1948
382 runs	...	Australia v. England (Adelaide)	1894-95
377 runs	...	Australia v. England (Sydney)	1920-21
365 runs	...	Australia v. England (Melbourne)	1936-37
338 runs	...	England v. Australia (Adelaide)	1932-33
326 runs	...	West Indies v. England (Lord's)	1950
322 runs	...	England v. Australia (Brisbane[2])	1936-37
312 runs	...	England v. South Africa (Cape Town) ...	1956-57
308 runs	...	Australia v. England (Melbourne)	1907-08
307 runs	...	Australia v. England (Sydney)	1924-25

RESULTS BY NARROW MARGINS

TIE

Australia v. West Indies (Brisbane[2]) 1960-61

WON BY ONE WICKET

England v. Australia (Oval)	1902
South Africa v. England (Johannesburg[1])	1905-06
England v. Australia (Melbourne)	1907-08
England v. South Africa (Cape Town)	1922-23
Australia v. West Indies (Melbourne)	1951-52

WON BY TWO WICKETS

England v. Australia (Oval)	1890
Australia v. England (Sydney)	1907-08
England v. South Africa (Durban[2])	1948-49
Australia v. West Indies (Melbourne)	1960-61
India v. Australia (Bombay)	1964-65

LESS THAN TWENTY RUNS

3	Australia v. England (Manchester)	1902
6	Australia v. England (Sydney)	1884-85
7	Australia v. England (Oval)	1882
10	England v. Australia (Sydney)	1894-95
11	Australia v. England (Adelaide)	1924-25
12	England v. Australia (Adelaide)	1928-29
13	England v. Australia (Sydney)	1886-87
17	South Africa v. England (Johannesburg[3])	1956-57
19	South Africa v. England (Johannesburg[1])	1909-10

England won the Durban[2] Test of the 1948-49 series by two wickets, scoring a leg-bye off the last possible ball of the match.

At Port of Spain in the 1934-35 series, West Indies took England's last second innings wicket with the fifth ball of the last possible over to win the match by 217 runs.

LONGEST MATCHES

10 days	South Africa v. England (Durban[2])	1938-39
9 days	West Indies v. England (Kingston)	1929-30
8 days	Australia v. England (Melbourne)	1928-29

MATCHES COMPLETED IN TWO DAYS

England (101 & 77) v. Australia (63 & 122) at The Oval	1882
England (53 & 62) v. Australia (116 & 60) at Lord's	1888
England (317) v. Australia (80 & 100) at The Oval	1888
England (172) v. Australia (81 & 70) at Manchester	1888
South Africa (84 & 129) v. England (148 & 67-2) at Port Elizabeth	1888-89
South Africa (47 & 43) v. England (292) at Cape Town	1888-89
England (100 & 95-8) v. Australia (92 & 102) at The Oval ...	1890
South Africa (93 & 30) v. England (185 & 226) at Port Elizabeth ...	1895-96
South Africa (115 & 117) v. England (265) at Cape Town	1895-96
England (176 & 14-0) v. South Africa (95 & 93) at The Oval ...	1912
Australia (448) v. South Africa (265 & 95) at Manchester	1912
England (112 & 147) v. Australia (232 & 30-0) at Nottingham ...	1921
Australia (328-8d) v. West Indies (99 & 107) at Melbourne ...	1930-31
South Africa (157 & 98) v. Australia (439) at Johannesburg[1] ...	1935-36
New Zealand (42 & 54) v. Australia (199-8d) at Wellington ...	1945-46

COMPLETE SIDE DISMISSED TWICE IN A DAY

England (65 & 72) v. Australia at Sydney on third day	1894-95
India (58 & 82) v. England at Manchester on third day	1952

MOST RUNS IN ONE DAY

(a) *BY ONE TEAM*

503-2	England v. South Africa	(Lord's)	1924	2nd day
494-6	Australia v. South Africa	(Sydney) ...	1910-11	1st day
475-2	Australia v. England	(Oval)	1934	1st day
471-8	England v. India	(Oval)	1936	1st day
458-3	Australia v. England	(Leeds)	1930	1st day
455-1	Australia v. England	(Leeds)	1934	2nd day

(b) *BY BOTH TEAMS*

588-6	England	(398-6)	v. India	(190-0)	Manchester	1936	2nd day
522-2	England	(503-2)	v. South Africa	(19-0)	Lord's	1924	2nd day
508-8	England	(221-2)	v. South Africa	(287-6)	Oval	1935	3rd day
496-4	England	(437-4)	v. Pakistan	(59-0)	Nottingham	1954	2nd day
473-4	England	(264-1)	v. South Africa	(209-3)	Oval	1929	3rd day
469-7	England	(366-3)	v. West Indies	(103-4)	Oval	1939	3rd day
464-11	Australia	(448)	v. South Africa	(16-1)	Manchester	1912	1st day

LEAST RUNS IN A FULL DAY'S PLAY

95	Australia (80) v. Pakistan (15-2) at Karachi	1956-57
104	Pakistan (104-5) v. Australia at Karachi	1959-60
106	England (92-2 to 198 out) v. Australia at Brisbane[2]	1958-59
112	Australia (138-6 to 187 out) v. Pakistan (63-1) at Karachi ...	1956-57
117	India (117-5) v. Australia at Madras[2]	1956-57
119	South Africa (7-0 to 126-2) v. Australia at Johannesburg[3] ...	1957-58
120	India (15-0 to 135-8) v. Australia at Calcutta	1956-57

BATSMEN'S MATCHES

(*Over* 60 *runs per wicket*)

Runs/Wkt	*Runs-Wkts*	*Match*	*Venue*	*Series*
109.3	(1093-10)	India v. New Zealand	New Delhi	1955-56
70.6	(1271-18)	England v. Australia	Manchester	1964
68.3	(1640-24)	West Indies v. Australia	Bridgetown	1964-65
66.9	(1406-21)	West Indies v. Pakistan	Kingston	1957-58
65.3	(1307-20)	England v. Australia	Manchester	1934
65.0	(1235-19)	India v. West Indies	Bombay	1948-49
64.7	(1036-16)	India v. New Zealand	Hyderabad	1955-56
63.6	(1528-24)	West Indies v. England	Port of Spain	1953-54
62.3	(1496-24)	England v. Australia	Nottingham	1938
62.0	(1116-18)	West Indies v. England	Bridgetown	1959-60
61.5	(1046-17)	India v. Pakistan	Madras[2]	1960-61

HIGHEST SCORES FOR EACH BATTING POSITION

No.					
1	364	L. Hutton	England v. Australia	Oval	1938
2	325	A. Sandham	England v. West Indies	Kingston	1929-30
3	365*	G. St. A. Sobers	West Indies v. Pakistan	Kingston	1957-58
4	307	R. M. Cowper	Australia v. England	Melbourne	1965-66
5	304	D. G. Bradman	Australia v. England	Leeds	1934
6	234	D. G. Bradman	Australia v. England	Sydney	1946-47
7	270	D. G. Bradman	Australia v. England	Melbourne	1936-37
8	209*	Imtiaz Ahmed	Pakistan v. New Zealand	Lahore[1]	1955-56
9	146	Asif Iqbal	Pakistan v. England	Oval	1967
10	117	W. W. Read	England v. Australia	Oval	1884
11	62*	A. E. E. Vogler	South Africa v. England	Cape Town	1905-06

MOST CENTURIES IN AN INNINGS

5	Australia v. West Indies at Kingston, 1954-55
4	England v. Australia at Nottingham, 1938
4	West Indies v. India at New Delhi, 1948-49

MOST CENTURIES IN A MATCH (BOTH TEAMS)

7	England (4) v. Australia (3) at Nottingham, 1938
7	West Indies (2) v. Australia (5) at Kingston, 1954-55

MOST CENTURIES IN A SERIES (ONE TEAM)

12	Australia v. West Indies	1954-55
11	England v. South Africa	1938-39
11	West Indies v. India	1948-49
11	Australia v. South Africa	1949-50

MOST CENTURIES IN A SERIES (BOTH TEAMS)

21	West Indies (9) v. Australia (12)	1954-55
17	Australia (9) v. England (8)	1928-29
17	South Africa (6) v. England (11)	1938-39
16	India (5) v. West Indies (11)	1948-49
15	Australia (10) v. England (5)	1946-47

TEAM UNCHANGED THROUGHOUT A COMPLETE SERIES

1881-82	4 Tests	England v. Australia in Australia
1884	3 Tests	Australia v. England in England
1884-85	5 Tests	England v. Australia in Australia
1893	3 Tests	Australia v. England in England
1905-06	5 Tests	South Africa v. England in South Africa
1964-65	3 Tests	Pakistan v. New Zealand in Pakistan

MOST PLAYERS ENGAGED BY ONE SIDE IN A SERIES

30 in 5 Tests	England v. Australia in England 1921
28 in 4 Tests	West Indies v. England in West Indies 1929-30
28 in 5 Tests	Australia v. England in Australia 1884-85
25 in 4 Tests	England v. West Indies in England 1950

South Africa used 20 players in the 3-match series of 1895-96 against England in South Africa.

MOST CONSECUTIVE WINS

8	Australia:	Sydney 1920-21 to Leeds 1921
7	England:	Melbourne 1884-85 to Sydney 1887-88
7	England:	Lord's 1928 to Adelaide 1928-29
6	England:	Oval 1888 to Oval 1890
6	England:	Leeds 1957 to Manchester 1958
6	West Indies:	Port of Spain 1961-62 to Manchester 1963

MOST CONSECUTIVE DEFEATS

8	South Africa:	Port Elizabeth 1888-89 to Cape Town 1898-99
8	England:	Sydney 1920-21 to Leeds 1921
7	Australia:	Melbourne 1884-85 to Sydney 1887-88
7	England:	Lord's 1950 to Adelaide 1950-51
6	South Africa:	Melbourne 1910-11 to Lord's 1912
6	New Zealand:	Johannesburg[2] 1953-54 to Lahore[1] 1955-56
6	India:	Nottingham 1959 to New Delhi 1959-60

MOST CONSECUTIVE MATCHES WITHOUT DEFEAT

25	Australia:	Wellington 1945-46 to Adelaide 1950-51
18	England:	Christchurch 1958-59 to Birmingham 1961
17	Australia:	Madras[2] 1956-57 to New Delhi 1959-60
16	Australia:	Sydney 1920-21 to Adelaide 1924-25
15	England:	Melbourne 1910-11 to Port Elizabeth 1913-14
13	India:	Port of Spain 1952-53 to Madras[2] 1955-56
12	England:	Oval 1938 to Oval 1946
12	Pakistan:	Manchester 1954 to Bridgetown 1957-58

MOST CONSECUTIVE MATCHES WITHOUT VICTORY

44	New Zealand:	Christchurch 1929-30 to Wellington 1955-56
28	South Africa:	Leeds 1935 to Port Elizabeth 1949-50
24	India:	Lord's 1932 to Kanpur 1951-52
22	Pakistan:	Lahore[1] 1958-59 to Christchurch 1964-65
22	New Zealand:	Auckland 1962-63 to date
16	South Africa:	Melbourne 1910-11 to Cape Town 1921-22
14	India:	Madras[2] 1956-57 to New Delhi 1959-60
13	India:	Madras[1] 1952-53 to Hyderabad 1955-56
12	South Africa:	Cape Town 1922-23 to Durban[2] 1927-28
12	England:	Leeds 1963 to Oval 1964

WINNING ALL FIVE TESTS IN A SERIES

1920-21	Australia v. England in Australia
1931-32	Australia v. South Africa in Australia
1959	England v. India in England
1961-62	West Indies v. India in West Indies

EACH BATSMAN REACHING DOUBLE FIGURES IN AN INNINGS

		Lowest Score
1894-95	England (475) v. Australia at Melbourne	11
1905-06	South Africa (385) v. England at Johannesburg[1]	10
1928-29	England (636) v. Australia at Sydney	11
1931-32	South Africa (358) v. Australia at Melbourne	10*
1947-48	Australia (575-9d) v. India at Melbourne	11
1952-53	India (397) v. Pakistan at Calcutta	11

NO BATSMAN ACHIEVING DOUBLE FIGURES IN A COMPLETED INNINGS

1924 South Africa (30—including 11 extras) v. England at Birmingham—the highest score being 7.

PLAYERS' RECORDS—BATTING

2000 RUNS IN TESTS

ENGLAND

				Opponents					
	M.	*I.*	*Runs*	*A*	*SA*	*WI*	*NZ*	*I*	*P*
W. R. Hammond	85	140	7249	2852	2188	639	1015	555	—
L. Hutton	79	138	6971	2428	1564	1661	777	522	19
K. F. Barrington ...	74	120	6348	1941	989	754	594	1355	715
M. C. Cowdrey ...	92	153	6346	1971	1021	1217	1034	653	450
D. C. S. Compton	78	131	5807	1842	2205	592	510	205	453
J. B. Hobbs ...	61	102	5410	3636	1562	212	—	—	—
H. Sutcliffe ...	54	84	4555	2741	1336	206	250	22	—
P. B. H. May ...	66	106	4537	1566	906	986	603	356	120
E. R. Dexter ...	60	98	4405	1261	585	866	477	467	749
T. W. Graveney ...	65	101	4033	738	234	1196	293	805	767
E. Hendren ...	51	83	3525	1740	876	909	—	—	—
F. E. Woolley ...	64	98	3283	1664	1354	—	235	30	—
M. Leyland ...	41	65	2764	1705	936	37	—	86	—
C. Washbrook ...	37	66	2569	996	938	255	234	146	—
W. J. Edrich ...	39	63	2440	1184	792	94	366	—	4
T. G. Evans ...	91	133	2439	783	511	625	142	315	63
L. E. G. Ames ...	47	72	2434	675	530	748	410	71	—
W. Rhodes ...	58	98	2325	1706	568	51	—	—	—
T. E. Bailey ...	61	91	2290	875	552	343	439	—	81
P. E. Richardson	34	56	2061	526	369	427	317	304	118

AUSTRALIA

				Opponents					
	M	*I*	*Runs*	*E*	*SA*	*WI*	*NZ*	*I*	*P*
D. G. Bradman ...	52	80	6996	5028	806	447	—	715	—
R. N. Harvey ...	79	137	6149	2416	1625	1054	—	775	279
R. B. Simpson ...	49	87	3837	1405	980	844	—	292	316
A. R. Morris ...	46	79	3533	2080	792	452	—	209	—
C. Hill	49	89	3412	2660	752	—	—	—	—
W. M. Lawry ...	40	73	3172	1639	792	368	—	284	89
V. T. Trumper ...	48	89	3164	2264	900	—	—	—	—
C. C. McDonald ...	47	83	3106	1043	786	880	—	223	174
A. L. Hassett ...	43	69	3073	1572	748	402	19	332	—
K. R. Miller ...	55	87	2958	1511	399	801	30	185	32
W. W. Armstrong	50	84	2863	2172	691	—	—	—	—
N. C. O'Neill ...	42	69	2779	1072	285	788	—	416	218
S. J. McCabe ...	39	62	2748	1922	621	205	—	—	—
W. Bardsley ...	41	66	2469	1487	982	—	—	—	—
W. M. Woodfull ...	35	54	2300	1684	421	195	—	—	—
P. J. Burge ...	42	68	2290	1179	331	229	—	457	94
S. E. Gregory ...	58	100	2282	2193	89	—	—	—	—
R. Benaud... ...	63	97	2201	767	684	462	—	144	144
C. G. Macartney ...	35	55	2131	1640	491	—	—	—	—
W. H. Ponsford ...	29	48	2122	1558	97	467	—	—	—

2000 Runs in Tests—*Cont.*

SOUTH AFRICA

	M	I	Runs	Opponents E	A	NZ
B. Mitchell ...	42	80	3471	2732	573	166
A. D. Nourse, Jnr.	34	62	2960	2037	923	—
H. W. Taylor ...	42	76	2936	2287	640	9
T. L. Goddard ...	38	73	2458	1193	1032	233
D. J. McGlew ...	34	64	2440	736	604	1100
J. H. B. Waite ...	50	86	2405	923	839	643
A. D. Nourse, Snr.	45	83	2234	1415	819	—
E. J. Barlow ...	26	50	2156	742	789	625
R. A. McLean ...	40	73	2120	1068	480	572

WEST INDIES

	M	I	Runs	Opponents E	A	NZ	I	P
G. St. A. Sobers ...	60	102	5514	2113	1013	81	1323	984
E. D. Weekes ...	48	81	4455	1313	714	478	1495	455
R. B. Kanhai ...	51	88	4150	1352	965	—	1260	573
F. M. M. Worrell...	51	87	3860	1979	918	233	730	—
C. L. Walcott ...	44	74	3798	1391	914	199	909	385
C. C. Hunte ...	44	78	3245	1005	927	—	670	643
G. A. Headley ...	22	40	2190	1852	336	—	2	—
J. B. Stollmeyer ...	32	56	2159	858	417	188	696	—

NEW ZEALAND

	M	I	Runs	Opponents E	SA	WI	I	P
J. R. Reid ...	58	108	3431	953	914	212	691	661
B. Sutcliffe ...	42	76	2727	1049	455	196	885	142

INDIA

	M	I	Runs	Opponents E	A	WI	NZ	P
P. R. Umrigar ...	59	94	3631	770	227	1372	351	911
V. L. Manjrekar ...	55	92	3209	1181	377	569	507	575
C. G. Borde ...	46	80	2634	746	316	871	371	330
P. Roy	43	79	2441	620	432	717	301	371
Vijay Hazare ...	30	52	2192	803	429	737	—	223
V. M. Mankad ...	44	72	2109	618	388	397	526	180

PAKISTAN

	M	I	Runs	Opponents E	A	WI	NZ	I
Hanif Mohammad	51	91	3812	993	548	736	565	970
Saeed Ahmed ...	35	68	2724	655	480	707	422	460
Imtiaz Ahmed ...	41	72	2079	488	131	423	284	753

BEST BATTING AVERAGES—Qualification 15 innings

	Tests	Inns	N.O.	Runs	H.S.	Avge.	100s	50s
D. G. Bradman (Australia) ...	52	80	10	6996	334	99.94	29	13
C. S. Dempster (New Zealand)...	10	15	4	723	136	65.72	2	5
S. G. Barnes (Australia)	13	19	2	1072	234	63.05	3	5
G. St. A. Sobers (West Indies) ...	60	102	13	5514	365*	61.95	17	21
G. A. Headley (West Indies) ...	22	40	4	2190	270*	60.83	10	5
H. Sutcliffe (England)	54	84	9	4555	194	60.73	16	23

Best Batting Averages—Qualification 15 innings—*Cont.*

	Tests	*Inns*	*N.O.*	*Runs*	*H.S.*	*Avge.*	*100s*	*50s*
K. F. Barrington (England) ...	74	120	14	6348	256	59.88	19	33
E. Paynter (England)	20	31	5	1540	243	59.23	4	7
E. D. Weekes (West Indies) ...	48	81	5	4455	207	58.61	15	19
K. S. Duleepsinhji (England) ...	12	19	2	995	173	58.52	3	5
W. R. Hammond (England) ...	85	140	16	7249	336*	58.45	22	24
R. G. Pollock (South Africa) ...	19	34	4	1739	209	57.96	6	8
J. B. Hobbs (England)	61	102	7	5410	211	56.94	15	28
A. C. Russell (England)	10	18	2	911	140	56.93	5	2
C. L. Walcott (West Indies) ...	44	74	7	3798	220	56.68	15	14
L. Hutton (England)	79	138	15	6971	364	56.67	19	33
E. Tyldesley (England)	14	20	2	990	122	55.00	3	6
A. D. Nourse, Jnr. (South Africa)	34	62	7	2960	231	53.81	9	14
A. Melville (South Africa) ...	11	19	2	894	189	52.58	4	3
C. F. Walters (England) ...	11	18	3	784	102	52.26	1	7
J. Ryder (Australia)	20	32	5	1394	201*	51.62	3	9
D. C. S. Compton (England) ...	78	131	15	5807	278	50.06	17	28

BATSMEN SCORING MOST CENTURIES

			Opponents						
	100s	*H.S.*	*E*	*A*	*SA*	*WI*	*NZ*	*I*	*P*
D. G. Bradman (Australia) ...	29	334	19	–	4	2	0	4	0
W. R. Hammond (England) ...	22	336*	–	9	6	1	4	2	0
R. N. Harvey (Australia) ...	21	205	6	–	8	3	0	4	0
K. F. Barrington (England) ...	19	256	–	5	2	2	3	3	4
L. Hutton (England)	19	364	–	5	4	5	3	2	0
M. C. Cowdrey (England) ...	18	182	–	4	3	4	2	3	2
D. C. S. Compton (England) ...	17	278	–	5	7	2	2	0	1
G. St. A. Sobers (West Indies) ...	17	365*	7	2	0	–	0	5	3
H. Sutcliffe (England)	16	194	–	8	6	0	2	0	0
J. B. Hobbs (England)	15	211	–	12	2	1	0	0	0
C. L. Walcott (West Indies) ...	15	220	4	5	0	–	1	4	1
E. D. Weekes (West Indies) ...	15	207	3	1	0	–	3	7	1
P. B. H. May (England)... ...	13	285*	–	3	3	3	3	1	0
Hanif Mohammad (Pakistan) ...	12	337	3	2	0	2	3	2	–
A. R. Morris (Australia)... ...	12	206	8	–	2	1	0	1	0
P. R. Umrigar (India)	12	223	3	0	0	3	1	–	5
A. L. Hassett (Australia) ...	10	198*	4	–	3	2	0	1	0
G. A. Headley (West Indies) ...	10	270*	8	2	0	–	0	0	0
R. B. Kanhai (West Indies) ...	10	256	2	4	0	–	0	3	1

Note: K. F. Barrington completed a unique record when he scored 142 against Pakistan at The Oval in 1967: he is the only player to have scored a hundred on each of England's six current Test Match grounds.

BATSMEN SCORING 50 FIFTIES

				Opponents			
	50s	*A*	*SA*	*WI*	*NZ*	*I*	*P*
K. F. Barrington (England)	52	17	8	5	4	12	6
L. Hutton (England) ...	52	19	11	11	7	4	–
M. C. Cowdrey (England)	51	15	10	10	9	5	2

HIGHEST AGGREGATES IN A SERIES

	Season	*M.*	*I.*	*N.O.*	*Runs*	*H.S.*	*Avge.*	*100s*	*50s*
D. G. Bradman (A v. E)	1930	5	7	0	974	334	139.14	4	–
W. R. Hammond (E v. A)	1928-29	5	9	1	905	251	113.12	4	–
R. N. Harvey (A v. SA)	1952-53	5	9	0	834	205	92.66	4	3
C. L. Walcott (WI v. A)	1954-55	5	10	0	827	155	82.70	5	2
G. St. A. Sobers (WI v. P)	1957-58	5	8	2	824	365*	137.33	3	3
D. G. Bradman (A v. E)	1936-37	5	9	0	810	270	90.00	3	1
D. G. Bradman (A v. SA)	1931-32	5	5	1	806	299*	201.50	4	–
E. D. Weekes (WI v. I)	1948-49	5	7	0	779	194	111.28	4	2
D. G. Bradman (A v. E)	1934	5	8	0	758	304	94.75	2	1
D. C. S. Compton (E v. SA)	1947	5	8	0	753	208	94.12	4	2
H. Sutcliffe (E v. A)	1924-25	5	9	0	734	176	81.55	4	2
G. A. Faulkner (SA v. A)	1910-11	5	10	0	732	204	73.20	2	5
G. St. A. Sobers (WI v. E)	1966	5	8	1	722	174	103.14	3	2
E. D. Weekes (WI v. I)	1952-53	5	8	1	716	207	102.28	3	2
D. G. Bradman (A v. I)	1947-48	5	6	2	715	201	178.75	4	1
G. St. A. Sobers (WI v. E)	1959-60	5	8	1	709	226	101.28	3	1
G. A. Headley (WI v. E)	1929-30	4	8	0	703	223	87.87	4	–
C. L. Walcott (WI v. E)	1953-54	5	10	2	698	220	87.25	3	3
A. R. Morris (A v. E)	1948	5	9	1	696	196	87.00	3	3
E. Hendren (E v. WI)	1929-30	4	8	2	693	205*	115.50	2	5
D. G. Bradman (A v. E)	1946-47	5	8	1	680	234	97.14	2	3
L. Hutton (E v. WI)	1953-54	5	8	1	677	205	96.71	2	3
J. B. Hobbs (E v. A)	1911-12	5	9	1	662	187	82.75	3	1
V. T. Trumper (A v. SA)	1910-11	5	9	2	661	214*	94.42	2	2
R. N. Harvey (A v. SA)	1949-50	5	8	3	660	178	132.00	4	1
E. Paynter (E v. SA)	1938-39	5	8	0	653	243	81.62	3	2
R. N. Harvey (A v. WI)	1954-55	5	7	1	650	204	108.33	3	1
Hanif Mohammad (P v. WI)	1957-58	5	9	0	628	337	69.77	1	3
C. C. Hunte (WI v. P)	1957-58	5	9	1	622	260	77.75	3	–
A. D. Nourse, Jnr. (SA v. E)	1947	5	9	0	621	149	69.00	2	5
B. Sutcliffe (NZ v. I)	1955-56	5	9	2	611	230*	87.28	2	1
W. R. Hammond (E v. SA)	1938-39	5	8	1	609	181	87.00	3	2
D. Lindsay (SA v. A)	1966-67	5	7	0	606	182	86.57	2	3
E. J. Barlow (SA v. A)	1963-64	5	10	2	603	201	75.37	3	1

HIGHEST INDIVIDUAL INNINGS

365*	G. St. A. Sobers: West Indies v. Pakistan (Kingston)	1957-58
364	L. Hutton: England v. Australia (Oval)	1938
337	Hanif Mohammad: Pakistan v. West Indies (Bridgetown) ...	1957-58
336*	W. R. Hammond: England v. New Zealand (Auckland) ...	1932-33
334	D. G. Bradman: Australia v. England (Leeds)	1930
325	A. Sandham: England v. West Indies (Kingston)	1929-30
311	R. B. Simpson: Australia v. England (Manchester)	1964
310*	J. H. Edrich: England v. New Zealand (Leeds)	1965
307	R. M. Cowper: Australia v. England (Melbourne)	1965-66
304	D. G. Bradman: Australia v. England (Leeds)	1934
299*	D. G. Bradman: Australia v. South Africa (Adelaide)... ...	1931-32
287	R. E. Foster: England v. Australia (Sydney)	1903-04
285*	P. B. H. May: England v. West Indies (Birmingham)... ...	1957
278	D. C. S. Compton: England v. Pakistan (Nottingham) ...	1954
270*	G. A. Headley: West Indies v. England (Kingston)	1934-35
270	D. G. Bradman: Australia v. England (Melbourne)	1936-37

Highest Individual Innings—*Cont.*

266 W. H. Ponsford: Australia v. England (Oval) 1934
261 F. M. M. Worrell: West Indies v. England (Nottingham) ... 1950
260 C. C. Hunte: West Indies v. Pakistan (Kingston) 1957-58
258 T. W. Graveney: England v. West Indies (Nottingham) ... 1957
256 R. B. Kanhai: West Indies v. India (Calcutta)... 1958-59
256 K. F. Barrington: England v. Australia (Manchester)... ... 1964
255* D. J. McGlew: South Africa v. New Zealand (Wellington) ... 1952-53
254 D. G. Bradman: Australia v. England (Lord's)... 1930
251 W. R. Hammond: England v. Australia (Sydney) 1928-29
246* G. Boycott: England v. India (Leeds) 1967
244 D. G. Bradman: Australia v. England (Oval) 1934
243 E. Paynter: England v. South Africa (Durban[2]) 1938-39
240 W. R. Hammond: England v. Australia (Lord's) 1938
237 F. M. M. Worrell: West Indies v. India (Kingston) 1952-53
236 E. A. B. Rowan: South Africa v. England (Leeds) 1951
234 D. G. Bradman: Australia v. England (Sydney) 1946-47
234 S. G. Barnes: Australia v. England (Sydney) 1946-47
232 D. G. Bradman: Australia v. England (Oval) 1930
232 S. J. McCabe: Australia v. England (Nottingham) 1938
231* W. R. Hammond: England v. Australia (Sydney) 1936-37
231 A. D. Nourse, Jnr.: South Africa v. Australia (Johannesburg[1]) 1935-36
231 V. M. Mankad: India v. New Zealand (Madras[2]) 1955-56
230* B. Sutcliffe: New Zealand v. India (New Delhi) 1955-56
227 W. R. Hammond: England v. New Zealand (Christchurch) ... 1932-33
226 D. G. Bradman: Australia v. South Africa (Brisbane[2]) ... 1931-32
226 G. St. A. Sobers: West Indies v. England (Bridgetown) ... 1959-60
225 R. B. Simpson: Australia v. England (Adelaide) 1965-66
223 G. A. Headley: West Indies v. England (Kingston) 1929-30
223 D. G. Bradman: Australia v. West Indies (Brisbane[1]) 1930-31
223 P. R. Umrigar: India v. New Zealand (Hyderabad) 1955-56
223 V. M. Mankad: India v. New Zealand (Bombay) 1955-56
220 C. L. Walcott: West Indies v. England (Bridgetown) 1953-54
219 W. J. Edrich: England v. South Africa (Durban[2]) 1938-39
219 D. Atkinson: West Indies v. Australia (Bridgetown) 1954-55
217 W. R. Hammond: England v. India (Oval) 1936
217 R. B. Kanhai: West Indies v. Pakistan (Lahore[1]) 1958-59
216* E. Paynter: England v. Australia (Nottingham) 1938
214* V. T. Trumper: Australia v. South Africa (Adelaide) 1910-11
212 D. G. Bradman: Australia v. England (Adelaide) 1936-37
211 W. L. Murdoch: Australia v. England (Oval) 1884
211 J. B. Hobbs: England v. South Africa (Lord's) 1924
210 W. M. Lawry: Australia v. West Indies (Bridgetown) 1964-65
209 C. A. Roach: West Indies v. England (Georgetown) 1929-30
209 Imtiaz Ahmed: Pakistan v. New Zealand (Lahore[1]) 1955-56
209 B. F. Butcher: West Indies v. England (Nottingham) 1966
209 R. G. Pollock: South Africa v. Australia (Cape Town) ... 1966-67
208 D. C. S. Compton: England v. South Africa (Lord's) 1947
208 A. D. Nourse, Jnr.: South Africa v. England (Nottingham) ... 1951
207 E. D. Weekes: West Indies v. India (Port of Spain) 1952-53
206* W. A. Brown: Australia v. England (Lord's) 1938
206 M. P. Donnelly: New Zealand v. England (Lord's) 1949
206 L. Hutton: England v. New Zealand (Oval) 1949
206 A. R. Morris: Australia v. England (Adelaide)... 1950-51
206 E. D. Weekes: West Indies v. England (Port of Spain) ... 1953-54

Highest Individual Innings—*Cont.*

205*	E. Hendren: England v. West Indies (Port of Spain)	1929-30
205*	J. Hardstaff, Jnr.: England v. India (Lord's)	1946
205	R. N. Harvey: Australia v. South Africa (Melbourne)... ...	1952-53
205	L. Hutton: England v. West Indies (Kingston)...	1953-54
205	E. R. Dexter: England v. Pakistan (Karachi)	1961-62
204	G. A. Faulkner: South Africa v. Australia (Melbourne) ...	1910-11
204	R. N. Harvey: Australia v. West Indies (Kingston)	1954-55
203*	Nawab of Pataudi, Jnr.: India v. England (New Delhi) ...	1963-64
203*	Hanif Mohammad: Pakistan v. New Zealand (Lahore[2]) ...	1964-65
203	H. L. Collins: Australia v. South Africa (Johannesburg[1]) ...	1921-22
202*	L. Hutton: England v. West Indies (Oval)	1950
201*	J. Ryder: Australia v. England (Adelaide)	1924-25
201	S. E. Gregory: Australia v. England (Sydney)	1894-95
201	D. G. Bradman: Australia v. India (Adelaide)...	1947-48
201	E. J. Barlow: South Africa v. Australia (Adelaide)	1963-64
201	R. B. Simpson: Australia v. West Indies (Bridgetown) ...	1964-65
201	S. M. Nurse: West Indies v. Australia (Bridgetown)	1964-65
200*	D. N. Sardesai: India v. New Zealand (Bombay)	1964-65
200	W. R. Hammond: England v. Australia (Melbourne)... ...	1928-29

A CENTURY ON DÉBUT

(*a*) *IN FIRST INNINGS*

Bannerman, C. ...	165*	Australia v. England (Melbourne) ...	1876-77
Foster, R. E. ...	287	England v. Australia (Sydney) ...	1903-04
Ganteaume, A. G....	112	West Indies v. England (Port of Spain)	1947-48
Grace, W. G. ...	152	England v. Australia (Oval)	1880
Graham, H. ...	107	Australia v. England (Lord's) ...	1893
Griffith, S. C. ...	140	England v. West Indies (Port of Spain)	1947-48
Gunn, G.	119	England v. Australia (Sydney) ...	1907-08
Hanumant Singh ...	105	India v. England (New Delhi) ...	1963-64
Hunte, C. C. ...	142	West Indies v. Pakistan (Bridgetown)	1957-58
Ibadulla, K. ...	166	Pakistan v. Australia (Karachi) ...	1964-65
Jackson, A. A. ...	164	Australia v. England (Adelaide) ...	1928-29
Kripal Singh, A.G.	100*	India v. New Zealand (Hyderabad)...	1955-56
May, P. B. H. ...	138	England v. South Africa (Leeds) ...	1951
Mills, J. W. E. ...	117	New Zealand v. England (Wellington)	1929-30
Milton, C. A. ...	104*	England v. New Zealand (Leeds) ...	1958
Pairaudeau, B. H....	115	West Indies v. India (Port of Spain)...	1952-53
Pataudi, Nawab of, Snr.	102	England v. Australia (Sydney) ...	1932-33
Ponsford, W. H. ...	110	Australia v. England (Sydney) ...	1924-25
Shodhan, D. H. ...	110	India v. Pakistan (Calcutta)	1952-53
Taylor, B. R. ...	105	New Zealand v. India (Calcutta) ...	1964-65
Valentine, B. H. ...	136	England v. India (Bombay[1])	1933-34
Walters, K. D. ...	155	Australia v. England (Brisbane[2]) ...	1965-66

(*b*) *IN SECOND INNINGS*

Amarnath, L. ...	118	India v. England (Bombay[1])	1933-34
Baig, A. A. ...	112	India v. England (Manchester) ...	1959
Burke, J. W. ...	101*	Australia v. England (Adelaide) ...	1950-51
Collins, H. L. ...	104	Australia v. England (Sydney) ...	1920-21
Duff, R. A. ...	104	Australia v. England (Melbourne) ...	1901-02

A Century on Début—*Cont.*

Gibb, P. A.	106	England v. South Africa (Johannesburg[1])	1938-39
Hartigan, R. J.	116	Australia v. England (Adelaide)	1907-08
Headley, G. A.	176	West Indies v. England (Bridgetown)	1929-30
Ranjitsinhji, K. S.	154*	England v. Australia (Manchester)	1896
Smith, O. G.	104	West Indies v. Australia (Kingston)	1954-55
Warner, P. F.	132*	England v. South Africa (Johannesburg[1])	1898-99

(*c*) *IN THE FIRST MATCH AGAINST A SPECIFIC COUNTRY*

(*having previously appeared in Test Cricket*)

Adhikari, H. R.	114*	India v. West Indies (New Delhi)	1948-49
Allen, G. O.	122	England v. New Zealand (Lord's)	1931
Ames, L. E. G.	137	England v. New Zealand (Lord's)	1931
Bakewell, A. H.	107	England v. West Indies (Oval)	1933
Bardsley, W.	132	Australia v. South Africa (Sydney)	1910-11
Barlow, E. J.	114	South Africa v. Australia (Brisbane[2])	1963-64
Barrington, K. F.	128	England v. West Indies (Bridgetown)	1959-60
Barrington, K. F.	139	England v. Pakistan (Lahore[2])	1961-62
Barrington, K. F.	126	England v. New Zealand (Auckland)	1962-63
Booth, B. C.	169	Australia v. South Africa (Brisbane[2])	1963-64
Boycott, G.	246*	England v. India (Leeds)	1967
Bradman, D. G.	226	Australia v. South Africa (Brisbane[2])	1931-32
Bradman, D. G.	185	Australia v. India (Brisbane[2])	1947-48
Braund, L. C.	104	England v. South Africa (Lord's)	1907
Burki, J.	138	Pakistan v. England (Lahore[2])	1961-62
Chipperfield, A. G.	109	Australia v. South Africa (Durban[2])	1935-36
Christiani, R. J.	107	West Indies v. India (New Delhi)	1948-49
Christy, J. A. J.	103	South Africa v. New Zealand (Christchurch)	1931-32
Compton, D. C. S.	102	England v. Australia (Nottingham)	1938
Compton, D. C. S.	120	England v. West Indies (Lord's)	1939
Compton, D. C. S.	163	England v. South Africa (Nottingham)	1947
Cowdrey, M. C.	154	England v. West Indies (Birmingham)	1957
Cowdrey, M. C.	159	England v. Pakistan (Birmingham)	1962
D'Oliveira, B. L.	109	England v. India (Leeds)	1967
Douglas, J. W. H. T.	119	England v. South Africa (Durban[1])	1913-14
Duleepsinhji, K. S.	173	England v. Australia (Lord's)	1930
Edrich, J. H.	120	England v. Australia (Lord's)	1964
Edrich, J. H.	310*	England v. New Zealand (Leeds)	1965
Gomez, G. E.	101	West Indies v. India (New Delhi)	1948-49
Graveney, T. W.	175	England v. India (Bombay)	1951-52
Guy, J. W.	102	New Zealand v. India (Hyderabad)	1955-56
Hanif Mohammad	337	Pakistan v. West Indies (Bridgetown)	1957-58
Hardstaff, J., Jnr.	114	England v. New Zealand (Lord's)	1937
Harvey, R. N.	112	Australia v. England (Leeds)	1948
Hassett, A. L.	112	Australia v. South Africa (Johannesburg[2])	1949-50
Hill, C.	142	Australia v. South Africa (Johannesburg[1])	1902-03

A Century on Début—*Cont.*

Hutton, L.	100	England v. Australia (Nottingham) ...	1938
Hutton, L.	196	England v. West Indies (Lord's) ...	1939
Kippax, A. P. ...	146	Australia v. West Indies (Adelaide) ...	1930-31
Knight, B. R. ...	125	England v. New Zealand (Auckland)	1962-63
Leyland, M. ...	137	England v. Australia (Melbourne) ...	1928-29
Loxton, S. J. E. ...	101	Australia v. South Africa (Johannesburg[2])	1949-50
McGlew, D. J. ...	255*	South Africa. v. New Zealand (Wellington)	1952-53
McMorris, E. D. A.	125	West Indies v. India (Kingston) ...	1961-62
Manjrekar, V. L.	118	India v. New Zealand (Hyderabad) ...	1955-56
Mitchell, B. ...	113	South Africa v. New Zealand (Christchurch)	1931-32
Murray, A. R. A. ...	109	South Africa v. New Zealand (Wellington)	1952-53
Murray, J. T. ...	112	England v. West Indies (Oval) ...	1966
Mushtaq Ali ...	106	India v. West Indies (Calcutta) ...	1948-49
O'Neill, N. C. ...	181	Australia v. West Indies (Brisbane[2]) ...	1960-61
Parfitt, P. H. ...	131*	England v. New Zealand (Auckland)	1962-63
Parks, J. M. ...	101*	England v. West Indies (Port of Spain)	1959-60
Pataudi, Nawab of, Jnr.	128*	India v. Australia (Madras[2])	1964-65
Paynter, E. ...	117 & 100	England v. South Africa (Johannesburg[1])	1938-39
Richardson, P. E. ...	117	England v. South Africa (Johannesburg[3])	1956-57
Richardson, P. E. ...	100	England v. New Zealand (Birmingham)	1958
Rigg, K. E. ...	127	Australia v. South Africa (Sydney) ...	1931-32
Robertson, J. D. ...	121	England v. New Zealand (Lord's) ...	1949
Saeed Ahmed ...	121	Pakistan v. India (Bombay)	1960-61
Sandham, A. ...	152	England v. West Indies (Bridgetown)	1929-30
Simpson, R. B. ...	153 & 115	Australia v. Pakistan (Karachi)...	1964-65
Simpson, R. T. ...	103	England v. New Zealand (Manchester)	1949
Smith, M. J. K. ...	100	England v. India (Manchester) ...	1959
Smith, O. G. ...	161	West Indies v. England (Birmingham)	1957
Sobers, G. St. A. ...	142*	West Indies v. India (Bombay) ...	1958-59
Spooner, R. H. ...	119	England v. South Africa (Lord's) ...	1912
Subba Row, R. ...	100	England v. West Indies (Georgetown)	1959-60
Subba Row, R. ...	112	England v. Australia (Birmingham) ...	1961
Sutcliffe, B.... ...	137*	New Zealand v. India (Hyderabad) ...	1955-56
Sutcliffe, H. ...	115	England v. Australia (Sydney) ...	1924-25
Sutcliffe, H. ...	117	England v. New Zealand (Oval) ...	1931
Tyldesley, E. ...	122	England v. West Indies (Lord's) ...	1928
Umrigar, P. R. ...	223	India v. New Zealand (Hyderabad) ...	1955-56
Vivian, H. G. ...	100	New Zealand v. South Africa (Wellington)	1931-32
Walcott, C. L. ...	152	West Indies v. India (New Delhi) ...	1948-49
Washbrook, C. ...	114	England v. West Indies (Lord's) ...	1950
Watkins, A. J. ...	138*	England v. India (New Delhi) ...	1951-52
Watson, W. ...	109	England v. Australia (Lord's) ...	1953
Watson, W. ...	116	England v. West Indies (Kingston) ...	1953-54
Weekes, E. D. ...	128	West Indies v. India (New Delhi) ...	1948-49
Weekes, E. D. ...	197	West Indies v. Pakistan (Bridgetown)	1957-58

A CENTURY IN EACH INNINGS OF A MATCH

136	130	W. Bardsley ...	Australia v. England (Oval)	1909
140	111	A. C. Russell ...	England v. South Africa (Durban[2]) ...	1922-23
176	127	H. Sutcliffe ...	England v. Australia (Melbourne) ...	1924-25
119*	177	W. R. Hammond	England v. Australia (Adelaide)	1928-29
104	109*	H. Sutcliffe ...	England v. South Africa (Oval)	1929
114	112	G. A. Headley ...	West Indies v. England (Georgetown) ...	1929-30
117	100	E. Paynter ...	England v. South Africa (Johannesburg[1])	1938-39
106	107	G. A. Headley ...	West Indies v. England (Lord's)	1939
147	103*	D. C. S. Compton	England v. Australia (Adelaide)	1946-47
122	124*	A. R. Morris ...	Australia v. England (Adelaide)	1946-47
189	104*	A. Melville ...	South Africa v. England (Nottingham) ...	1947
120	189*	B. Mitchell ...	South Africa v. England (Oval)	1947
132	127*	D. G. Bradman ...	Australia v. India (Melbourne)	1947-48
116	145	Vijay Hazare ...	India v. Australia (Adelaide)	1947-48
162	101	E. D. Weekes ...	West Indies v. India (Calcutta)	1948-49
118	101*	J. A. R. Moroney	Australia v. South Africa (Johannesburg[2])	1949-50
126	110	C. L. Walcott ...	West Indies v. Australia (Port of Spain)	1954-55
155	110	C. L. Walcott ...	West Indies v. Australia (Kingston) ...	1954-55
125	109*	G. St. A. Sobers ...	West Indies v. Pakistan (Georgetown) ...	1957-58
117	115	R. B. Kanhai ...	West Indies v. Australia (Adelaide) ...	1960-61
111	104	Hanif Mohammad	Pakistan v. England (Dacca)	1961-62
153	115	R. B. Simpson ...	Australia v. Pakistan (Karachi)	1964-65

CENTURIES IN MOST CONSECUTIVE INNINGS

FIVE

Weekes, E. D. ...	141	West Indies v. England (Kingston) ...	1947-48
	128	West Indies v. India (New Delhi) ...	1948-49
	194	West Indies v. India (Bombay) ...	1948-49
	162	West Indies v. India (Calcutta)... ...	1948-49
	101	West Indies v. India (Calcutta)... ...	1948-49

FOUR

Fingleton, J. H. ...	112	Australia v. South Africa (Cape Town)	1935-36
	108	Australia v. South Africa (Johannesburg[1])	1935-36
	118	Australia v. South Africa (Durban[2]) ...	1935-36
	100	Australia v. England (Brisbane[2]) ...	1936-37
Melville, A. ...	103	South Africa v. England (Durban[2]) ...	1938-39
	189	South Africa v. England (Nottingham)...	1947
	104*	South Africa v. England (Nottingham)...	1947
	117	South Africa v. England (Lord's) ...	1947

THREE

Bardsley, W. ...	136	Australia v. England (Oval)	1909
	130	Australia v. England (Oval)	1909
	132	Australia v. South Africa (Sydney) ...	1910-11
Bradman, D. G. ...	132	Australia v. India (Melbourne)... ...	1947-48
	127*	Australia v. India (Melbourne)... ...	1947-48
	201	Australia v. India (Adelaide)	1947-48
Compton, D. C. S.	163	England v. South Africa (Nottingham)...	1947
	208	England v. South Africa (Lord's) ...	1947
	115	England v. South Africa (Manchester)...	1947
Hazare, Vijay ...	122	India v. West Indies (Bombay)	1948-49
	164*	India v. England (New Delhi)	1951-52
	155	India v. England (Bombay)	1951-52
Headley, G. A. ...	270*	West Indies v. England (Kingston) ...	1934-35
	106	West Indies v. England (Lord's) ...	1939
	107	West Indies v. England (Lord's) ...	1939

Centuries in most Consecutive Innings—*Cont.*

Macartney, C. G.	133*	Australia v. England (Lord's)	1926
	151	Australia v. England (Leeds)	1926
	109	Australia v. England (Manchester) ...	1926
Morris, A. R. ...	155	Australia v. England (Melbourne) ...	1946-47
	122	Australia v. England (Adelaide) ...	1946-47
	124*	Australia v. England (Adelaide) ...	1946-47
Sobers, G. St. A. ...	365*	West Indies v. Pakistan (Kingston) ...	1957-58
	125	West Indies v. Pakistan (Georgetown) ...	1957-58
	109*	West Indies v. Pakistan (Georgetown) ...	1957-58
Sutcliffe, H. ...	115	England v. Australia (Sydney)	1924-25
	176	England v. Australia (Melbourne) ...	1924-25
	127	England v. Australia (Melbourne) ...	1924-25
Umrigar, P. R. ...	117	India v. Pakistan (Madras[2])	1960-61
	112	India v. Pakistan (New Delhi)	1960-61
	147*	India v. England (Kanpur)	1961-62
Weekes, E. D. ...	123	West Indies v. New Zealand (Dunedin)	1955-56
	103	West Indies v. New Zealand (Christchurch)	1955-56
	156	West Indies v. New Zealand (Wellington)	1955-56

CENTURY BEFORE LUNCH

ON FIRST DAY

V. T. Trumper ...	Australia v. England (Manchester)	1902
C. G. Macartney ...	Australia v. England (Leeds)	1926
D. G. Bradman ...	Australia v. England (Leeds)	1930

ON OTHER DAYS

K. S. Ranjitsinhji ...	England v. Australia (Manchester)	1896
C. Hill	Australia v. South Africa (Johannesburg[1]) ...	1902-03
J. B. Hobbs	England v. South Africa (Lord's)	1924
H. G. Owen-Smith ...	South Africa v. England (Leeds)	1929
W. R. Hammond ...	England v. New Zealand (Auckland) ...	1932-33
S. J. McCabe ...	Australia v. South Africa (Johannesburg[1]) ...	1935-36

FASTEST CENTURIES

70 min.	J. M. Gregory (119): Australia v. South Africa (Johannesburg[1]) ...	1921-22
75 min.	G. L. Jessop (104): England v. Australia (Oval)	1902
78 min.	R. Benaud (121): Australia v. West Indies (Kingston)	1954-55
80 min.	J. H. Sinclair (104): South Africa v. Australia (Cape Town) ...	1902-03
91 min.	J. Darling (160): Australia v. England (Sydney)	1897-98
91 min.	S. J. McCabe (189*): Australia v. South Africa (Johannesburg[1]) ...	1935-36
94 min.	V. T. Trumper (185*): Australia v. England (Sydney)	1903-04
95 min.	J. T. Brown (140): England v. Australia (Melbourne)	1894-95
95 min.	P. W. Sherwell (115): South Africa v. England (Lord's)	1907

FASTEST DOUBLE CENTURIES

214 min.	D. G. Bradman (334): Australia v. England (Leeds)	1930
223 min.	S. J. McCabe (232): Australia v. England (Nottingham)	1938
226 min.	V. T. Trumper (214*): Australia v. South Africa (Adelaide) ...	1910-11
234 min.	D. G. Bradman (254): Australia v. England (Lord's)	1930
240 min.	W. R. Hammond (336*): England v. New Zealand (Auckland) ...	1932-33
241 min.	S. E. Gregory (201): Australia v. England (Sydney)	1894-95
245 min.	D. C. S. Compton (278): England v. Pakistan (Nottingham) ...	1954

BATSMEN SCORING MAIDEN CENTURY IN A TEST MATCH

165*	†C. Bannerman: Australia v. England (Melbourne)	1876-77
153*	W. L. Murdoch: Australia v. England (Oval)	1880
147	P. S. McDonnell: Australia v. England (Sydney)	1881-82
102	H. J. H. Scott: Australia v. England (Oval)	1884
134*	H. Wood: England v. South Africa (Cape Town)	1891-92
107	†H. Graham: Australia v. England (Lord's)	1893
124	A. J. L. Hill: England v. South Africa (Cape Town) ...	1895-96
106	J. H. Sinclair: South Africa v. England (Cape Town) ...	1898-99
115	P. W. Sherwell: South Africa v. England (Lord's)	1907
116	†R. J. Hartigan: Australia v. England (Adelaide)	1907-08
129	H. G. Owen-Smith: South Africa v. England (Leeds) ...	1929
122	C. A. Roach: West Indies v. England (Bridgetown) ...	1929-30
140	†S. C. Griffith: England v. West Indies (Port of Spain) ...	1947-48
133	V. L. Manjrekar: India v. England (Leeds)	1952
122	C. C. Depeiza: West Indies v. Australia (Bridgetown) ...	1954-55
108	P. L. Winslow: South Africa v. England (Manchester) ...	1955
111	S. N. McGregor: New Zealand v. Pakistan (Lahore[1]) ...	1955-56
108	F. C. M. Alexander: West Indies v. Australia (Sydney) ...	1960-61
101	Nasim-ul-Ghani: Pakistan v. England (Lord's)	1962
105	†B. R. Taylor: New Zealand v. India (Calcutta)	1964-65

† on début in Test Cricket

MOST CONSECUTIVE FIFTIES

7 E. D. Weekes (West Indies): 141 (1947-48), 128, 194, 162, 101, 90, 56 (1948-49).
6 G. A. Headley (West Indies): 93, 53, 270* (1934-35), 106, 107, 51 (1939).
6 E. Hendren (England): 77, 205*, 56, 123, 61, 55 (1929-30).
6 A. Melville (South Africa): 67, 78, 103 (1938-39), 189, 104*, 117 (1947).
6 J. Ryder (Australia): 78*, 58, 56, 142 (1920-21), 201*, 88 (1924-25).
6 G. St. A. Sobers (West Indies): 52, 52, 80, 365*, 125, 109* (1957-58).
6 K. F. Barrington (England): 63, 132*, 101, 94, 126, 76 (1962-63).
6 E. R. Dexter (England): 85, 172 (1962), 70, 99, 93, 52 (1962-63).

FASTEST FIFTIES

61* in 34 min.	S. A. Durrani (61*): India v. England (Kanpur)	1963-64
	The exact time for reaching his fifty is not known. Durrani's innings was played in the dying minutes of a match certain to be drawn and against the bowling of batsman M. C. Cowdrey and wicket-keeper J. M. Parks.	
35 min.	J. H. Sinclair (104): South Africa v. Australia (Cape Town) ...	1902-03
35 min.	C. G. Macartney (56): Australia v. South Africa (Sydney) ...	1910-11
35 min.	J. W. Hitch (51*): England v. Australia (Oval)	1921
35 min.	J. M. Gregory (119): Australia v. South Africa (Johannesburg[1]) ...	1921-22
36 min.	J. J. Lyons (55): Australia v. England (Lord's)	1890
36 min.	J. Ryder (79): Australia v. England (Sydney)	1928-29
38 min.	J. T. Brown (140): England v. Australia (Melbourne)	1894-95
38 min.	R. Benaud (121): Australia v. West Indies (Kingston)	1954-55
40 min.	J. Darling (160): Australia v. England (Sydney)	1897-98
40 min.	V. T. Trumper(62): Australia v. England (Sheffield)	1902
42 min.	S. J. McCabe (189*): Australia v. South Africa (Johannesburg[1])...	1935-36
42 min.	T. G. Evans (73): England v. India (Nottingham)...	1959
43 min.	G. L. Jessop (104): England v. Australia (Oval)	1902
45 min.	V. T. Trumper (63): Australia v. South Africa (Johannesburg[1]) ...	1902-03
45 min.	G. L. Jessop (93): England v. South Africa (Lord's)	1907
45 min.	P. W. Sherwell (115): South Africa v. England (Lord's)	1907
45 min.	D. G. Bradman (152): Australia v. West Indies (Melbourne) ...	1930-31
45 min.	F. B. Smith (54*): New Zealand v. England (Leeds)	1949
45 min.	R. R. Lindwall (50): Australia v. England (Lord's)	1953

SLOWEST INDIVIDUAL INNINGS

Runs	Min.		
3	100	J. T. Murray (injured): England v. Australia (Sydney)	1962-63
8	120	T. E. Bailey: England v. South Africa (Leeds)	1955
10*	133	T. G. Evans: England v. Australia (Adelaide) ...	1946-47
18	194	W. R. Playle: New Zealand v. England (Leeds) ...	1958
20	195	Hanif Mohammad: Pakistan v. England (Lord's) ...	1954
21	210	P. G. Z. Harris: New Zealand v. Pakistan (Karachi) ...	1955-56
28*	250	J. W. Burke: Australia v. England (Brisbane[2])... ...	1958-59
31	266	K. D. Mackay: Australia v. England (Lord's)	1956
40	299	H. L. Collins: Australia v. England (Manchester) ...	1921
45	318	Shuja-ud-Din: Pakistan v. Australia (Lahore[2]) ...	1959-60
58	367	Ijaz Butt: Pakistan v. Australia (Karachi)	1959-60
68	455	T. E. Bailey: England v. Australia (Brisbane[2]) ...	1958-59
99	500	M. L. Jaisimha: India v. Pakistan (Kanpur)	1960-61
105	575	D. J. McGlew: South Africa v. Australia (Durban[2]) ...	1957-58
197*	682	F. M. M. Worrell: West Indies v. England (Bridgetown)	1959-60
337	999	Hanif Mohammad: Pakistan v. West Indies (Bridgetown)	1957-58

MOST CENTURIES IN A SERIES

FIVE:

C. L. Walcott ...	West Indies v. Australia	1954-55

FOUR:

H. Sutcliffe	England v. Australia	1924-25
W. R. Hammond ...	England v. Australia	1928-29
H. Sutcliffe	England v. South Africa	1929
G. A. Headley ...	West Indies v. England	1929-30
D. G. Bradman ...	Australia v. England	1930
D. G. Bradman ...	Australia v. South Africa	1931-32
D. C. S. Compton ...	England v. South Africa	1947
D. G. Bradman ...	Australia v. India	1947-48
E. D. Weekes ...	West Indies v. India	1948-49
R. N. Harvey ...	Australia v. South Africa	1949-50
R. N. Harvey ...	Australia v. South Africa	1952-53

YOUNGEST PLAYERS TO SCORE A CENTURY

Years	Days			
17	78	Mushtaq Mohammad	101	Pakistan v. India, New Delhi, 1960-61
18	251	Mushtaq Mohammad	100*	Pakistan v. England, Nottingham, 1962
19	121	H. G. Vivian ..	100	New Zealand v. S. Africa, Wellington, 1931-32
19	121	R. N. Harvey ..	153	Australia v. India, Melbourne, 1947-48
19	152	A. A. Jackson ..	164	Australia v. England, Adelaide, 1928-29
19	291	R. N. Harvey ..	112	Australia v. England, Leeds, 1948
19	318	R. G. Pollock ..	122	South Africa v. Australia, Sydney, 1963-64
19	332	R. G. Pollock ..	175	South Africa v. Australia, Melbourne, 1963-64
19	357	K. D. Walters ..	155	Australia v. England, Brisbane[2], 1965-66
20	14	K. D. Walters ..	115	Australia v. England, Melbourne, 1965-66
20	19	D. C. S. Compton ..	102	England v. Australia, Nottingham, 1938
20	58	Hanif Mohammad ..	142	Pakistan v. India, Bahawalpur, 1954-55
20	130	D. G. Bradman ..	112	Australia v. England, Melbourne, 1928-29
20	131	A. A. Baig	112	India v. England, Manchester, 1959
20	148	H. G. Owen-Smith ..	129	South Africa v. England, Leeds, 1929
20	154	Saeed Ahmed ..	150	Pakistan v. West Indies, Georgetown, 1957-58
20	230	G. A. Headley ..	176	West Indies v. England, Bridgetown, 1929-30

Youngest Players to Score a Century—*Cont.*

Years	*Days*	*Player*		
20	253	V. L. Manjrekar ..	133	India v. England, Leeds, 1952
20	317	C. Hill	188	Australia v. England, Melbourne, 1897-98
20	323	J. W. Hearne ..	114	England v. Australia, Melbourne, 1911-12
20	325	Hanif Mohammad ..	103	Pakistan v. New Zealand, Dacca, 1955-56
20	330	O. G. Smith	104	West Indies v. Australia, Kingston, 1954-55
20	351	R. G. Pollock ..	137	S. Africa v. England, Port Elizabeth, 1964-65

R. G. Pollock, South Africa, holds the unique record of scoring three Test centuries before his 21st birthday.

CENTURIES IN TEST CRICKET

ENGLAND (359)

Abel, R.	(2)	120	v. South Africa (Cape Town) ...	1888–89
		132*	v. Australia (Sydney)	1891–92
Allen, G. O. ...	(1)	122	v. New Zealand (Lord's) ...	1931
Ames, L. E. G. ...	(8)	105	v. West Indies (Port of Spain) ...	1929–30
		149	v. West Indies (Kingston) ...	1929–30
		137	v. New Zealand (Lord's) ...	1931
		103	v. New Zealand (Christchurch)	1932–33
		120	v. Australia (Lord's)	1934
		126	v. West Indies (Kingston) ...	1934–35
		148*	v. South Africa (Oval)	1935
		115	v. South Africa (Cape Town)	1938–39
Bailey, T. E. ...	(1)	134*	v. New Zealand (Christchurch)	1950–51
Bakewell, A. H. ...	(1)	107	v. West Indies (Oval) ...	1933
Barber, R. W. ...	(1)	185	v. Australia (Sydney)	1965–66
Barnes, W. ...	(1)	134	v. Australia (Adelaide) ...	1884–85
Barnett, C. J. ...	(2)	129	v. Australia (Adelaide) ...	1936–37
		126	v. Australia (Nottingham) ...	1938
Barrington, K. F.	(19)	128	v. West Indies (Bridgetown) ...	1959–60
		121	v. West Indies (Port of Spain) ...	1959–60
		139	v. Pakistan (Lahore[2])	1961–62
		151*	v. India (Bombay)	1961–62
		172	v. India (Kanpur)	1961–62
		113*	v. India (New Delhi)	1961–62
		132*	v. Australia (Adelaide) ...	1962–63
		101	v. Australia (Sydney)	1962-63
		126	v. New Zealand (Auckland) ...	1962-63
		256	v. Australia (Manchester) ...	1964
		148*	v. South Africa (Durban[2]) ...	1964-65
		121	v. South Africa (Johannesburg[3])	1964-65
		137	v. New Zealand (Birmingham)	1965
		163	v. New Zealand (Leeds) ...	1965
		102	v. Australia (Adelaide) ...	1965-66
		115	v. Australia (Melbourne) ...	1965-66
		148	v. Pakistan (Lord's)	1967
		109*	v. Pakistan (Nottingham) ...	1967
		142	v. Pakistan (Oval)	1967
Bowley, E. H. ...	(1)	109	v. New Zealand (Auckland) ...	1929-30
Boycott, G. ...	(3)	113	v. Australia (Oval)	1964
		117	v. South Africa (Port Elizabeth)	1964-65
		246*	v. India (Leeds)	1967

Centuries in Test Cricket—*Cont.*

Braund, L. C. ...	(3)	103*	v. Australia (Adelaide) ...	1901-02
		102	v. Australia (Sydney)	1903-04
		104	v. South Africa (Lord's) ...	1907
Briggs, J.	(1)	121	v. Australia (Melbourne) ...	1884-85
Brown, J. T. ...	(1)	140	v. Australia (Melbourne) ...	1894-95
Chapman, A. P. F.	(1)	121	v. Australia (Lord's)	1930
Compton, D. C. S.	(17)	102	v. Australia (Nottingham) ...	1938
		120	v. West Indies (Lord's) ...	1939
		147 103*	v. Australia (Adelaide) ...	1946-47
		163	v. South Africa (Nottingham) ...	1947
		208	v. South Africa (Lord's) ...	1947
		115	v. South Africa (Manchester) ...	1947
		113	v. South Africa (Oval)	1947
		184	v. Australia (Nottingham) ...	1948
		145*	v. Australia (Manchester) ...	1948
		114	v. South Africa (Johannesburg[2])	1948-49
		114	v. New Zealand (Leeds) ...	1949
		116	v. New Zealand (Lord's) ...	1949
		112	v. South Africa (Nottingham) ...	1951
		133	v. West Indies (Port of Spain)	1953-54
		278	v. Pakistan (Nottingham) ...	1954
		158	v. South Africa (Manchester) ...	1955
Cowdrey, M. C. ...	(18)	102	v. Australia (Melbourne) ...	1954-55
		101	v. South Africa (Cape Town) ...	1956-57
		154	v. West Indies (Birmingham) ...	1957
		152	v. West Indies (Lord's)... ...	1957
		100*	v. Australia (Sydney)	1958-59
		160	v. India (Leeds)	1959
		114	v. West Indies (Kingston) ...	1959-60
		119	v. West Indies (Port of Spain)	1959-60
		155	v. South Africa (Oval)	1960
		159	v. Pakistan (Birmingham) ...	1962
		182	v. Pakistan (Oval)	1962
		113	v. Australia (Melbourne) ...	1962-63
		128*	v. New Zealand (Wellington) ...	1962-63
		107	v. India (Calcutta)	1963-64
		151	v. India (New Delhi)	1963-64
		119	v. New Zealand (Lord's) ...	1965
		105	v. South Africa (Nottingham) ...	1965
		104	v. Australia (Melbourne) ...	1965-66
Denton, D. ...	(1)	104	v. South Africa (Johannesburg[1])	1909-10
Dexter, E. R. ...	(9)	141	v. New Zealand (Christchurch)	1958-59
		136*	v. West Indies (Bridgetown) ...	1959-60
		110	v. West Indies (Georgetown) ...	1959-60
		180	v. Australia (Birmingham) ...	1961
		126*	v. India (Kanpur)	1961-62
		205	v. Pakistan (Karachi)	1961-62
		172	v. Pakistan (Oval)	1962
		174	v. Australia (Manchester) ...	1964
		172	v. South Africa (Johannesburg[3])	1964-65
D'Oliveira, B. L. ...	(1)	109	v. India (Leeds)	1967
Douglas, J. W. H. T.	(1)	119	v. South Africa (Durban[1]) ...	1913-14
Duleepsinhji, K. S.	(3)	117	v. New Zealand (Auckland) ...	1929-30

Centuries in Test Cricket—*Cont.*

Duleepsinhji, K. S. (*cont.*)		173	v. Australia (Lord's)	1930
		109	v. New Zealand (Oval)... ...	1931
Edrich, J. H. ...	(4)	120	v. Australia (Lord's)	1964
		310*	v. New Zealand (Leeds) ...	1965
		109	v. Australia (Melbourne) ...	1965-66
		103	v. Australia (Sydney)	1965-66
Edrich, W. J. ...	(6)	219	v. South Africa (Durban[2]) ...	1938-39
		119	v. Australia (Sydney)	1946-47
		189	v. South Africa (Lord's) ...	1947
		191	v. South Africa (Manchester) ...	1947
		111	v. Australia (Leeds)	1948
		100	v. New Zealand (Oval)... ...	1949
Evans, T. G. ...	(2)	104	v. West Indies (Manchester) ...	1950
		104	v. India (Lord's)	1952
Fane, F. L. ...	(1)	143	v. South Africa (Johannesburg[1])	1905-06
Foster, R. E. ...	(1)	287	v. Australia (Sydney)	1903-04
Fry, C. B.	(2)	144	v. Australia (Oval)	1905
		129	v. South Africa (Oval)	1907
Gibb, P. A. ...	(2)	106	v. South Africa (Johannesburg[1])	1938-39
		120	v. South Africa (Durban[2]) ...	1938-39
Grace, W. G. ...	(2)	152	v. Australia (Oval)	1880
		170	v. Australia (Oval)	1886
Graveney, T. W. ...	(9)	175	v. India (Bombay)	1951-52
		111	v. Australia (Sydney)	1954-55
		258	v. West Indies (Nottingham) ...	1957
		164	v. West Indies (Oval) ...	1957
		153	v. Pakistan (Lord's)	1962
		114	v. Pakistan (Nottingham) ...	1962
		109	v. West Indies (Nottingham) ...	1966
		165	v. West Indies (Oval)	1966
		151	v. India (Lord's)	1967
Griffith, S. C. ...	(1)	140	v. West Indies (Port of Spain)...	1947-48
Gunn, G.	(2)	119	v. Australia (Sydney)	1907-08
		122*	v. Australia (Sydney)	1907-08
Gunn, W.	(1)	102*	v. Australia (Manchester) ...	1893
Hammond, W. R.	(22)	251	v. Australia (Sydney)	1928-29
		200	v. Australia (Melbourne) ...	1928-29
		119* / 177	v. Australia (Adelaide) ...	1928-29
		138*	v. South Africa (Birmingham)...	1929
		101*	v. South Africa (Oval)	1929
		113	v. Australia (Leeds)	1930
		136*	v. South Africa (Durban[2]) ...	1930-31
		100*	v. New Zealand (Oval)... ...	1931
		112	v. Australia (Sydney)	1932-33
		101	v. Australia (Sydney)	1932-33
		227	v. New Zealand (Christchurch)	1932-33
		336*	v. New Zealand (Auckland) ...	1932-33
		167	v. India (Manchester)	1936
		217	v. India (Oval)	1936
		231*	v. Australia (Sydney)	1936-37
		140	v. New Zealand (Lord's) ...	1937
		240	v. Australia (Lord's)	1938
		181	v. South Africa (Cape Town) ...	1938-39

Centuries in Test Cricket—*Cont.*

Hammond, W. R. (*cont.*)		120	v. South Africa (Durban[2]) ...	1938-39
		140	v. South Africa (Durban[2]) ...	1938-39
		138	v. West Indies (Oval)	1939
Hardstaff, J., Jnr....	(4)	114	v. New Zealand (Lord's) ...	1937
		103	v. New Zealand (Oval)... ...	1937
		169*	v. Australia (Oval)	1938
		205*	v. India (Lord's)	1946
Hayward, T. W. ...	(3)	122	v. South Africa (Johannesburg[1])	1895-96
		130	v. Australia (Manchester) ...	1899
		137	v. Australia (Oval)	1899
Hearne, J. W. ...	(1)	114	v. Australia (Melbourne) ...	1911-12
Hendren, E. ...	(7)	132	v. South Africa (Leeds) ...	1924
		142	v. South Africa (Oval)	1924
		127*	v. Australia (Lord's)	1926
		169	v. Australia (Brisbane[1])... ...	1928-29
		205*	v. West Indies (Port of Spain) ...	1929-30
		123	v. West Indies (Georgetown) ...	1929-30
		132	v. Australia (Manchester) ...	1934
Hill, A. J. L. ...	(1)	124	v. South Africa (Cape Town) ...	1895-96
Hobbs, J. B. ...	(15)	187	v. South Africa (Cape Town) ...	1909-10
		126*	v. Australia (Melbourne) ...	1911-12
		187	v. Australia (Adelaide)	1911-12
		178	v. Australia (Melbourne) ...	1911-12
		107	v. Australia (Lord's)	1912
		122	v. Australia (Melbourne) ...	1920-21
		123	v. Australia (Adelaide)	1920-21
		211	v. South Africa (Lord's) ...	1924
		115	v. Australia (Sydney)	1924-25
		154	v. Australia (Melbourne) ...	1924-25
		119	v. Australia (Adelaide)... ...	1924-25
		119	v. Australia (Lord's)	1926
		100	v. Australia (Oval)	1926
		159	v. West Indies (Oval)	1928
		142	v. Australia (Melbourne) ...	1928-29
Hutchings, K. L. ...	(1)	126	v. Australia (Melbourne) ...	1907-08
Hutton, L.... ...	(19)	100	v. New Zealand (Manchester)...	1937
		100	v. Australia (Nottingham) ...	1938
		364	v. Australia (Oval)	1938
		196	v. West Indies (Lord's)... ...	1939
		165*	v. West Indies (Oval)	1939
		122*	v. Australia (Sydney)	1946-47
		100	v. South Africa (Leeds) ...	1947
		158	v. South Africa (Johannesburg[2])	1948-49
		123	v. South Africa (Johannesburg[2])	1948-49
		101	v. New Zealand (Leeds) ...	1949
		206	v. New Zealand (Oval) ...	1949
		202*	v. West Indies (Oval)	1950
		156*	v. Australia (Adelaide) ...	1950-51
		100	v. South Africa (Leeds) ...	1951
		150	v. India (Lord's)	1952
		104	v. India (Manchester)	1952
		145	v. Australia (Lord's)	1953
		169	v. West Indies (Georgetown) ...	1953-54
		205	v. West Indies (Kingston) ...	1953-54

Centuries in Test Cricket—*Cont.*

Insole, D. J. ...	(1)	110*	v. South Africa (Durban[2]) ...	1956-57
Jackson, F. S. ...	(5)	103	v. Australia (Oval)	1893
		118	v. Australia (Oval)	1899
		128	v. Australia (Manchester) ...	1902
		144*	v. Australia (Leeds)	1905
		113	v. Australia (Manchester) ...	1905
Jardine, D. R. ...	(1)	127	v. West Indies (Manchester) ...	1933
Jessop, G. L. ...	(1)	104	v. Australia (Oval)	1902
Knight, B. R. ...	(2)	125	v. New Zealand (Auckland) ...	1962-63
		127	v. India (Kanpur)	1963-64
Legge, G. B. ...	(1)	196	v. New Zealand (Auckland) ...	1929-30
Leyland, M. ...	(9)	137	v. Australia (Melbourne) ...	1928-29
		102	v. South Africa (Lord's) ...	1929
		109	v. Australia (Lord's)	1934
		153	v. Australia (Manchester) ...	1934
		110	v. Australia (Oval)	1934
		161	v. South Africa (Oval)	1935
		126	v. Australia (Brisbane[2]) ...	1936-37
		111*	v. Australia (Melbourne) ...	1936-37
		187	v. Australia (Oval)	1938
MacLaren, A. C.	(5)	120	v. Australia (Melbourne) ...	1894-95
		109	v. Australia (Sydney)	1897-98
		124	v. Australia (Adelaide) ...	1897-98
		116	v. Australia (Sydney)	1901-02
		140	v. Australia (Nottingham) ...	1905
Makepeace, H. ...	(1)	117	v. Australia (Melbourne) ...	1920-21
Mann, F. G. ...	(1)	136*	v. South Africa (Port Elizabeth)	1948-49
May, P. B. H. ...	(13)	138	v. South Africa (Leeds) ...	1951
		135	v. West Indies (Port of Spain)...	1953-54
		104	v. Australia (Sydney)	1954-55
		112	v. South Africa (Lord's) ...	1955
		117	v. South Africa (Manchester) ...	1955
		101	v. Australia (Leeds)	1956
		285*	v. West Indies (Birmingham) ...	1957
		104	v. West Indies (Nottingham) ...	1957
		113*	v. New Zealand (Leeds) ...	1958
		101	v. New Zealand (Manchester)...	1958
		113	v. Australia (Melbourne) ...	1958-59
		124*	v. New Zealand (Auckland) ...	1958-59
		106	v. India (Nottingham)	1959
Mead, C. P. ...	(4)	102	v. South Africa (Johannesburg[1])	1913-14
		117	v. South Africa (Port Elizabeth)	1913-14
		182*	v. Australia (Oval)	1921
		181	v. South Africa (Durban[2]) ...	1922-23
Milburn, C. ...	(1)	126*	v. West Indies (Lord's)... ...	1966
Milton, C. A. ...	(1)	104*	v. New Zealand (Leeds) ...	1958
Murray, J. T. ...	(1)	112	v. West Indies (Oval)	1966
Parfitt, P. H. ...	(7)	111	v. Pakistan (Karachi)	1961-62
		101*	v. Pakistan (Birmingham) ...	1962
		119	v. Pakistan (Leeds)	1962
		101*	v. Pakistan (Nottingham) ...	1962
		131*	v. New Zealand (Auckland) ...	1962-63
		121	v. India (Kanpur)	1963-64
		122*	v. South Africa (Johannesburg[3])	1964-65

Centuries in Test Cricket—*Cont.*

Parks, J. M. ...	(2)	101*	v. West Indies (Port of Spain)...	1959-60
		108*	v. South Africa (Durban[2]) ...	1964-65
Pataudi, Nawab of, Snr.	(1)	102	v. Australia (Sydney)	1932-33
Paynter, E. ...	(4)	216*	v. Australia (Nottingham) ...	1938
		117 / 100	v. South Africa (Johannesburg[1])	1938-39
		243	v. South Africa (Durban[2]) ...	1938-39
Place, W.	(1)	107	v. West Indies (Kingston) ...	1947-48
Pullar, G.	(4)	131	v. India (Manchester)	1959
		175	v. South Africa (Oval)	1960
		119	v. India (Kanpur)	1961-62
		165	v. Pakistan (Dacca)	1961-62
Ranjitsinhji, K. S.	(2)	154*	v. Australia (Manchester) ...	1896
		175	v. Australia (Sydney)	1897-98
Read, W. W. ...	(1)	117	v. Australia (Oval)	1884
Rhodes, W. ...	(2)	179	v. Australia (Melbourne) ...	1911-12
		152	v. South Africa (Johannesburg[1])	1913-14
Richardson, P. E....	(5)	104	v. Australia (Manchester) ...	1956
		117	v. South Africa (Johannesburg[3])	1956-57
		126	v. West Indies (Nottingham) ...	1957
		107	v. West Indies (Oval)	1957
		100	v. New Zealand (Birmingham)	1958
Robertson, J. D. ...	(2)	133	v. West Indies (Port of Spain)...	1947-48
		121	v. New Zealand (Lord's) ...	1949
Robins, R. W. V....	(1)	108	v. South Africa (Manchester) ...	1935
Russell, A. C. ...	(5)	135*	v. Australia (Adelaide) ...	1920-21
		101	v. Australia (Manchester) ...	1921
		102*	v. Australia (Oval)	1921
		140 / 111	v. South Africa (Durban[2]) ...	1922-23
Sandham, A. ...	(2)	152	v. West Indies (Bridgetown) ...	1929-30
		325	v. West Indies (Kingston) ...	1929-30
Sharp, J.	(1)	105	v. Australia (Oval)	1909
Sheppard, D. S. ...	(3)	119	v. India (Oval)	1952
		113	v. Australia (Manchester) ...	1956
		113	v. Australia (Melbourne) ...	1962-63
Shrewsbury, A. ...	(3)	105*	v. Australia (Melbourne) ...	1884-85
		164	v. Australia (Lord's)	1886
		106	v. Australia (Lord's)	1893
Simpson, R. T. ...	(4)	103	v. New Zealand (Manchester)...	1949
		156*	v. Australia (Melbourne) ...	1950-51
		137	v. South Africa (Nottingham)	1951
		101	v. Pakistan (Nottingham) ...	1954
Smith, M. J. K. ...	(3)	100	v. India (Manchester)	1959
		108	v. West Indies (Port of Spain)...	1959-60
		121	v. South Africa (Cape Town) ...	1964-65
Spooner, R. H. ...	(1)	119	v. South Africa (Lord's) ...	1912
Steel, A. G. ...	(2)	135*	v. Australia (Sydney)	1882-83
		148	v. Australia (Lord's)	1884
Stoddart, A. E. ...	(2)	134	v. Australia (Adelaide) ...	1891-92
		173	v. Australia (Melbourne) ...	1894-95
Subba Row, R. ...	(3)	100	v. West Indies (Georgetown) ...	1959-60
		112	v. Australia (Birmingham) ...	1961
		137	v. Australia (Oval)	1961

Centuries in Test Cricket—*Cont.*

Sutcliffe, H. ...	(16)	122	v. South Africa (Lord's) ...	1924
		115	v. Australia (Sydney)	1924-25
		176 127	v. Australia (Melbourne) ...	1924-25
		143	v. Australia (Melbourne) ...	1924-25
		161	v. Australia (Oval)	1926
		102	v. South Africa (Johannesburg[1])	1927-28
		135	v. Australia (Melbourne) ...	1928-29
		114	v. South Africa (Birmingham)...	1929
		100	v. South Africa (Lord's) ...	1929
		104 109*	v. South Africa (Oval)	1929
		161	v. Australia (Oval)	1930
		117	v. New Zealand (Oval) ...	1931
		109*	v. New Zealand (Manchester)...	1931
		194	v. Australia (Sydney)	1932-33
Tate, M. W. ...	(1)	100*	v. South Africa (Lord's) ...	1929
Tyldesley, E. ...	(3)	122	v. South Africa (Johannesburg[1])	1927-28
		100	v. South Africa (Durban[2]) ...	1927-28
		122	v. West Indies (Lord's)...	1928
Tyldesley, J. T. ...	(4)	112	v. South Africa (Cape Town) ...	1898-99
		138	v. Australia (Birmingham) ...	1902
		100	v. Australia (Leeds)	1905
		112*	v. Australia (Oval)	1905
Ulyett, G.	(1)	149	v. Australia (Melbourne) ...	1881-82
Valentine, B. H. ...	(2)	136	v. India (Bombay[1])	1933-34
		112	v. South Africa (Cape Town) ...	1938-39
Walters, C. F. ...	(1)	102	v. India (Madras[1])	1933-34
Ward, A.	(1)	117	v. Australia (Sydney)	1894-95
Warner, P. F. ...	(1)	132*	v. South Africa (Johannesburg[1])	1898-99
Washbrook, C. ...	(6)	112	v. Australia (Melbourne) ...	1946-47
		143	v. Australia (Leeds)	1948
		195	v. South Africa (Johannesburg[2])	1948-49
		103*	v. New Zealand (Leeds) ...	1949
		114	v. West Indies (Lord's)... ...	1950
		102	v. West Indies (Nottingham) ...	1950
Watkins, A. J. ...	(2)	111	v. South Africa (Johannesburg[2])	1948-49
		138*	v. India (New Delhi)	1951-52
Watson, W. ...	(2)	109	v. Australia (Lord's)	1953
		116	v. West Indies (Kingston) ...	1953-54
Wood, H.	(1)	134*	v. South Africa (Cape Town) ...	1891-92
Woolley, F. E. ...	(5)	133*	v. Australia (Sydney)	1911-12
		115*	v. South Africa (Johannesburg[1])	1922-23
		134*	v. South Africa (Lord's) ...	1924
		123	v. Australia (Sydney)	1924-25
		154	v. South Africa (Manchester) ...	1929
Worthington, T. S.	(1)	128	v. India (Oval)	1936
Wyatt, R. E. S. ...	(2)	113	v. South Africa (Manchester) ...	1929
		149	v. South Africa (Nottingham)	1935

AUSTRALIA (*252*)

Archer, R. G. ...	(1)	128	v. West Indies (Kingston) ...	1954-55
Armstrong, W. W.	(6)	159*	v. South Africa (Johannesburg[1])	1902-03
		133*	v. England (Melbourne) ...	1907-08

Centuries in Test Cricket—*Cont.*

Player		Score	Opponent (Ground)	Season
Armstrong, W. W. (*cont.*)		132	v. South Africa (Melbourne) ...	1910-11
		158	v. England (Sydney)	1920-21
		121	v. England (Adelaide)	1920-21
		123*	v. England (Melbourne) ...	1920-21
Badcock, C. L. ...	(1)	118	v. England (Melbourne) ...	1936-37
Bannerman, C. ...	(1)	165*	v. England (Melbourne) ...	1876-77
Bardsley, W. ...	(6)	136 130	v. England (Oval)	1909
		132	v. South Africa (Sydney) ...	1910-11
		121	v. South Africa (Manchester) ...	1912
		164	v. South Africa (Lord's) ...	1912
		193*	v. England (Lord's)	1926
Barnes, S. G. ...	(3)	234	v. England (Sydney)	1946-47
		112	v. India (Adelaide)	1947-48
		141	v. England (Lord's)	1948
Benaud, R. ...	(3)	121	v. West Indies (Kingston) ...	1954-55
		122	v. South Africa (Johannesburg[3])	1957-58
		100	v. South Africa (Johannesburg[3])	1957-58
Bonnor, G. J. ...	(1)	128	v. England (Sydney)	1884-85
Booth, B. C. ...	(5)	112	v. England (Brisbane[2])	1962-63
		103	v. England (Melbourne) ...	1962-63
		169	v. South Africa (Brisbane[2]) ...	1963-64
		102*	v. South Africa (Sydney) ...	1963-64
		117	v. West Indies (Port of Spain) ...	1964-65
Bradman, D. G. ...	(29)	112	v. England (Melbourne) ...	1928-29
		123	v. England (Melbourne) ...	1928-29
		131	v. England (Nottingham) ...	1930
		254	v. England (Lord's)	1930
		334	v. England (Leeds)	1930
		232	v. England (Oval)	1930
		223	v. West Indies (Brisbane[1]) ...	1930-31
		152	v. West Indies (Melbourne) ...	1930-31
		226	v. South Africa (Brisbane[2]) ...	1931-32
		112	v. South Africa (Sydney) ...	1931-32
		167	v. South Africa (Melbourne) ...	1931-32
		299*	v. South Africa (Adelaide) ...	1931-32
		103*	v. England (Melbourne) ...	1932-33
		304	v. England (Leeds)	1934
		244	v. England (Oval)	1934
		270	v. England (Melbourne) ...	1936-37
		212	v. England (Adelaide)	1936-37
		169	v. England (Melbourne) ...	1936-37
		144*	v. England (Nottingham) ...	1938
		102*	v. England (Lord's)	1938
		103	v. England (Leeds)	1938
		187	v. England (Brisbane[2])	1946-47
		234	v. England (Sydney)	1946-47
		185	v. India (Brisbane[2])	1947-48
		132 127*	v. India (Melbourne)	1947-48
		201	v. India (Adelaide)	1947-48
		138	v. England (Nottingham) ...	1948
		173*	v. England (Leeds)	1948
Brown, W. A. ...	(4)	105	v. England (Lord's)	1934

Centuries in Test Cricket—*Cont.*

Brown, W. A. (*cont.*)		121	v. South Africa (Cape Town) ...	1935-36
		133	v. England (Nottingham) ...	1938
		206*	v. England (Lord's)	1938
Burge, P. J. ...	(4)	181	v. England (Oval)	1961
		103	v. England (Sydney)	1962-63
		160	v. England (Leeds)	1964
		120	v. England (Melbourne) ...	1965-66
Burke, J. W. ...	(3)	101*	v. England (Adelaide)	1950-51
		161	v. India (Bombay)	1956-57
		189	v. South Africa (Cape Town) ...	1957-58
Chipperfield, A. G.	(1)	109	v. South Africa (Durban[2]) ...	1935-36
Collins, H. L. ...	(4)	104	v. England (Sydney)	1920-21
		162	v. England (Adelaide)	1920-21
		203	v. South Africa (Johannesburg[1])	1921-22
		114	v. England (Sydney)	1924-25
Cowper, R. M. ...	(3)	143	v. West Indies (Port of Spain)...	1964-65
		102	v. West Indies (Bridgetown) ...	1964-65
		307	v. England (Melbourne) ...	1965-66
Darling, J.... ...	(3)	101	v. England (Sydney)	1897-98
		178	v. England (Adelaide)	1897-98
		160	v. England (Sydney)	1897-98
Duff, R. A. ...	(2)	104	v. England (Melbourne) ...	1901-02
		146	v. England (Oval)	1905
Favell, L. E. ...	(1)	101	v. India (Madras[2])	1959-60
Fingleton, J. H. ...	(5)	112	v. South Africa (Cape Town) ...	1935-36
		108	v. South Africa (Johannesburg[1])	1935-36
		118	v. South Africa (Durban[2]) ...	1935-36
		100	v. England (Brisbane[2])	1936-37
		136	v. England (Melbourne) ...	1936-37
Giffen, G.	(1)	161	v. England (Sydney)	1894-95
Graham, H. ...	(2)	107	v. England (Lord's)	1893
		105	v. England (Sydney)	1894-95
Gregory, J. M. ...	(2)	100	v. England (Melbourne) ...	1920-21
		119	v. South Africa (Johannesburg[1])	1921-22
Gregory, S. E. ...	(4)	201	v. England (Sydney)	1894-95
		103	v. England (Lord's)	1896
		117	v. England (Oval)	1899
		112	v. England (Adelaide)	1903-04
Hartigan, R. J. ...	(1)	116	v. England (Adelaide)	1907-08
Harvey, R. N. ...	(21)	153	v. India (Melbourne)	1947-48
		112	v. England (Leeds)	1948
		178	v. South Africa (Cape Town)...	1949-50
		151*	v. South Africa (Durban[2]) ...	1949-50
		100	v. South Africa (Johannesburg[2])	1949-50
		116	v. South Africa (Port Elizabeth)	1949-50
		109	v. South Africa (Brisbane[2]) ...	1952-53
		190	v. South Africa (Sydney) ...	1952-53
		116	v. South Africa (Adelaide) ...	1952-53
		205	v. South Africa (Melbourne) ...	1952-53
		122	v. England (Manchester) ...	1953
		162	v. England (Brisbane[2])... ...	1954-55
		133	v. West Indies (Kingston) ...	1954-55
		133	v. West Indies (Port of Spain)...	1954-55
		204	v. West Indies (Kingston) ...	1954-55

Centuries in Test Cricket—*Cont.*

Harvey, R. N. (*cont.*)		140	v. India (Bombay)	1956-57
		167	v. England (Melbourne) ...	1958-59
		114	v. India (New Delhi)	1959-60
		102	v. India (Bombay)	1959-60
		114	v. England (Birmingham) ...	1961
		154	v. England (Adelaide)	1962-63
Hassett, A. L. ...	(10)	128	v. England (Brisbane²) ...	1946-47
		198*	v. India (Adelaide)	1947-48
		137	v. England (Nottingham) ...	1948
		112	v. South Africa (Johannesburg²)	1949-50
		167	v. South Africa (Port Elizabeth)	1949-50
		132	v. West Indies (Sydney) ...	1951-52
		102	v. West Indies (Melbourne) ...	1951-52
		163	v. South Africa (Adelaide) ...	1952-53
		115	v. England (Nottingham) ...	1953
		104	v. England (Lord's)	1953
Hendry, H. L. ...	(1)	112	v. England (Sydney)	1928-29
Hill, C.	(7)	188	v. England (Melbourne) ...	1897-98
		135	v. England (Lord's)	1899
		119	v. England (Sheffield)	1902
		142	v. South Africa (Johannesburg¹)	1902-03
		160	v. England (Adelaide)	1907-08
		191	v. South Africa (Sydney) ...	1910-11
		100	v. South Africa (Melbourne) ...	1910-11
Horan, T.	(1)	124	v. England (Melbourne) ...	1881-82
Iredale, F. A. ...	(2)	140	v. England (Adelaide)	1894-95
		108	v. England (Manchester) ...	1896
Jackson, A. A. ...	(1)	164	v. England (Adelaide)	1928-29
Kelleway, C. E. ...	(3)	114	v. South Africa (Manchester) ...	1912
		102	v. South Africa (Lord's) ...	1912
		147	v. England (Adelaide)	1920-21
Kippax, A. F. ...	(2)	100	v. England (Melbourne) ...	1928-29
		146	v. West Indies (Adelaide) ...	1930-31
Lawry, W. M. ...	(8)	130	v. England (Lord's)	1961
		102	v. England (Manchester) ...	1961
		157	v. South Africa (Melbourne) ...	1963-64
		106	v. England (Manchester) ...	1964
		210	v. West Indies (Bridgetown) ...	1964-65
		166	v. England (Brisbane²) ...	1965-66
		119	v. England (Adelaide)	1965-66
		108	v. England (Melbourne) ...	1965-66
Lindwall, R. R. ...	(2)	100	v. England (Melbourne) ...	1946-47
		118	v. West Indies (Bridgetown) ...	1954-55
Loxton, S. J. E. ...	(1)	101	v. South Africa (Johannesburg²)	1949-50
Lyons, J. J. ...	(1)	134	v. England (Sydney)	1891-92
McCabe, S. J. ...	(6)	187*	v. England (Sydney)	1932-33
		137	v. England (Manchester) ...	1934
		149	v. South Africa (Durban²) ...	1935-36
		189*	v. South Africa (Johannesburg¹)	1935-36
		112	v. England (Melbourne) ...	1936-37
		232	v. England (Nottingham) ...	1938
Macartney, C. G.	(7)	137	v. South Africa (Sydney) ...	1910-11
		170	v. England (Sydney)	1920-21
		115	v. England (Leeds)	1921

Centuries in Test Cricket—*Cont.*

Macartney, C. G. (*cont.*)		116	v. South Africa (Durban[1]) ...	1921-22
		133*	v. England (Lord's)	1926
		151	v. England (Leeds)	1926
		109	v. England (Manchester) ...	1926
McCool, C. L. ...	(1)	104*	v. England (Melbourne) ...	1946-47
McDonald, C. C.	(5)	154	v. South Africa (Adelaide) ...	1952-53
		110	v. West Indies (Port of Spain)...	1954-55
		127	v. West Indies (Kingston) ...	1954-55
		170	v. England (Adelaide)	1958-59
		133	v. England (Melbourne) ...	1958-59
McDonnell, P. S.	(3)	147	v. England (Sydney)	1881-82
		103	v. England (Oval)	1884
		124	v. England (Adelaide)	1884-85
McLeod, C. E. ...	(1)	112	v. England (Melbourne) ...	1897-98
Miller, K. R. ...	(7)	141*	v. England (Adelaide)	1946-47
		145*	v. England (Sydney)	1950-51
		129	v. West Indies (Sydney) ...	1951-52
		109	v. England (Lord's)	1953
		147	v. West Indies (Kingston) ...	1954-55
		137	v. West Indies (Bridgetown) ...	1954-55
		109	v. West Indies (Kingston) ...	1954-55
Moroney, J. A. R.	(2)	118 101*	v. South Africa (Johannesburg[2])	1949-50
Morris, A. R. ...	(12)	155	v. England (Melbourne) ...	1946-47
		122 124*	v. England (Adelaide)	1946-47
		100*	v. India (Melbourne)	1947-48
		105	v. England (Lord's)	1948
		182	v. England (Leeds)	1948
		196	v. England (Oval)	1948
		111	v. South Africa (Johannesburg[2])	1949-50
		157	v. South Africa (Port Elizabeth)	1949-50
		206	v. England (Adelaide)	1950-51
		153	v. England (Brisbane[2]) ...	1954-55
		111	v. West Indies (Port of Spain)...	1954-55
Murdoch, W. L. ...	(2)	153*	v. England (Oval)	1880
		211	v. England (Oval)	1884
Noble, M. A. ...	(1)	133	v. England (Sydney)	1903-04
O'Neill, N. C. ...	(6)	134	v. Pakistan (Lahore[2])	1959-60
		163	v. India (Bombay)	1959-60
		113	v. India (Calcutta)	1959-60
		181	v. West Indies (Brisbane[2]) ...	1960-61
		117	v. England (Oval)	1961
		100	v. England (Adelaide)	1962-63
Pellew, C. E. ...	(2)	116	v. England (Melbourne) ...	1920-21
		104	v. England (Adelaide)	1920-21
Ponsford, W. H. ...	(7)	110	v. England (Sydney)	1924-25
		128	v. England (Melbourne) ...	1924-25
		110	v. England (Oval)	1930
		183	v. West Indies (Sydney) ...	1930-31
		109	v. West Indies (Brisbane[1]) ...	1930-31
		181	v. England (Leeds)	1934
		266	v. England (Oval)	1934
Ransford, V. S. ...	(1)	143*	v. England (Lord's)	1909

Centuries in Test Cricket—*Cont.*

Richardson, A. J....	(1)	100	v. England (Leeds)	1926
Richardson, V. Y.	(1)	138	v. England (Melbourne) ...	1924-25
Rigg, K. E. ...	(1)	127	v. South Africa (Sydney) ...	1931-32
Ryder, J.	(3)	142	v. South Africa (Cape Town) ...	1921-22
		201*	v. England (Adelaide)	1924-25
		112	v. England (Melbourne) ...	1928-29
Scott, H. J. H. ...	(1)	102	v. England (Oval)	1884
Simpson, R. B. ...	(6)	311	v. England (Manchester) ...	1964
		153 / 115	v. Pakistan (Karachi)	1964-65
		201	v. West Indies (Bridgetown) ...	1964-65
		225	v. England (Adelaide)	1965-66
		153	v. South Africa (Cape Town) ...	1966-67
Stackpole, K. R. ...	(1)	134	v. South Africa (Cape Town) ...	1966-67
Taylor, J. M. ...	(1)	108	v. England (Sydney)	1924-25
Trott, G. H. S. ...	(1)	143	v. England (Lord's)	1896
Trumper, V. T. ...	(8)	135*	v. England (Lord's)	1899
		104	v. England (Manchester) ...	1902
		185*	v. England (Sydney)	1903-04
		113	v. England (Adelaide)	1903-04
		166	v. England (Sydney)	1907-08
		159	v. South Africa (Melbourne) ...	1910-11
		214*	v. South Africa (Adelaide) ...	1910-11
		113	v. England (Sydney)	1911-12
Walters, K. D. ...	(2)	155	v. England (Brisbane[2])	1965-66
		115	v. England (Melbourne) ...	1965-66
Woodfull, W. M. ...	(7)	141	v. England (Leeds)	1926
		117	v. England (Manchester) ...	1926
		111	v. England (Sydney)	1928-29
		107	v. England (Melbourne) ...	1928-29
		102	v. England (Melbourne) ...	1928-29
		155	v. England (Lord's)	1930
		161	v. South Africa (Melbourne) ...	1931-32

SOUTH AFRICA (*99*)

Balaskas, X. C. ...	(1)	122*	v. New Zealand (Wellington) ...	1931-32
Barlow, E. J. ...	(4)	114	v. Australia (Brisbane[2]) ...	1963-64
		109	v. Australia (Melbourne) ...	1963-64
		201	v. Australia (Adelaide) ...	1963-64
		138	v. England (Cape Town) ...	1964-65
Bland, K. C. ...	(3)	126	v. Australia (Sydney)	1963-64
		144*	v. England (Johannesburg[3]) ...	1964-65
		127	v. England (Oval)	1965
Catterall, R. H. ...	(3)	120	v. England (Birmingham) ...	1924
		120	v. England (Lord's)	1924
		119	v. England (Durban[2])	1927-28
Christy, J. A. J. ...	(1)	103	v. New Zealand (Christchurch)	1931-32
Dalton, E. L. ...	(2)	117	v. England (Oval)	1935
		102	v. England (Johannesburg[1]) ...	1938-39
Endean, W. R. ...	(3)	162*	v. Australia (Melbourne) ...	1952-53
		116	v. New Zealand (Auckland) ...	1952-53
		116*	v. England (Leeds)	1955
Faulkner, G. A. ...	(4)	123	v. England (Johannesburg[1]) ...	1909-10
		204	v. Australia (Melbourne) ...	1910-11

Centuries in Test Cricket—*Cont.*

Batsman	No.	Score	Opponents (Ground)	Season
Faulkner, G. A. (*cont.*)		115	v. Australia (Adelaide)	1910-11
		122*	v. Australia (Manchester)	1912
Frank, C. N.	(1)	152	v. Australia (Johannesburg[1])	1921-22
Goddard, T. L.	(1)	112	v. England (Johannesburg[3])	1964-65
Hathorn, M.	(1)	102	v. England (Johannesburg[1])	1905-06
Lindsay, D.	(3)	182	v. Australia (Johannesburg[3])	1966-67
		137	v. Australia (Durban[2])	1966-67
		131	v. Australia (Johannesburg[3])	1966-67
McGlew, D. J.	(7)	255*	v. New Zealand (Wellington)	1952 53
		104*	v. England (Manchester)	1955
		133	v. England (Leeds)	1955
		108	v. Australia (Johannesburg[3])	1957-58
		105	v. Australia (Durban[2])	1957-58
		127*	v. New Zealand (Durban[2])	1961-62
		120	v. New Zealand (Johannesburg[3])	1961-62
McLean, R. A.	(5)	101	v. New Zealand (Durban[2])	1953-54
		142	v. England (Lord's)	1955
		100	v. England (Durban[2])	1956-57
		109	v. England (Manchester)	1960
		113	v. New Zealand (Cape Town)	1961-62
Melville, A.	(4)	103	v. England (Durban[2])	1938-39
		189 104*	v. England (Nottingham)	1947
		117	v. England (Lord's)	1947
Mitchell, B.	(8)	123	v. England (Cape Town)	1930-31
		113	v. New Zealand (Christchurch)	1931-32
		164*	v. England (Lord's)	1935
		128	v. England (Oval)	1935
		109	v. England (Durban[2])	1938-39
		120 189*	v. England (Oval)	1947
		120	v. England (Cape Town)	1948-49
Murray, A. R. A.	(1)	109	v. New Zealand (Wellington)	1952-53
Nourse, A. D. Snr.	(1)	111	v. Australia (Johannesburg[1])	1921-22
Nourse, A. D., Jnr.	(9)	231	v. Australia (Johannesburg[1])	1935-36
		120	v. England (Cape Town)	1938-39
		103	v. England (Durban[2])	1938-39
		149	v. England (Nottingham)	1947
		115	v. England (Manchester)	1947
		112	v. England (Cape Town)	1948-49
		129*	v. England (Johannesburg[2])	1948-49
		114	v. Australia (Cape Town)	1949-50
		208	v. England (Nottingham)	1951
Owen-Smith, H. G.	(1)	129	v. England (Leeds)	1929
Pithey, A. J.	(1)	154	v. England (Cape Town)	1964-65
Pollock, R. G.	(6)	122	v. Australia (Sydney)	1963-64
		175	v. Australia (Adelaide)	1963-64
		137	v. England (Port Elizabeth)	1964-65
		125	v. England (Nottingham)	1965
		209	v. Australia (Cape Town)	1966-67
		105	v. Australia (Port Elizabeth)	1966-67
Rowan, E. A. B.	(3)	156*	v. England (Johannesburg[2])	1948-49
		143	v. Australia (Durban[2])	1949-50
		236	v. England (Leeds)	1951

Centuries in Test Cricket—*Cont.*

Sherwell, P. W. ...	(1)	115	v. England (Lord's)	1907
Siedle, I. J. ...	(1)	141	v. England (Cape Town) ...	1930-31
Sinclair, J. H. ...	(3)	106	v. England (Cape Town) ...	1898-99
		101	v. Australia (Johannesburg[1]) ...	1902-03
		104	v. Australia (Cape Town) ...	1902-03
Snooke, S. J. ...	(1)	103	v. Australia (Adelaide) ...	1910-11
Taylor, H. W. ...	(7)	109	v. England (Durban[1])	1913-14
		176	v. England (Johannesburg[1]) ...	1922-23
		101	v. England (Johannesburg[1]) ...	1922-23
		102	v. England (Durban[2])	1922-23
		101	v. England (Johannesburg[1]) ...	1927-28
		121	v. England (Oval)	1929
		117	v. England (Cape Town) ...	1930-31
Van der Byl, P. G.	(1)	125	v. England (Durban[2])	1938-39
Viljoen, K. G. ...	(2)	111	v. Australia (Melbourne) ...	1931-32
		124	v. England (Manchester) ...	1935
Wade, W. W. ...	(1)	125	v. England (Port Elizabeth) ...	1948-49
Waite, J. H. B. ...	(4)	113	v. England (Manchester) ...	1955
		115	v. Australia (Johannesburg[3]) ...	1957-58
		134	v. Australia (Durban[2]) ...	1957-58
		101	v. New Zealand (Johannesburg[3])	1961-62
White, G. C. ...	(2)	147	v. England (Johannesburg[1]) ...	1905-06
		118	v. England (Durban[1])	1909-10
Winslow, P. L. ...	(1)	108	v. England (Manchester) ...	1955
Zulch, J. W. ...	(2)	105	v. Australia (Adelaide) ...	1910-11
		150	v. Australia (Sydney)	1910-11

WEST INDIES (121)

Alexander, F. C. M.	(1)	108	v. Australia (Sydney)	1960-61
Atkinson, D. ...	(1)	219	v. Australia (Bridgetown) ...	1954-55
Barrow, I. ...	(1)	105	v. England (Manchester) ...	1933
Butcher, B. F. ...	(5)	103	v. India (Calcutta)	1958-59
		142	v. India (Madras[2])	1958-59
		133	v. England (Lord's)	1963
		117	v. Australia (Port of Spain) ...	1964-65
		209*	v. England (Nottingham) ...	1966
Carew, G. ...	(1)	107	v. England (Port of Spain) ...	1947-48
Christiani, R. J. ...	(1)	107	v. India (New Delhi)	1948-49
Depeiza, C. C. ...	(1)	122	v. Australia (Bridgetown) ...	1954-55
Ganteaume, A. G.	(1)	112	v. England (Port of Spain) ...	1947-48
Gomez, G. E. ...	(1)	101	v. India (New Delhi)	1948-49
Headley, G. A. ...	(10)	176	v. England (Bridgetown) ...	1929-30
		114 / 112	v. England (Georgetown) ...	1929-30
		223	v. England (Kingston)	1929-30
		102*	v. Australia (Brisbane[1])... ...	1930-31
		105	v. Australia (Sydney)	1930-31
		169*	v. England (Manchester) ...	1933
		270*	v. England (Kingston)	1934-35
		106 / 107	v. England (Lord's)	1939
Holford, D. A. J.	(1)	105*	v. England (Lord's)	1966
Holt, J. K. ...	(2)	166	v. England (Bridgetown) ...	1953-54
		123	v. India (New Delhi)	1958-59

Centuries in Test Cricket—*Cont.*

Hunte, C. C. ...	(8)	142	v. Pakistan (Bridgetown) ...	1957-58
		260	v. Pakistan (Kingston)	1957-58
		114	v. Pakistan (Georgetown) ...	1957-58
		110	v. Australia (Melbourne) ...	1960-61
		182	v. England (Manchester) ...	1963
		108*	v. England (Oval)	1963
		135	v. England (Manchester) ...	1966
		101	v. India (Bombay)	1966-67
Kanhai, R. B. ...	(10)	256	v. India (Calcutta)	1958-59
		217	v. Pakistan (Lahore[1])	1958-59
		110	v. England (Port of Spain) ...	1959-60
		117 } 115 }	v. Australia (Adelaide) ...	1960-61
		138	v. India (Kingston)	1961-62
		139	v. India (Port of Spain) ...	1961-62
		129	v. Australia (Bridgetown) ...	1964-65
		121	v. Australia (Port of Spain) ...	1964-65
		104	v. England (Oval)	1966
McMorris, E. D. A.	(1)	125	v. India (Kingston)	1961-62
Martin, F. R. ...	(1)	123*	v. Australia (Sydney)	1930-31
Nurse, S. M. ...	(2)	201	v. Australia (Bridgetown) ...	1964-65
		137	v. England (Leeds)	1966
Pairaudeau, B. H.	(1)	115	v. India (Port of Spain) ...	1952-53
Rae, A. F. ...	(4)	104	v. India (Bombay)	1948-49
		109	v. India (Madras[1])	1948-49
		106	v. England (Lord's)	1950
		109	v. England (Oval)	1950
Roach, C. A. ...	(2)	122	v. England (Bridgetown) ...	1929-30
		209	v. England (Georgetown) ...	1929-30
Smith, O. G. ...	(4)	104	v. Australia (Kingston) ...	1954-55
		161	v. England (Birmingham) ...	1957
		168	v. England (Nottingham) ...	1957
		100	v. India (New Delhi)	1958-59
Sobers, G. St. A. ...	(17)	365*	v. Pakistan (Kingston)	1957-58
		125 } 109* }	v. Pakistan (Georgetown) ...	1957-58
		142*	v. India (Bombay)	1958-59
		198	v. India (Kanpur)	1958-59
		106*	v. India (Calcutta)	1958-59
		226	v. England (Bridgetown) ...	1959-60
		147	v. England (Kingston)	1959-60
		145	v. England (Georgetown) ...	1959-60
		132	v. Australia (Brisbane[2]) ...	1960-61
		168	v. Australia (Sydney)	1960-61
		153	v. India (Kingston)	1961-62
		104	v. India (Kingston)	1961-62
		102	v. England (Leeds)	1963
		161	v. England (Manchester) ...	1966
		163*	v. England (Lord's)	1966
		174	v. England (Leeds)	1966
Solomon, J. S. ...	(1)	100*	v. India (New Delhi)	1958-59
Stollmeyer, J. B. ...	(4)	160	v. India (Madras[1])	1948-49
		104	v. Australia (Sydney)	1951-52
		152	v. New Zealand (Auckland) ...	1951-52

Centuries in Test Cricket—*Cont.*

Stollmeyer, J. B. (*cont.*)		104*	v. India (Port of Spain) ...	1952-53
Walcott, C. L. ...	(15)	152	v. India (New Delhi)	1948-49
		108	v. India (Calcutta)	1948-49
		168*	v. England (Lord's)	1950
		115	v. New Zealand (Auckland) ...	1951-52
		125	v. India (Georgetown)	1952-53
		118	v. India (Kingston)	1952-53
		220	v. England (Bridgetown) ...	1953-54
		124	v. England (Port of Spain) ...	1953-54
		116	v. England (Kingston)	1953-54
		108	v. Australia (Kingston) ...	1954-55
		126 110	v. Australia (Port of Spain) ...	1954-55
		155 110	v. Australia (Kingston) ...	1954-55
		145	v. Pakistan (Georgetown) ...	1957-58
Weekes, E. D. ...	(15)	141	v. England (Kingston)	1947-48
		128	v. India (New Delhi)	1948-49
		194	v. India (Bombay)	1948-49
		162 101	v. India (Calcutta)	1948-49
		129	v. England (Nottingham) ...	1950
		207	v. India (Port of Spain) ...	1952-53
		161	v. India (Port of Spain) ...	1952-53
		109	v. India (Kingston)	1952-53
		206	v. England (Port of Spain) ...	1953-54
		139	v. Australia (Port of Spain) ...	1954-55
		123	v. New Zealand (Dunedin) ...	1955-56
		103	v. New Zealand (Christchurch)	1955-56
		156	v. New Zealand (Wellington) ...	1955-56
		197	v. Pakistan (Bridgetown) ...	1957-58
Weekes, K. H. ...	(1)	137	v. England (Oval)	1939
Worrell, F. M. M.	(9)	131*	v. England (Georgetown) ...	1947-48
		261	v. England (Nottingham) ...	1950
		138	v. England (Oval)	1950
		108	v. Australia (Melbourne) ...	1951-52
		100	v. New Zealand (Auckland) ...	1951-52
		237	v. India (Kingston)	1952-53
		167	v. England (Port of Spain) ...	1953-54
		191*	v. England (Nottingham) ...	1957
		197*	v. England (Bridgetown) ...	1959-60

NEW ZEALAND (29)

Barton, P. T. ...	(1)	109	v. South Africa (Port Elizabeth)	1961-62
Congdon, B. E. ...	(1)	104	v. England (Christchurch) ...	1965-66
Dempster, C. S. ...	(2)	136	v. England (Wellington) ...	1929-30
		120	v. England (Lord's)	1931
Donnelly, M. P. ...	(1)	206	v. England (Lord's)	1949
Dowling, G. T. ...	(1)	129	v. India (Bombay)	1964-65
Guy, J. W. ...	(1)	102	v. India (Hyderabad)	1955-56
Hadlee, W. A. ...	(1)	116	v. England (Christchurch) ...	1946-47
Harris, P. G. Z. ...	(1)	101	v. South Africa (Cape Town) ...	1961-62
McGregor, S. N. ...	(1)	111	v. Pakistan (Lahore[1])	1955-56
Mills, J. W. E. ...	(1)	117	v. England (Wellington) ...	1929-30

Centuries in Test Cricket—*Cont.*

Page, M. L. ...	(1)	104	v. England (Lord's)	1931
Rabone, G. O. ...	(1)	107	v. South Africa (Durban[2]) ...	1953-54
Reid, J. R. ...	(6)	135	v. South Africa (Cape Town) ...	1953-54
		119*	v. India (New Delhi)	1955-56
		120	v. India (Calcutta)	1955-56
		142	v. South Africa (Johannesburg[3])	1961-62
		100	v. England (Christchurch) ...	1962-63
		128	v. Pakistan (Karachi)	1964-65
Sinclair, B. W. ...	(3)	138	v. South Africa (Auckland) ...	1963-64
		130	v. Pakistan (Lahore[2])	1964-65
		114	v. England (Auckland)	1965-66
Sutcliffe, B. ...	(5)	101	v. England (Manchester) ...	1949
		116	v. England (Christchurch) ...	1950-51
		137*	v. India (Hyderabad)	1955-56
		230*	v. India (New Delhi)	1955-56
		151*	v. India (Calcutta)	1964-65
Taylor, B. R. ...	(1)	105	v. India (Calcutta)	1964-65
Vivian, H. G. ...	(1)	100	v. South Africa (Wellington) ...	1931-32
INDIA (74)				
Adhikari, H. R. ...	(1)	114*	v. West Indies (New Delhi) ...	1948-49
Amarnath, L. ...	(1)	118	v. England (Bombay[1])	1933-34
Apte, M. L. ...	(1)	163*	v. West Indies (Port of Spain) ...	1952-53
Baig, A. A. ...	(1)	112	v. England (Manchester) ...	1959
Borde, C. G. ...	(5)	109	v. West Indies (New Delhi) ...	1958-59
		177*	v. Pakistan (Madras[2])	1960-61
		109	v. New Zealand (Bombay) ...	1964-65
		121	v. West Indies (Bombay) ...	1966-67
		125	v. West Indies (Madras[1]) ...	1966-67
Contractor, N. J.	(1)	108	v. Australia (Bombay)	1959-60
Durrani, S. A. ...	(1)	104	v. West Indies (Port of Spain)	1961-62
Engineer, F. M. ...	(1)	109	v. West Indies (Madras[1]) ...	1966-67
Hanumant Singh	(1)	105	v. England (New Delhi) ...	1963-64
Hazare, Vijay ...	(7)	116 } 145 }	v. Australia (Adelaide) ...	1947-48
		134*	v. West Indies (Bombay) ...	1948-49
		122	v. West Indies (Bombay) ...	1948-49
		164*	v. England (New Delhi) ...	1951-52
		155	v. England (Bombay)	1951-52
		146*	v. Pakistan (Bombay)	1952-53
Jaisimha, M. L. ...	(2)	127	v. England (New Delhi) ...	1961-62
		129	v. England (Calcutta)	1963-64
Kripal Singh, A. G.	(1)	100*	v. New Zealand (Hyderabad) ...	1955-56
Kunderan, B. K. ...	(2)	192	v. England (Madras[2])	1963-64
		100	v. England (New Delhi) ...	1963-64
Manjrekar, V. L.	(7)	133	v. England (Leeds)	1952
		118	v. West Indies (Kingston) ...	1952-53
		118	v. New Zealand (Hyderabad) ...	1955-56
		177	v. New Zealand (New Delhi) ...	1955-56
		189*	v. England (New Delhi) ...	1961-62
		108	v. England (Madras[2])	1963-64
		102*	v. New Zealand (Madras[2]) ...	1964-65
Mankad, V. M. ...	(5)	116	v. Australia (Melbourne) ...	1947-48
		111	v. Australia (Melbourne) ...	1947-48

Centuries in Test Cricket—*Cont.*

Mankad, V. M. (*cont.*)		184	v. England (Lord's)	1952
		223	v. New Zealand (Bombay) ...	1955-56
		231	v. New Zealand (Madras[2]) ...	1955-56
Merchant, V. M.	(3)	114	v. England (Manchester) ...	1936
		128	v. England (Oval)	1946
		154	v. England (New Delhi) ...	1951-52
Modi, R. S. ...	(1)	112	v. West Indies (Bombay) ...	1948-49
Mushtaq Ali ...	(2)	112	v. England (Manchester) ...	1936
		106	v. West Indies (Calcutta) ...	1948-49
Nadkarni, R. G. ...	(1)	122*	v. England (Kanpur)	1963-64
Pataudi, Nawab of, Jnr.	(6)	103	v. England (Madras[2])	1961-62
		203*	v. England (New Delhi) ...	1963-64
		128*	v. Australia (Madras[2])	1964-65
		153	v. New Zealand (Calcutta) ...	1964-65
		113	v. New Zealand (New Delhi) ...	1964-65
		148	v. England (Leeds)	1967
Phadkar, D. G. ...	(2)	123	v. Australia (Adelaide) ...	1947-48
		115	v. England (Calcutta)	1951-52
Ramchand, G. S....	(2)	106*	v. New Zealand (Calcutta) ...	1955-56
		109	v. Australia (Bombay)	1956-57
Roy, P.	(5)	140	v. England (Bombay)	1951-52
		111	v. England (Madras[1])	1951-52
		150	v. West Indies (Kingston) ...	1952-53
		100	v. New Zealand (Calcutta) ...	1955-56
		173	v. New Zealand (Madras[2]) ...	1955-56
Sardesai, D. N. ...	(2)	200*	v. New Zealand (Bombay) ...	1964-65
		106	v. New Zealand (New Delhi) ...	1964-65
Shodhan, D. H. ...	(1)	110	v. Pakistan (Calcutta)	1952-53
Umrigar, P. R. ...	(12)	130*	v. England (Madras[1])	1951-52
		102	v. Pakistan (Bombay)	1952-53
		130	v. West Indies (Port of Spain)	1952-53
		117	v. West Indies (Kingston) ...	1952-53
		108	v. Pakistan (Peshawar) ...	1954-55
		223	v. New Zealand (Hyderabad)...	1955-56
		118	v. England (Manchester) ...	1959
		115	v. Pakistan (Kanpur)	1960-61
		117	v. Pakistan (Madras[2])	1960-61
		112	v. Pakistan (New Delhi) ...	1960-61
		147*	v. England (Kanpur)	1961-62
		172*	v. West Indies (Port of Spain)	1961-62

PAKISTAN (35)

Alim-ud-Din ...	(2)	103*	v. India (Karachi)	1954-55
		109	v. England (Karachi)	1961-62
Asif Iqbal	(1)	146	v. England (Oval)	1967
Burki, J.	(3)	138	v. England (Lahore[2])	1961-62
		140	v. England (Dacca)	1961-62
		101	v. England (Lord's)	1962
Hanif Mohammad	(12)	142	v. India (Bahawalpur) ...	1954-55
		103	v. New Zealand (Dacca) ...	1955-56
		337	v. West Indies (Bridgetown) ...	1957-58
		103	v. West Indies (Karachi) ...	1958-59
		101*	v. Australia (Karachi)	1959-60
		160	v. India (Bombay)	1960-61

Centuries in Test Cricket—*Cont.*

Hanif Mohammad (*cont.*)		111 } 104 }	v. England (Dacca)	1960-61
		104	v. Australia (Melbourne) ...	1964-65
		100*	v. New Zealand (Christchurch)	1964-65
		203*	v. New Zealand (Lahore[2]) ...	1964-65
		187*	v. England (Lord's)	1967
Ibadulla, K. ...	(1)	166	v. Australia (Karachi)	1964-65
Ilyas, M.	(1)	126	v. New Zealand (Karachi) ...	1964-65
Imtiaz Ahmed ...	(3)	209	v. New Zealand (Lahore[1]) ...	1955-56
		122	v. West Indies (Kingston) ...	1957-58
		135	v. India (Madras[2])	1960-61
Mushtaq Mohammad	(2)	101	v. India (New Delhi)	1960-61
		100*	v. England (Nottingham)	1962
Nasim-ul-Ghani ...	(1)	101	v. England (Lord's)	1962
Nazar Mohammad	(1)	124*	v. India (Lucknow)	1952-53
Saeed Ahmed ...	(5)	150	v. West Indies (Georgetown) ...	1957-58
		166	v. Australia (Lahore[2])	1959-60
		121	v. India (Bombay)	1960-61
		103	v. India (Madras[2])	1960-61
		172	v. New Zealand (Karachi) ...	1964-65
Waqar Hassan ...	(1)	189	v. New Zealand (Lahore[1]) ...	1955-56
Wazir Mohammad	(2)	106	v. West Indies (Kingston) ...	1957-58
		189	v. West Indies (Port of Spain)	1957-58

A CENTURY AND A 'DUCK' IN THE SAME MATCH

ENGLAND

L. C. Braund ...	102 & 0	v. Australia (Sydney)	1903-04
J. T. Tyldesley ...	0 & 100	v. Australia (Leeds)	1905
G. Gunn	122* & 0	v. Australia (Sydney)	1907-08
F. E. Woolley ...	0 & 123	v. Australia (Sydney)	1924-25
G. B. Legge	196 & 0	v. New Zealand (Auckland) ...	1929-30
D. C. S. Compton ...	145* & 0	v. Australia (Manchester) ...	1948
L. Hutton	101 & 0	v. New Zealand (Leeds)... ...	1949
P. B. H. May ...	0 & 112	v. South Africa (Lord's)... ...	1955
M. C. Cowdrey ...	119 & 0	v. West Indies (Port of Spain) ...	1959-60
D. S. Sheppard ...	0 & 113	v. Australia (Melbourne) ...	1962-63

AUSTRALIA

W. L. Murdoch ...	0 & 153*	v. England (Oval)	1880
G. H. S. Trott ...	0 & 143	v. England (Lord's)	1896
C. Hill	188 & 0	v. England (Melbourne)... ...	1897-98
D. G. Bradman ...	0 & 103*	v. England (Melbourne)... ...	1932-33
J. H. Fingleton ...	100 & 0	v. England (Brisbane[2])	1936-37
D. G. Bradman ...	138 & 0	v. England (Nottingham) ...	1948
S. G. Barnes	0 & 141	v. England (Lord's)	1948
R. N. Harvey ...	122 & 0	v. England (Manchester) ...	1953

SOUTH AFRICA

J. H. Sinclair ...	0 & 104	v. Australia (Cape Town) ...	1902-03
G. A. Faulkner ...	122* & 0	v. Australia (Manchester) ...	1912
R. H. Catterall ...	0 & 120	v. England (Birmingham) ...	1924
A. D. Nourse, Jnr. ...	0 & 231	v. Australia (Johannesburg[1]) ...	1935-36
E. J. Barlow	114 & 0	v. Australia (Brisbane[2])	1963-64

A Century and a 'Duck' in the same Match—*Cont.*

WEST INDIES

I. Barrow	105 & 0	v. England (Manchester) ...	1933
F. C. M. Alexander...	0 & 108	v. Australia (Sydney)	1960-61
S. M. Nurse	201 & 0	v. Australia (Bridgetown) ...	1964-65

NEW ZEALAND

Nil

INDIA

V. M. Mankad ...	111 & 0	v. Australia (Melbourne) ...	1947-48
P. Roy	140 & 0	v. England (Bombay)	1951-52
V. L. Manjrekar ...	133 & 0	v. England (Leeds)	1952
M. L. Apte	0 & 163*	v. West Indies (Port of Spain) ...	1952-53
V. L. Manjrekar ...	108 & 0	v. England (Madras[2])	1963-64

PAKISTAN

Imtiaz Ahmed ...	209 & 0	v. New Zealand (Lahore[1]) ...	1955-56
Imtiaz Ahmed ...	122 & 0	v. West Indies (Kingston) ...	1957-58
Hanif Mohammad ...	160 & 0	v. India (Bombay)	1960-61
J. Burki	140 & 0	v. England (Dacca)	1961-62

BATSMEN DISMISSED FOR A 'PAIR'

THRICE

R. Peel (England) v. Australia: at Adelaide and Sydney (1894-95) and at The Oval in 1896.

R. W. Blair (New Zealand) v. West Indies at Dunedin (1955-56), v. England at Christchurch (1962-63) and v. South Africa at Auckland (1963-64).

TWICE

A. V. Bedser (England); K. D. Mackay (Australia); R. J. Crisp, Q. McMillan and L. J. Tancred (South Africa); C. A. Roach and A. L. Valentine (West Indies).

ONCE

ENGLAND

G. F. Grace (1880)
W. Attewell (1891-92)
R. Peel (1894-95)
G. A. Lohmann (1895-96)
E. G. Arnold (1903-04)
A. E. Knight (1903-04)
E. G. Hayes (1905-06)
M. C. Bird (1909-10)
H. Strudwick (1921)
P. Holmes (1927-28)
C. I. J. Smith (1934-35)
J. T. Ikin (1946-47)
J. J. Warr (1950-51)
F. Ridgway (1951-52)
R. T. Spooner (1955)
J. H. Wardle (1956)
F. S. Trueman (1958-59)
T. E. Bailey (1958-59)
M. J. K. Smith (1961-62)
G. Pullar (1961-62)
D. L. Underwood (1966)
J. T. Murray (1967)

AUSTRALIA

P. S. McDonnell (1882-83)
T. W. Garrett (1882-83)
E. Evans (1886)
P. G. McShane (1887-88)
A. C. Bannerman (1888)
M. A. Noble (1899)
S. E. Gregory (1899)
C. E. McLeod (1901-02)
J. Darling (1902)
J. J. Kelly (1902)
H. Trumble (1903-04)
J. V. Saunders (1907-08)
V. T. Trumper (1907-08)
C. V. Grimmett (1930)
W. A. Oldfield (1931-32)
J. H. Fingleton (1932-33)
V. Y. Richardson (1932-33)
C. L. Badcock (1938)
I. W. Johnson (1946-47)
J. Iverson (1950-51)
J. A. R. Moroney (1950-51)
L. V. Maddocks (1956)
R. N. Harvey (1956)
A. T. W. Grout (1960-61)
R. Benaud (1961)
G. D. McKenzie (1963-64)

Batsmen Dismissed for a 'Pair'—*Cont.*

SOUTH AFRICA

C. Wimble (1891-92)
J. T. Willoughby (1895-96)
P. S. T. Jones (1902-03)
J. J. Kotze (1902-03)
A. E. E. Vogler (1910-11)
C. B. Llewellyn (1912)
T. A. Ward (1912)
J. L. Cox (1913-14)
C. E. Dixon (1913-14)
P. T. Lewis (1913-14)
A. E. Hall (1922-23)
G. A. L. Hearne (1922-23)
X. C. Balaskas (1935-36)
F. Nicholson (1935-36)
C. N. McCarthy (1948-49)
D. J. McGlew (1955)
W. R. Endean (1955)
P. S. Heine (1956-57)
C. Wesley (1960)

WEST INDIES

C. R. Browne (1929-30)
H. C. Griffith (1933)
E. Achong (1934-35)
J. Trim (1951-52)
A. P. Binns (1954-55)
O. G. Smith (1954-55)
S. Ramadhin (1957)
E. D. Weekes (1957)
F. C. M. Alexander (1957)
L. R. Gibbs (1958-59)
F. M. M. Worrell (1960-61)
J. S. Solomon (1961-62)
J. L. Hendriks (1966)

NEW ZEALAND

F. T. Badcock (1929-30)
K. C. James (1929-30)
J. A. Cowie (1937)
L. A. Butterfield (1945-46)
C. G. Rowe (1945-46)
L. S. M. Miller (1953-54)
M. B. Poore (1954-55)
I. A. Colquhoun (1954-55)
J. A. Hayes (1954-55)
A. R. MacGibbon (1955-56)
H. B. Cave (1955-56)
N. S. Harford (1958)
R. C. Motz (1961-62)
M. J. F. Shrimpton (1963-64)
A. E. Dick (1964-65)
G. A. Bartlett (1965-66)

INDIA

Vijay Hazare (1951-52)
P. Roy (1952)
G. S. Ramchand (1952)
P. G. Joshi (1952-53)
C. V. Gadkari (1952-53)
N. S. Tamhane (1958-59)
R. Surendranath (1959)
R. B. Desai (1959-60)
D. N. Sardesai (1961-62)

PAKISTAN

M. E. Z. Ghazali (1954)
Nasim-ul-Ghani (1957-58)
Wazir Mohammad (1957-58)
Imtiaz Ahmed (1961-62)
J. Burki (1964-65)

DISMISSED FOR A 'PAIR' BY THE SAME FIELDING COMBINATION

R. Peel, st Jarvis b Turner: England v. Australia (Sydney)	1894-95
J. Darling, c Braund b Barnes: Australia v. England (Sheffield) ...	1902
P. T. Lewis, c Woolley b Barnes: South Africa v. England (Durban[1])	1913-14
P. G. Joshi, c Worrell b Valentine: India v. West Indies (Bridgetown)	1952-53
K. D. Mackay, c Oakman b Laker: Australia v. England (Manchester)	1956
R. Benaud, b Trueman: Australia v. England (Leeds)	1961

Notes:

P. Roy (India v. England, 1952) and L. S. M. Miller (New Zealand v. South Africa, 1953-54) were each dismissed for four consecutive 'ducks'.

Three players—M. B. Poore, I. A. Colquhoun and J. A. Hayes—were dismissed for 'Pairs' in the Auckland match of the 1954-55 series between New Zealand and England.

CARRYING BAT THROUGH COMPLETED INNINGS

ENGLAND

R. Abel	132*(307)	v. Australia (Sydney)	1891-92
P. F. Warner ...	132*(237)	v. South Africa (Johannesburg[1])	1898-99
L. Hutton	202*(344)	v. West Indies (Oval)	1950
L. Hutton	156*(272)	v. Australia (Adelaide)	1950-51

AUSTRALIA

J. E. Barrett ...	67*(176)	v. England (Lord's)	1890
W. W. Armstrong...	159*(309)	v. South Africa (Johannesburg[1])	1902-03
W. Bardsley ...	193*(383)	v. England (Lord's)	1926
W. M. Woodfull ...	30* (66)†	v. England (Brisbane[1])	1928-29
W. M. Woodfull ...	73*(193)†	v. England (Adelaide)	1932-33
W. A. Brown ...	206*(422)	v. England (Lord's)	1938

SOUTH AFRICA

A. B. Tancred ...	26* (47)	v. England (Cape Town) ...	1888-89
J. W. Zulch ...	43*(103)	v. England (Cape Town) ...	1909-10
T. L. Goddard ...	56* (99)	v. Australia (Cape Town) ...	1957-58
D. J. McGlew ...	127*(292)	v. New Zealand (Durban[2]) ...	1961-62

WEST INDIES

F. M. M. Worrell...	191*(372)	v. England (Nottingham) ...	1957
C. C. Hunte ...	60*(131)	v. Australia (Port of Spain) ...	1964-65

PAKISTAN

Nazar Mohammad	124*(331)	v. India (Lucknow)	1952-53

L. Hutton (England) and W. M. Woodfull (Australia) are the only players to perform this feat twice in Test Matches.

W. A. Brown (Australia) holds the record for the highest score by a player carrying his bat through a Test innings: 206*. Australia's total of 422 on that occasion is the highest through which a player has carried his bat.

BATSMEN SCORING OVER 250 RUNS IN A DAY

309	D. G. Bradman (334), Australia v. England (Leeds)	1930
295	W. R. Hammond (336*), England v. New Zealand (Auckland)	1932-33
273	D. C. S. Compton (278), England v. Pakistan (Nottingham) ...	1954
271	D. G. Bradman (304), Australia v. England (Leeds)	1934

BATSMEN SCORING OVER 60% OF COMPLETED INNINGS TOTAL

67.3% (165*/245), C. Bannerman, Australia v. England (Melbourne), 1876-77
62.8% (100/159), J. R. Reid, New Zealand v. England (Christchurch), 1962-63
60.6% (74/122), V. T. Trumper, Australia v. England (Melbourne), 1903-04
60.1% (62/103), J. T. Tyldesley, England v. Australia (Melbourne), 1903-04

OVER 600 RUNS ADDED DURING A BATSMAN'S INNINGS

770	L. Hutton (364), England v. Australia (Oval)	1938
720	A. Sandham (325), England v. West Indies (Kingston) ...	1929-30
703	G. St. A. Sobers (365*), West Indies v. Pakistan (Kingston) ...	1957-58
646	R. B. Simpson (311), Australia v. England (Manchester) ...	1964
628	Hanif Mohammad (337), Pakistan v. West Indies (Bridgetown)	1957-58

(† denotes completed innings in which ten wickets did not fall, one or more batsmen being retired/absent hurt)

MOST RUNS OFF ONE OVER

EIGHT-BALL

25 (66061600) B. Sutcliffe and R. W. Blair, off H. J. Tayfield for New Zealand v. South Africa at Johannesburg[2] 1953-54

SIX-BALL

22 (116626) M. W. Tate and W. Voce, off A. E. Hall for England v. South Africa at Johannesburg[1] 1930-31

MOST SIXES OFF CONSECUTIVE BALLS

Three: W. R. Hammond (336*), England v. New Zealand at Auckland, off J. Newman 1932-33

MOST BOUNDARIES IN AN INNINGS

57: 5 sixes, 52 fours (238), J. H. Edrich (310*), England v. New Zealand at Leeds 1965

MOST SIXES IN AN INNINGS

10: W. R. Hammond (336*), England v. New Zealand at Auckland... 1932-33

RECORD PARTNERSHIPS FOR EACH WICKET

1st	413	V. M. Mankad & P. Roy, India v. New Zealand, Madras[2] ...	1955-56
2nd	451	W. H. Ponsford & D. G. Bradman, Australia v. England, Oval ...	1934
3rd	370	W. J. Edrich & D. C. S. Compton, England v. South Africa, Lord's	1947
4th	411	P. B. H. May & M. C. Cowdrey, England v. West Indies, Birmingham...	1957
5th	405	S. G. Barnes & D. G. Bradman, Australia v. England, Sydney ...	1946-47
6th	346	J. H. Fingleton & D. G. Bradman, Australia v. England, Melbourne	1936-37
7th	347	D. Atkinson & C. C. Depeiza, West Indies v. Australia, Bridgetown	1954-55
8th	246	L. E. G. Ames & G. O. Allen, England v. New Zealand, Lord's...	1931
9th	190	Asif Iqbal & Intikhab Alam, Pakistan v. England, Oval... ...	1967
10th	130	R. E. Foster & W. Rhodes, England v. Australia, Sydney ...	1903-04

HIGHEST SCORE REACHED AT THE FALL OF EACH WICKET

1st	413	India (537-3d) v. New Zealand (Madras[2])	1955-56
2nd	533	West Indies (790-3d) v. Pakistan (Kingston)	1957-58
3rd	602	West Indies (790-3d) v. Pakistan (Kingston)	1957-58
4th	667	England (849) v. West Indies (Kingston)	1929-30
5th	720	England (849) v. West Indies (Kingston)	1929-30
6th	770	England (903-7d) v. Australia (Oval)	1938
7th	876	England (903-7d) v. Australia (Oval)	1938
8th	813	England (849) v. West Indies (Kingston)	1929-30
9th	821	England (849) v. West Indies (Kingston)	1929-30
10th	849	England (849) v. West Indies (Kingston)	1929-30

LOWEST SCORE REACHED AT THE FALL OF EACH WICKET

1st	0	On several occasions.	
2nd	0	On several occasions.	
3rd	0	Australia (32-7d) v. England (Brisbane[2])	1950-51
		India (165) v. England (Leeds)	1952
4th	0	India (165) v. England (Leeds)	1952
5th	6	India (98) v. England (Oval)	1952
6th	7	Australia (70) v. England (Manchester)	1888
7th	18	Australia (60) v. England (Lord's)	1888
8th	22	New Zealand (26) v. England (Auckland)	1954-55
9th	26	New Zealand (26) v. England (Auckland)	1954-55
10th	26	New Zealand (26) v. England (Auckland)	1954-55

PARTNERSHIPS OF OVER 300

Runs	*Wkt.*		
451	2nd	W. H. Ponsford & D. G. Bradman: Australia v. England (Oval)	1934
446	2nd	C. C. Hunte & G. St. A. Sobers: West Indies v. Pakistan (Kingston)	1957-58
413	1st	V. M. Mankad & P. Roy: India v. New Zealand (Madras[2]) ...	1955-56
411	4th	P. B. H. May & M. C. Cowdrey: England v. West Indies (Birmingham)	1957
405	5th	S. G. Barnes & D. G. Bradman: Australia v. England (Sydney)	1946-47
399	4th	G. St. A. Sobers & F. M. M. Worrell: West Indies v. England (Bridgetown)	1959-60
388	4th	W. H. Ponsford & D. G. Bradman: Australia v. England (Leeds)	1934
382	2nd	L. Hutton & M. Leyland: England v. Australia (Oval)	1938
382	1st	W. M. Lawry & R. B. Simpson: Australia v. West Indies (Bridgetown)	1964-65
370	3rd	W. J. Edrich & D. C. S. Compton: England v. South Africa (Lord's)	1947
369	2nd	J. H. Edrich & K. F. Barrington: England v. New Zealand (Leeds)	1965
359	1st	L. Hutton & C. Washbrook: England v. South Africa (Johannesburg[2])	1948-49
347	7th	D. Atkinson & C. C. Depeiza: West Indies v. Australia (Bridgetown)	1954-55
346	6th	J. H. Fingleton & D. G. Bradman: Australia v. England (Melbourne)	1936-37
341	3rd	E. J. Barlow & R. G. Pollock: South Africa v. Australia (Adelaide)	1963-64
338	3rd	E. D. Weekes & F. M. M. Worrell: West Indies v. England (Port of Spain)	1953-54
323	1st	J. B. Hobbs & W. Rhodes: England v. Australia (Melbourne) ...	1911-12
319	3rd	A. Melville & A. D. Nourse, Jnr.: South Africa v. England (Nottingham)	1947
308	7th	Waqar Hassan & Imtiaz Ahmed: Pakistan v. New Zealand (Lahore[1])	1955-56
301	2nd	A. R. Morris & D. G. Bradman: Australia v. England (Leeds)	1948

MOST CENTURY PARTNERSHIPS IN ONE INNINGS

FOUR

England (382-2, 135-3, 215-6, 106-7) v. Australia (Oval)	1938
West Indies (267-4, 101-6, 118-7, 106-9) v. India (New Delhi)	1948-49
Pakistan (152-1, 112-2, 154-3, 121-4) v. West Indies (Bridgetown)	1957-58

THREE

England (151-1, 103-4, 131-6) v. Australia (Oval)	1893
Australia (171-4, 139-5, 154-9) v. England (Sydney)	1894-95
England (119-3, 122-4, 154-8) v. South Africa (Johannesburg[1])	1895-96
England (185-1, 131-2, 110-4) v. Australia (Oval)	1899
England (192-5, 115-9, 130-10) v. Australia (Sydney)	1903-04
Australia (123-1, 111-2, 187-6) v. England (Sydney)	1920-21
England (268-1, 142-2, 121*-3) v. South Africa (Lord's)	1924
Australia (161-4, 123-6, 100-9) v. England (Melbourne)	1924-25

Most Century Partnerships in One Innings—*Cont.*

England (126-1, 106-2, 133-7) v. Australia (Melbourne) 1924-25
England (182-1, 140-3, 116*-4) v. Australia (Lord's) 1926
England (173-1, 148-2, 249-4) v. West Indies (Kingston) 1929-30
Australia (162-1, 231-2, 192-3) v. England (Lord's) 1930
England (112-1, 188-2, 123-3) v. Australia (Sydney) 1932-33
England (134-2, 127-3, 138-8) v. India (Manchester) 1936
Australia (276-3, 106-4, 131-6) v. England (Brisbane[2]) 1946-47
Australia (236-2, 105-3, 142-4) v. India (Adelaide) 1947-48
England (168-1, 100-2, 155-3) v. Australia (Leeds) 1948
West Indies (197-1, 115-3, 189-5) v. New Zealand (Auckland) 1951-52
Australia (122-1, 103-3, 148-4) v. South Africa (Melbourne) 1952-53
Australia (108-1, 100-3, 206-6) v. West Indies (Bridgetown) 1954-55
Australia (295-3, 220-5, 137-8) v. West Indies (Kingston) 1954-55
West Indies (108-3, 217-4, 160*-6) v. India (Calcutta)... 1958-59
West Indies (255-2, 110-6, 127-7) v. India (Kingston) 1961-62
England (166-2, 107-3, 153*-6) v. Pakistan (Birmingham) 1962
England (111-2, 246-3, 143-5) v. Australia (Manchester) 1964
West Indies (110-3, 107-4, 173-5) v. England (Nottingham) 1966
England (139-2, 107-3, 252-4) v. India (Leeds) 1967

CENTURY PARTNERSHIP FOR SAME WICKET IN EACH INNINGS

1st WICKET

157 & 110 J. B. Hobbs & H. Sutcliffe: England v. Australia (Sydney) ... 1924-25
119 & 171 R. H. Catterall & B. Mitchell: South Africa v. England (Birmingham) 1929
131 & 191 P. G. Van der Byl with A. Melville (1st Inns) & B. Mitchell (2nd Inns): South Africa v. England (Durban[2]) 1938-39
137 & 100 L. Hutton & C. Washbrook: England v. Australia (Adelaide) ... 1946-47
168 & 129 L. Hutton & C. Washbrook: England v. Australia (Leeds) ... 1948

2nd WICKET

127 & 108 W. Rhodes & J. W. Hearne (1st Inns), J. B. Hobbs & G. Gunn (2nd Inns): England v. Australia (Melbourne) 1911-12
184 & 168 P. A. Gibb & E. Paynter: England v. South Africa (Johannesburg[1]) 1938-39
275 & 157 C. C. McDonald & A. L. Hassett (1st Inns) and A. R. Morris & R. N. Harvey (2nd Inns): Australia v. South Africa (Adelaide) 1952-53
125 & 165 A. L. Hassett & R. N. Harvey (1st Inns) and A. R. Morris & K. R. Miller (2nd Inns): Australia v. England (Lord's) ... 1953
269 & 135 G. St. A. Sobers with C. L. Walcott (1st Inns) & C. C. Hunte (2nd Inns): West Indies v. Pakistan (Georgetown) 1957-58

3rd WICKET

120 & 121 B. Mitchell & H. W. Taylor: South Africa v. Australia (Adelaide) 1931-32
245 & 104 J. Hardstaff, Jnr. with W. R. Hammond (1st Inns) & C. J. Barnett (2nd Inns): England v. New Zealand (Lord's) 1937
155 & 103 W. J. Edrich with A. V. Bedser (1st Inns) & D. C. S. Compton (2nd Inns): England v. Australia (Leeds) 1948
129 & 108 R. S. Modi & Vijay Hazare: India v. West Indies (Calcutta) ... 1948-49
242 & 127 C. L. Walcott & E. D. Weekes: West Indies v. Australia (Port of Spain) 1954-55
175 & 104 M. C. Cowdrey with E. R. Dexter (1st Inns) & D. S. Sheppard (2nd Inns): England v. Australia (Melbourne) 1962-63

Century Partnership for same Wicket in each Innings—*Cont.*

4th WICKET

117 & 113 G. Gunn with L. C. Braund (1st Inns) & J. Hardstaff, Snr. (2nd Inns): England v. Australia (Sydney) 1907-08

126 & 137 J. Ryder with A. A. Jackson (1st Inns) & A. F. Kippax (2nd Inns): Australia v. England (Adelaide) 1928-29

110 & 179 C. L. Walcott with F. M. M. Worrell (1st Inns) & G. St. A. Sobers (2nd Inns): West Indies v. Australia (Kingston) ... 1954-55

121 & 104 M. C. Cowdrey with P. B. H. May (1st Inns) & P. E. Richardson (2nd Inns): England v. New Zealand (Birmingham) ... 1958

5th WICKET

113 & 125 M. J. K. Smith & P. H. Parfitt: England v. New Zealand (Christchurch) 1965-66

SUMMARY OF CENTURY PARTNERSHIPS

For	*Opponents* E	A	SA	WI	NZ	I	P	*Total*
England	—	177	88	46	40	38	18	407
Australia	163	—	59	26	1	16	3	268
South Africa ...	75	38	—	—	16	—	—	129
West Indies	50	25	—	—	8	33	10	126
New Zealand ...	12	—	6	1	—	9	4	32
India	27	9	—	19	13	—	8	76
Pakistan	10	3	—	12	5	8	—	38
TOTAL	337	252	153	104	83	104	43	1076

For	*Wicket* 1st	2nd	3rd	4th	5th	6th	7th	8th	9th	10th	*Total*
England ...	80	80	68	62	45	39	18	7	6	2	407
Australia ...	41	56	49	49	31	16	11	10	3	2	268
South Africa	27	18	24	22	11	9	11	5	1	1	129
West Indies	12	19	24	26	20	17	7	—	1	—	126
New Zealand	7	2	7	4	7	1	3	1	—	—	32
India ...	9	13	17	12	9	9	3	2	1	1	76
Pakistan ...	6	9	8	5	3	3	1	1	1	1	38
TOTAL	182	197	197	180	126	94	54	26	13	7	1076

PLAYERS SHARING IN TEN OR MORE CENTURY PARTNERSHIPS

ENGLAND (24)

	Total	1st	2nd	3rd	4th	5th	6th	7th	8th	9th	10th
L. Hutton	41	17	13	7	1	–	2	1	–	–	–
M. C. Cowdrey ...	33	5	5	3	13	4	1	1	–	1	–
W. R. Hammond ...	33	1	6	12	11	2	1	–	–	–	–
H. Sutcliffe	33	21	10	1	–	–	1	–	–	–	–
J. B. Hobbs	32	24	6	1	–	–	–	1	–	–	–
K. F. Barrington ...	31	–	6	7	13	4	1	–	–	–	–
D. C. S. Compton ...	30	–	–	14	7	7	1	–	1	–	–

Players Sharing in Ten or More Century Partnerships—*Cont.*

	Total	1*st*	2*nd*	3*rd*	4*th*	5*th*	6*th*	7*th*	8*th*	9*th*	10*th*
E. R. Dexter	23	–	9	6	5	1	1	1	–	–	–
P. B. H. May ...	23	–	6	8	8	1	–	–	–	–	–
T. W. Graveney ...	21	–	6	5	4	4	1	–	1	–	–
W. Rhodes	17	9	4	2	–	–	1	–	–	–	1
E. Hendren	15	–	–	5	4	2	1	2	1	–	–
C. Washbrook ...	15	9	5	–	1	–	–	–	–	–	–
W. J. Edrich	14	–	7	7	–	–	–	–	–	–	–
M. Leyland	14	–	1	1	2	3	6	1	–	–	–
L. E. G. Ames ...	12	–	–	–	5	2	4	–	1	–	–
T. W. Hayward ...	12	6	2	2	1	–	–	1	–	–	–
G. Pullar	12	6	5	1	–	–	–	–	–	–	–
F. E. Woolley ...	12	–	1	3	1	3	2	1	–	1	–
A. C. Maclaren ...	10	4	3	1	1	1	–	–	–	–	–
P. H. Parfitt	10	–	–	–	5	3	2	–	–	–	–
P. E. Richardson ...	10	5	2	1	2	–	–	–	–	–	–
M. J. K. Smith ...	10	–	–	3	1	3	2	1	–	–	–
R. E. S. Wyatt ...	10	3	1	2	2	1	1	–	–	–	–

AUSTRALIA (20)

	Total	1*st*	2*nd*	3*rd*	4*th*	5*th*	6*th*	7*th*	8*th*	9*th*	10*th*
D. G. Bradman ...	35	–	14	11	3	6	1	–	–	–	–
R. N. Harvey ...	33	–	7	13	9	3	1	–	–	–	–
A. L. Hassett	21	–	4	8	7	1	–	–	1	–	–
A. R. Morris	19	8	4	5	1	1	–	–	–	–	–
C. Hill	17	–	8	3	3	1	–	1	1	–	–
R. B. Simpson ...	17	9	4	3	–	1	–	–	–	–	–
W. M. Woodfull ...	17	4	11	–	1	1	–	–	–	–	–
K. R. Miller	16	–	2	1	9	2	1	1	–	–	–
W. M. Lawry ...	15	9	2	2	1	1	–	–	–	–	–
W. Bardsley	13	4	3	4	1	1	–	–	–	–	–
C. G. Macartney ...	13	1	5	3	3	1	–	–	–	–	–
C. C. McDonald ...	13	8	3	2	–	–	–	–	–	–	–
N. C. O'Neill ...	13	–	1	5	6	1	–	–	–	–	–
V. T. Trumper ...	12	4	2	1	1	3	1	–	–	–	–
W. W. Armstrong ...	11	–	–	2	3	2	2	–	1	–	1
W. H. Ponsford ...	11	4	3	–	2	1	1	–	–	–	–
B. C. Booth	10	–	–	2	3	3	1	1	–	–	–
S. E. Gregory	10	1	–	1	3	3	1	–	–	1	–
C. E. Kelleway ...	10	–	2	2	1	–	4	–	1	–	–
S. J. McCabe ...	10	–	3	3	3	1	–	–	–	–	–

SOUTH AFRICA (8)

	Total	1*st*	2*nd*	3*rd*	4*th*	5*th*	6*th*	7*th*	8*th*	9*th*	10*th*
B. Mitchell	24	9	3	8	2	–	–	1	1	–	–
A. D. Nourse, Jnr. ...	15	–	–	8	4	1	1	1	–	–	–

Players Sharing in Ten or More Century Partnerships—*Cont.*

	Total	1*st*	2*nd*	3*rd*	4*th*	5*th*	6*th*	7*th*	8*th*	9*th*	10*th*
T. L. Goddard ...	13	9	3	–	1	–	–	–	–	–	–
H. W. Taylor ...	13	4	1	5	3	–	–	–	–	–	–
J. H. B. Waite ...	12	1	2	1	4	2	1	1	–	–	–
D. J. McGlew... ...	11	6	–	3	1	–	–	1	–	–	–
E. A. B. Rowan ...	11	1	5	3	1	1	–	–	–	–	–
R. H. Catterall ...	10	3	1	1	3	2	–	–	–	–	–

WEST INDIES (10)

	Total	1*st*	2*nd*	3*rd*	4*th*	5*th*	6*th*	7*th*	8*th*	9*th*	10*th*
G. St. A. Sobers ...	32	–	3	4	9	10	5	1	–	–	–
F. M. M. Worrell ...	22	–	2	4	9	3	4	–	–	–	–
R. B. Kanhai	21	2	5	8	3	2	1	–	–	–	–
E. D. Weekes	21	–	–	8	4	6	2	1	–	–	–
C. L. Walcott ...	17	–	1	2	10	2	2	–	–	–	–
C. C. Hunte	13	5	5	1	2	–	–	–	–	–	–
B. F. Butcher	12	–	–	3	4	3	2	–	–	–	–
J. B. Stollmeyer ...	12	5	3	4	–	–	–	–	–	–	–
G. A. Headley ...	11	–	7	3	–	–	–	1	–	–	–
O. G. Smith	11	–	1	1	3	2	3	1	–	–	–

NEW ZEALAND (2)

	Total	1*st*	2*nd*	3*rd*	4*th*	5*th*	6*th*	7*th*	8*th*	9*th*	10*th*
J. R. Reid	11	–	1	5	2	3	–	–	–	–	–
B. Sutcliffe	10	3	2	2	–	1	–	2	–	–	–

INDIA (5)

	Total	1*st*	2*nd*	3*rd*	4*th*	5*th*	6*th*	7*th*	8*th*	9*th*	10*th*
Vijay Hazare	14	–	–	7	4	–	2	1	–	–	–
C. G. Borde	13	–	–	–	4	5	3	1	–	–	–
V. L. Manjrekar ...	12	–	3	5	1	2	1	–	–	–	–
P. R. Umrigar ...	11	–	1	1	5	2	2	–	–	–	–
P. Roy	10	4	1	4	1	–	–	–	–	–	–

PAKISTAN (2)

	Total	1*st*	2*nd*	3*rd*	4*th*	5*th*	6*th*	7*th*	8*th*	9*th*	10*th*
Hanif Mohammad ...	17	4	6	3	2	–	1	–	1	–	–
Saeed Ahmed ...	13	–	6	6	1	–	–	–	–	–	–

CENTURY PARTNERSHIPS

ENGLAND

1st WICKET

		Venue	Series	A	SA	Opponents WI	NZ	I	P
L. Hutton	C. Washbrook	Johannesburg[2]	1948-49	—	359	—	—	—	—
J. B. Hobbs	W. Rhodes	Melbourne	1911-12	323	—	—	—	—	—
M. C. Cowdrey	G. Pullar	Oval	1960	—	290	—	—	—	—
J. B. Hobbs	H. Sutcliffe	Melbourne	1924-25	283	—	—	—	—	—
J. B. Hobbs	H. Sutcliffe	Lord's	1924	—	268	—	—	—	—
G. Boycott	R. W. Barber	Sydney	1965-66	234	—	—	—	—	—
J. B. Hobbs	W. Rhodes	Cape Town	1909-10	—	221	—	—	—	—
L. Hutton	C. J. Barnett	Nottingham	1938	219	—	—	—	—	—
C. Washbrook	R. T. Simpson	Nottingham	1950	—	—	212	—	—	—
G. Pullar	R. W. Barber	Dacca	1961-62	—	—	—	—	—	198
T. W. Hayward	F. S. Jackson	Oval	1899	185	—	—	—	—	—
J. B. Hobbs	H. Sutcliffe	Lord's	1926	182	—	—	—	—	—
M. C. Cowdrey	G. Pullar	Kingston	1959-60	—	—	177	—	—	—
P. E. Richardson	M. C. Cowdrey	Manchester	1956	174	—	—	—	—	—
G. Gunn	A. Sandham	Kingston	1929-30	—	—	173	—	—	—
J. B. Hobbs	H. Sutcliffe	Oval	1926	172	—	—	—	—	—
W. G. Grace	W. H. Scotton	Oval	1886	170	—	—	—	—	—
L. Hutton	C. Washbrook	Leeds	1948	168	—	—	—	—	—
R. E. S. Wyatt	W. R. Hammond	Durban[2]	1930-31	—	160	—	—	—	—
J. B. Hobbs	W. Rhodes	Johannesburg[1]	1909-10	—	159	—	—	—	—
P. E. Richardson	G. Pullar	Bombay	1961-62	—	—	—	—	159	—
A. C. Russell	G. Brown	Oval	1921	158	—	—	—	—	—
J. B. Hobbs	H. Sutcliffe	Sydney	1924-25	157	—	—	—	—	—
J. B. Hobbs	H. Sutcliffe	Leeds	1926	156	—	—	—	—	—
J. B. Hobbs	H. Sutcliffe	Oval	1928	—	—	155	—	—	—
T. W. Hayward	A. C. Maclaren	Sydney	1901-02	154	—	—	—	—	—
A. Sandham	A. C. Russell	Johannesburg[1]	1922-23	—	153	—	—	—	—
W. G. Grace	A. E. Stoddart	Oval	1893	151	—	—	—	—	—

Century Partnerships—*ENGLAND* (1*st wicket*)—*Cont.*

		Venue	*Series*	*Opponents* *A*	*SA*	*WI*	*NZ*	*I*	*P*
P. E. Richardson	M. C. Cowdrey	Nottingham	1956	151	—	—	—	—	—
T. W. Hayward	A. C. Maclaren	Adelaide	1901-02	149	—	—	—	—	—
T. W. Hayward	P. F. Warner	Adelaide	1903-04	148	—	—	—	—	—
J. B. Hobbs	W. Rhodes	Adelaide	1911-12	147	—	—	—	—	—
L. Hutton	R. T. Simpson	Oval	1949	—	—	—	147	—	—
W. G. A. Parkhouse	G. Pullar	Leeds	1959	—	—	—	—	146	—
T. W. Hayward	A. C. Maclaren	Nottingham	1905	145	—	—	—	—	—
J. B. Hobbs	H. Sutcliffe	Adelaide	1928-29	143	—	—	—	—	—
L. Hutton	J. D. Robertson	Lord's	1949	—	—	—	143	—	—
L. Hutton	D. S. Sheppard	Oval	1952	—	—	—	—	143	—
W. Rhodes	A. E. Relf	Johannesburg[1]	1913-14	—	141	—	—	—	—
L. Hutton	C. Washbrook	Leeds	1947	—	141	—	—	—	—
P. Holmes	H. Sutcliffe	Cape Town	1927-28	—	140	—	—	—	—
L. Hutton	C. Washbrook	Melbourne	1946-47	138	—	—	—	—	—
L. Hutton	C. Washbrook	Adelaide	1946-47	137	—	—	—	—	—
J. B. Hobbs	H. Sutcliffe	Birmingham	1924	—	136	—	—	—	—
J. B. Hobbs	W. Rhodes	Durban[1]	1913-14	—	133	—	—	—	—
L. Hutton	W. Watson	Kingston	1953-54	—	—	130	—	—	—
L. Hutton	J. D. Robertson	Kingston	1947-48	—	—	129	—	—	—
L. Hutton	C. Washbrook	Leeds	1948	129	—	—	—	—	—
D. Smith	A. Mitchell	Leeds	1935	—	128	—	—	—	—
J. B. Hobbs	H. Sutcliffe	Melbourne	1924-25	126	—	—	—	—	—
P. E. Richardson	W. Watson	Manchester	1958	—	—	—	126	—	—
J. B. Hobbs	H. Sutcliffe	Nottingham	1930	125	—	—	—	—	—
J. B. Bolus	J. G. Binks	Bombay	1963-64	—	—	—	—	125	—
C. F. Walters	H. Sutcliffe	Manchester	1934	123*	—	—	—	—	—
G. Ulyett	R. G. Barlow	Sydney	1881-82	122	—	—	—	—	—
T. W. Hayward	P. F. Warner	Melbourne	1903-04	122	—	—	—	—	—
L. Hutton	J. T. Ikin	Manchester	1951	—	121	—	—	—	—
G. Boycott	R. W. Barber	Durban[2]	1964-65	—	120	—	—	—	—

				A	SA	WI	NZ	I	P
J. B. Hobbs	H. Sutcliffe	Manchester	1928	—	—	119	—	—	—
H. Sutcliffe	R. E. S. Wyatt	Nottingham	1935	—	118	—	—	—	—
D. S. Sheppard	M. C. Cowdrey	Oval	1962	—	—	—	—	—	117
P. E. Richardson	T. E. Bailey	Durban[2]	1956-57	—	115	—	—	—	—
H. Sutcliffe	D. R. Jardine	Brisbane[2]	1932-33	114	—	—	—	—	—
D. S. Sheppard	G. Pullar	Brisbane[2]	1962-63	114	—	—	—	—	—
J. B. Hobbs	W. Rhodes	Lord's	1912	112	—	—	—	—	—
H. Sutcliffe	R. E. S. Wyatt	Sydney	1932-33	112	—	—	—	—	—
A. C. Maclaren	E. Wainwright	Sydney	1897-98	111	—	—	—	—	—
A. H. Bakewell	C. F. Walters	Madras[1]	1933-34	—	—	—	—	111	—
J. B. Hobbs	H. Sutcliffe	Sydney	1924-25	110	—	—	—	—	—
J. B. Hobbs	H. Sutcliffe	Manchester	1930	108	—	—	—	—	—
J. B. Hobbs	W. Rhodes	Oval	1912	107	—	—	—	—	—
L. Hutton	R. T. Simpson	Lord's	1952	—	—	—	—	106	—
J. B. Hobbs	C. B. Fry	Birmingham	1909	105*	—	—	—	—	—
J. B. Hobbs	H. Sutcliffe	Melbourne	1928-29	105	—	—	—	—	—
H. Sutcliffe	C. F. Walters	Oval	1934	104	—	—	—	—	—
L. Hutton	C. Washbrook	Manchester	1949	—	—	—	103	—	—
J. B. Bolus	J. H. Edrich	New Delhi	1963-64	—	—	—	—	101	—
J. B. Hobbs	W. Rhodes	Johannesburg[1]	1913-14	—	100	—	—	—	—
L. Hutton	C. J. Barnett	Manchester	1937	—	—	—	100	—	—
L. Hutton	C. Washbrook	Adelaide	1946-47	100	—	—	—	—	—
		TOTAL	80	41	18	7	5	7	2

2nd WICKET

		Venue	Series	A	SA	WI	NZ	I	P
						Opponents			
L. Hutton	M. Leyland	Oval	1938	382	—	—	—	—	—
J. H. Edrich	K. F. Barrington	Leeds	1965	—	—	—	369	—	—
P. A. Gibb	W. J. Edrich	Durban[2]	1938-39	—	280	—	—	—	—
P. E. Richardson	T. W. Graveney	Nottingham	1957	—	—	266	—	—	—
M. C. Cowdrey	E. R. Dexter	Oval	1962	—	—	—	—	—	248

Century Partnerships—*ENGLAND* (*2nd wicket*)—*Cont.*

		Venue	*Series*	*A*	*SA*	*WI*	*NZ*	*I*	*P*
						Opponents			
H. Sutcliffe	E. Tyldesley	Johannesburg[1]	1927-28	—	230	—	—	—	—
H. Sutcliffe	W. R. Hammond	Birmingham	1929	—	221	—	—	—	—
L. Hutton	W. J. Edrich	Oval	1949	—	—	—	218	—	—
M. C. Cowdrey	E. R. Dexter	Port of Spain	1959-60	—	—	191	—	—	—
H. Sutcliffe	W. R. Hammond	Sydney	1932-33	188	—	—	—	—	—
H. Sutcliffe	W. R. Hammond	Oval	1929	—	187*	—	—	—	—
P. A. Gibb	E. Paynter	Johannesburg[1]	1938-39	—	184	—	—	—	—
T. W. Graveney	P. B. H. May	Sydney	1954-55	182	—	—	—	—	—
H. Sutcliffe	K. S. Duleepsinhji	Oval	1931	—	—	—	178	—	—
P. A. Gibb	E. Paynter	Johannesburg[1]	1938-39	—	168	—	—	—	—
L. Hutton	T. W. Graveney	Lord's	1953	168	—	—	—	—	—
M. C. Cowdrey	E. R. Dexter	Birmingham	1962	—	—	—	—	—	166
G. Pullar	K. F. Barrington	New Delhi	1961-62	—	—	—	—	164	—
D. S. Sheppard	E. R. Dexter	Nottingham	1962	—	—	—	—	—	161
L. Hutton	P. B. H. May	Lord's	1952	—	—	—	—	158	—
A. Shrewsbury	W. Gunn	Lord's	1893	152	—	—	—	—	—
L. Hutton	W. J. Edrich	Sydney	1946-47	150	—	—	—	—	—
A. Sandham	R. E. S. Wyatt	Kingston	1929-30	—	—	148	—	—	—
C. Washbrook	W. J. Edrich	Melbourne	1946-47	147	—	—	—	—	—
G. Pullar	K. F. Barrington	Dacca	1961-62	—	—	—	—	—	147
P. E. Richardson	T. W. Graveney	Oval	1957	—	—	146	—	—	—
L. Hutton	R. T. Simpson	Nottingham	1951	—	144	—	—	—	—
A. C. Maclaren	K. S. Ranjitsinhji	Adelaide	1897-98	142	—	—	—	—	—
J. B. Hobbs	F. E. Woolley	Lord's	1924	—	142	—	—	—	—
G. Pullar	K. F. Barrington	Kanpur	1961-62	—	—	—	—	139	—
G. Boycott	K. F. Barrington	Leeds	1967	—	—	—	—	139	—
G. Ulyett	J. Selby	Melbourne	1881-82	137	—	—	—	—	—
A. C. Maclaren	T. W. Hayward	Sydney	1897-98	137	—	—	—	—	—
R. W. Barber	E. R. Dexter	Johannesburg[3]	1964-65	—	136	—	—	—	—
J. B. Hobbs	G. Gunn	Sydney	1907-08	134	—	—	—	—	—

A. E. Fagg	W. R. Hammond	Manchester	1936	—	—	—	—	134	—
L. Hutton	J. F. Crapp	Cape Town	1948-49	—	134	—	—	—	—
H. Sutcliffe	W. R. Hammond	Melbourne	1928-29	133	—	—	—	—	—
T. W. Graveney	P. B. H. May	Lord's	1955	—	132	—	—	—	—
T. W. Hayward	K. S. Ranjitsinhji	Oval	1899	131	—	—	—	—	—
L. Hutton	N. Oldfield	Oval	1939	—	—	131	—	—	—
L. Hutton	R. T. Simpson	Melbourne	1950-51	131	—	—	—	—	—
G. Pullar	M. C. Cowdrey	Manchester	1959	—	—	—	—	131	—
H. Sutcliffe	E. Tyldesley	Durban[2]	1927-28	—	130	—	—	—	—
J. B. Hobbs	E. Tyldesley	Oval	1928	—	—	129	—	—	—
L. Hutton	P. B. H. May	Leeds	1951	—	129	—	—	—	—
L. Hutton	J. Hardstaff, Jnr.	Manchester	1937	—	—	—	128	—	—
W. Rhodes	J. W. Hearne	Melbourne	1911-12	127	—	—	—	—	—
H. Sutcliffe	K. S. Duleepsinhji	Manchester	1931	—	—	—	126	—	—
W. Rhodes	R. H. Spooner	Lord's	1912	—	124	—	—	—	—
C. Washbrook	W. J. Edrich	Manchester	1948	124	—	—	—	—	—
D. S. Sheppard	E. R. Dexter	Melbourne	1962-63	124	—	—	—	—	—
H. Sutcliffe	W. R. Hammond	Sydney	1932-33	122	—	—	—	—	—
W. G. Grace	A. P. Lucas	Oval	1880	120	—	—	—	—	—
C. Washbrook	J. F. Crapp	Johannesburg[2]	1948-49	—	120	—	—	—	—
C. Washbrook	W. J. Edrich	Leeds	1949	—	—	—	118	—	—
D. S. Sheppard	J. T. Ikin	Oval	1952	—	—	—	—	118	—
W. E. Russell	M. C. Cowdrey	Auckland	1965-66	—	—	—	118	—	—
A. Shrewsbury	W. Barnes	Melbourne	1884-85	116	—	—	—	—	—
P. A. Gibb	E. Paynter	Durban[2]	1938-39	—	115	—	—	—	—
G. Boycott	T. W. Graveney	Lord's	1966	—	—	115	—	—	—
W. Rhodes	H. Makepeace	Melbourne	1920-21	113	—	—	—	—	—
J. B. Hobbs	G. Gunn	Melbourne	1911-12	112	—	—	—	—	—
E. H. Bowley	K. S. Duleepsinhji	Auckland	1929-30	—	—	—	111	—	—
G. Boycott	E. R. Dexter	Manchester	1964	111	—	—	—	—	—
R. Subba Row	E. R. Dexter	Manchester	1961	110	—	—	—	—	—
R. Subba Row	E. R. Dexter	Birmingham	1961	109	—	—	—	—	—
H. Gimblett	M. J. Turnbull	Lord's	1936	—	—	—	—	108*	—

Century Partnerships—*ENGLAND* (*2nd wicket*)—*Cont.*

		Venue	*Series*	*A*	*SA*	*WI*	*NZ*	*I*	*P*
						Opponents			
L. Hutton	P. B. H. May	Bridgetown	1953-54	—	—	107	—	—	—
A. C. Maclaren	J. T. Tyldesley	Sydney	1901-02	106	—	—	—	—	—
H. Sutcliffe	J. W. Hearne	Melbourne	1924-25	106	—	—	—	—	—
W. G. Grace	R. Abel	Lord's	1896	105	—	—	—	—	—
J. B. Hobbs	H. Makepeace	Adelaide	1920-21	105	—	—	—	—	—
A. Ward	A. E. Stoddart	Melbourne	1894-95	104	—	—	—	—	—
G. Pullar	K. F. Barrington	Bridgetown	1959-60	—	—	103	—	—	—
W. Rhodes	G. Gunn	Melbourne	1911-12	102	—	—	—	—	—
P. Holmes	E. Tyldesley	Durban[2]	1927-28	—	102	—	—	—	—
J. B. Hobbs	J. W. Hearne	Sydney	1920-21	100	—	—	—	—	—
C. Washbrook	W. J. Edrich	Leeds	1948	100	—	—	—	—	—
L. Hutton	P. B. H. May	Oval	1953	100	—	—	—	—	—
		TOTAL	80	34	17	9	8	8	4

3rd WICKET

		Venue	*Series*	*A*	*SA*	*WI*	*NZ*	*I*	*P*
						Opponents			
W. J. Edrich	D. C. S. Compton	Lord's	1947	—	370	—	—	—	—
L. Hutton	W. R. Hammond	Oval	1939	—	—	264	—	—	—
W. R. Hammond	D. R. Jardine	Adelaide	1928-29	262	—	—	—	—	—
E. R. Dexter	K. F. Barrington	Manchester	1964	246	—	—	—	—	—
R. E. S. Wyatt	F. E. Woolley	Manchester	1929	—	245	—	—	—	—
J. Hardstaff, Jnr.	W. R. Hammond	Lord's	1937	—	—	—	245	—	—
E. Paynter	W. R. Hammond	Durban[2]	1938-39	—	242	—	—	—	—
W. J. Edrich	D. C. S. Compton	Manchester	1947	—	228	—	—	—	—
A. Ward	J. T. Brown	Melbourne	1894-95	210	—	—	—	—	—
T. W. Graveney	P. B. H. May	Nottingham	1957	—	—	207	—	—	—
K. F. Barrington	T. W. Graveney	Lord's	1967	—	—	—	—	—	201
C. A. Milton	P. B. H. May	Leeds	1958	—	—	—	194*	—	—

K. F. Barrington	M. J. K. Smith	Lahore[2]	1961-62	—	—	—	—	—	192
E. R. Dexter	K. F. Barrington	Johannesburg[3]	1964-65	—	191	—	—	—	—
J. H. Edrich	K. F. Barrington	Melbourne	1965-66	178	—	—	—	—	—
M. C. Cowdrey	E. R. Dexter	Melbourne	1962-63	175	—	—	—	—	—
W. H. Scotton	W. Barnes	Adelaide	1884-85	175	—	—	—	—	—
R. Subba Row	M. J. K. Smith	Oval	1959	—	—	—	—	169	—
A. Sandham	E. Hendren	Bridgetown	1929-30	—	—	168	—	—	—
P. B. H. May	D. C. S. Compton	Port of Spain	1953-54	—	—	166	—	—	—
W. J. Edrich	A. V. Bedser	Leeds	1948	155	—	—	—	—	—
W. Rhodes	C. P. Mead	Johannesburg[1]	1913-14	—	152	—	—	—	—
J. F. Crapp	D. C. S. Compton	Johannesburg[2]	1948-49	—	150	—	—	—	—
L. Hutton	D. C. S. Compton	Georgetown	1953-54	—	—	150	—	—	—
W. R. Hammond	E. Paynter	Auckland	1932-33	—	—	—	149	—	—
R. Subba Row	E. R. Dexter	Georgetown	1959-60	—	—	148	—	—	—
E. R. Dexter	M. J. K. Smith	Karachi	1961-62	—	—	—	—	—	143
J. B. Hobbs	E. Hendren	Melbourne	1920-21	142	—	—	—	—	—
K. F. Barrington	T. W. Graveney	Oval	1967	—	—	—	—	—	141
F. E. Woolley	E. Hendren	Lord's	1926	140	—	—	—	—	—
A. C. Russell	C. P. Mead	Durban[2]	1922-23	—	139	—	—	—	—
A. Shrewsbury	F. S. Jackson	Lord's	1893	137	—	—	—	—	—
L. Hutton	W. R. Hammond	Oval	1938	135	—	—	—	—	—
W. R. Hammond	M. Leyland	Sydney	1936-37	129	—	—	—	—	—
R. T. Simpson	D. C. S. Compton	Christchurch	1950-51	—	—	—	129	—	—
E. Tyldesley	W. R. Hammond	Durban[2]	1927-28	—	127	—	—	—	—
W. R. Hammond	T. S. Worthington	Manchester	1936	—	—	—	—	127	—
G. Boycott	E. R. Dexter	Lord's	1965	—	—	—	126	—	—
W. R. Hammond	R. E. S. Wyatt	Sydney	1932-33	125*	—	—	—	—	—
P. B. H. May	D. C. S. Compton	Manchester	1955	—	124	—	—	—	—
W. J. Edrich	P. B. H. May	Brisbane[2]	1954-55	124	—	—	—	—	—
H. Sutcliffe	Nawab of Pataudi, Snr.	Sydney	1932-33	123	—	—	—	—	—
F. E. Woolley	E. Hendren	Lord's	1924	—	121*	—	—	—	—
T. W. Hayward	C. B. Fry	Johannesburg[1]	1895-96	—	119	—	—	—	—
W. R. Hammond	E. Hendren	Johannesburg[1]	1930-31	—	119	—	—	—	—

Century Partnerships—*ENGLAND* (*3rd wicket*)—*Cont.*

		Venue	*Series*	*A*	*SA*	*WI*	*NZ*	*I*	*P*
						Opponents			
J. H. Edrich	K. F. Barrington	Melbourne	1965-66	118	—	—	—	—	—
W. Place	J. Hardstaff, Jnr.	Kingston	1947-48	—	—	113	—	—	—
L. Hutton	D. C. S. Compton	Nottingham	1948	111	—	—	—	—	—
G. Pullar	P. B. H. May	Manchester	1961	111	—	—	—	—	—
P. A. Gibb	W. R. Hammond	Cape Town	1938-39	—	109	—	—	—	—
L. Hutton	D. C. S. Compton	Oval	1950	—	—	109	—	—	—
P. E. Richardson	P. B. H. May	Nottingham	1956	108	—	—	—	—	—
M. C. Cowdrey	T. W. Graveney	Birmingham	1962	—	—	—	—	—	107
G. Boycott	T. W. Graveney	Leeds	1967	—	—	—	—	107	—
J. T. Tyldesley	J. Sharp	Leeds	1909	106	—	—	—	—	—
W. J. Edrich	D. C. S. Compton	Nottingham	1947	—	106	—	—	—	—
J. G. Dewes	W. G. A. Parkhouse	Nottingham	1950	—	—	106	—	—	—
W. Rhodes	C. B. Fry	Oval	1909	104	—	—	—	—	—
J. Hardstaff, Jnr.	C. J. Barnett	Lord's	1937	—	—	—	104	—	—
M. C. Cowdrey	D. S. Sheppard	Melbourne	1962-63	104	—	—	—	—	—
W. J. Edrich	D. C. S. Compton	Leeds	1948	103	—	—	—	—	—
A. C. Maclaren	F. S. Jackson	Lord's	1902	102*	—	—	—	—	—
J. T. Brown	A. Ward	Sydney	1894-95	102	—	—	—	—	—
W. J. Edrich	D. C. S. Compton	Sydney	1946-47	102	—	—	—	—	—
L. Hutton	D. C. S. Compton	Leeds	1949	—	—	—	102	—	—
L. Hutton	D. C. S. Compton	Lord's	1953	102	—	—	—	—	—
P. B. H. May	D. J. Insole	Leeds	1955	—	101	—	—	—	—
T. W. Hayward	C. B. Fry	Oval	1905	100	—	—	—	—	—
		TOTAL	68	28	16	9	7	3	5

Although the 3rd wicket added 145 against Australia (2nd Test—Melbourne) in 1903-04, this consisted of two partnerships: J. T. Tyldesley added 89 with R. E. Foster (retired ill) and a further 56 with L. C. Braund.

4th WICKET

		Venue	Series	A	SA	Opponents WI	NZ	I	P
P. B. H. May	M. C. Cowdrey	Birmingham	1957	—	—	411	—	—	—
W. R. Hammond	T. S. Worthington	Oval	1936	—	—	—	—	266	—
G. Boycott	B. L. D'Oliveira	Leeds	1967	—	—	—	—	252	—
A. Sandham	L. E. G. Ames	Kingston	1929-30	—	—	249	—	—	—
L. Hutton	D. C. S. Compton	Lord's	1939	—	—	248	—	—	—
E. Hendren	L. E. G. Ames	Port of Spain	1929-30	—	—	237	—	—	—
W. R. Hammond	E. Paynter	Lord's	1938	222	—	—	—	—	—
K. F. Barrington	E. R. Dexter	Kanpur	1961-62	—	—	—	—	206	—
W. R. Hammond	L. E. G. Ames	Cape Town	1938-39	—	197	—	—	—	—
M. C. Cowdrey	K. F. Barrington	Leeds	1959	—	—	—	—	193	—
B. R. Knight	P. H. Parfitt	Kanpur	1963-64	—	—	—	—	191	—
E. R. Dexter	P. H. Parfitt	Karachi	1961-62	—	—	—	—	—	188
P. B. H. May	C. Washbrook	Leeds	1956	187	—	—	—	—	—
T. W. Graveney	P. H. Parfitt	Nottingham	1962	—	—	—	—	—	184
P. B. H. May	M. C. Cowdrey	Sydney	1958-59	182	—	—	—	—	—
T. W. Graveney	M. C. Cowdrey	Nottingham	1966	—	—	169	—	—	—
K. F. Barrington	M. C. Cowdrey	Auckland	1962-63	—	—	—	166	—	—
W. R. Hammond	E. Paynter	Durban[2]	1938-39	—	164	—	—	—	—
E. R. Dexter	K. F. Barrington	Birmingham	1961	161	—	—	—	—	—
K. F. Barrington	E. R. Dexter	Bombay	1961-62	—	—	—	—	161	—
D. B. Carr	A. J. Watkins	New Delhi	1951-52	—	—	—	—	158	—
G. Boycott	K. F. Barrington	Port Elizabeth	1964-65	—	157	—	—	—	—
P. B. H. May	D. C. S. Compton	Oval	1956	156	—	—	—	—	—
D. C. S. Compton	T. W. Graveney	Nottingham	1954	—	—	—	—	—	154
C. B. Fry	F. S. Jackson	Oval	1905	151	—	—	—	—	—
W. R. Hammond	M. Leyland	Oval	1935	—	151	—	—	—	—
W. R. Hammond	E. Hendren	Sydney	1928-29	145	—	—	—	—	—
K. F. Barrington	E. R. Dexter	Port of Spain	1959-60	—	—	142	—	—	—
D. C. S. Compton	W. Watson	Nottingham	1951	—	141	—	—	—	—
R. E. S. Wyatt	M. Leyland	Nottingham	1935	—	139	—	—	—	—
K. F. Barrington	M. C. Cowdrey	Birmingham	1965	—	—	—	136	—	—

Century Partnerships—*ENGLAND* (*4th wicket*)—*Cont.*

		Venue	Series	A	SA	WI	NZ	I	P
				Opponents					
K. F. Barrington	M. C. Cowdrey	Oval	1965	—	135	—	—	—	—
W. R. Hammond	L. E. G. Ames	Oval	1931	—	—	—	130	—	—
W. R. Hammond	R. E. S. Wyatt	Leeds	1935	—	129	—	—	—	—
D. C. S. Compton	J. Hardstaff, Jnr.	Oval	1937	—	—	—	125	—	—
P. B. H. May	K. F. Barrington	Nottingham	1959	—	—	—	—	125	—
T. W. Hayward	A. J. L. Hill	Johannesburg[1]	1895-96	—	122	—	—	—	—
D. C. S. Compton	W. Watson	Lord's	1951	—	122	—	—	—	—
T. W. Graveney	B. L. D'Oliveira	Lord's	1967	—	—	—	—	122	—
P. E. Richardson	M. C. Cowdrey	Johannesburg[3]	1956-57	—	121	—	—	—	—
P. B. H. May	M. C. Cowdrey	Birmingham	1958	—	—	—	121	—	—
W. R. Hammond	D. R. Jardine	Manchester	1928	—	—	120	—	—	—
J. B. Bolus	K. F. Barrington	Madras[2]	1963-64	—	—	—	—	119	—
G. Gunn	L. C. Braund	Sydney	1907-08	117	—	—	—	—	—
E. Hendren	A. P. F. Chapman	Lord's	1926	116*	—	—	—	—	—
P. B. H. May	M. C. Cowdrey	Sydney	1954-55	116	—	—	—	—	—
G. Gunn	J. Hardstaff, Snr.	Sydney	1907-08	113	—	—	—	—	—
L. C. Braund	J. Hardstaff, Snr.	Adelaide	1907-08	113	—	—	—	—	—
D. C. S. Compton	A. J. Watkins	Cape Town	1948-49	—	111*	—	—	—	—
C. B. Fry	A. C. Maclaren	Oval	1899	110	—	—	—	—	—
M. J. K. Smith	K. F. Barrington	Manchester	1959	—	—	—	—	109	—
J. H. Edrich	P. H. Parfitt	Leeds	1965	—	—	—	109	—	—
L. C. Braund	K. L. Hutchings	Melbourne	1907-08	108	—	—	—	—	—
P. B. H. May	M. C. Cowdrey	Manchester	1955	—	108	—	—	—	—
J. H. Edrich	M. C. Cowdrey	Melbourne	1965-66	105	—	—	—	—	—
K. S. Duleepsinhji	E. Hendren	Lord's	1930	104	—	—	—	—	—
W. R. Hammond	L. E. G. Ames	Sydney	1936-37	104	—	—	—	—	—
P. E. Richardson	M. C. Cowdrey	Birmingham	1958	—	—	—	104	—	—
A. Shrewsbury	A. Ward	Oval	1893	103	—	—	—	—	—
M. J. Turnbull	W. R. Hammond	Johannesburg[1]	1930-31	—	101	—	—	—	—

F. L. Fane	F. E. Woolley	Cape Town	1909-10	—	100	—	—	—	—
K. F. Barrington	P. H. Parfitt	Johannesburg[3]	1964-65	—	100	—	—	—	—
		TOTAL	62	18	16	7	7	11	3

5*th* *WICKET*

				Opponents					
		Venue	*Series*	*A*	*SA*	*WI*	*NZ*	*I*	*P*
W. R. Hammond	L. E. G. Ames	Christchurch	1932-33	—	—	—	242	—	—
D. C. S. Compton	N. W. D. Yardley	Nottingham	1947	—	237	—	—	—	—
E. Paynter	D. C. S. Compton	Nottingham	1938	206	—	—	—	—	—
R. E. Foster	L. C. Braund	Sydney	1903-04	192	—	—	—	—	—
D. C. S. Compton	T. E. Bailey	Nottingham	1954	—	—	—	—	—	192
E. Hendren	M. Leyland	Manchester	1934	191	—	—	—	—	—
G. B. Legge	M. S. Nichols	Auckland	1929-30	—	—	—	184	—	—
J. Hardstaff, Jnr.	P. A. Gibb	Lord's	1946	—	—	—	—	182	—
M. Leyland	L. E. G. Ames	Oval	1935	—	179	—	—	—	—
R. Subba Row	K. F. Barrington	Oval	1961	172	—	—	—	—	—
W. Watson	T. E. Bailey	Lord's	1953	163	—	—	—	—	—
A. C. Maclaren	R. Peel	Melbourne	1894-95	162	—	—	—	—	—
A. Shrewsbury	W. Barnes	Lord's	1886	161	—	—	—	—	—
M. Leyland	R. E. S. Wyatt	Adelaide	1932-33	156	—	—	—	—	—
C. P. Mead	P. G. H. Fender	Durban[2]	1922-23	—	154	—	—	—	—
T. W. Graveney	A. J. Watkins	Bombay	1951-52	—	—	—	—	148	—
D. R. Jardine	B. H. Valentine	Bombay[1]	1933-34	—	—	—	—	145	—
D. C. S. Compton	T. E. Bailey	Manchester	1955	—	144	—	—	—	—
K. F. Barrington	J. M. Parks	Manchester	1964	143	—	—	—	—	—
D. C. S. Compton	T. E. Bailey	Sydney	1954-55	134	—	—	—	—	—
C. Milburn	T. W. Graveney	Lord's	1966	—	—	130*	—	—	—
M. C. Cowdrey	K. F. Barrington	Oval	1964	126*	—	—	—	—	—
W. R. Hammond	D. R. Jardine	Melbourne	1928-29	126	—	—	—	—	—
F. S. Jackson	R. H. Spooner	Manchester	1905	125	—	—	—	—	—
M. J. K. Smith	P. H. Parfitt	Christchurch	1965-66	—	—	—	125	—	—

Century Partnerships—*ENGLAND* (5*th wicket*)—*Cont.*

		Venue	*Series*	*A*	*SA*	*WI* (*Opponents*)	*NZ*	*I*	*P*
D. C. S. Compton	J. Hardstaff, Jnr.	Adelaide	1946-47	118	—	—	—	—	—
P. B. H. May	M. C. Cowdrey	Melbourne	1958-59	118	—	—	—	—	—
P. H. Parfitt	M. C. Cowdrey	New Delhi	1963-64	—	—	—	—	115	—
P. F. Warner	F. E. Woolley	Lord's	1912	—	113	—	—	—	—
M. J. K. Smith	P. H. Parfitt	Christchurch	1965-66	—	—	—	113	—	—
R. Abel	W. Barnes	Oval	1888	112	—	—	—	—	—
J. W. Hearne	F. E. Woolley	Leeds	1912	—	111	—	—	—	—
D. C. S. Compton	T. W. Graveney	Port of Spain	1953-54	—	—	110	—	—	—
A. J. Watkins	C. J. Poole	Calcutta	1951-52	—	—	—	—	107	—
H. Makepeace	J. W. H. T. Douglas	Melbourne	1920-21	106	—	—	—	—	—
R. Abel	H. Wood	Cape Town	1888-89	—	105	—	—	—	—
R. T. Simpson	T. E. Bailey	Manchester	1949	—	—	—	105	—	—
M. C. Cowdrey	M. J. K. Smith	Lord's	1965	—	—	—	105	—	—
C. P. Mead	F. E. Woolley	Port Elizabeth	1913-14	—	104	—	—	—	—
B. L. D'Oliveira	D. B. Close	Lord's	1967	—	—	—	—	—	104
E. Tyldesley	P. G. H. Fender	Manchester	1921	102*	—	—	—	—	—
A. Sandham	E. Hendren	Oval	1924	—	101	—	—	—	—
K. F. Barrington	T. W. Graveney	Adelaide	1962-63	101*	—	—	—	—	—
E. R. Dexter	P. J. Sharpe	Birmingham	1963	—	—	101	—	—	—
D. B. Close	P. J. Sharpe	Oval	1963	—	—	101	—	—	—
		TOTAL	45	19	9	4	6	5	2

Although the 5th wicket added 115 against Australia in 1884-85 (5th Test—Melbourne), this consisted of two partnerships: A. Shrewsbury added 73 with W. Bates (retired hurt) and a further 42 with W. Flowers.

6th WICKET

		Venue	Series	A	SA	WI	NZ	I	P
						Opponents			
		Venue	*Series*	*A*	*SA*	*WI*	*NZ*	*I*	*P*
P. H. Parfitt	B. R. Knight	Auckland	1962-63	—	—	—	240	—	—
L. Hutton	J. Hardstaff, Jnr.	Oval	1938	215	—	—	—	—	—
K. F. Barrington	J. M. Parks	Durban[2]	1964-65	—	206*	—	—	—	—
D. C. S. Compton	T. E. Bailey	Lord's	1949	—	—	—	189	—	—
W. R. Hammond	L. E. G. Ames	Lord's	1938	186	—	—	—	—	—
H. Sutcliffe	R. E. S. Wyatt	Oval	1930	170	—	—	—	—	—
T. E. Bailey	T. G. Evans	Manchester	1950	—	—	161	—	—	—
T. W. Graveney	T. G. Evans	Lord's	1952	—	—	—	—	159	—
J. T. Tyldesley	R. H. Spooner	Oval	1905	158	—	—	—	—	—
L. E. G. Ames	J. Iddon	Kingston	1934-35	—	—	157	—	—	—
C. P. Mead	F. T. Mann	Durban[2]	1922-23	—	156	—	—	—	—
P. H. Parfitt	D. A. Allen	Birmingham	1962	—	—	—	—	—	153*
L. C. Braund	G. L. Jessop	Lord's	1907	—	145	—	—	—	—
M. Leyland	L. E. G. Ames	Manchester	1934	142	—	—	—	—	—
F. S. Jackson	L. C. Braund	Manchester	1902	141	—	—	—	—	—
E. Hendren	M. Leyland	Melbourne	1928-29	140	—	—	—	—	—
M. C. Cowdrey	J. M. Parks	Melbourne	1965-66	138	—	—	—	—	—
W. W. Read	F. S. Jackson	Oval	1893	131	—	—	—	—	—
M. Leyland	M. W. Tate	Lord's	1929	—	129	—	—	—	—
M. Leyland	L. E. G. Ames	Lord's	1934	129	—	—	—	—	—
A. P. F. Chapman	G. O. Allen	Lord's	1930	125	—	—	—	—	—
G. H. Hirst	K. S. Ranjitsinhji	Sydney	1897-98	124	—	—	—	—	—
J. W. H. T. Douglas	A. C. Russell	Adelaide	1920-21	124	—	—	—	—	—
F. E. Woolley	F. T. Mann	Johannesburg[1]	1922-23	—	124	—	—	—	—
C. P. Mead	L. H. Tennyson	Oval	1921	121	—	—	—	—	—
M. J. K. Smith	P. M. Walker	Lord's	1960	—	120	—	—	—	—
M. J. K. Smith	J. M. Parks	Cape Town	1964-65	—	117	—	—	—	—
W. W. Read	E. F. S. Tylecote	Sydney	1882-83	115	—	—	—	—	—
F. S. Jackson	W. Rhodes	Nottingham	1905	113*	—	—	—	—	—
J. T. Ikin	N. W. D. Yardley	Melbourne	1946-47	113	—	—	—	—	—
F. S. Jackson	G. L. Jessop	Oval	1902	109	—	—	—	—	—

Century Partnerships—*ENGLAND* (*6th wicket*)—*Cont.*

		Venue	*Series*	*A*	*SA*	*WI*	*NZ*	*I*	*P*
						Opponents			
W. G. Quaife	L. C. Braund	Adelaide	1901-02	108	—	—	—	—	—
L. Hutton	T. G. Evans	Kingston	1953-54	—	—	108	—	—	—
F. E. Woolley	M. Leyland	Leeds	1929	—	106	—	—	—	—
M. J. Horton	T. G. Evans	Nottingham	1959	—	—	—	—	106	—
M. Leyland	R. W. V. Robins	Manchester	1935	—	105	—	—	—	—
J. W. H. T. Douglas	P. G. H. Fender	Melbourne	1920-21	104	—	—	—	—	—
E. R. Dexter	R. W. Barber	Lahore[2]	1961-62	—	—	—	—	—	101*
F. G. Mann	R. O. Jenkins	Port Elizabeth	1948-49	—	100	—	—	—	—
		TOTAL	39	20	10	3	2	2	2

Although the 6th wicket added 121 against Australia in 1934 (5th Test—Melbourne), this consisted of two partnerships: M. Leyland added 85 with L. E. G. Ames (retired hurt) and a further 36 with O. Allen.

7th WICKET

		Venue	*Series*	*A*	*SA*	*WI*	*NZ*	*I*	*P*
						Opponents			
M. J. K. Smith	J. M. Parks	Port of Spain	1959-60	—	—	197	—	—	—
M. C. Cowdrey	T. G. Evans	Lord's	1957	—	—	174	—	—	—
F. E. Woolley	J. Vine	Sydney	1911-12	143	—	—	—	—	—
J. Sharp	K. L. Hutchings	Oval	1909	142	—	—	—	—	—
D. R. Jardine	R. W. V. Robins	Manchester	1933	—	—	140	—	—	—
W. W. Whysall	R. Kilner	Melbourne	1924-25	133	—	—	—	—	—
A. A. Lilley	L. C. Braund	Sydney	1901-02	124	—	—	—	—	—
E. R. Dexter	R. Swetman	Bridgetown	1959-60	—	—	123	—	—	—
J. B. Hobbs	E. Hendren	Adelaide	1924-25	117	—	—	—	—	—
J. W. H. T. Douglas	M. C. Bird	Durban[1]	1913-14	—	115	—	—	—	—
T. W. Hayward	A. A. Lilley	Manchester	1899	113	—	—	—	—	—
M. Leyland	R. W. V. Robins	Melbourne	1936-37	111	—	—	—	—	—
F. R. Brown	W. Voce	Christchurch	1932-33	—	—	—	108	—	—

		Venue	Series	A	SA	WI	NZ	I	P
J. Hardstaff, Jnr.	A. Wood	Oval	1938	106	—	—	—	—	—
L. Hutton	J. H. Wardle	Kingston	1953-54	—	—	105	—	—	—
W. Flowers	J. M. Read	Sydney	1884-85	102	—	—	—	—	—
R. Illingworth	R. Swetman	Oval	1959	—	—	—	—	102	—
E. Hendren	G. Geary	Nottingham	1934	101	—	—	—	—	—
		TOTAL	18	10	1	5	1	1	—

8th WICKET

						Opponents			
		Venue	*Series*	*A*	*SA*	*WI*	*NZ*	*I*	*P*
L. E. G. Ames	G. O. Allen	Lord's	1931	—	—	—	246	—	—
T. W. Graveney	J. T. Murray	Oval	1966	—	—	217	—	—	—
C. W. Wright	R. H. Bromley-Davenport	Johannesburg[1]	1895-96	—	154	—	—	—	—
R. W. V. Robins	H. Verity	Manchester	1936	—	—	—	—	138	—
E. Hendren	H. Larwood	Brisbane[1]	1928-29	124	—	—	—	—	—
D. C. S. Compton	A. V. Bedser	Manchester	1948	121	—	—	—	—	—
D. A. Allen	D. J. Brown	Christchurch	1965-66	—	—	—	107	—	—
		TOTAL	7	2	1	1	2	1	—

9th WICKET

						Opponents			
		Venue	*Series*	*A*	*SA*	*WI*	*NZ*	*I*	*P*
M. C. Cowdrey	A. C. Smith	Wellington	1962-63	—	—	—	163*	—	—
W. H. Scotton	W. W. Read	Oval	1884	151	—	—	—	—	—
F. E. Woolley	A. P. Freeman	Sydney	1924-25	128	—	—	—	—	—
T. E. Bailey	D. V. P. Wright	Christchurch	1950-51	—	—	—	117	—	—
R. E. Foster	A. E. Relf	Sydney	1903-04	115	—	—	—	—	—
G. Geary	G. G. Macaulay	Leeds	1926	108	—	—	—	—	—
		TOTAL	6	4	—	—	2	—	—

Century Partnerships—*ENGLAND—Cont.*

10th WICKET

		Venue	Series	A	SA	WI	NZ	I	P
R. E. Foster	W. Rhodes	Sydney	1903-04	130	—	—	—	—	—
K. Higgs	J. A. Snow	Oval	1966	—	—	128	—	—	—
		TOTAL	2	1	—	1	—	—	—

(Opponents: A, SA, WI, NZ, I, P)

AUSTRALIA

1st WICKET

		Venue	Series	E	SA	WI	NZ	I	P
W. M. Lawry	R. B. Simpson	Bridgetown	1964-65	—	—	382	—	—	—
R. B. Simpson	W. M. Lawry	Adelaide	1965-66	244	—	—	—	—	—
J. H. Fingleton	W. A. Brown	Cape Town	1935-36	—	233	—	—	—	—
W. M. Lawry	I. R. Redpath	Melbourne	1963-64	—	219	—	—	—	—
A. R. Morris	J. A. R. Moroney	Johannesburg[2]	1949-50	—	214	—	—	—	—
W. M. Lawry	R. B. Simpson	Manchester	1964	201	—	—	—	—	—
A. R. Morris	C. C. McDonald	Port of Spain	1954-55	—	—	191	—	—	—
C. C. McDonald	J. W. Burke	Cape Town	1957-58	—	190	—	—	—	—
W. Bardsley	S. E. Gregory	Oval	1909	180	—	—	—	—	—
W. H. Ponsford	A. A. Jackson	Adelaide	1930-31	—	—	172*	—	—	—
C. C. McDonald	J. W. Burke	Adelaide	1958-59	171	—	—	—	—	—
W. M. Woodfull	W. H. Ponsford	Lord's	1930	162	—	—	—	—	—
J. H. Fingleton	W. A. Brown	Durban[2]	1935-36	—	162	—	—	—	—
W. M. Woodfull	W. H. Ponsford	Oval	1930	159	—	—	—	—	—
C. C. McDonald	R. B. Simpson	Melbourne	1960-61	—	—	146	—	—	—
C. C. McDonald	J. W. Burke	Lord's	1956	137	—	—	—	—	—
W. M. Lawry	R. B. Simpson	Brisbane[2]	1962-63	136	—	—	—	—	—
V. T. Trumper	R. A. Duff	Manchester	1902	135	—	—	—	—	—
W. M. Woodfull	V. Y. Richardson	Brisbane[2]	1932-33	133	—	—	—	—	—
V. T. Trumper	R. A. Duff	Adelaide	1903-04	129	—	—	—	—	—
V. T. Trumper	M. A. Noble	Melbourne	1907-08	126	—	—	—	—	—

(Opponents: E, SA, WI, NZ, I, P)

		Venue	Series	E	SA	WI	NZ	I	P
S. G. Barnes	A. R. Morris	Sydney	1946-47	126	—	—	—	—	—
H. L. Collins	C. G. Macartney	Sydney	1920-21	123	—	—	—	—	—
S. G. Barnes	A. R. Morris	Lord's	1948	122	—	—	—	—	—
C. C. McDonald	A. R. Morris	Melbourne	1952-53	—	122	—	—	—	—
R. B. Simpson	W. M. Lawry	Melbourne	1965-66	120	—	—	—	—	—
R. B. Simpson	W. M. Lawry	Johannesburg[3]	1966-67	—	118	—	—	—	—
H. L. Collins	W. Bardsley	Melbourne	1920-21	117	—	—	—	—	—
S. G. Barnes	A. R. Morris	Oval	1948	117	—	—	—	—	—
C. E. McLeod	J. Worrall	Oval	1899	116	—	—	—	—	—
H. L. Collins	W. Bardsley	Melbourne	1920-21	116	—	—	—	—	—
A. R. Morris	M. Harvey	Adelaide	1946-47	116	—	—	—	—	—
W. M. Lawry	R. B. Simpson	Calcutta	1964-65	—	—	—	—	115	—
W. M. Lawry	R. B. Simpson	Manchester	1961	113	—	—	—	—	—
A. C. Bannerman	W. L. Murdoch	Melbourne	1881-82	110	—	—	—	—	—
C. C. McDonald	L. E. Favell	Bridgetown	1954-55	—	—	108	—	—	—
W. M. Woodfull	W. H. Ponsford	Manchester	1930	106	—	—	—	—	—
J. H. Fingleton	W. A. Brown	Johannesburg[1]	1935-36	—	105	—	—	—	—
W. Bardsley	T. J. E. Andrews	Lord's	1921	103	—	—	—	—	—
A. R. Morris	C. C. McDonald	Kingston	1954-55	—	—	102	—	—	—
V. T. Trumper	R. A. Duff	Cape Town	1902-03	—	100	—	—	—	—
		TOTAL	41	25	9	6	—	1	—

2nd WICKET

				Opponents					
		Venue	*Series*	*E*	*SA*	*WI*	*NZ*	*I*	*P*
W. H. Ponsford	D. G. Bradman	Oval	1934	451	—	—	—	—	—
A. R. Morris	D. G. Bradman	Leeds	1948	301	—	—	—	—	—
C. C. McDonald	A. L. Hassett	Adelaide	1952-53	—	275	—	—	—	—
W. M. Woodfull	D. G. Bradman	Melbourne	1931-32	—	274	—	—	—	—
S. G. Barnes	D. G. Bradman	Adelaide	1947-48	—	—	—	—	236	—
W. M. Woodfull	C. G. Macartney	Leeds	1926	235	—	—	—	—	—
W. M. Woodfull	D. G. Bradman	Lord's	1930	231	—	—	—	—	—

Century Partnerships—*AUSTRALIA* (*2nd wicket*)—*Cont.*

		Venue	*Series*	*E*	*SA*	*Opponents* *WI*	*NZ*	*I*	*P*
W. H. Ponsford	D. G. Bradman	Brisbane[1]	1930-31	—	—	229	—	—	—
W. Bardsley	C. Hill	Sydney	1910-11	—	224	—	—	—	—
W. M. Woodfull	H. L. Hendry	Sydney	1928-29	215	—	—	—	—	—
J. W. Burke	R. N. Harvey	Bombay	1956-57	—	—	—	—	204	—
W. A. Brown	S. J. McCabe	Manchester	1934	196	—	—	—	—	—
W. M. Woodfull	C. G. Macartney	Manchester	1926	192	—	—	—	—	—
W. M. Woodfull	D. G. Bradman	Leeds	1930	192	—	—	—	—	—
H. L. Collins	W. H. Ponsford	Sydney	1924-25	190	—	—	—	—	—
J. H. Fingleton	S. J. McCabe	Johannesburg[1]	1935-36	—	177	—	—	—	—
W. M. Woodfull	D. G. Bradman	Adelaide	1931-32	—	176	—	—	—	—
A. C. Bannerman	J. J. Lyons	Sydney	1891-92	174	—	—	—	—	—
S. G. Barnes	D. G. Bradman	Lord's	1948	174	—	—	—	—	—
W. A. Brown	D. G. Bradman	Nottingham	1938	170	—	—	—	—	—
J. A. R. Moroney	R. N. Harvey	Johannesburg[2]	1949-50	—	170	—	—	—	—
A. R. Morris	K. R. Miller	Lord's	1953	165	—	—	—	—	—
W. M. Woodfull	D. G. Bradman	Brisbane[2]	1931-32	—	163	—	—	—	—
W. M. Woodfull	D. G. Bradman	Melbourne	1930-31	—	—	162	—	—	—
W. A. Brown	S. J. McCabe	Durban[2]	1935-36	—	161	—	—	—	—
R. B. Simpson	R. N. Harvey	Sydney	1962-63	160	—	—	—	—	—
A. R. Morris	R. N. Harvey	Adelaide	1952-53	—	157	—	—	—	—
J. Darling	C. Hill	Adelaide	1897-98	148	—	—	—	—	—
C. E. Kelleway	C. G. Macartney	Lord's	1912	146	—	—	—	—	—
P. S. McDonnell	W. L. Murdoch	Oval	1884	143	—	—	—	—	—
V. T. Trumper	C. Hill	Adelaide	1903-04	143	—	—	—	—	—
W. M. Lawry	N. C. O'Neill	Sydney	1963-64	—	140	—	—	—	—
W. M. Lawry	R. M. Cowper	Bridgetown	1964-65	—	—	140	—	—	—
R. B. Simpson	R. M. Cowper	Port of Spain	1964-65	—	—	138	—	—	—
W. M. Woodfull	K. E. Rigg	Sydney	1931-32	—	137	—	—	—	—
V. T. Trumper	C. Hill	Adelaide	1901-02	136	—	—	—	—	—

F. A. Iredale	G. Giffen	Manchester	1896	131	—	—	—	—	—
C. C. McDonald	R. N. Harvey	Melbourne	1958-59	126	—	—	—	—	—
A. L. Hassett	R. N. Harvey	Lord's	1953	125	—	—	—	—	—
C. E. McLeod	C. Hill	Melbourne	1897-98	124	—	—	—	—	—
C. G. Macartney	H. V. Hordern	Sydney	1910-11	—	124	—	—	—	—
J. H. Fingleton	D. G. Bradman	Sydney	1936-37	124	—	—	—	—	—
H. L. Collins	C. G. Macartney	Lord's	1926	123	—	—	—	—	—
A. R. Morris	A. L. Hassett	Nottingham	1953	122	—	—	—	—	—
C. E. Kelleway	C. Hill	Sydney	1911-12	121	—	—	—	—	—
K. A. Archer	A. L. Hassett	Sydney	1950-51	121	—	—	—	—	—
R. B. Simpson	I. R. Redpath	Karachi	1964-65	—	—	—	—	—	119
R. B. Simpson	I. R. Redpath	Cape Town	1966-67	—	117	—	—	—	—
W. M. Woodfull	D. G. Bradman	Sydney	1932-33	115	—	—	—	—	—
H. L. Collins	J. Ryder	Johannesburg[1]	1921-22	—	113	—	—	—	—
H. L. Collins	W. Bardsley	Sydney	1920-21	111	—	—	—	—	—
S. G. Barnes	W. A. Brown	Wellington	1945-46	—	—	—	109	—	—
C. Hill	M. A. Noble	Nottingham	1905	106†	—	—	—	—	—
C. C. McDonald	R. N. Harvey	Adelaide	1958-59	105	—	—	—	—	—
J. A. R. Moroney	K. R. Miller	Cape Town	1949-50	—	104	—	—	—	—
W. Bardsley	C. Hill	Melbourne	1910-11	—	101	—	—	—	—
		TOTAL	56	32	16	4	1	2	1

† 128 runs were added for this wicket; V. T. Trumper (retired hurt) was replaced by M. A. Noble after 22 runs had been added.

Although the 2nd wicket added 134 against India in 1947-48 (5th Test—Melbourne), this consisted of two partnerships: W. A. Brown added 92 with D. G. Bradman (retired hurt) and a further 42 with K. R. Miller.

3rd WICKET

				Opponents					
		Venue	*Series*	*E*	*SA*	*WI*	*NZ*	*I*	*P*
C. C. McDonald	R. N. Harvey	Kingston	1954-55	—	—	295	—	—	—
D. G. Bradman	A. L. Hassett	Brisbane[2]	1946-47	276	—	—	—	—	—
D. G. Bradman	S. J. McCabe	Melbourne	1936-37	249	—	—	—	—	—

Century Partnerships—*AUSTRALIA* (*3rd wicket*)—*Cont.*

		Venue	*Series*	*E*	*SA*	*WI*	*NZ*	*I*	*P*
						Opponents			
W. Bardsley	C. E. Kelleway	Lord's	1912	—	242	—	—	—	—
D. G. Bradman	A. F. Kippax	Leeds	1930	229	—	—	—	—	—
R. M. Cowper	B. C. Booth	Port of Spain	1964-65	—	—	225†	—	—	—
R. N. Harvey	K. R. Miller	Kingston	1954-55	—	—	224	—	—	—
W. M. Lawry	R. M. Cowper	Melbourne	1965-66	212	—	—	—	—	—
H. L. Collins	J. M. Gregory	Johannesburg[1]	1921-22	—	209	—	—	—	—
W. L. Murdoch	H. J. H. Scott	Oval	1884	207	—	—	—	—	—
R. N. Harvey	N. C. O'Neill	Bombay	1959-60	—	—	—	—	207	—
W. Bardsley	C. E. Kelleway	Manchester	1912	—	202	—	—	—	—
A. R. Morris	R. N. Harvey	Brisbane[2]	1954-55	202	—	—	—	—	—
J. Darling	J. Worrall	Sydney	1897-98	193	—	—	—	—	—
D. G. Bradman	A. F. Kippax	Brisbane[1]	1930-31	—	—	193	—	—	—
D. G. Bradman	A. F. Kippax	Lord's	1930	192	—	—	—	—	—
A. R. Morris	A. L. Hassett	Adelaide	1946-47	189	—	—	—	—	—
A. R. Morris	R. N. Harvey	Port Elizabeth	1949-50	—	187	—	—	—	—
D. G. Bradman	A. L. Hassett	Melbourne	1947-48	—	—	—	—	169	—
W. W. Armstrong	C. Hill	Johannesburg[1]	1902-03	—	164	—	—	—	—
J. W. Burke	R. Benaud	Johannesburg[3]	1957-58	—	158	—	—	—	—
C. Hill	H. Carter	Adelaide	1911-12	157	—	—	—	—	—
R. N. Harvey	A. L. Hassett	Brisbane[2]	1952-53	—	155	—	—	—	—
D. G. Bradman	S. J. McCabe	Oval	1934	150	—	—	—	—	—
W. M. Lawry	N. C. O'Neill	Bridgetown	1964-65	—	—	126‡	—	—	—
R. N. Harvey	N. C. O'Neill	Birmingham	1961	146	—	—	—	—	—
C. G. Macartney	W. Bardsley	Sydney	1910-11	—	145	—	—	—	—
C. Hill	D. R. A. Gehrs	Sydney	1910-11	—	144	—	—	—	—
J. W. Burke	P. J. Burge	Bombay	1956	—	—	—	—	137	—
R. B. Simpson	B. C. Booth	Adelaide	1962-63	133	—	—	—	—	—

† 228 runs were added for this wicket; N. C. O'Neill (retired hurt) was replaced by B. C. Booth after 3 runs had been added.
‡ 147 runs were scored for this wicket, but W. M. Lawry retired hurt after 126 runs had been added.

		Venue	Series	E	SA	WI	NZ	I	P
J. Ryder	J. M. Gregory	Melbourne	1920-21	128*	—	—	—	—	—
R. N. Harvey	N. C. O'Neill	Melbourne	1958-59	118	—	—	—	—	—
R. B. Simpson	P. J. Burge	Karachi	1964-65	—	—	—	—	—	116
R. A. Duff	M. A. Noble	Oval	1905	115	—	—	—	—	—
V. T. Trumper	S. E. Gregory	Sydney	1907-08	114	—	—	—	—	—
C. C. McDonald	R. N. Harvey	Sydney	1952-53	—	113	—	—	—	—
K. E. Rigg	D. G. Bradman	Sydney	1931-32	—	111	—	—	—	—
A. R. Morris	R. N. Harvey	Adelaide	1950-51	110	—	—	—	—	—
D. G. Bradman	S. J. McCabe	Adelaide	1936-37	109	—	—	—	—	—
A. R. Morris	A. L. Hassett	Oval	1948	109	—	—	—	—	—
C. G. Macartney	T. J. E. Andrews	Oval	1921	108	—	—	—	—	—
R. N. Harvey	N. C. O'Neill	Sydney	1960-61	—	—	108	—	—	—
D. G. Bradman	A. L. Hassett	Adelaide	1947-48	—	—	—	—	105	—
R. B. Simpson	P. J. Burge	Adelaide	1963-64	—	104	—	—	—	—
R. N. Harvey	A. L. Hassett	Melbourne	1952-53	—	103	—	—	—	—
W. Bardsley	W. W. Armstrong	Melbourne	1910-11	—	102	—	—	—	—
C. G. Macartney	C. E. Pellew	Leeds	1921	101	—	—	—	—	—
D. G. Bradman	A. L. Hassett	Brisbane[2]	1947-48	—	—	—	—	101	—
R. N. Harvey	W. Watson	Bridgetown	1954-55	—	—	100	—	—	—
		TOTAL	49	22	14	7	—	5	1

4th WICKET

				Opponents					
		Venue	Series	E	SA	WI	NZ	I	P
W. H. Ponsford	D. G. Bradman	Leeds	1934	388	—	—	—	—	—
D. G. Bradman	A. A. Jackson	Oval	1930	243	—	—	—	—	—
A. L. Hassett	K. R. Miller	Sydney	1951-52	—	—	235	—	—	—
G. H. S. Trott	S. E. Gregory	Lord's	1896	221	—	—	—	—	—
C. G. Macartney	J. M. Gregory	Sydney	1920-21	198	—	—	—	—	—
C. E. Kelleway	W. W. Armstrong	Adelaide	1920-21	194	—	—	—	—	—
R. N. Harvey	N. C. O'Neill	Adelaide	1962-63	194	—	—	—	—	—
A. C. Bannerman	P. S. McDonnell	Sydney	1881-82	191	—	—	—	—	—

Century Partnerships—*AUSTRALIA* (*4th wicket*)—*Cont.*

		Venue	*Series*	*E*	*SA*	*Opponents* *WI*	*NZ*	*I*	*P*
A. F. Kippax	S. J. McCabe	Adelaide	1930-31	—	—	182	—	—	—
R. N. Harvey	G. B. Hole	Manchester	1953	173	—	—	—	—	—
R. M. Cowper	K. D. Walters	Melbourne	1965-66	172	—	—	—	—	—
F. A. Iredale	G. Giffen	Sydney	1894-95	171	—	—	—	—	—
R. N. Harvey	K. R. Miller	Sydney	1952-53	—	168	—	—	—	—
M. A. Noble	S. E. Gregory	Adelaide	1903-04	162	—	—	—	—	—
W. H. Ponsford	J. M. Taylor	Melbourne	1924-25	161	—	—	—	—	—
A. F. Kippax	J. Ryder	Melbourne	1928-29	161	—	—	—	—	—
R. N. Harvey	S. J. E. Loxton	Melbourne	1947-48	—	—	—	—	159	—
W. W. Armstrong	C. Hill	Melbourne	1910-11	—	154	—	—	—	—
N. C. O'Neill	P. J. Burge	Calcutta	1959-60	—	—	—	—	150	—
R. N. Harvey	I. D. Craig	Melbourne	1952-53	—	148	—	—	—	—
A. L. Hassett	K. R. Miller	Adelaide	1947-48	—	—	—	—	142	—
J. Ryder	A. F. Kippax	Adelaide	1928-29	137	—	—	—	—	—
R. N. Harvey	K. D. Mackay	New Delhi	1959-60	—	—	—	—	132	—
R. N. Harvey	G. B. Hole	Brisbane[2]	1954-55	131	—	—	—	—	—
C. Hill	M. A. Noble	Lord's	1899	130	—	—	—	—	—
J. W. Burke	K. D. Mackay	Cape Town	1957-58	—	130	—	—	—	—
W. M. Woodfull	A. J. Richardson	Leeds	1926	129	—	—	—	—	—
A. A. Jackson	J. Ryder	Adelaide	1928-29	126	—	—	—	—	—
B. C. Booth	R. M. Cowper	Bombay	1964-65	—	—	—	—	125	—
W. A. Brown	A. L. Hassett	Lord's	1938	124	—	—	—	—	—
R. N. Harvey	K. R. Miller	Melbourne	1951-52	—	—	124	—	—	—
N. C. O'Neill	P. J. Burge	Oval	1961	123	—	—	—	—	—
K. R. Miller	R. N. Harvey	Leeds	1948	121	—	—	—	—	—
D. G. Bradman	K. R. Miller	Brisbane[2]	1947-48	—	—	—	—	120	—
B. C. Booth	N. C. O'Neill	Brisbane[2]	1963-64	—	120	—	—	—	—
W. Bardsley	V. T. Trumper	Adelaide	1910-11	—	118	—	—	—	—
A. F. Kippax	S. J. McCabe	Melbourne	1931-32	—	114	—	—	—	—
A. R. Morris	A. L. Hassett	Port Elizabeth	1949-50	—	114	—	—	—	—

W. A. Brown	S. J. McCabe	Nottingham	1934	112	—	—	—	—	—
N. C. O'Neill	L. E. Favell	Sydney	1958-59	110	—	—	—	—	—
C. G. Macartney	J. M. Taylor	Leeds	1921	109	—	—	—	—	—
K. R. Miller	A. L. Hassett	Johannesburg[2]	1949-50	—	109	—	—	—	—
A. L. Hassett	K. R. Miller	Nottingham	1953	109	—	—	—	—	—
N. C. O'Neill	P. J. Burge	Sydney	1962-63	109	—	—	—	—	—
S. E. Gregory	C. Hill	Sheffield	1902	107	—	—	—	—	—
M. A. Noble	W. W. Armstrong	Sydney	1903-04	106	—	—	—	—	—
C. G. Macartney	J. Ryder	Durban[1]	1921-22	—	106	—	—	—	—
A. L. Hassett	K. R. Miller	Brisbane[2]	1946-47	106	—	—	—	—	—
W. M. Lawry	B. C. Booth	Oval	1964	106	—	—	—	—	—
		TOTAL	49	30	10	3	—	6	—

5th WICKET

				Opponents					
		Venue	*Series*	*E*	*SA*	*WI*	*NZ*	*I*	*P*
S. G. Barnes	D. G. Bradman	Sydney	1946-47	405	—	—	—	—	—
A. R. Morris	D. G. Bradman	Melbourne	1947-48	—	—	—	—	223*	—
K. R. Miller	R. G. Archer	Kingston	1954-55	—	—	220	—	—	—
R. B. Simpson	B. C. Booth	Manchester	1964	219	—	—	—	—	—
P. J. Burge	K. D. Walters	Melbourne	1956-66	198	—	—	—	—	—
W. M. Lawry	K. D. Walters	Brisbane[2]	1965-66	187	—	—	—	—	—
P. J. Burge	B. C. Booth	Oval	1961	185	—	—	—	—	—
D. G. Bradman	A. G. Fairfax	Melbourne	1928-29	183	—	—	—	—	—
W. H. Ponsford	W. M. Woodfull	Sydney	1930-31	—	—	183	—	—	—
C. L. Badcock	R. G. Gregory	Melbourne	1936-37	161	—	—	—	—	—
K. R. Miller	I. W. Johnson	Adelaide	1946-47	150	—	—	—	—	—
W. W. Armstrong	V. T. Trumper	Melbourne	1910-11	—	143	—	—	—	—
S. E. Gregory	J. Darling	Melbourne	1894-95	142	—	—	—	—	—
R. N. Harvey	S. J. E. Loxton	Cape Town	1949-50	—	140	—	—	—	—
G. Giffen	S. E. Gregory	Sydney	1894-95	139	—	—	—	—	—
D. G. Bradman	R. G. Gregory	Adelaide	1936-37	135	—	—	—	—	—

Century Partnerships—*AUSTRALIA* (*5th wicket*)—*Cont.*

		Venue	*Series*	*E*	*SA*	*WI*	*NZ*	*I*	*P*
R. N. Harvey	S. J. E. Loxton	Durban[2]	1949-50	—	135	—	—	—	—
S. J. McCabe	V. Y. Richardson	Sydney	1932-33	129	—	—	—	—	—
F. A. Iredale	G. H. S. Trott	Melbourne	1897-98	124	—	—	—	—	—
D. G. Bradman	A. L. Hassett	Nottingham	1948	120	—	—	—	—	—
W. Bardsley	V. T. Trumper	Oval	1909	118	—	—	—	—	—
D. G. Bradman	K. E. Rigg	Adelaide	1931-32	—	114	—	—	—	—
V. T. Trumper	C. Hill	Sydney	1907-08	108	—	—	—	—	—
T. Horan	G. Giffen	Melbourne	1881-82	107	—	—	—	—	—
G. H. S. Trott	H. Graham	Oval	1893	106	—	—	—	—	—
C. G. Macartney	W. W. Armstrong	Melbourne	1907-08	106	—	—	—	—	—
R. N. Harvey	S. J. E. Loxton	Leeds	1948	105	—	—	—	—	—
N. C. O'Neill	K. D. Mackay	Brisbane[2]	1960-61	—	—	103	—	—	—
J. Ryder	O. E. Nothling	Sydney	1928-29	102	—	—	—	—	—
B. C. Booth	R. Benaud	Brisbane[2]	1963-64	—	102	—	—	—	—
J. Darling	S. E. Gregory	Oval	1899	100	—	—	—	—	—
		TOTAL	31	22	5	3	—	1	—

6th WICKET

		Venue	*Series*	*E*	*SA*	*WI*	*NZ*	*I*	*P*
J. H. Fingleton	D. G. Bradman	Melbourne	1936-37	346	—	—	—	—	—
K. R. Miller	R. G. Archer	Bridgetown	1954-55	—	—	206	—	—	—
C. E. Kelleway	W. W. Armstrong	Sydney	1920-21	187	—	—	—	—	—
T. R. Veivers	B. N. Jarman	Bombay	1964-65	—	—	—	—	151	—
J. M. Gregory	W. W. Armstrong	Melbourne	1920-21	145	—	—	—	—	—
S. E. Gregory	H. Graham	Lord's	1893	142	—	—	—	—	—

		Venue	Series	E	SA	WI	NZ	I	P
R. M. Cowper	T. R. Veivers	Melbourne	1964-65	—	—	—	—	—	139
C. L. McCool	I. W. Johnson	Brisbane²	1946-47	131	—	—	—	—	—
C. E. Pellew	C. E. Kelleway	Adelaide	1920-21	126	—	—	—	—	—
V. Y. Richardson	C. E. Kelleway	Melbourne	1924-25	123	—	—	—	—	—
K. D. Walters	T. R. Veivers	Brisbane²	1965-66	119	—	—	—	—	—
V. T. Trumper	R. B. Minnett	Sydney	1911-12	109	—	—	—	—	—
C. E. Kelleway	V. S. Ransford	Melbourne	1910-11	—	107	—	—	—	—
R. N. Harvey	C. L. McCool	Durban²	1949-50	—	106*	—	—	—	—
W. H. Ponsford	A. F. Kippax	Sydney	1924-25	105	—	—	—	—	—
B. C. Booth	R. Benaud	Sydney	1963-64	—	100	—	—	—	—
		TOTAL	16	10	3	1	—	1	1

E

7th WICKET

		Venue	Series	E	SA	WI	NZ	I	P
				Opponents					
C. Hill	H. Trumble	Melbourne	1897-98	165	—	—	—	—	—
R. Benaud	G. D. McKenzie	Sydney	1963-64	—	160	—	—	—	—
K. R. Miller	I. W. Johnson	Sydney	1950-51	150	—	—	—	—	—
J. Ryder	T. J. E. Andrews	Adelaide	1924-25	134	—	—	—	—	—
R. Benaud	A. K. Davidson	Brisbane²	1960-61	—	—	134	—	—	—
K. R. Stackpole	G. D. Watson	Cape Town	1966-67	—	128	—	—	—	—
K. D. Mackay	R. Benaud	Lord's	1956	117	—	—	—	—	—
K. D. Mackay	A. K. Davidson	Sydney	1958-59	115	—	—	—	—	—
R. Benaud	A. T. W. Grout	Melbourne	1958-59	115	—	—	—	—	—
H. L. Collins	J. M. Gregory	Oval	1926	107	—	—	—	—	—
B. C. Booth	K. D. Mackay	Brisbane²	1962-63	103	—	—	—	—	—
		TOTAL	11	8	2	1	—	—	—

Century Partnerships—*AUSTRALIA—Cont.*

8th WICKET

		Venue	Series	*E*	*SA*	*WI*	*NZ*	*I*	*P*
C. Hill	R. J. Hartigan	Adelaide	1907-08	243	—	—	—	—	—
C. E. Pellew	J. M. Gregory	Melbourne	1920-21	173	—	—	—	—	—
G. J. Bonnor	S. P. Jones	Sydney	1884-85	154	—	—	—	—	—
D. Tallon	R. R. Lindwall	Melbourne	1946-47	154	—	—	—	—	—
R. Benaud	I. W. Johnson	Kingston	1954-55	—	—	137	—	—	—
C. E. Kelleway	W. A. Oldfield	Sydney	1924-25	116	—	—	—	—	—
H. Graham	A. E. Trott	Sydney	1894-95	112	—	—	—	—	—
W. W. Armstrong	H. Carter	Melbourne	1907-08	112	—	—	—	—	—
A. L. Hassett	R. R. Lindwall	Nottingham	1948	107	—	—	—	—	—
P. J. Burge	N. J. N. Hawke	Leeds	1964	105	—	—	—	—	—
		TOTAL	10	9	—	1	—	—	—

9th WICKET

		Venue	Series	*E*	*SA*	*WI*	*NZ*	*I*	*P*
S. E. Gregory	J. M. Blackham	Sydney	1894-95	154	—	—	—	—	—
J. Ryder	W. A. Oldfield	Adelaide	1924-25	108	—	—	—	—	—
A. E. V. Hartkopf	W. A. Oldfield	Melbourne	1924-25	100	—	—	—	—	—
		TOTAL	3	3	—	—	—	—	—

10th WICKET

		Venue	Series	*E*	*SA*	*WI*	*NZ*	*I*	*P*
J. M. Taylor	A. A. Mailey	Sydney	1924-25	127	—	—	—	—	—
R. A. Duff	W. W. Armstrong	Melbourne	1901-02	120	—	—	—	—	—
		TOTAL	2	2	—	—	—	—	—

SOUTH AFRICA

1st WICKET

		Venue	Series	Opponents E	A	NZ
B. Mitchell	I. J. Siedle	Cape Town	1930-31	260	—	—
B. Mitchell	J. A. J. Christy	Christchurch	1931-32	—	—	196
B. Mitchell	P. G. Van der Byl	Durban[2]	1938-39	191	—	—
D. J. McGlew	T. L. Goddard	Leeds	1955	176	—	—
D. J. McGlew	T. L. Goddard	Johannesburg[3]	1957-58	—	176	—
B. Mitchell	R. H. Catterall	Birmingham	1929	171	—	—
H. W. Taylor	J. W. Zulch	Johannesburg[1]	1913-14	153	—	—
D. J. McGlew	T. L. Goddard	Manchester	1955	147	—	—
D. J. McGlew	E. J. Barlow	Johannesburg[3]	1961-62	—	—	134
T. L. Goddard	E. J. Barlow	Johannesburg[3]	1964-65	134	—	—
A. Melville	P. G. Van der Byl	Durban[2]	1938-39	131	—	—
H. W. Taylor	J. W. Zulch	Port Elizabeth	1913-14	129	—	—
B. Mitchell	I. J. Siedle	Durban[2]	1930-31	127	—	—
B. Mitchell	R. H. Catterall	Birmingham	1929	119	—	—
T. L. Goddard	E. J. Barlow	Wellington	1963-64	—	—	117
T. L. Goddard	E. J. Barlow	Dunedin	1963-64	—	—	117
B. Mitchell	I. J. Siedle	Oval	1935	116	—	—
H. W. Taylor	J. M. Commaille	Cape Town	1927-28	115	—	—
T. L. Goddard	E. J. Barlow	Auckland	1963-64	—	—	115
T. L. Goddard	E. J. Barlow	Port Elizabeth	1964-65	114	—	—
D. J. McGlew	J. H. B. Waite	Durban[2]	1953-54	—	—	113
T. L. Goddard	E. J. Barlow	Port Elizabeth	1966-67	—	112	—
H. W. Taylor	R. H. Catterall	Durban[2]	1922-23	110	—	—
A. Melville	P. G. Van der Byl	Johannesburg[1]	1938-39	108	—	—
B. Mitchell	J. A. J. Christy	Wellington	1931-32	—	—	104
D. J. McGlew	R. J. Westcott	Johannesburg[2]	1953-54	—	—	104
B. Mitchell	E. A. B. Rowan	Port Elizabeth	1948-49	101	—	—
		TOTAL	27	17	2	8

Century Partnerships—*SOUTH AFRICA—Cont.*

2nd WICKET

		Venue	*Series*	*Opponents* *E*	*A*	*NZ*
E. A. B. Rowan	C. B. Van Ryneveld	Leeds	1951	198	—	—
L. J. Tancred	C. B. Llewellyn	Johannesburg[1]	1902-03	—	173	—
E. J. Barlow	A. J. Pithey	Cape Town	1964-65	172	—	—
R. H. Catterall	H. W. Taylor	Cape Town	1922-23	155	—	—
P. G. Van der Byl	E. A. B. Rowan	Cape Town	1938-39	147	—	—
A. Melville	K. G. Viljoen	Nottingham	1947	145*	—	—
P. W. Sherwell	M. Hathorn	Lord's	1907	139	—	—
J. W. Zulch	G. A. Faulkner	Adelaide	1910-11	—	135	—
T. L. Goddard	A. J. Pithey	Sydney	1963-64	—	124	—
B. Mitchell	E. A. B. Rowan	Durban[2]	1938-39	119	—	—
T. L. Goddard	A. J. Pithey	Johannesburg[3]	1964-65	115	—	—
E. A. B. Rowan	K. G. Viljoen	Johannesburg[2]	1948-49	113	—	—
T. L. Goddard	J. H. B. Waite	Johannesburg[3]	1956-57	112	—	—
J. H. B. Waite	W. R. Endean	Melbourne	1952-53	—	111	—
L. J. Tancred	G. C. White	Johannesburg[1]	1905-06	110	—	—
J. W. Zulch	G. A. Faulkner	Melbourne	1910-11	—	107	—
B. Mitchell	E. A. B. Rowan	Lord's	1935	104	—	—
B. Mitchell	J. A. J. Christy	Melbourne	1931-32	—	102	—
		TOTAL	18	12	6	—

3rd WICKET

		Venue	*Series*	*Opponents* *E*	*A*	*NZ*
E. J. Barlow	R. G. Pollock	Adelaide	1963-64	—	341	—
A. Melville	A. D. Nourse, Jnr.	Nottingham	1947	319	—	—
D. J. McGlew	J. H. B. Waite	Durban[2]	1957-58	—	231	—
B. Mitchell	A. D. Nourse, Jnr.	Cape Town	1948-49	190	—	—
B. Mitchell	A. D. Nourse, Jnr.	Oval	1947	184	—	—
E. A. B. Rowan	A. D. Nourse, Jnr.	Durban[2]	1949-50	—	167	—

E. A. B. Rowan	A. D. Nourse, Jnr.	Johannesburg[2]	1948-49	162*	—	—
J. W. Zulch	G. A. Faulkner	Sydney	1910-11	—	143	—
H. W. Taylor	A. D. Nourse, Snr.	Johannesburg[1]	1922-23	134	—	—
A. Bacher	R. G. Pollock	Durban[2]	1966-67	—	127*	—
R. H. Catterall	B. Mitchell	Johannesburg[1]	1930-31	122	—	—
B. Mitchell	H. W. Taylor	Adelaide	1931-32	—	121	—
G. C. White	A. D. Nourse, Snr.	Johannesburg[1]	1905-06	120	—	—
B. Mitchell	H. W. Taylor	Adelaide	1931-32	—	120	—
A. Melville	A. D. Nourse, Jnr.	Lord's	1947	118	—	—
B. Mitchell	A. D. Nourse, Jnr.	Johannesburg[1]	1938-39	116	—	—
B. Mitchell	E. A. B. Rowan	Johannesburg[1]	1938-39	116	—	—
D. J. McGlew	R. A. McLean	Johannesburg[3]	1961-62	—	—	112
G. A. Faulkner	A. D. Nourse, Snr.	Melbourne	1910-11	—	110	—
C. N. Frank	H. W. Taylor	Johannesburg[1]	1921-22	—	105	—
D. J. McGlew	R. A. McLean	Durban[2]	1961-62	—	—	103
B. Mitchell	A. D. Nourse, Jnr.	Port Elizabeth	1948-49	101	—	—
G. A. Faulkner	A. D. Nourse, Snr.	Johannesburg[1]	1909-10	100	—	—
H. W. Taylor	A. D. Nourse, Snr.	Durban[2]	1922-23	100	—	—
		TOTAL	24	13	9	2

4th WICKET

				Opponents		
		Venue	*Series*	*E*	*A*	*NZ*
H. W. Taylor	H. G. Deane	Oval	1929	214	—	—
C. N. Frank	A. D. Nourse, Snr.	Johannesburg[1]	1921-22	—	206	—
B. Mitchell	W. W. Wade	Port Elizabeth	1948-49	150	—	—
H. W. Taylor	R. H. Catterall	Cape Town	1930-31	148	—	—
A. D. Nourse, Snr.	G. C. White	Durban[1]	1909-10	143	—	—
K. J. Funston	R. A. McLean	Durban[2]	1953-54	—	—	135
B. Mitchell	A. D. Nourse, Jnr.	Johannesburg[1]	1935-36	—	129	—
A. J. Pithey	J. H. B. Waite	Melbourne	1963-64	—	128	—

Century Partnerships—*SOUTH AFRICA* (*4th wicket*)—*Cont.*

		Venue	*Series*	*Opponents* *E*	*A*	*NZ*
A. D. Nourse, Jnr.	K. G. Viljoen	Manchester	1947	121	—	—
S. J. Snooke	G. A. Faulkner	Cape Town	1909-10	120	—	—
E. A. B. Rowan	A. D. Nourse, Jnr.	Durban[2]	1935-36	—	118	—
A. J. Pithey	K. C. Bland	Cape Town	1964-65	117	—	—
T. L. Goddard	J. H. B. Waite	Oval	1960	115	—	—
G. C. White	G. A. Faulkner	Johannesburg[1]	1909-10	114	—	—
M. J. Susskind	R. H. Catterall	Lord's	1924	112	—	—
H. W. Taylor	W. V. S. Ling	Johannesburg[1]	1922-23	111	—	—
J. H. B. Waite	K. J. Funston	Adelaide	1952-53	—	108	—
J. F. W. Nicolson	R. H. Catterall	Durban[2]	1927-28	107	—	—
W. R. Endean	J. C. Watkins	Port Elizabeth	1953-54	—	—	107
A. D. Nourse, Jnr.	W. W. Wade	Johannesburg[2]	1948-49	106	—	—
J. H. B. Waite	W. R. Endean	Johannesburg[3]	1957-58	—	104	—
D. J. McGlew	R. A. McLean	Cape Town	1961-62	—	—	101
		TOTAL	22	13	6	3

5th WICKET

		Venue	*Series*	*Opponents* *E*	*A*	*NZ*
A. J. Pithey	J. H. B. Waite	Johannesburg[3]	1964-65	157	—	—
R. H. Catterall	H. B. Cameron	Durban[2]	1927-28	135	—	—
W. R. Endean	J. E. Cheetham	Auckland	1952-53	—	—	130
J. H. B. Waite	W. R. Endean	Johannesburg[3]	1957-58	—	129	—
A. D. Nourse, Jnr.	G. M. Fullerton	Nottingham	1951	121	—	—
H. R. Lance	D. Lindsay	Cape Town	1966-67	—	119	—
R. H. Catterall	J. M. Blanckenberg	Birmingham	1924	114	—	—
G. A. Faulkner	C. B. Llewellyn	Adelaide	1910-11	—	109	—

E. A. B. Rowan	R. A. McLean	Leeds	1951	108	—	—
H. J. Keith	R. A. McLean	Melbourne	1952-53	—	106*	—
A. Melville	K. G. Viljoen	Durban[2]	1938-39	104	—	—
		TOTAL	11	6	4	1

6th WICKET

				Opponents		
		Venue	*Series*	*E*	*A*	*NZ*
J. H. B. Waite	P. L. Winslow	Manchester	1955	171	—	—
K. C. Bland	G. D. Varnals	Johannesburg[3]	1964-65	124	—	—
K. C. Bland	D. Lindsay	Sydney	1963-64	—	118	—
R. G. Pollock	P. L. Van der Merwe	Port Elizabeth	1964-65	113	—	—
R. G. Pollock	P. L. Van der Merwe	Cape Town	1966-67	—	112	—
H. R. Lance	D. Lindsay	Johannesburg[3]	1966-67	—	110	—
R. A. McLean	H. J. Keith	Lord's	1955	109	—	—
A. D. Nourse, Jnr.	F. Nicholson	Johannesburg[1]	1935-36	—	106	—
R. A. McLean	S. O'Linn	Manchester	1960	102	—	—
		TOTAL	9	5	4	—

7th WICKET

				Opponents		
		Venue	*Series*	*E*	*A*	*NZ*
D. J. McGlew	A. R. A. Murray	Wellington	1952-53	—	—	246
D. Lindsay	P. L. Van der Merwe	Johannesburg[3]	1966-67	—	221	—
H. G. Deane	E. P. Nupen	Durban[2]	1927-28	123	—	—
G. C. White	A. D. Nourse, Snr.	Johannesburg[1]	1905-06	121	—	—
J. E. Cheetham	P. N. F. Mansell	Melbourne	1952-53	—	111	—
S. O'Linn	J. H. B. Waite	Nottingham	1960	109	—	—
K. G. Viljoen	E. L. Dalton	Johannesburg[1]	1938-39	108	—	—

Century Partnerships—*SOUTH AFRICA* (*7th wicket*)—*Cont.*

		Venue	*Series*	*Opponents* *E*	*A*	*NZ*
A. D. Nourse, Jnr.	R. E. Grieveson	Durban[2]	1938-39	107	—	—
X. C. Balaskas	C. L. Vincent	Wellington	1931-32	—	—	105
D. Lindsay	P. L. Van der Merwe	Durban[2]	1966-67	—	103	—
B. Mitchell	A. B. C. Langton	Lord's	1935	101	—	—
		TOTAL	11	6	3	2

8th WICKET

		Venue	*Series*	*Opponents* *E*	*A*	*NZ*
A. D. Nourse, Snr.	E. A. Halliwell	Johannesburg[1]	1902-03	—	124	—
B. Mitchell	L. Tuckett	Oval	1947	109*	—	—
K. G. Viljoen	Q. McMillan	Melbourne	1931-32	—	104	—
G. A. Faulkner	R. O. Schwarz	Sydney	1910-11	—	100	—
H. J. Tayfield	N. B. F. Mann	Cape Town	1949-50	—	100	—
		TOTAL	5	1	4	—

9th WICKET

		Venue	*Series*	*Opponents* *E*	*A*	*NZ*
E. L. Dalton	A. B. C. Langton	Oval	1935	137	—	—

10th WICKET

		Venue	*Series*	*Opponents* *E*	*A*	*NZ*
H. G. Owen-Smith	A. J. Bell	Leeds	1929	103	—	—

E*

WEST INDIES

1st WICKET

		Venue	Series	E	A	NZ	I	P
						Opponents		
J. B. Stollmeyer	A. F. Rae	Madras[1]	1948-49	—	—	—	239	—
J. B. Stollmeyer	A. F. Rae	Auckland	1951-52	—	—	197	—	—
G. Carew	A. G. Ganteaume	Port of Spain	1947-48	173	—	—	—	—
C. C. Hunte	J. K. Holt	New Delhi	1958-59	—	—	—	159	—
C. C. Hunte	B. A. Davis	Bridgetown	1964-65	—	145	—	—	—
C. A. Roach	E. A. C. Hunte	Georgetown	1929-30	144	—	—	—	—
J. B. Stollmeyer	A. F. Rae	Port of Spain	1952-53	—	—	—	142*	—
J. B. Stollmeyer	A. F. Rae	Bombay	1948-49	—	—	—	134	—
C. C. Hunte	R. B. Kanhai	Georgetown	1957-58	—	—	—	—	125
C. C. Hunte	R. B. Kanhai	Bridgetown	1957-58	—	—	—	—	122
C. C. Hunte	B. A. Davis	Port of Spain	1964-65	—	116	—	—	—
J. B. Stollmeyer	A. F. Rae	Nottingham	1950	103*	—	—	—	—
		TOTAL	12	3	2	1	4	2

2nd WICKET

		Venue	Series	E	A	NZ	I	P
						Opponents		
C. C. Hunte	G. St. A. Sobers	Kingston	1957-58	—	—	—	—	446
G. St. A. Sobers	C. L. Walcott	Georgetown	1957-58	—	—	—	—	269
E. D. A. McMorris	R. B. Kanhai	Kingston	1961-62	—	—	—	255	—
R. K. Nunes	G. A. Headley	Kingston	1929-30	228	—	—	—	—
J. K. Holt	F. M. M. Worrell	Bridgetown	1953-54	222	—	—	—	—
I. Barrow	G. A. Headley	Manchester	1933	200	—	—	—	—
C. A. Roach	G. A. Headley	Georgetown	1929-30	192	—	—	—	—
A. F. Rae	F. M. M. Worrell	Oval	1950	172	—	—	—	—
C. C. Hunte	R. B. Kanhai	Adelaide	1960-61	—	163	—	—	—
C. A. Roach	G. A. Headley	Bridgetown	1929-30	156	—	—	—	—
F. R. Martin	G. A. Headley	Sydney	1930-31	—	152	—	—	—
C. C. Hunte	R. B. Kanhai	Manchester	1963	151	—	—	—	—

Century Partnerships—*WEST INDIES* (*2nd wicket*)—*Cont.*

		Venue	*Series*	*E*	*A*	*Opponents* *NZ*	*I*	*P*
C. C. Hunte	G. St. A. Sobers	Georgetown	1957-58	—	—	—	—	135
J. B. Stollmeyer	J. K. Holt	Kingston	1953-54	134	—	—	—	—
E. D. A. McMorris	R. B. Kanhai	Port of Spain	1961-62	—	—	—	119	—
J. B. Stollmeyer	G. A. Headley	Lord's	1939	118	—	—	—	—
J. B. Stollmeyer	G. A. Headley	Oval	1939	113	—	—	—	—
C. C. Hunte	R. B. Kanhai	Oval	1963	113	—	—	—	—
J. K. Holt	O. G. Smith	Kingston	1954-55	—	102	—	—	—
		TOTAL	19	11	3	—	2	3

3rd WICKET

		Venue	*Series*	*E*	*A*	*Opponents* *NZ*	*I*	*P*
E. D. Weekes	F. M. M. Worrell	Port of Spain	1953-54	338	—	—	—	—
C. L. Walcott	E. D. Weekes	Port of Spain	1954-55	—	242	—	—	—
G. A. Headley	J. E. D. Sealy	Kingston	1934-35	202	—	—	—	—
R. B. Kanhai	S. M. Nurse	Bridgetown	1964-65	—	200	—	—	—
F. M. M. Worrell	E. D. Weekes	Kingston	1952-53	—	—	—	197	—
R. B. Kanhai	G. St. A. Sobers	Lahore[1]	1958-59	—	—	—	—	162
A. F. Rae	F. M. M. Worrell	Nottingham	1950	143	—	—	—	—
G. A. Headley	F. I. de Caires	Bridgetown	1929-30	142	—	—	—	—
R. B. Kanhai	B. F. Butcher	Georgetown	1964-65	—	135	—	—	—
E. D. A. McMorris	G. St. A. Sobers	Kingston	1959-60	133*†	—	—	—	—
J. B. Stollmeyer	E. D. Weekes	Port of Spain	1952-53	—	—	—	127*	—
C. L. Walcott	E. D. Weekes	Port of Spain	1954-55	—	127	—	—	—
S. M. Nurse	R. B. Kanhai	Melbourne	1960-61	—	123	—	—	—
C. C. Hunte	B. F. Butcher	Kingston	1964-65	—	116	—	—	—
J. B. Stollmeyer	E. D. Weekes	Auckland	1951-52	—	—	115	—	—
R. B. Kanhai	G. St. A. Sobers	Georgetown	1959-60	115	—	—	—	—

† 243 runs were added for this wicket, E. D. A. McMorris retiring hurt and being replaced by S. M. Nurse after 133 had been added.

				E	A	NZ	I	P
G. A. Headley	G. C. Grant	Sydney	1930-31	—	110	—	—	—
J. B. Stollmeyer	E. D. Weekes	Bombay	1948-49	—	—	—	110	—
G. St. A. Sobers	S. M. Nurse	Kingston	1959-60	110†	—	—	—	—
B. F. Butcher	R. B. Kanhai	Nottingham	1966	110	—	—	—	—
R. B. Kanhai	F. M. M. Worrell	Nottingham	1957	109	—	—	—	—
R. B. Kanhai	O. G. Smith	Calcutta	1958-59	—	—	—	108	—
A. F. Rae	E. D. Weekes	Lord's	1950	105	—	—	—	—
J. B. Stollmeyer	G. E. Gomez	Bridgetown	1947-48	104	—	—	—	—
		TOTAL	24	11	7	1	4	1

† 243 runs were added for this wicket, E. D. A. McMorris retiring hurt and being replaced by S. M. Nurse after 133 had been added.

4th WICKET

				Opponents				
		Venue	*Series*	*E*	*A*	*NZ*	*I*	*P*
G. St. A. Sobers	F. M. M. Worrell	Bridgetown	1959-60	399	—	—	—	—
F. M. M. Worrell	E. D. Weekes	Nottingham	1950	283	—	—	—	—
C. L. Walcott	G. E. Gomez	New Delhi	1948-49	—	—	—	267	—
R. B. Kanhai	B. F. Butcher	Calcutta	1958-59	—	—	—	217	—
F. M. M. Worrell	C. L. Walcott	Kingston	1952-53	—	—	—	213	—
G. St. A. Sobers	C. L. Walcott	Kingston	1957-58	—	—	—	—	188*
C. L. Walcott	G. St. A. Sobers	Kingston	1954-55	—	179	—	—	—
G. St. A. Sobers	F. M. M. Worrell	Brisbane[2]	1960-61	—	174	—	—	—
C. L. Walcott	B. H. Pairaudeau	Bridgetown	1953-54	165	—	—	—	—
E. D. Weekes	O. G. Smith	Dunedin	1955-56	—	—	162	—	—
B. F. Butcher	G. St. A. Sobers	Port of Spain	1964-65	—	160	—	—	—
S. M. Nurse	G. St. A. Sobers	Bridgetown	1964-65	—	146	—	—	—
R. B. Kanhai	G. St. A. Sobers	Leeds	1963	143	—	—	—	—
E. D. Weekes	C. L. Walcott	Georgetown	1952-53	—	—	—	130	—
F. M. M. Worrell	C. L. Walcott	Christchurch	1951-52	—	—	129	—	—
B. F. Butcher	O. G. Smith	New Delhi	1958-59	—	—	—	127	—
C. L. Walcott	F. M. M. Worrell	Georgetown	1954-55	—	125	—	—	—
F. I. de Caires	J. E. D. Sealy	Bridgetown	1929-30	124	—	—	—	—

Century Partnerships—*WEST INDIES* (*4th wicket*)—*Cont.*

		Venue	*Series*	*E*	*A*	*Opponents* *NZ*	*I*	*P*
C. C. Hunte	G. St. A. Sobers	Manchester	1963	120	—	—	—	—
G. St. A. Sobers	O. G. Smith	Bombay	1958-59	—	—	—	119	—
C. L. Walcott	F. M. M. Worrell	Kingston	1954-55	—	110	—	—	—
C. C. Hunte	C. H. Lloyd	Bombay	1966-67	—	—	—	110	—
R. B. Kanhai	F. M. M. Worrell	Adelaide	1960-61	—	107	—	—	—
B. F. Butcher	S. M. Nurse	Nottingham	1966	107	—	—	—	—
E. D. Weekes	C. L. Walcott	Port of Spain	1952-53	—	—	—	101	—
C. W. Smith	F. M. M. Worrell	Sydney	1960-61	—	101	—	—	—
		TOTAL	26	7	8	2	8	1

5th WICKET

		Venue	*Series*	*E*	*A*	*Opponents* *NZ*	*I*	*P*
S. M. Nurse	G. St. A. Sobers	Leeds	1966	265	—	—	—	—
E. D. Weekes	B. H. Pairaudeau	Port of Spain	1952-53	—	—	—	219	—
F. M. M. Worrell	C. L. Walcott	Auckland	1951-52	—	—	189	—	—
E. D. Weekes	O. G. Smith	Bridgetown	1957-58	—	—	—	—	185
B. F. Butcher	G. St. A. Sobers	Nottingham	1966	173	—	—	—	—
E. D. Weekes	R. J. Christiani	Bombay	1948-49	—	—	—	170	—
V. H. Stollmeyer	K. H. Weekes	Oval	1939	163	—	—	—	—
G. St. A. Sobers	B. F. Butcher	Bombay	1958-59	—	—	—	134	—
G. St. A. Sobers	S. M. Nurse	Sydney	1960-61	—	128	—	—	—
R. B. Kanhai	G. St. A. Sobers	Oval	1966	122	—	—	—	—
G. St. A. Sobers	F. M. M. Worrell	Georgetown	1959-60	121	—	—	—	—
E. D. Weekes	D. Atkinson	Wellington	1955-56	—	—	120	—	—
E. D. Weekes	K. R. Rickards	Kingston	1947-48	116	—	—	—	—
G. St. A. Sobers	B. F. Butcher	Kanpur	1958-59	—	—	—	114	—

R. B. Kanhai	S. M. Nurse	Calcutta	1966-67	—	—	—	105	—
C. H. Lloyd	G. St. A. Sobers	Bombay	1966-67	—	—	—	102*	—
C. L. Walcott	D. Atkinson	Port of Spain	1953-54	101	—	—	—	—
G. St. A. Sobers	O. G. Smith	Port of Spain	1957-58	—	—	—	—	101
F. M. M. Worrell	G. E. Gomez	Port of Spain	1947-48	100	—	—	—	—
E. D. Weekes	G. St. A. Sobers	Lord's	1957	100	—	—	—	—
		TOTAL	20	9	1	2	6	2

6th WICKET

				Opponents				
		Venue	*Series*	*E*	*A*	*NZ*	*I*	*P*
G. St. A. Sobers	D. A. J. Holford	Lord's	1966	274*	—	—	—	—
C. L. Walcott	G. E. Gomez	Lord's	1950	211	—	—	—	—
F. M. M. Worrell	O. G. Smith	Birmingham	1957	190	—	—	—	—
G. St. A. Sobers	J. S. Solomon	Kanpur	1958-59	—	—	—	163	—
G. St. A. Sobers	J. S. Solomon	Calcutta	1958-59	—	—	—	160*	—
C. L. Walcott	O. G. Smith	Kingston	1954-55	—	138	—	—	—
G. St. A. Sobers	D. A. J. Holford	Manchester	1966	127	—	—	—	—
G. C. Grant	E. L. Bartlett	Adelaide	1930-31	—	114	—	—	—
F. M. M. Worrell	F. C. M. Alexander	Adelaide	1960-61	—	113	—	—	—
G. St. A. Sobers	F. M. M. Worrell	Kingston	1961-62	—	—	—	110	—
B. F. Butcher	F. M. M. Worrell	Lord's	1963	110	—	—	—	—
G. E. Gomez	J. D. C. Goddard	Oval	1950	109	—	—	—	—
E. D. Weekes	A. P. Binns	Wellington	1955-56	—	—	106	—	—
D. Atkinson	O. G. Smith	Nottingham	1957	105	—	—	—	—
J. D. C. Goddard	E. D. Weekes	New Delhi	1948-49	—	—	—	101	—
B. F. Butcher	J. S. Solomon	Madras[2]	1958-59	—	—	—	101	—
R. B. Kanhai	J. S. Solomon	Lahore[1]	1958-59	—	—	—	—	100
		TOTAL	17	7	3	1	5	1

Century Partnerships—*WEST INDIES—Cont.*

7th WICKET

		Venue	Series	E	A	Opponents NZ	I	P
D. Atkinson	C. C. Depeiza	Bridgetown	1954-55	—	347	—	—	—
O. G. Smith	J. D. C. Goddard	Nottingham	1957	154	—	—	—	—
G. A. Headley	R. S. Grant	Kingston	1934-35	147	—	—	—	—
D. Atkinson	J. D. C. Goddard	Christchurch	1955-56	—	—	143	—	—
G. St. A. Sobers	I. Mendonca	Kingston	1961-62	—	—	—	127	—
E. D. Weekes	R. J. Christiani	New Delhi	1948-49	—	—	—	118	—
J. S. Solomon	F. C. M. Alexander	Kanpur	1958-59	—	—	—	100	—
		TOTAL	7	2	1	1	3	—

8th WICKET NO INSTANCE. HIGHEST PARTNERSHIP:

		Venue	Series	E	A	Opponents NZ	I	P
C. A. McWatt	J. K. Holt	Georgetown	1953-54	99	—	—	—	—

9th WICKET

		Venue	Series	E	A	Opponents NZ	I	P
R. J. Christiani	D. Atkinson	New Delhi	1948-49	—	—	—	106	—

10th WICKET NO INSTANCE. HIGHEST PARTNERSHIP:

		Venue	Series	E	A	Opponents NZ	I	P
F. M. M. Worrell	W. W. Hall	Port of Spain	1961-62	—	—	—	98*	—

NEW ZEALAND

1st WICKET

		Venue	*Series*	*E*	*SA*	*WI* (*Opponents*)	*I*	*P*
C. S. Dempster	J. W. E. Mills	Wellington	1929-30	276	—	—	—	—
G. T. Dowling	T. W. Jarvis	Lahore[2]	1964-65	—	—	—	—	136
B. Sutcliffe	W. A. Hadlee	Christchurch	1946-47	133	—	—	—	—
G. O. Rabone	M. E. Chapple	Cape Town	1953-54	—	126	—	—	—
B. Sutcliffe	V. J. Scott	Oval	1949	121	—	—	—	—
B. Sutcliffe	V. J. Scott	Leeds	1949	112	—	—	—	—
S. N. McGregor	J. G. Legatt	New Delhi	1955-56	—	—	—	101	—
		TOTAL	7	4	1	—	1	1

2nd WICKET

		Venue	*Series*	*E*	*SA*	*WI* (*Opponents*)	*I*	*P*
B. Sutcliffe	J. R. Reid	Christchurch	1950-51	131	—	—	—	—
B. Sutcliffe	J. W. Guy	New Delhi	1955-56	—	—	—	130	—
		TOTAL	2	1	—	—	1	—

3rd WICKET

		Venue	*Series*	*E*	*SA*	*WI* (*Opponents*)	*I*	*P*
B. Sutcliffe	J. R. Reid	New Delhi	1955-56	—	—	—	222*	—
J. W. Guy	J. R. Reid	Calcutta	1955-56	—	—	—	184	—
B. W. Sinclair	J. R. Reid	Lahore[2]	1964-65	—	—	—	—	178
G. T. Dowling	R. W. Morgan	Bombay	1964-65	—	—	—	134	—
C. S. Dempster	M. L. Page	Lord's	1931	118	—	—	—	—
B. Sutcliffe	J. R. Reid	Hyderabad	1955-56	—	—	—	108*	—
G. T. Dowling	J. R. Reid	Calcutta	1964-65	—	—	—	101	—
		TOTAL	7	1	—	—	5	1

Century Partnerships—*NEW ZEALAND—Cont.*

4th WICKET

		Venue	Series	E	SA	Opponents WI	I	P
B. W. Sinclair	S. N. McGregor	Auckland	1963-64	—	171	—	—	—
M. L. Page	R. C. Blunt	Lord's	1931	142	—	—	—	—
G. T. Dowling	J. R. Reid	Port Elizabeth	1961-62	—	125	—	—	—
B. E. Congdon	J. R. Reid	Wellington	1964-65	—	—	—	—	109
		TOTAL	4	1	2	—	—	1

5th WICKET

		Venue	Series	E	SA	Opponents WI	I	P
J. R. Reid	J. E. F. Beck	Cape Town	1953-54	—	174	—	—	—
S. N. McGregor	N. S. Harford	Lahore[1]	1955-56	—	—	—	—	150
P. G. Z. Harris	M. E. Chapple	Cape Town	1961-62	—	148	—	—	—
M. P. Donnelly	F. B. Smith	Leeds	1949	120	—	—	—	—
M. P. Donnelly	J. R. Reid	Manchester	1949	116	—	—	—	—
J. R. Reid	J. E. F. Beck	Auckland	1956	—	—	104	—	—
B. Sutcliffe	V. Pollard	Birmingham	1965	104	—	—	—	—
		TOTAL	7	3	2	1	—	1

6th WICKET

		Venue	Series	E	SA	Opponents WI	I	P
H. G. Vivian	F. T. Badcock	Wellington	1931-32	—	100	—	—	—

7th WICKET

		Venue	Series	E	SA	Opponents WI	I	P
B. Sutcliffe	B. R. Taylor	Calcutta	1964-65	—	—	—	163	—

		Venue	Series	E	SA	WI	I	P
T. W. Jarvis	B. Sutcliffe	New Delhi	1964-65	—	—	—	104	—
T. C. Lowry	H. M. McGirr	Auckland	1929-30	100	—	—	—	—
		TOTAL	3	1	—	—	2	—

8th WICKET

		Venue	Series	E	SA	Opponents WI	I	P
D. A. R. Maloney	A. W. Roberts	Lord's	1937	104	—	—	—	—

9th WICKET NO INSTANCE. HIGHEST PARTNERSHIP:

		Venue	Series	E	SA	Opponents WI	I	P
C. F. W. Allcott	I. B. Cromb	Wellington	1931-32	—	69	—	—	—

10th WICKET NO INSTANCE. HIGHEST PARTNERSHIP:

		Venue	Series	E	SA	Opponents WI	I	P
B. E. Congdon	F. J. Cameron	Karachi	1964-65	—	—	—	—	63

INDIA

1st WICKET

		Venue	Series	E	A	Opponents WI	NZ	P
V. M. Mankad	P. Roy	Madras[2]	1955-56	—	—	—	413	—
V. M. Merchant	Mushtaq Ali	Manchester	1936	203	—	—	—	—
D. N. Sardesai	F. M. Engineer	Madras[1]	1966-67	—	—	129	—	—
V. M. Merchant	Mushtaq Ali	Manchester	1946	124	—	—	—	—
V. M. Mankad	C. T. Sarwate	Melbourne	1947-48	—	124	—	—	—

Century Partnerships—*INDIA* (1*st wicket*)—*Cont.*

		Venue	*Series*	*E*	*A*	*Opponents* *WI*	*NZ*	*P*
P. Roy	N. J. Contractor	New Delhi	1959-60	—	121	—	—	—
M. L. Jaisimha	N. J. Contractor	New Delhi	1961-62	121	—	—	—	—
V. M. Mankad	P. Roy	Lord's	1952	106	—	—	—	—
P. Roy	V. M. Mankad	Calcutta	1951-52	103*	—	—	—	—
		TOTAL	9	5	2	1	1	—

2*nd WICKET*

		Venue	*Series*	*E*	*A*	*Opponents* *WI*	*NZ*	*P*
P. Roy	V. L. Manjrekar	Kingston	1952-53	—	—	237	—	—
F. M. Engineer	A. L. Wadekar	Leeds	1967	168	—	—	—	—
V. L. Mehra	S. A. Durrani	Port of Spain	1961-62	—	—	144	—	—
B. K. Kunderan	D. N. Sardesai	Madras[2]	1963-64	143	—	—	—	—
N. J. Contractor	P. R. Umrigar	New Delhi	1958-59	—	—	137	—	—
M. L. Jaisimha	V. L. Manjrekar	Bombay	1961-62	131	—	—	—	—
V. M. Mankad	H. R. Adhikari	Melbourne	1947-48	—	124	—	—	—
D. N. Sardesai	Hanumant Singh	New Delhi	1964-65	—	—	—	123	—
K. C. Ibrahim	R. S. Modi	New Delhi	1948-49	—	—	121	—	—
N. J. Contractor	A. A. Baig	Manchester	1959	109	—	—	—	—
M. L. Jaisimha	V. L. Manjrekar	Kanpur	1961-62	109	—	—	—	—
B. K. Kunderan	R. G. Nadkarni	Kanpur	1963-64	109	—	—	—	—
N. J. Contractor	R. F. Surti	New Delhi	1960-61	—	—	—	—	107
		TOTAL	13	6	1	4	1	1

3rd WICKET

		Venue	Series	E	A	WI	NZ	P
						Opponents		
P. R. Umrigar	V. L. Manjrekar	Hyderabad	1955-56	—	—	—	238	—
V. M. Merchant	Vijay Hazare	New Delhi	1951-52	211	—	—	—	—
V. M. Mankad	Vijay Hazare	Lord's	1952	211	—	—	—	—
P. Roy	Vijay Hazare	Bombay	1951-52	187	—	—	—	—
L. Amarnath	C. K. Nayudu	Bombay[1]	1933-34	186	—	—	—	—
R. S. Modi	Vijay Hazare	Bombay	1948-49	—	—	156	—	—
D. N. Sardesai	R. G. Nadkarni	Kanpur	1963-64	144	—	—	—	—
P. Roy	V. L. Manjrekar	Calcutta	1955-56	—	—	—	143	—
N. J. Contractor	A. A. Baig	Bombay	1959-60	—	133	—	—	—
P. Roy	V. L. Manjrekar	Dacca	1954-55	—	—	—	—	130*
R. S. Modi	Vijay Hazare	Calcutta	1948-49	—	—	129	—	—
B. K. Kunderan	Nawab of Pataudi, Jnr.	New Delhi	1963-64	125	—	—	—	—
P. Roy	V. L. Manjrekar	Bahawalpur	1954-55	—	—	—	—	123
M. L. Apte	Vijay Hazare	Bridgetown	1952-53	—	—	112	—	—
M. L. Jaisimha	V. L. Manjrekar	Bombay	1964-65	—	112	—	—	—
R. S. Modi	Vijay Hazare	Calcutta	1948-49	—	—	108	—	—
N. J. Contractor	Nawab of Pataudi, Jnr.	Madras[2]	1961-62	104	—	—	—	—
		TOTAL	17	7	2	4	2	2

4th WICKET

		Venue	Series	E	A	WI	NZ	P
						Opponents		
Vijay Hazare	V. L. Manjrekar	Leeds	1952	222	—	—	—	—
Vijay Hazare	P. R. Umrigar	Bombay	1952-53	—	—	—	—	183
P. R. Umrigar	A. G. Kripal Singh	Hyderabad	1955-56	—	—	—	171	—
V. M. Mankad	A. G. Kripal Singh	Bombay	1955-56	—	—	—	167	—
D. N. Sardesai	C. G. Borde	Bombay	1964-65	—	—	—	154	—
P. Roy	P. R. Umrigar	Kingston	1952-53	—	—	150	—	—
Vijay Hazare	L. Amarnath	Bombay	1948-49	—	—	144*	—	—
R. S. Modi	Vijay Hazare	Bombay	1948-49	—	—	139	—	—

Century Partnerships—*INDIA* (*4th wicket*)—*Cont.*

		Venue	*Series*	*E*	*A*	*Opponents* *WI*	*NZ*	*P*
C. G. Borde	Nawab of Pataudi, Jnr.	New Delhi	1964-65	—	—	—	138	—
M. L. Apte	P. R. Umrigar	Port of Spain	1952-53	—	—	135	—	—
C. G. Borde	H. R. Adhikari	New Delhi	1958-59	—	—	108	—	—
P. R. Umrigar	C. G. Borde	New Delhi	1960-61	—	—	—	—	107†
		TOTAL	12	1	—	5	4	2

† 123 runs were added for this wicket. C. G. Borde replaced N. J. Contractor who retired hurt after 16 runs had been added.

5th WICKET

		Venue	*Series*	*E*	*A*	*Opponents* *WI*	*NZ*	*P*
Nawab of Pataudi, Jnr.	C. G. Borde	New Delhi	1963-64	190*	—	—	—	—
P. R. Umrigar	C. G. Borde	Madras[2]	1960-61	—	—	—	—	177
C. G. Borde	S. A. Durrani	Bombay	1961-62	142	—	—	—	—
Hanumant Singh	Nawab of Pataudi, Jnr.	Leeds	1967	134	—	—	—	—
V. L. Manjrekar	C. G. Borde	New Delhi	1961-62	132	—	—	—	—
P. R. Umrigar	D. G. Phadkar	Port of Spain	1952-53	—	—	131	—	—
V. L. Manjrekar	G. S. Ramchand	New Delhi	1955-56	—	—	—	127	—
C. G. Borde	Nawab of Pataudi, Jnr.	Calcutta	1964-65	—	—	—	110	—
A. A. Baig	R. B. Kenny	Bombay	1959-60	—	109	—	—	—
		TOTAL	9	4	1	1	2	1

6th WICKET

		Venue	*Series*	*E*	*A*	*Opponents* *WI*	*NZ*	*P*
D. N. Sardesai	Hanumant Singh	Bombay	1964-65	—	—	—	193*	—
Vijay Hazare	D. G. Phadkar	Adelaide	1947-48	—	188	—	—	—
Nawab of Pataudi, Jnr.	C. G. Borde	Madras[2]	1964-65	—	142	—	—	—

C. G. Borde	H. R. Adhikari	New Delhi	1958-59	—	—	134	—	—
V. L. Manjrekar	R. G. Nadkarni	New Delhi	1955-56	—	—	—	123	—
P. R. Umrigar	D. K. Gaekwad	Port of Spain	1952-53	—	—	118	—	—
Vijay Hazare	D. G. Phadkar	Leeds	1952	105	—	—	—	—
D. G. Phadkar	P. R. Umrigar	Madras[1]	1951-52	104	—	—	—	—
C. G. Borde	S. A. Durrani	Bombay	1966-67	—	—	102	—	—
		TOTAL	9	2	2	3	2	—

7th WICKET

						Opponents		
		Venue	*Series*	*E*	*A*	*WI*	*NZ*	*P*
M. L. Apte	V. M. Mankad	Port of Spain	1952-53	—	—	153	—	—
C. G. Borde	S. A. Durrani	Bombay	1963-64	153	—	—	—	—
Vijay Hazare	H. R. Adhikari	Adelaide	1947-48	—	132	—	—	—
		TOTAL	3	1	1	1	—	—

8th WICKET

						Opponents		
		Venue	*Series*	*E*	*A*	*WI*	*NZ*	*P*
R. G. Nadkarni	F. M. Engineer	Madras[2]	1964-65	—	—	—	143	—
R. G. Nadkarni	F. M. Engineer	Madras[2]	1961-62	101	—	—	—	—
		TOTAL	2	1	—	—	1	—

9th WICKET

						Opponents		
		Venue	*Series*	*E*	*A*	*WI*	*NZ*	*P*
P. G. Joshi	R. B. Desai	Bombay	1960-61	—	—	—	—	149

Century Partnerships—*INDIA*—*Cont.*

10th WICKET

		Venue	Series	E	A	WI	NZ	P
H. R. Adhikari	Ghulam Ahmed	New Delhi	1952-53	—	—	—	—	109

PAKISTAN

1st WICKET

		Venue	Series	E	A	WI	NZ	I
K. Ibadulla	Abdul Kadir	Karachi	1964-65	—	249	—	—	—
Hanif Mohammad	Imtiaz Ahmed	Madras[2]	1960-61	—	—	—	—	162
Hanif Mohammad	Imtiaz Ahmed	Bridgetown	1957-58	—	—	152	—	—
Hanif Mohammad	Alim-ud-Din	Bahawalpur	1954-55	—	—	—	—	127
Hanif Mohammad	Alim-ud-Din	Dacca	1961-62	122	—	—	—	—
M. Ilyas	Naushad Ali	Karachi	1964-65	—	—	—	121	—
		TOTAL	6	1	1	1	1	2

2nd WICKET

		Venue	Series	E	A	WI	NZ	I
Hanif Mohammad	Saeed Ahmed	Bombay	1960-61	—	—	—	—	246
Hanif Mohammad	Saeed Ahmed	Karachi	1958-59	—	—	178	—	—
Hanif Mohammad	Waqar Hassan	Bombay	1952-53	—	—	—	—	165
Imtiaz Ahmed	Mushtaq Mohammad	Oval	1962	137	—	—	—	—
Hanif Mohammad	Saeed Ahmed	Port of Spain	1957-58	—	—	130	—	—
Imtiaz Ahmed	Saeed Ahmed	Kingston	1957-58	—	—	118	—	—
M. Ilyas	Saeed Ahmed	Rawalpindi	1964-65	—	—	—	114	—
Hanif Mohammad	Saeed Ahmed	Dacca	1961-62	113	—	—	—	—
Hanif Mohammad	Alim-ud-Din	Bridgetown	1957-58	—	—	112	—	—
		TOTAL	9	2	—	4	1	2

3rd WICKET

				Opponents				
		Venue	*Series*	*E*	*A*	*WI*	*NZ*	*I*
Saeed Ahmed	Wazir Mohammad	Port of Spain	1957-58	—	—	169	—	—
Saeed Ahmed	Shuja-ud-Din	Lahore[2]	1959-60	—	169	—	—	—
Hanif Mohammad	J. Burki	Dacca	1961-62	156	—	—	—	—
Hanif Mohammad	Saeed Ahmed	Bridgetown	1957-58	—	—	154	—	—
Saeed Ahmed	J. Burki	Lahore[2]	1961-62	138	—	—	—	—
Saeed Ahmed	Hanif Mohammad	Georgetown	1957-58	—	—	136	—	—
Saeed Ahmed	J. Burki	Karachi	1964-65	—	—	—	114	—
Imtiaz Ahmed	Wallis Mathias	Kingston	1957-58	—	—	101	—	—
		TOTAL	8	2	1	4	1	—

4th WICKET

				Opponents				
		Venue	*Series*	*E*	*A*	*WI*	*NZ*	*I*
Wazir Mohammad	Hanif Mohammad	Port of Spain	1957-58	—	—	154	—	—
J. Burki	Mushtaq Mohammad	Lahore[2]	1961-62	153	—	—	—	—
Maqsood Ahmed	A. H. Kardar	Lahore[1]	1954-55	—	—	—	—	136
Hanif Mohammad	Wazir Mohammad	Bridgetown	1957-58	—	—	121	—	—
Mushtaq Mohammad	Saeed Ahmed	Nottingham	1962	107	—	—	—	—
		TOTAL	5	2	—	2	—	1

5th WICKET

				Opponents				
		Venue	*Series*	*E*	*A*	*WI*	*NZ*	*I*
J. Burki	Nasim-ul-Ghani	Lord's	1962	197	—	—	—	—
Alim-ud-Din	A. H. Kardar	Karachi	1954-55	—	—	—	—	155
J. Burki	Mushtaq Mohammad	New Delhi	1960-61	—	—	—	—	136
		TOTAL	3	1	—	—	—	2

Century Partnerships—*PAKISTAN—Cont.*

6th WICKET

		Venue	Series	*E*	*A*	*WI* (Opponents)	*NZ*	*I*
Hanif Mohammad	Majid Jahangir	Lahore[2]	1964-65	—	—	—	217	—
Wazir Mohammad	A. H. Kardar	Kingston	1957-58	—	—	166	—	—
Wazir Mohammad	A. H. Kardar	Karachi	1956-57	—	104	—	—	—
		TOTAL	3	—	1	1	1	—

7th WICKET

		Venue	Series	*E*	*A*	*WI* (Opponents)	*NZ*	*I*
Waqar Hassan	Imtiaz Ahmed	Lahore[1]	1955-56	—	—	—	308	—

8th WICKET

		Venue	Series	*E*	*A*	*WI* (Opponents)	*NZ*	*I*
Hanif Mohammad	Asif Iqbal	Lord's	1967	130	—	—	—	—

9th WICKET

		Venue	Series	*E*	*A*	*WI* (Opponents)	*NZ*	*I*
Asif Iqbal	Intikhab Alam	Oval	1967	190	—	—	—	—

10th WICKET

		Venue	Series	*E*	*A*	*WI* (Opponents)	*NZ*	*I*
Zulfiqar Ahmed	Amir Elahi	Madras[1]	1952-53	—	—	—	—	104

PLAYERS' RECORDS—BOWLING

100 WICKETS IN TESTS

ENGLAND

	Tests	*Wkts.*	*Avge.*	*A*	*SA*	*WI*	*NZ*	*I*	*P*
						Opponents			
F. S. Trueman ...	67	307	21.57	79	27	86	40	53	22
J. B. Statham ...	70	252	24.82	69	69	42	20	25	27
A. V. Bedser ...	51	236	24.89	104	54	11	13	44	10
J. C. Laker ...	46	193	21.23	79	32	51	21	8	2
S. F. Barnes ...	27	189	16.43	106	83	—	—	—	—
G. A. R. Lock ...	47	170	24.94	31	15	35	47	26	16
M. W. Tate ...	39	155	26.13	83	53	13	6	—	—
H. Verity	40	144	24.37	59	31	9	7	38	—
F. J. Titmus ...	47	142	31.02	40	27	11	28	27	9
T. E. Bailey ...	61	132	29.21	42	28	29	32	—	1
W. Rhodes ...	58	127	26.96	109	8	10	—	—	—
D. A. Allen ...	39	122	30.96	28	21	15	13	21	24
J. Briggs	33	118	17.74	97	21	—	—	—	—
G. A. Lohmann ...	18	112	10.75	77	35	—	—	—	—
D. V. P. Wright ...	34	108	39.11	48	37	11	8	4	—
R. Peel	20	102	16.81	102	—	—	—	—	—
J. H. Wardle ...	28	102	20.39	24	46	7	5	—	20
C. Blythe	19	100	18.63	41	59	—	—	—	—

AUSTRALIA

	Tests	*Wkts.*	*Avge.*	*E*	*SA*	*WI*	*NZ*	*I*	*P*
						Opponents			
R. Benaud... ...	63	248	27.03	83	52	42	—	52	19
R. R. Lindwall ...	61	228	23.05	114	31	41	2	36	4
C. V. Grimmett ...	37	216	24.21	106	77	33	—	—	—
A. K. Davidson ...	44	186	20.58	84	25	33	—	30	14
K. R. Miller ...	55	170	22.97	87	30	40	2	9	2
G. D. McKenzie ...	37	161	28.18	76	40	17	—	13	15
W. A. Johnston ...	40	160	23.90	75	44	25	—	16	—
W. J. O'Reilly ...	27	144	22.59	102	34	—	8	—	—
H. Trumble ...	32	141	21.78	141	—	—	—	—	—
M. A. Noble ...	42	121	25.01	115	6	—	—	—	—
I. W. Johnson ...	45	109	29.19	42	22	22	—	19	4
G. Giffen	31	103	27.09	103	—	—	—	—	—
C. T. B. Turner ...	17	101	16.53	101	—	—	—	—	—

SOUTH AFRICA

	Tests	*Wkts.*	*Avge.*	*E*	*A*	*NZ*
					Opponents	
H. J. Tayfield	37	170	25.91	75	64	31
T. L. Goddard ...	38	114	26.51	63	44	7
N. A. T. Adcock ...	26	104	21.10	57	14	33
P. M. Pollock	24	101	25.22	32	37	32

WEST INDIES

	Tests	*Wkts.*	*Avge.*	*E*	*A*	*NZ*	*I*	*P*
					Opponents			
W. W. Hall	41	174	24.97	56	37	—	65	16
S. Ramadhin ...	43	158	28.96	80	22	32	15	9
L. R. Gibbs	34	151	23.46	47	37	—	42	25
G. St. A. Sobers ...	60	144	33.45	58	33	2	47	4
A. L. Valentine ...	36	139	30.32	40	43	23	30	3

100 Wickets in Tests—*Cont.*

NEW ZEALAND

No bowler has taken 100 wickets for New Zealand. J. R. Reid holds the record with 85 wickets.

INDIA

	Tests	Wkts.	Avge.	Opponents E	A	WI	NZ	P
V. M. Mankad ...	44	162	32.31	54	23	36	12	37
S. P. Gupte	36	149	29.54	24	8	49	34	34

PAKISTAN

	Tests	Wkts.	Avge.	Opponents E	A	WI	NZ	I
Fazal Mahmood ...	34	139	24.72	25	24	41	5	44

BEST BOWLING AVERAGES

(*Qualification:* 25 *wickets*)

	Tests	Balls	Mdns.	Runs	Wkts.	Avge.	5wI.	10wM.
G. A. Lohmann (England)	18	3821	364	1205	112	10.75	9	5
J. J. Ferris (Australia & England)	9	2302	251	775	61	12.70	6	1
W. Barnes (England)	21	2285	271	793	51	15.54	3	–
W. Bates (England)	15	2362	282	821	50	16.42	4	1
S. F. Barnes (England)	27	7873	358	3106	189	16.43	24	7
C. T. B. Turner (Australia) ...	17	5195	457	1670	101	16.53	11	2
R. Peel (England)	20	5216	444	1715	102	16.81	6	2
J. Briggs (England)	33	5332	389	2094	118	17.74	9	4
R. Appleyard (England)	9	1596	70	554	31	17.87	1	–
W. S. Lees (England)	5	1256	69	467	26	17.96	2	–
H. Ironmonger (Australia)	14	4695	328	1330	74	17.97	4	2
G. B. Lawrence (South Africa) ...	5	1334	61	512	28	18.28	2	–
F. R. Spofforth (Australia)	18	4185	416	1731	94	18.41	7	4
F. H. Tyson (England)	17	3452	98	1411	76	18.56	4	1
C. Blythe (England)	19	4438	231	1863	100	18.63	9	4
G. F. Bissett (South Africa)... ...	4	989	28	469	25	18.76	2	–
A. S. Kennedy (England)	5	1683	91	599	31	19.32	2	–
K. Higgs (England)	14	3761	174	1352	69	19.59	2	–
G. Ulyett (England)...	25	2623	299	1011	51	19.82	1	–

MOST FREQUENT WICKET-TAKERS

(*Qualification:* 25 *wickets*)

	Balls/wkt.	Tests	Balls	Mdns.	Runs	Wkts.	Avge.
G. A. Lohmann (England)	34.11	18	3821	364	1205	112	10.75
J. J. Ferris (Australia & England) ...	37.73	9	2302	251	775	61	12.70
G. F. Bissett (South Africa)... ...	39.56	4	989	28	469	25	18.76
B. J. T. Bosanquet (England) ...	39.56	7	989	10	604	25	24.16
S. F. Barnes (England)	41.65	27	7873	358	3106	189	16.43

MOST ECONOMICAL CAREER FIGURES

(*Qualification:* 2000 *balls*)

	Runs/100 balls	Tests	Balls	Mdns.	Runs	Wkts.	Avge
W. Attewell (England)	21.96	10	2850	326	626	27	23.18
C. Gladwin (England)	26.82	8	2129	89	571	15	38.06
T. L. Goddard (South Africa) ...	27.55	38	10976	648	3023	114	26.51
R. G. Nadkarni (India)	28.01	34	7486	560	2097	71	29.53
H. Ironmonger (Australia)	28.32	14	4695	328	1330	74	17.97
J. C. Watkins (South Africa) ...	29.09	15	2805	134	816	29	28.13
K. D. Mackay (Australia)	29.71	37	5972	266	1721	50	34.42
A. R. A. Murray (South Africa) ...	29.90	10	2374	111	710	18	39.44

TEN WICKETS IN A MATCH

ENGLAND (69)

			Opponents				
			A	*SA*	*WI*	*NZ*	*I*
1956	J. C. Laker	Manchester	19-90	—	—	—	—
1913-14	S. F. Barnes	Johannesburg[1]	—	17-159	—	—	—
1888-89	J. Briggs	Cape Town	—	15-28	—	—	—
1895-96	G. A. Lohmann	Port Elizabeth	—	15-45	—	—	—
1907	C. Blythe	Leeds	—	15-99	—	—	—
1934	H. Verity	Lord's	15-104	—	—	—	—
1903-04	W. Rhodes	Melbourne	15-124	—	—	—	—
1953	A. V. Bedser	Nottingham	14-99	—	—	—	—
1882-83	W. Bates	Melbourne	14-102	—	—	—	—
1913-14	S. F. Barnes	Durban[1]	—	14-144	—	—	—
1912	S. F. Barnes	Oval	—	13-57	—	—	—
1891-92	J. J. Ferris	Cape Town	—	13-91	—	—	—
1901-02	S. F. Barnes	Melbourne	13-163	—	—	—	—
1896	T. Richardson	Manchester	13-244	—	—	—	—
1928-29	J. C. White	Adelaide	13-256	—	—	—	—
1895-96	G. A. Lohmann	Johannesburg[1]	—	12-71	—	—	—
1956-57	J. H. Wardle	Cape Town	—	12-89	—	—	—
1951	R. Tattersall	Lord's	—	12-101	—	—	—
1890	F. Martin	Oval	12-102	—	—	—	—
1886	G. A. Lohmann	Oval	12-104	—	—	—	—
1951	A. V. Bedser	Manchester	—	12-112	—	—	—
1963	F. S. Trueman	Birmingham	—	—	12-119	—	—
1927-28	G. Geary	Johannesburg[1]	—	12-130	—	—	—
1891-92	J. Briggs	Adelaide	12-136	—	—	—	—
1929	A. P. Freeman	Manchester	—	12-171	—	—	—
1957	G. A. R. Lock	Oval	—	—	11-48	—	—
1958	G. A. R. Lock	Leeds	—	—	—	11-65	—
1888	R. Peel	Manchester	11-68	—	—	—	—
1886	J. Briggs	Lord's	11-74	—	—	—	—
1902	W. H. Lockwood	Manchester	11-76	—	—	—	—
1958-59	G. A. R. Lock	Christchurch	—	—	—	11-84	—
1961	F. S. Trueman	Leeds	11-88	—	—	—	—
1924	A. E. R. Gilligan	Birmingham	—	11-90	—	—	—
1946	A. V. Bedser	Manchester	—	—	—	—	11-93
1933	C. S. Marriott	Oval	—	—	11-96	—	—
1960	J. B. Statham	Lord's	—	11-97	—	—	—
1957	T. E. Bailey	Lord's	—	—	11-98	—	—
1909	C. Blythe	Birmingham	11-102	—	—	—	—
1912	S. F. Barnes	Lord's	—	11-110	—	—	—
1956	J. C. Laker	Leeds	11-113	—	—	—	—
1905-06	C. Blythe	Cape Town	—	11-118	—	—	—
1946	A. V. Bedser	Lord's	—	—	—	—	11-145
1929-30	W. Voce	Port of Spain	—	—	11-149	—	—
1963	F. S. Trueman	Lord's	—	—	11-152	—	—
1933-34	H. Verity	Madras[1]	—	—	—	—	11-153
1896	T. Richardson	Lord's	11-173	—	—	—	—
1924-25	M. W. Tate	Sydney	11-228	—	—	—	—
1912	F. E. Woolley	Oval	10-49	—	—	—	—
1936-37	W. Voce	Brisbane[2]	10-57	—	—	—	—
1887-88	R. Peel	Sydney	10-58	—	—	—	—
1896	J. T. Hearne	Oval	10-60	—	—	—	—
1936	G. O. Allen	Lord's	—	—	—	—	10-78
1886-87	G. A. Lohmann	Sydney	10-87	—	—	—	—
1928	A. P. Freeman	Manchester	—	—	10-93	—	—
1909-10	C. Blythe	Cape Town	—	10-104	—	—	—
1950-51	A. V. Bedser	Melbourne	10-105	—	—	—	—
1913-14	S. F. Barnes	Durban[1]	—	10-105	—	—	—

Ten Wickets in a Match—England—*Cont.*

			Opponents				
			A	*SA*	*WI*	*NZ*	*I*
1912	S. F. Barnes	Leeds	—	10-115	—	—	—
1951	J. C. Laker	Oval	—	10-119	—	—	—
1932-33	H. Larwood	Sydney	10-124	—	—	—	—
1954-55	F. H. Tyson	Sydney	10-130	—	—	—	—
1891-92	G. A. Lohmann	Sydney	10-142	—	—	—	—
1893	J. Briggs	Oval	10-148	—	—	—	—
1893	T. Richardson	Manchester	10-156	—	—	—	—
1947	D. V. P. Wright	Lord's	—	10-175	—	—	—
1934	K. Farnes	Nottingham	10-179	—	—	—	—
1929-30	G. T. S. Stevens	Bridgetown	—	—	10-195	—	—
1897-98	T. Richardson	Sydney	10-204	—	—	—	—
1929	A. P. Freeman	Leeds	—	10-207	—	—	—

AUSTRALIA (40)

			Opponents			
			E	*SA*	*WI*	*I*
1882	F. R. Spofforth	Oval	14-90	—	—	—
1931-32	C. V. Grimmett	Adelaide	—	14-199	—	—
1901-02	M. A. Noble	Melbourne	13-77	—	—	—
1878-79	F. R. Spofforth	Melbourne[1]	13-110	—	—	—
1935-36	C. V. Grimmett	Durban[2]	—	13-173	—	—
1920-21	A. A. Mailey	Melbourne	13-236	—	—	—
1887-88	C. T. B. Turner	Sydney	12-87	—	—	—
1896	H. Trumble	Oval	12-89	—	—	—
1959-60	A. K. Davidson	Kanpur	—	—	—	12-124
1902	H. Trumble	Oval	12-173	—	—	—
1911-12	H. V. Hordern	Sydney	12-175	—	—	—
1931-32	H. Ironmonger	Melbourne	—	11-24	—	—
1947-48	E. R. H. Toshack	Brisbane[2]	—	—	—	11-31
1930-31	H. Ironmonger	Melbourne	—	—	11-79	—
1924-25	C. V. Grimmett	Sydney	11-82	—	—	—
1909	C. G. Macartney	Leeds	11-85	—	—	—
1902	M. A. Noble	Sheffield	11-103	—	—	—
1956-57	R. Benaud	Calcutta	—	—	—	11-105
1882-83	F. R. Spofforth	Sydney	11-117	—	—	—
1934	W. J. O'Reilly	Nottingham	11-129	—	—	—
1881-82	G. E. Palmer	Sydney	11-165	—	—	—
1930-31	C. V. Grimmett	Adelaide	—	—	11-183	—
1960-61	A. K. Davidson	Brisbane[2]	—	—	11-222	—
1888	C. T. B. Turner	Lord's	10-63	—	—	—
1935-36	C. V. Grimmett	Cape Town	—	10-88	—	—
1964-65	G. D. McKenzie	Madras[2]	—	—	—	10-91
1935-36	C. V. Grimmett	Johannesburg[1]	—	10-110	—	—
1964-65	N. J. N. Hawke	Georgetown	—	—	10-115	—
1938	W. J. O'Reilly	Leeds	10-122	—	—	—
1882-83	G. E. Palmer	Melbourne	10-126	—	—	—
1902	H. Trumble	Manchester	10-128	—	—	—
1932-33	W. J. O'Reilly	Melbourne	10-129	—	—	—
1884-85	F. R. Spofforth	Sydney	10-144	—	—	—
1956	K. R. Miller	Lord's	10-152	—	—	—
1891-92	G. Giffen	Sydney	10-160	—	—	—
1911-12	H. V. Hordern	Sydney	10-161	—	—	—
1899	E. Jones	Lord's	10-164	—	—	—
1930	C. V. Grimmett	Nottingham	10-201	—	—	—
1936	L. O. Fleetwood-Smith	Adelaide	10-239	—	—	—
1920-21	A. A. Mailey	Adelaide	10-302	—	—	—

Ten Wickets in a Match—*Cont.*

SOUTH AFRICA (9)

			Opponents E	A	NZ
1952-53	H. J. Tayfield	Melbourne	—	13-165	—
1956-57	H. J. Tayfield	Johannesburg[3]	13-192	—	—
1905-06	S. J. Snooke	Johannesburg[1]	12-127	—	—
1909-10	A. E. E. Vogler	Johannesburg[1]	12-181	—	—
1922-23	A. E. Hall	Cape Town	11-112	—	—
1930-31	E. P. Nupen	Johannesburg[1]	11-150	—	—
1961-62	S. F. Burke	Cape Town	—	—	11-196
1965	P. M. Pollock	Nottingham	10-87	—	—
1902-03	C. B. Llewellyn	Johannesburg[1]	—	10-116	

WEST INDIES (9)

			Opponents E	A	I
1958-59	W. W. Hall	Kanpur	—	—	11-126
1950	S. Ramadhin	Lord's	11-152	—	—
1963	L. R. Gibbs	Manchester	11-157	—	—
1950	A. L. Valentine	Manchester	11-204	—	—
1947-48	W. F. Ferguson	Port of Spain	11-229	—	—
1947-48	H. H. H. Johnson	Kingston	10-96	—	—
1966	L. R. Gibbs	Manchester	10-106	—	—
1951-52	G. E. Gomez	Sydney	—	10-113	—
1950	A. L. Valentine	Oval	10-160	—	—

NEW ZEALAND (1)

			Opponents E
1937	J. A. Cowie	Manchester	10-140

INDIA (9)

			E	A	Opponents WI	NZ	P
1959-60	J. S. Patel	Kanpur	—	14-124	—	—	—
1952-53	V. M. Mankad	New Delhi	—	—	—	—	13-131
1964-65	S. Venkataraghavan	New Delhi	—	—	—	12-152	—
1966-67	B. S. Chandrasekhar	Bombay	—	—	12-235	—	—
1951-52	V. M. Mankad	Madras[1]	12-108	—	—	—	—
1964-65	R. G. Nadkarni	Madras[2]	—	11-122	—	—	—
1956-57	Ghulam Ahmed	Calcutta	—	10-130	—	—	—
1961-62	S. A. Durrani	Madras[2]	10-177	—	—	—	—
1958-59	S. P. Gupte	Kanpur	—	—	10-223	—	—

PAKISTAN (5)

			E	A	Opponents WI	NZ	I
1956-57	Fazal Mahmood	Karachi	—	13-114	—	—	—
1952-53	Fazal Mahmood	Lucknow	—	—	—	—	12-94
1954	Fazal Mahmood	Oval	12-99	—	—	—	—
1958-59	Fazal Mahmood	Dacca	—	—	12-100	—	—
1955-56	Zulfiqar Ahmed	Karachi	—	—	—	11-79	—

EIGHT WICKETS IN AN INNINGS

ENGLAND (18)

			A	SA	Opponents WI	NZ	I	P
1956	J. C. Laker	Manchester	10-53	—	—	—	—	—
1895-96	G. A. Lohmann	Johannesburg[1]	—	9-28	—	—	—	—
1956	J. C. Laker	Manchester	9-37	—	—	—	—	—
1913-14	S. F. Barnes	Johannesburg[1]	—	9-103	—	—	—	—
1895-96	G. A. Lohmann	Port Elizabeth	—	8-7	—	—	—	—

Eight Wickets in an Innings—England—*Cont.*

			Opponents					
			A	*SA*	*WI*	*NZ*	*I*	*P*
1888-89	J. Briggs	Cape Town	—	8-11	—	—	—	—
1912	S. F. Barnes	Oval	—	8-29	—	—	—	—
1952	F. S. Trueman	Manchester	—	—	—	—	8-31	—
1886-87	G. A. Lohmann	Sydney	8-35	—	—	—	—	—
1934	H. Verity	Lord's	8-43	—	—	—	—	—
1913-14	S. F. Barnes	Johannesburg[1]	—	8-56	—	—	—	—
1891-92	G. A. Lohmann	Sydney	8-58	—	—	—	—	—
1907	C. Blythe	Leeds	—	8-59	—	—	—	—
1903-04	W. Rhodes	Melbourne	8-68	—	—	—	—	—
1903-04	L. C. Braund	Melbourne	8-81	—	—	—	—	—
1897-98	T. Richardson	Sydney	8-94	—	—	—	—	—
1905	B. J. T. Bosanquet	Nottingham	8-107	—	—	—	—	—
1928-29	J. C. White	Adelaide	8-126	—	—	—	—	—

AUSTRALIA (4)

			Opponents					
			E	*SA*	*WI*	*NZ*	*I*	*P*
1920-21	A. A. Mailey	Melbourne	9-121	—	—	—	—	—
1909	F. Laver	Manchester	8-31	—	—	—	—	—
1894-95	A. E. Trott	Adelaide	8-43	—	—	—	—	—
1902	H. Trumble	Oval	8-65	—	—	—	—	—

SOUTH AFRICA (4)

			Opponents		
			E	*A*	*NZ*
1956-57	H. J. Tayfield	Johannesburg[3]	9-113	—	—
1961-62	G. B. Lawrence	Johannesburg[3]	—	—	8-53
1956-57	H. J. Tayfield	Durban[2]	8-69	—	—
1905-06	S. J. Snooke	Johannesburg[1]	8-70	—	—

WEST INDIES (2)

			Opponents				
			E	*A*	*NZ*	*I*	*P*
1961-62	L. R. Gibbs	Bridgetown	—	—	—	8-38	—
1950	A. L. Valentine	Manchester	8-104	—	—	—	—

INDIA (5)

			Opponents				
			E	*A*	*WI*	*NZ*	*P*
1959-60	J. S. Patel	Kanpur	—	9-69	—	—	—
1958-59	S. P. Gupte	Kanpur	—	—	9-102	—	—
1952-53	V. M. Mankad	New Delhi	—	—	—	—	8-52
1951-52	V. M. Mankad	Madras[1]	8-55	—	—	—	—
1964-65	S. Venkataraghavan	New Delhi	—	—	—	8-72	—

NEW ZEALAND & PAKISTAN

No bowler has taken eight wickets in an innings in an official Test. The best innings analysis for New Zealand is 6-40 by J. A. Cowie against Australia at Wellington in 1945-46.

The best innings analysis for Pakistan is 7-42 by Fazal Mahmood against India at Lucknow in 1952-53.

OUTSTANDING INNINGS ANALYSES

O	*M*	*R*	*W*		
51.2	23	53	10	J. C. Laker: England v. Australia (Manchester)... ...	1956
14.2	6	28	9	G. A. Lohmann: England v. S. Africa (Johannesburg[1])	1895-96
16.4	4	37	9	J. C. Laker: England v. Australia (Manchester)... ...	1956

Outstanding Innings Analyses—*Cont.*

O	*M*	*R*	*W*		
9.4	5	7	8	G. A. Lohmann: England v. S. Africa (Port Elizabeth)	1895-96
14.2	5	11	8	J. Briggs: England v. South Africa (Cape Town) ...	1888-89
19.1	11	17	7	J. Briggs: England v. South Africa (Cape Town) ...	1888-89
7.4	2	17	7	M. A. Noble: Australia v. England (Melbourne) ...	1901-02
11	3	17	7	W. Rhodes: England v. Australia (Birmingham) ...	1902
6.3	4	7	6	A. E. R. Gilligan: England v. South Africa (Birmingham)	1924
11.4	6	11	6	S. Haigh: England v. South Africa (Cape Town) ...	1898-99
14	7	13	6	H. J. Tayfield: S. Africa v. New Zealand (Johannesburg[2])	1953-54
18	11	15	6	C. T. B. Turner: Australia v. England (Sydney) ...	1886-87
2.3	1	2	5	E. R. H. Toshack: Australia v. India (Brisbane[2]) ...	1947-48
7.2	5	6	5	H. Ironmonger: Australia v. South Africa (Melbourne)	1931-32
12	8	5	4	Pervez Sajjad: Pakistan v. New Zealand (Rawalpindi)	1964-65
9	7	5	4	K. Higgs: England v. New Zealand (Christchurch) ...	1965-66
6.3	2	7	4	J. C. White: England v. Australia (Brisbane[1])	1928-29
5	2	7	4	J. H. Wardle: England v. Australia (Manchester) ...	1953
6	3	7	4	R. Appleyard: England v. New Zealand (Auckland) ...	1954-55
3.4	3	0	3	R. Benaud: Australia v. India (New Delhi)	1959-60

25 WICKETS IN A SERIES

ENGLAND				*Wickets & Opponents*				
	Series	*Venue*	*Tests*	*A*	*SA*	*WI*	*NZ*	*I*
S. F. Barnes	1913-14	SA	4	—	49	—	—	—
J. C. Laker	1956	E	5	46	—	—	—	—
A. V. Bedser	1953	E	5	39	—	—	—	—
M. W. Tate	1924-25	A	5	38	—	—	—	—
G. A. Lohmann	1895-96	SA	3	—	35	—	—	—
S. F. Barnes	1911-12	A	5	34	—	—	—	—
S. F. Barnes	1912	E	3	—	34	—	—	—
G. A. R. Lock	1958	E	5	—	—	—	34	—
F. S. Trueman	1963	E	5	—	—	34	—	—
H. Larwood	1932-33	A	5	33	—	—	—	—
T. Richardson	1894-95	A	5	32	—	—	—	—
F. R. Foster	1911-12	A	5	32	—	—	—	—
W. Rhodes	1903-04	A	5	31	—	—	—	—
A. S. Kennedy	1922-23	SA	5	—	31	—	—	—
J. N. Crawford	1907-08	A	5	30	—	—	—	—
A. V. Bedser	1950-51	A	5	30	—	—	—	—
A. V. Bedser	1951	E	5	—	30	—	—	—
F. S. Trueman	1952	E	4	—	—	—	—	29
F. H. Tyson	1954-55	A	5	28	—	—	—	—
R. Peel	1894-95	A	5	27	—	—	—	—
M. W. Tate	1924	E	5	—	27	—	—	—
J. B. Statham	1960	E	5	—	27	—	—	—
F. J. Titmus	1963-64	I	5	—	—	—	—	27
W. S. Lees	1905-06	SA	5	—	26	—	—	—
C. Blythe	1907	E	3	—	26	—	—	—
W. Voce	1936-37	A	5	26	—	—	—	—
J. H. Wardle	1956-57	SA	4	—	26	—	—	—
A. Fielder	1907-08	A	4	25	—	—	—	—
J. C. White	1928-29	A	5	25	—	—	—	—
F. S. Trueman	1960	SA	5	—	25	—	—	—

25 Wickets in a Series—*Cont.*

AUSTRALIA

	Series	Venue	Tests	*Wickets & Opponents* E	SA	WI	I
C. V. Grimmett	1935-36	SA	5	—	44	—	—
W. J. Whitty	1910-11	A	5	—	37	—	—
A. A. Mailey	1920-21	A	5	36	—	—	—
G. Giffen	1894-95	A	5	34	—	—	—
C. V. Grimmett	1930-31	A	5	—	—	33	—
C. V. Grimmett	1931-32	A	5	—	33	—	—
A. K. Davidson	1960-61	A	4	—	—	33	—
M. A. Noble	1901-02	A	5	32	—	—	—
H. V. Hordern	1911-12	A	5	32	—	—	—
J. V. Saunders	1907-08	A	5	31	—	—	—
H. Ironmonger	1931-32	A	4	—	31	—	—
R. Benaud	1958-59	A	5	31	—	—	—
R. Benaud	1957-58	SA	5	—	30	—	—
C. V. Grimmett	1930	E	5	29	—	—	—
G. D. McKenzie	1964	E	5	29	—	—	—
A. K. Davidson	1959-60	I	5	—	—	—	29
R. Benaud	1959-60	I	5	—	—	—	29
H. Trumble	1901-02	A	5	28	—	—	—
W. J. O'Reilly	1934	E	5	28	—	—	—
E. A. McDonald	1921	E	5	27	—	—	—
W. J. O'Reilly	1932-33	A	5	27	—	—	—
W. J. O'Reilly	1935-36	SA	5	—	27	—	—
R. R. Lindwall	1948	E	5	27	—	—	—
W. A. Johnston	1948	E	5	27	—	—	—
E. Jones	1899	E	5	26	—	—	—
H. Trumble	1902	E	3	26	—	—	—
R. R. Lindwall	1953	E	5	26	—	—	—
C. V. Grimmett	1934	E	5	25	—	—	—
W. J. O'Reilly	1936-37	A	5	25	—	—	—
A. K. Davidson	1957-58	SA	5	—	25	—	—

SOUTH AFRICA

	Series	Venue	Tests	*Wickets & Opponents* E	A	NZ
H. J. Tayfield	1956-57	SA	5	37	—	—
A. E. E. Vogler	1909-10	SA	5	36	—	—
H. J. Tayfield	1952-53	A	5	—	30	—
G. A. Faulkener	1909-10	SA	5	29	—	—
G. B. Lawrence	1961-62	SA	5	—	—	28
A. E. Hall	1922-23	SA	4	27	—	—
H. J. Tayfield	1955	E	5	26	—	—
N. A. T. Adcock	1960	E	5	26	—	—
T. L. Goddard	1966-67	SA	5	—	26	—
C. B. Llewellyn	1902-03	SA	3	—	25	—
R. O. Schwarz	1910-11	A	5	—	25	—
J. M. Blanckenberg	1922-23	SA	5	25	—	—
G. F. Bissett	1927-28	SA	4	25	—	—
T. L. Goddard	1955	E	5	25	—	—
P. M. Pollock	1963-64	A	5	—	25	—
J. T. Partridge	1963-64	A	5	—	25	—

25 Wickets in a Series—*Cont.*

WEST INDIES

	Series	Venue	Tests	Wickets & Opponents E	I
A. L. Valentine	1950	E	4	33	—
C. C. Griffith	1963	E	5	32	—
W. W. Hall	1958-59	I	5	—	30
A. L. Valentine	1952-53	WI	5	—	28
W. W. Hall	1961-62	WI	5	—	27
S. Ramadhin	1950	E	4	26	—
R. Gilchrist	1958-59	I	4	—	26
L. R. Gibbs	1963	E	5	26	—

INDIA

	Series	Venue	Tests	Wickets & Opponents E	WI	NZ	P
V. M. Mankad	1951-52	I	5	34	—	—	—
S. P. Gupte	1955-56	I	5	—	—	34	—
S. P. Gupte	1952-53	WI	5	—	27	—	—
V. M. Mankad	1952-53	I	5	—	—	—	25

HAT-TRICKS

F. R. Spofforth ...	Australia v. England (Melbourne[1]) ...	1878-79
W. Bates	England v. Australia (Melbourne)	1882-83
J. Briggs	England v. Australia (Sydney)	1891-92
G. A. Lohmann ...	England v. South Africa (Port Elizabeth) ...	1895-96
J. T. Hearne... ...	England v. Australia (Leeds)	1899
H. Trumble (2) ...	Australia v. England (Melbourne)	1901-02
	Australia v. England (Melbourne)	1903-04
T. J. Matthews (2)† ...	Australia v. South Africa (Manchester) ...	1912
M. J. C. Allom ...	England v. New Zealand (Christchurch) ... (His first appearance in Test Matches)	1929-30
T. W. Goddard ...	England v. South Africa (Johannesburg[1]) ...	1938-39
P. J. Loader	England v. West Indies (Leeds)	1957
L. F. Kline	Australia v. South Africa (Cape Town) ...	1957-58
W. W. Hall	West Indies v. Pakistan (Lahore[1])	1958-59
G. Griffin	South Africa v. England (Lord's)	1960
L. R. Gibbs	West Indies v. Australia (Adelaide) ...	1960-61

FOUR WICKETS IN FIVE BALLS

M. J. C. Allom ...	England v. New Zealand (Christchurch) ... (His first appearance in Test Matches)	1929-30

THREE WICKETS IN FOUR BALLS

F. R. Spofforth (2) ...	Australia v. England (Oval)	1882
	Australia v. England (Sydney)	1884-85
J. Briggs	England v. South Africa (Cape Town) ...	1888-89
E. P. Nupen	South Africa v. England (Johannesburg[1]) ...	1930-31
W. J. O'Reilly ...	Australia v. England (Manchester)... ...	1934
W. Voce	England v. Australia (Sydney)	1936-37
R. R. Lindwall ...	Australia v. England (Adelaide)	1946-47

† Matthews achieved the hat-trick in each innings

Three Wickets in Four Balls—*Cont.*

K. Cranston ... ... England v. South Africa (Leeds) 1947
(He took four wickets in a six-ball over)
R. Appleyard ... England v. New Zealand (Auckland) ... 1954-55
R. Benaud ... ... Australia v. West Indies (Georgetown) ... 1954-55
Fazal Mahmood ... Pakistan v. Australia (Karachi) 1956-57
J. W. Martin... ... Australia v. West Indies (Melbourne) ... 1960-61
L. R. Gibbs ... ... West Indies v. Australia (Sydney) 1960-61
K. D. Mackay ... Australia v. England (Birmingham) ... 1961
W. W. Hall ... ... West Indies v. India (Port of Spain) ... 1961-62

MOST WICKETS BY ONE BOWLER IN A DAY

15 (for 28), J. Briggs—England v. South Africa (Cape Town) ... 1888-89
14 (for 80, 15-104 in match), H. Verity—England v. Australia (Lord's) 1934

A WICKET WITH FIRST BALL IN TESTS

A. Coningham ... Australia v. England (Melbourne) 1894-95
G. G. Macaulay ... England v. South Africa (Cape Town) ... 1922-23
M. W. Tate ... ... England v. South Africa (Birmingham) ... 1924
T. Johnson ... ... West Indies v. England (Oval) 1939
R. Howorth ... ... England v. South Africa (Oval) 1947
Intikhab Alam ... Pakistan v. Australia (Karachi) 1959-60

TEN WICKETS IN DEBUT MATCH

12-102 F. Martin: England v. Australia (Oval) 1890
10-156 T. Richardson: England v. Australia (Manchester) ... 1893
11-112 A. E. Hall: South Africa v. England (Cape Town) ... 1922-23
11- 82 C. V. Grimmett: Australia v. England (Sydney) 1924-25
11- 96 C. S. Marriott: England v. West Indies (Oval) 1933
10-179 K. Farnes: England v. Australia (Nottingham) 1934
11-145 A. V. Bedser: England v. India (Lord's) 1946
10- 96 H. H. H. Johnson: West Indies v. England (Kingston) ... 1947-48
11-204 A. L. Valentine: West Indies v. England (Manchester) ... 1950
11-196 S. F. Burke: South Africa v. New Zealand (Cape Town) ... 1961-62

OVER 200 RUNS CONCEDED IN AN INNINGS

O	*M*	*R*	*W*		
87	11	298	1	L. O. Fleetwood-Smith: Australia v. England (Oval)	1938
80.2	13	266	5	O. C. Scott: West Indies v. England (Kingston)...	1929-30
54	5	259	0	Khan Mohammad: Pakistan v. West Indies (Kingston)	1957-58
85.2	20	247	2	Fazal Mahmood: Pakistan v. West Indies (Kingston)	1957-58
82	17	228	5	V. M. Mankad: India v. West Indies (Kingston)...	1952-53
71	8	204	6	I. A. R. Peebles: England v. Australia (Oval) ...	1930
75	16	202	3	V. M. Mankad: India v. West Indies (Bombay)...	1948-49
84	19	202	6	Haseeb Ahsan: Pakistan v. India (Madras[2]) ...	1960-61

OVER 300 RUNS CONCEDED IN A MATCH

O	*M*	*R*	*W*		
105.2	13	374	9	O. C. Scott: West Indies v. England (Kingston)...	1929-30
63	3	308	7	A. A. Mailey: Australia v. England (Sydney) ...	1924-25
61.3	6	302	10	A. A. Mailey: Australia v. England (Adelaide) ...	1920-21

BOWLERS UNCHANGED IN A COMPLETED INNINGS

ENGLAND

F. Morley (2-34) & R. G. Barlow (7-40) v. Australia (Sydney) 1882-83
G. A. Lohmann (7-36) & J. Briggs (3-28) v. Australia (Oval) 1886
G. A. Lohmann (5-17) & R. Peel (5-18) v. Australia (Sydney) 1887-88
J. Briggs (8-11) & A. J. Fothergill (1-30) v. South Africa (Cape Town) ... 1888-89
J. J. Ferris (7-37) & F. Martin (2-39) v. South Africa (Cape Town)... ... 1891-92
J. Briggs (6-19) & G. A. Lohmann (3-46) v. Australia (Adelaide) 1891-92
T. Richardson (6-39) & G. A. Lohmann (3-13) v. Australia (Lord's) ... 1896
S. Haigh (6-11) & A. E. Trott (4-19) v. South Africa (Cape Town) 1898-99
S. F. Barnes (6-42) & C. Blythe (4-64) v. Australia (Melbourne) 1901-02
G. H. Hirst (4-28) & C. Blythe (6-44) v. Australia (Birmingham) 1909
F. R. Foster (5-16) & S. F. Barnes (5-25) v. South Africa (Lord's) 1912
A. E. R. Gilligan (6-7) & M. W. Tate (4-12) v. South Africa (Birmingham) ... 1924
G. O. Allen (5-36) & W. Voce (4-16) v. Australia (Brisbane[2]) 1936-37

AUSTRALIA

G. E. Palmer (7-68) & E. Evans (3-64) v. England (Sydney)... 1881-82
F. R. Spofforth (5-30) & G. E. Palmer (4-32) v. England (Sydney) 1884-85
C. T. B. Turner (6-15) & J. J. Ferris (4-27) v. England (Sydney) 1886-87
C. T. B. Turner (5-36) & J. J. Ferris (5-26) v. England (Lord's) 1888
G. Giffen (5-26) & C. T. B. Turner (4-33) v. England (Sydney) 1894-95
H. Trumble (3-38) & M. A. Noble (7-17) v. England (Melbourne) 1901-02
M. A. Noble (5-54) & J. V. Saunders (5-43) v. England (Sydney) 1901-02

PAKISTAN

Fazal Mahmood (6-34) & Khan Mohammad (4-43) v. Australia (Karachi)... 1956-57

MOST BALLS BY ONE BOWLER IN A MATCH

774 S. Ramadhin: West Indies v. England (Birmingham)... ... 1957

MOST BALLS BY ONE BOWLER IN AN INNINGS

588 S. Ramadhin: West Indies v. England (Birmingham)... ... 1957

ONLY FOUR BOWLERS IN AN INNINGS OF OVER 300 RUNS

1893	England v. Australia (349) at The Oval
1921	Australia v. England (403-8d) at The Oval
1924	South Africa v. England (421-8) at The Oval
1928-29	Australia v. England (342-8d) at Brisbane[1]
1949	New Zealand v. England (372) at Leeds
1949	New Zealand v. England (482) at The Oval
1950-51	England v. Australia (426) at Sydney
1953	England v. Australia (318) at Manchester
1957-58	Pakistan v. West Indies (325 & 312) at Port of Spain
1959	India v. England (361) at The Oval
1963-64	New Zealand v. South Africa (371) at Auckland

ELEVEN BOWLERS IN AN INNINGS

1884 England v. Australia (551) at The Oval

PLAYERS' RECORDS—ALL-ROUND CRICKET

1000 RUNS AND 100 WICKETS

	Tests	Runs	Wkts.	Test in which Double was achieved
ENGLAND				
Bailey, T. E.	61	2290	132	47th
Rhodes, W.	58	2325	127	44th
Tate, W. M.	39	1198	155	33rd
Titmus, F. J.	47	1273	142	40th
AUSTRALIA				
Benaud, R.	63	2201	248	32nd
Davidson, A. K. ...	44	1328	186	34th
Giffen, G.	31	1238	103	30th
Johnson, I. W.	45	1000	109	45th
Lindwall, R. R. ...	61	1502	228	38th
Miller, K. R.	55	2958	170	33rd
Noble, M. A.	42	1997	121	27th
SOUTH AFRICA				
Goddard, T. L. ...	38	2458	114	36th
WEST INDIES				
Sobers, G. St. A. ...	60	5514	144	48th
INDIA				
Mankad, V. M. ...	44	2109	162	23rd

100 RUNS AND TEN WICKETS IN A MATCH

A. K. Davidson (44 & 80, 5-135 & 6-87) Australia v. West Indies at Brisbane[2] in 1960-61 (the tied Test).

250 RUNS AND 25 WICKETS IN A SERIES

Runs	*Avge.*	*Wkts.*	*Avge.*	*Player*	*Series*
475	52.77	34	24.11	G. Giffen: Australia v. England	1894-95
545	60.55	29	21.89	G. A. Faulkener: South Africa v. England	1909-10
329	54.83	30	21.93	R. Benaud: Australia v. South Africa ...	1957-58
294	32.66	26	16.23	T. L. Goddard: South Africa v. Australia	1966-67

PLAYERS' RECORDS—FIELDING

MOST CATCHES IN AN INNINGS

5	V. Y. Richardson	Australia v. South Africa (Durban[2]) ...	1935-36

MOST CATCHES IN A MATCH

6	A. Shrewsbury	England v. Australia (Sydney)	1887-88
6	A. E. E. Vogler	South Africa v. England (Durban[1]) ...	1909-10
6	F. E. Woolley	England v. Australia (Sydney)	1911-12
6	J. M. Gregory	Australia v. England (Sydney)	1920-21
6	B. Mitchell	South Africa v. Australia (Melbourne) ...	1931-32
6	V. Y. Richardson	Australia v. South Africa (Durban[2]) ...	1935-36
6	R. N. Harvey	Australia v. England (Sydney)	1962-63
6	M. C. Cowdrey	England v. West Indies (Lord's)	1963

MOST CATCHES IN A SERIES

15	J. M. Gregory	Australia v. England	1920-21
13	R. B. Simpson	Australia v. South Africa	1957-58
13	R. B. Simpson	Australia v. West Indies	1960-61

50 CATCHES IN A CAREER

Catches	*Player*	*For*	*Tests*	*Av./Test*
110	W. R. Hammond	E	85	1.29
105	M. C. Cowdrey	E	92	1.14
92	R. B. Simpson	A	49	1.87
79	G. St. A. Sobers...	WI	60	1.31
66	T. W. Graveney	E	65	1.01
65	R. Benaud	A	63	1.03
64	F. S. Trueman	E	67	0.95
64	F. E. Woolley	E	64	1.00
62	R. N. Harvey	A	79	0.78
60	W. Rhodes	E	58	1.03
57	L. Hutton	E	79	0.72
57	G. A. R. Lock	E	47	1.21
56	B. Mitchell	SA	42	1.33
53	K. F. Barrington	E	74	0.71

PLAYERS' RECORDS—WICKET-KEEPING

MOST DISMISSALS IN AN INNINGS

6	(all ct.)	A. T. W. Grout: Australia v. South Africa (Johannesburg[3])	1957-58
6	(all ct.)	D. Lindsay: South Africa v. Australia (Johannesburg[3])	1966-67
6	(all ct.)	J. T. Murray: England v. India (Lord's)	1967

MOST DISMISSALS IN A MATCH

9	(8ct. 1st.)	G. R. Langley: Australia v. England (Lord's) ...	1956

MOST DISMISSALS IN A SERIES

26	(23ct. 3st.)	J. H. B. Waite: South Africa v. New Zealand ...	1961-62
24	(22ct. 2st.)	D. L. Murray: West Indies v. England	1963
24	(all ct.)	D. Lindsay: South Africa v. Australia	1966-67
23	(16ct. 7st.)	J. H. B. Waite: South Africa v. New Zealand ...	1953-54
23	(22ct. 1st.)	F. C. M. Alexander: West Indies v. England ...	1959-60
23	(20ct. 3st.)	A. T. W. Grout: Australia v. West Indies	1960-61
23	(21ct. 2st.)	A. E. Dick: New Zealand v. South Africa	1961-62

MOST CATCHES IN A SERIES

24	D. Lindsay: South Africa v. Australia	1966-67

100 DISMISSALS IN A CAREER

219	(173ct. 46st.)	T. G. Evans (E)	in	91 Tests
187	(163ct. 24st.)	A. T. W. Grout (A)	„	51 „
141	(124ct. 17st.)	J. H. B. Waite (SA)	„	50 „
130	(78ct. 52st.)	W. A. Oldfield (A)	„	54 „
105	(94ct. 11st.)	J. M. Parks (E)	„	43 „

The dismissals total for Parks includes 2 catches made as a fielder.

WICKET-KEEPERS' DOUBLE

(100 *Dismissals & 1000 Runs*)

Evans, T. G....	219	2439
Oldfield, W. A.	130	1427
Parks, J. M.	105	1914
Waite, J. H. B.	141	2405

CENTURY AND SIX DISMISSALS IN AN INNINGS

D. Lindsay (6ct. & 182): South Africa v. Australia (Johannesburg[3]) 1966-67

500 RUNS IN A SERIES BY A WICKET-KEEPER

D. Lindsay	606 (avge. 86.57)	South Africa v. Australia ...	1966-67
B. K. Kunderan	525 (avge. 52.50)	India v. England	1963-64

NO BYES CONCEDED IN TOTAL OF OVER 500

659-8d	T. G. Evans: England v. Australia (Sydney)	1946-47
559-9d	W. W. Wade: South Africa v. England (Cape Town) ...	1938-39
551	J. J. Kelly: Australia v. England (Sydney)	1897-98
544-5d	Imtiaz Ahmed: Pakistan v. England (Birmingham) ...	1962
531	D. Lindsay: South Africa v. England (Johannesburg[3]) ...	1964-65
521	W. A. Oldfield: Australia v. England (Brisbane[1])	1928-29
520	J. H. B. Waite: South Africa v. Australia (Melbourne) ...	1952-53

HIGHEST NUMBER OF BYES CONCEDED IN AN INNINGS

37 F. E. Woolley (keeping wicket in place of L. E. G. Ames—injured): England v. Australia (Oval) 1934.

HIGHEST NUMBER OF EXTRAS IN AN INNINGS

57 Conceded by England v. New Zealand (Auckland) 1929-30. (31 byes, 16 leg byes, 10 no balls. Wicket-keeper: W. F. Cornford).

MOST LEG BYES IN AN INNINGS

22 Conceded by Australia v. England (Nottingham) 1932.

MOST WIDES IN AN INNINGS

9 Bowled by West Indies v. Australia (Kingston) 1954-55

MOST NO BALLS IN INNINGS

(From which no runs were scored by the batsman)

23 Bowled by West Indies v. India (Madras[2]) 1958-59

PLAYERS' RECORDS—THE CAPTAINS

RESULTS SUMMARY

ENGLAND (52)

	Tests as Captain	*Opponents* *A*	*SA*	*WI*	*NZ*	*I*	*P*	*Results* *W*	*L*	*D*	*Toss Won*
J. Lillywhite	2	2	–	–	–	–	–	1	1	–	–
Lord Harris	4	4	–	–	–	–	–	2	1	1	2
A. Shaw	4	4	–	–	–	–	–	–	2	2	4
A. N. Hornby	2	2	–	–	–	–	–	–	1	1	1
Hon. Ivo Bligh	4	4	–	–	–	–	–	2	2	–	3
A. Shrewsbury	7	7	–	–	–	–	–	5	2	–	4
A. G. Steel	4	4	–	–	–	–	–	3	1	–	2
W. W. Read	2	1	1	–	–	–	–	2	–	–	1
W. G. Grace	13	13	–	–	–	–	–	8	3	2	4
C. A. Smith	1	–	1	–	–	–	–	1	–	–	–
M. P. Bowden	1	–	1	–	–	–	–	1	–	–	1
A. E. Stoddart	8	8	–	–	–	–	–	3	4	1	2
T. C. O'Brien	1	–	1	–	–	–	–	1	–	–	–
Lord Hawke	4	–	4	–	–	–	–	4	–	–	4
A. C. MacLaren	22	22	–	–	–	–	–	4	11	7	11
P. F. Warner	10	5	5	–	–	–	–	4	6	–	5
Hon. F. S. Jackson ...	5	5	–	–	–	–	–	2	–	3	5
R. E. Foster	3	–	3	–	–	–	–	1	–	2	3
F. L. Fane	5	3	2	–	–	–	–	2	3	–	3
A. O. Jones	2	2	–	–	–	–	–	–	2	–	1
H. D. G. Leveson-Gower	3	–	3	–	–	–	–	1	2	–	–
J. W. H. T. Douglas ...	18	12	6	–	–	–	–	8	8	2	7
C. B. Fry	6	3	3	–	–	–	–	4	–	2	4
Hon. L. H. Tennyson ...	3	3	–	–	–	–	–	–	1	2	2
F. T. Mann	5	–	5	–	–	–	–	2	1	2	3
A. E. R. Gilligan	9	5	4	–	–	–	–	4	4	1	2
A. W. Carr	6	4	2	–	–	–	–	1	–	5	3
A. P. F. Chapman ...	17	9	5	3	–	–	–	9	2	6	9
R. T. Stanyforth	4	–	4	–	–	–	–	2	1	1	–

Results Summary—*Cont.*

	Tests as Captain	*Opponents*						*Results*			*Toss*
		A	*SA*	*WI*	*NZ*	*I*	*P*	*W*	*L*	*D*	*Won*
G. T. S. Stevens	1	–	1	–	–	–	–	–	1	–	–
J. C. White	4	1	3	–	–	–	–	1	1	2	3
A. H. H. Gilligan ...	4	–	–	–	4	–	–	1	–	3	2
Hon. F. S. G. Calthorpe	4	–	–	4	–	–	–	1	1	2	2
R. E. S. Wyatt	16	5	5	5	1	–	–	3	5	8	12
D. R. Jardine	15	5	–	2	4	4	–	9	1	5	7
C. F. Walters	1	1	–	–	–	–	–	–	1	–	–
G. O. Allen	11	5	–	3	–	3	–	4	5	2	6
R. W. V. Robins	3	–	–	–	3	–	–	1	–	2	2
W. R. Hammond ...	20	8	5	3	1	3	–	4	3	13	11
N. W. D. Yardley ...	14	6	5	3	–	–	–	4	7	3	9
K. Cranston	1	–	–	1	–	–	–	–	–	1	–
F. G. Mann	7	–	5	–	2	–	–	2	–	5	5
F. R. Brown	15	5	5	1	4	–	–	5	6	4	3
N. D. Howard	4	–	–	–	–	4	–	1	–	3	2
D. B. Carr	1	–	–	–	–	1	–	–	1	–	1
L. Hutton	23	10	–	5	2	4	2	11	4	8	7
D. S. Sheppard	2	–	–	–	–	–	2	1	–	1	1
P. B. H. May	41	13	10	8	7	3	–	20	10	11	26
M. C. Cowdrey	15	2	5	5	–	2	1	6	3	6	10
E. R. Dexter	30	10	–	5	3	5	7	9	7	14	13
M. J. K. Smith	25	5	8	1	6	5	–	5	3	17	11
D. B. Close	7	–	–	1	–	3	3	6	–	1	4
	439	198	102	50	37	37	15	171	117	151	223

Note: No player has captained England against every current opponent country.

AUSTRALIA (31)

	Tests as Captain	*Opponents*						*Results*				*Toss*
		E	*SA*	*WI*	*NZ*	*I*	*P*	*W*	*L*	*D*	*Tie*	*Won*
D. W. Gregory	3	3	–	–	–	–	–	2	1	–	–	2
W. L. Murdoch ...	16	16	–	–	–	–	–	5	7	4	–	7
T. Hogan	2	2	–	–	–	–	–	–	2	–	–	1
H. Massie	1	1	–	–	–	–	–	1	–	–	–	1
J. M. Blackham ...	8	8	–	–	–	–	–	3	3	2	–	4
H. Scott	3	3	–	–	–	–	–	–	3	–	–	1
P. S. McDonnell ...	6	6	–	–	–	–	–	1	5	–	–	2
G. Giffen	4	4	–	–	–	–	–	2	2	–	–	3
G. H. S. Trott ...	8	8	–	–	–	–	–	5	3	–	–	5
J. Darling	21	18	3	–	–	–	–	7	4	10	–	7
H. Trumble... ...	2	2	–	–	–	–	–	2	–	–	–	1
M. A. Noble ...	15	15	–	–	–	–	–	8	5	2	–	11
C. Hill	10	5	5	–	–	–	–	5	5	–	–	5
S. E. Gregory ...	6	3	3	–	–	–	–	2	1	3	–	1
W. W. Armstrong ...	10	10	–	–	–	–	–	8	–	2	–	4
H. L. Collins ...	11	8	3	–	–	–	–	5	2	4	–	7
W. Bardsley... ...	2	2	–	–	–	–	–	–	–	2	–	1
J. Ryder	5	5	–	–	–	–	–	1	4	–	–	2
W. M. Woodfull ...	25	15	5	5	–	–	–	14	7	4	–	12
V. Y. Richardson ...	5	–	5	–	–	–	–	4	–	1	–	1
D. G. Bradman ...	24	19	–	–	–	5	–	15	3	6	–	10
W. A. Brown ...	1	–	–	–	1	–	–	1	–	–	–	–
A. L. Hassett ...	24	10	10	4	–	–	–	14	4	6	–	18
A. R. Morris ...	2	1	–	1	–	–	–	–	2	–	–	2
I. W. Johnson ...	17	9	–	5	–	2	1	7	5	5	–	6
R. R. Lindwall ...	1	–	–	–	–	1	–	–	–	1	–	–
I. D. Craig	5	–	5	–	–	–	–	3	–	2	–	3
R. Benaud	28	14	1	5	–	5	3	12	4	11	1	11
R. N. Harvey ...	1	1	–	–	–	–	–	1	–	–	–	–
R. B. Simpson ...	27	8	9	5	–	3	2	6	7	14	–	13
B. C. Booth ...	2	2	–	–	–	–	–	–	1	1	–	1
	295	198	49	25	1	16	6	134	80	80	1	142

Results Summary—*Cont.*

SOUTH AFRICA (23)

	Tests as Captain	Opponents E	A	NZ	Results W	L	D	Toss Won
O. R. Dunell	1	1	–	–	–	1	–	1
W. H. Milton	2	2	–	–	–	2	–	1
E. A. Halliwell	3	2	1	–	–	3	–	1
A. Richards	1	1	–	–	–	1	–	–
M. Bissett	2	2	–	–	–	2	–	–
H. M. Taberer	1	–	1	–	–	–	1	1
J. H. Anderson	1	–	1	–	–	1	–	–
P. W. Sherwell	13	8	5	–	5	6	2	5
S. J. Snooke	5	5	–	–	3	2	–	3
F. Mitchell	3	1	2	–	–	3	–	2
L. J. Tancred	3	2	1	–	–	2	1	2
II. W. Taylor	18	15	3	–	1	10	7	11
H. G. Deane	12	12	–	–	2	4	6	9
E. P. Nupen	1	1	–	–	1	–	–	–
H. B. Cameron	9	2	5	2	2	5	2	3
H. F. Wade	10	5	5	–	1	4	5	5
A. Melville	10	10	–	–	–	4	6	4
A. D. Nourse, Jnr. ...	15	10	5	–	1	9	5	7
J. E. Cheetham	15	3	5	7	7	5	3	6
D. J. McGlew	14	8	1	5	4	6	4	4
C. B. Van Ryneveld ...	8	4	4	–	2	4	2	3
T. L. Goddard	13	5	5	3	1	2	10	4
P. L. Van der Merwe ...	8	3	5	–	4	1	3	4
	168	102	49	17	34	77	57	76

WEST INDIES (14)

	Tests as Captain	Opponents E	A	NZ	I	P	Results W	L	D	Tie	Toss Won
R. K. Nunes	4	4	–	–	–	–	–	3	1	–	2
E. L. G. Hoad	1	1	–	–	–	–	–	–	1	–	1
N. Betancourt	1	1	–	–	–	–	–	1	–	–	–
M. P. Fernandes	1	1	–	–	–	–	1	–	–	–	1
G. C. Grant	12	7	5	–	–	–	3	7	2	–	5
R. S. Grant	3	3	–	–	–	–	–	1	2	–	2
G. A. Headley	1	1	–	–	–	–	–	–	1	–	1
G. E. Gomez	1	1	–	–	–	–	–	–	1	–	–
J. D. C. Goddard ...	22	11	4	2	5	–	8	7	7	–	12
J. B. Stollmeyer	13	5	3	–	5	–	3	4	6	–	7
D. Atkinson	7	–	3	4	–	–	3	3	1	–	3
F. C. M. Alexander ...	18	5	–	–	5	8	7	4	7	–	9
F. M. M. Worrell... ...	15	5	5	–	5	–	9	3	2	1	9
G. St. A. Sobers	13	5	5	–	3	–	7	2	4	–	9
	112	50	25	6	23	8	41	35	35	1	61

NEW ZEALAND (10)

	Tests as Captain	Opponents E	A	SA	WI	I	P	Results W	L	D	Toss Won
T. C. Lowry	7	7	–	–	–	–	–	–	2	5	4
M. L. Page	7	5	–	2	–	–	–	–	3	4	4
W. A. Hadlee	8	7	1	–	–	–	–	–	2	6	5
B. Sutcliffe...	4	–	–	2	2	–	–	–	3	1	4
W. M. Wallace	2	–	–	2	–	–	–	–	1	1	–
G. O. Rabone	5	2	–	3	–	–	–	–	4	1	2
H. B. Cave	9	–	–	–	1	5	3	–	5	4	5
J. R. Reid	34	13	–	8	3	4	6	3	18	13	17
M. E. Chapple	1	1	–	–	–	–	–	–	–	1	–
B. W. Sinclair	2	2	–	–	–	–	–	–	–	2	2
	79	37	1	17	6	9	9	3	38	38	43

Results Summary—*Cont.*

INDIA (*14*)	*Tests as Captain*	*Opponents* *E*	*A*	*WI*	*NZ*	*P*	*Result* *W*	*L*	*D*	*Toss Won*
C. K. Nayudu	4	4	–	–	–	–	–	3	1	1
Vizianagram	3	3	–	–	–	–	–	2	1	1
Nawab of Pataudi, Snr.... ...	3	3	–	–	–	–	–	1	2	3
L. Amarnath	15	–	5	5	–	5	2	6	7	4
Vijay Hazare	14	9	–	5	–	–	1	5	8	8
V. M. Mankad	6	–	–	1	–	5	–	1	5	1
Ghulam Ahmed	3	–	–	2	1	–	–	2	1	1
P. R. Umrigar	8	–	3	1	4	–	2	2	4	6
H. R. Adhikari	1	–	–	1	–	–	–	–	1	1
D. K. Gaekwad	4	4	–	–	–	–	–	4	–	2
P. Roy	1	1	–	–	–	–	–	1	–	1
G. S. Ramchand	5	–	5	–	–	–	1	2	2	4
N. J. Contractor	12	5	–	2	–	5	2	2	8	7
Nawab of Pataudi, Jnr. ...	21	8	3	6	4	–	2	9	10	9
	100	37	16	23	9	15	10	40	50	49

PAKISTAN (5)	*Tests as Captain*	*Opponents* *E*	*A*	*WI*	*NZ*	*I*	*Result* *W*	*L*	*D*	*Toss Won*
A. H. Kardar	23	4	1	5	3	10	6	6	11	10
Fazal Mahmood	10	–	2	3	–	5	2	2	6	6
Imtiaz Ahmed	4	3	1	–	–	–	–	2	2	4
J. Burki	5	5	–	–	–	–	–	4	1	3
Hanif Mohammad	11	3	2	–	6	–	2	2	7	6
	53	15	6	8	9	15	10	16	27	29

CAPTAINS WHO INVITED THE OPPOSITION TO BAT

40 captains have between them invited the opposition to take first innings on 60 occasions. In only 18 instances has this decision resulted in the match being won and on 19 occasions it has brought defeat.

ENGLAND (15 *captains*, 22 *occasions*)

Captain	Opponents	Result	Margin
A. E. Stoddart ...	Australia (Sydney) 1894-95 ...	L	Inns. & 147
Lord Hawke ...	South Africa (Cape Town) 1895-96	W	Inns. & 33
A. C. MacLaren ...	Australia (Melbourne) 1901-02 ...	L	229 runs
A. O. Jones ...	Australia (Sydney) 1907-08 ...	L	49 runs
J. W. H. T. Douglas	Australia (Melbourne) 1911-12 ...	W	Inns. & 225
A. W. Carr ...	Australia (Leeds) 1926	D	
A. P. F. Chapman (2)	S. Africa (Johannesburg[1]) 1930-31	L	28 runs
	South Africa (Durban[2]) 1930-31 ...	D	
R. E. S. Wyatt (3)...	West Indies (Bridgetown) 1934-35...	W	4 wkts.
	W. Indies (Port of Spain) 1934-35	L	217 runs
	South Africa (Oval) 1935	D	
G. O. Allen... ...	India (Lord's) 1936...	W	9 wkts.
F. R. Brown ...	New Zealand (Manchester) 1949 ...	D	
L. Hutton (3) ...	Pakistan (Lord's) 1954	D	
	Australia (Brisbane[2]) 1954-55 ...	L	Inns. & 154
	New Zealand (Dunedin) 1954-55 ...	W	8 wkts.
P. B. H. May ...	Australia (Adelaide) 1958-59 ...	L	10 wkts.
E. R. Dexter (2) ...	New Zealand (Wellington) 1962-63	W	Inns. & 47
	Australia (Lord's) 1964	D	
M. J. K. Smith (2)	S. Africa (Johannesburg[3]) 1964-65	D	
	South Africa (Oval) 1965	D	
D. B. Close ...	Pakistan (Oval) 1967	W	8 wkts.

Captains who Invited the Opposition to Bat—*Cont.*

AUSTRALIA (*7 captains*, 12 *occasions*)

Captain	Opponent	Result	Margin
G. Giffen	England (Melbourne) 1894-95 ...	L	94 runs
M. A. Noble ...	England (Lord's) 1909	W	9 wkts.
A. L. Hassett (2) ...	West Indies (Sydney) 1951-52 ...	W	7 wkts.
	England (Leeds) 1953	D	
A. R. Morris ...	England (Sydney) 1954-55... ...	L	38 runs
I. W. Johnson ...	England (Sydney) 1954-55... ...	D	
R. Benaud (3) ...	England (Melbourne) 1958-59 ...	W	9 wkts.
	Pakistan (Dacca) 1959-60	W	8 wkts.
	West Indies (Melbourne) 1960-61	W	2 wkts.
R. B. Simpson (3) ...	Pakistan (Melbourne) 1964-65 ...	D	
	West Indies (Port of Spain) 1964-65	D	
	South Africa (Durban[2]) 1966-67 ...	L	8 wkts.

SOUTH AFRICA (5 *captains*, 9 *occasions*)

Captain	Opponent	Result	Margin
E. A. Halliwell ...	England (Port Elizabeth) 1895-96	L	288 runs
P. W. Sherwell (2)...	Australia (Melbourne) 1910-11 ...	L	530 runs
	Australia (Sydney) 1910-11 ...	L	7 wkts.
H. W. Taylor ...	England (Birmingham) 1924 ...	L	Inns. & 18
H. G. Deane (4) ...	England (Cape Town) 1927-28 ...	L	87 runs
	England (Johannesburg[1]) 1927-28	W	4 wkts.
	England (Durban[2]) 1927-28 ...	W	8 wkts.
	England (Oval) 1929	D	
P. L. Van der Merwe	Australia (Port Elizabeth) 1966-67	W	7 wkts.

WEST INDIES (3 *captains*, 3 *occasions*)

Captain	Opponent	Result	Margin
R. S. Grant... ...	England (Manchester) 1939 ...	D	
F. C. M. Alexander	Pakistan (Dacca) 1958-59	L	41 runs
F. M. M. Worrell ...	India (Bridgetown) 1961-62 ...	W	Inns. & 30

NEW ZEALAND (3 *captains*, 5 *occasions*)

Captain	Opponent	Result	Margin
T. C. Lowry ...	England (Manchester) 1931 ...	D	
B. Sutcliffe (2) ...	West Indies (Auckland) 1951-52 ...	D	
	S. Africa (Johannesburg[2]) 1953-54	L	9 wkts.
J. R. Reid (2) ...	South Africa (Auckland) 1963-64	D	
	Pakistan (Lahore[2]) 1964-65 ...	D	

INDIA (4 *captains*, 4 *occasions*)

Captain	Opponent	Result	Margin
Nawab of Pataudi, Snr.	England (Manchester) 1946 ...	D	
L. Amarnath	Pakistan (Calcutta) 1952-53 ...	D	
P. R. Umrigar ...	Australia (Calcutta) 1956-57 ...	L	94 runs
Nawab of Pataudi, Jnr.	Australia (Calcutta) 1964-65 ...	D	

PAKISTAN (3 *captains*, 5 *occasions*)

Captain	Opponent	Result	Margin
Fazal Mahmood ...	West Indies (Karachi) 1958-59	W	10 wkts.
J. Burki (2)	England (Leeds) 1962	L	Inns. & 117
	England (Nottingham) 1962 ...	D	
Hanif Mohammad (2)	New Zealand (Wellington) 1964-65	D	
	New Zealand (Rawalpindi) 1964-65	W	Inns. & 64

MOST CONSECUTIVE MATCHES AS CAPTAIN

England	35	P. B. H. May (Nottingham 1955—Leeds 1959)
Australia	25	W. M. Woodfull (Nottingham 1930—Oval 1934)
South Africa	18	H. W. Taylor (Durban[1] 1913-14—Oval 1924)
West Indies	18	F. C. M. Alexander (Bridgetown 1957-58—Port of Spain 1959-60)
New Zealand	34	J. R. Reid (Christchurch 1955-56—Leeds 1965)
India	21	Nawab of Pataudi, Jnr. (Bridgetown 1961-62—Birmingham 1967)
Pakistan	23	A. H. Kardar (New Delhi 1952-53 to Port of Spain 1957-58)

WINNING ALL FIVE TOSSES IN A SERIES

Hon. F. S. Jackson ...	England v. Australia in England	1905
M. A. Noble ...	Australia v. England in England	1909
H. G. Deane ...	South Africa v. England in South Africa ...	1927-28
J. D. C. Goddard ...	West Indies v. India in India	1948-49
A. L. Hassett ...	Australia v. England in England	1953
M. C. Cowdrey ...	England v. South Africa in England ...	1960
Nawab of Pataudi, Jnr.	India v. England in India	1963-64
G. St. A. Sobers ...	West Indies v. England in England ...	1966

Note: P. B. H. May (3) and M. C. Cowdrey (2) won all five tosses against West Indies in England's 1959-60 series.

CAPTAINS' TABLE

(*Qualification:* 13 *Tests*)

	For	*Played*	*Won* (2 pts.)	*Drawn* (1 pt.)	*Lost*	*Points*	%
D. R. Jardine ...	E	15	9	5	1	23	76.66
D. G. Bradman ...	A	24	15	6	3	36	75.00
A. L. Hassett ...	A	24	14	6	4	34	70.83
A. P. F. Chapman ...	E	17	9	6	2	24	70.58
W. G. Grace ...	E	13	8	2	3	18	69.23
G. St. A. Sobers ...	WI	13	7	4	2	18	69.23
F. M. M. Worrell ...	WI	15	9	2	3	20	66.66
L. Hutton	E	23	11	8	4	30	65.21
W. M. Woodfull ...	A	25	14	4	7	32	64.00
R. Benaud	A	28	12	11	4	35	62.50
P. B. H. May ...	E	41	20	11	10	51	62.19
M. A. Noble ...	A	15	8	2	5	18	60.00
M. C. Cowdrey ...	E	15	6	6	3	18	60.00
F. C. M. Alexander	WI	18	7	7	4	21	58.33
J. Darling	A	21	7	10	4	24	57.14
J. E. Cheetham ...	SA	15	7	3	5	17	56.66
I. W. Johnson ...	A	17	7	5	5	19	55.88
M. J. K. Smith ...	E	25	5	17	3	27	54.00
E. R. Dexter ...	E	30	9	14	7	32	53.33
W. R. Hammond ...	E	20	4	13	3	21	52.50
J. D. C. Goddard ...	WI	22	8	7	7	23	52.27
J. W. H. T. Douglas	E	18	8	2	8	18	50.00
A. H. Kardar ...	P	23	6	11	6	23	50.00
R. B. Simpson ...	A	27	6	14	7	26	48.14
F. R. Brown ...	E	15	5	4	6	14	46.66

Captains' Table—*Cont.*

	For	*Played*	*Won* (2 pts.)	*Drawn* (1 pt.)	*Lost*	*Points*	%
P. W. Sherwell ...	SA	13	5	2	6	12	46.15
J. B. Stollmeyer ...	WI	13	3	6	4	12	46.15
T. L. Goddard ...	SA	13	1	10	2	12	46.15
W. L. Murdoch ...	A	16	5	4	7	14	43.75
R. E. S. Wyatt ...	E	16	3	8	5	14	43.75
D. J. McGlew ...	SA	14	4	4	6	12	42.85
N. W. D. Yardley ...	E	14	4	3	7	11	39.28
L. Amarnath ...	I	15	2	7	6	11	36.66
Vijay Hazare ...	I	14	1	8	5	10	35.71
A. C. MacLaren ...	E	22	4	7	11	15	34.09
Nawab of Pataudi, Jnr.	I	21	2	10	9	14	33.33
J. R. Reid	NZ	34	3	13	18	19	27.94
H. W. Taylor ...	SA	18	1	7	10	9	25.00
A. D. Nourse, Jnr. ...	SA	15	1	5	9	7	23.33

INDIVIDUAL CAREER RECORDS

BATTING AND FIELDING

Complete Test Match career records for all players appearing in official Tests before 1st December, 1967:

ENGLAND (*437 Players*)

	Tests	*I.*	*N.O.*	*Runs*	*H.S.*	*Avge.*	100*s*	50*s*	*Ct.*	*St.*
Abel, R.	13	22	2	744	132*	37.20	2	2	13	—
Absolom, C. A.	1	2	0	58	52	29.00	—	1	—	—
Allen, D. A.	39	51	15	918	88	25.50	—	5	10	—
Allen, G. O.	25	33	2	750	122	24.19	1	3	20	—
Allom, M. J. C.	5	3	2	14	8*	14.00	—	—	—	—
Ames, L. E. G.	47	72	12	2434	149	40.56	8	7	75	23
Amiss, D. L.	4	6	1	125	45	25.00	—	—	4	—
Andrew, K. V.	2	4	1	29	15	9.66	—	—	1	—
Appleyard, R.	9	9	6	51	19*	17.00	—	—	4	—
Archer, A. G.	1	2	1	31	24*	31.00	—	—	—	—
Armitage, T.	2	3	0	33	21	11.00	—	—	—	—
Arnold, E. G.	10	15	3	160	40	13.33	—	—	8	—
Arnold, G. G.	2	2	0	73	59	36.50	—	1	1	—
Arnold, J.	1	2	0	34	34	17.00	—	—	—	—
Astill, W. E.	9	15	0	190	40	12.66	—	—	7	—
Attewell, W.	10	15	6	150	43*	16.66	—	—	9	—
Bailey, T. E.	61	91	14	2290	134*	29.74	1	10	32	—
Bakewell, A. H.	6	9	0	409	107	45.44	1	3	3	—
Barber, R. W.	27	43	3	1429	185	35.72	1	9	21	—
Barber, W.	2	4	0	83	44	20.75	—	—	1	—
Barlow, R. G.	17	30	4	591	62	22.73	—	2	14	—
Barnes, S. F.	27	39	9	242	38*	8.06	—	—	12	—
Barnes, W.	21	33	2	725	134	23.38	1	5	19	—
Barnett, C. J.	20	35	4	1098	129	35.41	2	5	14	—
Barratt, F.	5	4	1	28	17	9.33	—	—	2	—
Barrington, K. F.	74	120	14	6348	256	59.88	19	33	53	—
Barton, V. A.	1	1	0	23	23	23.00	—	—	—	—
Bates, W.	15	26	2	656	64	27.33	—	5	9	—
Bean, G.	3	5	0	92	50	18.40	—	1	4	—
Bedser, A. V.	51	71	15	714	79	12.75	—	1	26	—

Batting & Fielding—England—*Cont.*

	Tests	*I.*	*N.O.*	*Runs*	*H.S.*	*Avge.*	*100s*	*50s*	*Ct.*	*St.*
Berry, R.	2	4	2	6	4*	3.00	—	—	2	—
Binks, J. G.	2	4	0	91	55	22.75	—	1	8	—
Bird, M. C.	10	16	1	280	61	18.66	—	2	5	—
Bligh, Hon. Ivo	4	7	1	62	19	10.33	—	—	7	—
Blythe, C.	19	31	12	183	27	9.63	—	—	6	—
Board, J. H.	6	12	2	108	29	10.80	—	—	8	3
Bolus, J. B.	7	12	0	496	88	41.33	—	4	2	—
Booth, M. W.	2	2	0	46	32	23.00	—	—	—	—
Bosanquet, B. J. T.	7	14	3	147	27	13.36	—	—	9	—
Bowden, M. P.	2	2	0	25	25	12.50	—	—	1	—
Bowes, W. E.	15	11	5	28	10*	4.66	—	—	2	—
Bowley, E. H.	5	7	0	252	109	36.00	1	—	2	—
Boycott, G.	27	46	7	1613	246*	41.35	3	9	7	—
Bradley, W. M.	2	2	1	23	23*	23.00	—	—	—	—
Braund, L. C.	23	41	3	987	104	25.97	3	2	39	—
Brearley, W.	4	5	2	21	11*	7.00	—	—	—	—
Brennan, D. V.	2	2	0	16	16	8.00	—	—	—	1
Briggs, J.	33	50	5	815	121	18.11	1	2	12	—
Brockwell, W.	7	12	0	202	49	16.83	—	—	6	—
Bromley-Davenport, H. R.	4	6	0	128	84	21.33	—	1	1	—
Brookes, D.	1	2	0	17	10	8.50	—	—	1	—
Brown, A.	2	1	1	3	3*	—	—	—	1	—
Brown, D. J.	11	15	1	128	44	9.14	—	—	2	—
Brown, F. R.	22	30	1	734	79	25.31	—	5	22	—
Brown, G.	7	12	2	299	84	29.90	—	2	9	3
Brown, J. T.	8	16	3	470	140	36.15	1	1	7	—
Buckenham, C. P.	4	7	0	43	17	6.14	—	—	2	—
Butler, H. J.	2	2	1	15	15*	15.00	—	—	1	—
Butt, H. R.	3	4	1	22	13	7.33	—	—	1	1
Calthorpe, Hon. F. S. G.	4	7	0	129	49	18.42	—	—	2	—
Carr, A. W.	11	13	1	237	63	19.75	—	1	3	—
Carr, D. B.	2	4	0	135	76	33.75	—	1	—	—
Carr, D. W.	1	1	0	0	0	0.00	—	—	—	—
Cartwright, T. W.	5	7	2	26	9	5.20	—	—	2	—
Chapman, A. P. F.	26	36	4	925	121	28.90	1	5	32	—
Charlwood, H.	2	4	0	63	36	15.75	—	—	—	—
Chatterton, W.	1	1	0	48	48	48.00	—	—	—	—
Christopherson, S.	1	1	0	17	17	17.00	—	—	—	—
Clark, E. W.	8	9	5	36	10	9.00	—	—	—	—
Clay, J. C.	1	—	—	—	—	—	—	—	1	—
Close, D. B.	19	31	1	721	70	24.03	—	3	20	—
Coldwell, L. J.	7	7	5	9	6*	4.50	—	—	1	—
Compton, D. C. S.	78	131	15	5807	278	50.06	17	28	49	—
Cook, C.	1	2	0	4	4	2.00	—	—	—	—
Copson, W. H.	3	1	0	6	6	6.00	—	—	1	—
Cornford, W. F.	4	4	0	36	18	9.00	—	—	5	3
Coventry, Hon. C. J.	2	2	1	13	12	13.00	—	—	—	—
Cowdrey, M. C.	92	153	15	6346	182	45.98	18	33	105	—
Coxon, A.	1	2	0	19	19	9.50	—	—	—	—
Cranston, J.	1	2	0	31	16	15.50	—	—	1	—
Cranston, K.	8	14	0	209	45	14.92	—	—	3	—
Crapp, J. F.	7	13	2	319	56	29.00	—	3	7	—
Crawford, J. N.	12	23	2	469	74	22.33	—	2	13	—
Cuttell, W. R.	2	4	0	65	21	16.25	—	—	2	—
Dawson, E. W.	5	9	0	175	55	19.44	—	1	—	—
Dean, H.	3	4	2	10	8	5.00	—	—	2	—
Denton, D.	11	22	1	424	104	20.19	1	1	8	—
Dewes, J. G.	5	10	0	121	67	12.10	—	1	—	—
Dexter, E. R.	60	98	8	4405	205	48.94	9	27	27	—
Dipper, A. E.	1	2	0	51	40	25.50	—	—	—	—
Doggart, G. H. G.	2	4	0	76	29	19.00	—	—	3	—
D'Oliviera, B. L.	9	13	2	572	109	52.00	1	5	9	—

Batting & Fielding—England—*Cont.*

	Tests	*I.*	*N.O.*	*Runs*	*H.S.*	*Avge.*	*100s*	*50s*	*Ct.*	*St.*
Dollery, H. E.	4	7	0	72	37	10.28	—	—	1	—
Dolphin, A.	1	2	0	1	1	0.50	—	—	1	—
Douglas, J. W. H. T. ..	23	35	2	962	119	29.15	1	6	9	—
Druce, N. F.	5	9	0	252	64	28.00	—	1	5	—
Ducat, A.	1	2	0	5	3	2.50	—	—	1	—
Duckworth, G.	24	28	12	234	39*	14.62	—	—	45	15
Duleepsinhji, K. S.	12	19	2	995	173	58.52	3	5	10	—
Durston, F. J.	1	2	1	8	6*	8.00	—	—	—	—
Edrich, J. H.	21	30	2	1142	310*	40.78	4	1	11	—
Edrich, W. J.	39	63	2	2440	219	40.00	6	13	39	—
Elliott, H.	4	5	1	61	37*	15.25	—	—	8	3
Emmett, G. M.	1	2	0	10	10	5.00	—	—	—	—
Emmett, T.	7	13	1	160	48	13.33	—	—	9	—
Evans, A. J.	1	2	0	18	14	9.00	—	—	—	—
Evans, T. G.	91	133	14	2439	104	20.49	2	8	173	46
Fagg, A. E.	5	8	0	150	39	18.75	—	—	5	—
Fane, F. L.	14	27	1	682	143	26.23	1	3	6	—
Farnes, K.	15	17	5	58	20	4.83	—	—	1	—
Farrimond, W. F.	4	7	0	116	35	16.57	—	—	6	2
Fender, P. G. H.	13	21	1	380	60	19.00	—	2	14	—
Ferris, J. J.	1	1	0	16	16	16.00	—	—	—	—
Fielder, A.	6	12	5	78	20	11.14	—	—	4	—
Fishlock, L. B.	4	5	1	47	19*	11.75	—	—	1	—
Flavell, J. A.	4	6	2	31	14	7.75	—	—	—	—
Flowers, W.	8	14	0	254	56	18.14	—	1	2	—
Ford, F. G. J.	5	9	0	168	48	18.66	—	—	5	—
Foster, F. R.	11	15	1	330	71	23.57	—	3	11	—
Foster, R. E.	8	14	1	602	287	46.30	1	1	13	—
Fothergill, A. J.	2	2	0	33	32	16.50	—	—	—	—
Freeman, A. P.	12	16	5	154	50*	14.00	—	1	4	—
Fry, C. B.	26	41	3	1223	144	32.18	2	7	17	—
Gay, L. H.	1	2	0	37	33	18.50	—	—	3	1
Geary, G.	14	20	4	249	66	15.56	—	2	13	—
Gibb, P. A.	8	13	0	581	120	44.69	2	3	3	1
Gifford, N.	2	3	1	7	5	3.50	—	—	1	—
Gilligan, A. E. R.	11	16	3	209	39*	16.07	—	—	3	—
Gilligan, A. H. H.	4	4	0	71	32	17.75	—	—	—	—
Gimblett, H.	3	5	1	129	67*	32.25	—	1	1	—
Gladwin, C.	8	11	5	170	51*	28.33	—	1	2	—
Goddard, T. W.	8	5	3	13	8	6.50	—	—	3	—
Gover, A. R.	4	1	1	2	2*	—	—	—	1	—
Grace, E. M.	1	2	0	36	36	18.00	—	—	1	—
Grace, G. F.	1	2	0	0	0	0.00	—	—	2	—
Grace, W. G.	22	36	2	1098	170	32.29	2	5	39	—
Graveney, T. W.	65	101	12	4033	258	45.31	9	16	66	—
Greenhough, T.	4	4	1	4	2	1.33	—	—	1	—
Greenwood, A.	2	4	0	77	49	19.25	—	—	2	—
Grieve, B. A. F.	2	3	2	40	14*	40.00	—	—	—	—
Griffith, S. C.	3	5	0	157	140	31.40	1	—	5	—
Gunn, G.	15	29	1	1120	122*	40.00	2	7	15	—
Gunn, J.	6	10	2	85	24	10.62	—	—	3	—
Gunn, W.	11	20	2	392	102*	21.77	1	1	5	—
Haig, N. E.	5	9	0	126	47	14.00	—	—	4	—
Haigh, S.	11	18	3	113	25	7.53	—	—	8	—
Hallows, C.	2	2	1	42	26	42.00	—	—	—	—
Hammond, W. R.	85	140	16	7249	336*	58.45	22	24	110	—
Hardinge, H. T. W. ..	1	2	0	30	25	15.00	—	—	—	—
Hardstaff, J., Snr.	5	10	0	311	72	31.10	—	3	1	—

Batting & Fielding—England—*Cont.*

	Tests	*I.*	*N.O.*	*Runs*	*H.S.*	*Avge.*	*100s*	*50s*	*Ct.*	*St.*
Hardstaff, J., Jnr.	23	38	3	1636	205*	46.74	4	10	9	—
Harris, Lord	4	6	1	145	52	29.00	—	1	2	—
Hartley, J. C.	2	4	0	15	9	3.75	—	—	2	—
Hawke, Lord	5	8	1	55	30	7.85	—	—	3	—
Hayes, E. G.	5	9	1	86	35	10.75	—	—	2	—
Hayward, T. W.	35	60	2	1999	137	34.45	3	12	19	—
Hearne, A.	1	1	0	9	9	9.00	—	—	1	—
Hearne, F.	2	2	0	47	27	23.50	—	—	1	—
Hearne, G. G.	1	1	0	0	0	0.00	—	—	—	—
Hearne, J. T...	12	18	4	216	40	9.00	—	—	4	—
Hearne, J. W.	24	36	5	806	114	26.00	1	2	13	—
Hendren, E.	51	83	9	3525	205*	47.63	7	21	33	—
Heseltine, C.	2	2	0	18	18	9.00	—	—	3	—
Higgs, K.	14	17	3	183	63	13.07	—	1	3	—
Hill, A.	2	4	2	101	49	50.50	—	—	1	—
Hill, A. J. L.	3	4	0	251	124	62.75	1	1	1	—
Hilton, M. J...	4	6	1	37	15	7.40	—	—	1	—
Hirst, G. H.	24	38	3	790	85	22.57	—	5	18	—
Hitch, J. W.	7	10	3	103	51*	14.71	—	1	4	—
Hobbs, J. B.	61	102	7	5410	211	56.94	15	28	17	—
Hobbs, R. N. S.	4	5	3	26	15*	13.00	—	—	5	—
Hollies, W. E.	13	15	8	37	18*	5.28	—	—	2	—
Holmes, E. R. T.	5	9	2	114	85*	16.28	—	1	3	—
Holmes, P.	7	14	1	357	88	27.46	—	4	3	—
Hone, L.	1	2	0	13	7	6.50	—	—	2	—
Hopwood, J. L.	2	3	1	12	8	6.00	—	—	—	—
Hornby, A. N.	3	6	0	21	9	3.50	—	—	—	—
Horton, M. J.	2	2	0	60	58	30.00	—	1	2	—
Howard, N. D.	4	6	1	86	23	17.20	—	—	4	—
Howell, H.	5	8	6	15	5	7.50	—	—	—	—
Howorth, R.	5	10	2	145	45*	18.12	—	—	2	—
Humphries, J.	3	6	1	44	16	8.80	—	—	7	—
Hunter, J.	5	7	2	93	39*	18.60	—	—	8	3
Hutchings, K. L.	7	12	0	341	126	28.41	1	1	9	—
Hutton, L.	79	138	15	6971	364	56.67	19	33	57	—
Iddon, J.	5	7	1	170	73	28.33	—	2	—	—
Ikin, J. T.	18	31	2	606	60	20.89	—	3	31	—
Illingworth, R.	27	37	7	497	50	16.56	—	1	20	—
Insole, D. J.	9	17	2	408	110*	27.20	1	1	8	—
Jackson, H. L.	2	2	1	15	8	15.00	—	—	1	—
Jackson, Hon. F. S.	20	33	4	1415	144*	48.79	5	6	10	—
Jardine, D. R.	22	33	6	1296	127	48.00	1	10	26	—
Jenkins, R. O.	9	12	1	198	39	18.00	—	—	4	—
Jessop, G. L.	18	26	0	569	104	21.88	1	3	11	—
Jones, A. O.	12	21	0	291	34	13.85	—	—	15	—
Jones, I. J.	10	11	5	34	16	5.66	—	—	1	—
Jupp, H.	2	4	0	68	63	17.00	—	1	2	—
Jupp, V. W. C.	8	13	1	208	38	17.33	—	—	5	—
Keeton, W. W.	2	4	0	57	25	14.25	—	—	—	—
Kennedy, A. S.	5	8	2	93	41*	15.50	—	—	5	—
Kenyon, D.	8	15	0	192	87	12.80	—	1	5	—
Killick, E. T...	2	4	0	81	31	20.25	—	—	2	—
Kilner, R.	9	8	1	233	74	33.28	—	2	6	—
King, J. H.	1	2	0	64	60	32.00	—	1	—	—
Kinneir, S. P.	1	2	0	52	30	26.00	—	—	—	—
Knight, A. E.	3	6	1	81	70*	16.20	—	1	1	—
Knight, B. R.	22	27	4	616	127	26.78	2	—	11	—
Knight, D. J...	2	4	0	54	38	13.50	—	—	1	—
Knott, A. P.	2	2	0	28	28	14.00	—	—	12	1
Knox, N. A.	2	4	1	24	8*	8.00	—	—	—	—

Batting & Fielding—England—*Cont.*

	Tests	*I.*	*N.O.*	*Runs*	*H.S.*	*Avge.*	100*s*	50*s*	*Ct.*	*St.*
Laker, J. C.	46	63	15	676	63	14.08	—	2	12	—
Langridge, James	8	9	0	242	70	26.88	—	1	6	—
Larter, J. D. F.	10	7	2	16	10	3.20	—	—	5	—
Larwood, H.	21	28	3	485	98	19.40	—	2	15	—
Leadbeater, E.	2	2	0	40	38	20.00	—	—	3	—
Lee, H. W.	1	2	0	19	18	9.50	—	—	—	—
Lees, W. S.	5	9	3	66	25*	11.00	—	—	2	—
Legge, G. B.	5	7	1	299	196	49.83	1	—	1	—
Leslie, C. F. H.	4	7	0	106	54	15.14	—	1	1	—
Leveson-Gower, H. D. G. ..	3	6	2	95	31	23.75	—	—	1	—
Levett, W. H. V.	1	2	1	7	5	7.00	—	—	3	—
Leyland, M.	41	65	5	2764	187	46.06	9	10	13	—
Lilley, A. A.	35	52	8	903	84	20.52	—	4	70	22
Lillywhite, James	2	3	1	16	10	8.00	—	—	1	—
Loader, P. J...	13	19	6	76	17	5.84	—	—	2	—
Lock, G. A. R.	47	60	9	648	56	12.70	—	2	57	—
Lockwood, W. H.	12	16	3	231	52*	17.76	—	1	4	—
Lohmann, G. A.	18	26	2	213	62*	8.87	—	1	28	—
Lowson, F. A.	7	13	0	245	68	18.84	—	2	5	—
Lucas, A. P.	5	9	1	157	55	19.62	—	1	1	—
Lyttelton, Hon. A.	4	7	1	94	31	15.66	—	—	2	—
Macaulay, G. G.	8	10	4	112	76	18.66	—	1	5	—
MacBryan, J. C. W... ..	1	—	—	—	—	—	—	—	—	—
McConnon, J. E.	2	3	1	18	11	9.00	—	—	4	—
McGahey, C. P.	2	4	0	38	18	9.50	—	—	1	—
MacGregor, G.	8	11	3	96	31	12.00	—	—	14	3
McIntyre, A. J.	3	6	0	19	7	3.16	—	—	8	—
Mackinnon, F. A.	1	2	0	5	5	2.50	—	—	—	—
MacLaren, A. C.	35	61	4	1931	140	33.87	5	8	29	—
McMaster, J. E. P.	1	1	0	0	0	0.00	—	—	—	—
Makepeace, H.	4	8	0	279	117	34.87	1	2	—	—
Mann, F. G.	7	12	2	376	136*	37.60	1	—	3	—
Mann, F. T.	5	9	1	281	84	35.12	—	2	4	—
Marriott, C. S.	1	1	0	0	0	0.00	—	—	1	—
Martin, F.	2	2	0	14	13	7.00	—	—	2	—
Martin, J. W.	1	2	0	26	26	13.00	—	—	—	—
Mason, J. R...	5	10	0	129	32	12.90	—	—	3	—
Matthews, A. D. G... ..	1	1	1	2	2*	—	—	—	1	—
May, P. B. H.	66	106	9	4537	285*	46.77	13	22	42	—
Mead, C. P.	17	26	2	1185	182*	49.37	4	3	4	—
Mead, W.	1	2	0	7	7	3.50	—	—	1	—
Midwinter, W. E.	4	7	0	95	36	13.57	—	—	5	—
Milburn, C.	6	12	2	406	126*	40.60	1	1	5	—
Miller, A. M.	1	2	2	24	20*	—	—	—	—	—
Milligan, F. W.	2	4	0	58	38	14.50	—	—	1	—
Millman, G.	6	7	2	60	32*	12.00	—	—	13	2
Milton, C. A.	6	9	1	204	104*	25.50	1	—	5	—
Mitchell, A.	6	10	0	298	72	29.80	—	2	9	—
Mitchell, F.	2	4	0	88	41	22.00	—	—	2	—
Mitchell, T. B.	5	6	2	20	9	5.00	—	—	1	—
Mitchell-Innes, N. S. ..	1	1	0	5	5	5.00	—	—	—	—
Mold, A.	3	3	1	0	0*	0.00	—	—	1	—
Moon, L. J.	4	8	0	182	36	22.75	—	—	4	—
Morley, F.	4	6	2	6	2*	1.50	—	—	4	—
Mortimore, J. B.	9	12	2	243	73*	24.30	—	1	3	—
Moss, A. E.	9	7	1	61	26	10.16	—	—	1	—
Murdoch, W. L.	1	1	0	12	12	12.00	—	—	—	1
Murray, J. T.	21	28	5	506	112	22.00	1	2	52	3
Newham, W.	1	2	0	26	17	13.00	—	—	—	—
Nichols, M. S.	14	19	7	355	78*	29.58	—	2	12	—

Batting & Fielding—England—*Cont.*

	Tests	*I.*	*N.O.*	*Runs*	*H.S.*	*Avge.*	*100s*	*50s*	*Ct.*	*St.*
Oakman, A. S. M.	2	2	0	14	10	7.00	—	—	7	—
O'Brien, T. C.	5	8	0	59	20	7.37	—	—	4	—
O'Connor, J.	4	7	0	153	51	21.85	—	1	2	—
Oldfield, N.	1	2	0	99	80	49.50	—	1	—	—
Padgett, D. E. V.	2	4	0	51	31	12.75	—	—	—	—
Paine, G. A. E.	4	7	1	97	49	16.16	—	—	5	—
Palairet, L. C. H.	2	4	0	49	20	12.25	—	—	2	—
Palmer, C. H.	1	2	0	22	22	11.00	—	—	—	—
Palmer, K. E.	1	1	0	10	10	10.00	—	—	—	—
Parfitt, P. H.	33	44	5	1722	131*	44.15	7	5	37	—
Parker, C. W. L.	1	1	1	3	3*	—	—	—	—	—
Parkhouse, W. G. A.	7	13	0	373	78	28.69	—	2	3	—
Parkin, C. H.	10	16	3	160	36	12.30	—	—	3	—
Parks, J. H.	1	2	0	29	22	14.50	—	—	—	—
Parks, J. M.	43	64	7	1914	108*	33.57	2	9	94	11
Pataudi, Nawab of, Snr.	3	5	0	144	102	28.80	1	—	—	—
Paynter, E.	20	31	5	1540	243	59.23	4	7	7	—
Peate, E.	9	14	8	70	13	11.66	—	—	2	—
Peebles, I. A. R.	13	17	8	98	26	10.88	—	—	5	—
Peel, R.	20	33	4	427	83	14.72	—	3	17	—
Penn, F.	1	2	1	50	27*	50.00	—	—	—	—
Perks, R. T. D.	2	2	2	3	2*	—	—	—	1	—
Philipson, H.	5	8	1	63	30	9.00	—	—	8	3
Pilling, R.	8	13	1	91	23	7.58	—	—	10	4
Place, W.	3	6	1	144	107	28.80	1	—	—	—
Pollard, R.	4	3	2	13	10*	13.00	—	—	3	—
Poole, C. J.	3	5	1	161	69*	40.25	—	2	1	—
Pope, G. H.	1	1	1	8	8*	—	—	—	—	—
Pougher, A. D.	1	1	0	17	17	17.00	—	—	2	—
Price, J. S. E.	10	8	3	34	32	6.80	—	—	6	—
Price, W. F.	1	2	0	6	6	3.00	—	—	2	—
Pullar, G.	28	49	4	1974	175	43.86	4	12	2	—
Quaife, W. G.	7	13	1	228	68	19.00	—	1	4	—
Ranjitsinhji, K. S.	15	26	4	989	175	44.95	2	6	13	—
Read, H. D.	1	—	—	—	—	—	—	—	—	—
Read, J. M.	17	29	2	463	57	17.14	—	2	8	—
Read, W. W.	18	27	1	720	117	27.69	1	5	16	—
Relf, A. E.	13	21	3	416	63	23.11	—	1	14	—
Rhodes, H. J.	2	1	1	0	0*	—	—	—	—	—
Rhodes, W.	58	98	21	2325	179	30.19	2	11	60	—
Richardson, D. W.	1	1	0	33	33	33.00	—	—	1	—
Richardson, P. E.	34	56	1	2061	126	37.47	5	9	6	—
Richardson, T.	14	24	8	177	25*	11.06	—	—	5	—
Richmond, T. L.	1	2	0	6	4	3.00	—	—	—	—
Ridgway, F.	5	6	0	49	24	8.16	—	—	3	—
Robertson, J. D.	11	21	2	881	133	46.36	2	6	6	—
Robins, R. W. V.	19	27	4	612	108	26.60	1	4	12	—
Root, C. F.	3	—	—	—	—	—	—	—	1	—
Royle, V. P. F. A.	1	2	0	21	18	10.50	—	—	2	—
Rumsey, F. E.	5	5	3	30	21*	15.00	—	—	—	—
Russell, A. C.	10	18	2	911	140	56.93	5	2	8	—
Russell, W. E.	10	18	1	362	70	21.29	—	2	5	—
Sandham, A.	14	23	0	878	325	38.17	2	3	4	—
Schultz, S. S.	1	2	1	20	20	20.00	—	—	—	—
Scotton, W. H.	15	25	2	510	90	22.17	—	3	4	—
Selby, J.	6	12	1	256	70	23.27	—	2	1	—
Shackleton, D.	7	13	7	112	42	18.66	—	—	1	—
Sharp, J.	3	6	2	188	105	47.00	1	1	1	—

Batting & Fielding—England—*Cont.*

	Tests	*I.*	*N.O.*	*Runs*	*H.S*	*Avge.*	*100s*	*50s*	*Ct.*	*St.*
Sharpe, J. W.	3	6	4	44	26	22.00	—	—	2	—
Sharpe, P. J.	6	11	3	396	85*	49.50	—	3	4	—
Shaw, A.	7	12	1	111	40	10.09	—	—	4	—
Sheppard, D. S.	22	33	2	1172	119	37.80	3	6	12	—
Sherwin, M.	3	6	4	30	21*	15.00	—	—	5	2
Shrewsbury, A.	23	40	4	1277	164	35.47	3	4	29	—
Shuter, J.	1	1	0	28	28	28.00	—	—	—	—
Simpson, R. T.	27	45	3	1401	156*	33.35	4	6	5	—
Simpson-Hayward, G. H. ..	5	8	1	105	29*	15.00	—	—	1	—
Sims, J. M.	4	4	0	16	12	4.00	—	—	6	—
Sinfield, R. A.	1	1	0	6	6	6.00	—	—	—	—
Smailes, T. F.	1	1	0	25	25	25.00	—	—	—	—
Smith, A. C.	6	7	3	118	69*	29.50	—	1	20	—
Smith, C. A.	1	1	0	3	3	3.00	—	—	—	—
Smith, C. I. J.	5	10	0	102	27	10.20	—	—	1	—
Smith D.	2	4	0	128	57	32.00	—	1	1	—
Smith, D. R.	5	5	1	38	34	9.50	—	—	2	—
Smith, D. V.	3	4	1	25	16*	8.33	—	—	—	—
Smith, E. J.	11	14	1	113	22	8.69	—	—	17	3
Smith, H.	1	1	0	7	7	7.00	—	—	1	—
Smith, M. J. K.	47	72	6	2138	121	32.39	3	11	48	—
Smith, T. P. B.	4	5	0	33	24	6.60	—	—	1	—
Smithson, G. A.	2	3	0	70	35	23.33	—	—	—	—
Snow, J. A.	9	13	4	101	59*	11.22	—	1	3	—
Southerton, J.	2	3	1	7	6	3.50	—	—	2	—
Spooner, R. H.	10	15	0	481	119	32.06	1	4	4	—
Spooner, R. T.	7	14	1	354	92	27.23	—	3	10	2
Stanyforth, R. T.	4	6	1	13	6*	2.60	—	—	7	2
Staples, S. J.	3	5	0	65	39	13.00	—	—	—	—
Statham, J. B.	70	87	28	675	38	11.44	—	—	28	—
Steel, A. G.	13	20	3	600	148	35.29	2	—	5	—
Stevens, G. T. S.	10	17	0	263	69	15.47	—	1	9	—
Stewart, M. J.	8	12	1	385	87	35.00	—	2	6	—
Stoddart, A. E.	16	30	2	996	173	35.57	2	3	6	—
Storer, W.	6	11	0	215	51	19.54	—	1	11	—
Street, G. B.	1	2	1	11	7*	11.00	—	—	—	1
Strudwick, H.	28	42	13	230	24	7.93	—	—	60	12
Studd, C. T.	5	9	1	160	48	20.00	—	—	5	—
Studd, G. B.	4	7	0	31	9	4.42	—	—	8	—
Subba Row, R.	13	22	1	984	137	46.85	3	4	5	—
Sugg, F. H.	2	2	0	55	31	27.50	—	—	—	—
Sutcliffe, H.	54	84	9	4555	194	60.73	16	23	23	—
Swetman, R...	11	17	2	254	65	16.93	—	1	24	2
Tate, F. W.	1	2	1	9	5*	9.00	—	—	2	—
Tate, M. W.	39	52	5	1198	100*	25.48	1	5	11	—
Tattersall, R...	16	17	7	50	10*	5.00	—	—	8	—
Taylor, K.	3	5	0	57	24	11.40	—	—	1	—
Tennyson, Hon. L. H. ..	9	12	1	345	74*	31.36	—	4	6	—
Thompson, G. J.	6	10	1	273	63	30.33	—	2	5	—
Thomson, N. I.	5	4	1	69	39	23.00	—	—	3	—
Titmus, F. J.	47	65	11	1273	84*	23.57	—	9	34	—
Townsend, C. L.	2	3	0	51	38	17.00	—	—	—	—
Townsend, D. C. H... ..	3	6	0	77	36	12.83	—	—	1	—
Townsend, L. F.	4	6	0	97	40	16.16	—	—	1	—
Tremlett, M. F.	3	5	2	20	18*	6.66	—	—	—	—
Trott, A. E.	2	4	0	23	16	5.75	—	—	—	—
Trueman, F. S.	67	85	14	981	39*	13.81	—	—	64	—
Tufnell, N. C.	1	1	0	14	14	14.00	—	—	—	1
Turnbull, M. J.	9	13	2	224	61	20.36	—	1	1	—
Tyldesley, E...	14	20	2	990	122	55.00	3	6	2	—
Tyldesley, J. T.	31	55	1	1661	138	30.75	4	9	16	—
Tyldesley, R...	7	7	1	47	29	7.83	—	—	1	—
Tylecote, E. F. S.	6	9	1	152	66	19.00	—	1	5	5
Tyler, E. J.	1	1	0	0	0	0.00	—	—	—	—
Tyson, F. H.	17	24	3	230	37*	10.95	—	—	4	—

Batting & Fielding—England—*Cont.*

	Tests	*I.*	*N.O.*	*Runs*	*H.S.*	*Avge.*	100*s*	50*s*	*Ct.*	*St.*
Ulyett, G.	25	39	0	949	149	24.33	1	7	19	—
Underwood, D. L.	4	5	3	24	12*	12.00	—	—	3	—
Valentine, B. H.	7	9	2	454	136	64.85	2	1	2	—
Verity, H.	40	44	12	669	66*	20.90	—	3	30	—
Vernon, G. F.	1	2	1	14	11*	14.00	—	—	—	—
Vine, J.	2	3	2	46	36	46.00	—	—	—	—
Voce, W.	27	38	15	308	66	13.39	—	1	16	—
Waddington, A.	2	4	0	16	7	4.00	—	—	1	—
Wainwright, E.	5	9	0	132	49	14.66	—	—	2	—
Walker, P. M.	3	4	0	128	52	32.00	—	1	5	—
Walters, C. F.	11	18	3	784	102	52.26	1	7	6	—
Ward, A.	7	13	0	487	117	37.46	1	3	1	—
Wardle, J. H.	28	41	8	653	66	19.78	—	2	12	—
Warner, P. F.	15	28	2	622	132*	23.92	1	3	3	—
Warr, J. J.	2	4	0	4	4	1.00	—	—	—	—
Warren, A. R.	1	1	0	7	7	7.00	—	—	1	—
Washbrook, C.	37	66	6	2569	195	42.81	6	12	12	—
Watkins, A. J.	15	24	4	811	138*	40.55	2	4	17	—
Watson, W.	23	37	3	879	116	25.85	2	3	8	—
Webbe, A. J.	1	2	0	4	4	2.00	—	—	2	—
Wellard, A. W.	2	4	0	47	38	11.75	—	—	2	—
Wharton, A.	1	2	0	20	13	10.00	—	—	—	—
White, D. W.	2	2	0	0	0	0.00	—	—	—	—
White, J. C.	15	22	9	239	29	18.38	—	—	6	—
Whysall, W. W.	4	7	0	209	76	29.85	—	2	7	—
Wilkinson, L. L.	3	2	1	3	2	3.00	—	—	—	—
Wilson, C. E. M.	2	4	1	42	18	14.00	—	—	—	—
Wilson, D.	5	6	1	70	42	14.00	—	—	1	—
Wilson, E. R.	1	2	0	10	5	5.00	—	—	—	—
Wood, A.	4	5	1	80	53	20.00	—	1	10	1
Wood, G. E. C.	3	2	0	7	6	3.50	—	—	5	1
Wood, H.	4	4	1	204	134*	68.00	1	1	2	1
Wood, R.	1	2	0	6	6	3.00	—	—	—	—
Woods, S. M. J.	3	4	0	122	53	30.50	—	1	4	—
Woolley, F. E.	64	98	7	3283	154	36.07	5	23	64	—
Worthington, T. S.	9	11	0	321	128	29.18	1	1	8	—
Wright, C. W.	3	4	0	125	71	31.25	—	1	—	—
Wright, D. V. P.	34	39	13	289	45	11.11	—	—	10	—
Wyatt, R. E. S.	40	64	6	1839	149	31.70	2	12	17	—
Wynyard, E. G.	3	6	0	72	30	12.00	—	—	—	—
Yardley, N. W. D.	20	34	2	812	99	25.37	—	4	14	—
Young, H.	2	2	0	43	43	21.50	—	—	1	—
Young, J. A.	8	10	5	28	10*	5.60	—	—	5	—
Young, R. A.	2	4	0	27	13	6.75	—	—	6	—
Substitutes									43	1

AUSTRALIA (*241 Players*)

	Tests	*I.*	*N.O.*	*Runs*	*H.S.*	*Avge.*	100*s*	50*s*	*Ct.*	*St.*
A'Beckett, E. L.	4	7	0	143	41	20.42	—	—	4	—
Alexander, G.	2	4	0	52	33	13.00	—	—	2	—
Alexander, H. H.	1	2	1	17	17*	17.00	—	—	—	—
Allan, F. E.	1	1	0	5	5	5.00	—	—	—	—
Allan, P. J.	1	—	—	—	—	—	—	—	—	—
Allen, R.	1	2	0	44	30	22.00	—	—	2	—
Andrews, T. J. E.	16	23	1	592	94	26.90	—	4	12	—
Archer, K. A.	5	9	0	234	48	26.00	—	—	—	—
Archer, R. G.	19	30	1	713	128	24.58	1	2	20	—
Armstrong, W. W.	50	84	10	2863	159*	38.68	6	8	44	—

Batting & Fielding—Australia—*Cont.*

	Tests	*I.*	*N.O.*	*Runs*	*H.S.*	*Avge.*	*100s*	*50s*	*Ct.*	*St.*
Badcock, C. L.	7	12	1	160	118	14.54	1	—	3	—
Bannerman, A. C.	28	50	2	1105	94	23.02	—	8	21	—
Bannerman, C.	3	6	2	239	165*	59.75	1	—	—	—
Bardsley, W.	41	66	5	2469	193*	40.47	6	14	12	—
Barnes, S. G.	13	19	2	1072	234	63.05	3	5	14	—
Barnett, B. A.	4	8	1	195	57	27.85	—	1	3	2
Barrett, J. E.	2	4	1	80	67*	26.66	—	1	1	—
Benaud, R.	63	97	7	2201	122	24.45	3	9	65	—
Blackham, J. M.	35	62	11	800	74	15.68	—	4	36	24
Blackie, D. D. J.	3	6	3	24	11*	8.00	—	—	2	—
Bonnor, G. J.	17	30	0	512	128	17.06	1	2	16	—
Booth, B. C.	29	48	6	1773	169	42.21	5	10	17	—
Boyle, H. F.	12	16	4	153	36*	12.75	—	—	10	—
Bradman, D. G.	52	80	10	6996	334	99.94	29	13	32	—
Bromley, E. H.	2	4	0	38	26	9.50	—	—	2	—
Brown, W. A.	22	35	1	1592	206*	46.82	4	9	14	—
Bruce, W.	14	26	2	702	80	29.25	—	5	12	—
Burn, K. E.	2	4	0	41	19	10.25	—	—	—	—
Burge, P. J.	42	68	8	2290	181	38.16	4	12	22	—
Burke, J. W.	24	44	7	1280	189	34.59	3	5	18	—
Burton, F. J.	2	4	2	4	2*	2.00	—	—	1	1
Callaway, S. T.	3	6	1	87	41	17.40	—	—	—	—
Carkeek, W.	6	5	2	16	6*	5.33	—	—	6	—
Carter, H.	28	47	9	873	72	22.97	—	4	44	21
Chappell, I. M.	8	13	1	243	49	20.25	—	—	13	—
Charlton, P. C.	2	4	0	29	11	7.25	—	—	—	—
Chipperfield, A. G.	14	20	3	552	109	32.47	1	2	15	—
Collins, H. L.	19	31	1	1352	203	45.06	4	6	13	—
Coningham, A.	1	2	0	13	10	6.50	—	—	—	—
Connolly, A. N.	6	8	6	4	3*	2.00	—	—	3	—
Cooper, B. B.	1	2	0	18	15	9.00	—	—	2	—
Cooper, W. H.	2	3	1	13	7	6.50	—	—	1	—
Corling, G. E.	5	4	1	5	3	1.66	—	—	—	—
Cottam, W. J.	1	2	0	4	3	2.00	—	—	1	—
Cotter, A.	21	37	2	457	45	13.05	—	—	8	—
Coulthard, G.	1	1	1	6	6*	—	—	—	—	—
Cowper, R. M.	19	31	1	1385	307	46.16	3	7	10	—
Craig, I. D.	11	18	0	358	53	19.88	—	2	2	—
Crawford, P.	4	5	2	53	34	17.66	—	—	1	—
Darling, J.	34	60	2	1657	178	28.56	3	8	27	—
Darling, L. S.	12	18	1	474	85	27.88	—	3	8	—
Davidson, A. K.	44	61	7	1328	80	24.59	—	5	43	—
De Courcy, J. H.	3	6	1	81	41	16.20	—	—	3	—
Donnan, H.	5	10	1	75	15	8.33	—	—	1	—
Dooland, B.	3	5	1	76	29	19.00	—	—	3	—
Duff, R. A.	22	40	3	1316	146	35.56	2	6	14	—
Eady, C. J.	2	4	1	20	10*	6.66	—	—	2	—
Ebeling, H. I.	1	2	0	43	41	21.50	—	—	—	—
Edwards, J. D.	3	6	1	48	26	9.60	—	—	1	—
Emery, S. H.	4	2	0	6	5	3.00	—	—	2	—
Evans, E.	6	10	2	82	33	10.25	—	—	5	—
Fairfax, A. G.	10	12	4	410	65	51.25	—	4	15	—
Favell, L. E.	19	31	3	758	101	27.07	1	5	9	—
Ferris, J. J.	8	16	4	98	20*	8.16	—	—	4	—
Fingleton, J. H.	18	29	1	1189	136	42.46	5	3	13	—
Fleetwood-Smith, L. O.	10	11	5	54	16*	9.00	—	—	—	—
Freer, F. W.	1	1	1	28	28*	—	—	—	—	—

Batting & Fielding—Australia—*Cont.*

	Tests	*I.*	*N.O.*	*Runs*	*H.S.*	*Avge.*	*100s*	*50s*	*Ct.*	*St.*
Garrett, T. W.	19	33	6	339	51*	12.55	—	1	7	—
Gaunt, R. A.	3	4	2	6	3	3.00	—	—	1	—
Gehrs, D. R. A.	6	11	0	221	67	20.09	—	2	6	—
Giffen, G.	31	53	0	1238	161	23.35	1	6	24	—
Giffen, W. F.	3	6	0	11	3	1.83	—	—	1	—
Graham, H.	6	10	0	301	107	30.10	2	—	3	—
Gregory, D. W.	3	5	2	60	43	20.00	—	—	—	—
Gregory, E. J.	1	2	0	11	11	5.50	—	—	1	—
Gregory, J. M.	24	34	3	1146	119	36.96	2	7	37	—
Gregory, R. G.	2	3	0	153	80	51.00	—	2	1	—
Gregory, S. E.	58	100	7	2282	201	24.53	4	8	25	—
Grimmett, C. V.	37	50	10	557	50	13.92	—	1	17	—
Groube, T. U.	1	2	0	11	11	5.50	—	—	—	—
Grout, A. T. W.	51	67	8	890	74	15.08	—	3	163	24
Guest, C.	1	1	0	11	11	11.00	—	—	—	—
Hamence, R. A.	3	4	1	81	30*	27.00	—	—	1	—
Harry, J.	1	2	0	8	6	4.00	—	—	1	—
Hartigan, R. J.	2	4	0	170	116	42.50	1	—	1	—
Hartkopf, A. E. V.	1	2	0	80	80	40.00	—	1	—	—
Harvey, M.	1	2	0	43	31	21.50	—	—	—	—
Harvey, R. N.	79	137	10	6149	205	48.42	21	24	62	—
Hassett, A. L.	43	69	3	3073	198*	46.56	10	11	30	—
Hawke, N. J. N.	24	32	15	354	46*	20.82	—	—	9	—
Hazlitt, G. R.	9	12	4	89	34*	11.12	—	—	4	—
Hendry, H. L.	11	18	2	335	112	20.93	1	—	10	—
Hill, C.	49	89	2	3412	191	39.21	7	19	33	—
Hill, J. C.	3	6	3	21	8*	7.00	—	—	2	—
Hoare, D. G.	1	2	0	35	35	17.50	—	—	2	—
Hodges, J.	2	4	1	10	8	3.33	—	—	—	—
Hole, G. B.	18	33	2	789	66	25.45	—	6	21	—
Hopkins, A. J.	20	33	2	509	43	16.42	—	—	11	—
Horan, T.	15	27	2	471	124	18.84	1	1	6	—
Hordern, H. V.	7	13	2	254	50	23.09	—	1	6	—
Hornibrook, P. M.	6	7	1	60	26	10.00	—	—	7	—
Howell, W. P.	18	27	6	158	35	7.52	—	—	12	—
Hunt, W. A.	1	1	0	0	0	0.00	—	—	1	—
Hurwood, A.	2	2	0	5	5	2.50	—	—	2	—
Iredale, F. A.	14	23	1	807	140	36.68	2	4	16	—
Ironmonger, H.	14	21	5	42	12	2.62	—	—	3	—
Iverson, J.	5	7	3	3	1*	0.75	—	—	2	—
Jackson, A. A.	8	11	1	474	164	47.40	1	2	7	—
Jarman, B. N.	7	10	2	136	78	17.00	—	1	16	2
Jarvis, A. H.	11	21	3	303	82	16.83	—	1	9	8
Jennings, C. B.	6	8	2	107	32	17.83	—	—	5	—
Johnson, I. W.	45	66	12	1000	77	18.51	—	6	30	—
Johnson, L.	1	1	1	25	25*	—	—	—	2	—
Johnston, W. A.	40	49	25	273	29	11.37	—	—	16	—
Jones, E.	19	26	1	126	20	5.04	—	—	21	—
Jones, S. P.	12	24	4	432	87	21.60	—	1	12	—
Kelleway, C. E.	26	42	4	1422	147	37.42	3	6	24	—
Kelly, J. J.	36	56	17	664	46*	17.02	—	—	43	20
Kelly, T. J. D.	2	3	0	64	35	21.33	—	—	1	—
Kendall, T.	2	4	1	39	17*	13.00	—	—	2	—
Kippax, A. F.	22	34	1	1192	146	36.12	2	8	13	—
Kline, L. F.	13	16	9	58	15*	8.28	—	—	9	—

Batting & Fielding—Australia—*Cont.*

	Tests	*I.*	*N.O.*	*Runs*	*H.S.*	*Avge.*	*100s*	*50s*	*Ct.*	*St.*
Langley, G. R.	26	37	12	374	53	14.96	—	1	83	15
Laver, F.	15	23	6	196	45	11.52	—	—	8	—
Lawry, W. M.	40	73	6	3172	210	47.34	8	16	12	—
Lee, P. K.	2	3	0	57	42	19.00	—	—	1	—
Lindwall, R. R.	61	84	13	1502	118	21.15	2	5	26	—
Love, H. S. B.	1	2	0	8	5	4.00	—	—	3	—
Loxton, S. J. E.	12	15	0	554	101	36.93	1	3	7	—
Lyons, J. J.	14	27	0	731	134	27.07	1	3	3	—
McAlister, P. A.	8	16	1	252	41	16.80	—	—	10	—
Macartney, C. G.	35	55	4	2131	170	41.78	7	9	17	—
McCabe, S. J.	39	62	5	2748	232	48.21	6	13	42	—
McCool, C. L.	14	17	4	459	104*	35.30	1	1	14	—
McCormick, E. L.	12	14	5	54	17*	6.00	—	—	8	—
McDonald, C. C.	47	83	4	3106	170	39.31	5	17	14	—
McDonald, E. A.	11	12	5	116	36	16.57	—	—	3	—
McDonnell, P. S.	19	34	1	953	147	28.87	3	2	6	—
McIlwraith, J.	1	2	0	9	7	4.50	—	—	1	—
Mackay, K. D.	37	52	7	1507	89	33.48	—	13	17	—
McKenzie, G. D.	37	52	7	577	76	12.82	—	1	21	—
McKibbin, T. R.	5	8	2	88	28	14.66	—	—	4	—
McLaren, J. W.	1	2	2	0	0*	—	—	—	—	—
McLeod, C. E.	17	29	5	573	112	23.87	1	4	9	—
McLeod, R. W.	6	11	0	146	31	13.27	—	—	3	—
McShane, P. G.	3	6	1	26	12*	5.20	—	—	2	—
Maddocks, L. V.	7	12	2	177	69	17.70	—	1	18	1
Mailey, A. A.	21	29	9	222	46*	11.10	—	—	14	—
Marr, A. P.	1	2	0	5	5	2.50	—	—	—	—
Martin, J. W.	8	13	1	214	55	17.83	—	1	5	—
Massie, H. H.	9	16	0	249	55	15.56	—	1	5	—
Matthews, T. J.	8	10	1	153	53	17.00	—	1	7	—
Mayne, E. R.	4	4	1	64	25*	21.33	—	—	2	—
Mayne, L. R.	3	5	3	25	11*	12.50	—	—	2	—
Meckiff, I. W.	18	20	7	154	45*	11.84	—	—	9	—
Meuleman, K. D.	1	1	0	0	0	0.00	—	—	1	—
Midwinter, W. E.	8	14	1	174	37	13.38	—	—	5	—
Miller, K. R...	55	87	7	2958	147	36.97	7	13	38	—
Minnett, R. B.	9	15	0	391	90	26.06	—	3	—	—
Misson, F. M.	5	5	3	38	25*	19.00	—	—	6	—
Moroney, J. A. R.	7	12	1	383	118	34.81	2	1	—	—
Morris, A. R.	46	79	3	3533	206	46.48	12	12	15	—
Morris, S.	1	2	1	14	10*	14.00	—	—	—	—
Moses, H.	6	10	0	198	33	19.80	—	—	1	—
Moule, W. H.	1	2	0	40	34	20.00	—	—	1	—
Murdoch, W. L.	18	33	5	896	211	32.00	2	1	12	1
Musgrove, H.	1	2	0	13	9	6.50	—	—	—	—
Nagel, L. E.	1	2	1	21	21*	21.00	—	—	—	—
Nash, L. J.	2	2	0	30	17	15.00	—	—	6	—
Nitschke, H. C.	2	2	0	53	47	26.50	—	—	3	—
Noble, M. A...	42	73	7	1997	133	30.25	1	16	26	—
Noblet, G. J...	3	4	1	22	13*	7.33	—	—	1	—
Nothling, O. E.	1	2	0	52	44	26.00	—	—	—	—
O'Brien, L. P. J.	5	8	0	211	61	26.37	—	2	3	—
O'Connor, J. A.	4	8	1	86	20	12.28	—	—	3	—
Oldfield, W. A.	54	80	17	1427	65*	22.65	—	4	78	52
O'Neill, N. C.	42	69	8	2779	181	45.55	6	15	21	—
O'Reilly, W. J.	27	39	7	410	56*	12.81	—	1	7	—
Oxenham, R. K.	7	10	0	151	48	15.10	—	—	4	—
Palmer, G. E.	17	25	4	296	48	14.09	—	—	13	—
Park, R. L.	1	1	0	0	0	0.00	—	—	—	—

Batting & Fielding—Australia—*Cont.*

	Tests	*I.*	*N.O.*	*Runs*	*H.S.*	*Avge.*	100*s*	50*s*	*Ct.*	*St.*
Pellew, C. E.	10	14	1	484	116	37.23	2	1	4	—
Philpott, P. I.	8	10	1	93	22	10.33	—	—	5	—
Ponsford, W. H.	29	48	4	2122	266	48.22	7	6	21	—
Pope, R. J.	1	2	0	3	3	1.50	—	—	—	—
Ransford, V. S.	20	38	6	1211	143*	37.84	1	7	10	—
Redpath, I. R.	15	26	4	842	97	38.27	—	5	20	—
Reedman, J. C.	1	2	0	21	17	10.50	—	—	1	—
Renneberg, D. A.	5	8	5	13	9	4.33	—	—	2	—
Richardson, A. J.	9	13	0	403	100	31.00	1	2	1	—
Richardson, V. Y.	19	30	0	706	138	23.53	1	1	24	—
Rigg, K. E.	8	12	0	401	127	33.41	1	1	5	—
Ring, D. T.	13	21	2	426	67	22.42	—	4	5	—
Robertson, W. R.	1	2	0	2	2	1.00	—	—	—	—
Robinson, R. H.	1	2	0	5	3	2.50	—	—	1	—
Rorke, G.	4	4	2	9	7	4.50	—	—	1	—
Rutherford, J.	1	1	0	30	30	30.00	—	—	—	—
Ryder, J.	20	32	5	1394	201*	51.62	3	9	17	—
Saggers, R. A.	6	5	2	30	14	10.00	—	—	16	8
Saunders, J. V.	14	23	6	39	11*	2.29	—	—	5	—
Scott, H. J. H.	8	14	1	359	102	27.61	1	1	8	—
Sellers, R. H. D.	1	1	0	0	0	0.00	—	—	1	—
Shepherd, B. K.	9	14	2	502	96	41.83	—	5	2	—
Sievers, M. W. S.	3	6	1	67	25*	13.40	—	—	4	—
Simpson, R. B.	49	87	7	3837	311	47.96	6	23	92	—
Sincock, D. J.	3	4	1	80	29	26.66	—	—	2	—
Slater, K.	1	1	1	1	1*	—	—	—	—	—
Slight, J.	1	2	0	11	11	5.50	—	—	—	—
Smith, D.	2	3	1	30	24*	15.00	—	—	—	—
Spofforth, F. R.	18	29	6	217	50	9.43	—	1	11	—
Stackpole, K. R.	7	11	0	306	134	27.81	1	—	5	—
Stevens, G.	4	7	0	112	28	16.00	—	—	2	—
Taber, H. B.	5	9	1	94	30	11.75	—	—	19	1
Tallon, D.	21	26	3	394	92	17.13	—	2	50	8
Taylor, J. M.	20	28	0	997	108	35.60	1	8	11	—
Thomas, G.	8	12	1	325	61	29.54	—	3	3	—
Thompson, N.	2	4	0	67	41	16.75	—	—	3	—
Thoms, G.	1	2	0	44	28	22.00	—	—	—	—
Thurlow, H. M.	1	1	0	0	0	0.00	—	—	—	—
Toshack, E. R. H.	12	11	6	73	20*	14.60	—	—	4	—
Travers, J. F.	1	2	0	10	9	5.00	—	—	1	—
Tribe, G. E.	3	3	1	35	25*	17.50	—	—	—	—
Trott, A. E.	3	5	3	205	85*	102.50	—	2	4	—
Trott, G. H. S.	24	42	0	921	143	21.92	1	4	21	—
Trumble, H.	32	57	14	851	70	19.79	—	4	45	—
Trumble, J. W.	7	13	1	243	59	20.25	—	1	3	—
Trumper, V. T.	48	89	8	3164	214*	39.06	8	13	31	—
Turner, C. T. B.	17	32	4	323	29	11.53	—	—	8	—
Veivers, T. R.	21	30	4	813	88	31.26	—	7	7	—
Waite, M. G.	2	3	0	11	8	3.66	—	—	1	—
Wall, T. W.	18	24	5	121	20	6.36	—	—	11	—
Walters, F. H.	1	2	0	12	7	6.00	—	—	2	—
Walters, K. D.	5	7	1	410	155	68.33	2	1	1	—
Ward, F. A.	4	8	2	36	18	6.00	—	—	1	—
Watson, G. D.	3	5	0	76	50	15.20	—	1	—	—
Watson, W.	4	7	1	106	30	17.66	—	—	2	—
Whitty, W. J.	14	19	7	161	39*	13.41	—	—	4	—

Batting & Fielding—Australia—*Cont.*

	Tests	I.	N.O.	Runs	H.S.	Avge.	100s	50s	Ct.	St.
Wilson, J.	1	—	—	—	—	—	—	—	—	—
Woodfull, W. M.	35	54	4	2300	161	46.00	7	13	7	—
Woods, S. M. J.	3	6	0	32	18	5.33	—	—	1	—
Worrall, J.	11	22	3	478	76	25.15	—	5	13	—
Substitutes									36	—

SOUTH AFRICA (*230 Players*)

	Tests	I.	N.O.	Runs	H.S.	Avge.	100s	50s	Ct.	St.
Adcock, N. A. T.	26	39	12	146	24	5.40	—	—	4	—
Anderson, J. H.	1	2	0	43	32	21.50	—	—	1	—
Ashley, W. H.	1	2	0	1	1	0.50	—	—	—	—
Bacher, A.	8	15	1	462	70	33.00	—	4	8	—
Balaskas, X. C.	9	13	1	174	122*	14.50	1	—	5	—
Barlow, E. J.	26	50	2	2156	201	44.91	4	14	27	—
Baumgartner, N. V.	1	2	0	19	16	9.50	—	—	1	—
Beaumont, R.	5	9	0	70	31	7.77	—	—	2	—
Begbie, D. W.	5	7	0	138	48	19.71	—	—	2	—
Bell, A. J.	16	23	12	69	26*	6.27	—	—	6	—
Bisset, M.	3	6	2	103	35	25.75	—	—	2	1
Bissett, G. F.	4	4	2	38	23	19.00	—	—	—	—
Blanckenberg, J. M.	18	30	6	455	59	18.95	—	2	9	—
Bland, K. C.	21	39	5	1669	144*	49.08	3	9	10	—
Bock, G. E.	1	2	2	11	9*	—	—	—	—	—
Bond, G. E.	1	1	0	0	0	0.00	—	—	—	—
Botten, J. T.	3	6	0	65	33	10.83	—	—	1	—
Brann, W. H.	3	5	0	71	50	14.20	—	1	2	—
Briscoe, A. W.	2	3	0	33	16	11.00	—	—	1	—
Bromfield, H. D.	9	12	7	59	21	11.80	—	—	13	—
Brown, L. S.	2	3	0	17	8	5.66	—	—	—	—
Burger, C. G. de V.	2	4	1	62	37*	20.66	—	—	1	—
Burke, S. F.	2	4	1	42	20	14.00	—	—	—	—
Buys, I. D.	1	2	1	4	4*	4.00	—	—	—	—
Cameron, H. B.	26	45	4	1239	90	30.21	—	10	39	12
Campbell, T.	5	9	3	90	48	15.00	—	—	7	1
Carlstein, P. R.	8	14	1	190	42	14.61	—	—	3	—
Carter, C. P.	10	15	5	181	45	18.10	—	—	2	—
Catterall, R. H.	24	43	2	1555	120	37.92	3	11	12	—
Chapman, H. W.	2	4	1	39	17	13.00	—	—	1	—
Cheetham, J. E.	24	43	6	883	89	23.86	—	5	13	—
Christy, J. A. J.	10	18	0	618	103	34.33	1	5	3	—
Chubb, G. W. A.	5	9	3	63	15*	10.50	—	—	—	—
Cochran, J. A. K.	1	1	0	4	4	4.00	—	—	—	—
Coen, S. K.	2	4	2	101	41*	50.50	—	—	1	—
Commaille, J. M. M.	12	22	1	355	47	16.90	—	—	1	—
Conyngham, D. P.	1	2	2	6	3*	—	—	—	1	—
Cook, F. J.	1	2	0	7	7	3.50	—	—	—	—
Cooper, A. H. C.	1	2	0	6	6	3.00	—	—	1	—
Cox, J. L.	3	6	2	17	12*	4.25	—	—	1	—
Cripps, G.	1	2	0	21	18	10.50	—	—	—	—
Crisp, R. J.	9	13	1	123	35	10.25	—	—	3	—
Curnow, S. H.	7	14	0	168	47	12.00	—	—	5	
Dalton, E. L.	15	24	2	698	117	31.72	2	3	5	—
Davies, E. Q.	5	8	3	9	3	1.80	—	—	—	—
Dawson, O. C.	9	15	1	293	55	20.92	—	1	10	—
Deane, H. G.	17	27	2	628	93	25.12	—	3	8	—
Dixon, C. D.	1	2	0	0	0	0.00	—	—	1	—

Batting & Fielding—South Africa—*Cont.*

	Tests	*I.*	*N.O.*	*Runs*	*H.S.*	*Avge.*	100*s*	50*s*	*Ct.*	*St.*
Dower, R. R.	1	2	0	9	9	4.50	—	—	2	—
Draper, R. G.	2	3	0	25	15	8.33	—	—	—	—
Duckworth, C. A. R. ..	2	4	0	28	13	7.00	—	—	3	—
Dumbrill, R.	5	10	0	153	36	15.30	—	—	3	—
Duminy, J. P.	3	6	0	30	12	5.00	—	—	2	—
Dunell, O. R.	2	4	1	42	26*	14.00	—	—	1	—
Du Preez, J. H.	2	2	0	0	0	0.00	—	—	2	—
Du Toit, J. F.	1	2	2	2	2*	—	—	—	1	—
Dyer, D. V.	3	6	0	96	62	16.00	—	1	—	—
Elgie, M. K.	3	6	0	75	56	12.50	—	1	4	—
Endean, W. R.	28	52	4	1630	162*	33.95	3	8	41	—
Farrer, W. S...	6	10	2	221	40	27.62	—	—	2	—
Faulkner, G. A.	25	47	4	1754	204	40.79	4	8	20	—
Fellows-Smith, J. P. ..	4	8	2	166	35	27.66	—	—	2	—
Fichardt, C. G.	2	4	0	15	10	3.75	—	—	2	—
Finlason, C. E.	1	2	0	6	6	3.00	—	—	—	—
Floquet, C. E.	1	2	1	12	11*	12.00	—	—	—	—
Francis, H. H.	2	4	0	39	29	9.75	—	—	1	—
Francois, C. M.	5	9	1	252	72	31.50	—	1	5	—
Frank, C. N.	3	6	0	236	152	39.33	1	—	—	—
Frank, W. H. B.	1	2	0	7	5	3.50	—	—	—	—
Fuller, E. R. H.	7	9	1	64	17	8.00	—	—	3	—
Fullerton, G. M.	7	13	0	325	88	25.00	—	3	10	2
Funston, K. J.	18	33	1	824	92	25.75	—	5	7	—
Gleeson, R. A.	1	2	1	4	3	4.00	—	—	2	—
Glover, G. K.	1	2	1	21	18*	21.00	—	—	—	—
Goddard, T. L.	38	73	5	2458	112	36.14	1	18	46	—
Gordon, N.	5	6	2	8	7*	2.00	—	—	1	—
Graham, R.	2	4	0	6	4	1.50	—	—	2	—
Grieveson, R. E.	2	2	0	114	75	57.00	—	1	8	2
Griffin, G.	2	4	0	25	14	6.25	—	—	—	—
Hall, A. E.	7	8	2	11	5	1.83	—	—	4	—
Hall, G. G.	1	1	0	0	0	0.00	—	—	—	—
Halliwell, E. A.	8	15	0	188	57	12.53	—	1	9	2
Halse, C. G.	3	3	3	30	19*	—	—	—	1	—
Hands, P. A. M.	7	12	0	300	83	25.00	—	2	3	—
Hands, R. H. M.	1	2	0	7	7	3.50	—	—	—	—
Hanley, M. A.	1	1	0	0	0	0.00	—	—	—	—
Harris, T. A.	3	5	1	100	60	25.00	—	1	1	—
Hartigan, G. P. D.	5	10	0	114	51	11.40	—	1	—	—
Harvey, R. L.	2	4	0	51	28	12.75	—	—	—	—
Hathorn, M.	12	20	1	325	102	17.10	1	—	5	—
Hearne, F.	4	8	0	121	30	15.12	—	—	2	—
Hearne, G. A. L.	3	5	0	59	28	11.80	—	—	3	—
Heine, P. S.	14	24	3	209	31	9.95	—	—	8	—
Hime, C. F. W.	1	2	0	8	8	4.00	—	—	—	—
Hutchinson, P.	2	4	0	14	11	3.50	—	—	3	—
Innes, A. R.	2	4	0	14	13	3.50	—	—	2	—
Ironside, D. E. J.	3	4	2	37	13	18.50	—	—	1	—
Johnson, C. L.	1	2	0	10	7	5.00	—	—	1	—
Jones, P. S. T.	1	2	0	0	0	0.00	—	—	—	—

Batting & Fielding—South Africa—*Cont.*

	Tests	*I.*	*N.O.*	*Runs*	*H.S.*	*Avge.*	100*s*	50*s*	*Ct.*	*St.*
Keith, H. J.	8	16	1	318	73	21.20	—	2	9	—
Kempis, G. A.	1	2	1	0	0*	0.00	—	—	—	—
Kotze, J. J.	3	5	0	2	2	0.40	—	—	3	—
Kuys, F.	1	2	0	26	26	13.00	—	—	—	—
Lance, H. R.	10	17	1	452	70	28.25	—	4	5	—
Langton, A. B. C.	15	23	4	298	73*	15.68	—	2	8	—
Lawrence, G. B.	5	8	0	141	43	17.62	—	—	2	—
Le Roux, F. L.	1	2	0	1	1	0.50	—	—	—	—
Lewis, P. T.	1	2	0	0	0	0.00	—	—	—	—
Lindsay, J. D.	3	5	2	21	9*	7.00	—	—	4	1
Lindsay, D.	17	27	1	1021	182	39.26	3	4	47	2
Lindsay, N. V.	1	2	0	35	29	17.50	—	—	1	—
Ling, W. V. S.	6	10	0	168	38	16.80	—	—	1	—
Llewellyn, C. B.	15	28	1	544	90	20.14	—	4	7	—
Lundie, E. P.	1	2	1	1	1	1.00	—	—	—	—
McCarthy, C. N.	15	24	15	28	5	3.11	—	—	6	—
Macaulay, M. J.	1	2	0	33	21	16.50	—	—	—	—
McGlew, D. J.	34	64	6	2440	255*	42.06	7	10	18	—
McKinnon, A. H.	8	13	7	107	27	17.83	—	—	1	—
McLean, R. A.	40	73	3	2120	142	30.28	5	10	23	—
McMillan, Q.	13	21	4	306	50*	18.00	—	1	8	—
Mann, N. B. F.	19	31	1	400	52	13.33	—	1	3	—
Mansell, P. N. F.	13	22	2	355	90	17.75	—	2	15	—
Markham, L. A.	1	1	0	20	20	20.00	—	—	—	—
Marx, W. F. E.	3	6	0	125	36	20.83	—	—	—	—
Meintjes, D. J.	2	3	0	43	21	14.33	—	—	3	—
Melle, M. G.	7	12	4	68	17	8.50	—	—	4	—
Melville, A.	11	19	2	894	189	52.58	4	3	8	—
Middleton, J.	6	12	5	52	22	7.42	—	—	1	—
Mills, C.	1	2	0	25	21	12.50	—	—	2	—
Milton, W. H.	3	6	0	68	21	11.33	—	—	1	—
Mitchell, B.	42	80	9	3471	189*	48.88	8	21	56	—
Mitchell, F.	3	6	0	28	12	4.66	—	—	—	—
Morkel, D. P. B.	16	28	1	663	88	24.55	—	4	13	—
Murray, A. R. A.	10	14	1	289	109	22.23	1	1	3	—
Nel, J. D.	6	11	0	150	38	13.63	—	—	1	—
Newberry, C.	4	8	0	62	16	7.75	—	—	3	—
Newson, E. S.	3	5	1	30	16	7.50	—	—	3	—
Nicholson, F.	4	8	1	76	29	10.85	—	—	3	—
Nicolson, J. W. F.	3	5	0	179	78	35.80	—	1	—	—
Norton, N. O.	1	2	0	9	7	4.50	—	—	—	—
Nourse, A. D. Snr.	45	83	8	2234	111	29.78	1	15	43	—
Nourse, A. D. Jnr.	34	62	7	2960	231	53.81	9	14	12	—
Nupen, E. P.	17	31	7	348	69	14.50	—	2	9	—
Ochse, A. E.	2	4	0	16	8	4.00	—	—	—	—
Ochse, A. L.	3	4	1	11	4*	3.66	—	—	1	—
O'Linn, S.	7	12	1	297	98	27.00	—	2	4	—
Owen-Smith, H. G. ..	5	8	2	252	129	42.00	1	1	4	—
Palm, A. W.	1	2	0	15	13	7.50	—	—	1	—
Parker, G. M.	2	4	2	3	2*	1.50	—	—	—	—
Parkin, D. C.	1	2	0	6	6	3.00	—	—	1	—
Partridge, J. T.	11	12	5	73	13*	10.42	—	—	7	—
Pearce, O. C.	3	6	0	55	31	9.16	—	—	1	—
Pegler, S. J.	16	28	5	356	35*	15.47	—	—	5	—
Pithey, A. J.	17	27	1	819	154	31.50	1	4	3	—
Pithey, D. B.	8	12	1	138	55	12.54	—	1	6	—

Batting & Fielding—South Africa—*Cont.*

	Tests	*I.*	*N.O.*	*Runs*	*H.S.*	*Avge.*	100*s*	50*s*	*Ct.*	*St.*
Plimsoll, J. B.	1	2	1	16	8*	16.00	—	—	—	—
Pollock, P. M.	24	34	10	533	75*	22.20	—	2	6	—
Pollock, R. G.	19	34	4	1739	209	57.96	6	8	13	—
Poore, R. M.	3	6	0	76	20	12.66	—	—	3	—
Pothecary, J. E.	3	4	0	26	12	6.50	—	—	2	—
Powell, A. W.	1	2	0	16	11	8.00	—	—	2	—
Prince, C. F.	1	2	0	6	5	3.00	—	—	—	—
Procter, M. J.	3	3	0	17	16	5.66	—	—	—	—
Promnitz, H. L. E.	2	4	0	14	5	3.50	—	—	2	—
Quinn, N. A.	12	18	3	90	28	6.00	—	—	1	—
Reid, N.	1	2	0	17	11	8.50	—	—	—	—
Richards, A.	1	2	0	6	6	3.00	—	—	—	—
Richards, W. H.	1	2	0	4	4	2.00	—	—	—	—
Robertson, J. B.	3	6	1	51	17	10.20	—	—	2	—
Routledge, T.	4	8	0	72	24	9.00	—	—	2	—
Rowan, A. M. B.	15	23	6	290	41	17.05	—	—	7	—
Rowan, E. A. B.	26	50	5	1965	236	43.66	3	12	14	—
Rowe, G. A.	5	9	3	26	13*	4.33	—	—	4	—
Samuelson, S. V.	1	2	0	22	15	11.00	—	—	1	—
Schwarz, R. O.	20	35	8	374	61	13.85	—	1	18	—
Seccull, A. W.	1	2	1	23	17*	23.00	—	—	1	—
Seymour, M. A.	6	8	3	84	36	16.80	—	—	2	—
Shalders, W. A.	12	23	1	355	42	16.13	—	—	3	—
Shepstone, G. H.	2	4	0	38	21	9.50	—	—	2	—
Sherwell, P. W.	13	22	4	427	115	23.72	1	1	20	16
Siedle, I. J.	18	34	0	977	141	28.73	1	5	7	—
Sinclair, J. H.	25	47	1	1069	106	23.23	3	3	9	—
Smith, C. J. E.	3	6	1	106	45	21.20	—	—	2	—
Smith, F. W.	3	6	1	45	12	9.00	—	—	2	—
Smith, V. I.	9	16	6	39	11*	3.90	—	—	3	—
Snooke, S. D.	1	1	0	0	0	0.00	—	—	2	—
Snooke, S. J.	26	46	1	1008	103	22.40	1	5	24	—
Solomon, W. R.	1	2	0	4	2	2.00	—	—	1	—
Stewart, R. B.	1	2	0	13	9	6.50	—	—	2	—
Stricker, L. A.	13	24	0	342	48	14.25	—	—	3	—
Susskind, M. J.	5	8	0	268	65	33.50	—	4	1	—
Taberer, H. M.	1	1	0	2	2	2.00	—	—	—	—
Tancred, A. B.	2	4	1	87	29	29.00	—	—	2	—
Tancred, L. J.	14	26	1	530	97	21.20	—	2	3	—
Tancred, V. M.	1	2	0	25	18	12.50	—	—	—	—
Tapscott, L. E.	2	3	1	58	50*	29.00	—	1	—	—
Tapscott, L. G.	1	2	0	5	4	2.50	—	—	1	—
Tayfield, H. J.	37	60	9	862	75	16.90	—	2	26	—
Taylor, A. I.	1	2	0	18	12	9.00	—	—	—	—
Taylor, D.	2	4	0	85	36	21.25	—	—	—	—
Taylor, H. W.	42	76	4	2936	176	40.77	7	17	19	—
Theunissen, N.	1	2	1	2	2*	2.00	—	—	—	—
Thornton, G.	1	1	1	1	1*	—	—	—	1	—
Tomlinson, D. S.	1	1	0	9	9	9.00	—	—	—	—
Trimborn, P. H. J.	3	3	2	13	11*	13.00	—	—	5	—
Tuckett, L.	9	14	3	131	40*	11.90	—	—	9	—
Tuckett, L. R.	1	2	1	0	0*	0.00	—	—	2	—
Van der Byl, P. G.	5	9	0	460	125	51.11	1	2	1	—
Van der Merwe, E. A.	2	4	1	27	19	9.00	—	—	3	—
Van der Merwe, P. L.	15	23	2	533	76	25.38	—	3	11	—
Van Ryneveld, C. B.	19	33	6	724	83	26.81	—	3	14	—

Batting & Fielding—South Africa—*Cont.*

	Tests	I.	N.O.	Runs	H.S.	Avge.	100s	50s	Ct.	St.
Varnals, G. D.	3	6	0	97	23	16.16	—	—	—	—
Viljoen, K. G.	27	50	2	1365	124	28.43	2	9	5	—
Vincent, C. L.	25	38	12	526	60	20.23	—	2	27	—
Vintcent, C. H.	3	6	0	26	9	4.33	—	—	1	—
Vogler, A. E. E.	15	26	6	340	65	17.00	—	2	20	—
Wade, H. F...	10	18	2	327	40*	20.43	—	—	4	—
Wade, W. W.	11	19	1	511	125	28.38	1	3	14	3
Waite, J. H. B.	50	86	7	2405	134	30.44	4	16	124	17
Walter, K. A.	2	3	0	11	10	3.66	—	—	3	—
Ward, T. A.	23	42	9	459	64	13.90	—	2	19	12
Watkins, J. C.	15	27	1	612	92	23.53	—	3	12	—
Wesley, C.	3	5	0	49	35	9.80	—	—	1	—
Westcott, R. J.	5	9	0	166	62	18.44	—	1	—	—
White, G. C.	17	31	2	872	147	30.06	2	4	10	—
Willoughby, J. T.	2	4	0	8	5	2.00	—	—	—	—
Wimble, C. S.	1	2	0	0	0	0.00	—	—	—	—
Winslow, P. L.	5	9	0	186	108	20.66	1	—	1	—
Wynne, O. E.	6	12	0	219	50	18.25	—	1	3	—
Zulch, J. W.	16	32	2	985	150	32.83	2	4	4	—
Substitutes									20	—

WEST INDIES (*125 Players*)

	Tests	I.	N.O.	Runs	H.S	Avge.	100s	50s	Ct.	St.
Achong, E. E.	6	11	1	81	22	8.10	—	—	6	—
Alexander, F. C. M. ..	25	38	6	961	108	30.03	1	7	85	5
Allan, D. W.	5	7	1	75	40*	12.50	—	—	15	3
Asgarali, N. N.	2	4	0	62	29	15.50	—	—	—	—
Atkinson, D.	22	35	6	922	219	31.79	1	5	11	—
Atkinson, E. E.	8	9	1	126	37	15.75	—	—	2	—
Barrow, I.	11	19	2	276	105	16.23	1	—	17	5
Bartlett, E. L.	5	8	1	131	84	18.71	—	1	2	—
Betancourt, N.	1	2	0	46	33	23.00	—	—	—	—
Binns, A. P.	5	8	1	64	27	9.14	—	—	14	3
Birkett, L. S.	4	8	0	136	64	17.00	—	1	4	—
Browne, C. R.	4	8	1	176	70*	25.14	—	1	1	—
Butcher, B. F.	28	48	4	1944	209*	44.18	5	8	10	—
Butler, L.	1	1	0	16	16	16.00	—	—	—	—
Bynoe, M. R.	4	6	0	111	48	18.50	—	—	4	—
Cameron, F. J.	5	7	1	151	75*	25.16	—	1	—	—
Cameron, J. H.	2	3	0	6	5	2.00	—	—	—	—
Carew, G.	4	7	1	170	107	28.33	1	—	1	—
Carew, M. C.	3	6	1	59	40	11.80	—	—	—	—
Challenor, G.	3	6	0	101	46	16.83	—	—	—	—
Christiani, C. M.	4	7	2	98	32*	19.60	—	—	6	1
Christiani, R. J.	22	37	3	896	107	26.35	1	4	19	2
Clarke, C. B.	3	4	1	3	2	1.00	—	—	—	—
Constantine, L. N.	18	33	0	641	90	19.42	—	4	28	—
Da Costa, O. C.	5	9	1	153	39	19.12	—	—	5	—
Davis, B. A.	4	8	0	245	68	30.62	—	3	1	—
De Caires, F. I.	3	6	0	232	80	38.66	—	2	1	—
Depeiza, C. C.	5	8	2	187	122	31.16	1	—	6	4
Dewdney, D. T.	9	12	5	17	5*	2.42	—	—	—	—

Batting & Fielding—West Indies—*Cont.*

	Tests	*I.*	*N.O.*	*Runs*	*H.S.*	*Avge.*	100*s*	50*s*	*Ct.*	*St.*
Ferguson, W. F.	8	10	3	200	75	28.57	—	2	11	—
Fernandes, M. P.	2	4	0	49	22	12.25	—	—	—	—
Francis, G. N.	10	18	4	81	19*	5.78	—	—	7	—
Frederick, M.	1	2	0	30	30	15.00	—	—	—	—
Fuller, R. L.	1	1	0	1	1	1.00	—	—	—	—
Furlonge, H.	3	5	0	99	64	19.80	—	1	—	—
Ganteaume, A. G.	1	1	0	112	112	112.00	1	—	—	—
Gaskin, B. M.	2	3	0	17	10	5.66	—	—	1	—
Gibbs, G.	1	2	0	12	12	6.00	—	—	1	—
Gibbs, L. R.	34	47	10	255	22	6.89	—	—	21	—
Gilchrist, R.	13	14	3	60	12	5.45	—	—	4	—
Gladstone, G.	1	1	1	12	12*	—	—	—	—	—
Goddard, J. D. C.	27	39	11	859	83*	30.67	—	4	22	—
Gomez, G. E.	29	46	5	1243	101	30.31	1	8	18	—
Grant, G. C.	12	21	5	413	71*	25.81	—	3	10	—
Grant, R. S.	7	11	1	220	77	22.00	—	1	13	—
Grell, M. G.	1	2	0	34	21	17.00	—	—	1	—
Griffith, C. C.	19	27	8	341	54	17.94	—	1	11	—
Griffith, H. C.	13	23	5	91	18	5.05	—	—	4	—
Guillen, S. C.	5	6	2	104	54	26.00	—	1	9	2
Hall, W. W.	41	54	11	728	50*	16.90	—	2	10	—
Headley, G. A.	22	40	4	2190	270*	60.83	10	5	14	—
Hendriks, J. L.	11	16	3	239	64	18.38	—	1	24	3
Hoad, E. L. G.	4	8	0	98	36	12.25	—	—	1	—
Holford, D. A. J.	6	9	2	307	105*	43.85	1	1	6	—
Holt, J. K., Jnr.	17	31	2	1066	166	36.75	2	5	8	—
Hunte, C. C.	44	78	6	3245	260	45.06	8	13	17	—
Hunte, E. A. C.	3	6	1	166	58	33.20	—	2	5	—
Hylton, L. G.	6	8	2	70	19	11.66	—	—	1	—
Johnson, H. H. H.	3	4	0	38	22	9.50	—	—	—	—
Johnson, T.	1	1	1	9	9*	—	—	—	1	—
Jones, C. M.	4	7	0	63	19	9.00	—	—	3	—
Jones, P. E.	9	11	2	47	10*	5.22	—	—	4	—
Kanhai, R. B.	51	88	2	4150	256	48.25	10	18	28	—
Kentish, E. S. M.	2	2	1	1	1*	1.00	—	—	1	—
King, F.	14	17	3	116	21	8.28	—	—	5	—
King, L. A.	1	2	0	13	13	6.50	—	—	—	—
Lashley, P. D.	4	7	0	159	49	22.71	—	—	4	—
Legall, R.	4	5	0	50	23	10.00	—	—	8	1
Lloyd, C. H.	3	5	1	227	82	56.75	—	2	2	—
McMorris, E. D. A.	13	21	0	564	125	26.85	1	3	5	—
McWatt, C. A.	6	9	2	202	54	28.85	—	2	9	1
Madray, I. S.	2	3	0	3	2	1.00	—	—	1	—
Marshall, N. E.	1	2	0	8	8	4.00	—	—	—	—
Marshall, R. E.	4	7	0	143	30	20.42	—	—	1	—
Martin, F. R.	9	18	1	486	123*	28.58	1	—	2	—
Martindale, E. A.	10	14	3	58	22	5.27	—	—	4	—
Mendonca, I.	2	2	0	81	78	40.50	—	1	8	2
Merry, C. A.	2	4	0	34	13	8.50	—	—	1	—
Miller, R.	1	1	0	23	23	23.00	—	—	—	—
Mudie, G. H.	1	1	0	5	5	5.00	—	—	—	—
Murray, D. L.	5	8	2	93	34	15.50	—	—	22	2

Batting & Fielding—West Indies—*Cont.*

	Tests	I.	N.O.	Runs	H.S.	Avge.	100s	50s	Ct.	St.
Neblett, J. M.	1	2	1	16	11*	16.00	—	—	—	—
Nunes, R. K...	4	8	0	245	92	30.62	—	2	2	—
Nurse, S. M.	16	29	1	1183	201	42.25	2	7	15	—
Pairaudeau, B. H.	13	21	0	454	115	21.61	1	3	6	—
Passailaigue, C. C.	1	2	1	46	44	46.00	—	—	3	—
Pierre, L. R...	1	—	—	—	—	—	—	—	—	—
Rae, A. F.	15	24	2	1016	109	46.18	4	4	9	—
Ramadhin, S.	43	58	14	361	44	8.20	—	—	9	—
Rickards, K. R.	2	3	0	104	67	34.66	—	1	—	—
Roach, C. A.	16	32	1	952	209	30.70	2	6	5	—
Roberts, A.	1	2	0	28	28	14.00	—	—	—	—
Rodriguez, W. V.	4	6	0	96	50	16.00	—	1	3	—
St. Hill, E.	2	4	0	18	12	4.50	—	—	—	—
St. Hill, W. H.	3	6	0	117	38	19.50	—	—	1	—
Scarlett, R.	3	4	1	54	29*	18.00	—	—	2	—
Scott, A. P. H.	1	1	0	5	5	5.00	—	—	—	—
Scott, O. C.	8	13	3	171	35	17.10	—	—	—	—
Sealy, B. J.	1	2	0	41	29	20.50	—	—	—	—
Sealy, J. E. D.	11	19	2	478	92	28.11	—	3	6	1
Singh, C. K.	2	3	0	11	11	3.66	—	—	2	—
Small, J. A.	3	6	0	79	52	13.16	—	1	3	—
Smith, C. W...	5	10	1	222	55	24.66	—	1	4	1
Smith, O. G.	26	42	0	1331	168	31.69	4	6	9	—
Sobers, G. St. A.	60	102	13	5514	365*	61.95	17	21	79	—
Solomon, J. S.	27	46	7	1326	100*	34.00	1	9	14	—
Stayers, C.	4	4	1	58	35*	19.33	—	—	—	—
Stollmeyer, J. B.	32	56	5	2159	160	42.33	4	12	20	—
Stollmeyer, V. H.	1	1	0	96	96	96.00	—	1	—	—
Taylor, J.	3	5	3	4	4*	2.00	—	—	—	—
Trim, J.	4	5	1	21	12	5.25	—	—	2	—
Valentine, A. L.	36	51	21	141	14	4.70	—	—	13	—
Valentine, V. A.	2	4	1	35	19*	11.66	—	—	—	—
Walcott, C. L.	44	74	7	3798	220	56.68	15	14	54	11
Walcott, L. A.	1	2	1	40	24	40.00	—	—	—	—
Watson, C.	7	6	1	12	5	2.40	—	—	1	—
Weekes, E. D.	48	81	5	4455	207	58.61	15	19	49	—
Weekes, K. H.	2	3	0	173	137	57.66	1	—	—	—
White, W. A.	2	4	1	71	57*	23.66	—	1	1	—
Wight, C. V.	2	4	1	67	23	22.33	—	—	—	—
Wight, L.	1	1	0	21	21	21.00	—	—	—	—
Wiles, C. A.	1	2	0	2	2	1.00	—	—	—	—
Williams, E. A. V.	4	6	0	113	72	18.83	—	1	2	—
Wishart, K. L.	1	2	0	52	52	26.00	—	1	—	—
Worrell, F. M. M.	51	87	9	3860	261	49.48	9	22	43	—
Substitutes									22	—

NEW ZEALAND (*111 Players*)

	Tests	I.	N.O.	Runs	H.S.	Avge.	100s	50s	Ct.	St.
Alabaster, J. C.	15	25	2	193	24	8.39	—	—	4	—
Allcott, C. F. W.	6	7	2	113	33	22.60	—	—	3	—
Anderson, W. M.	1	2	0	5	4	2.50	—	—	1	—

Batting & Fielding—New Zealand—*Cont.*

	Tests	*I.*	*N.O.*	*Runs*	*H.S.*	*Avge.*	100*s*	50*s*	*Ct.*	*St.*
Badcock, F. T.	7	9	2	137	64	19.57	—	2	1	—
Barber, R. T.	1	2	0	17	12	8.50	—	—	1	—
Bartlett, G. A.	8	15	1	230	40	16.42	—	—	7	—
Barton, P. T.	7	14	0	285	109	20.35	1	1	4	—
Beard, D. D.	4	7	2	101	31	20.20	—	—	2	—
Beck, J. E. F.	8	15	0	394	99	26.26	—	3	—	—
Bell, W.	2	3	3	21	21*	—	—	—	1	—
Bilby, G. P.	2	4	0	55	28	13.75	—	—	3	—
Blair, R. W.	19	34	6	189	64*	6.75	—	1	5	—
Blunt, R. C.	9	13	1	330	96	27.50	—	1	5	—
Bolton, B. A.	2	3	0	59	33	19.66	—	—	1	—
Bradburn, W. P.	2	4	0	62	32	15.50	—	—	2	—
Burke, C. C.	1	2	0	4	3	2.00	—	—	—	—
Burtt, T. B.	10	15	3	252	42	21.00	—	—	2	—
Butterfield, L. A.	1	2	0	0	0	0.00	—	—	—	—
Cameron, F. J.	19	30	20	116	27*	11.60	—	—	2	—
Cave, H. B.	19	31	5	229	22*	8.80	—	—	8	—
Chapple, M. E.	14	27	1	497	76	19.11	—	3	10	—
Cleverley, D. C.	2	4	3	19	10*	19.00	—	—	—	—
Collinge, R. O.	10	14	2	209	54	17.41	—	1	5	—
Colquhoun, I. A.	2	4	2	1	1*	0.50	—	—	4	—
Congdon, B. E.	13	26	0	632	104	24.30	1	2	7	—
Cowie, J. A.	9	13	4	90	45	10.00	—	—	3	—
Cresswell, G. F.	3	5	3	14	12*	7.00	—	—	—	—
Cromb, I. B.	5	8	2	123	51*	20.50	—	1	1	—
Cunis, R. S.	4	8	4	59	16*	14.75	—	—	—	—
D'Arcy, J. W.	5	10	0	136	33	13.60	—	—	—	—
Dempster, C. S.	10	15	4	723	136	65.72	2	5	2	—
Dempster, E. W.	5	8	2	106	47	17.66	—	—	1	—
Dick, A. E.	17	30	4	370	50*	14.23	—	1	47	4
Dickinson, G. R.	3	5	0	31	11	6.20	—	—	3	—
Donnelly, M. P.	7	12	1	582	206	52.90	1	4	7	—
Dowling, G. T.	19	37	1	995	129	27.63	1	6	11	—
Dunning, J. A.	4	6	1	38	19	7.60	—	—	2	—
Emery, R. W. G.	2	4	0	46	28	11.50	—	—	—	—
Fisher, F. E.	1	2	0	23	14	11.50	—	—	—	—
Foley, H.	1	2	0	4	2	2.00	—	—	—	—
Freeman, D. L.	2	2	0	2	1	1.00	—	—	—	—
Gallichan, N. M.	1	2	0	32	30	16.00	—	—	—	—
Gedye, S. G.	4	8	0	193	55	24.12	—	2	—	—
Guillen, S. C.	3	6	0	98	41	16.33	—	—	4	1
Guy, J. W.	12	23	2	440	102	20.95	1	3	2	—
Hadlee, W. A.	11	19	1	543	116	30.16	1	2	6	—
Harford, N. S.	8	15	0	229	93	15.26	—	2	—	—
Harris, P. G. Z.	9	18	1	378	101	22.23	1	1	6	—
Harris, R. M.	2	3	0	31	13	10.33	—	—	—	—
Hayes, J. A.	15	22	7	73	19	4.86	—	—	3	—
Henderson, M.	1	2	1	8	6	8.00	—	—	1	—
Hough, K. W.	2	3	2	62	31*	62.00	—	—	1	—
James, K. C.	11	13	2	52	14	4.72	—	—	11	5
Jarvis, T. W.	6	11	1	302	77	30.20	—	2	2	—

Batting & Fielding—New Zealand—*Cont.*

	Tests	*I.*	*N.O.*	*Runs*	*H.S.*	*Avge.*	100*s*	50*s*	*Ct.*	*St.*
Kerr, J. L.	7	12	1	212	59	19.27	—	1	4	—
Leggat, I. B.	1	1	0	0	0	0.00	—	—	2	—
Leggat, J. G.	9	18	2	351	61	21.93	—	2	—	—
Lissette, A. F.	2	4	2	2	1*	1.00	—	—	1	—
Lowry, T. C.	7	8	0	223	80	27.87	—	2	8	—
MacGibbon, A. R.	26	46	5	814	66	19.85	—	3	13	—
McGirr, H. M.	2	1	0	51	51	51.00	—	1	—	—
McGregor, S. N.	25	47	2	892	111	19.82	1	3	9	—
McLeod, E. A.	1	2	1	18	16	18.00	—	—	—	—
McMahon, T. G.	5	7	4	8	4*	2.66	—	—	7	1
McRae, D. A. N.	1	2	0	8	8	4.00	—	—	—	—
Maloney, D. A. R.	3	6	0	156	64	26.00	—	1	3	—
Matheson, A. M.	2	1	0	7	7	7.00	—	—	2	—
Meale, T.	2	4	0	21	10	5.25	—	—	—	—
Merritt, W. E.	6	8	1	73	19	10.42	—	—	2	—
Meuli, E. M.	1	2	0	38	23	19.00	—	—	—	—
Miller, L. S. M.	13	25	0	346	47	13.84	—	—	1	—
Mills, J. W. E.	7	10	1	241	117	26.77	1	—	1	—
Moir, A. M.	17	30	8	326	41*	14.81	—	—	2	—
Mooney, F. L. H.	14	22	2	343	46	17.15	—	—	22	8
Morgan, R. W.	14	26	0	696	97	26.76	—	5	6	—
Morrison, B. D.	1	2	0	10	10	5.00	—	—	1	—
Motz, R. C.	22	40	3	415	60	11.21	—	3	7	—
Newman, J.	3	4	0	33	19	8.25	—	—	—	—
Overton, G. W. F.	3	6	1	8	3*	1.60	—	—	1	—
Page, M. L.	14	20	0	492	104	24.60	1	2	6	—
Petrie, E. C.	14	25	5	258	55	12.90	—	1	25	—
Playle, W. R.	8	15	0	151	65	10.06	—	1	4	—
Pollard, V.	13	24	3	515	81*	24.52	—	4	9	—
Poore, M. B.	14	24	1	354	45	15.39	—	—	1	—
Puna, N.	3	5	3	31	18*	15.50	—	—	1	—
Rabone, G. O.	12	20	2	562	107	31.22	1	2	5	—
Reid, J. R.	58	108	5	3431	142	33.31	6	22	43	1
Roberts, A. W.	5	10	1	248	66*	27.55	—	3	4	—
Rowe, C. G.	1	2	0	0	0	0.00	—	—	1	—
Scott, R. H.	1	1	0	18	18	18.00	—	—	—	—
Scott, V. J.	10	17	1	458	84	28.62	—	3	7	—
Shrimpton, M. J. F. ..	6	12	0	145	38	12.08	—	—	2	—
Sinclair, B. W.	19	36	1	1108	138	31.65	3	3	7	—
Sinclair, I. M.	2	4	1	25	18*	8.33	—	—	1	—
Smith, D.	1	1	0	4	4	4.00	—	—	—	—
Smith, F. B.	4	6	1	237	96	47.40	—	2	1	—
Snedden, C. A.	1	—	—	—	—	—	—	—	—	—
Sparling, J. T.	11	20	2	229	50	12.72	—	1	3	—
Sutcliffe, B.	42	76	8	2727	230*	40.10	5	15	20	—
Taylor, B. R..	9	17	3	359	105	25.64	1	2	2	—
Taylor, D. D.	3	5	0	159	77	31.80	—	1	2	—
Tindill, E. W.	5	9	1	73	37*	9.12	—	—	6	1
Truscott, P. B.	1	2	0	29	26	14.50	—	—	1	—

Batting & Fielding—New Zealand—*Cont.*

	Tests	I.	N.O.	Runs	H.S.	Avge.	100s	50s	Ct.	St.
Vivian, G. E.	1	2	0	44	43	22.00	—	—	—	—
Vivian, H. G.	7	10	0	421	100	42.10	1	5	4	—
Wallace, W. M.	13	21	0	439	66	20.90	—	5	5	—
Ward, J. T.	7	10	5	60	35*	12.00	—	—	15	1
Watt, L. A.	1	2	0	2	2	1.00	—	—	—	—
Weir, G. L.	11	16	2	416	74*	29.71	—	3	3	—
Whitelaw, P. E.	2	4	2	64	30	32.00	—	—	—	—
Yuile, B. W.	10	19	3	270	64	16.87	—	1	5	—
Substitutes									15	1

INDIA (*115 Players*)

	Tests	I.	N.O.	Runs	H.S.	Avge.	100s	50s	Ct.	St.
Adhikari, H. R.	21	36	8	872	114*	31.14	1	4	8	—
Ali, S. Nazir	2	4	0	30	13	7.50	—	—	—	—
Ali, S. Wazir	7	14	0	237	42	16.92	—	—	1	—
Amarnath, L.	24	40	4	878	118	24.38	1	4	13	—
Amar Singh, L.	7	14	1	292	51	22.46	—	1	3	—
Amir Elahi	1	2	0	17	13	8.50	—	—	—	—
Apte, A. L.	1	2	0	15	8	7.50	—	—	—	—
Apte, M. L.	7	13	2	542	163*	49.27	1	3	2	—
Baig, A. A.	10	18	0	428	112	23.77	1	2	6	—
Banerjee, S.	1	1	0	0	0	0.00	—	—	3	—
Banerjee, S. N.	1	2	0	13	8	6.50	—	—	—	—
Bedi, B. S.	5	10	1	70	15*	7.77	—	—	—	—
Bhandari, P.	3	4	0	77	39	19.25	—	—	1	—
Borde, C. G.	46	80	9	2634	177*	37.09	5	14	29	—
Chandrasekhar, B. S.	14	19	10	71	22	7.88	—	—	5	—
Chowdhury, N. R.	2	2	1	3	3*	3.00	—	—	—	—
Colah, S. H. M.	2	4	0	69	31	17.25	—	—	2	—
Contractor, N. J.	31	52	1	1611	108	31.58	1	11	18	—
Dani, H. T.	1	—	—	—	—	—	—	—	1	—
Desai, R. B.	26	41	11	359	85	11.96	—	1	9	—
Divecha, R. V.	5	5	0	60	26	12.00	—	—	5	—
Durrani, S. A.	23	40	2	935	104	24.60	1	5	11	—
Engineer, F. M.	15	27	1	749	109	28.80	1	4	20	3
Gadkari, C. V.	6	10	4	132	50*	22.00	—	1	6	—
Gaekwad, D. K.	11	20	1	350	52	18.42	—	1	5	—
Gaekwad, H. G.	1	2	0	22	14	11.00	—	—	—	—
Ghorpade, J. M.	8	15	0	229	41	15.26	—	—	4	—
Ghulam Ahmed	22	31	9	192	50	8.72	—	1	11	—
Gopalan, M. J.	1	2	1	18	11*	18.00	—	—	3	—
Gopinath, C. D.	8	12	1	242	50*	22.00	—	1	2	—
Guard, G. M.	2	2	0	11	7	5.50	—	—	2	—
Guha, S.	1	2	0	5	4	2.50	—	—	—	—
Gul Mahomed	8	15	0	166	34	11.06	—	—	3	—
Gupte, B. P.	3	3	2	28	17*	28.00	—	—	—	—
Gupte, S. P.	36	42	13	183	21	6.31	—	—	14	—

Batting & Fielding—India—*Cont.*

	Tests	*I.*	*N.O.*	*Runs*	*H.S.*	*Avge.*	100*s*	50*s*	*Ct.*	*St.*
Hafeez, A.	3	5	0	80	43	16.00	—	—	1	—
Hanumant Singh	13	22	2	672	105	33.60	1	5	11	—
Hardikar, M. S.	2	4	1	56	32*	18.66	—	—	3	—
Hazare, Vijay S.	30	52	6	2192	164*	47.65	7	9	11	—
Hindlekar, D. D.	4	7	2	71	26	14.20	—	—	3	—
Hussain, Dilawar	3	6	0	254	59	42.33	—	3	6	1
Ibrahim, K. C.	4	8	0	169	85	21.12	—	1	—	—
Indrajitsinhji, K. S.	3	5	1	32	23	8.00	—	—	5	3
Irani, J. K.	2	3	2	3	2*	3.00	—	—	2	1
Jahangir Khan, M.	4	7	0	39	13	5.57	—	—	4	—
Jai, L. P.	1	2	0	19	19	9.50	—	—	—	—
Jaisimha, M. L.	29	53	2	1741	129	34.13	2	11	12	—
Jamshedji, R. J.	1	2	2	5	4*	—	—	—	2	—
Jilani, M. Baqa	1	2	1	16	12	16.00	—	—	—	—
Joshi, P. G.	12	20	1	207	52*	10.89	—	1	18	9
Kardar, A. H., see Hafeez, A.										
Kenny, R. B..	5	10	1	245	62	27.22	—	3	1	—
Kishenchand, G.	5	10	0	89	44	8.90	—	—	1	—
Kripal Singh, A. G. ..	14	20	5	422	100*	28.13	1	2	4	—
Kumar, V. V.	2	2	0	6	6	3.00	—	—	2	—
Kunderan, B. K.	18	34	4	981	192	32.70	2	3	22	8
Lall Singh	1	2	0	44	29	22.00	—	—	1	—
Maka, E. S.	2	1	1	2	2*	—	—	—	2	1
Manjrekar, V. L.	55	92	10	3209	189*	39.13	7	15	19	2
Mankad, V. M.	44	72	5	2109	231	31.47	5	6	33	—
Mantri, M. K.	4	8	1	67	39	9.57	—	—	8	1
Meherhomji, K. R.	1	1	1	0	0*	—	—	—	1	—
Mehra, V. L.	8	14	1	329	62	25.30	—	2	1	—
Merchant, V. M.	10	18	0	859	154	47.72	3	3	7	—
Milkha Singh, A. G. ..	4	6	0	92	35	15.33	—	—	2	—
Modi, R. S.	10	17	1	736	112	46.00	1	6	3	—
Muddiah, V. M.	2	3	1	11	11	5.50	—	—	—	—
Mushtaq Ali	11	20	1	612	112	32.21	2	3	7	—
Nadkarni, R. G.	34	56	12	1274	122*	28.95	1	7	22	—
Naoomal Jeoomal	3	5	1	108	43	27.00	—	—	—	—
Navle, J. G..	2	4	0	42	13	10.50	—	—	1	—
Nayudu, C. K.	7	14	0	350	81	25.00	—	2	4	—
Nayudu, C. S.	11	19	3	147	36	9.18	—	—	3	—
Nissar, M.	6	11	3	55	14	6.87	—	—	2	—
Nyalchand, K.	1	2	1	7	6*	7.00	—	—	—	—
Palia, P. E.	2	4	1	29	16	9.66	—	—	—	—
Patankar, C. T.	1	2	1	14	13	14.00	—	—	3	1
Pataudi, Nawab of, Snr. ..	3	5	0	55	22	11.00	—	—	—	—
Pataudi, Nawab of, Jnr. ..	24	43	2	1643	203*	40.07	6	5	14	—
Patel, J. S.	7	10	1	25	12	2.77	—	—	2	—
Patiala, Yuvraj of	1	2	0	84	60	42.00	—	1	2	—
Patil, S. R.	1	1	1	14	14*	—	—	—	1	—
Phadkar, D. G.	31	45	7	1229	123	32.34	2	8	21	—
Prasanna, E. A. S.	6	12	2	110	24	11.00	—	—	2	—
Punjabi, P. L.	5	10	0	164	33	16.40	—	—	5	—

Batting & Fielding—India—*Cont.*

	Tests	*I.*	*N.O.*	*Runs*	*H.S.*	*Avge.*	*100s*	*50s*	*Ct.*	*St.*
Rai Singh	1	2	0	26	24	13.00	—	—	—	—
Rajindernath, V.	1	—	—	—	—	—	—	—	—	4
Rajinder Pal	1	2	1	6	3*	6.00	—	—	—	—
Ramaswami, C.	2	4	1	170	60	56.66	—	1	—	—
Ramchand, G. S.	33	53	5	1180	109	24.58	2	5	20	—
Ramji, L.	1	2	0	1	1	0.50	—	—	1	—
Rangachari, C. R.	4	6	3	8	8*	2.66	—	—	—	—
Rangnekar, K. M.	3	6	0	33	18	5.50	—	—	1	—
Ranjane, V. B.	7	9	3	40	16	6.66	—	—	1	—
Rege, M. R.	1	2	0	15	15	7.50	—	—	1	—
Roy, P.	43	79	4	2441	173	32.54	5	9	16	—
Sardesai, D. N.	18	33	3	1148	200*	38.26	2	7	4	—
Sarwate, C. T.	9	17	1	208	37	13.00	—	—	—	—
Saxena, R.	1	2	0	25	16	12.50	—	—	—	—
Sen, P.	14	18	4	165	25	11.78	—	—	20	11
Sengupta, A. K.	1	2	0	9	8	4.50	—	—	—	—
Shinde, S. G...	7	11	5	85	14	14.16	—	—	—	—
Shodhan, D. H.	3	4	1	181	110	60.33	1	—	1	—
Sohoni, S. W.	4	7	2	83	29*	16.60	—	—	2	—
Sood, M. M.	1	2	0	3	3	1.50	—	—	—	—
Subramanya, V.	5	9	0	131	61	14.55	—	1	5	—
Sunderram, G.	2	1	1	3	3*	—	—	—	—	—
Surendranath, R.	11	20	7	136	27	10.46	—	—	4	—
Surti, R. F.	15	26	3	525	64	22.82	—	3	10	—
Swamy, N. V.	1	—	—	—	—	—	—	—	—	—
Tamhane, N. S.	21	27	5	222	54*	10.09	—	1	35	16
Tarapore, K. K.	1	1	0	2	2	2.00	—	—	—	—
Umrigar, P. R.	59	94	8	3631	223	42.22	12	14	33	—
Venkataraghavan, S. ..	7	10	3	136	36*	19.42	—	—	6	—
Vizianagram, Maharaj Sir Vijaya	3	6	2	33	19*	8.25	—	—	1	—
Wadekar, A. L.	5	10	0	321	91	32.10	—	4	8	—
Substitutes									26	—

PAKISTAN (*56 Players*)

	Tests	*I.*	*N.O.*	*Runs*	*H.S.*	*Avge.*	*100s*	*50s*	*Ct.*	*St.*
Abbas, Ghulam	1	2	0	12	12	6.00	—	—	—	—
Afaq Hussain	2	4	4	64	33*	—	—	—	2	—
Agha Saadat Ali	1	1	1	8	8*	—	—	—	3	—
Akhtar, Javed	1	2	1	4	2*	4.00	—	—	—	—
Alim-ud-Din	25	45	2	1091	109	25.37	2	7	8	—
Amir Elahi	5	7	1	65	47	10.83	—	—	—	—
Anwar Hussain	4	6	0	42	17	7.00	—	—	—	—
Arif Butt	3	5	0	59	20	11.80	—	—	—	—
Asif Iqbal	11	19	1	570	146	31.66	1	3	7	—
Aslam, Mohammad ..	1	2	0	34	18	17.00	—	—	—	—
Bari, Wasim	3	5	0	29	13	5.80	—	—	5	1
Burki, Javed	24	46	3	1302	140	30.27	3	4	6	—
D'Souza, Antao	6	10	8	76	23*	38.00	—	—	3	—

Batting & Fielding—Pakistan—*Cont.*

	Tests	*I.*	*N.O.*	*Runs*	*H.S.*	*Avge.*	*100s*	*50s*	*Ct.*	*St.*
Farooq Hamid	1	2	0	3	3	1.50	—	—	—	—
Farooq, Mohammad ..	7	9	4	85	47	17.00	—	—	1	—
Fazal Mahmood	34	50	6	620	60	14.09	—	1	11	—
Ghazali, M. E. Z.	2	4	0	32	18	8.00	—	—	—	—
Gul Mahomed	1	2	1	39	27*	39.00	—	—	—	—
Hanif Mohammad	51	91	7	3812	337	45.38	12	15	34	—
Haseeb Ahsan	12	16	7	61	14	6.77	—	—	1	—
Ibadulla, Khalid	4	8	0	253	166	31.62	1	—	3	—
Ijaz Butt	8	16	2	279	58	19.92	—	1	5	—
Ilyas, Mohammad	8	15	0	399	126	26.60	1	2	4	—
Imtiaz Ahmed	41	72	1	2079	209	29.28	3	11	77	16
Intikhab Alam	20	35	6	611	61	21.06	—	4	11	—
Israr Ali	4	8	1	33	10	4.71	—	—	1	—
Kadir, Abdul	4	8	0	272	95	34.00	—	2	—	1
Kardar, A. H.	23	37	3	847	93	24.91	—	5	15	—
Khalid Hassan	1	2	1	17	10	17.00	—	—	—	—
Khalid Wazir, S.	2	3	1	14	9*	7.00	—	—	—	—
Khan Mohammad	13	17	7	100	26*	10.00	—	—	4	—
Mahmood Hussain	27	39	6	336	35	10.18	—	—	5	—
Majid Jahangir	7	11	0	185	80	16.81	—	1	9	—
Maqsood Ahmed	16	27	1	507	99	19.50	—	2	13	—
Mathias, Wallis	21	36	3	783	77	23.72	—	3	22	—
Miran Bux	2	3	2	1	1*	1.00	—	—	—	—
Mufasir-ul-Haq	1	1	1	8	8*	—	—	—	1	—
Munaf, Mohammad.. ..	4	7	2	63	19	12.60	—	—	—	—
Munir Malik	3	4	1	7	4	2.33	—	—	1	—
Mushtaq Mohammad ..	17	31	3	1014	101	36.21	2	6	3	—
Nasim-ul-Ghani	28	48	5	678	101	15.76	1	1	10	—
Naushad Ali	6	11	0	156	39	14.18	—	—	9	—
Nazar Mohammad	5	8	1	277	124*	39.57	1	1	7	—
Niaz Ahmed	1	2	2	1	1*	—	—	—	1	—
Pervez Sajjad	7	9	6	57	18	19.00	—	—	2	—
Rahman, S. F.	1	2	0	10	8	5.00	—	—	1	—
Saeed Ahmed	35	68	4	2724	172	42.56	5	15	9	—
Salah-ud-Din..	3	4	2	93	34*	46.50	—	—	2	—
Salim Altaf	2	3	2	9	7*	9.00	—	—	—	—
Shafqat Rana	1	2	0	24	24	12.00	—	—	—	—
Shahid Mahmood	1	2	0	25	16	12.50	—	—	—	—
Sharpe, D.	3	6	0	134	56	22.33	—	1	2	—
Shuja-ud-Din	19	32	6	395	47	15.19	—	—	8	—
Waqar Hassan	21	35	1	1071	189	31.50	1	6	10	—
Wazir Mohammad	20	33	4	801	189	27.62	2	3	5	—
Zulfiqar Ahmed	9	10	4	200	63*	33.33	—	1	5	—
Substitutes									9	—

BOWLING

ENGLAND

	Tests	*Balls*	*Mdns.*	*Runs*	*Wkts.*	*Avge.*	*5wI.*	*10wM.*
Allen, D. A.	39	11290	679	3778	122	30.96	4	—
Allen, G. O.	25	4392	116	2379	81	29.37	5	1
Allom, M. J. C.	5	810	28	265	14	18.92	1	—
Appleyard, R.	9	1596	70	554	31	17.87	1	—
Armitage, T.	2	12	0	15	0	—	—	—
Arnold, E. G.	10	1677	64	788	31	25.41	1	—
Arnold, G. G.	2	408	22	147	8	18.37	1	—
Astill, W. E.	9	2181	98	856	25	34.24	—	—
Attewell, W.	10	2850	326	626	27	23.18	—	—
Bailey, T. E.	61	9712	379	3856	132	29.21	5	1
Bakewell, A. H.	6	18	0	8	0	—	—	—
Barber, R. W.	27	3300	110	1719	39	44.07	—	—
Barber, W.	2	2	0	0	1	—	—	—
Barlow, R. G.	17	2456	315	767	34	22.55	3	—
Barnes, S. F.	27	7873	358	3106	189	16.43	24	7
Barnes, W.	21	2285	271	793	51	15.54	3	—
Barnett, C. J.	20	256	11	93	0	—	—	—
Barratt, F.	5	750	33	235	5	47.00	—	—
Barrington, K. F.	74	2193	87	1017	23	44.21	—	—
Bates, W.	15	2362	282	821	50	16.42	4	1
Bedser, A. V.	51	15941	572	5876	236	24.89	15	5
Berry, R.	2	653	47	228	9	25.33	1	—
Bird, M. C.	10	264	12	120	8	15.00	—	—
Blythe, C.	19	4438	231	1863	100	18.63	9	4
Bolus, J. B.	7	18	0	16	0	—	—	—
Booth, M. W.	2	312	8	130	7	18.57	—	—
Bosanquet, B. J. T.	7	989	10	604	25	24.16	2	—
Bowes, W. E.	15	3655	131	1519	68	22.33	6	—
Bowley, E. H.	5	252	7	116	0	—	—	—
Boycott, G.	27	784	36	339	7	48.42	—	—
Bradley, W. M.	2	625	49	233	6	38.83	1	—
Braund, L. C.	23	3693	144	1810	47	38.51	3	—
Brearley, W.	4	705	25	359	17	21.11	1	—
Briggs, J.	33	5332	389	2094	118	17.74	9	4
Brockwell, W.	7	582	31	309	5	61.80	—	—
Bromley-Davenport, H. R.	4	155	6	98	4	24.50	—	—
Brown, A.	2	321	9	148	3	49.33	—	—
Brown, D. J.	11	2149	71	908	31	29.29	1	—
Brown, F. R.	22	3260	117	1398	45	31.06	1	—
Brown, J. T.	8	35	0	22	0	—	—	—
Buckenham, C. P.	4	1182	25	593	21	28.23	1	—
Butler, H. J.	2	552	30	215	12	17.91	—	—
Calthorpe, Hon. F. S. G.	4	204	8	91	1	91.00	—	—
Carr, D. B.	2	210	6	140	2	70.00	—	—
Carr, D. W.	1	414	3	282	7	40.28	1	—
Cartwright, T. W.	5	1611	97	544	15	36.26	1	—
Chapman, A. P. F.	26	40	1	20	0	—	—	—
Christopherson, S.	1	136	13	69	1	69.00	—	—
Clark, E. W.	8	1931	71	899	32	28.09	1	—
Clay, J. C.	1	192	7	75	0	—	—	—
Close, D. B.	19	1212	56	532	18	29.55	—	—
Coldwell, L. J.	7	1662	60	610	22	27.72	1	—
Compton, D. C. S.	78	2722	70	1410	25	56.40	1	—
Cook, C.	1	180	4	127	0	—	—	—
Copson, W. H.	3	762	31	297	15	19.80	1	—
Cowdrey, M. C.	92	65	0	67	0	—	—	—
Coxon, A.	1	378	13	172	3	57.33	—	—
Cranston, K.	8	1010	37	461	18	25.61	—	—
Crawford, J. N.	12	2203	61	1150	39	29.48	3	—
Cuttell, W. R.	2	285	32	73	6	12.16	—	—

Bowling—England—*Cont.*

	Tests	*Balls*	*Mdns.*	*Runs*	*Wkts.*	*Avge.*	*5wI.*	*10wM.*
Dean, H.	3	447	23	153	11	13.90	—	—
Dexter, E. R.	60	5269	186	2278	66	34.51	—	—
D'Oliveira, B. L.	9	1470	85	503	12	41.91	—	—
Douglas, J. W. H. T.	23	2812	66	1486	45	33.02	1	—
Duleepsinhji, K. S.	12	6	0	7	0	—	—	—
Durston, F. J.	1	202	2	136	5	27.20	—	—
Edrich, J. H.	21	30	1	23	0	—	—	—
Edrich, W. J.	39	3234	80	1693	41	41.29	—	—
Emmett, T.	7	804	92	293	9	32.55	1	—
Farnes, K.	15	3932	103	1718	60	28.63	3	1
Fender, P. G. H.	13	2178	67	1185	29	40.86	2	—
Ferris, J. J.	1	272	27	91	13	7.00	2	1
Fielder, A.	6	1485	42	711	26	27.34	1	—
Flavell, J. A.	4	792	25	367	7	52.42	—	—
Flowers, W.	8	858	92	296	14	21.14	1	—
Ford, F. G. J.	5	210	6	129	1	129.00	—	—
Foster, F. R.	11	2441	108	926	45	20.57	4	—
Fothergill, A. J.	2	321	42	90	8	11.25	—	—
Freeman, A. P.	12	3732	142	1707	66	25.86	5	3
Fry, C. B.	26	10	1	3	0	—	—	—
Geary, G.	14	3810	181	1353	46	29.41	4	1
Gifford, N.	2	498	35	140	5	28.00	—	—
Gilligan, A. E. R.	11	2405	74	1046	36	29.05	2	1
Gladwin, C.	8	2129	89	571	15	38.06	—	—
Goddard, T. W.	8	1563	62	588	22	26.72	1	—
Gover, A. R.	4	816	26	359	8	44.87	—	—
Grace, W. G.	22	663	65	236	9	26.22	—	—
Graveney, T. W.	65	224	6	156	1	156.00	—	—
Greenhough, T.	4	1129	66	357	16	22.31	1	—
Gunn, G.	15	12	0	8	0	—	—	—
Gunn, J.	6	903	54	387	18	21.50	1	—
Haig, N. E.	5	1026	54	448	13	34.46	—	—
Haigh, S.	11	1294	61	622	24	25.91	1	—
Hammond, W. R.	85	7967	299	3140	83	37.83	2	—
Harris, Lord	4	32	1	29	0	—	—	—
Hartley, J. C.	2	192	2	115	1	115.00	—	—
Hayes, E. G.	5	90	1	52	1	52.00	—	—
Hayward, T. W.	35	869	42	514	14	36.71	—	—
Hearne, J. T.	12	2976	211	1082	49	22.08	4	1
Hearne, J. W.	24	2955	59	1462	30	48.73	1	—
Hendren, E.	51	47	0	31	1	31.00	—	—
Heseltine, C.	2	157	3	84	5	16.80	1	—
Higgs, K.	14	3761	174	1352	69	19.59	2	—
Hill, A.	2	340	37	130	6	21.66	—	—
Hill, A. J. L.	3	40	4	8	4	2.00	—	—
Hilton, M. J.	4	1238	69	471	14	33.64	1	—
Hirst, G. H.	24	3979	146	1770	59	30.00	3	—
Hitch, J. W.	7	462	5	325	7	46.42	—	—
Hobbs, J. B.	61	376	15	165	1	165.00	—	—
Hobbs, R. N. S.	4	979	59	333	10	33.30	—	—
Hollies, W. E.	13	3554	176	1332	44	30.27	5	—
Holmes, E. R. T.	5	108	4	76	2	38.00	—	—
Hopwood, J. L.	2	462	32	155	0	—	—	—
Hornby, A. N.	3	28	7	0	1	—	—	—
Horton, M. J.	2	238	18	59	2	29.50	—	—
Howorth, R.	5	1523	61	637	19	33.52	1	—

Bowling—England—*Cont.*

	Tests	*Balls*	*Mdns.*	*Runs*	*Wkts.*	*Avge.*	*5wI.*	*10wM.*
Howell, H.	5	918	23	559	7	79.85	—	—
Hutchings, K. L.	7	90	1	81	1	81.00	—	—
Hutton, L.	79	260	4	232	3	77.33	—	—
Iddon, J.	5	66	3	27	0	—	—	—
Ikin, J. T.	18	572	12	354	3	118.00	—	—
Illingworth, R.	27	5336	335	1682	58	29.00	1	—
Jackson, Hon. F. S.	20	1587	77	799	24	33.29	1	—
Jackson, H. L.	2	498	30	155	7	22.14	—	—
Jardine, D. R.	22	6	0	10	0	—	—	—
Jenkins, R. O.	9	2118	51	1098	32	34.31	1	—
Jessop, G. L.	18	672	28	354	10	35.40	—	—
Jones, A. O.	12	228	14	133	3	44.33	—	—
Jones, I. J.	10	2355	67	1113	30	37.10	1	—
Jupp, V. W. C.	8	1301	55	616	28	22.00	—	—
Kennedy, A. S.	5	1683	91	599	31	19.32	2	—
Kilner, R.	9	2368	79	734	24	30.58	—	—
King, J. H.	1	162	5	99	1	99.00	—	—
Knight, B. R.	22	4204	151	1776	53	33.50	—	—
Knox, N. A.	2	132	2	105	3	35.00	—	—
Laker, J. C.	46	12009	673	4099	193	21.23	9	3
Langridge, James	8	1074	51	413	19	21.73	2	—
Larter, J. D. F.	10	2172	88	941	37	25.43	2	—
Larwood, H.	21	4969	167	2216	78	28.41	4	1
Leadbeater, E.	2	289	9	218	2	109.00	—	—
Lees, W. S.	5	1256	69	467	26	17.96	2	—
Legge, G. B.	5	30	0	34	0	—	—	—
Leslie, C. F. H.	4	96	10	44	4	11.00	—	—
Leyland, M.	41	1103	35	585	6	97.50	—	—
Lilley, A. A.	35	25	1	23	1	23.00	—	—
Lillywhite, James	2	340	37	126	8	15.75	—	—
Loader, P. J.	13	2662	117	878	39	22.51	1	—
Lock, G. A. R.	47	12649	795	4240	170	24.94	9	3
Lockwood, W. H.	12	1973	100	884	43	20.55	5	1
Lohmann, G. A.	18	3821	364	1205	112	10.75	9	5
Lucas, A. P.	5	120	13	54	0	—	—	—
Lyttelton, Hon. A.	4	48	5	19	4	4.75	—	—
Macaulay, G. G.	8	1701	79	662	24	27.58	1	—
McConnon, J. E.	2	216	12	74	4	18.50	—	—
Marriott, C. S.	1	247	8	96	11	8.72	2	1
Martin, F.	2	410	30	141	14	10.07	2	1
Martin, J. W.	1	270	6	129	1	129.00	—	—
Mason, J. R.	5	324	13	149	2	74.50	—	—
Matthews, A. D. G.	1	180	8	65	2	32.50	—	—
Mead, W.	1	265	24	91	1	91.00	—	—
Midwinter, W. E.	4	776	79	272	10	27.20	—	—
Milligan, F. W.	2	45	2	29	0	—	—	—
Milton, C. A.	6	24	2	12	0	—	—	—
Mitchell, A.	6	6	0	4	0	—	—	—
Mitchell, T. B.	5	894	21	498	8	62.25	—	—
Mold, A.	3	491	32	234	7	33.42	—	—

Bowling—England—*Cont.*

	Tests	*Balls*	*Mdns.*	*Runs*	*Wkts.*	*Avge.*	5*wI.*	10*wM.*
Morley, F.	4	972	124	296	16	18.50	1	—
Mortimore, J. B.	9	2162	133	733	13	56.38	—	—
Moss, A. E.	9	1657	79	626	21	29.80	—	—
Nichols, M. S.	14	2565	98	1152	41	28.09	2	—
Oakman, A. S. M.	2	48	3	21	0	—	—	—
O'Connor, J.	4	162	6	72	1	72.00	—	—
Padgett, D. E. V.	2	12	0	8	0	—	—	—
Paine, G. A. E.	4	1044	39	467	17	27.47	1	—
Palmer, C. H.	1	30	1	15	0	—	—	—
Palmer, K. E.	1	378	7	189	1	189.00	—	—
Parfitt, P. H.	33	1290	68	556	12	46.33	—	—
Parker, C. W. L.	1	168	16	32	2	16.00	—	—
Parkin, C. H.	10	2095	55	1128	32	35.25	2	—
Parks, J. H.	1	126	9	36	3	12.00	—	—
Parks, J. M.	43	54	1	51	1	51.00	—	—
Peate, E.	9	2096	260	682	31	22.00	2	—
Peebles, I. A. R.	13	2882	78	1391	45	30.91	3	—
Peel, R.	20	5216	444	1715	102	16.81	6	2
Penn, F.	1	12	1	2	0	—	—	—
Perks, R. T. D.	2	829	17	355	11	32.27	2	—
Pollard, R.	4	1102	64	378	15	25.20	1	—
Poole, C. J.	3	30	1	9	0	—	—	—
Pope, G. H.	1	218	12	85	1	85.00	—	—
Pougher, A. D.	1	105	8	26	3	8.66	—	—
Price, J. S. E.	10	1969	59	1050	26	40.38	1	—
Pullar, G.	28	66	3	37	1	37.00	—	—
Quaife, W. G.	7	15	1	6	0	—	—	—
Ranjitsinhji, K. S.	15	97	6	39	1	39.00	—	—
Read, H. D.	1	270	14	200	6	33.33	—	—
Read, W. W.	18	60	2	63	0	—	—	—
Relf, A. E.	13	1764	91	624	25	24.96	1	—
Rhodes, H. J.	2	449	10	244	9	27.11	—	—
Rhodes, W.	58	8220	368	3425	127	26.96	6	1
Richardson, P. E.	34	120	9	48	3	16.00	—	—
Richardson, T.	14	4485	191	2220	88	25.22	11	4
Richmond, T. L.	1	114	3	86	2	43.00	—	—
Ridgway, F.	5	793	23	379	7	54.14	—	—
Robertson, J. D.	11	138	4	58	2	29.00	—	—
Robins, R. W. V.	19	3318	77	1758	64	27.46	1	—
Root, C. F.	3	642	47	194	8	24.25	—	—
Royle, V. P. F. A.	1	16	1	6	0	—	—	—
Rumsey, F. E..	5	1145	53	461	17	27.11	—	—
Russell, W. E.	10	144	9	44	0	—	—	—
Schultz, S. S.	1	35	3	26	1	26.00	—	—
Scotton, W. H.	15	20	1	20	0	—	—	—
Shackleton, D.	7	2078	96	768	18	42.66	—	—
Sharp, J.	3	183	3	111	3	37.00	—	—
Sharpe, J. W.	3	975	61	305	11	27.72	1	—
Shaw, A.	7	1099	155	285	12	23.75	1	—
Shrewsbury, A.	23	12	2	2	0	—	—	—
Simpson, R. T.	27	45	2	22	2	11.00	—	—
Simpson-Hayward, G. H. ..	5	898	18	420	23	18.26	2	—
Sims, J.	4	887	21	480	11	43.63	1	—
Sinfield, R. A.	1	378	16	123	2	61.50	—	—

Bowling—England—*Cont.*

	Tests	*Balls*	*Mdns.*	*Runs*	*Wkts.*	*Avge.*	*5wI.*	*10wM.*
Smailes, T. F.	1	120	3	62	3	20.66	—	—
Smith, C. A.	1	154	16	61	7	8.71	1	—
Smith, C. I. J.	5	930	40	392	15	26.13	1	—
Smith D. R.	5	972	47	359	6	59.83	—	—
Smith, D. V.	3	270	13	97	1	97.00	—	—
Smith, M. J. K.	47	214	4	128	1	128.00	—	—
Smith, T. P. B.	4	538	5	319	3	106.33	—	—
Snow, J. A.	9	2344	89	1067	33	32.33	—	—
Southerton, J.	2	263	24	107	7	15.28	—	—
Staples, S. J.	3	1149	50	435	15	29.00	—	—
Statham, J. B.	70	16026	590	6257	252	24.82	9	1
Steel, A. G.	13	1404	108	605	29	20.86	—	—
Stevens, G. T. S.	10	1186	24	648	20	32.40	2	1
Stoddart, A. E.	16	162	7	94	2	47.00	—	—
Storer, W.	6	168	5	108	2	54.00	—	—
Studd, C. T.	5	384	60	98	3	32.66	—	—
Subba Row, R.	13	6	0	2	0	—	—	—
Tate, F. W.	1	96	4	51	2	25.50	—	—
Tate, M. W.	39	12571	579	4051	155	26.13	7	1
Tattersall, R.	16	4186	208	1523	58	26.26	4	1
Taylor, K.	3	12	0	6	0	—	—	—
Tennyson, Hon. L. H.	9	6	0	1	0	—	—	—
Thompson, G. J.	6	1367	66	638	23	27.73	—	—
Thomson, N. I.	5	1488	68	568	9	63.11	—	—
Titmus, F. J.	47	13755	725	4406	142	31.02	7	—
Townsend, C. L.	2	140	5	75	3	25.00	—	—
Townsend, D. C. H.	3	6	0	9	0	—	—	—
Townsend, L. F.	4	399	22	205	6	34.16	—	—
Tremlett, M. F.	3	492	13	226	4	56.50	—	—
Trott, A. E.	2	474	37	198	17	11.64	1	—
Trueman, F. S.	67	15178	522	6625	307	21.57	17	3
Tyldesley, E.	14	3	0	2	0	—	—	—
Tyldesley, R.	7	1615	76	619	19	32.57	—	—
Tyler, E. J.	1	145	6	65	4	16.25	—	—
Tyson, F. H.	17	3452	98	1411	76	18.56	4	1
Ulyett, G.	25	2623	299	1011	51	19.82	1	—
Underwood, D. L.	4	810	52	301	9	33.44	1	—
Verity, H.	40	11143	604	3510	144	24.37	5	2
Voce, W.	27	6360	209	2733	98	27.88	3	2
Waddington, A.	2	276	7	119	1	119.00	—	—
Wainwright, E.	5	127	6	73	0	—	—	—
Walker, P. M.	3	78	3	34	0	—	—	—
Wardle, J. H.	28	6597	404	2080	102	20.39	5	1
Warr, J. J.	2	584	6	281	1	281.00	—	—
Warren, A. R.	1	236	9	113	6	18.83	1	—
Washbrook, C.	37	36	0	33	1	33.00	—	—
Watkins, A. J.	15	1364	45	554	11	50.36	—	—
Wellard, A. W.	2	456	9	237	7	33.85	—	—
White, D. W.	2	226	5	119	4	29.75	—	—
White, J. C.	15	4819	253	1581	49	32.26	3	1
Whysall, W. W.	4	16	0	9	0	—	—	—
Wilkinson, L. L.	3	573	9	271	7	38.71	—	—
Wilson, D.	5	1272	84	398	9	44.22	—	—
Wilson, E. R.	1	126	5	36	3	12.00	—	—
Woods, S. M. J.	3	195	8	129	5	25.80	—	—
Woolley, F. E.	64	6495	251	2815	83	33.91	4	1
Worthington, T. S.	9	633	18	316	8	39.50	—	—

Bowling—England—*Cont.*

	Tests	*Balls*	*Mdns.*	*Runs*	*Wkts.*	*Avge.*	*5wI.*	*10wM.*
Wright, D. V. P.	34	8141	176	4224	108	39.11	6	1
Wyatt, R. E. S.	40	1392	67	642	18	35.66	—	—
Wynyard, E. G.	3	24	0	17	0	—	—	—
Yardley, N. W. D.	20	1662	41	707	21	33.66	—	—
Young, H.	2	551	39	262	12	21.83	—	—
Young, J. A.	8	2368	119	757	17	44.52	—	—

AUSTRALIA

	Tests	*Balls*	*Mdns.*	*Runs*	*Wkts.*	*Avge.*	*5wI.*	*10wM.*
A'Beckett, E. L.	2	1062	47	317	3	105.66	—	—
Alexander, G.	2	168	13	93	2	46.50	—	—
Alexander, H. H.	1	276	3	154	1	154.00	—	—
Allan, F. E.	1	180	15	80	4	20.00	—	—
Allan, P. J.	1	192	6	83	2	41.50	—	—
Andrews, T. J. E.	16	156	5	116	1	116.00	—	—
Archer, R. G.	19	3570	160	1313	48	27.35	1	—
Armstrong, W. W.	50	8052	403	2923	87	33.59	3	—
Bannerman, A. C.	28	292	17	163	4	40.75	—	—
Barnes, S. G.	13	594	11	218	4	54.50	—	—
Benaud, R.	63	19093	805	6704	248	27.03	16	1
Blackie, D. D. J.	3	1260	51	444	14	31.71	1	—
Bonnor, G. J.	17	164	16	84	2	42.00	—	—
Booth, B. C.	29	436	27	146	3	48.66	—	—
Boyle, H. F.	12	1732	173	641	32	20.03	1	—
Bradman, D. G.	52	164	4	72	2	36.00	—	—
Bromley, E. H.	2	60	4	19	0	—	—	—
Bruce, W.	14	954	71	440	12	36.66	—	—
Burke, J. W.	24	814	40	230	8	28.75	—	—
Callaway, S. T.	3	471	33	142	6	23.66	1	—
Chappell, I. M.	8	1103	35	519	6	86.50	—	—
Charlton, P. C.	2	45	1	24	3	8.00	—	—
Chipperfield, A. G.	14	926	28	437	5	87.40	—	—
Collins, H. L.	19	654	31	252	4	63.00	—	—
Coningham, A.	1	186	9	76	2	38.00	—	—
Connolly, A. N.	6	1299	32	494	13	38.00	—	—
Cooper, W. H.	2	466	31	226	9	25.11	1	—
Corling, G. E.	5	1159	50	447	12	37.25	—	—
Cotter, A.	21	4633	86	2549	89	28.64	7	—
Cowper, R. M.	19	1559	70	659	15	43.93	—	—
Crawford, P.	4	438	27	107	7	15.28	—	—
Darling, L. S.	12	162	7	65	0	—	—	—
Davidson, A. K.	44	11665	432	3828	186	20.58	14	2
Donnan, H.	5	54	2	22	0	—	—	—
Dooland, B.	3	880	9	419	9	46.55	—	—
Duff, R. A.	22	180	8	85	4	21.25	—	—
Eady, C. J.	2	223	14	112	7	16.00	—	—
Ebeling, H. I.	1	186	9	89	3	29.66	—	—
Emery, S. H.	4	462	13	249	5	49.80	—	—
Evans, E.	6	1266	166	332	7	47.42	—	—
Fairfax, A. G.	10	1520	54	645	21	30.71	—	—
Ferris, J. J.	8	2030	224	684	48	14.25	4	—
Fleetwood-Smith, L. O.	10	3093	78	1570	42	37.38	2	1
Freer, F. W.	1	160	3	74	3	24.66	—	—

Bowling—Australia—*Cont.*

	Tests	*Balls*	*Mdns.*	*Runs*	*Wkts.*	*Avge.*	5*wI.*	10*wM.*
Garrett, T. W.	19	2708	297	970	36	26.94	2	—
Gaunt, R. A.	3	716	13	310	7	44.28	—	—
Gehrs. D. R. A.	6	6	0	4	0	—	—	—
Giffen, G.	31	6325	434	2791	103	27.09	7	1
Gregory, D. W.	3	20	1	9	0	—	—	—
Gregory, J. M.	24	5581	138	2648	85	31.15	4	—
Gregory, R. G.	2	24	0	14	0	—	—	—
Gregory, S. E.	58	30	0	33	0	—	—	—
Grimmett, C. V.	37	14573	734	5231	216	24.21	21	7
Guest, C.	1	144	0	59	0	—	—	—
Hartigan, R. J.	2	12	0	7	0	—	—	—
Hartkopf, A. E. V.	1	240	2	134	1	134.00	—	—
Harvey, R. N.	79	414	23	120	3	40.00	—	—
Hassett, A. L.	43	111	2	78	0	—	—	—
Hawke, N. J. N.	24	6433	216	2489	90	27.65	6	1
Hazlitt, G. R.	9	1563	73	623	23	27.08	1	—
Hendry, H. L.	11	1706	73	640	16	40.00	—	—
Hill, J. C.	3	606	29	273	8	34.12	—	—
Hoare, D. G.	1	232	0	156	2	78.00	—	—
Hodges, J.	2	136	9	84	6	14.00	—	—
Hole, G. B.	18	398	14	126	3	42.00	—	—
Hopkins, A. J.	20	1327	49	696	26	26.76	—	—
Horan, T.	15	373	45	143	11	13.00	1	—
Hordern, H. V.	7	2150	50	1075	46	23.36	5	2
Hornibrook, P. M.	6	1579	63	664	17	39.05	1	—
Howell, W. P.	18	3892	245	1409	49	28.75	1	—
Hunt, W. A.	1	96	2	39	0	—	—	—
Hurwood, A.	2	517	28	170	11	15.45	—	—
Iredale, F. A.	14	12	0	3	0	—	—	—
Ironmonger, H.	14	4695	328	1330	74	17.97	4	2
Iverson, J.	5	1108	29	320	21	15.23	1	—
Johnson, I. W.	45	8773	328	3182	109	29.19	3	—
Johnson, L.	1	282	10	74	6	12.33	—	—
Johnston, W. A.	40	11048	370	3825	160	23.90	7	—
Jones, E.	19	3754	161	1857	64	29.01	3	1
Jones, S. P.	12	262	26	112	6	18.66	—	—
Kelleway, C. E.	26	4363	141	1683	52	32.36	1	—
Kendall, T.	2	563	56	215	14	15.35	1	—
Kippax, A. F.	22	72	5	19	0	—	—	—
Kline, L. F.	13	2385	112	776	34	22.82	1	—
Laver, F.	15	2367	122	961	37	25.97	2	—
Lawry, W. M.	40	8	1	0	0	—	—	—
Lee, P. K.	2	436	18	212	5	42.40	—	—
Lindwall, R. R.	61	13666	417	5257	228	23.05	12	—
Loxton, S. J. E.	12	906	19	349	8	43.62	—	—
Lyons, J. J.	14	316	17	149	6	24.83	1	—
Macartney, C. G.	35	3615	175	1240	45	27.55	2	1
McCabe, S. J.	39	3746	127	1543	36	42.86	—	—
McCool, C. L.	14	2512	45	958	36	26.61	3	—
McCormick, E. L.	12	2107	50	1079	36	29.97	—	—
McDonald, C. C.	47	8	0	3	0	—	—	—
McDonald, E. A.	11	2885	90	1431	43	33.27	2	—
McDonnell, P. S.	19	52	1	53	0	—	—	—
Mackay, K. D.	37	5792	266	1721	50	34.42	2	—

Bowling—Australia—*Cont.*

	Tests	*Balls*	*Mdns.*	*Runs*	*Wkts.*	*Avge.*	5*wI.*	10*wM.*
McKenzie, G. D.	37	10905	327	4538	161	28.18	12	1
McKibbin, T. R.	5	1032	41	496	17	29.17	—	—
McLaren, J. W.	1	144	3	70	1	70.00	—	—
McLeod, C. E.	17	3374	172	1325	33	40.15	2	—
McLeod, R. W.	6	1089	67	384	12	32.00	1	—
McShane, P. G.	3	108	9	48	1	48.00	—	—
Mailey, A. A.	21	6117	116	3358	99	33.91	6	2
Marr, A. P.	1	48	6	14	0	—	—	—
Martin, J. W.	8	1834	57	832	17	48.94	—	—
Matthews, T. J.	8	1111	46	419	16	26.18	—	—
Mayne, E. R.	4	6	0	1	0	—	—	—
Mayne, L. R.	3	492	11	261	9	29.00	—	—
Meckiff, I. W..	18	3780	118	1415	45	31.44	2	—
Midwinter, W. E.	8	949	102	333	14	23.78	1	—
Miller, K. R.	55	10474	338	3905	170	22.97	7	1
Minnett, R. B.	9	589	26	290	11	26.36	—	—
Misson, F. M.	5	1197	30	616	16	38.50	—	—
Morris, A. R.	46	111	1	50	2	25.00	—	—
Morris, S.	1	136	14	73	2	36.50	—	—
Moule, W. H.	1	51	4	23	3	7.66	—	—
Nagel, L. E.	1	262	9	110	2	55.00	—	—
Nash, L. J.	2	311	12	126	10	12.60	—	—
Noble, M. A.	42	7109	361	3027	121	25.01	9	2
Noblet, G. J.	3	774	25	183	7	26.14	—	—
Nothling, O. E.	1	276	15	72	0	—	—	—
O'Connor, J. A.	4	692	24	340	13	26.15	1	—
O'Neill, N. C.	42	1392	49	667	17	39.23	—	—
O'Reilly, W. J.	27	10024	585	3254	144	22.59	11	3
Oxenham, R. K.	7	1796	112	522	14	37.28	—	—
Palmer, G. E.	17	4519	452	1678	78	21.51	6	2
Park, R. L.	1	6	0	9	0	—	—	—
Pellew, C. E.	10	78	3	34	0	—	—	—
Philpott, P. I.	8	2268	67	1000	26	38.46	1	—
Ransford, V. S.	20	43	3	28	1	28.00	—	—
Redpath, I. R.	15	42	1	28	0	—	—	—
Reedman, J. C.	1	57	2	24	1	24.00	—	—
Renneberg, D. A.	5	1068	34	528	11	48.00	1	—
Richardson, A. J.	9	1812	91	521	12	43.41	—	—
Ring, D. T.	13	3024	69	1305	35	37.28	2	—
Robertson, W. R.	1	44	3	24	0	—	—	—
Rorke, G.	4	703	27	203	10	20.30	—	—
Rutherford, J.	1	36	2	15	1	15.00	—	—
Ryder, J.	20	1897	73	743	17	43.70	—	—
Saunders, J. V.	14	3565	116	1797	79	22.74	6	—
Scott, H. J. H.	8	28	1	26	0	—	—	—
Sellers, R. H. D.	1	30	1	17	0	—	—	—
Shepherd, B. K.	9	26	1	9	0	—	—	—
Sievers, M. W. S.	3	602	25	161	9	17.88	1	—
Simpson, R. B.	49	5155	205	2139	47	45.51	1	—
Sincock, D. J.	3	724	9	410	8	51.25	—	—
Slater, K.	1	256	9	101	2	50.50	—	—
Stackpole, K. R.	7	526	17	246	3	82.00	—	—
Spofforth, F. R.	18	4185	416	1731	94	18.41	7	4

Bowling—Australia—*Cont.*

	Tests	*Balls*	*Mdns.*	*Runs*	*Wkts.*	*Avge.*	*5wI.*	*10wM.*
Taylor, J. M.	20	114	5	45	1	45.00	—	—
Thompson, N.	2	112	16	31	1	31.00	—	—
Thurlow, H. M.	1	234	7	86	0	—	—	—
Toshack, E. R. H.	12	3140	155	989	47	21.04	4	1
Travers, J. F.	1	48	2	14	1	14.00	—	—
Tribe, G. E.	3	760	9	330	2	165.00	—	—
Trott, A. E.	3	474	17	192	9	21.33	1	—
Trott, G. H. S.	24	1890	47	1019	29	35.13	—	—
Trumble, H.	32	8099	452	3072	141	21.78	9	3
Trumble, J. W.	7	600	59	222	10	22.20	—	—
Trumper, V. T.	48	546	19	315	8	39.37	—	—
Turner, C. T. B.	17	5195	457	1670	101	16.53	11	2
Veivers, T. R.	21	4191	196	1375	33	41.66	—	—
Waite, M. G.	2	552	23	190	1	190.00	—	—
Wall, T. W.	18	4752	154	2010	56	35.89	3	—
Walters, K. D.	5	632	8	283	9	31.44	—	—
Ward, F. A.	4	1268	30	574	11	52.18	1	—
Watson, G. D...	3	312	9	162	3	54.00	—	—
Watson, W.	4	6	0	5	0	—	—	—
Whitty, W. J.	14	3357	163	1373	65	21.12	3	—
Wilson, J.	1	216	17	64	1	64.00	—	—
Woods, S. M. J.	3	217	18	121	5	24.20	—	—
Worrall, J.	11	255	29	127	1	127.00	—	—

SOUTH AFRICA

	Tests	*Balls*	*Mdns.*	*Runs*	*Wkts.*	*Avge.*	*5wI.*	*10wM.*
Adcock, N. A. T.	26	6423	217	2195	104	21.10	5	—
Ashley, W. H.	1	173	18	95	7	13.57	1	—
Balaskas, X. C.	9	1584	28	806	22	36.63	1	—
Barlow, E. J.	26	2481	88	1105	29	38.10	1	—
Baumgartner, N. V.	1	166	3	99	2	49.50	—	—
Beaumont, R.	5	6	1	0	0	—	—	—
Begbie, D. W.	5	160	0	130	1	130.00	—	—
Bell, A. J.	16	3342	89	1567	48	32.64	4	—
Bissett, G. F.	4	989	28	469	25	18.76	2	—
Blanckenberg, J. M.	18	3888	132	1817	60	30.28	4	—
Bland, K. C.	21	400	19	125	2	62.50	—	—
Bock, G. E.	1	138	2	91	0	—	—	—
Bond, G. E.	1	16	0	16	0	—	—	—
Botten, J. T.	3	828	37	337	8	42.12	—	—
Bromfield, H. D.	9	1810	101	599	17	35.23	1	—
Brown, L. S.	2	318	7	189	3	63.00	—	—
Burke, S. F.	2	660	37	257	11	23.36	2	1
Buys, I. D.	1	144	4	52	0	—	—	—
Carter, C. P.	10	1475	47	694	28	24.78	2	—
Catterall, R. H.	24	342	7	162	7	23.14	—	—
Chapman, H. W.	2	126	1	104	1	104.00	—	—
Cheetham, J. E.	24	6	0	2	0	—	—	—
Christy, J. A. J.	10	138	4	92	2	46.00	—	—
Chubb, G. W. A.	5	1424	63	577	21	27.47	2	—
Cochran, J. A. K.	1	138	5	47	0	—	—	—
Coen, S. K.	2	12	0	7	0	—	—	—
Conyngham, D. P.	1	366	22	103	2	51.50	—	—
Cox, J. L.	3	576	24	245	4	61.25	—	—
Cripps, G.	1	15	0	23	0	—	—	—
Crisp, R. J.	9	1428	30	747	20	37.35	1	—

Bowling—South Africa—*Cont.*

	Tests	*Balls*	*Mdns.*	*Runs*	*Wkts.*	*Avge.*	*5wI.*	*10wM.*
Dalton, E. L.	15	864	7	500	12	41.66	—	—
Davies, E. Q.	5	768	7	481	7	68.71	—	—
Dawson, O. C.	9	1294	41	578	10	57.80	—	—
Dixon, C. D.	1	240	6	118	3	39.33	—	—
Dumbrill, R.	5	816	40	336	9	37.33	—	—
Duminy, J. P.	3	60	0	39	1	39.00	—	—
Du Preez, J. H.	2	144	12	51	3	17.00	—	—
Du Toit, J. F.	1	85	5	47	1	47.00	—	—
Elgie, M. K.	3	66	2	46	0	—	—	—
Faulkner, G. A.	25	4227	124	2180	82	26.58	4	—
Fellows-Smith, J. P.	4	114	1	61	0	—	—	—
Finlason, C. E.	1	12	0	7	0	—	—	—
Floquet, C. E.	1	48	2	24	0	—	—	—
Francois, C. M.	5	684	36	225	6	37.50	—	—
Frank, W. H. B.	1	58	3	52	1	52.00	—	—
Fuller, E. R. H.	7	1898	61	668	22	30.36	1	—
Glover, G. K.	1	65	4	28	1	28.00	—	—
Goddard, T. L.	38	10976	648	3023	114	26.51	5	—
Gordon, N.	5	1966	28	807	20	40.35	2	—
Graham, R.	2	240	13	127	3	42.33	—	—
Griffin, G.	2	432	14	192	8	24.00	—	—
Hall, A. E.	7	2361	107	886	40	22.15	3	1
Hall, G. G.	1	186	7	94	1	94.00	—	—
Halse, C. G.	3	587	8	260	6	43.33	—	—
Hands, P. A. M.	7	37	0	18	0	—	—	—
Hanley, M. A.	1	232	7	88	1	88.00	—	—
Hartigan, G. P. D.	5	252	7	141	1	141.00	—	—
Hearne, F.	4	62	0	40	2	20.00	—	—
Heine, P. S.	14	3890	107	1455	58	25.08	4	—
Hime, C. F. W.	1	55	4	31	1	31.00	—	—
Innes, A. R.	2	128	8	89	5	17.80	1	—
Ironside, D. E. J.	3	985	41	275	15	18.33	1	—
Johnson, C. L.	1	140	12	57	0	—	—	—
Keith, H. J.	8	108	1	63	0	—	—	—
Kempis, G. A.	1	168	17	76	4	19.00	—	—
Kotze, J. J.	3	413	8	243	6	40.50	—	—
Kuys, F.	1	60	4	31	2	15.50	—	—
Lance, H. R.	10	768	28	402	11	36.54	—	—
Langton, A. B. C.	15	4199	104	1818	40	45.45	1	—
Lawrence, G. B.	5	1334	61	512	28	18.28	2	—
Le Roux, F. L.	1	54	3	24	0	—	—	—
Ling, W. V. S.	6	18	0	20	0	—	—	—
Llewellyn, C. B.	15	2292	55	1421	48	29.60	4	1
Lundie, E. P.	1	286	9	107	4	26.75	—	—
Macaulay, M. J.	1	276	17	73	2	36.50	—	—
McCarthy, C. N.	15	3499	63	1510	36	41.94	2	—
McGlew, D. J.	34	32	0	23	0	—	—	—
McKinnon, A. H.	8	2546	153	925	26	35.57	—	—

Bowling—South Africa—*Cont.*

	Tests	*Balls*	*Mdns.*	*Runs*	*Wkts.*	*Avge.*	5*wI.*	10*wM.*
McLean, R. A.	40	4	0	1	0	—	—	—
McMillan, O.	13	2021	38	1243	36	34.52	2	—
Mann, N. B. F.	19	5796	260	1920	58	33.10	1	—
Mansell, P. N. F.	13	1506	31	736	11	66.90	—	—
Markham, L. A.	1	104	1	72	1	72.00	—	—
Marx, W. F. E.	3	228	1	144	4	36.00	—	—
Meintjes, D. J.	2	246	7	115	6	19.16	—	—
Melle, M. G.	7	1667	20	851	26	32.73	2	—
Middleton, J.	6	1064	61	442	24	18.41	2	—
Mills, C.	1	140	7	83	2	41.50	—	—
Milton, W. H...	3	79	5	48	2	24.00	—	—
Mitchell, B.	42	2519	26	1379	27	51.07	1	—
Morkel, D. P. B.	16	1704	55	821	18	45.61	—	—
Murray, A. R. A.	10	2374	111	710	18	39.44	—	—
Newberry, C.	4	558	15	268	11	24.36	—	—
Newson, E. S.	3	874	18	265	4	66.25	—	—
Nicolson, J. W. F.	3	24	0	17	0	—	—	—
Norton, N. O.	1	90	4	47	4	11.75	—	—
Nourse, A. D., Snr.	45	3234	120	1553	41	37.87	—	—
Nourse, A. D., Jnr.	34	20	1	9	0	—	—	—
Nupen, E. P.	17	4159	133	1788	50	35.76	5	1
Ochse, A. L.	3	649	10	362	10	36.20	—	—
Owen-Smith, H. G.	5	156	0	113	0	—	—	—
Parker, G. M.	2	366	3	273	8	34.12	1	—
Parkin, D. C.	1	130	4	82	3	27.33	—	—
Partridge, J. T.	11	3684	135	1373	44	31.20	3	—
Pearce, O. C.	3	144	3	106	3	35.33	—	—
Pegler, S. J.	16	2989	84	1572	47	33.44	2	—
Pithey, A. J.	17	12	0	5	0	—	—	—
Pithey, D. B.	8	1424	67	577	12	48.08	1	—
Plimsoll, J. B.	1	237	9	143	3	47.66	—	—
Pollock, P. M.	24	5836	229	2548	101	25.22	8	1
Pollock, R. G.	19	396	15	196	4	49.00	—	—
Poore, R. M.	3	9	0	4	1	4.00	—	—
Pothecary, J. E.	3	828	32	354	9	39.33	—	—
Powell, A. W.	1	20	1	10	1	10.00	—	—
Procter, M. J.	3	656	28	263	15	17.53	—	—
Promnitz, H. L. E.	2	528	30	161	8	20.12	1	—
Quinn, N. A.	12	2922	103	1145	35	32.71	1	—
Reid, N.	1	126	3	63	2	31.50	—	—
Robertson, J. B.	3	738	26	321	6	53.50	—	—
Rowan, A. M. B.	15	5193	136	2084	54	38.59	4	—
Rowan, E. A. B.	26	19	1	7	0	—	—	—
Rowe, G. A.	5	998	50	456	15	30.40	1	—
Samuelson, S. V.	1	108	2	64	0	—	—	—
Schwarz, R. O.	20	2639	66	1417	55	25.76	2	—
Seccull, A. W.	1	60	2	37	2	18.50	—	—
Seymour, M. A.	6	1272	27	520	7	74.28	—	—
Shalders, W. A.	12	48	3	6	1	6.00	—	—
Shepstone, G. H.	2	115	9	47	0	—	—	—
Siedle, I. J.	18	19	1	7	1	7.00	—	—
Sinclair, J. H.	25	3598	110	1996	63	31.68	1	—

Bowling—South Africa—*Cont.*

	Tests	Balls	Mdns.	Runs	Wkts.	Avge.	5wI.	10wM.
Smith, V. I.	9	1655	55	769	12	64.08	—	—
Snooke, S. J.	26	1620	62	702	35	20.05	1	1
Stricker, L. A.	13	174	3	105	1	105.00	—	—
Taberer, H. M.	1	60	2	48	1	48.00	—	—
Tapscott, L. E.	2	12	1	2	0	—	—	—
Tayfield, H. J.	37	13568	602	4405	170	25.91	14	2
Taylor, H. W.	42	342	18	156	5	31.20	—	—
Theunissen, N.	1	80	5	51	0	—	—	—
Thornton, G.	1	24	0	20	1	20.00	—	—
Tomlinson, D. S.	1	60	0	38	0	—	—	—
Trimborn, P. H. J.	3	523	26	166	7	23.71	—	—
Tuckett, L.	9	2104	46	980	19	51.57	2	—
Tuckett, L. R.	1	120	4	69	0	—	—	—
Van der Merwe, P. L.	15	79	7	22	1	22.00	—	—
Van Ryneveld, C. B.	19	1554	27	671	17	39.47	—	—
Varnals, G. D.	3	12	1	2	0	—	—	—
Viljoen, K. G.	27	48	1	23	0	—	—	—
Vincent, C. L.	25	5863	194	2631	84	31.32	3	—
Vintcent, C. H.	3	369	23	193	4	48.25	—	—
Vogler, A. E. E.	15	2764	96	1455	64	22.73	5	1
Walter, K. A.	2	494	20	197	6	32.83	—	—
Watkins, J. C.	15	2805	134	816	29	28.13	—	—
Westcott, R. J.	5	32	0	22	0	—	—	—
White, G. C.	17	498	14	301	9	33.44	—	—
Willoughby, J. T.	2	275	12	159	6	26.50	—	—
Zulch, J. W.	16	24	0	28	0	—	—	—

WEST INDIES

	Tests	Balls	Mdns.	Runs	Wkts.	Avge.	5wI.	10wM.
Achong, E. E.	6	918	34	378	8	47.25	—	—
Atkinson, D.	22	5201	312	1647	47	35.04	3	—
Atkinson, E. E.	8	1634	77	589	25	23.56	1	—
Birkett, L. S.	4	126	1	71	1	71.00	—	—
Browne, C. R.	4	840	38	288	6	48.00	—	—
Butcher, B. F.	28	36	1	17	0	—	—	—
Butler, L.	1	240	7	151	2	75.50	—	—
Bynoe, M. R.	4	30	4	5	1	5.00	—	—
Cameron, F. J.	5	786	34	278	3	92.66	—	—
Cameron, J. H.	2	232	6	88	3	29.33	—	—
Carew, G.	4	18	2	2	0	—	—	—
Carew, M. C.	3	18	0	11	1	11.00	—	—
Christiani, R. J.	22	234	1	108	3	36.00	—	—
Clarke, C. B.	3	456	2	261	6	43.50	—	—
Constantine, L. N.	18	3553	125	1746	58	30.10	2	—
Da Costa, O. C.	5	372	13	175	3	58.33	—	—
De Caires, F. I.	3	12	0	9	0	—	—	—
Depeiza, C. C.	5	30	0	15	0	—	—	—
Dewdney, D. T.	9	1641	67	807	21	38.42	1	—

Bowling—West Indies—*Cont.*

	Tests	*Balls*	*Mdns.*	*Runs*	*Wkts.*	*Avge.*	*5wI.*	*10wM.*
Ferguson, W. F.	8	2556	90	1165	34	34.26	3	1
Francis, G. N.	10	1619	54	763	23	33.17	—	—
Fuller, R. L.	1	48	2	12	0	—	—	—
Gaskin, B. M.	2	474	24	158	2	79.00	—	—
Gibbs, G.	1	24	1	7	0	—	—	—
Gibbs, L. R.	34	10912	573	3543	151	23.46	11	2
Gilchrist, R.	13	3227	124	1521	57	26.68	1	—
Gladstone, G.	1	300	5	189	1	189.00	—	—
Goddard, J. D. C.	27	2931	148	1050	33	31.81	1	—
Gomez, G. E.	29	5236	284	1590	58	27.41	1	1
Grant, G. C.	12	24	0	18	0	—	—	—
Grant, R. S.	7	986	32	353	11	32.09	—	—
Grell, M. G.	1	30	1	17	0	—	—	—
Griffith, C. C.	19	3764	129	1830	71	25.77	4	—
Griffith, H. C.	13	2663	89	1243	44	28.25	2	—
Hall, W. W.	41	8952	274	4346	174	24.97	9	1
Headley, G. A.	22	398	7	230	0	—	—	—
Holford, D. A. J.	6	897	22	464	10	46.40	—	—
Holt, J. K., Jnr.	17	30	2	20	1	20.00	—	—
Hunte, C. C.	44	270	11	110	2	55.00	—	—
Hylton, L. G.	6	966	32	418	16	26.12	—	—
Johnson, H. H. H.	3	789	37	238	13	18.30	2	1
Johnson, T.	1	240	3	129	3	43.00	—	—
Jones, C. M.	4	102	11	11	0	—	—	—
Jones, P. E.	9	1842	64	751	25	30.04	1	—
Kanhai, R. B.	51	42	4	11	0	—	—	—
Kentish, E. S. M.	2	540	30	178	8	22.25	1	—
King, F.	14	2869	139	1159	29	39.96	1	—
King, L. A.	1	192	7	64	7	9.14	1	—
Lashley, P. D.	4	18	2	1	1	1.00	—	—
Lloyd, C. H.	3	258	12	90	2	45.00	—	—
McWatt, C. A.	6	24	1	16	1	16.00	—	—
Madray, I. S.	2	210	6	108	0	—	—	—
Marshall, N. E.	1	279	21	63	2	31.50	—	—
Marshall, R. E.	4	52	2	15	0	—	—	—
Martin, F. R.	9	1346	27	619	8	77.37	—	—
Martindale, E. A.	10	1605	40	804	37	21.72	3	—
Miller, R.	1	96	8	28	0	—	—	—
Mudie, G. H.	1	174	12	40	3	13.33	—	—
Neblett, J. M.	1	216	11	75	1	75.00	—	—
Nurse, S. M.	16	24	1	7	0	—	—	—
Pairaudeau, B. H.	13	6	0	3	0	—	—	—
Passailaigue, C. C.	1	12	0	15	0	—	—	—
Pierre, L. R.	1	42	0	28	0	—	—	—
Ramadhin, S.	43	13939	813	4577	158	28.96	10	1
Roach, C. A.	16	222	5	103	2	51.50	—	—
Rodriguez, W. V.	4	303	5	195	3	65.00	—	—

Bowling—West Indies—*Cont.*

	Tests	*Balls*	*Mdns.*	*Runs*	*Wkts.*	*Avge.*	*5wI.*	*10wM.*
St. Hill, E.	2	558	29	221	3	73.66	—	—
St. Hill, W. H.	3	18	0	9	0	—	—	—
Scarlett, R.	3	804	53	209	2	104.50	—	—
Scott, A. P. H.	1	264	9	140	0	—	—	—
Scott, O. C.	8	1405	17	925	22	42.04	1	—
Sealy, B. J.	1	30	1	10	1	10.00	—	—
Sealy, J. E. D.	11	156	4	94	3	31.33	—	—
Singh, C. K.	2	506	35	165	5	33.00	—	—
Small, J. A.	3	366	11	184	3	61.33	—	—
Smith, O. G.	26	4431	229	1625	48	33.85	1	—
Sobers, G. St. A.	60	12610	552	4818	144	33.45	4	—
Solomon, J. S.	27	696	39	268	4	67.00	—	—
Stayers, C.	4	636	20	364	9	40.44	—	—
Stollmeyer, J. B.	32	990	32	507	13	39.00	—	—
Taylor, J.	3	672	33	273	10	27.30	1	—
Trim, J.	4	794	28	291	18	16.16	1	—
Valentine, A. L.	36	12961	789	4215	139	30.32	8	2
Valentine, V. A.	2	288	14	104	1	104.00	—	—
Walcott, C. L.	44	1194	72	408	11	37.09	—	—
Walcott, L. A.	1	48	1	32	1	32.00	—	—
Watson, C.	7	1458	47	724	19	38.10	—	—
Weekes, E. D.	48	128	3	77	1	77.00	—	—
White, W. A.	2	491	26	152	3	50.66	—	—
Wight, C. V.	2	30	1	6	0	—	—	—
Williams, E. A. V.	4	796	34	241	9	26.77	—	—
Worrell, F. M. M.	51	7147	275	2673	69	38.73	2	—

NEW ZEALAND

	Tests	*Balls*	*Mdns.*	*Runs*	*Wkts.*	*Avge.*	*5wI.*	*10wM.*
Alabaster, J. C.	15	2780	122	1315	36	36.52	—	—
Allcott, C. F. W.	6	1206	41	541	6	90.16	—	—
Badcock, F. T.	7	1608	66	610	16	38.12	—	—
Bartlett, G. A.	8	1337	45	596	14	42.57	—	—
Beard, D. D.	4	812	38	302	9	33.55	—	—
Bell, W.	2	491	13	235	2	117.50	—	—
Blair, R. W.	19	3525	113	1515	43	35.23	—	—
Blunt, R. C.	9	933	34	472	12	39.33	—	—
Burke, C. C.	1	66	2	30	2	15.00	—	—
Burtt, T. B.	10	2611	119	1170	33	35.45	3	—
Butterfield, L. A.	1	78	6	24	0	—	—	—
Cameron, F. J.	19	4570	219	1849	61	30.31	3	—
Cave, H. B.	19	4080	244	1467	34	43.14	—	—
Chapple, M. E.	14	248	17	84	1	84.00	—	—
Cleverley, D. C.	2	222	3	130	0	—	—	—
Collinge, R. O.	10	1983	83	862	30	28.73	—	—
Congdon, B. E.	13	462	24	219	5	43.80	—	—
Cowie, J. A.	9	2028	65	969	45	21.53	4	1
Cresswell, G. F.	3	644	30	292	13	22.46	1	—
Cromb, I. B.	5	960	36	442	8	55.25	—	—
Cunis, R. S.	4	963	35	375	9	41.66	—	—

Bowling—New Zealand—*Cont.*

	Tests	*Balls*	*Mdns.*	*Runs*	*Wkts.*	*Avge.*	*5wI.*	*10wM.*
Dempster, C. S.	10	5	0	10	0	—	—	—
Dempster, E. W.	5	544	17	219	2	109.50	—	—
Dickinson, G. R.	3	451	13	245	8	30.62	—	—
Donnelly, M. P.	7	30	0	20	0	—	—	—
Dowling, G. T.	19	36	2	19	1	19.00	—	—
Dunning, J. A.	4	830	20	493	5	98.60	—	—
Emery, R. W. G.	2	46	0	52	2	26.00	—	—
Fisher, F. E.	1	204	6	78	1	78.00	—	—
Freeman, D. L.	2	240	3	169	1	169.00	—	—
Gallichan, N. M.	1	264	11	113	3	37.66	—	—
Harris, P. G. Z.	9	42	2	14	0	—	—	—
Hayes, J. A.	15	2681	87	1217	30	40.56	—	—
Henderson, M.	1	90	3	64	2	32.00	—	—
Hough, K. W...	2	462	22	175	6	29.16	—	—
Jarvis, T. W.	6	6	0	3	0	—	—	—
Leggat, I. B.	1	24	0	6	0	—	—	—
Lissette, A. F.	2	288	16	124	3	41.33	—	—
Lowry, T. C.	7	12	1	5	0	—	—	—
MacGibbon, A. R.	26	5605	230	2160	70	30.85	1	—
McGirr, H. M.	2	180	5	115	1	115.00	—	—
McLeod, E. A.	1	12	0	5	0	—	—	—
McRae, D. A. N.	1	84	3	44	0	—	—	—
Matheson, A. M.	2	282	9	136	2	68.00	—	—
Merritt, W. E.	6	936	10	617	12	51.41	—	—
Miller, L. S. M.	13	2	0	1	0	—	—	—
Moir, A. M.	17	2638	92	1418	28	50.64	2	—
Moloney, D. A. R.	3	12	1	9	0	—	—	—
Mooney, F. L. H.	14	8	1	0	0	—	—	—
Morgan, R. W.	14	751	25	444	3	148.00	—	—
Morrison, B. D.	1	186	5	129	2	64.50	—	—
Motz, R. C.	22	4697	192	2050	61	33.60	1	—
Newman, J.	3	425	11	254	2	127.00	—	—
Overton, G. W. F.	3	730	23	258	9	28.66	—	—
Page, M. L.	14	381	11	231	5	46.20	—	—
Pollard, V.	13	1722	89	777	14	55.50	—	—
Poore, M. B.	14	788	24	367	9	40.77	—	—
Puna, N.	3	480	20	240	4	60.00	—	—
Rabone, G. O.	12	1385	48	633	16	39.56	1	—
Reid, J. R.	58	7719	441	2840	85	33.41	1	—
Roberts, A. W.	5	459	19	209	7	29.85	—	—
Scott, R. H.	1	138	3	74	1	74.00	—	—
Scott, V. J.	10	18	0	14	0	—	—	—

Bowling—New Zealand—*Cont.*

	Tests	*Balls*	*Mdns.*	*Runs*	*Wkts.*	*Avge.*	*5wI.*	*10wM.*
Shrimpton, M. J. F.	6	12	1	1	0	—	—	—
Sinclair, B. W.	19	60	3	32	2	16.00	—	—
Sinclair, I. M.	2	233	9	120	1	120.00	—	—
Smith, D.	1	120	0	113	1	113.00	—	—
Snedden, C. A.	1	96	4	46	0	—	—	—
Sparling, J. T...	11	708	32	327	5	65.40	—	—
Sutcliffe, B.	42	544	10	346	4	86.50	—	—
Taylor, B. R.	9	1628	56	816	30	27.20	2	—
Vivian, G. E.	1	90	3	51	1	51.00	—	—
Vivian, H. G.	7	1311	44	633	17	37.23	—	—
Wallace, W. M.	13	6	0	5	0	—	—	—
Weir, G. L.	11	342	7	209	7	29.85	—	—
Yuile, B. W.	10	1699	116	712	19	37.47	—	—

INDIA

	Tests	*Balls*	*Mdns.*	*Runs*	*Wkts.*	*Avge.*	*5wI.*	*10wM.*
Adhikari, H. R.	21	170	2	82	3	27.33	—	—
Ali, S. Nazir	2	138	0	83	4	20.75	—	—
Ali, S. Wazir	7	30	1	25	0	—	—	—
Amarnath, L.	24	4241	195	1481	45	32.91	2	—
Amar Singh, L.	7	2182	95	858	28	30.64	2	—
Apte, M. L.	7	6	0	3	0	—	—	—
Baig, A. A.	10	18	0	15	0	—	—	—
Banerjee, S.	1	306	3	181	5	36.20	—	—
Banerjee, S. N.	1	273	8	127	5	25.40	—	—
Bedi, B. S.	5	1082	57	464	14	33.14	—	—
Bhandari, P.	3	78	2	39	0	—	—	—
Borde, C. G.	46	5707	237	2416	52	46.46	1	—
Chandrasekhar, B. S. ..	14	4374	218	1768	61	28.98	2	1
Chowdhury, N. R.	2	516	21	205	1	205.00	—	—
Contractor, N. J.	31	186	6	82	1	82.00	—	—
Dani, H. T.	1	60	5	19	1	19.00	—	—
Desai, R. B.	26	5327	172	2624	72	36.44	2	—
Divecha, R. V.	5	1044	44	361	11	32.81	—	—
Durrani, S. A.	23	5918	294	2437	71	34.32	3	1
Gadkari, C. V.	6	102	4	45	0	—	—	—
Gaekwad, D. K.	11	12	0	12	0	—	—	—
Gaekwad, H. G.	1	222	21	47	0	—	—	—
Ghorpade, J. M.	8	150	1	131	0	—	—	—
Ghulam, Ahmed	22	5650	253	2052	68	30.17	4	1
Gopalan, M. J.	1	114	7	39	1	39.00	—	—
Gopinath C. D.	8	48	2	11	1	11.00	—	—
Guha, S.	1	288	10	115	0	—	—	—
Guard, G.	2	396	16	182	3	60.66	—	—
Gul Mahomed	8	77	4	24	2	12.00	—	—
Gupte, B. P.	3	678	28	349	3	116.33	—	—
Gupte, S. P.	36	11284	598	4402	149	29.54	12	1

Bowling—India—*Cont.*

	Tests	*Balls*	*Mdns.*	*Runs*	*Wkts.*	*Avge.*	*5wI.*	*10wM.*
Hanumant Singh	13	66	0	51	0	—	—	—
Hardikar, M. S.	2	108	7	55	1	55.00	—	—
Hazare, Vijay S.	30	2840	97	1220	20	61.00	—	—
Jahangir Khan, M.	4	606	28	255	4	63.75	—	—
Jaisimha, M. L.	29	1621	80	655	8	81.87	—	—
Jamshedji, R. J.	1	210	4	137	3	45.66	—	—
Jilani, M. Baqa	1	90	4	55	0	—	—	—
Kripal Singh, A. G.	14	1524	75	584	10	58.40	—	—
Kumar, V. V.	2	598	46	202	7	28.85	1	—
Kunderan, B. K.	18	24	0	13	0	—	—	—
Manjrekar, V. L.	55	204	17	43	1	43.00	—	—
Mankad, V. M.	44	14686	777	5235	162	32.31	8	2
Mehra, V. L.	8	36	1	6	0	—	—	—
Merchant, V. M.	10	54	0	40	0	—	—	—
Milkha Singh, A. G.	4	6	0	2	0	—	—	—
Modi, R. S.	10	30	1	14	0	—	—	—
Muddiah, V. M.	2	312	16	134	3	44.66	—	—
Mushtaq Ali	11	378	9	202	3	67.33	—	—
Nadkarni, R. G.	34	7486	560	2097	71	29.53	3	1
Naoomal Jeoomal	3	108	0	68	2	34.00	—	—
Nayudu, C. K.	7	858	24	386	9	42.88	—	—
Nayudu, C. S.	11	522	6	359	2	179.50	—	—
Nissar, M.	6	1211	34	707	25	28.28	3	—
Nyalchand, K.	1	384	33	97	3	32.33	—	—
Palia, P. E.	2	42	3	13	0	—	—	—
Pataudi, Nawab of, Jnr. ..	24	114	5	80	1	80.00	—	—
Patel, J. S.	7	1665	94	636	29	21.93	2	1
Patil, S. R.	1	138	7	51	2	25.50	—	—
Phadkar, D. G.	31	5975	275	2285	62	36.85	3	—
Prasanna, E. A. S.	6	1827	71	815	18	45.27	—	—
Rajinder Pal	1	78	4	22	0	—	—	—
Ramchand, G. S.	33	4976	258	1900	41	46.34	1	—
Ramji, L.	1	138	5	64	0	—	—	—
Rangachari, C. R.	4	846	11	493	9	54.77	1	—
Ranjane, V. B.	7	1265	33	649	19	34.15	—	—
Roy, P...	43	104	4	66	1	66.00	—	—
Sardesai, D. N.	18	48	2	33	0	—	—	—
Sarwate, C. T.	9	658	5	374	3	124.66	—	—
Saxena, R.	1	12	0	11	0	—	—	—
Shinde, S. G.	7	1515	60	717	12	59.75	1	—
Shodhan, D. H.	3	60	3	26	0	—	—	—
Sohoni, S. W.	4	532	20	202	2	101.00	—	—
Subramanya, V.	5	372	15	149	3	49.66	—	—
Sunderram, G.	2	396	12	164	3	54.66	—	—
Surendranath, R.	11	2602	145	1053	26	40.50	2	—
Surti, R. F.	15	2200	71	1101	18	61.16	—	—
Swamy, N. V.	1	108	5	45	0	—	—	—
Tarapore, K. K.	1	114	2	72	0	—	—	—

Bowling—India—*Cont.*

	Tests	Balls	Mdns.	Runs	Wkts.	Avge.	5wI.	10wM.
Umrigar, P. R.	59	4738	258	1475	35	42.14	2	—
Venkataraghavan, S.	7	2139	151	657	24	27.37	1	1
Wadekar, A. L.	5	25	0	26	0	—	—	—

PAKISTAN

	Tests	Balls	Mdns.	Runs	Wkts.	Avge.	5wI.	10wM.
Afaq Hussain	2	240	7	106	1	106.00	—	—
Akhtar, Javed	1	96	5	52	0	—	—	—
Alim-ud-Din	25	84	0	76	1	76.00	—	—
Amir Elahi	5	400	5	248	7	35.42	—	—
Anwar Hussain	4	36	1	29	1	29.00	—	—
Arif Butt	3	666	26	288	14	20.57	1	—
Asif Iqbal	11	2378	123	897	39	23.00	2	—
Burki, Javed	24	42	2	23	0	—	—	—
D'Souza, Antao	6	1587	56	745	17	43.82	1	—
Farooq Hamid	1	184	1	107	1	107.00	—	—
Farooq, Mohammad	7	1422	50	682	21	32.47	—	—
Fazal Mahmood	34	9870	548	3437	139	24.72	13	4
Ghazali, M. E. Z.	2	48	1	18	0	—	—	—
Hanif Mohammad	51	176	6	91	1	91.00	—	—
Haseeb Ahsan	12	2847	100	1330	27	49.25	2	—
Ibadulla, Khalid	4	336	21	99	1	99.00	—	—
Ilyas, Mohammad	8	78	1	62	0	—	—	—
Imtiaz Ahmed	41	6	1	0	0	—	—	—
Intikhab Alam	20	3617	125	1564	31	50.45	—	—
Israr Ali	4	318	12	165	6	27.50	—	—
Kardar, A. H.	23	2712	147	953	21	45.38	—	—
Khalid Hassan	1	126	1	116	2	58.00	—	—
Khan Mohammad	13	3169	152	1294	54	23.96	4	—
Mahmood Hussain	27	5983	231	2628	68	38.64	2	—
Majid Jahangir	7	828	23	356	9	39.55	—	—
Maqsood Ahmed	16	462	21	191	3	63.66	—	—
Mathias, Wallis	21	24	0	20	0	—	—	—
Miran Bux	2	348	22	115	2	57.50	—	—
Mufasir-ul-Haq	1	222	13	84	3	28.00	—	—
Munaf, Mohammad	4	769	31	341	11	31.00	—	—
Munir Malik	3	684	19	358	9	39.77	1	—
Mushtaq Mohammad ..	17	482	20	224	9	24.88	—	—
Nasim-ul-Ghani	28	4460	204	1959	52	37.67	2	—
Nazar Mohammad	5	12	1	4	0	—	—	—
Niaz Ahmed	1	222	10	72	2	36.00	—	—

Bowling—Pakistan—*Cont.*

	Tests	Balls	Mdns.	Runs	Wkts.	Avge.	5wI.	10wM.
Pervez Sajjad	7	1506	82	505	22	22.95	1	—
Rahman, S. F.	1	204	3	99	1	99.00	—	—
Saeed Ahmed	35	1251	55	507	12	42.25	—	—
Salah-ud-Din	3	546	27	187	7	26.71	—	—
Salim Altaf	2	453	21	180	4	45.00	—	—
Shafqat Rana	1	6	0	1	0	—	—	—
Shahid Mahmood	1	36	1	23	0	—	—	—
Shuja-ud-Din	19	2358	128	801	20	40.05	—	—
Waqar Hassan	21	6	0	10	0	—	—	—
Wazir Mohammad	20	24	0	15	0	—	—	—
Zulfiqar Ahmed	9	1285	84	365	20	18.25	2	1

COMBINED RECORDS OF PLAYERS APPEARING FOR TWO COUNTRIES

BATTING AND FIELDING

	M.	I.	N.O.	Runs	H.S.	Avge.	100s	50s	Ct.	St.
Amir Elahi (India & Pakistan) ..	6	9	1	82	47	10.25	—	—	—	—
J. J. Ferris (Australia & England) ..	9	17	4	114	20*	8.76	—	—	4	—
S. C. Guillen (West Indies & New Zealand)	8	12	2	202	54	20.20	—	1	13	3
Gul Mahomed (India & Pakistan) ..	9	17	1	205	34	12.81	—	—	3	—
F. Hearne (England & South Africa)	6	10	0	168	30	16.80	—	—	3	—
A. H. Kardar (India & Pakistan) ..	26	42	3	927	93	23.76	—	5	16	—
W. E. Midwinter (England & Australia)	12	21	1	269	37	13.45	—	—	10	—
F. Mitchell (England & South Africa)	5	10	0	116	41	11.60	—	—	2	—
W. L. Murdoch (Australia & England)	19	34	5	908	211	31.31	2	1	12	2
Nawab of Pataudi, Snr. (England & India)	6	10	0	199	102	19.90	1	—	—	—
A. E. Trott (Australia & England) ..	5	9	3	228	85*	38.00	—	2	4	—
S. M. J. Woods (Australia & England)	6	10	0	154	53	15.40	—	1	5	—

BOWLING

	M.	Balls	Mdns.	Runs	Wkts.	Avge.	5wI.	10wM.
Amir Elahi	6	400	5	248	7	35.42	—	—
J. J. Ferris	9	2302	251	775	61	12.70	6	1
Gul Mahomed	9	77	4	24	2	12.00	—	—
F. Hearne	6	62	0	40	2	20.00	—	—
A. H. Kardar	26	2712	147	953	21	45.38	—	—
W. E. Midwinter	12	1725	181	605	24	25.20	1	—
A. E. Trott	5	948	54	390	26	15.00	2	—
S. M. J. Woods	6	412	26	250	10	25.00	—	—

SERIES RECORDS

HIGHEST INDIVIDUAL RUN AGGREGATES

ENGLAND v. AUSTRALIA

	Tests	I.	N.O.	Runs	H.S.	Avge.	100s.	50s.
D. G. Bradman (A)	37	63	7	5028	334	89.78	19	13
J. B. Hobbs (E)	41	71	4	3636	187	54.26	12	15
W. R. Hammond (E)	33	58	3	2852	251	51.85	9	7
H. Sutcliffe (E)..	27	46	5	2741	194	66.85	8	16
C. Hill (A)	41	76	1	2660	188	35.46	4	16
L. Hutton (E)	27	49	6	2428	364	56.46	5	14
R. N. Harvey (A)	37	68	5	2416	167	38.34	6	12
V. T. Trumper (A)	40	74	5	2264	185*	32.81	6	9
S. E. Gregory (A)	52	92	7	2193	201	25.80	4	8
W. W. Armstrong (A) ..	42	71	9	2172	158	35.03	4	5
A. R. Morris (A)	24	43	2	2080	206	50.73	8	8

ENGLAND v. SOUTH AFRICA

	Tests	I.	N.O.	Runs	H.S.	Avge.	100s.	50s.
B. Mitchell (SA)	30	57	7	2732	189*	54.64	7	16
H. W. Taylor (SA)	30	54	3	2287	176	44.84	7	12
D. C. S. Compton (E).. ..	24	42	1	2205	208	53.78	7	11
W. R. Hammond (E)	24	42	7	2188	181	62.51	6	14
A. D. Nourse, Jnr. (SA) ..	24	43	6	2037	208	55.05	7	9

ENGLAND v. WEST INDIES

	Tests	I.	N.O.	Runs	H.S.	Avge.	100s.	50s.
G. St. A. Sobers (WI) ..	21	36	3	2113	226	64.03	7	7
F. M. M. Worrell (WI) ..	25	42	6	1979	261	54.97	6	7
G. A. Headley (WI)	16	29	3	1852	270*	71.23	8	5
L. Hutton (E)	13	24	3	1661	205	79.09	5	6

ENGLAND v. NEW ZEALAND

	Tests	I.	N.O.	Runs	H.S.	Avge.	100s.	50s.
B. Sutcliffe (NZ)	16	28	2	1049	116	40.34	2	8
M. C. Cowdrey (E)	17	22	5	1034	128*	60.82	2	7
W. R. Hammond (E)	9	11	2	1015	336*	112.77	4	1

ENGLAND v. INDIA

	Tests	I.	N.O.	Runs	H.S.	Avge.	100s.	50s.
K. F. Barrington (E)	14	21	3	1355	172	75.27	3	9
V. L. Manjrekar (I)	17	29	2	1181	189*	43.74	3	5

ENGLAND v. PAKISTAN

	Tests	I.	N.O.	Runs	H.S.	Avge.	100s.	50s.
Hanif Mohammad (P).. ..	15	29	1	993	187*	35.46	3	3
T. W. Graveney (E)	10	8	—	767	153	95.87	2	5

AUSTRALIA v. SOUTH AFRICA

	Tests	I.	N.O.	Runs	H.S.	Avge.	100s.	50s.
R. N. Harvey (A)	15	23	3	1625	205	81.25	8	5
T. L. Goddard (SA)	15	28	4	1032	93	43.00	—	8

AUSTRALIA v. WEST INDIES

	Tests	I.	N.O.	Runs	H.S.	Avge.	100s.	50s.
R. N. Harvey (A)	14	25	1	1054	204	43.91	3	3
G. St. A. Sobers (WI) ..	14	28	3	1013	168	40.52	2	4

SOUTH AFRICA v. NEW ZEALAND

	Tests	I.	N.O.	Runs	H.S.	Avge.	100s.	50s.
D. J. McGlew (SA)	12	21	4	1100	255*	64.70	3	5
J. R. Reid (NZ)	15	28	1	914	142	33.85	2	5

Highest Individual Run Aggregates—*Cont.*

WEST INDIES v. INDIA

	Tests	*I.*	*N.O.*	*Runs*	*H.S.*	*Avge.*	*100s.*	*50s.*
E. D. Weekes (WI)	10	15	1	1495	207	106.78	7	4
P. R. Umrigar (I)	16	30	3	1362	172*	50.44	3	10
G. St. A Sobers (WI)	13	20	5	1323	198	88.20	5	6
R. B. Kanhai (WI)	13	19	—	1260	256	66.31	3	5

WEST INDIES v. PAKISTAN

	Tests	*I.*	*N.O.*	*Runs*	*H.S.*	*Avge.*	*100s.*	*50s.*
G. St. A. Sobers (WI)	8	13	2	984	365*	89.45	3	4

INDIA v. PAKISTAN

	Tests	*I.*	*N.O.*	*Runs*	*H.S.*	*Avge.*	*100s.*	*50s.*
Hanif Mohammad (P).. ..	15	26	2	970	160	40.41	2	6
P. R. Umrigar (I)	15	19	2	911	117	53.58	5	2

HIGHEST INDIVIDUAL WICKET AGGREGATES

ENGLAND v. AUSTRALIA

	Tests	*Balls*	*Mdns.*	*Runs*	*Wkts.*	*Avge.*	*5wI.*	*10wM.*
H. Trumble (A)	31	7895	448	2945	141	20.88	9	3
M. A. Noble (A)	39	6845	353	2862	115	24.88	9	2
R. R. Lindwall (A)	29	6720	216	2559	114	22.44	6	—
W. Rhodes (E)	41	5785	237	2616	109	24.00	6	1
S. F. Barnes (E)	20	5749	264	2288	106	21.58	12	1
C. V. Grimmett (A).. ..	22	9224	426	3439	106	32.44	11	2
A. V. Bedser (E)	21	7065	208	2859	104	27.49	7	2
G. Giffen (A)	31	6325	434	2791	103	27.09	7	1
W. J. O'Reilly (A)	19	7864	439	2587	102	25.36	8	3
R. Peel (E)	20	5216	444	1715	102	16.81	6	2
C. T. B. Turner (A).. ..	17	5179	457	1670	101	16.53	11	2

ENGLAND v. SOUTH AFRICA

	Tests	*Balls*	*Mdns.*	*Runs*	*Wkts.*	*Avge.*	*5wI.*	*10wM.*
S. F. Barnes (E)	7	2124	94	818	83	9.85	12	6
H. J. Tayfield (SA)	15	5286	297	1658	75	22.10	7	1
C. L. Vincent (SA)	18	4441	154	1967	72	27.31	3	—
J. B. Statham (E)	16	3931	154	1426	69	20.66	4	1
G. A. Faulkner (SA) ..	17	3086	104	1472	68	21.64	4	—
T. L. Goddard (SA) ..	20	5807	366	1622	63	25.76	3	—
A. E. E. Vogler (SA) ..	13	2736	91	1279	60	21.31	5	1

ENGLAND v. WEST INDIES

	Tests	*Balls*	*Mdns.*	*Runs*	*Wkts.*	*Avge.*	*5wI.*	*10wM.*
F. S. Trueman (E)	18	4581	176	2018	86	23.46	6	2
S. Ramadhin (WI)	18	7154	464	2201	80	27.51	5	1
G. St. A. Sobers (WI) ..	21	4677	175	1908	58	32.89	2	—
W. W. Hall (WI)	15	3539	110	1768	56	31.57	2	—
J. C. Laker (E)	13	4090	239	1549	51	30.37	1	—
L. N. Constantine (WI) ..	13	2788	110	1339	50	26.78	2	—

ENGLAND v. NEW ZEALAND

	Tests	*Balls*	*Mdns.*	*Runs*	*Wkts.*	*Avge.*	*5wI.*	*10wM.*
G. A. R. Lock (E)	7	1505	122	367	47	7.80	5	2
F. S. Trueman (E)	11	2167	113	762	40	19.05	2	—
J. A. Cowie (NZ)	8	1902	57	929	39	23.82	3	1
T. E. Bailey (E)	12	1876	70	866	32	27.06	2	—

ENGLAND v. INDIA

	Tests	*Balls*	*Mdns.*	*Runs*	*Wkts.*	*Avge.*	*5wI.*	*10wM.*
V. M. Mankad (I)	11	4101	259	1249	54	23.12	3	1
F. S. Trueman (E)	9	1784	78	787	53	14.84	2	—
A. V. Bedser (E)	7	1867	90	577	44	13.11	4	2
H. Verity (E)	6	1601	105	615	38	16.18	1	1

Highest Individual Wicket Aggregates—*Cont.*

ENGLAND v. PAKISTAN

	Tests	Balls	Mdns.	Runs	Wkts.	Avge.	5wI.	10wM.
J. B. Statham (E)	7	1255	66	491	27	18.18	—	—
Fazal Mahmood (P) ..	7	2046	98	838	25	33.52	2	1

AUSTRALIA v. SOUTH AFRICA

	Tests	Balls	Mdns.	Runs	Wkts.	Avge.	5wI.	10wM.
C. V. Grimmett (A).. ..	10	3913	248	1199	77	15.57	8	4
H. J. Tayfield (SA).. ..	15	6027	181	2208	64	34.50	4	1
R. Benaud (A)	13	4136	115	1413	52	27.17	5	—
W. J. Whitty (A)	8	2055	89	875	50	17.50	3	—

AUSTRALIA v. WEST INDIES

	Tests	Balls	Mdns.	Runs	Wkts.	Avge.	5wI.	10wM.
A. Valentine (WI)	13	3949	123	1573	43	36.58	3	—
R. Benaud (A)	11	3290	105	1279	42	30.45	1	—
R. R. Lindwall (A)	10	1980	44	1127	41	27.48	2	—
K. R. Miller (A)	10	1907	53	1028	40	25.70	3	—

AUSTRALIA v. INDIA

	Tests	Balls	Mdns.	Runs	Wkts.	Avge.	5wI.	10wM.
R. Benaud (A)	8	2947	200	956	52	18.38	5	1

WEST INDIES v. INDIA

	Tests	Balls	Mdns.	Runs	Wkts.	Avge.	5wI.	10wM.
W. W. Hall (WI)	13	2810	112	1221	65	18.78	4	1
S. P. Gupte (I)	10	3852	158	1716	49	35.02	4	1
G. St. A. Sobers (WI) ..	13	2957	145	1115	47	23.72	1	—
L. R. Gibbs (WI)	9	2998	164	948	42	22.57	2	—

WEST INDIES v. PAKISTAN

	Tests	Balls	Mdns.	Runs	Wkts.	Avge.	5wI.	10wM.
Fazal Mahmood (P) ..	8	2779	141	1097	41	26.75	3	1
Nasim-ul-Ghani (P).. ..	8	1699	81	721	30	24.03	2	—

INDIA v. PAKISTAN

	Tests	Balls	Mdns.	Runs	Wkts.	Avge.	5wI.	10wM.
Fazal Mahmood (P) ..	14	3677	227	1082	44	24.59	4	1
Mahmood Hussain (P) ..	14	3106	130	1293	39	32.32	2	—
V. M. Mankad (I)	9	3173	230	913	37	24.67	4	1

RECORDS FOR INDIVIDUAL SERIES

ENGLAND v. AUSTRALIA

(*The Ashes*)

HIGHEST INNINGS TOTALS

England in England ...	903-7d at The Oval	1938
England in Australia ...	636 at Sydney	1928-29
Australia in England ...	729-6d at Lord's	1930
Australia in Australia ...	659-8d at Sydney	1946-47

LOWEST INNINGS TOTALS

England in England ...	52 at The Oval	1948
England in Australia ...	45 at Sydney	1886-87
Australia in England ...	36 at Birmingham	1902
Australia in Australia ...	42 at Sydney	1887-88

Highest Match Aggregate ...	1753-40 wkts at Adelaide	1920-21
Lowest Match Aggregate ...	291-40 wkts at Lord's	1888

Records for Individual Series—England v. Australia—*Cont.*

HIGHEST INDIVIDUAL INNINGS

England in England ...	364 L. Hutton (Oval)	1938
England in Australia ...	287 R. E. Foster (Sydney)	1903-04
Australia in England ...	334 D. G. Bradman (Leeds)	1930
Australia in Australia ...	307 R. M. Cowper (Melbourne) ...	1965-66

BEST INNINGS BOWLING ANALYSIS

England in England ...	10-53	J. C. Laker (Manchester) ...	1956
England in Australia ...	8-35	G. A. Lohmann (Sydney) ...	1886-87
Australia in England ...	8-31	F. Laver (Manchester)... ...	1909
Australia in Australia ...	9-121	A. A. Mailey (Melbourne) ...	1920-21

HIGHEST RUN AGGREGATE BY A BATSMAN IN A SERIES

England in England ...	562 (av. 62.44) D. C. S. Compton ...	1948
England in Australia ...	905 (av. 113.12) W. R. Hammond ...	1928-29
Australia in England ...	974 (av. 139.14) D. G. Bradman ...	1930
Australia in Australia ...	810 (av. 90.00) D. G. Bradman ...	1936-37

HIGHEST WICKET AGGREGATE BY A BOWLER IN A SERIES

England in England ...	46 (av. 9.60) J. C. Laker	1956
England in Australia ...	38 (av. 23.18) M. W. Tate	1924-25
Australia in England ...	29 (av. 31.89) C. V. Grimmett ...	1930
	29 (av. 22.55) G. D. McKenzie ...	1964
Australia in Australia ...	36 (av. 26.27) A. A. Mailey	1920-21

RECORD WICKET PARTNERSHIPS—ENGLAND

1st	323	J. B. Hobbs & W. Rhodes at Melbourne	1911-12
2nd	382	L. Hutton & M. Leyland at The Oval	1938
3rd	262	W. R. Hammond & D. R. Jardine at Adelaide ...	1928-29
4th	222	W. R. Hammond & E. Paynter at Lord's	1938
5th	206	E. Paynter & D. C. S. Compton at Nottingham ...	1938
6th	215	L. Hutton & J. Hardstaff, Jnr. at The Oval	1938
7th	143	F. E. Woolley & J. Vine at Sydney	1911-12
8th	124	E. Hendren & H. Larwood at Brisbane[1]	1928-29
9th	151	W. H. Scotton & W. W. Read at The Oval	1884
10th	130	R. E. Foster & W. Rhodes at Sydney	1903-04

RECORD WICKET PARTNERSHIPS—AUSTRALIA

1st	244	R. B. Simpson & W. M. Lawry at Adelaide	1965-66
2nd	451	W. H. Ponsford & D. G. Bradman at The Oval ...	1934
3rd	276	D. G. Bradman & A. L. Hassett at Brisbane[2]	1946-47
4th	388	W. H. Ponsford & D. G. Bradman at Leeds	1934
5th	405	S. G. Barnes & D. G. Bradman at Sydney	1946-47
6th	346	J. H. Fingleton & D. G. Bradman at Melbourne ...	1936-37
7th	165	C. Hill & H. Trumble at Melbourne	1897-98
8th	243	C. Hill & R. J. Hartigan at Adelaide	1907-08
9th	154	S. E. Gregory & J. M. Blackham at Sydney	1894-95
10th	127	J. M. Taylor & A. A. Mailey at Sydney	1924-25

Records for Individual Series—*Cont.*

ENGLAND v. SOUTH AFRICA

HIGHEST INNINGS TOTALS

England in England ...	554-8d at Lord's	1947
England in South Africa ...	654-5 at Durban[2]	1938-39
South Africa in England ...	538 at Leeds	1951
South Africa in South Africa	530 at Durban[2]	1938-39

LOWEST INNINGS TOTALS

England in England ...	76 at Leeds	1907
England in South Africa ...	92 at Cape Town	1898-99
South Africa in England ...	30 at Birmingham	1924
South Africa in South Africa	30 at Port Elizabeth	1895-96

Highest Match Aggregate ...	1981-35 wkts at Durban[2]	1938-39
Lowest Match Aggregate ...	378-30 wkts at The Oval	1912

HIGHEST INDIVIDUAL INNINGS

England in England ...	211 J. B. Hobbs (Lord's)	1924
England in South Africa ...	243 E. Paynter (Durban[2])	1938-39
South Africa in England ...	236 E. A. B. Rowan (Leeds) ...	1951
South Africa in South Africa	176 H. W. Taylor (Johannesburg[1])	1922-23

BEST INNINGS BOWLING ANALYSIS

England in England ...	8-29 S. F. Barnes (Oval)	1912
England in South Africa ...	9-28 G. A. Lohmann (Johannesburg[1])	1895-96
South Africa in England ...	7-65 S. J. Pegler (Lord's)	1912
South Africa in South Africa	9-113 H. J. Tayfield (Johannesburg[3])	1956-57

HIGHEST RUN AGGREGATE BY A BATSMAN IN A SERIES

England in England ...	753 (av. 94.12) D. C. S. Compton ...	1947
England in South Africa ...	653 (av. 81.62) E. Paynter	1938-39
South Africa in England ...	621 (av. 69.00) A. D. Nourse, Jnr....	1947
South Africa in South Africa	582 (av. 64.66) H. W. Taylor ...	1922-23

HIGHEST WICKET AGGREGATE BY A BOWLER IN A SERIES

England in England ...	34 (av. 8.29) S. F. Barnes	1912
England in South Africa ...	49 (av. 10.93) S. F. Barnes ...	1913-14
South Africa in England ...	26 (av. 21.84) H. J. Tayfield ...	1955
	26 (av. 22.57) N. A. T. Adcock ...	1960
South Africa in South Africa	37 (av. 17.18) H. J. Tayfield ...	1956-57

RECORD WICKET PARTNERSHIPS—ENGLAND

1st	359	L. Hutton & C. Washbrook at Johannesburg[2]	1948-49
2nd	280	P. A. Gibbs & W. J. Edrich at Durban[2]	1938-39
3rd	370	W. J. Edrich & D. C. S. Compton at Lord's	1947
4th	197	W. R. Hammond & L. E. G. Ames at Cape Town ...	1938-39
5th	237	D. C. S. Compton & N. W. D. Yardley at Nottingham	1947
6th	206*	K. F. Barrington & J. M. Parks at Durban[2]	1964-65
7th	115	J. W. H. T. Douglas & M. C. Bird at Durban[1] ...	1913-14

Records for Individual Series—England v. South Africa—*Cont.*

8th	154	C. W. Wright & H. R. Bromley-Davenport at Johannesburg[1]	1895-96
9th	71	H. Wood & J. T. Hearne at Cape Town	1891-92
10th	92	A. C. Russell & A. E. R. Gilligan at Durban[2]	1922-23

RECORD WICKET PARTNERSHIPS—SOUTH AFRICA

1st	260	I. J. Siedle & B. Mitchell at Cape Town	1930-31
2nd	198	E. A. B. Rowan & C. B. Van Ryneveld at Leeds ...	1951
3rd	319	A. Melville & A. D. Nourse, Jnr. at Nottingham ...	1947
4th	214	H. W. Taylor & H. G. Deane at The Oval	1929
5th	157	A. J. Pithey & J. H. B. Waite at Johannesburg[3] ...	1964-65
6th	171	J. H. B. Waite & P. L. Winslow at Manchester	1955
7th	123	H. G. Deane & E. P. Nupen at Durban[2]	1927-28
8th	109*	B. Mitchell & L. Tuckett at The Oval	1947
9th	137	E. L. Dalton & A. B. C. Langton at The Oval ...	1935
10th	103	H. G. Owen-Smith & A. J. Bell at Leeds	1929

ENGLAND v. WEST INDIES
(The Wisden Trophy)

HIGHEST INNINGS TOTALS

England in England	619-6d at Nottingham	1957
England in West Indies ...	849 at Kingston	1929-30
West Indies in England ...	558 at Nottingham	1950
West Indies in West Indies ...	681-8d at Port of Spain	1953-54

LOWEST INNINGS TOTALS

England in England	103 at The Oval	1950
England in West Indies ...	103 at Kingston	1934-35
West Indies in England ...	86 at The Oval	1957
West Indies in West Indies ...	102 at Bridgetown...	1934-35

Highest Match Aggregate ...	1815-34 wkts at Kingston... ...	1929-30
Lowest Match Aggregate... ...	309-29 wkts at Bridgetown ...	1934-35

HIGHEST INDIVIDUAL INNINGS

England in England	285*	P. B. H. May (Birmingham)	1957
England in West Indies ...	325	A. Sandham (Kingston) ...	1929-30
West Indies in England ...	261	F. M. M. Worrell (Nottingham)	1950
West Indies in West Indies ...	270*	G. A. Headley (Kingston) ...	1934-35

BEST INNINGS BOWLING ANALYSIS

England in England	7-44	T. E. Bailey (Lord's) ...	1957
	7-44	F. S. Trueman (Birmingham)	1963
England in West Indies ...	7-34	T. E. Bailey (Kingston) ...	1953-54
West Indies in England ...	8-104	A. L. Valentine (Manchester)	1950
West Indies in West Indies ...	7-69	W. W. Hall (Kingston) ...	1959-60

HIGHEST RUN AGGREGATE BY A BATSMAN IN A SERIES

England in England	489 (av. 97.80) P. B. H. May ...	1957
England in West Indies ...	693 (av. 115.50) E. Hendren ...	1929-30
West Indies in England ...	722 (av. 103.14) G. St. A. Sobers	1966
West Indies in West Indies ...	709 (av. 101.28) G. St. A. Sobers	1959-60

Records for Individual Series—England v. West Indies—*Cont.*

HIGHEST WICKET AGGREGATE BY A BOWLER IN A SERIES

England in England	34 (av. 17.47)	F. S. Trueman ...	1963
England in West Indies ...	21 (av. 26.14)	F. S. Trueman ...	1959-60
West Indies in England ...	33 (av. 20.42)	A. L. Valentine ...	1950
West Indies in West Indies ...	23 (av. 24.65)	W. F. Ferguson ...	1947-48
	23 (av. 24.30)	S. Ramadhin ...	1953-54

RECORD WICKET PARTNERSHIPS—ENGLAND

1st	212	C. Washbrook & R. T. Simpson at Nottingham ...	1950
2nd	266	P. E. Richardson & T. W. Graveney at Nottingham ...	1957
3rd	264	L. Hutton & W. R. Hammond at The Oval	1939
4th	411	P. B. H. May & M. C. Cowdrey at Birmingham ...	1957
5th	130*	C. Milburn & T. W. Graveney at Lord's	1966
6th	161	T. E. Bailey & T. G. Evans at Manchester	1950
7th	197	M. J. K. Smith & J. M. Parks at Port of Spain ...	1959-60
8th	217	T. W. Graveney & J. T. Murray at The Oval ...	1966
9th	89	P. J. Sharpe & G. A. R. Lock at Birmingham ...	1963
10th	128	K. Higgs & J. A. Snow at The Oval	1966

RECORD WICKET PARTNERSHIPS—WEST INDIES

1st	173	G. Carew & A. G. Ganteaume at Port of Spain ...	1947-48
2nd	228	R. K. Nunes & G. A. Headley at Kingston	1929-30
3rd	338	E. D. Weekes & F. M. M. Worrell at Port of Spain	1953-54
4th	399	G. St. A. Sobers & F. M. M. Worrell at Bridgetown ...	1959-60
5th	265	S. M. Nurse & G. St. A. Sobers at Leeds	1966
6th	274*	G. St. A. Sobers & D. A. J. Holford at Lord's	1966
7th	154	O. G. Smith & J. D. C. Goddard at Nottingham ...	1957
8th	99	C. A. McWatt & J. K. Holt at Georgetown	1953-54
9th	36	C. C. Griffith & W. W. Hall at The Oval	1966
10th	55	F. M. M. Worrell & S. Ramadhin at Nottingham ...	1957

ENGLAND v. NEW ZEALAND

(The W. J. Jordan Trophy)

HIGHEST INNINGS TOTALS

England in England	546-4d at Leeds	1965
England in New Zealand ...	562-7d at Auckland	1962-63
New Zealand in England ...	484 at Lord's	1949
New Zealand in New Zealand	440 at Wellington	1929-30

LOWEST INNINGS TOTALS

England in England	187 at Manchester...	1937
England in New Zealand ...	181 at Christchurch	1929-30
New Zealand in England ...	47 at Lord's	1958
New Zealand in New Zealand	26 at Auckland	1954-55

Highest Match Aggregate ...	1293-34 wkts at Lord's	1931
Lowest Match Aggregate ...	390-30 wkts at Lord's	1958

Records for Individual Series—England v. New Zealand—*Cont.*

HIGHEST INDIVIDUAL INNINGS

England in England	310*	J. H. Edrich (Leeds) ...	1965
England in New Zealand ...	336*	W. R. Hammond (Auckland)	1932-33
New Zealand in England ...	206	M. P. Donnelly (Lord's) ...	1949
New Zealand in New Zealand	136	C. S. Dempster (Wellington)	1929-30

BEST INNINGS BOWLING ANALYSIS

England in England	7-35	G. A. R. Lock (Manchester)	1958
England in New Zealand ...	7-75	F. S. Trueman (Christchurch)	1962-63
New Zealand in England ...	6-67	J. A. Cowie (Manchester) ...	1937
New Zealand in New Zealand	6-83	J. A. Cowie (Christchurch)	1946-47

HIGHEST RUN AGGREGATE BY A BATSMAN IN A SERIES

England in England	469 (av. 78.16)	L. Hutton ...	1949
England in New Zealand ...	563 (av. 563.00)	W. R. Hammond	1932-33
New Zealand in England ...	462 (av. 77.00)	M. P. Donnelly ...	1949
New Zealand in New Zealand	341 (av. 85.25)	C. S. Dempster ...	1929-30

HIGHEST WICKET AGGREGATE BY A BOWLER IN A SERIES

England in England	34 (av. 7.47)	G. A. R. Lock ...	1958
England in New Zealand ...	17 (av. 9.34)	K. Higgs	1965-66
New Zealand in England ...	20 (av. 19.45)	A. R. MacGibbon	1958
New Zealand in New Zealand	9 (av. 19.00)	R. C. Blunt ...	1929-30

RECORD WICKET PARTNERSHIPS—ENGLAND

1st	147	L. Hutton & R. T. Simpson at The Oval	1949
2nd	369	J. H. Edrich & K. F. Barrington at Leeds	1965
3rd	245	J. Hardstaff, Jnr. & W. R. Hammond at Lord's ...	1937
4th	166	K. F. Barrington & M. C. Cowdrey at Auckland ...	1962-63
5th	242	W. R. Hammond & L. E. G. Ames at Christchurch ...	1932-33
6th	240	P. H. Parfitt & B. R. Knight at Auckland	1962-63
7th	108	F. R. Brown & W. Voce at Christchurch	1932-33
8th	246	L. E. G. Ames & G. O. Allen at Lord's	1931
9th	163*	M. C. Cowdrey & A. C. Smith at Wellington	1962-63
10th	41	K. F. Barrington & F. E. Rumsey at Birmingham ...	1965

RECORD WICKET PARTNERSHIPS—NEW ZEALAND

1st	276	C. S. Dempster & J. W. E. Mills at Wellington ...	1929-30
2nd	131	B. Sutcliffe & J. R. Reid at Christchurch	1950-51
3rd	118	C. S. Dempster & M. L. Page at Lord's	1931
4th	142	M. L. Page & R. C. Blunt at Lord's	1931
5th	120	M. P. Donnelly & F. B. Smith at Leeds	1949
6th	99	W. A. Hadlee & M. L. Page at Manchester	1937
7th	104	B. Sutcliffe & V. Pollard at Birmingham	1965
8th	104	D. A. R. Moloney & A. W. Roberts at Lord's... ...	1937
9th	64	J. A. Cowie & T. B. Burtt at Christchurch	1946-47
10th	57	F. L. H. Mooney & J. A. Cowie at Leeds	1949

Records for Individual Series—*Cont.*

ENGLAND v. INDIA

HIGHEST INNINGS TOTALS

England in England	571-8d at Manchester	1936
England in India	559-8d at Kanpur	1963-64
India in England	510 at Leeds	1967
India in India	485-9d at Bombay	1951-52

LOWEST INNINGS TOTALS

England in England	134 at Lord's	1936
England in India	183 at Madras[1]	1951-52
India in England	58 at Manchester	1952
India in India	121 at Kanpur	1951-52

Highest Match Aggregate	1350-28 wkts at Leeds	1967
Lowest Match Aggregate	482-31 wkts at Lord's	1936

HIGHEST INDIVIDUAL INNINGS

England in England	246*	G. Boycott (Leeds)	1967
England in India	175	T. W. Graveney (Bombay)	1951-52
India in England	184	V. M. Mankad (Lord's)	1952
India in India	203*	Nawab of Pataudi, Jnr. (New Delhi)	1963-64

BEST INNINGS BOWLING ANALYSIS

England in England	8-31	F. S. Trueman (Manchester)	1952
England in India	7-49	H. Verity (Madras[1])	1933-34
India in England	6-35	L. Amar Singh (Lord's)	1936
India in India	8-55	V. M. Mankad (Madras[1])	1951-52

HIGHEST RUN AGGREGATE BY A BATSMAN IN A SERIES

England in England	399	(av. 79.80)	L. Hutton	1952
England in India	594	(av. 99.00)	K. F. Barrington	1961-62
India in England	333	(av. 55.50)	Vijay Hazare	1952
India in India	586	(av. 83.71)	V. L. Manjrekar	1961-62

HIGHEST WICKET AGGREGATE BY A BOWLER IN A SERIES

England in England	29	(av. 13.31)	F. S. Trueman	1952
England in India	27	(av. 27.66)	F. J. Titmus	1963-64
India in England	17	(av. 34.64)	S. P. Gupte	1959
India in India	34	(av. 16.79)	V. M. Mankad	1951-52

RECORD WICKET PARTNERSHIPS—ENGLAND

1st	159	P. E. Richardson & G. Pullar at Bombay	1961-62
2nd	164	G. Pullar & K. F. Barrington at New Delhi	1961-62
3rd	169	R. Subba Row & M. J. K. Smith at The Oval	1959
4th	266	W. R. Hammond & T. S. Worthington at The Oval	1936
5th	182	J. Hardstaff, Jnr. & P. A. Gibb at Lord's	1946
6th	159	T. W. Graveney & T. G. Evans at Lord's	1952
7th	102	R. Illingworth & R. Swetman at The Oval	1959

Records for Individual Series—England v. India—*Cont.*

8th	138	R. W. V. Robins & H. Verity at Manchester	1936
9th	81	R. W. Barber & G. A. R. Lock at Kanpur	1961-62
10th	57	J. T. Murray & R. N. S. Hobbs at Birmingham ...	1967

RECORD WICKET PARTNERSHIPS—INDIA

1st	203	V. M. Merchant & Mushtaq Ali at Manchester ...	1936
2nd	168	F. M. Engineer & A. L. Wadekar at Leeds	1967
3rd	211	V. M. Merchant & Vijay Hazare at New Delhi ...	1951-52
		V. M. Mankad & Vijay Hazare at Lord's	1952
4th	222	Vijay Hazare & V. L. Manjrekar at Leeds	1952
5th	190*	Nawab of Pataudi, Jnr. & C. G. Borde at New Delhi	1963-64
6th	105	Vijay Hazare & D. G. Phadkar at Leeds	1952
7th	153	C. G. Borde & S. A. Durrani at Bombay	1963-64
8th	101	R. G. Nadkarni & F. M. Engineer at Madras[2] ...	1961-62
9th	54	G. S. Ramchand & S. G. Shinde at Lord's	1952
10th	51	R. G. Nadkarni & B. S. Chandrasekhar at Calcutta ...	1963-64

ENGLAND v. PAKISTAN

HIGHEST INNINGS TOTALS

England in England	558-6d at Nottingham	1954
England in Pakistan	507 at Karachi	1961-62
Pakistan in England	355 at Lord's	1962
Pakistan in Pakistan	404-8 at Karachi	1961-62

LOWEST INNINGS TOTALS

England in England	130 at The Oval	1954
England in Pakistan	380 at Lahore[2]	1961-62
Pakistan in England	87 at Lord's	1954
Pakistan in Pakistan	200 at Lahore[2]	1961-62

Highest Match Aggregate	1176-34 wkts at Lahore[2]	1961-62
Lowest Match Aggregate ...	325-22 wkts at Lord's	1954

HIGHEST INDIVIDUAL INNINGS

England in England	278	D. C. S. Compton (Nottingham)	1954
England in Pakistan	205	E. R. Dexter (Karachi) ...	1961-62
Pakistan in England	187*	Hanif Mohammad (Lord's)	1967
Pakistan in Pakistan	140	Javed Burki (Dacca) ...	1961-62

BEST INNINGS BOWLING ANALYSIS

England in England	7-56	J. H. Wardle (Oval) ...	1954
England in Pakistan	5-30	D. A. Allen (Dacca)... ...	1961-62
Pakistan in England	6-46	Fazal Mahmood (Oval) ...	1954
Pakistan in Pakistan	5-112	Antao D'Souza (Karachi) ...	1961-62

HIGHEST RUN AGGREGATE BY A BATSMAN IN A SERIES

England in England	453 (av. 90.60)	D. C. S. Compton	1954
England in Pakistan	303 (av. 101.00)	E. R. Dexter ...	1961-62
Pakistan in England	401 (av. 44.55)	Mushtaq Mohammad	1962
Pakistan in Pakistan	407 (av. 67.83)	Hanif Mohammad	1961-62

Records for Individual Series—England v. Pakistan—*Cont.*

HIGHEST WICKET AGGREGATE BY A BOWLER IN A SERIES

England in England	22 (av. 19.69) F. S. Trueman ...	1962
England in Pakistan	13 (av. 25.69) D. A. Allen ...	1961-62
Pakistan in England	20 (av. 20.40) Fazal Mahmood ...	1954
Pakistan in Pakistan	9 (av. 22.88) Antao D'Souza ...	1961-62

RECORD WICKET PARTNERSHIPS—ENGLAND

1st	198	G. Pullar & R. W. Barber at Dacca	1961-62
2nd	248	M. C. Cowdrey & E. R. Dexter at The Oval	1962
3rd	201	K. F. Barrington & T. W. Graveney at Lord's... ...	1967
4th	188	E. R. Dexter & P. H. Parfitt at Karachi	1961-62
5th	192	D. C. S. Compton & T. E. Bailey at Nottingham ...	1954
6th	153	P. H. Parfitt & D. A. Allen at Birmingham	1962
7th	67	P. H. Parfitt & J. T. Murray at Leeds	1962
8th	99	P. H. Parfitt & D. A. Allen at Leeds	1962
9th	76	T. W. Graveney & F. S. Trueman at Lord's	1962
10th	51	D. A. Allen & J. B. Statham at Leeds	1962

RECORD WICKET PARTNERSHIPS—PAKISTAN

1st	122	Hanif Mohammad & Alim-ud-Din at Dacca	1961-62
2nd	137	Imtiaz Ahmed & Mushtaq Mohammad at The Oval...	1962
3rd	156	Hanif Mohammad & Javed Burki at Dacca	1961-62
4th	153	Javed Burki & Mushtaq Mohammad at Lahore[2] ...	1961-62
5th	197	Javed Burki & Nasim-ul-Ghani at Lord's	1962
6th	81	Imtiaz Ahmed & Mushtaq Mohammad at Karachi ...	1961-62
7th	51	Saeed Ahmed & Nasim-ul-Ghani at Nottingham ...	1962
8th	130	Hanif Mohammad & Asif Iqbal at Lord's	1967
9th	190	Asif Iqbal & Intikhab Alam at The Oval	1967
10th	52	Afaq Hussain & Haseeb Ahsan at Lahore[2]	1961-62

AUSTRALIA v. SOUTH AFRICA

HIGHEST INNINGS TOTALS

Australia in Australia	578 at Melbourne	1910-11
Australia in South Africa ...	549-7d at Port Elizabeth	1949-50
South Africa in Australia ...	595 at Adelaide	1963-64
South Africa in South Africa ...	620 at Johannesburg[3]	1966-67

LOWEST INNINGS TOTALS

Australia in Australia	153 at Melbourne	1931-32
Australia in South Africa ...	76 at Durban[2]	1949-50
South Africa in Australia ...	36 at Melbourne	1931-32
South Africa in South Africa ...	85 at Johannesburg[1] and Cape Town	1902-03

Highest Match Aggregate ...	1646-40 wkts at Adelaide ...	1910-11
Lowest Match Aggregate ...	234-29 wkts at Melbourne ...	1931-32

HIGHEST INDIVIDUAL INNINGS

Australia in Australia	299*	D. G. Bradman (Adelaide)	1931-32
Australia in South Africa ...	203	H. L. Collins (Johannesburg[1])	1921-22
South Africa in Australia ...	204	G. A. Faulkner (Melbourne)	1910-11
South Africa in South Africa ...	231	A. D. Nourse, Jnr. (Johannesburg[1]) ...	1935-36

Records for Individual Series—Australia v. South Africa—*Cont.*

BEST INNINGS BOWLING ANALYSIS

Australia in Australia	7-83 C. V. Grimmett (Adelaide)...	1931-32
Australia in South Africa ...	7-34 J. V. Saunders (Johannesburg[1])	1902-03
South Africa in Australia ...	7-81 H. J. Tayfield (Melbourne)	1952-53
South Africa in South Africa ...	7-23 H. J. Tayfield (Durban[2]) ...	1949-50

HIGHEST RUN AGGREGATE BY A BATSMAN IN A SERIES

Australia in Australia	834 (av. 92.66) R. N. Harvey ...	1952-53
Australia in South Africa ...	660 (av. 132.00) R. N. Harvey ...	1949-50
South Africa in Australia ...	732 (av. 73.20) G. A. Faulkner ...	1910-11
South Africa in South Africa ...	606 (av. 86.57) D. Lindsay ...	1966-67

HIGHEST WICKET AGGREGATE BY A BOWLER IN A SERIES

Australia in Australia	37 (av. 17.08) W. J. Whitty ...	1910-11
Australia in South Africa ...	44 (av. 14.59) C. V. Grimmett ...	1935-36
South Africa in Australia ...	30 (av. 28.10) H. J. Tayfield ...	1952-53
South Africa in South Africa ...	26 (av. 16.23) T. L. Goddard ...	1966-67

RECORD WICKET PARTNERSHIPS—AUSTRALIA

1st	233	J. H. Fingleton & W. A. Brown at Cape Town ...	1935-36
2nd	275	C. C. McDonald & A. L. Hassett at Adelaide	1952-53
3rd	242	W. Bardsley & C. E. Kelleway at Lord's	1912
4th	168	R. N. Harvey & K. R. Miller at Sydney	1952-53
5th	143	W. W. Armstrong & V. T. Trumper at Melbourne ...	1910-11
6th	107	C. E. Kelleway & V. S. Ransford at Melbourne ...	1910-11
7th	160	R. Benaud & G. D. McKenzie at Sydney	1963-64
8th	83	A. G. Chipperfield & C. V. Grimmett at Durban[2] ...	1935-36
9th	78	D. G. Bradman & W. J. O'Reilly at Adelaide ...	1931-32
	78	K. D. Mackay & I. W. Meckiff at Johannesburg[3] ...	1957-58
10th	82	V. S. Ransford & W. J. Whitty at Melbourne	1910-11

RECORD WICKET PARTNERSHIPS—SOUTH AFRICA

1st	176	D. J. McGlew & T. L. Goddard at Johannesburg[3] ...	1957-58
2nd	173	L. J. Tancred & C. B. Llewellyn at Johannesburg[1] ...	1902-03
3rd	341	E. J. Barlow & R. G. Pollock at Adelaide	1963-64
4th	206	C. N. Frank & A. D. Nourse, Snr. at Johannesburg[1] ...	1921-22
5th	129	J. H. B. Waite & W. R. Endean at Johannesburg[3] ...	1957-58
6th	118	K. C. Bland & D. Lindsay at Sydney	1963-64
7th	221	D. Lindsay & P. L. Van der Merwe at Johannesburg[3]	1966-67
8th	124	A. D. Nourse, Snr. & E. A. Halliwell at Johannesburg[1]	1902-03
9th	85	R. G. Pollock & P. M. Pollock at Cape Town ...	1966-67
10th	53	S. J. Pegler & L. A. Stricker at Adelaide	1910-11

AUSTRALIA v. WEST INDIES

(*The Sir Frank Worrell Trophy*)

HIGHEST INNINGS TOTALS

Australia in Australia	558 at Brisbane[1]	1930-31
Australia in West Indies ...	758-8d at Kingston	1954-55
West Indies in Australia ...	453 at Brisbane[2]	1960-61
West Indies in West Indies ...	573 at Bridgetown...	1964-65

Records for Individual Series—Australia v. West Indies—*Cont.*

LOWEST INNINGS TOTALS

Australia in Australia ...	82 at Adelaide	1951-52
Australia in West Indies	144 at Georgetown	1964-65
West Indies in Australia	78 at Sydney	1951-52
West Indies in West Indies	131 at Port of Spain	1964-65

Highest Match Aggregate ...	1661-36 wkts at Bridgetown ...	1954-55
Lowest Match Aggregate... ...	534-28 wkts at Melbourne ...	1930-31

HIGHEST INDIVIDUAL INNINGS

Australia in Australia ...	223 D. G. Bradman (Brisbane[1]) ...	1930-31
Australia in West Indies	210 W. M. Lawry (Bridgetown)...	1964-65
West Indies in Australia	168 G. St. A. Sobers (Sydney) ...	1960-61
West Indies in West Indies	219 D. Atkinson (Bridgetown) ...	1954-55

BEST INNINGS BOWLING ANALYSIS

Australia in Australia ...	7-23 H. Ironmonger (Melbourne)	1930-31
Australia in West Indies	7-44 I. W. Johnson (Georgetown)	1954-55
West Indies in Australia	7-55 G. E. Gomez (Sydney) ...	1951-52
West Indies in West Indies	6-29 L. R. Gibbs (Georgetown) ...	1964-65

HIGHEST RUN AGGREGATE BY A BATSMAN IN A SERIES

Australia in Australia ...	522 (av. 52.20) N. C. O'Neill ...	1960-61
Australia in West Indies	650 (av. 108.33) R. N. Harvey ...	1954-55
West Indies in Australia	503 (av. 50.30) R. B. Kanhai ...	1960-61
West Indies in West Indies	827 (av. 82.70) C. L. Walcott ...	1954-55

HIGHEST WICKET AGGREGATE BY A BOWLER IN A SERIES

Australia in Australia ...	33 (av. 17.96) C. V. Grimmett ...	1930-31
	33 (av. 18.54) A. K. Davidson ...	1960-61
Australia in West Indies	24 (av. 21.83) N. J. N. Hawke ...	1964-65
West Indies in Australia	24 (av. 28.79) A. L. Valentine ...	1951-52
West Indies in West Indies	18 (av. 30.83) L. R. Gibbs ...	1964-65

RECORD WICKET PARTNERSHIPS—AUSTRALIA

1st	382	W. M. Lawry & R. B. Simpson at Bridgetown ...	1964-65
2nd	229	W. H. Ponsford & D. G. Bradman at Brisbane[1] ...	1930-31
3rd	295	C. C. McDonald & R. N. Harvey at Kingston ...	1954-55
4th	235	A. L. Hassett & K. R. Miller at Sydney	1951-52
5th	220	K. R. Miller & R. G. Archer at Kingston	1954-55
6th	206	K. R. Miller & R. G. Archer at Bridgetown	1954-55
7th	134	R. Benaud & A. K. Davidson at Brisbane[2]	1960-61
8th	137	R. Benaud & I. W. Johnson at Kingston	1954-55
9th	97	K. D. Mackay & J. W. Martin at Melbourne	1960-61
10th	66*	K. D. Mackay & L. F. Kline at Adelaide	1960-61

RECORD WICKET PARTNERSHIPS—WEST INDIES

1st	145	C. C. Hunte & B. A. Davis at Bridgetown	1964-65
2nd	163	C. C. Hunte & R. B. Kanhai at Adelaide	1960-61
3rd	242	C. L. Walcott & E. D. Weekes at Port of Spain ...	1954-55
4th	179	C. L. Walcott & G. St. A Sobers at Kingston	1954-55

Records for Individual Series—Australia v. West Indies—*Cont.*

5th	128	G. St. A. Sobers & S. M. Nurse at Sydney	1960-61
6th	138	C. L. Walcott & O. G. Smith at Kingston	1954-55
7th	347	D. Atkinson & C. C. Depeiza at Bridgetown	1954-55
8th	74	F. C. M. Alexander & L. R. Gibbs at Sydney ...	1960-61
9th	86	F. C. M. Alexander & W. W. Hall at Brisbane[2] ...	1960-61
10th	31	W. W. Hall & A. L. Valentine at Brisbane[2]	1960-61

AUSTRALIA v. INDIA

HIGHEST INNINGS TOTALS

Australia in Australia	674 at Adelaide	1947-48
Australia in India	523-7d at Bombay	1956-57
India in Australia	381 at Adelaide	1947-48
India in India	341 at Bombay	1964-65

LOWEST INNINGS TOTALS

Australia in Australia	107 at Sydney	1947-48
Australia in India	105 at Kanpur	1959-60
India in Australia	58 at Brisbane[2]	1947-48
India in India	135 at New Delhi	1959-60

Highest Match Aggregate ...	1332-30 wkts at Adelaide	1947-48
Lowest Match Aggregate ...	356-27 wkts at Sydney	1947-48

HIGHEST INDIVIDUAL INNINGS

Australia in Australia	201	D. G. Bradman (Adelaide)	1947-48
Australia in India	163	N. C. O'Neill (Bombay) ...	1959-60
India in Australia	145	Vijay Hazare (Adelaide) ...	1947-48
India in India	128*	Nawab of Pataudi, Jnr. (Madras[2])	1964-65

BEST INNINGS BOWLING ANALYSIS

Australia in Australia	7-38	R. R. Lindwall (Adelaide) ...	1947-48
Australia in India	7-43	R. R. Lindwall (Madras[2]) ...	1956-57
India in Australia	4-29	Vijay Hazare (Sydney) ...	1947-48
India in India	9-69	J. S. Patel (Kanpur)... ...	1959-60

HIGHEST RUN AGGREGATE BY A BATSMAN IN A SERIES

Australia in Australia	715 (av. 178.75)	D. G. Bradman	1947-48
Australia in India	376 (av. 62.66)	N. C. O'Neill ...	1959-60
India in Australia	429 (av. 47.66)	Vijay Hazare ...	1947-48
India in India	438 (av. 43.80)	N. J. Contractor...	1959-60

HIGHEST WICKET AGGREGATE BY A BOWLER IN A SERIES

Australia in Australia	18 (av. 16.88)	R. R. Lindwall ...	1947-48
Australia in India	29 (av. 15.17)	A. K. Davidson ...	1959-60
	29 (av. 19.58)	R. Benaud ...	1959-60
India in Australia	13 (av. 28.15)	L. Amarnath ...	1947-48
India in India	19 (av. 17.21)	J. S. Patel	1959-60

Records for Individual Series—Australia v. India—*Cont.*

RECORD WICKET PARTNERSHIPS—AUSTRALIA

1st	115	W. M. Lawry & R. B. Simpson at Calcutta	1964-65
2nd	236	S. G. Barnes & D. G. Bradman at Adelaide	1947-48
3rd	207	R. N. Harvey & N. C. O'Neill at Bombay	1959-60
4th	159	R. N. Harvey & S. J. E. Loxton at Melbourne ...	1947-48
5th	223*	A. R. Morris & D. G. Bradman at Melbourne... ...	1947-48
6th	151	T. R. Veivers & B. N. Jarman at Bombay	1964-65
7th	64	T. R. Veivers & J. W. Martin at Madras[2]	1964-65
8th	73	T. R. Veivers & G. D. McKenzie at Madras[2]	1964-65
9th	87	I. W. Johnson & P. Crawford at Madras[2]	1956-57
10th	33	A. L. Hassett & E. R. H. Toshack at Adelaide ...	1947-48

RECORD WICKET PARTNERSHIPS—INDIA

1st	124	V. M. Mankad & C. T. Sarwate at Melbourne ...	1947-48
2nd	124	V. M. Mankad & H. R. Adhikari at Melbourne ...	1947-48
3rd	133	N. J. Contractor & A. A. Baig at Bombay	1959-60
4th	66	Vijay Hazare & Gul Mahomed at Adelaide	1947-48
5th	109	A. A. Baig & R. B. Kenny at Bombay	1959-60
6th	188	Vijay Hazare & D. G. Phadkar at Adelaide	1947-48
7th	132	Vijay Hazare & H. R. Adhikari at Adelaide	1947-48
8th	38	Hanumant Singh & R. G. Nadkarni at Madras[2] ...	1964-65
	38	Nawab of Pataudi, Jnr. & R. G. Nadkarni at Bombay	1964-65
9th	45	D. G. Phadkar & P. Sen at Melbourne...	1947-48
10th	39	C. G. Borde & B. S. Chandrasekhar at Calcutta ...	1964-65

SOUTH AFRICA v. NEW ZEALAND

HIGHEST INNINGS TOTALS

South Africa in South Africa ...	464 at Johannesburg[3]	1961-62
South Africa in New Zealand	524-8d at Wellington	1952-53
New Zealand in South Africa	505 at Cape Town	1953-54
New Zealand in New Zealand	364 at Wellington	1931-32

LOWEST INNINGS TOTALS

South Africa in South Africa ...	148 at Johannesburg[2]	1953-54
South Africa in New Zealand	223 at Dunedin	1963-64
New Zealand in South Africa	79 at Johannesburg[2]	1953-54
New Zealand in New Zealand	138 at Dunedin	1963-64

Highest Match Aggregate ...	1122-39 wkts at Cape Town ...	1961-62
Lowest Match Aggregate ...	535-31 wkts at Johannesburg[2] ...	1953-54

HIGHEST INDIVIDUAL INNINGS

South Africa in South Africa ...	127*	D. J. McGlew (Durban[2]) ...	1961-62
South Africa in New Zealand	255*	D. J. McGlew (Wellington)	1952-53
New Zealand in South Africa	142	J. R. Reid (Johannesburg[3])	1961-62
New Zealand in New Zealand	138	B. W. Sinclair (Auckland) ...	1963-64

Records for Individual Series—South Africa v. New Zealand—*Cont.*

BEST INNINGS BOWLING ANALYSIS

South Africa in South Africa ...	8-53 G. B. Lawrence (Johannesburg[3]) ...	1961-62
South Africa in New Zealand	6-47 P. M. Pollock (Wellington)	1963-64
New Zealand in South Africa	6-68 G. O. Rabone (Cape Town)	1953-54
New Zealand in New Zealand	6-60 J. R. Reid (Dunedin) ...	1963-64

HIGHEST RUN AGGREGATE BY A BATSMAN IN A SERIES

South Africa in South Africa ...	426 (av. 60.85) D. J. McGlew ...	1961-62
South Africa in New Zealand	323 (av. 161.50) D. J. McGlew ...	1952-53
New Zealand in South Africa	546 (av. 60.64) J. R. Reid ...	1961-62
New Zealand in New Zealand	264 (av. 44.00) B. W. Sinclair ...	1963-64

HIGHEST WICKET AGGREGATE BY A BOWLER IN A SERIES

South Africa in South Africa ...	28 (av. 18.28) G. B. Lawrence ...	1961-62
South Africa in New Zealand	16 (av. 20.18) Q. McMillan ...	1931-32
New Zealand in South Africa	22 (av. 20.63) A. R. MacGibbon	1953-54
	22 (av. 28.04) J. C. Alabaster ...	1961-62
New Zealand in New Zealand	12 (av. 23.16) J. R. Reid	1963-64
	12 (av. 27.16) R. W. Blair ...	1963-64

RECORD WICKET PARTNERSHIPS—SOUTH AFRICA

1st	196	J. A. J. Christy & B. Mitchell at Christchurch... ...	1931-32
2nd	76	J. A. J. Christy & H. B. Cameron at Wellington ...	1931-32
3rd	112	D. J. McGlew & R. A. McLean at Johannesburg[3] ...	1961-62
4th	135	K. J. Funston & R. A. McLean at Durban[2]	1953-54
5th	130	W. R. Endean & J. E. Cheetham at Auckland ...	1952-53
6th	79	E. L. Dalton & D. P. B. Morkel at Christchurch ...	1931-32
7th	246	D. J. McGlew & A. R. A. Murray at Wellington ...	1952-53
8th	95	J. E. Cheetham & H. J. Tayfield at Cape Town ...	1953-54
9th	60	P. M. Pollock & N. A. T. Adcock at Port Elizabeth ...	1961-62
10th	47	D. J. McGlew & H. D. Bromfield at Port Elizabeth ...	1961-62

RECORD WICKET PARTNERSHIPS—NEW ZEALAND

1st	126	G. O. Rabone & M. E. Chapple at Cape Town ...	1953-54
2nd	44	S. N. McGregor & J. T. Sparling at Cape Town ...	1961-62
3rd	94	M. E. Chapple & B. Sutcliffe at Cape Town	1953-54
4th	171	B. W. Sinclair & S. N. McGregor at Auckland ...	1963-64
5th	174	J. R. Reid & J. E. F. Beck at Cape Town	1953-54
6th	100	H. G. Vivian & F. T. Badcock at Wellington	1931-32
7th	84	J. R. Reid & G. A. Bartlett at Johannesburg[2]	1961-62
8th	73	P. G. Z. Harris & G. A. Bartlett at Durban[2]	1961-62
9th	69	C. F. W. Alcott & I. B. Cromb at Wellington	1931-32
10th	49*	A. E. Dick & F. J. Cameron at Cape Town	1961-62

WEST INDIES v. INDIA

HIGHEST INNINGS TOTALS

West Indies in West Indies ...	631-8d at Kingston	1961-62
West Indies in India	644-8d at New Delhi	1958-59
India in West Indies	444 at Kingston	1952-53
India in India	454 at New Delhi	1948-49

Records for Individual Series—West Indies v. India—*Cont.*

LOWEST INNINGS TOTALS

West Indies in West Indies ...	228 at Bridgetown	1952-53
West Indies in India	222 at Kanpur	1958-59
India in West Indies	98 at Port of Spain	1961-62
India in India	124 at Calcutta	1958-59

Highest Match Aggregate ...	1424-33 wkts at Kingston ...	1952-53
Lowest Match Aggregate... ...	605-30 wkts at Port of Spain ...	1961-62

HIGHEST INDIVIDUAL INNINGS

West Indies in West Indies ...	237	F. M. M. Worrell (Kingston)	1952-53
West Indies in India	256	R. B. Kanhai (Calcutta) ...	1958-59
India in West Indies	172*	P. R. Umrigar (Port of Spain)	1961-62
India in India	134*	Vijay Hazare (Bombay) ...	1948-49

BEST INNINGS BOWLING ANALYSIS

West Indies in West Indies ...	8-38	L. R. Gibbs (Bridgetown)...	1961-62
West Indies in India	6-50	W. W. Hall (Kanpur) ...	1958-59
India in West Indies	7-162	S. P. Gupte (Port of Spain)	1952-53
India in India	9-102	S. P. Gupte (Kanpur) ...	1958-59

HIGHEST RUN AGGREGATE BY A BATSMAN IN A SERIES

West Indies in West Indies ...	716 (av. 102.28) E. D. Weekes ...	1952-53
West Indies in India	779 (av. 111.28) E. D. Weekes ...	1948-49
India in West Indies	560 (av. 62.22) P. R. Umrigar ...	1952-53
India in India	560 (av. 56.00) R. S. Modi ...	1948-49

HIGHEST WICKET AGGREGATE BY A BOWLER IN A SERIES

West Indies in West Indies ...	28 (av. 29.57) A. L. Valentine ...	1952-53
West Indies in India	30 (av. 17.66) W. W. Hall ...	1958-59
India in West Indies	27 (av. 29.22) S. P. Gupte ...	1952-53
India in India	22 (av. 42.13) S. P. Gupte ...	1958-59

RECORD WICKET PARTNERSHIPS—WEST INDIES

1st	239	J. B. Stollmeyer & A. F. Rae at Madras[1]	1948-49
2nd	255	E. D. A. McMorris & R. B. Kanhai at Kingston ...	1961-62
3rd	197	F. M. M. Worrell & E. D. Weekes at Kingston ...	1952-53
4th	267	C. L. Walcott & G. E. Gomez at New Delhi	1948-49
5th	219	E. D. Weekes & B. H. Pairaudeau at Port of Spain ...	1952-53
6th	163	G. St. A. Sobers & J. S. Solomon at Kanpur	1958-59
7th	127	G. St. A. Sobers & I. Mendonca at Kingston	1961-62
8th	80	F. M. M. Worrell & R. B. Kanhai at Kingston ...	1961-62
9th	106	R. J. Christiani & D. Atkinson at New Delhi	1948-49
10th	98*	F. M. M. Worrell & W. W. Hall at Port of Spain ...	1961-62

RECORD WICKET PARTNERSHIPS—INDIA

1st	129	D. N. Sardesai & F. M. Engineer at Madras[1]	1966-67
2nd	237	P. Roy & V. L. Manjrekar at Kingston	1952-53
3rd	156	R. S. Modi & Vijay Hazare at Bombay	1948-49
4th	150	P. Roy & P. R. Umrigar at Kingston	1952-53
5th	131	P. R. Umrigar & D. G. Phadkar at Port of Spain ...	1952-53
6th	134	C. G. Borde & H. R. Adhikari at New Delhi	1958-59

Records for Individual Series—West Indies v. India—*Cont.*

7th	153	M. L. Apte & V. M. Mankad at Port of Spain ...	1952-53
8th	94	R. G. Nadkarni & F. M. Engineer at Kingston ...	1961-62
9th	95	B. K. Kunderan & S. Venkataraghavan at Bombay ...	1966-67
10th	51	P. R. Umrigar & B. K. Kunderan at Port of Spain ...	1961-62

INDIA v. PAKISTAN

HIGHEST INNINGS TOTALS

India in India	539-9d at Madras[2]...	1960-61
India in Pakistan	251 at Lahore[1]	1954-55
Pakistan in India	448-8d at Madras[2]...	1960-61
Pakistan in Pakistan	328 at Lahore[1]	1954-55

LOWEST INNINGS TOTALS

India in India	106 at Lucknow	1952-53
India in Pakistan	145 at Karachi	1954-55
Pakistan in India	150 at New Delhi	1952-53
Pakistan in Pakistan	158 at Dacca	1954-55

Highest Match Aggregate ...	1046-17 wkts at Madras[2]	1960-61
Lowest Match Aggregate ...	617-27 wkts at Karachi	1954-55

HIGHEST INDIVIDUAL INNINGS

India in India	177* C. G. Borde (Madras[2]) ...	1960-61
India in Pakistan	108 P. R. Umrigar (Peshawar)...	1954-55
Pakistan in India	160 Hanif Mohammad (Bombay)	1960-61
Pakistan in Pakistan	142 Hanif Mohammad (Bahawalpur) ...	1954-55

BEST INNINGS BOWLING ANALYSIS

India in India	8-52 V. M. Mankad (New Delhi)	1952-53
India in Pakistan	6-49 G. S. Ramchand (Karachi)	1954-55
Pakistan in India	7-42 Fazal Mahmood (Lucknow)	1952-53
Pakistan in Pakistan	6-67 Mahmood Hussain (Dacca)	1954-55

HIGHEST RUN AGGREGATE BY A BATSMAN IN A SERIES

India in India	382 (av. 63.66) P. R. Umrigar ...	1960-61
India in Pakistan	272 (av. 34.00) P. Roy	1954-55
Pakistan in India	460 (av. 51.11) Saeed Ahmed ...	1960-61
Pakistan in Pakistan	332 (av. 41.50) Alim-ud-Din ...	1954-55

HIGHEST WICKET AGGREGATE BY A BOWLER IN A SERIES

India in India	25 (av. 20.56) V. M. Mankad ...	1952-53
India in Pakistan	21 (av. 22.61) S. P. Gupte ...	1954-55
Pakistan in India	20 (av. 25.51) Fazal Mahmood ...	1952-53
Pakistan in Pakistan	22 (av. 15.86) Khan Mohammad	1954-55

RECORD WICKET PARTNERSHIPS—INDIA

1st	84	M. L. Jaisimha & N. J. Contractor at Madras[2] ...	1960-61
2nd	107	N. J. Contractor & R. F. Surti at New Delhi	1960-61
3rd	130*	P. Roy & V. L. Manjrekar at Dacca	1954-55
4th	183	Vijay Hazare & P. R. Umrigar at Bombay	1952-53

Records for Individual Series—India v. Pakistan—*Cont.*

5th	177	P. R. Umrigar & C. G. Borde at Madras[2]	1960-61
6th	82	C. G. Borde & R. G. Nadkarni at Bombay	1960-61
7th	86	D. G. Phadkar & D. H. Shodhan at Calcutta	1952-53
8th	82	G. S. Ramchand & N. S. Tamhane at Bahawalpur ...	1954-55
9th	149	P. G. Joshi & R. B. Desai at Bombay	1960-61
10th	109	H. R. Adhikari & Ghulam Ahmed at New Delhi ...	1952-53

RECORD WICKET PARTNERSHIPS—PAKISTAN

1st	162	Hanif Mohammad & Imtiaz Ahmed at Madras[2] ...	1960-61
2nd	246	Hanif Mohammad & Saeed Ahmed at Bombay ...	1960-61
3rd	82	Hanif Mohammad & Javed Burki at Calcutta... ...	1960-61
4th	136	Maqsood Ahmed & A. H. Kardar at Lahore[1]	1954-55
5th	155	Alim-ud-Din & A. H. Kardar at Karachi	1954-55
6th	84	Wazir Mohammad & Imtiaz Ahmed at Lahore[1] ...	1954-55
7th	88	Mushtaq Mohammad & Intikhab Alam at Calcutta ...	1960-61
8th	63	Nazar Mohammad & Zulfiqar Ahmed at Lucknow ...	1952-53
9th	31	A. H. Kardar & Khan Mohammad at New Delhi ...	1952-53
10th	104	Zulfiqar Ahmed & Amir Elahi at Madras[1]	1952-53

MISCELLANEOUS RECORDS

MOST CONSECUTIVE TEST APPEARANCES

59 G. St. A. Sobers (West Indies): Port of Spain 1954-55 to date.
58 J. R. Reid (New Zealand): Manchester 1949 to Leeds 1965.
52 F. E. Woolley (England): Oval 1909 to Oval 1926.
52 P. B. H. May (England): Oval 1953 to Leeds 1959.
51 R. B. Kanhai (West Indies): Birmingham 1957 to date.
48 V. T. Trumper (Australia): Nottingham 1899 to Sydney 1911-12.

The most consecutive appearances for the other countries are:—

South Africa: 45 A. D. Nourse, Snr.—Johannesburg[1] 1902-03 to Oval 1924.
India: 41 P. R. Umrigar—New Delhi 1951-52 to Manchester 1959.
Pakistan: 39 Imtiaz Ahmed—New Delhi 1952-53 to Lord's 1962.

MOST TEST APPEARANCES

	Player	*Caps*	*No. of players with 50 caps*
England:	M. C. Cowdrey	92	18
Australia:	R. N. Harvey	79	9
South Africa:	J. H. B. Waite	50	1
West Indies:	G. St. A. Sobers	60	3
New Zealand:	J. R. Reid	58	1
India:	P. R. Umrigar	59	2
Pakistan:	Hanif Mohammad	51	1
			35

PLAYERS WHO HAVE REPRESENTED TWO COUNTRIES (12)

Amir Elahi	...	India (1947-48) and Pakistan (1952-53)
J. J. Ferris	...	Australia (1886-87 to 1890) and England (1891-92)
S. C. Guillen	...	West Indies (1951-52) and New Zealand (1955-56)

Players who have Represented Two Countries (12)—*Cont.*

Gul Mahomed ...	India (1946 to 1952-53) and Pakistan (1956-57)
F. Hearne ...	England (1888-89) and South Africa (1891 to 1895-96)
A. H. Kardar ...	India (1946) and Pakistan (1952-53 to 1957-58)
W. E. Midwinter	Australia (1876-77 to 1886-87) and England (1881-82)
F. Mitchell ...	England (1898-99) and South Africa (1912)
W. L. Murdoch ...	Australia (1876-77 to 1890) and England (1891-92)
Nawab of Pataudi, Snr.	England (1932-33 to 1934) and India (1946)
A. E. Trott ...	Australia (1894-95) and England (1898-99)
S. M. J. Woods ...	Australia (1888) and England (1895-96)

YOUNGEST TEST PLAYERS

Years	*Days*	*Player*	*Debut Match*
15	124	Mushtaq Mohammad	Pakistan v. West Indies, Lahore[1], 1958-59
16	248	Nasim-ul-Ghani ...	Pakistan v. West Indies, Bridgetown, 1957-58
16	352	Khalid Hassan ...	Pakistan v. England, Nottingham, 1954
17	122	J. E. D. Sealy ...	West Indies v. England, Bridgetown, 1929-30
17	239	I. D. Craig ...	Australia v. South Africa, Melbourne, 1952-53
17	245	G. St. A. Sobers ...	West Indies v. England, Kingston, 1953-54
17	265	V. L. Mehra ...	India v. New Zealand, Bombay, 1955-56
17	300	Hanif Mohammad	Pakistan v. India, New Delhi, 1952-53
18	26	Majid Jahangir ...	Pakistan v. Australia, Karachi, 1964-65
18	31	M. R. Bynoe ...	West Indies v. Pakistan, Lahore[1], 1958-59
18	41	Salah-ud-Din ...	Pakistan v. New Zealand, Rawalpindi, 1964-65
18	44	Khalid Wazir ...	Pakistan v. England, Lord's, 1954
18	105	J. B. Stollmeyer ...	West Indies v. England, Lord's, 1939
18	149	D. B. Close ...	England v. New Zealand, Manchester, 1949
18	173	A. Roberts	West Indies v. New Zealand, Auckland, 1955-56
18	186	Haseeb Ahsan ...	Pakistan v. West Indies, Bridgetown, 1957-58
18	197	D. L. Freeman ...	New Zealand v. England, Christchurch, 1932-33
18	232	T. W. Garrett ...	Australia v. England, Melbourne, 1876-77
18	249	B. S. Chandrasekhar	India v. England, Bombay, 1963-64
18	267	H. G. Vivian ...	New Zealand v. England, Oval, 1931

OLDEST TEST PLAYERS ON DEBUT

Years	*Days*	*Player*	*Debut Match*
49	119	J. Southerton ...	England v. Australia, Melbourne, 1876-77
47	275	Miran Bux	Pakistan v. India, Lahore[1], 1954-55
46	273	D. D. J. Blackie ...	Australia v. England, Sydney, 1928-29
41	337	E. R. Wilson ...	England v. Australia, Sydney, 1920-21
41	275	H. Ironmonger ...	Australia v. England, Brisbane[1], 1928-29
41	28	R. J. Jamshedji ...	India v. England, Bombay[1], 1933-34
40	346	C. A. Wiles... ...	West Indies v. England, Manchester, 1933
40	110	H. W. Lee	England v. South Africa, Johannesburg[1], 1930-31
40	56	G. W. A. Chubb ...	South Africa v. England, Nottingham, 1951
40	37	C. Ramaswami ...	India v. England, Manchester, 1936
39	361	G. Challenor ...	West Indies v. England, Lord's, 1928
39	360	A. Wood	England v. Australia, Oval, 1938
39	306	B. M. Gaskin ...	West Indies v. England, Bridgetown, 1947-48

RELATED TEST PLAYERS

FATHER AND SON

Gregory, E. J. and S. E. (Australia)
Hardstaff, J., Snr. and Jnr. (England)
Hearne, F. (England and South Africa) and G. A. L. (South Africa)
Jahangir Khan (India) and Majid Jahangir (Pakistan)
Lindsay, J. D. and D. (South Africa)
Mann, F. T. and F. G. (England)—both captained England
Nourse, A. D., Snr. and Jnr. (South Africa)
Parks, J. H. and J. M. (England)
Scott, O. C. and A. P. H. (West Indies)
Tate, F. W. and M. W. (England)
Townsend, C. L. and D. C. H. (England)
Tuckett, L. R. and L. (South Africa)
Vivian, H. G. and G. E. (New Zealand)

BROTHERS

There are many instances of two brothers playing for their country but only four families have provided three:—
Grace, E. M., G. F. and W. G. (England)
Hearne, A., F. and G. G. (England)
Mohammad, Hanif, Mushtaq and Wazir (Pakistan)
Tancred, A. B., L. J. and V. M. (South Africa)

All three brothers Grace played in the very first Test to be played in England (Oval, 1880)—no other family has provided three players in one match.

There are two instances of brothers captaining their country:—

Gilligan, A. E. R. and A. H. H. (England)
Grant, G. C. and R. S. (West Indies)

PLAYERS ON FIELD ENTIRE MATCH

Nazar Mohammad — Pakistan v. India (Lucknow) 1952-53
He carried his bat for 124* through an innings total of 331 in 8 hours 35 minutes. The match ended after 15 minutes play on the fourth day.

D. J. McGlew ... South Africa v. New Zealand (Wellington) ... 1952-53
He scored 255* out of a total of 524-8d and the match ended after 3½ days.

J. H. Edrich ... England v. New Zealand (Leeds) 1967
He scored 310* out of a total of 546-4d and the match ended after 15 minutes play on the fifth day.

UMPIRES

Only six umpires have officiated in more than 25 Test Matches.

Tests	*Umpire*	*Venue of Tests*	*First Series*	*Last Series*
48	F. Chester	England	1924	1955
33	R. W. Crockett	Australia	1901-02	1924-25
29	J. Phillips	Australia (13)	1884-85	1897-98
		England (11)	1893	1905
		South Africa (5)	1905-06	1905-06
29	F. S. Lee	England	1949	1962
27	J. S. Buller	England	1956	to date
26	C. S. Elliott	England	1957	to date

ENGLAND TEST SELECTORS

In the following list England's opponents are given in brackets, the chairman is listed first, and the captain – normally a co-opted member – is excluded. The first professional member was L. E. G. Ames (1950).

1899 (Australia)—Lord Hawke, W. G. Grace, H. W. Bainbridge.
1902 (Australia)—Lord Hawke, G. MacGregor, H. W. Bainbridge.
1905 (Australia)—Lord Hawke, J. A. Dixon, P. F. Warner.
1907 (South Africa)—Lord Hawke, H. K. Foster, C. H. B. Marsham.
1909 (Australia)—Lord Hawke, C. B. Fry, H. D. G. Leveson-Gower.
1911 (Trials)—Lord Hawke, P. F. Warner, G. L. Jessop.
1912 (Triangular Tournament)—J. Shuter, C. B. Fry, H. K. Foster.
1921 (Australia)—H. K. Foster, R. H. Spooner, J. Daniell.
1924 (South Africa)—H. D. G. Leveson-Gower, J. Sharp, J. Daniell.
1926 (Australia)—P. F. Warner, P. A. Perrin, A. E. R. Gilligan.
J. B. Hobbs and W. Rhodes were co-opted as professional members.
1927 (Trials)—H. D. G. Leveson-Gower, J. W. H. T. Douglas, A. W. Carr.
1928 (West Indies)—H. D. G. Leveson-Gower, J. W. H. T. Douglas, A. W. Carr.
1929 (South Africa)—H. G. D. Leveson-Gower, J. C. White, N. E. Haig.
1930 (Australia)—H. D. G. Leveson-Gower, J. C. White, F. T. Mann.
1931 (New Zealand)—P. F. Warner, P. A. Perrin, T. A. Higson.
1932 (India)—P. F. Warner, P. A. Perrin, T. A. Higson.
1933 (West Indies)—Lord Hawke, P. A. Perrin, T. A. Higson.
1934 (Australia)—Hon. F. S. Jackson, P. A. Perrin, T. A. Higson.
1935 (South Africa)—P. F. Warner, P. A. Perrin, T. A. Higson.
1936 (India)—P. F. Warner, P. A. Perrin, T. A. Higson.
1937 (New Zealand)—Sir Pelham Warner, P. A. Perrin, T. A. Higson.
E. R. T. Holmes was a co-opted member.
1938 (Australia)—Sir Pelham Warner, P. A. Perrin, A. B. Sellers, M. J. Turnbull.
1939 (West Indies)—P. A. Perrin, A. B. Sellers, M. J. Turnbull, A. J. Holmes.
1946 (India)—Sir F. S. Jackson, A. B. Sellers, A. J. Holmes, R. W. V. Robins.
1947 (South Africa)—A. J. Holmes, R. W. V. Robins, J. C. Clay.
1948 (Australia)—A. J. Holmes, R. W. V. Robins, J. C. Clay.
1949 (New Zealand)—A. J. Holmes, A. B. Sellers, R. W. V. Robins, T. N. Pearce.
1950 (West Indies)—R. E. S. Wyatt, A. B. Sellers, T. N. Pearce, L. E. G. Ames.
1951 (South Africa)—N. W. D. Yardley, R. E. S. Wyatt, F. R. Brown, L. E. G. Ames.
1952 (India)—N. W. D. Yardley, R. E. S. Wyatt, F. R. Brown, L. E. G. Ames.
1953 (Australia)—F. R. Brown, N. W. D. Yardley, R. E. S. Wyatt, L. E. G. Ames.
1954 (Pakistan)—H. S. Altham, R. W. V. Robins, R. E. S. Wyatt, L. E. G. Ames.
1955 (South Africa)—G. O. Allen, W. Wooller, A. B. Sellers, L. E. G. Ames.
1956 (Australia)—G. O. Allen, W. Wooller, C. Washbrook, L. E. G. Ames.
1957 (West Indies)—G. O. Allen, W. Wooller, C. Washbrook, H. E. Dollery.
1958 (New Zealand)—G. O. Allen, W. Wooller, L. E. G. Ames, H. E. Dollery.
1959 (India)—G. O. Allen, W. Wooller, D. J. Insole, H. Sutcliffe.
1960 (South Africa)—G. O. Allen, W. Wooller, D. J. Insole, H. Sutcliffe.
1961 (Australia)—G. O. Allen, W. Wooller, D. J. Insole, H. Sutcliffe.
1962 (Pakistan)—R. W. V. Robins, D. J. Insole, A. V. Bedser, W. Watson.
1963 (West Indies)—R. W. V. Robins, D. J. Insole, A. V. Bedser, W. Watson.
1964 (Australia)—R. W. V. Robins, D. J. Insole, A. V. Bedser, W. Watson.
1965 (New Zealand, South Africa)—D. J. Insole, A. V. Bedser, P. B. H. May, D. Kenyon.
1966 (West Indies)—D. J. Insole, A. V. Bedser, P. B. H. May, D. Kenyon.
1967 (India, Pakistan)—D. J. Insole, A. V. Bedser, P. B. H. May, D. Kenyon.

COUNTIES PROVIDING ENGLAND PLAYERS

437 players have represented England in the 439 matches played up to the end of 1967 – a total of 4829 caps.

Eight players have represented more than one county during their Test careers. These players are asterisked (*) in the following summary and their number of caps listed separately for each of their counties.

DERBYSHIRE: 15 *Players* – 53 *Caps*

Carr, D. B. ... 2
Chatterton, W. ... 1
Copson, W. H. ... 3
Elliott, H. ... 4
Gladwin, C. ... 8
Humphries, J. ... 3
Jackson, H. L. ... 2
Mitchell, T. B. ... 5
Pope, G. H. ... 1
Rhodes, H. J. ... 2
Smith, D. ... 2
Storer, W. ... 6
Townsend, L. F.... 4
Warren, A. R. ... 1
Worthington, T. S. 9

ESSEX: 16 *Players* – 190 *Caps*

Bailey, T. E. ... 61
Buckenham, C. P. 4
Douglas, J. W. H. T. 23
Fane, F. L. ... 14
Farnes, K. ... 15
Hobbs, R. N. S.... 4
Insole, D. J. ... 9
Knight, B. R. ... 22
McGahey, C. P. ... 2
Mead, W.... ... 1
Nichols, M. S. ... 14
O'Connor, J. ... 4
Read, H. D. ... 1
Russell, A. C. ... 10
Smith, T. P. B. ... 4
Young, H. ... 2

GLAMORGAN: 8 *Players* – 48 *Caps*

Clay, J. C. ... 1
Jones, I. J. ... 10
Matthews, A. D. G. 1
McConnon, J. E. 2
Parkhouse, W. G. A. 7
Turnbull, M. J. ... 9
Walker, P. M. ... 3
Watkins, A. J. ... 15

GLOUCESTERSHIRE: 24 *Players* – 289 *Caps*

Allen, D. A. ... 39
Barnett, C. J. ... 20
Board, J. H. ... 6
Cook, C. 1
Cranston, J. ... 1
Crapp, J. F. ... 7
Dipper, A. E. ... 1
Emmett, G. M. ... 1
Ferris, J. J. ... 1
Goddard, T. W. ... 8
Grace, E. M. ... 1
Grace, G. F. ... 1
Grace, W. G. ... 22
Graveney, T. W.* 48
Hammond, W. R. 85
Jessop, G. L. ... 18
Midwinter, W. E. 4
Milton, C. A. ... 6
Mortimore, J. B. 9
Parker, C. W. L. 1
Sinfield, R. A. ... 1
Smith, D. R. ... 5
Smith, H. ... 1
Townsend, C. L. 2

HAMPSHIRE: 12 *Players* – 63 *Caps*

Arnold, J. ... 1
Barton, V. A. ... 1
Brown G.... ... 7
Fry, C. B.* ... 6
Heseltine, C. ... 2
Hill, A. J. L. ... 3
Kennedy, A. S. ... 5
Mead, C. P. ... 17
Shackleton, D. ... 7
Tennyson, Hon. L. H. 9
White, D. W. ... 2
Wynyard, E. G.... 3

Counties Providing England Players—*Cont.*

KENT: 38 *Players* – 477 *Caps*

Absolom, C. A.	1	Fielder, A.	6	Martin, F.	2
Ames, L. E. G.	47	Freeman, A. P.	12	Martin J. W.	1
Bligh, Hon. Ivo	4	Hardinge, H. T. W.	1	Mason, J. R.	5
Blythe, C.	19	Harris, Lord	4	Penn, F.	1
Bradley, W. M.	2	Hearne, A.	1	Richardson, P. E.*	9
Brown, A.	2	Hearne, F.	2	Ridgway, F.	5
Carr, D. W.	1	Hearne, G. G.	1	Tylecote, E. F. S.	6
Chapman, A. P. F.	26	Hutchings, K. L.	7	Underwood, D. L.	4
Christopherson, S.	1	Knott, A. P.	2	Valentine, B. H.	7
Cowdrey, M. C.	92	Legge, G. B.	5	Wood, G. E. C.	3
Evans, A. J.	1	Levett, W. H. V.	1	Woolley, F. E.	64
Evans, T. G.	91	Mackinnon, F. A.	1	Wright, D. V. P.	34
Fagg, A. E.	5	Marriott, C. S.	1		

LANCASHIRE: 46 *Players* – 499 *Caps*

Barber, R. W.*	9	Hornby, A. N.	3	Schultz, S. S.	1
Barlow, R. G.	17	Howard, N. D.	4	Sharp, J.	3
Barnes, S. F.*	4	Iddon, J.	5	Spooner, R. H.	10
Berry, R.	2	Ikin, J. T.	18	Statham, J. B.	70
Brearley, W.	4	MacLaren, A. C.	35	Steel, A. G.	13
Briggs, J.	33	Makepeace, H.	4	Sugg, F. H.	2
Cranston, K.	8	Mold, A.	3	Tattersall, R.	16
Cuttell, W. R.	2	Oldfield, N.	1	Tyldesley, E.	14
Dean, H.	3	Parkin, C. H.	10	Tyldesley, J. T.	31
Duckworth, G.	24	Paynter, E.	20	Tyldesley, R.	7
Farrimond, W. F.	4	Pilling, R.	8	Ward, A.	7
Greenhough, T.	4	Place, W.	3	Washbrook, C.	37
Hallows, C.	2	Pollard, R.	4	Wharton, A.	1
Higgs, K.	14	Pullar, G.	28	Wilkinson, L. L.	3
Hilton, M. J.	4	Royle, V. P. F. A.	1	Wood, R.	1
Hopwood, J. L.	2				

LEICESTERSHIRE: 8 *Players* – 40 *Caps*

Astill, W. E.	9	King, J. H.	1	Pougher, A. D.	1
Dawson, E. W.	5	Knight, A. E.	3	Watson, W. *	6
Geary, G.	14	Palmer, C. H.	1		

MIDDLESEX: 44 *Players* – 548 *Caps*

Allen, G. O.	25	Lyttelton, Hon. A.	4	Russell, W. E.	10
Bosanquet, B. J. T.	7	MacGregor, G.	8	Sims, J. M.	4
Bromley-Davenport, H. R.	4	Mann, F. G.	7	Smith, C. I. J.	5
Compton, D. C. S.	78	Mann, F. T.	5	Stevens, G. T. S.	10
Dewes, J. G.	5	Moon, L. J.	4	Stoddart, A. E.	16
Durston, F. J.	1	Moss, A. E.	9	Studd, C. T.	5
Edrich, W. J.	39	Murray, J. T.	21	Studd, G. B.	4
Ford, F. G. J.	5	O'Brien, T. C.	5	Titmus, F. J.	47
Haig, N. E.	5	Parfitt, P. H.	33	Trott, A. E.	2
Hearne, J. T.	12	Peebles, I. A. R.	13	Vernon, G. F.	1
Hearne, J. W.	24	Philipson, H.	5	Warner, P. F.	15
Hendren, E.	51	Price, J. S. E.	10	Warr, J. J.	2
Killick, E. T.	2	Price, W. F.	1	Webbe, A. J.	1
Lee, H. W.	1	Robertson, J. D.	11	Young, J. A.	8
Leslie, C. F. H.	4	Robins, R. W. V.	19		

Counties Providing England Players—*Cont.*

NORTHAMPTONSHIRE: 11 *Players* – 91 *Caps*

Player	Caps	Player	Caps	Player	Caps
Andrew, K. V. ...	2	Clark, E. W. ...	8	Subba Row, R. ...	13
Bakewell, A. H. ...	6	Jupp, V. W. C.*	6	Thompson, G. J.	6
Brookes, D. ...	1	Larter, J. D. F. ...	10	Tyson, F. H. ...	17
Brown, F. R. * ...	16	Milburn, C. ...	6		

NOTTINGHAMSHIRE: 29 *Players* – 291 *Caps*

Player	Caps	Player	Caps	Player	Caps
Attewell, W. ...	10	Hardstaff, J. Snr.	5	Selby, J.	6
Barnes, W. ...	21	Hardstaff, J. Jnr.	23	Shaw, A. ...	7
Barratt, F. ...	5	Jones, A. O. ...	12	Sherwin, M. ...	3
Bolus, J. B. ...	7	Keeton, W. W. ...	2	Shrewsbury, A. ...	23
Butler, H. J. ...	2	Larwood, H. ...	21	Simpson, R. T. ...	27
Carr, A. W. ...	11	Millman, G. ...	6	Staples, S. J. ...	3
Flowers, W. ...	8	Morley, F. ...	4	Voce, W. ...	27
Gunn, G.... ...	15	Poole, C. J. ...	3	Whysall, W. W....	4
Gunn, J.	6	Richmond, T. L....	1	Wright, C. W. ...	3
Gunn, W. ...	11	Scotton, W. H. ...	15		

SOMERSET: 14 *Players* – 63 *Caps*

Player	Caps	Player	Caps	Player	Caps
Braund, L. C. ...	23	Mitchell-Innes, N. S.	1	Tyler, E. J. ...	1
Fothergill, A. J. ...	2	Palairet, L. C. H.	2	Wellard, A. W. ...	2
Gay, L. H. ...	1	Palmer, K. E. ...	1	White, J. C. ...	15
Gimblett, H. ...	3	Rumsey, F. E. ...	5	Woods, S. M. J....	3
MacBryan, J. C. W.	1	Tremlett, M. F.	3		

SURREY: 47 *Players* – 710 *Caps*

Player	Caps	Player	Caps	Player	Caps
Abel, R.	13	Hayes, E. G.... ...	5	Lucas, A. P. ...	5
Allom, M. J. C. ...	5	Hayward, T. W. ...	35	May, P. B. H. ...	66
Arnold, G. G. ...	2	Hitch, J. W.... ...	7	McIntyre, A. J.	3
Barrington, K. F....	74	Hobbs, J. B. ...	61	Read, J. M. ...	17
Bedser, A. V. ...	51	Holmes, E. R. T. ...	5	Read, W. W. ...	18
Bird, M. C. ...	10	Jardine, D. R. ...	22	Richardson, T....	14
Bowden, M. P. ...	2	Jupp, H.	2	Sandham, A. ...	14
Brockwell, W. ...	7	Knight, D. J. ...	2	Sharpe, J. W. ...	3
Brown, F. R.* ...	6	Knox, N. A.... ...	2	Shuter, J. ...	1
Crawford, J. N. ...	12	Laker, J. C.	46	Southerton, J. ...	2
Druce, N. F. ...	5	Lees, W. S.	5	Stewart, M. J. ...	8
Ducat, A.	1	Leveson-Gower, H. D. G.	3	Strudwick, H. ...	28
Edrich, J. H. ...	21	Loader, P. J. ...	13	Swetman, R. ...	11
Fender, P. G. H....	13	Lock, G. A. R. ...	47	Tufnell, N. C. ...	1
Fishlock, L. B. ...	4	Lockwood, W. H. ...	12	Wood, H. ...	4
Gover, A. R. ...	4	Lohmann, G. A. ...	18		

SUSSEX: 33 *Players* – 304 *Caps*

Player	Caps	Player	Caps	Player	Caps
Bean, G.	3	Griffith, S. C. ...	3	Relf, A. E. ...	13
Bowley, E. H. ...	5	Hartley, J. C. ...	2	Sheppard, D. S....	22
Butt, H. R. ...	3	Jupp, V. W. C.*	2	Smith, C. A. ...	1
Charlwood, H. ...	2	Langridge, Jas. ...	8	Smith, D. V. ...	3
Cornford, W. F. ...	4	Lillywhite, Jas. ...	2	Snow, J. A. ...	9

Counties Providing England Players—*Cont.*

Dexter, E. R. ... 60
Doggart, G. H. G. 2
Duleepsinhji, K. S. 12
Fry, C. B.* ... 20
Gilligan, A. E. R. 11
Gilligan, A. H. H. 4
Murdoch, W. L. 1
Newham, W. ... 1
Oakman, A. S. M. 2
Parks, J. H. ... 1
Parks, J. M. ... 43
Ranjitsinhji, K. S. 15
Street, G. B. ... 1
Tate, F. W. ... 1
Tate, M. W. ... 39
Thomson, N. I. ... 5
Vine, J. 2
Young, R. A. ... 2

WARWICKSHIRE: 18 *Players* – 233 *Caps*

Amiss, D. L. ... 4
Barber, R. W.* ... 18
Brown, D. J. ... 11
Calthorpe, Hon. F. S. G. 4
Cartwright, T. W. 5
Dollery, H. E. ... 4
Foster, F. R. ... 11
Hollies, W. E. ... 13
Howell, H. ... 5
Kinneir, S. P. ... 1
Lilley, A. A. ... 35
Paine, G. A. E. ... 4
Quaife, W. G. ... 7
Smith, A. C. ... 6
Smith, E. J. ... 11
Smith, M. J. K. ... 47
Spooner, R. T. ... 7
Wyatt, R. E. S. ... 40

WORCESTERSHIRE: 18 *Players* – 131 *Caps*

Arnold, E. G. ... 10
Coldwell, L. J. ... 7
D'Oliveira, B. L. ... 9
Flavell, J. A. ... 4
Foster, R. E. ... 8
Gifford, N. ... 2
Graveney, T. W.* 17
Horton, M. J. ... 2
Howorth, R. ... 5
Jenkins, R. O. ... 9
Kenyon, D. ... 8
Nawab of Pataudi, Snr. 3
Perks, R. T. D. ... 2
Richardson, D. W. 1
Richardson, P. E.* 25
Root, C. F. ... 3
Simpson-Hayward, G. H. 5
Walters, C. F. ... 11

YORKSHIRE: 56 *Players* – 765 *Caps*

Appleyard, R. ... 9
Armitage, T. ... 2
Barber, W. ... 2
Bates, W. 15
Binks, J. G. ... 2
Booth, M. W. ... 2
Bowes, W. E. ... 15
Boycott, G. ... 27
Brennan, D. V. ... 2
Brown, J. T. ... 8
Close, D. B. ... 19
Coxon, A. 1
Denton, D. ... 11
Dolphin, A. ... 1
Emmett, T. ... 7
Gibb, P. A. ... 8
Greenwood, A. ... 2
Haigh, S. 11
Hawke, Lord ... 5
Hill, A. 2
Hirst, G. H. ... 24
Holmes, P. ... 7
Hunter, J. ... 5
Hutton, L. ... 79
Illingworth. R. ... 27
Jackson, Hon. F. S. 20
Kilner, R. ... 9
Leadbeater, E. ... 2
Leyland, M. ... 41
Lowson, F. A. ... 7
Macaulay, G. G. 8
Milligan, F. W. ... 2
Mitchell, A. ... 6
Mitchell, F. ... 2
Padgett, D. E. V. 2
Peate, E. ... 9
Peel, R. 20
Rhodes, W. ... 58
Sharpe, P. J. ... 6
Smailes, T. F. ... 1
Smithson, G. A. 2
Stanyforth, R. T. 4
Sutcliffe, H. ... 54
Taylor, K. ... 3
Trueman, F. S. ... 67
Ulyett, G. ... 25
Verity, H. ... 40
Waddington, A. ... 2
Wainwright, E. ... 5
Wardle, J. H. ... 28
Watson, W.* ... 17
Wilson, C. E. M. 2
Wilson, D. ... 5
Wilson, E. R. ... 1
Wood, A. ... 4
Yardley, N. W. D. 20

MISCELLANEOUS: 8 *Players* – 34 *Caps*

Archer, A. G. ... 1
Barnes, S. F.* 23
Coventry, Hon. C. J. 2
Grieve, B. A. F.... 2
Hone, L. ... 1
McMaster, J. E. P. 1
Miller, A. M. ... 1
Townsend, D. C. H. 3

COUNTIES PROVIDING ENGLAND'S CAPTAINS

Derbyshire... ...	(1):	Carr, D. B. (1)
Essex	(23):	Douglas, J. W. H. T. (18), Fane, F. L. (5)
Gloucestershire ...	(33):	Grace, W. G. (13), Hammond, W. R. (20)
Hampshire ...	(9):	Fry, C. B. (6), Tennyson, Hon. L. H. (3)
Kent	(40):	Bligh, Hon. Ivo (4), Chapman, A. P. F. (17), Cowdrey, M. C. (15), Harris, Lord (4)
Lancashire... ...	(33):	Cranston, K. (1), Hornby, A. N. (2), Howard, N. D. (4), McLaren, A. C. (22), Steel, A. G. (4)
Middlesex	(46):	Allen, G. O. (11), Mann, F. G. (7), Mann F. T. (5), O'Brien, T. C. (1), Robins, R. W. V. (3), Stevens, G. T. S. (1), Stoddart, A. E. (8), Warner, P. F. (10)
Northamptonshire	(15):	Brown, F. R. (15)
Nottinghamshire ...	(19):	Carr, A. W. (6), Jones, A. O. (2), Shaw, A. (4), Shrewsbury, A. (7)
Somerset	(4):	White, J. C. (4)
Surrey	(62):	Bowden, M. P. (1), Jardine, D. R. (15), Leveson-Gower, H. D. G. (3), May, P. B. H. (41), Read, W. W. (2)
Sussex	(48):	Dexter, E. R. (30), Gilligan, A. E. R. (9), Gilligan, A. H. (4), Lillywhite, Jas. (2), Sheppard, D. S. (2), Smith, C. A. (1)
Warwickshire ...	(45):	Calthorpe, Hon. F. S. G. (4), Smith, M. J. K. (25), Wyatt, R. E. S. (16)
Worcestershire ...	(4) :	Foster, R. E. (3) Walters, C. F. (1)
Yorkshire	(57):	Close, D. B. (7), Hawke, Lord (4), Hutton, L. (23), Jackson, Hon. F. S. (5), Stanyforth, R. T. (4), Yardley, N. W. D. (14)

First-Class Cricket Records

TEAM RECORDS

HIGHEST INNINGS TOTALS

1107	Victoria v. New South Wales (Melbourne)	1926-27
1059	Victoria v. Tasmania (Melbourne)	1922-23
918	New South Wales v. South Australia (Sydney)	1900-01
912-8d	Holkar v. Mysore (Indore)	1945-46
910-6d	Railways v. Dera Ismail Khan (Lahore)	1964-65
903-7d	England v. Australia (Oval)	1938
887	Yorkshire v. Warwickshire (Birmingham)	1896
849	England v. West Indies (Kingston)	1929-30
843	Australians v. Oxford & Cambridge Univs. P. & P. (Portsmouth)	1893
839	New South Wales v. Tasmania (Sydney)	1898-99
826-4	Maharashtra v. Western India States (Poona)	1948-49
821-7d	South Australia v. Queensland (Adelaide)	1939-40
815	New South Wales v. Victoria (Sydney)	1908-09
811	Surrey v. Somerset (Oval)	1899
807	New South Wales v. South Australia (Adelaide)	1899-00
805	New South Wales v. Victoria (Melbourne)	1905-06
803-4d	Kent v. Essex (Brentwood)	1934
803	Non-Smokers v. Smokers (East Melbourne)	1886-87
802	New South Wales v. South Australia (Sydney)	1920-21
801	Lancashire v. Somerset (Taunton)	1895

INNINGS TOTALS OF 600 AND OVER

These are listed under the respective teams for England and Australia, the highest total being given when no total of 600 has been scored.

IN ENGLAND

Derbyshire	645	v.	Hampshire (Derby)	1898
Essex	692	v.	Somerset (Taunton)	1895
	673	v.	Leicestershire (Leicester)	1899
	616-5d	v.	Surrey (Oval)	1904
	609-4d	v.	Derbyshire (Leyton)	1912
	604-7d	v.	Northamptonshire (Northampton)	1921
Glamorgan	587-8d	v.	Derbyshire (Cardiff)	1951
Gloucestershire	653-6d	v.	Glamorgan (Bristol)	1928
	643-5d	v.	Nottinghamshire (Bristol)	1946
	636	v.	Nottinghamshire (Nottingham)	1904
	634	v.	Nottinghamshire (Bristol)	1898
	627-2d	v.	Oxford U. (Oxford)	1930
	625-6d	v.	Worcestershire (Dudley)	1934
	608-7d	v.	Sussex (Cheltenham)	1934
	603-6d	v.	Glamorgan (Bristol)	1934
Hampshire	672-7d	v.	Somerset (Taunton)	1899
	642-9d	v.	Somerset (Taunton)	1901
	616-7d	v.	Warwickshire (Portsmouth)	1920
Kent	803-4d	v.	Essex (Brentwood)	1934
	621-6d	v.	Essex (Tonbridge)	1922
	615	v.	Derbyshire (Derby)	1908
	610	v.	Hampshire (Bournemouth)	1906
	607-6d	v.	Gloucestershire (Cheltenham)	1910
	602-7d	v.	Worcestershire (Dudley)	1938
	601-8d	v.	Somerset (Taunton)	1908

Innings Totals of 600 and Over—*Cont.*

Lancashire	801	v.	Somerset (Taunton)	1895
	676-7d	v.	Hampshire (Manchester)	1911
	640-8d	v.	Sussex (Hove)	1937
	627	v.	Nottinghamshire (Nottingham)	1905
	601-8d	v.	Sussex (Hove)	1905
Leicestershire	701-4d	v.	Worcestershire (Worcester)	1906
	609-8d	v.	Sussex (Leicester)	1900
	603	v.	Sir Julien Cahn's XI (Nottingham)	1935
Middlesex	642-3d	v.	Hampshire (Southampton)	1923
	637-4d	v.	Leicestershire (Leicester)	1947
	632-8d	v.	Sussex (Hove)	1937
	623-5d	v.	Worcestershire (Worcester)	1949
	621-9d	v.	Nottinghamshire (Nottingham)	1931
	612-8d	v.	Nottinghamshire (Lord's)	1921
	608-7d	v.	Hampshire (Lord's)	1919
Northamptonshire	557-6d	v.	Sussex (Hove)	1914
Nottinghamshire	739-7d	v.	Leicestershire (Nottingham)	1903
	726	v.	Sussex (Nottingham)	1895
	674	v.	Sussex (Hove)	1893
	662-8d	v.	Essex (Nottingham)	1947
	661	v.	Derbyshire (Derby)	1901
	656-3d	v.	Warwickshire (Coventry)	1928
	642-7d	v.	Sussex (Hove)	1901
	607	v.	Gloucestershire (Bristol)	1899
	602	v.	Kent (Nottingham)	1904
Somerset	675-9d	v.	Hampshire (Bath)	1924
	630	v.	Yorkshire (Leeds)	1901
Surrey	811	v.	Somerset (Oval)	1899
	742	v.	Hampshire (Oval)	1909
	706-4d	v.	Nottinghamshire (Nottingham)	1947
	698	v.	Sussex (Oval)	1888
	650	v.	Oxford U. (Oval)	1888
	645-9d	v.	New Zealanders (Oval)	1949
	634	v.	Lancashire (Oval)	1898
	634	v.	Warwickshire (Oval)	1906
	631	v.	Sussex (Oval)	1885
	619-5d	v.	Northamptonshire (Northampton)	1920
	617-6d	v.	Oxford U. (Oval)	1928
	617	v.	Kent (Oval)	1897
	616-5d	v.	Northamptonshire (Oval)	1921
	614	v.	Oxford U. (Oval)	1889
	611-9d	v.	Derbyshire (Derby)	1904
	609	v.	Warwickshire (Oval)	1898
	602	v.	Warwickshire (Oval)	1897
Sussex	705-8d	v.	Surrey (Hastings)	1902
	686-8	v.	Leicestershire (Leicester)	1900
	670-9d	v.	Northamptonshire (Hove)	1921
	631-4d	v.	Northamptonshire (Northampton)	1938
	611	v.	Essex (Leyton)	1905
	600-7d	v.	Surrey (Oval)	1903
Warwickshire	657-6d	v.	Hampshire (Birmingham)	1899
	645-7d	v.	Worcestershire (Dudley)	1914
	635	v.	Derbyshire (Birmingham)	1900
	614-8d	v.	Essex (Birmingham)	1904
	605	v.	Leicestershire (Leicester)	1899
	603-9d	v.	Worcestershire (Birmingham)	1920
Worcestershire	633	v.	Warwickshire (Worcester)	1906
	627-9d	v.	Kent (Worcester)	1905
Yorkshire	887	v.	Warwickshire (Birmingham)	1896
	704	v.	Surrey (Oval)	1899
	681-5d	v.	Sussex (Sheffield)	1897
	662	v.	Derby (Chesterfield)	1898
	660	v.	Leicestershire (Leicester)	1896

Innings Totals of 600 and Over—*Cont.*

Team	Total		Opponent (Venue)	Year
Oxford University	651	v.	Sussex (Hove)	1895
	644-8d	v.	Leveson-Gower's XI (Eastbourne)	1921
	612	v.	Middlesex (Prince's)	1876
Cambridge University	703-9d	v.	Sussex (Hove)	1890
	611	v.	Sussex (Hove)	1919
	609-8d	v.	M.C.C. (Lord's)	1913
M.C.C.	607	v.	Cambridge U. (Lord's)	1902
England (Test matches)	903-7d	v.	Australia (Oval)	1938
	658-8d	v.	Australia (Nottingham)	1938
	627-9d	v.	Australia (Manchester	1934
	619-6d	v.	West Indies (Nottingham)	1957
	611	v.	Australia (Manchester)	1964
Australians	843	v.	Oxford and Cambridge U. P. & P. (Portsmouth)	1893
	774-7d	v.	Gloucestershire (Bristol)	1948
	729-6d	v.	England (Lord's)	1930
	721	v.	Essex (Southend)	1948
	708-5d	v.	Cambridge U. (Cambridge)	1938
	708-7d	v.	Hampshire (Southampton)	1921
	701	v.	England (Oval)	1934
	695	v.	England (Oval)	1930
	694-6	v.	Leicestershire (Leicester)	1956
	679-7d	v.	Oxford U. (Oxford)	1938
	676	v.	Kent (Canterbury)	1921
	675	v.	Nottinghamshire (Nottingham)	1921
	656-8d	v.	England (Manchester)	1964
	650-8d	v.	Cambridge U. (Cambridge)	1919
	643	v.	Sussex (Hove)	1882
	632	v.	Surrey (Oval)	1948
	629	v.	Surrey (Oval)	1934
	625	v.	Derbyshire (Derby)	1896
	624-4d	v.	Sussex (Hove)	1899
	621	v.	Northamptonshire (Northampton)	1921
	620	v.	Hampshire (Southampton)	1905
	610-5d	v.	Gentlemen of England (Lord's)	1948
	609-4d	v.	Somerset (Bath)	1905
	609-6d	v.	Essex (Leyton)	1909
	609	v.	Northamptonshire (Northampton)	1905
South Africans	692	v.	Cambridge U. (Cambridge)	1901
	611	v.	Nottinghamshire (Nottingham)	1904
West Indians	730-3	v.	Cambridge U. (Cambridge)	1950
	682-2d	v.	Leicestershire (Leicester)	1950
	665	v.	Middlesex (Lord's)	1939
New Zealanders	546	v.	Sussex (Hove)	1937
Indians	533-3d	v.	Sussex (Hove)	1946
Pakistan	456-6	v.	Somerset (Taunton)	1967
Gentlemen	578	v.	Players (Oval)	1904
Players	651-7d	v.	Gentlemen (Oval)	1934
	647	v.	Gentlemen (Oval)	1899
	608-8d	v.	Gentlemen (Oval)	1921

Other innings totals of over 600 *in England:*

676-8d	Oxford Harlequins v. West Indians (Eastbourne)	1928
636-7d	Free Foresters v. Cambridge U. (Cambridge)	1938
633	London County v. M.C.C. (Crystal Palace)	1901
631-5d	Rest of England v. Warwickshire (Champion County) (Oval)	1911
603-5d	Rest of England v. Middlesex (Champion County) (Oval)	1920
603-8d	Rest of England v. Lancashire (Champion County) (Oval)	1928

IN AUSTRALIA

Team	Total		Opponent (Venue)	Year
New South Wales	918	v.	South Australia (Sydney)	1900-01
	839	v.	Tasmania (Sydney)	1898-99
	815	v.	Victoria (Sydney)	1908-09

Innings Totals of 600 and Over—*Cont.*

Team	Total		Opponent (Venue)	Season
New South Wales (*cont.*)	807	v.	South Australia (Adelaide)	1899-00
	805	v.	Victoria (Melbourne)	1905-06
	802	v.	South Australia (Sydney)	1920-21
	786	v.	South Australia (Adelaide)	1922-23
	775	v.	Victoria (Sydney)	1881-82
	770	v.	South Australia (Adelaide)	1920-21
	763	v.	Queensland (Brisbane)	1906-07
	761-8d	v.	Queensland (Sydney)	1929-30
	713-6d	v.	Victoria (Sydney)	1928-29
	713	v.	South Australia (Adelaide)	1908-09
	708	v.	Victoria (Sydney)	1925-26
	705	v.	Victoria (Melbourne)	1925-26
	691	v.	Queensland (Brisbane)	1905-06
	690	v.	South Australia (Adelaide)	1919-20
	686	v.	Queensland (Sydney)	1904-05
	684	v.	South Australia (Sydney)	1923-24
	681	v.	South Australia (Sydney)	1903-04
	675	v.	Victoria (Sydney)	1913-14
	672-8d	v.	Victoria (Sydney)	1933-34
	661	v.	Queensland (Brisbane)	1963-64
	645	v.	Rest (except Victoria) (Sydney)	1924-25
	642	v.	South Australia (Sydney)	1925-26
	640	v.	Queensland (Sydney)	1899-00
	639	v.	Western Australia (Sydney)	1925-26
	639	v.	Queensland (Sydney)	1927-28
	629-8d	v.	M.C.C. (Sydney)	1929-30
	624	v.	South Australia (Adelaide)	1903-04
	619	v.	M.C.C. (Sydney)	1924-25
	614-5d	v.	Tasmania (Hobart)	1912-13
	614-6d	v.	Queensland (Sydney)	1933-34
	614	v.	Victoria (Sydney)	1924-25
	610	v.	South Australia (Adelaide)	1930-31
	602	v.	Queensland (Brisbane)	1932-33
	601-9d	v.	South Australia (Adelaide)	1964-65
Queensland	687	v.	New South Wales (Brisbane)	1930-31
	613	v.	New South Wales (Brisbane)	1963-64
South Australia	821-7d	v.	Queensland (Adelaide)	1939-40
	688	v.	Tasmania (Adelaide)	1935-36
	644-7d	v.	Queensland (Adelaide)	1934-35
	642-8d	v.	Queensland (Adelaide)	1935-36
	614-8d	v.	Western Australia (Adelaide)	1929-30
	612	v.	Western Australia (Adelaide)	1925-26
	610	v.	Victoria (Melbourne)	1939-40
	603	v.	New South Wales (Adelaide)	1946-47
	600-8d	v.	New South Wales (Adelaide)	1938-39
Tasmania	458	v.	Indians (Launceston)	1947-48
Victoria	1107	v.	New South Wales (Melbourne)	1926-27
	1059	v.	Tasmania (Melbourne)	1922-23
	793	v.	Queensland (Melbourne)	1927-28
	724	v.	South Australia (Melbourne)	1920-21
	699	v.	South Australia (Melbourne)	1907-08
	697	v.	South Australia (Adelaide)	1945-46
	660	v.	Tasmania (Melbourne)	1909-10
	649	v.	South Australia (Melbourne)	1926-27
	647	v.	Tasmania (Melbourne)	1951-52
	646-8d	v.	South Australia (Adelaide)	1927-28
	639	v.	South Australia (Adelaide)	1920-21
	637	v.	South Australia (Melbourne)	1927-28
	633-4d	v.	Queensland (Melbourne)	1962-63
	626	v.	Tasmania (Launceston)	1908-09
	620	v.	South Australia (Adelaide)	1921-22
	617-6d	v.	M.C.C. (Melbourne)	1922-23
	614	v.	South Australia (Melbourne)	1910-11
	605	v.	South Australia (Melbourne)	1919-20
	604	v.	South Australia (Melbourne)	1925-26
	602	v.	New Zealanders (Melbourne)	1898-99

Innings Totals of 600 and Over—*Cont.*

Team	Total	Opponent	Season
Western Australia	554-7d	v. Queensland (Perth)	1966-67
M.C.C.	734-7d	v. New South Wales (Sydney)	1928-29
	660-8d	v. South Australia (Adelaide)	1907-08
	634-9d	v. South Australia (Adelaide)	1932-33
	633-7d	v. Australian XI (Melbourne)	1962-63
	627	v. South Australia (Adelaide)	1920-21
	626	v. New South Wales (Sydney)	1924-25
England	636	v. Australia (Sydney)	1928-29
Australia	674	v. India (Adelaide)	1947-48
	659-8d	v. England (Sydney)	1946-47
	645	v. England (Brisbane)	1946-47
	604	v. England (Melbourne)	1936-37
	601-8d	v. England (Brisbane)	1954-55
	600	v. England (Melbourne)	1924-25
South Africans	595	v. Australia (Adelaide)	1963-64
West Indians	495	v. Victoria (Melbourne)	1930-31
New Zealanders	459	v. South Australia (Adelaide)	1953-54
Indians	475-7d	v. Tasmania (Launceston)	1947-48
Pakistanis	490-6d	v. South Australia (Adelaide)	1964-65

Other innings totals of over 600 *in Australia:*

803	Non-Smokers v. Smokers (East Melbourne)	1886-87
769	MacLaren's XI v. New South Wales (Sydney)	1901-02
663	Ryder's XI v. Woodfull's XI (Sydney)	1929-30
648	Australian XI v. Rest of Australia (Melbourne)	1908-09
624	Shrewsbury's XI v. Victoria (Melbourne)	1887-88
619	Australian XI v. Rest of Australia (Melbourne)	1883-84
609	Stoddart's XI v. South Australia (Adelaide)	1894-95

IN SOUTH AFRICA

676	M.C.C. v. Griqualand West (Kimberley)	1938-39
664-6d	Natal v. Western Province (Durban)	1936-37
654-5	England v. South Africa (Durban)	1938-39
620	South Africa v. Australia (Johannesburg)	1966-67
620	Australians v. Griqualand West (Kimberley)	1966-67
618-4d	South Africa v. Rest of South Africa (Johannesburg)	1964-65
609	Transvaal v. Orange Free State (Johannesburg)	1934-35
608-6d	Transvaal v. Natal (Johannesburg)	1939-40
608	England v. South Africa (Johannesburg)	1948-49
603	Griqualand West v. Western Province (Kimberley)	1929-30
602	Griqualand West v. Rhodesia (Kimberley)	1929-30
601	Western Province v. Border (Cape Town)	1929-30

IN THE WEST INDIES

849	England v. West Indies (Kingston)	1929-30
790-3d	West Indies v. Pakistan (Kingston)	1957-58
758-8d	Australia v. West Indies (Kingston)	1954-55
753	Barbados v. Jamaica (Bridgetown)	1951-52
750-8d	Trinidad v. British Guiana (Port of Spain)	1946-47
726-7d	Barbados v. Trinidad (Bridgetown)	1926-27
715-9d	Barbados v. British Guiana (Bridgetown)	1926-27
702-5d	Jamaica v. Lord Tennyson's XI (Kingston)	1931-32
698	Barbados v. Trinidad (Bridgetown)	1948-49
692-9d	British Guiana v. Barbados (Georgetown)	1951-52
686-6d	Barbados v. British Guiana (Bridgetown)	1949-50
681-8d	West Indies v. England (Port of Spain)	1953-54
673	Barbados v. Trinidad (Georgetown)	1922-23
668	Australia v. West Indies (Bridgetown)	1954-55
664	Barbados v. Jamaica (Georgetown)	1961-62
657-8d	Pakistan v. West Indies (Bridgetown)	1957-58
650-3d	Barbados v. Trinidad (Bridgetown)	1943-44
650-6d	Australia v. West Indies (Bridgetown)	1964-65

Innings Totals of 600 and Over—*Cont.*

641-6	M.C.C. v. Berbice (Blairmont)	1959-60
641-5d	Guyana v. Barbados (Georgetown)	1966-67
631-8d	West Indies v. India (Kingston)	1961-62
629	British Guiana v. Barbados (Georgetown)	1937-38
627	British Guiana v. Trinidad (Georgetown)	1937-38
623-5d	Barbados v. Trinidad (Bridgetown)	1919-20
619-3d	Barbados v. Trinidad (Port of Spain)	1945-46
610	British Guiana v. Barbados (Georgetown)	1929-30
609	Jamaica v. Tennyson's XI (Kingston)	1927-28
609	British Guiana v. Jamaica (Georgetown)	1952-53
607	M.C.C. v. British Guiana (Georgetown)	1953-54
606-7d	Barbados v. Indians (Bridgetown)	1952-53
605-5d	M.C.C. v. British Guiana (Georgetown)	1929-30
601-5d	British Guiana v. Jamaica (Georgetown)	1956-57
601-9d	Barbados v. British Guiana (Georgetown)	1946-47
601	M.C.C. v. Barbados (Bridgetown)	1934-35
600-9d	Australia v. West Indies (Port of Spain)	1954-55

IN NEW ZEALAND

752-8d	New South Wales v. Otago (Dunedin)	1923-24
693-9d	Auckland v. Canterbury (Auckland)	1939-40
663	Australians v. New Zealand XI (Auckland)	1920-21
658	Australians v. Auckland (Auckland)	1913-14
653-5d	M.C.C. v. New Zealand XI (Dunedin)	1935-36
653	Australians v. Canterbury (Christchurch)	1913-14
643	Auckland v. Canterbury (Auckland)	1919-20
610-6d	Australians v. New Zealand XI (Auckland)	1913-14
602-8d	Otago v. Canterbury (Dunedin)	1928-29

IN INDIA

912-8d	Holkar v. Mysore (Indore)	1945-46
826-4	Maharashtra v. Kathiawar (Poona)	1948-49
798	Maharashtra v. Northern India (Poona)	1940-41
784	Baroda v. Holkar (Baroda)	1946-47
764	Bombay v. Holkar (Bombay)	1944-45
760	Bengal v. Assam (Calcutta)	1951-52
757	Holkar v. Hyderabad (Indore)	1950-51
735	Bombay v. Maharashtra (Bombay)	1943-44
725-8d	Bombay v. Maharashtra (Bombay)	1950-51
714-8d	Bombay v. Maharashtra (Poona)	1948-49
703	Bengal Cyclone XI v. Bijapur Famine XI (Bombay)	1942-43
675	Maharashtra v. Bombay (Poona)	1940-41
673	Bijapur Famine XI v. Bengal Cyclone XI (Bombay)	1942-43
658-8d	Southern Punjab v. Northern India (Patiala)	1945-46
657-9d	Bombay v. Maharashtra (Bombay)	1956-57
654	Cricket Club of India v. Nayudu's XI (Bombay)	1944-45
652	Bombay v. Hyderabad (Bombay)	1947-48
651	Bombay v. Maharashtra (Poona)	1948-49
650-9d	Maharashtra v. Baroda (Poona)	1939-40
650	Bombay v. Maharashtra (Poona)	1940-41
645	Bombay v. Baroda (Bombay)	1945-46
644-8d	West Indies v. India (New Delhi)	1958-59
638-8d	Bombay v. Sind (Bombay)	1947-48
635-6d	Hyderabad v. Bengal (Hyderabad)	1964-65
634-9d	Bombay v. Madras (Bombay)	1956-57
632-7d	Bombay v. Maharashtra (Bombay)	1947-48
631	West Indies v. India (New Delhi)	1948-49
629-6d	West Indies v. India (Bombay)	1948-49
629	Gujerat v. Maharashtra (Kolaphur)	1951-52
620	Bombay v. Northern India (Bombay)	1944-45
620	Bombay v. Baroda (Bombay)	1948-49
618	Holkar v. Bengal (Indore)	1942-43
615-4d	Cricket Club of India v. Services XI (Bombay)	1944-45
615	Holkar v. Delhi and District (Delhi)	1949-50
615	Rajasthan v. Vidarbha (Udaipur)	1957-58

Innings Totals of 600 and Over—*Cont.*

615	Hyderabad v. Uttar Pradesh (Hyderabad)	1964-65
614-5d	West Indies v. India (Calcutta)	1958-59
613-7d	Northern India v. N.W.F.P. (Lahore)	1941-42
613-7d	Commonwealth XI v. North Zone (Patiala)	1949-50
612-6d	India in England 1946 v. Rest of India (Calcutta)	1946-47
611	Commonwealth XI v. West Zone (Poona)	1949-50
608-8d	Commonwealth XI v. Indian XI (New Delhi)	1949-50
604	Maharashtra v. Bombay (Poona)	1948-49
603	M.C.C. v. Madras (Madras)	1933-34
602-7d	Bombay v. Mysore (Bombay)	1966-67

IN PAKISTAN

910-6d	Railways v. Dera Ismail Khan (Lahore)	1964-65
824	Lahore Greens v. Bahawalpur (Lahore)	1965-66
772-7d	Karachi v. Bahawalpur (Karachi)	1958-59
762	Karachi Whites v. Karachi Blues (Karachi)	1956-57
702	Punjab U. v. Sind U. (Karachi)	1958-59
671	Karachi Whites v. Quetta (Karachi)	1963-64
634-4d	Karachi Blues v. Hyderabad (Karachi)	1964-65
633	Lahore v. Punjab U. (Lahore)	1960-61
632-8d	Karachi Blues v. Bahawalpur (Karachi)	1964-65
630-9d	Commonwealth XI v. Pakistan (Lahore)	1963-64
616	Lahore Greens v. Railways (Lahore)	1964-65

HIGHEST SECOND INNINGS TOTALS

770	New South Wales v. South Australia (Adelaide)	1920-21
764	Bombay v. Holkar (Bombay)	1944-45
761-8d	New South Wales v. Queensland (Sydney)	1929-30
726-7d	Barbados v. Trinidad (Bridgetown)	1926-27
724	Victoria v. South Australia (Melbourne)	1920-21
714-8d	Bombay v. Maharashtra (Poona)	1948-49
703-9d	Cambridge University v. Sussex (Hove)	1890

HIGH SCORING MEMORABILIA

1895 Somerset, in consecutive innings, conceded totals of 692 against Essex and 801 against Lancashire, both at Taunton.

1920-21 South Australia conceded the following totals during the season: 639 (Victoria at Adelaide), 512-5d (M.C.C. at Adelaide), 310 & 724 (Victoria at Melbourne), 802 (N.S.W. at Sydney), 304 & 770 (N.S.W. at Adelaide), and 627 (M.C.C. at Adelaide).

1921 During their tour of England the Australians scored three successive totals of over 500: 621 v. Northants. (Northampton), 675 v. Notts. (Nottingham), and 506 v. Warwicks. (Birmingham).

1921 Northants. conceded the following totals in successive innings: 616-5d (Surrey at The Oval), 604-7d (Essex at Leyton), 621 (Australians at Northampton), and 545-9d (Essex at Leyton).

1925-26 N.S.W. totalled 642 and 592 against South Australia at Sydney.

1948-49 Bombay (651 & 714-8d) and Maharashtra (407 & 604) produced the highest match aggregate on record: 2376 for 38 wickets.

LOWEST INNINGS TOTALS

12	Oxford University v. M.C.C. (Oxford) (i)	1877
12	Northamptonshire v. Gloucestershire (Gloucester)	1907
13	Wellington v. Nelson (Nelson)	1862-63
13	Auckland v. Canterbury (Auckland) (ii)	1877-78
13	Nottinghamshire v. Yorkshire (Nottingham)	1901
15	M.C.C. v. Surrey (Lord's)	1839
15	Victoria v. M.C.C. (Melbourne)	1903-04
15	Northamptonshire v. Yorkshire (Northampton) (iii)	1908
15	Hampshire v. Warwickshire (Birmingham) (iv)	1922
16	M.C.C. v. Surrey (Lord's) (v)	1872

Lowest Innings Totals—*Cont.*

16	Derbyshire v. Nottinghamshire (Nottingham)	1879
16	Surrey v. Nottinghamshire (Oval)	1880
16	Warwickshire v. Kent (Tonbridge)	1913
16	Trinidad v. Barbados (Bridgetown)	1941-42
16	Border v. Natal (East London) 1st innings	1959-60
17	Gentlemen of Kent v. Gentlemen of England (Lord's)	1850
17	Gloucestershire v. Australians (Cheltenham)	1896
18	The B's v. England (Lord's)	1831
18	Kent v. Sussex (Gravesend)	1867
18	Tasmania v. Victoria (Melbourne)	1868-69
18	Australians v. M.C.C. (Lord's)	1896
18	Border v. Natal (East London) 2nd innings	1959-60
19	Sussex v. Surrey (Godalming)	1830
19	Sussex v. Nottinghamshire (Hove)	1873
19	M.C.C. v. Australians (Lord's)	1878
19	Wellington v. Nelson (Nelson)	1885-86

(i) Oxford University were dismissed for 35 in their second innings, batting one short in each innings.
(ii) The highest individual score was 2 and there were 8 extras.
(iii) Northamptonshire were dismissed for 27 in their first innings.
(iv) Hampshire followed-on, scored 521 and won the match by 155 runs.
(v) Seven wickets fell before the first run was scored, the 8th wicket fell at 2, and the 9th wicket at 8.

IN ENGLAND

Derbyshire	16	v. Nottinghamshire (Nottingham)	1879
	20	v. Yorkshire (Sheffield)	1939
	23	v. Yorkshire (Hull)	1921
	26	v. M.C.C. (Lord's)	1880
	26	v. Yorkshire (Derby)	1880
	30	v. Nottinghamshire (Chesterfield)	1913
Essex	30	v. Yorkshire (Leyton)	1901
Glamorgan	22	v. Lancashire (Liverpool)	1924
	26	v. Lancashire (Cardiff)	1958
Gloucestershire	17	v. Australians (Cheltenham)	1896
	22	v. Somerset (Bristol)	1920
	25	v. Somerset (Cheltenham)	1891
Hampshire	15	v. Warwickshire (Birmingham)	1922
	23	v. Derbyshire (Burton-upon-Trent)	1958
	30	v. Worcestershire (Worcester)	1903
	30	v. Nottinghamshire (Southampton)	1932
Kent	18	v. Sussex (Gravesend)	1867
	20	v. Surrey (Oval)	1870
	21	v. England (Lord's)	1834
	23	v. Sussex (Brighton)	1828
	23	v. England (Bromley)	1840
	25	v. Derbyshire (Wirksworth)	1874
	25	v. M.C.C. (Lord's)	1879
	27	v. Sussex (Town Malling)	1836
	27	v. M.C.C. (Lord's)	1856
	28	v. Gloucestershire (Moreton in the Marsh)	1888
	30	v. England (Bromley)	1840
Lancashire	25	v. Derbyshire (Manchester)	1871
	27	v. Surrey (Manchester)	1958
	28	v. Australians (Liverpool)	1896
	30	v. Yorkshire (Holbeck)	1868
Leicestershire	25	v. Kent (Leicester)	1912
	26	v. Kent (Leicester)	1911
	28	v. Australians (Leicester)	1899
	30	v. M.C.C. (Lord's)	1899
Middlesex	20	v. M.C.C. (Lord's)	1864
	24	v. M.C.C. (Lord's)	1815
	25	v. Surrey (Oval)	1885

Lowest Innings Totals—*Cont.*

Middlesex (*cont.*)	29	v. Derbyshire (Chesterfield)	1957
Northamptonshire	12	v. Gloucestershire (Gloucester)	1907
	15	v. Yorkshire (Northampton)	1908
	27	v. Yorkshire (Northampton)	1908
	27	v. Yorkshire (Kettering)	1933
Nottinghamshire	13	v. Yorkshire (Nottingham)	1901
	21	v. M.C.C. (Lord's)	1891
	23	v. M.C.C. (Nottingham)	1883
	24	v. Yorkshire (Sheffield)	1888
Somerset	25	v. Gloucestershire (Bristol)	1947
Surrey	16	v. Nottinghamshire (Oval)	1880
	26	v. Nottinghamshire (Nottingham)	1876
	27	v. Gloucestershire (Cheltenham)	1874
Sussex	19	v. Surrey (Godalming)	1830
	19	v. Nottinghamshire (Hove)	1873
	20	v. Yorkshire (Hull)	1922
	22	v. Kent (Sevenoaks)	1828
	23	v. M.C.C. (Lord's)	1838
	23	v. M.C.C. (Lord's)	1856
	23	v. Warwickshire (Worthing)	1964
	24	v. Yorkshire (Hove)	1878
	24	v. Lancashire (Manchester)	1890
	25	v. M.C.C. (Lord's)	1843
	29	v. M.C.C. (Lord's)	1861
	29	v. Gloucestershire (Cheltenham)	1878
	29	v. Lancashire (Liverpool)	1907
Warwickshire	16	v. Kent (Tonbridge)	1913
	28	v. Derbyshire (Derby)	1937
Worcestershire	24	v. Yorkshire (Huddersfield)	1903
	25	v. Yorkshire (Hull)	1906
	25	v. Surrey (Oval)	1954
	25	v. Kent (Tunbridge Wells)	1960
	28	v. Yorkshire (Bradford)	1907
Yorkshire	23	v. Hampshire (Middlesbrough)	1965
	26	v. Surrey (Oval)	1909
	30	v. Kent (Sheffield)	1865
Oxford University	12	v. M.C.C. (Oxford)	1877
Cambridge University	28	v. M.C.C. (Lord's)	1845
	30	v. Yorkshire (Cambridge)	1928
M.C.C.	15	v. Surrey (Lord's)	1839
	16	v. Surrey (Lord's)	1872
	19	v. Australians (Lord's)	1878
	24	v. Oxford U. (Lord's)	1846
	27	v. Yorkshire (Lord's)	1902
	29	v. The B's (Lord's)	1832
	29	v. North (Lord's)	1848
	30	v. Lancashire (Lord's)	1886

Other totals of 30 *and less in England:*

17	Gentlemen of Kent v. Gentlemen of England (Lord's)	1850
18	The B's v. England (Lord's)	1831
18	Australians v. M.C.C. (Lord's)	1896
23	Australians v. Yorkshire (Leeds)	1902
24	Players v. Gentlemen (Lord's)	1829
25	Ireland v. Scotland (Dublin)	1965
26	Slow Bowlers v. Fast Bowlers (Lord's)	1849
26	England v. M.C.C. (Lord's)	1877
26	England XI v. Australians (Aston, Birmingham)	1884
27	England v. Sussex (Brighton)	1827
27	Lord Sheffield's XI v. Australians (Sheffield Park)	1890
27	Rest v. England (Bradford—Test Trial)	1950
28	England XI v. Australians (Stoke)	1888
29	Gentlemen of Kent v. Gentlemen of England (Lord's)	1849

Lowest Innings Totals—*Cont.*

30 England v. Sussex (Brighton) 1833
30 England v. Kent (Bromley) 1841
30 Gentlemen of England v. Gentlemen of Kent (Canterbury) 1859
30 United North of England XI v. United South of England XI (Northampton) .. 1872
30 South Africa v. England (Birmingham) 1924
30 Ireland v. New Zealanders (Dublin) 1937

IN AUSTRALIA

15 Victoria v. M.C.C. (Melbourne) 1903-04
18 Tasmania v. Victoria (Melbourne) 1868-69
23 South Australia v. Victoria (Melbourne) 1882-83
27 South Australia v. New South Wales (Sydney) 1955-56
28 Victoria v. New South Wales (Melbourne) 1855-56
31 Victoria v. New South Wales (Melbourne) 1906-07
32 Australian XI v. Vernon's XI (Sydney) 1887-88
34 Victoria v. New South Wales (Melbourne) 1875-76
35 Victoria v. New South Wales (Melbourne) 1887-88
35 Victoria v. New South Wales (Sydney) 1926-27
36 Tasmania v. Victoria (Melbourne) 1870-71
36 South Africa v. Australia (Melbourne) 1931-32
37 New South Wales v. Victoria (Sydney) 1868-69
37 Victoria v. New South Wales (Sydney) 1875-76
38 Victoria v. New South Wales (Sydney) 1856-57
38 Victoria v. New South Wales (Sydney) 1858-59
38 Rest of Australia v. Australian XI (Sydney) 1888-89
38 Western Australia v. Victoria (Melbourne) 1892-93
39 Tasmania v. Victoria (Hobart) 1889-90
40 Queensland v. Victoria (Brisbane) 1902-03

IN SOUTH AFRICA

16 Border v. Natal (East London) 1st innings 1959-60
18 Border v. Natal (East London) 2nd innings 1959-60
23 Border v. Natal (East London) 1920-21
29 Griqualand West v. Transvaal (Johannesburg) 1950-51
30 South Africa v. England (Port Elizabeth) 1895-96
31 Griqualand West v. Natal (Johannesburg) 1906-07
34 Griqualand West v. Transvaal (Port Elizabeth) 1902-03
34 Border v. Eastern Province (East London) 1946-47
35 South Africa v. England (Cape Town) 1898-99
36 Eastern Province v. Transvaal (Port Elizabeth) 1937-38
37 Orange Free State v. Transvaal (Bloemfontein) 1936-37
37 Eastern Province v. Western Province (Port Elizabeth) 1933-34
40 Eastern Province v. Orange Free State (Durban) 1910-11
40 Orange Free State v. Transvaal B (Johannesburg) 1960-61

IN WEST INDIES

16 Trinidad v. Barbados (Bridgetown) 1941-42
22 British Guiana v. Barbados (Bridgetown) 1864-65
33 British Guiana v. Barbados (Bridgetown) 1864-65
33 Priestley's XI v. Trinidad (Port of Spain) 1896-97
33 Jamaica v. Bennett's XI (Kingston) 1901-02
33 West Indian XI v. Bennett's XI (Georgetown) 1901-02
35 Trinidad v. Barbados (Port of Spain) 1893-94

IN NEW ZEALAND

13 Wellington v. Nelson (Nelson) 1862-63
13 Auckland v. Canterbury (Auckland) 1877-78
19 Wellington v. Nelson (Nelson) 1885-86
22 1st inns }
22 2nd inns } Wellington v. Auckland (Auckland) 1862-63
22 Wellington v. Canterbury (Wellington) 1903-04
25 Canterbury v. Otago (Christchurch) 1866-67

Lowest Innings Totals—*Cont.*

26	New Zealand v. England (Auckland)	1954-55
27	Canterbury v. Otago (Dunedin)	1896-97
28	Hawke's Bay v. Auckland (Auckland)	1910-11
29	Wellington v. Nelson (Nelson)	1879-80
30	Wellington v. Nelson (Nelson)	1883-84
31	Wellington v. Nelson (Nelson)	1862-63
31	Wellington v. Nelson (Nelson)	1887-88
32	Canterbury v. Otago (Dunedin)	1863-64
32	Canterbury v. Otago (Christchurch)	1866-67
32	Nelson v. Wellington (Wellington)	1866-67
32	Nelson v. Wellington (Wellington)	1870-71
32	Wellington v. Canterbury (Wellington)	1877-78
32	Hawke's Bay v. Wellington (Wellington)	1883-84
33	Nelson v. Wellington (Wellington)	1866-67
33	Nelson v. Auckland (Nelson)	1882-83
34	Wellington v. Canterbury (Wellington)	1886-87
34	Otago v. Wellington (Dunedin)	1956-57
35	Nelson v. Wellington (Nelson)	1862-63
35	Wellington v. Auckland (Wellington)	1873-74
35	Otago v. Auckland (Christchurch)	1884-85
36	Wellington v. Nelson (Nelson)	1885-86
36	Otago v. New South Wales (Dunedin)	1889-90
37	Nelson v. Wellington (Wellington)	1863-64
37	Wellington v. Nelson (Nelson)	1876-77
37	Canterbury v. Southland (Invercargill)	1920-21
37	Canterbury v. Wellington (Wellington)	1925-26
38	Canterbury v. Otago (Christchurch)	1873-74
39	Wellington v. Auckland (Wellington)	1859-60
39	Taranaki v. Hawke's Bay (Napier)	1891-92
40	Otago v. Canterbury (Dunedin)	1869-70
40	Nelson v. Auckland (Nelson)	1873-74
40	Tasmania v. Otago (Dunedin)	1883-84

IN INDIA

21	Muslims v. Europeans (Poona)	1915-16
22	Southern Punjab v. Northern India (Amritsar)	1934-35
23	Sind v. Southern Punjab (Patiala)	1938-39
23	Jammu & Kashmir v. Delhi (Srinagar) 1st innings	1960-61
24	Europeans v. Parsis (Bombay)	1894-95
25	Saurashtra v. Bombay (Bombay)	1951-52
27	Kerala v. Mysore (Bangalore)	1963-64
28	Mysore v. Bombay (Bangalore)	1951-52
28	Jammu & Kashmir v. Delhi (Srinagar) 2nd innings	1960-61
30	Europeans v. Parsis (Poona)	1895-96
31	East Punjab v. Railways (Jullundur)	1958-59
32	Rajputana v. M.C.C. (Ajmer)	1933-34
33	Parsis v. Europeans (Poona)	1918-19
33	Railways v. Services (New Delhi)	1958-59
35	Orissa v. Bihar (Patna)	1958-59
35	Patiala v. Services (New Delhi)	1958-59
37	Europeans v. Parsis (Poona)	1913-14
36	Kerala v. Madras (Salem)	1961-62
37	Parsis v. Europeans (Poona)	1898-99
37	Parsis v. Europeans (Poona)	1909-10
37	Delhi v. United Provinces (Agra)	1934-35
37	Baroda v. Nawanagar (Jamnagar)	1937-38
37	Jammu & Kashmir v. Services (New Delhi)	1959-60
38	Mysore v. Madras (Madras)	1936-37
38	Jammu & Kashmir v. Delhi (New Delhi)	1963-64
39	Muslims v. Europeans (Poona)	1915-16
39	Maharashtra v. Nawanagar (Jamnagar)	1941-42
39	East Zone v. West Indians (Jorhat)	1958-59
40	Europeans v. Parsis (Bombay)	1904-05
40	Delhi v. N.W.F.P. (Peshawar)	1938-39
40	Railways v. Delhi (New Delhi)	1961-62
40	Kerala v. Mysore (Bangalore)	1965-66

Lowest Innings Totals—*Cont.*

IN PAKISTAN

27	Dera Ismail Khan v. Railways (Lahore) 2nd innings	1964-65
29	Dacca University & Board v. Dacca (Dacca) (*one absent*)	1964-65
30	Quetta v. Karachi B (Karachi)	1957-58
32	Dera Ismail Khan v. Railways (Lahore) 1st innings	1964-65
33	East Pakistan Whites v. Services (Dacca)	1956-57
39	Dacca University v. Bahawalpur (Bahawalpur)	1957-58

LOW SCORING MEMORABILIA

1862-63 Wellington scored only 184 runs in 6 completed innings: 13 & 51 v. Nelson (Nelson), 22 & 22 v. Auckland (Auckland), and 31 & 45 v. Nelson (Nelson)

1899 Although totalling only 86 against Somerset (Lord's), Middlesex dismissed the visitors for 35 and 44 to win by an innings and 7 runs in about three hours' playing time.

1924 Set 58 runs to win by Lancashire at Leeds, Yorkshire were all out for 33. This is the smallest target to be set a defeated side in the County Championship.

1946-47 Set 42 runs to win by Eastern Province at East London, Border were dismissed for only 34. This is the lowest target in first-class cricket for a losing team to be set.

1960-61 After declaring at 385-3, Delhi needed only two bowlers and 105 minutes to twice dismiss Jammu & Kashmir (23 & 28) in their Ranji Trophy match at Srinagar.

1964-65 Railways declared at 910-6, the highest total ever scored in Pakistan, and then dismissed their Ayub Zonal Trophy opponents, Dera Ismail Khan, for 32 & 27. Their victory margin of an innings and 851 runs is the record for all first-class cricket.

1965 F. S. Trueman hit 26 runs off one over from D. Shackleton in Yorkshire's first innings against Hampshire at Middlesbrough; this was three runs more than the entire Yorkshire team scored in the second innings.

LOWEST MATCH AGGREGATES BY ONE TEAM

34	(16 & 18)	Border v. Natal (East London)	1959-60
42	(27 & 15)	Northamptonshire v. Yorkshire (Northampton)	1908
44	(22 & 22)	Wellington v. Auckland (Auckland)	1862-63
47	(12 & 35)	Oxford U. v. M.C.C. (Oxford)	1877
51	(23 & 28)	Jammu & Kashmir v. Delhi (Srinagar)	1960-61
52	(33 & 19)	M.C.C. v. Australians (Lord's)	1878
53	(18 & 35)	The B's v. England (Lord's)	1831
53	(23 & 30)	Kent v. England (Bromley)	1840
55	(36 & 19)	Wellington v. Nelson (Nelson)	1885-86
57	(35 & 22)	Sussex v. Kent (Sevenoaks)	1828
57	(25 & 32)	Canterbury v. Otago (Christchurch)	1866-67
59	(35 & 24)	Sussex v. Yorkshire (Hove)	1878
59	(35 & 24)	Sussex v. Lancashire (Manchester)	1890
59	(32 & 27)	Dera Ismail Khan v. Railways (Lahore)	1964-65

HIGHEST FOURTH INNINGS TOTALS

654-5	(set 696 runs)	England v. South Africa (Durban)	1938-39
604	(lost 354 runs)	Maharashtra v. Bombay (Poona)	1948-49
576-8	(set 672 runs)	Trinidad v. Barbados (Port of Spain)	1945-46
572	(lost 20 runs)	New South Wales v. South Australia (Sydney)	1907-08
529-9	(set 579 runs)	Combined XI v. South Africans (Perth)	1963-64
518	(lost 234 runs)	Victoria v. Queensland (Brisbane)	1926-27
507-7	(and won)	Cambridge U. v. M.C.C. (Lord's)	1896
502-6	(and won)	Middlesex v. Nottinghamshire (Nottingham)	1925
502-8	(and won)	Players v. Gentlemen (Lord's)	1900
495	(lost 145 runs)	Otago v. Wellington (Dunedin)	1923-24
492	(lost 374 runs)	Holkar v. Bombay (Bombay)	1944-45
473-6	(and won)	Canterbury v. Auckland (Christchurch)	1930-31
472	(lost 79 runs)	New South Wales v. Australian XI (Sydney)	1905-06
466	(lost 86 runs)	New South Wales v. West Indians (Sydney)	1930-31
463-8	(set 568 runs)	Hampshire v. Kent (Southampton)	1911
460	(lost 5 runs)	Surrey v. M.C.C. (Lord's)	1938
458	(lost 276 runs)	Auckland v. Wellington (Wellington)	1927-28
456	(lost 50 runs)	Queensland v. Victoria (Melbourne)	1928-29

Highest Fourth Innings Totals—*Cont.*

447	(lost 111 runs)	Orange Free State v. Transvaal (Bloemfontein)	1926-27
446-6	(and won)	New South Wales v. South Australia (Adelaide)	1926-27
442	(lost 45 runs)	South Africans v. New South Wales (Sydney)	1910-11
435-7	(and won)	Victoria v. New South Wales (Melbourne)	1931-32
430-3	(set 448 runs)	New South Wales v. South Africans (Sydney)	1931-32
428-5	(and won)	Sussex v. Northamptonshire (Kettering)	1939
428-6	(and won)	Surrey & Kent v. Middlesex & Essex (Kingston)	1947
427-4	(and won)	Cambridge U. v. Surrey (Oval)	1925
427-9	(and won)	Commonwealth XI v. Bengal Chief Minister's XI (Calcutta)	1964-65
425	(lost 121 runs)	Hassett's XI v. Morris's XI (Melbourne)	1953-54
424-4	(set 508 runs)	Hampshire v. Worcestershire (Worcester)	1926
423-7	(set 451 runs)	South Africa v. England (Oval)	1947
422-9	(set 499 runs)	M.C.C. v. Victoria (Melbourne)	1907-08
420-5	(and won)	Free Foresters v. Oxford U. (Oxford)	1921
419-6	(and won)	Nottinghamshire v. Leicestershire (Nottingham)	1926
416-6	(and won)	Kent v. Surrey (Blackheath)	1934
415	(lost 26 runs)	Victoria v. New South Wales (Sydney)	1935-36
413	(lost 76 runs)	Australians v. Transvaal (Johannesburg)	1966-67
412-4	(and won)	I. Zingari v. Gentlemen of England (Lord's)	1904
412-5	(and won)	M.C.C. v. Oxford U. (Lord's)	1923
412-8	(and won)	Gentlemen v. Players (Lord's)	1904
412	(lost 84 runs)	South Australia v. New South Wales (Sydney)	1912-13
412	(lost 22 runs)	President's XI v. West Indies (Nagpur)	1966-67
411	(lost 193 runs)	England v. Australia (Sydney)	1924-25
409-7	(and won)	Victoria v. South Australia (Adelaide)	1924-25
409-8	(and won)	Rest of Australia v. New South Wales (Sydney)	1933-34
408-5	(set 836 runs)	West Indies v. England (Kingston)	1929-30
406	(lost 17 runs)	South Australia v. New South Wales (Adelaide)	1921-22
404-3	(and won)	Australia v. England (Leeds)	1948
404-5	(and won)	Lancashire v. Hampshire (Southampton)	1910
404	(lost 50 runs)	M.C.C. v. Cambridge U. (Lord's)	1959
403-7	(and won)	Oxford U. v. Worcestershire (Worcester)	1904
403-8	(and won)	Lancashire v. Nottinghamshire (Manchester)	1910
403	(lost 385 runs)	South Australia v. Victoria (Melbourne)	1920-21
402-9	(set 403 runs)	Bradman's XI v. Hassett's XI (Melbourne)	1948-49
401-4	(and won)	New South Wales v. Queensland (Brisbane)	1928-29
401-6	(and won)	Gentlemen of England v. Cambridge U. (Eastbourne)	1908

HIGHEST FOURTH INNINGS TOTAL WITHOUT LOSS

233-0	(and won)	Lancashire v. Sussex (Eastbourne)	1947

W. Place (106) and C. Washbrook (121*) in 115 minutes.*

LARGEST MARGINS OF VICTORY

LARGEST INNINGS VICTORIES

Inns & 851 runs	Railways (910-6d) v. Dera Ismail Khan (Lahore)	1964-65
Inns & 666 runs	Victoria (1059) v. Tasmania (Melbourne)	1922-23
Inns & 656 runs	Victoria (1107) v. New South Wales (Melbourne)	1926-27
Inns & 605 runs	New South Wales (918) v. South Australia (Sydney)	1900-01
Inns & 579 runs	England (903-7d) v. Australia (Oval)	1938
Inns & 527 runs	New South Wales (713) v. South Australia (Adelaide)	1908-09
Inns & 517 runs	Australians (675) v. Nottinghamshire (Nottingham)	1921
Inns & 487 runs	New South Wales (839) v. Tasmania (Sydney)	1898-99
Inns & 487 runs	Australians (679-7d) v. Oxford U. (Oxford)	1938
Inns & 485 runs	Surrey (698) v. Sussex (Oval)	1888
Inns & 484 runs	Australians (621) v. Northamptonshire (Northampton)	1921
Inns & 479 runs	Karachi (772-7d) v. Bahawalpur (Karachi)	1958-59
Inns & 468 runs	Surrey (742) v. Hampshire (Oval)	1909
Inns & 456 runs	Shrewsbury's XI (634) v. Victoria (Melbourne)	1887-88

LARGEST VICTORIES BY RUNS MARGINS

685 runs	New South Wales (235 & 761-8d) v. Queensland (Sydney)	1929-30
675 runs	England (521 & 342-8d) v. Australia (Brisbane)	1928-29
638 runs	New South Wales (304 & 770) v. South Australia (Adelaide)	1920-21

Largest Margins of Victory—*Cont.*

571 runs Victoria (304 & 649) v. South Australia (Adelaide) 1926-27
562 runs Australia (701 & 327) v. England (Oval) 1934
541 runs New South Wales (642 & 593) v. South Australia (Sydney) 1925-26
540 runs Bengal (479 & 321-9d) v. Orissa (Cuttack) 1953-54
531 runs Bombay (596 & 442-5d) v. Holkar (Bombay) 1951-52
530 runs Australia (328 & 578) v. South Africa (Melbourne) 1910-11
512 runs Wellington (447 & 374) v. Auckland (Wellington) 1926-27

VICTORY WITHOUT LOSING A WICKET

1956 Lancashire (166-0d & 66-0) beat Leicestershire (108 & 122) by 10 wickets (Manchester).
1957-58 Karachi A (277-0d) beat Sind A (92 & 108) by an innings & 77 runs (Karachi).
1960-61 Railways (236-0d & 16-0) beat Jammu & Kashmir (92 & 159) by 10 wickets (Srinagar).

VICTORY AFTER FOLLOWING-ON

1888 Lancashire (205 & 172) beat Oxford U. (315 & 42) by 20 runs at Manchester.
1894-95 England (325 & 437) beat Australia (586 & 166) by 10 runs at Sydney.
1901 Somerset (87 & 630) beat Yorkshire (325 & 113) by 279 runs at Leeds.
1902-03 South Australia (304 & 454) beat Lord Hawke's XI (553 & 108) by 97 runs at Adelaide.
1922 Hampshire (15 & 521) beat Warwickshire (223 & 158) by 155 runs at Birmingham.
1926-27 Barbados (175 & 726-7d) beat Trinidad (559 & 217) by 125 runs at Bridgetown.
1932-33 Natal (115 & 458) beat Transvaal (370 & 190) by 13 runs at Durban.
1962-63 Transvaal B. (293 & 362) beat North-Eastern Transvaal (468 & 87) by 100 runs, the last N.E. Transvaal batsman being dismissed by the last possible ball of the match.
1965-66 New South Wales (108 & 450) beat Queensland (307 & 224) by 27 runs at Brisbane.

VARIATION IN INNINGS TOTALS

There are only seven instances of a side's two innings in a match varying in total by 500 runs or more:

551 Barbados (175 & 726-7d) v. Trinidad (Bridgetown) 1926-27
551 Pakistan (106 & 657-8d) v. West Indies (Bridgetown) 1957-58
543 Somerset (87 & 630) v. Yorkshire (Leeds) 1901
531 Free Foresters (65 & 596-8d) v. Cambridge U. (Cambridge) 1919
524 Cambridge U. (179 & 703-9d) v. Sussex (Hove) 1890
506 Hampshire (15 & 521) v. Warwickshire (Birmingham) 1922
500 Essex (597 & 97) v. Derbyshire (Chesterfield) 1904

HIGHEST MATCH AGGREGATES

Runs-Wkts.

2376-38 Bombay v. Maharashtra (Poona) 1948-49
2078-40 Bombay v. Holkar (Bombay) 1944-45
1981-35 South Africa v. England (Durban) 1938-39
1929-39 New South Wales v. South Australia (Sydney) 1925-26
1911-34 New South Wales v. Victoria (Sydney) 1908-09
1905-40 Otago v. Wellington (Dunedin) 1923-24
1815-34 West Indies v. England (Kingston) 1929-30
1801-40 Hassett's XI v. Morris's XI (Melbourne) 1953-54
1753-40 Australia v. England (Adelaide) 1920-21
1752-34 New South Wales v. Queensland (Sydney) 1926-27
1744-40 New South Wales v. South Africans (Sydney) 1910-11
1739-40 New South Wales v. Stoddart's XI (Sydney) 1897-98
1723-31 England v. Australia (Leeds) 1948
1716-40 New South Wales v. South Australia (Sydney) 1907-08
1704-39 Ryder's XI v. Woodfull's XI (Sydney) 1929-30
1683-40 Victoria v. South Australia (Melbourne) 1920-21
1677-37 Barbados v. Trinidad (Bridgetown) 1926-27
1672-39 Bradman's XI v. Hassett's XI (Melbourne) 1948-49

Highest Match Aggregates—*Cont.*

Runs-Wkts.		
1661-36	West Indies v. Australia (Bridgetown)	1954-55
1647-30	Bengal Cyclone XI v. Bijapur Famine XI (Bombay)	1942-43
1646-40	Australia v. South Africa (Adelaide)	1910-11
1640-25	West Indies v. Australia (Bridgetown)	1964-65
1635-31	Trinidad v. Barbados (Port of Spain)	1945-46
1619-40	Australia v. England (Melbourne)	1924-25
1615-40	New South Wales v. Victoria (Sydney)	1907-08
1611-40	Australia v. England (Sydney)	1924-25
1611-24	Holkar v. Mysore (Indore)	1945-46
1607-22	New South Wales v. M.C.C. (Sydney)	1929-30
1605-38	New South Wales v. Queensland (Sydney)	1927-28
1601-29	England v. Australia (Lord's)	1930
1587-40	British Guiana v. Barbados (Georgetown)	1929-30
1581-39	South Australia v. New South Wales (Adelaide)	1921-22
1573-36	South Australia v. New South Wales (Adelaide)	1926-27
1571-38	British Guiana v. Trinidad (Georgetown)	1937-38
1570-40	New South Wales v. South Australia (Sydney)	1912-13
1568-34	South Australia v. New South Wales (Adelaide)	1965-66
1567-37	Auckland v. Wellington (Auckland)	1936-37
1562-37	Australia v. England (Melbourne)	1946-47
1560-37	New South Wales v. Queensland (Sydney)	1928-29
1560-39	Bengal Chief Minister's XI v. Commonwealth XI (Calcutta)	1964-65
1558-30	Victoria v. New South Wales (Melbourne)	1926-27
1558-37	Delhi v. Holkar (New Delhi)	1949-50
1555-40	Holkar v. Gujerat (Indore)	1950-51
1554-35	Australia v. England (Melbourne)	1928-29
1554-40	Wellington v. Auckland (Wellington)	1922-23
1553-33	Australian XI v. Rest of Australia (Sydney)	1898-99
1545-34	Bombay v. Holkar (Bombay)	1951-52
1541-35	Australia v. England (Sydney)	1903-04
1541-28	New South Wales v. M.C.C. (Sydney)	1924-25
1533-33	New South Wales v. Victoria (Sydney)	1924-25
1531-39	Wellington v. Auckland (Wellington	1923-24
1528-24	West Indies v. England (Port of Spain)	1953-54
1522-36	Barbados v. Trinidad (Bridgetown)	1948-49
1516-37	Barbados v. British Guiana (Bridgetown)	1949-50
1514-40	Australia v. England (Sydney)	1894-95
1513-29	New South Wales v. Victoria (Sydney)	1927-28
1510-38	South Australia v. New South Wales (Adelaide)	1920-21
1504-39	Victoria v. Tasmania (Melbourne)	1912-13
1503-37	South Australia v. Victoria (Adelaide)	1924-25
1502-40	Queensland v. New South Wales (Brisbane)	1926-27
1502-28	M.C.C. v. New Zealanders (Lord's)	1927
1502-29	Australia v. England (Adelaide)	1946-47
1501-37	Canterbury v. Otago (Christchurch)	1931-32
1500-35	South Australia v. New South Wales (Adelaide)	1929-30

Aggregates of over 1400 *runs in England:*

1723-31	England v. Australia (Leeds), 5-day match	1849
1601-29	England v. Australia (Lord's), 4-day match	1930
1502-28	M.C.C. v. New Zealanders (Lord's)	1927
1499-31	Pearce's XI v. Australians (Scarborough)	1961
1496-24	England v. Australia (Nottingham)	1938
1494-37	England v. Australia (Oval)	1934
1492-33	Worcestershire v. Oxford U. (Worcester)	1904
1477-32	Hampshire v. Oxford U. (Southampton)	1913
1477-33	England v. South Africa (Oval)	1947
1475-27	Northamptonshire v. Surrey (Northampton)	1920
1469-30	Surrey v. Cambridge U. (Oval)	1921
1458-31	England v. South Africa (Nottingham)	1947
1451-36	Sussex v. Kent (Hastings)	1929
1446-33	Hampshire v. Kent (Southampton)	1911
1443-34	Middlesex v. Gloucestershire (Lord's)	1938
1427-21	Sussex v. Surrey (Hastings)	1902
1426-30	Cambridge U. v. Free Foresters (Cambridge)	1934
1425-16	Worcestershire v. Leicestershire (Worcester)	1906

Highest Match Aggregates—*Cont.*

Runs-Wkts.		
1424-30	Hampshire v. Worcestershire (Bournemouth)	1905
1423-37	North v. South (Torquay)	1955
1422-34	Kent v. Essex (Gravesend)	1938
1422-27	England v. West Indies (Nottingham)	1957
1417-32	North v. South (Kingston)	1947
1414-24	Essex v. Kent (Brentwood)	1934
1410-28	Sussex v. Oxford U. (Hove)	1895
1409-25	Surrey v. Middlesex (Oval)	1919
1409-29	Oxford U. v. M.C.C. (Oxford)	1919
1406-37	Navy & Army v. Oxford & Cambridge U. (Portsmouth)	1911
1405-24	Leicestershire v. Middlesex (Leicester)	1947
1402-40	Sussex v. Cambridge U. (Hove)	1891

LOWEST MATCH AGGREGATES

Lowest aggregates for a completed match:

Runs-Wkts.		
105-31	M.C.C. v. Australians (Lord's)	1878
134-30	England v. The B's (Lord's)	1831
147-40	Kent v. Sussex (Sevenoaks)	1828
149-30	England v. Kent (Lord's)	1858
151-30	Canterbury v. Otago (Christchurch)	1866-67
153-37	M.C.C. v. Sussex (Lord's)	1843
153-31	Otago v. Canterbury (Dunedin)	1896-97
156-30	Nelson v. Wellington (Nelson)	1885-86
158-22	Surrey v. Worcestershire (Oval)	1954
159-31	Nelson v. Wellington (Nelson)	1887-88
165-30	Yorkshire v. Nottinghamshire (Sheffield)	1888
165-30	Middlesex v. Somerset (Lord's)	1899
167-40	Nelson v. Wellington (Nelson)	1862-63
169-35	Wellington v. Nelson (Wellington)	1870-71
171-29	Oxford U. v. M.C.C. (Oxford)	1877
175-35	M.C.C. v. Surrey (Lord's)	1872
175-29	Essex v. Yorkshire (Leyton)	1901
176-32	Otago v. Tasmania (Dunedin)	1883-84
177-40	Nelson v. Wellington (Nelson)	1862-63
181-33	M.C.C. v. North (Lord's)	1848
183-33	Gentlemen of Kent v. M.C.C. (Chislehurst)	1838
183-37	Victoria v. New South Wales (Melbourne)	1855-56
183-30	Lancashire v. Derbyshire (Manchester)	1871
183-40	Nelson v. Wellington (Nelson)	1883-84
184-40	Fast Bowlers v. Slow Bowlers (Lord's)	1849
184-30	Gentlemen of England v. Gentlemen of Kent (Lord's)	1850
185-30	Kent v. England (Canterbury)	1846
186-40	Wellington v. Nelson (Wellington)	1866-67
187-36	M.C.C. v. Sussex (Lord's)	1890
188-32	England v. Kent (Lord's)	1834
188-30	Gentlemen v. Players (Lord's)	1837
188-30	M.C.C. v. Sussex (Lord's)	1838
188-30	M.C.C. v. Oxford U. (Lord's)	1863
188-32	Orissa v. Bihar (Patna)	1958-59
191-40	Oxford U. v. Australians (Oxford)	1886
193-37	Victoria v. New South Wales (Melbourne)	1855-56
193-31	Oxford U. v. M.C.C. (Oxford)	1868
193-29	Yorkshire v. Worcestershire (Bradford)	1900
195-40	Wellington v. Auckland (Auckland)	1862-63
197-30	England v. Surrey (Lord's)	1805
197-31	M.C.C. v. Sussex (Lord's)	1856
198-30	Kent v. England (Bromley)	1841
198-36	M.C.C. v. Sussex (Lord's)	1862
198-22	Eastern Province v. Transvaal (Port Elizabeth)	1937-38

Lowest aggregates for a match in which all 40 *wickets fell:*

147-40	Kent v. Sussex (Sevenoaks)	1828
167-40	Nelson v. Wellington (Nelson)	1862-63
177-40	Nelson v. Wellington (Nelson)	1862-63

Lowest Match Aggregates—*Cont.*

Runs-Wkts.

183-40 Nelson v. Wellington (Nelson) 1883-84
184-40 Fast Bowlers v. Slow Bowlers (Lord's) 1849
186-40 Wellington v. Nelson (Wellington) 1866-67
191-40 Oxford U. v. Australians (Oxford) 1886
195-40 Wellington v. Auckland (Auckland) 1862-63
210-40 M.C.C. v. Middlesex (Lord's) 1815
210-40 England v. Kent (Lord's) 1841
210-40 M.C.C. v. Kent (Lord's) 1856
210-40 M.C.C. v. Kent (Lord's) 1879
211-40 Nelson v. Wellington (Nelson) 1879-80
223-40 Lancashire v. Yorkshire (Manchester) 1893
226-40 Otago v. Canterbury (Dunedin) 1863-64

TIE MATCHES

Before 1948 a match was considered to be tied if the scores were level after the fourth innings, even if the side batting last had wickets in hand when stumps were drawn on the final day. Law 22 was amended in 1948 by Note 4 which states: 'A "Draw" is regarded as a "Tie" when the scores are equal at the conclusion of play but only if the match has been played out.' Tied matches played before 1948 but which would not have qualified as such under this amendment are marked §.

M.C.C. (69 & 107) v. Oxford & Cambridge U. (115 & 61) at Lord's 1839
Surrey (112 & 160) v. Kent (127 & 145) at the Oval 1847
Surrey (204 & 93) v. M.C.C. (175 & 122) at the Oval 1868
Surrey (93 & 186) v. Middlesex (112 & 167) at the Oval 1868
Wellington (63 & 118) v. Nelson (111 & 70) at Wellington 1873-74
Surrey (215 & 245) v. Middlesex (138 & 322) at the Oval 1876
Gentlemen (235 & 149) v. Players (203 & 181) at the Oval 1883
Surrey (97 & 124) v. Lancashire (147 & 74) at the Oval 1894
Worcestershire (224 & 209) v. South Africans (293 & 140) at Worcester 1901
Middlesex (272 & 225) v. South Africans (287 & 210) at Lord's 1904
Surrey (125 & 161) v. Kent (202 & 84) at the Oval 1905
§Lancashire (253 & 168-7) v. England XI (193 & 228-6d) at Blackpool 1905
Lancashire had three wickets to fall with two balls to go, but insufficient time remained for another batsman to go in.
M.C.C. (371 & 69) v. Leicestershire (239 & 201) at Lord's 1907
Jamaica (173 & 227) v. M.C.C. (269 & 131) at Kingston 1910-11
Somerset (243 & 103) v. Sussex (242 & 104) at Taunton 1919
The last Sussex batsman, H. J. Heygate, was not allowed to bat under Law 45.
§Orange Free State (100 & 349) v. Eastern Province (225 & 224-8) at Bloemfontein 1925-26
Eastern Province had two wickets in hand. The match was ruled as an Eastern Province win on first innings for the Currie Cup.
§Essex (178 & 137-9) v. Somerset (208 & 107) at Chelmsford 1926
The ninth Essex wicket fell half a minute before time, and M.C.C. ruled that the match ranked as a tie.
Gloucestershire (72 & 202) v. Australians (157 & 117) at Bristol 1930
§Victoria (327 & 177-3) v. M.C.C. (321 & 183-9d) at Melbourne 1932-33
The third Victorian wicket fell to the last ball of the match with one run needed for victory.
Worcestershire (130 & 142) v. Somerset (131 & 141) at Kidderminster 1939
Southern Punjab (167 & 146) v. Baroda (106 & 207) at Patiala 1945-46
Essex (267 & 239) v. Northamptonshire (215 & 291) at Ilford.. 1947
Hampshire (363 & 224-7d) v. Lancashire (367-9d & 220) at Bournemouth 1947
§Bradman's XI (434 & 402-9) v. Hassett's XI (406 & 430) at Melbourne 1948-49
Hampshire (180 & 152) v. Kent (162 & 170) at Southampton 1950
Sussex (123 & 131) v. Warwickshire (138 & 116) at Hove 1952
Essex (261 & 231) v. Lancashire (266 & 226-7d) at Brentwood 1952
Northamptonshire (182 & 226) v. Middlesex (96 & 312) at Peterborough 1953
Yorkshire (351-4d & 113) v. Leicestershire (328 & 136) at Huddersfield 1954
Sussex (172 & 120) v. Hampshire (153 & 139) at Eastbourne 1955
Victoria (244 & 197) v. New South Wales (281 & 160) at Melbourne (St. Kilda) .. 1956-57
Pearce's XI (313-7d & 258) v. New Zealanders (268 & 303-8d) at Scarborough .. 1958
Essex (364-6d) & 176-8d) v. Gloucestershire (329 & 211) at Leyton 1959
Australia (505 & 232) v. West Indies (453 & 284) at Brisbane. 1960-61
The only instance in Test Matches.
Bahawalpur (123 & 282) v. Lahore B. (127 & 278) at Bahawalpur 1961-62
Hampshire (277 & 173) v. Middlesex (327-5d & 123-9d) at Portsmouth 1967

MATCHES COMPLETED IN ONE DAY

1831 The B's (18 & 35) v. England (81) at Lord's on June 13th.
1837 Cambridge U. (81 & 54-2) v. M.C.C. (70 & 64) at Cambridge on May 18th.
1840 M.C.C. (125) v. Oxford U. (34 & 86) at Lord's on July 9th.
1848 M.C.C. (54 & 81-8) v. Cambridge U. (70 & 64) at Lord's on June 19th.
1848 M.C.C. (167 & 19-3) v. Surrey (56 & 128) at Lord's on July 17th.
1849 Gentlemen of Kent (87 & 29) v. Gentlemen of England (85 & 32-5) at Lord's on July 2nd.
1850 Gentlemen of Kent (59 & 17) v. Gentlemen of England (108) at Lord's on July 1st.
1850 North (131) v. South (36 & 76) at Lord's on July 15th.
1853 Gentlemen of Kent (69 & 65) v. Gentlemen of England (184) at Lord's on July 4th.
1854 M.C.C. (154) v. Surrey (60 & 47) at Lord's on June 12th.
1856 M.C.C. (88 & 11-1) v. Sussex (75 & 23) at Lord's on June 2nd.
1857 Surrey (166) v. Sussex (35 & 31) at the Oval on July 16th.
1858 Kent (33 & 41) v. England (73 & 2-0) at Lord's on July 5th.
1862-63 Auckland (82 & 69) v. Wellington (22 & 22) at Auckland on December 6th.
1863 M.C.C. (31 & 53) v. Oxford U. (104) at Lord's on June 18th.
1866-67 Canterbury (25 & 32) v. Otago (94) at Christchurch on February 7th.
1868 North of Thames (73 & 56) v. South of Thames (106 & 25-1) at Lord's on June 8th.
1872 M.C.C. (16 & 71) v. Surrey (49 & 39-5) at Lord's on May 14th.
1874 Middlesex (61 & 47) v. Oxford U. (123) at Prince's on June 18th.
1875 North (90 & 72) v. South (123 & 41-0) at Lord's on May 17th.
1877 Oxford U. (12 & 35) v. M.C.C. (124) at Oxford on May 24th.
1878 M.C.C. (33 & 19) v. Australians (41 & 12-1) at Lord's on May 27th.
1880 Oxford U. (53 & 75) v. M.C.C. (85 & 41-9) at Oxford on May 28th.
1884 England XI (82 & 26) v. Australians (76 & 33-6) at Aston, Birmingham on May 26th.
1886 M.C.C. (30 & 92) v. Lancashire (53 & 71-4) at Lord's on May 18th.
1887 North (99 & 46-4) v. South (61 & 82) at Lord's on May 30th.
1888 Lancashire (35 & 63) v. Surrey (123) at Manchester on August 2nd.
1889-90 Auckland (62 & 68) v. Otago (48 & 83-2) at Auckland on December 26th.
1891 M.C.C. (127) v. Nottinghamshire (21 & 69) at Lord's on June 1st.
1892 Lancashire (116 & 32-2) v. Somerset (88 & 58) at Manchester on August 9th.
1893-94 Auckland (93 & 102) v. New South Wales (185 & 14-1) at Auckland on January 20t
1894 M.C.C. (103) v. Sussex (42 & 59) at Lord's on May 2nd.
1894 Lancashire (231) v. Somerset (31 & 132) at Manchester on July 17th.
1894 Yorkshire (173) v. Somerset (74 & 94) at Huddersfield on July 19th.
1897 Leicestershire (35 & 35) v. Surrey (164) at Leicester on June 10th.
1898 Hampshire (42 & 36) v. Yorkshire (157) at Southampton on May 27th. (H. Baldwin's benefit.)
1899 Middlesex (86) v. Somerset (35 & 44) at Lord's on May 23rd. (W. Flowers's benefit.)
1900 Yorkshire (99) v. Worcestershire (43 & 51) at Bradford on May 7th.
1903 M.C.C. (150 & 10-1) v. London County (72 & 87) at Lord's on May 20th.
1906-07 Transvaal (180 & 4-0) v. Orange Free State (118 & 64) at Johannesburg on December 30th.
1908 Middlesex (92 & 24-3) v. Philadelphians (58 & 55) at Lord's on July 20th.
1909 Gloucestershire (33 & 81) v. Middlesex (145) at Bristol on August 26th.
1912-13 Eastern Province (209) v. Orange Free State (57 & 121) at Port Elizabeth on December 26th.
1919 Kent (261-6d) v. Sussex (60 & 78) at Tonbridge on June 21st.
1925 Lancashire (130 & 20-1) v. Somerset (74 & 73) at Manchester on May 21st.
1934-35 Madras (130) v. Mysore (48 & 59) at Madras on November 4th.
1937 Ireland (79 & 30) v. New Zealanders (64 & 46-2) at Dublin on September 11th.
1947 Derbyshire (231) v. Somerset (68 & 38) at Chesterfield on June 11th.
1950 Lancashire (239) v. Sussex (101 & 51) at Manchester on July 12th.
1953 Surrey (146) v. Warwickshire (45 & 52) at the Oval on May 16th.
1953 Somerset (55 & 79) v. Lancashire (158) at Bath on June 6th. (H. T. F. Buse's benefit).
1960 Kent (187) v. Worcestershire (25 & 61) at Tunbridge Wells on June 15th.

Lancashire have beaten Somerset in a single day on four occasions: 1892, 1894, 1925 *and* 1953.

TEAMS SCORING FOUR OR MORE CENTURIES IN AN INNINGS

SIX

HOLKAR (912-8d) v. MYSORE (Indore) 1945-46
K. V. Bhandarkar 142, C. T. Sarwate 101, M. M. Jagdale 164, C. K. Nayudu 101, B. B. Nimbalkar 172, R. Pratapsingh 100.

Teams Scoring Four or More Centuries—*Cont.*

FIVE

New South Wales (918) v. South Australia (Sydney) 1900-01
F. A. Iredale 118, M. A. Noble 153, S. E. Gregory 168, R. A. Duff 119, L. O. S. Poidevin 140*.
Australia (758-8d) v. West Indies (Kingston) 1954-55
C. C. McDonald 127, R. N. Harvey 204, K. R. Miller 109, R. G. Archer 128, R. Benaud 121.

FOUR

Yorkshire (887) v. Warwickshire (Birmingham) 1896
R. Peel 210*, F. S. Jackson 117, E. Wainwright 126, Lord Hawke 166.
Derbyshire (645) v. Hampshire (Derby) 1898
L. G. Wright 134, W. Storer 100, W. Chatterton 142, G. Davidson 108.
Lancashire (580) v. Somerset (Manchester) 1904
A. C. MacLaren 151, J. T. Tyldesley 103, A. H. Hornby 114, W. R. Cuttell 101.
M.C.C. (660-8d) v. South Australia (Sydney) 1907-08
A. O. Jones 119, J. Hardstaff, Snr. 135, L. C. Braund 160, J. N. Crawford 114.
Kent (601-8d) v. Somerset (Taunton) 1908
James Seymour 129, F. E. Woolley 105, A. P. Day 118, E. Humphreys 149.
Australian XI (610-6d) v. New Zealand XI (Auckland) 1913-14
E. L. Waddy 140, C. E. Dolling 104, W. W. Armstrong 110*, J. N. Crawford 134.
New South Wales (690) v. South Australia (Adelaide) 1919-20
W. Bardsley 106, J. Bogle 200, T. J. E. Andrews 103, C. E. Kelleway 121*.
Middlesex (543-4d) v. Sussex (Lord's) 1920
P. F. Warner 139, H. W. Lee 119, J. W. Hearne 116*, N. E. Haig 131. The first four batsmen in the order.
New South Wales (786) v. South Australia (Adelaide) 1922-23
J. M. Taylor 159, A. F. Kippax 170, H. L. Hendry 146, W. A. Oldfield 118.
Victoria (617-6d) v. M.C.C. (Melbourne) 1922-23
H. S. B. Love 192, R. L. Park 101, V. S. Ransford 118*, A. E. Liddicut 102.
Middlesex (642-3d) v. Hampshire (Southampton) 1923
H. L. Dales 103, H. W. Lee 107, J. W. Hearne 232, E. Hendren 177*. The first four batsmen in the order.
New South Wales (645) v. Rest of Australia (except Victoria) (Sydney) 1924-25
H. L. Collins 106, J. M. Taylor 111, A. F. Kippax 115, C. E. Kelleway 101.
Victoria (1107) v. New South Wales (Melbourne) 1926-27
W. M. Woodfull 133, W. H. Ponsford 352, H. L. Hendry 100, J. Ryder 295. The first four batsmen in the order.
Barbados (715-9d) v. British Guiana (Bridgetown) 1926-27
P. H. Tarilton 120, G. Challenor 104, E. L. G. Hoad 115, C. A. Browne 131*.
New South Wales (571) v. New Zealanders (Sydney) 1927-28
J. M. Gregory 152, T. J. E. Andrews 134, A. F. Kippax 119, A. A. Jackson 104.
New South Wales (533) v. Victoria (Sydney) 1927-28
A. F. Kippax 134, J. G. Morgan 110, W. A. Oldfield 101, C. O. Nicholls 110.
Nottinghamshire (656-3d) v. Warwickshire (Coventry) 1928
G. Gunn 148, W. W. Whysall 132, W. Walker 146*, F. Barratt 139*.
M.C.C. (502) v. Tasmania (Launceston) 1932-33
H. Sutcliffe 101, Nawab of Pataudi, Snr. 109, L. E. G. Ames 107, E. Paynter 102.
Victoria (558) v. New South Wales (Melbourne) 1934-35
L. P. O'Brien 126, K. E. Rigg 111, L. S. Darling 106, E. H. Bromley 102.
South Australia (644-7d) v. Queensland (Adelaide) 1934-35
V. Y. Richardson 185, H. C. Nitschke 116, A. R. Lonergan 137, C. L. Badcock 137. The first four batsmen in the order.
Auckland (590) v. Canterbury (Auckland) 1937-38
P. E. Whitelaw 108, A. J. Postles 103, V. J. Scott 122, A. M. Matheson 112.
Australians (708-5d) v. Cambridge University (Cambridge) 1938
J. H. Fingleton 111, D. G. Bradman 137, C. L. Badcock 186, A. L. Hassett 220*.
England (658-8d) v. Australia (Nottingham) 1938
L. Hutton 100, C. J. Barnett 126, E. Paynter 216*, D. C. S. Compton 102.
Sussex (631-4d) v. Northamptonshire (Northampton) 1938
John Langridge 227, J. H. Parks 106, G. Cox 101, H. T. Bartlett 101*.
M.C.C. (676) v. Griqualand West (Kimberley) 1938-39
L. Hutton 149, W. J. Edrich 109, E. Paynter 158, N. W. D. Yardley 142.
South Australia (821-7d) v. Queensland (Adelaide) 1939-40
K. L. Ridings 151, D. G. Bradman 138, C. L. Badcock 236, M. G. Waite 137.
Cricket Club of India (654) v. Nayudu's XI (Bombay) 1944-45
V. M. Mankad 121, V. M. Merchant 130, Vijay Hazare 168, R. S. Cooper 127*.

Teams Scoring Four or More Centuries—*Cont.*

BOMBAY (645) v. BARODA (Bombay) 1945-46
K. C. Ibrahim 132, V. M. Merchant 171, U. M. Merchant 136, K. M. Rangnekar 113.
INDIANS (533-3d) v. SUSSEX (Hove) 1946
V. M. Merchant 205, V. M. Mankad 105, Nawab of Pataudi, Snr. 110*, L. Amarnath 106. The only four batsmen to go to the wicket.
SURREY (706-4d) v. NOTTINGHAMSHIRE (Nottingham) 1947
D. G. W. Fletcher 194, H. S. Squires 154, J. F. Parker 108*, E. R. T. Holmes 122*.
BOMBAY (632-7d) v. MAHARASHTRA (Bombay) 1947-48
K. C. Ibrahim 159, P. J. Dickinson 122, M. M. Dalvi 143, M. N. Raiji 130.
AUSTRALIANS (721) v. ESSEX (Southend) 1948
W. A. Brown 153, D. G. Bradman 187, S. J. E. Loxton 120, R. A. Saggers 104*.
WEST INDIES (631) v. INDIA (New Delhi) 1948-49
C. L. Walcott 152, C. E. Gomez 101, E. D. Weekes 128, R. J. Christiani 107.
BENGAL (760) v. ASSAM (Calcutta) 1951-52
P. Roy 146, S. Bose 145, A. D. Gupte 117, C. S. Nayudu 119.
BRITISH GUIANA (601-5d) v. JAMAICA (Georgetown) 1956-57
B. H. Pairaudeau 111, R. B. Kanhai 129, B. F. Butcher 154*, J. S. Solomon 114*.
PUNJAB UNIVERSITY (702) v. SIND UNIVERSITY (Karachi) 1958-59
Saeed Ahmed 140, Khalid Aziz 106, Mohammad Yusuf 115, Zafar Altaf 111.
AUSTRALIANS (449-3d) v. CAMBRIDGE UNIVERSITY (Cambridge) 1961
W. M. Lawry 100, C. C. McDonald 100, B. C. Booth 113, K. D. Mackay 106*. The first four batsmen in the order.
SOUTH AFRICA (618-4d) v. REST OF SOUTH AFRICA (Johannesburg) 1964-65
A. J. Pithey 110, R. G. Pollock 123, K. C. Bland 151*, D. Lindsay 107*.
RAILWAYS (910-6d) v. DERA ISMAIL KHAN (Lahore) 1964-65
Ijaz Hussain 124, Javed Baber 200, Pervez Akhtar 337*, Mohammad Sharif 106*.

TEAMS SCORING SEVEN FIFTIES IN AN INNINGS

AUSTRALIANS (679-7d) v. OXFORD UNIVERSITY (Oxford) 1938
J. H. Fingleton 124, W. A. Brown 72, D. G. Bradman 58, S. J. McCabe 110, A. G. Chipperfield 53, A. L. Hassett 146, M. G. Waite 54. The first seven batsmen in the order.
M.C.C. (641-6) v. BERBICE (Blairmont) 1959-60
G. Pullar 65, M. J. K. Smith 50, J. M. Parks 183, K. F. Barrington 103, R. Illingworth 100, E. R. Dexter 54, R. Subba Row 58*. The first seven batsmen in the order.

MATCHES DOMINATED BY BATTING

(*Qualification:* 1200 *runs, average* 60)

Avge.		
189	Cambridge U. (594-4d) v. West Indians (730-3) at Cambridge	1950
89	Worcs. (380 & 344-2) v. Leics. (701-4d) at Worcester	1906
81	Leics. (609-8d) v. Sussex (686-8) at Leicester	1900
75	Glos. (643-5d) v. Notts. (467 & 168-2) at Bristol	1946
73	Surrey (551-7) v. Yorkshire (704) at The Oval	1899
72	N.S.W. (349 & 364-3) v. M.C.C. (734-7d) at Sydney	1928-29
72	N.S.W. (629-8d & 305-3d) v. M.C.C. (469 & 204-2) at Sydney	1929-30
72	Notts. (401 & 201-4) v. Surrey (706-4d) at Nottingham	1947
71	Guyana (641-5d & 244-5) v. Barbados (552) at Georgetown	1966-67
70	British Guiana (601-5d & 60-1) v. Jamaica (469) at Georgetown	1956-57
70	England (611) v. Australia (656-8d & 4-0) at Manchester	1964
69	Pakistan (580) v. Commonwealth XI (630-9d & 250-2) at Lahore	1963-64
67	Sussex (705-8d & 170-4) v. Surrey (552) at Hastings	1902
67	O.F.S. (552) v. Natal (402 & 452-1) at Bloemfontein	1926-27
67	Glamorgan (196 & 557-4) v. Glos. (505-5d) at Newport	1939
67	Holkar (912-8d) v. Mysore (190 & 509-6) at Indore	1945-46
67	Notts (191 & 519-5) v. Derby (496-3d) at Nottingham	1947
66	Somerset (560-8d) v. Sussex (236 & 466-1) at Taunton	1901
66	Surrey (475-9d & 162-2) v. Australians (629) at The Oval	1934
66	Maharashtra (675) v. Bombay (650) at Poona	1940-41
65	England (627-9d & 123-0d) v. Australia (491 & 66-1) at Manchester	1934
65	India (273 & 333-3) v. West Indies (629-6d) at Bombay	1948-49
65	West Indies (573 & 242-5) v. Australia (650-6d & 175-4d) at Bridgetown	1964-65
64	N.S.W. (713-6d) v. Victoria (265 & 510-7) at Sydney	1928-29

Matches Dominated by Batting—*Cont.*

Avge.		
63	West Indies (681-8d & 212-4d) v. England (537 & 98-3) at Port of Spain ..	1953-54
63	Somerset (361-5d & 272-6) v. Surrey (358-4d & 273-5d) at Taunton	1961
62	Essex (453 & 242-1) v. Sussex (611) at Leyton	1905
62	England (658-8d) v. Australia (411 & 427-6) at Nottingham	1938
62	Hants. (594-6d) v. Glos. (317 & 403-5) at Southampton	1911
62	Maharashtra (798) v. Kathiawar (442) at Poona	1940-41
62	Bombay (651 & 714-8d) v. Maharashtra (407 & 604) at Poona	1948-49
62	Mahood's XI (499-8d & 104-1d) v. Cannon's XI (365-5d & 101-3) at Karachi ..	1953-54
61	Sussex (415-5d & 281) v. South Africans (555-6d & 45-0) at Hove	1947
61	Queensland (613 & 27-1) v. N.S.W. (661) at Brisbane	1963-64
60	Cambridge U. (533) v. Free Foresters (636-7d & 223-6) at Cambridge ..	1938

SIMILARITY OF DISMISSAL

Instances of the same combination of fielder and/or bowler dismissing several batsmen in the same match, with the fielding side listed first: –

HAT TRICKS

st W. H. Brain b C. L. Townsend: Glos. v. Somerset (Cheltenham) 1895
c G. J. Thompson b S. G. Smith: Northants. v. Warwicks. (Birmingham) 1914
lbw b H. Fisher: Yorks. v. Somerset (Sheffield) 1932
c G. Dawkes b H. L. Jackson: Derby. v. Worcs. (Kidderminster) 1958
lbw b J. A. Flavell: Worcs. v. Lancs. (Manchester) 1963

FIRST SIX WICKETS TO FALL IN AN INNINGS

c or st D. Gamsy: Natal v. Orange Free State (Pietermaritzburg) 1960-61
c G. C. Becker: Western Australia v. Victoria (Melbourne) 1965-66

FIRST FIVE WICKETS TO FALL IN AN INNINGS

c or st H. R. Butt: Sussex v. Notts. (Hove) 1905
c G. M. Lee: Notts v. Hants. (Southampton) 1913
c or st H. Elliott: Derby. v. Sussex (Buxton) 1934
c or st K. C. James: Northants. v. Cambridge U. (Cambridge) 1939
c or st J. Ducker: South Australia v. Queensland (Adelaide) 1952-53
c R. T. Spooner: Warwicks. v. Notts. (Birmingham) 1957
c or st R. Julian: Leics. v. Kent (Leicester) 1963

FIRST FOUR WICKETS TO FALL IN AN INNINGS

st M. Turner b J. Buchanan: Gentlemen of England v. Oxford U. (Oxford) 1870
c V. E. Walker b E. Rutter: Middx. v. Surrey (Prince's) 1873
st J. P. Whiteside b F. Geeson: Leics. v. Essex (Leicester) 1901
c T. W. Oates: Notts v. Kent (Catford) 1901
c H. L. Simms b A. E. Relf: Sussex v. Derby (Hove) 1908
c H. R. Murrell: Middx. v. Notts. (Nottingham) 1921
All cleaned bowled for 1: Lancs. v. Essex (Colchester) 1928
c or st W. F. Cornford: Sussex v. Surrey (Oval) 1930
c W. R. Hammond b C. W. L. Parker: Glos. v. Notts. (Bristol) 1933
c A. F. Wensley: Sussex v. Surrey (Horsham) 1934
c F. E. Woolley: Kent v. Notts. (Canterbury) 1934
c or st D. D. Hindlekar: Indians v. Oxford U. (Oxford) 1936
c J. Firth: Leics. v. Essex (Colchester) 1953
c B. T. Swift: Cambridge U. v. Hants (Bournemouth) 1957
c or st G. Millman: Notts. v. Surrey (Oval) 1957
c A. Wilson: Lancs. v. Hants. (Manchester) 1958
c M. F. Tremlett: Somerset v. Lancs. (Weston-super-Mare) 1958
c D. Gamsy: Natal v. Rhodesia (Salisbury) 1960-61
c K. V. Andrew: Northants. v. Sussex (Northampton) 1961

FIRST THREE WICKETS TO FALL IN AN INNINGS

run out: South Australia v. Vernon's XI (Adelaide) 1887-88
st N. C. Tufnell b J. H. B. Lockhart: Cambridge U. v. Australians (Cambridge) .. 1909
c H. L. V. Day b G. S. Boyes: Hants v. Glos. (Southampton) 1922
c G. B. Legge b M. A. McCanlis: Oxford U. v. Cambridge U. (Lord's) 1926

Similarity of Dismissal—*Cont.*

c or st W. H. Livsey b G. Brown: Hants. v. Kent (Southampton) 1926
st W. F. Price b J. W. Hearne: Middx. v. Yorks. (Lord's) 1927
c C. F. Root b C. V. Tarbox, 0: Worcs. v. Essex (Worcester) 1927
st F. L. H. Mooney b T. B. Burtt: New Zealanders v. Leveson-Gowers' XI (Scarborough) 1949
run out: South Australia v. Western Australia (Adelaide) 1954-55

SIX BATSMEN IN SUCCESSION IN COURSE OF AN INNINGS

c A. S. Brown: Glos. v. Notts. (Nottingham) 1966

FIVE BATSMEN IN SUCCESSION IN COURSE OF AN INNINGS

c T. W. Oates b A. W. Hallam: Notts v. Middx. (Nottingham) 1906
c W. R. Hammond b C. W. L. Parker: Glos. v. Surrey (Cheltenham) 1928
c or st P. Corrall: Leics. v. Sussex (Hove) 1936
c or st W. H. V. Levett: Kent v. Glamorgan (Neath) 1939

FOUR BATSMEN IN SUCCESSION IN COURSE OF AN INNINGS

c or st W. F. Farrimond: Lancs. v. Kent (Manchester) 1930
c V. Y. Richardson: Australia v. South Africa (Durban) 1935-36
c John Langridge b James Langridge: Sussex v. Lancs. (Manchester) 1936

SEVEN OUT OF EIGHT WICKETS TO FALL

c or st W. F. Farrimond (www.wwww): Lancs. v. Kent (Manchester) 1930
c A. S. Brown (.wwwwww.w): Glos. v. Notts. (Nottingham) 1966

SEVEN OUT OF NINE WICKETS TO FALL

c W. F. Price (.www.w.www): Middx. v. Yorks. (Lord's) 1937

SIX OUT OF EIGHT SUCCESSIVE WICKETS TO FALL

c or st W. H. V. Levett: Kent v. Northants. (Northampton) 1934
c or st P. Corrall: Leics. v. Sussex (Hove) 1936
c or st M. H. Matthews: Oxford U. v. Surrey (Oval) 1937
c K. C. James: Northants. v. Glamorgan (Swansea) 1937

SIX OUT OF SEVEN SUCCESSIVE WICKETS TO FALL, INCLUDING FIVE IN FIVE

c W. R. Hammond (wwwww.w): Glos. v. Surrey (Cheltenham) 1928
c or st H. Elliott (wwwww.w): Derby v. Lancs. (Manchester) 1935
c or st W. H. V. Levett (wwwww.w): Kent v. Glamorgan (Neath) 1939

FIVE DISMISSALS IN ONE INNINGS (OUTSTANDING CASES)

c F. G. J. Ford (only 7 wkts fell): Cambridge U. v. M.C.C. (Lord's) 1888
c or st D. Hunter b W. Rhodes (last 5 wkts): Yorks. v. Surrey (Bradford) 1898
c T. W. Oates b A. W. Hallam (in 34 balls): Notts. v. Middx. (Nottingham) .. 1906
st N. C. Tufnell b J. H. B. Lockhart: Cambridge U. v. Yorks. (Cambridge) .. 1909
c G. Brown b A. Jaques: Hants. v. Somerset (Bath) 1914
c J. F. Sheppard b D. MacAndrews: Queensland v. N.S.W. (Brisbane) 1914-15
c J. H. Nicholson b V. W. C. Jupp: Northants. v. Worcs. (Dudley) 1928
c V. Y. Richardson (....w.wwww): Australia v. South Africa (Durban) 1935-36
c T. N. Pierce b J. E. D. Sealy: Trinidad v. Barbados (Bridgetown) 1941-42
c and b R. E. East: Essex v. Glos. (Ilford) 1966
c Ealham b D. L. Underwood: Kent v. Glos. (Folkestone) 1966

(*All in the same place topographically: four off right-handed batsmen at long-off and the other at long-on off a left hander*).

UNUSUAL DISMISSALS

Although there are nine ways in which a batsman can lose his wicket, three of them occur very rarely: handled ball, hit the ball twice, and obstructing the field. There have been few instances of a substitute wicket-keeper making a stumping, or of a bowler running-out a non-striking batsman for backing up before the ball has been bowled and these are listed also.

Unusual Dismissals—*Cont.*

HANDLED BALL

Before the introduction of Law 33b in 1899, a batsman could be dismissed 'handled ball' for removing a ball lodged in his clothing. The instances in 1872, 1893, and 1894-95 occurred before this amendment which ruled such a ball to be 'dead'.

J. Grundy (15): M.C.C. v. Kent (Lord's) 1857
G. Bennett (0): Kent v. Sussex (Hove) 1872
W. H. Scotton (18): Smokers v. Non-Smokers (East Melbourne) 1886-87
C. W. Wright (4): Nottinghamshire v. Gloucestershire (Bristol) 1893
E. Jones (9): South Australia v. Victoria (Melbourne) 1894-95
A. D. Nourse, Snr. (1): South Africans v. Sussex (Hove) 1907
E. T. Benson (29): M.C.C. v. Auckland (Auckland) 1929-30
A. W. Gilbertson (7): Otago v. Auckland (Auckland) 1952-53
W. R. Endean (3): South Africa v. England (Cape Town) 1956-57
P. J. Burge (11): Queensland v. New South Wales (Sydney) 1958-59
Dildar Awan (8): Services v. Lahore (Lahore) 1959-60
Mahmood-ul-Hasan (50): Karachi U. v. Railways & Quetta (Karachi) 1960-61
Ali Reza (52): Karachi Greens v. Hyderabad (Karachi) 1961-62
Mohammad Yusuf (35): Rawalpindi v. Peshawar (Peshawar) 1962-63
A. Rees (14): Glamorgan v. Middlesex (Lord's) 1965

HIT THE BALL TWICE

H. E. Bull (29): M.C.C. v. Oxford U. (Lord's) 1864
H. Charlwood (73): Sussex v. Surrey (Hove) 1872
I. J. Salmon (13): Wellington v. Hawke's Bay (Wellington) 1873-74
R. G. Barlow (20): North v. South (Lord's) 1878
P. S. Wimble (0): Transvaal v. Griqualand West (Kimberley) 1892-93
G. B. Nicholls (10): Somerset v. Gloucestershire (Bristol) 1896
A. A. Lilley (13): Warwickshire v. Yorkshire (Birmingham) 1897
J. H. King (13): Leicestershire v. Surrey (Oval) 1906
A. P. Binns (151): Jamaica v. British Guiana (Georgetown) 1956-57

OBSTRUCTING THE FIELD

C. A. Absolom (38): Cambridge U. v. Surrey (Oval) 1868
T. Straw (8): Worcestershire v. Warwickshire (Worcester) 1899
T. Straw (3): Worcestershire v. Warwickshire (Birmingham) 1901
J. P. Whiteside (0): Leicestershire v. Lancashire (Leicester) 1901
L. Hutton (27): England v. South Africa (Oval) 1951
J. A. Hayes (0): Canterbury v. Central Districts (Christchurch) 1954-55
D. D. Deshpande (6): Madhya Pradesh v. Uttar Pradesh (Benares) 1956-57
K. Ibadulla (0): Warwickshire v. Hampshire (Coventry) 1963
Kaiser (3): Dera Ismail Khan v. Railways (Lahore) 1964-65

RUN OUT BY THE BOWLER

(while backing up before the ball had been bowled)

G. Jones (6) by (name unknown): Surrey v. Australians (Oval) 1878
C. W. Wright (13) by G. P. Harrison: Cambridge U. v. Yorks. (Cambridge) .. 1883
E. J. Tyler (25) by A. Hearne: Somerset v. Kent (Taunton) 1894
T. W. Reese (15) by A. Downes: Canterbury v. Otago (Christchurch) 1894-95
J. Hardstaff, Jnr. (2) by Khadim Hussain: Lord Tennyson's XI v. Sind (Karachi) .. 1937-38
W. A. Brown (30) by V. M. Mankad: Australian XI v. Indians (Sydney) 1947-48
W. A. Brown (18) by V. M. Mankad: Australia v. India (Sydney) 1947-48
R. Routledge (1) by J. P. Fellows-Smith: Middlesex v. Oxford U. (Oxford) 1953
G. E. Barker (33) by W. Wooller: Essex v. Glamorgan (Cardiff) 1956
G. G. Arnold (71) by Saeed Ahmed: M.C.C. v. Central Zone (Sahiwal) 1966-67

STUMPED BY A SUBSTITUTE

N. C. Tufnell (sub for H. Strudwick) st S. J. Snooke: England v. South Africa (Durban) 1909-10
N. C. Tufnell (sub for W. Findlay) st G. C. Drysdale: M.C.C. v. Argentine (Buenos Aires) 1911-12
F. E. Kapadia (sub for B. E. Kapadia) st G. S. Boyes: Bombay v. M.C.C. (Bombay) 1926-27
Naik (sub for A. Rangabashyam) st E. L. Grant: Indians v. Europeans (Madras) .. 1927-28
L. E. G. Ames (sub for R. T. Stanyforth) st J. S. Mackenzie: M.C.C. v. British Guiana (Georgetown) .. 1929-30

Unusual Dismissals—*Cont.*

A. M. Taylor (sub for C. L. Browne) st L. R. Pierre: Barbados v. Trinidad (Port of Spain) .. 1941-42
Parthasarathy (sub for P. Sen) st D. C. S. Compton: Governor's XI v. Services XI (Calcutta) .. 1944-45
R. T. Spooner (sub for J. T. Kendall) st I. J. M. Lumsden: Warwicks. v. Scotland (Birmingham) .. 1948
H. W. Stephenson (sub for A. T. Barlow) st M. D. Mohoni: Commonwealth v. Governor's XI (Nagpur) .. 1950-51
P. Rochford (sub for D. V. Brennan) st T. E. Bailey: Yorks. v. M.C.C. (Scarborough) .. 1951
M. Fitchett (sub for I. H. McDonald) st J. Grove: Victoria v. South Australia (Adelaide) .. 1952-53
L. A. Johnson (sub for K. V. Andrew) st P. M. Walker: Northants. v. Glamorgan (Northampton) .. 1959
E. Legard (sub for A. C. Smith) st A. M. Zuill: Warwickshire v. Scotland (Birmingham) 1962
N. L. Majendie (sub for A. L. Mason) st B. Whittingham: Oxford U. v. Nottinghamshire (Oxford) .. 1963
D. L. Murray (sub for D. W. Allan) st J. Cotton: West Indians v. M.C.C. (Lord's) .. 1963
C. J. Saunders (sub for Asif Ahmed) st D. Brown: Oxford U. v. Gloucestershire (Bristol) .. 1964
B. E. Congdon (sub for A. E. Dick) st Pervez Sajjad: New Zealand v. Pakistan (Lahore) 1964-65

MEMORABILIA

J. Potter (Australians) was bowled by the seventh ball of G. Cross's over v. Leicestershire (Leicester) 1964.

PLAYERS' RECORDS—BATTING

HIGHEST INDIVIDUAL INNINGS

499	Hanif Mohammad: Karachi v. Bahawalpur (Karachi)	1958-59
452*	D. G. Bradman: New South Wales v. Queensland (Sydney)	1929-30
443*	B. B. Nimbalkar: Maharashtra v. Kathiawar (Poona)	1948-49
437	W. H. Ponsford: Victoria v. Queensland (Melbourne)	1927-28
429	W. H. Ponsford: Victoria v. Tasmania (Melbourne)	1922-23
424	A. C. MacLaren: Lancashire v. Somerset (Taunton)	1895
385	B. Sutcliffe: Otago v. Canterbury (Christchurch)	1952-53
383	C. W. Gregory: New South Wales v. Queensland (Brisbane)	1906-07
369	D. G. Bradman: South Australia v. Tasmania (Adelaide)	1935-36
365*	C. Hill: South Australia v. New South Wales (Adelaide)	1900-01
365*	G. St. A. Sobers: West Indies v. Pakistan (Kingston)	1957-58
364	L. Hutton: England v. Australia (Oval)	1938
359*	V. M. Merchant: Bombay v. Maharashtra (Bombay)	1943-44
359	R. B. Simpson: New South Wales v. Queensland (Brisbane)	1963-64
357*	R. Abel: Surrey v. Somerset (Oval)	1899
357	D. G. Bradman: South Australia v. Victoria (Melbourne)	1935-36
355	B. Sutcliffe: Otago v. Auckland (Dunedin)	1949-50
352	W. H. Ponsford: Victoria v. New South Wales (Melbourne)	1926-27
345	C. G. Macartney: Australians v. Nottinghamshire (Nottingham)	1921
344*	G. A. Headley: Jamaica v. Lord Tennyson's XI (Kingston)	1931-32
344	W. G. Grace: M.C.C. v. Kent (Canterbury)	1876
343*	P. A. Perrin: Essex v. Derbyshire (Chesterfield)	1904
341	G. H. Hirst: Yorkshire v. Leicestershire (Leicester)	1905
340*	D. G. Bradman: New South Wales v. Victoria (Sydney)	1928-29
338*	R. C. Blunt: Otago v. Canterbury (Christchurch)	1931-32
338	W. W. Read: Surrey v. Oxford U. (Oval)	1888
337*	Pervez Akhtar: Railways v. Dera Ismail Khan (Lahore)	1964-65
337	Hanif Mohammad: Pakistan v. West Indies (Bridgetown)	1957-58
336*	W. R. Hammond: England v. New Zealand (Auckland)	1932-33
336	W. H. Ponsford: Victoria v. South Australia (Melbourne)	1927-28
334	D. G. Bradman: Australia v. England (Leeds)	1930
333	K. S. Duleepsinhji: Sussex v. Northamptonshire (Hove)	1930

Highest Individual Innings—*Cont.*

332	W. H. Ashdown: Kent v. Essex (Brentwood)	1934
331*	J. D. Robertson: Middlesex v. Worcestershire (Worcester)	1949
325*	H. L. Hendry: Victoria v. New Zealanders (Melbourne)	1925-26
325	C. L. Badcock: South Australia v. Victoria (Adelaide)	1935-36
325	A. Sandham: England v. West Indies (Kingston)	1929-30
324	J. B. Stollmeyer: Trinidad v. British Guiana (Port of Spain)	1946-47
323	A. L. Wadekar: Bombay v. Mysore (Bombay)	1966-67
322	E. Paynter: Lancashire v. Sussex (Hove)	1937
321	W. L. Murdoch: New South Wales v. Victoria (Sydney)	1881-82
319	Gul Mahomed: Baroda v. Holkar (Baroda)	1946-47
318*	W. G. Grace: Gloucestershire v. Yorkshire (Cheltenham)	1876
317	W. R. Hammond: Gloucestershire v. Nottinghamshire (Gloucester)	1936
316*	Vijay Hazare: Maharashtra v. Baroda (Poona)	1939-40
316*	J. B. Hobbs: Surrey v. Middlesex (Lord's)	1926
316	R. H. Moore: Hampshire v. Warwickshire (Bournemouth)	1937
315*	T. W. Hayward: Surrey v. Lancashire (Oval)	1898
315*	P. Holmes: Yorkshire v. Middlesex (Lord's)	1925
315*	A. F. Kippax: New South Wales v. Queensland (Sydney)	1927-28
314*	C. L. Walcott: Barbados v. Trinidad (Port of Spain)	1945-46
313	H. Sutcliffe: Yorkshire v. Essex (Leyton)	1932
312*	W. W. Keeton: Nottinghamshire v. Middlesex (Oval)	1939
312*	J. M. Brearley: M.C.C. Under-25 v. North Zone (Peshawar)	1966-67
311	J. T. Brown: Yorkshire v. Sussex (Sheffield)	1897
311	R. B. Simpson: Australia v. England (Manchester)	1964
310*	J. H. Edrich: England v. New Zealand (Leeds)	1965
310	H. Gimblett: Somerset v. Sussex (Eastbourne)	1948
309	Vijay Hazare: Rest v. Hindus (Bombay)	1943-44
308*	F. M. M. Worrell: Barbados v. Trinidad (Bridgetown)	1943-44
307	M. C. Cowdrey: M.C.C. v. South Australia (Adelaide)	1962-63
307	R. M. Cowper: Australia v. England (Melbourne)	1965-66
306*	A. Ducat: Surrey v. Oxford U. (Oval)	1919
306*	E. A. B. Rowan: Transvaal v. Natal (Johannesburg)	1939-40
305*	F. E. Woolley: M.C.C. v. Tasmania (Hobart)	1911-12
305*	F. R. Foster: Warwickshire v. Worcestershire (Dudley)	1914
305*	W. H. Ashdown: Kent v. Derbyshire (Dover)	1935
304*	P. H. Tarilton: Barbados v. Trinidad (Bridgetown)	1919-20
304*	A. D. Nourse, Snr.: Natal v. Transvaal (Johannesburg)	1919-20
304*	E. D. Weekes: West Indians v. Cambridge U. (Cambridge)	1950
304	R. M. Poore: Hampshire v. Somerset (Taunton)	1899
304	D. G. Bradman: Australia v. England (Leeds)	1934
303*	W. W. Armstrong: Australians v. Somerset (Bath)	1905
302*	P. Holmes: Yorkshire v. Hampshire (Portsmouth)	1920
302*	W. R. Hammond: Gloucestershire v. Glamorgan (Bristol)	1934
302	W. R. Hammond: Gloucestershire v. Glamorgan (Newport)	1939
301*	E. Hendren: Middlesex v. Worcestershire (Dudley)	1933
301	W. G. Grace: Gloucestershire v. Sussex (Bristol)	1896
300*	V. T. Trumper: Australians v. Sussex (Hove)	1899
300*	F. Watson: Lancashire v. Surrey (Manchester)	1928
300*	Imtiaz Ahmed: Prime Minister's XI v. Commonwealth (Bombay)	1950-51
300	J. T. Brown: Yorkshire v. Derbyshire (Chesterfield)	1898
300	D. C. S. Compton: M.C.C. v. North-Eastern Transvaal (Benoni)	1948-49
300	R. Subba Row: Northamptonshire v. Surrey (Oval)	1958

HIGHEST INDIVIDUAL INNINGS FOR AND AGAINST EACH TEAM

(*Complete details of each innings over* 200 *can be found by reference to the list of double centuries*).

ENGLAND:

	For		Against	
Derbyshire	274	G. Davidson	343*	P. A. Perrin (Essex)
Essex	343*	P. A. Perrin	332	W. H. Ashdown (Kent)
Glamorgan	287*	E. Davies	302*	W. R. Hammond (Glos.)
Gloucestershire	318*	W. G. Grace	296	A. O. Jones (Notts.)
Hampshire	316	R. H. Moore	302*	P. Holmes (Yorks.)
Kent	332	W. H. Ashdown	344	W. G. Grace (M.C.C.)
Lancashire	424	A. C. MacLaren	315*	T. W. Hayward (Surrey)
Leicestershire	252*	S. Coe	341	G. H. Hirst (Yorks.)

Highest Individual Innings For and Against Each Team—*Cont.*

	For		Against	
Middlesex	331*	J. D. Robertson	316*	J. B. Hobbs (Surrey)
Northamptonshire ..	300	R. Subba Row	333	K. S. Duleepsinhji (Sussex)
Nottinghamshire ..	312*	W. W. Keeton	345	C. G. Macartney (Australians)
Somerset	310	H. Gimblett	424	A. C. MacLaren (Lancs.)
Surrey	357*	R. Abel	300*	F. Watson (Lancs.)
			300	R. Subba Row (Northants.)
Sussex	333	K. S. Duleepsinhji	322	E. Paynter (Lancs.)
Warwickshire ..	305*	F. R. Foster	316	R. H. Moore (Hants.)
Worcestershire.. ..	276	F. L. Bowley	331*	J. D. Robertson (Middx.)
Yorkshire	341	G. H. Hirst	318*	W. G. Grace (Glos.)
M.C.C.	344	W. G. Grace	281*	W. H. Ponsford (Australians)
Oxford U.	281	K. J. Key	338	W. W. Read (Surrey)
Cambridge U. ..	254*	K. S. Duleepsinhji	304*	E. D. Weekes (West Indians)
England (Tests) ..	364	L. Hutton	334	D. G. Bradman (Australia)
Australians	345	C. G. Macartney	364	L. Hutton (England)
South Africans ..	239	M. Hathorn	229	G. J. Bryan (Combined Services)
West Indians	304*	E. D. Weekes	285*	P. B. H. May (England)
New Zealanders ..	243	B. Sutcliffe	310*	J. H. Edrich (England)
Indians	252*	P. R. Umrigar	246*	G. Boycott (England)
Pakistan	191	Hanif Mohammad	278	D. C. S. Compton (England)

AUSTRALIA:

	For		Against	
New South Wales ..	452*	D. G. Bradman	365*	C. Hill (South Australia)
Queensland	283	P. J. Burge	452*	D. G. Bradman (New South Wales)
South Australia ..	369	D. G. Bradman	336	W. H. Ponsford (Victoria)
Tasmania	274	C. L. Badcock	429	W. H. Ponsford (Victoria)
Victoria	437	W. H. Ponsford	357	D. G. Bradman (South Australia)
Western Australia ..	236*	R. B. Simpson	247*	R. B. Simpson (New South Wales)
M.C.C./England ..	307	M. C. Cowdrey	307	R. M. Cowper (Australia)
Australia (Tests) ..	307	R. M. Cowper	287	R. E. Foster (England)
South Africans ..	209	E. J. Barlow	299*	D. G. Bradman (Australia)
West Indians	252	R. B. Kanhai	223	D. G. Bradman (Australia)
New Zealanders ..	160	J. R. Reid	325*	H. L. Hendry (Victoria)
Indians	228*	L. Amarnath	201	D. G. Bradman (Australia)
Pakistanis	154	Mohammad Ilyas	125	G. Thomas (New South Wales)

SOUTH AFRICA:

	For		Against	
Border	207	W. S. Farrer	261*	S. S. L. Steyn (Western Province)
Eastern Province ..	284	E. A. B. Rowan	247	W. R. Endean (Transvaal)
Griqualand West ..	215	K. G. Viljoen	284	E. A. B. Rowan (Eastern Province)
Natal	304*	A. D. Nourse, Snr.	306*	E. A. B. Rowan (Transvaal)
North-Eastern Transvaal	237	P. L. Corbett	300	D. C. S. Compton (M.C.C.)
Orange Free State ..	258	C. Richardson	279*	P. Holmes (M.C.C.)
Rhodesia	179	B. J. Carew	222*	A. L. Wilmot (Eastern Province)
Transvaal	306*	E. A. B. Rowan	304*	A. D. Nourse, Snr. (Natal)
Western Province ..	271*	J. E. Cheetham	240	A. D. Nourse, Jnr. (Natal)
M.C.C./England ..	300	D. C. S. Compton	176*	J. W. Zulch (Transvaal)
			176	H. W. Taylor (South Africa)
Australians	243	R. B. Simpson	235	A. Bacher (Transvaal)
New Zealanders ..	203	J. R. Reid	147*	W. S. Farrer (South African Colts)

WEST INDIES:

	For		Against	
Barbados	314*	C. L. Walcott	281*	W. R. Hammond (M.C.C.)
Berbice	201*	J. S. Solomon	183	J. M. Parks (M.C.C.)
British Guiana/Guyana	268	H. P. Bayley	324	J. B. Stollmeyer (Trinidad)
Jamaica	344*	G. A. Headley	275	W. A. Farmer (Barbados)
Leeward Islands ..	100	O. Williams	188	R. M. Cowper (Australians)
Trinidad	324	J. B. Stollmeyer	314*	C. L. Walcott (Barbados)
Windward Islands ..	86	H. Bristol	176	B. A. Davis (Trinidad)
Windward & Leeward Is.	113*	I. Shillingford	197	C. Wiltshire (British Guiana)
English teams	325	A. Sandham	344*	G. A. Headley (Jamaica)
Australians	210	W. M. Lawry	219	D. Atkinson (West Indies)
Indians	172*	P. R. Umrigar	253	E. D. Weekes (Barbados)
Pakistanis	337	Hanif Mohammad	365*	G. St. A. Sobers (West Indies)

Highest Individual Innings For and Against Each Team—*Cont.*

NEW ZEALAND:

	For		Against	
Auckland	290	W. N. Carson	355	B. Sutcliffe (Otago)
Canterbury	226	B. F. Hastings	385	B. Sutcliffe (Otago)
Central Districts	163	L. B. Reade	264	B. Sutcliffe (Otago)
Northern Districts	136	E. C. Petrie	296	J. R. Reid (Wellington)
Otago	385	B. Sutcliffe	290	W. N. Carson (Auckland)
Wellington	296	J. R. Reid	206	G. T. Dowling (Canterbury)
			206	M. L. Page (Canterbury)
M.C.C./England	336*	W. R. Hammond	197	B. Sutcliffe (Otago)
Australians	293	V. T. Trumper	198	W. A. Hadlee (Otago)
South Africans	255*	D. J. McGlew	165	M. E. Chapple (Canterbury)
West Indians	156	E. D. Weekes	114	L. S. M. Miller (Wellington)
Pakistanis	142	Saeed Ahmed	127*	W. J. Mitchell (Northern Districts)

Records for teams in India and Pakistan are restricted to those for touring teams as the home teams of these two countries have had numerous changes of title.

INDIA:

M.C.C./England	183	J. D. Robertson	203*	Nawab of Pataudi, Jnr. (India)
Australians	284	N. C. O'Neill	128*	Nawab of Pataudi, Jnr. (India)
West Indians	256	R. B. Kanhai	223*	L. Amarnath (North Zone)
New Zealanders	230*	B. Sutcliffe	231	V. M. Mankad (India)
Pakistanis	222	Hanif Mohammad	177*	C. G. Borde (India)

PAKISTAN:

M.C.C./England	312*	J. M. Brearley	147	Shuja-ud-Din (Pakistan Services XI)
Australians	153	R. B. Simpson	166	Saeed Ahmed (Pakistan)
			166	K. Ibadulla (Pakistan)
West Indians	217	R. B. Kanhai	131	Imtiaz Ahmed (Pakistan)
New Zealanders	150*	J. R. Reid	209	Imtiaz Ahmed (Pakistan)
Indians	151	P. R. Umrigar	163	Hanif Mohammad (Combined Schools)

HIGHEST MAIDEN CENTURIES

337*	Pervez Akhtar: Railways v. Dera Ismail Khan (Lahore)	1964-65
292*	V. T. Trumper: New South Wales v. Tasmania (Sydney)	1898-99
290	W. N. Carson: Auckland v. Otago (Dunedin)	1936-37
282	H. L. Collins: New South Wales v. Tasmania (Hobart)	1912-13
275	W. A. Farmer: Barbados v. Jamaica (Bridgetown)	1951-52
274	G. Davidson: Derbyshire v. Lancashire (Manchester)	1896
271	R. Maddocks: Victoria v. Tasmania (Melbourne)	1951-52
268	C. R. Maxwell: Cahn's XI v. Leicestershire (Nottingham)	1935
268	H. P. Bayley: British Guiana v. Barbados (Georgetown)	1937-38
264	P. Vaulkhard: Derbyshire v. Nottinghamshire (Nottingham)	1946
264*	R. Flockton: New South Wales v. South Australia (Sydney)	1959-60
262*	L. Wight: British Guiana v. Barbados (Georgetown)	1951-52
261*	S. S. L. Steyn: Western Province v. Border (Cape Town)	1929-30
261	I. R. Redpath: Victoria v. Queensland (Melbourne)	1962-63
253	L. S. Birkett: Trinidad v. British Guiana (Georgetown)	1929-30

DOUBLE CENTURIES

MOST IN A SEASON

Six	D. G. Bradman	1930	334	254	252*	236	232	205*
Five	K. S. Ranjitsinhji	1900	275	222	220	215*	202	
	E. D. Weekes	1950	232	304*	279	246*	200*	
Four	C. B. Fry	1901	244	241	219*	209		
	E. Hendren	1929-30	254*	223*	211*	205* (West Indies)		
	W. R. Hammond	1933	264	239	231	206		
	W. R. Hammond	1934	302*	290	265*	217		
	V. M. Merchant	1944-45	221*	217	278	201 (India)		

Double Centuries—*Cont.*

TWO IN SUCCESSIVE INNINGS

W. W. Read (Surrey) in 1887—247 and 244*.
K. S. Ranjitsinhji (Sussex) in 1900—222 and 215*.
K. S. Ranjitsinhji (Sussex) in 1901—285* and 204.
F. A. Tarrant (Middlesex) in 1914—250* and 200.
T. F. Shepherd (Surrey) in 1921—212 and 210*.
W. H. Ponsford (Victoria) in 1927-28—437 and 202.
W. R. Hammond (England) in 1928-29—251 and 200 (both in Test matches).
E. Hendren (M.C.C. in West Indies) in 1929-30—223* and 211*.
E. Hendren (M.C.C. in West Indies) in 1929-30—205* and 254*.
D. G. Bradman (New South Wales) in 1931-32—226 and 219.
W. R. Hammond (England) in 1932-33—227 and 336* (both in Test matches).
A. H. Bakewell (Northamptonshire) in 1933—246 and 257.
Nawab of Pataudi, Snr. (Worcestershire) in 1933—231* and 222.
D. G. Bradman (Australia) in 1934—304 and 244 (both in Test matches).
W. H. Ponsford (Australians) in 1934—229* and 281*.
D. G. Bradman (South Australia) in 1935-36—233 and 357.
W. R. Hammond (Gloucestershire) in 1933—231 and 264.
D. G. Bradman (South Australia) in 1935-36 and 1936-37—369 and 212.
A. E. Fagg (Kent) in 1938—244 and 202* (both in same match).
V. M. Merchant (Hindus) in 1941-42—243* and 221.
V. M. Merchant (Hindus & Bombay) in 1944-45—221* and 217.
R. S. Modi (Bombay) in 1944-45—210 and 245*.
E. D. Weekes (West Indians) in 1950—232 and 304*.
E. D. Weekes (West Indians) in 1950—246* and 200*.
F. M. M. Worrell (West Indians) in 1950—241* and 261.
E. D. Weekes (Barbados) in 1952-53—207 and 253.
R. B. Simpson (Western Australia) in 1959-60—236* and 230*.
P. J. Burge (Queensland) in 1963-64—283 and 205*.
R. B. Simpson (Combined XI & New South Wales) in 1963-64—246 and 247*.
K. F. Barrington (England & Surrey) in 1964—256 and 207.

NEAREST TO THREE IN SUCCESSIVE INNINGS

W. G. Grace (Gloucestershire) in 1876—344, 177 and 318*.
C. Hill (South Australia) in 1909-10—176, 205 and 185.
E. Hendren (M.C.C. in West Indies) in 1929-30—205*, 254* and 171.
V. M. Merchant (Hindus) in 1941-42—170*, 243*, 221 and 153*.
R. B. Simpson (New South Wales & Combined XI) in 1963-64—359, 4, 246, 247*.

PLAYERS SCORING DOUBLE CENTURIES IN FIRST-CLASS CRICKET

Player	No.	Score	Match	Season
Abel, R.	(9)	217	Surrey v. Essex (Oval)	1895
		231	Surrey v. Essex (Oval)	1896
		250	Surrey v. Warwickshire (Oval)	1897
		215	Surrey v. Nottinghamshire (Oval)	1897
		219	Surrey v. Kent (Oval)	1898
		357*	Surrey v. Somerset (Oval)	1899
		221	Surrey v. Worcestershire (Oval)	1900
		247	Players v. Gentlemen (Oval)	1901
		205*	Surrey v. Middlesex (Oval)	1901
Abell, G. E. B.	(1)	210	Northern India v. Army (Lahore)	1934-35
Ackerman, H. L. ..	(1)	200*	North-Eastern Transvaal v. Western Province (Cape Town)	1966-67
Adhikari, H. R. ..	(1)	230*	Services v. Rajasthan (Ajmer)	1951-52
Akash Lal	(1)	209*	Delhi v. Jammu & Kashmir (Srinagar) ..	1964-65
Allen, B. O.	(1)	220	Gloucestershire v. Hampshire (Bournemouth)	1947
Alley, W. E.	(3)	209*	Commonwealth v. West Zone (Poona) ..	1949-50
		206*	Commonwealth v. Cricket Club of India (Bombay)	1949-50
		221*	Somerset v. Warwickshire (Nuneaton) ..	1961
Amarnath, L.	(4)	241	Hindus v. Rest (Bombay)	1938-39
		262	India in England v. Rest of India (Calcutta) ..	1946-47
		228*	Indians v. Victoria (Melbourne)	1947-48
		223*	North Zone v. West Indians (Patiala) ..	1948-49
Ames, L. E. G. ..	(9)	200	Kent v. Surrey (Blackheath)	1928
		210	Kent v. Warwickshire (Tonbridge)	1933

Double Centuries—*Cont.*

Ames, L. E. G. (*cont.*)		295	Kent v. Gloucestershire (Folkestone)	1933
		201	Players v. Gentlemen (Folkestone)	1933
		202*	Kent v. Essex (Brentwood)	1934
		201*	Kent v. Worcestershire (Gillingham)	1937
		201	Kent v. Worcestershire (Worcester)	1939
		212*	Kent v. Nottinghamshire (Gravesend)	1947
		212	Kent v. Gloucestershire (Dover)	1948
Andrews, C. W.	(1)	253	Queensland v. New South Wales (Sydney)	1934-35
Andrews, T. J. E.	(2)	247*	New South Wales v. Victoria (Sydney)	1919-20
		224	New South Wales v. M.C.C. (Sydney)	1924-25
Armstrong, W. W.	(7)	200	Victoria v. Queensland (Melbourne)	1904-05
		303*	Australians v. Somerset (Bath)	1905
		248*	Australians v. Gentlemen (Lord's)	1905
		231	Victoria v. South Australia (Melbourne)	1907-08
		250	Victoria v. South Australia (Melbourne)	1911-12
		202*	Victoria v. Queensland (Melbourne)	1913-14
		245	Victoria v. South Australia (Melbourne)	1920-21
Arnold, E. G.	(2)	200*	Worcestershire v. Warwickshire (Birmingham)	1909
		215	Worcestershire v. Oxford U. (Oxford)	1910
Arnold, J.	(1)	227	Hampshire v. Glamorgan (Cardiff)	1932
Ashdown, W. H.	(2)	332	Kent v. Essex (Brentwood)	1934
		305*	Kent v. Derbyshire (Dover)	1935
Ashton, H.	(1)	236*	Cambridge U. v. Free Foresters (Cambridge)	1920
Atkinson, D.	(1)	219	West Indies v. Australia (Bridgetown)	1954-55
Avery, A. V.	(4)	210	Essex v. Surrey (Oval)	1946
		214*	Essex v. Worcestershire (Clacton)	1948
		224	Essex v. Northamptonshire (Northampton)	1952
		208*	Essex v. Glamorgan (Westcliff)	1953
Bacher, A.	(1)	235	Transvaal v. Australians (Johannesburg)	1966-67
Badcock, C. L.	(4)	274	Tasmania v. Victoria (Launceston)	1933-34
		325	South Australia v. Victoria (Adelaide)	1935-36
		271*	South Australia v. New South Wales (Adelaide)	1938-39
		236	South Australia v. Queensland (Adelaide)	1939-40
Baig, A. A.	(2)	221*	Oxford U. v. Free Foresters (Oxford)	1959
		224*	South Zone v. North Zone (New Delhi)	1966-67
Bailey, T. E.	(1)	205	Essex v. Sussex (Eastbourne)	1947
Bakewell, A. H.	(4)	204	Northamptonshire v. Somerset (Bath)	1930
		246	Northamptonshire v. Nottinghamshire (Northampton)	1933
		257	Northamptonshire v. Glamorgan (Swansea)	1933
		241*	Northamptonshire v. Derbyshire (Chesterfield)	1936
Balaskas, X. C.	(2)	206	Griqualand West v. Rhodesia (Kimberley)	1929-30
		200*	Rest of South Africa v. Western Province (Cape Town)	1932-33
Baldwin, C.	(1)	234	Surrey v. Kent (Oval)	1897
Barber, W.	(2)	248	Yorkshire v. Kent (Leeds)	1934
		255	Yorkshire v. Surrey (Sheffield)	1935
Bardsley, W.	(7)	264	Australian XI v. Rest (Melbourne)	1908-09
		219	Australians v. Essex (Leyton)	1909
		211	Australians v. Gloucestershire (Bristol)	1909
		235	New South Wales v. South Australia (Sydney)	1920-21
		235	New South Wales v. South Australia (Adelaide)	1920-21
		209	Australians v. Hampshire (Southampton)	1921
		200*	New South Wales v. Auckland (Auckland)	1923-24
Barling, T. H.	(2)	269	Surrey v. Hampshire (Southampton)	1933
		233*	Surrey v. Nottinghamshire (Oval)	1946
Barlow, E. J.	(3)	209	South Africans v. Combined XI (Perth)	1963-64
		201	South Africa v. Australia (Adelaide)	1963-64
		212	Transvaal v. Rhodesia (Johannesburg)	1966-67
Barnes, S. G.	(2)	200	New South Wales v. Queensland (Brisbane)	1945-46
		234	Australia v. England (Sydney)	1946-47
Barnett, C. J.	(4)	204*	Gloucestershire v. Leicestershire (Leicester)	1936
		259	M.C.C. v. Queensland (Brisbane)	1936-37
		232	Gloucestershire v. Lancashire (Gloucester)	1937
		228*	Gloucestershire v. Leicestershire (Gloucester)	1947
Barrett, E. I. M.	(1)	215	Hampshire v. Gloucestershire (Southampton)	1920
Barrick, D.	(1)	211	Northamptonshire v. Essex (Northampton)	1952

Double Centuries—*Cont.*

Barrington, K. F.	(3)	219*	M.C.C. v. Australian XI (Melbourne)	1962-63
		256	England v. Australia (Manchester)	1964
		207	Surrey v. Nottinghamshire (Oval)	1964
Barton, V. A.	(1)	205	Hampshire v. Sussex (Hove)	1900
Bates, L. A.	(2)	200	Warwickshire v. Worcestershire (Birmingham)	1928
		211	Warwickshire v. Gloucestershire (Gloucester)	1932
Bates, W. E.	(1)	200*	Glamorgan v. Worcestershire (Kidderminster)	1927
Bayley, H. P.	(1)	268	British Guiana v. Barbados (Georgetown)	1937-38
Beames, P. J.	(1)	226*	Victoria v. Tasmania (Launceston)	1938-39
Begbie, D. W.	(1)	207*	Transvaal v. Orange Free State (Johannesburg)	1937-38
Bell, J. T.	(2)	225	Glamorgan v. Worcestershire (Dudley)	1926
		209*	Wales v. M.C.C. (Lord's)	1927
Berry, L. G.	(2)	207	Leicestershire v. Worcestershire (Ashby de la Zouch)	1928
		232	Leicestershire v. Sussex (Leicester)	1930
Bhandari, P.	(1)	227	Delhi v. Patiala (Patiala)	1957-58
Bhandarkar, K. V.	(1)	205	Maharashtra v. Kathiawar (Poona)	1948-49
Bird, M. C.	(1)	200	M.C.C. v. Orange Free State (Bloemfontein)	1913-14
Birkett, L. S.	(1)	253	Trinidad v. British Guiana (Georgetown)	1929-30
Blunt, R. C.	(3)	221	Otago v. Canterbury (Dunedin)	1928-29
		225*	New Zealanders v. Gentlemen (Eastbourne)	1931
		338*	Otago v. Canterbury (Christchurch)	1931-32
Board, J. H.	(1)	214	Gloucestershire v. Somerset (Bristol)	1900
Bogle, J.	(1)	200	New South Wales v. South Australia (Adelaide)	1919-20
Bokhari, I. A.	(1)	203	Lahore v. Punjab U. (Lahore)	1960-61
Bolus, J. B.	(1)	202*	Nottinghamshire v. Glamorgan (Nottingham)	1963
Bonitto, N.	(1)	207*	Jamaica v. British Guiana (Georgetown)	1952-53
Booth, B. C.	(1)	214*	Australians v. Central Districts (Palmerston North)	1966-67
Booth, M. W.	(1)	210	Yorkshire v. Worcestershire (Worcester)	1911
Bosanquet, B. J. T.	(1)	214	Rest of England v. Yorkshire (Oval)	1908
Bowell, A.	(1)	204	Hampshire v. Lancashire (Bournemouth)	1914
Bowley, E. H.	(4)	228	Sussex v. Northamptonshire (Hove)	1921
		220	Sussex v. Gloucestershire (Hove)	1927
		280*	Sussex v. Gloucestershire (Hove)	1929
		283	Sussex v. Middlesex (Hove)	1933
Bowley, F. L.	(3)	217	Worcestershire v. Leicestershire (Stourbridge)	1905
		201	Worcestershire v. Gloucestershire (Worcester)	1913
		276	Worcestershire v. Hampshire (Dudley)	1914
Bowring, T.	(1)	228	Oxford U. v. Gentlemen of England (Oxford)	1908
Boycott, G.	(2)	246*	England v. India (Leeds)	1967
		220*	Yorkshire v. Northamptonshire (Sheffield)	1967
Bradman, D. G.	(37)	340*	New South Wales v. Victoria (Sydney)	1928-29
		225	Woodfull's XI v. Ryder's XI (Sydney)	1929-30
		452*	New South Wales v. Queensland (Sydney)	1929-30
		236	Australians v. Worcestershire (Worcester)	1930
		252*	Australians v. Surrey (Oval)	1930
		254	Australia v. England (Lord's)	1930
		334	Australia v. England (Leeds)	1930
		232	Australia v. England (Oval)	1930
		205*	Australians v. Kent (Canterbury)	1930
		258	New South Wales v. South Australia (Adelaide)	1930-31
		223	Australia v. West Indies (Brisbane)	1930-31
		220	New South Wales v. Victoria (Sydney)	1930-31
		226	Australia v. South Africa (Brisbane)	1931-32
		219	New South Wales v. South Africans (Sydney)	1931-32
		299*	Australia v. South Africa (Adelaide)	1931-32
		238	New South Wales v. Victoria (Sydney)	1932-33
		200	New South Wales v. Queensland (Brisbane)	1933-34
		253	New South Wales v. Queensland (Sydney)	1933-34
		206	Australians v. Worcestershire (Worcester)	1934
		304	Australia v. England (Leeds)	1934
		244	Australia v. England (Oval)	1934
		233	South Australia v. Queensland (Adelaide)	1935-36
		357	South Australia v. Victoria (Melbourne)	1935-36
		369	South Australia v. Tasmania (Adelaide)	1935-36
		212	Bradman's XI v. Richardson's XI (Sydney)	1936-37

Double Centuries—*Cont.*

Player	No.	Score	Match	Season
Bradman, D. G. (*cont.*)		270	Australia v. England (Melbourne)	1936-37
		212	Australia v. England (Adelaide)	1936-37
		246	South Australia v. Queensland (Adelaide)	1937-38
		258	Australians v. Worcestershire (Worcester)	1938
		278	Australians v. M.C.C. (Lord's)	1938
		202	Australians v. Somerset (Taunton)	1938
		225	South Australia v. Queensland (Adelaide)	1938-39
		251*	South Australia v. New South Wales (Adelaide)	1939-40
		267	South Australia v. Victoria (Melbourne)	1939-40
		209*	South Australia v. Western Australia (Perth)	1939-40
		234	Australia v. England (Sydney)	1946-47
		201	Australia v. India (Adelaide)	1947-48
Braund, L. C.	(1)	257*	Somerset v. Worcestershire (Worcester)	1913
Brearley, J. M.	(2)	312*	M.C.C. Under-25 v. North Zone (Peshawar)	1966-67
		223	M.C.C. Under-25 v. Pakistan Under-25 (Dacca)	1966-67
Brockwell, W.	(1)	225	Surrey v. Hampshire (Oval)	1897
Brookes, D.	(6)	200	Northamptonshire v. Worcestershire (Kidderminster)	1946
		210	Northamptonshire v. Leicestershire (Leicester)	1947
		257	Northamptonshire v. Gloucestershire (Bristol)	1949
		204*	Northamptonshire v. Essex (Northampton)	1952
		210*	Northamptonshire v. Somerset (Northampton)	1954
		203*	Northamptonshire v. Somerset (Taunton)	1956
Brown, F. R.	(1)	212	Surrey v. Middlesex (Oval)	1932
Brown, G.	(3)	232*	Hampshire v. Yorkshire (Leeds)	1920
		230	Hampshire v. Essex (Bournemouth)	1920
		204	Hampshire v. Yorkshire (Portsmouth)	1927
Brown, J. T.	(3)	203	Yorkshire v. Middlesex (Lord's)	1896
		311	Yorkshire v. Sussex (Sheffield)	1897
		300	Yorkshire v. Derbyshire (Chesterfield)	1898
Brown, S. M.	(2)	200	Middlesex v. Kent (Canterbury)	1949
		232*	Middlesex v. Somerset (Lord's)	1951
Brown, W. A.	(5)	205	New South Wales v. Victoria (Sydney)	1933-34
		206*	Australia v. England (Lord's)	1938
		265*	Australians v. Derbyshire (Chesterfield)	1938
		215	Queensland v. Victoria (Brisbane)	1938-39
		200	Australians v. Cambridge U. (Cambridge)	1948
Bryan, G. J.	(1)	229	Combined Services v. South Africans (Portsmouth)	1924
Bryan, J. L.	(2)	231	Cambridge U. v. Surrey (Oval)	1921
		236	Kent v. Hampshire (Canterbury)	1923
Buckle, W. H.	(1)	207	Queensland v. Western Australia (Brisbane)	1964-65
Burge, P. J.	(5)	210	Queensland v. Victoria (Brisbane)	1956-57
		240	Queensland v. South Australia (Adelaide)	1960-61
		283	Queensland v. New South Wales (Brisbane)	1963-64
		205*	Queensland v. Western Australia (Brisbane)	1963-64
		242*	Queensland v. New South Wales (Sydney)	1964-65
Burke, J. W.	(1)	220	New South Wales v. South Australia (Adelaide)	1956-57
Burki, J.	(3)	202*	Lahore A v. Combined Us. (Lahore)	1962-63
		227	Karachi Whites v. Khairpur (Karachi)	1963-64
		210	Pakistan v. Ceylon (Karachi)	1966-67
Burnup, C. J.	(1)	200	Kent v. Lancashire (Manchester)	1900
Butcher, B. F.	(1)	209*	West Indies v. England (Nottingham)	1966
Byrne, J. F.	(1)	222	Warwickshire v. Lancashire (Birmingham)	1905
Callaway, N.	(1)	207	New South Wales v. Queensland (Sydney)	1914-15
Calthorpe, Hon. F. S. G.	(1)	209	Warwickshire v. Hampshire (Birmingham)	1921
Carlstein, P. R.	(2)	203	Transvaal v. Western Province (Johannesburg)	1962-63
		229	Transvaal v. Cavaliers (Johannesburg)	1962-63
Carr, A. W.	(2)	204	Nottinghamshire v. Essex (Leyton)	1921
		206	Nottinghamshire v. Leicestershire (Leicester)	1925
Carson, W. N.	(1)	290	Auckland v. Otago (Dunedin)	1936-37
Cartwright, T. W.	(1)	210	Warwickshire v. Middlesex (Nuneaton)	1962
Challenor, G.	(2)	237*	Barbados v. Jamaica (Bridgetown)	1924-25
		220	Barbados v. Trinidad (Bridgetown)	1926-27
Chaplin, H. P.	(1)	213*	Sussex v. Nottinghamshire (Hove)	1914
Chapman, A. P. F.	(1)	260	Kent v. Lancashire (Maidstone)	1927
Chappell, I. M.	(1)	205*	South Australia v. Queensland (Brisbane)	1963-64

Double Centuries—*Cont.*

Charlesworth, C. ..	(2)	216	Warwickshire v. Derbyshire (Blackwell) ..	1910
		206	Warwickshire v. Yorkshire (Dewsbury) ..	1914
Cheetham, J. E. ..	(1)	271*	Western Province v. Orange Free State (Bloemfontein)	1950-51
Chowdhari, Y. M. ..	(1)	211	Delhi v. Patiala (New Delhi)	1955-56
Clarke, A. J.	(1)	206*	Border v. Eastern Province (Port Elizabeth) ..	1925-26
Coe, S.	(1)	252*	Leicestershire v. Northamptonshire (Leicester)	1914
Collins, H. L.	(3)	282	New South Wales v. Tasmania (Hobart) ..	1912-13
		235	A.I.F. v. South African XI (Johannesburg) ..	1919-20
		203	Australia v. South Africa (Johannesburg) ..	1921-22
Compton, D. C. S. ..	(9)	214*	Middlesex v. Derbyshire (Lord's)	1939
		249*	Holkar v. Bombay (Bombay)	1944-45
		202	Middlesex v. Cambridge U. (Cambridge) ..	1946
		235	Middlesex v. Surrey (Lord's)	1946
		208	England v. South Africa (Lord's)	1947
		246	Middlesex v. Rest (Oval)	1947
		252*	Middlesex v. Somerset (Lord's)	1948
		300	M.C.C. v. North-Eastern Transvaal (Benoni) ..	1948-49
		278	England v. Pakistan (Nottingham)	1954
Constable, B.	(1)	205*	Surrey v. Somerset (Oval)	1952
Cook, T. E.	(3)	278	Sussex v. Hampshire (Hove)	1930
		214	Sussex v. Worcestershire (Eastbourne) ..	1933
		220	Sussex v. Worcestershire (Worcester)	1934
Cooper E.	(1)	216*	Worcestershire v. Warwickshire (Dudley) ..	1938
Corbett, P. L.	(1)	237	North-Eastern Transvaal v. Transvaal B (Johannesburg)	1962-63
Cowdrey, M. C. ..	(3)	204*	Kent v. Cambridge U. (Cambridge)	1956
		250	Kent v. Essex (Blackheath)	1959
		307	M.C.C. v. South Australia (Adelaide) ..	1962-63
Cowper, R. M. ..	(2)	307	Australia v. England (Melbourne)	1965-66
		201*	Australians v. Orange Free State (Bloemfontein)	1966-67
Cox, A.	(1)	204	Canterbury v. Otago (Christchurch)	1925-26
Cox, G.	(4)	232	Sussex v. Northamptonshire (Kettering) ..	1939
		234*	Sussex v. Indians (Hove)	1946
		205*	Sussex v. Glamorgan (Hove)	1947
		212*	Sussex v. Yorkshire (Leeds)	1949
Craig, E. J.	(1)	208*	Cambridge U. v. Steven's XI (Eastbourne) ..	1961
Craig, I. D.	(1)	213*	New South Wales v. South Africans (Sydney)	1952-53
Crawford, J. N... ..	(1)	232	Surrey v. Somerset (Oval)	1908
Crawley, A. M... ..	(1)	204	Oxford U. v. Northamptonshire (Wellingborough)	1929
Crawley, L. G.	(1)	222	Essex v. Glamorgan (Swansea)	1928
Creese, W. L.	(1)	241	Hampshire v. Northamptonshire (Northampton)	1939
Croom, A. J.	(1)	211	Warwickshire v. Worcestershire (Birmingham)	1934
Curnow, S. H. ..	(1)	224	North v. South (Cape Town)	1932-33
Cutmore, J. A.	(1)	238*	Essex v. Gloucestershire (Bristol)	1927
Dacre, C. C.	(1)	223	Gloucestershire v. Worcestershire (Worcester)	1930
Darling, J.	(1)	210	South Australia v. Queensland (Brisbane) ..	1898-99
Davidson, G.	(1)	274	Derbyshire v. Lancashire (Manchester) ..	1896
Davies, D.	(1)	216	Glamorgan v. Somerset (Newport)	1939
Davies, E.	(2)	287*	Glamorgan v. Gloucestershire (Newport) ..	1939
		215	Glamorgan v. Essex (Brentwood)	1948
Davies, P. C.	(1)	220	North-Eastern Transvaal v. Orange Free State (Bloemfontein)	1955-56
Davis, P.	(1)	237	Northamptonshire v. Somerset (Northampton)	1947
De Courcy, J. H. ..	(1)	204	Australians v. Combined Services (Kingston) ..	1953
De Saram, F. C. ..	(1)	208	Oxford U. v. Leveson-Gower's XI (Reigate) ..	1934
De Villiers, D. I. ..	(1)	200*	Orange Free State v. Border (Johannesburg) ..	1923-24
Dempster, C. S. ..	(2)	212	New Zealanders v. Essex (Leyton)	1931
		207*	Leicestershire v. Cahn's XI (Nottingham)	1935
Denton, D.	(3)	200*	Yorkshire v. Warwickshire (Birmingham) ..	1912
		221	Yorkshire v. Kent (Tunbridge Wells) ..	1912
		209*	Yorkshire v. Worcestershire (Worcester) ..	1920
Denton, W. H.	(1)	230*	Northamptonshire v. Essex (Leyton)	1913
Deodhar, D. B. ..	(1)	246	Maharashtra v. Bombay (Poona)	1940-41
Devey, J.	(1)	246	Warwickshire v. Derbyshire (Birmingham) ..	1900
Dewes, J. G.	(2)	204*	Cambridge U. v. Essex (Cambridge)	1949
		212	Cambridge U. v. Sussex (Hove)	1950

Double Centuries—*Cont.*

Dexter, E. R.	(1)	205	England v. Pakistan (Karachi)	1961-62
Diamond, A.	(1)	210*	New South Wales v. Victoria (Sydney) ..	1906-07
Dipper, A. E.	(3)	252*	Gloucestershire v. Glamorgan (Cheltenham) ..	1923
		247	Gloucestershire v. Oxford U. (Bristol) ..	1924
		212	Gloucestershire v. Worcestershire (Bristol) ..	1927
Dixon, J. A.	(1)	268*	Nottinghamshire v. Sussex (Nottingham) ..	1897
Doggart, G. H. G. ..	(2)	215*	Cambridge U. v. Lancashire (Cambridge) ..	1948
		219*	Cambridge U. v. Essex (Cambridge)	1949
Doll, C. C. T.	(1)	224*	M.C.C. v. London County (Crystal Palace) ..	1901
Dollery, H. E.	(2)	200	Warwickshire v. Gloucestershire (Gloucester) ..	1949
		212	Warwickshire v. Leicestershire (Birmingham) ..	1952
Donnelly, M. P. ..	(2)	208*	M.C.C. v. Yorkshire (Scarborough)	1948
		206	New Zealand v. England (Lord's)	1949
Douglas, J.	(1)	204	Middlesex v. Gloucestershire (Bristol)	1903
Douglas, J. W. H. T. ..	(1)	210*	Essex v. Derbyshire (Leyton)	1921
Dowling, G. T. ..	(1)	206	Canterbury v. Wellington (Christchurch) ..	1962-63
Druce, N. F.	(1)	227*	Cambridge U. v. Thornton's XI (Cambridge)	1897
Ducat, A. ..	(8)	306*	Surrey v. Oxford U. (Oval)	1919
		271	Surrey v. Hampshire (Southampton)	1919
		203	Surrey v. Sussex (Oval)	1920
		290*	Surrey v. Essex (Leyton)	1921
		204*	Surrey v. Northamptonshire (Northampton) ..	1921
		235	Surrey v. Leicestershire (Oval)	1926
		208	Surrey v. Essex (Leyton)	1928
		218	Surrey v. Nottinghamshire (Nottingham) ..	1930
Duckfield, R.	(1)	280*	Glamorgan v. Surrey (Oval)	1936
Duff, R. A.	(1)	271	New South Wales v. South Australia (Sydney) ..	1903-04
Duleepsinhji, K. S. ..	(4)	254*	Cambridge U. v. Middlesex (Cambridge) ..	1927
		202	Sussex v. Essex (Leyton)	1929
		246	Sussex v. Kent (Hastings)	1929
		333	Sussex v. Northamptonshire (Hove)	1930
Dyson, A. H.	(1)	208	Glamorgan v. Surrey (Oval)	1932
Edrich, J. H.	(4)	216	Surrey v. Nottinghamshire (Nottingham) ..	1962
		205*	Surrey v. Gloucestershire (Bristol)	1965
		310*	England v. New Zealand (Leeds)	1965
		226*	Surrey v. Middlesex (Oval)	1967
Edrich, W. J.	(9)	245	Middlesex v. Nottinghamshire (Lord's) ..	1938
		219	England v. South Africa (Durban)	1938-39
		222*	Middlesex v. Northamptonshire (Northampton)	1946
		225	Middlesex v. Warwickshire (Birmingham) ..	1947
		257	Middlesex v. Leicestershire (Leicester)	1947
		267*	Middlesex v. Northamptonshire (Northampton)	1947
		239	Middlesex v. Oxford U. (Oxford)	1952
		211	Middlesex v. Essex (Lord's)	1953
		208*	Middlesex v. Derbyshire (Chesterfield) ..	1956
Eggar, J. D.	(1)	219	Derbyshire v. Yorkshire (Bradford)	1949
Elliott, C. S.	(1)	215	Derbyshire v. Nottinghamshire (Nottingham) ..	1947
Endean, W. R. ..	(3)	235	Transvaal v. Orange Free State (Johannesburg)	1954-55
		247	Transvaal v. Eastern Province (Johannesburg)	1955-56
		204*	Transvaal A v. Border (Johannesburg) ..	1959-60
Fagg, A. E.	(6)	257	Kent v. Hampshire (Southampton)	1936
		244	Kent v. Essex (Colchester) 1st innings ..	1938
		202*	Kent v. Essex (Colchester) 2nd innings	1938
		203	Kent v. Middlesex (Dover)	1948
		221	Kent v. Nottinghamshire (Nottingham) ..	1951
		269*	Kent v. Nottinghamshire (Nottingham) ..	1953
Fane, F. L.	(2)	207	Essex v. Leicestershire (Leicester)	1899
		217	Essex v. Surrey (Oval)	1911
Farmer, W. A.	(1)	275	Barbados v. Jamaica (Bridgetown)	1951-52
Farrer, W. S.	(1)	207	Border v. Orange Free State (Bloemfontein) ..	1965-66
Fasih-ud-Din	(1)	237	Quetta v. East Pakistan (Karachi)	1962-63
Faulkner, G. A. ..	(1)	204	South Africa v. Australia (Melbourne) ..	1910-11
Fishlock, L. B.	(2)	253	Surrey v. Leicestershire (Leicester)	1948
		210	Surrey v. Somerset (Oval)	1949
Flockton, R.	(1)	264*	New South Wales v. South Australia (Adelaide)	1959-60
Foster, F. R.	(2)	200	Warwickshire v. Surrey (Birmingham) ..	1911
		305*	Warwickshire v. Worcestershire (Dudley) ..	1914

Double Centuries—*Cont.*

Player	No.	Score	Match	Season
Foster, H. K.	(2)	216	Worcestershire v. Somerset (Worcester)	1903
		215	Worcestershire v. Warwickshire (Worcester)	1908
Foster, R. E.	(2)	287	England v. Australia (Sydney)	1903-04
		246*	Worcestershire v. Kent (Worcester)	1905
Freeman, J. R.	(1)	286	Essex v. Northamptonshire (Northampton)	1921
Fry, C. B.	(16)	229	Sussex v. Surrey (Hove)	1900
		241	Sussex v. Cambridge U. (Hove)	1901
		219*	Sussex v. Oxford U. (Eastbourne)	1901
		244	Sussex v. Leicestershire (Leicester)	1901
		209	Sussex v. Yorkshire (Hove)	1901
		234	Sussex v. Yorkshire (Bradford)	1903
		232*	Gentlemen v. Players (Lord's)	1903
		200	Sussex v. Surrey (Hove)	1903
		226	Sussex v. Derbyshire (Hove)	1904
		211	Sussex v. Hampshire (Hove)	1904
		229	Sussex v. Yorkshire (Hove)	1904
		201*	Sussex v. Nottinghamshire (Hove)	1905
		233	Sussex v. Nottinghamshire (Nottingham)	1905
		214	Sussex v. Worcestershire (Hove)	1908
		258*	Hampshire v. Gloucestershire (Southampton)	1911
		203*	Hampshire v. Oxford U. (Southampton)	1912
Gaekwad, D. K.	(3)	218	Baroda v. Bombay (Sholapur)	1957-58
		249*	Baroda v. Maharashtra (Poona)	1959-60
		201*	Baroda v. Gujerat (Baroda)	1961-62
Gale, R. A.	(1)	200	Middlesex v. Glamorgan (Newport)	1962
Gardner, F. C.	(1)	215*	Warwickshire v. Somerset (Taunton)	1950
Gibb, P. A.	(1)	204	Cambridge U. v. Free Foresters (Cambridge)	1938
Gibb, P. J. M.	(1)	203	Transvaal v. North-Eastern Transvaal (Johannesburg)	1952-53
Gibbons, H. H.	(2)	200*	Worcestershire v. West Indians (Worcester)	1928
		212*	Worcestershire v. Northamptonshire (Dudley)	1939
Gibbs, G.	(1)	216	British Guiana v. Barbados (Georgetown)	1951-52
Giffen, G.	(4)	203	South Australia v. Vernon's XI (Adelaide)	1887-88
		237	South Australia v. Victoria (Melbourne)	1890-91
		271	South Australia v. Victoria (Adelaide)	1891-92
		205	South Australia v. New South Wales (Adelaide)	1893-94
Gilbert, W. R.	(1)	205*	England XI v. Cambridge U. (Cambridge)	1876
Gillingham, F. H.	(1)	201	Essex v. Middlesex (Lord's)	1904
Gimblett, H.	(2)	231	Somerset v. Middlesex (Taunton)	1946
		310	Somerset v. Sussex (Eastbourne)	1948
Girdhari, S. K.	(1)	229*	Assam v. Orissa (Cuttack)	1957-58
Goddard, J. D. C.	(1)	218*	Barbados v. Trinidad (Bridgetown)	1943-44
Goddard, T. L.	(2)	200	Natal v. Rhodesia (Durban)	1959-60
		222	North-Eastern Transvaal v. Western Province (Cape Town)	1966-67
Gomez, G. E.	(2)	216*	Trinidad v. Barbados (Port of Spain)	1942-43
		213*	Trinidad v. Barbados (Port of Spain)	1945-46
Goonesena, G.	(1)	211	Cambridge U. v. Oxford U. (Lord's)	1957
Gopinath, C. D.	(1)	234	Madras v. Mysore (Coimbatore)	1958-59
Grace, W. G.	(13)	224*	England v. Surrey (Oval)	1866
		215	Gentlemen v. Players (Oval)	1870
		268	South v. North (Oval)	1871
		217	Gentlemen v. Players (Brighton)	1871
		344	M.C.C. v. Kent (Canterbury)	1876
		318*	Gloucestershire v. Yorkshire (Cheltenham)	1876
		261	South v. North (Prince's)	1877
		221*	Gloucestershire v. Middlesex (Clifton)	1885
		215	Gloucestershire v. Sussex (Hove)	1888
		288	Gloucestershire v. Somerset (Bristol)	1895
		257	Gloucestershire v. Kent (Gravesend)	1895
		243*	Gloucestershire v. Sussex (Hove)	1896
		301	Gloucestershire v. Sussex (Bristol)	1896
Graveney, T. W.	(7)	201	Gloucestershire v. Sussex (Worthing)	1950
		201	Gloucestershire v. Oxford U. (Oxford)	1951
		211	Gloucestershire v. Kent (Gillingham)	1953
		231	M.C.C. v. British Guiana (Georgetown)	1953-54
		222	Gloucestershire v. Derbyshire (Chesterfield)	1954

Double Centuries—*Cont.*

Graveney, T. W. (*cont.*)		200	Gloucestershire v. Glamorgan (Newport)	1956
		258	England v. West Indies (Nottingham)	1957
Gray, J. R.	(1)	213*	Hampshire v. Derbyshire (Portsmouth)	1962
Greenidge, G. A.	(1)	205	Barbados v. Jamaica (Bridgetown)	1966-67
Gregory, C. W.	(1)	383	New South Wales v. Queensland (Brisbane)	1906-07
Gregory, R. J.	(1)	243	Surrey v. Somerset (Oval)	1938
Gregory, S. E.	(2)	201	Australia v. England (Sydney)	1894-95
		201	New South Wales v. Victoria (Sydney)	1907-08
Greig, J. G.	(2)	249*	Hampshire v. Lancashire (Liverpool)	1901
		216	England XII v. Indian XII (Bombay)	1915-16
Grewal, S. S.	(1)	211	Services v. Southern Punjab (Patiala)	1950-51
Grieves, K. J.	(3)	224	Lancashire v. Cambridge U. (Cambridge)	1957
		202*	Lancashire v. Indians (Blackpool)	1959
		216	Lancashire v. Cambridge U. (Manchester)	1960
Gul Mahomed	(1)	319	Baroda v. Holkar (Baroda)	1946-47
Gunasekara, C. I.	(1)	212	Ceylon v. Madras (Colombo)	1958-59
Gunn, G.	(1)	220	Nottinghamshire v. Derbyshire (Nottingham)	1923
Gunn, J.	(1)	294	Nottinghamshire v. Leicestershire (Nottingham)	1903
Gunn, W.	(8)	203	M.C.C. v. Yorkshire (Lord's)	1885
		205*	Nottinghamshire v. Sussex (Nottingham)	1887
		228	Players v. Australians (Lord's)	1890
		219	Nottinghamshire v. Sussex (Nottingham)	1895
		207*	Nottinghamshire v. Derbyshire (Derby)	1896
		230	Nottinghamshire v. Derbyshire (Nottingham)	1897
		236*	Nottinghamshire v. Surrey (Oval)	1898
		273	Nottinghamshire v. Derbyshire (Derby)	1901
Hadow, W. H.	(1)	217	Middlesex v. M.C.C. (Lord's)	1871
Hallam, M. R.	(4)	200	Leicestershire v. Derbyshire (Leicester)	1959
		210*	Leicestershire v. Glamorgan (Leicester)	1959
		203*	Leicestershire v. Sussex (Worthing)	1961
		200*	Leicestershire v. Nottinghamshire (Nottingham)	1962
Hallebone, J.	(1)	202	Victoria v. Tasmania (Melbourne)	1951-52
Hallows, C.	(3)	227	Lancashire v. Warwickshire (Manchester)	1921
		233*	Lancashire v. Hampshire (Liverpool)	1927
		232	Lancashire v. Sussex (Manchester)	1928
Hamer, A.	(1)	227	Derbyshire v. Nottinghamshire (Nottingham)	1955
Hammond, W. R.	(36)	250*	Gloucestershire v. Lancashire (Manchester)	1925
		238*	M.C.C. v. West Indian XI (Bridgetown)	1925-26
		205*	Gloucestershire v. Surrey (Oval)	1928
		218*	Gloucestershire v. Glamorgan (Bristol)	1928
		244	Gloucestershire v. Essex (Chelmsford)	1928
		225	M.C.C. v. New South Wales (Sydney)	1928-29
		251	England v. Australia (Sydney)	1928-29
		200	England v. Australia (Melbourne)	1928-29
		238*	Gloucestershire v. Warwickshire (Birmingham)	1929
		211*	Gloucestershire v. Oxford U. (Oxford)	1930
		264	Gloucestershire v. Lancashire (Liverpool)	1932
		203	M.C.C. v. Victoria (Melbourne)	1932-33
		227	England v. New Zealand (Christchurch)	1932-33
		336*	England v. New Zealand (Auckland)	1932-33
		206	Gloucestershire v. Leicestershire (Leicester)	1933
		239	Gloucestershire v. Glamorgan (Gloucester)	1933
		231	Gloucestershire v. Derbyshire (Cheltenham)	1933
		264	Gloucestershire v. West Indians (Bristol)	1933
		290	Gloucestershire v. Kent (Tunbridge Wells)	1934
		217	Gloucestershire v. Nottinghamshire (Bristol)	1934
		265*	Gloucestershire v. Worcestershire (Dudley)	1934
		302*	Gloucestershire v. Glamorgan (Bristol)	1934
		281*	M.C.C. v. Barbados (Bridgetown)	1934-35
		252	Gloucestershire v. Leicestershire (Leicester)	1935
		217	England v. India (Oval)	1936
		317	Gloucestershire v. Nottinghamshire (Gloucester)	1936
		231*	England v. Australia (Sydney)	1936-37
		217	Gloucestershire v. Leicestershire (Gloucester)	1937
		237	Gloucestershire v. Derbyshire (Bristol)	1933
		240	England v. Australia (Lord's)	1938
		271	Gloucestershire v. Lancashire (Bristol)	1988

Double Centuries—*Cont.*

Hammond, W. R. (*cont.*)		302	Gloucestershire v. Glamorgan (Newport) ..	1939
		207	Gloucestershire v. Essex (Westcliff)	1939
		211*	Gloucestershire v. Nottinghamshire (Bristol) ..	1946
		214	Gloucestershire v. Somerset (Bristol)	1946
		208	M.C.C. v. Western Australia (Perth)	1946-47
Hanif Mohammad ..	(7)	203*	Pakistan v. Bombay (Bombay)	1952-53
		230*	Karachi v. Sind (Karachi)	1954-55
		228	Karachi Whites v. Karachi Blues (Karachi) ..	1956-57
		337	Pakistan v. West Indies (Bridgetown)	1957-58
		499	Karachi v. Bahawalpur (Karachi)	1958-59
		222	Pakistanis v. Combined Us. (Poona)	1960-61
		203*	Pakistan v. New Zealand (Lahore)	1964-65
Hanumant Singh ..	(3)	200*	Rajasthan v. Uttar Pradesh (Udaipur) ..	1961-62
		210	Central Zone v. South Zone (Hyderabad) ..	1964-65
		213*	Rajasthan v. Bombay (Bombay)	1966-67
Hardikar, M. S. ..	(2)	204	Bombay v. Gujerat (Bombay)	1956-57
		207*	Bombay v. Services (Bombay)	1964-65
Hardinge, H. T. W. ..	(4)	207	Kent v. Surrey (Blackheath)	1921
		249*	Kent v. Leicestershire (Leicester)	1922
		263*	Kent v. Gloucestershire (Gloucester)	1928
		205	Kent v. Warwickshire (Tunbridge Wells) ..	1928
Hardstaff, J., Snr. ..	(1)	213*	Nottinghamshire v. Sussex (Hove)	1914
Hardstaff, J., Jnr. ..	(10)	230*	M.C.C. v. Australian XI (Sydney)	1935-36
		214*	Nottinghamshire v. Somerset (Nottingham) ..	1937
		266	Nottinghamshire v. Leicestershire (Leicester) ..	1937
		243	Nottinghamshire v. Middlesex (Nottingham) ..	1937
		213	Lord Tennyson's XI v. Madras (Madras) ..	1937-38
		205*	England v. India (Lord's)	1946
		200*	Nottinghamshire v. Somerset (Nottingham) ..	1947
		202	Nottinghamshire v. Worcestershire (Dudley) ..	1947
		221*	Nottinghamshire v. Warwickshire (Nottingham)	1947
		247	Nottinghamshire v. Northamptonshire (Nottingham)	1951
Harris, C. B.	(2)	234	Nottinghamshire v. Middlesex (Nottingham) ..	1933
		239*	Nottinghamshire v. Hampshire (Nottingham) ..	1950
Hartley, A.	(1)	234	Lancashire v. Somerset (Manchester) ..	1910
Harvey, R. N.	(7)	205	Australia v. South Africa (Melbourne) ..	1952-53
		202*	Australians v. Leicestershire (Leicester) ..	1953
		204	Australia v. West Indies (Kingston)	1954-55
		225	Australians v. M.C.C. (Lord's)	1956
		209	Victoria v. New South Wales (Sydney) ..	1956-57
		229	New South Wales v. Queensland (Sydney) ..	1960-61
		231*	New South Wales v. South Australia (Sydney)	1962-63
Hassett, A. L.	(8)	220*	Australians v. Cambridge U. (Cambridge) ..	1938
		211*	Victoria v. South Australia (Melbourne) ..	1938-39
		200	Victoria v. Queensland (Brisbane)	1946-47
		204	Victoria v. Queensland (Brisbane)	1947-48
		200*	Australians v. Gentlemen (Lord's)	1948
		205	Victoria v. Queensland (Brisbane)	1948-49
		232	Victoria v. M.C.C. (Melbourne)	1950-51
		229	Victoria v. South Australia (Melbourne) ..	1951-52
Hastings, B. F.	(1)	226	Canterbury v. New Zealand Under-23 (Christchurch)	1964-65
Hathorn, M.	(1)	239	South Africans v. Cambridge U. (Cambridge)	1901
Hayes, E. G.	(4)	273*	Surrey v. Derbyshire (Derby)	1904
		218	Surrey v. Oxford U. (Oval)	1906
		202	Surrey v. Middlesex (Oval)	1907
		276	Surrey v. Hampshire (Oval)	1909
Hayward, T. W. ..	(8)	229*	Surrey v. Derbyshire (Derby)	1896
		315*	Surrey v. Lancashire (Oval)	1898
		273	Surrey v. Yorkshire (Oval)	1899
		203	Players v. Gentlemen (Oval)	1904
		219	Surrey v. Northamptonshire (Oval)	1906
		208	Surrey v. Warwickshire (Oval)	1906
		204*	Surrey v. Warwickshire (Oval)	1909
		202	Surrey v. Derbyshire (Oval)	1911
Hazare, Vijay S. ..	(10)	316*	Maharashtra v. Baroda (Poona)	1939-40

Double Centuries—*Cont.*

Player		Score	Match	Season
Hazare, Vijay S. (*cont.*)		264	Bengal Cyclone XI v. Bijapur Famine XI (Bombay)	1942-43
		248	Rest v. Muslims (Bombay)	1943-44
		309	Rest v. Hindus (Bombay)	1943-44
		223	India States v. Rest of India (Poona)	1943-44
		200*	Cricket Club of India v. Services XI (Bombay)	1944-45
		244*	Indians v. Yorkshire (Sheffield)	1946
		288	Baroda v. Holkar (Baroda)	1946-47
		204*	Baroda v. Gujerat (Ahmedabad)	1954-55
		203	Baroda v. Services (Baroda)	1957-58
Headley, G. A.	(9)	211	Jamaica v. Tennyson's XI (Kingston)	1927-28
		223	West Indies v. England (Kingston)	1929-30
		344*	Jamaica v. Lord Tennyson's XI (Kingston)	1931-32
		224*	West Indians v. Somerset (Taunton)	1933
		200*	West Indians v. Derbyshire (Derby)	1933
		270*	West Indians v. England (Kingston)	1934-35
		227	West Indians v. Middlesex (Lord's)	1939
		234*	West Indians v. Nottinghamshire (Nottingham)	1939
		203*	Jamaica v. Barbados (Kingston)	1946-47
Healy, G. E.	(1)	218	Victoria v. Tasmania (Melbourne)	1909-10
Hearne, J. W.	(11)	234*	Middlesex v. Somerset (Lord's)	1911
		204	Middlesex v. Lancashire (Lord's)	1914
		218*	Middlesex v. Hampshire (Lord's)	1919
		215*	Middlesex v. Warwickshire (Birmingham)	1920
		202	Middlesex v. Warwickshire (Birmingham)	1921
		201	Middlesex v. Gloucestershire (Gloucester)	1922
		221*	Middlesex v. Warwickshire (Birmingham)	1922
		232	Middlesex v. Hampshire (Southampton)	1923
		245*	Middlesex v. Gloucestershire (Bristol)	1927
		223*	Middlesex v. Somerset (Taunton)	1928
		285*	Middlesex v. Essex (Leyton)	1929
Hendren, E.	(22)	214	M.C.C. v. Yorkshire (Lord's)	1919
		201	Middlesex v. Hampshire (Lord's)	1919
		232	Middlesex v. Nottinghamshire (Lord's)	1920
		271	M.C.C. v. Victoria (Melbourne)	1920-21
		277*	Middlesex v. Kent (Lord's)	1922
		200*	Middlesex v. Essex (Leyton)	1923
		234	Middlesex v. Worcestershire (Lord's)	1925
		240	Middlesex v. Kent (Tonbridge)	1925
		206*	Middlesex v. Nottinghamshire (Nottingham)	1925
		213	Middlesex v. Yorkshire (Lord's)	1926
		201*	Middlesex v. Essex (Leyton)	1927
		200	Middlesex v. Hampshire (Lord's)	1928
		209*	Middlesex v. Warwickshire (Birmingham)	1928
		223*	M.C.C. v. Barbados (Bridgetown)	1929-30
		211*	M.C.C. v. Barbados (Bridgetown)	1929-30
		205*	England v. West Indies (Port of Spain)	1929-30
		254*	M.C.C. v. British Guiana (Georgetown)	1929-30
		232	Middlesex v. Nottinghamshire (Nottingham)	1931
		203	Middlesex v. Northamptonshire (Lord's)	1931
		301*	Middlesex v. Worcestershire (Dudley)	1933
		222*	Middlesex v. Essex (Leyton)	1933
		202	M.C.C. v. Surrey (Lord's)	1936
Hendry, H. L.	(1)	325*	Victoria v. New Zealanders (Melbourne)	1925-26
Hewett, H. T.	(1)	201	Somerset v. Yorkshire (Taunton)	1892
Hiddleston, J. S.	(2)	212	Wellington v. Canterbury (Wellington)	1925-26
		204	Wellington v. Auckland (Wellington)	1925-26
Hill, C.	(4)	206*	South Australia v. New South Wales (Sydney)	1895-96
		200	South Australia v. Stoddart's XI (Adelaide)	1897-98
		365*	South Australia v. New South Wales (Adelaide)	1900-01
		205	South Australia v. New South Wales (Adelaide)	1909-10
Hill, N. W.	(1)	201*	Nottingham v. Sussex (Worksop)	1961
Hirst, G. H.	(4)	214	Yorkshire v. Worcestershire (Worcester)	1901
		341	Yorkshire v. Leicestershire (Leicester)	1905
		232*	Yorkshire v. Surrey (Oval)	1905
		218	Yorkshire v. Sussex (Hastings)	1911
Hobbs, J. B.	(16)	205	Surrey v. Hampshire (Oval)	1909

Double Centuries—*Cont.*

Player		Score	Match	Season
Hobbs, J. B. (*cont.*)		215*	Surrey v. Essex (Leyton)	1914
		226	Surrey v. Nottinghamshire (Oval)	1914
		202	Surrey v. Yorkshire (Lord's)	1914
		205*	Surrey v. A.I.F. (Oval)	1919
		215	Rest v. Middlesex (Oval)	1920
		211	England v. South Africa (Lord's)	1924
		203*	Surrey v. Nottinghamshire (Nottingham)	1924
		215	Surrey v. Warwickshire (Birmingham)	1925
		266*	Players v. Gentlemen (Scarborough)	1925
		261	Surrey v. Oxford U. (Oval)	1926
		200	Surrey v. Hampshire (Southampton)	1926
		316*	Surrey v. Middlcsex (Lord's)	1926
		200*	Surrey v. Warwickshire (Birmingham)	1928
		204	Surrey v. Somerset (Oval)	1929
		221	Surrey v. West Indians (Oval)	1933
Holdsworth, R. L.	(1)	202	Oxford U. v. Free Foresters (Oxford)	1921
Hole, G. B.	(1)	226	South Australia v. Queensland (Adelaide)	1953-54
Holmes, E. R. T.	(2)	236	Oxford U. v. Free Foresters (Oxford)	1927
		206	Surrey v. Derbyshire (Chesterfield)	1935
Holmes, P.	(12)	302*	Yorkshire v. Hampshire (Portsmouth)	1920
		277*	Yorkshire v. Northamptonshire (Harrogate)	1921
		209	Yorkshire v. Warwickshire (Birmingham)	1922
		220*	Yorkshire v. Warwickshire (Huddersfield)	1922
		202*	Thornton's XI v. South Africans (Scarborough)	1924
		315*	Yorkshire v. Middlesex (Lord's)	1925
		244	M.C.C. v. Jamaica (Kingston)	1925-26
		279*	M.C.C. v. Orange Free State (Bloemfontein)	1927-28
		275	Yorkshire v. Warwickshire (Bradford)	1928
		285	Yorkshire v. Nottinghamshire (Nottingham)	1929
		250	Yorkshire v. Warwickshire (Birmingham)	1931
		224*	Yorkshire v. Essex (Leyton)	1932
Hopkins, A. J.	(1)	218	New South Wales v. South Australia (Adelaide)	1908-09
Hopwood, J. L.	(1)	220	Lancashire v. Gloucestershire (Bristol)	1934
Horner, N. F.	(1)	203*	Warwickshire v. Surrey (Oval)	1960
Horsfall, R.	(1)	206	Essex v. Kent (Blackheath)	1951
Horton, M. J.	(2)	212	Worcestershire v. Essex (Leyton)	1959
		233	Worcestershire v. Somerset (Worcester)	1962
Hosie, A. L.	(1)	200	Europeans v. Hindus (Bombay)	1924-25
Hudson, R. E. H.	(1)	217	Army v. R.A.F. (Oval)	1932
Humphreys, E.	(2)	208	Kent v. Gloucestershire (Catford)	1909
		200*	Kent v. Lancashire (Tunbridge Wells)	1910
Hunte, C. C.	(3)	260	West Indies v. Pakistan (Kingston)	1957-58
		263	Barbados v. Jamaica (Georgetown)	1961-62
		206	West Indians v. Somerset (Taunton)	1966
Hutton, L.	(11)	271*	Yorkshire v. Derbyshire (Sheffield)	1937
		364	England v. Australia (Oval)	1938
		202	M.C.C. v. Eastern Province (Port Elizabeth)	1938-39
		280*	Yorkshire v. Hampshire (Sheffield)	1939
		270*	Yorkshire v. Hampshire (Bournemouth)	1947
		201	Yorkshire v. Lancashire (Manchester)	1949
		269*	Yorkshire v. Northamptonshire (Wellingborough)	1949
		206	England v. New Zealand (Oval)	1949
		202*	England v. West Indies (Oval)	1950
		241	Players v. Gentlemen (Scarborough)	1953
		205	England v. West Indies (Kingston)	1953-54
Ibrahim, K. C.	(5)	230*	Bombay v. Western India States (Bombay)	1941-42
		250	Bijapur Famine XI v. Bengal Cyclone XI (Bombay)	1942-43
		218*	Ibrahim's XI v. Raiji's XI (Bombay)	1947-48
		234*	Ibrahim's XI v. Mantri's XI (Bombay)	1947-48
		219	Bombay v. Baroda (Bombay)	1948-49
Iddon, J.	(5)	222	Lancashire v. Leicestershire (Liverpool)	1929
		201	Lancashire v. Sussex (Manchester)	1932
		204*	Lancashire v. Warwickshire (Birmingham)	1933
		200*	Lancashire v. Nottinghamshire (Manchester)	1934
		217*	Lancashire v. Worcestershire (Manchester)	1939
Imtiaz Ahmed	(4)	300*	Prime Minister's XI v. Commonwealth (Bombay)	1950-51

Double Centuries—*Cont.*

Name	No.	Score	Match	Season
Imtiaz Ahmed (*cont.*)		213*	Pakistan v. Central Zone (Nagpur)	1952-53
		209	Pakistan v. New Zealand (Lahore)	1955-56
		251	Services v. Karachi Blues (Karachi)	1961-62
Insole, D. J.	(1)	219*	Essex v. Yorkshire (Colchester)	1949
Iremonger, J.	(4)	210	Nottinghamshire v. Kent (Nottingham)	1903
		272	Nottinghamshire v. Kent (Nottingham)	1904
		239	Nottinghamshire v. Essex (Nottingham)	1905
		200*	Nottinghamshire v. Gloucestershire (Nottingham)	1906
Jaisimha, M. L.	(1)	259	Hyderabad v. Bengal (Hyderabad)	1964-65
Jakeman, F.	(1)	258*	Northamptonshire v. Essex (Northampton)	1951
James, R.	(1)	210	South Australia v. Queensland (Adelaide)	1947-48
Jardine, D. R.	(1)	214	M.C.C. v. Tasmania (Launceston)	1928-29
Javed Masood	(1)	215	East Pakistan v. Hyderabad (Hyderabad)	1962-63
Javed Baber	(1)	200	Railways v. Dera Ismail Khan (Lahore)	1964-65
Jeacocke, A.	(1)	201*	Surrey v. Sussex (Oval)	1922
Jephson, D. L. A.	(1)	213	Surrey v. Derbyshire (Oval)	1900
Jessop, G. L.	(5)	233	Rest of England v. Yorkshire (Lord's)	1901
		286	Gloucestershire v. Sussex (Hove)	1903
		206	Gloucestershire v. Nottinghamshire (Nottingham)	1904
		234	Gloucestershire v. Somerset (Bristol)	1905
		240	Gloucestershire v. Sussex (Bristol)	1907
Jones, A. O.	(4)	250	Nottinghamshire v. Gloucestershire (Bristol)	1899
		249	Nottinghamshire v. Sussex (Hove)	1901
		296	Nottinghamshire v. Gloucestershire (Nottingham)	1903
		274	Nottinghamshire v. Essex (Leyton)	1905
Jones, W. E.	(2)	207	Glamorgan v. Kent (Gravesend)	1948
		212*	Glamorgan v. Essex (Brentwood)	1948
Jupp, V. W. C.	(1)	217*	Sussex v. Worcestershire (Worcester)	1914
Kanga, H. D.	(1)	233	Parsis v. Europeans (Poona)	1905-06
Kanhai, R. B.	(3)	256	West Indies v. India (Calcutta)	1958-59
		217	West Indies v. Pakistan (Lahore)	1958-59
		252	West Indians v. Victoria (Melbourne)	1960-61
Keeton, W. W.	(7)	200*	Nottinghamshire v. Cambridge U. (Cambridge)	1932
		242	Nottinghamshire v. Glamorgan (Nottingham)	1932
		261	Nottinghamshire v. Gloucestershire (Nottingham)	1934
		223	Nottinghamshire v. Worcestershire (Worksop)	1934
		312*	Nottinghamshire v. Middlesex (Oval)	1939
		210	Nottinghamshire v. Yorkshire (Sheffield)	1949
		208	Nottinghamshire v. Glamorgan (Nottingham)	1949
Kenny, R. B.	(1)	218	Bombay v. Madras (Bombay)	1956-57
Kenyon, D.	(7)	238*	Worcestershire v. Yorkshire (Worcester)	1953
		202*	Worcestershire v. Hampshire (Portsmouth)	1954
		253*	Worcestershire v. Leicestershire (Worcester)	1954
		259	Worcestershire v. Yorkshire (Kidderminster)	1956
		200*	Worcestershire v. Nottinghamshire (Worcester)	1957
		229	Worcestershire v. Hampshire (Portsmouth)	1959
		201	Worcestershire v. Glamorgan (Stourbridge)	1960
Key, K. J.	(1)	281	Oxford U. v. Middlesex (Chiswick Park)	1887
Khanna, A. K.	(1)	218	Services v. Delhi (New Delhi)	1952-53
Killick, E. H.	(1)	200	Sussex v. Yorkshire (Hove)	1901
Killick, E. T.	(3)	200*	Cambridge U. v. Glamorgan (Cambridge)	1929
		201	Cambridge U. v. Essex (Cambridge)	1929
		206	Middlesex v. Warwickshire (Lord's)	1931
Kilner, N.	(1)	228	Warwickshire v. Worcestershire (Worcester)	1935
Kilner, R.	(1)	206*	Yorkshire v. Derbyshire (Sheffield)	1920
King, J. H.	(2)	227*	Leicestershire v. Worcestershire (Coalville)	1914
		205	Leicestershire v. Hampshire (Leicester)	1923
Kinneir, S. P.	(2)	215*	Warwickshire v. Lancashire (Birmingham)	1901
		268*	Warwickshire v. Hampshire (Birmingham)	1911
Kippax, A. F.	(7)	248	New South Wales v. South Australia (Sydney)	1923-24
		212*	New South Wales v. Victoria (Sydney)	1924-25
		271*	New South Wales v. Victoria (Sydney)	1925-26
		217*	New South Wales v. Victoria (Sydney)	1926-27
		315*	New South Wales v. Queensland (Sydney)	1927-28
		260*	New South Wales v. Victoria (Melbourne)	1928-29
		250	Australians v. Sussex (Hove)	1934
Kishenchand, G.	(1)	218	North Zone v. South Zone (Bombay)	1946-47

Double Centuries—*Cont.*

Player	No.	Score	Match	Season
Knight, A. E. ..	.. (2)	229*	Leicestershire v. Worcestershire (Worcester) ..	1903
		203	Leicestershire v. M.C.C. (Lord's)	1904
Knott, C. H. ..	.. (1)	261*	Harlequins v. West Indians (Eastbourne) ..	1928
Koch, L. B. ..	.. (1)	216*	Orange Free State v. Natal (Bloemfontein) ..	1952-53
Kortlang, B. J. ..	.. (1)	214*	Wellington v. Auckland (Wellington)	1925-26
Kripal Singh, A. G.	.. (1)	208	Madras v. Travancore-Cochin (Ernakulam) ..	1954-55
Kunderan, B. K.	.. (1)	205	Railways v. Jammu & Kashmir (New Delhi)	1959-60
Langridge, John	.. (8)	250*	Sussex v. Glamorgan (Hove)	1933
		232*	Sussex v. Northamptonshire (Peterborough) ..	1934
		227	Sussex v. Northamptonshire (Northampton) ..	1938
		215	Sussex v. Glamorgan (Eastbourne)	1938
		202	Sussex v. Leicestershire (Hastings)	1939
		234*	Sussex v. Derbyshire (Ilkeston)	1949
		241	Sussex v. Somerset (Worthing)	1950
		200*	Sussex v. Derbyshire (Derby)	1951
Lashley, P. D. ..	.. (2)	200*	Barbados v. British Guiana (Bridgetown) ..	1958-59
		204	Barbados v. Guyana (Georgetown)	1966-67
Lawry, W. M. ..	.. (3)	266	Victoria v. New South Wales (Sydney) ..	1960-61
		246	Victoria v. South Australia (Melbourne) ..	1964-65
		210	Australia v. West Indies (Bridgetown) ..	1964-65
Lee, G. M. ..	.. (1)	200*	Nottinghamshire v. Leicestershire (Nottingham)	1913
Lee, H. W. ..	.. (4)	221*	Middlesex v. Hampshire (Southampton) ..	1920
		243*	Middlesex v. Nottinghamshire (Lord's) ..	1921
		200	Middlesex v. Oxford U. (Oxford)	1929
		225	Middlesex v. Surrey (Oval)	1929
Lee, I. S. ..	.. (1)	268	Victoria v. Tasmania (Melbourne)	1933-34
Lewis, A. E. ..	.. (1)	201*	Somerset v. Kent (Taunton)	1909
Lewis, A. R. ..	.. (1)	223	Glamorgan v. Kent (Gravesend)	1966
Leyland, M. ..	.. (5)	204*	Yorkshire v. Middlesex (Sheffield)	1927
		247	Yorkshire v. Worcestershire (Worcester) ..	1928
		211*	Yorkshire v. Lancashire (Leeds)	1930
		210*	Yorkshire v. Kent (Dover)	1933
		263	Yorkshire v. Essex (Hull)	1936
Lindsay, D. ..	.. (1)	216	North-Eastern Transvaal v. Transvaal B (Johannesburg)	1966-67
Livingston, T. L.	.. (4)	201*	Northamptonshire v. South Africans (Northampton)	1951
		210	Northamptonshire v. Somerset (Weston-super-Mare)	1951
		200	Northamptonshire v. Kent (Maidstone) ..	1954
		207*	Northamptonshire v. Nottinghamshire (Nottingham)	1954
Livingstone, D. A.	.. (1)	200	Hampshire v. Surrey (Southampton)	1962
Llewellyn, C. B.	.. (1)	216	Hampshire v. South Africans (Southampton) ..	1901
Lockwood, E. ..	.. (1)	208	Yorkshire v. Kent (Gravesend)	1883
Longrigg, E. F.	.. (1)	205	Somerset v. Leicestershire (Taunton)	1930
Lowndes, W. G. L. F.	.. (1)	216	Oxford U. v. Leveson-Gower's XI (Eastbourne)	1921
Lowson, F. A. ..	.. (1)	259*	Yorkshire v. Worcestershire (Worcester) ..	1953
Loxton, S. J. E.	.. (1)	232*	Victoria v. Queensland (Melbourne)	1946-47
Lucas, F. M. ..	.. (1)	215*	Sussex v. Gloucestershire (Hove)	1885
Lucas, J. H. ..	.. (1)	216*	Barbados v. Trinidad (Bridgetown)	1948-49
Lyon, M. D. ..	.. (2)	219	Somerset v. Derbyshire (Burton upon Trent) ..	1924
		210	Somerset v. Gloucestershire (Taunton) ..	1930
McAlister, P. A.	.. (1)	224	Victoria v. New Zealanders (Melbourne) ..	1898-99
Macartney, C. G.	.. (4)	208	Australians v. Essex (Leyton)	1912
		201	New South Wales v. Victoria (Sydney) ..	1913-14
		345	Australians v. Nottinghamshire (Nottingham)	1921
		221	New South Wales v. Canterbury (Christchurch)	1923-24
McCabe, S. J. ..	.. (3)	229*	New South Wales v. Queensland (Brisbane) ..	1931-32
		240	Australians v. Surrey (Oval)	1934
		232	Australia v. England (Nottingham)	1938
McCorkell, N. ..	.. (1)	203	Hampshire v. Gloucestershire (Gloucester) ..	1951
McDonald, C. C.	.. (2)	207	Victoria v. New South Wales (Sydney) ..	1951-52
		229	Victoria v. South Australia (Adelaide) ..	1953-54
McDonnell, P. S.	.. (1)	239	New South Wales v. Victoria (Melbourne) ..	1886-87
McGahey, C. P.	.. (3)	225	Essex v. Nottinghamshire (Leyton)	1904
		277	Essex v. Derbyshire (Leyton)	1905

Double Centuries—*Cont.*

Name		Score	Match	Season
McGahey, C. P. (*cont.*)		230	Essex v. Northamptonshire (Northampton)	1908
McGlew, D. J.	(2)	255*	South Africa v. New Zealand (Wellington)	1952-53
		213*	Natal v. Border (Durban)	1957-58
Mackay, J. R. M.	(1)	203	New South Wales v. Queensland (Brisbane)	1905-06
Mackay, K. D.	(2)	223	Queensland v. Victoria (Brisbane)	1953-54
		203	Queensland v. New South Wales (Sydney)	1955-56
McKenzie, C.	(1)	211	Victoria v. Western Australia (Perth)	1909-10
MacLaren, A. C.	(6)	228	Stoddart's XI v. Victoria (Melbourne)	1894-95
		424	Lancashire v. Somerset (Taunton)	1895
		226*	Lancashire v. Kent (Canterbury)	1896
		244	Lancashire v. Kent (Canterbury)	1897
		204	Lancashire v. Gloucestershire (Liverpool)	1903
		200*	M.C.C. v. New Zealand XI (Wellington)	1922-23
McLean, A. R.	(1)	213	South Australia v. Queensland (Adelaide)	1949-50
McLean, R. A.	(1)	207	South Africans v. Worcestershire (Worcester)	1960
McMorris, E. D. A.	(1)	218	Jamaica v. Guyana (Georgetown)	1966-67
Maddocks, R.	(1)	271	Victoria v. Tasmania (Melbourne)	1951-52
Mahendra Kumar	(1)	205	Hyderabad v. Uttar Pradesh (Hyderabad)	1964-65
Majid Jahangir	(1)	241	Lahore Greens v. Bahawalpur (Lahore)	1965-66
Makepeace, H.	(2)	203	Lancashire v. Worcestershire (Worcester)	1923
		200*	Lancashire v. Northamptonshire (Liverpool)	1923
Manjrekar, V. L.	(2)	204*	Indians v. Oxford U. (Oxford)	1959
		283	Vizianagram XI v. Tata Sports Club XI (Hyderabad)	1963-64
Mankad, V. M.	(3)	223	India v. New Zealand (Bombay)	1955-56
		231	India v. New Zealand (Madras)	1955-56
		221	Rajasthan v. Vidarbha (Udaipur)	1957-58
Mantri, M. K.	(1)	200	Bombay v. Maharashtra (Poona)	1948-49
Marks, A. E.	(1)	201	New South Wales v. Queensland (Sydney)	1935-36
Marshall, R. E.	(2)	212	Hampshire v. Somerset (Bournemouth)	1961
		228*	Hampshire v. Pakistanis (Bournemouth)	1962
Martin, F. R.	(1)	204*	Jamaica v. Tennyson's XI (Kingston)	1926-27
Marx, W. F. E.	(1)	240	Transvaal v. Griqualand West (Johannesburg)	1920-21
Massie, H. H.	(1)	206	Australians v. Oxford U. (Oxford)	1882
Matthews, T. G.	(1)	201	Gloucestershire v. Surrey (Clifton)	1871
Maxwell, C. R.	(1)	268	Cahn's XI v. Leicestershire (Nottingham)	1935
May, P. B. H.	(5)	227*	Cambridge U. v. Hampshire (Cambridge)	1950
		211*	Surrey v. Nottinghamshire (Nottingham)	1954
		207	Surrey v. Cambridge U. (Oval)	1954
		206	M.C.C. v. Rhodesia (Salisbury)	1956-57
		285*	England v. West Indies (Birmingham)	1957
Maynard, A.	(1)	200*	Trinidad v. M.C.C. (Port of Spain)	1934-35
Mayne, E. R.	(1)	209	Victoria v. Queensland (Melbourne)	1923-24
Mead, C. P.	(13)	207*	Hampshire v. Warwickshire (Southampton)	1911
		223	Players v. Gentlemen (Scarborough)	1911
		213	Hampshire v. Yorkshire (Southampton)	1914
		207	Hampshire v. Essex (Leyton)	1919
		280*	Hampshire v. Nottinghamshire (Southampton)	1921
		224	Hampshire v. Sussex (Horsham)	1921
		235	Hampshire v. Worcestershire (Worcester)	1922
		211*	Hampshire v. Warwickshire (Southampton)	1922
		222	Hampshire v. Warwickshire (Birmingham)	1923
		213*	Hampshire v. Worcestershire (Bournemouth)	1925
		200*	Hampshire v. Essex (Southampton)	1927
		233	M.C.C. Australian XI v. Hawke's XI (Scarborough)	1929
		227	Hampshire v. Derbyshire (Ilkeston)	1933
Merchant, U. M.	(1)	217	Bombay v. Hyderabad (Bombay)	1947-48
Merchant, V. M.	(11)	243*	Hindus v. Muslims (Bombay)	1941-42
		221	Hindus v. Parsis (Bombay)	1941-42
		250*	Hindus v. Rest (Bombay)	1943-44
		359*	Bombay v. Maharashtra (Bombay)	1943-44
		221*	Hindus v. Parsis (Bombay)	1944-45
		217	Bombay v. Western India States (Bombay)	1944-45
		278	Bombay v. Holkar (Bombay)	1944-45
		201	Cricket Club of India v. Services XI (Bombay)	1944-45

Double Centuries—*Cont.*

Player	No.	Score	Match	Season
Merchant, V. M. (*cont.*)		234*	Bombay v. Sind (Bombay)	1945-46
		242*	Indians v. Lancashire (Manchester)	1946
		205	Indians v. Sussex (Hove)	1946
Meuleman, K. D.	(2)	206	Victoria v. Tasmania (Melbourne)	1947-48
		234*	Western Australia v. South Australia (Perth)	1956-57
Meyer, R. J. O.	(1)	202*	Somerset v. Lancashire (Taunton)	1936
Midlane, F. A.	(1)	222*	Wellington v. Otago (Wellington)	1914-15
Milburn, C.	(1)	203	Northamptonshire v. Essex (Clacton)	1966
Miller, K. R.	(7)	206*	Victoria v. New South Wales (Sydney)	1946-47
		202*	Australians v. Leicestershire (Leicester)	1948
		201*	New South Wales v. Queensland (Brisbane)	1950-51
		214	New South Wales v. M.C.C. (Sydney)	1950-51
		220*	Australians v. Worcestershire (Worcester)	1953
		262*	Australians v. Combined Services (Kingston)	1953
		281*	Australians v. Leicestershire (Leicester)	1956
Minnett, R. B.	(1)	216*	New South Wales v. Victoria (Sydney)	1911-12
Mitchell, N. F.	(1)	220	Victoria v. Tasmania (Melbourne)	1926-27
Mitchell-Innes, N. S.	(1)	207	Oxford U. v. Leveson-Gower's XI (Reigate)	1936
Modi, R. S.	(4)	215	Parsis v. Europeans (Bombay)	1944-45
		210	Bombay v. Western India States (Bombay)	1944-45
		245*	Bombay v. Baroda (Baroda)	1944-45
		203	Indian XI v. Australian Services (Madras)	1945-46
Moore, D. N.	(1)	206	Gloucestershire v. Oxford U. (Oxford)	1930
Moore, H. I.	(1)	206*	Nottinghamshire v. Indians (Nottingham)	1967
Moore, R. H.	(1)	316	Hampshire v. Warwickshire (Bournemouth)	1937
Mordaunt, G. J.	(1)	264*	Oxford U. v. Sussex (Hove)	1895
Morkel, D. P. B.	(2)	208*	Western Province v. Natal (Cape Town)	1929-30
		251	Cahn's XI v. South Americans (Nottingham)	1932
Moroney, J. A. R.	(1)	217	Morris' XI v. Hassett's XI (Sydney)	1948-49
Morris, A. R.	(4)	290	Australians v. Gloucestershire (Bristol)	1948
		206	Australia v. England (Adelaide)	1950-51
		253	New South Wales v. Queensland (Brisbane)	1951-52
		210	New South Wales v. Victoria (Melbourne)	1951-52
Morrison, J. S. F.	(1)	233*	Cambridge U. v. M.C.C. (Cambridge)	1914
Moses, H.	(1)	297*	New South Wales v. Victoria (Sydney)	1887-88
Murdoch, W. L.	(5)	321	New South Wales v. Victoria (Sydney)	1881-82
		286*	Australians v. Sussex (Hove)	1882
		279*	Australian XI v. Rest (Melbourne)	1883-84
		211	Australia v. England (Oval)	1884
		226	Sussex v. Cambridge U. (Hove)	1895
Mushtaq Ali	(1)	233	Holkar v. United Provinces (Indore)	1947-48
Mushtaq Mohammad	(2)	229*	Karachi Whites v. East Pakistan (Karachi)	1961-62
		281	P.I.A. v. Railways (Lahore)	1962-63
Nadkarni, R. G.	(3)	201*	Maharashtra v. Saurashtra (Poona)	1957-58
		283*	Bombay v. Delhi (Bombay)	1960-61
		219	Bombay v. Rajasthan (Jaipur)	1962-63
Naoomal Jeoomal	(1)	203*	Sind v. Nawanagar (Karachi)	1938-39
Nayudu, C. K.	(1)	200	Holkar v. Baroda (Indore)	1945-46
Nel, J. D.	(1)	217*	Western Province v. Eastern Province (Port Elizabeth)	1952-53
Newham, W.	(1)	201*	Sussex v. Somerset (Hove)	1896
Nichol, M.	(1)	262*	Worcestershire v. Hampshire (Bournemouth)	1930
Nicholls, D.	(1)	211	Kent v. Derbyshire (Folkestone)	1963
Nicholls, R. B.	(1)	217	Gloucestershire v. Oxford U. (Oxford)	1962
Nichols, M. S.	(1)	205	Essex v. Hampshire (Southend)	1936
Nicolson, J. F. W.	(1)	252*	Natal v. Orange Free State (Bloemfontein)	1926-27
Nimbalkar, B. B.	(2)	443*	Maharashtra v. Kathiawar (Poona)	1948-49
		219	Holkar v. Bengal (Calcutta)	1952-53
Noble, M. A.	(7)	200	New South Wales v. South Australia (Adelaide)	1899-00
		284	Australians v. Sussex (Hove)	1902
		230	New South Wales v. South Australia (Sydney)	1903-04
		267	Australians v. Sussex (Hove)	1905
		281	New South Wales v. Victoria (Melbourne)	1905-06
		213	New South Wales v. South Australia (Adelaide)	1908-09
		213	New South Wales v. Victoria (Sydney)	1908-09
Norman, M. E. J. C.	(1)	221*	Leicestershire v. Cambridge U. (Cambridge)	1967
Nourse, A. D., Snr.	(7)	212	Natal v. Griqualand West (Johannesburg)	1906-07

Double Centuries—*Cont.*

Player	No.	Score	Match	Season
Nourse, A. D., Snr. (*cont.*)		200*	Natal v. Western Province (Cape Town)	1907-08
		201*	South Africans v. South Australia (Adelaide)	1910-11
		213*	South Africans v. Hampshire (Bournemouth)	1912
		304*	Natal v. Transvaal (Johannesburg)	1919-20
		204	Transvaal v. Griqualand West (Johannesburg)	1925-26
		219*	Western Province v. Natal (Cape Town)	1932-33
Nourse, A. D., Jnr.	(6)	231	South Africa v. Australia (Johannesburg)	1935-36
		260*	Natal v. Transvaal (Johannesburg)	1936-37
		240	Natal v. Western Province (Durban)	1936-37
		205*	South Africans v. Warwickshire (Birmingham)	1947
		214*	Natal v. Griqualand West (Durban)	1947-48
		208	South Africa v. England (Nottingham)	1951
Nunes, R. K.	(1)	200*	Jamaica v. Tennyson's XI (Kingston)	1926-27
Nurse, S. M.	(3)	213	Barbados v. M.C.C. (Bridgetown)	1959-60
		210	Barbados v. Trinidad (Bridgetown)	1962-63
		201	West Indies v. Australia (Bridgetown)	1964-65
Oakman, A. S. M.	(1)	229*	Sussex v. Nottinghamshire (Worksop)	1961
O'Brien, T. C.	(1)	202	Middlesex v. Sussex (Hove)	1895
O'Connor, J.	(2)	237	Essex v. Somerset (Leyton)	1933
		248	Essex v. Surrey (Brentwood)	1934
Ollivierre, C. A.	(1)	229	Derbyshire v. Essex (Chesterfield)	1904
O'Neill, N. C.	(2)	233	New South Wales v. Victoria (Sydney)	1957-58
		284	Australians v. President's XI (Ahmedabad)	1959-60
Outschoorn, L.	(2)	215*	Worcestershire v. Northamptonshire (Worcester)	1949
		200*	Worcestershire v. Scotland (Dundee)	1951
Page, M. L.	(1)	206	Canterbury v. Wellington (Wellington)	1931-32
Paine, A. I.	(1)	220	Western Province v. Griqualand West (Johannesburg)	1896-97
Palairet, L. C. H.	(2)	292	Somerset v. Hampshire (Southampton)	1896
		203	Somerset v. Worcestershire (Worcester)	1904
Palia, P. E.	(1)	216	United Provinces v. Maharashtra (Poona)	1939-40
Palmer, C. H.	(1)	201	Leicestershire v. Northamptonshire (Northampton)	1953
Pandit, B.	(1)	262*	Kerala v. Andhra (Pulghat)	1959-60
Parfitt, P. H.	(1)	200*	Middlesex v. Nottinghamshire (Nottingham)	1964
Park, R. L.	(1)	228	Victoria v. South Australia (Melbourne)	1919-20
Parker, G. W.	(1)	210	Gloucestershire v. Kent (Dover)	1937
Parker, J. F.	(2)	204*	Surrey v. Derbyshire (Oval)	1947
		255	Surrey v. New Zealanders (Oval)	1949
Parkhouse, W. G. A.	(1)	201	Glamorgan v. Kent (Swansea)	1956
Parks, H. W.	(1)	200*	Sussex v. Essex (Chelmsford)	1931
Parks, J. M.	(1)	205*	Sussex v. Somerset (Hove)	1955
Parsons, J. H.	(1)	225	Warwickshire v. Glamorgan (Birmingham)	1927
Passailaigue, C. C.	(1)	261*	Jamaica v. Lord Tennyson's XI (Kingston)	1931-32
Pataudi, Nawab of, Snr.	(5)	238*	Oxford U. v. Cambridge U. (Lord's)	1931
		224*	Worcestershire v. Kent (Worcester)	1933
		231*	Worcestershire v. Essex (Worcester)	1933
		222	Worcestershire v. Somerset (Weston-super-Mare)	1933
		214*	Worcestershire v. Glamorgan (Worcester)	1934
Pataudi, Nawab of, Jnr.	(1)	203*	India v. England (New Delhi)	1963-64
Paynter, E.	(7)	208*	Lancashire v. Northamptonshire (Northampton)	1935
		266	Lancashire v. Essex (Manchester)	1937
		322	Lancashire v. Sussex (Hove)	1937
		291	Lancashire v. Hampshire (Southampton)	1938
		216*	England v. Australia (Nottingham)	1938
		243	England v. South Africa (Durban)	1938-39
		222	Lancashire v. Derbyshire (Manchester)	1939
Peach, H. A.	(1)	200*	Surrey v. Northamptonshire (Northampton)	1920
Pearce, T. N.	(1)	211*	Essex v. Leicestershire (Westcliff)	1948
Peel, R.	(1)	210*	Yorkshire v. Warwickshire (Birmingham)	1896
Pellew, C. E.	(1)	271	South Australia v. Victoria (Adelaide)	1919-20
Perrin, P. A.	(3)	205	Essex v. Kent (Leyton)	1900
		343*	Essex v. Derbyshire (Chesterfield)	1904
		245	Essex v. Derbyshire (Leyton)	1912
Pervez Akhtar	(1)	337*	Railways v. Dera Ismail Khan (Lahore)	1964-65
Phadkar, D. G.	(1)	217	Bombay v. Maharashtra (Bombay)	1950-51
Place, W.	(3)	266*	Lancashire v. Oxford U. (Oxford)	1947
		200	Lancashire v. Somerset (Taunton)	1948

Double Centuries—*Cont.*

Place, W. (*cont.*)		226*	Lancashire v. Nottinghamshire (Nottingham)	1949
Pollock, R. G.	(3)	209*	Eastern Province XI v. Cavaliers (Port Elizabeth)	1962-63
		203*	South Africans v. Kent (Canterbury)	1965
		209	South Africa v. Australia (Cape Town)	1966-67
Ponsford, W. H.	(13)	429	Victoria v. Tasmania (Melbourne)	1922-23
		248	Victoria v. Queensland (Melbourne)	1923-24
		214	Victoria v. South Australia (Adelaide)	1926-27
		352	Victoria v. New South Wales (Melbourne)	1926-27
		437	Victoria v. Queensland (Melbourne)	1927-28
		202	Victoria v. New South Wales (Melbourne)	1927-28
		336	Victoria v. South Australia (Melbourne)	1927-28
		275*	Victoria v. South Australia (Melbourne)	1928-29
		220*	Australians v. Oxford U. (Oxford)	1930
		200	Victoria v. New South Wales (Sydney)	1932-33
		229*	Australians v. Cambridge U. (Cambridge)	1934
		281*	Australians v. M.C.C. (Lord's)	1934
		266	Australia v. England (Oval)	1934
Poole, C. J.	(2)	222*	Nottinghamshire v. Indians (Nottingham)	1952
		219	Nottinghamshire v. Derbyshire (Ilkeston)	1952
Poore, R. M.	(1)	304	Hampshire v. Somerset (Taunton)	1899
Pope, G. H.	(1)	207*	Derbyshire v. Hampshire (Portsmouth)	1948
Potter, J.	(1)	221	Victoria v. New South Wales (Melbourne)	1965-66
Pretty, H. C.	(1)	200	Northamptonshire v. Derbyshire (Chesterfield)	1906
Prideaux, R. M.	(1)	202*	Northamptonshire v. Oxford U. (Oxford)	1963
Punjabi, P. H.	(1)	224*	Gujerat v. Saurashtra (Rajkot)	1959-60
Quaife, W. G.	(4)	207*	Warwickshire v. Hampshire (Birmingham)	1899
		223*	Warwickshire v. Essex (Leyton)	1900
		200*	Warwickshire v. Essex (Birmingham)	1904
		255*	Warwickshire v. Surrey (Oval)	1905
Quin, S. O.	(1)	210	Victoria v. Tasmania (Melbourne)	1933-34
Ram Prakash	(1)	209*	Northern India v. Maharashtra (Poona)	1940-41
Ramchand, G. S.	(1)	230*	Bombay v. Maharashtra (Bombay)	1950-51
Rangnekar, K. M.	(3)	202	Bombay v. Maharashtra (Poona)	1940-41
		200*	West Zone v. East Zone (Bombay)	1946-47
		217	Holkar v. Hyderabad (Indore)	1950-51
Ranjitsinhji, K. S.	(14)	260	Sussex v. M.C.C. (Lord's)	1897
		222	Sussex v. Somerset (Hove)	1900
		215*	Sussex v. Cambridge U. (Cambridge)	1900
		202	Sussex v. Middlesex (Hove)	1900
		275	Sussex v. Leicestershire (Leicester)	1900
		220	Sussex v. Kent (Hove)	1900
		285*	Sussex v. Somerset (Taunton)	1901
		204	Sussex v. Lancashire (Hove)	1901
		219	Sussex v. Essex (Hove)	1901
		230	Sussex v. Essex (Leyton)	1902
		234*	Sussex v. Surrey (Hastings)	1902
		204	Sussex v. Surrey (Oval)	1903
		207*	Sussex v. Lancashire (Hove)	1904
		200	Sussex v. Surrey (Oval)	1908
Raphael, J. E.	(1)	201	Oxford U. v. Yorkshire (Oxford)	1904
Ratcliffe, A.	(1)	201	Cambridge U. v. Oxford U. (Lord's)	1931
Read, W. W.	(3)	247	Surrey v. Lancashire (Manchester)	1887
		244*	Surrey v. Cambridge U. (Oval)	1887
		338	Surrey v. Oxford U. (Oval)	1888
Redpath, I. R.	(2)	261	Victoria v. Queensland (Melbourne)	1962-63
		202	Australians v. Western Australia (Perth)	1963-64
Reid, J. R.	(4)	283	Wellington v. Otago (Wellington)	1951-52
		201	Otago v. Canterbury (Dunedin)	1957-58
		203	New Zealanders v. Western Province (Cape Town)	1961-62
		296	Wellington v. Northern Districts (Wellington)	1962-63
Relf, R. R.	(3)	210	Sussex v. Kent (Canterbury)	1907
		272*	Sussex v. Worcestershire (Eastbourne)	1909
		225	Sussex v. Lancashire (Eastbourne)	1920
Reynolds, R.	(1)	203*	Queensland v. South Australia (Adelaide)	1957-58
Rhodes, W.	(3)	201	Yorkshire v. Somerset (Taunton)	1905

Double Centuries—*Cont.*

Player	No.	Score	Match	Season
Rhodes, W. (*cont.*)		210	M.C.C. v. South Australia (Adelaide)	1920-21
		267*	Yorkshire v. Leicestershire (Leeds)	1921
Richardson, A. J.	(4)	280	South Australia v. M.C.C. (Adelaide)	1922-23
		200*	South Australia v. M.C.C. (Adelaide)	1924-25
		227	South Australia v. Western Australia (Adelaide)	1925-26
		232	South Australia v. Queensland (Adelaide)	1926-27
Richardson, C.	(1)	258	Orange Free State v. Transvaal B (Johannesburg)	1959-60
Richardson, V. Y.	(2)	231	South Australia v. M.C.C. (Adelaide)	1928-29
		203	South Australia v. Victoria (Adelaide)	1932-33
Riches, N. V. H.	(1)	239*	Wales v. Ireland (Belfast)	1926
Roach, C. A.	(1)	209	West Indies v. England (Georgetown)	1929-30
Robertson, J. D.	(4)	229	Middlesex v. Hampshire (Lord's)	1947
		331*	Middlesex v. Worcestershire (Worcester)	1949
		201*	Middlesex v. Somerset (Taunton)	1951
		201*	Middlesex v. Essex (Lord's)	1957
Rock, H. O.	(1)	235	New South Wales v. Victoria (Sydney)	1924-25
Roller, W. E.	(1)	204	Surrey v. Sussex (Oval)	1885
Rowan, E. A. B.	(5)	306*	Transvaal v. Natal (Johannesburg)	1939-40
		284	Eastern Province v. Griqualand West (Port Elizabeth)	1945-46
		277*	Transvaal v. Griqualand West (Johannesburg)	1950-51
		202*	South Africans v. Northamptonshire (Northampton)	1951
		236	South Africa v. England (Leeds)	1951
Roy, P.	(1)	202*	Bengal v. Orissa (Cuttack)	1963-64
Russell, A. C.	(2)	201	M.C.C. v. South Australia (Adelaide)	1920-21
		273	Essex v. Northamptonshire (Leyton)	1921
Ryder, J.	(3)	242	Victoria v. South Australia (Melbourne)	1921-22
		201*	Australia v. England (Adelaide)	1924-25
		295	Victoria v. New South Wales (Melbourne)	1926-27
Sandham, A.	(11)	292*	Surrey v. Northamptonshire (Oval)	1921
		209*	Surrey v. Somerset (Oval)	1921
		200	Surrey v. Essex (Leyton)	1923
		230	Surrey v. Essex (Oval)	1927
		282*	Surrey v. Lancashire (Manchester)	1928
		248*	Surrey v. Glamorgan (Cardiff)	1928
		325	England v. West Indies (Kingston)	1929-30
		204	Surrey v. Warwickshire (Birmingham)	1930
		215	Surrey v. Somerset (Taunton)	1932
		219	Surrey v. Australians (Oval)	1934
		239	Surrey v. Glamorgan (Oval)	1937
Santall, F. R.	(1)	201*	Warwickshire v. Northamptonshire (Northampton)	1933
Sardesai, D. N.	(2)	222	A.C.C. XI v. Indian Starlets XI (Hyderabad)	1964-65
		200*	India v. New Zealand (Bombay)	1964-65
Sarwate, C. T.	(3)	235	Holkar v. Delhi (New Delhi)	1949-50
		246	Holkar v. Bengal (Calcutta)	1950-51
		234	Holkar v. Gujerat (Indore)	1950-51
Sathasivam, M.	(1)	215	All Ceylon v. South India (Madras)	1946-47
Scott, S. W.	(1)	224	Middlesex v. Gloucestershire (Lord's)	1892
Scott, V. J.	(2)	204	Auckland v. Otago (Dunedin)	1947-48
		203	New Zealanders v. Combined Services (Gillingham)	1949
Sellers, A. B.	(1)	204	Yorkshire v. Cambridge U. (Cambridge)	1936
Seymour, James	(3)	204	Kent v. Hampshire (Tonbridge)	1907
		218*	Kent v. Essex (Leyton)	1911
		214	Kent v. Essex (Tunbridge Wells)	1914
Shahid Mahmood	(1)	220	Karachi U. v. Peshawar U. (Karachi)	1958-59
Shakoor Ahmed	(1)	280	Lahore Greens v. Railways (Lahore)	1964-65
Sharp, A. T.	(1)	216	Leicestershire v. Derbyshire (Chesterfield)	1911
Sharp, J.	(1)	211	Lancashire v. Leicestershire (Manchester)	1912
Sharpe, P. J.	(2)	202	Minor Counties v. Indians (Stoke)	1959
		203*	Yorkshire v. Cambridge U. (Cambridge)	1960
Sheahan, A. P.	(1)	202	Victoria v. South Australia (Melbourne)	1966-67
Shepherd, B. K.	(3)	212*	Western Australia v. Queensland (Perth)	1961-62
		219	Western Australia v. Victoria (Melbourne)	1962-63
		215*	Western Australia v. Victoria (Perth)	1964-65

Double Centuries—*Cont.*

Player		Score	Match	Season
Shepherd, T. F.	(5)	212	Surrey v. Lancashire (Oval)	1921
		210*	Surrey v. Kent (Blackheath)	1921
		207*	Surrey v. Kent (Blackheath)	1925
		277*	Surrey v. Gloucestershire (Oval)	1927
		234	Surrey v. Cambridge U. (Oval)	1930
Sheppard, D. S.	(3)	204	Sussex v. Glamorgan (Eastbourne)	1949
		227	Cambridge U. v. West Indians (Cambridge)	1950
		239*	Cambridge U. v. Worcestershire (Worcester)	1952
Shiell, A. B.	(1)	202*	South Australia v. M.C.C. (Adelaide)	1965-66
Shipman, A.	(1)	226	Leicestershire v. Kent (Tonbridge)	1928
Shodhan, D. H.	(1)	261	Baroda v. Maharashtra (Ahmedabad)	1957-58
Shrewsbury, A.	(10)	207	Nottinghamshire v. Surrey (Oval)	1882
		209	Nottinghamshire v. Sussex (Hove)	1884
		224*	Nottinghamshire v. Middlesex (Lord's)	1885
		227*	Nottinghamshire v. Gloucestershire (Moreton-in-the-Marsh)	1886
		236	Non-Smokers v. Smokers (East Melbourne)	1886-87
		267	Nottinghamshire v. Middlesex (Nottingham)	1887
		232	Shrewsbury's XI v. Victoria (Melbourne)	1887-88
		206	Shrewsbury's XI v. Australian XI (Sydney)	1887-88
		267	Nottinghamshire v. Sussex (Nottingham)	1890
		212	Nottinghamshire v. Middlesex (Lord's)	1892
Siedle, I. J.	(3)	212*	Natal v. Border (Durban)	1928-29
		265*	Natal v. Orange Free State (Durban)	1929-30
		207	Natal v. Western Province (Durban)	1936-37
Simpson, R. B.	(11)	236*	Western Australia v. New South Wales (Perth)	1959-60
		230*	Western Australia v. Queensland (Perth)	1959-60
		221*	Western Australia v. West Indians (Perth)	1960-61
		205	New South Wales v. Western Australia (Perth)	1962-63
		359	New South Wales v. Queensland (Brisbane)	1963-64
		246	Combined XI v. South Africans (Perth)	1963-64
		247*	New South Wales v. Western Australia (Sydney)	1963-64
		311	Australia v. England (Manchester)	1964
		201	Australia v. West Indies (Bridgetown)	1964-65
		225	Australia v. England (Adelaide)	1965-66
		243	Australians v. North-Eastern Transvaal (Pretoria)	1966-67
Simpson, R. T.	(10)	201	Nottinghamshire v. Warwickshire (Nottingham)	1946
		200*	Nottinghamshire v. Surrey (Nottingham)	1949
		238	Nottinghamshire v. Lancashire (Manchester)	1949
		230*	Nottinghamshire v. Glamorgan (Swansea)	1950
		243*	Nottinghamshire v. Worcestershire (Nottingham)	1950
		259	M.C.C. v. New South Wales (Sydney)	1950-51
		201	Nottinghamshire v. Oxford U. (Oxford)	1951
		212	Nottinghamshire v. Essex (Clacton)	1951
		216	Nottinghamshire v. Sussex (Nottingham)	1952
		200	Nottinghamshire v. Warwickshire (Nottingham)	1952
Sinfield, R. A.	(1)	209*	Gloucestershire v. Glamorgan (Cardiff)	1935
Smith, D.	(2)	225	Derbyshire v. Hampshire (Chesterfield)	1935
		202*	Derbyshire v. Nottinghamshire (Nottingham)	1937
Smith, D. V.	(1)	206*	Sussex v. Nottinghamshire (Nottingham)	1950
Smith, M. J. K.	(3)	201*	Oxford U. v. Cambridge U. (Lord's)	1954
		200*	Warwickshire v. Worcestershire (Birmingham)	1959
		204	Cavaliers v. Natal (Durban)	1960-61
Smith, S. G.	(2)	204	Northamptonshire v. Gloucestershire (Northampton)	1910
		256	Auckland v. Canterbury (Auckland)	1919-20
Sobers, G. St. A.	(5)	219*	West Indians v. Nottinghamshire (Nottingham)	1957
		365*	West Indies v. Pakistan (Kingston)	1957-58
		226	West Indies v. England (Bridgetown)	1959-60
		251	South Australia v. New South Wales (Adelaide)	1961-62
		204	Barbados v. British Guiana (Bridgetown)	1965-66
Sohoni, S. W.	(1)	218*	Maharashtra v. Western India (Rajkot)	1940-41
Solomon, J. S.	(1)	201*	Berbice v. M.C.C. (Blairmont)	1959-60
Spooner, R. H.	(5)	247	Lancashire v. Nottinghamshire (Nottingham)	1903
		215	Lancashire v. Essex (Leyton)	1904
		240	Lancashire v. Somerset (Bath)	1906
		200*	Lancashire v. Yorkshire (Manchester)	1910

Double Centuries—*Cont.*

Spooner, R. H. (*cont.*)		224	Lancashire v. Surrey (Oval)	1911
Squires, H. S.	(3)	200*	Surrey v. Cambridge U. (Oval)	1931
		236	Surrey v. Lancashire (Oval)	1933
		210	Surrey v. Derbyshire (Oval)	1949
Stevens, G.	(1)	259*	South Australia v. New South Wales (Sydney)	1958-59
Stewart, M. J.	(2)	200*	Surrey v. Essex (Oval)	1962
		227*	Surrey v. Middlesex (Oval)	1964
Steyn, S. S. L.	(1)	261*	Western Province v. Border (Cape Town)	1929-30
Stoddart, A. E.	(2)	215*	Middlesex v. Lancashire (Manchester)	1891
		221	Middlesex v. Somerset (Lord's)	1900
Stollmeyer, J. B.	(5)	210	Trinidad v. Barbados (Bridgetown)	1943-44
		324	Trinidad v. British Guiana (Port of Spain)	1946-47
		244*	West Indies v. South Zone (Madras)	1948-49
		261	Trinidad v. Jamaica (Port of Spain)	1949-50
		208	Trinidad v. Barbados (Bridgetown)	1950-51
Storer, H.	(2)	209	Derbyshire v. Essex (Derby)	1929
		232	Derbyshire v. Essex (Derby)	1933
Storer, W.	(1)	216*	Derbyshire v. Leicestershire (Chesterfield)	1899
Strydom, S.	(1)	234	Orange Free State v. Transvaal B. (Vereeniging)	1965-66
Subba Row, R.	(2)	260*	Northamptonshire v. Lancashire (Northampton)	1955
		300	Northamptonshire v. Surrey (Oval)	1958
Subramanya, V.	(1)	213*	Mysore v. Madras (Madras)	1966-67
Sudhir Das	(1)	221*	Bihar v. Assam (Jamshedpur)	1957-58
Sugg, F. H.	(1)	220	Lancashire v. Gloucestershire (Bristol)	1896
Surti, R. F.	(1)	246*	Rajasthan v. Uttar Pradesh (Udaipur)	1959-60
Sutcliffe, B.	(8)	208*	North Island v. South Island (Dunedin)	1947-48
		243	New Zealanders v. Essex (Southend)	1949
		355	Otago v. Auckland (Dunedin)	1949-50
		275	Otago v. Auckland (Auckland)	1950-51
		385	Otago v. Canterbury (Christchurch)	1952-53
		230*	New Zealand v. India (New Delhi)	1955-56
		264	Otago v. Central Districts (Dunedin)	1959-60
		201	Otago v. Northern Districts (Hamilton)	1960-61
Sutcliffe, H.	(17)	232	Yorkshire v. Surrey (Oval)	1922
		213	Yorkshire v. Somerset (Dewsbury)	1924
		255*	Yorkshire v. Essex (Southend)	1924
		235	Yorkshire v. Middlesex (Leeds)	1925
		206	Yorkshire v. Warwickshire (Dewsbury)	1925
		200	Yorkshire v. Leicestershire (Leicester)	1926
		227	England v. Rest (Bristol)	1927
		228	Yorkshire v. Sussex (Eastbourne)	1928
		230	Yorkshire v. Kent (Folkestone)	1931
		313	Yorkshire v. Essex (Leyton)	1932
		270	Yorkshire v. Sussex (Leeds)	1932
		205	Yorkshire v. Warwickshire (Birmingham)	1933
		203	Yorkshire v. Surrey (Oval)	1934
		200*	Yorkshire v. Worcestershire (Sheffield)	1935
		212	Yorkshire v. Leicestershire (Leicester)	1935
		202	Yorkshire v. Middlesex (Scarborough)	1936
		234*	Yorkshire v. Leicestershire (Hull)	1939
Suttle, K. G.	(1)	204*	Sussex v. Kent (Tunbridge Wells)	1962
Tarilton, P. H.	(1)	304*	Barbados v. Trinidad (Bridgetown)	1919-20
Tarrant, F. A.	(4)	206	Victoria v. New South Wales (Sydney)	1907-08
		207*	Middlesex v. Yorkshire (Bradford)	1911
		250*	Middlesex v. Essex (Leyton)	1914
		200	Middlesex v. Worcestershire (Lord's)	1914
Tate, M. W.	(1)	203	Sussex v. Northamptonshire (Hove)	1921
Tayfield, A.	(1)	205	Transvaal v. Eastern Province (Port Elizabeth)	1961-62
Taylor, H. W.	(1)	250*	Natal v. Transvaal (Johannesburg)	1912-13
Taylor, K.	(1)	203*	Yorkshire v. Warwickshire (Birmingham)	1961
Tennyson, Hon. L. H.	(1)	217	Hampshire v. West Indians (Southampton)	1928
Thomas, G.	(1)	229	New South Wales v. Victoria (Melbourne)	1965-66
Thompson, F. C.	(1)	275*	Queensland v. New South Wales (Brisbane)	1930-31
Timms, J. E.	(1)	213	Northamptonshire v. Worcestershire (Stourbridge)	1934
Townsend, C. L.	(2)	224*	Gloucestershire v. Essex (Clifton)	1899
		214	Gloucestershire v. Worcestershire (Cheltenham)	1906

Double Centuries—*Cont.*

Townsend, L. F. ..	(1)	233	Derbyshire v. Leicestershire (Loughborough)..	1933
Trimble, S. C.	(2)	252*	Queensland v. New South Wales (Sydney) ..	1963-64
		220	Queensland v. South Australia (Adelaide) ..	1964-65
Trumper, V. T. ..	(8)	292*	New South Wales v. Tasmania (Sydney) ..	1898-99
		253	New South Wales v. New Zealanders (Sydney)	1898-99
		300*	Australians v. Sussex (Hove)	1899
		208	New South Wales v. Queensland (Sydney) ..	1899-00
		230	New South Wales v. Victoria (Sydney) ..	1900-01
		214*	Australia v. South Africa (Adelaide)	1910-11
		201*	New South Wales v. South Australia (Sydney)	1912-13
		293	Australians v. Canterbury (Christchurch) ..	1913-14
Tunnicliffe, J.	(1)	243	Yorkshire v. Derbyshire (Chesterfield).. ..	1898
Turnbull, M. J. ..	(3)	205	Glamorgan v. Nottinghamshire (Cardiff) ..	1932
		200*	Glamorgan v. Northamptonshire (Swansea) ..	1933
		233	Glamorgan v. Worcestershire (Swansea) ..	1937
Tyldesley, E.	(7)	244	Lancashire v. Warwickshire (Birmingham) ..	1920
		236	Lancashire v. Surrey (Oval)	1923
		226	Lancashire v. Sussex (Manchester)	1926
		242	Lancashire v. Leicestershire (Leicester) ..	1928
		256*	Lancashire v. Warwickshire (Manchester) ..	1930
		225*	Lancashire v. Worcestershire (Worcester) ..	1932
		239	Lancashire v. Glamorgan (Cardiff)	1934
Tyldesley, J. T... ..	(13)	200	Lancashire v. Derbyshire (Manchester) ..	1898
		249	Lancashire v. Leicestershire (Leicester) ..	1899
		221	Lancashire v. Nottinghamshire (Nottingham)	1901
		248	Lancashire v. Worcestershire (Liverpool) ..	1903
		210	Lancashire v. Somerset (Bath)	1904
		225	Lancashire v. Nottinghamshire (Nottingham)..	1904
		250	Lancashire v. Nottinghamshire (Nottingham)..	1905
		295*	Lancashire v. Kent (Manchester)	1906
		209	Lancashire v. Warwickshire (Birmingham) ..	1907
		243	Lancashire v. Leicestershire (Leicester) ..	1908
		210	Lancashire v. Surrey (Oval)	1913
		253	Lancashire v. Kent (Canterbury)	1914
		272	Lancashire v. Derbyshire (Chesterfield) ..	1919
Umrigar, P. R... ..	(9)	229*	Indians v. Oxford U. (Oxford)..	1952
		204	Indians v. Lancashire (Manchester)	1952
		204	Indians v. Kent (Canterbury)	1952
		223	India v. New Zealand (Hyderabad)	1955-56
		245	Bombay v. Saurashtra (Poona)	1957-58
		213	Bombay v. Gujerat (Khadakvasla)	1957-58
		252*	Indians v. Cambridge U. (Cambridge) ..	1959
		203	Indians v. Somerset (Taunton)	1959
		202*	Indians v. Northamptonshire (Northampton)..	1959
Valentine, B. H. ..	(2)	242	Kent v. Leicestershire (Oakham)	1938
		201	Kent v. Nottinghamshire (Nottingham) ..	1939
Vaulkhard, P.	(1)	264	Derbyshire v. Nottinghamshire (Nottingham)	1946
Versfeld, B. J. ..	(1)	201*	Natal v. Transvaal (Durban)	1965-66
Viljoen, K. G.	(3)	215	Griqualand West v. Western Province (Kimberley)	1929-30
		200*	Orange Free State v. Transvaal ((Bloemfontein)	1933-34
		201	South Africans v. Sussex (Hove)	1947
Vine, J.	(1)	202	Sussex v. Northamptonshirc (Hastings) ..	1920
Wade, W. W.	(1)	208	Natal v. Eastern Province (Pietermaritzburg)..	1939-40
Wadekar, A. L... ..	(3)	235	Bombay v. Rajasthan (Bombay)	1961-62
		229	West Zone v. East Zone (Calcutta)	1964-65
		323	Bombay v. Mysore (Bombay)	1966-67
Wainwright, E... ..	(1)	228	Yorkshire v. Surrey (Oval)	1899
Waite, J. H. B. ..	(1)	219	Eastern Province v. Griqualand West (Kimberley)	1950-51
Walcott, C. L.	(4)	314*	Barbados v. Trinidad (Port of Spain)	1945-46
		211*	Barbados v. British Guiana (Bridgetown) ..	1949-50
		209	Barbados v. Trinidad (Bridgetown)	1950-51
		220	West Indies v. England (Bridgetown)	1953-54
Walford, M. M. ..	(2)	201*	Oxford U. v. M.C.C. (Lord's)	1938
		264	Somerset v. Hampshire (Weston-super-Mare)..	1947
Walker, L.	(1)	222	London County v. M.C.C. (Crystal Palace) ..	1901
Wallace, W. M. ..	(1)	211	Auckland v. Canterbury (Auckland)	1939-40

Double Centuries—*Cont.*

Wallis Mathias	(2)	228	Karachi Blues v. Hyderabad (Karachi)	1964-65
		278*	Karachi Blues v. Railway Greens (Karachi)	1965-66
Walters, C. F.	(1)	226	Worcestershire v. Kent (Gravesend)	1933
Walters, K. D.	(1)	253	New South Wales v. South Australia (Adelaide)	1964-65
Waqar Hassan	(1)	201*	Cannon's XI v. Mahood's XI (Karachi)	1953-54
Ward, A.	(1)	219	Stoddart's XI v. South Australia (Adelaide)	1894-95
Warner, P. F.	(3)	211	Lord Hawke's XI v. Otago (Dunedin)	1902-03
		204	M.C.C. v. Sussex (Lord's)	1905
		244	Rest of England v. Warwickshire (Oval)	1911
Washbrook, C.	(7)	228	Lancashire v. Oxford U. (Oxford)	1935
		219*	Lancashire v. Gloucestershire (Bristol)	1938
		204*	Lancashire v. Sussex (Manchester)	1947
		251*	Lancashire v. Surrey (Manchester)	1947
		200	Lancashire v. Hampshire (Manchester)	1948
		209*	Lancashire v. Warwickshire (Birmingham)	1951
		211*	Lancashire v. Somerset (Manchester)	1952
Watson, F.	(4)	223	Lancashire v. Northamptonshire (Manchester)	1928
		300*	Lancashire v. Surrey (Manchester)	1928
		236	Lancashire v. Sussex (Hove)	1928
		207	Lancashire v. Worcestershire (Worcester)	1929
Watson, W.	(3)	257	M.C.C. v. British Guiana (Georgetown)	1953-54
		214*	Yorkshire v. Worcestershire (Worcester)	1955
		217*	Leicestershire v. Somerset (Taunton)	1961
Watson, W.	(1)	206	New South Wales v. Western Australia (Perth)	1956-57
Wazir Ali, S.	(2)	268*	Indian U. Occasionals v. Viceroy's XI (Calcutta)	1935-36
		222*	Southern Punjab v. Bengal (Calcutta)	1938-39
Webbe, A. J.	(1)	243*	Middlesex v. Yorkshire (Huddersfield)	1887
Weekes, E. D.	(9)	236*	Barbados v. British Guiana (Bridgetown)	1949-50
		232	West Indians v. Surrey (Oval)	1950
		304*	West Indians v. Cambridge U. (Cambridge)	1950
		279	West Indians v. Nottinghamshire (Nottingham)	1950
		246*	West Indians v. Hampshire (Southampton)	1950
		200*	West Indians v. Leicestershire (Leicester)	1950
		207	West Indies v. India (Port of Spain)	1952-53
		253	Barbados v. Indians (Bridgetown)	1952-53
		206	West Indies v. England (Port of Spain)	1953-54
Wells, C. M.	(1)	244	Middlesex v. Nottinghamshire (Nottingham)	1899
White, R. C.	(1)	205	Transvaal B. v. Griqualand West (Johannesburg)	1965-66
Whysall, W. W.	(3)	209	Nottinghamshire v. Essex (Leyton)	1926
		244	Nottinghamshire v. Gloucestershire (Nottingham)	1929
		248	Nottinghamshire v. Northamptonshire (Nottingham)	1930
Wight, L.	(1)	262*	British Guiana v. Barbados (Georgetown)	1951-52
Wight, P. B.	(2)	222*	Somerset v. Kent (Taunton)	1959
		215	Somerset v. Yorkshire (Taunton)	1962
Williams, E. S. B.	(2)	209	Army v. Oxford U. (Oxford)	1925
		228	Army v. Royal Navy (Lord's)	1928
Wilmot, A. L.	(1)	222*	Eastern Province v. Rhodesia (Salisbury)	1965-66
Wilson, B. B.	(1)	208	Yorkshire v. Sussex (Bradford)	1914
Wilson, J. V.	(2)	223*	Yorkshire v. Scotland (Edinburgh)	1951
		230	Yorkshire v. Derbyshire (Sheffield)	1952
Winrow, H.	(1)	204*	Nottinghamshire v. Derbyshire (Nottingham)	1947
Wood, C. J. B.	(2)	200*	Leicestershire v. Hampshire (Leicester)	1905
		225	Leicestershire v. Worcestershire (Worcester)	1906
Woodfull, W. M.	(7)	212*	Victoria v. Canterbury (Christchurch)	1924-25
		236	Victoria v. South Australia (Melbourne)	1925-26
		201	Australians v. Essex (Leyton)	1926
		284	Australians v. New Zealand XI (Auckland)	1927-28
		275*	Victoria v. M.C.C. (Melbourne)	1928-29
		216	Australians v. Cambridge U. (Cambridge)	1930
		228*	Australians v. Glamorgan (Swansea)	1934
Woods, S. M. J.	(1)	215	Somerset v. Sussex (Hove)	1895
Woolley, C. N.	(1)	204*	Northamptonshire v. Worcestershire (Northampton)	1921
Woolley, F. E.	(9)	305*	M.C.C. v. Tasmania (Hobart)	1911-12
		224*	Kent v. Oxford U. (Oxford)	1913
		270	Kent v. Middlesex (Canterbury)	1923

Double Centuries—*Cont.*

Woolley, F. E. (*cont.*)		202	Rest of England v. Yorkshire (Oval)	1924
		215	Kent v. Somerset (Gravesend)	1925
		217	Kent v. Northamptonshire (Northampton)	1926
		219	M.C.C. v. New South Wales (Sydney)	1929-30
		224	Kent v. New Zealanders (Canterbury)	1931
		229	Kent v. Surrey (Oval)	1935
Worrell, F. M. M.	(7)	308*	Barbados v. Trinidad (Bridgetown)	1943-44
		255*	Barbados v. Trinidad (Port of Spain)	1945-46
		223*	Commonwealth v. Indian XI (Kanpur)	1949-50
		241*	West Indians v. Leicestershire (Leicester)	1950
		261	West Indies v. England (Nottingham)	1950
		285	Commonwealth v. Ceylon (Colombo)	1950-51
		237	West Indies v. India (Kingston)	1952-53
Worthington, T. S.	(2)	200*	Derbyshire v. Worcestershire (Chesterfield)	1933
		238*	Derbyshire v. Sussex (Derby)	1937
Wyatt, R. E. S.	(2)	232	Warwickshire v. Derbyshire (Birmingham)	1937
		201*	Warwickshire v. Lancashire (Birmingham)	1937
Wynne, O. E.	(1)	200*	Transvaal v. Border (Johannesburg)	1946-47
Wynyard, E. G.	(2)	268	Hampshire v. Yorkshire (Southampton)	1896
		225	Hampshire v. Somerset (Taunton)	1899
Young, R. A.	(1)	220	Sussex v. Essex (Leyton)	1905
Zafar Altaf	(1)	268	Lahore Greens v. Bahawalpur (Lahore)	1965-66
Ziebell, K. P.	(1)	212*	Queensland v. Victoria (Melbourne)	1966-67

CENTURY WITH A RUNNER

Amir Ashraf	113	Railways & Quetta v. Karachi U. (Karachi)	1960-61

(He strained a thigh muscle in the first over of his innings)

A CENTURY ON DÉBUT IN FIRST-CLASS CRICKET

Allsopp, A.	117	New South Wales v. M.C.C. (Sydney)	1929-30
Asif Ahmed	148	Combined Universities v. East Pakistan (Karachi)	1959-60
Barker, G. E.	107*	Essex v. Canadians (Clacton)	1954
Barrass, A. E. O.	113	Western Australia v. Victoria (Perth)	1938-39
Bernau, E. H. L.	117	Wellington v. Auckland (Wellington)	1922-23
Biggs, M.	108	Queensland v. South Australia (Brisbane)	1930-31
Bilby, G. P.	132	Wellington v. Central Districts (Wellington)	1962-63
Bill, O. W.	115	New South Wales v. Tasmania (Sydney)	1929-30
Bisgood, B. L.	116*	Somerset v. Worcestershire (Worcester)	1907
Bloomfield, H. O.	107*	Surrey v. Northamptonshire (Northampton)	1921
Bogle, J.	145	New South Wales v. Victoria (Sydney)	1918-19
Bradman, D. G.	118	New South Wales v. South Australia (Adelaide)	1927-28
Briggs, R.	121	New South Wales v. Western Australia (Perth)	1952-53
Brook-Smith, W.	112*	Auckland v. Hawke's Bay (Auckland)	1904-05
Browne, C. F.	137	Barbados v. Trinidad (Bridgetown)	1919-20
Bryan, G. J.	124	Kent v. Nottinghamshire (Nottingham)	1920
Byrne, J. F.	100	Warwickshire v. Leicestershire (Birmingham)	1897
Callaway, N.	207	New South Wales v. Queensland (Sydney)	1914-15
Chadwick, D.	129	Western Australia v. Queensland (Brisbane)	1963-64
Chambers, J. L.	132	Victoria v. Tasmania (Melbourne)	1949-50
Chapman, A. P. F.	118	Cambridge U. v. Essex (Cambridge)	1920
Cheshire, F. W.	107	Border v. Orange Free State (Johannesburg)	1923-24
Chidgey, G. J.	113	Free Foresters v. Cambridge U. (Cambridge)	1962
Clark, E. A.	100*	Middlesex v. Cambridge U. (Cambridge)	1959
Contractor, N. J.	152 & 102*	Gujerat v. Baroda (Baroda)	1952-53
Day, S. H.	101*	Kent v. Gloucestershire (Cheltenham)	1897
De Saram, F. C.	176	Oxford U. v. Gloucestershire (Oxford)	1934
Dillon, E. W.	108	London County v. Worcestershire (Crystal Palace)	1900
Doggart, G. H. G.	215*	Cambridge U. v. Lancashire (Cambridge)	1948
Draper, R. G.	114	Eastern Province v. Orange Free State (Port Elizabeth)	1945-46
Dyer, D. V.	185	Natal v. Eastern Province (Pietermaritzburg)	1939-40
Ebden, C. H. M.	137	Cambridge U. v. Leveson Gower's XI (Cambridge)	1902
Ellis, M.	118	Victoria v. South Australia (Melbourne)	1902-03
Fairbairn, A.	108	Middlesex v. Somerset (Taunton)	1947
Favell, L. E.	164	South Australia v. New South Wales (Adelaide)	1951-52

A Century on Début in First-Class Cricket—*Cont.*

Fernley, D. L.	106	Eastern Province v. North-Eastern Transvaal (Pretoria)	1954-55
Forssberg, E. B.	143	New South Wales v. Queensland (Sydney)	1920-21
Francis, J.	135	Victoria v. Tasmania (Launceston)	1932-33
Frank, C. N.	108	Transvaal v. A.I.F. (Johannesburg)	1919-20
Freakes, H. D.	122*	Eastern Province v. Natal (Johannesburg)	1931-32
Gill, J. R.	106	Ireland v. M.C.C. (Dublin)	1948
Gimblett, H.	123	Somerset v. Essex (Frome)	1935
Gooden, N. L.	102	South Australia v. Western Australia (Adelaide)	1912-13
Gordon-Stewart, C. S.	121	Victoria v. New South Wales (Melbourne)	1869-70
Grangel, H.	108	Victoria v. Tasmania (Melbourne)	1935-36
Gwynne, L.	138	New South Wales v. South Australia (Adelaide)	1924-25
Hall, P. M.	101	Oxford U. v. Free Foresters (Oxford)	1919
Hallebone, J.	202	Victoria v. Tasmania (Melbourne)	1951-52
Hamence, R. A.	121	South Australia v. Tasmania (Adelaide)	1935-36
Hamilton, C. P.	121	Army v. West Indians (Aldershot)	1933
Harbottle, M. N.	156	Army v. Oxford U. (Camberley)	1938
Harris, T. A.	114*	Griqualand West v. Orange Free State (Kimberley)	1933-34
Hearn, P.	124	Kent v. Warwickshire (Gillingham)	1947
Higgs, K. A.	101	Sussex v. Worcestershire (Hove)	1920
Hilder, A. L.	103*	Kent v. Essex (Gravesend)	1924
Hone, B. W.	137	South Australia v. Victoria (Adelaide)	1928-29
Human, J. H.	158*	Cambridge U. v. Leveson-Gower's XI (Eastbourne)	1932
Hyett, F.	108*	Victoria v. Tasmania (Melbourne)	1914-15
Kanitkar, H. S.	151*	Maharashtra v. Saurashtra (Poona)	1963-64
Kerr, C.	122	Auckland v. Wellington (Auckland)	1941-42
Kerr, E. A. D.	112	Victoria v. Tasmania (Launceston)	1946-47
Khurshid Ahmed	101	Pakistan v. Central Zone (Nagpur)	1952-53
King, C. H.	135	British Guiana v. Trinidad (Georgetown)	1895-96
Krishna, S.	108	Mysore v. Kerala (Mysore)	1961-62
Lacey, S.	102	Transvaal v. Rhodesia (Salisbury)	1945-46
Leadbeater, L.	128	New South Wales v. Tasmania (Sydney)	1929-30
Leslie, C. F. H.	111*	Oxford U. v. M.C.C. (Oxford)	1881
Levy, R. M.	129	Queensland v. Victoria (Brisbane)	1928-29
Loxton, J. F. C.	100	Queensland v. Western Australia (Perth)	1966-67
Loxton, S. J. E.	232*	Victoria v. Queensland (Melbourne)	1946-47
Lukeman, E.	118	New South Wales v. South Australia (Adelaide)	1946-47
Lyons, R.	102	Queensland v. Victoria (Brisbane)	1955-56
McIlwraith, J.	133	Victoria v. New South Wales (Melbourne)	1885-86
MacLaren, A. C.	108	Lancashire v. Sussex (Hove)	1890
MacLeod, D. N.	117	Central Districts v. Wellington (Wanganui)	1956-57
McLeod, D.	107	Victoria v. Tasmania (Hobart)	1894-95
McPetrie, W.	123	Victoria v. Tasmania (Melbourne)	1904-05
Majid Jahangir	111*	Lahore B. v. Khairpur (Lahore)	1961-62
Maqsood, Ahmed	144	Southern Punjab v. Northern India (Lahore)	1944-45
Marks, N.	180	New South Wales v. South Australia (Sydney)	1958-59
Marlow, F. W.	144	Sussex v. M.C.C. (Lord's)	1891
Martin, F. C.	145	Western Province v. Eastern Province (Cape Town)	1929-30
Martin, F. R.	195	Jamaica v. Barbados (Bridgetown)	1925-26
Marx, W. F. E.	240	Transvaal v. Griqualand West (Johannesburg)	1920-21
Maynard, A.	200*	Trinidad v. M.C.C. (Port of Spain)	1934-35
Miller, K. R.	181	Victoria v. Tasmania (Melbourne)	1937-38
Miller, N.	124	Surrey v. Sussex (Hove)	1899
Mitchell, W. J.	127*	Northern Districts v. Pakistanis (Hamilton)	1964-65
Morris, A. R.	148 & 111	New South Wales v. Queensland (Sydney)	1940-41
Morton, H. G. S.	135*	Queensland v. Victoria (Melbourne)	1904-05
Moyes, A. G.	104	South Australia v. Western Australia (Adelaide)	1912-13
Mullarkey, D.	130	New South Wales v. Queensland (Brisbane)	1923-24
Murray-Wood, W.	106*	Oxford U. v. Gloucestershire (Oxford)	1936
Nichol, M.	104	Worcestershire v. West Indians (Worcester)	1928
Nicholson, W. G.	101	Scotland v. Ireland (Dublin)	1929
Nutt, R. H.	102	New South Wales v. South Australia (Adelaide)	1931-32
Oakley, H. H.	108	Victoria v. South Australia (Melbourne)	1930-31
O'Halloran, J.	128*	Victoria v. New South Wales (Melbourne)	1896-97
Ongley, J. A.	110	Wellington v. Otago (Wellington)	1938-39
Parija, L.	103	Orissa v. Assam (Cuttack)	1952-53
Passailaigue, C. C.	183	Jamaica v. M.C.C. (Kingston)	1929-30
Patel, Y. B.	101*	Mysore v. Hyderabad (Hyderabad)	1961-62

A Century on Début in First-Class Cricket—*Cont.*

Player	Score	Match	Season
Payne, C. A. L.	101	M.C.C. v. Derbyshire (Lord's)	1905
Persaud, C. S.	174	British Guiana v. Barbados (Georgetown)	1937-38
Pinch, F. B.	138*	Glamorgan v. Worcestershire (Swansea)	1921
Poddar, P. C.	141	Bengal v. Assam (Gauhati)	1960-61
Pretty, H. C.	124	Surrey v. Nottinghamshire (Oval)	1899
Pye, L. W.	166	New South Wales v. Queensland (Brisbane)	1896-97
Rhys, H. R. J.	149	Free Foresters v. Cambridge U. (Cambridge)	1929
Ricketts, J.	195*	Lancashire v. Surrey (Oval)	1867
Rock, H. O.	127	New South Wales v. South Australia (Sydney)	1924-25
Roy, N.	102	Bengal v. Assam (Gauhati)	1960-61
Roy, P.	112*	Bengal v. United Provinces (Calcutta)	1946-47
Saldana, N. F.	142	Maharashtra v. Saurashtra (Nasik)	1965-66
Sampath, C.	123	Trinidad v. Barbados (Bridgetown)	1948-49
Scott, J. G. C.	137	Sussex v. Oxford U. (Eastbourne)	1907
Scott, V. J.	122	Auckland v. Canterbury (Auckland)	1937-38
Sealy, J. E. D.	100	Barbados v. M.C.C. (Bridgetown)	1929-30
Sen Gupta, A. K.	100*	Services v. West Indians (Poona)	1958-59
Shepherd, B. K.	103*	Western Australia v. Queensland (Perth)	1955-56
Shepherd, D. R.	108	Gloucestershire v. Oxford U. (Oxford)	1965
Siedle, J. R.	127	Western Province v. Eastern Province (Cape Town)	1955-56
Slack, J. K. E.	135	Cambridge U. v. Middlesex (Cambridge)	1954
Smith, K. F. H.	141*	Wellington v. Central Districts (Wellington)	1953-54
Snedden, C. A.	119	Auckland v. Hawke's Bay (Auckland)	1920-21
Solomon, J. S.	114*	British Guiana v. Jamaica (Georgetown)	1956-57
Stocks, F. W.	114	Nottinghamshire v. Kent (Nottingham)	1946
Talbot, R. O.	105	Canterbury v. Otago (Dunedin)	1922-23
Tennyson, Hon. L. H.	110	M.C.C. v. Oxford U. (Lord's)	1913
Tindill, E. W.	106	Wellington v. Auckland (Auckland)	1932-33
Trevor, A. H.	103	Sussex v. Kent (Hove)	1880
Tuck, G. S.	125	Royal Navy v. New Zealanders (Portsmouth)	1927
Tyson, C.	100*	Yorkshire v. Hampshire (Southampton)	1921
Waddy, E. F.	129*	New South Wales v. South Australia (Adelaide)	1904-05
Walker, I. D.	102	Middlesex v. Surrey (Oval)	1862
Watson, G.	175	Canterbury v. Otago (Christchurch)	1880-81
Watt, D. G.	105	Otago v. Canterbury (Christchurch)	1943-44
Weekes, K. H.	106	Jamaica v. Oxford & Cambridge Us. (Kingston)	1938-39
Whitehead, R.	131*	Lancashire v. Nottinghamshire (Manchester)	1908
Whitehead, T. H.	107*	Eastern Province v. Orange Free State (Port Elizabeth)	1921-22
Williams, O.	100	Leeward Islands v. Jamaica (Kingston)	1958-59
Wilson, E. R.	117*	Webbe's XI v. Cambridge U. (Cambridge)	1899
Winslow, L.	124	Sussex v. Gloucestershire (Hove)	1875
Wood, B. B.	108	Canterbury v. Wellington (Wellington)	1907-08
Wootton, S. C.	105	Victoria v. Tasmania (Hobart)	1923-24

CENTURY IN SECOND MATCH NOT HAVING BATTED IN THEIR FIRST

Player	Score	Match	Season
Harvey, P. F.	125*	Nottinghamshire v. Derbyshire (Nottingham)	1947
Saxena, R.	113*	Delhi v. Southern Punjab (New Delhi)	1960-61

CENTURY IN FIRST THREE INNINGS

Player	Score	Match	Season
Solomon, J. S.	114*	British Guiana v. Jamaica (Georgetown)	1956-57
	108	British Guiana v. Barbados (Georgetown)	1956-57
	121	British Guiana v. Pakistanis (Georgetown)	1957-58

CENTURY IN FIRST TWO INNINGS

Player	Score	Match	Season
Marks, N.	180	New South Wales v. South Australia (Sydney)	1958-59
	103	New South Wales v. Victoria (Melbourne)	1958-59
Poddar, P. C.	141	Bengal v. Assam (Gauhati)	1960-61
	104	Bengal v. Orissa (Calcutta)	1960-61

In his first two first-class matches, D. Chadwick (Western Australia) scored 129 v. Queensland (Brisbane) and 58 & 114 v. Victoria (Melbourne).

CENTURY IN ONLY FIRST-CLASS MATCH

Callaway, N.	207	New South Wales v. Queensland (Sydney)	1914-15
Gill, J. R.	106	Ireland v. M.C.C. (Dublin)	1948
Grangel, H.	108	Victoria v. Tasmania (Melbourne)	1935-36
Hardbottle, M. N.	156	Army v. Oxford U. (Camberley)	1938
Wootton, S.C.	105	Victoria v. Tasmania (Hobart)	1923-24

CENTURY IN FIRST MATCH FOR A COUNTY OR UNIVERSITY

(*Having previously played in first-class cricket*)

Abercrombie, C. H.	126	Hampshire v. Oxford U. (Southampton)	1913
Baldry, D. O.	151	Hampshire v. Glamorgan (Portsmouth)	1959
Bartlett, H. T.	122	Sussex v. Cambridge U. (Worthing)	1937
Barton, M. R.	124	Surrey v. M.C.C. (Lord's)	1948
Dixon, E. J. H.	123	Northamptonshire v. Somerset (Northampton)	1939
Evans, A. J.	102	Kent v. Northamptonshire (Northampton)	1921
Fiddian-Green, C. A.	108	Worcestershire v. Essex (Worcester)	1931
Gibb, P. A.	157*	Yorkshire v. Nottinghamshire (Sheffield)	1935
Miller, K. R.	102*	Nottinghamshire v. Cambridge U. (Nottingham)	1959
Moore, D. N.	206	Gloucestershire v. Oxford U. (Oxford)	1930
Ranjitsinhji, K. S.	150	Sussex v. M.C.C. (Lord's)	1895
Sarel, W. G. M.	103	Sussex v. Oxford U. (Hove)	1919
Walford, M. M.	141*	Somerset v. Indians (Taunton)	1946
White, R. C.	125	Cambridge U. v. Surrey (Cambridge)	1962
Wight, P. B.	109*	Somerset v. Australians (Taunton)	1953

CENTURY ON DÉBUT IN OTHER COUNTRIES

Players who have scored a century for an international team in their first match in a particular country overseas are included in the appropriate list for their home country; e.g. S. M. Nurse's century for E. W. Swanton's XI in Calcutta is included under West Indian teams in India.

A. R. Morris holds the unique record of scoring a century in his first match in each of the four countries in which he played first-class cricket: Australia, England, South Africa and West Indies. He did not play in New Zealand, India or Pakistan.

ENGLISH TEAMS

IN AUSTRALIA

J. T. Brown	115	Stoddart's XI v. South Australia (Adelaide)	1894-95
A. C. MacLaren	228	Stoddart's XI v. Victoria (Melbourne)	1894-95
K. S. Ranjitsinhji	189	Stoddart's XI v. South Australia (Adelaide)	1897-98
G. Gunn	119	England v. Australia (Sydney)	1907-08
F. R. Foster	158	M.C.C. v. South Australia (Adelaide)	1911-12
A. C. Russell	156	M.C.C. v. South Australia (Adelaide)	1920-21
R. Kilner	103	M.C.C. v. Western Australia (Perth)	1924-25
D. R. Jardine	109	M.C.C. v. Western Australia (Perth)	1928-29
Nawab of Pataudi, Snr.	166	M.C.C. v. Western Australia (Perth)	1932-33
D. B. Close	108*	M.C.C. v. Western Australia (Perth)	1950-51
R. W. Barber	126	M.C.C. v. Western Australia (Perth)	1965-66
J. M. Parks	107*	M.C.C. v. Western Australia (Perth)	1965-66

IN SOUTH AFRICA

J. B. Hobbs	114	M.C.C. v. Western Province (Cape Town)	1909-10
G. B. Legge	120	M.C.C. v. Orange Free State (Bloemfontein)	1927-28
E. Paynter	158	M.C.C. v. Griqualand West (Kimberley)	1938-39
N. W. D. Yardley	142	M.C.C. v. Griqualand West (Kimberley)	1938-39
F. G. Mann	112	M.C.C. v. Western Province (Cape Town)	1948-49
P. B. H. May	162	M.C.C. v. Western Province (Cape Town)	1956-57
K. F. Barrington	111	Surrey v. Rhodesia (Salisbury)	1959-60
W. Watson	100	Commonwealth XI v. Rhodesia (Kitwe)	1962-63
R. W. Barber	108	M.C.C. v. Rhodesia (Salisbury)	1964-65

Century on Début in Other Countries—*Cont.*

IN WEST INDIES

E. Humphreys	106	M.C.C. v. Barbados (Bridgetown)	1912-13
E. Tyldesley	101	Tennyson's XI v. Jamaica (Kingston)	1926-27
C. P. Mead	103*	Tennyson's XI v. Jamaica (Kingston)	1927-28
E. Hendren	223*	M.C.C. v. Barbados (Bridgetown)	1929-30
A. Mitchell	101*	Yorkshire v. Jamaica (Kingston)	1935-36
R. C. M. Kimpton	113	Oxford & Cambridge Us. v. Jamaica (Kingston)	1938-39
W. Watson	161	M.C.C. v. Jamaica (Kingston)	1953-54
J. M. Parks	183	M.C.C. v. Berbice (Berbice)	1959-60
B. L. D'Oliveira	101	Worcestershire v. Jamaica (Montego Bay)	1965-66

IN NEW ZEALAND

C. H. Titchmarsh	154	M.C.C. v. Auckland (Auckland)	1922-23
L. E. G. Ames	103	England v. New Zealand (Christchurch)	1932-33
W. R. Hammond	227	England v. New Zealand (Christchurch)	1932-33
C. Washbrook	133	M.C.C. v. Wellington (Wellington)	1946-47
N. W. D. Yardley	126	M.C.C. v. Otago (Dunedin)	1946-47
T. W. Graveney	101	M.C.C. v Canterbury (Christchurch)	1954-55
K. F. Barrington	126	England v New Zealand (Auckland)	1962-63
P. H. Parfitt	131*	England v. New Zealand (Auckland)	1962-63
B. R. Knight	125	England v. New Zealand (Auckland)	1962-63

IN INDIA

C. J. Barnett	122	M.C.C. v. Sind (Karachi)	1933-34
D. R. Jardine	101*	M.C.C. v. Sind (Karachi)	1933-34
W. J. Edrich	140*	Lord Tennyson's XI v. Sind (Karachi)	1937-38
Lord Tennyson	118	Lord Tennyson's XI v. Sind (Karachi)	1937-38
G. M. Emmett	104	Commonwealth v. Cricket Club of India (Bombay)	1950-51
T. W. Graveney	101	M.C.C. v. Combined Universities (Bombay)	1951-52
K. F. Barrington	149*	M.C.C. v. Combined Universities (Poona)	1961-62

AUSTRALIAN TEAMS

IN ENGLAND

H. H. Massie	206	Australians v. Oxford U. (Oxford)	1882
M. A. Noble	116*	Australians v. South of England (Crystal Palace)	1899
W. M. Woodfull	201	Australians v. Essex (Leyton)	1926
D. G. Bradman	236	Australians v. Worcestershire (Worcester)	1930
A. G. Chipperfield	175	Australians v. Essex (Chelmsford)	1934
K. R. Miller	105	Australian Services v. England XI (Lord's)	1945
A. R. Morris	138	Australians v. Worcestershire (Worcester)	1948
G. B. Hole	112	Australians v. Worcestershire (Worcester)	1953
R. G. Archer	108	Australians v. Worcestershire (Worcester)	1953

IN SOUTH AFRICA

C. Hill	142	Australia v. South Africa (Johannesburg)	1902-03
W. A. Brown	148	Australians v. Natal (Durban)	1935-36
J. H. Fingleton	121	Australians v. Natal (Durban)	1935-36
J. A. R. Moroney	106	Australians v. Natal (Durban)	1949-50
A. R. Morris	153	Australians v. Natal (Durban)	1949-50
I. D. Craig	113	Australians v. Rhodesia (Salisbury)	1957-58
R. Benaud	117*	Australians v. Rhodesia (Salisbury)	1957-58
A. K. Davidson	100*	Australians v. Rhodesia (Salisbury)	1957-58
I. R. Redpath	139*	Australians v. Rhodesia (Salisbury)	1966-67
		(Carried his bat through innings of 307)	

IN WEST INDIES

A. R. Morris	157	Australians v. Jamaica (Kingston)	1954-55
R. B. Simpson	111	Australians v. Jamaica (Kingston)	1964-65
R. M. Cowper	121	Australians v. Jamaica (Kingston)	1964-65
N. C. O'Neill	125	Australians v. Jamaica (Kingston)	1964-65

Century on Début in Other Countries—*Cont.*

IN NEW ZEALAND

E. R. Mayne	102	Australians v. Canterbury (Christchurch)	1909-10
E. L. Waddy	130	Australians v. Auckland (Auckland)	1913-14
V. S. Ransford	159	Australians v. Auckland (Auckland)	1913-14
J. L. Ellis	103	Victoria v. Otago (Dunedin)	1924-25
S. G. Barnes	107	Australians v. Auckland (Auckland)	1945-46
K. R. Miller	139	Australians v. Auckland (Auckland)	1945-46
A. L. Hassett	121	Australians v. Auckland (Auckland)	1945-46
P. J. Burge	105	Australians v. Canterbury (Christchurch)	1956-57
B. C. Booth	105	Australians v. Auckland (Auckland)	1959-60
J. H. Shaw	120	Australians v. Auckland (Auckland)	1959-60

IN INDIA AND CEYLON

O. W. Bill	101	Australians v. Ceylon (Colombo)	1935-36
E. A. Williams	100*	Australians v. Prince's XI (New Delhi)	1945-46
R. B. Simpson	104	International XI v. C.C. of India President's XI (Bombay)	1961-62

IN PAKISTAN

R. B. Simpson	167	International XI v. Pakistan Cricket Board XI (Karachi)	1961-62

SOUTH AFRICAN TEAMS

IN ENGLAND

M. Hathorn	103	South Africans v. Hampshire (Southampton)	1901
H. B. Cameron	102	South Africans v. Worcestershire (Worcester)	1929

IN AUSTRALIA

A. D. Nourse, Snr.	201*	South Africans v. South Australia (Adelaide)	1910-11
L. A. Stricker	146	South Africans v. South Australia (Adelaide)	1910-11
J. A. J. Christy	102	South Africans v. Western Australia (Perth)	1931-32
D. J. McGlew	182	South Africans v. Western Australia (Perth)	1952-53
D. Lindsay	104	South Africans v South Australia (Adelaide)	1963-64

IN NEW ZEALAND

B. Mitchell	123	South Africans v. Auckland (Auckland)	1931-32
H. W. Taylor	113	South Africans v. Auckland (Auckland)	1931-32
D. J. McGlew	255*	South Africa v. New Zealand (Wellington)	1952-53
A. R. A. Murray	100*	South Africans v. Canterbury (Christchurch)	1952-53

WEST INDIAN TEAMS

IN AUSTRALIA

G. St. A. Sobers	119	West Indians v. Western Australia (Perth)	1960-61
R. B. Kanhai	103	West Indians v. Australian XI (Perth)	1960-61

IN NEW ZEALAND

R. E. Marshall	102*	West Indians v. Otago (Dunedin)	1951-52

IN INDIA

E. D. Weekes	172*	West Indians v. North Zone (Patiala)	1948-49
F. M. M. Worrell	109	Commonwealth v. Indian Universities (Bombay)	1949-50
S. M. Nurse	106 & 135*	Swanton's XI v. Indian XI (Calcutta)	1963-64

NEW ZEALAND TEAMS

IN ENGLAND

C. C. Dacre	107	New Zealanders v. M.C.C. (Lord's)	1927
T. C. Lowry	106	New Zealanders v. M.C.C. (Lord's)	1927

Century on Début in Other Countries—*Cont.*

IN AUSTRALIA

B. Sutcliffe ..	.. 142	New Zealanders v. Western Australia (Perth)	.. 1953-54
L. S. M. Miller	.. 142	New Zealanders v. South Australia (Adelaide)	.. 1953-54

IN SOUTH AFRICA

J. R. Reid ..	.. 111	New Zealanders v. Western Province (Cape Town)	.. 1953-54

IN INDIA

B. R. Taylor ..	.. 105	New Zealand v. India (Calcutta)	.. 1964-65

IN PAKISTAN

J. R. Reid ..	.. 150*	New Zealanders v. Chief Commissioner's XI (Karachi)	1955-56

INDIAN TEAMS

IN ENGLAND

S. Wazir Ali ..	.. 108*	Indians v. Glamorgan (Cardiff)	.. 1932
A. A. Baig ..	.. 102	Indians v. Middlesex (Lord's)	.. 1959

IN WEST INDIES

Vijay Hazare ..	.. 153*	Indians v. Trinidad (Port of Spain)	.. 1952-53

PAKISTANI TEAMS

IN ENGLAND

Alim-ud-Din ..	.. 142	Pakistan v. Worcestershire (Worcester) ..	.. 1954
Maqsood Ahmed	.. 111	Pakistan v. Worcestershire (Worcester) ..	.. 1954

IN AUSTRALIA

Mohammad Ilyas	.. 126	Pakistanis v. Queensland (Brisbane)	.. 1964-65

IN WEST INDIES

Wazir Mohammad	.. 134	Pakistanis v. Barbados (Bridgetown)	.. 1957-58

IN INDIA

Hanif Mohammad	.. 121 & 109*	Pakistanis v. North Zone (Amritsar) ..	.. 1952-53
Khurshid Ahmed	.. 101	Pakistanis v. Central Zone (Nagpur) ..	.. 1952-53
Mushtaq Mohammad	125*	Pakistanis v. Combined Universities (Poona) ..	.. 1960-61
Wallis Mathias	.. 103*	Pakistanis v. Combined Universities (Poona) ..	.. 1960-61

DOUBLE CENTURY IN EACH INNINGS OF A MATCH

Fagg, A. E.	244	202*	Kent v. Essex (Colchester)	1938

A CENTURY IN EACH INNINGS OF A MATCH

Adhikari, H.R. ..	(1)	129	151*	Baroda v. Nawanagar (Jamnagar) ..	.. 1945-46
Allan, J. M... ..	(1)	121*	105	Kent v. Northamptonshire (Northampton) ..	1955
Alley, W. E. ..	(1)	183*	134*	Somerset v. Surrey (Taunton)	1961
Amarnath, L. ..	(1)	130	107	Indians v. Essex (Brentwood)	1936
Ames, L. E. G. ..	(3)	132	145*	Kent v. Northamptonshire (Dover)	1933
		119	127	Kent v. Surrey (Blackheath)	1937
		112	119	Kent v. Gloucestershire (Bristol)	1950
Armstrong, W. W.	(1)	157*	245	Victoria v. South Australia (Melbourne) ..	1920-21
Arnold, E. G. ..	(1)	101*	128	Worcestershire v. Cambridge U. (Cambridge)	1903
Ashdown, W. H. ..	(1)	121	103	Kent v. Middlesex (Lord's)	1931
Avery, A. V. ..	(1)	117	100	Essex v. Glamorgan (Ebbw Vale)	1949

A Century in Each Innings of a Match—*Cont.*

Badcock, C. L. ..	(1)	120	102	South Australia v. Victoria (Melbourne) ..	1940-41
Bardsley, W. ..	(1)	136	130	Australia v. England (Oval)	1909
Barrington, K. F. ..	(1)	186	118*	Surrey v. Warwickshire (Birmingham) ..	1959
Bates, L. A. ..	(1)	116	144	Warwickshire v. Kent (Coventry)	1927
Bates, W. E. ..	(1)	105	111	Glamorgan v. Essex (Leyton)	1927
Berry, L. G... ..	(1)	165	111*	Leicestershire v. Essex (Clacton)	1947
Booth, B. J. ..	(1)	109	104	Leicestershire v. Middlesex (Lord's)	1965
Bosanquet, B. J. T...	(2)	136	139	Middlesex v. Leicestershire (Lord's)	1900
		103	100*	Middlesex v. Sussex (Lord's)	1905
Boycott, G.	(1)	103	105	Yorkshire v. Nottinghamshire (Sheffield) ..	1966
Bradman, D. G. ..	(4)	131	133*	New South Wales v. Queensland (Brisbane)	1928-29
		124	225	Woodfull's XI v. Ryder's XI (Sydney) ..	1929-30
		107	113	South Australia v. Queensland (Brisbane) ..	1937-38
		132	127*	Australia v. India (Melbourne)	1947-48
Brann, G.	(1)	105	101	Sussex v. Kent (Hove)	1892
Brookes, D.	(1)	112	154*	Northamptonshire v. Sussex (Eastbourne) ..	1946
Burke, J. W. ..	(1)	138	125*	Australians v. Somerset (Taunton)	1956
Burki, J.	(1)	144*	109*	Oxford U. v. Essex (Brentwood)	1960
Carpenter, H. ..	(1)	127	104	Essex v. Kent (Leyton)	1901
Carr, D. B.	(1)	156*	109	Derbyshire v. Kent (Canterbury)	1959
Charlesworth, C. ..	(1)	100	101*	Warwickshire v. Surrey (Birmingham) ..	1913
Chinnery, H. B. ..	(1)	105	165	M.C.C. v. Oxford U. (Oxford)	1901
Christiani, R. J. ..	(1)	131*	100*	West Indians v. Middlesex (Lord's)	1950
Compton, D. C. S.	(3)	124	100	Middlesex v. Lancashire (Manchester) ..	1946
		147	103*	England v. Australia (Adelaide)	1946-47
		135	125*	M.C.C. S.A. XI v. Leveson-Gower's XI (Scarborough)	1948
Contractor, N.J. ..	(1)	152	102*	Gujerat v. Baroda (Baroda)	1952-53
Cooper, E.	(1)	191	106*	Worcestershire v. Northamptonshire (Kidderminster)	1946
Cowdrey, M. C. ..	(3)	110	103	M.C.C. v. New South Wales (Sydney) ..	1954-55
		115*	103*	Kent v. Essex (Gillingham)	1955
		149	121	Kent v. Australians (Canterbury)	1961
Cunningham, K. G.	(1)	107	101*	South Australia v. Western Australia (Adelaide)	1966-67
Dacre, C. C. ..	(2)	127*	101*	Auckland v. Victoria (Auckland)	1924-25
		119	125*	Gloucestershire v. Worcestershire (Worcester)	1933
Dalton, E. L. ..	(1)	157	116*	South Africans v. Kent (Canterbury)	1929
Daniell, J.	(1)	174*	108	Somerset v. Essex (Taunton)	1925
Dempster. C. S. ..	(1)	133	154*	Leicestershire v. Gloucestershire (Gloucester)	1937
Denton, D.	(3)	107	109*	Yorkshire v. Nottinghamshire (Nottingham)	1906
		133	121	Yorkshire v. M.C.C. (Scarborough)	1908
		139	138	M.C.C. v. Transvaal (Johannesburg)	1909-10
Deodhar, D. B. ..	(1)	105	141	Maharashtra v. Nawanagar (Poona) ..	1944-45
Dewes, J. G. ..	(1)	128	101	Middlesex v. Sussex (Hove)	1950
Dipper, A. E. ..	(1)	117	103	Gloucestershire v. Sussex (Horsham)	1922
Doggart, G. H. G...	(1)	140	105	Sussex v. Oxford U. (Oxford)	1954
Draper, R. G. ..	(1)	129	177	Griqualand West v. Border (Kimberley) ..	1952-53
Duleepsinhji, K. S...	(3)	115	246	Sussex v. Kent (Hastings)	1929
		116	102*	Sussex v. Middlesex (Lord's)	1930
		125	103*	Gentlemen v. Players (Lord's)..	1930
Eady, C. J.	(1)	116	112*	Tasmania v. Victoria (Hobart)	1894-95
Edrich, J. H. ..	(1)	112	124	Surrey v. Nottinghamshire (Nottingham) ..	1959
Edwards, A. ..	(1)	103	105	Western Australia v. Queensland (Perth) ..	1950-51
Emmett, G. M. ..	(2)	115	103*	Gloucestershire v. Leicestershire (Leicester) ..	1947
		110	102*	Gloucestershire v. Somerset (Bristol)	1951
Enthoven, H. J. ..	(1)	123	115	Middlesex v. Sussex (Lord's)	1930
Fagg, A. E... ..	(2)	244	202*	Kent v. Essex (Colchester)	1938
		136	117*	Kent v. Essex (Maidstone)	1948
Favell, L. E. ..	(2)	112	114	South Australia v. New South Wales (Sydney)	1956-57
		104	145	South Australia v. Western Australia (Adelaide)	1958-59
Fellows-Smith, J.P.	(1)	100*	102*	Transvaal v. Commonwealth (Johannesburg)..	1959-60
Fishlock, L. B. ..	(4)	131*	100*	Surrey v. Sussex (Oval)	1936
		113	105	Surrey v. Yorkshire (Oval)	1937
		129	112	Surrey v. Leicestershire (Leicester)	1946
		111	118	Surrey v. Nottinghamshire (Nottingham) ..	1949
Fordham, C. B. ..	(1)	140	100*	Minor Counties v. Oxford U. (Oxford) ..	1933
Foster, M. K. ..	(1)	141	106	Worcestershire v. Hampshire (Worcester) ..	1926

A Century in Each Innings of a Match—*Cont.*

Player		1st	2nd	Match	Season
Foster, R. E.	(3)	134	101*	Worcestershire v. Hampshire (Worcester)	1899
		128	100*	Oxford U. v. Webbe's XI (Oxford)	1900
		102*	136	Gentlemen v. Players (Lord's)	1900
Foster, W. L.	(1)	140	172*	Worcestershire v. Hampshire (Worcester)	1899
Fredericks, R.	(1)	127	115	Guyana v. Barbados (Georgetown)	1966-67
Fry, C. B.	(5)	108	123*	Sussex v. Middlesex (Hove)	1898
		125	229	Sussex v. Surrey (Hove)	1900
		138	101*	Sussex v. Kent (Hove)	1903
		156	106	Sussex v. M.C.C. (Lord's)	1905
		123	112	Hampshire v. Kent (Canterbury)	1911
Gaekwad, D. K.	(1)	128	101*	Baroda v. Gujerat (Baroda)	1949-50
Gardner, F. C.	(1)	113	101*	Warwickshire v. Essex (Ilford)	1950
Gedye, S. G.	(1)	104	101	Auckland v. Central Districts (Auckland)	1963-64
Gehrs, D. R. A.	(1)	148*	100*	South Australia v. Western Australia (Fremantle)	1905-06
Gibbons, H. H.	(1)	111*	100*	Worcestershire v. Hampshire (Worcester)	1939
Gimblett, H.	(2)	115	127*	Somerset v. Hampshire (Taunton)	1949
		146	116	Somerset v. Derbyshire (Taunton)	1952
Gomez, G. E.	(1)	148	108*	Trinidad v. British Guiana (Georgetown)	1953-54
Grace, W. G.	(3)	130	102*	South of Thames v. North of Thames (Canterbury)	1868
		101	103*	Gloucestershire v. Kent (Clifton)	1887
		148	153	Gloucestershire v. Yorkshire (Clifton)	1888
Graveney, T. W.	(4)	103	105*	Gloucestershire v. Northamptonshire (Bristol)	1951
		153	120	Howard's XI v. President's XI (Bombay)	1956-57
		106	101*	Gloucestershire v. Warwickshire (Birmingham)	1957
		164	107*	Commonwealth XI v. Pakistan (Lahore)	1963-64
Gregory, J. M.	(1)	122	102	A.I.F. v. New South Wales (Sydney)	1919-20
Greig, J. G.	(1)	115	130	Hampshire v. Worcestershire (Worcester)	1905
Gunn, G.	(3)	132	109*	Nottinghamshire v. Yorkshire (Nottingham)	1913
		169	185*	Nottinghamshire v. Surrey (Nottingham)	1919
		100	110	Nottinghamshire v. Warwickshire (Nottingham)	1927
Hall, I. W.	(1)	101	101	Derbyshire v. Kent (Folkestone)	1965
Hallam, M. R.	(3)	210	157*	Leicestershire v. Glamorgan (Leicester)	1959
		203*	143*	Leicestershire v. Sussex (Worthing)	1961
		107*	149*	Leicestershire v. Worcestershire (Leicester)	1965
Hallows, C.	(2)	112*	103*	Lancashire v. Leicestershire (Ashby de la Zouch)	1924
		123	101*	Lancashire v. Warwickshire (Birmingham)	1928
Hamence, R. A.	(2)	130	103*	South Australia v. Victoria (Melbourne)	1940-41
		132	101*	South Australia v. New South Wales (Adelaide)	1946-47
Hammond, W. R.	(7)	108	128	Gloucestershire v. Surrey (Oval)	1927
		139	143	Gloucestershire v. Surrey (Cheltenham)	1928
		119*	177	England v. Australia (Adelaide)	1928-29
		122	111*	Gloucestershire v. Worcestershire (Worcester)	1933
		104	136	M.C.C. v. South Australia (Adelaide)	1936-37
		110	123	Gloucestershire v. Derbyshire (Burton-upon-Trent)	1938
		121	102	England XI v. Dominions XI (Lord's)	1945
Hanif Mohammad	(3)	121	109*	Pakistan v. North Zone (Amritsar)	1952-53
		133	146	Karachi Whites v. Karachi Greens (Karachi)	1961-62
		111	104	Pakistan v. England (Dacca)	1961-62
Hanumant Singh	(1)	109	213*	Rajasthan v. Bombay (Bombay)	1966-67
Harbinson, W. K.	(1)	130	109*	Cambridge U. v. Glamorgan (Cambridge)	1929
Hardinge, H. T. W.	(4)	153	126	Kent v. Essex (Leyton)	1908
		175	109	Kent v. Hampshire (Southampton)	1911
		117	105*	Kent v. Hampshire (Dover)	1913
		207	102*	Kent v. Surrey (Blackheath)	1921
Hardstaff, J., Snr.	(1)	118	106*	Nottinghamshire v. Derbyshire (Nottingham)	1911
Hardstaff, J., Jnr.	(1)	100*	114*	Nottinghamshire v. Northamptonshire (Nottingham)	1949
Hassett, A. L.	(2)	122	122	Victoria v. New South Wales (Sydney)	1939-40
		187	124*	Australian Services v. Prince's XI (New Delhi)	1945-46
Hayward, T. W.	(3)	106	112	Surrey v. Sussex (Hove)	1904
		144*	100	Surrey v. Nottinghamshire (Nottingham)	1906
		143	125	Surrey v. Leicestershire (Leicester)	1906
Hazare, Vijay	(3)	127	162*	Baroda v. Maharashtra (Poona)	1944-45
		116	145	India v. Australia (Adelaide)	1947-48

A Century in Each Innings of a Match—*Cont.*

Player		1st	2nd	Match	Season
Hazare, Vijay (*cont.*)		130	101	Baroda v. Holkar (Baroda)	1949-50
Headley, G. A.	(2)	114	112	West Indies v. England (Georgetown)	1929-30
		106	107	West Indies v. England (Lord's)	1939
Hearne, J. W.	(1)	104	101*	Middlesex v. Glamorgan (Lord's)	1931
Hendren, E.	(4)	119	102	M.C.C. v. Kent (Folkestone)	1927
		189	100*	Middlesex v. Warwickshire (Birmingham)	1931
		101	101	Middlesex v. Kent (Lord's)	1933
		104	101	Middlesex v. Surrey (Lord's)	1936
Hill A. J. L.	(1)	124	118*	Hampshire v. Somerset (Southampton)	1905
Hill, N. W.	(1)	101	102	Nottinghamshire v. Lancashire (Nottingham)	1959
Hirst, G. H.	(1)	111	117*	Yorkshire v. Somerset (Bath)	1906
Hobbs, J. B.	(6)	160	100	Surrey v. Warwickshire (Birmingham)	1909
		104	143*	Surrey v. Cambridge U. (Oval)	1925
		101	101*	Surrey v. Somerset (Taunton)	1925
		112	104	Surrey v. Hampshire (Oval)	1927
		137	111*	Surrey v. Glamorgan (Oval)	1930
		113	119*	Surrey v. Essex (Oval)	1932
Holmes, P.	(1)	126	111*	Yorkshire v. Lancashire (Manchester)	1920
Howell, M.	(1)	115	102	Oxford U. v. Leveson-Gower's XI (Eastbourne)	1919
Human, J. H.	(1)	110	122	Cambridge U. v. Surrey (Oval)	1933
Hutchings, K. L.	(1)	109	109*	Kent v. Worcestershire (Worcester)	1907
Hutton, L.	(3)	197	104	Yorkshire v. Essex (Southend)	1947
		165	100	Yorkshire v. Sussex (Hove)	1949
		103	137	Yorkshire v. M.C.C. (Scarborough)	1952
Ingle, R.A.	(1)	117	100*	Somerset v. Middlesex (Taunton)	1928
Insole, D. J.	(1)	111	118	Essex v. Kent (Gillingham)	1955
Jackson, A. A.	(1)	131	122	New South Wales v. South Australia (Sydney)	1927-28
Jessop, G. L.	(4)	104	139	Gloucestershire v. Yorkshire (Bradford)	1900
		143	133*	Gloucestershire v. Somerset (Bath)	1908
		161	129	Gloucestershire v. Hampshire (Bristol)	1909
		153	123*	Gloucestershire v. Hampshire (Southampton)	1911
Johnson, P. R.	(1)	164	131	Somerset v. Middlesex (Taunton)	1908
Johnston, A. C.	(1)	175	100*	Hampshire v. Warwickshire (Coventry)	1912
Jones, A.	(1)	187*	105*	Glamorgan v. Somerset (Glastonbury)	1963
Jones, A. O.	(1)	137	100	Nottinghamshire v. Lancashire (Nottingham)	1903
Kadri, S. M.	(1)	105	114	Bombay v. Western India States (Poona)	1935-36
Kanhai, R. B.	(1)	117	115	West Indies v. Australia (Adelaide)	1960-61
Keith, H. J.	(1)	111	113*	South Africans v. Victoria (Melbourne)	1952-53
Kelly, P. C.	(1)	119	108*	Western Australia v. M.C.C. (Perth)	1965-66
Kenny, A.	(1)	164	100*	Victoria v. Queensland (Brisbane)	1909-10
Kimpton, R. C. M.	(1)	101	106	Oxford U. v. Gloucestershire (Oxford)	1936
King, J. H.	(2)	104	109*	Players v. Gentlemen (Lord's)	1904
		111	100*	Leicestershire v. Northamptonshire (Leicester)	1913
Kinneir, S. P.	(1)	124	110	Warwickshire v. Sussex (Chichester)	1911
Kippax, A. F.	(2)	127	131	New South Wales v. Queensland (Brisbane)	1926-27
		158	102*	Australians v. Sussex (Hove)	1930
Knight, D. J.	(1)	114	101	Surrey v. Yorkshire (Oval)	1919
Lambert, W.	(1)	107*	157	Sussex v. Epsom (Lord's)	1817
Lance, H. R.	(1)	101	122	Transvaal v. Eastern Province (Johannesburg)	1966-67
Langridge, John	(2)	115	129	Sussex v. Lancashire (Manchester)	1949
		146	146*	Sussex v. Derbyshire (Worthing)	1949
Lee, F. S.	(1)	109*	107	Somerset v. Worcestershire (Worcester)	1938
Lee, H. W.	(2)	163	126	Middlesex v. Surrey (Oval)	1919
		124	105*	Middlesex v. Lancashire (Lord's)	1929
Lester, E.	(2)	126	142	Yorkshire v. Northamptonshire (Northampton)	1947
		125*	132	Yorkshire v. Lancashire (Manchester)	1948
Livingstone, D. A.	(1)	117	105*	Hampshire v. Kent (Canterbury)	1964
Llewellyn, C. B.	(2)	102	100	Hampshire v. Derbyshire (Derby)	1905
		130	101*	Hampshire v. Sussex (Hove)	1909
Lonergan, A. R.	(1)	115	100	South Australia v. Victoria (Melbourne)	1933-34
Lyon, B. H.	(1)	115	101*	Gloucestershire v. Essex (Bristol)	1930
Macartney, C. G.	(2)	119	126	New South Wales v. South Africans (Sydney)	1910-11
		142	121	Australians v. Sussex (Hove)	1912
McCabe, S. J.	(1)	106	103*	New South Wales v. Victoria (Sydney)	1931-32
McGahey, C. P.	(1)	114	145*	Essex v. Gloucestershire (Leyton)	1901
Mackay, J. R. M.	(1)	105	102*	New South Wales v. South Australia (Sydney)	1905-06
MacLaren, A. C.	(1)	142	100	Stoddart's XI v. New South Wales (Sydney)	1897-98

A Century in Each Innings of a Match—*Cont.*

May, P. B. H.	(3)	167	103*	Surrey v. Essex (Southend)	1951
		174	100*	M.C.C. v. Yorkshire (Scarborough)	1952
		140	114	M.C.C. v. Australian XI (Sydney)	1958-59
Mead, C. P.	(3)	109	100*	Hampshire v. Leicestershire (Leicester)	1911
		102	113*	Hampshire v. Leicestershire (Southampton)	1913
		113	224	Hampshire v. Sussex (Horsham)	1921
Melville, A.	(1)	189	104*	South Africa v. England (Nottingham)	1947
Merchant, U. M.	(1)	143	156	Bombay v. Maharashtra (Poona)	1948-49
Miller, K. R.	(1)	100	101	Hassett's XI v. Morris's XI (Melbourne)	1953-54
Milton, C. A.	(2)	150	100*	Gloucestershire v. Sussex (Eastbourne)	1961
		110*	102*	Gloucestershire v. Kent (Bristol)	1962
Mitchell, A.	(1)	100*	100*	Leveson-Gower's XI v. M.C.C. Australian XI (Scarborough)	1933
Mitchell, B.	(1)	120	189*	South Africa v. England (Oval)	1947
Moroney, J. A. R.	(1)	118	101*	Australia v. South Africa (Johannesburg)	1949-50
Morris, A. R.	(2)	148	111	New South Wales v. Queensland (Sydney)	1940-41
		122	124*	Australia v. England (Adelaide)	1946-47
Mushtaq Ali	(1)	109	130	Holkar v. Bombay (Bombay)	1944-45
Needham, E.	(1)	107*	104	Derbyshire v. Essex (Leyton)	1908
Newman, J. A.	(1)	102	102*	Hampshire v. Surrey (Oval)	1927
Noble, M. A.	(1)	176	123	New South Wales v. Victoria (Sydney)	1907-08
Nourse, A. D., Jnr.	(1)	147	108*	South Africans v. Surrey (Oval)	1935
Nurse, S. M.	(1)	106	135*	Swanton's XI v. Indian XI (Calcutta)	1963-64
O'Connor, J.	(1)	138	120*	Essex v. Gloucestershire (Bristol)	1930
O'Connor, L. P. D.	(1)	103	143*	Queensland v. New South Wales (Sydney)	1926-27
O'Keefe, F. A.	(1)	177	141	Rest v. Australian XI (Sydney)	1921-22
Onyons, B. A.	(1)	105	127	Victoria v. Queensland (Brisbane)	1928-29
Ord, J. S.	(1)	107*	101	Warwickshire v. Nottinghamshire (Nottingham)	1948
Parfitt, P. H.	(2)	105	101*	Middlesex v. Nottinghamshire (Nottingham)	1961
		122	114	Middlesex v. Pakistan (Lord's)	1962
Parkhouse, W. G. A.	(1)	121	148	Glamorgan v. Somerset (Cardiff)	1950
Parks, H. W.	(1)	114*	105*	Sussex v. Essex (Leyton)	1933
Parks, J. M.	(1)	101	100*	Sussex v. Worcestershire (Worcester)	1957
Pataudi, Nawab of, Snr.	(1)	165	100	Oxford U. v. Surrey (Oval)	1931
Pataudi, Nawab of, Jnr.	(2)	106	103*	Oxford U. v. Yorkshire (Oxford)	1961
		130	107*	Delhi v. Services (New Delhi)	1964-65
Paynter, E.	(2)	125	113*	Lancashire v. Warwickshire (Birmingham)	1938
		117	100	England v. South Africa (Johannesburg)	1938-39
Perrin, P. A.	(4)	170	102*	Essex v. Nottinghamshire (Nottingham)	1903
		140	103*	Essex v. Middlesex (Lord's)	1905
		112	100*	Essex v. Nottinghamshire (Nottingham)	1911
		126	101*	Essex v. Kent (Leyton)	1919
Phadkar, D. G.	(1)	131	160	Bombay v. Maharashtra (Poona)	1948-49
Pinch, C.	(2)	110	100	South Australia v. Western Australia (Perth)	1956-57
		102	102	South Australia v. Victoria (Melbourne)	1957-58
Place, W.	(1)	105	132*	Lancashire v. Nottinghamshire (Manchester)	1947
Ponsford, W. H.	(1)	110	110*	Victoria v. New South Wales (Sydney)	1923-24
Poore, R. M.	(1)	104	119*	Hampshire v. Somerset (Portsmouth)	1899
Prideaux, R. M.	(2)	102	106	Cambridge U. v. Somerset (Taunton)	1960
		106	100	Northamptonshire v. Nottinghamshire (Nottingham)	1966
Quaife, W. G.	(1)	124	109	Warwickshire v. Surrey (Oval)	1913
Rae, A. F.	(1)	111	128	Jamaica v. Barbados (Kingston)	1946-47
Ranjitsinhji, K. S.	(1)	100	125*	Sussex v. Yorkshire (Hove)	1896
Ransford, V. S.	(1)	182	110	Victoria v. New South Wales (Sydney)	1908-09
Ratcliffe, A.	(1)	130	104*	Cambridge U. v. Surrey (Oval)	1932
Rege, M. R.	(1)	133	100	Maharashtra v. Bombay (Poona)	1948-49
Reid, J. R.	(1)	101	118*	New Zealanders v. Orange Free State (Bloemfontein)	1961-62
Rhodes, W.	(2)	128	115	Yorkshire v. M.C.C. (Scarborough)	1911
		119	109	M.C.C. v. New South Wales (Sydney)	1911-12
Richardson, B. A.	(1)	126	105	Warwickshire v. Cambridge U. (Birmingham)	1967
Richardson, P. E.	(1)	111	115	Kent v. Australians (Canterbury)	1964
Richardson, V. Y.	(1)	100	125	South Australia v. New South Wales (Sydney)	1924-25
Rigg. K. E.	(1)	100	167*	Victoria v. New South Wales (Melbourne)	1936-37
Robertson, J. D.	(1)	147	137	Middlesex v. Sussex (Lord's)	1948

A Century in Each Innings of a Match—*Cont.*

Player		1st	2nd	Match	Season
Roy, P.	(2)	170	143	Bengal v. Orissa (Cuttack)	1953-54
		112	118	Bengal v. Hyderabad (Calcutta)	1962-63
Russell, A. C.	(3)	115	118	Essex v. Surrey (Oval)	1922
		140	111	England v. South Africa (Durham)	1922-23
		131	104	Essex v. Lancashire (Liverpool)	1928
Saeed Ahmed	(1)	105	102	P.I.A. v. North Zone (Lahore)	1961-62
Sandham, A.	(1)	137	104	M.C.C. v. New South Wales (Sydney)	1924-25
Seymour, James	(2)	108	136*	Kent v. Worcestershire (Maidstone)	1904
		143	105*	Kent v. Essex (Leyton)	1923
Shepherd, T. F.	(1)	121	101*	Surrey v. Leicestershire (Oval)	1926
Sheppard, D. S.	(1)	143	126	Cambridge U. v. Middlesex (Cambridge)	1951
Shrewsbury, A.	(1)	101	127*	Nottinghamshire v. Gloucestershire (Nottingham)	1902
Simpson, R. B.	(2)	153	115	Australia v. Pakistan (Karachi)	1964-65
		121	142*	New South Wales v. South Australia (Sydney)	1964-65
Simpson, R. T.	(1)	143	102*	Nottinghamshire v. Leicestershire (Nottingham)	1949
Smith, A. C.	(1)	145	124	Oxford U. v. Hampshire (Bournemouth)	1959
Smith, H.	(1)	120	102*	Gloucestershire v. Hampshire (Southampton)	1919
Sobers, G. St. A.	(1)	125	109*	West Indies v. Pakistan (Georgetown)	1957-58
Solomon, J. S.	(1)	107	100*	British Guiana v. Trinidad (Georgetown)	1963-64
Squires, H. S.	(1)	131	102	Surrey v. Oxford U. (Oval)	1932
Stephens, S.	(1)	108	181	Victoria v. Tasmania (Launceston)	1913-14
Stevens, G.	(1)	164	111	South Australia v. New South Wales (Sydney)	1957-58
Stewart, W. J.	(1)	155	125	Warwickshire v. Lancashire (Blackpool)	1959
Stoddart, A. E.	(1)	195*	124	Middlesex v. Nottinghamshire (Lord's)	1893
Storer, H.	(1)	119	100	Derbyshire v. Sussex (Derby)	1929
Storer, W.	(1)	100	100*	Derbyshire v. Yorkshire (Derby)	1896
Sutcliffe, B.	(4)	197	128	Otago v. M.C.C. (Dunedin)	1946-47
		118	125	Otago v. Canterbury (Dunedin)	1947-48
		141	135	Auckland v. Canterbury (Auckland)	1948-49
		243	100*	New Zealanders v. Essex (Southend)	1949
Sutcliffe, H.	(4)	176	127	England v. Australia (Melbourne)	1924-25
		107	109*	Yorkshire v. M.C.C. (Scarborough)	1926
		111	100*	Yorkshire v. Nottinghamshire (Nottingham)	1928
		104	109*	England v. South Africa (Oval)	1929
Thomson, K.	(1)	102	102*	Canterbury v. Otago (Dunedin)	1966-67
Timms, J. E.	(1)	101	114*	Northamptonshire v. Sussex (Kettering)	1939
Tompkin, M.	(1)	156	107*	Leicestershire v. Middlesex (Leicester)	1952
Trimble, S. C.	(1)	113	136*	Queensland v. Victoria (Brisbane)	1963-64
Trumper, V. T.	(1)	109	119	Australians v. Essex (Leyton)	1902
Tyldesley, E.	(2)	165	123*	Lancashire v. Essex (Leyton)	1921
		109	108*	Lancashire v. Glamorgan (Cardiff)	1930
Tyldesley, J. T.	(3)	106	100*	Lancashire v. Warwickshire (Birmingham)	1897
		121	100*	North v. South (Hastings)	1900
		136	101	Lancashire v. Hampshire (Manchester)	1910
Uttley, K. F. M.	(1)	132	138	Otago v. Auckland (Auckland)	1937-38
Virgin, R.	(1)	124	125*	Somerset v. Warwickshire (Birmingham)	1965
Waite, J. H. B.	(1)	159*	134*	Transvaal v. Natal (Durban)	1959-60
Walcott, C. L.	(2)	126	110	West Indies v. Australia (Trinidad)	1954-55
		155	110	West Indies v. Australia (Kingston)	1954-55
Warner, P. F.	(1)	116	113*	Rest v. Nottinghamshire (Oval)	1907
Washbrook, C.	(1)	176	121*	Lancashire v. Sussex (Eastbourne)	1947
Weekes, E. D.	(1)	162	101	West Indies v. India (Calcutta)	1948-49
Wharton, A.	(1)	129	108	Leicestershire v. Middlesex (Leicester)	1961
Whitelaw, P. E.	(1)	115	155	Auckland v. Wellington (Auckland)	1934-35
Whysall, W. W.	(2)	100	167*	Nottinghamshire v. Gloucestershire (Nottingham)	1926
		117	101*	Nottinghamshire v. Hampshire (Nottingham)	1930
Wilcox, D. R.	(1)	104	129	Essex v. Kent (Westcliff)	1937
Winlaw, R. de W. K.	(1)	108	109*	Cambridge U. v. Glamorgan (Cardiff)	1934
Wood, C. J. B.	(1)	107*	117*	Leicestershire v. Yorkshire (Bradford)	1911
Woolley, F. E.	(1)	104	148*	Kent v. Somerset (Tunbridge Wells)	1911
Worthington, T. S.	(1)	103	110*	Derbyshire v. Nottinghamshire (Ilkeston)	1938
Wright, L. G.	(1)	176	122	Derbyshire v. Warwickshire (Birmingham)	1905
Young, D. M.	(1)	121	117*	Gloucestershire v. Northamptonshire (Kettering)	1955
Zulch, J. W.	(1)	185	125	Transvaal v. Orange Free State (Bloemfontein)	1920-21

CENTURY IN EACH INNINGS—MEMORABILIA

BOTH CENTURIES IN ONE DAY

K. S. Ranjitsinhji scored 100 and 125* for Sussex v. Yorkshire at Hove on August 22nd, 1896, starting the day with his first innings overnight score at 0*.

CARRYING BAT THROUGH COMPLETED INNINGS

C. J. B. Wood for Leicestershire v. Yorkshire at Bradford in 1911: 107* out of 309, and 117* out of 296.

ON FIRST-CLASS DEBUT

A. R. Morris	148	111	New South Wales v. Queensland (Sydney) ..	1940-41
N. J. Contractor	152	102*	Gujerat v. Baroda (Baroda)	1952-53

IN SUCCESSIVE MATCHES

T. W. Hayward (Surrey) v. Nottinghamshire at Nottingham and v. Leicestershire at Leicester in 1906—four centuries in six days.

3 BATSMEN IN A MATCH

U. M. Merchant, D. G. Phadkar and M. R. Rege—Bombay v. Maharashtra (Poona) 1948-49.

NEAR-MISSES

C. B. Fry, who achieved the feat five times, missed by one run on three occasions for Sussex at Hove: 99 & 123 v. Hampshire in 1898, 99 & 127* v. Leicestershire in 1903, and 125 & 99* v. Worcestershire in 1907.

A. H. Dyson scored 96 and 104* for Glamorgan v. Essex at Neath in 1934. He hit his wicket in cutting the boundary which would have given him his first innings century.

CENTURIES BY NUMBER ELEVEN BATSMEN

163	T. P. B. Smith ..	Essex v. Derbyshire (Chesterfield)	1947
126	W. C. Smith	M.C.C. v. Barbados (Bridgetown)	1912-13
121	S. N. Banerjee.. ..	Indians v. Surrey (Oval)	1946
		(He added 249 for the last wicket with the No. 10, C. T. Sarwate who made 124—the only instance of Nos. 10 and 11 scoring centuries in the same innings.)*	
112*	A. Fielder	Kent v. Worcestershire (Stourbridge)..	1909
106*	T. Hastings ..	Victoria v. South Australia (Melbourne)	1902-03
101	A. E. R. Gilligan ..	Cambridge U. v. Sussex (Hove)	1919

BATSMEN SCORING 400 RUNS IN A MATCH

499	(499)	Hanif Mohammad: Karachi v. Bahawalpur (Karachi)	1958-59
455	(3 & 452*)	D. G. Bradman: N.S.W. v. Queensland (Sydney)	1929-30
446	(244 & 202*)	A. E. Fagg: Kent v. Essex (Colchester)	1938
443	(443*)	B. B. Nimbalkar: Maharashtra v. Kathiawar (Poona)	1948-49
437	(437)	W. H. Ponsford: Victoria v. Queensland (Melbourne)	1927-28
429	(429)	W. H. Ponsford: Victoria v. Tasmania (Melbourne)	1922-23
424	(424)	A. C. MacLaren: Lancashire v. Somerset (Taunton)	1895
402	(157* & 245)	W. W. Armstrong: Victoria v. South Australia (Melbourne) ..	1920-21

The highest match aggregate in Tests is 375 (325 & 50)—A. Sandham: England v. West Indies (Kingston), 1929-30.

THREE OR MORE CENTURIES IN SUCCESSIVE INNINGS

SIX CENTURIES

Bradman, D. G. (South Australia) in 1938-39—118 Bradman's XI v. Rigg's XI (Melbourne), 143 v. N.S.W. (Adelaide), 225 v. Queensland (Adelaide), 107 v. Victoria (Melbourne), 186 v. Queensland (Brisbane), 135* v. N.S.W. (Sydney).

Fry, C. B. (Sussex) in 1901—106 v. Hants. (Portsmouth), 209 v. Yorks. (Hove), 149 v. Middx. (Hove), 105 v. Surrey (Oval, 140 v. Essex (Hove), 105 Rest of England v. Yorks. (Lord's).

FIVE CENTURIES IN SUCCESSIVE INNINGS

Weekes, E. D. (West Indians) in 1955-56—156 v. Auckland (Auckland), 148 v. Canterbury (Christchurch), 123 v. New Zealand (Dunedin), 119* v. Wellington (Wellington), 103 v. New Zealand (Christchurch).

FOUR CENTURIES IN SUCCESSIVE INNINGS

Bradman, D. G. (N.S.W.) in 1931-32—135 for N.S.W. (Sydney), 226 for Australia (Brisbane), 219 for N.S.W. (Sydney), 112 for Australia (Sydney): all v. South Africa.

Bradman, D. G. (Australians) in 1948 and 1948-49—150 v. Gentlemen of England (Lord's), 143 v. South of England (Hastings), 153 v. Leveson-Gower's XI (Scarborough). (His last three innings in England). 123 Bradman's XI v. Hassett's XI (Melbourne) 1948-49.

Compton, D. C. S. (Middx.) in 1946-47—124 M.C.C. v. Combined XI (Hobart), 163 M.C.C. v. Tasmania (Launceston), 147 & 103* England v. Australia (Adelaide).

Contractor, N. J. (Gujerat) in 1957-58—102 v. Bombay (Khadakvasla), 135 v. Saurashtra (Poona), 167 v. Baroda (Sangli), 110 v. Maharashtra (Poona).

Duleepsinhji, K. S. (Sussex) in 1931—161* v. Worcs. (Dudley), 109 England v. New Zealand (Oval), 103 v. Middx. (Hove), 127 v. Hants. (Hastings).

Fry, C. B. (Hants.) in 1911—123 & 112 v. Kent (Canterbury), 258* v. Glos. (Southampton), 102* Rest of England v. Warwicks. (Oval).

Hammond, W. R. (M.C.C.) in 1936-37—141 v. Western Australia (Perth), 107 v. Combined XI (Perth), 104 & 136 v. South Australia (Adelaide).

Hammond, W. R. (Glos.) in 1945 and 1946—121 & 102 England XI v. Dominions XI (Lord's) 1945, 132 v. Oxford U. (Oxford), 134 v. Lancs. (Gloucester) 1946.

Hardinge, H. T. W. (Kent) in 1913—154* v. Leics. (Canterbury), 117 & 105* v. Hants. (Dover), 107 v. Northants. (Dover).

Hayward, T. W. (Surrey) in 1906—144* & 100 v. Notts. (Nottingham), 143 & 125 v. Leics. (Leicester). All scored within six days.

Hobbs, J. B. (Surrey) in 1920—110 v. Sussex (Oval), 134 v. Leics. (Leicester), 101 v. Warwicks. (Birmingham), 112 v. Yorks. (Sheffield).

Hobbs, J. B. (Surrey) in 1925—104 & 143* v. Cambridge U. (Oval), 111 v. Somerset (Oval), 215 v. Warwicks. (Birmingham). (His two previous innings were 107 & 87 v. Essex (Oval).)

Langridge, John (Sussex) in 1949—115* v. Cambridge U. (Cambridge), 115 & 129 v. Lancs. (Manchester), 120 v. Glos. (Chichester).

Macartney, C. G. (Australians) in 1921—105 v. Hants. (Southampton), 193 v. Northants. (Northampton), 345 v. Notts. (Nottingham), 115 v. England (Leeds).

May, P. B. H. (M.C.C.) in 1956-57—162 v. Western Province (Cape Town), 118 v. Eastern Province (Port Elizabeth), 124* v. Rhodesia (Bulawayo), 206 v. Rhodesia (Salisbury).

Merchant, V. M. (Bombay & India) in 1941-42—170* Bombay v. Nawanagar (Jamnagar), 243* Hindus v. Rest (Bombay), 221 Hindus v. Parsis (Bombay), 153* Bombay v. Sind (Bombay).

Mitchell, A. (Yorks.) in 1933—150* v. Worcs. (Worcester), 107 v. M.C.C. (Scarborough), 100* & 100* Leveson-Gower's XI v. M.C.C. Australian XI (Scarborough).

Pataudi, Nawab of, Snr. (Oxford U.) in 1931—183* v. Army (Folkestone), 165 & 100 v. Surrey (Oval), 138 v. Leveson-Gower's XI (Eastbourne).

Roy, P. (Bengal) in 1962-63—178 v. Bihar, 136 v. Orissa, 112 & 118 v. Hyderabad (all at Calcutta).

Saeed Ahmed (P.I.A.) in 1961-62—149 East Pakistan Governor's XI v. Commonwealth XI (Dacca), 127* v. East Zone (Dacca), 105 & 102 v. North Zone (Lahore).

Sutcliffe, H. (Yorks.) in 1931—120* v. Middx. (Lord's), 107 v. Hants. (Portsmouth), 230 v. Kent (Folkestone), 183 v. Somerset (Dewsbury).

Sutcliffe, H. (Yorks.) in 1939—163 v. Lancs. (Manchester), 116 v. Hants. (Sheffield), 234* v. Leics. (Hull), 175 v. Middx. (Lord's).

Tyldesley, E. (Lancs.) in 1926—131 v. Surrey (Oval), 131 Players v. Gentlemen (Lord's), 106 v. Essex (Nelson), 126 v. Somerset (Taunton).

Whysall, W. W. (Notts.) in 1930—117 & 101* v. Hants. (Nottingham), 120 v. Australians (Nottingham), 158 v. Warwicks. (Birmingham).

Woolley, F. E. (Kent) in 1929—155 v. Derby (Chesterfield), 108 v. Somerset (Tonbridge), 131 v. Yorks. (Tonbridge), 117 v. Hants. (Folkestone).

THREE CENTURIES IN SUCCESSIVE INNINGS

Abel, R. (Surrey) in 1896—138 v. Warwicks. (Oval), 152 v. Leics. (Oval), 231 v. Essex (Oval).

Ames, L. E. G. (Kent) in 1932—130 v. Middx. (Tunbridge Wells), 149 v. Northants. (Tunbridge Wells), 120 v. Surrey (Blackheath).

Ames, L. E. G. (Kent) in 1937—125 v. Worcs. (Worcester), 119 & 127 v. Surrey (Blackheath).

Balaskas, X. C. (Griqualand West) in 1929-30—206 v. Rhodesia (Kimberley), 132 v. Eastern Province (Kimberley), 101 v. Western Province (Kimberley).

Bardsley, W. (N.S.W.) in 1910-11—191* v. South Australia (Sydney), 132 Australia v. South Africa (Sydney), 124 v. Victoria (Melbourne).

Three Centuries in Successive Innings—*Cont.*

Bardsley, W. (Australians) in 1926—127 v. Derby (Chesterfield), 193* v. England (Lord's), 112 v. Northants. (Northampton).

Bradman, D. G. (N.S.W.) in 1929-30—157 v. M.C.C. (Sydney), 124 & 225 Woodfull's XI v. Ryder's XI (Sydney).

Bradman, D. G. (N.S.W.) in 1933-34 and 1934—253 v. Queensland (Sydney), 128 v. Victoria (Sydney) in 1933-34, 206 Australians v. Worcs. (Worcester) in 1934.

Bradman, D. G. (Australians) in 1934—140 v. Yorks. (Sheffield), 304 v. England (Leeds), 244 v. England (Oval).

Bradman, D. G. (South Australia) in 1935-36—117 v. N.S.W. (Adelaide), 233 v. Queensland (Adelaide), 357 v. Victoria (Melbourne).

Bradman, D. G. (Australians) in 1937-38 and 1938—144 v. Tasmania (Hobart), 102 v. Western Australia (Perth) 1937-38, 258 v. Worcs. (Worcester) 1938.

Bradman, D. G. (South Australia) in 1946-47—119 v. Victoria (Adelaide), 187 Australia v. England (Brisbane), 234 Australia v. England (Sydney).

Bradman, D. G. (Australia) in 1947-48—132 & 127* v. India (Melbourne), 201 v. India (Adelaide).

Brown, W. A. (Australians) in 1948—200 v. Cambridge U. (Cambridge), 153 v. Essex (Southend), 108 v. Oxford U. (Oxford).

Cameron, H. B. (Transvaal) in 1933-34 and 1934-35—110 v. Western Province (Cape Town) 1933-34, 182 v. Griqualand West (Johannesburg), 112 v. Natal (Durban) 1934-35.

Chinnery, H. B. (Middx.) in 1901—105 & 165 M.C.C. v. Oxford U. (Oxford), 100 v. Glos. (Lord's).

Christy, J. A. J. (Transvaal) in 1927-28 and 1928-29—103 v. Rhodesia (Bulawayo), 175 v. Rhodesia (Salisbury) 1927-28, 141 v. Natal (Durban) 1928-29.

Compton, D. C. S. (Middx.) in 1947—112 v. Worcs. (Lord's), 110 v. Sussex (Lord's), 154 v. South Africans (Lord's).

Compton, D. C. S. (M.C.C.) in 1948-49—121 v. Cape Province (Cape Town), 150* v. Griqualand West (Kimberley), 106 v. Natal (Durban).

Cox, G. (Sussex) in 1947—103 v. Lancs. (Eastbourne), 142 v. Glos. (Hove), 132 v. South Africans (Hove).

Croom, A. J. (Warwicks.) in 1931—109 v. Kent (Birmingham), 105 v. Northants. (Peterborough), 159 v. Notts. (Birmingham).

Dalton, E. L. (South Africans) in 1929—157 & 116* v. Kent (Canterbury), 102 v. Sussex (Hove).

Davies, D. (Glamorgan) in 1928—126* v. Sussex (Swansea), 103 v. Northants. (Northampton), 165* v. Sussex (Eastbourne).

Dempster, C. S. (Leics.) in 1937—110 v. Sussex (Leicester), 133 & 154* v. Glos. (Gloucester).

Dempster, C. S. (Leics.) in 1938—105 v. Australians (Leicester), 110 v. Hants. (Southampton), 187 v. Oxford U. (Oxford).

Denton, D. (M.C.C.) in 1909-10—139 & 138 v. Transvaal (Johannesburg), 104 England v. South Africa (Johannesburg).

Ducat, A. (Surrey) in 1921—290* v. Essex (Leyton), 134 v. Northants. (Oval), 120 v. Warwicks. (Birmingham).

Ducat, A. (Surrey) in 1928—179* v. Warwicks. (Oval), 101* v. Sussex (Horsham), 208 v. Essex (Leyton).

Duleepsinhji, K. S. (Sussex) in 1932—116 v. Worcs. (Horsham), 126 v. Surrey (Hove), 128 South v. North (Manchester).

Edrich, J. H. (Surrey) in 1965—139 v. New Zealanders (Oval), 121* v. Oxford U. (Oxford), 205* v. Glos. (Bristol).

Fiddian-Green, C. A. (Cambridge U.) in 1922—103 v. Essex (Colchester), 113 v. Sussex (Hove), 120 v. Leveson-Gower's XI (Eastbourne).

Fishlock, L. B. (Surrey) in 1937—113 & 105 v. Yorks. (Oval), 127 v. Middx. (Lord's).

Foster, R. E. (Oxford U.) in 1900—128 & 100* v. Webbe's XI (Oxford), 169 v. London County (Oxford).

Fry, C. B. (Sussex) in 1900—125 & 229 v. Surrey (Hove), 110 v. Middx. (Hove).

Grace, W. G. (Glos.) in 1871—118 Gentlemen of South v. Gentlemen of North (West Brompton), 178 South v. North (Lord's), 162 Gentlemen of England v. Cambridge U. (Cambridge).

Grace, W. G. (Glos.) in 1872—112 Gentlemen v. Players (Lord's), 117 Gentlemen v. Players (Oval), 170* England v. Notts. & Yorks. (Lord's).

Grace, W. G. (Glos.) in 1873—134 Gentlemen of South v. Players of South (Oval), 163 Gentlemen v. Players (Lord's), 158 Gentlemen v. Players (Oval).

Grace, W. G. (Glos.) in 1874—121 Kent & Glos. v. England (Canterbury), 123 M.C.C. v. Kent (Canterbury), 127 v. Yorks. (Clifton).

Grace, W. G. (Glos.) in 1876—344 M.C.C. v. Kent (Canterbury), 177 v. Notts. (Clifton), 318* v. Yorks. (Cheltenham).

Hallows, C. (Lancs.) in 1927 and 1928—120 v. Rest of England (Oval) 1927, 100 v. Northants. (Manchester), 101 v. Glamorgan (Manchester) 1928.

Three Centuries in Successive Innings—*Cont.*

Hamence, R. A. (South Australia) in 1946-47—116 v. Victoria (Adelaide), 132 & 101* v. N.S.W. (Adelaide).

Hammond, W. R. (Glos.) in 1927—135 v. Yorks. (Gloucester), 108 & 128 v. Surrey (Oval).

Hammond, W. R. (M.C.C.) in 1928-29—119* & 177 England v. Australia (Adelaide), 114 v. Victoria (Melbourne).

Hammond, W. R. (Glos.) in 1937—140 England v. New Zealand (Lord's) 108 v. New Zealanders (Bristol), 112 v. Hants. (Bristol).

Hammond, W. R. (Glos.) in 1938—110 & 123 v. Derby (Burton-on-Trent), 240 England v. Australia (Lord's).

Hanif Mohammad (Karachi A.) in 1956-57 and 1957-58—228 Karachi Whites v. Karachi Blues (Karachi) 1956-57, 123 v. Sind B. (Karachi), 146* v. Sind A. (Karachi) 1957-58.

Hanif Mohammad (Karachi) in 1958-59—129 v. Hyderabad (Hyderabad), 499 v. Bahawalpur (Karachi), 130 v. Services (Karachi).

Hanif Mohammad (Karachi Whites) in 1961-62—133 & 146 v. Karachi Greens (Karachi), 189 v. Hyderabad (Karachi).

Harvey, R. N. (Australians) in 1953—141 v. Glos. (Bristol), 118 v. Northants. (Northampton), 122 v. England (Manchester).

Hassett, A. L. (Australians) in 1938—146 v. Oxford U. (Oxford), 148 v. Leics. (Leicester), 220* v. Cambridge U. (Cambridge).

Hassett, A. L. (Victoria) in 1939-40—122 & 122 v. N.S.W. (Sydney), 136 Rest of Australia v. N.S.W. (Sydney).

Hassett, A. L. (Australians) in 1948—200* v. Gentlemen of England (Lord's), 103 v. Somerset (Taunton), 151 v. South of England (Hastings).

Hayward, T. W. (Surrey) in 1899—273 v. Yorks. (Oval), 137 England v. Australia (Oval), 158 v. Somerset (Taunton).

Hazare, Vijay (India) in 1943-44—309 Rest v. Hindus (Bombay), 101 Baroda v. Bombay (Bombay), 233 Indian States v. Rest of India (Poona).

Hazare, Vijay (India) in 1949-50 and 1950—130 & 101 Baroda v. Holkar (Baroda) 1949-50, 114 Commonwealth XI v. England XI (Kingston) 1950.

Headley, G. A. (West Indians) in 1939—106 & 107 v. England (Lord's), 234* v. Notts. (Nottingham).

Hendren, E. (M.C.C.) in 1929-30—205 England v. West Indies (Port of Spain), 254* M.C.C. v. British Guiana (Georgetown), 171 M.C.C. v. British Guiana (Georgetown).

Hendren, E. (Middx.) in 1931—232 v. Notts. (Nottingham), 189 & 100* v. Warwicks. (Birmingham).

Hendren, E. (Middx.) in 1933—111 v. Surrey (Lord's), 101 & 101 v. Kent (Lord's).

Hendry, H. L. (Victoria) in 1926-27—177 v. South Australia (Adelaide), 140 v. Queensland (Melbourne), 100 v. N.S.W. (Melbourne).

Hill, C. (South Australia) in 1909-10—176 v. Victoria (Adelaide), 205 v. N.S.W. (Adelaide). 185 v. Victoria (Melbourne).

Hirst, G. H. (Yorks.) in 1899—186 v. Surrey (Oval), 131 v. Hants. (Bradford), 138 v. Notts, (Nottingham).

Hobbs, J. B. (Surrey) in 1914—122 v. Kent (Blackheath), 226 v. Notts. (Oval), 126 v. Worcs. (Worcester).

Hobbs, J. B. (Surrey) in 1926—261 v. Oxford U. (Oval), 119 England v. Australia (Lord's), 200 v. Hants. (Southampton).

Hobbs, J. B. (Surrey) in 1932—113 & 119* v. Essex (Oval), 123 v. Somerset (Taunton).

Howell, M. (Oxford U.) in 1919—115 & 102 v. Leveson-Gower's XI (Eastbourne), 170 v. Cambridge U. (Lord's).

Hutton, L. (Yorks.) in 1937—136 v. Kent (Tonbridge), 271* v. Derby (Sheffield), 153 v. Leics. (Hull).

Hutton, L. (Yorks.) in 1947—197 & 104 v. Essex (Southend), 270* v. Hants. (Bournemouth).

Hutton, L. (Yorks.) in 1952—120 v. Kent (Canterbury), 103 & 137 v. M.C.C. (Scarborough).

Iremonger, J. (Notts.) in 1904—189* v. Middx. (Lord's), 272 v. Kent (Nottingham), 142 v. Derby (Chesterfield).

Jardine, D. R. (Surrey) in 1927—120 Oxford Harlequins v. Oxford U. (Oxford), 147 v. Leics. (Leicester), 143 v. Lancs. (Manchester).

Jardine, D. R. (M.C.C.) in 1928-29—109 v. Western Australia (Perth), 104 v. Victoria (Melbourne), 140 v. N.S.W. (Sydney).

Johnson, P. R. (Somerset) in 1908—164 & 131 v. Middx. (Taunton), 117 v. Hants. (Southampton).

Keeton, W. W. (Notts.) in 1933—110 v. Hants. (Southampton), 168 v. Middx. (Nottingham), 110 v. Yorks. (Bradford).

Keeton, W. W. (Notts.) in 1949—109* v. Hants. (Nottingham), 208 v. Glamorgan (Nottingham), 134 v. Lancs. (Manchester).

Kippax, A. F. (N.S.W.) in 1925-26 and 1926-27—271* v. Victoria (Sydney) 1925-26, 127 & 131 v. Queensland (Brisbane) 1926-27.

Three Centuries in Successive Innings—*Cont.*

Knight, D. J. (Surrey) in 1919—114 & 101 v. Yorks. (Oval), 146 v. Lancs. (Manchester).
Lee, F. S. (Somerset) in 1938—109* & 107 v. Worcs. (Worcester), 141 v. Surrey (Taunton).
Lester, E. (Yorks.) in 1947—127 v. Derby (Scarborough), 126 & 142 v. Northants. (Northampton).
Leyland, M. (Yorks.) in 1934—104* v. M.C.C. (Lord's), 100 v. Oxford U. (Oxford), 126 v. Glamorgan (Swansea).
Macartney, C. G. (N.S.W.) in 1910-11—119 & 126 v. South Africans (Sydney), 137 Australia v. South Africa (Sydney).
Macartney, C. G. (Australians) in 1912—127 v. Northants. (Northampton), 208 v. Essex (Leyton), 123 v. Surrey (Oval).
Macartney, C. G. (N.S.W.) in 1923-24—120 v. Wellington (Wellington), 120 v. Otago (Dunedin), 221 v. Canterbury (Christchurch).
Mackay, J. R. M. (N.S.W.) in 1905-06—194 v. Victoria (Melbourne), 105 & 102* v. South Australia (Sydney).
MacLaren, A. C. (Lancs.) in 1895—152 v. Notts. (Manchester), 108 v. Middx. (Lord's), 135 v. Leics. (Leicester).
MacLaren, A. C. (A. E. Stoddart's XI) in 1897-98—142 & 100 v. N.S.W. (Sydney), 109 England v. Australia (Sydney).
Mason, J. R. (Kent) in 1904—138 v. Yorks. (Tunbridge Wells), 126 v. Somerset (Beckenham), 133 v. Essex (Colchester).
Mason, J. R. (Kent) in 1909—179* v. Sussex (Hove), 111 v. Somerset (Taunton), 152* v. Surrey (Oval).
May, P. B. H. (Surrey) in 1952—197 v. Leics. (Leicester), 174 & 100* M.C.C. v. Yorks. (Scarborough).
May, P. B. H. (Surrey) in 1958—155 v. Yorks. (Oval), 101 England v. New Zealand (Manchester), 112* v. New Zealanders (Oval).
McCabe, S. J. (N.S.W.) in 1931-32—229* v. Queensland (Brisbane), 106 & 103* v. Victoria (Sydney).
Mead, C. P. (Hants.) in 1921—280* v. Notts. (Southampton), 113 & 224 v. Sussex (Horsham).
Mead, C. P. (Hants.) in 1922—152 v. Kent (Southampton), 235 v. Worcs. (Worcester), 105 v. Leics. (Southampton).
Mead, C. P. (Hants.) in 1923—132 v. Worcs. (Worcester), 222 v. Warwicks. (Birmingham), 147 v. Sussex (Hove).
Mead, C. P. (Hants.) in 1933—135 v. Kent (Canterbury), 152 v. Notts. (Southampton), 113* v. Lancs. (Manchester).
Melville, A. (South Africans) in 1947—189 & 104* v. England (Nottingham), 117 v. England (Lord's).
Merchant, V. M. (India) in 1943-44—250* Hindus v. Rest (Bombay), 141 Bombay v. Baroda (Bombay), 359* Bombay v. Maharashtra (Bombay).
Mitchell, B. (South Africans) in 1947—131 v. Lancs. (Manchester), 120 & 189* v. England (Oval).
Moroney, J. A. R. (Australians) in 1949-50—118 & 101* v. South Africa (Johannesburg), 133 v. Natal (Pietermaritzberg).
Morris, A. R. (Australians) in 1949-50—102* v. Griqualand West (Kimberley), 157 v. South Africa (Port Elizabeth), 103 v. Western Province (Cape Town).
Nichol, M. (Worcs.) in 1933—116 v. Hants. (Bournemouth), 165* v. Glamorgan (Worcester), 154 v. Yorks. (Worcester).
Noble, M. A. (N.S.W.) in 1898-99—101 v. South Australia (Sydney), 100 v. Victoria (Sydney), 111 Australian XI v. Rest of Australia (Adelaide).
Nourse, A. D., Jnr. (South Africans) in 1935—147 & 108* v. Surrey (Oval), 148 v. Oxford U. (Oxford).
Nourse, A. D. Jnr. (Natal) in 1950-51—124 v. Border (Pietermaritzburg), 121 v. O.F.S. (Bloemfontein), 114 v. Western Province (Durban).
O'Connor, L. P. D. (Queensland) in 1926-27—196 v. N.S.W. (Brisbane), 103 & 143* v. N.S.W. (Sydney).
O'Keefe, F. A. (Victoria) in 1921-22—180 v. South Australia (Adelaide), 177 & 141 Rest of Australia v. Australian XI (Sydney).
Onyons, B. A. (Victoria) in 1928-29—131 v. N.S.W. (Sydney), 105 & 127 v. Queensland (Brisbane).
Pairaudeau, B. H. (British Guiana) in 1952-53—101 v. Jamaica (Georgetown), 126 v. Jamaica (Georgetown), 115 West Indies v. India (Port of Spain).
Parfitt, P. H. (Middx.) in 1962—122 & 144 v. Pakistanis (Lord's), 101* England v. Pakistan (Nottingham).
Parkhouse, W. G. A. (Glamorgan) 1950—121 & 148 v. Somerset (Cardiff), 127 v. Combined Services (Cardiff).
Pataudi, Nawab of, Jnr. (Oxford U.) in 1961—106 & 103* v. Yorks. (Oxford), 144 v. Middx. (Oxford).

Three Centuries in Successive Innings—*Cont.*

Paynter, E. (Lancs.) in 1936—123* v. Notts. (Nottingham), 177 v. Glamorgan (Manchester), 119 v. Northants. (Manchester).

Perrin, P. A. (Essex) in 1903—170 & 102* v. Notts. (Nottingham), 102* v. Derby (Leyton).

Phadkar, D. G. (Bombay), in 1948-49—134* v. Madras (Madras), 131 & 160 v. Maharashtra (Poona).

Place, W. (Lancs.) in 1947—171 v. Essex (Clacton), 105 & 132* v. Notts. (Manchester).

Ponsford, W. H. (Victoria) in 1921-22 and 1922-23—162 v. Tasmania (Melbourne) 1921-22, 429 v. Tasmania (Melbourne), 108 v. South Australia (Adelaide) 1922-23. (His 3rd, 4th and 5th innings in first-class cricket.)

Ponsford, W. H. (Victoria) in 1923-24—159 v. South Australia (Melbourne), 110 & 110* v. N.S.W. (Sydney).

Ponsford, W. H. (Victoria) in 1926-27—151 v. Queensland (Melbourne), 352 v. N.S.W. (Melbourne), 108 v. South Australia (Melbourne).

Ponsford, W. H. (Victoria) in 1927-28—133 v. South Australia (Adelaide), 437 v. Queensland (Melbourne), 202 v. N.S.W. (Melbourne).

Ponsford, W. H. (Victoria) in 1930-31—109* v. N.S.W. (Melbourne), 183 Australia v. West Indies (Sydney), 109 v. West Indies (Brisbane).

Poore, R. M. (Hants.) in 1899—104 & 119* v. Somerset (Portsmouth), 111 v. Lancs. (Southampton).

Prideaux, R. M. (Northants.) in 1966—135* v. Cambridge U. (Cambridge), 106 & 100 v. Notts. (Nottingham).

Quaife, W. G. (Warwicks.) in 1901—118* v. Yorks. (Birmingham), 108 London County v. Cambridge U. (Crystal Palace), 117* v. Derby (Derby).

Quaife, W. G. (Warwicks.) in 1913—124 & 109 v. Surrey (Oval), 107 v. Northants. (Birmingham).

Ranjitsinhji, K. S. (Sussex) in 1896—165 v. Lancs. (Hove), 100 & 125* v. Yorks. (Hove).

Ranjitsinhji, K. S. (Sussex) in 1900—127 v. Glos. (Hove), 222 v. Somerset (Hove), 215* v. Cambridge U. (Cambridge).

Reid, J. R. (New Zealanders) in 1961-62—101 & 118* v. O.F.S. (Bloemfontein), 165 v. South African Colts XI (East London).

Rhodes, W. (M.C.C.) in 1911-12—179 England v. Australia (Melbourne), 119 & 109 v. N.S.W. (Sydney).

Richardson, P. E. (Worcs.) in 1956—134 v. Notts. (Worcester), 104 England v. Australia (Manchester), 147 v. Essex (Worcester).

Robertson, J. D. (Middx.) in 1947—140 v. Kent (Canterbury), 127 v. Surrey (Oval), 110 v. Kent (Lord's).

Robertson, J. D. (Middx.) in 1954—123 v. Glamorgan (Lord's), 101 v. Northants. (Northampton), 101 v. Worcs. (Worcester).

Rowan, E. A. B. (Transvaal) in 1952-53—157 v. Border (Johannesburg), 196 v. N.-E. Transvaal (Johannesburg), 102 v. Griqualand West (Kimberley).

Roy, P. (Bengal) in 1957-58—154 v. Assam (Calcutta), 114 v. Orissa (Cuttack), 114 v. Bihar (Patna).

Siedle, I. J. (Natal) in 1936-37—105 v. Border (Durban), 111 v. Eastern Province (Pietermaritzburg), 207 v. Western Province (Durban).

Simpson, R. T. (Notts.) in 1959—108* v. Surrey (Oval), 132 v. Sussex (Nottingham), 100 v. Indians (Nottingham).

Sobers, G. St. A. (West Indies) in 1957-58—365* v. Pakistan (Kingston), 125 & 109* v. Pakistan (Georgetown).

Solomon, J. S. (British Guiana) in 1956-57 and 1957-58—114* v. Jamaica (Georgetown), and 108 v. Barbados (Georgetown) 1956-57; 121 v. Pakistanis (Georgetown) 1957-58. (His first three innings in first-class cricket).

Squires, H. S. (Surrey) in 1932—103 v. Cambridge U. (Oval), 131 & 102 v. Oxford U. (Oval).

Stevens, G. (South Australia) in 1957-58—164 & 111 v. N.S.W. (Sydney), 143 v. Queensland (Brisbane).

Stewart, W. J. (Warwicks.) in 1959—156 v. Essex (Coventry), 155 & 125 v. Lancs. (Blackpool).

Storer, W. (Derby) in 1896—100 & 100* v. Yorks. (Derby), 142* v. Leics. (Leicester).

Sutcliffe, B. (Otago) in 1947-48—103 v. Auckland (Auckland), 118 & 135 v. Canterbury (Dunedin).

Sutcliffe, B. (Auckland) in 1948-49—141 & 135 v. Canterbury (Auckland), 140 New Zealand XI v. Rest (Christchurch).

Sutcliffe, H. (M.C.C.) in 1924-25—115 England v. Australia (Sydney), 176 & 127 England v. Australia (Melbourne).

Sutcliffe, H. (Yorks.) in 1928—111 v. Derby (Derby), 111 & 100* v. Notts. (Nottingham).

Sutcliffe, H. (Yorks.) in 1931—117 England v. New Zealand (Oval), 195 v. Lancs. (Sheffield), 187 v. Leics. (Leicester).

Tate, M. W. (Sussex) in 1927—113 v. Cambridge U. (Cambridge), 122 v. Worcs. (Hove), 101 v. Hants. (Portsmouth).

Three Centuries in Successive Innings—*Cont.*

Tyldesley, E. (Lancs.) in 1928—159 v. Kent (Manchester), 242 v. Leics. (Leicester), 118 v. Sussex (Hove).

Tyldesley, E. (Lancs.) in 1934—239 v. Glamorgan (Cardiff), 107 v. Australians (Manchester), 134 v. Glos. (Bristol).

Tyldesley, J. T. (Lancs.) in 1897—106 & 100* v. Warwicks. (Birmingham), 174 v. Sussex (Manchester).

Tyldesley, J. T. (Lancs.) in 1904—103 v. Somerset (Manchester), 225 v. Notts. (Nottingham), 196 v. Worcs. (Worcester).

Weekes, E. D. (West Indians) in 1950—246* v. Hants. (Southampton), 200* v. Leics. (Leicester), 129 v. England (Nottingham).

White, R. C. (Transvaal B. & Transvaal) in 1965-66 and 1966-67—205 v. Griqualand West (Johannesburg), and 117 v. Western Province (Johannesburg) 1965-66; 103 v. Rhodesia (Salisbury) 1966-67.

Wilson, J. V. (Yorks.) in 1955—109* v. Somerset (Taunton), 132* v. Warwicks. (Birmingham), 132 v. Essex (Bradford).

Wright, L. G. (Derby) in 1905—195 v. Northants. (Derby), 176 & 122 v. Warwicks. (Birmingham).

Zulch, J. W. (Transvaal) in 1920-21—124 v. Eastern Province (Port Elizabeth), 185 & 125 v. O.F.S. (Bloemfontein).

5 *CENTURIES IN* 6 *INNINGS*

H. T. W. Hardinge—154*-117-105*-107-3-110	1913
J. B. Hobbs—107-87-104-143*-111-215	1925
E. Tyldesley—144*-226-51-131-131-106	1926
C. Hallows—120-100-101-51*-123-101*	1927 & 1928
Nawab of Pataudi, Snr.—183*-165-100-138-68-238*	1931
D. G. Bradman—135-226-219-112-2-167	1931-32
E. Hendren—111-101-101-12-105-154	1933
D. G. Bradman—144-102-258-58-137-278	1937-38 & 1938
V. M. Merchant—109-137-12-170*-243*-221	1940-41 & 1941-42
W. R. Hammond—121-102-132-134-59*-143	1945 & 1946

6 *CENTURIES IN* 7 *INNINGS*

E. Tyldesley—144*-226-51-131-131-106-126	1926
V. M. Merchant—109-137-12-170*-243*-221-153	1940-41 & 1941-42
W. R. Hammond—121-102-132-134-59*-143-104	1945 & 1946

7 *CENTURIES IN* 9 *INNINGS*

C. B. Fry—119*-36-88-106-209-149-105-140-105	1901
E. Tyldesley—144-69-144*-226-51-131-131-106-126	1926
D. G. Bradman—135-226-219-112-2-167-23-167-299*	1931-32
D. G. Bradman—144-102-258-58-137-278-2-143-145*	1937-38 & 1938
D. G. Bradman—202-17-67-118-143-225-107-186-135*	1938 & 1938-39
D. G. Bradman—132-127*-201-57-115-107-81-146-187	1947-48 & 1948

8 *CENTURIES IN* 11 *INNINGS*

D. G. Bradman—103-16-202-17-67-118-143-225-107-186-135*	1938 & 1938-39

8 *CENTURIES IN* 12 *INNINGS*

E. Tyldesley—144-69-144*-226-51-131-131-106-126-81-44-139	1926
W. H. Ponsford—214-54-151-353-108-84-12-116-131-7-133-437	1926-27 & 1927-28
D. G. Bradman—140-304-244-77-19-149*-132-15-50-117-233-357	1934 & 1935-36
D. G. Bradman—118-143-225-107-186-135*-5-76-64-251*-90*-138	1938-39 & 1939-40
V. M. Merchant—140-192-4-32-88*-109-137-12-170*-243*-221-153*	1939 to 1942

MOST FIFTIES IN SUCCESSIVE INNINGS

10 *CONSECUTIVE FIFTIES*

E. Tyldesley—144-69-144*-226-51-131-131-126-106-81	1926
D. G. Bradman—132-127*-201-57*-115-107-81-146-187-98	1947-48

Most Fifties in Successive Innings—*Cont.*

9 CONSECUTIVE FIFTIES

T. W. Hayward—61*-70*-63-144*-100-143-125-54-69 1906
Vijay Hazare—264-81-97-248-59-309-101-223-87 .. .. .. 1942-43 & 1943-44
R. B. Simpson—98-236*-230*-79-98-161*-67-80-52 1959-60
J. H. Edrich—139-121*-205*-55-96-188-92-105-310* 1965

8 CONSECUTIVE FIFTIES

C. B. Fry—135-68-72-125-229-110-96-105 1900
C. B. Fry—88-106-209-149-105-140-105-82 .. .. 1901 & 1902
C. P. Mead—162-78-62*-132-222-147-58-80* 1923
W. R. Hammond—101-75*-59-64-227-336*-55-51 .. .. 1932-33 & 1933
D. G. Bradman—85-79-144-102-258-58-137-278 .. ..1937-38 & 1938
B. Sutcliffe—71-74-111-62*-197-128-58-75 .. .. 1946-47 & 1947-48

7 CONSECUTIVE FIFTIES

E. Tyldesley—96-174*-66-58-65-82-67 1919
W. W. Whysall—54-117-101*-120-158-60-64 1930
W. R. Hammond—84*-54-81-100-53-75-70 1930-31
D. G. Bradman—67-118-143-225-107-186-135* 1938-39
S. G. Barnes—137-132-55-185-79-51-200 .. .. 1940-41 & 1945-46
R. S. Cooper—73-58*-62-68-127*-52-104 1944-45
W. R. Hammond—121-102-132-134-59*-143-104 .. .. 1945 & 1946
W. J. Edrich—57-50-54*-189-70-102-191 1947
A. R. Morris—60-105-62-290-51*-54-109.. 1948
L. Hutton—125-62*-134-61-78-174-83 1948-49
R. T. Simpson—54-143-102*-96-63*-80-54 1949
L. Hutton—147-52-54-101-54-75-52 .. .. 1949 & 1950
D. J. McGlew—85-66-53-118-68-51-69 1955
G. Pullar—62-57*-107-51-76*-76-105 1959
R. E. Marshall—51-56-104-63-63-75-63 1959
P. H. Parfitt—63-122-114-101*-56-92-54 1962
R. B. Simpson—125-138-55-57-95-105*-52* 1964

Other good sequences broken by scores of less than 50

H. Sutcliffe—59-119-176-127-33-59-188-88-143 1924-25
D. R. Jardine—91-157-86-40-83-109-104-140 .. .. 1928 & 1928-29
H. H. Gibbons—43-93-7-88-104-157-70*-100-129 1934
H. Gimblett—53-108-93-103-108-23-108-57-129 1939
W. A. Brown—99-12-174*-95-168-1-81-215-87-137 1939-40
S. G. Barnes—137-132-55-185-79-51-200-25-115-146-34-154-102 .. 1940-41 & 1945-46
V. M. Merchant—109-137-12-170*-243*-221-153 1941-42
B. Sutcliffe—21-71-74-111-62*-197-128-58-75-12-98-103-118-125-7-108* 1946-47 & 1947-48
D. C. S. Compton—123*-84-82-135-125*-34-30*-121-150*-106-9-300-84-72-28-114-1-151*-108 .. ..1948 & 1948-49
G. St. A. Sobers—49-183*-0-52-52-80-365*-125-109* .. ..1957 & 1957-58

MOST RUNS BEFORE BEING DISMISSED

(*Most runs by a batsman in a sequence of not-out innings before being dismissed*)

709	K. C. Ibrahim (Bombay) in 1947-48	218*, 36*, 234*, 77*, 144
634	V. M. Merchant (Hindus) in 1941-42	170*, 243*, 221
630	E. Hendren (M.C.C.) in 1929-30	205*, 254*, 171
575	E. D. Weekes (West Indians) in 1950	246*, 200*, 129
558	F. Jakeman (Northants.) in 1951	80*, 258*, 176*, 44
545	R. B. Simpson (Western Australia) in 1959-60	236*, 230*, 79
517	D. G. Bradman (N.S.W.) in 1933-34	187*, 77*, 253
514	E. Hendren (M.C.C.) in 1929-30	223*, 211*, 80
510	W. H. Ponsford (Australians) in 1934	229*, 281*, 0
502	F. M. M. Worrell (West Indians) in 1950	241*, 261
490	G. St. A. Sobers (West Indies) in 1957-58	365*, 125
474	W. G. Quaife (Warwicks.) in 1898	60*, 117*, 157*, 24*, 52*, 61*, 3

W. A. Johnston headed the batting averages for the Australians' 1953 Tour of England by being dismissed only once in 17 innings in which he scored 102 runs. V. H. Cannings (Hants.) caught and bowled him in his fourth innings and he remained undefeated throughout his last 13 innings.

J. C. Dye (Kent), another Number Eleven batsman, was not dismissed until F. J. Titmus had him lbw in the eleventh innings of his first-class career by which time he had accrued 20 runs (1962 and 1963).

3000 RUNS IN AN ENGLISH SEASON

	Season	*Inns.*	*N.O.*	*Runs*	*H.S.*	*Avge.*	*100s*
D. C. S. Compton (Middx.) ..	1947	50	8	3816	246	90.85	18
W. J. Edrich (Middx.)	1947	52	8	3539	267*	80.43	12
T. W. Hayward (Surrey)	1906	61	8	3518	219	66.37	13
L. Hutton (Yorks.)	1949	56	6	3429	269*	68.58	12
F. E. Woolley (Kent)	1928	59	4	3352	198	60.94	12
H. Sutcliffe (Yorks.)	1932	52	7	3336	313	74.13	14
W. R. Hammond (Glos.)	1933	54	5	3323	264	67.81	13
E. Hendren (Middx.)	1928	54	7	3311	209*	70.44	13
R. Abel (Surrey)	1901	68	8	3309	247	55.15	7
W. R. Hammond (Glos.)	1937	55	5	3252	217	65.04	13
M. J. K. Smith (Warwicks.) ..	1959	67	11	3245	200*	57.94	8
E. Hendren (Middx.)	1933	65	9	3186	301*	56.89	11
C. P. Mead (Hants.)	1921	52	6	3179	280*	69.10	10
T. W. Hayward (Surrey)	1904	63	5	3170	203	54.65	11
K. S. Ranjitsinhji (Sussex) ..	1899	58	8	3159	197	63.18	8
C. B. Fry (Sussex)	1901	43	3	3147	244	78.67	13
K. S. Ranjitsinhji (Sussex)	1900	40	5	3065	275	87.57	11
L. E. G. Ames (Kent)	1933	57	5	3058	295	58.80	9
J. T. Tyldesley (Lancs.)	1901	60	5	3041	221	55.29	9
C. P. Mead (Hants)	1928	50	10	3027	180	75.67	13
J. B. Hobbs (Surrey)	1925	48	5	3024	266*	70.32	16
E. Tyldesley (Lancs.)	1928	48	10	3024	242	79.57	10
W. E. Alley (Somerset)	1961	64	11	3019	221*	56.96	11
W. R. Hammond (Glos.)	1938	42	2	3011	271	75.27	15
E. Hendren (Middx.)	1923	51	12	3010	200*	77.17	13
H. Sutcliffe (Yorks.)	1931	42	11	3006	230	96.96	13
J. H. Parks (Sussex)	1937	63	4	3003	168	50.89	11
H. Sutcliffe (Yorks.)	1928	44	5	3002	228	76.97	13

2000 RUNS IN AN ENGLISH SEASON

		Season	*Inns.*	*N.O.*	*Runs*	*H.S.*	*Avge.*	*100s*
Abel, R. (Surrey)	(8)	1895	50	4	2057	217	44.71	5
		1896	55	3	2218	231	42.65	5
		1897	50	3	2099	250	44.65	6
		1898	45	3	2053	219	48.88	7
		1899	53	3	2685	357*	53.70	7
		1900	49	3	2592	221	56.34	12
		1901	68	8	3309	247	55.15	7
		1902	64	8	2299	179	41.05	9
Alley, W. E. (Somerset)	(1)	1961	64	11	3019	221*	56.96	11
Ames, L. E. G. (Kent)	(6)	1932	50	7	2482	180	57.72	9
		1933	57	5	3058	295	58.80	9
		1934	43	6	2113	202*	57.10	5
		1937	52	4	2347	201*	48.89	7
		1947	42	7	2272	212*	64.91	7
		1949	47	2	2125	160	47.22	7
Armstrong, N. F. (Leics.)	(1)	1933	54	5	2113	164	43.12	4
Arnold, J. (Hants.)	(1)	1934	52	5	2261	160	48.10	7
Ashdown, W. H. (Kent)	(2)	1928	55	3	2247	178	43.21	3
		1934	51	2	2030	332	41.42	6
Atkinson, G. (Somerset)	(2)	1961	57	1	2078	146	37.10	3
		1962	63	5	2075	133	35.77	4
Bailey, T. E. (Essex)	(1)	1959	55	12	2011	146	46.76	6
Bakewell, A. H. (Northants.)	(1)	1933	47	1	2149	257	46.71	7

2000 Runs in an English Season—*Cont.*

		Season	Inns.	N.O.	Runs	H.S.	Avge.	100s
Barber, W. (Yorks.)	(1)	1935	55	4	2147	255	42.09	4
Bardsley, W. (Australians)	(3)	1909	49	4	2072	219	46.04	6
		1912	52	6	2365	184*	51.41	8
		1921	41	4	2005	209	54.18	8
Barling, T. H. (Surrey)	(1)	1946	52	6	2014	233*	43.78	6
Barnett, C. J. (Glos.)	(4)	1933	59	3	2280	154	40.71	6
		1934	58	4	2348	194	43.48	6
		1936	58	3	2098	204*	38.14	6
		1937	65	3	2489	232	40.14	5
Barrington, K. F. (Surrey)	(3)	1959	52	6	2499	186	54.32	6
		1961	42	7	2070	163	59.14	4
		1967	40	10	2059	158*	68.63	6
Berry, L. G. (Leics.)	(1)	1937	51	4	2446	184*	52.04	7
Bolus, J. B. (Notts.)	(1)	1963	57	4	2190	202*	41.32	5
Bond, J. D. (Lancs.)	(1)	1962	67	8	2125	157	36.01	5
Bowley, E. H. (Sussex)	(4)	1923	66	5	2180	120	35.73	2
		1927	41	3	2062	220	54.26	4
		1928	53	1	2359	188	45.36	6
		1929	57	3	2360	280*	43.70	5
Boycott, G. (Yorks.)	(1)	1964	44	4	2110	177	52.75	6
Bradman, D. G. (Australians) ..	(4)	1930	36	6	2960	334	98.66	10
		1934	27	3	2020	304	84.16	7
		1938	26	5	2429	278	115.66	13
		1948	31	4	2428	187	89.92	11
Brearley, J. M. (Middx)	(1)	1964	54	5	2178	169	44.44	5
Brookes, D. (Northants.)	(6)	1946	48	5	2191	200	50.95	7
		1947	55	2	2217	210	41.83	6
		1949	54	5	2163	257	44.14	7
		1950	45	6	2000	171	51.28	5
		1952	54	7	2229	204*	47.42	6
		1955	58	5	2012	177	37.96	3
Brown, G. (Hants.)	(1)	1926	53	2	2040	146	40.00	6
Brown, S. M. (Middx.)	(1)	1947	60	5	2078	155	37.78	4
Burnup, C. J. (Kent)	(1)	1902	55	3	2048	161	39.38	6
Carr, A. W. (Notts.)	(1)	1925	49	4	2338	206	51.95	8
Carr, D. B. (Derby)	(1)	1959	60	8	2292	156*	44.07	5
Compton, D. C. S. (Middx.)	(6)	1939	50	6	2468	214*	56.09	8
		1946	45	6	2403	235	61.61	10
		1947	50	8	3816	246*	90.85	18
		1948	47	7	2451	252*	61.27	9
		1949	56	4	2530	182	48.65	9
		1951	40	6	2193	172	64.50	8
Cook, T. E. (Sussex)	(1)	1934	45	6	2132	220	54.66	4
Cowdrey, M. C. (Kent)	(2)	1959	44	4	2008	250	50.20	6
		1965	43	10	2093	196*	63.42	5
Cox, G. (Sussex)	(2)	1947	56	2	2032	205*	37.62	8
		1950	55	7	2369	165*	49.35	6
Crapp, J. F. (Glos.)	(1)	1949	48	4	2014	140	45.77	7
Davies, E. (Glamorgan)	(1)	1937	52	2	2012	140	40.24	3
Denton, D. (Yorks.)	(5)	1904	55	3	2088	119	40.15	3
		1905	60	3	2405	172	42.19	8
		1906	60	4	2287	157*	40.83	7
		1911	57	4	2232	137*	42.11	6
		1912	54	4	2127	211	42.54	6
Dewes, J. G. (Middx.)	(1)	1950	45	4	2432	212	59.31	9
Dexter, E. R. (Sussex)	(3)	1959	53	8	2055	127	45.66	7
		1960	53	2	2217	157	43.47	7
		1962	47	7	2148	172	53.70	5
Dipper, A. E. (Glos.)	(5)	1923	57	6	2048	252*	40.15	3
		1926	63	6	2147	135	37.66	2
		1927	53	8	2246	212	49.91	7
		1928	49	6	2365	188	55.00	7
		1929	50	3	2218	153	47.19	3
Dodds, T. C. (Essex)	(1)	1947	58	2	2147	157	38.33	1
Doggart, G. H. G. (Sussex)	(1)	1949	51	6	2063	219*	45.84	5
Dollery, H. E. (Warwicks.)	(2)	1949	48	4	2084	200	47.36	6

2000 Runs in an English Season—*Cont.*

		Season	Inns.	N.O.	Runs	H.S.	Avge.	100s
Dollery, H. E. (*cont.*)		1952	51	2	2073	212	42.30	4
Donnelly, M. P. (New Zealanders) ..	(1)	1949	45	8	2287	206	61.81	5
Ducat, A. (Surrey)	(1)	1930	48	6	2067	218	49.21	5
Duleepsinhji, K. S. (Sussex)	(3)	1929	51	3	2545	246	53.02	8
		1930	48	3	2562	333	56.93	9
		1931	51	2	2684	162	54.79	12
Edrich, G. A. (Lancs.)	(1)	1952	53	3	2067	162	41.34	4
Edrich, J. H. (Surrey)	(3)	1962	55	7	2482	216	51.70	7
		1965	44	7	2319	310*	62.67	8
		1967	47	5	2077	226*	49.45	5
Edrich, W. J. (Middx.)	(9)	1937	53	5	2154	175	44.87	3
		1938	51	6	2378	245	52.84	6
		1939	45	1	2186	161	49.68	7
		1947	52	8	3539	267*	80.43	12
		1948	55	6	2428	168*	49.55	9
		1949	62	5	2253	182	39.52	5
		1951	58	4	2086	118	38.62	2
		1952	63	4	2281	239	38.66	6
		1953	60	2	2557	211	47.35	5
Emmett, G. M. (Glos.)	(3)	1949	51	2	2005	116	40.91	3
		1951	56	5	2019	146	39.58	3
		1953	62	2	2115	141	35.25	4
Fagg, A. E. (Kent)	(5)	1938	53	6	2456	244	52.25	9
		1947	56	5	2203	184	43.19	5
		1948	48	3	2423	203	53.84	8
		1950	54	3	2034	156	39.88	6
		1951	51	1	2081	221	41.62	6
Fishlock, L. B. (Surrey)	(6)	1936	53	13	2129	133*	53.22	5
		1938	53	1	2121	165	40.78	4
		1946	46	2	2221	172	50.47	5
		1948	56	2	2106	253	39.00	5
		1949	56	3	2426	210	45.77	7
		1950	59	5	2417	147	44.75	6
Foster, R. E. (Worcs.)	(1)	1901	44	2	2128	136	50.66	6
Fry, C. B. (Sussex)	(6)	1899	55	1	2366	181	43.81	5
		1900	41	3	2325	229	61.18	9
		1901	43	3	3147	244	78.67	13
		1903	40	7	2683	234	81.30	9
		1904	42	2	2824	229	70.60	10
		1905	44	4	2801	233	70.02	10
Gale, R. A. (Middx.)	(1)	1962	58	1	2211	200	38.78	4
Gibbons, H. H. (Worcs.)	(3)	1933	57	4	2008	155	37.88	4
		1934	57	6	2654	157	52.03	8
		1938	55	6	2120	178	43.26	6
Gimblett, H. (Somerset)	(2)	1949	52	4	2093	156	43.60	5
		1952	55	1	2134	169	39.51	5
Grace, W. G. (Glos.)	(6)	1871	39	4	2739	268	78.25	10
		1873	38	8	2139	192*	71.30	7
		1876	46	4	2622	344	62.42	7
		1887	46	8	2062	183*	54.26	6
		1895	48	2	2346	288	51.00	9
		1896	54	4	2135	301	42.70	4
Graveney, T. W. (Glos. & Worcs.) ..	(7)	1951	50	3	2291	201	48.74	8
		1952	51	7	2066	171	48.04	6
		1955	51	2	2117	159	43.20	5
		1956	54	6	2397	200	49.93	9
		1957	53	5	2361	258	49.18	8
		1962	48	6	2269	164*	54.02	9
		1964	51	7	2385	164	54.20	5
Gray, J. R. (Hants.)	(3)	1959	57	5	2170	176*	41.73	6
		1961	66	3	2034	136	32.28	2
		1962	61	6	2224	213*	40.43	5
Green, D. M. (Lancs.)	(1)	1965	63	1	2037	85	32.85	–
Gregory, R. J. (Surrey)	(2)	1934	49	3	2379	180	51.71	8
		1937	50	3	2166	154	46.08	7
Grieves, K. J. (Lancs.)	(1)	1959	58	4	2253	202*	41.72	4

2000 Runs in an English Season—*Cont.*

	Season	Inns.	N.O.	Runs	H.S.	Avge.	100s
Gunn, W. (Notts.) .. .. .. (1)	1893	51	3	2057	156	42.85	7
Hallam, M. R. (Leics.) .. .. (3)	1957	62	2	2068	176	34.46	6
	1959	62	1	2070	210*	33.93	4
	1961	65	8	2262	203*	39.68	5
Hallows, C. (Lancs.) .. .. .. (3)	1925	51	6	2354	163	52.31	8
	1927	44	13	2343	233*	75.58	7
	1928	46	5	2645	232	64.51	11
Hammond, W. R. (Glos.) .. .. (12)	1927	47	4	2969	197	69.04	12
	1928	48	5	2825	244	65.69	9
	1929	47	9	2456	238*	64.63	10
	1930	44	6	2032	211*	53.47	5
	1932	49	4	2528	264	56.17	8
	1933	54	5	3323	264	67.81	13
	1934	35	4	2366	302*	76.32	8
	1935	58	5	2616	252	49.35	7
	1936	42	5	2107	317	56.94	5
	1937	55	5	3252	217	65.04	13
	1938	42	2	3011	271	75.27	15
	1939	46	7	2479	302	63.56	7
Hardinge, H. T. W. (Kent) .. .. (5)	1913	56	7	2037	168	41.57	7
	1921	52	7	2339	207	51.97	9
	1922	48	8	2207	249*	55.17	7
	1926	52	5	2234	176	47.53	7
	1928	46	5	2446	263*	59.65	5
Hardstaff, J., Jnr. (Notts.) .. .. (4)	1937	46	2	2540	266	57.72	8
	1939	46	7	2129	159	54.58	5
	1947	44	7	2396	221*	64.75	7
	1949	40	9	2251	162*	72.61	8
Harvey, R. N. (Australians) .. .. (1)	1953	35	4	2040	202*	65.80	10
Hayes, E. G. (Surrey) .. .. .. (2)	1906	56	5	2309	218	45.27	7
	1909	65	5	2161	276	36.01	3
Hayward, T. W. (Surrey) .. .. (10)	1899	49	4	2647	273	58.82	7
	1900	57	7	2693	193	53.86	10
	1901	58	8	2535	181	50.70	2
	1903	64	3	2177	156*	35.68	3
	1904	63	5	3170	203	54.65	11
	1905	64	6	2592	129*	44.68	5
	1906	61	8	3518	219	66.37	13
	1907	58	6	2353	161	45.25	7
	1908	52	1	2337	175	45.82	5
	1911	51	6	2149	202	47.75	5
Headley, G. A. (West Indians) .. (1)	1933	38	3	2320	224*	66.28	7
Headley, R. G. A. (Worcs.) .. .. (1)	1961	69	5	2040	150*	31.87	4
Hearne, J. W. (Middx.) .. .. (4)	1913	49	3	2036	189	44.26	6
	1914	43	8	2116	204	60.45	8
	1920	46	7	2148	215*	55.07	6
	1932	52	3	2151	176	43.89	6
Hedges, B. (Glamorgan) .. .. (1)	1961	65	2	2026	141	32.15	3
Hendren, E. (Middx.) .. .. (15)	1920	47	6	2520	232	61.46	6
	1921	53	5	2013	113	41.93	7
	1922	38	7	2072	277*	66.83	7
	1923	51	12	3010	200*	77.17	13
	1924	48	11	2100	142	56.75	5
	1925	50	6	2601	240	59.11	8
	1926	53	11	2643	213	62.92	9
	1927	43	5	2784	201*	73.26	13
	1928	54	7	3311	209*	70.44	13
	1929	63	9	2213	156	40.98	5
	1931	54	9	2548	232	56.62	7
	1932	47	7	2041	194	51.02	5
	1933	65	9	3186	301*	56.89	11
	1934	55	6	2213	135	45.16	7
	1936	58	2	2654	202	47.39	9
Hill, N. W. (Notts.) .. .. .. (2)	1959	57	2	2129	167	38.70	6
	1961	60	4	2239	201*	39.98	6
Hirst, G. H. (Yorks.) .. .. .. (3)	1904	50	4	2501	157	54.36	9

2000 Runs in an English Season—*Cont.*

	Season	Inns.	N.O.	Runs	H.S.	Avge.	100s
Hirst, G. H. (*cont.*)	1905	52	10	2266	341	53.95	6
	1906	58	6	2385	169	45.86	6
Hobbs, J. B. (Surrey) .. .. .. (17)	1907	63	6	2135	166*	37.45	4
	1909	54	2	2114	205	40.65	6
	1911	60	3	2376	154*	41.68	4
	1912	60	6	2042	111	37.81	3
	1913	57	5	2605	184	50.09	9
	1914	48	2	2697	226	58.63	11
	1919	49	6	2594	205*	60.32	8
	1920	50	2	2827	215	58.89	11
	1922	46	5	2552	168	62.24	10
	1923	59	4	2087	136	37.94	5
	1924	43	7	2094	211	58.16	6
	1925	48	5	3024	266*	70.32	16
	1926	41	3	2949	316*	77.60	10
	1928	38	7	2542	200*	82.00	12
	1929	39	5	2263	204	66.55	10
	1930	43	2	2103	146*	51.29	5
	1931	49	6	2418	153	56.23	10
Holmes, P. (Yorks.) .. .. .. (7)	1920	51	6	2254	302*	50.08	7
	1923	54	3	2001	199	39.23	3
	1925	52	9	2453	315*	57.04	6
	1926	50	4	2006	143	43.60	4
	1927	47	9	2174	180	57.21	6
	1928	43	5	2220	275	58.42	6
	1930	52	6	2003	132*	43.54	4
Horton, H. (Hants.) .. .. .. (3)	1959	59	8	2428	140*	47.60	4
	1960	59	9	2170	131	43.40	7
	1961	65	4	2329	160*	38.18	4
Horton, M. J. (Worcs.) .. .. (1)	1959	58	3	2468	212	44.87	4
Hutton, L. (Yorks.) .. .. .. (9)	1937	58	7	2888	271*	56.62	10
	1939	52	6	2883	280*	62.67	12
	1947	44	4	2585	270*	64.62	11
	1948	48	7	2654	176*	64.73	10
	1949	56	6	3429	269*	68.58	12
	1950	40	3	2128	202*	57.51	6
	1951	47	8	2145	194*	55.00	7
	1952	45	3	2567	189	61.11	11
	1953	44	5	2458	241	63.02	8
Ibadulla, K. (Warwicks.) .. .. (1)	1962	64	2	2098	119	33.83	6
Iddon, J. (Lancs.) .. .. .. (1)	1934	51	6	2381	200*	52.91	6
Insole, D. J. (Essex) .. .. .. (3)	1951	57	9	2032	186*	42.33	3
	1955	62	5	2427	142	42.57	9
	1959	50	5	2045	180	45.44	5
Jessop, G. L. (Glos.) .. .. .. (2)	1900	58	3	2210	179	40.18	6
	1901	58	1	2323	233	40.75	5
Jones, A. O. (Notts.) .. .. .. (1)	1901	51	2	2292	249	46.77	5
Jupp, V. W. C. (Sussex) .. .. (1)	1921	60	4	2169	179	38.73	7
Keeton, W. W. (Notts.) .. .. (6)	1932	51	3	2062	242	42.95	7
	1933	56	3	2258	168	42.60	6
	1934	46	0	2006	261	43.60	3
	1937	52	8	2004	136	45.54	4
	1946	48	2	2021	160	43.93	5
	1949	38	1	2049	210	55.37	6
Kenyon, D. (Worcs.) .. .. .. (7)	1950	58	3	2351	163	42.74	6
	1951	59	6	2145	145	40.47	6
	1952	60	2	2489	171	42.91	7
	1953	58	3	2439	238*	44.38	6
	1954	58	7	2636	253*	51.68	6
	1955	64	3	2296	131	37.63	5
	1957	62	3	2231	200*	37.81	6
Kilner, N. (Warwicks.) .. .. (1)	1933	50	2	2159	197	44.97	6
Langridge, James (Sussex) .. .. (1)	1937	58	7	2082	150*	40.82	1
Langridge, John (Sussex) .. .. (11)	1933	51	6	2056	250*	45.68	4
	1934	52	6	2256	232*	49.04	4
	1935	56	4	2035	195	39.13	4

2000 Runs in an English Season—*Cont.*

		Season	Inns.	N.O.	Runs	H.S.	Avge.	100s
Langridge, John (*cont.*)		1937	63	3	2514	175	41.90	10
		1938	54	4	2347	227	46.94	5
		1939	51	0	2106	202	41.29	6
		1947	57	5	2023	138*	38.90	3
		1949	53	5	2914	234*	60.70	12
		1950	65	5	2412	241	40.20	5
		1951	53	3	2041	200*	40.82	5
		1952	60	4	2082	140	37.17	6
Lawry, W. M. (Australians)	(1)	1961	39	6	2019	165	61.18	9
Lee, F. S. (Somerset)	(1)	1938	51	6	2019	162	44.86	7
Lenham, L. J. (Sussex)	(1)	1961	68	6	2016	107	32.51	2
Lewis, A. R. (Glamorgan)	(2)	1962	60	6	2188	151	40.51	5
		1966	61	8	2198	223	41.47	5
Leyland, M. (Yorks.)	(3)	1930	50	7	2175	211*	50.58	6
		1933	50	4	2317	210*	50.36	7
		1934	44	4	2142	182	53.55	7
Livingston, T. L. (Northants.) ..	(3)	1954	48	7	2269	207*	55.34	6
		1955	58	5	2172	172*	40.98	5
		1956	47	6	2006	188*	48.92	2
Lowson, F. A. (Yorks.)	(1)	1950	56	5	2152	141*	42.19	5
Macartney, C. G. (Australians) ..	(2)	1912	49	1	2187	208	45.56	6
		1921	41	2	2317	345	59.41	8
McCabe, S. J. (Australians)	(1)	1934	37	7	2078	240	69.26	8
Makepeace, H. (Lancs.)	(2)	1923	53	6	2310	203	49.14	6
		1926	54	5	2340	180	48.75	5
Marshall, R. E. (Hants.)	(6)	1955	60	4	2115	110*	37.76	3
		1958	57	3	2118	193	39.22	5
		1959	63	1	2532	150	40.83	4
		1960	62	5	2380	168	41.75	5
		1961	62	2	2607	212	43.45	5
		1962	52	3	2124	228*	43.34	6
May, P. B. H. (Surrey)	(5)	1951	43	9	2339	178*	68.79	9
		1952	47	7	2498	197	62.45	10
		1953	59	9	2554	159	51.08	8
		1957	41	3	2347	285*	61.76	7
		1958	41	6	2231	174	63.74	8
Mead, C. P. (Hants.)	(11)	1911	52	5	2562	223	54.51	9
		1913	60	8	2627	171*	50.51	9
		1914	53	5	2476	213	51.58	7
		1921	52	6	3179	280*	69.10	10
		1922	50	10	2391	235	59.77	8
		1923	52	8	2604	222	59.18	7
		1926	45	8	2326	177*	62.86	10
		1927	41	9	2385	200*	74.53	8
		1928	50	10	3027	180	75.67	13
		1933	44	6	2576	227	67.78	10
		1934	46	8	2011	198	52.92	6
Merchant, V. M. (Indians)	(1)	1946	41	9	2385	242*	74.53	7
Milton, C. A. (Glos.)	(1)	1967	49	4	2089	145	46.42	7
Mitchell, A. (Yorks.)	(1)	1933	51	12	2300	158	58.97	8
Mitchell, B. (South Africans)	(1)	1947	37	4	2014	189*	61.03	8
Nichol, M. (Worcs.)	(1)	1933	54	5	2154	165*	43.95	8
Nicholls, R. B. (Glos.)	(1)	1962	58	2	2059	217	36.76	4
Noble, M. A. (Australians)	(1)	1905	46	2	2053	267	46.65	6
Oakman, A. S. M. (Sussex)	(2)	1961	67	4	2307	229*	36.61	6
		1962	63	9	2008	177	37.18	3
O'Connor, J. (Essex)	(4)	1928	53	4	2325	157	47.44	6
		1929	54	3	2288	168*	44.86	9
		1933	52	5	2077	237	44.19	6
		1934	49	7	2350	248	55.95	9
Oldfield, N. (Northants.)	(1)	1949	47	3	2192	168	49.81	4
Padgett, D. E. V. (Yorks.)	(1)	1959	61	8	2181	161*	41.15	4
Palmer, C. H. (Leics.)	(1)	1952	56	4	2071	127	39.82	4
Parfitt, P. H. (Middx.)	(3)	1961	59	8	2007	165*	39.35	8
		1962	51	4	2121	138	45.12	8
		1966	57	8	2018	114*	41.18	2

2000 Runs in an English Season—*Cont.*

		Season	*Inns.*	*N.O.*	*Runs*	*H.S.*	*Avge.*	*100s*
Parkhouse, W. G. A. (Glamorgan) ..	(1)	1959	49	3	2243	154	48.76	6
Parks, H. W. (Sussex)	(1)	1947	57	2	2122	170	38.58	5
Parks, J. H. (Sussex)	(1)	1937	63	4	3003	168	50.89	11
Parks, J. M. (Sussex)	(3)	1955	63	8	2314	205*	42.07	5
		1957	55	6	2171	132*	44.30	4
		1959	56	11	2313	157*	51.40	6
Paynter, E. (Lancs.)	(4)	1932	55	1	2035	159	37.68	5
		1936	54	10	2016	177	45.81	4
		1937	58	4	2904	322	53.77	5
		1938	52	6	2691	291	58.50	8
Place, W. (Lancs.)	(1)	1947	47	7	2501	266*	62.52	10
Pullar, G. (Lancs.)	(2)	1959	55	7	2647	161	55.14	8
		1961	61	7	2344	165*	43.40	5
Quaife, W. G. (Warwicks.)	(1)	1905	52	14	2060	255*	54.21	6
Ranjitsinhji, K. S. (Sussex)	(5)	1896	55	7	2780	171*	57.91	10
		1899	58	8	3159	197	63.18	8
		1900	40	5	3065	275	87.57	11
		1901	40	5	2468	285*	70.51	8
		1904	34	6	2077	207*	74.17	8
Rhodes, W. (Yorks.)	(2)	1909	59	7	2094	199	40.26	5
		1911	64	5	2261	128	38.32	5
Richardson, P. E. (Worcs. & Kent) ..	(4)	1953	61	3	2294	171	39.55	3
		1961	58	1	2152	171	37.75	4
		1962	54	0	2081	162	38.53	4
		1963	56	2	2110	172	39.07	5
Robertson, J. D. (Middx.)	(9)	1946	58	3	2114	128	38.43	5
		1947	57	4	2760	229	52.07	12
		1948	54	7	2366	154	50.34	7
		1949	57	1	2244	331*	40.07	7
		1950	59	3	2093	138*	37.37	4
		1951	56	4	2917	201*	56.09	7
		1952	64	2	2337	162	37.69	2
		1955	64	0	2070	137	32.34	1
		1957	59	2	2155	201*	37.80	4
Rogers, N. H. (Somerset)	(1)	1952	58	3	2244	164	40.80	3
Russell, A. C. (Essex)	(5)	1920	56	1	2432	197	44.21	3
		1921	44	3	2236	273	54.53	8
		1922	50	3	2575	172	54.78	9
		1925	47	4	2081	150	48.39	7
		1928	42	7	2243	182	64.08	8
Russell, W. E. (Middx.)	(3)	1960	63	9	2051	182	37.98	2
		1961	62	1	2014	156	33.01	4
		1964	56	5	2342	193	45.92	5
Sandham, A. (Surrey)	(8)	1921	48	5	2117	292*	49.23	5
		1924	37	2	2082	169	59.48	7
		1925	47	6	2255	181	55.00	5
		1927	46	6	2315	230	57.87	7
		1928	47	4	2532	282*	58.88	8
		1929	52	2	2565	187	51.30	6
		1930	50	4	2295	204	49.89	6
		1931	50	8	2209	175	52.59	9
Seymour, James (Kent)	(1)	1913	60	6	2088	124	38.66	5
Sharp, J. (Lancs.)	(1)	1911	55	3	2099	184*	40.36	4
Sharp, P. J. (Yorks.)	(1)	1962	64	9	2252	138	40.94	7
Shepherd, T. F. (Surrey)	(1)	1927	45	6	2145	277*	55.00	8
Sheppard, D. S. (Sussex)	(3)	1951	43	3	2014	183	52.60	7
		1952	39	4	2262	239*	64.62	10
		1953	57	7	2270	186*	45.40	7
Simpson, R. T. (Notts.)	(5)	1949	46	6	2525	238	63.12	6
		1950	47	6	2576	243*	62.82	8
		1952	54	1	2222	216	41.92	5
		1953	60	5	2505	157	45.54	7
		1959	55	5	2033	132	40.66	5
Smith, D. (Derby)	(1)	1935	61	6	2175	225	39.54	2
Smith, D. V. (Sussex)	(1)	1957	54	5	2088	166	42.61	5
Smith, M. J. K. (Warwicks.)	(6)	1957	63	5	2125	127	36.63	3

2000 Runs in an English Season—*Cont.*

		Season	*Inns.*	*N.O.*	*Runs*	*H.S.*	*Avge.*	*100s*
Smith, M. J. K. (*cont.*)		1958	51	3	2126	160	44.29	3
		1959	67	11	3245	200*	57.94	8
		1960	63	7	2551	169*	45.55	4
		1961	67	5	2587	145	41.72	5
		1962	64	12	2290	163	44.03	5
Spooner, R. H. (Lancs.)	(1)	1911	45	0	2312	224	51.37	7
Stewart, M. J. (Surrey)	(1)	1962	55	9	2045	200*	44.45	5
Stewart, W. J. (Warwicks.)	(1)	1962	62	9	2318	182*	43.73	7
Stoddart, A. E. (Middx.)	(1)	1893	50	1	2072	195*	42.28	4
Stott, W. B. (Yorks.)	(1)	1959	56	2	2034	144*	37.66	3
Sutcliffe, B. (New Zealanders) ..	(1)	1949	49	5	2627	243	59.70	7
Sutcliffe, H. (Yorks.)	(15)	1922	48	5	2020	232	46.97	4
		1923	60	6	2220	139	41.11	3
		1924	52	8	2142	255*	48.68	6
		1925	51	8	2308	235	53.67	7
		1926	47	9	2528	200	66.52	8
		1927	49	6	2414	227	56.13	6
		1928	44	5	3002	228	76.97	13
		1929	46	4	2189	150	52.11	9
		1930	44	8	2312	173	64.22	6
		1931	42	11	3006	230	96.96	13
		1932	52	7	3336	313	74.13	14
		1933	52	5	2211	205	47.04	7
		1934	44	3	2023	203	49.34	4
		1935	54	3	2494	212	48.90	8
		1937	54	5	2162	189	44.12	4
Suttle, K. G. (Sussex)	(1)	1962	65	6	2326	204*	39.42	3
Tarrant, F. A. (Middx.)	(1)	1911	48	4	2030	207*	46.13	5
Todd, L. J. (Kent)	(1)	1947	55	5	2312	173	46.24	7
Tompkin, M. (Leics.)	(1)	1955	62	3	2190	131	37.11	3
Townsend, C. L. (Glos.)	(1)	1899	54	7	2440	224*	51.91	9
Townsend, L. F. (Derby)	(1)	1933	59	8	2268	233	44.47	6
Tremlett, M. F. (Somerset)	(1)	1951	59	0	2101	185	35.61	2
Trumper, V. T. (Australians) ..	(1)	1902	53	0	2570	128	48.49	11
Tyldesley, E. (Lancs.)	(6)	1922	57	5	2168	178	41.69	4
		1923	60	6	2040	236	37.77	4
		1926	51	7	2826	226	64.22	10
		1928	48	10	3024	242	79.57	10
		1932	48	7	2420	225*	59.02	8
		1934	51	8	2487	239	57.83	8
Tyldesley, J. T. (Lancs.)	(5)	1901	60	5	3041	221	55.29	9
		1904	44	5	2439	225	62.53	8
		1906	52	3	2270	295*	46.32	4
		1907	63	5	2132	209	36.75	5
		1910	51	2	2265	158	46.22	7
Walters, C. F. (Worcs.)	(2)	1933	52	3	2404	226	50.08	9
		1934	48	4	2048	178	46.54	4
Warner, P. F. (Middx.)	(1)	1911	51	5	2123	244	46.15	5
Washbrook, C. (Lancs.)	(2)	1946	43	8	2400	182	68.57	9
		1947	47	8	2662	251*	68.25	11
Watson, F. (Lancs.)	(3)	1928	46	4	2583	300*	61.05	9
		1929	50	4	2137	207	46.45	6
		1930	47	2	2031	135	45.13	3
Watson, W. (Leics.)	(1)	1959	50	10	2212	173	55.30	7
Weekes, E. D. (West Indians) ..	(1)	1950	33	4	2310	304*	79.65	7
Wharton, A. (Lancs.)	(1)	1959	59	6	2157	199	40.69	4
Whysall, W. W. (Notts.)	(5)	1926	56	5	2138	209	41.92	6
		1927	50	5	2069	184	45.97	5
		1928	51	2	2573	166	52.51	9
		1929	56	3	2716	244	51.24	7
		1930	47	3	2174	248	49.40	8
Wight, P. B. (Somerset)	(2)	1960	62	5	2375	155*	41.66	7
		1962	55	9	2030	215	44.13	4
Wilson, J. V. (Yorks.)	(1)	1951	51	9	2027	223*	48.26	6
Wilson, R. C. (Kent)	(1)	1964	49	5	2038	156	46.31	4
Wood, C. J. B. (Leics.)	(1)	1901	52	3	2033	156	41.48	3

2000 Runs in an English Season—*Cont.*

		Season	*Inns.*	*N.O.*	*Runs*	*H.S.*	*Avge.*	100s
Woolley, F. E. (Kent)	(13)	1914	52	2	2272	160*	45.44	6
		1921	50	1	2101	174	42.87	6
		1922	47	3	2022	188	45.95	5
		1923	56	5	2091	270	41.00	5
		1924	49	2	2344	202	49.87	8
		1925	43	4	2190	215	56.15	5
		1926	50	3	2183	217	46.44	6
		1928	59	4	3352	198	60.94	12
		1929	55	5	2804	176	56.08	11
		1930	50	5	2023	120	44.95	5
		1931	51	4	2301	224	48.95	5
		1934	56	1	2643	176	48.05	10
		1935	56	0	2339	229	41.76	6
Wyatt, R. E. S. (Warwicks.)	(5)	1928	52	10	2408	177	57.33	6
		1929	55	6	2630	161*	53.67	10
		1933	50	10	2379	187*	59.47	8
		1935	55	9	2019	149	43.89	4
		1937	54	5	2625	232	53.57	9
Young, D. M. (Glos.)	(2)	1955	63	1	2106	170	33.96	4
		1959	57	4	2179	148	41.11	6

Note: D. M. Green is the only player to score 2000 runs in a season without hitting a century. His highest innings in 1965 when he scored 2037 runs was only 85, but twenty of his innings were of 40 or more.

Three players have scored 2000 runs in a season while making only one century: James Langridge in 1937, T. C. Dodds in 1947, and J. D. Robertson in 1955.

1000 RUNS IN A SEASON IN AUSTRALIA

		Season	*Inns.*	*N.O.*	*Runs*	*H.S.*	*Avge.*	100s
Amarnath, L. (Indians)	(1)	1947-48	23	3	1162	228*	58.10	5
Armstrong, W. W. (Victoria) ..	(2)	1907-08	16	2	1033	231	73.78	5
		1920-21	15	3	1069	245	89.08	5
Barber, R. W. (M.C.C.)	(1)	1965-66	22	2	1001	185	50.05	3
Bardsley, W. (N.S.W.)	(1)	1910-11	19	1	1233	191*	68.50	3
Barlow, E. J. (South Africans) ..	(1)	1963-64	25	2	1523	209	66.21	6
Barnes, S. G. (N.S.W.)	(1)	1940-41	14	0	1050	185	75.00	6
Barnett, C. J. (M.C.C.)	(1)	1936-37	25	0	1375	259	55.00	5
Barrington, K. F. (M.C.C.) ..	(1)	1965-66	22	5	1451	219*	83.35	5
Booth, B. C. (N.S.W.)	(1)	1963-64	17	4	1180	169*	90.76	5
Bradman, D. G. (N.S.W. and South Australia)	(12)	1928-29	24	6	1690	340*	93.88	7
		1929-30	16	2	1586	452*	113.28	5
		1930-31	18	0	1422	258	79.00	5
		1931-32	13	1	1403	299*	116.91	7
		1932-33	21	2	1171	238	61.63	3
		1933-34	11	2	1192	253	132.44	5
		1935-36	9	0	1173	369	130.33	4
		1936-37	19	1	1552	270	86.22	6
		1937-38	18	2	1437	246	89.81	7
		1939-40	15	3	1475	267	122.91	5
		1946-47	14	1	1032	234	79.38	4
		1947-48	12	2	1296	201	129.60	8
Brown, W. A. (Queensland) ..	(1)	1938-39	11	1	1057	215	105.70	3
Burge, P. J. (Queensland)	(2)	1960-61	22	1	1115	240	53.09	2
		1963-64	17	2	1144	283	76.26	3
Chappell, I. M. (South Australia)	(1)	1965-66	19	2	1019	134	59.94	4
Compton, D. C. S. (M.C.C.) ..	(1)	1946-47	25	3	1432	163	65.09	5
Cowdrey, M. C. (M.C.C.) ..	(1)	1962-63	24	3	1028	307	48.95	2
Cowper, R. M. (Victoria)	(1)	1965-66	21	2	1418	307	74.63	4
Dexter, E. R. (M.C.C.)	(1)	1962-63	24	1	1023	102	44.47	1
Endean, W. R. (South Africans) ..	(1)	1952-53	27	3	1281	181*	53.37	2
Faulkner, G. A. (South Africans)	(1)	1910-11	27	1	1534	204	59.00	3
Goddard, T. L. (South Africans) ..	(1)	1963-64	20	3	1054	194	62.00	1
Hammond, W. R. (M.C.C.) ..	(2)	1928-29	18	1	1553	251	91.35	7
		1936-37	20	2	1206	231*	67.00	5

1000 Runs in a Season in Australia—*Cont.*

	Season	Inns.	N.O.	Runs	H.S.	Avge.	100s
Hardstaff, J., Snr. (M.C.C.) .. (1)	1907-08	28	2	1360	135	52.30	3
Harvey, R. N. (Victoria and N.S.W.) (4)	1950-51	25	1	1099	146	45.79	3
	1952-53	27	1	1659	205	63.80	5
	1954-55	24	2	1009	162	45.86	1
	1962-63	22	2	1107	231*	55.35	3
Hassett, A. L. (Victoria) .. .. (2)	1946-47	18	1	1213	200	71.35	5
	1950-51	25	3	1423	232	64.68	4
Hazare, Vijay (Indians) .. .. (1)	1947-48	23	1	1056	145	48.00	4
Headley, G. A. (West Indians) .. (1)	1930-31	25	1	1066	131	44.41	4
Hendren, E. (M.C.C.) .. .. (3)	1920-21	20	1	1178	271	62.00	3
	1924-25	22	3	1233	168	64.89	4
	1928-29	17	1	1033	169	64.56	3
Hill, C. (South Australia).. .. (2)	1897-98	19	1	1186	200	65.89	5
	1901-02	20	0	1035	107	50.17	1
Hutton, L. (M.C.C.) .. .. (2)	1946-47	21	3	1267	151*	70.38	3
	1950-51	21	4	1199	156*	70.52	5
Jardine, D. R. (M.C.C.) .. .. (1)	1928-29	19	1	1168	214	64.88	6
Kanhai, R. B. (West Indians) .. (1)	1960-61	18	1	1093	252	64.29	4
Kippax, A. F. (N.S.W.) .. .. (2)	1926-27	13	1	1039	217*	86.58	5
	1928-29	19	2	1079	260*	63.47	4
Lawry, W. M. (Victoria) .. .. (3)	1960-61	20	1	1042	266	54.84	2
	1963-64	24	4	1340	187*	67.00	4
	1965-66	21	1	1445	166	72.25	6
MacLaren, A. C. .. .. .. (1)	1897-98	20	1	1037	142	54.57	5
May, P. B. H. (M.C.C.) .. .. (1)	1958-59	22	1	1197	140	57.00	5
Miller, K. R. (Victoria and N.S.W.) (2)	1946-47	19	3	1202	206*	75.12	4
	1950-51	20	3	1332	214	78.35	5
Morris, A. R. (N.S.W.) .. .. (3)	1946-47	20	2	1234	155	68.55	5
	1948-49	17	1	1069	177	66.81	6
	1950-51	22	1	1221	206	58.14	6
Noble, M. A. (N.S.W.) .. .. (1)	1907-08	19	1	1071	176	59.50	3
Nourse, A. D., Snr. (South Africans) (1)	1910-11	29	5	1454	201*	60.58	5
O'Neill, N. C. (N.S.W.) .. .. (2)	1957-58	14	2	1005	233	83.75	4
	1960-61	27	3	1288	181	53.66	5
Pollock, R. G. (South Africans) .. (1)	1963-64	20	1	1018	175	53.57	5
Ponsford, W. H. (Victoria) .. (2)	1926-27	10	0	1229	352	122.90	6
	1927-28	8	0	1217	437	152.12	4
Ranjitsinhji, K. S. .. .. .. (1)	1897-98	22	3	1157	189	60.89	3
Rhodes, W. (M.C.C.) .. .. (1)	1911-12	24	4	1098	179	54.90	4
Ryder, J. (Victoria) .. .. (1)	1928-29	17	2	1045	175	69.66	3
Shepherd, B. K. (Western Australia) (2)	1962-63	21	2	1001	219	52.68	2
	1963-64	23	1	1087	149	49.40	3
Simpson, R. B. (Western Australia (3)	1960-61	26	2	1542	221*	64.25	4
and N.S.W.)	1962-63	24	2	1337	205	60.77	5
	1963-64	25	2	1524	359	66.26	4
Sobers, G. St. A. (South Australia) (2)	1962-63	18	2	1006	196	62.87	3
	1963-64	14	0	1128	195	80.57	6
Sutcliffe, H. (M.C.C.) .. .. (2)	1924-25	18	0	1250	188	69.44	5
	1932-33	19	1	1318	194	73.22	5
Thomas, G. (N.S.W.) .. .. (1)	1965-66	20	1	1171	229	58.55	4
Trimble, S. C. (Queensland) .. (1)	1963-64	14	2	1006	252*	83.83	5
Trumper, V. T. (N.S.W.).. .. (1)	1910-11	20	2	1246	214*	69.22	3
Walters, K. D. (N.S.W.) .. .. (1)	1965-66	21	2	1332	168	70.11	6

Only seven Australian batsmen have scored 1000 runs in a purely domestic sesaon: S. G. Barnes, D. G. Bradman, W. A. Brown, A. F. Kippax, A. R. Morris, N. C. O'Neill and W. H. Ponsford.

1000 RUNS IN A SEASON IN SOUTH AFRICA

	Season	Inns.	N.O.	Runs	H.S.	Avge.	100s
J. R. Reid (New Zealanders)	1961-62	30	2	1915	203	68.39	7
D. C. S. Compton (M.C.C.)	1948-49	26	5	1781	300	84.80	8
R. N. Harvey (Australians)	1949-50	25	5	1526	178	76.30	8
J. B. Hobbs (M.C.C.)	1913-14	22	2	1489	170	74.45	5

1000 Runs in a Season in South Africa—*Cont.*

	Season	*Inns.*	*N.O.*	*Runs*	*H.S.*	*Avge.*	*100s*
L. Hutton (M.C.C.)	1948-49	21	1	1477	174	73.85	5
A. R. Morris (Australians)	1949-50	27	3	1411	157	58.79	8
R. B. Simpson (Australians)	1966-67	26	4	1344	243	61.09	3
J. A. R. Moroney (Australians)	1949-50	27	3	1331	160*	55.45	6
P. B. H. May (M.C.C.)	1956-57	24	1	1270	206	55.21	6
J. B. Hobbs (M.C.C.)	1909-10	20	1	1194	187	62.84	3
J. H. Fingleton (Australians)	1935-36	19	4	1192	167	79.46	6
L. Hutton (M.C.C.)	1938-39	19	1	1168	202	64.88	5
B. Sutcliffe (New Zealanders)	1953-54	27	2	1155	196	46.20	1
G. Boycott (M.C.C.)	1964-65	25	5	1135	193*	56.75	4
E. Tyldesley (M.C.C.)	1927-28	21	2	1130	161	59.47	4
K. F. Barrington (M.C.C.)	1964-65	18	5	1128	169*	86.76	4
C. Washbrook (M.C.C.)	1948-49	23	2	1124	195	53.52	3
R. M. Cowper (Australians)	1966-67	25	2	1116	201*	48.52	2
P. Holmes (M.C.C.)	1927-28	22	3	1112	279*	58.52	3
E. Paynter (M.C.C.)	1938-39	14	0	1072	243	76.57	5
W. A. Brown (Australians)	1935-36	19	2	1065	148	62.64	2
K. C. Bland (Rhodesia)	1964-65	18	3	1048	151*	69.86	3
W. R. Hammond (M.C.C.)	1930-31	19	2	1045	136*	61.47	3
I. R. Redpath (Australians)	1966-67	23	3	1045	154	52.25	2
J. W. Burke (Australians)	1957-58	19	3	1041	189	65.06	4
M. C. Cowdrey (M.C.C.)	1956-57	27	1	1035	173	39.80	2
H. Sutcliffe (M.C.C.)	1927-28	23	3	1030	102	51.50	2
W. R. Hammond (M.C.C.)	1938-39	18	1	1025	181	60.29	4
D. Lindsay (North-Eastern Transvaal) ..	1966-67	14	0	1014	216	72.42	4
J. R. Reid (New Zealanders)	1953-54	27	0	1012	175	37.48	3

Highest aggregates by home batsmen:

	Season	*Inns.*	*N.O.*	*Runs*	*H.S.*	*Avge.*	*100s*
K. C. Bland (Rhodesia)	1964-65	18	3	1048	151*	69.86	3
D. Lindsay (North-Eastern Transvaal) ..	1966-67	14	0	1014	216	72.42	4
A. J. Pithey (Rhodesia)	1964-65	16	2	957	154	68.35	2
D. J. McGlew (Natal)	1957-58	21	2	953	213*	50.16	3
E. A. B. Rowan (Transvaal)	1952-53	12	0	899	196	74.91	3
W. S. Farrer (Border)	1962-63	17	3	888	107*	63.42	2
A. D. Nourse, Jnr. (Natal)	1948-49	16	3	877	129*	67.46	3
A. D. Nourse, Jnr. (Natal)	1947-48	11	2	864	214*	96.00	4
P. R. Carlstein (Transvaal)	1962-63	13	1	852	229	71.00	3
A. D. Nourse, Jnr. (Natal)	1936-37	6	1	846	260*	169.20	4
R. G. Pollock (Eastern Province) ..	1962-63	15	3	836	209*	69.66	3
T. L. Goddard (North-Eastern Transvaal)	1966-67	17	0	830	222	48.82	1
H. W. Taylor (Natal)	1913-14	14	2	824	109	68.66	2
B. J. Versfeld (Natal)	1965-66	13	3	824	201	82.40	3
A. D. Nourse, Jnr. (Natal)	1946-47	12	0	775	192	64.58	2
A. Bacher (Transvaal)	1966-67	17	1	770	235	48.12	1
M. J. Susskind (Transvaal)	1931-32	13	1	769	124	64.08	4
A. D. Nourse, Snr. (Natal)	1921-22	16	2	768	143	54.85	3
E. A. B. Rowan (Transvaal)	1950-51	9	2	765	277*	109.28	3
E. J. Barlow (Eastern Province)	1964-65	16	0	761	138	47.56	1

OVER 700 RUNS IN THE WEST INDIES

	Season	*Inns.*	*N.O.*	*Runs*	*H.S.*	*Avge.*	*100s*
E. Hendren (M.C.C.)	1929-30	18	5	1765	254	135.76	6
A. Sandham (M.C.C.)	1929-30	20	0	1281	325	64.05	6
M. C. Cowdrey (M.C.C.)	1959-60	18	2	1014	173	63.37	5
G. St. A. Sobers (Barbados)	1957-58	10	3	1007	365*	143.85	4
E. D. Weekes (Barbados)	1952-53	9	1	969	253	121.12	4
C. L. Walcott (Barbados)	1954-55	13	0	945	155	72.69	5
E. R. Dexter (M.C.C.)	1959-60	18	2	908	136*	56.75	3
W. Watson (M.C.C.)	1953-54	16	3	892	257	68.61	4
G. A. Headley (Jamaica)	1929-30	11	0	891	223	81.00	4
Hanif Mohammad (Pakistanis)	1957-58	16	1	867	337	57.80	2
G. St. A. Sobers (Barbados)	1959-60	9	1	863	226	107.87	4
R. M. Cowper (Australians)	1964-65	15	1	854	188	61.00	4

Over 700 Runs in the West Indies—*Cont.*

	Season	Inns.	N.O.	Runs	H.S.	Avge.	100s
Wazir Mohammad (Pakistanis)	1957-58	16	4	850	189	70.83	4
K. F. Barrington (M.C.C.)	1959-60	19	1	830	128	46.11	3
L. E. G. Ames (M.C.C.)	1929-30	19	2	818	149	48.11	4
P. R. Umrigar (Indians)	1952-53	16	3	813	130	62.53	2
P. Holmes (M.C.C.)	1925-26	17	0	797	244	46.88	1
W. M. Lawry (Australians)	1964-65	15	3	791	210	65.91	2
W. R. Hammond (M.C.C.)	1934-35	17	3	789	281*	56.35	3
R. N. Harvey (Australians)	1954-55	12	2	789	204	78.90	3
Saeed Ahmed (Pakistanis)	1957-58	16	0	784	150	49.00	1
R. B. Simpson (Australians)	1964-65	14	1	784	201	60.31	3
L. Hutton (M.C.C.)	1953-54	12	2	780	205	78.00	2
G. Pullar (M.C.C.)	1959-60	18	2	777	141	48.56	1
G. St. A. Sobers (Barbados)	1964-65	14	2	734	183*	61.16	2
W. R. Hammond (M.C.C.)	1925-26	18	3	732	238*	48.80	2
G. A. Headley (Jamaica)	1931-32	4	2	723	344*	361.50	3
C. L. Walcott (Barbados)	1953-54	12	2	723	220	72.30	3
G. Gunn (M.C.C.)	1929-30	17	0	707	178	41.59	1
C. C. Hunte (Barbados)	1957-58	11	1	706	260	70.60	3

OVER 600 RUNS IN NEW ZEALAND

	Season	Inns.	N.O.	Runs	H.S.	Avge.	100s
E. D. Weekes (West Indians)	1955-56	10	1	940	156	104.44	6
G. T. Dowling (Canterbury)	1966-67	18	2	871	102*	54.43	1
B. Sutcliffe (Otago)	1952-53	13	0	859	385	66.07	1
B. Sutcliffe (Otago)	1950-51	12	0	798	275	66.50	4
W. M. Woodfull (Australians)	1927-28	9	3	781	284	130.16	3
B. Sutcliffe (Otago)	1947-48	8	1	747	208*	106.71	4
B. Sutcliffe (Otago)	1959-60	17	1	747	264	46.88	2
J. R. Reid (Wellington)	1959-60	16	1	724	165*	48.26	2
B. Sutcliffe (Auckland & Otago)	1946-47	8	1	722	197	103.14	3
W. M. Woodfull (Victoria)	1924-25	9	5	710	212*	177.50	3
R. M. Prideaux (M.C.C.)	1960-61	18	2	710	160	44.37	1
J. T. Sparling (Auckland)	1959-60	20	1	705	105	37.11	1
B. W. Sinclair (Wellington)	1965-66	17	2	700	114	46.66	1
B. Sutcliffe (Otago)	1949-50	9	0	698	355	77.55	2
J. R. Reid (Wellington)	1962-63	14	1	681	296	52.38	2
L. S. M. Miller (Wellington)	1955-56	16	1	679	144	45.26	2
Saeed Ahmed (Pakistanis)	1964-65	17	0	675	142	39.70	2
B. Sutcliffe (Otago)	1960-61	13	3	665	201	66.50	1
J. L. Kerr (Canterbury)	1935-36	13	2	655	146*	59.54	3
C. G. Macartney (Australians)	1923-24	8	1	641	221	91.57	3
B. W. Sinclair (Wellington)	1963-64	15	1	641	138	45.78	2
R. W. Morgan (Auckland)	1964-65	15	2	633	112*	48.69	1
B. F. Hastings (Canterbury)	1964-65	10	0	629	226	62.90	2
V. T. Trumper (Australians)	1913-14	9	0	628	293	89.51	1
Hanif Mohammad (Pakistanis)	1964-65	16	2	627	100*	44.78	1
W. Bardsley (N.S.W.)	1923-24	7	2	623	200*	124.00	1
S. G. Gedye (Auckland)	1963-64	20	0	621	104	31.05	2
J. S. Hiddleston (Wellington)	1923-24	12	0	619	163	51.58	2
C. S. Dempster (Wellington)	1927-28	12	1	616	145	56.00	1
P. F. Warner (Lord Hawke's XI)	1902-03	10	1	615	211	68.33	2
R. V. de W. Worker (Otago)	1923-24	12	0	606	172	50.50	2

1000 RUNS IN A SEASON IN INDIA, PAKISTAN AND CEYLON

		Season	Inns.	N.O.	Runs	H.S.	Avge.	100s
Alim-ud-Din	(1)	1961-62	22	2	1020	131*	51.00	4
Alley, W. E. (Commonwealth)	(1)	1949-50	28	9	1255	209*	66.05	3
Barrington, K. F. (M.C.C.)	(1)	1961-62	26	7	1329	172	69.94	5
Borde, C. G.	(2)	1964-65	28	3	1604	168	64.16	6
		1966-67	26	4	1480	155*	67.27	5
Butcher, B. F. (West Indians)	(1)	1958-59	29	5	1133	142	47.20	2
Dexter, E. R. (M.C.C.)	(1)	1961-62	27	5	1053	205	47.86	2
Emmett, G. M. (Commonwealth)	(1)	1950-51	37	5	1296	104	40.50	2

1000 Runs in a Season in India, Pakistan and Ceylon—*Cont.*

		Season	*Inns.*	*N.O.*	*Runs*	*H.S.*	*Avge.*	*100s*
Engineer, F. M.	(1)	1964-65	23	1	1050	142	47.72	2
Fishlock, L. B. (Commonwealth) ..	(1)	1950-51	32	2	1123	138	37.43	3
Gimblett, H. (Commonwealth) ..	(1)	1950-51	38	6	1269	111	39.65	1
Graveney, T. W. (M.C.C.)	(1)	1951-52	32	7	1393	175	55.72	6
Grieves, K. J. (Commonwealth) ..	(1)	1950-51	32	4	1193	155	42.60	2
Hanif Mohammad	(2)	1952-53	20	5	1010	203*	67.33	4
		1961-62	21	0	1250	189	59.52	5
Hanumant Singh	(3)	1963-64	26	4	1234	179	56.09	5
		1964-65	30	6	1270	210	52.91	3
		1966-67	27	4	1586	213*	68.95	6
Hazare, Vijay	(4)	1943-44	7	0	1066	309	152.28	4
		1948-49	21	3	1310	146	72.77	6
		1949-50	19	3	1364	195	85.24	5
		1950-51	20	3	1140	186	67.05	5
Holt, J. K., Jnr.	(1)	1958-59	27	4	1001	123	43.52	3
Hunte, C. C. (West Indians) ..	(1)	1958-59	32	3	1127	137	38.86	1
Ibrahim, K. C.	(1)	1947-48	11	4	1171	234*	167.28	4
Ikin, J. T. (Commonwealth) ..	(1)	1950-51	33	5	1292	111	46.14	2
Imtiaz Ahmed	(1)	1961-62	24	1	1142	251	49.65	4
Jaisimha, M. L.	(3)	1959-60	23	2	1143	164	54.42	4
		1962-63	22	3	1003	124	52.78	3
		1964-65	31	0	1416	259	45.67	5
Kanhai, R. B. (West Indians) ..	(1)	1958-59	28	2	1518	256	58.38	4
Kunderan, B. K.	(1)	1963-64	29	1	1079	192	38.53	3
Livingston, T. L. (Commonwealth)	(1)	1949-50	25	5	1020	123	51.00	3
Lowson, F. A. (M.C.C.)	(1)	1951-52	28	5	1016	138	44.17	1
Manjrekar, V. L.	(1)	1963-64	21	2	1077	283	56.68	5
Merchant, V. M.	(1)	1944-45	15	3	1323	275	110.25	5
Meuleman, K. D. (Commonwealth)	(1)	1953-54	26	4	1158	131	52.63	3
Modi, R. S.	(1)	1944-45	15	3	1386	245*	115.50	6
Mushtaq Mohammad	(1)	1961-62	20	2	1112	229*	61.77	4
Nadkarni, R. G.	(1)	1962-63	19	2	1190	219	70.00	2
Parfitt, P. H. (M.C.C.)	(1)	1961-62	29	4	1043	166*	41.72	3
Parsons, J. H. (M.C.C.)	(1)	1926-27	28	2	1289	160	49.58	2
Pataudi, Nawab of, Jnr.	(2)	1963-64	31	1	1031	203*	34.36	2
		1964-65	27	3	1416	154	59.00	7
Pullar, G. (M.C.C.)	(1)	1961-62	25	1	1046	165	43.58	3
Rae, A. F. (West Indians)	(1)	1948-49	25	0	1150	160	46.00	6
Reid, J. R. (New Zealanders) ..	(1)	1955-56	25	6	1024	150*	53.89	3
Richardson, P. E. (M.C.C.) ..	(1)	1961-62	30	3	1003	147	37.14	1
Robertson, J. D. (M.C.C.)	(1)	1951-52	31	3	1173	183	41.89	3
Sandham, A. (M.C.C.)	(1)	1926-27	30	2	1756	150	62.71	7
Sardesai, D. N.	(3)	1963-64	29	2	1197	110	44.33	2
		1964-65	27	4	1428	222	62.08	6
		1966-67	20	1	1190	199	62.63	4
Sobers, G. St. A. (West Indians) ..	(1)	1958-59	26	5	1419	198	67.57	5
Stollmeyer, J. B. (West Indians) ..	(1)	1948-49	22	5	1091	244*	64.17	2
Sutcliffe, B. (New Zealanders) ..	(1)	1955-56	28	4	1031	230*	42.95	3
Tate, M. W. (M.C.C.)	(1)	1926-27	33	0	1193	133	36.15	3
Umrigar, P. R.	(2)	1955-56	14	2	1028	223	85.66	3
		1962-63	19	2	1065	124*	62.64	4
Wadekar, A. L.	(2)	1965-66	24	4	1325	185	66.25	6
		1966-67	23	1	1321	323	60.04	3
Walcott, C. L. (West Indians) ..	(1)	1948-49	22	4	1366	152	75.88	5
Weekes, E. D. (West Indians) ..	(1)	1948-49	19	4	1350	194	90.00	6
Worrell, F. M. M. (Commonwealth)	(2)	1949-50	26	4	1640	223*	74.54	5
		1950-51	33	3	1900	285	63.33	5
Wyatt, R. E. S. (M.C.C.) ..	(1)	1926-27	37	4	1747	138	52.93	5

MOST CENTURIES IN A SEASON

In 1871, W. G. Grace became the first player to score ten centuries in an English season. No player has reached this aggregate overseas but the home record has progressed as follows: 12—R. Abel (1900), 13—C. B. Fry (1901), 16—J. B. Hobbs (1925) and 18—D. C. S. Compton (1947).

Most Centuries in a Season—*Cont.*

UNITED KINGDOM

18	D. C. S. Compton (Middx.) ..	1947	13	H. Sutcliffe (Yorks.)	1928
16	J. B. Hobbs (Surrey)	1925	13	H. Sutcliffe (Yorks.)	1931
15	W. R. Hammond (Glos.) ..	1938	12	R. Abel (Surrey)	1900
14	H. Sutcliffe (Yorks.)	1932	12	K. S. Duleepsinhji (Sussex) ..	1931
13	D. G. Bradman (Australians) ..	1938	12	W. J. Edrich (Middx.) ..	1947
13	C. B. Fry (Sussex)	1901	12	W. R. Hammond (Glos.) ..	1927
13	W. R. Hammond (Glos.) ..	1933	12	J. B. Hobbs (Surrey)	1928
13	W. R. Hammond (Glos.) ..	1937	12	L. Hutton (Yorks.)	1939
13	T. W. Hayward (Surrey) ..	1906	12	L. Hutton (Yorks.)	1949
13	E. Hendren (Middx.)	1923	12	John Langridge (Sussex) ..	1949
13	E. Hendren (Middx.)	1927	12	J. D. Robertson (Middx.) ..	1947
13	E. Hendren (Middx.)	1928	12	F. E. Woolley (Kent) ..	1928
13	C. P. Mead (Hants.)	1928			

OVERSEAS

Australia .. 8—D. G. Bradman (1947-48), 7—D. G. Bradman (1928-29, 1931-32 and 1937-38), W. R. Hammond (1928-29).
South Africa .. 8—D. C. S. Compton (1948-49), R. N. Harvey, A. R. Morris (1949-50).
West Indies .. 6—E. Hendren (1929-30), A. Sandham (1929-30).
New Zealand .. 6—E. D. Weekes (1955-56).
India .. .. 7—A. Sandham (1926-27), Nawab of Pataudi, Jnr. (1964-65).
Pakistan .. .. 5—Hanif Mohammad (1961-62).

LEADING HOME BATSMEN OF THE ENGLISH SEASON 1894-1967

(*Qualifications: highest average*—20 *innings*)

Season		*Inns.*	*N.O.*	*Runs*	*H.S.*	*Avge.*	100*s*
1894	W. Brockwell (Surrey)	45	6	1491	128	38.23	5
1895	A. C. MacLaren (Lancs.)	24	0	1229	424	51.20	4
1896	K. S. Ranjitsinhji (Sussex)	55	7	2780	171*	57.91	10
1897	N. F. Druce (Cambridge U. & Surrey) ..	20	2	928	227*	51.55	3
1898	W. G. Quaife (Warwicks.)	28	8	1219	157*	60.95	3
1899	R. M. Poore (Hants.)	21	4	1551	304	91.23	7
1900	K. S. Ranjitsinhji (Sussex)	40	5	3065	275	87.57	11
1901	C. B. Fry (Sussex)	43	3	3147	244	78.67	13
1902	A. Shrewsbury (Notts.)	32	7	1250	127*	50.00	4
1903	C. B. Fry (Sussex)	40	7	2683	234	81.30	9
1904	K. S. Ranjitsinhji (Sussex)	34	6	2077	207*	74.17	8
1905	C. B. Fry (Sussex)	44	4	2801	233	70.02	10
1906	C. J. Burnup (Kent)	21	3	1207	179	67.05	4
1907	C. B. Fry (Sussex)	34	3	1449	187	46.74	4
1908	B. J. T. Bosanquet (Middx.)	22	2	1081	214	54.05	3
1909	A. P. Day (Kent)	24	1	1014	177	44.08	3
1910	J. T. Tyldesley (Lancs.)	51	2	2265	158	46.22	7
1911	C. B. Fry (Hants.)	26	2	1728	258*	72.00	7
1912	C. B. Fry (Hants.)	31	3	1592	203*	56.85	5
1913	C. P. Mead (Hants.)	60	8	2627	171*	50.51	9
1914	J. W. Hearne (Middx.)	43	8	2116	204	60.45	8
1919	G. Gunn (Notts.)	25	2	1451	185*	63.08	5
1920	E. Hendren (Middx.)	47	6	2520	232	61.46	6
1921	C. P. Mead (Hants.)	52	6	3179	280*	69.10	10
1922	E. Hendren (Middx.)	38	7	2072	277	66.83	7
1923	E. Hendren (Middx.)	51	12	3010	200*	77.17	13
1924	A. Sandham (Surrey)	37	2	2082	169	59.48	7
1925	J. B. Hobbs (Surrey)	48	5	3024	266*	70.32	16
1926	J. B. Hobbs (Surrey)	41	3	2949	316*	77.60	10
1927	C. Hallows (Lancs.)	44	13	2343	233*	75.58	7
1928	J. B. Hobbs (Surrey)	38	7	2542	200*	82.00	12
1929	J. B. Hobbs (Surrey)	39	5	2263	204	66.55	10
1930	H. Sutcliffe (Yorks.)	44	8	2312	173	64.22	6
1931	H. Sutcliffe (Yorks.)	42	11	3006	230	96.96	13
1932	H. Sutcliffe (Yorks.)	52	7	3336	313	74.13	14

Leading Home Batsmen of the English Season—*Cont.*

Season		*Inns.*	*N.O.*	*Runs*	*H.S.*	*Avge.*	*100s*
1933	W. R. Hammond (Glos.)	54	5	3323	264	67.81	13
1934	W. R. Hammond (Glos.)	35	4	2366	302*	76.32	8
1935	W. R. Hammond (Glos.)	58	5	2616	252	49.35	7
1936	W. R. Hammond (Glos.)	42	5	2107	317	56.94	5
1937	W. R. Hammond (Glos.)	55	5	3252	217	65.04	13
1938	W. R. Hammond (Glos.)	42	2	3011	271	75.27	15
1939	W. R. Hammond (Glos.)	46	7	2479	302	63.56	8
1946	W. R. Hammond (Glos.)	26	5	1783	214	84.90	7
1947	D. C. S. Compton (Middx.)	50	8	3816	246	90.85	18
1948	C. Washbrook (Lancs.)	31	4	1900	200	70.37	7
1949	J. Hardstaff, Jnr. (Notts.)	40	9	2251	162*	72.61	8
1950	R. T. Simpson (Notts.)	47	6	2576	243*	62.82	8
1951	P. B. H. May (Cambridge U. & Surrey)	43	9	2339	178*	68.79	9
1952	D. S. Sheppard (Cambridge U. & Sussex)	39	4	2262	239*	64.62	10
1953	L. Hutton (Yorks.)	44	5	2458	241	63.02	8
1954	D. C. S. Compton (Middx.)	28	2	1524	278	58.62	4
1955	P. B. H. May (Surrey)	42	5	1902	125	51.40	5
1956	T. W. Graveney (Glos.)	54	6	2397	200	49.93	9
1957	P. B. H. May (Surrey)	41	3	2347	285*	61.76	7
1958	P. B. H. May (Surrey)	41	6	2231	174	63.74	8
1959	M. J. K. Smith (Warwicks.)	67	11	3245	200*	57.94	8
1960	R. Subba Row (Northants.)	32	5	1503	147*	55.66	4
1961	K. F. Barrington (Surrey)	42	7	2070	163	59.14	4
1962	R. T. Simpson (Notts.)	20	4	867	105	54.18	2
1963	M. J. K. Smith (Warwicks.)	39	6	1566	144*	47.45	3
1964	K. F. Barrington (Surrey)	35	5	1872	256	62.40	4
1965	M. C. Cowdrey (Kent)	43	10	2093	196*	63.42	5
1966	T. W. Graveney (Worcs.)	40	6	1777	166	52.26	4
1967	K. F. Barrington (Surrey)	40	10	2059	158*	68.63	6

The following touring players achieved a higher average than that of the leading English batsman of the season:

1909	W. Bardsley (Australians)	49	4	2072	219	46.04	6
1930	D. G. Bradman (Australians)	36	6	2960	334	98.66	10
1934	D. G. Bradman (Australians)	27	3	2020	304	84.16	7
1934	W. H. Ponsford (Australians)	27	4	1784	281*	77.56	5
1938	D. G. Bradman (Australians)	26	5	2429	278	115.66	13
1939	G. A. Headley (West Indians)	30	6	1745	234*	72.70	6
1948	D. G. Bradman (Australians)	31	4	2428	187	89.92	11
1948	A. L. Hassett (Australians)	27	6	1563	200*	74.42	7
1948	A. R. Morris (Australians)	29	2	1922	290	71.18	7
1950	E. D. Weekes (West Indians)	33	4	2310	304*	79.65	7
1950	F. M. M. Worrell (West Indians) ..	31	5	1775	261	68.26	6
1953	R. N. Harvey (Australians)	35	4	2040	202*	65.80	10
1955	D. J. McGlew (South Africans)	34	2	1871	161	58.46	5
1956	K. D. Mackay (Australians)	28	7	1103	163*	52.52	3
1961	W. M. Lawry (Australians)	39	6	2019	165	61.18	9
1961	N. C. O'Neill (Australians)	37	4	1981	162	60.03	7
1963	G. St. A. Sobers (West Indians) ..	34	6	1333	112	47.60	4
1966	G. St. A. Sobers (West Indians) ..	25	3	1349	174	61.31	4

HIGHEST BATTING AVERAGES IN AN ENGLISH SEASON

(*Qualifications:* 12 *innings—average* 70.00)

D. G. Bradman achieved the unique distinction of averaging over 80 on each of his four tours of England: 98.66 in 1930, 84.16 in 1934, 115.66 in 1938, and 89.92 in 1948. On each visit he exceeded the average of the leading home batsman of the season.

	Season	*Inns.*	*N.O.*	*Runs*	*H.S.*	*Avge.*	*100s*
D. G. Bradman (Australians)	1938	26	5	2429	278	115.66	13
W. A. Johnston (Australians)	1953	17	16	102	28*	102.00	—
D. G. Bradman (Australians)	1930	36	6	2960	334	98.66	10

Highest Batting Averages in an English Season—*Cont.*

	Season	*Inns.*	*N.O.*	*Runs*	*H.S.*	*Avge.*	*100s*
H. Sutcliffe (Yorks.)	1931	42	11	3006	230	96.96	13
R. M. Poore (Hants.)	1899	21	4	1551	304	91.23	7
D. R. Jardine (Surrey)	1927	14	3	1002	147	91.09	5
D. C. S. Compton (Middx.) ..	1947	50	8	3816	246	90.85	18
D. G. Bradman (Australians)	1948	31	4	2428	187	89.92	11
K. S. Ranjitsinhji (Sussex)	1900	40	5	3065	275	87.57	11
D. R. Jardine (Surrey)	1928	17	4	1133	193	87.15	3
W. R. Hammond (Glos.)	1946	26	5	1783	214	84.90	7
D. G. Bradman (Australians)	1934	27	3	2020	304	84.16	7
J. B. Hobbs (Surrey)	1928	38	7	2542	200*	82.00	12
C. B. Fry (Sussex)	1903	40	7	2683	234	81.30	9
W. J. Edrich (Middx.)	1947	52	8	3539	267*	80.43	12
E. D. Weekes (West Indians)	1950	33	4	2310	304*	79.65	7
E. Tyldesley (Lancs.)	1928	48	10	3024	242	79.57	10
Nawab of Pataudi, Snr. (Worcs.) ..	1934	15	3	945	214*	78.75	3
A. Shrewsbury (Notts.)	1887	23	2	1653	267	78.71	8
C. B. Fry (Sussex)	1901	43	3	3147	244	78.67	13
W. G. Grace (Glos.)	1871	39	4	2739	268	78.25	10
J. B. Hobbs (Surrey)	1926	41	3	2949	316*	77.60	10
W. H. Ponsford (Australians)	1934	27	4	1784	281*	77.56	5
E. Hendren (Middx.)	1923	51	12	3010	200*	77.17	13
H. Sutcliffe (Yorks.)	1928	44	5	3002	228	76.97	13
W. R. Hammond (Glos.)	1934	35	4	2366	302*	76.32	8
C. P. Mead (Hants.)	1928	50	10	3027	180	75.67	13
C. Hallows (Lancs.)	1927	44	13	2343	233*	75.58	7
W. R. Hammond (Glos.)	1938	42	2	3011	271	75.27	15
C. P. Mead (Hants.)	1927	41	9	2385	200*	74.53	8
V. M. Merchant (Indians)	1946	41	9	2385	242*	74.53	7
A. L. Hassett (Australians)	1948	27	6	1563	200*	74.42	7
K. S. Ranjitsinhji (Sussex)	1904	34	6	2077	207*	74.17	8
H. Sutcliffe (Yorks.)	1932	52	7	3336	313	74.13	14
E. Hendren (Middx.)	1927	43	5	2784	201*	73.26	13
G. A. Headley (West Indians) ..	1939	30	6	1745	234*	72.70	6
J. Hardstaff, Jnr. (Notts.)	1949	40	9	2251	162*	72.61	8
K. R. Miller (Australian services) ..	1945	13	3	725	185	72.50	3
C. B. Fry (Hants.)	1911	26	2	1728	258*	72.00	7
W. G. Grace (Glos.)	1873	38	8	2139	192*	71.30	7
A. R. Morris (Australians)	1948	29	2	1922	290	71.18	7
C. B. Fry (Sussex)	1904	42	2	2824	229	70.60	10
K. S. Ranjitsinhji (Sussex)	1901	40	5	2468	285*	70.51	8
E. Hendren (Middx.)	1928	54	7	3311	209*	70.44	13
C. Washbrook (Lancs.)	1948	31	4	1900	200	70.37	7
J. B. Hobbs (Surrey)	1925	48	5	3024	266*	70.32	16
C. B. Fry (Sussex)	1905	44	4	2801	233	70.02	10

1000 RUNS WITH AVERAGE UNDER 20

A few players have managed to reach an aggregate of 1000 runs in an English season without attaining an average of 20.

	Season	*Inns.*	*N.O.*	*Runs*	*H.S.*	*Avge.*
A. H. H. Gilligan (Sussex)	1923	70	3	1186	68	17.70
J. J. Lyons (Australians)	1890	59	1	1029	99	17.74
G. H. S. Trott (Australians)	1888	61	2	1081	73	18.32
A. W. Wellard (Somerset)	1937	60	4	1049	91*	18.73
D. Kirby (Leics.)	1962	53	0	1007	118	19.00
J. E. Timms (Northants.)	1932	55	1	1032	97	19.11
A. F. T. White (Worcs.)	1947	54	2	1001	79	19.25
W. E. Bates (Glamorgan)	1931	52	0	1001	74	19.25
G. Ulyett (Yorks.)	1886	52	0	1005	78	19.32
M. W. Tate (Sussex)	1922	56	2	1050	88	19.44
J. T. Murray (Middx.)	1957	57	5	1025	120	19.71
C. H. Bull (Worcs.)	1936	54	0	1066	108	19.74
J. Lawrence (Somerset)	1953	52	1	1015	89	19.90
F. J. Titmus (Middx.)	1957	56	3	1056	70	19.92
J. B. Mortimore (Glos.)	1964	58	2	1118	95	19.96

BATSMEN SCORING 1000 RUNS IN A MONTH

Month	*Season*		*Inns.*	*N.O.*	*Runs*	*H.S.*	*Avge.*
May	1895	W. G. Grace (Glos.)	10	1	1016	288	112.88
	1927	W. R. Hammond (Glos.)	14	0	1042	192	74.42
	1928	C. Hallows (Lancs.)	11	3	1000	232	125.00
June	1899	K. S. Ranjitsinhji (Sussex)	15	2	1037	197	79.76
	1901	C. B. Fry (Sussex)	11	2	1130	244	125.55
	1904	J. Iremonger (Notts.)	11	1	1010	272	101.00
	1921	C. P. Mead (Hants.)	13	1	1159	280*	96.58
	1925	E. Hendren (Middx.)	12	2	1122	240	112.20
	1925	J. B. Hobbs (Surrey)	14	1	1112	215	85.53
	1925	P. Holmes (Yorks.)	12	2	1021	315*	102.10
	1932	H. Sutcliffe (Yorks.)	14	3	1193	313	108.45
	1949	L. Hutton (Yorks.)	16	2	1294	201	92.42
July	1900	K. S. Ranjitsinhji (Sussex)	12	1	1059	275	96.27
	1912	D. Denton (Yorks.)	14	2	1023	221	85.25
	1923	C. P. Mead (Hants.)	13	6	1070	222	152.85
	1926	E. Tyldesley (Lancs.)	9	1	1024	226	128.00
	1938	A. E. Fagg (Kent)	15	1	1016	244	72.57
	1946	C. Washbrook (Lancs.)	14	3	1079	162	98.09
	1947	W. J. Edrich (Middx.)	11	3	1047	267*	130.87
	1959	M. J. K. Smith (Warwicks.)	15	2	1209	200*	93.00
August	1871	W. G. Grace (Glos.)	11	0	1024	268	93.09
	1876	W. G. Grace (Glos.)	11	1	1278	344	127.80
	1899	K. S. Ranjitsinhji (Sussex)	14	1	1011	161	77.76
	1901	C. B. Fry (Sussex)	12	1	1116	209	101.45
	1932	H. Sutcliffe (Yorks.)	13	1	1006	194	83.83
	1932	M. Leyland (Yorks.)	13	1	1013	166	84.41
	1933	E. Hendren (Middx.)	18	2	1110	222*	69.37
	1933	W. R. Hammond (Glos.)	13	3	1060	264	106.00
	1933	W. W. Keeton (Notts.)	15	2	1102	136*	84.76
	1936	W. R. Hammond (Glos.)	16	3	1281	317	98.53
	1936	E. Hendren (Middx.)	14	0	1026	156	73.28
	1937	J. Hardstaff, Jnr. (Notts.)	11	1	1150	266	115.00
	1947	D. C. S. Compton (Middx.)	12	3	1039	178	115.44
	1949	L. Hutton (Yorks.)	15	1	1050	269*	75.00
December	1927	W. H. Ponsford (Victoria)	5	0	1146	437	229.20

The following batsmen performed this feat twice in the same season:—

1899	K. S. Ranjitsinhji	June and August
1901	C. B. Fry	June and August
1932	H. Sutcliffe	June and August
1949	L. Hutton	June and August

1000 RUNS DURING MAY

Only three players have scored 1000 runs within the month of May, although three others have reached 1000 runs before June with the inclusion of some innings played in April. W. G. Grace was the first player to achieve this distinction in May, 1895, and he also scored his one hundredth century that month. 32 years elapsed before W. R. Hammond emulated Grace, and C. Hallows repeated the feat the following season in 1928. A decision to delay the start of the county championship until mid-May from the 1969 season will mean that only touring players and members of the University teams will have any real chance of equalling this record.

W. G. Grace (Gloucestershire) in 1895. (May 9th to May 30th, 22 days)—13, 103, 18, 25, 288, 52, 257, 73*, 18, 169—1016 runs.

W. R. Hammond (Gloucestershire) in 1927. (May 7th to May 31st, 25 days)—27, 135, 108, 128, 17, 11, 99, 187, 4, 30, 83, 7, 192, 14—1042 runs. Hammond scored his 1000th run on May 28th, equalling Grace's record of 22 days.

C. Hallows (Lancashire) in 1928. (May 5th to May 31st, 27 days)—100, 101, 51*, 123, 101*, 22, 74, 104, 58, 34*, 232—1000 runs.

The following players scored 1000 runs before June but only with the aid of some runs made in April:

T. W. Hayward (Surrey) in 1900. (April 16th to May 31st)—120*, 55, 108, 131*, 55, 193, 120, 5, 6, 3, 40, 146, 92—1074 runs.
D. G. Bradman (Australians) in 1930. (April 30th to May 31st)—236, 185*, 78, 9, 48*, 66, 4, 44, 252*, 32, 47*—1001 runs.
D. G. Bradman (Australians) in 1938. (April 30th to May 31st)—258, 58, 137, 278, 2, 143, 145*, 5, 30*—1056 runs. Bradman actually scored his 1000th run on May 27th.
W. J. Edrich (Middlesex) in 1938. (April 30th to May 31st)—104, 37, 115, 63, 20*, 182, 71, 31, 53*, 45, 15, 245, 0, 9, 20*—1010 runs, all scored at Lord's.

EARLIEST DATES FOR REACHING RUN AGGREGATES

1000 runs	27 May 1938	D. G. Bradman (Australians).
	28 May 1927	W. R. Hammond (Gloucestershire).
	30 May 1895	W. G. Grace (Gloucestershire).
	31 May 1900	T. W. Hayward (Surrey).
	31 May 1928	C. Hallows (Lancashire).
	31 May 1930	D. G. Bradman (Australians).
	31 May 1938	W. J. Edrich (Middlesex).
2000 runs	5 July 1906	T. W. Hayward (Surrey).
	6 July 1927	W. R. Hammond (Gloucestershire).
	11 July 1930	D. G. Bradman (Australians).
	11 July 1949	John Langridge (Sussex).
	12 July 1921	C. P. Mead (Hampshire).
	14 July 1937	W. R. Hammond (Gloucestershire).
3000 runs	20 August 1906	T. W. Hayward (Surrey).
	20 August 1937	W. R. Hammond (Gloucestershire).
	21 August 1959	M. J. K. Smith (Warwickshire).
	26 August 1921	C. P. Mead (Hampshire).
	27 August 1947	D. C. S. Compton (Middlesex).
	28 August 1947	W. J. Edrich (Middlesex).

MOST RUNS ADDED DURING A BATSMAN'S INNINGS

The following batsmen were at the wicket whilst over 700 runs were added during an innings in a first-class match. R. Abel carried his bat through the innings when setting the record:

811	R. Abel (357*): Surrey v. Somerset (Oval)	1899
801	W. H. Ponsford (429): Victoria v. Tasmania (Melbourne)	1922-23
792	A. C. MacLaren (424): Lancashire v. Somerset (Taunton)	1895
792	W. H. Ponsford (437): Victoria v. Queensland (Melbourne)	1927-28
772	Hanif Mohammad (499): Karachi v. Bahawalpur (Karachi)	1958-59
770	L. Hutton (364): England v. Australia (Oval)	1938
745	B. B. Nimbalkar (443*): Maharashtra v. Kathiawar (Poona)	1948-49
739	D. G. Bradman (452*): New South Wales v. Queensland (Sydney) ..	1929-30
720	A. Sandham (325): England v. West Indies (Kingston)	1929-30
702	G. A. Headley (344*): Jamaica v. Lord Tennyson's XI (Kingston).. ..	1931-32

1000 RUNS IN DÉBUT SEASON

The following batsmen scored 1000 runs in the season in which they made their first appearance in first-class cricket. The age at which they made that initial appearance is given:

	Age	*Season*	*Inns.*	*N.O.*	*Runs*	*H.S.*	*Avge.*	*100s*
A. E. Relf (Sussex)	25	1900	48	3	1059	96	23.53	—
A. P. Day (Kent)	20	1905	39	4	1149	107*	32.82	2
J. B. Hobbs (Surrey)	22	1905	54	3	1317	155	25.82	2
R. A. Young (Camb. U. & Sussex)	19	1905	33	0	1170	220	35.45	3
H. L. Wilson (Sussex)	31	1913	47	1	1352	109	29.39	1
H. Sutcliffe (Yorks.)	24	1919	45	4	1839	174	44.85	5

1000 Runs in Début Season—*Cont.*

	Age	*Season*	*Inns.*	*N.O.*	*Runs*	*H.S.*	*Avge.*	*100s*
H. L. V. Day (Hants.)	23	1922	27	0	1062	107	39.33	1
D. N. Moore (Glos.)	19	1930	34	2	1317	206	41.15	3
F. C. de Saram (Oxford U.) ..	21	1934	23	1	1119	208	50.86	3
N. Oldfield (Lancs.)	24	1935	40	7	1066	111*	32.30	2
D. C. S. Compton (Middx.) ..	17	1936	32	3	1004	100*	34.62	1
J. F. Crapp (Glos.)	23	1936	48	8	1052	168	26.30	1
K. Cranston (Lancs.)	29	1947	41	4	1228	155*	33.18	1
D. J. Insole (Camb. U. & Essex) ..	21	1947	41	5	1237	161*	34.36	2
G. H. G. Doggart (Camb. U. & Sussex)	23	1948	37	3	1169	215*	34.38	3
W. G. A. Parkhouse (Glamorgan) ..	22	1948	49	1	1204	117	25.08	2
D. B. Close (Yorks.)	18	1949	50	10	1098	88*	27.45	—
F. A. Lowson (Yorks.)	23	1949	55	5	1799	104	35.98	1
D. M. Green (Oxford U. & Lancs.)	19	1959	45	3	1049	125	24.97	1
D. Kirby (Camb. U. & Leics.) ..	20	1959	53	2	1102	109	21.60	1
P. J. Watts (Northants.)	18	1959	41	2	1118	113	28.66	2
B. S. Crump (Northants.)	22	1960	36	7	1000	90	34.48	—
S. E. J. Russell (Middx.)	22	1960	39	3	1119	129	31.08	1
E. J. Craig (Camb. U. & Lancs.) ..	19	1961	41	5	1528	208*	42.44	5
J. M. Brearley (Camb. U. & Middx.)	19	1961	40	6	1222	145*	35.94	2

Several other players reached 1000 runs in their first full season having played only a few innings in their début season:

C. P. Mead (Hants.)—1014 runs (26.68) in 1906 after one match in 1905.
T. C. Dodds (Essex)—1050 runs (25.60) in 1946 after one match in India in 1943-44.
D. G. W. Fletcher (Surrey)—1857 runs (43.18) in 1947 after one match in 1946.
R. C. White (Camb. U. & Glos.)—1696 runs (29.24) in 1962 after one match in South Africa in 1960-61.
K. W. R. Fletcher (Essex)—1310 runs (26.20) in 1963 after two matches in 1962.
A. W. Greig (Sussex)—1299 runs (24.50) in 1967 after one match (in South Africa) in 1965-66 and two in 1966.

CARRYING BAT THROUGH A COMPLETED INNINGS

Opening batsmen who have remained at the wickets undefeated throughout a completed innings with all ten of their partners dismissed in turn.

In BOTH innings of the same match

H. Jupp ..	43*	(95)	109*	(193)	Surrey v. Yorks. (Oval)	1874
S. P. Kinneir ..	70*	(239)	69*	(166)	Warwicks. v. Leics. (Leicester) ..	1907
C. J. B. Wood	107*	(309)	117*	(296)	Leics. v. Yorks. (Bradford) ..	1911
V. M. Merchant	135*	(271)	77*	(161)	Indians v. Lancs. (Liverpool) ..	1936

In one innings, being last out in the other

H. Jupp ..	53	(102)	51*	(113)	Surrey v. Notts. (Oval)	1873
F. S. Lee ..	109*	(196)	107	(205)	Somerset v. Worcs. (Worcester) ..	1938

In one innings († denotes completed innings in which ten wickets did not fall, one or more batsmen being retired/absent hurt)

Abel, R.	(8)	88*	(198)	Surrey v. Gloucestershire (Cheltenham) ..	1885
		151*	(425)	Surrey v. Middlesex (Lord's)	1890
		132*	(307)	England v. Australia (Sydney)	1891-92
		136*	(300)	Surrey v. Middlesex (Oval)	1894
		168*	(363)	Players v. Gentlemen (Oval)	1894
		357*	(811)	Surrey v. Somerset (Oval)	1899
		153*	(302)	Players v. Gentlemen (Oval)	1900
		151*	(263)	Surrey v. Sussex (Oval)	1902
Adams, W. W. ..	(1)	14*	(40)	Northamptonshire v. Yorkshire (Northampton)	1920
Alderman, A. E.	(1)	124*	(291)	Derbyshire v. Hampshire (Portsmouth) ..	1934
Amiss, D. L. ..	(1)	160*	(315)	†Warwickshire v. West Indians (Birmingham)	1966
Anson, T. A. ..	(1)	22*	(54)	M.C.C. v. North (Burton-on-Trent)	1840

Carrying Bat Through a Completed Innings—*Cont.*

Player	No.	Score	Total	Match	Season
Anstruther, W.	(1)	23*	(93)	Sussex v. Surrey (Oval)	1878
Anwar Arif	(1)	37*	(102)	N.W. Frontier Province v. Punjab (Peshawar)	1954-55
Armstrong, W. W.	(1)	159*	(309)	Australia v. South Africa (Johannesburg)	1902-03
Ashdown, W. H.	(4)	150*	(303)	Kent v. Surrey (Oval)	1926
		100*	(236)	Kent v. Sussex (Tunbridge Wells)	1928
		83*	(223)	Kent v. Gloucestershire (Maidstone)	1930
		305*	(560)	Kent v. Derbyshire (Dover)	1935
Ashton, H.	(1)	236*	(484)	Cambridge U. v. Free Foresters (Cambridge)	1920
Atkinson, G.	(1)	30*	(73)	Yorkshire v. Nottinghamshire (Bradford)	1865
Atkinson, G.	(1)	46*	(94)	†Somerset v. Yorkshire (Hull)	1965
Atkinson, J.	(1)	144*	(277)	Tasmania v. Victoria (Hobart)	1927-28
Avery, A. V.	(3)	84*	(180)	Essex v. Derbyshire (Southend)	1939
		83*	(165)	Essex v. Gloucestershire (Brentwood)	1946
		92*	(154)	Essex v. Nottinghamshire (Nottingham)	1954
Bagshaw, H.	(1)	114*	(218)	Derbyshire v. Surrey (Oval)	1897
Bailey, J.	(1)	70*	(139)	Hampshire v. West Indians (Bournemouth)	1939
Bainbridge, H. W.	(1)	65*	(113)	Warwickshire v. Kent (Birmingham)	1894
Baker, A.	(1)	55*	(110)	Surrey v. Gloucestershire (Bristol)	1905
Bakewell, A. H.	(3)	83*	(166)	Northamptonshire v. New Zealanders (Peterborough)	1931
		90*	(169)	Northamptonshire v. Essex (Leyton)	1931
		120*	(211)	Northamptonshire v. Leicestershire (Leicester)	1936
Bannerman, A. C.	(7)	71*	(171)	Australians v. Orleans Club (Twickenham)	1878
		45*	(83)	Australian XI v. Shrewsbury's XI (Sydney)	1887-88
		93*	(319)	Australians v. Cambridge U. P. & P. (Leyton)	1888
		39*	(168)	Australians v. England XI (Harrogate)	1888
		45*	(151)	New South Wales v. Victoria (Melbourne)	1890-91
		7*	(60)	Australians v. Kent (Canterbury)	1893
		79*	(258)	Australians v. Philadelphians (Philadelphia)	1893-94
Bardsley, W.	(5)	143*	(271)	Australians v. Cochrane's XI (Bray)	1909
		191*	(361)	New South Wales v. South Australia (Sydney)	1910-11
		50*	(213)	New South Wales v. Victoria (Sydney)	1914-15
		200*	(352)	New South Wales v. Auckland (Auckland)	1923-24
		193*	(383)	Australia v. England (Lord's)	1926
Barker, G. E.	(1)	36*	(80)	Essex v. Kent (Westcliff)	1966
Barlow, R. G.	(11)	26*	(116)	Lancashire v. Kent (Maidstone)	1874
		34*	(187)	Lancashire v. Nottinghamshire (Nottingham)	1876
		34*	(99)	Lancashire v. M.C.C. (Lord's)	1878
		10*	(47)	Lancashire v. Yorkshire (Manchester)	1880
		66*	(269)	Lancashire v. Australians (Manchester)	1882
		5*	(69)	Lancashire v. Nottinghamshire (Nottingham)	1882
		44*	(93)	Lancashire v. Nottinghamshire (Liverpool)	1882
		58*	(240)	Lancashire v. Gloucestershire (Clifton)	1882
		62*	(183)	Lancashire v. Gloucestershire (Clifton)	1885
		51*	(215)	Lancashire v. Kent (Maidstone)	1889
		29*	(131)	Lancashire v. Surrey (Oval)	1890
Barnes, W.	(1)	118*	(236)	M.C.C. v. Oxford U. (Lord's)	1880
Barnett, C. J.	(1)	228*	(363)	Gloucestershire v. Leicestershire (Gloucester)	1947
Barnett, C. S.	(1)	62*	(235)	Gloucestershire v. Worcestershire (Cheltenham)	1913
Barnett, E. P.	(1)	52*	(141)	Gloucestershire v. Yorkshire (Bradford)	1905
Barrett, J. E.	(2)	67*	(176)	Australia v. England (Lord's)	1890
		61*	(134)	Australians v. Thornton's XI (Barnes)	1890
Barton, W. E.	(1)	76*	(50)	Auckland v. Otago (Dunedin)	1882-83
Barua, M. P.	(1)	87*	(148)	Assam v. Bengal (Jorhat)	1966-67
Bates, L. A.	(2)	96*	(207)	Warwickshire v. Surrey (Oval)	1921
		50*	(125)	Warwickshire v. Yorkshire (Huddersfield)	1922
Bates, W. E.	(2)	200*	(390)	Glamorgan v. Worcestershire (Kidderminster)	1927
		73*	(160)	Glamorgan v. Northamptonshire (Swansea)	1928
Bean, G.	(1)	145*	(264)	Sussex v. Nottinghamshire (Hove)	1891
Beldam, G. W.	(1)	12*	(51)	Middlesex v. Sussex (Lord's)	1902
Bell, J. T.	(2)	72*	(164)	Glamorgan v. Essex (Cardiff)	1926
		209*	(395)	Wales v. M.C.C. (Lord's)	1927
Berry, A.	(1)	23*	(147)	†Cambridgeshire v. Nottinghamshire (Nottingham)	1862
Berry, L. G.	(4)	75*	(177)	Leicestershire v. Nottinghamshire (Leicester)	1932
		58*	(126)	Leicestershire v. Derbyshire (Chesterfield)	1939
		45*	(121)	Leicestershire v. South Africans (Leicester)	1947
		109*	(236)	Leicestershire v. Somerset (Leicester)	1949

Carrying Bat Through a Completed Innings—*Cont.*

Player		Score	Total	Match	Season
Blunt, R. C. ..	(2)	137*	(336)	Canterbury v. Wellington (Wellington) ..	1919-20
		131*	(204)	Otago v. Canterbury (Dunedin)	1926-27
Bokul, M. H. ..	(1)	90*	(159)	East Pakistan v. Combined Us. (Karachi) ..	1959-60
Bolus, J. B. ..	(1)	136*	(299)	Nottinghamshire v. Derbyshire (Nottingham)	1963
Booth, B. J. ..	(1)	62*	(140)	Lancashire v. Derbyshire (Liverpool)	1963
Bowley, E. H. ..	(4)	110*	(245)	Sussex v. Glamorgan (Swansea)	1922
		93*	(188)	Sussex v. Hampshire (Hove)	1923
		71*	(119)	Sussex v. Worcestershire (Hove)	1926
		94*	(206)	Sussex v. Nottinghamshire (Hastings) ..	1926
Bowley, F. L. ..	(1)	104*	(267)	Worcestershire v. Middlesex (Lord's)	1911
Bradburn, W. P...	(2)	45*	(87)	Northern Districts v. Wellington (Wellington)	1960-61
		37*	(57)	Northern Districts v. Wellington (Hamilton)	1961-62
Braund, L. C. ..	(4)	28*	(97)	Somerset v. Middlesex (Lord's)	1907
		42*	(113)	Somerset v. Yorkshire (Taunton)	1907
		67*	(226)	Somerset v. Middlesex (Taunton)	1907
		58*	(148)	Somerset v. Worcestershire (Taunton) ..	1914
Brearley, J. M. ..	(1)	90*	(197)	M.C.C. v. Yorkshire (Lord's)	1965
Brockwell, W. ..	(1)	76*	(158)	Surrey v. Leicestershire (Leicester) ..	1898
Brookes, D. ..	(5)	80*	(170)	Northamptonshire v. Leicestershire (Northampton)	1946
		166*	(347)	Northamptonshire v. Kent (Northampton) ..	1950
		102*	(185)	Northamptonshire v. Kent (Northampton) ..	1952
		139*	(300)	Rest v. South (Hastings)	1953
		113*	(252)	Northamptonshire v. Glamorgan (Ebbw Vale)	1958
Brown, G. ..	(2)	103*	(188)	Hampshire v. Middlesex (Bournemouth) ..	1926
		150*	(294)	Hampshire v. Surrey (Oval)	1933
Brown, S. M. ..	(1)	96*	(153)	Middlesex v. Cambridge U. (Cambridge) ..	1948
Brown, W. A. ..	(2)	206*	(422)	Australia v. England (Lord's)	1938
		174*	(311)	Queensland v. South Australia (Adelaide) ..	1938-39
Bruce, Hon. C. N.	(1)	64*	(120)	Oxford U. v. Worcestershire (Oxford) ..	1907
Bryan, J. L. ..	(2)	82*	(157)	Kent v. Yorkshire (Tunbridge Wells)	1921
		93*	(186)	Kent v. Middlesex (Lord's)	1929
Bull, C. H. ..	(1)	57*	(156)	Worcestershire v. Lancashire (Kidderminster)	1935
Bull. D. F. ..	(1)	167*	(336)	Queensland v. Victoria (Melbourne)	1965-66
Burke, J. W. ..	(2)	162*	(360)	New South Wales v. Victoria (Melbourne) ..	1949-50
		132*	(281)	New South Wales v. Victoria (Melbourne) ..	1956-57
Burnup, C. J. ..	(1)	103*	(209)	Kent v. Surrey (Oval)	1899
Bush, J. E. ..	(1)	52*	(146)	Oxford v. Surrey (Guildford)	1952
Cadman, S. ..	(3)	36*	(71)	Derbyshire v. Hampshire (Derby)	1912
		73*	(155)	Derbyshire v. Leicestershire (Leicester) ..	1914
		19*	(53)	Derbyshire v. Leicestershire (Leicester) ..	1920
Carew, M. C. ..	(1)	65*	(135)	Trinidad v. Barbados (Port of Spain)	1966-67
Carris, H. E. ..	(1)	35*	(92)	Middlesex v. Yorkshire (Bradford)	1929
Chalk, F. G. H. ..	(1)	115*	(215)	Kent v. Yorkshire (Dover)	1939
Challenor, G. ..	(1)	155*	(305)	West Indians v. Surrey (Oval)	1923
Chatterton, W. ..	(1)	109*	(238)	M.C.C. v. Lancashire (Lord's)	1892
Clark, T. H. ..	(1)	81*	(135)	Surrey v. Yorkshire (Oval)	1956
Claxton, N. ..	(1)	199*	(378)	South Australia v. Victoria (Melbourne) ..	1905-06
Cobcroft, L. T. ..	(1)	85*	(239)	New South Wales v. Wellington (Wellington)	1895-96
Collins, D. C. ..	(1)	53*	(131)	Wellington v. Canterbury (Christchurch) ..	1906-07
Collins, G. G. ..	(1)	18*	(67)	Kent v. Northamptonshire (Gravesend) ..	1924
Collins, J. C. ..	(1)	128*	(187)	Fiji v. Hawke's Bay (Napier)	1894-95
Cook, G. G. ..	(2)	36*	(74)	Queensland v. Victoria (Melbourne) ..	1932-33
		169*	(400)	Queensland v. M.C.C. (Brisbane)	1946-47
Cook, G. W. ..	(1)	61*	(134)	Cambridge U. v. Yorkshire (Cambridge) ..	1957
Cooper, E. ..	(2)	104*	(273)	Worcestershire v. Lancashire (Manchester) ..	1939
		69*	(154)	Worcestershire v. Warwickshire (Dudley) ..	1951
Cowdrey, M. C. ..	(1)	65*	(169)	Kent v. Gloucestershire (Cheltenham) ..	1956
Croom, A. J. ..	(4)	131*	(311)	Warwickshire v. Northamptonshire (Birmingham)	1929
		58*	(120)	Warwickshire v. Gloucestershire (Cheltenham)	1930
		102*	(204)	Warwickshire v. Lancashire (Manchester) ..	1931
		69*	(133)	Warwickshire v. Leicestershire (Hinckley) ..	1936
Cutmore, J. A. ..	(1)	31*	(64)	Essex v. Yorkshire (Dewsbury)	1933
Dadu Sattar ..	(1)	48*	(88)	East Pakistan B. v. Dacca U. (Dacca) ..	1957-58
Daft, H. B. ..	(1)	77*	(240)	Nottinghamshire v. Surrey (Oval)	1896
Daft, R.	(1)	12*	(48)	Nottinghamshire v. Lancashire (Nottingham)	1877
Daniell, J. ..	(3)	24*	(82)	Somerset v. Kent (Gravesend)	1903
		129*	(312)	Somerset v. Hampshire (Southampton) ..	1911

Carrying Bat Through a Completed Innings—*Cont.*

Player		Score	Total	Match	Season
Daniell, J. (*cont.*)		174*	(318)	Somerset v. Essex (Taunton)	1925
Darnton, T.	(1)	81*	(144)	Yorkshire v. All England XI (Sheffield)	1865
Davey, D. C.	(1)	62*	(106)	Natal v. Griqualand West (Kimberley)	1888-89
Davies, D.	(1)	100*	(161)	Glamorgan v. Worcestershire (Worcester)	1923
Davies, D. D.	(1)	40*	(95)	Border v. Transvaal (Port Elizabeth)	1902-03
Davies, E.	(3)	75*	(142)	Glamorgan v. South Africans (Cardiff)	1935
		155*	(340)	Glamorgan v. Somerset (Weston-super-mare)	1935
		107*	(180)	Over 32 v. Under 32 (Hastings)	1950
Davis, B. A.	(1)	188*	(338)	North Trinidad v. South Trinidad (Port of Spain)	1966-67
Dawson, E. W.	(1)	126*	(256)	Leicestershire v. Essex (Leyton)	1928
Dean, J.	(1)	46*	(102)	Sussex v. M.C.C. (Brighton)	1850
Dempster, C. S.	(2)	167*	(345)	New Zealanders v. Glamorgan (Cardiff)	1927
		28*	(62)	Leicestershire v. Yorkshire (Bradford)	1938
Denton, W. H.	(2)	230*	(476)	Northamptonshire v. Essex (Leyton)	1913
		108*	(305)	Northamptonshire v. Gloucestershire (Northampton)	1914
Dewes, J. G.	(1)	101*	(203)	Middlesex v. Surrey (Oval)	1955
Dillon, E. W.	(1)	38*	(86)	Kent v. Nottinghamshire (Gravesend)	1902
Dipper, A. E.	(11)	168*	(343)	Gloucestershire v. Somerset (Taunton)	1914
		37*	(104)	Gloucestershire v. Lancashire (Manchester)	1919
		99*	(185)	Gloucestershire v. Worcestershire (Cheltenham)	1919
		120*	(175)	Gloucestershire v. Warwickshire (Birmingham)	1920
		22*	(72)	Gloucestershire v. Leicestershire (Ashby)	1922
		37*	(138)	Gloucestershire v. Kent (Cheltenham)	1922
		87*	(192)	Gloucestershire v. Warwickshire (Bristol)	1923
		126*	(211)	Gloucestershire v. West Indians (Bristol)	1923
		85*	(210)	Gloucestershire v. Northamptonshire (Northampton)	1926
		66*	(119)	Gloucestershire v. Kent (Bristol)	1929
		64*	(192)	Gloucestershire v. Glamorgan (Swansea)	1930
Donnan, H.	(1)	160*	(374)	New South Wales v. South Australia (Adelaide)	1898-99
Dunn, A.	(1)	42*	(136)	Griqualand West v. Western Province (Kimberley)	1946-47
Dyer, D. V.	(1)	49*	(96)	Natal v. Transvaal (Durban)	1945-46
Dyson, A. H.	(5)	75*	(156)	Glamorgan v. Northamptonshire (Kettering)	1931
		109*	(204)	Glamorgan v. Middlesex (Cardiff)	1932
		191*	(352)	Glamorgan v. Lancashire (Cardiff)	1934
		110*	(210)	Glamorgan v. Cahn's XI (Newport)	1938
		99*	(196)	Glamorgan v. Gloucestershire (Newport)	1939
Edrich, J. H.	(1)	79*	(122)	Surrey v. Northamptonshire (Oval)	1963
Edrich, W. J.	(1)	140*	(303)	Lord Tennyson's XI v. Sind (Karachi)	1937-38
Elliott, C. S.	(1)	51*	(126)	Derbyshire v. Leicestershire (Ashby)	1948
Ellis, R. T.	(1)	50*	(107)	Sussex v. Australians (Hove)	1880
Emmett. G. M.	(1)	104*	(156)	Gloucestershire v. Oxford U. (Oxford)	1948
Fagg, A. E.	(3)	37*	(127)	Kent v. Gloucestershire (Gillingham)	1938
		117*	(230)	Kent v. Essex (Maidstone)	1948
		71*	(134)	Kent v. Surrey (Oval)	1950
Felix, N.	(1)	30*	(43)	Married v. Single (Lord's)	1831
Ferris, J. J.	(2)	62*	(170)	Gentlemen v. Players (Scarborough)	1892
		34*	(77)	Gloucestershire v. Sussex (Bristol)	1894
Fiddian-Green, C. A.	(1)	60*	(123)	†Warwickshire v. Hampshire (Southampton)	1922
Fillary, E. W. J.	(1)	28*	(146)	Kent v. Yorkshire (Dover)	1964
Fingleton, J. H.	(1)	119*	(361)	New South Wales v. M.C.C. (Sydney)	1932-33
Fishlock, L. B.	(1)	81*	(141)	Surrey v. Australians (Oval)	1948
Fishwick, T. S.	(1)	85*	(181)	Warwickshire v. Lancashire (Manchester)	1907
Fletcher, D. G. W.	(1)	127*	(271)	Surrey v. Yorkshire (Bradford)	1947
Freakes, H. D.	(1)	122*	(190)	Eastern Province v. Natal (Johannesburg)	1931-32
Freeman, J. R.	(2)	67*	(206)	Essex v. Lancashire (Colchester)	1922
		113*	(283)	Essex v. Oxford U. (Chelmsford)	1926
Fry, C. B.	(3)	104*	(197)	Sussex v. Middlesex (Lord's)	1898
		179*	(311)	Sussex v. Yorkshire (Hove)	1898
		170*	(254)	Sussex v. Nottinghamshire (Nottingham)	1901
Gardner, F. C.	(4)	140*	(283)	Warwickshire v. Worcestershire (Birmingham)	1949
		73*	(133)	Warwickshire v. Glamorgan (Swansea)	1950
		184*	(286)	Warwickshire v. Lancashire (Liverpool)	1952
		62*	(149)	Warwickshire v. Glamorgan (Birmingham)	1954

Carrying Bat Through a Completed Innings—*Cont.*

Player	No.	Score	Total	Match	Season
Gehrs, D. R. A. ..	(1)	148*	(235)	South Australia v. Western Australia (Fremantle)	1905-06
Gibb, P. A. ..	(1)	80*	(163)	Cambridge U. v. Australians (Cambridge) ..	1938
Gibbes, W. R. L.	(1)	75*	(193)	Wellington v. Canterbury (Christchurch) ..	1911-12
Gibbons, H. H. ..	(2)	70*	(165)	Worcestershire v. Warwickshire (Kidderminster)	1934
		83*	(148)	Worcestershire v. Lancashire (Kidderminster)	1935
Gilbert, W. R. ..	(2)	205*	(383)	England XI v. Cambridge U. (Cambridge) ..	1876
		40*	(110)	Gloucestershire v. Lancashire (Clifton) ..	1885
Goddard, T. L. ..	(1)	56*	(99)	South Africa v. Australia (Cape Town) ..	1957-58
Godsell, R. T. ..	(1)	98*	(269)	Gloucestershire v. Nottinghamshire (Bristol) ..	1905
Grace, E. M. ..	(1)	192*	(344)	M.C.C. v. Gentlemen of Kent (Canterbury) ..	1862
Grace, W. G. ..	(17)	138*	(215)	M.C.C. v. Surrey (Oval)	1869
		117*	(183)	M.C.C. v. Nottinghamshire (Lord's)	1870
		189*	(310)	Single v. Married (Lord's)	1871
		81*	(141)	W. G. Grace's XI v. Kent (Maidstone) ..	1871
		170*	(290)	England v. Nottinghamshire & Yorkshire (Lord's)	1872
		192*	(311)	South v. North (Oval)	1873
		318*	(528)	Gloucestershire v. Yorkshire (Cheltenham) ..	1876
		221*	(348)	Gloucestershire v. Middlesex (Clifton) ..	1885
		81*	(128)	M.C.C. v. Sussex (Lord's)	1887
		113*	(186)	Gloucestershire v. Nottinghamshire (Clifton) ..	1887
		37*	(87)	Gloucestershire v. Lancashire (Bristol) ..	1889
		127*	(282)	Gloucestershire v. Middlesex (Cheltenham) ..	1889
		190*	(231)	Gloucestershire v. Kent (Maidstone)	1890
		159*	(284)	Sheffield's XI v. Victoria (Melbourne) ..	1891-92
		61*	(105)	Gloucestershire v. Surrey (Oval)	1893
		243*	(463)	Gloucestershire v. Sussex (Hove)	1896
		102*	(238)	Gloucestershire v. Lancashire (Bristol) ..	1896
Gray, J. R. ..	(2)	118*	(208)	Hampshire v. Essex (Portsmouth)	1956
		118*	(214)	Hampshire v. Somerset (Bournemouth) ..	1964
Greig, J. G. ..	(2)	79*	(170)	Europeans v. Parsis (Bombay)	1894-95
		249*	(487)	Hampshire v. Lancashire (Liverpool)	1901
Griffiths, E. L. ..	(1)	24*	(123)	Gloucestershire v. Nottinghamshire (Nottingham)	1885
Grimshaw, I. ..	(1)	36*	(182)	Yorkshire v. Kent (Maidstone)	1881
Gunn, G. ..	(8)	91*	(188)	Nottinghamshire v. Yorkshire (Nottingham) ..	1909
		52*	(146)	Nottinghamshire v. Essex (Leyton) ..	1911
		62*	(176)	Nottinghamshire v. Yorkshire (Dewsbury) ..	1913
		64*	(144)	Nottinghamshire v. Middlesex (Lord's) ..	1913
		117*	(283)	Nottinghamshire v. Middlesex (Lord's) ..	1921
		67*	(155)	Nottinghamshire v. Gloucestershire (Cheltenham)	1926
		109*	(267)	Nottinghamshire v. Sussex (Eastbourne) ..	1929
		85*	(186)	Nottinghamshire v. Kent (Nottingham) ..	1931
Gwynne, L. H. ..	(1)	153*	(274)	Dublin U. v. Leicestershire (Leicester) ..	1895
Hall, L.	(15)	31*	(94)	Yorkshire v. Sussex (Hove)	1878
		124*	(331)	Yorkshire v. Sussex (Hove)	1883
		128*	(285)	Yorkshire v. Sussex (Sheffield)	1884
		32*	(81)	Yorkshire v. Kent (Sheffield)	1885
		79*	(285)	Yorkshire v. Surrey (Sheffield)	1885
		37*	(96)	Yorkshire v. Derbyshire (Derby)	1885
		50*	(173)	Yorkshire v. Sussex (Huddersfield)	1886
		74*	(172)	Yorkshire v. Kent (Canterbury)	1886
		119*	(334)	Yorkshire v. Gloucestershire (Dewsbury) ..	1887
		82*	(218)	Yorkshire v. Sussex (Hove)	1887
		105*	(261)	North v. South (Scarborough)	1887
		34*	(104)	Yorkshire v. Surrey (Oval)	1888
		129*	(461)	Yorkshire v. Gloucestershire (Clifton) ..	1888
		85*	(259)	Yorkshire v. Middlesex (Lord's)	1889
		41*	(106)	Yorkshire v. Nottinghamshire (Sheffield) ..	1891
Hallam, M. R. ..	(1)	152*	(231)	Leicestershire v. Gloucestershire (Leicester) ..	1961
Hallows, C. ..	(6)	109*	(230)	Lancashire v. Sussex (Manchester) ..	1921
		110*	(183)	Lancashire v. Leicestershire (Manchester) ..	1921
		179*	(393)	Lancashire v. Essex (Southend)	1923
		158*	(297)	Lancashire v. Leicestershire (Leicester) ..	1925
		65*	(103)	Lancashire v. Derbyshire (Nelson)	1925
		152*	(305)	Lancashire v. Yorkshire (Manchester) ..	1929
Hamer, A. ..	(4)	35*	(90)	Derbyshire v. Gloucestershire (Bristol) ..	1950
		147*	(272)	Derbyshire v. Yorkshire (Leeds)	1954

Carrying Bat Through a Completed Innings—*Cont.*

Player	No.	Score	Total	Match	Season
Hamer, A. (*cont.*)		112*	(208)	Derbyshire v. Surrey (Oval)	1957
		57*	(105)	Derbyshire v. Gloucestershire (Bristol)	1958
Hamid Nagra	(1)	122*	(266)	Sargodha v. Railways (Lyallpur)	1963-64
Hamilton, L. A.	(1)	117*	(205)	Kent v. Australians (Canterbury)	1890
Hanif Mohammad	(2)	147*	(252)	Bahawalpur v. Sind (Bahawalpur)	1953-54
		142*	(241)	Pakistan v. Essex (Southend)	1954
Hardinge, H. T. W.	(11)	113*	(220)	Rest v. England (Lord's)	1911
		123*	(203)	Kent v. Essex (Tonbridge)	1911
		79*	(169)	Kent v. Yorkshire (Leeds)	1919
		172*	(339)	Kent v. Essex (Canterbury)	1919
		62*	(163)	Kent v. Hampshire (Canterbury)	1920
		118*	(196)	Kent v. M.C.C. (Lord's)	1921
		249*	(440)	Kent v. Leicestershire (Leicester)	1922
		71*	(161)	Kent v. Gloucestershire (Tunbridge Wells)	1923
		54*	(96)	Kent v. Oxford U. (Oxford)	1924
		30*	(55)	Kent v. Somerset (Tonbridge)	1926
		49*	(122)	Kent v. Essex (Southend)	1930
Harris, C. B.	(2)	117*	(246)	Nottinghamshire v. Yorkshire (Leeds)	1934
		239*	(401)	Nottinghamshire v. Hampshire (Nottingham)	1950
Harris, Lord	(1)	80*	(148)	Kent v. Yorkshire (Gravesend)	1883
Harris, L. M.	(1)	41*	(65)	Otago v. Tasmania (Dunedin)	1883-84
Harvey, J. F.	(1)	23*	(67)	†Derbyshire v. Surrey (Oval)	1964
Hawke, Lord	(1)	107*	(229)	M.C.C. v. Oxford U. (Lord's)	1902
Hayman, H. B.	(1)	104*	(213)	Middlesex v. Kent (Catford)	1898
Hayward, T. W.	(8)	156*	(287)	Surrey v. Philadelphians (Oval)	1903
		188*	(321)	Surrey v. Kent (Canterbury)	1904
		129*	(286)	Surrey v. Australians (Oval)	1905
		144*	(225)	Surrey v. Nottinghamshire (Nottingham)	1906
		114*	(190)	Surrey v. Lancashire (Oval)	1907
		146*	(278)	Players v. Gentlemen (Lord's)	1907
		90*	(156)	Surrey v. Somerset (Taunton)	1909
		96*	(178)	Surrey v. Australians (Oval)	1909
Haywood, R.	(1)	131*	(251)	Northamptonshire v. Sussex (Hove)	1921
Hearn, P.	(1)	12*	(32)	Kent v. Hampshire (Southampton)	1952
Hearne, A.	(6)	43*	(189)	Kent v. Somerset (Catford)	1892
		116*	(256)	Kent v. Gloucestershire (Canterbury)	1892
		22*	(76)	Kent v. Gloucestershire (Gravesend)	1895
		55*	(114)	Kent v. Sussex (Tonbridge)	1899
		79*	(172)	Kent v. Worcestershire (Canterbury)	1903
		90*	(294)	Kent v. Gloucestershire (Tonbridge)	1904
Hearne, J. W.	(1)	152*	(390)	Middlesex v. Leicestershire (Leicester)	1931
Hearne, W.	(1)	58*	(126)	M.C.C. v. Oxford U. (Oxford)	1879
Henty, E.	(1)	32*	(81)	Kent v. Yorkshire (Dewsbury)	1870
Hill, N. W.	(1)	23*	(57)	Nottinghamshire v. Sussex (Eastbourne)	1962
Hillyer, W.	(1)	11*	(67)	Players v. Gentlemen (Lord's)	1842
Hobbs, J. B.	(7)	60*	(155)	Surrey v. Warwickshire (Birmingham)	1907
		154*	(292)	Players v. Gentlemen (Lord's)	1911
		117*	(190)	M.C.C. v. Londesborough's XI (Scarborough)	1911
		205*	(344)	Surrey v. A. I. F. (Oval)	1919
		172*	(294)	Surrey v. Yorkshire (Leeds)	1921
		153*	(300)	Surrey v. Yorkshire (Oval)	1931
		161*	(320)	Players v. Gentlemen (Lord's)	1932
Hofmeyr, M. B.	(2)	95*	(247)	Oxford U. v. New Zealanders (Oxford)	1949
		64*	(169)	Oxford U. v. Cambridge U. (Lord's)	1949
Holdsworth, R. L.	(1)	100*	(227)	N. W. Frontier Province v. Southern Punjab (Patiala)	1938-39
Holland, J.	(1)	46*	(95)	Leicestershire v. Surrey (Leicester)	1894
Holloway, R. A.	(1)	61*	(122)	Otago v. Central Districts (Nelson)	1962-63
Holmes, P.	(3)	145*	(270)	Yorkshire v. Northamptonshire (Northampton)	1920
		175*	(377)	Yorkshire v. New Zealanders (Bradford)	1927
		110*	(219)	Yorkshire v. Northamptonshire (Bradford)	1929
Holt, J. K., Jnr.	(1)	103*	(196)	West Indians v. Cricket Club of India (Bombay)	1958-59
Hooker, W.	(1)	8*	(19)	Sussex v. Surrey (Godalming)	1830
Hopkins, A. J.	(1)	91*	(159)	Rest v. Australian XI (Sydney)	1908-09
Hopkins, H. O.	(1)	142*	(314)	Oxford U. v. Army (Oxford)	1922
Hopwood, J. L.	(2)	60*	(153)	Lancashire v. Somerset (Nelson)	1931

Carrying Bat Through a Completed Innings—*Cont.*

Hopwood, J. L. (*cont.*)		73*	(128)	Lancashire v. South Africans (Manchester) ..	1935
Hornby, A. N. ..	(2)	23*	(56)	Lancashire v. Yorkshire (Manchester) ..	1876
		121*	(194)	M.C.C. v. Cambridge U. (Lord's)	1882
Horton, M. J. ..	(1)	53*	(91)	Worcestershire v. Lancashire (Manchester) ..	1966
Howard, T. ..	(1)	47*	(202)	Western Australia v. South Australia (Fremantle)	1905-06
Howell, M. ..	(1)	15*	(73)	Surrey v. Kent (Blackheath)	1920
Humphrey, R. ..	(1)	30*	(60)	Surrey v. Nottinghamshire (Oval)	1872
Humphrey, T. ..	(1)	43*	(95)	Surrey v. Sussex (Brighton)	1867
Hunte, C. C. ..	(1)	60*	(131)	West Indies v. Australia (Port of Spain) ..	1964-65
Hussain, Dilawar	(1)	101*	(249)	Indians v. Warwickshire (Birmingham) ..	1936
Hutton, L. ..	(4)	99*	(200)	Yorkshire v. Leicestershire (Sheffield) ..	1948
		78*	(153)	Yorkshire v. Worcestershire (Sheffield) ..	1949
		202*	(344)	England v. West Indies (Oval)	1950
		156*	(272)	England v. Australia (Adelaide)	1950-51
Ibrahim, K. C. ..	(2)	218*	(380)	Ibrahim's XI v. Raiji's XI (Bombay) ..	1947-48
		234*	(398)	Ibrahim's XI v. Mantri's (Bombay)	1947-48
Ijaz Butt	(1)	151*	(234)	North Zone v. Lahore (Lahore)	1961-62
Ikin, J. T. ..	(3)	119*	(261)	†Lancashire v. Middlesex (Manchester) ..	1949
		96*	(227)	Commonwealth v. Indian XI (Calcutta) ..	1950-51
		125*	(197)	Lancashire v. Surrey (Oval)	1951
Imtiaz Ahmed ..	(1)	166*	(351)	North Zone v. P. I. A. (Lahore)	1961-62
Iremonger, J. ..	(1)	189*	(377)	Nottinghamshire v. Middlesex (Lord's) ..	1904
Jackson, F. S. ..	(1)	59*	(162)	Yorkshire v. Cambridge U. (Cambridge) ..	1897
Jadeja Mulubha..	(1)	75*	(160)	Saurashtra v. Baroda (Baroda)	1958-59
Jagdale, A. ..	(1)	149*	(312)	Madhya Pradesh v. Uttar Pradesh (Agra) ..	1966-67
Javed Baber ..	(1)	114*	(239)	Railways v. Karachi B. (Lahore)	1962-63
Jena, B.	(1)	38*	(83)	Orissa v. Bihar (Jamshedpur)	1961-62
Johnstone, C. P...	(1)	78*	(206)	M.C.C. v. Cambridge U. (Lord's)	1939
Jones, A.	(1)	166*	(364)	Glamorgan v. Nottinghamshire (Nottingham)	1967
Jones, A. O. ..	(1)	125*	(239)	Nottinghamshire v. Australians (Nottingham)	1909
Jones, S. P. ..	(1)	134*	(266)	Australian XI v. Shrewsbury's XI (Sydney)..	1887-88
Jordaan, H. ..	(1)	83*	(183)	N. E. Transvaal v. Western Province (Cape Town)	1946-47
Jupp, H.	(11)	90*	(222)	Surrey v. Yorkshire (Sheffield)	1868
		27*	(95)	Surrey v. Lancashire (Manchester)	1870
		50*	(88)	Surrey v. Gloucestershire (Clifton)	1870
		50*	(98)	South v. North (Lord's)	1873
		51*	(113)	Surrey v. Nottinghamshire (Oval)	1873
		43*	(95)	Surrey v. Yorkshire (Oval) 1st innings ..	1874
		109*	(193)	Surrey v. Yorkshire (Oval) 2nd innings ..	1874
		37*	(74)	Surrey v. Yorkshire (Sheffield)	1876
		73*	(268)	Surrey v. Kent (Oval)	1876
		91*	(264)	Surrey v. Kent (Oval)	1877
		117*	(284)	Surrey v. Yorkshire (Sheffield)	1880
Keeton, W. W. ..	(1)	99*	(190)	Nottinghamshire v. Kent (Nottingham) ..	1937
Kelly, P. C. ..	(1)	82*	(147)	Western Australia v. South Australia (Perth)	1964-65
Kennedy, A. S. ..	(1)	152*	(344)	Hampshire v. Nottinghamshire (Nottingham)	1921
Kenyon, D. ..	(1)	103*	(215)	Worcestershire v. Hampshire (Bournemouth)	1955
Kerr, J. L. ..	(1)	146*	(243)	Canterbury v. M.C.C. (Christchurch) ..	1935-36
Kher, D. R. ..	(1)	56*	(106)	Maharashtra v. Bombay (Bombay)	1961-62
Kilner, N. ..	(1)	40*	(119)	Warwickshire v. Kent (Tunbridge Wells) ..	1928
Kinneir, S. P. ..	(3)	70*	(239)	Warwickshire v. Leicestershire (Leicester) 1st inns.	1907
		69*	(166)	Warwickshire v. Leicestershire (Leicester) 2nd inns.	1907
		65*	(164)	Warwickshire v. Somerset (Taunton)	1908
Kitcat, S. A. P. ..	(1)	18*	(70)	Gloucestershire v. Yorkshire (Hull)	1901
Knight, A. E. ..	(5)	91*	(155)	†Leicestershire v. Surrey (Oval)	1903
		61*	(131)	Leicestershire v. Nottinghamshire (Nottingham)	1908
		137*	(345)	Leicestershire v. Warwickshire (Birmingham)	1909
		66*	(182)	Leicestershire v. Hampshire (Portsmouth) ..	1911
		74*	(182)	Leicestershire v. Surrey (Leicester)	1911
Langdon, T. ..	(1)	78*	(151)	Gloucestershire v. South Africans (Bristol) ..	1907
Langridge, John ..	(3)	108*	(218)	Sussex v. Nottinghamshire (Hove)	1948
		48*	(101)	Sussex v. Lancashire (Manchester)	1950
		111*	(191)	Sussex v. Somerset (Hove)	1952
Langridge, R. J.	(1)	137*	(222)	Sussex v. Leicestershire (Leicester)	1963
Lawry, W. M. ..	(1)	150*	(309)	Victoria v. South Australia (Melbourne) ..	1961-62

Carrying Bat Through a Completed Innings—*Cont.*

Lee, C.	(1)	96*	(211)	Derbyshire v. Middlesex (Chesterfield) ..	1956
Lee, F. S... ..	(3)	134*	(236)	Somerset v. Sussex (Taunton)	1931
		59*	(116)	Somerset v. Australians (Taunton)	1934
		109*	(196)	Somerset v. Worcestershire (Worcester) ..	1938
Lee, H. W. ..	(1)	80*	(212)	Middlesex v. Essex (Leyton)	1920
Lee, J. W. ..	(2)	135*	(352)	Somerset v. Kent (Taunton)	1934
		54*	(160)	Somerset v. Cambridge U. (Cambridge) ..	1935
Lenham, L. J. ..	(2)	66*	(147)	Sussex v. Surrey (Hove)	1957
		51*	(161)	Sussex v. Glamorgan (Margam)	1960
Lillywhite, W. ..	(2)	42*	(89)	Sussex v. M.C.C. (Lord's)	1839
		18*	(38)	M.C.C. v. Cambridge U. (Cambridge) ..	1845
Lockwood, E. ..	(2)	67*	(115)	Players v. Gentlemen (Oval)	1874
		68*	(121)	England XI v. Cambridge U. (Cambridge) ..	1879
Lowson, F. A. ..	(1)	76*	(218)	Yorkshire v. M.C.C. (Lord's)	1951
Lucas, A. P. ..	(3)	36*	(121)	Surrey v. Gloucestershire (Clifton)	1877
		43*	(126)	M.C.C. v. Lancashire (Lord's)	1881
		47*	(149)	Gentlemen v. Players (Oval)	1883
Luckhurst, B. W.	(1)	126*	(253)	Kent v. Sussex (Tunbridge Wells)	1967
McGlew, D. J. ..	(4)	114*	(251)	South Africans v. Hampshire (Southampton)	1951
		64*	(95)	South Africans v. Pearce's XI (Scarborough)	1951
		54*	(147)	Natal v. Australians (Durban)	1957-58
		127*	(292)	South Africa v. New Zealand (Durban) ..	1961-62
McKenzie, U. M.	(1)	115*	(292)	British Guiana v. Trinidad (Port of Spain) ..	1943-44
Mackinnon, F. A.	(1)	33*	(64)	Kent v. Yorkshire (Bradford)	1881
McMorris, E. D. A.	(3)	190*	(383)	West Indians v. Middlesex (Lord's)	1963
		103*	(185)	Jamaica v. Cavaliers (Kingston)	1963-64
		127*	(236)	Jamaica v. Trinidad (Port of Spain)	1965-66
Makepeace, H. ..	(4)	39*	(88)	Lancashire v. Kent (Maidstone)	1913
		71*	(185)	Lancashire v. Cambridge U. (Cambridge) ..	1921
		106*	(208)	Lancashire v. Nottinghamshire (Nottingham)	1923
		92*	(159)	Lancashire v. Nottinghamshire (Nottingham)	1926
Mantri, M. K. ..	(1)	64*	(229)	Bombay v. Gujerat (Ahmedabad)	1950-51
Marlow, F. W. ..	(2)	43*	(123)	Sussex v. Surrey (Oval)	1891
		144*	(268)	Sussex v. M.C.C. (Lord's)	1891
Marshal, A. ..	(1)	66*	(114)	Queensland v. New Zealanders (Brisbane) ..	1913-14
Maynard, E. A. J.	(1)	28*	(55)	Derbyshire v. Lancashire (Derby)	1882
Mayne, E. R. ..	(1)	154*	(345)	Victoria v. New South Wales (Sydney) ..	1923-24
Mead, C. P. ..	(3)	88*	(223)	Hampshire v. Warwickshire (Leamington) ..	1909
		120*	(234)	Hampshire v. Yorkshire (Huddersfield) ..	1911
		117*	(221)	Hampshire v. Nottinghamshire (Nottingham)	1935
Mehra, V. L. ..	(1)	87*	(206)	East Punjab v. Delhi (Jullunder)	1957-58
Merchant, V. M.	(4)	135*	(271)	Indians v. Lancashire (Liverpool) 1st innings	1936
		77*	(161)	Indians v. Lancashire (Liverpool)2nd innings	1936
		86*	(197)	Indians v. Warwickshire (Birmingham) ..	1946
		184*	(317)	Bombay v. Commonwealth (Bombay) ..	1950-51
Midlane, F. A. ..	(2)	14*	(60)	†Wellington v. Canterbury (Christchurch) ..	1910-11
		222*	(498)	Wellington v. Otago (Wellington)	1914-15
Midwinter, W. E.	(1)	16*	(76)	Australians v. Nottinghamshire (Nottingham)	1878
Mills, G.	(1)	106*	(235)	Auckland v. Wellington (Auckland)	1895-96
Mills, I.	(1)	88*	(156)	Auckland v. Otago (Dunedin)	1893-94
Millyard, G. ..	(1)	10*	(47)	Sussex v. Kent (Brighton)	1841
Milton, C. A. ..	(3)	51*	(117)	Gloucestershire v. Lancashire (Bristol) ..	1955
		28*	(69)	Gloucestershire v. Middlesex (Gloucester) ..	1956
		138*	(253)	Gloucestershire v. Leicestershire (Bristol) ..	1966
Miller, L. S. M. ..	(1)	81*	(154)	Wellington v. Otago (Dunedin)	1956-57
Mitchell, B. ..	(1)	103*	(198)	South Africans v. M.C.C. (Lord's)	1947
Mitchell, R. A. H.	(1)	125*	(204)	M.C.C. v. Kent (Canterbury)..	1872
Mitford, Capt. ..	(1)	65*	(97)	Army v. M.C.C. (Pretoria)	1905-06
Moon, L, J. ..	(1)	62*	(136)	Middlesex v. Essex (Leyton)	1903
Moore, D. N. ..	(1)	101*	(217)	South of England v. M.C.C. (Folkestone) ..	1930
Morgan, T. R. ..	(4)	22*	(68)	†Glamorgan v. Yorkshire (Cardiff)	1922
		14*	(47)	Glamorgan v. Nottinghamshire (Cardiff) ..	1922
		13*	(42)	Glamorgan v. Lancashire (Swansea)	1922
		87*	(188)	†Glamorgan v. Leicestershire (Leicester) ..	1923
Morris, E. B. ..	(1)	106*	(297)	Natal v. Orange Free State (Johannesburg) ..	1906-07
Morton, A. ..	(2)	28*	(62)	Derbyshire v. Yorkshire (Bradford)	1910
		105*	(204)	Derbyshire v. Leicestershire (Derby)	1920

Carrying Bat Through a Completed Innings—*Cont.*

Player		Score	Total	Match	Season
Moulder, E. R. D.	(1)	104*	(264)	West Indian XI v. M.C.C. (Georgetown) ..	1912-13
Murdoch, W. L.	(2)	82*	(177)	New South Wales v. Harris's XI (Sydney) ..	1878-79
		107*	(240)	Australians v. Orleans Club (Twickenham) ..	1882
Muttaqi Hasan ..	(2)	72*	(153)	Hyderabad v. Karachi Greens (Karachi) ..	1961-62
		98*	(180)	Hyderabad v. East Pakistan (Hyderabad) ..	1962-63
Nazar Mohammad	(1)	124*	(311)	Pakistan v. India (Lucknow)	1952-53
Needham, E. ..	(2)	58*	(111)	Derbyshire v. Surrey (Derby)	1908
		107*	(195)	Derbyshire v. Essex (Leyton)	1908
Newham, W. ..	(1)	110*	(174)	Sussex v. Lancashire (Manchester)	1894
Nicholls, R. B. ..	(1)	26*	(87)	Gloucestershire v. Hampshire (Bristol) ..	1966
Nicholson, W. G.	(1)	63*	(143)	Gentlemen of South v. Gentlemen of North (Lord's)	1862
Nitschke, H. C. ..	(1)	130*	(246)	South Australia v. New South Wales (Sydney)	1933-34
North, M. K. ..	(1)	32*	(73)	British Guiana v. Lucas's XI (Georgetown) ..	1894-95
Northway, R. P.	(1)	21*	(43)	Somerset v. Yorkshire (Bradford) ..	1930
Norton, W. S. ..	(1)	64*	(143)	Gentlemen of Kent & Sussex v. Gentlemen of England (Canterbury) ..	1857
Oakman, A. S. M.	(1)	137*	(238)	Sussex v. Lancashire (Hove)	1956
Oliver, L. ..	(1)	75*	(146)	Derbyshire v. Warwickshire (Birmingham) ..	1912
Oscroft, E. ..	(1)	53*	(94)	Nottinghamshire v. Surrey (Nottingham) ..	1865
Padgett, D. E. V.	(1)	115*	(230)	Yorkshire v. Gloucestershire (Bristol) ..	1962
Palairet, L. C. H.	(4)	75*	(197)	Oxford U. v. Sussex (Hove)	1892
		22*	(58)	Somerset v. Lancashire (Manchester) ..	1892
		51*	(122)	Somerset v. Kent (Taunton)	1893
		113*	(172)	Somerset v. Middlesex (Taunton)	1895
Parkhouse, W. G. A.	(1)	60*	(152)	Glamorgan v. Lancashire (Swansea)	1954
Parks, H. W. ..	(2)	49*	(105)	Sussex v. Yorkshire (Eastbourne)	1946
		119*	(221)	Sussex v. Lancashire (Eastbourne)	1947
Parks, J. H. ..	(2)	33*	(137)	Sussex v. Glamorgan (Swansea)	1936
		144*	(262)	Sussex v. Cambridge U. (Cambridge) ..	1937
Parsons, A. B. D.	(1)	30*	(71)	Surrey v. Leicestershire (Oval)	1961
Parsons, J. H. ..	(1)	161*	(347)	Warwickshire v. Gloucestershire (Nuneaton) ..	1913
Patterson, G. S. ..	(1)	109*	(234)	Philadelphians v. Mitchell's XI (Philadelphia)	1895-96
Patterson, W. H.	(1)	107*	(306)	Oxford U. v. Cambridge U. (Lord's)	1881
Payne, C... ..	(3)	53*	(165)	Sussex v. Kent (Brighton)	1865
		135*	(367)	Kent v. Surrey (Gravesend)	1866
		37*	(79)	Sussex v. Middlesex (Brighton)	1868
Payton, W. E. G.	(1)	33*	(84)	Combined Services v. Oxford U. (Oxford) ..	1947
Pearson, F. ..	(4)	154*	(342)	Worcestershire v. Surrey (Dudley)	1912
		67*	(152)	Worcestershire v. Sussex (Eastbourne) ..	1914
		151*	(275)	Worcestershire v. Warwickshire (Worcester)	1921
		68*	(123)	Worcestershire v. Hampshire (Southampton)	1923
Phebey, A. H. ..	(4)	89*	(209)	Kent v. Worcestershire (Kidderminster) ..	1951
		54*	(126)	Kent v. Middlesex (Lord's)	1951
		85*	(181)	Kent v. Australians (Canterbury)	1953
		50*	(127)	Kent v. Northamptonshire (Northampton) ..	1954
Phillips, G. ..	(1)	8*	(13)	Wellington v. Nelson (Nelson)	1862-63
Pichamuthu, D. V.	(1)	93*	(208)	Bihar v. Orissa (Cuttack)	1959-60
Picknell, G. ..	(1)	27*	(64)	Sussex v. Surrey (Oval)	1850
Pickerill, J. ..	(1)	143*	(325)	North-Eastern Transvaal v. Rhodesia (Pretoria)	1951-52
Pilkington, H. C.	(1)	77*	(169)	Oxford U. v. M.C.C. (Lord's)	1899
Pinch, C... ..	(1)	146*	(259)	†South Australia v. Victoria (Melbourne) ..	1950-51
Place, W... ..	(1)	101*	(244)	Lancashire v. Warwickshire (Manchester) ..	1950
Playle, W. R. ..	(1)	89*	(139)	Auckland v. Northern Districts (Auckland) ..	1959-60
Ponniah, C. E. M.	(1)	98*	(206)	Cambridge U. v. Leicestershire (Leicester) ..	1967
Ponsford, W. H...	(2)	143*	(283)	Australians v. Glamorgan (Swansea) ..	1926
		109*	(185)	Victoria v. New South Wales (Melbourne) ..	1930-31
Poore, R. M. ..	(1)	49*	(97)	Hampshire v. Somerset (Bath)	1898
Prentice, F. T. ..	(1)	36*	(89)	Leicestershire v. Worcestershire (Hinckley) ..	1937
Quaife, B. W. ..	(1)	31*	(112)	Warwickshire v. Kent (Stourbridge)	1931
Quaife, W. ..	(1)	40*	(81)	Sussex v. Lancashire (Manchester)	1887
Quaife, W. G. ..	(1)	178*	(475)	†Warwickshire v. Hampshire (Southampton) ..	1897
Radcliffe, O. G...	(2)	104*	(207)	Gloucestershire v. Middlesex (Lord's) ..	1886
		101*	(214)	Gloucestershire v. Kent (Canterbury) ..	1889
Raghinath, R. ..	(1)	68*	(169)	Kerala v. Mysore (Palghat)	1958-59
Ram, D... ..	(1)	31*	(79)	Kerala v. Madras (Madurai)	1957-58
Rawlin, J. T. ..	(1)	122*	(290)	M.C.C. v. London County (Crystal Palace)	1902

Carrying Bat Through a Completed Innings—*Cont.*

Read, W. W. ..	(2)	196*	(413)	Surrey v. Sussex (Oval)	1892
		142*	(368)	Vernon's XI v. Victoria (Melbourne) ..	1887-88
Redpath, I. R. ..	(1)	139*	(307)	Australians v. Rhodesia (Salisbury)	1966-67
Rees, J. S. ..	(1)	21*	(54)	South Australia v. Western Australia (Perth)	1905-06
Relf, R. R. ..	(1)	272*	(433)	Sussex v. Worcestershire (Eastbourne) ..	1909
Reynolds, R. ..	(1)	125*	(281)	Queensland v. Western Australia (Perth) ..	1958-59
Rhodes, W. ..	(3)	98*	(184)	Yorkshire v. M.C.C. (Lord's)	1903
		85*	(152)	Yorkshire v. Essex (Leyton)	1910
		79*	(165)	Capped v. Uncapped (Hastings)	1923
Rice, R. W. ..	(2)	38*	(101)	Gloucestershire v. Yorkshire (Cheltenham) ..	1900
		58*	(147)	Gloucestershire v. Essex (Clifton)	1901
Richardson, P. E.	(2)	91*	(155)	Worcestershire v. Hampshire (Worcester) ..	1955
		59*	(105)	M.C.C. v. Pakistan XI (Dacca)	1955-56
Riches, N. V. H.	(2)	177*	(347)	Glamorgan v. Leicestershire (Leicester) ..	1921
		85*	(161)	Glamorgan v. Yorkshire (Leeds)	1922
Ricketts, J. ..	(1)	195*	(429)	Lancashire v. Surrey (Oval) *Début Match* ..	1867
Rippon, A. D. E.	(1)	87*	(194)	Somerset v. Kent (Taunton)	1914
Rippon, A. E. S...	(2)	19*	(66)	†Somerset v. Sussex (Bath)	1920
		90*	(165)	Somerset v. Hampshire (Southampton) ..	1921
Rodrigo, M. ..	(1)	135*	(318)	Ceylon v. West Indies (Colombo)	1948-49
Rogers, N. H. ..	(5)	32*	(68)	†Hampshire v. Leicestershire (Loughborough)	1953
		56*	(126)	M.C.C. v. Surrey (Lord's)	1954
		172*	(327)	Hampshire v. Gloucestershire (Bristol) ..	1954
		125*	(221)	Hampshire v. Somerset (Glastonbury) ..	1954
		101*	(182)	England XI v. Pakistan (Hastings)	1954
Rothery, J. W. ..	(1)	53*	(258)	Yorkshire v. Worcestershire (Worcester) ..	1907
Roy, A. Guha ..	(1)	84*	(180)	Assam v. West Bengal (Calcutta)	1951-52
Russell, A. C. ..	(1)	89*	(161)	Essex v. Northamptonshire (Northampton) ..	1913
Ryder, J... ..	(1)	93*	(188)	Victoria v. New South Wales (Sydney) ..	1914-15
Sandham, A. ..	(7)	123*	(323)	Surrey v. Hampshire (Portsmouth)	1922
		155*	(330)	Surrey v. Somerset (Oval)	1923
		96*	(158)	Surrey v. Cambridge U. (Oval)	1924
		159*	(271)	Cahn's XI v. West Indian XI (Kingston) ..	1928-29
		125*	(282)	Surrey v. Northamptonshire (Northampton)..	1930
		113*	(221)	Surrey v. Hampshire (Bournemouth).. ..	1931
		169*	(333)	Surrey v. Hampshire (Oval)	1933
Scotton, W. H. ..	(4)	110*	(223)	Nottinghamshire v. Surrey (Nottingham) ..	1886
		35*	(92)	Nottinghamshire v. Lancashire (Manchester)	1887
		17*	(58)	Nottinghamshire v. Yorkshire (Sheffield) ..	1888
		9*	(28)	England XI v. Australians (Stoke)	1888
Serrurier, L. R...	(1)	74*	(162)	Western Province v. M.C.C. (Cape Town) ..	1927-28
Sewell, C. O. H...	(1)	88*	(127)	Gloucestershire v. Yorkshire (Sheffield) ..	1898
Shakoor Ahmed ..	(1)	150*	(263)	Lahore Greens v. Karachi Blues (Karachi) ..	1965-66
Shaw, E. D. ..	(1)	78*	(189)	Oxford U. v. Australians (Oxford)	1882
Shipman, A. ..	(1)	100*	(212)	Leicestershire v. Lancashire (Manchester) ..	1935
Shrewsbury, A. ..	(8)	224*	(415)	Nottinghamshire v. Middlesex (Lord's) ..	1885
		227*	(430)	Nottinghamshire v. Gloucestershire (Moreton-in-the-Marsh)..	1886
		54*	(90)	North v. South (Lord's)	1890
		81*	(167)	Players v. Gentlemen (Lord's)..	1891
		151*	(345)	Sherwins' XI v. Hall's XI (Bradford) ..	1891
		111*	(226)	Nottinghamshire v. Kent (Canterbury) ..	1892
		151*	(325)	Players v. Gentlemen (Oval)	1892
		125*	(277)	Nottinghamshire v. Gloucestershire (Nottingham)	1896
Shuter, J... ..	(1)	45*	(92)	Surrey v. Nottinghamshire (Oval)	1878
Siedle, I. J. ..	(1)	132*	(297)	South Africans v. M.C.C. (Lord's)	1935
Simpson, R. B. ..	(1)	161*	(294)	Western Australia v. New South Wales (Sydney)	1959-60
Simpson, R. T. ..	(2)	119*	(237)	M.C.C. v. Natal (Durban)	1948-49
		230*	(352)	Nottinghamshire v. Glamorgan (Swansea) ..	1950
Sinfield, R. A. ..	(5)	161*	(374)	Gloucestershire v. Oxford U. (Oxford) ..	1931
		39*	(104)	Gloucestershire v. Sussex (Cheltenham) ..	1931
		100*	(290)	Gloucestershire v. Sussex (Bristol)	1935
		38*	(106)	Gloucestershire v. Derbyshire (Buxton) ..	1937
		69*	(165)	Gloucestershire v. Worcestershire (Bristol) ..	1939
Smith, C. H. ..	(1)	47*	(129)	Sussex v. Surrey (Oval)	1868
Smith, D... ..	(2)	140*	(265)	Derbyshire v. Hampshire (Chesterfield) ..	1937

Carrying Bat Through a Completed Innings—*Cont.*

Smith, D. (*cont.*)		57*	(112)	Derbyshire v. Kent (Ilkeston)	1939
Smith, D. V.	(1)	147*	(256)	Sussex v. West Indians (Hove)	1957
Smith, H. O.	(1)	124*	(264)	Tasmania v. South Africans (Launceston)	1910-11
Smith, M. J. K.	(1)	76*	(137)	Oxford U. v. Hampshire (Bournemouth)	1955
Snary, H. C.	(1)	124*	(291)	Leicestershire v. Indians (Leicester)	1932
Spooner, R. T.	(1)	98*	(210)	Warwickshire v. Worcestershire (Worcester)	1952
Stoddart, A. E.	(2)	216*	(372)	Middlesex v. Lancashire (Manchester)	1891
		195*	(327)	Middlesex v. Nottinghamshire (Lord's)	1893
Stollmeyer, J. B.	(1)	45*	(84)	West Indians v. Somerset (Taunton)	1939
Stott, W. B.	(1)	144*	(262)	Yorkshire v. Worcestershire (Worcester)	1959
Studd, G. B.	(1)	106*	(187)	Cambridge U. v. Lancashire (Liverpool)	1881
Sutcliffe, H.	(7)	125*	(307)	Yorkshire v. Essex (Southend)	1920
		104*	(170)	†Yorkshire v. Hampshire (Leeds)	1932
		110*	(307)	†North v. South (Manchester)	1932
		114*	(202)	Yorkshire v. Rest of England (Oval)	1933
		187*	(401)	Yorkshire v. Worcestershire (Bradford)	1934
		135*	(262)	Yorkshire v. Glamorgan (Neath)	1935
		125*	(322)	Yorkshire v. Oxford U. (Oxford)	1939
Suttle, K. G.	(2)	97*	(166)	Sussex v. Lancashire (Liverpool)	1964
		89*	(161)	Sussex v. Leicestershire (Leicester)	1966
Tancred, A. B.	(1)	26*	(47)	South Africa v. England (Cape Town)	1888-89
Tancred, L. J.	(1)	61*	(135)	South Africans v. M.C.C. (Lord's)	1907
Tarrant, F. A.	(6)	51*	(114)	M.C.C. v. Kent (Lord's)	1907
		48*	(162)	M.C.C. v. Oxford U. (Oxford)	1908
		55*	(145)	Middlesex v. Gloucestershire (Bristol)	1909
		140*	(262)	Middlesex v. Sussex (Lord's)	1910
		207*	(378)	Middlesex v. Yorkshire (Bradford)	1911
		81*	(159)	Middlesex v. Lancashire (Liverpool)	1913
Tayfield, A.	(1)	133*	(261)	Transvaal v. Eastern Province (Port Elizabeth)	1955-56
Taylor, C. H.	(1)	105*	(274)	Oxford U. v. Worcestershire (Oxford)	1925
Taylor, H. W.	(1)	83*	(124)	Natal v. M.C.C. (Pietermaritzburg)	1913-14
Taylor, K. A.	(1)	81*	(222)	Warwickshire v. Yorkshire (Birmingham)	1948
Thompson, G. J.	(1)	103*	(270)	Northamptonshire v. Cambridge U. (Cambridge)	1906
Thompson, W. K.	(1)	74*	(225)	Natal v. Transvaal (Durban)	1904-05
Timms, J. E.	(1)	82*	(156)	Northamptonshire v. Derbyshire (Chesterfield)	1935
Tindill, E. W.	(1)	47*	(111)	Wellington v. Otago (Dunedin)	1946-47
Todd, L. J.	(1)	133*	(265)	Kent v. Leicestershire (Tunbridge Wells)	1946
Townsend, A. F.	(1)	102*	(228)	Derbyshire v. Lancashire (Manchester)	1948
Troup, W.	(1)	127*	(388)	Gloucestershire v. Worcestershire (Bristol)	1902
Ulyett, G.	(2)	146*	(248)	Yorkshire v. M.C.C. (Scarborough)	1884
		199*	(399)	Yorkshire v. Derbyshire (Sheffield)	1887
Van der Berg, J. H.	(1)	55*	(188)	Eastern Province v. Transvaal (Johannesburg)	1926-27
Varnals, G. D.	(1)	151*	(267)	Eastern Province v. Border (East London)	1957-58
Vials, G. A. T.	(1)	62*	(105)	Northamptonshire v. Surrey (Northampton)	1910
Vine, J.	(9)	75*	(178)	Sussex v. Middlesex (Eastbourne)	1902
		62*	(241)	Sussex v. Somerset (Hove)	1906
		80*	(218)	Sussex v. Somerset (Bath)	1906
		78*	(222)	Sussex v. Middlesex (Lord's)	1907
		67*	(186)	Sussex v. Essex (Hove)	1907
		37*	(160)	Sussex v. Gloucestershire (Bristol)	1909
		19*	(100)	Sussex v. Lancashire (Liverpool)	1910
		23*	(98)	Sussex v. Kent (Tonbridge)	1910
		72*	(153)	Sussex v. Worcestershire (Hove)	1910
Virgin, R.	(1)	96*	(167)	Somerset v. Glamorgan (Weston-super-Mare)	1964
Walker, D. F.	(1)	107*	(236)	Oxford U. v. Gloucestershire (Oxford)	1933
Walker, I. D.	(1)	47*	(126)	Middlesex v. Surrey (Lord's)	1884
Walters, C. F.	(1)	53*	(100)	Worcestershire v. Glamorgan (Pontypridd)	1931
Ward, A.	(5)	140*	(281)	Lancashire v. Gloucestershire (Bristol)	1893
		45*	(97)	Lancashire v. Australians (Manchester)	1893
		75*	(168)	Lancashire v. Leicestershire (Manchester)	1895
		109*	(337)	Lancashire v. Hampshire (Southampton)	1899
		83*	(262)	Lancashire v. Middlesex (Lord's)	1899
Warne, F.	(1)	43*	(153)	Worcestershire v. Middlesex (Lord's)	1937
Warne, T.	(1)	61*	(129)	Victoria v. MacLaren's XI (Melbourne)	1901-02
Warner, E. W.	(3)	141*	(279)	Orange Free State v. Griqualand West (Kimberley)	1936-37
		102*	(210)	Orange Free State v. Border (Bethlehem)	1936-37

Carrying Bat Through a Complete Innings—*Cont.*

Player		Score	Total	Match	Season
Warner, E. W. (*cont.*)		87*	(235)	Orange Free State v. Eastern Province (Bloemfontein)	1937-38
Warner, P. F.	(10)	46*	(75)	Middlesex v. Gloucestershire (Lord's)	1898
		132*	(237)	England v. South Africa (Johannesburg)	1898-99
		197*	(400)	Middlesex v. Somerset (Lord's)	1901
		73*	(168)	Middlesex v. Yorkshire (Lord's)	1901
		65*	(130)	Middlesex v. Nottinghamshire (Nottingham)	1907
		59*	(139)	Middlesex v. Nottinghamshire (Lord's)	1907
		64*	(95)	M.C.C. v. Yorkshire (Lord's)	1908
		64*	(124)	M.C.C. v. Kent (Lord's)	1908
		102*	(201)	Middlesex v. Surrey (Lord's)	1909
		145*	(279)	Middlesex v. Hampshire (Lord's)	1910
Washbrook, C.	(1)	49*	(124)	Lancashire v. Worcestershire (Manchester)	1935
Watson, W.	(1)	79*	(132)	Leicestershire v. Yorkshire (Leicester)	1959
Webbe, A. J.	(8)	62*	(118)	Middlesex v. Yorkshire (Sheffield)	1882
		97*	(201)	Middlesex v. Nottinghamshire (Prince's)	1875
		44*	(134)	Middlesex v. Nottinghamshire (Nottingham)	1876
		83*	(196)	Middlesex v. Surrey (Oval)	1884
		63*	(119)	Middlesex v. Oxford U. (Chiswick Park)	1887
		243*	(527)	Middlesex v. Yorkshire (Huddersfield)	1887
		192*	(412)	Middlesex v. Kent (Canterbury)	1887
		37*	(82)	M.C.C. v. Kent (Lord's)	1888
Wells, G.	(2)	38*	(81)	Sussex v. Kent (Brighton)	1858
		55*	(73)	Sussex v. M.C.C. (Lord's)	1860
Wessels, N.	(1)	111*	(209)	Orange Free State v. Eastern Province (Bloemfontein)	1959-60
White, E. A.	(1)	48*	(103)	Kent v. Middlesex (Islington)	1868
Whitehead, H.	(1)	130*	(271)	Leicestershire v. Lancashire (Leicester)	1907
Whitelaw, P. E.	(1)	99*	(183)	Auckland & Wellington v. M.C.C. (Auckland)	1936-37
Whitfield, H. J.	(1)	41*	(109)	Sussex v. Surrey (Oval)	1884
Whittington, T. A. R.	(1)	115*	(318)	M.C.C. v. Jamaica (Kingston)	1910-11
Whysall, W. W.	(2)	109*	(242)	Nottinghamshire v. Kent (Canterbury)	1924
		111*	(238)	Nottinghamshire v. Essex (Nottingham)	1929
Wight, P. B.	(1)	222*	(450)	Somerset v. Kent (Taunton)	1959
Wilkinson, A. J.	(1)	84*	(209)	Gents. of Middlesex v. Gents. of England (Islington)	1865
Wilson, H. L.	(2)	42*	(104)	†Sussex v. Somerset (Taunton)	1919
		108*	(215)	Sussex v. Warwickshire (Hove)	1924
Wood, A. M.	(1)	73*	(149)	Philadelphians v. Cambridge U. (Cambridge)	1897
Wood, C. J. B.	(17)	21*	(98)	Leicestershire v. Yorkshire (Dewsbury)	1898
		46*	(262)	Leicestershire v. Sussex (Leicester)	1903
		118*	(322)	Leicestershire v. Yorkshire (Leicester)	1903
		160*	(419)	Leicestershire v. Yorkshire (Leicester)	1905
		200*	(507)	Leicestershire v. Hampshire (Leicester)	1905
		56*	(112)	Leicestershire v. Lancashire (Leicester)	1906
		105*	(303)	Leicestershire v. Essex (Southend)	1906
		110*	(220)	Leicestershire v. Northamptonshire (Northampton)	1906
		84*	(159)	Leicestershire v. Lancashire (Leicester)	1908
		38*	(116)	Leicestershire v. Derbyshire (Derby)	1910
		78*	(270)	Leicestershire v. Kent (Leicester)	1911
		54*	(151)	Leicestershire v. Northamptonshire (Leicester)	1911
		54*	(164)	Leicestershire v. Warwickshire (Hinckley)	1911
		107*	(309)	Leicestershire v. Yorkshire (Bradford) 1st innings	1911
		117*	(296)	Leicestershire v. Yorkshire (Bradford) 2nd innings	1911
		38*	(179)	Leicestershire v. Lancashire (Leicester)	1913
		164*	(392)	Leicestershire v. Warwickshire (Hinckley)	1913
Woodfull, W. M.	(4)	116*	(281)	Australians v. England XI (Blackpool)	1926
		30*	(66)	†Australia v. England (Brisbane)	1928-29
		67*	(164)	Victoria v. M.C.C. (Melbourne)	1928-29
		73*	(193)	†Australia v. England (Adelaide)	1932-33
Woolley, C. N.	(3)	62*	(113)	Northamptonshire v. Sussex (Hove)	1923
		59*	(130)	Northamptonshire v. Sussex (Hastings)	1925
		38*	(102)	Northamptonshire v. Yorkshire (Bradford)	1929
Worrell, F. M. M.	(1)	191*	(372)	West Indies v. England (Nottingham)	1957
Worthington, T. S.	(1)	156*	(376)	M.C.C. Australian Team v. Rest (Lord's)	1937
Wright, H.	(1)	26*	(63)	Leicestershire v. Hampshire (Southampton)	1914
Wright, L. G.	(3)	59*	(112)	Derbyshire v. Essex (Leyton)	1899
		58*	(136)	Derbyshire v. Essex (Leyton)	1903

Carrying Bat Through a Completed Innings—*Cont.*

Wright, L. G. (*cont.*)		50*	(104)	Derbyshire v. Leicestershire (Leicester) ..	1906
Wright, R. L. ..	(1)	96*	(201)	Northamptonshire v. Lancashire (Northampton)	1923
Wright, W. ..	(1)	127*	(371)	Northamptonshire v. Gloucestershire (Nottingham)	1883
Yarde, D. K. ..	(1)	27*	(85)	Baroda v. Nawanagar (Jamnagar)	1937-38
Zulch, J. W. ..	(1)	43*	(103)	South Africa v. England (Cape Town) ..	1909-10

R. Abel (Surrey) holds the record for the highest score by a player carrying his bat through a completed innings: 357* v. Somerset at The Oval in 1899. Surrey's total of 811 on that occasion is the highest through which a player has carried his bat.

FAST SCORING

The following times were taken from the moment that the batsman reached the wicket at the start of his innings.

FAST FIFTIES

min.		
51*— 8	C. C. Inman (57): Leics. v. Notts. (Nottingham)	1965
50*—11	C. I. J. Smith (66): Middx. v. Glos. (Bristol)	1938
50*—14	S. J. Pegler (50): South Africans v. Tasmania (Launceston)	1910-11
52*—14	F. T. Mann (53): Middx. v. Notts. (Lord's)	1921
50*—14	H. B. Cameron (56): Transvaal v. O.F.S. (Johannesburg)	1934-35
50*—14	C. I. J. Smith (52): Middx. v. Kent (Maidstone)	1935
50*—15	G. L. Jessop (61): Glos. v. Somerset (Bristol)	1904
53*—15	G. L. Jessop (92): Glos. v. Hants. (Cheltenham)	1907
50*—15	F. R. Foster (63): Warwicks. v. Middx. (Birmingham)	1914
50*—15	H. R. Murrell (50): Middx. v. Hants. (Southampton)	1921
50*—15	C. C. Dacre (64): New Zealanders v. Glos. (Cheltenham)	1927
50*—15	G. F. Earle (59): Somerset v. Glos. (Taunton)	1929
50*—15	G. Cox (51): Sussex v. Cambridge U. (Hove)	1934
50*—15	J. Hardstaff, Jnr. (77): Notts v. Glos. (Bristol)	1937
53*—15	R. Smith (78): Essex v. Notts. (Brentwood)	1949
51*—15	D. J. Shepherd (51): Glamorgan v. Australians (Swansea)	1961

FAST CENTURIES

100*—35	P. G. H. Fender (113*): Surrey v. Northants. (Northampton)	1920
101 —40	G. L. Jessop (101): Glos. v. Yorks. (Harrogate)	1897
100*—42	G. J. Jessop (191): Gentlemen of South v. Players of South (Hastings) ..	1907
100*—43	A. H. Hornby (106): Lancs. v. Somerset (Manchester)	1905
100*—45	E. M. Sprot (125*): Hants. v. Glos. (Bristol)	1911
100*—45	W. Voce (129): Notts. v. Glamorgan (Nottingham)	1931
100*—48	A. W. Carr (124): Notts. v. Sussex (Hove)	1925
100 —50	K. L. Hutchings (100): Kent v. Glos. (Catford)	1909
100*—50	D. R. A. Gehrs (119): South Australia v. Western Australia (Adelaide) ..	1912-13
100*—51	J. Hardstaff, Jnr. (126): Notts. v. Kent (Canterbury)	1937
100 —52	L. N. Constantine (100): West Indians v. Tasmania (Launceston) ..	1930-31
100*—52	R. M. Prideaux (118): South v. North (Blackpool)	1961
100*—53	G. L. Jessop (139): Glos. v. Surrey (Bristol)	1911
100*—53	M. G. Francis (115*): O.F.S. v. Griqualand West (Bloemfontein) ..	1927-28
100*—54	J. E. Raphael (111): Oxford U. v. Worcs. (Worcester)	1904
100*—54	J. N. Crawford (114): M.C.C. v. South Australia (Adelaide)	1907-08
100*—55	F. G. J. Ford (112): Middx. v. Philadelphians (Lord's)	1897
100*—55	A. P. Day (100*): Kent v. Hants. (Southampton)	1911
100*—55	G. L. Tapscott (111): Rest v. Transvaal (Johannesburg)	1911-12
100*—55	G. L. Jessop (116): Londesborough's XI v. Kent (Scarborough)	1913
102*—55	Hon. L. H. Tennyson (102*): Hants. v. Glos. (Southampton)	1927
100*—57	G. L. Jessop (124): Glos. v. Middx. (Lord's)	1901
101 —57	V. T. Trumper (101): N.S.W. v. Victoria (Sydney)	1905-06
100*—57	H. T. Bartlett (157): Sussex v. Australians (Hove)	1938
100*—59	G. L. Jessop (139): Glos. v. Yorks. (Bradford)	1900
100*—60	E. C. Streatfeild (145): Cambridge U. P. & P. v. Australians (Leyton) ..	1890
100*—60	J. J. Lyons (149): Australians v. M.C.C. (Lord's)	1893
100*—60	G. L. Jessop (112*): Rest v. Stoddart's XI (Hastings)	1898
100*—60	G. L. Jessop (126): Glos. v. Notts. (Nottingham)	1899
100*—60	G. L. Jessop (109): Glos. v. Middx. (Lord's)	1900

Fast Centuries—*Cont.*

min.		
100*—60	G. L. Jessop (169): M.C.C. v. Leics. (Lord's)	1901
100*—60	W. S. Lees (130): Surrey v. Hants. (Aldershot)	1905
100*—60	S. J. Snooke (121): Western Province v. Griqualand West (Johannesburg)	1906-07
100*—60	C. C. Page (164*): Middx. v. Somerset (Lord's)	1908
101 —60	G. N. Foster (101): Oxford U. v. Gentlemen of England (Eastbourne)	1908
101*—60	C. B. Llewellyn (101*): Hants. v. Sussex (Hove)	1909
100*—60	G. L. Jessop (165): Glos. v. Worcs. (Stourbridge)	1910
100*—60	P. J. Heather (109*): Transvaal v. Border (Durban)	1910-11
100*—60	H. L. Simms (126): Sussex v. Notts. (Hove)	1912
100*—60	K. O. Goldie (104): England XII v. Indian XII (Bombay)	1915-16
100*—60	W. V. S. Ling (187): Griqualand West v. O.F.S. (Pretoria)	1923-24
100*—60	A. W. Carr (100*): Notts. v. Northants. (Northampton)	1928
103 —60	L. N. Constantine (103): West Indians v. Middx. (Lord's)	1928
103 —60	C. R. Browne (103): West Indians v. Kent (Canterbury)	1928
100*—60	E. T. Killick (200*): Cambridge U. v. Glamorgan (Cambridge)	1929
101 —60	C. J. Barnett (101): Glos. v. Hants. (Southampton)	1937
100*—60	G. Cox (142): Sussex v. Yorks. (Hove)	1938
100*—60	C. J. Poole (154*): Notts. v. Leics. (Nottingham)	1949

FASTEST 150

150*—63	G. L. Jessop (191): Gentlemen of South v. Players of South (Hastings)	1907

FAST DOUBLE CENTURIES

200*—120	G. L. Jessop (286): Glos. v. Sussex (Hove)	1903
200*—130	G. L. Jessop (234): Glos. v. Somerset (Bristol)	1905
200*—131	V. T. Trumper (293): Australians v. Canterbury (Christchurch)	1913-14
200*—135	S. M. J. Woods (215): Somerset v. Sussex (Hove)	1895
200*—135	G. L. Jessop (233): Rest v. Yorks. (Lord's)	1901
200*—135	C. R. Maxwell (268): Cahn's XI v. Leics. (Nottingham)	1935
200*—140	G. L. Jessop (206): Glos. v. Notts. (Nottingham)	1904
200*—144	D. C. S. Compton (300): M.C.C. v. N-E. Transvaal (Benoni)	1948-49
200*—145	J. S. F. Morrison (233*): Cambridge U. v. M.C.C. (Cambridge)	1914
200*—145	C. G. Macartney (345): Australians v. Notts. (Nottingham)	1921
200*—150	H. K. Foster (216): Worcs. v. Somerset (Worcester)	1903
200*—150	M. M. Walford (201*): Oxford U. v. M.C.C. (Lord's)	1938

FAST TRIPLE CENTURIES

300 —181	D. C. S. Compton (300): M.C.C. v. N-E. Transvaal (Benoni)	1948-49
300*—205	F. E. Woolley (305*): M.C.C. v. Tasmania (Hobart)	1911-12
300*—205	C. G. Macartney (345): Australians v. Notts. (Nottingham)	1921
300*—213	D. G. Bradman (369): South Australia v. Tasmania (Adelaide)	1935-36

FAST INNINGS

(*The fastest completed innings graded by their duration in minutes*)

66 — 18	C. I. J. Smith: Middx. v. Glos. (Bristol)	1938
69 — 20	C. I. J. Smith :Middx. v. Sussex (Lord's)	1938
69 — 26	C. I. J. Smith: Middx. v. Somerset (Lord's)	1936
75 — 30	R. T. D. Perks: Worcs. v. Notts. (Nottingham)	1938
78 — 32	R. Smith: Essex v. Notts. (Brentwood)	1949
101 — 40	G. L. Jessop: Glos. v. Yorks. (Harrogate)	1897
113*— 42	P. G. H. Fender: Surrey v. Northants. (Northampton)	1920
114 — 58	J. N. Crawford: M.C.C. v. South Australia (Adelaide)	1907-08
119 — 60	D. R. A. Gehrs: South Australia v. Western Australia (Adelaide)	1912-13
124 — 70	A. W. Carr: Notts. v. Sussex (Hove)	1925
129 — 75	W. Voce: Notts. v. Glamorgan (Nottingham)	1931
139 — 80	P. G. H. Fender: Surrey v. Somerset (Oval)	1931
139*— 84	F. Barratt: Notts. v. Warwicks. (Coventry)	1928
147*— 89	Majid Jahangir: Pakistanis v. Glamorgan (Swansea)	1967
189 — 90	E. Alletson: Notts. v. Sussex (Hove)	1911
191 — 90	G. L. Jessop: Gentlemen of South v. Players of South (Hastings)	1907
206 —145	G. L. Jessop: Glos. v. Notts. (Nottingham)	1904
215 —150	S. M. J. Woods: Somerset v. Sussex (Hove)	1895
233 —150	G. L. Jessop: Rest v. Yorks. (Lord's)	1901

Fast Innings—*Cont.*

min.			
286 —175	G. L. Jessop: Glos. v. Sussex (Hove)	1903
293 —180	V. T. Trumper: Australians v. Canterbury (Christchurch)	1913-14
300 —181	D. C. S. Compton: M.C.C. v. N.E. Transvaal (Benoni)	1948-49
305*—210	F. E. Woolley: M.C.C. v. Tasmania (Hobart)	1911-12
345 —235	C. G. Macartney: Australians v. Notts. (Nottingham)	1921
369 —253	D. G. Bradman: South Australia v. Tasmania (Adelaide)	1935-36
383 —345	C. W. Gregory: N.S.W. v. Queensland (Brisbane)	1906-07
452*—415	D. G. Bradman: N.S.W. v. Queensland (Sydney)	1929-30

FASTEST PARTNERSHIPS

(The fastest partnerships graded by their duration in minutes)

runs	*wkt.*	*min.*		
113	9th	30	A. H. Hornby & W. Findlay: Lancs. v. Somerset (Manchester)	1905
116	5th	35	C. J. Burnup & E. Humphreys: Kent v. Somerset (Taunton)	1906
152	10th	40	E. Alletson & W. Riley: Notts. v. Sussex (Hove)	1911
171*	6th	42	P. G. H. Fender & H. A. Peach: Surrey v. Northants. (Northampton)	1920
181	7th	65	G. N. Foster & W. B. Burns: Worcs. v. Hants. (Worcester)	1905
202*	2nd	75	G. H. Hirst & W. Rhodes: Yorks. v. Somerset (Bath)	1906
236	6th	85	E. R. T. Holmes & R. E. C. Butterworth: Oxford U. v. Free Foresters (Oxford)	1927
255	3rd	90	J. S. F. Morrison & H. G. H. Mulholland: Cambridge U. v. M.C.C. (Cambridge)	1914
267*	5th	99	K. C. Bland & D. Lindsay: South Africa v. The Rest (Johannesburg)	1964-65
291	4th	105	C. G. Macartney & C. E. Pellew: Australians v. Notts. (Nottingham)	1921
295	2nd	130	A. Hartley & J. T. Tyldesley: Lancs. v. Somerset (Manchester)	1910
336	5th	145	W. H. Ponsford & H. S. B. Love: Victoria v. Tasmania (Melbourne)	1922-23
371	2nd	165	J. B. Hobbs & E. G. Hayes: Surrey v. Hants. (Oval)	1909
433	8th	180	V. T. Trumper & A. Sims: Australians v. Canterbury (Christchurch)	1913-14
487*	6th	245	G. A. Headley & C. C. Passailaigue: Jamaica v. Lord Tennyson's XI (Kingston)	1931-32
574*	4th	335	C. L. Walcott & F. M. M. Worrell: Barbados v. Trinidad (Port of Spain)	1945-46

BATSMEN REACHING 50 *WITH FEWEST SCORING STROKES*

Eleven Scoring Strokes

A. E. Harragin (50): West Indies v. W. G. Grace's XI (Crystal Palace) 1906
—5 sixes, 4 fours, 2 twos.

D. A. Sparks (57*): Orange Free State v. M.C.C. (Bloemfontein) 1938-39
—reached 50* with 6 sixes, 3 fours and 2 singles.

D. J. Shepherd (51): Glamorgan v. Australians (Swansea) 1961
—reached 51* out of 55 with 6 sixes, 3 fours, 1 two and 1 single.

C. C. Inman (57*): Leicestershire v. Nottinghamshire (Nottingham) 1965
—reached 51* out of 51 in 8 minutes (a record) off 12 balls with 5 sixes, 5 fours and 1 single. With Nottinghamshire giving away runs in hope of a declaration, Inman hit 12 slow full tosses from N. W. Hill to or over the mid-wicket boundary: 440064/466664.

Twelve Scoring Strokes

C. I. J. Smith (52): Middlesex v. Kent (Maidstone) 1935
—reached 50* in 14 minutes with 4 sixes, 6 fours, and 2 singles.

C. I. J. Smith (66): Middlesex v. Gloucestershire (Bristol) 1938
—reached 50* in 11 minutes with 6 sixes, 2 fours, 2 twos and 2 singles.

Thirteen Scoring Strokes

K. M. Rangnekar (102): Maharashtra v. Western India States (Poona) 1939-40
—reached 50* off his first 17 balls with 11 fours and 2 threes.

D. J. Shepherd (73): Glamorgan v. Derbyshire (Cardiff) 1961
—reached 52* out of 57, off 16 balls in 16 minutes with 6 sixes, 2 fours, 3 twos and 2 singles: 0016662422604166—including 26 off an over from E. Smith.

Batsmen Reaching 50 with Fewest Scoring Strokes

A. R. Windows (69): Cambridge U. v. Nottinghamshire (Nottingham) .. 1962
—reached 50* with 2 sixes, 9 fours and 2 singles.

K. F. Barrington (51*) Surrey v. Warwickshire (Oval) 1963
—reached 51* in 25 minutes with 3 sixes, 7 fours, 1 three and 2 singles.

A CENTURY BEFORE LUNCH

Although the playing time in the pre-lunch period may vary between 90 and 150 minutes, the only qualification for inclusion in these records is the scoring of one hundred runs during that session.

On the First Day of a Match

W. G. Grace (134): Gentlemen of South v. Players of South (Oval) 1873
H. H. Massie (206): Australians v. Oxford U. (Oxford) 1882
(*Scored 100* out of 145 at lunch in first innings in England*)
R. Abel (152): Surrey v. Leicestershire (Oval) 1896
W. Brockwell (102): Surrey v. Derbyshire (Oval) 1899
T. S. Fishwick (131): Warwickshire v. Gloucestershire (Bristol) 1900
V. T. Trumper (104): Australia v. England (Manchester) 1902
T. S. Fishwick (113): Warwickshire v. Leicestershire (Leicester) 1904
J. Douglas (114): Middlesex v. Somerset (Taunton) 1904
E. H. D. Sewell (107): Essex v. Warwickshire (Birmingham) 1904
(*Scored out of 142 for first wicket in 80 minutes.*)
J. W. Rothery (118): Yorkshire v. Hampshire (Bournemouth) 1905
V. T. Trumper (108): Australians v. Gloucestershire (Bristol) 1905
W. H. B. Evans (139*): Oxford U. v. M.C.C. (Lord's) 1905
R. H. Spooner (164): Lancashire v. Nottinghamshire (Nottingham) 1905
H. K. Foster (180): Worcestershire v. Somerset (Worcester) 1905
J. B. Hobbs (125): Surrey v. Worcestershire (Worcester) 1906
T. W. Hayward (135): Surrey v. Leicestershire (Oval) 1906
(*Scored 125* out of 184-0 at lunch*)
C. L. Townsend (214): Gloucestershire v. Worcestershire (Cheltenham) 1906
(*Scored 130* out of 214-2 at lunch*)
R. H. Spooner (240): Lancashire v. Somerset (Bath) 1906
P. F. Warner (149): Middlesex v. Surrey (Oval) 1907
G. H. Simpson-Hayward (105): Worcestershire v. Oxford U. (Oxford) 1908
(*Went in to bat at No. 6 and scored 105 out of 140 in 80 minutes.*)
J. B. Hobbs (205): Surrey v. Hampshire (Oval) 1909
T. W. Hayward (106): Surrey v. Warwickshire (Oval) 1910
A. O. Jones (103): Nottinghamshire v. Gloucestershire (Nottingham) 1911
J. B. Hobbs (107): Surrey v. Gloucestershire (Bristol) 1913
F. L. Bowley (177): Worcestershire v. Warwickshire (Birmingham) 1913
J. B. Hobbs (100): Surrey v. Yorkshire (Bradford) 1914
F. L. Bowley (276): Worcestershire v. Hampshire (Dudley) 1914
J. B. Hobbs (102): Surrey v. Lancashire (Manchester) 1919
J. B. Hobbs (134): Surrey v. Leicestershire (Leicester) 1920
P. V. Williams (146): Army v. Royal Navy (Lord's) 1920
F. L. Bowley (131): Worcestershire v. Essex (Leyton) 1920
J. W. Zulch (185): Transvaal v. Orange Free State (Bloemfontein) 1920-21
A. J. Richardson (280): South Australia v. M.C.C. (Adelaide) 1922-23
(*The first time the feat had been achieved in Australia*).
A. Ducat (115): Surrey v. Cambridge U. (Oval) 1923
J. B. Hobbs (104): Surrey v. Gloucestershire (Oval) 1925
J. S. Hiddleston (212): Wellington v. Canterbury (Wellington) 1925-26
C. G. Macartney (151): Australia v. England (Leeds) 1926
A. Sandham (150): M.C.C. v. Europeans (Rawalpindi) 1926-27
M. W. Tate (133): M.C.C. v. Parsis & Europeans (Bombay) 1926-27
J. B. Hobbs (131): Surrey v. Nottinghamshire (Oval) 1927
M. W. Tate (101): Sussex v. Hampshire (Portsmouth) 1927
(*Scored out of 144 for first wicket in 68 minutes.*)
J. M. Gregory (152): New South Wales v. New Zealanders (Sydney) 1927-28
K. S. Duleepsinhji (121): Sussex v. Glamorgan (Eastbourne) 1928
(*Scored 102* out of 137 in 65 minutes.*)
H. H. Gibbons (107): Worcestershire v. Hampshire (Southampton) 1928
H. T. W. Hardinge (114): Kent v. Hampshire (Dover) 1928
K. S. Duleepsinhji (115): Sussex v. Kent (Hastings) 1929

A Century Before Lunch

D. G. Bradman (334): Australia v. England (Leeds) 1930
F. E. Woolley (110): Kent v. Surrey (Blackheath) 1930
C. A. Roach (180): West Indians v. Surrey (Oval) 1933
W. W. Keeton (110): Nottinghamshire v. Yorkshire (Bradford) 1933
D. G. Bradman (132): Australians v. Leveson-Gower's XI (Scarborough) 1934
W. R. Hammond (116): M.C.C. v. Trinidad (Port of Spain) 1934-35
W. G. L. F. Lowndes (118): Hampshire v. Kent (Portsmouth) 1935
W. R. Hammond (252): Gloucestershire v. Leicestershire (Leicester) 1935
H. Gimblett (106): Somerset v. Northamptonshire (Kettering) 1936
A. H. Dyson (104): Glamorgan v. Kent (Swansea) 1937
(*Achieved on first day of season.*)
R. H. Moore (316): Hampshire v. Warwickshire (Bournemouth) 1937
E. Paynter (322): Lancashire v. Sussex (Hove) 1937
J. H. Parks (104): Sussex v. Nottinghamshire (Hove) 1937
A. E. Fagg (244): Kent v. Essex (Colchester) 1938
F. E. Woolley (136): Kent v. Worcestershire (Tonbridge) 1938
J. D. Robertson (154): Middlesex v. Warwickshire (Lord's) 1939
H. Gimblett (114): Somerset v. Cambridge U. (Bath) 1946
S. M. Brown (118): Middlesex v. Essex (Westcliff) 1946
J. D. Robertson (118): Middlesex v. Nottinghamshire (Nottingham) 1947
R. G. Draper (122): Eastern Province v. Griqualand West (Kimberley) 1947-48
A. R. Morris (290): Australians v. Gloucestershire (Bristol) 1948
H. Gimblett (111): Commonwealth v. Governor's XI (Nagpur) 1950-51
E. A. B. Rowan (176): Transvaal v. Rhodesia (Salisbury) 1950-51
R. G. Draper (127): Griqualand West v. Orange Free State (Bloemfontein) 1951-52
Imtiaz Ahmed (103): Pakistan v. East Zone (Jamshedpur) 1952-53
R. G. Draper (145): Griqualand West v. Rhodesia (Salisbury) 1952-53
R. G. Draper (129): Griqualand West v. Border (Kimberley) 1952-53
R. T. Simpson (101): M.C.C. v. Yorkshire (Scarborough) 1953
L. Hutton (241): Players v. Gentlemen (Scarborough) 1953
R. T. Simpson (125): Commonwealth v. Holkar (Indore) 1953-54
F. M. M. Worrell (110): Commonwealth v. North Zone (Amritsar) 1953-54
R. T. Simpson (147): Nottinghamshire v. Somerset (Nottingham) 1954
W. R. Endean (235): Transvaal v. Orange Free State (Johannesburg) 1954-55
(*Score 197* at lunch after three hours' play.*)
O. C. Dawson (139): Border v. Rhodesia (East London) 1954-55
K. N. Kirton (124): Border v. Rhodesia (East London) 1954-55
(*The above two instances were on same day in same match.*)
L. B. Koch (111): Orange Free State v. Western Province (Bloemfontein) 1954-55
D. J. McGlew (121): Natal v. Orange Free State (Bloemfontein) 1954-55
P. N. F. Mansell (111): Rhodesia v. Griqualand West (Kimberley) 1954-55
D. O'Connell-Jones (121): Rhodesia v. Orange Free State (Salisbury) 1955-56
F. Seyfried (144): North-Eastern Transvaal v. Orange Free State (Bloemfontein) .. 1955-56
K. N. Kirton (111): Border v. North-Eastern Transvaal (Benoni) 1955-56
E. R. Dexter (185): Cambridge U. v. Lancashire (Cambridge) 1957
J. D. Robertson (119): Middlesex v. Sussex (Lord's) 1957
P. E. Richardson (116): Worcestershire v. Derbyshire (Derby) 1957
W. J. Stewart (151): Warwickshire v. Combined Services (Birmingham) 1959
(*Scored 131* out of 180-1 at lunch.*)
G. Pullar (103): Rest of England v. Yorkshire (Oval) 1959
Hanif Mohammad (222): Pakistanis v. Combined Universities (Poona) 1960-61
C. C. McDonald (100): Australians v. Cambridge U. (Cambridge) 1961
G. E. Barker (181*): Essex v. Kent (Colchester) 1961
J. H. Edrich (110): Pearce's XI v. Australians (Scarborough) 1961
Mushtaq Mohammad (229*): Karachi Whites v. East Pakistan (Karachi) 1961-62
D. M. Green (121): Lancashire v. Glamorgan (Cardiff) 1964
P. E. Richardson (124): Kent v. Hampshire (Canterbury) 1964
R. W. Barber (138): Warwickshire v. Australians (Birmingham) 1964
R. E. Marshall (163): Hampshire v. Glamorgan (Cardiff) 1964
R. M. Cowper (110): Australians v. Pearce's XI (Scarborough) 1964
B. Awasthy (142): Services v. Jammu & Kashmir (New Delhi) 1965-66
C. Milburn (113): Northamptonshire v. Nottinghamshire (Nottingham) 1966
C. Milburn (203): Northamptonshire v. Essex (Clacton) 1966

On Other Days

J. Briggs (186): Lancashire v. Surrey (Liverpool) 1885
(*Score taken from 81* to 186 on second morning.*)

A Century Before Lunch—*Cont.*

W. W. Read (109): Gentlemen of England v. Australians (Lord's) 1888
(*Achieved on second morning.*)
L. C. H. Palairet (181): Somerset v. Oxford U. (Oxford) 1894
(*Score taken from 80* to 181 on third morning.*)
K. S. Ranjitsinhji (154*): England v. Australia (Manchester) 1896
(*Score taken from 41* to 154* on third morning.*)
R. Abel (193): Surrey v. Derbyshire (Oval) 1900
(*101* at lunch on second day.*)
K. S. Ranjitsinhji (234*): Sussex v. Surrey (Hastings) 1902
(*Scored 180 runs in 150 minutes on second morning, taking his score from 54* to 234*.*)
C. Hill (142): Australia v. South Africa (Johannesburg) 1902-03
(*Score taken from 28* to 138* on third morning.*)
E. H. D. Sewell (106*): Essex v. Surrey (Oval) 1904
(*Achieved on second day.*)
S. J. Snooke (157): South Africans v. Somerset (Bath) 1907
(*Innings started on third morning.*)
F. H. Gillingham (194): Essex v. Gloucestershire (Leyton) 1908
(*Score taken from 60* to 194* on second morning.*)
F. A. Tarrant (250*): Middlesex v. Essex (Leyton) 1914
J. W. Hearne (106*): Middlesex v. Essex (Leyton) 1914
(*Achieved in same match, Tarrant taking his score from 140* to 250* on second morning, while the total was advanced from 245 to 464.*)
J. L. Bryan (106): Kent v. Lancashire (Maidstone) 1921
(*Achieved on second morning.*)
C. G. Macartney (120): New South Wales v. Wellington (Wellington) 1923-24
(*Innings started on third morning, 112* at lunch.*)
C. G. Macartney (120): New South Wales v. Otago (Dunedin) 1923-24
(*Score taken from 19* to 120 on third morning in 91 minutes.*)
A. Punch (176): New South Wales v. Otago (Dunedin) 1923-24
(*Score taken from 59* to 175* on third morning.*)
A. E. R. Gilligan (112): Gentlemen v. Players (Oval) 1924
(*Achieved on third morning.*)
J. B. Hobbs (211): England v. South Africa (Lord's) 1924
(*Score taken from 12* to 114* on second morning.*)
A. P. F. Chapman (136): Kent v. Hampshire (Canterbury) 1926
(*104 runs scored on second morning.*)
C. C. Dacre (109): Auckland v. Otago (Dunedin) 1926-27
(*105 runs scored in 102 minutes on third morning.*)
N. E. Haig (104*): Middlesex v. Nottinghamshire (Nottingham) 1927
(*Achieved on third morning—only available play in match.*)
W. R. Hammond (187): Gloucestershire v. Lancashire (Manchester) 1927
(*131 out of 186 scored on third morning.*)
W. Vorrath (103): Otago v. Wellington (Dunedin) 1927-28
(*Achieved on third morning.*)
T. F. Shepherd (132): Surrey v. Warwickshire (Oval) 1928
(*109* in 85 minutes on second morning.*)
F. E. Woolley (198): Kent v. Derbyshire (Maidstone) 1928
(*Score taken from 52* to 170* on third morning.*)
E. Hendren (174): Rest of England v. Lancashire (Oval) 1928
(*Score taken from 42* to 174 on third morning.*)
R. C. Blunt (221): Otago v. Canterbury (Dunedin) 1928-29
(*Score taken from 104* to 210* on third morning.*)
H. G. Owen-Smith (129): South Africa v. England (Leeds) 1929
(*Score taken from 27* to 129 on third morning.*)
E. T. Killick (200*): Cambridge U. v. Glamorgan (Cambridge) 1929
(*Achieved on third morning.*)
K. S. Duleepsinhji (202): Sussex v. Essex (Leyton) 1929
(*Achieved on third morning of match, score 122* at lunch*)
D. G. Bradman (452*): New South Wales v. Queensland (Sydney) 1929-30
(*Score taken from 205* to 310* on third morning.*)
J. L. Powell (164): Canterbury v. Otago (Christchurch) 1929-30
(*Achieved on second morning.*)
F. T. Badcock (105): Otago v. Canterbury (Christchurch) 1931-32
(*Achieved on third morning.*)
W. R. Hammond (336*): England v. New Zealand (Auckland) 1932-33
(*Score taken from 41* to 152* on second morning.*)

A Century Before Lunch—*Cont.*

F. E. Woolley (161): Kent v. Derbyshire (Canterbury) 1933
(Score taken from 21 to 131* on second morning.)*
F. R. Santall (201*): Warwickshire v. Northamptonshire (Northampton) 1933
(Score taken from 28 to 201* in 116 minutes on third morning.)*
P. E. Whitelaw (155): Auckland v. Wellington (Auckland) 1934-35
(Innings started on third morning; 102 at lunch)*
W. R. Hammond (163): Gloucestershire v. Kent (Canterbury) 1935
(Achieved on second morning.)
S. J. McCabe (189*): Australia v. South Africa (Johannesburg) 1935-36
(Score taken from 59 to 159* on fourth morning.)*
J. N. Grover (121): Oxford U. v. Cambridge U. (Lord's) 1937
(Score taken from 14 to 121* on second day.)*
B. P. King (124): Worcestershire v. Hampshire (Worcester) 1938
(Achieved on second morning.)
D. Tallon (152): Combined XI v. New South Wales (Brisbane) 1940-41
(Achieved on third morning.)
Vijay Hazare (309): Rest v. Hindus (Bombay) 1943-44
(Achieved on third morning.)
K. R. Miller (185): Dominions XI v. England XI (Lord's) 1945
(Score taken from 61 to 185 on third morning.)*
Mushtaq Ali (108): Prince's XI v. Australian Services (New Delhi) 1945-46
(Achieved on second morning.)
A. P. Singleton (152): Worcestershire v. Hampshire (Southampton) 1946
(Achieved on second morning.)
B. P. King (145): Lancashire v. Gloucestershire (Gloucester) 1946
(Score taken from 34 to 145 on third morning.)*
D. G. Bradman (133*): Australians v. Lancashire (Manchester) 1948
(Score taken from 25 to 133* in 150 minutes on second morning.)*
W. J. Edrich (128): Gentlemen v. Australians (Lord's) 1948
(Achieved on third morning of match, 104 at lunch.)*
A. R. Morris (108*): New South Wales v. Queensland (Sydney) 1948-49
(Achieved on third morning.)
D. C. S. Compton (300): M.C.C. v. North-Eastern Transvaal (Benoni) 1948-49
(Score taken from 120 to 300 in 90 minutes on second morning.)*
F. B. Smith (146): Canterbury v. Auckland (Auckland) 1948-49
(Score taken from 13 to 116* on third morning.)*
L. G. Berry (141): Leicestershire v. Sussex (Hove) 1949
(Score taken from 9 to 115* on second morning.)*
T. N. Pearce (111*): Essex v. Kent (Ilford) 1949
(Score taken from 4 to 111* on third morning.)*
A. E. G. Rhodes (126): Derbyshire v. Nottinghamshire (Ilkeston) 1949
(Achieved on third morning.)
B. Sutcliffe (100*): New Zealanders v. Essex (Southend) 1949
(Achieved on third morning.)
L. Hutton (141): Yorkshire v. Somerset (Huddersfield) 1950
(Score taken from 2 to 102* on second morning.)*
G. Dews (101*): Worcestershire v. Hampshire (Dudley) 1950
(Score taken from 1 to 101* on third morning.)*
J. R. Reid (283): Wellington v. Otago (Wellington) 1951-52
(Score taken from 80 to 180* on third morning.)*
G. M. Emmett (117): Gloucestershire v. Nottinghamshire (Bristol) 1952
(Achieved on second day of match, 106 at lunch.)*
R. G. Broadbent (108): Worcestershire v. Leicestershire (Leicester) 1952
(Achieved on third day.)
W. H. H. Sutcliffe (171*): Yorkshire v. Worcestershire (Worcester) 1952
(Score taken from 70 to 171* on second day.)*
R. N. Harvey (180): Australians v. Glamorgan (Swansea) 1953
(Score taken from 20 to 152* on second morning.)*
S. C. Guillen (197): Canterbury v. Fiji (Christchurch) 1953-54
(Scored 122 runs on second morning.)
D. J. Insole (114*): Essex v. Nottinghamshire (Southend) 1955
T. E. Bailey (114*): Essex v. Nottinghamshire (Southend) 1955
(These two instances were achieved on the third day, Insole 9 and Bailey 12* at the start of play.)*
A. C. Walton (116*): Oxford U. v. Sussex (Oxford) 1956
(Achieved on second morning, reaching his century in 61 minutes.)
J. W. Burke (125*): Australians v. Somerset (Taunton) 1956
(Score taken from 10 to 125* on third morning.)*

A Century Before Lunch—*Cont.*

P. E. Richardson (134): Worcestershire v. Nottinghamshire (Worcester) 1956
(*Score taken from 12* to 122* on third morning.*)

N. F. Horner (129*): Warwickshire v. Leicestershire (Birmingham) 1956
(*Achieved on third day, no play being possible on previous days.*)

R. E. Marshall (163): Hampshire v. Glamorgan (Portsmouth) 1957
(*Achieved on second morning of match, score 104* at lunch.*)

D. C. S. Compton (109): Middlesex v. Essex (Leyton) 1957
(*Score taken from 1* to 104* on second morning.*)

M. C. Cowdrey (165): Kent v. Nottinghamshire (Nottingham) 1957
(*Achieved on second morning.*)

L. E. Favell (190): Australians v. Griqualand West (Kimberley) 1957-58
(*Score taken from 53* to 167* on third morning.*)

R. A. Gale (106): Middlesex v. Kent (Gravesend) 1959
(*Achieved on third morning.*)

W. J. Stewart (155): Warwickshire v. Lancashire (Blackpool) 1959
(*Achieved on second morning of match, score 107* at lunch.*)

M. J. K. Smith (200*): Warwickshire v. Worcestershire (Birmingham) 1959
(*Score taken from 77* to 200* on third morning.*)

M. J. K. Smith (182*): Warwickshire v. Gloucestershire (Stroud) 1959
(*Score taken from 12* to 124* on third morning.*)

J. Pressdee (107*): Glamorgan v. Kent (Dartford) 1959
(*Achieved on third morning.*)

W. R. Endean (204*): Transvaal v. Border (Johannesburg) 1959-60
(*Score taken from 96* to 204* on second morning.*)

M. K. Elgie (162*): Natal v. Border (East London) 1959-60
(*Score taken from 15* to 162* on second morning.*)

K. F. H. Smith (108): Central Districts v. Wellington (Wanganui) 1959-60
(*Score taken from 8* to 108 on second morning.*)

B. Sutcliffe (264): Otago v. Central Districts (Dunedin) 1959-60
(*Score taken from 156* to 264 on second morning.*)

E. R. Dexter (107): M.C.C. v. Leeward Islands (St. John's, Antigua) 1959-60
(*Achieved in 85 minutes on third morning.*)

E. R. Dexter (133): Sussex v. Somerset (Taunton) 1960
(*Achieved on third morning.*)

R. E. Marshall (111): Hampshire v. Leicestershire (Bournemouth) 1960
(*Score taken from 0* to 111 on third morning.*)

K. F. Barrington (111): Players v. Gentlemen (Scarborough) 1960
(*Score taken from 8* to 111 on third morning.*)

B. Sutcliffe (201): Otago v. Northern Districts (Hamilton) 1960-61
(*Score taken from 15* to 115* on second morning.*)

W. E. Alley (221*): Somerset v. Warwickshire (Nuneaton) 1961
(*Score taken from 12* to 146* out of 185 runs added on third morning.*)

B. L. Reynolds (155): Northamptonshire v. Cambridge U. (Northampton) 1961
(*Score taken from 7* to 127* on third morning.*)

R. N. Harvey (140): Australians v. Nottinghamshire (Nottingham) 1961
(*Score taken from 11* to 134* on second morning.*)

L. J. Lenham (102*): Sussex v. Middlesex (Hove) 1961
(*Achieved on third morning.*)

J. Pressdee (115): Glamorgan v. Sussex (Cardiff) 1961
(*Scored 102* before lunch on third day.*)

E. R. Dexter (117): Sussex v. Pakistanis (Hove) 1962
(*Scored 12* to 117* on second morning.*)

A. S. M. Oakman (177): Sussex v. Nottinghamshire (Eastbourne) 1962
(*Score taken from 10* to 120* on second morning.*)

W. J. Stewart (182*): Warwickshire v. Leicestershire (Hinckley) 1962
(*Scored 103* before lunch on third day.*)

B. R. Knight (165): Essex v. Middlesex (Brentwood) 1962
(*Score taken from 16* to 122* on second morning.*)

A. W. Catt (162): Kent v. Leicestershire (Maidstone) 1962
(*Score taken from 0* to 121* on second morning.*)

R. M. Prideaux (109): Gentlemen v. Players (Lord's) 1962
(*Score taken from 7* to 109 on third morning.*)

Ijaz Butt (129*): Pakistanis v. Kent (Canterbury) 1962
(*Scored 105* before lunch on third day.*)

J. R. Reid (296): Wellington v. Northern Districts (Wellington) 1962-63
(*Score taken from 0* to 174* in 142 minutes of second morning.*)

K. J. Grieves (123): Lancashire v. West Indians (Manchester) 1963
(*Achieved in 113 minutes on third morning.*)

A Century Before Lunch—*Cont.*

P. E. Richardson (131): Kent v. Leicestershire (Leicester) 1963
(*Score taken from 26* to 131 on second morning.*)
R. B. Simpson (125): Australians v. Somerset (Taunton) 1964
(*Achieved in 140 minutes on third day.*)
R. E. Marshall (106): Hampshire v. Derbyshire (Bournemouth) 1964
(*Achieved on second morning.*)
B. L. Reynolds (141): Northamptonshire v. Lancashire (Manchester) 1964
(*Scored 137* before lunch on third day.*)
M. C. Cowdrey (100*): Kent v. Hampshire (Canterbury) 1964
(*Achieved on third morning.*)
N. Rosendorff (178): Orange Free State v. North-Eastern Transvaal (Pretoria) .. 1964-65
(*Score taken from 55* to 178 in 120 minutes on second morning.*)
J. R. Reid (126): Wellington v. Northern Districts (Wellington) 1964-65
(*Scored 120* before lunch on second day.*)
M. R. Hallam (149*): Leicestershire v. Worcestershire (Leicester) 1965
(*Achieved century before lunch on third day.*)
K. G. Suttle (102): Sussex v. Gloucestershire (Eastbourne) 1965
(*Achieved on third morning.*)
C. Milburn (152*): Northamptonshire v. Gloucestershire (Northampton) .. 1965
(*Score taken from 47* to 152* on second morning.*)
C. Milburn (137): Northamptonshire v. Sussex (Hove) 1966
(*Score taken from 7* to 111* on second morning.*)
R. B. Kanhai (192*): West Indians v. Oxford U. (Oxford) 1966
(*Score taken from 50* to 192* in 150 minutes on third morning.*)
J. M. Parks (119): Sussex v. Lancashire (Hove) 1966
(*Score taken from 14* to 119 on third morning.*)
Majid Jahangir (147*): Pakistanis v. Glamorgan (Swansea) 1967
(*Achieved out of 222 runs added in 89 minutes on third morning.*)

MOST RUNS IN PRE-LUNCH SESSION

197 W. R. Endean (235): Transvaal v. Orange Free State (Johannesburg) 1954-55
(*In three hours on first morning of match.*)
180 K. S. Ranjitsinhji (234*): Sussex v. Surrey (Hastings) 1902
(*Score taken from 54* to 234* in 150 minutes on second day.*)
180 D. C. S. Compton (300): M.C.C. v. North-Eastern Transvaal (Benoni) 1948-49
(*Score taken from 120* to 300 in 90 minutes on second day.*
174 J. R. Reid (296): Wellington v. Northern Districts (Wellington) 1962-63
(*In 142 minutes on second morning.*)
173 F. R. Santall (201*): Warwickshire v. Northamptonshire (Northampton) .. 1933
(*Score taken from 28* to 201* in 116 minutes on third day.*)
164 J. L. Powell (164): Canterbury v. Otago (Christchurch) 1929-30
(*In 130 minutes on second morning of match.*)

BATSMEN SCORING 300 *RUNS IN A DAY*

345 C. G. Macartney (345): Australians v. Nottinghamshire (Nottingham) 1921
(*Scored out of 540 in 235 minutes on the first day.*)
334 W. H. Ponsford (352): Victoria v. New South Wales (Melbourne) 1926-27
(*Scored out of 573 in 322 minutes on the second day.*)
333 K. S. Ranjitsinhji (333): Sussex v. Northamptonshire (Hove) 1930
(*Scored out of 513 in 330 minutes on the first day.*)
331 J. D. Robertson (331*): Middlesex v. Worcestershire (Worcester) 1949
(*Scored out of 623 in 390 minutes on the first day.*)
322 E. Paynter (322): Lancashire v. Sussex (Hove) 1937
(*Scored out of 546 in 300 minutes on the first day.*)
318 C. W. Gregory (383): New South Wales v. Queensland (Brisbane) 1906-07
(*Score taken from 48* to 366* on the second day in 345 minutes.*)
316 R. H. Moore (316): Hampshire v. Warwickshire (Bournemouth) 1937
(*Scored out of 509 in 380 minutes on the first day.*)
315 R. C. Blunt (338*): Otago v. Canterbury (Christchurch) 1931-32
(*Scored out of 540 in 320 minutes on the third day.*)
312 J. M. Brearley (312*): M.C.C. Under-25 v. North Zone (Peshawar) 1966-67
(*Scored out of 514 in 330 minutes on the first day.*)
309 D. G. Bradman (334): Australia v. England (Leeds) 1930
(*Scored out of 456 in 340 minutes on the first day.*)

Batsmen Scoring 300 Runs in a Day—*Cont.*

307 W. H. Ashdown (332): Kent v. Essex (Brentwood) 1934
Scored out of 623 in 360 minutes of the first day.)

306 A. Ducat (306*): Surrey v. Oxford U. (Oval) 1919
(*Scored in 280 minutes on the first day.*)

305 F. R. Foster (305*): Warwickshire v. Worcestershire (Dudley) 1914
(*Scored out of 448 in 260 minutes on the second day.*)

TEAMS SCORING 600 *RUNS IN A DAY*

600 *Runs by One Team*

721-10	Australians (721) v. Essex at Southend	1948
651-2	West Indians (682-2d) v. Leicestershire at Leicester	1950
649-8	New South Wales (752-8d) v. Otago at Dunedin	1923-24
645-4	Surrey (742) v. Hampshire at The Oval	1909
644-8	Oxford U. (644-8d) v. Leveson-Gower's XI at Eastbourne	1921
640-8	Lancashire (640-8d) v. Sussex at Hove	1937
636-7	Free Foresters (636-7d) v. Cambridge U. at Cambridge	1938
625-6	Gloucestershire (625-6d) v. Worcestershire at Dudley	1934
623-2	Kent (803-4d) v. Essex at Brentwood	1934
623-5	Middlesex (623-5d) v. Worcestershire at Worcester	1949
621-6	Lancashire (676-6d) v. Hampshire at Manchester	1911
621-8	Australians (658) v. Auckland at Auckland	1913-14
618-4	South Africa (618-4d) v. Rest of South Africa at Johannesburg	1964-65
616-5	Surrey (616-5d) v. Northamptonshire at The Oval	1921
608-7	Australians (675) v. Nottinghamshire at Nottingham	1921
608-7	Players (651-7d) v. Gentlemen at The Oval	1934
607-3	Hampshire (672-7d) v. Somerset at Taunton	1899
607-6	Kent (607-6d) v. Gloucestershire at Cheltenham	1910
607-4	Surrey (619-5d) v. Northamptonshire at Northampton	1920
603-5	Rest of England (603-5d) v. Middlesex at the Oval	1920

600 *Runs Aggregate by Both Teams*

685	North (169-8d & 255-7) v. South (261-8d) at Blackpool	1961
666	Northamptonshire (59-2) v. Surrey (607-4) at Northampton	1920
663	Leicestershire (160-2) v. Middlesex (503-4) at Leicester	1947
649	Hampshire (570-8) v. Somerset (79-3) at Taunton	1901
647	Sussex (115) v. Surrey (532-6d) at The Oval	1919
639	Hampshire (245-7 & 63-0) v. Gloucestershire (331-4d) at Southampton	1919
626	Leicestershire (291) v. Nottinghamshire (335-4) at Nottingham	1919
626	Surrey (337-2) v. Hampshire (289) at Southampton	1919
622	Essex (99-2) v. Sussex (523) at Leyton	1919
619	Rest of England (603-5) v. Middlesex (16-2) at The Oval	1920
616	Transvaal (557) v. Orange Free State (59-6) at Johannesburg	1929-30
613	Worcestershire (6-1 & 47-1) v. Essex (560-5d) at Leyton	1921
610	Kent (544) v. Essex (66-3) at Gravesend	1938
608	Somerset (329-6) v. Oxford U. (279) at Oxford	1901
604	Natal (553) v. Orange Free State (51-3) at Bloemfontein	1954-55
603	Kent (532-8) v. Leicestershire (71-1) at Maidstone	1962
602	Lancashire (408) v. Essex (194-3) at Manchester	1919
601	Surrey (361-5) v. Middlesex (240) at The Oval	1919

The longer hours of play in South African two-day matches have produced the following instances of sides aggregating 600 runs in a day:—

720—15 wkts	Orange Free State (412-5) v. Border (308) at Bloemfontein	1920-21
665—20 wkts	Transvaal (326) v. Rest of South Africa (339) at Johannesburg	1911-12
661—20 wkts	Griqualand West (460) v. Border (201) at Kimberley	1920-21
645—16 wkts	Transvaal (450-9) v. Orange Free State (195-7) at Johannesburg	1920-21
644—12 wkts	Natal (587) v. Eastern Province (57-2) at Durban	1939-40
641—12 wkts	Transvaal (499) v. Sherwell's XI (142-2) at Johannesburg	1913-14
606— 9 wkts	Griqualand West (378-5) v. Orange Free State (228-4) at Pretoria	1923-24

Fast Scoring—*Cont.*

FAST SCORING BY TEAMS

(Qualification: 200 runs at the rate of 110 runs per 100 balls)

Runs per 100 balls			
156	219—2	Kent v. Gloucestershire (Dover)	1937
132	279—1	Nottinghamshire v. Leicestershire (Nottingham)	1949
127	218—5	Yorkshire v. Sussex (Hove)	1959
125	219—3	Karachi A. v. Quetta (Karachi)	1962-63
123	267—4d	Hampshire v. Essex (Bournemouth)	1919
121	460	Griqualand West v. Border (Kimberley)	1920-21
115	313	Gentlemen of South v. Players of South (Hastings)	1907
111	234—3	Kent v. Surrey (Oval)	1939
110	358—5d	Kent v. Somerset (Taunton)	1906
110	448	New South Wales v. Tasmania (Hobart)	1909-10
110	500	Australian XI v. Tasmania (Hobart)	1960-61

MOST RUNS FROM ONE HIT

Ten

S. H. Hill-Wood off C. J. Burnup: Derby v. M.C.C. (Lord's) 1900
(*Recorded under the 'net-system' of scoring in trial use in 1900*)

Nine

Hon. F. Ponsonby off name unknown: M.C.C. v. Cambridge U. (Cambridge) .. 1842
T. A. Raynes off name unknown: Gentlemen of Surrey & Sussex v. Gentlemen of England (Lord's) 1856
T. Hearne off name unknown: Middlesex v. Surrey (Oval) 1870
R. Daft off I. D. Walker: Players v. Gentlemen (Oval) 1872
C. Hill off T. Richardson: Australians v. Surrey (Oval) 1902
J. A. Cuffe off name unknown: Worcestershire v. Philadelphians (Worcester) .. 1903
R. A. Duff off W. Brearley: Australians v. Gentlemen (Crystal Palace) 1905
Hon. J. B. Coventry off C. W. L. Parker: Worcestershire v. Gloucestershire (Worcester) 1923
A. Ducat off J. H. Parks: Surrey v. Sussex (Oval) 1929
A. Staples off E. W. Clark: Nottinghamshire v. Northamptonshire (Kettering) .. 1932
J. D. Robertson off H. S. Squires: M.C.C. v. Surrey (Lord's) 1948
W. J. Edrich off V. H. Broderick: Middlesex v. Northamptonshire (Lord's) 1949

The highest scoring strokes, all-run and without the assistance of overthrows, have been:

9 Hon. F. Ponsonby off name unknown: M.C.C. v. Cambridge U. (Cambridge) .. 1842
6 C. C. Case off P. G. H. Fender: Somerset v. Surrey (Oval) 1925
(Two balls later, in the same over, Case hit and ran a five)
6 T. G. Evans off T. E. Bailey: Players v. Gentlemen (Lord's) 1949

MOST RUNS OFF ONE OVER

Four-Ball Overs

22 (6466) H. J. H. Scott off S. Wade: Australians v. Yorks (Sheffield) 1886
20 (6446) C. I. Thornton off D. Buchanan: Cambridge U. v. Gentlemen (Cambridge) 1871
20 (6446) G. J. Bonnor off A. P. Lucas: Australians v. I. Zingari (Scarborough) .. 1882

Five-Ball Overs

21 (54444) E. Jones & W. P. Howell off E. R. Wilson: Australians v. Cambridge U. (Cambridge) 1899
21 (66414) A. E. Trott & C. M. Wells off E. J. Tyler: Middx. v. Somerset (Taunton) 1899

Six-Ball Overs

34 (46604446) E. Alletson off E. H. Killick: Notts. v. Sussex (Hove) 1911
(*The over included two no-balls*)
32 (664664) C. Smart off G. Hill: Glamorgan v. Hants. (Cardiff) 1935
32 (466664) C. C. Inman off N. W. Hill: Leics. v. Notts. (Nottingham) 1965
31 (666661) A. W. Wellard off F. E. Woolley: Somerset v. Kent (Wells) 1938
30 (466464) D. G. Bradman off A. P. Freeman: Australians v. England XI (Folkestone) 1934

Most Runs Off One Over—*Cont.*

Runs	Balls	Details	Year
30	(444666)	H. B. Cameron off H. Verity: South Africans v. Yorks. (Sheffield) ..	1935
30	(066666)	A. W. Wellard off T. R. Armstrong: Somerset v. Derby (Wells) ..	1936
30	(446646)	P. L. Winslow off J. T. Ikin: South Africans v. Lancs. (Manchester)	1955
30	(066666)	D. Lindsay off W. T. Greensmith: South African Fezela XI v. Essex (Chelmsford)	1961
30	(466266)	D. Wilson off R. N. S. Hobbs: Yorks. v. M.C.C. (Scarborough) ..	1966
30	(606666)	Majid Jahangir off R. Davis: Pakistanis v. Glamorgan (Swansea) ..	1967
28	(444646)	G. L. Jessop off L. C. Braund: Glos. v. Somerset (Bristol)	1904
28	(466246)	G. L. Jessop off R. D. Burrows: Glos. v. Worcs. (Stourbridge) ..	1910
28	(666046)	H. L. Hazell off H. Verity: Somerset v. Yorks. (Bath)	1936
28	(664444)	H. T. Bartlett off T. P. B. Smith: Gentlemen v. Players (Lord's) ..	1938
28	(066646)	J. H. de Courcy off W. T. Greensmith: Australians v. Essex (Southend)	1953
28	(644446)	J. E. McConnon off N. I. Thomson: Glamorgan v. Sussex (Cardiff) ..	1955
28	(066664)	D. W. White off J. D. Piachand: Hants. v. Oxford U. (Oxford) ..	1960
27	(664641)	H. L. Simms off J. Gunn: Sussex v. Notts. (Hove)	1912
27	(466443)	J. M. Allan off V. E. Jackson: Oxford U. v. Leics. (Oxford)	1955
27	(346662)	D. E. V. Padgett & J. V. Wilson off J. M. Allan: Yorks. v. Kent (Scarborough)	1956
26	(66644)	B. E. Gordon off name unknown: Border v. Eastern Province (Kingwilliamstown)	1903-04
26	(66644)	C. Hill off K. M. Ollivier: Australians v. New Zealand XI (Wellington)	1904-05
26	(646442)	A. Cotter off J. V. Saunders: N.S.W. v. Victoria (Melbourne) ..	1905-06
26	(444446)	G. L. Jessop off A. E. Relf: Gentlemen of South v. Players of South (Hastings)	1907
26	(66644)	G. L. Jessop off D. W. Carr: Londesborough's XI v. Kent (Scarborough)	1913
26	(444626)	G. F. Earle off F. E. Woolley: Somerset v. Kent (Gravesend) ..	1925
26	(644444)	A. H. H. Gilligan off J. T. Bell: Sussex v. Glamorgan (Eastbourne) ..	1928
26	(026666)	J. H. Parsons off O. C. Scott: Warwicks. v. West Indies (Birmingham)	1928
26	(666440)	A. M. Crawley off V. W. C. Jupp: Oxford U. v. Northants. (Wellingborough)	1929
26	(66644)	H. W. Stephenson off R. O. Jenkins: Somerset v. Worcs. (Kidderminster)	1954
26	(466046)	G. Cox off R. T. D. Perks: Sussex v. Worcs. (Dudley)	1955
26	(46444400)	P. J. Burge off A. K. Walker: Australians v. Notts. (Nottingham) .. (*The over included two no-balls.*)	1956
26	(626606)	J. A. Flavell off D. J. Shepherd: Worcs. v. Glamorgan (Swansea) ..	1956
26	(46664)	T. G. Evans off I. W. Johnson: Pearce's XI v. Australians (Scarborough)	1956
26	(666242)	D. J. Shepherd off E. Smith: Glamorgan v. Derby. (Cardiff)	1961
26	(664442)	B. N. Jarman off D. A. Allen: Australians v. Pearce's XI (Scarborough)	1961
26	(431666)	K. F. Barrington & B. R. Knight off S. A. Durrani: M.C.C. v. Rajasthan (Jaipur)	1960-61
26	(440666)	F. S. Trueman off D. Shackleton: Yorks. v. Hants. (Middlesbrough)	196
26	(606626)	A. A. Johnson off P. I. Pocock: Notts. v. Surrey (Nottingham) ..	1966

C. C. Inman, playing for Leicestershire v. Nottinghamshire (Nottingham) 1965, hit 50 runs off two successive overs of deliberate slow full-tosses from N. W. Hill: 440064 and 466664.

Eight-Ball Overs

Runs	Balls	Details	Year
32	(34166066)	D. K. Carmody (41) and I. D. Craig (366066) off I. W. Johnson: Morris's XI v. Hassett's XI (Melbourne)	1953-54
31	(62460661)	J. Mercer off R. Howorth: Glamorgan v. Worcs. (Cardiff)	1939
29	(14466440)	H. Jordaan (1) and P. G. Van der Byl (446644) off J. Buchanan: Western Province v. Eastern Province (Cape Town)	1937-38

MOST SIXES IN AN INNINGS

Before the scoring laws were amended in 1910, it was usually necessary to hit the ball right out of the ground to score a six, and not just over the boundary line as now.

Fifteen

J. R. Reid (296): Wellington v. Northern Districts (Wellington) 1962-63

Thirteen

Majid Jahangir (147*): Pakistanis v. Glamorgan (Swansea) 1967

Most Sixes in an Innings—*Cont.*

Eleven

C. K. Nayudu (153): Hindus v. M.C.C. (Bombay) 1926-27
C. J. Barnett (194): Gloucestershire v. Somerset (Bath) 1934
R. Benaud (135): Australians v. Pearce's XI (Scarborough) 1953

Ten

H. L. Simms (126): Sussex v. Nottinghamshire (Hove) 1912
A. M. Crawley (204): Oxford U. v. Northamptonshire (Wellingborough) 1929
W. R. Hammond (336*): England v. New Zealand (Auckland) 1932-33
H. Sutcliffe (113): Yorkshire v. Northamptonshire (Kettering) 1933
W. J. Stewart (155): Warwickshire v. Lancashire (Blackpool) 1959

Nine

C. I. Thornton (124): Kent v. Sussex (Tunbridge Wells) 1869
P. J. Heather (109*): Transvaal v. Border (Durban) 1910-11
M. C. Bird (151): Surrey v. Sussex (Hove) 1911
H. Gimblett (141): Somerset v. Hampshire (Wells) 1937
E. Paynter (158): M.C.C. v. Griqualand West (Kimberley) 1938-39
G. J. Whittaker (148): Surrey v. Northamptonshire (Northampton) 1949
D. V. Smith (166): Sussex v. Gloucestershire (Hove) 1957

Eight

C. I. Thornton (107*): Gentlemen of England v. I Zingari (Scarborough) 1886
K. G. MacLeod (128): Lancashire v. Somerset (Bath) 1909
E. Alletson (189): Nottinghamshire v. Sussex (Hove) 1911
F. E. Woolley (215): Kent v. Somerset (Gravesend) 1925
A. W. Carr (206): Nottinghamshire v. Leicestershire (Leicester) 1925
G. F. Earle (130): M.C.C. v. Hindus (Bombay) 1926-27
C. C. Dacre (176): New Zealand v. Derbyshire (Derby) 1927
E. R. T. Holmes (236): Oxford U. v. Free Foresters (Oxford) 1927
G. M. Lee (141*): Derbyshire v. Northamptonshire (Northampton) (*All off V. W. C. Jupp*) 1931
H. Sutcliffe (132): Yorkshire v. Gloucestershire (Bradford) 1932
C. I. J. Smith (66): Middlesex v. Gloucestershire (Bristol) 1938
I. L. Bula (102): Fiji v. Canterbury (Christchurch) 1953-54
F. M. M. Worrell (101): A. E. R. Gilligan's XI v. New Zealanders (Hastings) .. 1958
P. Marner (95): Lancashire v. New Zealanders (Blackpool) 1958
W. J. Stewart (104): Warwickshire v. Somerset (Street) 1961
D. B. Close (161): Yorkshire v. Northamptonshire (Northampton) 1963

HITS FOR SIX OFF CONSECUTIVE BALLS

Five Sixes Off Five Balls

A. W. Wellard off T. R. Armstrong: Somerset v. Derby (Wells) 1936
A. W. Wellard off F. E. Woolley: Somerset v. Kent (Wells) 1938
D. Lindsay off W. T. Greensmith: South African Fezela XI v. Essex (Chelmsford) .. 1961

Four Sixes Off Four Balls

R. E. Foster off W. G. Grace: Oxford U. v. London County (Oxford) 1900
E. R. T. Holmes off J. C. Masterman and I. P. F. Campbell: Oxford U. v. Free Foresters (Oxford) 1927
J. H. Parsons off O. C. Scott: Warwicks. v. West Indians (Birmingham) .. 1928
A. Jepson off J. H. Wardle: Notts. v. Yorks. (Bradford) 1952
R. Benaud off R. Tattersall: Australians v. Pearce's XI (Scarborough) 1953
D. W. White off J. D. Piachaud: Hants. v. Oxford U. (Oxford) 1960
C. C. Inman off N. W. Hill: Leics. v. Notts. (Nottingham) 1965
Majid Jahangir off R. Davis: Pakistanis v. Glamorgan (Swansea) 1967

Three Sixes Off Three Balls

C. Hill off K. M. Ollivier: Australians v. New Zealand XI (Wellington) 1904-05
C. P. Carter off R. W. Sievwright: South Africans v. Scotland (Edinburgh) 1912
E. Alletson off W. Rhodes: Notts. v. Yorks. (Dewsbury) 1913
F. Barratt off W. Rhodes: Notts. v. Yorks. (Sheffield) 1919
F. T. Mann off M. W. Tate: Middx. v. Sussex (Hove) 1920
A. W. Carr off F. E. Woolley: Gentlemen v. Players (Scarborough) 1922

Hits for six off Consecutive Balls—*Cont.*

E. P. Hewetson off T. S. Jennings: Oxford U. v. Surrey (Oval)	1923
A. G. Liddell off R. W. V. Robins: Northants v. Cambridge U. (Northampton)	1928
F. Barratt off V. W. C. Jupp: Notts. v. Northants. (Northampton)	1928
E. Hendren off J. Iddon: Rest of England v. Lancs. (Oval)	1928
L. N. Constantine off W. W. Whysall: West Indians v. Notts. (Nottingham)	1928
C. Wright off R. W. V. Robins: Kent v. Middx. (Dover)	1929
A. M. Crawley off V. W. C. Jupp: Oxford U. v. Northants. (Wellingborough)	1929
J. M. Hutchinson off C. F. Root: Derby v. Worcs. (Derby)	1931
G. M. Lee off V. W. C. Jupp: Derby v. Northants. (Northampton)	1931
E. T. Killick off T. W. Goddard: Middx. v. Glos. (Clifton)	1932
W. R. Hammond off J. Newman: England v. New Zealand (Auckland)	1932-33
G. Pearce off E. L. G. Hoad: Sussex v. West Indians (Hove)	1933
H. B. Cameron off R. Howorth: South Africans v. Worcs. (Worcester)	1935
H. B. Cameron off H. Verity: South Africans v. Yorks. (Sheffield)	1935
A. V. Pope off J. W. Lee: Derby v. Somerset (Derby)	1935
H. Larwood off G. S. Boyes: Notts. v. Hants. (Nottingham)	1935
A. E. Watt off R. A. Sinfield: Kent v. Glos. (Gravesend)	1936
W. Voce off T. W. Goddard: Notts. v. Glos. (Nottingham)	1936
H. Gimblett off P. F. Jackson: Somerset v. Worcs. (Yeovil)	1936
R. T. D. Perks off A. P. Freeman: Worcs. v. Kent (Worcester)	1936
R. T. D. Perks off W. Murray-Wood: Works. v. Oxford U. (Oxford)	1936
H. L. Hazell off H. Verity: Somerset v. Yorks. (Bath)	1936
J. C. Clay off James Langridge: Glamorgan v. Sussex (Hastings)	1937
D. G. Bradman off S. L. Putman: Australian XI v. Tasmania (Hobart)	1937-38
C. I. J. Smith off R. A. Sinfield: Middx. v. Glos. (Bristol)	1938
L. L. Wilkinson off R. Howorth: Lancs. v. Worcs (Manchester)	1938
A. E. Watt off S. H. Martin: Kent v. Worcs. (Gillingham)	1939
A. W. Wellard off D. V. P. Wright: Somerset v. Kent (Maidstone)	1939
H. T. Bartlett off E. P. Robinson: Sussex v. Yorks. (Bradford)	1947
K. R. Miller off C. J. Knott: Australians v. Hants. (Southampton)	1948
R. T. D. Perks off J. M. Sims: Worcs. v. Middx. (Lord's)	1948
K. J. Grieves off G. O. Rabone: Lancs. v. New Zealanders (Manchester)	1949
G. J. Whittaker off V. H. Broderick: Surrey v. Northants. (Northampton)	1949
A. W. Wellard off W. E. Hollies: Somerset v. Warwicks. (Birmingham)	1949
G. Lambert off R. O. Jenkins: Glos. v. Worcs. (Dudley)	1949
H. Gimblett off J. E. McConnon: Somerset v. Glamorgan (Ebbw Vale)	1951
C. J. Scott off E. Smith: Glos. v. Derby (Buxton)	1952
W. S. Surridge off J. T. Ikin: South v. North (Kingston)	1952
R. T. Simpson off R. Illingworth: M.C.C. v. Yorks. (Scarborough)	1953
J. H. de Courcy off W. T. Greensmith: Australians v. Essex (Southend)	1953
J. V. Wilson off J. M. Allan: Yorks. v. Kent (Scarborough)	1956
T. G. Evans off I. W. Johnson: Pearce's XI v. Australians (Scarborough)	1956
T. W. Graveney off R. Maragh: Duke of Norfolk's XI v. Jamaica (Kingston)	1956-57
V. M. Mankad off R. R. Shelke: Rajasthan v. Vidarbha (Udaipur)	1957-58
D. B. Close off T. Greenhough: Yorks. v. M.C.C. (Lord's)	1959
J. B. Mortimore off J. S. Manning: England XI v. Commonwealth (Hastings)	1959
D. M. Young off J. D. Piachaud: Glos. v. Oxford U. (Bristol)	1960
L. J. Coldwell off E. A. Bedser: Worcs. v. Surrey (Oval)	1961
D. J. Shepherd off E. Smith: Glamorgan v. Derby. (Cardiff)	1961
K. F. Barrington off S. A. Durrani: M.C.C. v. Rajasthan (Jaipur)	1960-61
R. C. White off I. Davison: Glos. v. Notts. (Nottingham)	1963
D. Wilson off F. J. Titmus: Yorks v. M.C.C. (Scarborough)	1965
D. Keynon off B. A. Langford: Worcs. v. Somerset (Kidderminster)	1965
F. S. Trueman off D. Shackleton: Yorks. v. Hants. (Middlesbrough)	1965
A. S. Brown off B. A. Langford: Glos. v. Somerset (Taunton)	1967

MOST SIXES IN A MATCH

Seventeen

W. J. Stewart Warwickshire v. Lancashire (Blackpool) 1959
10 in a first innings of 155 and 7 in a second innings of 125.

MOST SIXES IN A SEASON

72	A. W. Wellard	Somerset	1935
57	A. W. Wellard	Somerset	1936
57	A. W. Wellard	Somerset	1938

Most Sixes in a Season—*Cont.*

51	A. W. Wellard	Somerset	1933
49	J. H. Edrich	Surrey	1965
48	A. W. Carr	Nottinghamshire	1925
46	F. Barratt	Nottinghamshire	1928

MOST BOUNDARIES IN AN INNINGS

6s	*5s*	*4s*		
—	—	68	P. A. Perrin (343*): Essex v. Derby (Chesterfield)	1904
1	—	64	A. C. MacLaren (424): Lancs. v. Somerset (Taunton)	1895
—	—	64	Hanif Mohammad (499): Karachi v. Bahawalpur (Karachi)	1958-59
5	—	52	J. H. Edrich (310*): England v. New Zealand (Leeds)	1965
—	—	55	C. W. Gregory (383): N.S.W. v. Queensland (Brisbane)	1906-07
1	—	53	G. H. Hirst (341): Yorks. v. Leics. (Leicester)	1905
—	—	52	A. D. Nourse, Snr. (304*): Natal v. Transvaal (Johannesburg)	1919-20
4	—	48	D. G. Bradman (369): South Australia v. Tasmania (Adelaide)	1935-36
—	—	51	W. G. Grace (344): M.C.C. v. Kent (Canterbury)	1876
15	—	35	J. R. Reid (296): Wellington v. Northern Districts (Wellington)	1962-63
4	—	47	C. G. Macartney (345): Australians v. Notts. (Nottingham)	1921
1	—	49	B. B. Nimbalkar (443*): Maharashtra v. Kathiawar (Poona)	1948-49
3	—	46	B. Sutcliffe (385): Otago v. Canterbury (Christchurch)	1952-53
—	—	49	P. Holmes (275): Yorks. v. Warwicks. (Bradford)	1928
—	—	49	D. G. Bradman (452*): N.S.W. v. Queensland (Sydney)	1929-30
—	3	47	A. Ducat (306*): Surrey v. Oxford U. (Oval)	1919
4	—	44	C. R. Maxwell (268): Cahn's XI v. Leics. (Nottingham)	1935
—	—	48	J. T. Brown (300): Yorks. v. Derby (Chesterfield)	1898
—	—	48	J. Tunnicliffe (243): Yorks. v. Derby (Chesterfield)	1898
—	1	46	W. W. Read (338): Surrey v. Oxford U. (Oval)	1888
3	—	44	V. T. Trumper (293): Australians v. Canterbury (Christchurch)	1913-14
5	—	42	D. C. S. Compton (300): M.C.C. v. N-E. Transvaal (Benoni)	1948-49
2	—	45	D. P. B. Morkel (251): Cahn's XI v. South Americans (Nottingham)	1932
1	—	46	P. Holmes (277*): Yorks. v. Northants. (Harrogate)	1921
—	—	47	W. H. Ashdown (305*): Kent v. Derby (Dover)	1935
1	7	38	R. Abel (357*): Surrey v. Somerset (Oval)	1899
1	—	45	W. H. Ashdown (332): Kent v. Essex (Brentwood)	1934
—	—	46	D. G. Bradman (334): Australia v. England (Leeds)	1930
3	—	43	R. H. Moore (316): Hants. v. Warwicks. (Bournemouth)	1937
—	—	45	R. M. Poore (304): Hants v. Somerset (Taunton)	1899
2	—	43	D. G. Bradman (304): Australia v. England (Leeds)	1934
2	—	43	F. E. Woolley (305*): M.C.C. v. Tasmania (Hobart)	1911-12
—	1	44	F. R. Foster (305*): Warwicks. v. Worcs. (Dudley)	1914
—	—	45	J. T. Brown (311): Yorks. v. Sussex (Sheffield)	1897

HIGHEST PROPORTION OF BOUNDARIES IN AN INNINGS

6s	*4s*		*Inns.*		
5	3	(42)	42	A. E. Watt: Kent v. Notts. (Nottingham)	1933
1	9	(42)	42	H. L. Johnson: Derby v. Hants. (Southampton)	1960
4	5	(44)	44	P. Marner: Lancs. v. Notts. (Southport)	1960
1	10	(46)	51*	C. A. Rowland: Wales v. Minor Counties (Colwyn Bay)	1930
3	7	(46)	51*	P. G. Van der Byl: Western Province v. Eastern Province (Cape Town)	1937-38
3	7	(46)	51*	K. F. Barrington: Surrey v. Warwicks. (Oval)	1963
6	3	(48)	51	D. J. Shepherd: Glamorgan v. Australians (Swansea)	1961
—	12	(48)	52	P. G. H. Fender: Surrey v. Glamorgan (Oval)	1924
4	6	(48)	52	C. I. J. Smith: Middx. v. Kent (Maidstone)	1935
—	12	(48)	52	B. L. D'Oliveira: M.C.C. v. Cambridge U. (Lord's)	1964
—	12	(48)	52	R. A. McLean: The Rest v. South Africa (Johannesburg)	1964-65
4	6	(48)	53	F. T. Mann: Middx. v. Notts. (Lord's)	1921
4	6	(48)	53	J. Oakes: Sussex v. Middx. (Lord's)	1949
1	11	(50)	54*	J. H. de Courcy: Australians v. Hants. (Southampton)	1953
—	13	(52)	55	V. W. C. Jupp: Northants. v. Notts. (Nottingham)	1928
7	3	(54)	57*	D. A. Sparks: O.F.S. v. M.C.C. (Bloemfontein)	1938-39
4	8	(56)	61	O. W. Herman: Hants. v. Somerset (Wells)	1937
5	7	(58)	62	D. M. Sayer: Oxford U. v. Notts. (Oxford)	1959
3	10	(58)	62	D. L. Hays: Cambridge U. v. Glamorgan (Cardiff)	1966

Highest Proportion of Boundaries in an Innings—*Cont.*

6s	*4s*		*Inns.*		
2	12	(60)	62	J. B. Statham: Lancs. v. Leics. (Manchester)	1955
4	9	(60)	66	E. Lewis: Glamorgan v. Cambridge U. (Pontypridd)	1965
4	9	(60)	69*	K. J. Grieves: Lancs. v. Kent (Manchester)	1963
—	17	(68)	70	T. R. Veivers: Queensland v. Western Australia (Brisbane)	1965-66
—	17	(68)	77	P. F. Warner: Middx. v. Somerset (Taunton)	1907
4	11	(68)	79	T. R. Veivers: Australians v. Kent (Canterbury)	1964
6	9	(72)	79	O. G. Smith: West Indians v. Ames's XI (Hastings)	1957
7	8	(74)	81	C. G. Pepper: N.S.W. v. Queensland (Brisbane)	1939-40
—	19	(76)	82	A. E. Wilson: Glos. v. Worcs. (Cheltenham)	1953
5	12	(78)	86	L. C. Eastman: Essex v. Glamorgan (Westcliff)	1937
—	21	(84)	88	B. R. Knight: Essex v. Warwicks. (Birmingham)	1962
—	21	(84)	99	E. R. Dexter: Sussex v. Kent (Tunbridge Wells)	1959
—	22	(88)	102	R. C. M. Kimpton: Oxford U. v. Lancs. (Oxford)	1936
5	15	(90)	106*	P. Marner: Lancs. v. Warwicks. (Southport)	1962
8	12	(96)	107*	C. I. Thornton: Gentlemen v. I Zingari (Scarborough)	1886
—	24	(96)	114	A. J. Watkins: Glamorgan v. Worcs. (Swansea)	1953
—	25	(100)	115	G. J. Bonnor: Australians v. Yorks. (Bradford)	1888
5	19	(106)	118	R. M. Prideaux: South v. North (Blackpool)	1961
1	25	(106)	120	K. J. Key: Leveson-Gowers' XI v. Oxford U. (Oxford)	1902
—	27	(108)	135	M. C. Cowdrey: Kent v. Notts. (Tunbridge Wells)	1961
3	26	(122)	137	R. W. Hooker: Middx. v. Kent (Gravesend)	1959
—	32	(128)	162	F. T. Delves: Victoria v. Tasmania (Launceston)	1908-09
2	29	(128)	162	I. R. Redpath: Australians v. Oxford U. (Oxford)	1964
4	26	(128)	165	J. R. Reid: New Zealanders v. South African Colts XI (East London)	1961-62
1	31	(130)	176	M. R. Hallam: Leics. v. Kent (Leicester)	1957
8	21	(132)	176	C. C. Dacre: New Zealanders v. Derby (Derby)	1927
1	33	(138)	182	G. Thomas: N.S.W. v. Queensland (Brisbane)	1965-66
8	23	(140)	189	E. Alletson: Notts. v. Sussex (Hove)	1911
5	30	(150)	191	G. L. Jessop: Gentlemen of South v. Players of South (Hastings)	1907
2	35	(152)	196	K. R. Stackpole: Hawke's XI v. Trimble's XI (Launceston)	1964-65
4	32	(152)	208*	W. J. Edrich: Middx. v. Derby (Chesterfield)	1956
8	27	(156)	215	F. E. Woolley: Kent v. Somerset (Gravesend)	1925
6	34	(172)	221	W. E. Alley: Somerset v. Warwicks. (Nuneaton)	1961
—	48	(192)	243	J. Tunnicliffe: Yorks. v. Derby (Chesterfield)	1898
4	44	(200)	268	C. R. Maxwell: Cahn's XI v. Leics. (Nottingham)	1935
15	35	(230)	296	J. R. Reid: Wellington v. Northern Districts (Wellington)	1962-63
5	52	(238)	310*	J. H. Edrich: England v. New Zealand (Leeds)	1965
—	68	(272)	343*	P. A. Perrin: Essex v. Derby (Chesterfield)	1904

SLOW SCORING

SLOWEST INNINGS

	Min.		
3	—100	J. T. Murray (injured): England v. Australia (Sydney)	1962-63
4	—120	P. Corrall: Leicestershire v. Cambridge U. (Cambridge)	1930
6	—132	K. Howard: Lancashire v. Derbyshire (Manchester)	1964
10*	—133	T. G. Evans: England v. Australia (Adelaide)	1946-47
5	—150	R. G. Barlow: Lancashire v. Sussex (Manchester)	1876
5*	—150	R. G. Barlow: Lancashire v. Nottinghamshire (Nottingham)	1882
12*	—165	L. Hall: Yorkshire v. Kent (Canterbury)	1885
16*	—180	W. E. Midwinter: Australians v. Nottinghamshire (Nottingham)	1878
17	—205	R. G. Barlow: Lancashire v. Nottinghamshire (Manchester)	1888
21	—210	P. G. Z. Harris: New Zealand v. Pakistan (Karachi)	1955-56
22	—220	L. Hall: Yorkshire v. Nottinghamshire (Nottingham)	1888
26	—240	A. Haygarth: Gentlemen v. Players (Lord's)	1846
26	—251	T. E. Bailey: M.C.C. v. South African XI (Pretoria)	1956-57
31	—266	K. D. Mackay: Australia v. England (Lord's)	1956
34	—300	F. P. Fenner: England v. Kent (Canterbury)	1841
45	—318	Shuja-ud-Din: Pakistan v. Australia (Lahore)	1959-60
45*	—330	A. C. Bannerman: New South Wales v. Victoria (Melbourne)	1890-91
21	—332	Vijay Hazare: Rest v. Hindus (Bombay)	1943-44
58	—367	Ijaz Butt: Pakistan v. Australia (Karachi)	1959-60
60	—390	D. N. Sardesai: India v. West Indies (Bridgetown)	1961-62

Slowest Innings—*Cont.*

Min.		
80 —395	T. E. Bailey: England v. South Africa (Durban)	1956-57
88 —420	B. Mitchell: South Africa v. England (Birmingham)	1929
90 —444	P. Roy: India v. West Indies (Bombay)	1958-59
91 —448	A. C. Bannerman: Australia v. England (Sydney)	1891-92
31 —450	T. Pierpoint: Sussex v. Kent (Sevenoaks)	1827
68 —455	T. E. Bailey: England v. Australia (Brisbane)	1958-59
100 —479	A. Dunn: Griqualand West v. Eastern Province (Kimberley)	1947-48
99 —500	M. L. Jaisimha: India v. Pakistan (Kanpur)	1960-61
134 —513	J. H. B. Waite: South Africa v. Australia (Durban)	1957-58
124*—517	Nazar Mohammad: Pakistan v. India (Lucknow)	1952-53
117 —525	P. E. Richardson: England v. South Africa (Johannesburg)	1956-57
138*—540	A. J. Watkins: England v. India (New Delhi)	1951-52
105 —575	D. J. McGlew: South Africa v. Australia (Durban)	1957-58
142 —630	Hanif Mohammad: Pakistan XI v. M.C.C. (Lahore)	1955-56
197*—682	F. M. M. Worrell: West Indies v. England (Bridgetown)	1959-60

AN HOUR BEFORE SCORING FIRST RUN

—timed from the moment the batsman reached the wicket at the start of his innings.

Min.		
97	T. G. Evans (10*): England v. Australia (Adelaide)	1946-47
75	J. Vine (57): Sussex v. Nottinghamshire (Hove)	1901
74	J. T. Murray (3*): England v. Australia (Sydney) *(Handicapped by an injured shoulder)*	1962-63
73	B. J. Versfeld (201*): Natal v. Transvaal (Durban)	1965-66
72	F. H. Vigar (3*): Essex v. Hampshire (Portsmouth)	1946
70	W. Humphreys (0*): Sussex v. Kent (Hove)	1892
68	D. Ward (0): Glamorgan v. Gloucestershire (Newport)	1956
67	J. W. Prodger (4): Kent v. Surrey (Blackheath)	1958
65	R. G. Barlow (0): Shrewsbury's XI v. New South Wales (Sydney)	1886-87
65	Shuja-ud-Din (45): Pakistan v. Australia (Lahore)	1959-60
65	A. Buss (5*): Sussex v. Yorkshire (Bradford)	1965
64	R. McDonald (7): Western Province v. Natal (Pietermaritzburg)	1955-56
63	R. W. Barber (22): Lancashire v. Kent (Gravesend)	1959
62	D. J. McGlew (0): Natal v. Transvaal (Johannesburg)	1955-56
61	H. D. Davies (0*): Glamorgan v. Middlesex (Lord's)	1960
61	M. J. Harris (2): Middlesex v. Leicestershire (Loughborough)	1965
60	R. G. Barlow (34*): Lancashire v. Nottinghamshire (Nottingham)	1876
60	J. N. Fowke (19*): Auckland v. Canterbury (Christchurch)	1893-94
60	E. Smith (0*): Yorkshire v. Essex (Leyton)	1905
60	S. O'Linn (11): South Africans v. Kent (Canterbury)	1960
60	K. Howard (2): Lancashire v. Warwickshire (Manchester)	1963
60	A. M. Beddow (39): Lancashire v. Somerset (Taunton)	1965

AN HOUR WITHOUT ADDING TO A SCORE

Min.		
90	B. Mitchell (58): South Africa v. Australia (Brisbane)	1931-32
80	R. G. Barlow (5*): Lancashire v. Nottinghamshire (Nottingham)	1882
80	Hanif Mohammad (142): Pakistan XI v. M.C.C. (Lahore)	1955-56
79	T. E. Bailey (8): England v. South Africa (Leeds)	1955
75	J. Vine (57): Sussex v. Nottinghamshire (Hove)	1901
72	T. E. Bailey (64*): M.C.C. v. Australians (Lord's)	1953
70	L. Hall (12*): Yorkshire v. Kent (Canterbury)	1885
70	A. C. Bannerman (45*): New South Wales v. Victoria (Melbourne)	1890-91
67	W. H. Scotton (34): England v. Australia (Oval)	1886
65	J. Vine (4): Sussex v. Gloucestershire (Hove)	1902
65	A. S. M. Oakman (40): Sussex v. Lancashire (Hastings)	1960
65	W. B. Stott (22): Yorkshire v. Surrey (Sheffield)	1960
63	W. R. Endean (18): South Africa v. England (Johannesburg)	1956-57
63	R. A. Evans (110): Griqualand West v. M.C.C. (Kimberley)	1956-57
63	W. R. Playle (18): New Zealand v. England (Leeds)	1958
62	R. Illingworth (53): Yorkshire v. Lancashire (Sheffield)	1955
62	K. F. Barrington (137): England v. New Zealand (Birmingham)	1965
60	A. P. Lucas (20): Gentlemen v. Players (Oval)	1882

An Hour Without Adding to Score—*Cont.*

Min.		
60	W. H. Scotton (46): Nottinghamshire v. Gloucestershire (Nottingham)	1885
60	L. Hall (22): Yorkshire v. Nottinghamshire (Nottingham)	1888
60	S. Haigh (31): Yorkshire v. Leicestershire (Leicester)	1905
60	R. Aird (26): Hampshire v. Yorkshire (Leeds)	1923
60	D. R. Jardine (24): England v. Australia (Brisbane)	1932-33
60	B. Mitchell (73): South Africa v. England (Johannesburg)	1938-39
60	A. Tayfield (38): Transvaal v. M.C.C. (Johannesburg)	1956-57
60	T. E. Bailey (80): England v. South Africa (Durban)	1956-57
60	M. J. Horton (5*): Worcestershire v. Warwickshire (Dudley)	1957

INNINGS WITH FEW BOUNDARIES

Innings Without Boundaries

74*	H. A. Pawson: Oxford U. v. Somerset (Bath)	1948
72	R. A. Sinfield: Gloucestershire v. Sussex (Cheltenham)	1937
67	E. A. B. Rowan: South Africa v. England (Durban)	1938-39
56	W. Bardsley: Australia v. South Africa (Nottingham)	1912
51	J. L. Hopwood: Lancashire v. Gloucestershire (Gloucester)	1935

Innings With Only One Four

118	W. M. Woodfull: Australians v. Surrey (Oval)	1926
102	A. Shipman: Leicestershire v. Essex (Leyton)	1925
97*	T. N. Pearce: Essex v. Northamptonshire (Colchester)	1935

Innings With Only Two Fours

132	N. W. Hill: Nottinghamshire v. Lancashire (Manchester)	1967
120	P. A. Gibb: England v. South Africa (Durban)	1938-39
116	C. A. Milton: M.C.C. v. Victoria (Melbourne)	1958-59
115	A. R. Morris: Australian XI v. M.C.C. (Melbourne)	1946-47
112	G. Gunn: Nottinghamshire v. Essex (Leyton)	1924
100	Mushtaq Ali: Holkar v. Hyderabad (Indore)	1950-51

N. W. Hill's innings included only one boundary in the first hundred runs.

L. Marks (N.S.W.) scored 185 with only two fours and a five v. South Australia (Adelaide) 1964-65.

SLOWEST FIFTIES

Min.		
361	T. E. Bailey (68): England v. Australia (Brisbane)	1958-59
313	D. J. McGlew (70): South Africa v. Australia (Johannesburg)	1957-58
302	D. N. Sardesai (60): India v. West Indies (Bridgetown)	1961-62
282	E. D. A. McMorris (73): West Indies v. England (Kingston)	1959-60
280	P. E. Richardson (117): England v. South Africa (Johannesburg)	1956-57
270	T. E. Bailey (134*): England v. New Zealand (Christchurch)	1950-51
268	Hanif Mohammad (142): Pakistan XI v. M.C.C. (Lahore)	1955-56
253	B. Mitchell (99): South Africa v. England (Port Elizabeth)	1948-49
250	Hanif Mohammad (111): Pakistan v. England (Dacca)	1961-62

SLOWEST CENTURIES

Min.		
545	D. J. McGlew (105): South Africa v. Australia (Durban)	1957-58
525	Hanif Mohammad (142): Pakistan XI v. M.C.C. (Lahore)	1955-56
488	P. E. Richardson (117): England v. South Africa (Johannesburg)	1956-57
479	A. Dunn (100): Griqualand West v. Eastern Province (Kimberley)	1947-48
468	Hanif Mohammad (142): Pakistan v. India (Bahawalpur)	1954-55
460	Hanif Mohammad (111): Pakistan v. England (Dacca)	1961-62
435	J. W. Guy (102): New Zealand v. India (Hyderabad)	1955-56
434	M. C. Cowdrey (154): England v. West Indies (Birmingham)	1957
420	W. H. Denton (102): Northamptonshire v. Derbyshire (Derby)	1914
414	J. H. B. Waite (134): South Africa v. Australia (Durban)	1957-58

Slow Scoring—*Cont.*

SLOWEST DOUBLE CENTURIES

Min.		
570	S. G. Barnes (234): Australia v. England (Sydney)	1946-47
559	B. J. Versfeld (201*): Natal v. Transvaal (Durban)	1965-66

FEWEST RUNS IN A DAY

95	Australia (80) v. Pakistan (15-2) at Karachi	1956-57
104	Pakistan (0-0 to 104-5) v. Australia at Karachi	1959-60
105	Queensland (30-1 to 135-5) v. M.C.C. at Brisbane	1958-59
106	England (92-2 to 198) v. Australia at Brisbane	1958-59
107	Pakistan XI (66-0 to 173-1) v. M.C.C. at Lahore	1955-56
110	Combined XI (159-2 to 260) v. M.C.C. (9-1) at Perth	1958-59
112	Australia (138-6 to 187) v. Pakistan (63-1) at Karachi	1956-57
117	India (117-5) v. Australia at Madras	1956-57
119	South Africa (7-0 to 126-2) v. Australia at Johannesburg	1957-58
120	India (115-0 to 135-8) v. Australia at Calcutta	1956-57
122	England (110-9 to 110) v. South Africa (122-7) at Port Elizabeth	1956-57
122	Australia (156-6 to 186) v. England (92-2) at Brisbane	1958-59
122	Australia (282-6 to 306 & 9-0) v. England (87) at Melbourne	1958-59
124	Pakistan (74-4 to 134) v. Australia (64-1) at Dacca	1959-60
124	India (226-6 to 291) v. Australia (59-2) at Kanpur	1959-60
125	New Zealand (125) v. England at Dunedin	1954-55
127	India (162-3 to 245) v. Pakistan (44-1) at Peshawar	1954-55
127	West Indies (291-2 to 353) v. England (65-0) at Kingston	1959-60
128	England (53-2 to 181-9) v. West Indies at Bridgetown	1953-54
129	Pakistan (129-6) v. India at Peshawar	1954-55
129	India (46-1 to 149 & 26-2) v. Australia at Madras	1959-60
130	South Africa (200-7 to 243) v. New Zealand (79 & 8-1) at Johannesburg	1953-54
130	India (115-5 to 148) v. Pakistan (97-1) at Dacca	1954-55
130	West Indies (349-7 to 386) v. New Zealand (93-5) at Christchurch	1955-56
134	England (333-1 to 439) v. Pakistan (28-0) at Dacca	1961-62
136	South Africa (138-5 to 164) v. England (110-9) at Port Elizabeth	1956-57
138	Australia (138-6) v. Pakistan at Karachi	1956-57
138	South Africa (138-5) v. England at Port Elizabeth	1956-57
140	New Zealand (8-1 to 148-6) v. South Africa at Johannesburg	1953-54

The lowest in England is 142-7 in 335 minutes (25 minutes lost for rain) by England on the first day of the Test match v. Australia at Leeds in 1953.

Australia scored only 121 runs for the loss of eight wickets in five hours (one hour lost through early finish) v. England (Manchester) 1956.

SLOW SCORING IN A MATCH

528 runs in four days—Pakistan v. Australia (Karachi) 1956-57—95 runs on first day, 184 on second, 138 on third and 112 on fourth.

538 runs in four days of complete match—South Africa v. England (Port Elizabeth) 1956-57—138 on first day, 136 on second, 122 on third, and 142 on fourth.

518 runs on first four days of match—Australia v. England (Brisbane) 1958-59—142 on first day, 148 on second, 122 on third and 106 on fourth.

LONGEST INDIVIDUAL INNINGS

	Min.		
337	—999	Hanif Mohammad: Pakistan v. West Indies (Bridgetown)	1957-58
364	—800	L. Hutton: England v. Australia (Oval)	1938
311	—762	R. B. Simpson: Australia v. England (Manchester)	1964
307	—727	R. M. Cowper: Australia v. England (Melbourne)	1956-66
262*	—708	L. Wight: British Guiana v. Barbados (Georgetown)	1951-52
197*	—682	F. M. M. Worrell: West Indies v. England (Bridgetown)	1959-60
256	—683	K. F. Barrington: England v. Australia (Manchester)	1964
226	—647	G. St. A. Sobers: West Indies v. England (Bridgetown)	1959-60
219	—645	K. C. Ibrahim: Bombay v. Baroda (Bombay)	1948-49
234	—642	S. G. Barnes: Australia v. England (Sydney)	1946-47
359*	—640	V. M. Merchant: Bombay v. Maharashtra (Bombay)	1943-44
499	—640	Hanif Mohammad: Karachi v. Bahawalpur (Karachi)	1958-59

Longest Individual Innings—*Cont.*

Min.		
297*—630	H. Moses: N.S.W. v. Victoria (Sydney)	1887-88
275*—630	F. C. Thompson: Queensland v. N.S.W. (Brisbane)	1930-31
142 —630	Hanif Mohammad: Pakistan XI v. M.C.C. (Lahore)	1955-56
288 —628	Vijay Hazare: Baroda v. Holkar (Baroda)	1946-47
437 —621	W. H. Ponsford: Victoria v. Queensland (Melbourne)	1927-28
267 —615	A. Shrewsbury: Notts. v. Middx. (Nottingham)	1887
365*—608	G. St. A. Sobers: West Indies v. Pakistan (Kingston)	1957-58
325 —600	A. Sandham: England v. West Indies (Kingston)	1929-30

Hanif Mohammad batted for 893 minutes in scoring 111 (500 mins.) and 104 (393 mins.) for Pakistan v. England at Dacca in 1961-62.

H. Sutcliffe batted for 810 minutes in scoring 176 (431 mins.) and 127 (379 mins.) for England v. Australia at Melbourne in 1924-25.

B. Mitchell batted for 801 minutes in scoring 120 (381 mins.) and 189* (420 mins.) for South Africa v. England at The Oval in 1947.

MONOPOLISING THE SCORING

The most outstanding scoring monopoly occurred in the Bombay Pentangular Tournament of 1943-44 when Vijay Hazare, playing against the Hindus, scored 309 (79.85%) of the Rest's second innings total of 387 after his team had followed-on 448 runs behind. Hazare's 309 runs were scored out of 373 while he was at the wicket and he contributed 266 to a sixth wicket partnership of 300 with his younger brother, Vivek.

Percentages in this section are calculated only to the lower whole unit, 79.8% being shown as 79%

LOWEST INNINGS TOTALS TO INCLUDE INDIVIDUAL MILESTONES

A Fifty

66	Indians v. Yorkshire (Harrogate) 1932	S. Nazir Ali	52

A Century

144	Kent v. Warwickshire (Folkestone) 1931	F. E. Woolley	103*

A Double-Century

298	Gloucestershire v. Glamorgan (Newport) 1956	T. W. Graveney	200

A Triple-Century

387	Rest v. Hindus (Bombay) 1943-44	Vijay Hazare	309

BATSMEN SCORING 70% OF INNINGS TOTAL

%	*Score Inns.*		
79	(309 —387)	Vijay Hazare: Rest v. Hindus (Bombay)	1943-44
79	(126 —159)	W. G. Grace: United South v. United North (Hull)	1876
78	(18 — 23)	J. Noel: South Australia v. Victoria (Melbourne)	1882-83
78	(45 — 57)	A. N. Hornby: M.C.C. v. Sussex (Lord's)	1890
78	(63*— 80)	C. O. H. Sewell: Glos. v. Sussex (Hove)	1913
78	(52 — 66)	S. Nazir Ali: Indians v. Yorks. (Harrogate)	1932
77	(385 —500)	B. Sutcliffe: Otago v. Canterbury (Christchurch)	1952-53
75	(82 —109)	W. Beldham: Surrey v. England (Lord's)	1801
75	(55*— 73)	G. Wells: Sussex v. M.C.C. (Lord's)	1860
75	(69 — 92)	F. G. Rogers: Glos. v. Hants. (Southampton)	1924
75	(127*—169)	W. J. Edrich: Middx. v. Glos. (Lord's)	1946
75	(85 —112)	G. E. Barker: Essex v. Yorks. (Sheffield)	1962
74	(20 — 27)	W. G. Grace: Sheffield's XI v. Australians (Sheffield Park)	1890
73	(50 — 68)	A. Morton: Derby v. Yorks. (Chesterfield)	1914
72	(150 —206)	D. C. S. Compton: Middx. v. Sussex (Lord's)	1955
71	(103*—144)	F. E. Woolley: Kent v. Warwicks. (Folkestone)	1931
70	(122 —173)	W. G. Grace: South v. North (Sheffield)	1869
70	(70 —100)	E. Smith: Oxford U. v. M.C.C. (Oxford)	1891

Monopolising the Scoring—*Cont.*

%	*Score*	*Inns.*		
70	(92	—131)	C. E. de Trafford: Leics. v. Yorks. (Leicester)	1894
70	(67*	— 95)	W. Flowers: Notts. v. M.C.C. (Lord's)	1894
70	(97	—137)	F. H. B. Champain: Glos. v. Lancs. (Bristol)	1897
70	(161	—229)	F. E. Woolley: Kent v. Derby (Canterbury)	1933
70	(141	—199)	A. H. Bakewell: Northants. v. Worcs. (Northampton)	1935
70	(130	—184)	L. Amarnath: Indians v. Essex (Brentwood)	1936
70	(74*	—105)	R. E. S. Wyatt: Warwicks. v. Leics. (Birmingham)	1939
70	(296	—422)	J. R. Reid: Wellington v. Northern Districts (Wellington)	1962-63

BATSMEN SCORING 50% *OF TOTAL IN EACH INNINGS*

Score	*Total*	*Score*	*Total*		
62*	(121)	92	(168)	James Broadbridge: Sussex v. Hants. (Petworth)	1825
80*	(148)	79	(150)	Lord Harris: Kent v. Yorks. (Gravesend)	1883
56	(102)	42	(81)	J. T. Tyldesley: Lancs. v. Australians (Manchester)	1899
88	(159)	106	(212)	C. B. Fry: Sussex v. Hants. (Portsmouth)	1901
176	(336)	122	(197)	L. G. Wright: Derby v. Warwicks. (Birmingham)	1905
35	(63)	111	(205)	C. N. Woolley: Northants. v. Derby (Northampton)	1922
109*	(196)	107	(205)	F. S. Lee: Somerset v. Worcs. (Worcester)	1938
129	(244)	112	(212)	L. B. Fishlock: Surrey v. Leics. (Leicester)	1946
97	(188)	175	(337)	P. B. H. May: Combined Services v. Worcs. (Worcester)	1949
154	(270)	34	(63)	M. C. Cowdrey: Oxford U. v. Surrey (Oval)	1953
100	(153)	67	(107)	T. W. Graveney: Glos. v. Essex (Romford)	1956
156*	(257)	109	(191)	D. B. Carr: Derby v. Kent (Canterbury)	1959

BATSMEN MONOPOLISING SCORING DURING THEIR INNINGS

The leading instances of a batsman monopolising the scoring during his stay at the wicket, with the batsman's innings listed first and the runs scored during his stay at the wicket second.

39 — 39	J. N. Crawford: Surrey v. Somerset (Taunton)	1919
39 — 39	B. D. Wells: Notts. v. Essex (Westcliff)	1961
40 — 41	G. L. Jessop: Glos. v. Middx. (Lord's)	1907
43 — 44	A. B. Hipkin: Essex v. Yorks. (Leyton)	1929
45 — 46	P. S. McDonnell: Australians v. Shaw's XI (Leeds)	1882
50 — 51	E. A. McDonald: Lancs. v. Glos. (Manchester)	1926
53 — 54	M. Tompkin: Leics. v. Yorks. (Leicester)	1947
53 — 54	G. C. Gill: Somerset v. Hants. (Bath)	1902
56 — 57	C. I. J. Smith: Middx. v. Yorks. (Scarborough)	1936
61*— 63	P. G. H. Fender: Surrey v. Sussex (Eastbourne)	1926
63 — 65	G. L. Jessop: Glos. v. Yorks. (Cheltenham)	1895
66 — 66	G. L. Jessop: Glos. v. Sussex (Bristol)	1901
69 — 70	P. S. McDonnell: Australians v. Oxford & Cambridge U.P. & P. (Portsmouth)	1888
72 — 75	V. T. Hill: Somerset v. Middx. (Lord's)	1900
73*— 80	A. W. Wellard: Somerset v. Glamorgan (Cardiff)	1938
76 — 82	G. L. Jessop: Glos. v. Notts. (Bristol)	1901
82 — 86	P. S. McDonnell: Australians v. North of England (Manchester)	1888
84 — 89	G. E. Winter: Cambridge U. v. Surrey (Oval)	1899
93 —104	L. B. Fishlock: Surrey v. Australians (Oval)	1938
93 —108	E. R. Dexter: Sussex v. Warwicks. (Birmingham)	1960
95 —109	W. P. Howell: N.S.W. v. Stoddart's XI (Sydney)	1897-98
96 —110	M. F. Tremlett: Somerset v. Glos. (Bristol)	1948
103 —116	D. C. S. Compton: Rest v. England (Canterbury)	1946
109 —120	G. L. Jessop: Glos. v. Middx. (Lord's)	1900
114*—129	K. G. Suttle: Sussex v. Worcs. (Eastbourne)	1952
122 —131	F. R. Brown: Gentlemen v. Players (Lord's)	1950
130*—145	C. K. Nayudu: Indians v. Somerset (Taunton)	1932
143 —173	S. M. J. Woods: Somerset v. Sussex (Eastbourne)	1898
149 —181	J. J. Lyons: Australians v. M.C.C. (Lord's)	1893
153 —187	C. K. Nayudu: Hindus v. M.C.C. (Bombay)	1926-27
163 —201	W. Rashleigh: Kent v. Middx. (Tonbridge)	1896
164 —203	G. L. Jessop: Glos. v. Sussex (Gloucester)	1908
164 —203	H. G. Gaekwad: Holkar v. Bihar (Jamshedpur)	1951-52
171*—206	G. L. Jessop: Cambridge U. v. Yorks. (Cambridge)	1899

Monopolising the Scoring—*Cont.*

174 —220	Hon. F. S. G. Calthorpe: Warwicks. v. Lancs. (Birmingham)	1925
183 —224	J. B. Hobbs: Surrey v. Warwicks. (Oval)	1914
192 —227	W. R. Hammond: Glos. v. Hants. (Southampton)	1927
200*—258	A. D. Nourse, Snr.: Natal v. Western Province (Cape Town)	1907-08
206 —265	H. H. Massie: Australians v. Oxford U. (Oxford)	1882
215 —282	S. M. J. Woods: Somerset v. Sussex (Hove)	1895
220 —293	K. S. Ranjitsinhji: Sussex v. Kent (Hove)	1900
233 —300	S. J. McCabe: Australia v. England (Nottingham)	1938
239 —310	P. S. McDonnell: N.S.W. v. Victoria (Melbourne)	1886-87
286 —355	G. L. Jessop: Glos. v. Sussex (Hove)	1903
309 —373	Vijay Hazare: Rest v. Hindus (Bombay)	1943-44
317 —462	W. R. Hammond: Glos. v. Notts. (Gloucester)	1936
336*—492	W. R. Hammond: England v. New Zealand (Auckland)	1932-33
385 —500	B. Sutcliffe: Otago v. Canterbury (Christchurch)	1952-53

BATSMEN MONOPOLISING A PARTNERSHIP

307 —10th	A. F. Kippax (238) & J. E. H. Hooker (62) (7 ex): N.S.W. v. Victoria (Sydney)	1928-29
300 — 6th	Vijay Hazare (266) & Vivek Hazare (21) (13 ex): Rest v. Hindus (Bombay)	1943-44
184 —10th	R. C. Blunt (146) & W. Hawkesworth (21) (17 ex): Otago v. Canterbury (Christchurch)	1931-32
152 —10th	E. Alletson (142) & W. Riley (10): Notts. v. Sussex (Hove)	1911
138 —10th	R. I. Jefferson (115) & D. A. D. Sydenham (15) (8 ex): Surrey v. Northants. (Northampton)	1963
128 — 9th	G. C. Cooper (109) & F. Pountain (16) (3 ex): Sussex v. Warwicks. (Birmingham)	1960
127 — 3rd	C. Milburn (111) & Mushtaq Mohammad (14) (2 ex): Northants v. Leics. (Leicester)	1966
119*— 9th	K. G. Suttle (109) & P. A. Kelland (5) (5 ex): Sussex v. Worcs. (Eastbourne)	1952
116 —10th	C. I. J. Smith (98) & I. A. R. Peebles (14) (4 ex): Middx. v. Kent (Canterbury)	1939
107 —10th	H. J. Enthoven (102) & W. F. Price (3) (2 ex): Middx. v. Sussex (Lord's)	1930
107 — 8th	B. L. D'Oliveira (101) & B. M. Brain (4) (2 ex): Worcs. v. Notts. (Worcester)	1966
104 —10th	F. R. Brown (91) & J. F. Parker (12) (1 ex): Surrey v. Kent (Blackheath)	1932
101 —10th	W. W. Whysall (84) & W. Voce (17): Notts. v. Glos. (Nottingham) ..	1929
100*—10th	D. Tallon (91) & G. J. Noblet (9): Bradman's XI v. Hassett's XI (Melbourne)	1948-49
100 — 2nd	S. Jayasinghe (91) & B. J. Booth (9): Leics. v. Northants. (Northampton)	1964
96 —10th	C. T. Ashton (91) & G. M. Louden (3) (2 ex): Essex v. Middx. (Leyton)	1922
88 — 7th	H. T. W. Hardinge (80) & W. H. Ashdown (4) (4 ex): Kent v. Leics. (Leicester)	1922
86 — 1st	P. S. McDonnell (82) & A. C. Bannerman (4): Australians v. North (Manchester)	1888
86 —10th	S. H. Day (82) & C. D. Dewe (4): Cambridge U. v. Sussex (Hove) ..	1901
84 —10th	H. A. Peach (78) & S. Fenley (5) (1 ex): Surrey v. Lancs. (Oval) ..	1928
80 —10th	J. N. Crawford (73) & T. Rushby (2) (5 ex): Surrey v. A.I.F. (Oval)	1919
79 —10th	D. C. S. Compton (78) & L. H. Gray (1): Middx. v. Essex (Lord's) ..	1939
77 —10th	S. J. McCabe (72) & L. O. Fleetwood-Smith (5): Australia v. England (Nottingham)	1938
75 —10th	R. W. V. Robins (75) & J. A. Young (0): M.C.C. v. Yorks. (Scarborough)	1946
71 —10th	R. W. V. Robins (68) & L. H. Gray (1) (2 ex): Middx. v. Essex (Chelmsford)	1937
69 —10th	H. J. Enthoven (61) & R. S. Machin (0) (8 ex): Cambridge U. v. Free Foresters (Cambridge)	1926
69 —10th	A. H. Kardar (64) & W. E. Hollies (4) (1 ex): Warwicks. v. Middx. (Lord's)	1950
67 —10th	R. W. V. Robins (65) & N. F. Turner (0) (2 ex): Middx. v. Yorks. (Lord's)	1937
67*— 8th	M. J. Turnbull (64) & A. H. Fabian (3): Cambridge U. v. Yorks. (Cambridge)	1929
60 — 8th	S. J. Storey (54) & D. J. S. Taylor (3) (3 ex): Surrey v. Northants. (Oval)	1967
59 —10th	A. K. Davidson (58) & D. Ford (0) (1 ex): N.S.W. v. Victoria (Sydney)	1961-62
57 —10th	C. I. J. Smith (56) & L. H. Gray (1): Middx. v. Yorks. (Scarborough) ..	1936
57 — 8th	T. R. Veivers (52) & J. W. Martin (5): Australians v. Kent (Canterbury)	1964
55 — 9th	D. J. Shepherd (51) & D. L. Evans (4): Glamorgan v. Australians (Swansea)	1961

Monopolising the Scoring—*Cont.*

55	—10th	J. A. Snow (53) & D. L. Bates (1) (1 ex): Sussex v. Somerset (Eastbourne)	1966
51	—10th	P. R. Umrigar (47) & B. K. Kunderan (4): India v. West Indies (Port of Spain)	1961-62
50	—10th	H. J. Enthoven (45) & L. G. Irvine (5): Cambridge U. v. Australians (Cambridge)	1926
50	—10th	W. J. Edrich (49) & L. H. Gray (1): Middx. v. Surrey (Lord's)	1939

PLAYERS' RECORDS—PARTNERSHIPS

WORLD RECORD FOR EACH WICKET

1st	555	P. Holmes & H. Sutcliffe: Yorks. v. Essex (Leyton)	1932
2nd	455	K. V. Bhandarkar & B. B. Nimbalkar: Maharashtra v. Kathiawar (Poona)	1948-49
3rd	445	P. E. Whitelaw & W. N. Carson: Auckland v. Otago (Dunedin)	1936-37
4th	577	Gul Mahomed & Vijay Hazare: Baroda v. Holkar (Baroda)	1946-47
5th	405	S. G. Barnes & D. G. Bradman: Australia v. England (Sydney)	1946-47
6th	487*	G. A. Headley & C. C. Passailaigue: Jamaica v. Tennyson's XI (Kingston)	1931-32
7th	347	D. Atkinson & C. C. Depeiza: West Indians v. Australia (Bridgetown)	1954-55
8th	433	V. T. Trumper & A. Sims: Australians v. Canterbury (Christchurch)	1913-14
9th	283	A. R. Warren & J. Chapman: Derby v. Warwicks. (Blackwell)	1910
10th	307	A. F. Kippax & J. E. H. Hooker: N.S.W. v. Victoria (Melbourne)	1928-29

Australian batsmen hold three records, English, West Indian and Indian batsmen two each and New Zealand batsmen one.

RECORDS BY ENGLISH BATSMEN

1st	555	P. Holmes & H. Sutcliffe: Yorks. v. Essex (Leyton)	1932
2nd	429*	J. G. Dewes & G. H. G. Doggart: Cambridge U. v. Essex (Cambridge)	1949
3rd	424*	W. J. Edrich & D. C. S. Compton: Middx. v. Somerset (Lord's)	1948
4th	448	R. Abel & T. W. Hayward: Surrey v. Yorks. (Oval)	1899
5th	393	E. G. Arnold & W. B. Burns: Worcs. v. Warwicks. (Birmingham)	1909
6th	411	R. M. Poore & E. G. Wynyard: Hants. v. Somerset (Taunton)	1899
7th	344	K. S. Ranjitsinhji & W. Newham: Sussex v. Essex (Leyton)	1902
8th	292	R. Peel & Lord Hawke: Yorks. v. Warwicks. (Birmingham)	1896
9th	283	A. R. Warren & J. Chapman: Derby v. Warwicks. (Blackwell)	1910
10th	235	F. E. Woolley & A. Fielder: Kent v. Worcs. (Stourbridge)	1909

RECORDS BY AUSTRALIAN BATSMEN

1st	456	W. H. Ponsford & E. R. Mayne: Victoria v. Queensland (Melbourne)	1923-24
2nd	451	W. H. Ponsford & D. G. Bradman: Australia v. England (Oval)	1934
3rd	389	W. H. Ponsford & S. J. McCabe: Australians v. M.C.C. (Lord's)	1934
4th	424	I. S. Lee & S. O. Quin: Victoria v. Tasmania (Melbourne)	1933-34
5th	405	S. G. Barnes & D. G. Bradman: Australia v. England (Sydney)	1946-47
6th	428	W. W. Armstrong & M. A. Noble: Australians v. Sussex (Hove)	1902
7th	335	C. W. Andrews & E. C. Bensted: Queensland v. N.S.W. (Sydney)	1934-35
8th	433	V. T. Trumper & A. Sims: Australians v. Canterbury (Christchurch)	1913-14
9th	232	C. Hill & E. Walkley: South Australia v. N.S.W. (Adelaide)	1900-01
10th	307	A. F. Kippax & J. E. H. Hooker: N.S.W. v. Victoria (Melbourne)	1928-29

RECORDS BY SOUTH AFRICAN BATSMEN

1st	424	J. F. W. Nicolson & I. J. Siedle: Natal v. O.F.S. (Bloemfontein)	1926-27
2nd	305	S. K. Coen & J. M. M. Commaille: O.F.S. v. Natal (Bloemfontein)	1926-27
3rd	341	E. J. Barlow & R. G. Pollock: South Africa v. Australia (Adelaide)	1963-64
4th	342	E. A. B. Rowan & P. J. M. Gibb: Transvaal v. N.-E. Transvaal (Johannesburg)	1952-53
5th	327	H. B. Cameron & A. W. Briscoe: Transvaal v. Griqualand West (Johannesburg)	1934-35

Records by South African Batsmen—*Cont.*

6th	244*	J. M. M. Commaille & A. W. Palm: Western Province v. Griqualand West (Johannesburg)	1923-24
7th	299	B. Mitchell & A. Melville: Transvaal v. Griqualand West (Kimberley)	1946-47
8th	222	S. S. L. Steyn & D. P. B. Morkel: Western Province v. Border (Cape Town)	1929-30
9th	221	N. V. Lindsay & G. R. McCubbin: Transvaal v. Rhodesia (Bulawayo)	1922-23
10th	174	H. R. Lance & D. Mackay-Coghill: Transvaal v. Natal (Johannesburg)	1965-66

RECORDS BY WEST INDIAN BATSMEN

1st	390	L. Wight & G. Gibbs: British Guiana v. Barbados (Georgetown)	1951-52
2nd	446	C. C. Hunte & G. St. A. Sobers: West Indies v. Pakistan (Kingston)	1957-58
3rd	434	J. B. Stollmeyer & G. E. Gomez: Trinidad v. British Guiana (Port of Spain)	1946-47
4th	574*	C. L. Walcott & F. M. M. Worrell: Barbados v. Trinidad (Port of Spain)	1945-46
5th	283	N. L. Bonitto & A. P. Binns: Jamaica v. British Guiana (Georgetown)	1952-53
6th	487*	G. A. Headley & C. C. Passailaigue: Jamaica v. Tennyson's XI (Kingston)	1931-32
7th	347	D. Atkinson & C. C. Depeiza: West Indies v. Australia (Bridgetown)	1954-55
8th	255	E. A. V. Williams & E. A. Martindale: Barbados v. Trinidad (Bridgetown)	1935-36
9th	134	W. W. Hall & F. C. M. Alexander: Weekes' XI v. Walcott's XI (Port of Spain)	1956-57
10th	138	E. L. G. Hoad & H. C. Griffith: West Indians v. Sussex (Hove)	1933

RECORDS BY NEW ZEALAND BATSMEN

1st	373	B. Sutcliffe & L. A. Watt: Otago v. Auckland (Auckland)	1950-51
2nd	301	C. S. Dempster & C. F. W. Allcott: New Zealanders v. Warwicks. (Birmingham)	1927
3rd	445	P. E. Whitelaw & W. N. Carson: Auckland v. Otago (Dunedin)	1936-37
4th	324	W. M. Wallace & J. R. Reid: New Zealanders v. Cambridge U. (Cambridge)	1949
5th	266	B. Sutcliffe & W. S. Haig: Otago v. Auckland (Dunedin)	1949-50
6th	187*	J. E. F. Beck & L. C. Butler: Wellington v. Central Districts (New Plymouth)	1961-62
7th	265	J. L. Powell & N. Dorreen: Canterbury v. Otago (Christchurch)	1929-30
8th	190*	J. W. E. Mills & C. F. W. Allcott: New Zealanders v. Civil Service (Chiswick)	1927
9th	239	H. B. Cave & I. B. Leggat: Central Districts v. Otago (Dunedin)	1952-53
10th	184	R. C. Blunt & W. Hawkesworth: Otago v. Canterbury (Christchurch)	1931-32

RECORDS BY INDIAN BATSMEN

1st	413	V. M. Mankad & P. Roy: India v. New Zealand (Madras)	1955-56
2nd	455	K. V. Bhandarkar & B. B. Nimbalkar: Maharashtra v. Kathiawar (Poona)	1948-49
3rd	410	R. S. Modi & L. Amarnath: India in England v. Rest (Calcutta)	1946-47
4th	577	Gul Mahomed & Vijay Hazare: Baroda v. Holkar (Baroda)	1946-47
5th	360	U. M. Merchant & M. N. Raiji: Bombay v. Hyderabad (Bombay)	1947-48
6th	371	V. M. Merchant & R. S. Modi: Bombay v. Maharashtra (Bombay)	1943-44
7th	274	K. C. Ibraham & K. M. Rangnekar: Bijapur XI v. Bengal XI (Bombay)	1942-43
8th	236	C. T. Sarwate & R. P. Singh: Holkar v. Delhi (New Delhi)	1949-50
9th	245	Vijay Hazare & N. D. Nagarwalla: Maharashtra v. Baroda (Poona)	1939-40
10th	249	C. T. Sarwate & S. N. Banerjee: Indians v. Surrey (Oval)	1946

RECORDS BY PAKISTANI BATSMEN

1st	277	Hanif Mohammad & Alim-ud-Din: Karachi A. v. Sind A. (Karachi)	1957-58
2nd	269	Nazar Mohammad & Murawat Hussain: Pakistan v. Ceylon (Colombo)	1948-49
3rd	388	Salah-ud-Din & Wallis Mathias: Karachi Blues v. Hyderabad (Karachi)	1964-65
4th	346	Zafar Altaf & Majid Jahangir: Lahore Greens v. Bahawalpur (Lahore)	1965-66
5th	216	Wallis Mathias & Nasim-ul-Ghani: Karachi A. v. East Pakistan (Karachi)	1962-63
6th	217	Hanif Mohammad & Majid Jahangir: Pakistan v. New Zealand (Lahore)	1964-65
7th	308	Waqar Hassan & Imtiaz Ahmed: Pakistan v. New Zealand (Lahore)	1955-56
8th	171	Majid Jahangir & Zulfiqar Ali: Lahore Board v. P.I.A. (Lahore)	1964-65
9th	190	Asif Iqbal & Intikhab Alam: Pakistan v. England (Oval)	1966
10th	144	Shakoor Ahmed & Pervez Sajjad: Lahore Greens v. Karachi Blues (Karachi)	1965-66

HIGHEST SCORE AT THE FALL OF EACH WICKET

1st	wicket	555	Yorkshire (555-1d) v. Essex (Leyton)	1932
2nd	wicket	594	Victoria (1107) v. N.S.W. (Melbourne)	1926-27
3rd	wicket	667	Kent (803-4d) v. Essex (Brentwood)	1934
4th	wicket	801	Maharashtra (826-4) v. Kathiawar (Poona)	1948-49
5th	wicket	720	England (849) v. West Indies (Kingston)	1929-30
6th	wicket	834	Victoria (1107) v. N.S.W. (Melbourne)	1926-27
7th	wicket	956	Victoria (1059) v. Tasmania (Melbourne)	1922-23
8th	wicket	1043	Victoria (1107) v. N.S.W. (Melbournc)	1926-27
9th	wicket	1046	Victoria (1107) v. N.S.W. (Melbourne)	1926-27
10th	wicket	1107	Victoria (1107) v. N.S.W. (Melbourne)	1926-27

WICKET PARTNERSHIPS OF OVER 400

(*Details of opponents and venue are given in the appropriate wicket partnership section*).

577 —4th	Gul Mahomed & Vijay Hazare for Holkar	1946-47
574*—4th	C. L. Walcott & F. M. M. Worrell for Barbados	1945-46
555 —1st	P. Holmes & H. Sutcliffe for Yorkshire	1932
554 —1st	J. T. Brown & J. Tunnicliffe for Yorkshire	1898
502*—4th	F. M. M. Worrell & J. D. C. Goddard for Barbados	1943-44
490 —1st	E. H. Bowley & John Langridge for Sussex	1933
487*—6th	G. A. Headley & C. C. Passailaigue for Jamaica	1931-32
456 —1st	E. R. Mayne & W. H. Ponsford for Victoria	1923-24
455 —2nd	K. V. Bhandarkar & B. B. Nimbalkar for Maharashtra	1948-49
451 —2nd	W. H. Ponsford & D. G. Bradman for Australia	1934
448 —4th	R. Abel & T. W. Hayward for Surrey	1899
446 —2nd	C. C. Hunte & G. St. A. Sobers for West Indies	1957-58
445 —3rd	P. E. Whitelaw & W. N. Carson for Auckland	1936-37
434 —3rd	J. B. Stollmeyer & G. E. Gomez for Trinidad	1946-47
433 —8th	V. T. Trumper & A. Sims for Australians	1913-14
429*—2nd	J. G. Dewes & G. H. G. Doggart for Cambridge U.	1949
428 —1st	J. B. Hobbs & A. Sandham for Surrey	1926
428 —6th	W. W. Armstrong & M. A. Noble for Australians	1902
424 —1st	J. F. W. Nicolson & I. J. Siedle for Natal	1926-27
424*—3rd	W. J. Edrich & D. C. S. Compton for Middlesex	1948
424 —4th	I. S. Lee & S. O. Quin for Victoria	1933-34
413 —1st	V. M. Mankad & P. Roy for India	1955-56
411 —6th	R. M. Poore & E. G. Wynyard for Hampshire	1899
411 —4th	P. B. H. May & M. C. Cowdrey for England	1957
410 —3rd	R. S. Modi & L. Amarnath for India in England	1946-47
410 —4th	G. Abraham & B. Pandit for Kerala	1959-60
405 —5th	S. G. Barnes & D. G. Bradman for Australia	1946-47
402 —4th	W. Watson & T. W. Graveney for M.C.C.	1953-54

F. M. M. Worrell is the only batsman to have shared in two partnerships of over 500 runs. The only other players to appear twice in the above list are D. G. Bradman and W. H. Ponsford.

HIGHEST PARTNERSHIPS

The minimum qualification for inclusion in the following lists is: 1st-4th wickets: 250 runs; 5th & 6th wickets: 225 runs; 7th wicket: 200 runs; 8th & 9th wickets: 150 runs; 10th wicket: 100 runs.

So-called 'partnerships', fulfilling the above qualification but involving three or more players when one of the original partners has retired hurt, etc., are omitted from these lists for reasons given in the Preface.

FIRST WICKET

555	P. Holmes & H. Sutcliffe: Yorks. v. Essex (Leyton)	1932
554	J. T. Brown & J. Tunnicliffe: Yorks. v. Derby (Chesterfield)	1898
490	E. H. Bowley & John Langridge: Sussex v. Middx. (Hove)	1933
456	W. H. Ponsford & E. R. Mayne: Victoria v. Queensland (Melbourne)	1923-24
428	J. B. Hobbs & A. Sandham: Surrey v. Oxford U. (Oval)	1926
424	J. F. W. Nicolson & I. J. Siedle: Natal v. O.F.S. (Bloemfontein)	1926-27

Highest Partnerships-First Wicket—*Cont.*

413	V. M. Mankad & P. Roy: India v. New Zealand (Madras)	1955-56
395	D. M. Young & R. B. Nicholls: Glos. v. Oxford U. (Oxford)	1962
391	A. O. Jones & A. Shrewsbury: Notts. v. Glos. (Bristol)	1899
390	L. Wight & G. Gibbs: British Guiana v. Barbados (Georgetown)	1951-52
382	W. M. Lawry & R. B. Simpson: Australia v. West Indies (Bridgetown)	1964-65
380	C. J. B. Wood & H. Whitehead: Leics. v. Worcs. (Worcester)	1906
379	R. Abel & W. Brockwell: Surrey v. Hants. (Oval)	1897
378	J. T. Brown & J. Tunnicliffe: Yorks. v. Sussex (Sheffield)	1897
377*	N. F. Horner & K. Ibadulla: Warwicks. v. Surrey (Oval)	1960
375	W. M. Woodfull & W. H. Ponsford: Victoria v. N.S.W. (Melbourne)	1926-27
373	B. Sutcliffe & L. A. Watt: Otago v. Auckland (Auckland)	1950-51
368	A. C. MacLaren & R. H. Spooner: Lancs. v. Glos. (Liverpool)	1903
368	E. H. Bowley & J. H. Parks: Sussex v. Glos. (Hove)	1929
364	R. Abel & D. L. A. Jephson: Surrey v. Derby (Oval)	1900
361	N. Oldfield & V. H. Broderick: Northants. v. Scotland (Peterborough)	1953
359	L. Hutton & C. Washbrook: England v. South Africa (Johannesburg)	1948-49
355	A. F. Rae & J. B. Stollmeyer: West Indians v. Sussex (Hove)	1950
352	T. W. Hayward & J. B. Hobbs: Surrey v. Warwicks. (Oval)	1909
350*	C. Washbrook & W. Place: Lancs v. Sussex (Manchester)	1947
349	J. G. Dewes & D. S. Sheppard: Cambridge U. v. Sussex (Hove)	1950
347	P. Holmes & H. Sutcliffe: Yorks. v. Hants. (Portsmouth)	1920
346	L. C. H. Palairet & H. T. Hewett: Somerset v. Yorks. (Taunton)	1892
343	J. G. Dewes & D. S. Sheppard: Cambridge U. v. West Indians (Cambridge)	1950
338	T. Bowring & H. Teesdale: Oxford U. v. Gentlemen of England (Oxford)	1908
337	C. C. McDonald & K. D. Meuleman: Victoria v. South Australia (Adelaide)	1949-50
333	J. F. Byrne & S. P. Kinneir: Warwicks v. Lancs. (Birmingham)	1905
330	B. Mitchell & E. A. B. Rowan: South Africans v. Surrey (Oval)	1935
323	J. B. Hobbs & W. Rhodes: England v. Australia (Melbourne)	1911-12
323	P. Holmes & H. Sutcliffe: Yorks. v. Lancs. (Sheffield)	1931
322	H. Storer & J. Bowden: Derby v. Essex (Derby)	1929
322	G. Gunn & A. Sandham: M.C.C. v. Jamaica (Kingston)	1929-30
318	W. W. Keeton & R. T. Simpson: Notts. v. Lancs. (Manchester)	1949
315	H. Sutcliffe & L. Hutton: Yorks. v. Leics. (Hull)	1937
315	H. Sutcliffe & L. Hutton: Yorks. v. Hants. (Sheffield)	1939
314	A. C. MacLaren & T. W. Hayward: MacLaren's XI v. N.S.W. (Sydney)	1901-02
313	T. W. Hayward & J. B. Hobbs: Surrey v. Worcs. (Worcester)	1913
313	A. J. Richardson & L. T. Gun: South Australia v. Western Australia (Adelaide)	1925-26
312	G. F. Dakin & C. G. Rushmere: Eastern Province v. Western Province (Cape Town)	1962-63
312	W. E. Russell & M. J. Harris: Middx. v. Pakistanis (Lord's)	1967
310	J. D. Robertson & S. M. Brown: Middx. v. Notts. (Lord's)	1947
309	F. L. Bowley & H. K. Foster: Worcs. v. Derby (Derby)	1901
309	P. Holmes & H. Sutcliffe: Yorks. v. Warwicks. (Birmingham)	1931
308	R. B. Simpson & G. Thomas: N.S.W. v. Western Australia (Sydney)	1963-64
306	L. A. Cuff & J. D. Lawrence: Canterbury v. Auckland (Christchurch)	1893-94
306	P. F. Warner & J. Douglas: Middx. v. Notts. (Nottingham)	1904
306	F. L. Bowley & F. Pearson: Worcs. v. Glos. (Worcester)	1913
305	John Langridge & H. W. Greenwood: Sussex v. Essex (Hove)	1935
303	G. L. Wilson & F. W. Marlow: Sussex v. Oxford U. (Hove)	1895
303	A. O. Jones & J. Iremonger: Notts. v. Glos. (Nottingham)	1904
299	D. V. Smith & M. J. K. Smith: M.C.C. v. Surrey (Lord's)	1958
298	V. T. Trumper & R. A. Duff: N.S.W. v. South Australia (Sydney)	1902-03
295	C. J. Barnett & A. E. Fagg: M.C.C. v. Queensland (Brisbane)	1936-37
295	John Langridge & J. H. Parks: Sussex v. Leics. (Hove)	1938
293	V. M. Merchant & V. M. Mankad: Indians v. Sussex (Hove)	1946
293	R. M. Prideaux & C. Milburn: Northants. v. Essex (Clacton)	1966
292	G. Challenor & P. H. Tarilton: Barbados v. Trinidad (Bridgetown)	1926-27
290	J. B. Hobbs & T. W. Hayward: Surrey v. Yorks. (Lord's)	1914
290	P. Holmes & H. Sutcliffe: Yorks. v. Middx. (Leeds)	1928
290	D. Kenyon & P. E. Richardson: Worcs. v. Glos. (Dudley)	1953
290	G. Pullar & M. C. Cowdrey: England v. South Africa (Oval)	1960
288	H. W. Bainbridge & W. G. Quaife: Warwicks. v. Hants. (Southampton)	1897
287	C. B. Fry & J. Vine: Sussex v. Hants. (Hove)	1904
286	R. E. H. Hudson & C. P. Hamilton: Army v. West Indians (Aldershot)	1933
286	B. Sutcliffe & D. D. Taylor: Auckland v. Canterbury (Auckland)	1948-49
286	J. B. Stollmeyer & A. G. Ganteaume: Trinidad v. Jamaica (Port of Spain)	1949-50
286	L. Hutton & F. A. Lowson: Yorks. v. South Africans (Sheffield)	1951

Highest Partnerships-First Wicket—*Cont.*

285 I. J. Siedle & H. F. Wade: Natal v. Eastern Province (Pietermaritzburg) .. 1936-37
284 J. W. H. T. Douglas & A. E. Knight: England XI v. Australians (Blackpool) 1909
284 R. T. Simpson & R. J. Giles: Notts. v. Oxford U. (Oxford) 1951
283 W. G. Grace & B. B. Cooper: Gentlemen of South v. Players of South (Oval) .. 1869
283 J. B. Hobbs & H. Sutcliffe: England v. Australia (Melbourne) 1924-25
283 A. E. Fagg & P. R. Sunnucks: Kent v. Essex (Colchester) 1938
282* G. Wilson & W. W. Hill-Wood: M.C.C. v. Victoria (Melbourne) 1922-23
281 G. Pullar & M. C. Cowdrey: M.C.C. v. British Guiana (Georgetown) .. 1959-60
281* W. B. Stott & K. Taylor: Yorks. v. Sussex (Hove) 1960
279 P. Holmes & H. Sutcliffe: Yorks. v. Northants. (Northampton) 1919
279 C. F. Walters & H. H. Gibbons: Worcs. v. Essex (Chelmsford) 1934
278 A. A. Jackson & W. H. Ponsford: Ryder's XI v. Woodfull's XI (Sydney) .. 1929-30
278* C. F. Walters & H. H. Gibbons: Worcs. v. Leics. (Worcester) 1934
278 A. M. Taylor & R. E. Marshall: Barbados v. Trinidad (Bridgetown) 1948-49
277 T. H. Fowler & H. Wrathall: Glos. v. London County (Crystal Palace) .. 1903
277 G. T. S. Stevens & E. T. Killick: Middx. v. Warwicks. (Lord's) 1931
277 W. W. Keeton & C. B. Harris: Notts. v. Middx. (Nottingham) 1933
277 D. Kenyon & L. Outschoorn: Worcs. v. Kent (Gravesend) 1954
277* Hanif Mohammad & Alim-ud-Din: Karachi A v. Sind A (Karachi) 1957-58
277 M. R. Hallam & H. D. Bird: Leics. v. South Africans (Leicester) 1960
276 C. S. Dempster & J. W. E. Mills: New Zealand v. England (Wellington) .. 1929-30
276* R. B. Simpson & N. C. O'Neill: N.S.W. v. South Australia (Sydney) 1964-65
274 H. K. Foster & F. L. Bowley: Worcs. v. Hants. (Portsmouth) 1907
274 P. Holmes & H. Sutcliffe: Yorks. v. Somerset (Hull) 1923
274 P. Holmes & H. Sutcliffe: Yorks. v. Glos. (Gloucester) 1927
274 A. H. Dyson & E. Davies: Glamorgan v. Leics. (Leicester) 1937
274 E. A. B. Rowan & A. I. Taylor: Transvaal v. Border (Johannesburg) 1952-53
273 Nazar Mohammad & Jagdish Lal: Northern India v. N.W.F.P. (Lahore) .. 1941-42
272 P. Holmes & H. Sutcliffe: Yorks. v. Leics. (Hull) 1925
272 A. J. Croom & N. Kilner: Warwicks. v. Worcs. (Birmingham) 1934
272 G. Pullar & B. J. Booth: Lancs. v. Oxford U. (Oxford) 1962
270* R. Abel & W. Brockwell: Surrey v. Kent (Oval) 1900
270 C. Hallows & H. Makepeace: Lancs. v. Worcs. (Worcester) 1922
270 A. V. Avery & T. C. Dodds: Essex v. Surrey (Oval) 1946
270 N. J. Contractor & S. P. Gaekwad: West Zone v. East Zone (Bombay) .. 1963-64
269* P. Holmes & H. Sutcliffe: North v. South (Sheffield) 1927
269 R. T. Simpson & W. W. Keeton: Notts v. Kent (Nottingham) 1951
269 Imtiaz Ahmed & Shuja-ud-Din: Services v. Karachi Blues (Karachi) 1961-62
269 F. M. Engineer & S. G. Adhikari: Bombay v. Bengal (Calcutta) 1962-63
268 J. B. Hobbs & H. Sutcliffe: England v. South Africa (Lord's) 1924
268 P. Holmes & H. Sutcliffe: Yorks. v. Essex (Leyton) 1928
268 E. Paynter & C. Washbrook: Lancs. v. Sussex (Hove) 1937
268 P. C. Davies & F. Seyfried: N-E. Transvaal v. O.F.S. (Bloemfontein) 1955-56
267 V. T. Trumper & R. A. Duff: N.S.W. v. Victoria (Sydney) 1902-03
267 W. Barber & L. Hutton: Yorks v. Kent (Leeds) 1934
266 A. Shrewsbury & A. E. Stoddart: England v. M.C.C. (Lord's) 1887
266 A. Sandham & A. Jeacocke: Surrey v. Northants. (Oval) 1921
266 N. Kilner & E. J. Smith: Warwicks. v. Middx. (Lord's) 1927
265 R. Abel & W. Brockwell: Surrey v. Warwicks. (Oval) 1898
265* P. Holmes & H. Sutcliffe: Yorks. v. Surrey (Oval) 1926
265 L. G. Brown & F. T. Prentice: Leics. v. New Zealanders (Leicester) 1937
265 W. A. Brown & G. G. Cook: Queensland v. N.S.W. (Sydney) 1938-39
264 J. B. Hobbs & A. Sandham: Surrey v. Somerset (Taunton) 1932
263 J. B. Hobbs & H. Sutcliffe: Players v. Gentlemen (Lord's) 1926
262 L. Hutton & W. J. Edrich: M.C.C. v. Griqualand West (Kimberley) 1938-39
262 F. G. Mann & J. R. Thompson: Cambridge U. v. Leics. (Cambridge) 1939
261 E. L. G. Hoad & P. H. Tarilton: Barbados v. M.C.C. (Bridgetown) 1929-30
261 D. J. McGlew & T. L. Goddard: Natal v. Rhodesia (Bulawayo) 1957-58
260 F. Watson & C. Hallows: Lancs. v. Hants. (Liverpool) 1927
260 B. Mitchell & I. J. Siedle: South Africa v. England (Cape Town) 1930-31
260 L. B. Fishlock & E. A. Bedser: Surrey v. Somerset (Oval) 1949
259 Hon. H. G. H. Mulholland & D. C. Collins: Cambridge U. v. Indians (Cambridge) 1911
259 A. R. Morris & J. A. R. Moroney: Australians v. Natal (Durban) 1949-50
258 A. E. Lewis & L. C. H. Palairet: Somerset v. Sussex (Taunton) 1901
258 John Langridge & J. H. Parks: Sussex v. Surrey (Horsham) 1934

Highest Partnerships-First Wicket—*Cont.*

258 E. A. B. Rowan & R. Connell: Eastern Province v. Griqualand West (Port Elizabeth) 1945-46
258 A. F. Rae & E. D. A. McMorris: Jamaica v. Trinidad (Georgetown) 1959-60
256 A. J. Richardson & V. Y. Richardson: South Australia v. M.C.C. (Adelaide) 1922-23
256 D. J. McGlew & T. L. Goddard: South Africans v. Glamorgan (Cardiff) .. 1960
256 S. C. Trimble & R. Reynolds: Queensland v. South Australia (Adelaide) .. 1963-64
255 C. F. Walters & H. H. Gibbons: Worcs. v. Lancs. (Worcester) 1933
255 V. Y. Richardson & H. C. Nitschke: South Australia v. Queensland (Adelaide) 1934-35
255 A. H. Dyson & E. Davies: Glamorgan v. Glos. (Newport) 1939
255 R. C. E. Pratt & M. J. Stewart: Surrey v. Cambridge U. (Guildford) 1956
255 E. J. Barlow & A. J. Pithey: South Africans v. Combined XI (Perth) 1963-64
253 P. Holmes & H. Sutcliffe: Yorks. v. Lancs. (Sheffield) 1919
253* J. B. Hobbs & A. Sandham: Surrey v. West Indians (Oval) 1928
252 R. R. Relf & J. Vine: Sussex v. Notts. (Hove) 1912
252 G. Gunn & W. W. Whysall: Notts v. Kent (Nottingham) 1924
252 B. Sutcliffe & V. J. Scott: New Zealand XI v. Rest (Christchurch) 1948-49
251 L. J. Todd & A. E. Fagg: Kent v. Leics. (Maidstone) 1949
251 P. Roy & S. Bose: Bengal v. Assam (Calcutta) 1951-52
250 R. A. Sinfield & C. J. Barnett: Glos. v. Glamorgan (Cardiff) 1935

SECOND WICKET

455 K. V. Bhandarkar & B. B. Nimbalkar : Maharashtra v. Kathiawar (Poona) .. 1948-49
451 W. H. Ponsford & D. G. Bradman: Australia v. England (Oval) 1934
446 C. C. Hunte & G. St. A. Sobers: West Indies v. Pakistan (Kingston) 1957-58
429* J. G. Dewes & G. H. G. Doggart: Cambridge U. v. Essex (Cambridge) .. 1949
398 A. Shrewsbury & W. Gunn: Notts. v. Sussex (Nottingham) 1890
385 E. H. Bowley & M. W. Tate: Sussex v. Northants. (Hove) 1921
382 L. Hutton & M. Leyland: England v. Australia (Oval) 1938
380 F. A. Tarrant & J. W. Hearne: Middx. v. Lancs. (Lord's) 1914
378 L. Marks & K. D. Walters: N.S.W. v. South Australia (Adelaide) 1964-65
374 R. B. Simpson & R. M. Cowper: Australians v. N-E. Transvaal (Pretoria) .. 1966-67
371 J. B. Hobbs & E. G. Hayes: Surrey v. Hants. (Oval) 1909
371 F. Watson & E. Tyldesley: Lancs v. Surrey (Manchester) 1928
369 J. H. Edrich & K. F. Barrington: England v. New Zealand (Leeds) 1965
368 W. Rhodes & A. C. Russell: M.C.C. v. South Australia (Adelaide) 1920-21
368 A. C. MacLaren & A. Paul: Lancs. v. Somerset (Taunton) 1895
358 B. J. Kortlang & C. McKenzie: Victoria v. Western Australia (Perth) 1909-10
356 J. M. Brearley & D. L. Amiss: M.C.C. v. Pakistan (Decca) 1966-67
352 W. H. Ashdown & F. E. Woolley: Kent v. Essex (Brentwood) 1934
349 C. B. Fry & E. H. Killick: Sussex v. Yorks. (Hove) 1901
349 C. S. Elliott & J. D. Eggar: Derby v. Notts. (Nottingham) 1947
346 W. Barber & M. Leyland: Yorks v. Middx. (Sheffield) 1932
344 J. Devey & S. P. Kinneir: Warwicks. v. Derby (Birmingham) 1900
344 A. Sandham & R. J. Gregory: Surrey v. Glamorgan (Oval) 1937
343 F. A. Lowson & J. V. Wilson: Yorks v. Oxford U. (Oxford) 1956
336 F. Watson & E. Tyldesley: Lancs. v. Worcs. (Worcester) 1929
334 A. A. Jackson & D. G. Bradman: N.S.W. v. South Australia (Adelaide) .. 1930 31
333 G. M. Lee & A. W. Carr: Notts v. Leics. (Nottingham) 19-13
333 P. Holmes & E. Oldroyd: Yorks. v. Warwicks. (Birmingham) 1922
331* W. K. Harbinson & E. T. Killick: Cambridge U. v. Glamorgan (Cambridge) 1929
327 F. Watson & E. Tyldesley: Lancs. v. Indians (Manchester) 1932
325 G. Brann & K. S. Ranjitsinhji: Sussex v. Surrey (Oval) 1899
324 I. D. Walker & Hon. A. Lyttelton: Middx. v. Glos. (Clifton) 1883
324 S. M. Brown & W. J. Edrich: Middx. v. Warwicks. (Birmingham) 1954
323 I. D. Craig & R. N. Harvey: N.S.W. v. Queensland (Sydney) 1960-61
321 G. Brown & E. I. M. Barrett: Hants. v. Glos. (Southampton) 1920
319 H. W. Lee & G. O. Allen: Middx. v. Surrey (Oval) 1929
318 R. E. H. Hudson & C. P. Hamilton: Army v. Royal Air Force (Oval) 1932
318 M. C. Cowdrey & A. S. M. Oakman: M.C.C. v. O.F.S. (Bloemfontein) .. 1956-57
318 C. W. Smith & S. M. Nurse: Barbados v. Trinidad (Bridgetown) 1962-63
317 H. Sutcliffe & C. Hallows: England v. Rest (Bristol) 1927
316 J. L. Hopwood & E. Tyldesley: Lancs v. Glos. (Bristol) 1934
316* M. J. Stewart & K. F. Barrington: Surrey v. Essex (Oval) 1962
315 A. Thompson & W. J. Edrich: Middx. v. Worcs. (Dudley) 1952
314 H. Sutcliffe & E. Oldroyd: Yorks v. Essex (Southend) 1924
314 W. H. Ponsford & H. L. Hendry: Victoria v. Queensland (Melbourne) .. 1927-28

Highest Partnerships-Second Wicket—*Cont.*

314 H. W. Lee & E. Hendren: Middx. v. Hants. (Lord's) 1928
312 A. Shrewsbury & W. Gunn: Notts. v. Sussex (Hove) 1891
307 H. T. W. Hardinge & James Seymour: Kent v. Worcs. (Kidderminster) .. 1922
307 John Langridge & H. W. Parks: Sussex v. Kent (Tonbridge) 1939
306 F. Watson & E. Tyldesley: Lancs. v. Sussex (Hove) 1928
306 C. L. Badcock & W. Horrocks: Combined XI v. M.C.C. (Perth) 1936-37
305 J. W. Rothery & D. Denton: Yorks. v. Derby (Chesterfield) 1910
305 J. M. M. Commaille & S. K. Coen: O.F.S. v. Natal (Bloemfontein) 1926-27
305 F. Watson & J. Iddon: Lancs. v. Somerset (Taunton) 1934
304 W. Bardsley & M. A. Noble: N.S.W. v. Victoria (Sydney) 1908-09
304 G. E. B. Abell & Agha Ahmed Raza: Northern India v. Army (Lahore) .. 1934-35
302 W. Watson & J. V. Wilson: Yorks. v. Derby (Scarborough) 1948
301 C. S. Dempster & C. F. W. Allcott: New Zealanders v. Warwicks. (Birmingham) 1927
301 A. R. Morris & D. G. Bradman: Australia v. England (Leeds) 1948
299 E. L. Bowley & J. T. Murray: South Australia v. Queensland (Adelaide) .. 1923-24
299 A. Sandham & A. Ducat: Surrey v. Lancs. (Manchester) 1928
299* T. L. Livingstone & D. Barrick: Northants v. Sussex (Northampton) 1953
296 E. J. Smith & L. A. Bates: Warwicks. v. Kent (Coventry) 1927
296 W. H. Ponsford & D. G. Bradman: Australian XI v. Tasmania (Hobart) .. 1929-30
295 A. Hartley & J. T. Tyldesley: Lancs. v. Somerset (Manchester) 1910
295 J. B. Stollmeyer & K. B. Trestrail: Trinidad v. Jamaica (Port of Spain) .. 1949-50
294 W. A. Brown & D. G. Bradman: N.S.W. v. Queensland (Brisbane) .. 1933-34
294 A. V. Avery & P. A. Gibb: Essex v. Northants. (Northampton) 1952
293 L. E. Favell & R. B. Simpson: Australians v. Griqualand West (Kimberley) .. 1957-58
292* K. S. Ranjitsinhji & C. B. Fry: Sussex v. Somerset (Taunton) 1901
292 J. T. Ikin & G. A. Edrich: Lancs. v. Oxford U. 1951
291 A. Sandham & H. S. Squires: Surrey v. Yorks. (Oval) 1933
289 A. Shrewsbury & W. Barnes: Notts. v. Surrey (Oval) 1882
288 H. Sutcliffe & A. Mitchell: Yorks. v. Lancs. (Manchester) 1939
287 W. Watson & A. Wharton: Leics. v. Lancs. (Leicester) 1961
286 J. C. W. MacBryan & M. D. Lyon: Somerset v. Derby (Burton) 1924
284 P. J. Sharpe & F. R. Bailey: Minor Counties v. Indians (Stoke) 1959
283 A. J. Hopkins & M. A. Noble: N.S.W. v. South Australia (Adelaide) 1908-09
283 H. W. Taylor & R. A. Blake: Natal v. Griqualand West (Durban) 1910-11
283 I. J. Siedle & A. Melville: Natal v. Border (Durban) 1928-29
283 H. Sutcliffe & Nawab of Pataudi Snr.: M.C.C. v. Combined XI (Perth) .. 1932-33
283 V. L. Mehra & B. K. Kunderan: Railways v. Jammu & Kashmir (New Delhi) 1959-60
282 D. Brooks & T. L. Livingstone: Northants. v. Kent (Maidstone) 1954
282 J. Rutherford & R. N. Harvey: Australians v. M.C.C. (Lord's) 1956
281 W. G. Grace & J. M. Cotterill: South v. North (Prince's) 1877
281 A. Sandham & A Ducat: Surrey v. Notts. (Nottingham) 1930
281 W. M. Woodfull & W. A. Brown: Australians v. Lancs. (Manchester) 1934
281 John Langridge & H. W. Parks: Sussex v. Glamorgan (Eastbourne) 1938
281 C. L. Walcott & F. M. M. Worrell: West Indies v. Tasmania (Hobart) .. 1951-52
280 L. Hall & F. Lee: Yorks. v. Lancs. (Bradford) 1887
280 G. Brown & E. I. M. Barrett: Hants. v. Warwicks. (Portsmouth) 1920
280 P. A. Gibb & W. J. Edrich: England v. South Africa (Durban) 1938-39
280 J. W. Burke & R. N. Harvey: Australians v. Warwicks. (Birmingham) .. 1956
277 C. J. B. Wood & G. W. Beldam: London County v. Surrey (Oval) 1901
277 W. J. Edrich & D. C. S. Compton: Middx. v. Leics. (Leicester) 1947
277 S. G. Adhikari & H. D. Amroliwalla: Bombay v. Maharashtra (Poona) .. 1960-61
276 W. Bardsley & C. G. Macartney: Australians v. Leics. (Leicester) 1921
276 J. B. Hobbs & R. J. Gregory: Surrey v. Hants. (Southampton) 1926
275 A. E. Fagg & F. G. H. Chalk: Kent v. Worcs. (Dudley) 1938
275 C. C. McDonald & A. L. Hassett: Australia v. South Africa (Adelaide) .. 1952-53
274 A. Shrewsbury & W. Gunn: Notts. v. Sussex (Hove) 1893
274 W. M. Woodfull & D. G. Bradman: Australia v. South Africa (Melbourne) .. 1931-32
274 H. H. Gibbons & Nawab of Pataudi Snr.: Worcs. v. Kent (Worcester) .. 1933
274 H. H. Gibbons & Nawab of Pataudi Snr.: Worcs. v. Glamorgan (Worcester) .. 1934
273 J. L. Hopwood & E. Tyldesley: Lancs. v. Glamorgan (Cardiff) 1934
273 L. J. Todd & L. E. G. Ames: Kent v. Essex (Maidstone) 1947
272 R. Abel & E. G. Hayes: Surrey v. Worcs. (Oval) 1900
271 M. Harvey & K. R. Miller: Victoria v. N.S.W. (Melbourne) 1946-47
271 C. Washbrook & G. A. Edrich: Lancs. v. Sussex (Manchester) 1951
270 H. L. Collins & T. J. E. Andrews: N.S.W. v. M.C.C. (Sydney) 1924-25
270 W. M. Woodfull & C. G. Macartney: Australians v. Essex (Leyton) 1926
270 D. N. Sardesai & A. L. Wadekar: Bombay v. Mysore (Bombay) 1966-67

Highest Partnerships-Second Wicket—*Cont.*

269	Nazar Mohammad & Murrawat Hussain: Pakistan v. Ceylon (Colombo)	1948-49
269	G. St. A. Sobers & C. L. Walcott: West Indies v. Pakistan (Georgetown)	1957-58
268	J. R. M. Mackay & M. A. Noble: N.S.W. v. Victoria (Melbourne)	1905-06
267	V. M. Mankad & R. F. Surti: Rajasthan v. Uttar Pradesh (Udaipur)	1959-60
266	P. E. Richardson & T. W. Graveney: England v. West Indies (Nottingham)	1957
266*	K. Taylor & D. E. V. Padgett: Yorks. v. Oxford U. (Oxford)	1962
265	A. Ward & J. T. Tyldesley: Lancs. v. Derby (Derby)	1901
265	G. Gunn & W. Walker: Notts. v. Hants. (Bournemouth)	1928
265	D. Brookes & W. Barron: Northants. v. Cambridge U. (Cambridge)	1948
265	A. R. Morris & K. R. Miller: N.S.W. v. M.C.C. (Sydney)	1950-51
263	G. B. Y. Cox & H. B. G. Austin: Barbados v. Trinidad (Bridgetown)	1897-98
262	J. M. Gregory & T. J. E. Andrews: N.S.W. v. New Zealanders (Sydney)	1927-28
262	H. T. W. Hardinge & F. E. Woolley: Kent v. Warwicks. (Tunbridge Wells)	1928
262	W. P. J. Donaldson & K. R. Miller: N.S.W. v. Western Australia (Sydney)	1947-48
262	R. Virgin & M. J. Kitchen: Somerset v. Pakistanis (Taunton)	1967
261	E. W. Dillon & James Seymour: Kent v. Somerset (Taunton)	1905
261	A. R. Morris & S. G. Barnes: N.S.W. v. Queensland (Sydney)	1940-41
261*	L. Hutton & J. V. Wilson: Yorks. v. Scotland (Hull)	1949
261	N. W. Hill & J. D. Clay: Notts. v. Yorks. (Nottingham)	1959
260	A. E. Fagg & F. E. Woolley: Kent v. Northants. (Northampton)	1934
259	T. W. Hayward & E. G. Hayes: Surrey v. Yorks. (Oval)	1911
259	John Langridge & A. Melville: Sussex v. Indians (Hove)	1936
259	D. Brookes & T. L. Livingston: Northants v. Leics. (Northampton)	1950
259*	R. T. Spooner & T. W. Graveney: M.C.C. v. Pakistan (Lahore)	1951-52
258	H. Sutcliffe & E. Oldroyd: Yorks. v. Kent (Folkstone)	1931
256	W. G. Grace & W. Chatterton: M.C.C. v. Cambridge U. (Cambridge)	1894
256	W. W. Whysall & W. Walker: Notts. v. Hants. (Nottingham)	1930
256	H. F. Wade & E. A. B. Rowan: South Africans v. Glamorgan (Cardiff)	1935
256	C. T. M. Pugh & T. W. Graveney: Glos. v. Derby (Chesterfield)	1960
256	Salim Asghar & Mohammad Arif: Rawalpindi v. Peshawar (Rawalpindi)	1963-64
255	A. Ward & A. E. Stoddart: Stoddart's XI v. Queensland (Brisbane)	1894-95
255	V. Y. Richardson & D. E. Pritchard: South Australia v. M.C.C. (Adelaide)	1928-29
255	H. T. W. Hardinge & F. E. Woolley: Kent v. Derby (Chesterfield)	1929
255	E. D. A. McMorris & R. B. Kanhai: West Indies v. India (Kingston)	1961-62
255	D. L. Amiss & J. A. Jameson: Warwicks. v. Oxford U. (Birmingham)	1964
254*	L. G. Berry & N. F. Armstrong: Leics v. Parkinson's XI (Blackpool)	1935
254*	W. M. Lawry & R. M. Cowper: Combined XI v. M.C.C. (Hobart)	1965-66
253	B. B. Wilson & D. Denton: Yorks. v. Warwicks. (Birmingham)	1912
253	C. T. Sarwate & L. Amarnath: Indians v. Tasmania (Launceston)	1947-48
253	J. W. Burke & K. D. Mackay: Australians v. Eastern Province (Port Elizabeth)	1957-58
253	J. W. Burke & R. N. Harvey: N.S.W. v. Queensland (Brisbane)	1958-59
252	G. Brann & K. S. Ranjitsinhji: Sussex v. Glos. (Bristol)	1899
252	W. Tyldesley & J. T. Tyldesley: Lancs. v. Derby (Derby)	1911
252	W. A. Baker & E. M. Beechey: Wellington v. Auckland (Wellington)	1918-19
252	W. M. Lawry & J. Potter: Victoria v. N.S.W. (Sydney)	1960-61
251	J. C. W. MacBryan & A. Young: Somerset v. Glamorgan (Taunton)	1923
251	C. J. Barnett & W. R. Hammond: Glos. v. Sussex (Cheltenham)	1934
251*	R. T. Simpson & C. J. Poole: Notts. v. Leics. (Nottingham)	1949
250	F. L. Bowley & H. K. Foster: Worcs. v. Somerset (Worcester)	1903
250	A. C. Johnston & C. P. Mead: Hants. v. Warwicks. (Coventry)	1912
250	H. T. W. Hardinge & James Seymour: Kent v. Essex (Leyton)	1923
250	D. J. McGlew & M. K. Elgie: Natal v. Border (Durban)	1957-58

THIRD WICKET

445	P. E. Whitelaw & W. N. Carson: Auckland v. Otago (Dunedin)	1936-37
434	J. B. Stollmeyer & G. E. Gomez: Trinidad v. British Guiana (Port of Spain)	1946-47
424*	W. J. Edrich & D. C. S. Compton: Middx. v. Somerset (Lord's)	1948
410	R. S. Modi & L. Amarnath: India in England v. Rest (Calcutta)	1946-47
399	R. T. Simpson & D. C. S. Compton: M.C.C. v. N-E. Transvaal (Benoni)	1948-49
389	W. H. Ponsford & S. J. McCabe: Australians v. M.C.C. (Lord's)	1934
388	Salah-ud-Din & Wallis Mathias: Karachi Blues v. Hyderabad (Karachi)	1964-65
375	J. W. Hearne & E. Hendren: Middx. v. Hants. (Southampton)	1923
373	V. M. Merchant & R. S. Modi: Bombay v. Western India States (Bombay)	1944-45
370	W. J. Edrich & D. C. S. Compton: England v. South Africa (Lord's)	1947
369	W. Gunn & J. Gunn: Notts. v. Leics. (Nottingham)	1903
363	D. G. Bradman & A. F. Kippax: N.S.W. v. Queensland (Sydney)	1933-34

Highest Partnerships-Third Wicket—*Cont.*

362	W. Bardsley & C. G. Macartney: Australians v. Essex (Leyton)	1912
356	D. G. Bradman & R. A. Hamence: South Australia v. Tasmania (Adelaide)	1935-36
355	W. Bardsley & V. S. Ransford: Australians v. Essex (Leyton)	1909
353	A. Ducat & E. G. Hayes: Surrey v. Hants. (Southampton)	1919
350	F. M. M. Worrell & E. D. Weekes: West Indians v. Cambridge U. (Cambridge)	1950
345	W. Bardsley & J. M. Taylor: N.S.W. v. South Australia (Adelaide)	1920-21
345	V. M. Merchant & H. R. Adhikari: Hindus v. Rest (Bombay)	1943-44
344	G. Brown & C. P. Mead: Hants. v. Yorks. (Portsmouth)	1927
343	P. A. Gibb & R. Horsfall: Essex v. Kent (Blackheath)	1951
341	E. J. Barlow & R. G. Pollock: South Africa v. Australia (Adelaide)	1963-64
340*	F. M. M. Worrell & E. D. Weekes: West Indians v. Leics. (Leicester)	1950
338	E. D. Weekes & F. M. M. Worrell: West Indies v. England (Port of Spain)	1953-54
336	W. R. Hammond & B. H. Lyon: Glos. v. Leics. (Leicester)	1933
335	D. K. Gaekwad & C. G. Borde: Baroda v. Maharashtra (Poona)	1959-60
333	R. M. Taylor & J. O'Connor: Essex v. Northants. (Colchester)	1937
330	A. E. Dipper & W. R. Hammond: Glos. v. Lancs. (Manchester)	1925
328	H. Carpenter & C. P. McGahey: Essex. v. Surrey (Oval)	1904
327	S. P. Kinneir & W. G. Quaife: Warwicks. v. Lancs. (Birmingham)	1901
323	C. P. McGahey & P. A. Perrin: Essex v. Kent (Leyton)	1900
323*	H. Sutcliffe & M. Leyland: Yorks. v. Glamorgan (Huddersfield)	1928
321*	A. Hearne & J. R. Mason: Kent v. Notts. (Nottingham)	1899
320	W. W. Armstrong & M. A. Noble: Australians v. Somerset (Bath)	1905
320	T. L. Livingston & F. Jakeman: Northants. v. South Africans (Northampton)	1951
319	A. Melville & A. D. House, Jnr.: South Africa v. England (Nottingham)	1947
318	G. A. Faulkner & A. D. Nourse, Snr.: South Africans v. N.S.W. (Sydney)	1910-11
318	T. W. Graveney & J. F. Crapp: Glos. v. Kent (Gillingham)	1953
317	A. Ducat & T. F. Shepherd: Surrey v. Essex (Leyton)	1928
316*	W. Watson & A. Wharton: Leics. v. Somerset (Taunton)	1961
315	L. G. Crawley & W. V. Fox: Worcs. v. Northants. (Worcester)	1923
315	C. L. Badcock & A. L. Hassett: Australians v. Leics. (Leicester)	1938
315	K. M. Tewari & V. L. Manjrekar: Uttar Pradesh v. Madhya Pradesh (Indore)	1957-58
314	M. J. Horton & T. W. Graveney: Worcs. v. Somerset (Worcester)	1962
313	Umar Khan & Prithiviraj: Western India v. Bombay (Rajkot)	1943-44
313	E. Davies & W. E. Jones: Glamorgan v. Essex (Brentwood)	1948
312	P. A. Perrin & C. P. McGahey: Essex v. Derby (Leyton)	1912
310	A. Shrewsbury & W. Gunn: Non-Smokers v. Smokers (East Melbourne)	1886-87
309*	C. B. Fry & A. C. MacLaren: Gentlemen v. Players (Lord's)	1903
306	R. Abel & F. C. Holland: Surrey v. Cambridge U. (Oval)	1895
306	E. Paynter & N. Oldfield: Lancs. v. Hants. (Southampton)	1938
306	S. M. Nurse & G. St. A. Sobers: Barbados v. M.C.C. (Bridgetown)	1959-60
305	W. E. Roller & W. W. Read: Surrey v. Lancs. (Manchester)	1887
304	W. J. Edrich & D. C. S. Compton: Middx. v. Glos. (Lord's)	1938
304	A. H. Phebey & R. C. Wilson: Kent v. Glamorgan (Blackheath)	1960
303	H. K. Foster & R. E. Foster: Worcs. v. Kent (Worcester)	1907
301	E. T. Killick & E. Hendren: Middx. v. Sussex (Hove)	1928
301	H. Sutcliffe & M. Leyland: Yorks. v. Middx. (Lord's)	1939
301*	Atma Singh & H. T. Dani: Services v. Bengal (New Delhi)	1957-58
300	G. Atkinson & P. B. Wight: Somerset v. Glamorgan (Bath)	1960
298	K. S. Ranjitsinhji & E. H. Killick: Sussex v. Lancs. (Hove)	1901
298	J. B. Hobbs & E. Hendren: Players v. Gentlemen (Scarborough)	1925
297	P. B. Wight & W. E. Alley: Somerset v. Surrey (Taunton)	1961
297	J. H. Edrich & K. F. Barrington: Surrey v. Middx. (Oval)	1967
296	R. H. Spooner & J. Hallows: Lancs. v. Essex (Leyton)	1904
296	W. J. Edrich & E. Hendren: M.C.C. v. Surrey (Lord's)	1936
296	W. J. Edrich & D. C. S. Compton: Middx. v. Surrey (Lord's)	1946
295	C. C. McDonald & R. N. Harvey: Australia v. West Indies (Kingston)	1954-55
295	K. D. Mackay & P. J. Burge: Queensland v. South Australia (Adelaide)	1960-61
294	J. M. Parks & James Langridge: Sussex v. Kent (Tunbridge Wells)	1951
292	A. C. Johnston & C. P. Mead: Hants. v. Warwicks. (Southampton)	1911
291	A. E. Knight & J. H. King: Leics. v. M.C.C. (Lord's)	1904
291	P. A. Perin & F. H. Gillingham: Essex v. Cambridge U. (Cambridge)	1910
290*	J. S. Solomon & B. F. Butcher: Berbice v. M.C.C. (Blairmont)	1959-60
290	A. L. Wadekar & V. H. Bhosle: West Zone v. East Zone (Calcutta)	1964-65
287*	W. J. Edrich & D. C. S. Compton: Middx. v. Surrey (Oval)	1947
286	J. W. Hearne & E. Hendren: Middx. v. Somerset (Taunton)	1928
284	E. T. Killick & G. C. Grant: Cambridge U. v. Essex (Cambridge)	1929
283	H. T. W. Hardinge & F. E. Woolley: Kent v. South Africans (Canterbury)	1924

Highest Partnerships-Third Wicket—*Cont.*

283	J. M. Parks & K. F. Barrington: M.C.C. v. Berbice (Blairmont)	1959-60
283	R. C. Wilson & S. E. Leary: Kent v. Northants. (Kettering)	1963
281	W. G. Grace & L. Walker: London County v. M.C.C. (Crystal Palace)	1901
281	K. E. Rigg & L. S. Darling: Victoria v. South Australia (Adelaide)	1932-33
281	T. L. Livingstone & R. Subba Row: Northants. v. Notts. (Nottingham)	1955
280	James Seymour & F. E. Woolley: Kent v. Lancs. (Dover)	1922
280	O. W. Bill & A. F. Kippax: N.S.W. v. Queensland (Brisbane)	1930-31
280	C. Richardson & D. Schonegevel: O.F.S. v. Transvaal B (Johannesburg)	1959-60
280	T. L. Goddard & R. A. McLean: South Africans v. Northants. (Northampton)	1960
279	H. Makepeace & E. Tyldesley: Lancs. v. Notts. (Manchester)	1926
279*	E. Tyldesley & J. Iddon: Lancs. v. Worcs. (Worcester)	1932
279	H. H. Gibbons & S. H. Martin: Worcs. v. Northants. (Stourbridge)	1934
279	D. S. Sheppard & G. Cox: Sussex v. Yorks. (Hastings)	1953
278	A. Ward & F. H. Sugg: Lancs. v. Somerset (Taunton)	1898
278	C. J. B. Wood & A. E. Knight: Leics. v. Hants. (Southampton)	1905
278	T. N. Pearce & M. P. Donnelly: M.C.C. v. Yorks. (Scarborough)	1948
277	W. A. Hill & R. E. S. Wyatt: Warwicks. v. Northants. (Northampton)	1939
276	W. L. Murdoch & G. H. S. Trott: Australians v. Cambridge U. P. & P. (Leyton)	1890
276	M. N. Harbottle & R. E. H. Hudson: Army v. Oxford U. (Camberley)	1938
276	D. G. Bradman & A. L. Hassett: Australia v. England (Brisbane)	1946-47
273	F. L. Fane & G. J. V. Weigall: M.C.C. v. Cambridge U. (Lord's)	1901
273	H. T. W. Hardinge & F. E. Woolley: Kent v. Hants. (Southampton)	1922
273	F. C. de Saram & N. S. Mitchell-Innes: Oxford U. v. Glos. (Oxford)	1934
273	W. R. Hammond & B. O. Allen: Glos v. Leics. (Leicester)	1935
273	W. Place & G. A. Edrich: Lancs. v. Essex (Clacton)	1947
273	V. L. Manjrekar & B. R. Irani: Bombay v. Pakistan (Bombay)	1952-53
273	Hanif Mohammad & V. L. Manjrekar: Mahmood's XI v. Cannon's XI (Karachi)	1953-54
272	C. P. Mead & E. Hendren: M.C.C. Australian XI v. Hawke's XI (Scarborough)	1929
272	D. G. Bradman & A. F. Kippax: N.S.W. v. Queensland (Sydney)	1929-30
272	H. Horton & D. A. Livingstone: Hants. v. Middx. (Bournemouth)	1966
271	E. Paynter & N. Oldfield: Lancs. v. Sussex (Hove)	1937
269*	G. Brown and C. P. Mead: Hants. v. Yorks. (Leeds)	1920
269	B. O. Allen & W. R. Hammond: Glos. v. Worcs. (Cheltenham)	1937
268	H. O. Rock & A. F. Kippax: N.S.W. v. Victoria (Sydney)	1924-25
268	N. F. Armstrong & C. S. Dempster: Leics. v. Glos. (Gloucester)	1937
268	Vijay Hazare & R. S. Modi: West Zone v. North Zone (Bombay)	1946-47
267	R. J. Gregory & T. H. Barling: Surrey v. Notts. (Oval)	1946
267	W. J. Edrich & S. M. Brown: Middx. v. Oxford U. (Oxford)	1952
267*	R. E. Marshall & D. A. Livingstone: Hants. v. Pakistanis (Bournemouth)	1962
267	P. R. Carlstein & J. H. B. Waite: Transvaal v. Cavaliers (Johannesburg)	1962-63
266	R. Aird & C. P. Mead: Hants. v. Sussex (Hastings)	1924
266	C. B. Harris & J. Hardstaff, Jnr.: Notts. v. Glos. (Nottingham)	1936
266	C. C. Hunte & G. St. A. Sobers: West Indies v. Universities XI (Nagpur)	1958-59
264	F. E. Woolley & J. W. Hearne: M.C.C. v. Tasmania (Hobart)	1911-12
264*	C. B. Fry & E. I. M. Barrett: Hants v. Oxford U. (Southampton)	1912
264	J. Vine & R. R. Relf: Sussex v. Oxford U. (Hove)	1913
264	L. Hutton & W. R. Hammond: England v. West Indies (Oval)	1939
263	D. F. Pope & A. C. Russell: Essex v. Sussex (Hove)	1930
263	D. G. W. Fletcher & H. S. Squires: Surrey v. Notts. (Nottingham)	1947
262	L. C. H. Palairet & C.A. Bernard: Somerset v. Hants. (Southampton)	1900
262	W. R. Hammond & D. R. Jardine: England v. Australia (Adelaide)	1928-29
261	A. Ducat & T. F. Shepherd: Surrey v. Leics. (Oval)	1926
261	B. Constable & P. B. H. May: Surrey v. Notts. (Nottingham)	1958
260	W. W. Keeton & J. Hardstaff, Jnr.: Notts. v. Yorks. (Sheffield)	1949
259	C. L. Townsend & W. Troup: Glos. v. Essex (Clifton)	1899
259	L. E. G. Ames & L. J. Todd: Kent v. Glos. (Folkestone)	1933
259	J. Arnold & C. P. Mead: Hants. v. Derby (Portsmouth)	1934
258*	J. T. Brown & F. Mitchell: Yorks. v. Warwicks. (Bradford)	1901
258	E. S. B. Williams & G. J. Bryan: Army v. Royal Navy (Lord's)	1928
258*	E. D. Weekes & C. L. Walcott: West Indians v. Ceylon (Colombo)	1948-49
258	D. S. Sheppard & G. Cox: Sussex v. Glamorgan (Eastbourne)	1949
256	W. W. Whysall & A. W. Carr: Notts. v. Leics. (Leicester)	1928
255*	W. G. Grace & E. M. Knapp: Glos. v. Surrey (Clifton)	1873
255	C. B. Fry & K. S. Ranjitsinhji: Sussex v. Yorks. (Sheffield)	1904
255	J. S. F. Morrison & Hon. H. G. H. Mulholland: Cambridge U. v. M.C.C. (Cambridge)	1914
255	J. W. Hearne & E. Hendren: Middx. v. Somerset (Taunton)	1934

Highest Partnerships-Third Wicket—*Cont.*

255 L. Amarnath & Vijay Hazare: Indians v. Tasmania (Hobart) 1947-48
255 O. C. Dawson & K. N. Kirton: Border v. Rhodesia (East London) 1954-55
254 B. Chowdhury & P. Roy: Bengal v. Bihar (Calcutta) 1962-63
253 C. Hill & D. R. A. Gehrs: South Australia v. Victoria (Adelaide) 1909-10
253 H. T. W. Hardinge & F. E. Woolley: Kent v. Lancs. (Dover) 1926
252 C. L. Townsend & C. O. H. Sewell: Glos. v. Worcs. (Cheltenham) 1906
252 D. G. Bradman & K. R. Miller: Australian XI v. Indians (Sydney) 1947-48
252 D. E. V. Padgett & D. B. Close: Yorks. v. Notts. (Nottingham) 1959
252 G. E. Barker & J. Milner: Essex v. Leics. (Leicester) 1959
250* H. T. W. Hardinge & James Seymour: Kent v. Worcs. (Tonbridge) 1921
250 J. O'Connor & A. C. Russell: Essex v. Leics. (Leyton) 1927
250 E. H. Bowley & K. S. Duleepsinhji: Sussex v. Surrey (Oval) 1931
250 C. H. Bull & H. H. Gibbons: Worcs. v. Northants. (Kidderminster) 1937
250 R. J. Christiani & J. L. Thomas: British Guiana v. Barbados (Georgetown) .. 1946-47
250 M. K. Mantri & U. M. Merchant: Bombay v. Maharashtra (Poona) 1948-49

FOURTH WICKET

577 Gul Mahomed & Vijay Hazare: Baroda v. Holkar (Baroda) 1946-47
574* C. L. Walcott & F. M. M. Worrell: Barbados v. Trinidad (Port of Spain) .. 1945-46
502* F. M. M. Worrell & J. D. C. Goddard: Barbados v. Trinidad (Bridgetown) .. 1943-44
448 R. Abel & T. W. Hayward: Surrey v. Yorks. (Oval) 1899
424 I. S. Lee & S. O. Quin: Victoria v. Tasmania (Melbourne) 1933-34
411 P. B. H. May & M. C. Cowdrey: England v. West Indies (Birmingham) .. 1957
410 G. Abraham & B. Pandit: Kerala v. Andhra (Pulghat) 1959-60
402 W. Watson & T. W. Graveney: M.C.C. v. British Guiana (Georgetown) .. 1953-54
399 G. St. A. Sobers & F. M. M. Worrell: West Indies v. England (Bridgetown) .. 1959-60
388 W. H. Ponsford & D. G. Bradman: Australia v. England (Leeds) 1934
382 Vijay Hazare & V. M. Merchant: C. C. of India v. Services XI (Bombay) .. 1944-45
381 H. P. Bayley & C. S. Persaud: British Guiana v. Barbados (Georgetown) .. 1937-38
377 K. R. Miller & J. H. de Courcy: Australians v. Combined Services (Kingston) 1953
366* P. R. Umrigar & Vijay Hazare: Indians v. Oxford U. (Oxford) 1952
361 A. O. Jones & J. Gunn: Notts. v. Essex (Leyton) 1905
346 Zafar Altaf & Majid Jahangir: Lahore Greens v. Bahawalpur (Lahore) .. 1965-66
342* S. W. Sohoni & Vijay Hazare: Maharashtra v. Western India States (Rajkot) .. 1940-41
342 E. A. B. Rowan & P. J. M. Gibb: Transvaal v. N-E. Transvaal (Johannesburg) 1952-53
334 R. Abel & T. W. Hayward: Surrey v. Somerset (Oval) 1899
333 W. R. Hammond & E. Hendren: M.C.C. v. N.S.W. (Sydney) 1928-29
330 W. Barnes & W. Gunn: M.C.C. v. Yorks. (Lord's) 1885
328 P. Vaulkhard & D. Smith: Derby v. Notts. (Nottingham) 1946
326* James Langridge & G. Cox: Sussex v. Yorks. (Leeds) 1949
325 J. W. Hearne & E. Hendren: Middx. v. Hants. (Lord's) 1919
324 J. T. Tyldesley & A. C. MacLaren: Lancs. v. Notts. (Nottingham) 1904
324 J. R.Reid & W. M. Wallace: New Zealanders v. Cambridge U. (Cambridge) 1949
323 A. W. Carr & W. Payton: Notts. v. Kent (Nottingham) 1923
323 N. C. O'Neill & B. C. Booth: N.S.W. v. Victoria (Sydney) 1957-58
322 Vijay Hazare & V. M. Mankad: Indians v. Yorks. (Sheffield) 1946
322 D. K. Gaekwad & Vijay Hazare: Baroda v. Bombay (Sholapur) 1957-58
321 W. R. Hammond & W. L. Neale: Glos. v. Leics. (Gloucester) 1937
319 R. E. S. Wyatt & H. E. Dollery: Warwicks. v. Lancs. (Birmingham) 1937
315 M.A. Noble & S. E. Gregory: N.S.W. v. Victoria (Sydney) 1907-08
315 W. G. Quaife & J. H. Parsons: Warwicks. v. Glamorgan (Birmingham) .. 1927
312 D. Denton & G. H. Hirst: Yorks. v. Hants. (Southampton) 1914
308 G. Davidson & W. Storer: Derby v. Lancs. (Manchester) 1896
304 D. C. S. Compton & F. G. Mann: Middx. v. Surrey (Lord's) 1947
303* Vijay Hazare & H. R. Adhikari: Baroda v. Maharashtra (Poona) 1944-45
302 Vijay Hazare & Gul Mohamed: Bengal Cyclone XI v. Bijapur Famine XI (Bombay) 1942-43
302 U. M. Merchant & D. G. Phadkar: Bombay v. Maharashtra (Poona) 1948-49
301 L. P. O'Brien & L. S. Darling: Victoria v. Queensland (Brisbane) 1932-33
301 T. E. Bailey & P. B. H. May: M.C.C. v. Rhodesia (Salisbury) 1956-57
300 E. Tyldesley & J. Iddon: Lancs. v. Leics. (Leicester) 1928
299 P. Holmes & R. Kilner: Yorks. v. Northants. (Harrogate) 1921
299 W. M. Wallace & M. P. Donnelly: New Zealanders v. Leics. (Leicester) .. 1949
298 A. V. Avery & R. Horsfall: Essex v. Worcs. (Clacton) 1948
297 H. T. W. Hardinge & A. P. F. Chapman: Kent v. Hants. (Southampton) .. 1926

Highest Partnerships-Fourth Wicket—*Cont.*

297 D. N. Sardesai & P. R. Umrigar: Associated Cement Co. XI v. Indian Starlets (Hyderabad) 1964-65
296 K. L. Hutchings & F. E. Woolley: Kent v. Northants. (Gravesend) 1908
295 P. J. Burge & T. R. Veivers: Queensland v. South Australia (Brisbane) .. 1962-63
294 I. D. Walker & G. F. Grace: Gentlemen of South v. Gentlemen of North (Beeston) 1870
294 T. L. Goddard & H. L. Ackerman: N-E. Transvaal v. Western Province (Cape Town) 1966-67
293 R. A. Duff & M. A. Noble: N.S.W. v. South Australia (Sydney) 1903-04
293 T. H. Barling & H. S. Squires: Surrey v. Oxford U. (Oval) 1932
293 P. R. Umrigar & G. Kishenchand: Gujerat v. Maharashtra (Kolhapur) .. 1951-52
291 C. G. Macartney & C. E. Pellew: Australians v. Notts. (Nottingham) .. 1921
289 A. Ducat & T. F. Shepherd: Surrey v. Glos. (Oval) 1927
283 F. M. M. Worrell & E. D. Weekes: West Indies v. England (Nottingham) .. 1950
282 A. C. Wilkinson & A. P. F. Chapman: M.C.C. v. Canterbury (Christchurch) 1922-23
282 J. Hardstaff, Jnr. & D. C. S. Compton: M.C.C. v. Tasmania (Launceston) .. 1946-47
281 T. E. Cook & James Langridge: Sussex v. Surrey (Oval) 1930
279 R. E. Marshall & C. L. Walcott: West Indians v. Surrey (Oval) 1950
278 E. Hendren & L. E. G. Ames: M.C.C. v. British Guiana (Georgetown) .. 1929-30
278 A. W. Roberts & M. L. Page: Canterbury v. Wellington (Wellington) .. 1931-32
278 G. Boycott & M. J. K. Smith: M.C.C. v. Eastern Province (Port Elizabeth) .. 1964-65
277 H. H. Gibbons & B. W. Quaife: Worcs. v. Middx. (Worcester) 1931
277 D. G. Bradman & C. L. Badcock: Australians v. Worcs. (Worcester) 1938
276 P. G. T. Kingsley & N. M. Ford: Oxford U. v. Surrey (Oval) 1930
275 R. de W. K. Winlaw & J. H. Human: Cambridge U. v. Essex (Cambridge) .. 1934
275 C. L. Badcock & A. L. Hassett: Australians v. Cambridge U. (Cambridge) .. 1938
275 F. C. Gardner & H. E. Dollery: Warwicks. v. Somerset (Coventry) 1953
274* R. Flockton & G. Thomas: N.S.W. v. South Australia (Sydney) 1959-60
271 B. B. Wilson & W. Rhodes: Yorks. v. Sussex (Bradford) 1914
271 J. O'Connor & T. N. Pearce: Essex v. Lancs. (Clacton) 1931
271 T. W. Graveney & B. L. D'Oliveira: Worcs. v. Essex (Worcester) 1966
270 J. B. Hobbs & D. R. Jardine: Surrey v. Middx. (Lord's) 1926
270 C. S. Dempster & G. S. Watson: Leics. v. Yorks. (Hull) 1937
268 H. Carpenter & T. M. Russell: Essex v. Derby (Derby) 1900
268* E. Tyldesley & J. Iddon: Lancs. v. Glamorgan (Swansea) 1933
267 C. L. Walcott & G. E. Gomez: West Indies v. India (New Delhi) 1948-49
266* W. Payton & J. Gunn: Notts. v. Glos. (Nottingham) 1911
266 W. R. Hammond & T. S. Worthington: England v. India (Oval) 1936
266 G. Cox & James Langridge: Sussex v. Lancs. (Hove) 1939
265 H. B. Cameron & Q. McMillan: Transvaal v. O.F.S. (Cape Town) 1928-29
265 F. E. Woolley & M. J. Turnbull: M.C.C. v. N.S.W. (Sydney) 1929-30
265 P. A. Gibb & J. R. Thompson: Cambridge U. v. Free Foresters (Cambridge) 1938
265 N. Rosendorff & S. Strydom: O.F.S. v. Transvaal B (Vereeniging) 1965-66
264 I. D. Craig & W. Watson: N.S.W. v. Western Australia (Perth) 1956-57
263 G. Lavis & C. Smart: Glamorgan v. Worcs. (Cardiff) 1934
263 J. Hardstaff, Jnr. & F. W. Stocks: Notts. v. Northants. (Nottingham) 1951
262 I. S. Lee & R. G. Gregory: Victoria v. M.C.C. (Melbourne) 1936-37
260 C. F. Walters & C. H. Bull: Worcs. v. Kent (Gravesend) 1933
259 A. Drake & G. H. Hirst: Yorks. v. Sussex (Hastings) 1911
259 C. P. Mead & Hon L. H. Tennyson: Hants. v. Leics. (Portsmouth) 1921
259* D. V. Smith & James Langridge: Sussex v. Notts. (Nottingham) 1950
259 Hanif Mohammad & Wallis Mathias: Karachi v. Bahawalpur (Karachi) .. 1958-59
258 J. Tunnicliffe & G. H. Hirst: Yorks. v. Hants. (Portsmouth) 1904
258 M. C. Datar & M. R. Rege: Maharashtra v. Bombay (Poona) 1948-49
256 R. Abel & F. C. Holland: Surrey v. Essex (Oval) 1895
256 A. E. Knight & H. Whitehead: Leics. v. Sussex (Leicester) 1900
256 E. Hendren & F. T. Mann: Middx. v. Essex (Leyton) 1923
256 A. C. Russell & P. A. Perrin: Essex v. Worcs. (Worcester) 1923
256 C. F. Walters & M. Nichol: Worcs. v. Hants. (Bournemouth) 1933
256 G. Cox & C. Oakes: Sussex v. Northants. (Northampton) 1950
256 H. R. Adhikari & H. T. Dani: Services v. Southern Punjab (Patiala) 1959-60
256* P. J. Burge & G. Bizzell: Queensland v. Western Australia (Brisbane) 1963-64
255* Hanif Mohammad & Raees Mohammad: Karachi v. Sind (Karachi) 1954-55
255 R. Pinnock & E. D. A. McMorris: Jamaica v. Guyana (Georgetown) 1966-67
254 F. Chester & G. N. Foster: Worcs. v. Middx. (Lord's) 1913
254 K. G. Viljoen & J. C. Newton: O.F.S. v. Transvaal (Bloemfontein) 1933-34
254 J. R. Reid & L. S. M. Miller: New Zealanders v. Natal (Durban) 1953-54
253 R. E. S. Wyatt & H. E. Dollery: Warwicks. v. Derby (Birmingham) 1937

Highest Partnerships-Fourth Wicket—*Cont.*

253	I. M. McLachlan & G. St. A. Sobers: South Australia v. South Africans (Adelaide)	1963-64
252	G. Boycott & B. L. D'Oliveria: England v. India (Leeds)	1967
251*	G. A. Edrich & K. J. Grieves: Lancs. v. Notts. (Manchester)	1951
251	H. I. Moore & D. L. Murray: Notts. v. Indians (Nottingham)	1967
250	H. H. Gibbons & M. Nichol: Worcs. v. Warwicks. (Dudley)	1929
250	T. H. Clark & R. C. E. Pratt: Surrey v. Kent (Oval)	1953
250	H. L. Johnson & D. C. Morgan: Derby v. Somerset (Chesterfield)	1964

FIFTH WICKET

405	S. G. Barnes & D. G. Bradman: Australia v. England (Sydney)	1946-47
397	W. Bardsley & C. E. Kelleway: N.S.W. v. South Australia (Sydney)	1920-21
393	E. G. Arnold & W. B. Burns: Worcs. v. Warwicks. (Birmingham)	1909
360	U. M. Merchant & M. N. Raiji: Bombay v. Hyderabad (Bombay)	1947-48
347	D. Brookes & D. Barrick: Northants. v. Essex (Northampton)	1952
344	M. C. Cowdrey & T. W. Graveney: M.C.C. v. South Australia (Adelaide)	1962-63
343	R. Maddocks & J. Hallebone: Victoria v, Tasmania (Melbourne)	1951-52
340	E. Wainwright & G. H. Hirst: Yorks. v. Surrey (Oval)	1899
338	R. S. Lucas & T. C. O'Brien: Middx. v. Sussex (Hove)	1895
336	W. H. Ponsford & H. S. B. Love: Victoria v. Tasmania (Melbourne)	1922-23
332	E. Hendren & W. F. Price: Middx v. Worcs. (Dudley)	1933
332	M. L. Jaisimha & Mahendra Kumar: Hyderabad v. Bengal (Hyderabad)	1964-65
329	F. Mitchell & E. Wainwright: Yorks. v. Leics. (Leicester)	1899
327	P. Holmes & W. E. Astill: M.C.C. v. Jamaica (Kingston)	1925-26
327	H. B. Cameron & A. W. Briscoe: Transvaal v. Griqualand West (Johannesburg)	1934-35
325	V. M. Merchant & K. M. Rangnekar: Bombay v. Sind (Bombay)	1945-46
308	J. N. Crawford & F. C. Holland: Surrey v. Somerset (Oval)	1908
301*	C. E. Pellew & C. B. Willis: A.I.F. v. Worcs. (Worcester)	1919
301*	R. B. Simpson & K. D. Meuleman: Western Australia v. N.S.W. (Perth)	1959-60
301	F. M. M. Worrell & W. H. H. Sutcliffe: Commonwealth v. Ceylon (Colombo)	1950-51
300	D. W. Begbie & A. W. Briscoe: Transvaal v. O.F.S. (Johannesburg)	1937-38
297	J. H. Parks & H. W. Parks: Sussex v. Hants (Portsmouth)	1937
291	A. D. Nourse, Snr. & J. M. Blanckenberg: Natal v. Western Province (Johannesburg)	1923-24
290	M. M. Sood & R. Saxena: Delhi v. Southern Punjab (New Delhi)	1960-61
289*	Nawab of Pataudi, Snr. & L. E. G. Ames: England v. Rest (Lord's)	1934
288	H. A. Peach & A. Ducat: Surrey v. Northants. (Northampton)	1920
287	R. Abel & W. H. Lockwood: Surrey v. Lancs. (Oval)	1899
287	J. O'Connor & C. T. Ashton: Essex v. Surrey (Brentwood)	1934
286	M. A. Noble & S. E. Gregory: N.S.W. v. South Australia (Adelaide)	1899-00
285	E. Hendren & J. H. Human: Middx. v. Surrey (Oval)	1935
283	N. L. Bonitto & A. P. Binns: Jamaica v. British Guiana (Georgetown)	1952-53
281	C. L. Badcock & M. G. Waite: South Australia v. Queensland (Adelaide)	1939-40
279	B. Versfeld & M. J. Procter: Natal v. Transvaal (Durban)	1965-66
277	F. E. Woolley & L. E. G. Ames: Kent v. New Zealanders (Canterbury)	1931
276	W. Rhodes & R. Kilner: Yorks. v. Northants. (Northampton)	1921
276	A. G. Kripal Singh & R. B. Alagannan: Madras v. Travancore-Cochin (Ernakulam)	1954-55
275	M. A. Noble & J. Darling: Australians v. Sussex (Hove)	1905
273	L. Hutton & N. W. D. Yardley: Yorks. v. Hants. (Bournemouth)	1947
270	L. C. Braund & J. Hardstaff, Snr.: M.C.C. v. South Australia (Adelaide)	1907-08
268	W. G. Quaife & W. Quaife: Warwicks. v. Essex (Leyton)	1900
268	R. Lloyd & I. M. McLachlan: South Australia v. Queensland (Adelaide)	1960-61
267*	K. C. Bland & D. Lindsay: South Africa v. Rest of South Africa (Johannesburg)	1964-65
266	A. Shrewsbury & W. Gunn: Notts. v. Sussex (Hove)	1884
266	C. E. Pellew & C. B. Willis: A.I.F. v. Leics. (Leicester)	1919
266	R. E. S. Wyatt & A. J. Croom: Warwicks. v. Somerset (Birmingham)	1928
266	B. Sutcliffe & W. S. Haig: Otago v. Auckland (Dunedin)	1949-50
265	S. M. Nurse & G. St. A. Sobers: West Indies v. England (Leeds)	1966
264	M. Robinson & S. W. Montgomery: Glamorgan v. Hants. (Bournemouth)	1949
264	A. R. Morris & R. Benaud: N.S.W. v. Queensland (Brisbane)	1953-54
263	J. M. Taylor & A. F. Kippax: N.S.W. v. South Australia (Adelaide)	1922-23
263	A. L. Wadekar & G. S. Ramchand: Bombay v. Rajasthan (Bombay)	1961-62
262	A. Jeacocke & W. J. Abel: Surrey v. Cambridge U. (Oval)	1923
262	W. H. Ponsford & W. A. Brown: Australians v. Cambridge U. (Cambridge)	1934
262	K. G. Viljoen & H. B. Cameron: South Africans v. Derby (Ilkeston)	1935
261	W. G. Grace & W. O. Moberley: Glos. v. Yorks. (Cheltenham)	1876

Highest Partnerships-Fifth Wicket—*Cont.*

261 H. H. Gibbons & C. H. Palmer: Worcs. v. Northants. (Dudley) 1939
256* R. Abel & D. L. A. Jephson: Surrey v. Glos. (Oval) 1898
256 C. G. Macartney & N. Callaway: N.S.W. v. Queensland (Sydney) 1914-15
256* A. A. Baig & C. A. Fry: Oxford U. v. Free Foresters (Oxford) 1959
255 G. E. Healy & F. Vaughan: Victoria v. Tasmania (Melbourne) 1909-10
255* J. A. Jameson & T. W. Cartwright: Warwicks. v. New Zealanders (Birmingham) 1965
254 E. Humphreys & A. P. Day: Kent v. Lancs. (Tunbridge Wells) 1910
251 R. B. Kanhai & J. S. Solomon: British Guiana v. Barbados (Georgetown) .. 1956-57
250 T. W. Hayward & D. L. A. Jephson: Surrey v. Derby (Oval) 1901
249 R. A. McLean & A. L. Upton: Natal v. O.F.S. (Pietermaritzburg) 1954-55
247 J. Hardstaff, Jnr. & A. Staples: Notts. v. Middx. (Nottingham) 1937
247* J. F. Parker & E. R. T. Holmes: Surrey v. Notts. (Nottingham) 1947
247 P. R. Umrigar & M. S. Hardikar: Bombay v. Saurashtra (Poona) 1957-58
246 K. S. Ranjitsinhji & A. Collins: Sussex v. Kent (Hove) 1900
245* H. Sutcliffe & W. Barber: Yorks. v. Northants. (Northampton) 1939
245 J. F. Crapp & A. E. Wilson: Glos. v. Worcs. (Dudley) 1953
245 K. C. Ibrahim & D. B. Satha: Ibrahim's XI v. Mantri's XI (Bombay) .. 1947-48
244 H. Winrow & T. B. Reddick: Notts. v. Kent (Nottingham) 1947
244 J. R. Reid & M. E. Chapple: New Zealanders v. Western Province (Cape Town) 1961-62
243 W. E. Alley & F. W. Freer: Commonwealth v. C.C. of India (Bombay) .. 1949-50
242 W. R. Hammond & L. E. G. Ames: England v. New Zealand (Christchurch) 1932-33
242 W. R. Hammond & B. O. Allen: Glos. v. Somerset (Bristol) 1946
241* F. E. Woolley & D. W. Jennings: Kent v. Somerset (Tunbridge Wells) .. 1911
240 J. C. White & C. C. Case: Somerset v. Glos. (Taunton).. 1927
239 M. M. Naidu & C. S. Nayudu: Baroda v. Rajputana (Baroda) 1942-43
237 L. O. S. Poidevin & L. W. Pye: N.S.W. v. Queensland (Sydney) 1904-05
237 D. C. S. Compton & N. W. D. Yardley: England v. South Africa (Nottingham) 1947
236 G. J. Thompson & R. Haywood: Northants. v. Yorks. (Dewsbury) 1911
236 W. W. Keeton & A. W. Carr: Notts. v. Essex (Nottingham) 1932
236 D. C. H. Townsend & F. G. H. Chalk: Oxford U. v. Free Foresters (Oxford) 1933
235 B. J. T. Bosanquet & F. A. Tarrant: Rest of England v. Yorks. (Oval) .. 1908
235* W. M. Woodfull & V. S. Ransford: Victoria v. New Zealand XI (Christchurch) 1924-25
235 G. Hill & D. F. Walker: Hants. v. Sussex (Portsmouth) 1937
235* N. Oldfield & A. E. Nutter: Lancs. v. Notts. (Manchester) 1939
234 P. F. Warner & C. B. Fry: Rest of England v. Warwicks. (Oval) 1911
234 D. G. Bradman & O. W. Bill: N.S.W. v. Victoria (Sydney) 1930-31
234* V. J. Scott & J. B. Morris: Auckland v. Central Districts (Auckland) 1951-52
234 J. M. Brearley & J. A. Ormrod: M.C.C. Under-25 v. North Zone (Peshawar) 1966-67
233 D. A. R. Moloney & J. L. Kerr: New Zealanders v. England XI (Folkestone) 1937
232 H. W. Taylor & R. H. Catterall: South Africans v. Combined Services (Portsmouth) 1924
232 A. D. Nourse, Jnr. & D. F. Dowling: Natal v. Griqualand West (Durban) .. 1947-48
232 M. J. K. Smith & K. F. Barrington: M.C.C. v. Transvaal (Johannesburg) .. 1964-65
231 C. B. Llewellyn & E. I. M. Barrett: Hants. v. Derby (Southampton) 1903
231 K. D. Mackay & R. G. Archer: Queensland v. Victoria (Brisbane) 1953-54
230 C. Baldwin & D. L. A. Jephson: Surrey v. Kent (Oval).. 1897
230 James Seymour & J. R. Mason: Kent v. Somerset (Taunton) 1907
230 J. Iddon & M. Halliday: Lancs. v. Surrey (Oval) 1928
230 K. R. Miller & P. J. Burge: Australians v. Leics. (Leicester) 1956
230 C. Baldwin & D. L. A. Jephson: Surrey v. Kent (Oval) 1897
228 C. S. Baker & A. A. Lilley: Warwicks. v. Worcs. (Worcester) 1907
228 G. A. Headley & C. A. Merry: West Indians v. Warwicks. (Birmingham) .. 1933
228 J. Hardstaff, Jnr. & F. W. Stocks: Notts. v. Northants. (Northampton) .. 1952
227 W. G. Grace & P. C. Crutchley: M.C.C. v. Kent (Canterbury) 1876
227 A. D. Nourse, Snr. & S. S. L. Steyn: Western Province v. Natal (Cape Town).. 1932-33
227 R. C. Wilson & M. C. Cowdrey: Kent v. Northants (Tunbridge Wells) .. 1955
226* R. McDonald & F. Geeson: Leics. v. Derby (Glossop) 1901
226 R. T. Dick & C. W. Travers: O.F.S. v. Griqualand West (Bloemfontein) .. 1934-35
226* T. E. Cook & A. J. Holmes: Sussex v. Leics. (Leicester).. 1937
225 V. M. Merchant & K. M. Rangnekar: Hindus v. Parsis (Bombay) 1941-42

SIXTH WICKET

487* G. A. Headley & C. C. Passailaigue: Jamaica v. Lord Tennyson's XI (Kingston) 1931-32
428 W. W. Armstrong & M. A. Noble: Australians v. Sussex (Hove) 1902
411 R. M. Poore & E. G. Wynyard: Hants. v. Somerset (Taunton) 1899

Highest Partnerships-Sixth Wicket—*Cont.*

376	R. Subba Row & A. Lightfoot: Northants. v. Surrey (Oval)	1958
371	V. M. Merchant & R. S. Modi: Bombay v. Maharashtra (Bombay)	1943-44
346	J. H. Fingleton & D. G. Bradman: Australia v. England (Melbourne)	1936-37
332	N. Marks & G. Thomas: N.S.W. v. South Australia (Sydney)	1958-59
323	E. Hendren & J. W. H. T. Douglas: M.C.C. v. Victoria (Melbourne)	1920-21
320	J. H. Board & G. L. Jessop: Glos. v. Sussex (Hove)	1903
316*	H. R. Adhikari & A. K. Khanna: Services v. Rajasthan (Ajmer)	1951-52
313	J. A. Newman & Hon. L. H. Tennyson: Hants. v. West Indians (Southampton)	1928
303*	H. Winrow & P. F. Harvey: Notts. v. Derby (Nottingham)	1947
300	Vijay Hazare & Vivek Hazare: Rest v. Hindus (Bombay)	1943-44
298	A. Sandham & H. S. Harrison: Surrey v. Sussex (Oval)	1913
294	D. R. Jardine & P. G. H. Fender: Surrey v. Yorks. (Bradford)	1928
289	S. J. E. Loxton & D. T. Ring: Victoria v. Queensland (Melbourne)	1946-47
285	W. R. Hammond & B. H. Lyon: Glos. v. Surrey (Oval)	1928
284	A. P. F. Chapman & G. B. Legge: Kent v. Lancs. (Maidstone)	1927
280*	B. F. Butcher & J. S. Solomon: British Guiana v. Jamaica (Georgetown)	1956-57
279	A. L. Hassett & E. A. Williams: Australian Services v. Prince's XI (New Delhi)	1945-46
278	J. Iddon & H. R. W. Butterworth: Lancs. v. Sussex (Manchester)	1932
277	O. G. Smith & A. P. Binns: Jamaica v. Australians (Kingston)	1954-55
276	M. Leyland & E. Robinson: Yorks. v. Glamorgan (Swansea)	1926
274*	G. St. A. Sobers & D. A. J. Holford: West Indies v. England (Lord's)	1966
270	R. T. Simpson & A. Jepson: Notts. v. Worcs. (Nottingham)	1950
269	V. T. Trumper & C. Hill: Australians v. New Zealand XI (Wellington)	1904-05
265	W. E. Alley & K. E. Palmer: Somerset v. Northants. (Northampton)	1961
262	A. Kenny & B. J. Kortlang: Victoria v. Queensland (Brisbane)	1909-10
262	A. T. Sharp & G. H. S. Fowke: Leics. v. Derby (Chesterfield)	1911
260	J. N. Crawford & Lord Dalmeny: Surrey v. Leics. (Oval)	1905
260	A. C. MacLaren & R. Whitehead: Lancs. v. Worcs. (Worcester)	1910
260	A. Wharton & K. Cranston: Lancs. v. Warwicks. (Birmingham)	1948
259	D. Brookes & E. Davis: Northants. v. Leics. (Leicester)	1947
258	V. T. Trumper & F. A. Iredale: N.S.W. v. Tasmania (Sydney)	1898-99
255	K. S. Duleepsinhji & M. W. Tate: Sussex v. Northants. (Hove)	1930
255	G. St. A. Sobers & B. N. Jarman: South Australia v. Western Australia (Perth)	1963-64
254	E. Smith & C. E. de Trafford: North v. South (Hastings)	1893
253	A. F. Kippax & J. G. Morgan: N.S.W. v. Queensland (Sydney)	1927-28
251	C. P. Mead & J. A. Newman: Hants. v. Warwicks. (Bournemouth)	1928
248	T. J. E. Andrews & W. W. Armstrong: Australians v. South (Hastings)	1921
247*	W. Payton & W. A. Flint: Notts. v. Northants. (Nottingham)	1927
245	J. L. Bryan & C. T. Ashton: Cambridge U. v. Surrey (Oval)	1921
244*	J. M. M. Commaille & A. W. Palm: Western Province v. Griqualand West (Johannesburg)	1923-24
244	R. Benaud & A. K. Davidson: Australians v. Natal (Pietermaritzburg)	1957-58
243	W. R. Hammond & James Langridge: M.C.C. v. South Australia (Adelaide)	1946-47
241	A. A. Lilley & W. Smith: London County v. Cambridge U. (Crystal Palace)	1901
241	N. J. Contractor & D. H. Shodhan: Gujerat v. Baroda (Baroda)	1952-53
240	P. H. Parfitt & B. R. Knight: England v. New Zealand (Auckland)	1962-63
238	R. McDonald & O. Cowley: Queensland v. Hawke's Bay (Napier)	1896-97
236	E. R. T. Holmes & R. E. C. Butterworth: Oxford U. v. Free Foresters (Oxford)	1927
234	D. C. S. Compton & P. B. H. May: M.C.C. v. South Australia (Adelaide)	1954-55
233	M. W. Booth & G. H. Hirst: Yorks. v. Worcs. (Worcester)	1911
233	J. N. Crawford & W. W. Armstrong: Australians v. New Zealand XI (Auckland)	1913-14
233	C. H. Knott & R. H. Bettington: Harlequins v. West Indians (Eastbourne)	1928
233	R. Mayes & W. Murray-Wood: Kent v. Sussex (Tunbridge Wells)	1952
231	V. F. S. Crawford & T. Jayes: Leics. v. Hants. (Leicester)	1908
230	W. E. Jones & B. L. Muncer: Glamorgan v. Worcs. (Worcester)	1953
229	W. Rhodes & N. Kilner: Yorks. v. Leics. (Leeds)	1921
228	M. J. Turnbull & F. J. Seabrook: Cambridge U. v. Sussex (Cambridge)	1928
227	N. W. D. Yardley & H. T. Bartlett: M.C.C. v. O.F.S. (Bloemfontein)	1938-39
227	C. T. Radley & F. J. Titmus: Middx. v. South Africans (Lord's)	1965
226	K. C. Ibraham & J. B. Khot: Bombay v. Western India States (Bombay)	1941-42
226*	Vijay Hazare & V. M. Mankad: Indians v. Middx. (Lord's)	1946
226*	W. R. Hammond & G. M. Emmett: Glos. v. Notts. (Bristol)	1946
226	G. Cox & G. Potter: Sussex v. Worcs. (Worcester)	1954
225	E. Wainwright & Lord Hawke: Yorks. v. Hants. (Southampton)	1899
225	V. M. Merchant & H. R. Adhikari: Hindus v. Rest (Bombay)	1943-44

Highest Partnerships—*Cont.*

SEVENTH WICKET

347 D. Atkinson & C. C. Depeiza: West Indies v. Australia (Bridgetown) 1954-55
344 K. S. Ranjitsinhji & W. Newman: Sussex v. Essex (Leyton) 1902
340 K. J. Key & H. Philipson: Oxford U. v. Middx. (Chiswick Park) 1887
336 F. C. W. Newman & C. R. Maxwell: Cahn's XI v. Leics. (Nottingham) .. 1935
335 C. W. Andrews & E. C. Bensted: Queensland v. N.S.W. (Sydney) 1934-35
325 G. Brown & C. H. Abercrombie: Hants. v. Essex (Leyton) 1913
323 E. Hendren & L. F. Townsend: M.C.C. v. Barbados (Bridgetown) 1929-30
308 Waqar Hassan & Imtiaz Ahmed: Pakistan v. New Zealand (Lahore) 1955-56
299 B. Mitchell & A. Melville: Transvaal v. Griqualand West (Kimberley) .. 1946-47
289 G. Goonesena & G. W. Cook: Cambridge U. v. Oxford U. (Lord's) 1957
274 K. C. Ibrahim & K. M. Rangnekar: Bijapur XI v. Bengal XI (Bombay) .. 1942-43
273* W. W. Armstrong & J. Darling: Australians v. Gentlemen of England (Lord's) 1905
271* E. Hendren & F. T. Mann: Middx. v. Notts. (Nottingham) 1925
270 C. P. Mead & J. P. Parker: Hants. v. Kent (Canterbury) 1926
268 A. H. Kardar & Imtiaz Ahmed: North Zone v. Australian Services (Lahore) 1945-46
265 J. L. Powell & N. Dorreen: Canterbury v. Otago (Christchurch) 1929-30
262* D. P. B. Morkel & A. W. Palm: Western Province v. Natal (Cape Town) .. 1929-30
261 J. W. H. T. Douglas & J. R. Freeman: Essex v. Lancs. (Leyton) 1914
257 J. T. Morgan & F. R. Brown: Cambridge U. v. Surrey (Oval) 1930
255 C. H. Knott & A. J. Evans: Harlequins v. West Indians (Eastbourne) .. 1928
255 G. Thomas & R. Benaud: N.S.W. v. Victoria (Melbourne) 1961-62
254 D. C. F. Burton & W. Rhodes: Yorks. v. Hants. (Dewsbury) 1919
252 S. K. Girdhari & A. G. Roy: Assam v. Orissa (Cuttack) 1957-58
250 H. E. Dollery & J. S. Ord: Warwicks. v. Kent (Maidstone) 1953
249 W. L. Murdoch & J. H. Hunt: Gentlemen v. Players (Oval) 1904
248 W. G. Grace & E. L. Thomas: Glos. v. Sussex (Hove) 1896
248 A. P. Day & E. Humphreys: Kent v. Somerset (Taunton) 1908
248* Pervez Akhtar & Mohammad Sharif: Railways v. Dera Ismail Khan (Lahore) 1964-65
247 P. Holmes & W. Rhodes: Yorks. v. Notts. (Nottingham) 1929
246 J. F. Ireland & K. G. McLeod: Cambridge U. v. Gentlemen (Eastbourne) .. 1908
246 D. J. McGlew & A. R. A. Murray: South Africa v. New Zealand (Wellington) 1952-53
245 J. Sharp & A. H. Hornby: Lancs v. Leics. (Manchester) 1912
244 W. R. Patrick & C. F. W. Allcott: New Zealanders v. N.S.W. (Sydney) .. 1925-26
244 T. W. Cartwright & A. C. Smith: Warwicks. v. Middx. (Nuneaton) 1962
244 Javed Masood & Sukumar Guha: East Pakistan v. Hyderabad (Hyderabad) .. 1962-63
241* G. H. Pope & A. E. G. Rhodes: Derby v. Hants. (Portsmouth) 1948
240 S. M. J. Woods & V. T. Hill: Somerset v. Kent (Taunton) 1898
240 A. D. Nourse, Jnr. & L. W. Payn: Natal v. Transvaal (Johannesburg) 1936-37
238 Dr. Macdonald & O. Cowley: Queensland v. Hawke's Bay (Farndon, H. B.) 1896-97
232 W. Bruce & H. Trumble: Australians v. Oxford & Cambridge Us. P. &. P. (Portsmouth) 1893
229 W. W. Timms & F. A. Walden: Northants. v. Warwicks. (Northampton) .. 1926
229 K. J. Schnieder & W. A. Oldfield: Australians v. Canterbury (Christchurch) .. 1927-28
224 C. F. Browne & K. Mason: Barbados v. Trinidad (Bridgetown) 1919-20
224 V. J. Scott & A. M. Matheson: Auckland v. Canterbury (Auckland) 1937-38
222 G. J. Thompson & R. Haywood: Northants v. Glos. (Northampton) 1911
221 D. Lindsay & P. L. van der Merwe: South Africa v. Australia (Johannesburg) 1966-67
220* J. T. Murray & D. Bennett: Middx. v. Yorks. (Leeds) 1964
218 T. E. Cook & A. F. Wensley: Sussex v. Worcs. (Eastbourne) 1933
218 J. H. Cameron & E. A. V. Williams: West Indians v. Oxford U. (Oxford) .. 1939
216 D. B. Deodhar & M. N. Paranjpe: Maharashtra v. Nawanagar (Poona) .. 1944-45
215 E. Robinson & D. C. F. Burton: Yorks. v. Leics. (Leicester) 1921
213* K. Vasudevamurthy & D. Gupta: Mysore v. Kerala (Mangalore) 1959-60
213 S. J. Diwadkar & A. V. Mankad: Bombay v. Rajasthan (Bombay) 1963-64
212 W. A. Tester & J. Jones: Players of South v. Gentlemen of South (Oval) .. 1885
208 C. G. Macartney & A. J. Hopkins: N.S.W. v. Queensland (Sydney) 1906-07
207 G. Kishenchand & Fazal Mahmood: North Zone v. South Zone (Bombay) .. 1946-47
206 A. H. Hornby & W. R. Cuttell: Lancs. v. Somerset (Manchester) 1904
205 Mahendra Kumar & Wahid Yar Khan: Hyderabad v. Uttar Pradesh (Hyderabad) 1964-65
204 M. J. Smedley & R. A. White: Notts. v. Surrey (Oval) 1967
203 M. E. Z. Ghazali & Qamar Yusuf: Services v. Karachi (Karachi) 1953-54
202 A. E. Lawton & R. T. Crawford: Gentlemen v. Oxford U. (Eastbourne) .. 1910
202 S. J. E. Loxton & B. A. Barnett: Commonwealth v. Bombay (Bombay) .. 1953-54
201 R. H. Howitt & R. Bagguley: Notts. v. Sussex (Nottingham) 1895
200 T. F. Shepherd & J. W. Hitch: Surrey v. Kent (Blackheath) 1921
200 F. Watson & M. L. Taylor: Lancs. v. Oxford U. (Oxford) 1930

Highest Partnerships—*Cont.*

EIGHTH WICKET

433 V. T. Trumper & A. Sims: Australians v. Canterbury (Christchurch) 1913-14
292 R. Peel & Lord Hawke: Yorks. v. Warwicks. (Birmingham) 1896
270 V. T. Trumper & E. P. Barbour: N.S.W. v. Victoria (Sydney) 1912-13
263 D. R. Wilcox & R. M. Taylor: Essex v. Warwicks. (Southend) .. 1946
255 E. A. V. Williams & E. A. Martindale: Barbados v. Trinidad (Bridgetown) .. 1935-36
246 L. E. G. Ames & G. O. Allen: England v. New Zealand (Lord's) 1931
243 C. Hill & R. J. Hartigan: Australia v. England (Adelaide) 1907-08
239 W. R. Hammond & A. E. Wilson: Glos. v. Lancs. (Bristol) 1938
237 W. V. D. Dickinson & R. St. L. Fowler: Army v. M.C.C. (Lord's) 1920
236 R. A. Duff & A. J. Hopkins: N.S.W. v. Hawke's XI (Sydney) 1902-03
236 C. T. Sarwate & R. P. Singh: Holkar v. Delhi (New Delhi) 1949-50
229* C. L. A. Smith & G. Brann: Sussex v. Kent (Hove) 1902
228 A. J. Croom & R. E. S. Wyatt: Warwicks. v. Worcs. (Dudley) 1925
222 S. S. L. Steyn & D. P. B. Morkel: Western Province v. Border (Cape Town) .. 1929-30
220 G. F. H. Hearne & R. Winrow: Notts v. Somerset (Nottingham) 1935
218 C. G. Macartney & J. D. Scott: N.S.W. v. Queensland (Sydney) 1913-14
217 C. K. Nayudu & N. D. Marshall: Indians v. Warwicks. (Birmingham) .. 1932
217 T. W. Graveney & J. T. Murray: England v. West Indies (Oval) 1966
216 C. A. Browne & E. L. Bartlett: Barbados v. British Guiana (Bridgetown) .. 1926-27
215 W. W. Armstrong & R. L. Park: Victoria v. South Australia (Melbourne) .. 1919-20
214 J. A. Cutmore & T. P. B. Smith: Essex v. Indians (Brentwood) 1936
210 V. M. Merchant & R. S. Cooper: Bombay v. Maharashtra (Bombay) 1943-44
210 M. M. Dalvi & V. R. Amladi: Bombay v. Sind (Bombay) 1947-48
209 G. Stannard & H. E. Roberts: Sussex v. Worcs. (Hove) 1920
209 K. M. Rangnekar & J. N. Bhaya: Holkar v. Hyderabad (Indore) 1950-51
204 T. W. Hayward & L. C. Braund: Surrey v. Lancs. (Oval) 1898
204 W. A. Oldfield & C. O. Nicholls: N.S.W. v. Victoria (Sydney) 1927-28
204 A. Shukla & Saghir Ahmed: Uttar Pradesh v. Rajasthan (Udaipur) 1961-62
203 G. Kishenchand & V. Desai: Gujerat v. Services (Ahmedabad) 1950-51
202 D. Davies & J. J. Hills: Glamorgan v. Sussex (Eastbourne) 1928
198 R. W. McLeod & F. Laver: Victoria v. South Australia (Adelaide) 1892-93
198 K. F. Barrington & J. C. Laker: Surrey v. Glos. (Oval) 1954
197 T. H. Barling & A. V. Bedser: Surrey v. Somerset (Taunton) 1947
195 W. Payton & T. W. Oates: Notts. v. Kent (Nottingham) 1920
193 W. W. Armstrong & A. E. Liddicut: Victoria v. South Australia (Melbourne) 1920-21
192 C. Hill & W. F. Giffen: South Australia v. Stoddart's XI (Adelaide) 1894-95
192 W. L. Neale & A. E. Wilson: Glos. v. Middx. (Lord's) 1938
191* W. Rhodes & G. G. Macaulay: Yorks. v. Essex (Harrogate) 1922
190* J. W. E. Mills & C. F. W. Allcott: New Zealanders v. Civil Services (Chiswick) .. 1927
189 W. N. Carson & A. M. Matheson: Auckland v. Wellington (Auckland) .. 1938-39
188 H. S. Bush & V. F. S. Crawford: Surrey v. Lancs. (Manchester) 1902
188 R. L. Holdsworth & A. E. R. Gilligan: Sussex v. Lancs. (Eastbourne) 1927
187 J. D. Henderson & W. A. Edward: Scotland v. Ireland (Paisley) 1954
185* J. D. Nel & J. H. Ferrandi: Western Province v. Eastern Province (Port Elizabeth) 1952-53
184 M. S. Nichols & T. P. B. Smith: Essex v. Kent (Gravesend) 1938
183 D. J. Insole & R. Smith: Essex v. Worcs. (Worcester) 1951
183 T. E. Bailey & C. Griffiths: Essex v. Kent (Tunbridge Wells) 1952
182 R. Abel & W. E. Roller: Surrey v. Kent (Oval) 1883
182 G. N. Wyatt & H. Phillips: Sussex v. Australians (Hove) 1884
182* M. H. C. Doll & H. R. Murrell: Middx. v. Notts. (Lord's) 1913
182 A. H. M. Jackson & W. Carter: Derby v. Leics. (Leicester) 1922
180 W. Barber & T. F. Smailes: Yorks. v. Sussex (Leeds) 1935
179* G. Leach & C. L. A. Smith: Sussex v. Derby (Hove) 1909
179 L. D. Kemp & S. O. Quin: Victoria v. Tasmania (Hobart) 1932-33
178 C. P. Mead & C. P. Brutton: Hants v. Worcs. (Bournemouth) 1925
177 W. G. Quaife & A. Whittle: Warwicks v. Essex (Birmingham) 1904
176 H. W. Parks & A. F. Wensley: Sussex v. Cambridge U. (Cambridge) 1936
175 E. Pooley & J. Southerton: Surrey v. M.C.C. (Oval) 1871
175 A. J. Bowden & A. D. Fisher: N.S.W. v. Queensland (Sydney) 1907-08
174 W. E. Jones & G. Lavis: Glamorgan v. Essex (Cardiff) 1947
174 O. C. Dawson & L. A. Markham: Natal v. O.F.S. (Durban) 1947-48
173 J. M. Gregory & C. E. Pellew: Australia v. England (Melbourne) 1920-21
173 B. Constable & J. C. Laker: Surrey v. Cambridge U. (Guildford) 1949
172 V. T. Trumper & J. J. Kelly: N.S.W. v. Tasmania (Sydney) 1898-99
172 W. E. Astill & A. E. R. Gilligan: M.C.C. v. Yorks. (Scarborough) 1923
172 J. F. Crapp & L. M. Cranfield: Glos. v. Cambridge U. (Cambridge) 1947

Highest Partnerships-Eighth Wicket—*Cont.*

171 R. James & R. R. Lindwall: N.S.W. v. Queensland (Sydney) 1945-46
171 A. J. McIntyre & E. R. T. Holmes: Surrey v. Hants. (Guildford) 1948
171 Majid Jahangir & Zulfiqar Ali: Lahore Board v. P.I.A. (Lahore) 1964-65
170 H. Moses & J. R. Wood: N.S.W. v. Victoria (Sydney) 1887-88
169 S. E. Gregory & A. L. Newell: N.S.W. v. Stoddart's XI (Sydney) 1897-98
168 P. Cartwright & C. L. A. Smith: Sussex v. Leics. (Leicester) 1909
168 E. H. Bowley & T. O. Jameson: Tennyson's XI v. Rhodesia (Bulawayo) .. 1924-25
167 F. Barratt & A. Staples: Notts. v. Surrey (Oval) 1928
167 J. L. Ellis & H. I. Ebeling: Victoria v. South Australia (Adelaide) 1928-29
166 J. Pettiford & F. W. Freer: Commonwealth v. Indian XI (Bombay) 1949-50
165 S. Haigh & Lord Hawke: Yorks. v. Surrey (Oval) 1902
165* J. N. Crawford & A. Eckhold: Otago v. Wellington (Wellington) 1914-15
164 M. R. Hallam & C. T. Spencer: Leics. v. Essex (Leicester) 1964
164 J. T. Murray & B. R. Knight: M.C.C. v. South Australia (Adelaide) 1965-66
163 W. Reeves & C. P. Buckenham: Essex v. Sussex (Leyton) 1906
163 G. G. Macaulay & A. Waddington: Yorks. v. Worcs. (Leeds) 1927
162 C. P. Mead & W. K. Pearce: Hants v. Glamorgan (Southampton) 1923
162 Masood-ul-Hasan & Intikhab Alam: Karachi Whites v. Quetta (Karachi) .. 1963-64
161 F. M. Lucas & G. Brann: Sussex v. Australians (Hove) 1886
161 H. Moses & T. W. Garrett: N.S.W. v. Victoria (Sydney) 1890-91
161 E. Smith & W. Rhodes: Yorks. v. M.C.C. (Scarborough) 1901
161 H. S. Squires & G. S. Mobey: Surrey v. Cambridge U. (Oval) 1932
161 D. G. Bradman & M. G. Waite: South Australia v. Queensland (Adelaide) .. 1937-38
161 S. S. Grewal & Inderjit: Services v. Southern Punjab (Patiala) 1950-51
161 D. N. F. Slade & C. C. Griffith: Commonwealth XI v. Pakistan (Karachi) .. 1963-64
161 B. N. Jarman & C. E. Griffiths: South Australia v. N.S.W. (Adelaide) .. 1965-66
160 H. Philipson & A. C. M. Croome: Oxford U. v. M.C.C. (Lord's) 1889
160 H. W. Parks & A. E. R. Gilligan: Sussex v. Kent (Hastings) 1928
160 O. S. Wight & R. L. Hunte: British Guiana v. Barbados (Georgetown) .. 1929-30
158 J. Pettiford & R. A. Saggers: N.S.W. v. Queensland (Brisbane) 1947-48
157 P. A. Turner & A. D. Nourse, Snr.: Natal v. Eastern Province (Johannesburg) 1896-97
157 A. C. McLaren & J. F. McLean: M.C.C. v. New Zealand XI (Wellington) .. 1922-23
157 A. L. Hilder & C. Wright: Kent v. Essex (Gravesend) 1924
157 A. Hamer & E. Smith: Derby v. Notts. (Nottingham) 1955
156 T. Langdon & J. H. Board: Glos. v. Middx. (Bristol) 1903
156 G. C. White & R. O. Schwarz: South Africans v. Glos. (Bristol) 1907
156 S. F. Hird & C. J. Hill: N.S.W. v. Queensland (Sydney) 1932-33
156 W. T. Greensmith & F. Rist: Essex v. Kent (Blackheath) 1953
155 A. Morton & W. Horsley: Derby v. Essex (Leyton) 1924
155 F. R. Brown & A. E. Nutter: Northants. v. Glamorgan (Northampton) .. 1952
154 G. J. Bonnor & S. P. Jones: Australia v. England (Sydney) 1884-85
154 C. W. Wright & H. R. Bromley-Davenport: England v. South Africa (Johannesburg) 1895-96
154 F. T. Badcock & K. C. James: Wellington v. Canterbury (Christchurch) .. 1926-27
154 D. Tallon & R. R. Lindwall: Australia v. England (Melbourne) 1946-47
153 L. Amarnath & C. S. Nayudu: Indians v. Victoria (Melbourne) 1947-48
152 W. Rhodes & J. W. Rothery: Yorks. v. Hants. (Portsmouth) 1904
152* R. J. O. Meyer & S. A. Block: Free Foresters v. Cambridge U. (Cambridge) .. 1938
152 F. H. Vigar & R. Smith: Essex v. Derby (Colchester) 1948
151 W. Rhodes & Lord Hawke: Yorks. v. Somerset (Taunton) 1905
151 W. Payton & H. Larwood: Notts. v. Northants. (Nottingham) 1925
151* K. J. Grieves & K. C. Gulliver: N.S.W. v. Australian Services (Sydney) .. 1945-46
150 A. Ward & C. R. Hartley: Lancs. v. Leics. (Leicester) 1900
150 E. A. Halliwell & G. C. White: South Africans v. Leics. (Leicester) 1904
150 H. L. Wilson & G. Stannard: Sussex v. Warwicks. (Hove) 1920
150 G. Geary & T. E. Sidwell: Leics. v. Surrey (Oval) 1926

NINTH WICKET

283 A. R. Warren & J. Chapman: Derby v. Warwicks. (Blackwell) 1910
251 J. W. H. T. Douglas & S. N. Hare: Essex v. Derby (Leyton) 1921
245 Vijay Hazare & N. D. Nagarwalla: Maharashtra v. Baroda (Poona) 1939-40
239 H. B. Cave & I. B. Leggat: Central Districts v. Otago (Dunedin) 1952-53
232 C. Hill & E. Walkley: South Australia v. N.S.W. (Adelaide) 1900-01
231 P. Sen & J. Mitter: Bengal v. Bihar (Jamshedpur) 1950-51
230 D. A. Livingstone & A. T. Castell: Hants. v. Surrey (Southampton) 1962
226 C. E. Kelleway & W. A. Oldfield: N.S.W. v. Victoria (Melbourne) 1925-26

Highest Partnerships-Ninth Wicket—*Cont.*

225	W. W. Armstrong & E. A. Windsor: Australian XI v. Rest (Sydney)	1907-08
221	E. F. Waddy & W. P. Howell: N.S.W. v. South Australia (Adelaide)	1904-05
221	N. V. Lindsay & G. R. McCubbin: Transvaal v. Rhodesia (Bulawayo)	1922-23
217	A. D. Nourse, Snr. & B. C. Cooley: Natal v. Western Province (Johannesburg)	1906-07
203*	J. J. Hills & J. C. Clay: Glamorgan v. Worcs. (Swansea)	1929
200	E. B. Forssberg & H. S. B. Love: N.S.W. v. Queensland (Sydney)	1920-21
200	G. W. Cook & C. S. Smith: Cambridge U. v. Lancs. (Liverpool)	1957
197	C. P. Mead & W. R. Shirley: Hants. v. Warwicks. (Birmingham)	1923
193	W. G. Grace & S. A. P. Kitcat: Glos. v. Sussex (Bristol)	1896
193	G. O. Allen & N. E. Haig: Gentlemen v. Players (Oval)	1925
192	G. H. Hirst & S. Haigh: Yorks. v. Surrey (Bradford)	1898
190	Asif Iqbal & Intikhab Alam: Pakistan v. England (Oval)	1967
184	A. C. Russell & L. C. Eastman: Essex v. Middx. (Lord's)	1920
183	C. Greetham & H. W. Stephenson: Somerset v. Leics. (Weston-super-Mare)	1963
181	J. A. Cuffe & R. D. Burrows: Worcs. v. Glos. (Worcester)	1907
181	A. Bacher & J. T. Botten: South Africans v. Leics. (Leicester)	1965
179	C. P. McGahey & C. P. Buckenham: Essex v. Notts. (Leyton)	1904
178	H. W. Parks & A. F. Wensley: Sussex v. Derby (Horsham)	1930
177	G. Brown & W. H. Livsey: Hants. v. Warwicks. (Birmingham)	1922
176*	R. Moorhouse & G. H. Hirst: Yorks. v. Glos. (Bristol)	1894
173	S. Haigh & W. Rhodes: Yorks. v. Sussex (Hove)	1902
173	P. Roy & S. K. Girdhari: Bengal Governor's XI v. West Indians (Calcutta)	1948-49
172	R. G. Barlow & W. Flowers: Players v. Australians (Nottingham)	1886
171	D. P. B. Morkel & N. A. Quinn: South Africans v. Western Australia (Perth)	1931-32
170	T. W. Garrett & T. R. McKibbin: N.S.W. v. South Australia (Sydney)	1896-97
169	C. B. Willis & W. A. Oldfield: Australians v. Notts. (Nottingham)	1919
168	L. G. Crawley & F. Watson: M.C.C. v. Jamaica (Kingston)	1925-26
168	E. R. T. Holmes & E. W. Brookes: Surrey v. Hants. (Oval)	1936
167	W. McIntyre & G. Wootton: Notts. v. Kent (Nottingham)	1869
167	H. Verity & T. F. Smailes: Yorks. v. Somerset (Hull)	1936
164	W. A. Oldfield & E. S. White: N.S.W. v. South Australia (Sydney)	1936-37
163*	M. C. Cowdrey & A. C. Smith: England v. New Zealand (Wellington)	1962-63
162	W. Rhodes & S. Haigh: Yorks. v. Lancs. (Manchester)	1904
161	E. Smith & W. Rhodes: Yorks. v. Sussex (Sheffield)	1900
161	B. R. Edrich & F. Ridgway: Kent v. Sussex (Tunbridge Wells)	1949
161	G. J. Whittaker & W. S. Surridge: Surrey v. Glamorgan (Oval)	1951
161	J. W. Ghorpade & C. Williams: Baroda v. Bombay (Baroda)	1961-62
160	R. T. Crawford & W. W. Odell: Leics. v. Worcs. (Leicester)	1902
160	K. S. Ranjitsinhji & F. W. Tate: Sussex v. Surrey (Hastings)	1902
160	P. S. Arnott & C. V. Single: N.S.W. v. Western Australia (Sydney)	1912-13
160	J. W. H. T. Douglas & H. W. F. Franklin: Essex v. Middx. (Leyton)	1923
160*	E. Hendren & T. J. Durston: Middx. v. Essex (Leyton)	1927
160	D. R. Wilcox & R. Smith: Essex v. Yorks. (Southend)	1947
159	H. V. Page & W. O. Vizard: Glos. v. Notts. (Cheltenham)	1883
159	Saeed Ahmed & Rathod: Western India States v. Sind (Karachi)	1939-40
158	F. Marchant & E. B. Shine: Kent v. Warwicks. (Tonbridge)	1897
157	C. P. Mead & W. H. Livsey: Hants. v. Notts. (Southampton)	1921
157	H. M. Garland-Wells & C. K. Hill-Wood: Oxford U. v. Kent (Oxford)	1928
157	H. G. Gaekwad & K. Bhatnagar: Holkar v. Bihar (Jamshedpur)	1948-49
156	A. Street & F. E. Smith: Surrey v. Leics. (Leicester)	1895
156	T. W. Hayward & J. T. Hearne: Players v. Gentlemen (Lord's)	1896
156	H. Wrathall & W. S. A. Brown: Glos. v. Warwicks. (Birmingham)	1898
156	M. W. Payne & G. H. M. Cartwright: Free Foresters v. Cambridge U. (Cambridge)	1927
156	R. Subba Row & S. Starkie: Northants. v. Lancs. (Northampton)	1955
156	S. K. Sahu & U. M. Kumre: Vidarbha v. Uttar Pradesh (Nagpur)	1959-60
155	F. R. Brown & M. J. C. Allom: Surrey v. Middx. (Oval)	1932
154	S. E. Gregory & J. M. Blackham: Australia v. England (Sydney)	1894-95
154	G. W. Stephens & A. J. Croom: Warwicks. v. Derby (Birmingham)	1925
153	J. S. Shepherd & R. M. Rutherford: Otago v. Southland (Dunedin)	1913-14
152	E. Martin & H. R. Murrell: Middx. v. Essex (Leyton)	1919
152*	A. T. W. Grout & W. Walmsley: Queensland v. N.S.W. (Sydney)	1956-57
151	W. H. Scotton & W. W. Read: England v. Australia (Oval)	1884
150	A. E. Relf & S. Haigh: Londesborough's XI v. Australians (Scarborough)	1912

TENTH WICKET

307	A. F. Kippax & J. E. H. Hooker: N.S.W. v. Victoria (Melbourne)	1928-29
249	C. T. Sarwate & S. N. Banerjee: Indians v. Surrey (Oval)	1946

Highest Partnerships-Tenth-Wicket—*Cont.*

235 F. E. Woolley & A. Fielder: Kent v. Worcs. (Stourbridge) 1909

230 R. W. Nicholls & W. Roche: Middx. v. Kent (Lord's) 1899

218 F. H. Vigar & T. P. B. Smith: Essex v. Derby (Chesterfield) 1947

211 M. Ellis & T. Hastings: Victoria v. South Australia (Melbourne) 1902-03

192 A. Bowell & W. H. Livsey: Hants. v. Worcs. (Bournemouth) 1921

184 R. C. Blunt & W. Hawkesworth: Otago v. Canterbury (Christchurch) 1931-32

177 J. H. Naumann & A. E. R. Gilligan: Cambridge U. v. Sussex (Hove) 1919

174 H. R. Lance & D. Mackay-Coghill: Transvaal v. Natal (Johannesburg) 1965-66

173 J. Briggs & R. Pilling: Lancs. v. Surrey (Liverpool) 1885

173 A. Ducat & A. Sandham: Surrey v. Essex (Leyton) 1921

169 R. B. Minnett & C. McKew: N.S.W. v. Victoria (Sydney) 1911-12

167 A. F. Somerset & W. C. Smith: M.C.C. v. Barbados (Bridgetown) 1912-13

157 J. Parnham & J. White: North v. South (Lord's) 1886

157 A. C. Russell & A. B. Hipkin: Essex v. Somerset (Taunton) 1926

157 W. E. Astill & W. H. Marlow: Leics. v. Glos. (Cheltenham) 1933

156 H. R. Butt & G. R. Cox: Sussex v. Cambridge U. (Cambridge) 1908

154 F. Buttesworth & J. Lanigan: Western Australia v. Victoria (Perth) 1921-22

154* N. A. McDonald & K. C. Martin: Natal B v. Griqualand West (Kimberley) 1965-66

152 E. Alleston & W. Riley: Notts. v. Essex (Hove) 1911

149 F. H. Hollins & B. A. Collins: Oxford U. v. M.C.C. (Oxford) 1901

149 K. Farnes & T. H. Wade: Essex v. Somerset (Taunton) 1936

148 Lord Hawke & D. Hunter: Yorks. v. Kent (Sheffield) 1898

148 B. Bellamy & V. Murdin: Northants. v. Glamorgan (Northampton) 1925

147 E. M. Sprot & A. E. Fielder: Hants. v. Glos. (Bristol) 1911

147 C. G. Macartney & S. C. Everett: Australian XI v. Tasmania (Hobart) 1925-26

145 G. A. Rotherham & J. H. Naumann: Cambridge U. v. A.I.F. (Cambridge) 1919

144 S. Wazir Ali & J. G. Navle: Indians v. Scotland (Dundee) 1932

144 Shakoor Ahmed & Pervez Sajjad: Lahore Greens v. Karachi Blues (Karachi) 1965-66

143 H. Gibbs & J. J. Bridges: Somerset v. Essex (Weston-super-Mare) 1919

141 J. T. Tyldesley & W. Worsley: Lancs. v. Notts. (Nottingham) 1905

141 J. R. Mason & C. Blythe: Kent v. Surrey (Oval) 1909

140 S. J. Staples & L. B. Richmond: Notts. v. Derby (Worksop) 1922

140* G. S. Boyes & A. E. Thomas: Players v. Gentlemen (Folkestone) 1930

139 P. R. Johnson & R. C. Robertson-Glasgow: Somerset v. Surrey (Oval) 1926

138 K. C. James & W. S. Brice: Wellington v. Otago (Wellington) 1926-27

138 E. L. G. Hoad & H. C. Griffith: West Indians v. Sussex (Hove) 1933

138 Yadvendrasinhji & Mubarak Ali: Nawanagar v. Bengal (Bombay) 1936-37

138 R. I. Jefferson & D. A. D. Sydenham: Surrey v. Northants. (Northampton) 1963

136 J. O'Halloran & A. E. Johns: Victoria v. South Australia (Melbourne) 1896-97

136 K. S. Ranjitsinhji & P. R. May: London County v. M.C.C. (Crystal Palace) 1903

136 G. Challenor & G. N. Francis: West Indians v. Surrey (Oval) 1923

136 H. Larwood & W. Voce: Notts. v. Sussex (Nottingham) 1931

136 J. S. Patel & H. A. Nakhuda: Gujerat v. Holkar (Indore) 1950-51

135 T. W. Hayward & H. Young: Players v. Gentlemen (Oval) 1899

135 W. A. Oldfield & A. A. Mailey: N.S.W. v. South Australia (Adelaide) 1923-24

134 A. E. R. Gilligan & M. Falcon: Gentlemen v. Players (Oval) 1924

134 H. G. Gaekwad & M. Salim Khan: Holkar v. Delhi (New Delhi) 1949-50

134 Wallis Mathias & Afaq Hussain: Karachi A v. Karachi B (Karachi) 1962-63

133* A. Sandham & W. J. Abel: Surrey v. Middx. (Oval) 1919

133 G. A. Bartlett & I. A. Colquhoun: Central Districts v. Auckland (Auckland) 1959-60

133* G. Inderdev & V. K. Tewari: Delhi v. Jammu & Kashmir (New Delhi) 1961-62

132 R. W. McLeod & C. H. Ross: Victoria v. South Australia (Adelaide) 1899-00

132 V. A. Valentine & H. G. Griffith: West Indians v. Middx. (Lord's) 1933

131 D. L. A. Jephson & F. Stedman: Surrey v. Lancs. (Oval) 1900

131 E. Tyldesley & R. Whitehead: Lancs. v. Warwicks. (Birmingham) 1914

131 W. R. Gouldsworthy & J. G. Bessant: Glos. v. Somerset (Bristol) 1923

131* C. Smart & W. D. Hughes: Glamorgan v. South Africans (Cardiff) 1935

130 G. W. Beldham & C. Headlam: Middx v. Surrey (Lord's) 1902

130 R. E. Foster & W. Rhodes: England v. Australia (Sydney) 1903-04

130 H. Strudwick & J. W. Hitch: Surrey v. Warwicks. (Birmingham) 1911

130 G. R. Cox & G. Stannard: Sussex v. Essex (Hove) 1919

130 N. J. Venkatesen & C. R. Rangachari: Madras v. Madhya Pradesh (Madras) 1951-52

129 E. G. Goatly & F. Stedman: Surrey v. South Africans (Oval) 1904

129 F. Caulfield & L. R. Tuckett: O.F.S. v. Western Province (Bloemontein) 1925-26

128 W. Mudie & T. Sewell: Surrey v. Kent (Oval) 1859

128 H. D. G. Leveson-Gower & G. K. Molineux: Gentlemen v. Oxford U. (Eastbourne) 1908

Highest Partnerships-Tenth Wicket—*Cont.*

128 F. R. Santall & W. Sanders: Warwicks. v. Yorks. (Birmingham) 1930
128 K. Higgs & J. A. Snow: England v. West Indies (Oval) 1966
127 C. P. Mead & G. S. Boyes: Hants. v. Worcs. (Worcester) 1922
127 J. M. Taylor & A. A. Mailey: Australia v. England (Sydney) 1924-25
126 J. W. Hearne & H. Strudwick: Jessop's XI v. Warner's XI (Sheffield) .. 1911
126 R. E. S. Wyatt & J. H. Mayer: Warwicks. v. Surrey (Oval) 1927
125 A. L. Hosie & W. L. Budd: Hants. v. Glamorgan (Bournemouth) 1935
124 W. A. Oldfield & A. A. Mailey: Australians v. Warwicks. (Birmingham) .. 1921
124 Salah-ud-Din & Niaz Ahmed: Pakistanis v. Minor Counties (Swindon) .. 1967
123 H. B. Massey & L. Beard: Wellington v. Otago (Wellington) 1927-28
123 R. Duckfield & J. C. Clay: Glamorgan v. Leics. (Cardiff) 1933
123 B. Dooland & A. K. Walker: Notts. v. Somerset (Nottingham) 1956
122 W. G. Ward & N. Dodds: Tasmania v. Victoria (Hobart) 1898-99
122 J. W. Hitch & H. Strudwick: Players v. Gentlemen (Oval) 1914
122 W. Reeves & G. M. Louden: Essex v. Surrey (Leyton) 1919
122 W. R. Hammond & C. I. J. Smith: M.C.C. v. Barbados (Bridgetown) .. 1934-35
121 W. Bates & E. Peate: Under 30 v. Over 30 (Lord's) 1882
121 J. T. Brown & D. Hunter: Yorks. v. Liverpool & District (Liverpool) .. 1894
121 W. L. Murdoch & J. Gilman: London County v. Cambridge U. (Crystal Palace) 1900
120 R. A. Duff & W. W. Armstrong: Australia v. England (Melbourne) 1901-02
120 A. J. Hopkins & W. McIntyre: N.S.W. v. Queensland (Sydney) 1906-07
120 G. Lavis & J. Mercer: Glamorgan v. Surrey (Oval) 1934
119 W. B. Burns & G. A. Wilson: Worcs. v. Somerset (Worcester) 1906
119 C. D. McIver & C. U. Peat: Leveson-Gower's XI v. Cambridge U. (Eastbourne) 1921
119* W. H. Ponsford & A. J. Richardson: Australians v. M.C.C. (Lord's) 1926
119* E. A. Watts & J. V. Daley: Surrey v. Hants. (Bournemouth) 1936
119 W. N. Carson & J. A. Cowie: Auckland v. Otago (Auckland) 1937-38
118 C. T. Calvert & T. Sewell: Surrey v. Sussex (Brighton) 1868
118 Lord Hawke & D. Hunter: Yorks. v. Kent (Leeds) 1896
118 C. H. Abercrombie & H. A. H. Smith: Hants. v. Worcs. (Dudley) 1913
118 A. Hurwood & P. M. Hornibrook: Australians v. Sussex (Hove) 1930
118 R. J. L. Hammond & J. H. G. Deighton: Combined Services v. Essex (Chelmsford) 1950
117* R. Dare & R. O. Prouton: Hants. v. Worcs. (Bournemouth) 1952
117 V. Subramanya & B. S. Chandrasekhar: Mysore v. Madras (Madras) 1966-67
116 C. I. J. Smith & I. A. R. Peebles: Middx. v. Kent (Canterbury) 1939
115 W. Drysdale & Tandy: Europeans v. Parsis (Poona) 1900-01
115 L. G. Fuller & L. R. Tuckett: O.F.S. v. Western Province (Bloemfontein) .. 1925-26
115 B. W. Malcolm & T. Bhattacharjee: Bengal v Madras (Calcutta) 1938-39
115 A. J. Watkins & D. J. Shepherd: Glamorgan v. Northants. (Northampton) .. 1958
115 R. E. Hitchcock & R. B. Edmonds: Warwicks. v. Northants. (Northampton) .. 1964
113 J. G. Greig & C. Robson: Hants. v. Lancs. (Liverpool) 1901
113 G. R. Cox & H. R. Butt: Sussex v. Hants. (Chichester) 1906
113* E. W. Whitfield & J. F. Parker: Surrey v. Indians (Oval) 1932
113 F. L. H. Mooney & D. Knapp: Wellington v. Auckland (Wellington) .. 1943-44
113 Wallis Mathias & Arshad Bashir: Karachi Blues v. Railway Greens (Karachi) 1961-62
112 J. J. Kelly & F. Laver: Australians v. Glos. (Bristol) 1905
112 A. E. Dipper & G. Dennett: Glos. v. Sussex (Gloucester) 1908
112 A. E. Relf & H. E. Roberts: Sussex v. Lancs. (Hove) 1914
112 C. E. Kelleway & H. Carter: N.S.W. v. South Australia (Adelaide) 1920-21
112 J. W. Lee & W. T. Luckes: Somerset v. Kent (Taunton) 1934
112 J. T. Botten & M. J. Macaulay: South African Colts v. M.C.C. (Benoni) .. 1964-65
111 A. Ward & A. Mold: Lancs. v. Leics. (Manchester) 1895
111 M. A. Noble & W. P. Howell: N.S.W. v. Victoria (Sydney) 1896-97
111 J. Gunn & W. A. Flint: Notts. v. Middx. (Nottingham) 1919
111* A. P. F. Chapman & F. T. Mann: South v. North (Folkestone) 1927
111 J. F. Parker & A. R. Gover: Surrey v. Indians (Oval) 1936
111 Gulraiz Wali & Shanwar: Punjab U. v. Railways (Lahore) 1964-65
110 J. S. E. Hood & C. E. Green: Cambridge U. v. M.C.C. (Lord's) 1867
110 J. R. Sheffield & T. H. Wade: Essex v. Warwicks. (Chelmsford) 1929
110* A. G. Marshall & G. Hunt: Somerset v. Hants. (Taunton) 1930
110* F. W. Stocks & E. A. Meads: Notts. v. Worcs. (Nottingham) 1946
110 N. Chanmugam & P. I. Pieris: Ceylon v. West Indians (Colombo) 1966-67
109 W. Gunn & R. G. Hardstaff: Notts. v. Derby (Derby) 1896
109 A. L. Newell & W. P. Howell: N.S.W. v. Stoddart's XI (Sydney) 1897-98
109 G. Dewhurst & C. Fraser: Trinidad v. Barbados (Georgetown) 1922-23
109 D. C. S. Compton & O. P. Rawal: Holkar v. Bombay (Bombay) 1944-45
109 H. R. Adhikari & Ghulam Ahmed: India v. Pakistan (New Delhi) 1952-53

Highest Partnerships-Tenth Wicket—*Cont.*

108	Lord Hawke & L. Whitehead: Yorks. v. Lancs. (Manchester)	1903
108	R. G. Nadkarni & S. R. Patil: Maharashtra v. Bombay (Bombay)	1953-54
107	A. Jaques & W. H. Livsey: Hants. v. Worcs. (Southampton)	1914
107	J. A. Small & G. N. Francis: West Indians v. Harlequins (Eastbourne) ..	1928
107	H. J. Enthoven & W. F. Price: Middx. v. Sussex (Lord's)	1930
107	R. C. Motz & F. J. Cameron: New Zealanders v. Worcs. (Worcester).. ..	1965
106	G. Wootton & R. S. Forster: M.C.C. v. Sussex (Brighton)	1863
106	H. Wrathall & J. H. Board: Glos. v. Surrey (Oval)	1899
106	E. R. Wilson & C. E. Hatfeild: M.C.C. v. Argentine (Hurlingham)	1911-12
106	G. Brown & A. S. Kennedy: Hants. v. Yorks. (Bournemouth)	1913
106	R. C. Robertson-Glasgow & V. R. Price: Oxford U. v. Somerset (Oxford) ..	1922
106	F. W. Gilligan & M. S. Nichols: Essex v. Kent (Canterbury)	1926
106	E. S. Sim & H. J. O'Reilly: Rhodesia v. Griqualand West (Kimberley) ..	1929-30
106	E. Hendren & G. E. Hart: Middx. v. Somerset (Taunton)	1935
106	A. B. Sellers & D. V. Brennan: Yorks. v. Worcs. (Worcester)	1948
106	D. Bennett & H. W. Tilly: M.C.C. v. Oxford U. (Lord's)	1955
105	W. Brockwell & T. Richardson: Surrey v. Glos. (Oval)	1893
105	L. W. Pye & A. J. Bowden: N.S.W. v. Queensland (Sydney)	1899-00
105	R. W. Cherry & R. C. Torrance: Otago v. Canterbury (Christchurch) ..	1925-26
105*	W. Walmsley & J. Freeman: Queensland v. N.S.W. (Brisbane)	1957-58
105	A. Wilson & R. Tattersall: Lancs. v. Leics. (Manchester)	1958
104	W. O. Reid & J. T. Hings: Transvaal v. Natal (Pietermaritzburg)	1894-95
104	W. S. A. Brown & F. G. Roberts: Glos. v. Sussex (Bristol)	1903
104	G. Brown & J. Mercer: M.C.C. v. Hindus-Muslims XI (Bombay)	1926-27
104	K. C. James & H. B. Massey: Wellington v. Australians (Wellington).. ..	1927-28
104	F. R. Brown & J. F. Parker: Surrey v. Kent (Blackheath)	1932
104	L. Michael & E. Pynor: South Australia v. Victoria (Adelaide)	1949-50
104	Zulfiqar Ahmed & Amir Elahi: Pakistan v. India (Madras)	1952-53
103	L. S. D'Ade & S. Rudder: Trinidad v. Priestley's XI (Port of Spain)	1896-97
103	P. A. McAlister & F. A. Tarrant: Victoria v. New Zealanders (Melbourne) ..	1898-99
103	James Seymour & A. Fielder: Kent v. Worcs. (Maidstone)	1904
103	A. Dolphin & E. Smith: Yorks. v. Essex (Leyton)	1919
103	W. Voce & S. J. Staples: Notts. v. Leics. (Leicester)	1933
103	H. G. Owen-Smith & A. J. Bell: South Africa v. England (Leeds)	1929
102	D. Denton & D. Hunter: Yorks. v. Cambridge U. (Cambridge)	1895
102	James Seymour & A. Fielder: Kent v. Essex (Leyton)	1911
102	P. T. Eckersley & W. E. Phillipson: Lancs. v. Sussex (Manchester)	1933
102	H. G. Gaekwad & O. P. Rawal: Holkar v. Baroda (Indore)	1945-46
101	A. J. L. Hill & E. C. Streatfeild: Cambridge U. v. Yorks. (Cambridge) ..	1890
101	C. R. Hartley & A. Mold: Lancs. v. Glos. (Gloucester)	1901
101	G. Giffen & J. F. Travers: South Australia v. Victoria (Adelaide) ..	1902-03
101	H. D. G. Leveson-Gower & R. H. Fox: Leveson-Gower's XI v. Oxford U. (Oxford)	1904
101*	J. W. H. T. Douglas & B. Tremlin: Essex v. Derby (Leyton)	1914
101	W. W. Armstrong & G. Truman: Victoria v. South Australia (Melbourne) ..	1918-19
101	F. G. Travers & B. Howlett: Europeans v. Muslims (Bombay)	1925-26
101	W. W. Whysall & W. Voce: Notts. v. Glos. (Nottingham)	1929
101	A. E. Wilson & T. W. Goddard: Glos. v. Somerset (Bristol)	1939
100	G. E. Palmer & W. H. Cooper: Victoria v. N.S.W. (Sydney)	1881-82
100	P. H. Tarilton & H. W. Ince: Barbados v. M.C.C. (Bridgetown)	1912-13
100	E. L. Dalton & A. L. Ochse: South Africans v. Kent (Canterbury)	1929
100	S. N. Banerjee & C. S. Nayudu: Indians v. Hants. (Bournemouth)	1936
100	W. A. Sime & W. Voce: Notts. v. Cambridge U. (Cambridge)	1935
100*	D. Tallon & G. J. Noblet: Bradman's XI v. Hassett's XI (Melbourne) ..	1948-49

ELEVENTH WICKET

80	H. Whitfield & P. H. Morton: Cambridge U. v. Surrey (Oval)	1878

A CENTURY FIRST-WICKET PARTNERSHIP IN EACH INNINGS

123	108	L. Hall & G. Ulyett: Yorks. v. Sussex (Hove)	1885
139	147*	J. T. Brown & J. Tunnicliffe: Yorks. v. Middx. (Lord's)	1896
135	148	C. B. Fry & G. Brann: Sussex v. Middx. (Lord's)	1899
131	142	W. G. Grace & C. J. B. Wood: London County v. Surrey (Crystal Palace)	1901
108	100	C. J. Burnup & E. Humphreys: Kent v. South Africans (Beckenham) ..	1901

A Century First-Wicket Partnership in Each Innings—*Cont.*

114	109	R. Abel & D. L. A. Jephson: Surrey v. Sussex (Hove)	1901
134	144*	A. O. Jones & J. Iremonger: Notts. v. Surrey (Oval)	1901
170	179	C. B. Fry & J. Vine: Sussex v. Leics. (Hove)	1903
113	119*	V. T. Trumper & R. A. Duff: N.S.W. v. Victoria (Sydney)	1903-04
102	303	A. O. Jones & J. Iremonger: Notts. v. Glos. (Nottingham)	1904
106	125	T. W. Hayward & J. B. Hobbs: Surrey v. Cambridge U. (Oval) ..	1907
147	105	T. W. Hayward & J. B. Hobbs: Surrey v. Middx. (Lord's)	1907
		(*These two instances were recorded in the same week.*)	
105	118	T. W. Hayward & J. B. Hobbs: Surrey v. Oxford U. (Oval)	1908
103	100	A. Hartley & W. Tyldesley: Lancs. v. Hants. (Southampton)	1910
122	121	V. T. Trumper & W. Bardsley: N.S.W. v. South Africans (Sydney) ..	1910-11
141	193	A. H. Hornby & H. Makepeace: Lancs. v. Notts. (Nottingham)	1912
127	136	A. E. Dipper & C. S. Barnett: Glos. v. Somerset (Bristol)	1913
191	104	A. C. Russell & F. Loveday: Essex v. Lancs. (Leyton)	1921
122	140	F. H. Gillingham & A. C. Russell: Essex v. Surrey (Oval)	1922
154	155	J. S. Shepherd & R. V. de R. Worker: Otago v. Wellington (Dunedin) ..	1923-24
157	110	J. B. Hobbs & H. Sutcliffe: England v. Australia (Sydney)	1924-25
114	116	H. Makepeace & C. Hallows: Lancs. v. Australians (Liverpool)	1926
105	265*	P. Holmes & H. Sutcliffe: Yorks. v. Surrey (Oval)	1926
109	100	J. A. Newman & H. L. Dales: Calthorpe's XI v. Tennyson's XI (Folkestone)	1926
202	107*	F. Watson & C. Hallows: Lancs. v. Glamorgan (Manchester)	1928
184	210*	P. Holmes & H. Sutcliffe: Yorks. v. Notts. (Nottingham)	1928
106	368	E. H. Bowley & J. H. Parks: Sussex v. Glos. (Hove)	1929
119	171	R. H. Catterall & B. Mitchell: South Africa v. England (Birmingham) ..	1929
129	109	N. E. Haig & H. W. Lee: Middx. v. Leics. (Lord's)	1930
102	113	D. Ayling & A. L. S. Jackson: South Americans v. Cahn's XI (Nottingham)	1932
125	128	W. W. Keeton & C. B. Harris: Notts. v. Kent (Nottingham)	1933
119	121	A. W. Snowden & A. H. Bakewell: Northants. v. Warwicks. (Birmingham)	1934
		(*Both stands were made on the same day.*)	
119	146	J. W. Lee & F. S. Lee: Somerset v. Sussex (Eastbourne)	1934
101	127	W. H. Ashdown & A. E. Fagg: Kent v. Glamorgan (Cardiff)	1935
111	109	J. H. Parks & H. E. Hammond: Sussex v. Hants. (Portsmouth)	1936
109	102	N. Kilner & A. J. Croom: Warwicks. v. Worcs. (Worcester)	1937
108	126*	E. Paynter & C. Washbrook: Lancs. v. Notts. (Nottingham)	1937
102	100	N. McCorkell & J. Arnold: Hants. v. Kent (Southampton)	1938
116	105	F. S. Lee & H. Gimblett: Somerset v. Sussex (Taunton)	1939
152	169	I. S. Lee & B. A. Barnett: Victoria v. Queensland (Brisbane)	1939-40
127	172	V. H. Stollmeyer & J. B. Stollmeyer: Trinidad v. Barbados (Port of Spain)	1940-41
224	105*	V. H. Stollmeyer & J. B. Stollmeyer: Trinidad v. Barbados (Port of Spain)	1941-42
123	136	D. Brookes & P. Davis: Northants. v. Lancs. (Northampton)	1946
137	100	L. Hutton & C. Washbrook: England v. Australia (Adelaide)	1946-47
110	117	L. Hutton & W. Watson: Yorks. v. Lancs. (Manchester)	1947
121	116	A. H. Dyson & E. Davies: Glamorgan v. Sussex (Cardiff)	1947
121	176	J. D. Robertson & S. M. Brown: Middx. v. Essex (Colchester)	1947
124	139	L. G. Berry & G. Lester: Leics. v. Middx. (Leicester)	1948
168	129	L. Hutton & C. Washbrook: England v. Australia (Leeds)	1948
220	286	B. Sutcliffe & D. D. Taylor: Auckland v. Canterbury (Auckland) ..	1948-49
122	151*	W. W. Keeton & C. B. Harris: Notts. v. Northants. (Northampton) ..	1950
199	109	J. D. Robertson & S. M. Brown: Middx. v. Somerset (Lord's)	1951
166	108	B. C. Khanna & R. Balasundaram: Uttar Pradesh v. Madhya Pradesh (Nagpur)	1952-53
101	118	C. Washbrook & J. T. Ikin: Lancs. v. Hants. (Manchester)	1953
107	132	A. E. Fagg & A. H. Phebey: Kent v. Glos. (Gloucester)	1954
106	104	D. V. Smith & A. S. M. Oakman: M.C.C. v. Oxford U. (Lord's) ..	1956
122	230	W. B. Stott & K. Taylor: Yorks. v. Notts. (Nottingham)	1957
172	112	G. Atkinson & R. Virgin: Somerset v. Cambridge U. (Taunton)	1960
198	137	R. M. Prideaux & A. R. Lewis: Cambridge U. v. Somerset (Taunton) ..	1960
152	110	M. J. Stewart & J. H. Edrich: Surrey v. Somerset (Taunton)	1960
123	106	N. F. Horner & K. Ibadulla: Warwicks. v. Northants. (Northampton) ..	1961
161	139*	I. D. Craig & R. B. Simpson: N.S.W. v. Victoria (Sydney)	1961-62
136	138	J. B. Bolus & K. Taylor: Yorks. v. Cambridge U. (Cambridge)	1962
170	103	B. J. Booth & K. Tebay: Lancs. v. Worcs. (Manchester)	1963
105	104	G. Boycott & K. Taylor: Yorks. v. Leics. (Sheffield)	1963
116	114*	J. H. Hampshire & K. Taylor: Yorks. v. Oxford U. (Oxford)	1964

(*Hampshire retired ill at 114; D. E. V. Padgett & Taylor added a further 37 runs for this wicket in the second innings.*)

A Century First-Wicket Partnership in Each Innings—*Cont.*

157	142	W. M. Lawry & I. R. Redpath: Victoria v. South Australia (Melbourne)	1964-65
136	101	B. J. Booth & D. J. Constant: Leics. v. Oxford U. (Oxford)	1965
141	127*	C. Milburn & R. M. Prideaux: Northants v. Sussex (Hove)	1966

A. Sandham, playing for Surrey v. Essex (Leyton) 1925, shared in opening stands of 216 with J. B. Hobbs in the first innings and 181 with A. Jeacocke in the second.

F. W. Shipston, playing for Nottinghamshire v. Gloucestershire (Bristol) 1932, shared in two century stands—113 with G. Gunn in the first innings and 139 with C. B. Harris in the second.

A. S. M. Oakman, playing for Sussex v. Oxford U. (Oxford) 1956, shared in two century stands—109 with D. V. Smith in the first innings and 100 with A. A. K. Lawrence in the second.

W. M. Lawry, playing for Australians v. M.C.C. (Lord's) 1961, shared in opening stands totalling 123 (53* and 70) in the first innings with C. C. McDonald (retired hurt) and R. N. Harvey, and another of 186* with R. B. Simpson in the second.

Playing for N.S.W. v. Western Australia (Sydney) 1963-64, R. B. Simpson and G. Thomas shared an opening partnership of 308 in the first innings, and B. C. Booth and N. C. O'Neill shared in one of 127 in the second.

PLAYERS' RECORDS—BOWLING

MOST WICKETS IN A SEASON

250 *WICKETS IN ENGLAND*

	Season	*Balls in an over*	*Overs*	*Mdns.*	*Runs*	*Wkts.*	*Avge.*
A. P. Freeman	1928	(6-ball)	1976.1	423	5489	304	18.05
A. P. Freeman	1933	(6-ball)	2039	651	4549	298	15.26
T. Richardson	1895	(5-ball)	1690.1	463	4170	290	14.37
C. T. B. Turner	1888	(4-ball)	2427.2	1127	3307	283	11.68
A. P. Freeman	1931	(6-ball)	1618	360	4307	276	15.60
A. P. Freeman	1930	(6-ball)	1914.3	472	4632	275	16.84
T. Richardson	1897	(5-ball)	1603.4	495	3945	273	14.45
A. P. Freeman	1929	(6-ball)	1670.5	381	4879	267	18.27
W. Rhodes	1900	(6-ball)	1553	455	3606	261	13.81
J. T. Hearne	1896	(5-ball)	2003.1	818	3670	257	14.28
A. P. Freeman	1932	(6-ball)	1565.5	404	4149	253	16.39
W. Rhodes	1901	(6-ball)	1565	505	3797	251	15.12

150 *WICKETS IN ENGLAND*

	Season	*Overs*	*Mdns.*	*Runs*	*Wkts.*	*Avge.*
Appleyard, R. (Yorks) .. .. (2)	1951	1323.1	391	2829	200	14.14
	1954	1026.3	315	2221	154	14.42
Astill, W. E. (Leics.) .. .. (1)	1921	1226.3	316	3212	153	20.99
Attewell, W. (Notts.) .. .. (2)	1890	1581.2	820	1874	151	12.41
	1891	1514.3	706	2132	153	13.93
Bedser, A. V. (Surrey) .. .. (2)	1952	1184.4	296	2530	154	16.42
	1953	1253	340	2702	162	16.67
Blythe, C. (Kent) .. .. .. (7)	1907	1136.1	291	2822	183	15.42
	1908	1366.4	386	3326	197	16.88
	1909	1273.5	343	3128	215	14.54
	1910	1041.3	274	2497	175	14.26
	1912	919.3	241	2183	178	12.26
	1913	1120.2	289	2729	167	16.34
	1914	1008.4	280	2583	170	15.19
Booth, M. W. (Yorks.) .. .. (2)	1913	1156.2	185	3342	181	18.46
	1914	983.5	178	2803	157	17.85
Bowes, W. E. (Yorks.) .. .. (3)	1932	1194.2	271	2877	190	15.14
	1933	1010.4	226	2828	159	17.78
	1935	1286.5	342	2981	193	15.44
Bradley, W. M. (Kent) .. .. (1)	1899	1257	414	2981	156	19.10

150 Wickets in a Season—*Cont.*

		Season	*Overs*	*Mdns.*	*Runs*	*Wkts.*	*Avge.*
Braund, L. C. (Somerset)	(1)	1902	1100	250	3407	172	19.80
Brearley, W. (Lancs.)	(2)	1905	1049.4	191	3486	181	19.25
		1908	856.2	165	2636	163	16.17
Briggs, J. (Lancs.)	(5)	1888	1450.2	763	1679	160	10.49
		1890	1113.2	456	1950	158	12.34
		1893	1364	488	2639	166	15.89
		1896	1741.4	592	3253	165	19.71
		1897	1288	387	2560	155	16.51
Clay, J. C. (Glamorgan)	(1)	1937	1103.3	229	3052	176	17.34
Coldwell, L. J. (Worcs.)	(1)	1962	1104	253	2722	152	17.90
Cook, L. (Lancs.)	(2)	1920	1069.4	275	2322	156	14.88
		1921	1402	293	3472	151	22.99
Copson, W. H. (Derby)	(1)	1936	946.4	239	2135	160	13.34
Cox, G. R. (Sussex)	(2)	1905	1557.3	456	3179	170	21.87
		1907	1218.2	359	2900	164	17.68
Dean, H. (Lancs.)	(2)	1911	1295.5	324	3191	183	17.43
		1912	1060	356	2216	162	13.67
Dennett, G. (Glos.)	(6)	1905	1161.3	280	3421	163	20.98
		1906	1145.5	256	3093	175	17.69
		1907	1216.2	305	3227	201	16.05
		1908	1317.1	409	3148	153	20.57
		1909	1039.5	242	2977	156	19.08
		1913	1175.1	289	3139	153	20.51
Dooland, B. (Notts.)	(3)	1953	1332.3	461	2852	172	16.58
		1954	1287.1	408	3035	196	15.48
		1955	1245.3	327	3452	150	23.01
Drake, A. (Yorks.)	(1)	1914	1017.2	283	2428	158	15.36
Faulkner, G. A. (South Africans)	(1)	1912	1015.1	207	2514	163	15.42
Ferris, J. J. (Australians)	(2)	1888	2085.1	937	2934	199	14.74
		1890	1545.1	628	2657	186	14.28
Fender, P. G. H. (Surrey)	(2)	1922	1116	208	3329	157	21.20
		1923	1324.2	307	3558	178	19.98
Fielder, A. (Kent)	(2)	1906	1159.3	234	3756	186	20.19
		1907	977.3	197	2773	172	16.12
Flavell, J. A. (Worcs.)	(1)	1961	1245.2	300	3043	171	17.79
Freeman, A. P. (Kent)	(14)	1921	1017.2	217	3086	166	18.59
		1923	990	262	2642	157	16.82
		1922	1101.1	270	2839	194	14.63
		1924	1035.2	250	2518	167	15.07
		1926	1353.5	327	3740	180	20.77
		1927	1220.1	269	3330	181	18.39
		1928	1976.1	423	5489	304	18.05
		1929	1670.5	381	4879	267	18.27
		1930	1914.3	472	4632	275	16.84
		1931	1618	360	4307	276	15.60
		1932	1565.5	404	4149	253	16.39
		1933	2039	651	4549	298	15.26
		1934	1744.4	440	4753	205	23.18
		1935	1503.2	320	4562	212	21.51
Geary, G. (Leics.)	(1)	1929	1495.2	500	2980	152	19.60
Giffen, G. (Australians)	(1)	1886	1673.2	710	2674	154	17.36
Gilligan, A. E. R. (Sussex)	(1)	1923	1075.4	235	2853	163	17.50
Gladwin, C. (Derby)	(1)	1952	1258.2	402	2917	152	19.19
Goddard, T. W. (Glos.)	(10)	1929	1285.1	357	3015	184	16.38
		1932	1316	343	3258	170	19.16
		1933	1371.5	414	3187	183	17.41
		1935	1553	384	4073	200	20.36
		1936	1425.2	323	3106	153	20.30
		1937	1478.1	359	4158	248	16.76
		1939	819	139	2973	200	14.86
		1946	1310.2	358	3095	177	17.48
		1947	1451.2	344	4119	238	17.30
		1949	1187.2	326	3069	160	19.18
Gover, A. R. (Surrey)	(2)	1936	1159.2	185	3547	200	17.73
		1937	1219.4	191	3816	201	18.98

150 Wickets in a Season—*Cont.*

	Season	Overs	Mdns.	Runs	Wkts.	Avge.
Grace, W. G. (Glos.) .. .. .. (3)	1875	1689.1	698	2468	191	12.92
	1877	1801	772	2291	179	12.79
	1878	1420	586	2204	152	14.50
Haigh, S. (Yorks.) .. .. (3)	1900	958.3	259	2416	163	14.82
	1902	799	219	1984	158	12.55
	1906	971.3	209	2540	174	14.59
Hallam, A. W. (Notts.) .. .. .. (1)	1907	937.1	302	2133	168	12.69
Hearne, J. T. (Middx.) .. .. .. (6)	1892	1360.3	527	2510	163	15.39
	1893	1741.4	667	3492	212	16.47
	1894	1486	600	2739	195	14.04
	1896	2003.1	818	3670	257	14.28
	1897	1619.3	647	3066	173	17.72
	1898	1802.2	781	3120	222	14.05
Hilton, M. J. (Lancs.) .. .. .. (1)	1956	1199.5	558	2207	158	13.96
Hirst, G. H. (Yorks.) .. .. .. (6)	1895	1262.1	429	2560	150	17.06
	1901	1135.3	261	2999	183	16.38
	1906	1306.1	271	3434	208	16.50
	1907	1167.4	269	2859	188	15.20
	1908	1121.5	290	2445	174	14.05
	1910	1021.2	252	2426	164	14.79
Hitch, J. W. (Surrey) .. .. .. (3)	1911	965.1	160	3477	151	23.02
	1913	958.4	169	3228	174	18.55
	1919	1052	207	3430	161	21.30
Hollies, W. E. (Warwicks.) .. .. (2)	1946	1528	433	2871	184	15.60
	1949	1627.4	484	3413	166	20.56
Howell, H. (Warwicks.) .. .. .. (2)	1920	1050.3	222	2885	161	17.91
	1923	1090.4	197	3126	152	20.56
Howorth, R. (Worcs.) .. .. .. (1)	1947	1254	375	2929	164	17.85
Humphreys, W. (Sussex) .. .. .. (1)	1893	813.4	122	2598	150	17.32
Jackson, H. L. (Derby) .. .. .. (1)	1960	1082.2	310	2179	160	13.61
Jenkins, R. O. (Worcs.) .. .. .. (1)	1949	1146.1	187	3879	183	21.19
Jupp, V. W. C. (Northants.) .. .. (1)	1928	1023	192	3345	166	20.15
Kennedy, A. S. (Hants.) .. .. .. (6)	1914	1289.4	331	3243	162	20.01
	1920	1179.4	279	3093	169	18.30
	1921	1427	316	4009	186	21.55
	1922	1346.4	366	3444	205	16.80
	1923	1376.5	370	3599	184	19.55
	1929	1178.5	344	2773	154	18.00
Kilner, R. (Yorks.) .. .. .. (1)	1923	1259.5	507	2040	158	12.91
Laker, J. C. (Surrey) .. .. .. (1)	1950	1409.5	522	2544	166	15.32
Langridge, James (Sussex) .. .. (1)	1933	1228.3	355	2617	158	16.56
Larwood, H. (Notts.) .. .. .. (1)	1932	866.4	203	2084	162	12.86
Lees, W. S. (Surrey) .. .. .. (2)	1905	1388.2	387	3476	193	18.01
	1906	1258.5	321	3402	168	20.25
Llewellyn, C. B. (Hants.) .. .. (2)	1902	1129.4	314	3164	170	18.61
	1910	951.3	161	2930	152	19.27
Lock, G. A. R. (Surrey) .. .. .. (4)	1955	1407.4	497	3109	216	14.39
	1956	1058.2	437	1932	155	12.46
	1957	1194.1	449	2550	212	12 02
	1958	1014.4	382	2055	170	12.08
Lockwood, W. H. (Surrey) .. .. (3)	1892	890.2	292	2052	151	13.58
	1893	931.2	267	2517	150	16.78
	1894	894.2	244	2233	150	14.88
Lohmann, G. A. (Surrey) .. .. (7)	1886	1715	809	2425	160	15.15
	1887	1634.2	737	2404	154	15.61
	1888	1649.1	783	2280	209	10.90
	1889	1614.1	646	2714	202	13.83
	1890	1759.1	737	2998	220	13.62
	1891	1189.3	445	2065	177	11.66
	1892	1213.4	431	2316	151	15.33
Macaulay, G. G. (Yorks.) .. .. (3)	1923	1042.4	245	2297	166	13.83
	1924	1220.4	343	2514	190	13.23
	1925	1338.2	307	3268	211	15.48
McDonald, E. A. (Lancs.) .. .. (4)	1925	1249.4	282	3828	205	18.67
	1926	1177.4	222	3541	175	20.23
	1927	1137.3	223	3586	150	23.90
	1928	1254.1	266	3754	190	19.75

150 Wickets in a Season—*Cont.*

		Season	Overs	Mdns.	Runs	Wkts.	Avge.
Martin, F. (Kent)	(1)	1890	1702.2	711	2481	190	13.05
Mead, W. (Essex)	(1)	1895	1206	390	2605	179	14.50
Mitchell, T. B. (Derby)	(2)	1934	986.1	202	3064	159	19.27
		1935	919.5	142	3448	171	20.16
Mold, A. (Lancs.)	(4)	1893	1282.4	426	2817	166	16.97
		1894	1288.3	456	2548	207	12.30
		1895	1629	598	3400	213	15.96
		1896	1116.1	373	2719	150	18.12
Morley, F. (Notts.)	(2)	1878	1916.1	1017	2265	190	11.92
		1880	1712.1	872	2077	174	11.93
Muncer, B. L. (Glamorgan)	(1)	1948	1289.2	381	2748	159	17.28
Newman, J. A. (Hants.)	(3)	1910	1012.1	192	2879	156	18.45
		1921	1234.1	260	3817	177	21.56
		1926	1277	267	3904	154	24.70
Nichols, M. S. (Essex)	(2)	1935	972.3	196	2610	157	16.62
		1938	1228.1	264	3408	171	19.92
Paine, G. A. E. (Warwicks.)	(1)	1934	1285.5	463	2664	156	17.07
Parker, C. W. L. (Glos.)	(10)	1921	1178.5	381	2893	164	17.64
		1922	1294.5	445	2712	206	13.16
		1923	1420.2	520	3229	173	18.77
		1924	1303.5	411	2913	204	14.27
		1925	1512.3	478	3311	222	14.91
		1926	1739.5	556	3920	213	18.40
		1927	1727.4	540	3849	193	19.94
		1928	1474.2	470	3602	162	22.23
		1930	1016.3	301	2299	179	12.84
		1931	1320.4	386	3125	219	14.26
Parkin, C. H. (Lancs.)	(4)	1922	1309.3	348	3300	189	17.46
		1923	1356.2	356	3543	209	16.94
		1924	1162.5	357	2735	200	13.67
		1925	1075.1	281	2935	152	19.30
Peate, E. (Yorks.)	(2)	1881	1712	731	2195	173	12.68
		1882	1562.1	864	2466	214	11.52
Peel, R. (Yorks.)	(3)	1888	1648.1	830	2091	171	12.23
		1890	1552.4	714	2239	172	13.01
		1895	1691.1	714	2695	180	14.96
Pegler, S. J. (South Africans)	(1)	1912	1286.5	352	2885	189	15.26
Perks, R. T. D. (Worcs.)	(1)	1939	828	112	3057	159	19.22
Pritchard, T. L. (Warwicks.)	(1)	1948	1271.3	276	3225	172	18.75
Relf, A. E. (Sussex)	(2)	1908	1301.3	428	2648	151	17.53
		1910	1360.3	448	3108	158	19.67
Rhodes, W. (Yorks.)	(10)	1898	1240	482	2249	154	14.60
		1899	1518.4	543	3062	179	17.10
		1900	1553	455	3606	261	13.81
		1901	1565	505	3797	251	15.12
		1902	1306.3	405	2801	213	13.15
		1903	1378	425	2813	193	14.57
		1905	1241.3	310	3085	182	16.95
		1907	1067.1	231	2757	177	15.57
		1919	1048.3	305	2365	164	14.42
		1920	1028.4	291	2123	161	13.18
Richardson, T. (Surrey)	(7)	1893	993.4	288	2680	174	15.40
		1894	936.3	293	2024	196	10.32
		1895	1690.1	463	4170	290	14.37
		1896	1656.2	526	4015	246	16.32
		1897	1603.4	495	3945	273	14.48
		1898	1223.4	342	3147	161	19.54
		1901	1301.4	271	3697	159	23.25
Richmond, L. B. (Notts.)	(2)	1920	949.4	162	2981	150	19.87
		1922	862.2	209	2279	169	13.48
Robins, R. W. V. (Middx.)	(1)	1929	1154.4	159	3489	162	21.53
Robinson, E. P. (Yorks.)	(1)	1946	1138.2	354	2498	167	14.95
Root, C. F. (Worcs.)	(3)	1923	1263.3	353	3498	170	20.52
		1924	1007.3	281	2508	153	16.39
		1925	1493.2	416	3770	219	17.21

150 Wickets in a Season—*Cont.*

	Season	Overs	Mdns.	Runs	Wkts.	Avge.
Shackleton, D. (Hants.) .. .. .. (6)	1953	1219.4	328	3070	150	20.46
	1955	1220.2	438	2138	159	13.72
	1957	1217.3	446	2429	155	15.67
	1958	1320.2	505	2549	165	15.44
	1961	1501.5	532	3017	158	19.09
	1962	1717.1	678	3467	172	20.15
Shaw, A. (Notts.) .. .. (4)	1875	1755.1	1023	1495	160	9.34
	1876	2631.2	1528	2601	190	13.68
	1878	2465	1468	2044	189	10.81
	1880	1995	1251	1512	177	8.54
Shepherd, D. J. (Glamorgan) .. .. (1)	1956	1226.5	433	2719	177	15.36
Sims, J. M. (Middx.) .. .. .. (1)	1939	775.4	72	3228	159	20.30
Sinfield, R. A. (Glos.) .. .. .. (1)	1936	1501	461	3082	161	19.14
Smith, C. I. J. (Middx.) .. .. .. (1)	1934	1398	346	3248	172	18.88
Smith, H. A. (Leics.) .. .. .. (1)	1935	1103.2	230	2950	150	19.66
Smith, T. P. B. (Essex) .. .. .. (2)	1937	995.3	186	3039	155	19.60
	1947	1606	287	4667	172	27.13
Smith, W. C. (Surrey) .. .. .. (2)	1910	1423.3	420	3225	247	13.05
	1911	1283.4	368	3223	160	20.14
Southerton, J. (Surrey) .. .. .. (4)	1868	1096.2	238	2093	150	13.95
	1870	1876.1	709	3074	210	14.63
	1871	1633.1	643	2375	151	15.72
	1872	1570.1	629	2209	169	13.07
Spofforth, F. R. (Australians) .. .. (1)	1884	1577	653	2774	207	13.25
Steel, A. G. (Lancs.) .. .. .. (1)	1878	1223	447	1547	164	9.43
Tarrant, F. A. (Middx.) .. .. .. (2)	1907	1085.5	244	2874	183	15.70
	1908	1124.2	297	2819	169	16.68
Tate, F. W. (Sussex) .. .. .. (1)	1902	1183.2	359	2828	180	15.71
Tate, M. W. (Sussex) .. .. .. (6)	1923	1608.5	331	3061	219	13.97
	1924	1469.5	465	2818	205	13.74
	1925	1694.3	472	3415	228	14.97
	1928	1584.2	491	3184	165	19.29
	1929	1420.1	393	2903	156	18.60
	1932	1380.1	440	2494	160	15.58
Tattersall, R. (Lancs.) .. .. .. (2)	1950	1404.4	502	2623	193	13.59
	1953	1186	345	2974	164	18.13
Thompson, G. J. (Northants.) .. .. (1)	1909	905.5	228	2392	163	14.67
Titmus, F. J. (Middx.) .. .. .. (1)	1955	1449.5	522	3117	191	16.31
Tribe, G. E. (Northants.) .. .. .. (1)	1955	1289	342	3366	176	19.12
Trott, A. E. (Middx.) .. .. .. (3)	1899	1772.4	587	4086	239	17.09
	1900	1547.1	363	4923	211	23.33
	1901	1289.1	289	3835	176	21.78
Trueman, F. S. (Yorks.) .. .. .. (4)	1955	996.5	214	2454	153	16.03
	1960	1068.4	274	2447	175	13.98
	1961	1190.1	302	3000	155	19.35
	1962	1141.5	273	2717	153	17.75
Turner, C. T. B. (Australians) .. .. (2)	1888	2427.2	1127	3307	283	11.68
	1890	1501.1	655	2544	179	14.21
Tyldesley, R. (Lancs.) .. .. .. (2)	1924	1075.3	346	2574	184	13.98
	1929	1114.3	350	2399	154	15.57
Underwood, D. L. (Kent) .. .. (1)	1966	1104.5	475	2167	157	13.80
Verity, H. (Yorks.) .. .. .. (9)	1931	1137.3	356	2542	188	13.52
	1932	1117.5	401	2250	162	13.88
	1933	1195.4	428	2553	190	13.43
	1934	1282.1	500	2645	150	17.63
	1935	1297.2	453	3032	221	14.36
	1936	1289.3	463	2847	216	13.81
	1937	1386.2	487	3168	202	15.68
	1938	1191.4	424	2476	158	15.67
	1939	936.3	270	2509	191	13.13
Wainwright, E. (Yorks.) .. .. .. (1)	1894	1087.3	413	2114	166	12.73
Walsh, J. E. (Leics.) .. .. .. (2)	1947	1032.1	135	3477	152	22.87
	1948	1175.3	193	3405	174	19.56
Wardle, J. H. (Yorks.) .. .. .. (6)	1948	1283.4	483	2923	150	19.48
	1950	1627.1	741	2909	174	16.71
	1952	1857	810	3460	177	19.54

150 Wickets in a Season—*Cont.*

		Season	Overs	Mdns.	Runs	Wkts.	ge
Wardle, J. H. (*cont.*)		1954	1262	520	2449	155	15.80
		1955	1486.4	572	3149	195	16.14
		1956	1230.2	464	2482	153	16.22
Wass, T. G. (Notts.)	(1)	1907	885	218	2328	163	14.28
Wellard, A. W. (Somerset)	(2)	1937	1276.1	220	3675	156	23.55
		1938	1233.4	241	3491	172	20.29
White, J. C. (Somerset)	(1)	1929	1556.1	631	2648	168	15.76
Wilkinson, L. L. (Lancs.)	(1)	1938	1251.2	240	3531	151	23.38
Woods, S, M. J. (Somerset)	(1)	1892	1055.4	319	2576	153	16.83
Woolley, F. E. (Kent)	(3)	1920	1135.4	315	2633	185	14.23
		1921	1163.1	367	2697	167	16.14
		1922	1233.1	370	2995	163	18.37
Wright, D. V. P. (Kent)	(2)	1947	1175.5	252	3739	177	21.12
		1950	929.3	187	3140	151	20.79
Young, J. A. (Middx.)	(4)	1947	1291.1	416	2765	159	17.38
		1949	1453.3	526	2948	150	19.65
		1951	1680.2	741	2976	157	18.95
		1952	1448.1	511	3241	163	19.88

OVERSEAS BOWLERS

HIGHEST WICKET AGGREGATES IN A SEASON

60 *WICKETS IN AUSTRALIA*	Season	Overs	Mdns.	Runs	Wkts.	Avge.
C. T. B. Turner (N.S.W.)	1887-88	1066.3	473	1441	106	13.59
G. Giffen (South Australia)	1894-95	808.5	195	2097	93	22.54
C. V. Grimmett (South Australia)	1929-30	471.7	52	1943	82	23.69
R. Benaud (N.S.W.)	1958-59	559.5	146	1579	82	19.25
A. A. Mailey (N.S.W.)	1920-21	2986*	45	1825	81	22.53
M. W. Tate (M.C.C.)	1924-25	502.2	93	1464	77	19.01
C. V. Grimmett (South Australia)	1931-32	588.4	166	1535	77	19.93
E. Jones (South Australia)	1897-98	575.1	121	1653	76	21.75
C. V. Grimmett (South Australia)	1930-31	449.9	99	1417	74	19.14
C. V. Grimmett (South Australia)	1939-40	442.7	57	1654	73	22.65
C. V. Grimmett (South Australia)	1928-29	5252*	134	2432	71	34.25
C. T. B. Turner (N.S.W.)	1886-87	536.1	273	538	70	7.68
W. J. Whitty (South Australia)	1910-11	493.3	99	1419	70	20.27
H. J. Tayfield (South Africans)	1952-53	608.4	123	1954	70	27.91
T. Richardson (Stoddart's XI)	1894-95	592.2	148	1616	69	23.42
H. Ironmonger (Victoria)	1930-31	379.5	112	972	68	14.29
J. N. Crawford (M.C.C.)	1907-08	566	115	1663	66	25.19
J. V. Saunders (Victoria)	1907-08	555.4	113	1587	66	24.04
C. V. Grimmett (South Australia)	1933-34	420.5	68	1441	66	21.83
W. Rhodes (M.C.C.)	1903-04	423.3	112	1055	65	16.23
J. C. White (M.C.C.)	1928-29	5213*	223	1471	65	22.63
L. O. Fleetwood-Smith (Victoria)	1937-38	395.1	29	1436	64	22.43
W. J. O'Reilly (N.S.W.)	1937-38	310.7	91	784	64	12.25
G. A. Lohmann (Shrewsbury's XI)	1887-88	659.1	354	755	63	11.98
H. Ironmonger (Victoria)	1931-32	491.5	178	1168	63	18.53
F. R. Foster (M.C.C.)	1911-12	485.1	110	1252	62	20.19
W. J. O'Reilly (N.S.W.)	1932-33	642.5	237	1237	62	19.95
L. C. Braund (MacLaren's XI)	1901-02	623.5	147	1779	61	29.16
V. M. Mankad (Indians)	1947-48	494.3	76	1595	61	26.14

(**Number of balls bowled* as both six and eight ball overs were bowled)

50 *WICKETS IN SOUTH AFRICA*	Season	Overs	Mdns.	Runs	Wkts.	Avge.
R. Benaud (Australians)	1957-58	743.6	185	2056	106	19.39
S. F. Barnes (M.C.C.)	1913-14	460.2	129	1117	104	10.74
W. J. O'Reilly (Australians)	1935-36	662.5	250	1289	95	13.56
C. V. Grimmett (Australians)	1935-36	663.1	229	1362	92	14.80
J. H. Wardle (M.C.C.)	1956-57	380.3	94	1103	90	12.25
J. C. Alabaster (New Zealanders)	1961-62	749	180	2219	86	25.80

Overseas Bowlers-South Africa—*Cont.*

	Season	*Overs*	*Mdns.*	*Runs*	*Wkts.*	*Avge.*
R. C. Motz (New Zealanders)	1961-62	579.4	155	1439	81	17.77
I. W. Johnson (Australians)	1949-50	414.6	77	1276	77	16.57
A. K. Davidson (Australians)	1957-58	430.5	101	1090	72	15.13
R. O. Jenkins (M.C.C.)	1948-49	406.7	64	1508	71	21.23
I. A. R. Peebles (M.C.C.)	1930-31	444.4	80	1274	66	19.30
A. S. Kennedy (Tennyson's XI)	1924.25	480.2	121	1287	65	19.80
J. T. Partridge (Rhodesia)	1962-63	472.5	165	1068	64	16.68
J. T. Botten (N-E. Transvaal)	1958-59	261.3	68	667	63	10.58
F. J. Cameron (New Zealanders)	1961-62	633.2	203	1412	62	22.77
A. S. Kennedy (M.C.C.)	1922-23	478.5	168	1024	61	16.78
G. Geary (Tennyson's XI)	1924-25	408	104	955	59	16.18
A. E. E. Vogler (Transvaal)	1909-10	317.3	50	1109	58	19.12
P. G. H. Fender (M.C.C.)	1922-23	380.1	81	1136	58	19.58
C. Blythe (M.C.C.)	1905-06	481.2	167	1046	57	18.35
W. A. Johnston (Australians)	1949-50	335.2	77	770	56	13.75
G. A. R. Lock (M.C.C.)	1956-57	352.7	120	833	56	14.87
H. J. Tayfield (Natal)	1956-57	450.1	153	1036	56	18.50
A. E. E. Volger (Eastern Province) ..	1906-07	190.1	40	580	55	10.54
J. J. Kotze (Western Province)	1906-07	196.1	38	585	54	10.83
H. J. Tayfield (Natal)	1953-54	401.7	160	850	54	15.74
L. F. Kline (Australians)	1957-58	423	122	1103	54	20.42
C. Blythe (M.C.C.)	1909-10	404.1	129	820	53	15.47
J. E. Waddington (Griqualand West) ..	1952-53	303.6	59	893	53	16.84
A. E. Hall (Transvaal)	1926.27	277.4	60	650	52	12.50
P. N. F. Mansell (Rhodesia)	1951-52	295.5	49	917	52	17.63
D. V. P. Wright (M.C.C.)	1938-39	343.4	35	1453	51	28.49
D. V. P. Wright (M.C.C.)	1948-49	378.1	53	1544	51	30.27
C. L. McCool (Australians)	1949-50	314.2	56	976	51	19.13
J. R. Reid (New Zealanders)	1953-54	350.4	89	986	51	19.33
F. J. Titmus (M.C.C.)	1964-65	593.1	188	1240	51	24.31
A. P. Freeman (M.C.C.)	1927-28	325.3	73	965	50	19.30
R. R. Lindwall (Australians)	1949-50	292.4	53	729	50	14.58
H. J. Tayfield (Natal)	1951-52	387.2	121	889	50	17.78
V. I. Smith (Natal)	1952-53	335.5	63	892	50	17.84
A. R. MacGibbon (New Zealanders) ..	1953-54	343.6	70	983	50	19.66
J. C. Laker (M.C.C.)	1956-57	388.7	121	875	50	17.50

35 *WICKETS IN WEST INDIES*

	Season	Overs	Mdns.	Runs	Wkts.	Avge.
E. M. Dowson (Bennett's XI)	1901-02	404.5	121	997	80	12.46
G. J. Thompson (Brackley's XI)	1904-05	353.5	81	1048	75	13.97
E. R. Wilson (Bennett's XI)	1901-02	414.1	144	767	67	11.44
J. W. Hearne (M.C.C.)	1910-11	398.4	62	1450	67	21.64
C. E. Goodman (Barbados)	1896-97	304.2	71	676	57	11.85
H. R. Bromley-Davenport (Lucas's XI) ..	1894-95	317.2	95	561	56	10.01
B. J. T. Bosanquet (Bennett's XI)	1901-02	338.3	92	906	55	16.47
A. E. Stoddart (Priestley's XI)	1896-97	303.4	128	520	53	9.81
F. W. Bush (Lucas's XI)	1894-95	284.4	90	610	51	11.96
S. P. Gupte (Indians)	1952-53	510	147	1182	50	23.64
P. I. Philpott (Australians)	1964-65	447.1	99	1207	49	24.63
S. G. Smith (Trinidad)	1901-02	220.5	36	568	48	11.83
S. G. Smith (M.C.C.)	1910-11	300.2	57	845	47	17.97
A. Cumberbatch (Trinidad)	1896-97	223.3	74	529	45	11.75
W. Voce (M.C.C.)	1929-30	387.2	68	1188	44	27.00
W. Williams (Priestley's XI)	1896-97	202.3	55	464	43	10.79
C. R. Browne (Barbados)	1910-11	220.2	51	555	41	13.53
E. Humphreys (M.C.C.)	1912-13	249.1	57	660	40	16.73
G. A. E. Paine (M.C.C.)	1934-35	369	103	957	40	23.92
L. R. Gibbs (British Guiana)	1961-62	438.1	132	937	40	23.42
W. Rhodes (M.C.C.)	1929-30	501.1	172	947	39	24.28
A. L. Valentine (Jamacia)	1952-53	580.5	220	1202	38	31.63
W. E. Astill (M.C.C.)	1929-30	494.1	131	1171	37	31.64
F. S. Trueman (M.C.C.)	1959-60	342.3	86	883	37	23.86
J. Woods (Trinidad)	1896-97	173	53	349	36	9.69
J. C. Laker (M.C.C.)	1947-48	388.5	116	971	36	26.97
S. M. J. Woods (Priestley's XI)	1896-97	226.2	75	501	35	14.31

Overseas Bowlers—*Cont.*

45 *WICKETS IN NEW ZEALAND*

	Season	Overs	Mdns.	Runs	Wkts.	Avge.
G. J. Thompson (Hawke's XI)	1902-03	297	104	668	57	11.71
S. T. Callaway (Canterbury)	1903-04	224.5	73	474	54	8.77
R. W. Blair (Wellington)	1956-57	325.1	105	784	53	14.79
W. W. Armstrong (Australians)	1913-14	307.4	81	789	52	15.17
S. Austin (New South Wales)	1893-94	1751†	86	612	52	11.76
J. W. H. T. Douglas (M.C.C.)	1906-07	239.3	51	663	50	13.26
J. V. Saunders (Wellington)	1913-14	267	65	893	49	18.22
R. W. Blair (Wellington)	1957-58	302.2	103	606	49	12.36
J. C. Alabaster (Otago)	1960-61	426.3	127	961	49	19.61
R. W. Blair (Wellington)	1963-64	408.1	135	856	49	17.46
J. A. Hayes (Auckland)	1957-58	244.3	49	568	48	11.83
W. Lankham (Auckland)	1882-83	257.2	128	294	48	6.12
B. W. Yuile (Central Districts)	1966-67	462.4	212	802	48	16.70
W. Robertson (Canterbury)	1893-94	261.2	66	570	47	12.12
P. M. Hornibrook (Australians)	1920-21	170	33	573	47	12.19
C. V. Grimmett (Australians)	1927-28	319.4	65	795	47	16.91
R. W. Blair (Central Districts)	1955-56	280.5	54	882	47	18.76
J. C. Alabaster (Otago)	1959-60	313	78	824	47	17.53
K. W. Hough (Auckland)	1958-59	414.3	151	701	46	15.23
B. W. Yuile (Central Districts)	1964-65	505.3	264	787	46	17.10
F. J. Cameron (Otago)	1964-65	405	129	940	46	20.43
P. R. May (M.C.C.)	1906-07	248.4	47	719	45	15.97
H. Ironmonger (Australians)	1920-21	198.3	40	593	45	13.17
R. W. Barber (M.C.C.)	1960-61	381.3	91	1070	45	23.77

† 1751 balls bowled (85.3 five ball overs, 220.3 six-ball overs)

60 *WICKETS IN INDIA, PAKISTAN AND CEYLON*

	Season	Overs	Mdns.	Runs	Wkts.	Avge.
M. W. Tate (M.C.C.)	1926-27	727.1	211	1599	116	13.78
G. E. Tribe (Commonwealth)	1949-50	787.2	215	1805	99	18.23
B. S. Chandrasekhar	1966-67	610.3	148	1682	89	18.89
W. W. Hall (West Indians)..	1958-59	519.2	167	1312	87	15.08
R. K. Oxenham (Australians)	1935-36	323.3	149	586	86	6.81
G. Geary (M.C.C.)	1926-27	528.1	148	1162	81	14.34
G. A. R. Lock (M.C.C.)	1955-56	577	296	869	81	10.79
S. Ramadhin (Commonwealth)	1950-51	754.3	261	1553	79	19.65
H. Verity (M.C.C.)	1933-34	482.2	179	1180	78	15.12
G. E. Tribe (Commonwealth)	1950-51	592	127	1619	67	21.30
B. P. Gupte	1962-63	452.5	76	1459	76	19.19
W. E. Astill (M.C.C.)	1926-27	567.4	151	1556	71	21.91
L. Amar Singh	1937-38	473.2	120	1019	71	14.35
G. E. Gomez (West Indians)	1948-49	729	238	1328	71	18.70
R. Gilchrist (West Indians)	1958-59	386.5	117	964	71	13.57
S. P. Gupte	1954-55	571.2	201	1095	69	15.86
R. G. Nadkarni	1963-64	824.3	450	1095	68	16.10
C. S. Nayudu	1944-45	568.2	92	1708	65	26.27
R. B. Desai	1958-59	325	87	940	63	14.92
B. S. Chandrasekhar	1963-64	478	133	1131	63	17.95
M. Nissar	1935-36	333.2	76	846	62	13.64
S. Venkataraghavan..	1964-65	557.2	197	989	62	15.95
E. A. S. Prasanna	1966-67	505.4	119	1420	61	23.27
B. Dooland (Commonwealth)	1950-51	545.4	131	1480	60	24.66
V. M. Mankad	1950-51	633	166	1539	60	25.65
B. P. Gupte	1963-64	585.5	144	1722	60	28.70

OUTSTANDING BOWLING AVERAGES

Before 1900, it was quite usual for bowlers to take a hundred wickets at a cost of less than thirteen runs each but, since the turn of the century, this feat has become comparatively rare. Accordingly, the following list includes all instances of 100 wickets for an average of less than 13 this century, together with those of 100 wickets for less than 11 runs apiece before 1900.

BEFORE 1900

	Seasons	*Overs*	*Mdns.*	*Runs*	*Wkts.*	*Avge.*
A. Shaw (Notts.)	1880	1995	1251	1512	177	8.54
A. Shaw (Notts.)	1875	1755.1	1023	1495	160	9.34
A. G. Steel (Lancs.)	1878	1223	447	1547	164	9.43
A. Shaw (Notts.)	1879	1501	870	1232	129	9.55
E. Willsher (Kent)	1868	979.2	529	1128	113	9.98
T. Richardson (Surrey)	1894	936.3	293	2024	196	10.32
J. Briggs (Lancs)	1888	1450.2	763	1679	160	10.49
A. Shaw (Notts.)	1878	2465	1486	2044	189	10.81
G. A. Lohmann (Surrey)	1888	1649.1	783	2280	209	10.90

SINCE 1900

	Seasons	*Overs*	*Mdns.*	*Runs*	*Wkts.*	*Avge.*
H. L. Jackson (Derby)	1958	829	295	1572	143	10.99
H. J. Rhodes (Derby)	1965	646.5	187	1314	119	11.04
W. Rhodes (Yorks.)	1923	929	345	1547	134	11.54
A. Booth (Yorks.)	1946	917.2	423	1289	111	11.61
R. O. Schwarz (South Africans)	1907	711.3	153	1616	137	11.79
G. A. R. Lock (Surrey)	1957	1194.1	449	2550	212	12.02
H. Larwood (Notts.)	1931	651.3	142	1553	129	12.03
G. A. R. Lock (Surrey)	1958	1014.4	382	2055	170	12.08
W. Rhodes (Yorks.)	1922	814.1	312	1451	119	12.19
C. Blythe (Kent)	1912	919.3	241	2183	178	12.26
J. B. Statham (Lancs.)	1958	894.2	275	1648	134	12.29
J. B. Statham (Lancs.)	1960	844.1	274	1662	135	12.31
S. Haigh (Yorks.)	1912	813.4	245	1541	125	12.32
D. L. Underwood (Kent)	1967	979.1	459	1686	136	12.39
A. B. Jackson (Derby)	1965	807.5	262	1491	120	12.42
G. A. R. Lock (Surrey)	1956	1058.2	437	1932	155	12.46
J. B. Statham (Lancs.)	1965	771	205	1716	137	12.52
S. Haigh (Yorks.)	1902	799	219	1984	158	12.55
A. W. Hallam (Notts.)	1907	937.1	302	2133	168	12.69
S. G. Smith (Northants.)	1912	559	165	1269	100	12.69
J. T. Hearne (Middx.)	1910	752	253	1523	119	12.79
S. Haigh (Yorks.)	1907	591.3	146	1308	102	12.82
C. C. Griffith (West Indians)	1963	701.2	192	1527	119	12.83
C. W. L. Parker (Glos.)	1930	1016.3	301	2299	179	12.84
H. Larwood (Notts.)	1932	866.4	203	2084	162	12.86
R. Kilner (Yorks.)	1923	1259.5	507	2040	158	12.91
H. Larwood (Notts.)	1936	679.1	165	1544	119	12.97

LEADING HOME BOWLERS OF THE ENGLISH SEASON

(*Qualification:* 100 *wickets—lowest average*)

Season		*Overs*	*Mdns.*	*Runs*	*Wkts.*	*Avge.*
1894	T. Richardson (Surrey)	936.3	293	2024	196	10.32
1895	C. L. Townsend (Glos.)	746.1	178	1827	131	13.94
1896	J. T. Hearne (Middx.)	2003.1	818	3670	257	14.28
1897	T. Richardson (Surrey)	1603.4	495	3945	273	14.45
1898	J. T. Hearne (Middx.)	1802.2	781	3120	222	14.05
1899	A. E. Trott (Middx.)	1772.4	587	4086	239	17.09
1900	W. Rhodes (Yorks.)	1553	455	3606	261	13.81
1901	W. Rhodes (Yorks.)	1565	505	3797	251	15.12
1902	S. Haigh (Yorks.)	799	219	1984	158	12.55
1903	W. Mead (Essex)	971.3	355	1791	131	13.67
1904	J. T. Hearne (Middx.)	1153.3	330	2732	145	18.84
1905	S. Haigh (Yorks.)	831.5	220	1983	120	15.37

Leading Home Bowlers of the English Season—*Cont.*

Season		*Overs*	*Mdns.*	*Runs*	*Wkts.*	*Avge.*
1906	S. Haigh (Yorks.)	971.3	209	2540	174	14.59
1907	A. W. Hallam (Notts.)	937.1	302	2133	168	12.69
1908	S. Haigh (Yorks.)	623.2	176	1380	103	13.39
1909	S. Haigh (Yorks.)	844.2	205	1702	122	13.95
1910	J. T. Hearne (Middx.)	752	253	1523	119	12.79
1911	G. J. Thompson (Northants.)	735.5	199	1899	113	16.71
1912	C. Blythe (Kent)	919.3	241	2183	178	12.26
1913	C. Blythe (Kent)	1120.2	289	2729	167	16.34
1914	C. Blythe (Kent)	1008.4	280	2583	170	15.19
1919	W. Rhodes (Yorks.)	1048.3	305	2365	164	14.42
1920	W. Rhodes (Yorks.)	1028.4	291	2123	161	13.18
1921	W. Rhodes (Yorks.)	963	316	1872	141	13.27
1922	W. Rhodes (Yorks.)	814.1	312	1451	119	12.19
1923	W. Rhodes (Yorks.)	929	345	1547	134	11.54
1924	G. G. Macaulay (Yorks.)	1220.4	343	2514	190	13.23
1925	C. W. L. Parker (Glos.)	1512.3	478	3311	222	14.91
1926	W. Rhodes (Yorks.)	892.4	315	1709	115	14.86
1927	H. Larwood (Notts.)	629.2	147	1695	100	16.95
1928	H. Larwood (Notts.)	834.5	204	2003	138	14.51
1929	R. Tyldesley (Lancs.)	1114.3	350	2399	154	15.57
1930	C. W. L. Parker (Glos.)	1016.3	301	2299	179	12.84
1931	H. Larwood (Notts.)	651.3	142	1553	129	12.03
1932	H. Larwood (Notts.)	866.4	203	2084	162	12.86
1933	H. Verity (Yorks.)	1195.4	428	2553	190	13.43
1934	G. A. E. Paine (Warwicks.)	1285.5	463	2664	156	17.07
1935	H. Verity (Yorks.)	1279.2	453	3032	211	14.36
1936	H. Larwood (Notts.)	679.1	165	1544	119	12.97
1937	H. Verity (Yorks.)	1386.2	487	3168	202	15.68
1938	W. E. Bowes (Yorks.)	932.3	294	1844	121	15.23
1939	H. Verity (Yorks.)	936.3	270	2509	191	13.13
1946	A. Booth (Yorks.)	917.2	423	1289	111	11.61
1947	T. W. Goddard (Glos.)	1451.2	344	4119	238	17.30
1948	C. Gladwin (Derby)	954.5	266	2174	128	16.98
1949	T. W. Goddard (Glos.)	1187.2	326	3069	160	19.18
1950	R. Tattersall (Lancs.)	1404.4	502	2623	193	13.59
1951	R. Appleyard (Yorks.)	1323.1	391	2829	200	14.14
1952	A. V. Bedser (Surrey)	1184.4	296	2530	154	16.42
1953	H. L. Jackson (Derby)	741.4	229	1574	103	15.28
1954	R. Appleyard (Yorks.)	1026.3	315	2221	154	14.42
1955	D. Shackleton (Hants.)	1220.2	438	2183	159	13.72
1956	G. A. R. Lock (Surrey)	1058.2	437	1932	155	12.46
1957	G. A. R. Lock (Surrey)	1194.1	449	2550	212	12.02
1958	H. L. Jackson (Derby)	829	295	1572	143	10.99
1959	J. B. Statham (Lancs.)	977.4	267	2087	139	15.01
1960	J. B. Statham (Lancs.)	844.1	274	1662	135	12.31
1961	J. A. Flavell (Worcs.)	1245.2	300	3043	171	17.79
1962	D. A. D. Sydenham (Surrey)	989.2	295	2030	115	17.65
1963	F. S. Trueman (Yorks.)	844.3	206	1955	129	15.15
1964	T. W. Cartwright (Warwicks.)	1146.2	502	2141	134	15.97
1965	H. J. Rhodes (Derby)	646.5	187	1314	119	11.04
1966	D. L. Underwood (Kent)	1104.5	475	2167	157	13.80
1967	D. L. Underwood (Kent.)	979.1	495	1686	136	12.39

The following touring bowlers achieved a better average than the leading English bowler of that season:

		Overs	*Mdns.*	*Runs*	*Wkts.*	*Avge*
1896	T. R. McKibbin (Australians)	647.1	198	1441	101	14.26
1907	R. O. Schwarz (South Africans)	711.3	153	1616	137	11.79
1934	W. J. O'Reilly (Australians)	870	320	1858	109	17.04
1948	W. A. Johnston (Australians)	850.1	279	1675	102	16.42
1963	C. C. Griffith (West Indians)	701.2	192	1527	119	12.83

MOST BALLS BOWLED BY A BOWLER IN A SEASON

	Balls	Season	Overs	Mdns.	Runs	Wkts.	Avge.
A. P. Freeman (Kent)	12234	1933	2039	651	4549	298	15.26
A. P. Freeman (Kent)	11857	1928	1976.1	423	5489	304	18.05
A. P. Freeman (Kent)	11487	1930	1914.3	472	4632	275	16.84
J. H. Wardle (Yorks.)	11142	1952	1857	810	3460	177	19.54
A. Shaw (Notts.)	10526	1876	2631.2	1528	2601	190	13.68
A. P. Freeman (Kent)	10468	1934	1744.4	440	4753	205	23.18
C. W. L. Parker (Glos.)	10439	1926	1739.5	556	3920	213	18.40
C. W. L. Parker (Glos.)	10366	1927	1727.4	540	3849	193	19.94
D. Shackleton (Hants.)	10303	1962	1717.1	678	3467	172	20.15
M. W. Tate (Sussex)	10167	1925	1694.3	472	3415	228	14.97
J. A. Young (Middx.)	10082	1951	1680.2	741	2976	157	18.95
A. P. Freeman (Kent)	10025	1929	1670.5	381	4879	267	18.27
J. T. Hearne (Middx.)	10016	1896	2003.1	818	3670	257	14.28

MOST RUNS OFF A BOWLER IN A SEASON

	Season	Overs	Mdns.	Runs	Wkts.	Avge.
A. P. Freeman (Kent)	1928	1976.1	423	5489	304	18.50
A. E. Trott (Middx.)	1900	1547.1	363	4923	211	23.33
A. P. Freeman (Kent)	1929	1670.5	381	4879	267	18.27
A. P. Freeman (Kent)	1934	1744.4	440	4753	205	23.18
T. P. B. Smith (Essex)	1947	1606	287	4667	172	27.13
R. Smith (Essex)	1947	1557	324	4658	125	37.26
A. P. Freeman (Kent)	1930	1914.3	472	4632	275	16.84
A. P. Freeman (Kent)	1935	1503.2	320	4562	212	21.51
A. P. Freeman (Kent)	1933	2039	651	4549	298	15.26
A. P. Freeman (Kent)	1931	1618	360	4307	276	15.60
T. Richardson (Surrey)	1895	1690.1	463	4170	290	14.37
T. W. Goddard (Glos.)	1937	1478.1	359	4158	248	16.76
A. P. Freeman (Kent)	1932	1565.5	404	4149	253	16.39
T. W. Goddard (Glos.)	1947	1451.2	344	4119	238	17.30
A. E. Trott (Middx.)	1899	1772.4	587	4086	239	17.09
T. W. Goddard (Glos.)	1935	1553	384	4073	200	20.36
T. Richardson (Surrey)	1896	1656.2	526	4015	246	16.79
A. S. Kennedy (Hants.)	1921	1427	316	4009	186	21.55

THE MOST EXPENSIVE 100 WICKETS IN A SEASON

	Seasons	Overs	Mdns.	Runs	Wkts.	Avge.
R. Smith (Essex)	1947	1557	324	4658	125	37.26
R. Smith (Essex)	1950	1267	298	3547	102	34.77
O. W. Herman (Hants.)	1938	1098	198	3263	101	32.30
C. W. L. Parker (Glos.)	1934	1417.2	344	3724	117	31.82
R. Smith (Essex)	1949	1185.5	252	3290	104	31.62
L. C. Braund (Somerset)	1901	988.3	161	3675	120	30.62
J. K. Nye (Sussex)	1939	769.1	56	3367	110	30.60
R. Smith (Essex)	1948	1241	316	3157	104	30.35
J. A. Newman (Hants.)	1928	1118	199	3394	112	30.30
D. W. White (Hants.)	1964	1011	185	3149	104	30.27
K. Higgs (Lancs.)	1961	1098.1	237	3080	102	30.19

FOUR WICKETS WITH CONSECUTIVE BALLS

J. Wells	Kent v. Sussex (Brighton)	1862
G. Ulyett	Lord Harris' XI v. N.S.W. (Sydney)	1878-79
J. B. Hide	Sussex v. M.C.C. (Lord's)	1890
F. Shacklock	Notts. v. Somerset (Nottingham)	1893
A. D. Downes	Otago v. Auckland (Dunedin)	1893-94
F. Martin	M.C.C. v. Derby (Lord's)	1895
A. Mold	Lancs. v. Notts. (Nottingham)	1895

Four Wickets with Consecutive Balls—*Cont.*

W. Brearley	Lancs. v. Somerset (Manchester)	(*a*) 1905
S. Haigh	M.C.C. v. Army XI (Pretoria)	1905-06
A. E. Trott	Middx. v. Somerset (Lord's)	(*b*) 1907
F. A. Tarrant	Middx. v. Glos. (Bristol)	1907
A. Drake	Yorks. v. Derby (Chesterfield)	1914
S. G. Smith	Northants v. Warwicks. (Birmingham)	1914
H. A. Peach	Surrey v. Sussex (Oval)	1924
A. F. Borland	Natal v. Griqualand West (Kimberley)	1926-27
J. E. H. Hooker	N.S.W. v. Victoria (Sydney)	(*a*) 1928-29
R. Tyldesley	Lancs. v. Derby (Derby)	(*a*) 1929
R. J. Crisp	Western Province v. Griqualand West (Johannesburg)	1931-32
R. J. Crisp	Western Province v. Natal (Durban)	1933-34
A. R. Gover	Surrey v. Worcs. (Worcester)	1935
W. H. Copson	Derby v. Warwicks. (Derby) (*Last 4 balls of innings*)	1937
W. A. Henderson	N-E. Transvaal v. O.F.S. (Bloemfontein)	1937-38
F. Ridgway	Kent v. Derby (Folkestone)	1951
A. K. Walker	Notts. v. Leics. (Leicester)	(*c*) 1956
S. N. Mohol	Combined XI v. President's XI (Poona)	1965-66

(*a*) Not all in the same innings.
(*b*) Hat-trick performed in same innings—Trott's benefit match.
(*c*) Wicket with last ball of first innings and hat-trick with first three balls in second innings.

HAT TRICKS

IN BOTH INNINGS OF A MATCH

A. Shaw	Notts. v. Glos. (Nottingham)	1884
T. J. Matthews	Australia v. South Africa (Manchester)	1912
C. W. L. Parker	Glos. v. Middx. (Bristol)	1924
R. O. Jenkins	Worcs. v. Surrey (Worcester)	1949

UNUSUAL SIMILARITIES OF DISMISSAL

All stumped W. H. Brain	C. L. Townsend: Glos. v. Somerset (Cheltenham)	1893
All caught G. J. Thompson	S. G. Smith: Northants v. Warwicks. (Birmingham)	1914
(*Smith then took another wicket to perform the four in four balls feat.*)		
All l.b.w.	H. Fisher: Yorks. v. Somerset (Sheffield)	1932
	J. A. Flavell: Worcs. v. Lancs. (Manchester)	1963
All caught wicket G. Dawkes	H. L. Jackson: Derby v. Worcs. (Kidderminster)	1958

MOST HAT-TRICKS IN A CAREER

7—D. V. P. Wright.
6—T. W. Goddard, C. W. L. Parker
5—S. Haigh, V. W. C. Jupp, A. E. G. Rhodes, F. A. Tarrant.
4—J. T. Hearne, J. C. Laker, G. A. R. Lock, G.G. Macaulay, T.J. Mathews, T. Richardson, F. S. Trueman.

BOWLERS WHO HAVE DONE THE HAT-TRICK

Abdul Wahab	(1)	Punjab v. N.W.F.P. (Peshawar)	1954-55
A'Court, D. G.	(1)	Glos. v. Derby (Gloucester)	1961
Alabaster, G. D.	(1)	Northern Districts v. Canterbury (Hamilton)	1962-63
Allom, M. J. C.	(1)	England v. New Zealand (Christchurch)	1929-30
Amjad Hussain	(1)	Lahore B v. Bahawalpur (Bahawalpur)	1962-63
Anderson, I. D. E.	(1)	Natal v. Griqualand West (Durban)	1934-35
Andrews, W. H. R.	(1)	Somerset v. Surrey (Oval)	1937
Appleyard, R.	(1)	Yorks. v. Glos. (Sheffield)	1956
Armstrong, W. W.	(1)	Victoria v. N.S.W. (Melbourne)	1902-03
Arnott, T.	(1)	Glamorgan v. Somerset (Cardiff)	1926
Arshad Khan	(1)	Dacca U. v. East Pakistan B. (Dacca)	1957-58
Bailey, T. E.	(1)	Essex v. Glamorgan (Newport)	1950
Baird, H. H. C.	(1)	Navy & Army v. Oxford & Cambridge Us. (Aldershot)	1910
Banerjee, S.	(1)	East Zone v. West Zone (Bombay)	1948-49
Banerjee, Shute N.	(1)	Bihar v. Delhi (Jamshedpur)	1948-49
Bannister, J. D.	(1)	Warwicks. v. Yorks. (Sheffield)	1955

Hat Tricks—*Cont.*

Bowler	No.	Match	Season
Baqa Jilani, M.	(1)	Northern India v. Southern Punjab (Amritsar)	1934-35
Barber, R. W.	(1)	Warwicks. v. Glamorgan (Birmingham)	1963
Barclay, F.	(1)	Auckland v. Canterbury (Auckland)	1903-04
Barlow, R. G.	(3)	Lancs. v. Derby (Derby)	1881
		Players v. Gentlemen (Oval)	1884
		Lancs. v. Notts. (Manchester)	1886
Barnes, S. F.	(1)	England v. Rest (Oval)	1912
Barratt, E.	(1)	North v. South (Prince's)	1872
Bartlett, G. A.	(1)	Central Districts v. Northern Districts (Hamilton)	1959-60
Bates, W.	(1)	England v. Australia (Melbourne)	1882-83
Beaumont, J.	(1)	South v. North (Hastings)	1889
Bedser, A. V.	(1)	Surrey v. Essex (Oval)	1953
Beesley, R.	(1)	Border v. Griqualand West (Queenstown)	1946-47
Benskin, W. E.	(2)	Leics. v. Essex (Southend)	1906
		Scotland v. Oxford U. (Oxford)	1913
Bennett, J. H.	(1)	Canterbury v. Wellington (Wellington)	1911-12
Bettington, R. H. B.	(1)	Oxford U. v. Essex (Oxford)	1920
Best, W. F.	(1)	Kent v. Somerset (Taunton)	1891
Birkenshaw, J.	(1)	Leics. v. Worcs. (Worcester)	1967
Blackman, W.	(1)	Sussex v. Surrey (Hove)	1881
Blair, R. W.	(1)	Wellington v. Northern Districts (Wellington)	1962-63
Blythe, C.	(2)	Kent v. Surrey (Blackheath)	1910
		Kent v. Derby (Gravesend)	1910
Booth, M. W.	(2)	Yorks. v. Worcs. (Bradford)	1911
		Yorks. v. Essex (Leyton)	1912
Borland, A. F.	(2)	Natal v. Griqualand West (Kimberley) (4 in 4)	1926-27
		Natal v. Transvaal (Johannesburg)	1931-32
Bosanquet, B. J. T.	(1)	Bennett's XI v. Barbados (Bridgetown)	1901-02
Bowes, W. E.	(1)	M.C.C. v. Cambridge U. (Lord's)	1928
Boyes, G. S.	(2)	Hants. v. Surrey (Portsmouth)	1925
		Hants. v. Warwicks. (Birmingham)	1926
Bradley, W. M.	(3)	Kent v. Essex (Leyton)	1899
		Kent v. Yorks. (Tonbridge)	1899
		Kent v. Somerset (Blackheath)	1900
Braund, L. C.	(1)	Somerset v. Worcs. (Worcester)	1906
Brearley, W.	(1)	Lancs. v. Somerset (Manchester) (4 in 4)	1905
Bridges, J. J.	(1)	Somerset v. Derby (Burton upon Trent)	1924
Briggs, J.	(2)	North v. South (Scarborough)	1891
		England v. Australia (Sydney)	1891-92
Brockwell, W.	(1)	Surrey v. Yorks. (Sheffield)	1900
Bromley-Davenport, H. R.	(1)	Lucas's XI v. British Guaina (Georgetown)	1894-95
Brown, J. T.	(1)	Yorks. v. Derby (Derby)	1896
Browne, C. R.	(1)	British Guiana v. Barbados (Georgetown)	1937-38
Browne, H. E.	(1)	Europeans v. Parsis (Poona)	1895-96
Buchanan, D.	(1)	Gentlemen v. Cambridge U. (Cambridge)	1874
Budgen, E. A.	(1)	O.F.S. v. Griqualand West (Kimberley)	1921-22
Bullough, J.	(1)	Lancs. v. Derby (Derby)	1914
Burns, W. B.	(1)	Worcs. v. Glos. (Worcester)	1913
Buss, A.	(2)	Sussex v. Cambridge U. (Cambridge)	1965
		Sussex v. Derby (Hove)	1965
Butler, H. J.	(3)	Notts. v. Surrey (Nottingham)	1937
		Notts. v. Leics. (Worksop)	1937
		Notts. v. Hants. (Nottingham)	1939
Cameron, F. J.	(1)	Otago v. Northern Districts (Hamiliton)	1962-63
Carey, P. A. D.	(1)	Sussex v. Glamorgan (Hove)	1947
Carter, R. G. M.	(1)	Worcs. v. Lancs. (Worcester)	1965
Cartwright, G. H. M.	(1)	Free Foresters v. Cambridge U. (Cambridge)	1920
Chowdhury, N. R.	(1)	Gen. Stewart's XI v. Governor Bengal's XI (Calcutta)	1944-45
Clark, E. W.	(1)	Northants. v. West Indians (Northampton)	1923
Cobden, F. C.	(1)	Cambridge U. v. Oxford U. (Lord's)	1870
Coldwell, L. J.	(2)	Worcs. v. Leics. (Stourbridge)	1957
		Worcs. v. Essex (Brentwood)	1965
Constantine, L. N.	(1)	West Indians v. Northants. (Northampton)	1928
Cooke, R.	(1)	Warwicks v. Kent (Tunbridge Wells)	1925
Copson, W. H.	(3)	Derby v. Lancs. (Burton upon Trent)	1937
		Derby v. Warwicks. (Derby) (4 in 4)	1937
		Derby v. Oxford U. (Oxford)	1939

Hat Tricks—*Cont.*

Bowler	No.	Match	Season
Cotton, J.	(1)	Leics. v. Surrey (Oval)	1965
Cousens, P.	(1)	Essex v. Combined Services (Chelmsford)	1950
Cox, A. L.	(1)	Northants. v. Lancs. (Northampton)	1930
Coxon, A.	(1)	Yorks. v. Worcs. (Leeds)	1946
Crisp, R. J.	(3)	Western Province v. Griqualand West (Johannesburg) (4 in 4)	1931-32
		Western Province v. Transvaal (Johannesburg)	1931-32
		Western Province v. Natal (Durban) (4 in 4)	1933-34
Crossland, J.	(1)	Lancs. v. Surrey (Oval)	1881
Cuffe, J. A.	(1)	Worcs. v. Hants. (Bournemouth)	1910
Davidson, A. K.	(1)	N.S.W. v. Western Australia (Perth)	1962-63
Davidson, F.	(1)	Derby v. Notts. (Derby)	1898
Davidson, G.	(2)	Derby v. Lancs. (Derby)	1895
		Derby v. M.C.C. (Lord's)	1898
Davies, E.	(1)	Glamorgan v. Leics. (Leicester)	1937
Davies, P. H.	(1)	Oxford U. v. Middx. (Oxford)	1914
Davies, R. E.	(1)	Natal v. Western Province (Cape Town)	1934-35
Dawson, O. C.	(1)	South Africans v. Northants. (Northampton)	1947
Dean, T. A.	(1)	Hants. v. Worcs. (Bournemouth)	1939
Dench, C. E.	(1)	Notts. v. Glos. (Bristol)	1899
Dennett, G.	(2)	Glos. v. Northants. (Gloucester)	1907
		Glos. v. Surrey (Bristol)	1913
Dewdney, D. T.	(1)	West Indians v. Hants. (Southampton)	1957
Deyes, G.	(1)	Yorks. v. Gentlemen of Ireland (Bray)	1907
Dildar Awan	(1)	Services v. Sargodha (Lyallpur)	1961-62
Dilley, M. R.	(2)	Northants. v. Notts. (Nottingham)	1961
		Northants. v. Sussex (Hove)	1961
Divecha, R. V.	(1)	Indians v. Surrey (Oval)	1952
Dixon, J. A.	(1)	Notts. v. Lancs. (Nottingham)	1887
Dollery, K. R.	(2)	Warwicks. v. Glos. (Bristol)	1953
		Warwicks. v. Kent (Coventry)	1956
Dooland, B.	(1)	South Australia v. Victoria (Melbourne)	1945-46
Douglas, J. W. H. T.	(3)	Essex v. Yorks. (Leyton)	1905
		M.C.C. v. N.S.W. (Sydney)	1920-21
		Essex v. Sussex (Leyton)	1923
Downes, A.	(1)	Otago v. Auckland (Dunedin) (4 in 4)	1893-94
Drake, A.	(2)	Yorks. v. Essex (Huddersfield)	1912
		Yorks. v. Derby (Chesterfield) (4 in 4)	1914
Drybrough, C. D.	(1)	Middx. v. Northants. (Northampton)	1964
Durston, T. J.	(2)	Middx. v. Cambridge U. (Cambridge)	1922
		Middx. v. Oxford U. (Oxford)	1923
Easter, J. N. C.	(1)	Oxford U. v. Northants. (Oxford)	1967
Ebeling, H. I.	(1)	Victoria v. Queensland (Melbourne)	1928-29
Enthoven, H. J.	(2)	Gentlemen v. Players (Lord's)	1926
		Middx. v. Australians (Lord's)	1934
Evans, H.	(1)	Derby v. Sussex (Hove)	1881
Evans, W. H. B.	(1)	Oxford U. v. Notts. (Oxford)	1905
Fannin, H. A.	(1)	Hawke's Bay v. Taranaki (Napier)	1897-98
Farnes, K.	(1)	Essex v. Notts. (Clacton)	1939
Farrands, F. H.	(1)	M.C.C. v. Cambridge U. (Cambridge)	1872
Faulkner, G. A.	(2)	Transvaal v. Western Province (Cape Town)	1906-07
		Transvaal v. Border (Cape Town)	1908-09
Fender, P. G. H.	(2)	Surrey v. Somerset (Oval)	1914
		Surrey v. Glos. (Oval)	1924
Field, F. E.	(1)	Warwicks, v. Hants. (Birmingham)	1911
Fisher, H.	(1)	Yorks. v. Somerset (Sheffield)	1932
Flanagan, M.	(1)	M.C.C. v. Surrey (Lord's)	1876
Flavell, J. A.	(3)	Worcs. v. Kent (Kidderminster)	1951
		Worcs. v. Cambridge U. (Cambridge)	1953
		Worcs. v. Lancs. (Manchester)	1963
Fletcher, A.	(1)	Yorks. v. M.C.C. (Lord's)	1892
Flowers, W.	(2)	Notts. v. Kent (Maidstone)	1888
		M.C.C. v. Oxford U. (Oxford)	1892
Foster, D. G.	(1)	Warwicks. v. Hants. (Birmingham)	1929
Freeman, A. P.	(3)	Kent v. Middx. (Canterbury)	1920
		M.C.C. v. South Australia (Adelaide)	1922-23
		Kent v. Surrey (Blackheath)	1934

Hat Tricks—*Cont.*

Freeman, G.	(1)	Yorks. v. Lancs. (Holbeck, Leeds)	1868
Frith, C.	(1)	Otago v. Canterbury (Dunedin)	1884-85
Fry, C. B.	(1)	Oxford U. v. M.C.C. (Lord's)	1894
Fulljames, R. E. G.	(1)	R. A. F. v. Royal Navy (Oval)	1928
Furlong, B. D. M.	(1)	N.Z. Under-23 XI v. Canterbury (Christchurch)	1964-65
Geary, G.	(1)	Leics. v. Glos. (Bristol)	1922
Ghias-ud-Din	(1)	Bahawalpur v. Khairpur (Bahawalpur)	1961-62
Gibbs, K.	(1)	O.F.S. v. Eastern Province (Bloemfontein)	1952-53
Gibbs, L. R.	(1)	West Indies v. Australia (Adelaide)	1960-61
Gibson, D.	(1)	Surrey v. Northants. (Northampton)	1961
Giffen, G.	(3)	Australians v. Lancs. (Manchester)	1884
		South Australia v. Vernon's XI (Adelaide)	1887-88
		Australians v. England XI (Wembley Park)	1896
Gifford, N.	(1)	Worcs. v. Derby (Chesterfield)	1965
Gilbert, G. H. B.	(1)	N.S.W. v. Victoria (Melbourne)	1857-58
Gilligan, A. E. R.	(1)	Sussex v. Surrey (Oval)	1923
Gladwin, C.	(2)	M.C.C. v. N-E. Transvaal (Benoni)	1948-49
		Derby v. New Zealanders (Derby)	1958
Goddard, T. L.	(1)	Natal v. Border (East London)	1959-60
Goddard, T. W.	(6)	Glos. v. Sussex (Eastbourne)	1924
		Glos. v. Glamorgan (Swansea)	1930
		England v. South Africa (Johannesburg)	1938-39
		M.C.C. v. Rhodesia (Salisbury)	1938-39
		Glos. v. Glamorgan (Swansea)	1947
		Glos. v. Somerset (Bristol)	1947
Gopalan, M. J.	(1)	Madras v. Ceylon (Madras)	1932-33
Gordon, N.	(1)	Transvaal v. Border (East London)	1937-38
Gothard, E. J.	(1)	Derby v. Middx. (Derby)	1947
Gover, A. R.	(1)	Surrey v. Worcs. (Worcester) (4 in 4)	1935
Grace, W. G.	(1)	M.C.C. v. Kent (Canterbury)	1874
Gregson, W. R.	(1)	Lancs. v. Leics. (Blackpool)	1906
Griffin, G.	(1)	South Africa v. England (Lord's)	1960
Grimmett, C. V.	(1)	South Australia v. Queensland (Brisbane)	1928-29
Grove, C. W.	(1)	Warwicks. v. Somerset (Taunton)	1947
Gunn, J.	(2)	Notts. v. Middx. (Lord's)	1899
		Notts. v. Derby (Chesterfield)	1904
Haigh, S.	(5)	Yorks. v. Derby (Bradford)	1897
		Lord Hawke's XI v. Cape Province (Cape Town)	1898-99
		Yorks. v. Somerset (Sheffield)	1902
		M.C.C. v. Army XI (Pretoria) (4 in 4)	1905-06
		Yorks. v. Lancs. (Manchester)	1909
Halfyard, D. J.	(2)	Kent v. Worcs. (Folkestone)	1957
		Kent v. Leics. (Gillingham)	1958
Hall, W. W.	(1)	West Indies v. Pakistan (Lahore)	1958-59
Hallam, A. W.	(1)	Notts. v. Leics. (Nottingham)	1907
Hammersley, W. J.	(1)	M.C.C. v. Surrey (Oval)	1848
Hammond, H. E.	(1)	Sussex v. Warwicks. (Hove)	1946
Harman, R.	(1)	Surrey v. Kent (Blackheath)	1963
Harvey, E.	(1)	Cambridge U. v. M.C.C. (Lord's)	1872
Haslip, S. M.	(1)	Middx. v. Notts. (Nottingham)	1919
Hay, H.	(1)	South Australia v. Hawke's XI (Adelaide) (*on debut*)	1902-03
Hayward, T. W.	(2)	Surrey v. Glos. (Oval)	1899
		Surrey v. Derby. (Chesterfield)	1899
Hayward, Thomas	(1)	Players v. Gentlemen (Lord's)	1870
Hazare, Vijay	(1)	Baroda v. Maharashtra (Poona)	1941-42
Hearne, A.	(2)	Kent v. Glos. (Clifton)	1900
		M.C.C. v. Yorks. (Lord's)	1888
Hearne, G. G.	(1)	Kent v. Lancs. (Manchester)	1875
Hearne, J. T.	(4)	Middx. v. Kent (Tonbridge)	1896
		England v. Australia (Leeds)	1899
		Middx. v. Essex (Lord's)	1902
		Middx. v. Warwicks. (Lord's)	1912
Hearne, J. W.	(3)	Middx. v. Essex (Lord's)	1911
		Middx. v. Kent (Lord's)	1914
		Middx. v. Essex (Leyton)	1922
Hearne, T.	(1)	Middx. v. Kent (Islington)	1868
Hearne, W.	(1)	Kent v. Lancs. (Tonbridge)	1894

Hat Tricks—*Cont.*

Bowler	No.	Match	Season
Henderson, W. A.	(1)	N-E. Transvaal v. O.F.S. (Bloemfontein) (4 in 4)	1937-38
Herman, O. W.	(1)	Hants. v. Glamorgan (Portsmouth)	1938
Hesketh-Prichard, H.	(1)	M.C.C. v. Philadelphians (Haverford)	1907-08
Hide, J. B.	(1)	Sussex v. M.C.C. (Lord's) (4 in 4)	1890
Higgs, K.	(1)	Lancs. v. Essex (Blackpool)	1960
Hill, A.	(3)	Yorks. v. United South XI (Bradford)	1874
		Players v. Gentlemen (Lord's)	1874
		Yorks. v. Surrey (Oval)	1880
Hilton, J.	(1)	Somerset v. Hants. (Weston-super-Mare)	1955
Hipkin, A. B.	(1)	Essex v. Lancs. (Blackpool)	1924
Hirst, G. H.	(2)	Yorks. v. Leics. (Leicester)	1895
		Yorks. v. Leics. (Hull)	1907
Hitch, J. W.	(2)	Surrey v. Cambridge U. (Oval)	1911
		Surrey v. Warwicks. (Oval)	1914
Hooker, J. E. H.	(1)	N.S.W. v. Victoria (Sydney) (4 in 4)	1928-29
Hopkins, A. J.	(2)	Australians v. Cambridge U. (Cambridge)	1902
		N.S.W. v. South Australia (Sydney)	1903-04
Horsley, W.	(1)	Derby v. A.I.F. (Derby)	1919
Horton, M. J.	(1)	Worcs. v. Somerset (Bath)	1956
Howard, T. H.	(1)	N.S.W. v. Queensland (Sydney)	1902-03
Howell, W. P.	(2)	Australians v. Western Province (Cape Town)	1902-03
		Australians v. New Zealand XI (Wellington)	1904-05
Howorth, R.	(1)	Worcs. v. Warwicks. (Birmingham)	1950
Huggins, J. H.	(1)	Glos. v. Notts. (Nottingham)	1903
Humphreys, W.	(2)	Sussex v. Australians (Hove)	1880
		Sussex v. Australians (Hove)	1884
Hutton, R. A.	(1)	M.C.C. Under-25 v. North Zone (Peshawar)	1966-67
Ikin, J. T.	(1)	Lancs. v. Somerset (Taunton)	1949
Iqbal Sheikh, M.	(1)	Lahore Greens v. Multan (Lahore)	1964-65
Ireland, J. F.	(1)	Cambridge U. v. Oxford U. (Lord's)	1911
Ironmonger, H.	(1)	Victoria v. M.C.C. (Melbourne)	1924-25
Jackson, H. L.	(2)	Derby v. Worcs. (Kidderminster)	1958
		Derby v. Worcs. (Derby)	1960
Jackson, P. F.	(1)	Worcs. v. Glamorgan (Neath)	1936
Jackson, V. E.	(2)	Leics. v. Derby (Derby)	1946
		Leics. v. Surrey (Leicester)	1950
Jameson, J. A.	(1)	Warwicks. v. Glos. (Birmingham)	1965
Jayes, T.	(2)	Leics. v. Northants. (Leicester)	1906
		Leics. v. Kent (Maidstone)	1907
Jenkins, R. O.	(3)	Worcs. v. Surrey (Oval)	1948
		Worcs. v. Surrey (Worcester) 1st inns.	1949
		Worcs. v. Surrey (Worcester) 2nd inns.	1949
Jephson, D. L. A.	(1)	Surrey v. Middx. (Oval)	1904
Jhanji, S.	(1)	Uttar Pradesh v. Vidharba (Nagpur)	1963-64
Jones, I. J.	(1)	Glamorgan v. Yorks. (Harrogate)	1962
Jones, J. F.	(1)	Wellington v. Central Districts (Wellington)	1953-54
Jupp, V. W. C.	(5)	Sussex v. Surrey (Hove)	1911
		Sussex v. Essex (Leyton)	1919
		Sussex v. Essex (Colchester)	1921
		Northants. v. Glamorgan (Swansea)	1925
		Northants v.. Glos (Bristol)	1931
Kennedy, A. S.	(3)	Hants. v. Glos. (Southampton)	1920
		Hants. v. Somerset (Bournemouth)	1920
		Hants. v. Glos. (Southampton)	1924
Kermode, A.	(1)	Lancs. v. Leics. (Leicester)	1906
Khanna, N.	(1)	Southern Punjab v. Jammu & Kashmir (Patiala)	1959-60
Khot, J. B.	(1)	Bombay v. Baroda (Bombay)	1943-44
King, J. H.	(2)	Leics. v. Sussex (Hove)	1903
		Leics. v. Somerset (Weston-super-Mare)	1920
Kline, L. F.	(1)	Australia v. South Africa (Cape Town)	1957-58
Knott, C. J.	(1)	Gentlemen v. Players (Lord's)	1950
Kotze, J. J.	(2)	Transvaal v. Griqualand West (Port Elizabeth)	1902-03
		Western Province v. Eastern Province (Cape Town)	1904-05
Kulkarni, U. N.	(1)	Bombay v. Gujerat (Vallabh Vidyanagar)	1963-64
Laker, J. C.	(4)	Warner's XI v. South of England (Hastings)	1947
		Surrey v. Glos. (Gloucester)	1951
		Surrey v. Warwicks. (Oval)	1953

Hat Tricks—*Cont.*

Bowler	No.	Match	Season
Laker, J. C. (*cont.*)		Surrey v. Cambridge U. (Guildford)	1953
Langridge, James	(1)	Sussex v. Derby (Derby)	1939
Larwood, H.	(2)	Notts. v. Cambridge U. (Cambridge)	1926
		Notts. v. Glamorgan (Nottingham)	1931
Lawrence, J.	(1)	Somerset v. Yorks. (Taunton)	1948
Lees, W. S.	(1)	Surrey v. Hants. (Southampton)	1897
Lewis, C.	(1)	Kent v. Notts. (Nottingham)	1939
Leyland, M.	(1)	Yorks. v. Surrey (Sheffield)	1935
Loader, P. J.	(2)	England v. West Indies (Leeds)	1957
		Surrey v. Leics. (Oval)	1963
Lock, G. A. R.	(4)	Surrey v. Somerset (Weston-super-Mare)	1955
		M.C.C. v. Bahawalpur XI (Bahawalpur)	1955-56
		M.C.C. v. Combined XI (Multan)	1955-56
		Leics. v. Hants. (Portsmouth)	1967
		(*First hat-trick in England to be completed on a Sunday*)	
Lockwood, W. H.	(3)	Surrey v. Cambridge U. (Cambridge)	1893
		Surrey v. Derby (Oval)	1901
		Surrey v. Yorks. (Sheffield)	1903
Lohmann, G. A.	(1)	England v. South Africa (Port Elizabeth)	1895-96
Lomax, J. G.	(1)	Somerset v. Notts. (Weston-super-Mare)	1958
Longfield, T. C.	(1)	Bengal v. Bihar (Calcutta)	1937-38
Louden, G. M.	(1)	Essex v. Somerset (Southend)	1921
Lowe, R. G. H.	(1)	Cambridge U. v. Oxford U. (Lord's)	1926
Macaulay, G. G.	(4)	Yorks. v. Warwicks. (Birmingham)	1923
		Yorks. v. Leics. (Hull)	1930
		Yorks. v. Glamorgan (Cardiff)	1933
		Yorks. v. Lancs. (Manchester)	1933
Macaulay, M. J.	(1)	South Africans v. Kent (Canterbury)	1965
McCarthy, C. N.	(1)	South Africans v. Sussex (Hove)	1951
McConnon, J. E.	(1)	Glamorgan v. South Africans (Swansea)	1951
McDonald, E. A.	(3)	Lancs. v. Sussex (Hove)	1925
		Lancs. v. Kent (Dover)	1926
		Lancs. v. Warwicks. (Birmingham)	1930
McGlew, D. J.	(1)	Natal v. Transvaal (Durban)	1963-64
McKibbin, T. R.	(1)	Australians v. Lancs. (Liverpool)	1896
Maile, J. H.	(1)	Western Province v. Rhodesia (Salisbury)	1958-59
Marlar, R. G.	(1)	Cambridge U. v. Essex (Cambridge)	1952
Marlow, J.	(1)	Derby v. Kent (Derby)	1884
Marriott, C. S.	(1)	M.C.C. v. Madras (Madras)	1933-34
Martin, F.	(2)	Kent v. Surrey (Oval)	1890
		M.C.C. v. Derby (Lord's) (4 in 4)	1895
Matthews, T. J.	(4)	Victoria v. Tasmania (Launceston)	1908-09
		Australia v. South Africa (Manchester) 1st inns	1912
		Australia v. South Africa (Manchester) 2nd inns	1912
		Australians v. Philadelphians (Germantown)	1912-13
Melle, B. G.	(1)	Oxford U. v. Scotland (Oxford)	1913
Melville, A.	(1)	Oxford U. v. Leveson-Gower's XI (Eastbourne)	1932
Mercer, J.	(1)	Glamorgan v. Surrey (Oval)	1932
Merchant, V. M.	(1)	Pereira's XI v. Mehta's XI (Bombay)	1946-47
Middleton, F. S.	(1)	Wellington v. Hawke's Bay (Wellington)	1919-20
Mills, P. T.	(1)	Glos. v. Hants. (Clifton)	1920
Mohol, S. N.	(1)	Combined XI v. President's XI (Poona) (4 in 4)	1965-66
Moir, A. M.	(1)	Otago v. Canterbury (Christchurch)	1950-51
Mold, A.	(2)	Lancs. v. Somerset (Manchester)	1894
		Lancs. v. Notts. (Nottingham) (4 in 4)	1895
Moore, F. W.	(1)	Lancs. v. Essex (Chelmsford)	1956
More, R. E.	(1)	Bosanquet's XI v. Philadelphians (Philadelphia)	1901-02
Morton, F. L.	(1)	Victoria v. Tasmania (Melbourne)	1931-32
Morton, P. H.	(1)	Cambridge U. v. Oxford U. (Lord's)	1880
Moss, A. E.	(1)	Middx. v. Glos. (Lord's)	1956
Mubarak Ali	(1)	Nawanagar v. Western India States (Poona)	1936-37
Muddiah, V. M.	(1)	Services v. East Punjab (New Delhi)	1955-56
Mulcock, E. T.	(1)	Canterbury v. Otago (Christchurch)	1937-38
Munden, V. S.	(1)	Leics. v. Derby (Ashby-de-la-Zouch)	1953
Murdin, V.	(1)	Northants. v. Kent (Northampton)	1920
Murray, R. M.	(1)	Wellington v. Otago (Wellington)	1949-50
Narottam, D.	(1)	Kathiawar v. Baroda (Dhrol)	1947-48

Hat Tricks—*Cont.*

Nayudu, C. S.	(1)	Indians v. Surrey (Oval)	1946
Needham, P. G.	(1)	Transvaal v. Eastern Province (Johannesburg)	1951-52
Newman, J. A.	(1)	Hants. v. Australians (Southampton)	1909
Newstead, J. T.	(1)	Yorks. v. Worcs. (Bradford)	1907
Nichols, M. S.	(1)	Essex v. Yorks. (Leeds)	1931
Noble, M. A.	(1)	N.S.W. v. Tasmania (Sydney)	1898-99
Nyalchand, S.	(1)	Saurashtra v. Baroda (Dharangadhra)	1961-62
Oakman, A. S. M.	(1)	Sussex v. Somerset (Hove)	1952
O'Connor, J.	(1)	Essex v. Worcs. (Worcester)	1925
Odell, W. W.	(2)	London County v. M.C.C. (Lord's)	1904
		Leics. v. Northants. (Leicester)	1908
Oliff, C.	(1)	Auckland v. Wellington (Auckland)	1912-13
Orchard, S. A.	(1)	Canterbury v. Auckland (Auckland)	1909-10
Orton, C. T.	(1)	Europeans v. Muslims (Bombay)	1938-39
Overton, G. W. F.	(1)	Otago v. Canterbury (Christchurch)	1946-47
Owen-Smith, H. G.	(2)	Oxford U. v. Leveson-Gower's XI (Eastbourne)	1931
		Gentlemen v. Players (Folkestone)	1935
Oxenham, R. K.	(1)	Australians v. Ceylon (Colombo)	1935-36
Paine, G. E. A.	(2)	Warwicks. v. Middx. (Lord's)	1932
		Warwicks. v. Glamorgan (Cardiff)	1933
Palmer, G. E.	(2)	Australians v. Sussex (Hove)	1882
		Victoria v. South Australia (Melbourne)	1882-83
Parakh, M. D.	(1)	Parsis v. Hindus (Bombay)	1912-13
Parker, C. W. L.	(6)	Glos. v. Yorks. (Bristol)	1922
		Glos. v. Middx. (Bristol) 1st inns	1924
		Glos. v. Middx. (Bristol) 2nd inns	1924
		Glos. v. Surrey (Oval)	1924
		Glos. v. Yorks. (Hull)	1926
		Glos. v. Essex (Chelmsford)	1930
Partridge, R. J.	(1)	Northants. v. Notts. (Nottingham)	1946
Peach, H. A.	(1)	Surrey v. Sussex (Oval) (4 in 4)	1924
Pearson, F.	(1)	Worcs. v. Surrey (Worcester)	1914
Peate, E.	(2)	Yorks. v. Kent (Sheffield)	1882
		Yorks. v. Glos. (Moreton-in-the-Marsh)	1884
Peebles, I. A. R.	(1)	Middx. v. Glos. (Lord's)	1932
Peel, R.	(1)	Yorks. v. Kent (Halifax)	1897
Pegler, S. J.	(1)	South Africans v. Yorks. (Huddersfield)	1912
Pepper, C. G.	(1)	Commonwealth v. Holkar (Indore)	1949-50
Perks. R. T. D.	(2)	Worcs. v. Kent (Stourbridge)	1931
		Worcs. v. Warwicks. (Birmingham)	1933
Phillips, R. R.	(1)	Border v. Eastern Province (Port Elizabeth)	1939-40
Pieris, P. I.	(1)	Cambridge U. v. Jardine's XI (Eastbourne)	1958
Platts, J.	(1)	Derby v. Yorks. (Derby)	1880
Plowden, H. M.	(1)	Cambridge U. v. M.C.C. (Cambridge)	1862
Pollard, R.	(2)	Lancs. v. Glamorgan (Preston)	1939
		Lancs. v. Warwicks. (Blackpool)	1947
Pope, G. H.	(1)	Derby v. Notts. (Ilkeston)	1947
Pougher, A. D.	(1)	M.C.C. v. Cambridge U. (Lord's)	1887
Preece, C. A.	(1)	Worcs. v. Warwicks. (Birmingham)	1924
Pritchard, T. L.	(3)	Warwicks. v. Leics. (Birmingham)	1948
		Warwicks. v. Kent (Maidstone)	1949
		Warwicks. v. Glamorgan (Birmingham)	1951
Rajinder Pal	(1)	Delhi v. Southern Punjab (Chandigarh)	1965-66
Ramadhin, S.	(1)	West Indies v. Hyderabad (Hyderabad)	1958-59
Rangachari, C. R.	(1)	Indians v. Tasmania (Hobart)	1947-48
Ranjane, V. R.	(1)	Maharashtra v. Saurashtra (Khadakvasla)	1956-57
Rao, J. S.	(3)	Services v. Jammu & Kashmir (New Delhi) (*On début in first-class cricket*)	1963-64
		Services v. Northern Punjab (Amritsar)	1963-64
		Services v. Northern Punjab (Amritsar) (*Two hat-tricks in the same innings and three hat-tricks in two consecutive matches*)	1963-64
Read, H. D.	(1)	Essex v. Glos. (Bristol)	1935
Read, W. W.	(1)	Gentlemen v. Sherwin's Notts XI (Scarborough)	1891
Reid, R. E.	(1)	Wellington v. Otago (Dunedin)	1958-59
Relf, A. E.	(1)	Sussex v. Worcs. (Hove)	1902
Rhodes, A. E. G.	(5)	Derby v. Ireland (Buxton)	1947

Hat Tricks—*Cont.*

Rhodes, A. E. G. (*cont.*)		M.C.C. v. Surrey (Lord's)	1948
		Derby v. Essex (Colchester)	1948
		Derby v. Oxford U. (Oxford)	1950
		Derby v. Sussex (Derby)	1951
Rhodes, H. J.	(1)	Derby v. Oxford U. (Buxton)	1961
Rhodes, W.	(1)	Yorks. v. Derby (Derby)	1920
Richardson, T.	(4)	Surrey v. Glos. (Oval)	1893
		Surrey v. Leics. (Oval)	1896
		Surrey v. Warwicks. (Oval)	1898
		Surrey v. Sussex (Hove)	1898
Richmond, L. B.	(1)	Notts. v. Lancs. (Nottingham)	1926
Ridgway, F.	(2)	Kent v. Derby (Folkestone) (4 in 4)	1951
		Kent v. Oxford U. (Oxford)	1958
Robins, D.	(1)	South Australia v. N.S.W. (Adelaide)	1965-66
Robins, R. W. V.	(2)	Middx. v. Leics. (Lord's)	1929
		Middx. v. Somerset (Lord's)	1937
Robinson, E.	(2)	Yorks. v. Sussex (Hull)	1928
		Yorks. v. Kent (Gravesend)	1930
Robinson, E. P.	(1)	Yorks. v. Kent (Leeds)	1939
Robson, E.	(2)	Somerset v. Hants. (Bath)	1898
		Somerset v. Yorks. (Taunton)	1902
Roller, W. E.	(1)	Surrey v. Sussex (Oval)	1885
Rorke, G.	(1)	N.S.W. v. Queensland (Sydney)	1958-59
Rought-Rought, R. C.	(1)	Cambridge U. v. Sussex (Hove)	1932
Rylott, A.	(1)	M.C.C. v. Derby (Lord's)	1884
Sadler, W.	(1)	Surrey v. Cambridge U. (Oval)	1923
Sarwate, C. T.	(1)	Holkar v. Bihar (Jamshedpur)	1948-49
Savage, J. S.	(1)	Leics. v. Somerset (Loughborough)	1961
Sayer, D. M.	(2)	Oxford U. v. Kent (Oxford)	1958
		Kent v. Glamorgan (Maidstone)	1964
Sedgwick, H.	(1)	Yorks. v. Worcs. (Hull) (*On debut*)	1906
Sen, P.	(1)	Bengal v. Orissa (Cuttack)	1954-55
Shacklock, F.	(1)	Notts. v. Somerset (Nottingham) (4 in 4)	1893
Shaw, A.	(3)	Notts. v. Derby (Derby)	1875
		Notts. v. Glos. (Nottingham) 1st inns	1884
		Notts. v. Glos. (Nottingham) 2nd inns	1884
Shepherd, D. J.	(1)	Glamorgan v. Northants. (Swansea)	1964
Shepherd, T. F.	(1)	Surrey v. Glos. (Oval)	1926
Shepstone, G. H.	(1)	Transvaal v. Border (Port Elizabeth)	1902-03
Shipman, W.	(1)	Leics. v. Derby (Leicester)	1909
Shuja-ud-Din	(1)	Services v. Rawalpindi (Lahore)	1961-62
Simms, H. L.	(1)	Europeans v. Muslims (Poona)	1915-16
Sims, J. M.	(1)	Middx. v. South Africans (Lord's)	1947
Smales, K.	(1)	Notts. v. Lancs. (Nottingham)	1955
Smith, A. C.	(1)	Warwicks. v. Essex (Clacton)	1965
		(*Unique instance of this feat by a player who kept wicket in the same match.*)	
Smith, C. I. J.	(1)	Middx. v. Lancs. (Manchester)	1939
Smith, D. V.	(2)	M.C.C. v. Oxford U. (Lord's)	1956
		Sussex v. Cambridge U. (Cambridge)	1958
Smith, S. G.	(2)	Northants. v. Leics. (Leicester)	1912
		Northants. v. Warwicks. (Birmingham) (4 in 4)	1914
Smith, V. I.	(2)	Natal v. Border (Pietermaritzburg)	1946-47
		South Africans v. Derby (Derby)	1947
Smith, W. C.	(2)	Surrey v. Hants. (Oval)	1908
		Surrey v. Northants. (Oval)	1910
Somers-Cox, A.	(1)	Barbados v. Priestley's XI (Bridgetown)	1896-97
Southerton, J.	(1)	South v. North (Sheffield)	1869
Spofforth, F. R.	(3)	Australians v. M.C.C. (Lord's)	1878
		Australia v. England (Melbourne)	1878-79
		Australians v. South (Oval)	1884
Statham, J. B.	(3)	Lancs. v. Sussex (Manchester)	1956
		M.C.C. v. Transvaal (Johannesburg)	1956-57
		Lancs. v. Leics. (Manchester)	1958
Steel, A. G.	(1)	Cambridge U. v. Oxford U. (Lord's)	1879
Stephenson, H. H.	(1)	England v. Kent (Lord's)	1858
Storey, S. J.	(1)	Surrey v. Glamorgan (Swansea)	1965

Hat Tricks—*Cont.*

Bowler	No.	Match	Year
Sully, H.	(1)	Northants. v. Lancs. (Wellingborough)	1967
Tariq Cheema	(1)	Lahore Board v. Railways (Lahore)	1964-65
Tarrant, F. A.	(5)	Middx. v. Glos. (Bristol) (4 in 4)	1907
		M.C.C. v. Cambridge U. (Cambridge)	1908
		Middx. v. Surrey (Lord's)	1909
		Middx. v. Glos. (Bristol)	1909
		Middx. v. Somerset (Bath)	1911
Tate, F. W.	(1)	Sussex v. Surrey (Oval)	1901
Tate, M. W.	(3)	Sussex v. Middx. (Lord's)	1926
		Rest of England v. Lancs. (Oval)	1926
		Sussex v. Northants. (Peterborough)	1934
Tattersall, R.	(1)	Lancs. v. Notts. (Manchester)	1953
Tayfield, H. J.	(2)	Natal v. Transvaal (Durban)	1946-47
		South Africans v. Victoria (Melbourne)	1952-53
Taylor, M. N. S.	(1)	Notts. v. Kent (Dover)	1965
Thomas, A. E.	(1)	Northants. v. Leics. (Northampton)	1927
Thompson, G. J.	(1)	Northants. v. Lancs. (Manchester)	1907
Thompson, R. G.	(1)	Warwicks. v. Sussex (Horsham)	1956
Thorbourn, D.	(1)	Jamaica v. Leeward Islands (Kingston)	1958-59
Titmus, F. J.	(1)	Middx. v. Somerset (Weston-super-Mare)	1966
Toone, P.	(1)	Essex v. Kent (Leyton)	1920
Townsend, C. L.	(1)	Glos. v. Somerset (Cheltenham)	1893
Townsend, L. F.	(1)	Derby v. Northants. (Northampton)	1931
Treanor, J.	(1)	N.S.W. v. Queensland (Brisbane)	1954-55
Tremlin, B.	(1)	Essex v. Derby (Derby)	1914
Trott, A. E.	(2)	Middx. v. Somerset (Lord's) (4 in 4) } same inns.	1907
		Middx. v. Somerset (Lord's) }	
Trueman, F. S.	(4)	Yorks. v. Notts. (Nottingham)	1951
		Yorks. v. Notts. (Scarborough)	1955
		Yorks. v. M.C.C. (Lord's)	1958
		Yorks. v. Notts. (Bradford)	1963
Trumble, H.	(3)	Australians v. Glos. (Cheltenham)	1896
		Australia v. England (Melbourne)	1901-02
		Australia v. England (Melbourne)	1903-04
Turner, C. T. B.	(1)	N.S.W. v. Victoria (Melbourne)	1886-87
Tyldesley, James	(2)	Lancs. v. Derby (Manchester	1920
		Lancs. v. Worcs. (Manchester)	1922
Tyldesley, R.	(1)	Lancs. v. Derby (Derby) (4 in 4)	1929
Tyler, E. J.	(1)	Somerset v. Yorks. (Taunton)	1895
Ulyett, G.	(2)	Lord Harris's XI v. N.S.W. (Sydney) (4 in 4)	1878-79
		Yorks. v. Lancs. (Sheffield)	1883
Verity, H.	(2)	Yorks. v. Notts. (Leeds)	1932
		M.C.C. Australian XI v. Leveson-Gower's XI (Scarborough)	1937
Waddington, A.	(1)	Yorks. v. Northants. (Northampton)	1920
Wainwright, E.	(1)	Yorks. v. Sussex (Dewsbury)	1894
Waite, M. G.	(1)	South Australia v. M.C.C. (Adelaide)	1935-36
Walker, A. K.	(2)	N.S.W. v. Queensland (Sydney)	1948-49
		Notts. v. Leics. (Leicester) (4 in 4)	1956
Walker, Ashley	(1)	Cambridge U. v. Surrey (Oval)	1865
Walsh, J. E.	(1)	Leics. v. Notts. (Loughborough)	1949
Ward, A. S.	(1)	Griqualand West v. O.F.S. (Kimberley)	1926-27
Warr, J. J.	(1)	Middx. v. Leics. (Loughborough)	1956
Wass, T. G.	(1)	Notts. v. Essex (Nottingham)	1908
Weighell, W. B.	(1)	Cambridge U. v. M.C.C. (Lord's)	1866
Wellard, A. W.	(1)	Somerset v. Leics. (Leicester)	1929
Wells, Joseph	(1)	Kent v. Sussex (Brighton) (4 in 4)	1862
Wells, W.	(1)	Northants. v. Notts. (Northampton)	1910
Wensley, A. F.	(1)	Sussex v. Middx. (Lord's)	1935
Whateley, E. G.	(1)	Oxford U. v. Philadelphians (Oxford)	1903
White, D. W.	(2)	Hants. v. Sussex (Portsmouth)	1961
		Hants. v. Sussex (Hove)	1962
White, G. C.	(1)	South Africans v. Kent (Canterbury)	1904
White, J. C.	(1)	Somerset v. Middx. (Lord's)	1923
Whitehead, R.	(1)	Lancs. v. Surrey (Manchester)	1912
Wilkinson, L. L.	(1)	Lancs. v. Sussex (Hove)	1938
Willsher, E.	(1)	Players of South v. Gentlemen of South (Oval)	1868

Hat Tricks—*Cont.*

Wilson, D.	(3)	Yorks. v. Notts. (Middlesbrough)	1959
		Yorks. v. Notts. (Worksop)	1966
		Yorks. v. Kent (Harrogate)	1966
Wilson, E. R.	(1)	Gentlemen v. Players (Scarborough)	1919
Wilson, G. A.	(3)	Worcs. v. London County (Worcester)	1900
		Worcs. v. Surrey (Worcester)	1901
		Worcs. v. Australians (Worcester)	1905
Wiltshire, G. G. M.	(1)	Glos. v. Yorks. (Leeds)	1958
Woods, S. M. J.	(1)	Cambridge U. v. Thornton's XI (Cambridge)	1888
Woolley, C. N.	(1)	Northants. v. Essex (Northampton)	1920
Woolley, F. E.	(1)	Kent v. Surrey (Blackheath)	1919
Wooster, G.	(1)	Northants. v. Dublin U. (Northampton)	1925
Wootton, G.	(1)	M.C.C. v. Sussex (Lord's)	1863
Wright, C.	(1)	Kent v. Warwicks. (Tunbridge Wells)	1925
Wright, D. V. P.	(7)	Kent v. Worcs. (Worcester)	1937
		Kent v. Notts. (Nottingham)	1937
		Kent v. Glos. (Gillingham)	1938
		M.C.C. v. Border (East London)	1938-39
		Kent v. Glos. (Bristol)	1939
		Kent v. Sussex (Hastings)	1947
		Kent v. Hants. (Canterbury)	1949
Wyatt, R. E. S.	(1)	M.C.C. v. Ceylon (Colombo)	1926-27
Young, H.	(1)	Essex v. Leics. (Leyton)	1907
Young, J. A.	(2)	Middx. v. Northants. (Northampton)	1946
		Middx. v. Lancs. (Lord's)	1951

FIVE WICKETS WITH SIX SUCCESSIVE BALLS

W. H. Copson	Derbyshire v. Warwickshire (Derby)	1937
W. A. Henderson	North-Eastern Transvaal v. Orange Free State (Bloemfontein)	1937-38

FOUR WICKETS WITH FIVE SUCCESSIVE BALLS

J. Southerton	Surrey v. Lancashire (Oval)	1869
S. E. Butler	Oxford U. v. M.C.C. (Oxford)	1871
W. F. Neilson	Canterbury v. Otago (Christchurch)	1876-77
W. Flowers	Shaw's XI v. Emmett's XI (Bradford)	1881
G. A. Lohmann	Surrey v. Lancashire (Manchester)	1888
A. Downes	Otago v. Canterbury (Dunedin)	1891-92
J. T. Hearne	Middlesex v. Essex (Lord's)	1902
F. S. Jackson	Yorkshire v. Australians (Leeds)	1902
T. H. Howard	New South Wales v. Queensland (Sydney)	1902-03
W. P. Howell	Australians v. Western Province (Cape Town)	1902-03
G. A. Wilson	Worcestershire v. Gloucestershire (Cheltenham)	1903
G. J. Thompson	Northamptonshire v. Leicestershire (Leicester)	1905
W. R. Gregson	Lancashire v. Leicestershire (Blackpool)	1906
C. Blythe	Kent v. Surrey (Blackheath)	1910
J. W. Hitch	Surrey v. Cambridge U. (Oval)	1911
S. J. Pegler	South Africans v. M.C.C. (Lord's)	1912
H. B. Fawcus	Army v. Royal Navy (Lord's)	1913
M. F. S. Jewell	Worcestershire v. Gloucestershire (Cheltenham)	1919
C. W. L. Parker	Gloucestershire v. Warwickshire (Bristol)	1920
A. Waddington	Yorkshire v. Northamptonshire (Northampton)	1920
W. E. Benskin	Leicestershire v. Derbyshire (Leicester)	1921
C. W. L. Parker	Gloucestershire v. Yorkshire (Bristol)	1922
M. W. Tate	England v. Rest—Trial match (Lord's)	1923
L. Cook	Sharp's XI v. Tennyson's XI (Blackpool)	1923
R. Cooke	Warwickshire v. Kent (Tunbridge Wells)	1925
P. G. H. Fender	Surrey v. Middlesex (Lord's)	1927
G. O. Allen	Middlesex v. Lancashire (Lord's)	1929
M. J. C. Allom	England v. New Zealand (Christchurch)	1920-30
A. L. Cox	Northamptonshire v. Lancashire (Northampton)	1930
R. J. Crisp	Western Province v. Transvaal (Johannesburg)	1931-32
M. P. Gopalan	Madras v. Ceylon (Madras)	1932-33

Four Wickets with Five Successive Balls—*Cont.*

G. G. Macaulay	Yorkshire v. Lancashire (Manchester)	1933
T. A. Dean	Hampshire v. Worcestershire (Bournemouth)	1939
W. H. Copson	Derbyshire v. Oxford U. (Oxford)	1939
James Langridge	Sussex v. Somerset (Weston-super-Mare)	1948
J. Lawrence	Somerset v. Yorkshire (Taunton)	1948
C. Gladwin	M.C.C. v. North-Eastern Transvaal (Benoni)	1948-49
A. J. Watkins	Glamorgan v. Derbyshire (Chesterfield)	1954
A. Brown	Kent v. Nottinghamshire (Folkestone)	1959
D. W. White	M.C.C. v. Services XI (Calcutta)	1961-62
C. D. Drybrough	Middlesex v. Somerset (Weston-super-Mare)	1962
J. B. Mortimore	Gloucestershire v. Lancashire (Cheltenham)	1962
R. Harman	Surrey v. Kent (Blackheath)	1963
C. D. Drybrough	Middlesex v. Northamptonshire (Northampton)	1964

OUTSTANDING SPELLS OF WICKET-TAKING

Instances of bowlers taking five or more wickets within a short spell of bowling.

Wkts. Balls		
10 in 42	A. Drake: Yorks. v. Somerset (Weston-super-Mare)	1914
10 in 52	H. Verity: Yorks. v. Notts. (Leeds)	1932
9 in 38	A. Drake: Yorks. v. Somerset (Weston-super-Mare)	1914
9 in 39	H. Verity: Yorks. v. Notts. (Leeds)	1932
9 in 39	H. Verity: Yorks. v. Kent (Sheffield)	1936
9 in 39	Ahad Khan: Railways v. Dera Ismail Khan (Lahore)	1964-65
9 in 44	T. W. Wall: South Australia v. N.S.W. (Sydney)	1932-33
9 in 47	A. P. Freeman: Kent v. Sussex (Hove)	1922
8 in 23	A. Drake: Yorks. v. Somerset (Weston-super-Mare)	1914
8 in 24	G. E. Tribe: Northants. v. Yorks. (Northampton)	1958
8 in 32	S. Ramadhin: West Indians v. Glos. (Cheltenham)	1950
8 in 34	H. Verity: Yorks. v. Notts. (Leeds)	1932
8 in 34	J. E. D. Sealy: Barbados v. Trinidad (Bridgetown)	1941-42
8 in 36	G. Dennett: Glos. v. Northants. (Gloucester)	1907
8 in 36	T. B. Mitchell: Derby v. Worcs. (Stourbridge)	1934
8 in 36	H. Verity: Yorks. v. Kent (Sheffield)	1936
8 in 39	A. P. Freeman: Kent v. Sussex (Hove)	1922
8 in 39	W. H. R. Andrews: Somerset v. Surrey (Oval)	1937
8 in 40	W. G. Grace: Glos. v. Yorks. (Clifton)	1877
7 in 15	H. Verity: Yorks. v. Notts. (Leeds)	1932
7 in 17	W. G. Grace: Glos. v. Notts. (Cheltenham)	1877
7 in 19	R. Tattersall: Lancs. v. Notts. (Manchester)	1953
7 in 20	A. Mold: Lancs. v. Somerset (Manchester)	1894
7 in 20	J. H. King: Leics. v. Yorks. (Leicester)	1911
7 in 20	A. Drake: Yorks. v. Somerset (Weston-super-Mare)	1914
7 in 20	P. G. H. Fender: Surrey v. Middlesex (Oval)	1927
7 in 22	R. Appleyard: Yorks. v. Somerset (Taunton)	1954
7 in 22	J. C. Laker: England v. Australia (Manchester)	1956
7 in 23	W. H. Copson: Derby v. Warwicks. (Derby)	1937
7 in 24	W. Rhodes: Thornton's XI v. Australians (Scarborough)	1899
7 in 24	F. E. Woolley: Kent v. Surrey (Oval)	1911
7 in 24	H. Verity: Yorks. v. Kent (Sheffield)	1936
7 in 25	J. W. Hearne: Middx. v. Essex (Lord's)	1910
7 in 25	V. W. C. Jupp: Northants. v. Glamorgan (Swansea)	1925
7 in 25	T. W. Durnell: Warwicks. v. Northants. (Birmingham)	1927
7 in 25	R. J. Crisp: Western Province v. Griqualand West (Johannesburg)	1931-32
7 in 25	A. P. Freeman: Kent v. Somerset (Taunton)	1935
7 in 26	S. Ramadhin: West Indians v. Glos. (Cheltenham)	1950
7 in 26	M. G. Melle: Transvaal v. Griqualand West (Johannesburg)	1950-51
7 in 28	A. Cotter: Australians v. Worcs. (Worcester)	1905
7 in 28	W. Rhodes: Yorks. v. Essex (Leyton)	1929
7 in 29	J. E. D. Sealy: Barbados v. Trinidad (Bridgetown)	1941-42
7 in 29	T. E. Bailey: Essex v. Glamorgan (Brentwood)	1950
7 in 30	T. G. Wass: Notts. v. Sussex (Hove)	1902

Outstanding Spells of Wicket-Taking—*Cont.*

Wkts. Balls		
6 in 12	P. G. H. Fender: Surrey v. Middx. (Lord's)	1927
6 in 12	R. J. Crisp: Western Province v. Griqualand West (Johannesburg)	1931-32
6 in 13	T. B. Mitchell: Derby v. Middx. (Derby)	1934
6 in 13	H. Verity: Yorks. v. Kent (Sheffield)	1936
6 in 13	W. H. Copson: Derby v. Warwicks. (Derby)	1937
6 in 14	S. E. Butler: Oxford U. v. Cambridge U. (Lord's)	1871
6 in 14	A. S. Kennedy: Hants. v. Warwicks. (Portsmouth)	1927
6 in 14	H. Verity: Yorks. v. Notts. (Leeds)	1932
6 in 15	P. G. H. Fender: Surrey v. Middx. (Lord's)	1927
5 in 6	W. H. Copson: Derby v. Warwicks. (Derby)	1937
5 in 6	W. A. Henderson: N-E. Transvaal v. O.F.S. (Bloemfontein)	1937-38
5 in 7	J. Briggs: Lancs. v. Sussex (Manchester)	1890
5 in 7	E. Wainwright: Yorks. v. Sussex (Dewsbury)	1894
5 in 7	P. H. Clark: Philadelphians v. Bosanquet's XI (Philadelphia)	1901-02
5 in 7	P. G. H. Fender: Surrey v. Middx. (Lord's)	1927
5 in 7	T. W. Goddard: Glos. v. Glamorgan (Swansea)	1930
5 in 7	T. W. Goddard: Glos. v. Somerset (Bristol)	1947
5 in 8	J. W. H. T. Douglas: Essex v. Yorks. (Leyton) (WW 000WWW)	1905
5 in 8	R. J. Crisp: Western Province v. Griqualand West (Johannesburg)	1931-32
5 in 9	C. F. Root: Worcs. v. Glos. (Cheltenham)	1924
5 in 9	V. W. C. Jupp: Northants. v. Worcs. (Dudley)	1928
5 in 9	J. E. Walsh: Leics. v. Notts. (Nottingham)	1946
5 in 9	D. Shackleton: Hants. v. Leics. (Leicester)	1950
5 in 9	T. E. Bailey: Pearce's XI v. Indians (Scarborough)	1952
5 in 10	S. Haigh: Yorks. v. Derby (Bradford)	1897
5 in 10	C. Blythe: Kent v. Surrey (Blackheath)	1910
5 in 10	J. N. Fraser: Oxford U. v. Leveson-Gower's XI (Eastbourne)	1912
5 in 10	C. W. L. Parker: Glos. v. Warwicks. (Bristol)	1920
5 in 10	H. Verity: Yorks. v. Kent (Sheffield)	1936

ALL TEN WICKETS IN AN INNINGS

O.	*M.*	*R.*		
			E. Hinkly: Kent v. England (Lord's)	1848
			J. Wisden: North v. South (Lord's)	1850
43	17	74	V. E. Walker: England v. Surrey (Oval)	1859
32.2	7	69	E. M. Grace: M.C.C. v. Gentlemen of Kent (Canterbury)	1862
44.2		104	V. E. Walker: Middx. v. Lancs. (Manchester)	1865
			G. Wootton: All England XI v. Yorks. (Sheffield)	1865
24.1	11	38	S. E. Butler: Oxford U. v. Cambridge U. (Lord's)	1871
60.2	22	129	James Lillywhite: South v. North (Canterbury)	1872
36.2	8	73	A. Shaw: M.C.C. v. North (Lord's)	1874
29	11	43	E. Barratt: Players v. Australians (Oval)	1878
26	10	66	G. Giffen: Australian XI v. Rest (Sydney)	1883-84
36.2	17	49	W. G. Grace: M.C.C. v. Oxford U. (Oxford)	1886
52.3	25	59	G. Burton: Middx. v. Surrey (Oval)	1888
21.3	10	28	A. E. Moss: Canterbury v. Wellington (Christchurch) (*On début*)	1889-90
31	6	69	S. M. J. Woods: Cambridge U. v. Thornton's XI (Cambridge)	1890
15.3	3	45	T. Richardson: Surrey v. Essex (Oval)	1894
27	11	32	H. Pickett: Essex v. Leics. (Leyton)	1895
34.3	15	49	E. J. Tyler: Somerset v. Surrey (Taunton)	1895
23.2	14	28	W. P. Howell: Australians v. Surrey (Oval)	1899
25.2	0	48	C. H. G. Bland: Sussex v. Kent (Tonbridge)	1899
14.2	5	42	A. E. Trott: Middx. v. Somerset (Taunton)	1900
28.5	7	55	J. Briggs: Lancs. v. Worcs. (Manchester)	1900
24.5	1	90	A. Fielder: Players v. Gentlemen (Lord's)	1906
19.4	7	40	G. Dennett: Glos. v. Essex (Bristol)	1906
12	2	26	A. E. E. Vogler: Eastern Province v. Griqualand West (Johannesburg)	1906-07
16	7	30	C. Blythe: Kent v. Northants. (Northampton)	1907
8.5	0	35	A. Drake: Yorks. v. Somerset (Weston-super-Mare)	1914
19	2	40	W. Bestwick: Derby v. Glamorgan (Cardiff)	1921
28.4	5	66	A. A. Mailey: Australians v. Glos. (Cheltenham)	1921
42.2	11	76	J. C. White: Somerset v. Worcs. (Worcester)	1921
17.5	4	43	T. Rushby: Surrey v. Somerset (Taunton)	1921
40.3	13	79	C. W. L. Parker: Glos. v. Somerset (Bristol)	1921

All Ten Wickets in an Innings—*Cont.*

O.	*M.*	*R.*		
19.3	4	65	G. G. Collins: Kent v. Notts. (Dover)	1922
25.1	5	51	H. Howell: Warwicks. v. Yorks. (Birmingham)	1923
22.4	10	37	A. S. Kennedy: Players v. Gentlemen (Oval)	1927
25.3	10	40	G. O. Allen: Middx. v. Lancs. (Lord's)	1929
42	9	131	A. P. Freeman: Kent v. Lancs. (Maidstone)	1929
16.2	8	18	G. Geary: Leics. v. Glamorgan (Pontypridd)	1929
22.3	8	37	C. V. Grimmett: Australians v. Yorks. (Sheffield)	1930
30.4	8	53	A. P. Freeman: Kent v. Essex (Southend)	1930
18.4	6	36	H. Verity: Yorks. v. Warwicks. (Leeds)	1931
36.1	9	79	A. P. Freeman: Kent v. Lancs. (Manchester)	1931
39	6	127	V. W. C. Jupp: Northants. v. Kent (Tunbridge Wells)	1932
19.4	16	10	H. Verity: Yorks. v. Notts. (Leeds)	1932
12.4	2	36	T. W. Wall: South Australia v. N.S.W. (Sydney)	1932-33
19.1	4	64	T. B. Mitchell: Derby v. Leics. (Leicester)	1935
26	10	51	J. Mercer: Glamorgan v. Worcs. (Worcester)	1936
28.4	4	113	T. W. Goddard: Glos. v. Worcs. (Cheltenham)	1937
17.1	5	47	T. F. Smailes: Yorks. v. Derby (Sheffield)	1939
24.1	8	67	E. A. Watts: Surrey v. Warwicks. (Birmingham)	1939
20.4	4	49	W. E. Hollies: Warwicks. v. Notts. (Birmingham)	1946
18.4	2	90	J. M. Sims: East v. West (Kingston)	1948
18.4	2	66	J. K. Graveney: Glos. v. Derby (Chesterfield)	1949
39.4	9	90	T. E. Bailey: Essex v. Lancs. (Clacton)	1949
36.2	9	102	R. Berry: Lancs. v. Worcs. (Blackpool)	1953
24.2	7	78	S. P. Gupte: Bombay v. Pakistan Services (Bombay)	1954-55
46	18	88	J. C. Laker: Surrey v. Australians (Oval)	1956
41.3	20	66	K. Smales: Notts. v. Glos. (Stroud)	1956
29.1	18	54	G. A. R. Lock: Surrey v. Kent (Blackheath)	1956
51.2	23	53	J. C. Laker: England v. Australia (Manchester)	1956
19	11	20	P. Chatterjee: Bengal v. Assam (Jorhat)	1956-57
23.3	11	41	J. D. Bannister: Warwicks. v. Combined Services (Birmingham)	1959
30.3	8	78	A. J. G. Pearson: Cambridge U. v. Leics. (Loughborough)	1961
34.2	19	49	N. I. Thomson: Sussex v. Warwicks. (Worthing)	1964
15.6	3	61	P. J. Allan: Queensland v. Victoria (Melbourne)	1965-66

Only one bowler went on to take 17 wickets in a match, C. Blythe taking 17 wickets in a day at a personal cost of 48 runs, for Kent v. Northamptonshire (Northampton) 1907.

NINE OR TEN WICKETS IN AN INNINGS

Ahad Khan	(1)	9-7	Railways v. Dera Ismail Khan (Lahore)	1964-65
Allan, P. J.	(1)	10-61	Queensland v. Victoria (Melbourne)	1965-66
Allen, G. O.	(1)	10-40	Middx. v. Lancs. (Lord's)	1929
Allom, M. J. C.	(1)	9-55	Cambridge U. v. Army (Cambridge)	1927
Appleby, A.	(1)	9-25	Lancs. v. Sussex (Hove)	1877
Arkwright, H. A.	(3)	9-43	M.C.C. v. Gentlemen of Kent (Canterbury)	1861
		9-53	M.C.C. v. Gentlemen of Kent (Canterbury)	1861
		9-79	M.C.C. v. Gentlemen of Kent (Canterbury)	1864
Arnold, E. G.	(1)	9-64	Worcs. v. Oxford U. (Oxford)	1905
Astill, W. E.	(1)	9-41	Leics. v. Warwicks. (Birmingham)	1923
Attewell, W.	(1)	9-23	Notts. v. Sussex (Nottingham)	1886
Bailey, T. E.	(1)	10-90	Essex v. Lancs. (Clacton)	1949
Bannister, J. D.	(2)	9-35	Warwicks. v. Yorks. (Sheffield)	1955
		10-41	Warwicks. v. Combined Services (Birmingham)	1959
Baring, A. E. G.	(1)	9-26	Hants. v. Essex (Colchester)	1931
Barlow, R. G.	(1)	9-39	Lancs. v. Sussex (Manchester)	1886
Barnes, S. F.	(1)	9-103	England v. South Africa (Johannesburg)	1913-14
Barratt, E.	(1)	10-43	Players v. Australians (Oval)	1878
Bennett, G.	(1)	9-113	Kent v. Sussex (Brighton)	1871
Berry, R.	(1)	10-102	Lancs. v. Worcs. (Blackpool)	1953
Bestwick, W.	(2)	10-40	Derby v. Glamorgan (Cardiff)	1921
		9-65	Derby v. Warwicks. (Birmingham)	1921
Blair, R. W.	(2)	9-75	Wellington v. Canterbury (Wellington)	1956-57
		9-72	Wellington v. Auckland (Wellington)	1956-57
Blanckenberg, J. M.	(1)	9-78	Western Province v. Transvaal (Johannesburg)	1920-21
Bland, C. H. G.	(1)	10-48	Sussex v. Kent (Tonbridge)	1899
Blythe, C.	(6)	9-67	Kent v. Essex (Canterbury)	1903
		9-30	Kent v. Hants. (Tonbridge)	1904

Nine or Ten Wickets in an Innings—*Cont.*

Player		Analysis	Match	Year
Blythe, C. (*cont.*)		10-30	Kent v. Northants. (Northampton) ..	1907
		9-42	Kent v. Leics. (Leicester)	1909
		9-44	Kent v. Northants. (Northampton) ..	1909
		9-97	Kent v. Surrey (Lord's)	1914
Bosanquet, B. J. T. ..	(2)	9-31	Oxford U. v. Sussex (Oxford)	1900
		9-107	M.C.C. v. South Africans (Lord's)	1904
Botten, J. T.	(2)	9-23	N-E. Transvaal v. Griqualand West (Pretoria)	1958-59
		9-29	N-E. Transvaal v. Rhodesia (Pretoria) ..	1963-64
Bowditch, M. H. ..	(1)	9-52	Western Province v. Natal (Cape Town) ..	1965-66
Bowes, W. E.	(1)	9-121	Yorks. v. Essex (Scarborough)	1932
Bowley, E. H.	(1)	9-114	Sussex v. Derby (Hove)	1929
Boyce, K. D.	(1)	9-61	Essex v. Cambridge U. (Brentwood) ..	1966
Boyes, G. S.	(1)	9-57	Hants. v. Somerset (Yeovil)	1938
Bradley, W. M.	(1)	9-87	Kent v. Hants. (Tonbridge)	1901
Braund, L. C.	(1)	9-41	Somerset v. Yorks. (Sheffield)	1902
Brearley, W.	(2)	9-47	Lancs. v. Somerset (Manchester)	1905
		9-80	Lancs. v. Yorks. (Manchester)	1909
Brice, W. S.	(1)	9-67	Wellington v. Auckland (Wellington) ..	1918-19
Briggs, J.	(4)	9-29	Lancs. v. Derby (Derby)	1885
		9-88	Lancs. v. Sussex (Manchester)	1888
		9-31	Londesborough's XI v. Australians (Scarborough)	1890
		10-55	Lancs. v. Worcs. (Manchester)	1900
Broderick, V. H. ..	(1)	9-35	Northants. v. Sussex (Horsham)	1948
Buchanan, D.	(1)	9-82	Gentlemen v. Players (Oval)	1868
Bull, F. G.	(1)	9-93	Essex v. Surrey (Oval)	1897
Burton, G.	(1)	10-59	Middx. v. Surrey (Oval)	1888
Butler, S. E.	(1)	10-38	Oxford U. v. Cambridge U. (Lord's) ..	1871
Caffyn, W.	(1)	9-29	Surrey & Sussex v. England (Oval) ..	1857
Chatterjee, P.	(1)	10-20	Bengal v. Assam (Jorhat)	1956-57
Chester, J.	(1)	9-	M.C.C. v. Cambridge U. (Cambridge) ..	1850
Clarke, W.	(2)	9-	Notts. v. Kent (Town Malling)	1840
		9-29	Notts. v. Kent (Nottingham)	1845
Clay, J. C.	(3)	9-54	Glamorgan v. Northants. (Llanelly) ..	1935
		9-59	Glamorgan v. Essex (Westcliff)	1937
		9-66	Glamorgan v. Worcs. (Swansea)	1937
Collins, G. G.	(1)	10-65	Kent v. Notts. (Dover)	1922
Connolly, A. N.	(1)	9-67	Victoria v. Queensland (Brisbane)	1964-65
Conway, A. J.	(1)	9-38	Worcs. v. Glos. (Moreton-in-the-Marsh) ..	1914
Cook, C.	(1)	9-42	Glos. v. Yorks. (Bristol)	1947
Cooke, F. H.	(1)	9-73	Otago v. Canterbury (Christchurch) ..	1884-85
Cornford, J.	(1)	9-53	Sussex v. Northants. (Rushden)	1949
Cottam, R. M. H. ..	(1)	9-25	Hants. v. Lancs. (Manchester)	1965
Cotton, J.	(1)	9-29	Leics. v. Indians (Leicester)	1967
Cowan, M. J.	(1)	9-43	Yorks. v. Warwicks. (Birmingham) ..	1960
Cox, G. R.	(1)	9-50	Sussex v. Warwicks. (Horsham)	1926
Crisp, R. J.	(1)	9-64	Western Province v. Natal (Durban) ..	1933-34
Cuffe, J. A.	(1)	9-38	Worcs. v. Yorks. (Bradford)	1907
Davidson, G.	(2)	9-42	Derby v. Glos. (Derby)	1886
		9-39	Derby v. Warwicks. (Derby)	1895
Dean, H.	(6)	9-46	Lancs. v. Derby (Chesterfield)	1907
		9-35	Lancs. v. Warwicks. (Liverpool)	1909
		9-31	Lancs. v. Somerset (Manchester)	1909
		9-77	Lancs. v. Somerset (Bath)	1910
		9-109	Lancs. v. Leics. (Leicester)	1911
		9-62	Lancs. v. Yorks. (Liverpool)	1913
Dean, J.	(1)	9-34	M.C.C. v. Notts. (Nottingham)	1843
Deas, L. M.	(1)	9-91	Europeans v. Hindus (Bombay)	1905-06
Dennett, G.	(2)	10-40	Glos. v. Essex (Bristol)	1906
		9-63	Glos. v. Surrey (Bristol)	1913
Dent, T. H.	(1)	9-47	Hawke's Bay v. Wellington (Napier) ..	1900-01
Douglas, J. W. H. T. ..	(2)	9-105	Gentlemen v. Players (Lord's)	1914
		9-47	Essex v. Derby (Leyton)	1921
Drake, A.	(1)	10-35	Yorks. v. Somerset (Weston-super-Mare) ..	1914
Dwyer, E. B.	(2)	9-35	Sussex v. Derby (Hove)	1906
		9-44	Sussex v. Middx. (Hove)	1906
Eden, T.	(1)	9-43	Nelson v. Wellington (Wellington)	1875-76
Emmett, T.	(2)	9-34	Yorks. v. Notts. (Dewsbury)	1868

Nine or Ten Wickets in an Innings—*Cont.*

Player	No.	Figures	Match	Season
Emmett, T. (*cont.*)		9-23	Yorks. v. Cambridgeshire (Hunslet, Leeds)	1869
Evans, A. H.	(1)	9-59	England XI v. Daft's XI (Lord's)	1880
Fazal Mahmood	(1)	9-43	Punjab v. Services (Lahore)	1956-57
Fee, F.	(1)	9-26	Ireland v. Scotland (Dublin)	1957
Field, F. E.	(1)	9-104	Warwicks. v. Leics. (Leicester)	1899
Fielder, A.	(2)	10-90	Players v. Gentlemen (Lord's)	1906
		9-108	Kent v. Lancs. (Canterbury)	1907
Fisher, A. H.	(1)	9-50	Otago v. Queensland (Dunedin)	1896-97
Flanagan, M.	(1)	9-78	M.C.C. v. Surrey (Lord's)	1876
Flavell, J. A.	(3)	9-122	Worcs. v. Sussex (Hastings)	1954
		9-30	Worcs. v. Kent (Dover)	1955
		9-56	Worcs. v. Middx. (Kidderminster)	1964
Fleetwood-Smith, L. O.	(2)	9-36	Victoria v. Tasmania (Melbourne)	1932-33
		9-135	Victoria v. South Australia (Melbourne)	1937-38
Foster, F. R.	(1)	9-118	Warwicks. v. Yorks. (Birmingham)	1911
Foster, T.	(1)	9-59	Yorks. v. M.C.C. (Lord's)	1894
Freeman, A. P.	(8)	9-87	Kent v. Sussex (Hastings)	1921
		9-11	Kent v. Sussex (Hove)	1922
		9-104	Kent v. West Indians (Canterbury)	1928
		10-131	Kent v. Lancs. (Maidstone)	1929
		9-50	Kent v. Derby (Ilkeston)	1930
		10-53	Kent v. Essex (Southend)	1930
		10-79	Kent v. Lancs. (Manchester)	1931
		9-61	Kent v. Warwicks. (Folkestone)	1932
Geary, G.	(2)	9-33	Leics. v. Lancs. (Ashby-de-la-Zouch)	1926
		10-18	Leics. v. Glamorgan (Pontypridd)	1929
Ghulam Ahmed	(1)	9-53	Hyderabad v. Madras (Secunderabad)	1947-48
Giffen, G.	(5)	10-66	Australian XI v. Rest (Sydney)	1883-84
		9-91	South Australia v. Victoria (Adelaide)	1885-86
		9-60	Australians v. Derby (Derby)	1886
		9-96	South Australia v. Victoria (Adelaide)	1891-92
		9-147	South Australia v. Victoria (Adelaide)	1892-93
Gill, G.	(1)	9-89	Leics. v. Warwicks. (Birmingham)	1905
Gladwin, C.	(3)	9-119	Derby v. Lancs. (Buxton)	1947
		9-64	North v. South (Kingston)	1951
		9-41	Derby v. Worcs. (Stourbridge)	1952
Goddard, T. W.	(9)	9-21	Glos. v. Cambridge U. (Cheltenham)	1929
		9-37	Glos. v. Leics. (Bristol)	1934
		10-113	Glos. v. Worcs. (Cheltenham)	1937
		9-55	Glos. v. Worcs. (Bristol)	1939
		9-38	Glos. v. Kent (Bristol)	1939
		9-44	Glos. v. Somerset (Bristol)	1939
		9-82	Glos. v. Surrey (Cheltenham)	1946
		9-41	Glos. v. Notts. (Bristol)	1947
		9-61	Glos. v. Derby (Bristol)	1949
Gomez, G. E.	(1)	9-24	West Indians v. South Zone (Madras)	1948-49
Grace, E. M.	(1)	10-69	M.C.C. v. Gentlemen of Kent (Canterbury)	1862
Grace, W. G.	(5)	10-92	M.C.C. v. Kent (Canterbury)	1873
		9-48	South v. North (Loughborough)	1875
		9-55	Glos. v. Notts. (Cheltenham)	1877
		9-20	M.C.C. v. Notts. (Lord's)	1885
		10-49	M.C.C. v. Oxford U. (Oxford)	1886
Graveney, J. K.	(1)	10-66	Glos. v. Derby (Chesterfield)	1949
Gregory, J. M.	(1)	9-32	A.I.F. v. Natal (Durban)	1919-20
Greswell, W. T.	(1)	9-62	Somerset v. Hants. (Weston-super-Mare)	1928
Griffith, G.	(1)	9-130	Surrey v. Lancs. (Oval)	1867
Grimmett, C. V.	(3)	10-37	Australians v. Yorks. (Sheffield)	1930
		9-74	Australians v. Cambridge U. (Cambridge)	1934
		9-180	South Australia v. Queensland (Adelaide)	1934-35
Grove, C. W.	(1)	9-39	Warwicks. v. Sussex (Birmingham)	1952
Grundy, J.	(1)	9-19	Notts. v. Kent (Nottingham)	1864
Gupte, B. P.	(1)	9-55	West Zone v. South Zone (Calcutta)	1962-63
Gupte, S. P.	(2)	10-78	Bombay v. Pakistan Services (Bombay)	1954-55
		9-102	India v. West Indies (Kanpur)	1958-59
Gyaneshwar, T.	(1)	9-34	Delhi v. Jammu & Kashmir (New Delhi)	1961-62
Hagemann, A. F.	(1)	9-32	Border v. Griqualand West (Kimberley)	1960-61
Haigh, S.	(1)	9-25	Yorks. v. Glos. (Leeds)	1912

Nine or Ten Wickets in an Innings—*Cont.*

Halfyard, D. J.	(2)	9-39	Kent v. Glamorgan (Neath)	1957
		9-61	Kent v. Worcs. (Maidstone)	1959
Hall, G. G.	(1)	9-122	South African Us. v. Western Province (Cape Town)	1960-61
Hallows, J.	(1)	9-37	Lancs. v. Glos. (Gloucester)	1904
Hammond, W. R.	(1)	9-23	Glos. v. Worcs. (Cheltenham)	1928
Hargreave, S.	(1)	9-35	Warwicks. v. Surrey (Oval)	1903
Harry, F.	(1)	9-44	Lancs. v. Warwicks. (Manchester)	1906
Hay, H.	(1)	9-67	South Australia v. Lord Hawke's XI (Adelaide)	1902-03
Heap, J. S.	(1)	9-43	Lancs. v. Northants. (Northampton)	1910
Hearne, J. T.	(8)	9-32	Middx. v. Notts. (Nottingham)	1891
		9-41	M.C.C. v. Notts. (Lord's)	1892
		9-43	M.C.C. v. Lancs. (Lord's)	1894
		9-73	M.C.C. v. Australians (Lord's)	1896
		9-54	M.C.C. v. Oxford U. (Oxford)	1897
		9-68	Middx. v. Lancs. (Manchester)	1898
		9-71	M.C.C. v. Yorks. (Lord's)	1900
		9-78	Middx. v. Yorks. (Bradford)	1908
Hearne, J. W.	(3)	9-82	Middx. v. Surrey (Lord's)	1911
		9-65	Middx. v. Somerset (Lord's)	1920
		9-61	Middx. v. Derby (Chesterfield)	1933
Hinkly, E.	(1)	10-	Kent v. England (Lord's)	1848
Hirst, G. H.	(4)	9-45	Yorks. v. Middx. (Sheffield)	1907
		9-23	Yorks. v. Lancs. (Leeds)	1910
		9-41	Yorks. v. Worcs. (Worcester)	1911
		9-69	Yorks. v. M.C.C. (Lord's)	1912
Hollies, W. E.	(3)	9-93	Warwicks. v. Glamorgan (Birmingham)	1939
		10-49	Warwicks. v. Notts. (Birmingham)	1946
		9-56	Warwicks. v. Northants. (Birmingham)	1950
Hopwood, J. L.	(2)	9-33	Lancs. v. Leics. (Manchester)	1933
		9-69	Lancs. v. Worcs. (Blackpool)	1934
Horton, M. J.	(1)	9-56	Worcs. v. South Africans (Worcester)	1955
Howell, H.	(3)	10-51	Warwicks. v. Yorks. (Birmingham)	1923
		9-35	Warwicks. v. Somerset (Taunton)	1924
		9-32	Warwicks. v. Hants. (Birmingham)	1925
Howell, W. P.	(3)	10-28	Australians v. Surrey (Oval)	1899
		9-23	Australians v. Western Province (Cape Town)	1902-03
		9-52	N.S.W. v. Victoria (Melbourne)	1902-03
Huddleston, W.	(1)	9-36	Lancs. v. Notts. (Liverpool)	1906
Huggins, J. H.	(1)	9-34	Glos. v. Sussex (Bristol)	1904
Hulme, J.	(1)	9-27	Derby v. Yorks. (Sheffield)	1894
Iddon, J.	(1)	9-42	Lancs. v. Yorks. (Sheffield)	1937
Illingworth, R.	(1)	9-42	Yorks. v. Worcs. (Worcester)	1957
Israr Ali	(1)	9-58	Bahawalpur v. Punjab A (Bahawalpur)	1957-58
Jackson, J.	(3)	9-27	Kent v. England (Lord's)	1858
		9-35	Kent v. England (Canterbury)	1858
		9-49	Notts. v. Surrey (Oval)	1860
Jackson, H. L.	(2)	9-60	Derby v. Lancs. (Manchester)	1952
		9-17	Derby v. Cambridge U. (Cambridge)	1959
Jackson, P. F.	(1)	9-45	Worcs. v. Somerset (Dudley)	1935
James, A. E.	(1)	9-60	Sussex v. Yorks. (Hove)	1955
Jayes, T.	(1)	9-78	Leics. v. Derby (Leicester)	1905
Jupp, V. W. C.	(1)	10-127	Northants. v. Kent (Tunbridge Wells)	1932
Kannan, K. S.	(1)	9-50	Madras v. Hyderabad (Secunderabad)	1947-48
Kennedy, A. S.	(3)	9-33	Hants. v. Lancs. (Liverpool)	1920
		10-37	Players v. Gentlemen (Oval)	1927
		9-46	Hants. v. Derby (Portsmouth)	1929
Khalid Qureshi	(1)	9-28	Lahore v. Board of Education (Lahore)	1960-61
King, J. B.	(2)	9-25	Philadelphians v. Warner's XI (Belmont)	1897-98
		9-62	Philadelphians v. Lancs. (Manchester)	1903
Knutton, H. J.	(1)	9-100	England XI v. Australians (Bradford)	1902
Laker, J. C.	(3)	10-88	Surrey v. Australians (Oval)	1956
		9-37	England v. Australia (Manchester) 1st innings	1956
		10-53	England v. Australia (Manchester) 2nd innings	1956
Lampard, A. W.	(1)	9-42	A.I.F. v. Lancs. (Manchester)	1919
Langford, B. A.	(1)	9-26	Somerset v. Lancs. (Weston-super-Mare)	1958
Langridge, James	(1)	9-34	Sussex v. Yorks. (Sheffield)	1934

Nine or Ten Wickets in an Innings—*Cont.*

Bowler	No.	Analysis	Match	Season
Larwood, H.	(1)	9-41	Notts. v. Kent (Nottingham)	1931
Lees, W. S.	(1)	9-81	Surrey v. Sussex (Eastbourne)	1905
Lillywhite, James	(3)	9-29	Sussex v. M.C.C. (Lord's)	1862
		9-73	Sussex v. Kent (Folkestone)	1863
		10-129	South v. North (Canterbury)	1872
Lillywhite, W.	(4)	9-	Sussex v. Hants. & Surrey (Bramshill)	1826
		9-	Players v. Gentlemen (Lord's)	1837
		9-	Slow Bowlers v. Fast Bowlers (Lord's)	1841
		9-	M.C.C. v. Cambridge U. (Cambridge)	1846
Lipscombe, R.	(1)	9-88	Kent v. M.C.C. (Lord's)	1871
Llewelyn, C. B.	(1)	9-55	London County v. Cambridge U. (Crystal Palace)	1902
Loader, P. J.	(2)	9-28	Surrey v. Kent (Blackheath)	1953
		9-17	Surrey v. Warwicks. (Oval)	1958
Lock, G. A. R.	(2)	10-54	Surrey v. Kent (Blackheath)	1956
		9-77	Surrey v. Oxford U. (Guildford)	1960
Lockwood, W. H.	(3)	9-105	Surrey v. Glos. (Cheltenham)	1899
		9-94	Surrey v. Essex (Oval)	1900
		9-59	Surrey v. Essex (Leyton)	1902
Lohmann, G. A.	(2)	9-67	Surrey v. Sussex (Hove)	1889
		9-28	England v. South Africa (Johannesburg)	1895-96
McBeath, D. J.	(1)	9-56	Canterbury v. Auckland (Christchurch)	1918-19
McCormick, E. L.	(1)	9-40	Victoria v. South Australia (Adelaide)	1936-37
McIntyre, M.	(1)	9-33	Notts. v. Surrey (Oval)	1872
McKibbin, T. R.	(1)	9-68	N.S.W. v. Queensland (Brisbane)	1894-95
McMillan, Q.	(1)	9-53	South Africans v. South Australia (Adelaide)	1931-32
McNally, J. P.	(1)	9-91	Griqualand West v. Border (Kimberley)	1951-52
McShane, P. G.	(1)	9-45	Rest v. Australian XI (Sydney)	1880-81
Mailey, A. A.	(3)	9-121	Australia v. England (Melbourne)	1920-21
		10-66	Australians v. Glos. (Cheltenham)	1921
		9-86	Australians v. Lancs. (Liverpool)	1926
Marchant, J. W.	(1)	9-21	Wellington v. Hawke's Bay (Wellington)	1873-74
Marlar, R. G.	(1)	9-46	Sussex v. Lancs. (Hove)	1955
Marsham, C. D.	(1)	9-64	Gents of England v. Gents of M.C.C. (Lord's)	1855
Matthews, F. C. L.	(1)	9-50	Notts. v. Northants. (Nottingham)	1923
Mead, W.	(3)	9-52	Essex v. Hants. (Southampton)	1895
		9-75	Essex v. Leics. (Leyton)	1896
		9-40	Essex v. Hants. (Southampton)	1900
Mee, R. J.	(1)	9-54	Notts. v. Sussex (Nottingham)	1893
Melle, M. G.	(1)	9-22	South Africans v. Tasmania (Launceston)	1952-53
Mercer, J.	(2)	9-24	Wales v. Scotland (Perth)	1923
		10-51	Glamorgan v. Worcs. (Worcester)	1936
Meyer, R. J. O.	(1)	9-160	Europeans v. Muslims (Bombay)	1927-28
Mistri, K. B.	(1)	9-81	Parsis v. Europeans (Poona)	1906-07
Mitchell, T. B.	(1)	10-64	Derby v. Leics. (Leicester)	1935
Mold, A.	(4)	9-41	Lancs. v. Yorks. (Huddersfield)	1890
		9-43	Thornton's XI v. Australians (Barnes)	1890
		9-29	Lancs. v. Kent (Tonbridge)	1892
		9-62	Lancs. v. Kent (Manchester)	1895
Morton, A.	(1)	9-71	Derby v. Notts. (Blackwell)	1911
Moss, A. E.	(1)	10-28	Canterbury v. Wellington (Christchurch) *(On début)*	1889-90
Muncer, B. L.	(2)	9-97	Glamorgan v. Surrey (Cardiff)	1947
		9-62	Glamorgan v. Essex (Brentwood)	1948
Mycroft, W.	(1)	9-80	Derby v. Lancs. (Derby)	1875
Mynn, A.	(1)	9-	Gents of Kent v. Gents of M.C.C. (Lord's)	1842
Napier, G. G.	(1)	9-17	Europeans v. Parsis (Poona)	1909-10
Nash, J.	(1)	9-93	Glamorgan v. Sussex (Swansea)	1922
Neill, R.	(2)	9-75	Auckland v. Canterbury (Auckland)	1891-92
		9-86	Auckland v. Canterbury (Auckland)	1897-98
Newman, J. A.	(1)	9-131	Hants. v. Essex (Bournemouth)	1921
Nichols, M. S.	(4)	9-59	Essex v. Hants. (Chelmsford)	1927
		9-116	Essex v. Middx. (Leyton)	1930
		9-32	Essex v. Notts. (Nottingham)	1936
		9-37	Essex v. Glos. (Gloucester)	1938
Nicholson, A. G.	(1)	9-62	Yorks. v. Sussex (Eastbourne)	1967
Nixon, T.	(1)	9-	M.C.C. v. Middx. (Lord's)	1851

Nine or Ten Wickets in an Innings—*Cont.*

Nupen, E. P.	(1)	9-48	Transvaal v. Griqualand West (Johannesburg)	1931-32
O'Reilly, W. J.	(3)	9-50	N.S.W. v. Victoria (Melbourne)	1933-34
		9-38	Australians v. Somerset (Taunton)	1934
		9-41	N.S.W. v. South Australia (Adelaide)	1937-38
Oxenham, R. K.	(1)	9-18	Australians v. Ceylon (Colombo)	1935-36
Pallett, H. J.	(1)	9-55	Warwicks. v. Essex (Leyton)	1894
Palmer, K. E.	(1)	9-57	Somerset v. Notts. (Nottingham)	1963
Parker, C. W. L.	(9)	9-35	Glos. v. Leics. (Cheltenham)	1920
		10-79	Glos. v. Somerset (Bristol)	1921
		9-87	Glos. v. Derby (Gloucester)	1922
		9-36	Glos. v. Yorks. (Bristol)	1922
		9-44	Glos. v. Essex (Gloucester)	1925
		9-118	Glos. v. Surrey (Gloucester)	1925
		9-103	Glos. v. Somerset (Bristol)	1927
		9-46	Glos. v. Northants. (Northampton)	1927
		9-44	Glos. v. Warwicks. (Cheltenham)	1930
Parkin, C. H.	(2)	9-85	Players v. Gentlemen (Oval)	1920
		9-32	Lancs. v. Leics. (Ashby-de-la-Zouch)	1924
Partridge, R. J.	(1)	9-66	Northants. v. Warwicks. (Kettering)	1934
Patel, J. S.	(1)	9-69	India v. Australia (Kanpur)	1959-60
Pearson, A. J. G.	(1)	10-78	Cambridge U. v. Leics. (Loughborough)	1961
Pearson, F.	(1)	9-41	Foster's XI v. Oxford U. (Oxford)	1913
Peel, R.	(1)	9-22	Yorks. v. Somerset (Leeds)	1895
Perks, R. T. D.	(2)	9-40	Worcs. v. Glamorgan (Stourbridge)	1939
		9-42	Worcs. v. Glos. (Cheltenham)	1946
Pickett, H.	(1)	10-32	Essex v. Leics. (Leyton)	1895
Pougher, A. D.	(1)	9-34	England XI v. Surrey (Oval)	1895
Powys, W. N.	(1)	9-42	Cambridge U. v. M.C.C. (Cambridge)	1871
Pressdee, J. S.	(1)	9-43	Glamorgan v. Yorks. (Swansea)	1965
Preston, J. M.	(1)	9-28	Yorks. v. M.C.C. (Scarborough)	1888
Quilty, J.	(1)	9-55	South Australia v. Victoria (Adelaide)	1881-82
Raikes, T. B.	(1)	9-38	Oxford U. v. Army (Oxford)	1924
Ranjane, V. R.	(1)	9-35	Maharashtra v. Saurashtra (Khadakvasla)	1956-57
Relf, A. E.	(1)	9-95	Sussex v. Warwicks. (Hove)	1910
Rhodes, W.	(3)	9-28	Yorks. v. Essex (Leyton)	1899
		9-24	Thornton's XI v. Australians (Scarborough)	1899
		9-39	Yorks. v. Essex (Leyton)	1929
Richardson, T.	(4)	9-47	Surrey v. Yorks. (Sheffield)	1893
		10-45	Surrey v. Essex (Oval)	1894
		9-49	Surrey v. Sussex (Oval)	1895
		9-70	Surrey v. Hants. (Oval)	1895
Richmond, L. B.	(2)	9-21	Notts. v. Hants. (Nottingham)	1922
		9-55	Notts. v. Northants. (Nottingham)	1925
Ringrose, W.	(1)	9-76	Yorks. v. Australians (Bradford)	1905
Robertson, W.	(1)	9-98	Canterbury v. Wellington (Christchurch)	1894-95
Robertson-Glasgow, R. C.	(1)	9-38	Somerset v. Middx. (Lord's)	1924
Robinson, E.	(1)	9-36	Yorks. v. Lancs. (Bradford)	1920
Root, C. F.	(3)	9-40	Worcs. v. Essex (Worcester)	1924
		9-81	Worcs. v. Kent (Tunbridge Wells)	1930
		9-23	Worcs. v. Lancs. (Worcester)	1931
Rowan, A. M. B.	(1)	9-19	Transvaal v. Australians (Johannesburg)	1949-50
Rushby, T.	(1)	10-43	Surrey v. Somerset (Taunton)	1921
Rylott, A.	(1)	9-30	M.C.C. v. Cambridge U. (Cambridge)	1873
Sajjad Ahmed	(1)	9-80	Peshawar v. Services (Peshawar)	1958-59
Sarwate, C. T.	(1)	9-61	Holkar v. Mysore (Indore)	1945-46
Shackleton, D.	(4)	9-77	Hants. v. Glamorgan (Newport)	1953
		9-59	Hants. v. Glos. (Bristol)	1958
		9-81	Hants. v. Glos. (Bristol)	1959
		9-30	Hants. v. Warwicks. (Portsmouth)	1960
Sharp, J.	(1)	9-77	Lancs. v. Worcs. (Worcester)	1901
Sharpe, J. W.	(1)	9-47	Surrey v. Middx. (Oval)	1891
Shaw, A.	(1)	10-73	M.C.C. v. North (Lord's)	1874
Shaw, J. C.	(1)	9-84	Notts. v. Glos. (Nottingham)	1871
Shepherd, D. J.	(2)	9-47	Glamorgan v. Northants. (Cardiff)	1954
		9-48	Glamorgan v. Yorks. (Swansea)	1965
Shipman, W.	(1)	9-83	Leics. v. Surrey (Oval)	1910

Nine or Ten Wickets in an Innings—*Cont.*

Bowler	No.	Figures	Match	Season
Sims, J. M.	(2)	9-92	Middx. v. Lancs. (Manchester)	1934
		10-90	East v. West (Kingston)	1948
Sinfield, R. A.	(1)	9-111	Glos. v. Middx. (Lord's)	1936
Smailes, T. F.	(1)	10-47	Yorks. v. Derby (Sheffield)	1939
Smales, K.	(1)	10-66	Notts. v. Glos. (Stroud)	1956
Smith, E.	(1)	9-64	Derby v. Scotland (Edinburgh)	1955
Smith, S. G.	(1)	9-34	West Indian XI v. Bennett's XI (Port of Spain)	1901-02
Smith, T. P. B.	(4)	9-121	M.C.C. v. N.S.W. (Sydney)	1946-47
		9-77	Essex v. Middx. (Colchester)	1947
		9-117	Essex v. Notts. (Southend)	1948
		9-108	Essex v. Kent (Maidstone)	1948
Smith, V. I.	(1)	9-88	Natal v. Border (Pietermaritzburg)	1946-47
Smith, W. C.	(1)	9-31	Surrey v. Hants. (Oval)	1904
Sobers, G. St. A.	(1)	9-49	West Indians v. Kent (Canterbury)	1966
Southerton, J.	(1)	9-30	South v. North (Lord's)	1875
Spencer, C. T.	(1)	9-63	Leics. v. Yorks. (Huddersfield)	1954
Spofforth, F. R.	(2)	9-53	Australians v. Lancs. (Manchester)	1878
		9-18	Australians v. Oxford U. (Oxford)	1886
Staples, S. J.	(1)	9-141	Notts. v. Kent (Canterbury)	1927
Steel, A. G.	(1)	9-63	Lancs. v. Yorks. (Manchester)	1878
Stephenson, J. W. A.	(1)	9-46	Gentlemen v. Players (Lord's)	1936
Sydenham, D. A. D.	(1)	9-70	Surrey v. Glos. (Oval)	1964
Tarrant, F. A.	(7)	9-57	Middx. v. Yorks. (Leeds)	1906
		9-54	Middx. v. Lancs. (Manchester)	1906
		9-41	Middx. v. Glos. (Bristol)	1907
		9-59	Middx. v. Notts. (Lord's)	1907
		9-105	Middx. v. Lancs. (Manchester)	1914
		9-35	England XII v. Indian XII (Bombay)	1915-16
		9-99	Europeans v. Parsis (Bombay)	1916-17
Tate, F. W.	(1)	9-73	Sussex v. Leics. (Leicester)	1902
Tate, M. W.	(1)	9-71	Sussex v. Middx. (Lord's)	1926
Tattersall, R.	(1)	9-40	Lancs. v. Notts. (Manchester)	1953
Tayfield, H. J.	(1)	9-113	South Africa v. England (Johannesburg)	1956-57
Thomas, A. E.	(1)	9-30	Northants v. Yorks. (Bradford)	1920
Thompson, G. J.	(2)	9-85	Hawke's XI v. South Australia (Adelaide)	1902-03
		9-64	Northants. v. Derby (Northampton)	1906
Thompson, R. G.	(1)	9-65	Warwicks. v. Notts. (Birmingham)	1952
Thomson, N. I.	(1)	10-49	Sussex v. Warwicks. (Worthing)	1964
Titmus, F. J.	(2)	9-52	Middx. v. Cambridge U. (Cambridge)	1962
		9-57	Middx. v. Lancs. (Lord's)	1964
Townsend, C. L.	(2)	9-48	Glos. v. Middx. (Lord's)	1898
		9-128	Glos. v. Warwicks. (Cheltenham)	1898
Travers, J. F.	(1)	9-30	South Australia v. Victoria (Melbourne)	1900-01
Tremlin, B.	(1)	9-126	Essex v. Derby (Leyton)	1905
Tribe, G. E.	(4)	9-45	Queensland v. Victoria (Brisbane)	1945-46
		9-50	Commonwealth v. Governor's XI (Calcutta)	1949-50
		9-45	Northants. v. Yorks. (Bradford)	1955
		9-43	Northants. v. Worcs. (Northampton)	1958
Trott, A. E.	(1)	10-42	Middx. v. Somerset (Taunton)	1900
Trumble, H.	(1)	9-39	Australians v. South of England (Bournemouth)	1902
Turner, C. T. B.	(2)	9-15	Australians v. England XI (Stoke)	1888
		9-37	Australians v. England XI (Hastings)	1888
Tyler, E. J.	(3)	9-33	Somerset v. Notts. (Taunton)	1892
		10-49	Somerset v. Surrey (Taunton)	1895
		9-83	Somerset v. Sussex (Hastings)	1907
Underwood, D. L.	(2)	9-28	Kent v. Sussex (Hastings)	1964
		9-37	Kent v. Essex (Westcliff)	1966
Verity, H.	(9)	9-60	Yorks. v. Glamorgan (Swansea)	1930
		10-36	Yorks. v. Warwicks. (Leeds)	1931
		10-10	Yorks. v. Notts. (Leeds)	1932
		9-44	Yorks. v. Essex (Leyton)	1933
		9-59	Yorks. v. Kent (Dover)	1933
		9-12	Yorks. v. Kent (Sheffield)	1936
		9-48	Yorks. v. Essex (Westcliff)	1936
		9-43	Yorks. v. Warwicks. (Leeds)	1937
		9-62	Yorks. v. M.C.C. (Lord's)	1939
Vogler, A. E. E.	(2)	9-44	M.C.C. v. West Indians (Lord's)	1906

Nine or Ten Wickets in an Innings—*Cont.*

Vogler, A. E. E. (*cont.*)		10-26	Eastern Province v. Griqualand West (Johannesburg)	1906-07
Waddington, J. E.	(1)	9-105	Griqualand West v. Eastern Province (Port Elizabeth)	1954-55
Wadkar, R. D.	(1)	9-38	Bombay v. Western India States (Jamnagar)	1937-38
Wainwright, E.	(1)	9-66	Yorks. v. Middx. (Sheffield)	1894
Walker, G. G.	(1)	9-68	Derby v. Leics. (Leicester)	1895
Walker, V. E.	(3)	10-74	England v. Surrey (Oval)	1859
		9-62	Middx. v. Sussex (Islington)	1864
		10-104	Middx. v. Lancs. (Manchester)	1865
Wall, T. W.	(1)	10-36	South Australia v. N.S.W. (Sydney)	1932-33
Walsh, J. E.	(1)	9-101	Cahn's XI v. Glamorgan (Newport)	1938
Wardle, J. H.	(2)	9-48	Yorks. v. Sussex (Hove)	1954
		9-25	Yorks. v. Lancs. (Manchester)	1954
Warr, J. J.	(1)	9-65	Middx. v. Kent (Lord's)	1956
Wass, T. G.	(2)	9-91	Notts. v. Surrey (Oval)	1902
		9-67	Notts. v. Derby (Blackwell)	1911
Watson, A.	(1)	9-117	Lancs. v. Derby (Manchester)	1874
Watts, E. A.	(1)	10-67	Surrey v. Warwicks. (Birmingham)	1939
Wells, G.	(1)	9-105	Sussex v. Surrey (Brighton)	1860
Wensley, A. F.	(1)	9-36	Auckland v. Otago (Auckland)	1929-30
White, D. W.	(1)	9-44	Hants. v. Leics. (Portsmouth)	1966
White, J. C.	(5)	9-46	Somerset v. Glos. (Bristol)	1914
		10-76	Somerset v. Worcs. (Worcester)	1921
		9-58	Somerset v. Warwicks. (Birmingham)	1922
		9-71	Somerset v. Sussex (Eastbourne)	1931
		9-51	Somerset v. Glamorgan (Bath)	1932
Williams, A. C.	(1)	9-29	Yorks. v. Hants. (Dewsbury)	1919
Wilson, G. A.	(1)	9-75	Worcs. v. Oxford U. (Oxford)	1904
Wisden, J.	(2)	10-	North v. South (Lord's)	1850
		9-	Under 36 v. Over 36 (Lord's)	1850
Woodcock, A.	(1)	9-28	Leics. v. M.C.C. (Lord's)	1899
Woods, S. M. J.	(1)	10-69	Cambridge U. v. Thornton's XI (Cambridge)	1890
Wootton, G.	(3)	9-37	M.C.C. v. Oxford U. (Lord's)	1865
		10-	All England XI v. Yorks. (Sheffield)	1865
		9-45	M.C.C. v. England (Lord's)	1868
Wright, D. V. P.	(2)	9-47	Kent v. Glos. (Bristol)	1939
		9-51	Kent v. Leics. (Maidstone)	1949
Wright, W.	(1)	9-72	Kent v. M.C.C. (Lord's)	1889
Young, J. A.	(1)	9-55	England XI v. Commonwealth (Hastings)	1952
Yuile, B. W.	(1)	9-100	Central Districts v. Canterbury (New Plymouth)	1965-66

SEVENTEEN OR MORE WICKETS IN A MATCH

NINETEEN WICKETS

O. M. R. W.		
68 —27— 90—19	J. C. Laker: England v. Australia (Manchester)	1956

EIGHTEEN WICKETS

O. M. R. W.		
48 — — 96—18	H. A. Arkwright: M.C.C. v. Gentlemen of Kent (Canterbury)	1861

(*This was a twelve-a-side match.*)

SEVENTEEN WICKETS

O. M. R. W.		
76.1—36— 89—17	W. G. Grace: Glos. v. Notts. (Cheltenham)	1877
116.2—41—201—17	G. Giffen: South Australia v. Victoria (Adelaide)	1885-86
69 —37— 50—17	C. T. B. Turner: Australians v. England XI (Hastings)	1888
77.3—32—119—17	W. Mead: Essex v. Hants. (Southampton)	1895
26.3— 6— 54—17	W. P. Howell: Australians v. Western Province (Cape Town)	1902-03
35.2— 7—137—17	W. Brearley: Lancs. v. Somerset (Manchester)	1905
31.1—14— 48—17	C. Blythe: Kent v. Northants. (Northampton)	1907
47.4—10— 91—17	H. Dean: Lancs. v. Yorks. (Liverpool)	1913

Seventeen or More Wickets in a Match—*Cont.*

O. M. R. W.		
65.3—16—159—17	S. F. Barnes: England v. South Africa (Johannesburg) ..	1913-14
33.5—10— 67—17	A. P. Freeman: Kent v. Sussex (Hove)	1922
30 — 6— 89—17	F. C. L. Matthews: Notts. v. Northants. (Nottingham) ..	1923
48.3—23— 56—17	C. W. L. Parker: Glos. v. Essex (Gloucester)	1925
75.3—36—106—17	G. R. Cox: Sussex v. Warwicks. (Horsham) *(Aged 51)* ..	1926
41.4—12— 92—17	A. P. Freeman: Kent v. Warwicks. (Folkestone)	1932
41.1—13— 91—17	H. Verity: Yorks. v. Essex (Leyton)	1933
62.5—11—212—17	J. C. Clay: Glamorgan v. Worcs. (Swansea)	1937
31.6— 3—106—17	T. W. Goddard: Glos. v. Kent (Bristol)	1939

SIXTEEN OR MORE WICKETS IN A DAY

17-48	C. Blythe: Kent v. Northants. (Northampton)	1907
17-91	H. Verity: Yorks. v. Essex (Leyton)	1933
17-106	T. W. Goddard: Glos. v. Kent (Bristol)	1939
16-38	T. Emmett: Yorks. v. Cambridgeshire (Hunslet)	1869
16-38	A. E. E. Vogler: Eastern Province v. Griqualand West (Johannesburg) ..	1906-07
16-52	J. Southerton: South v. North (Lord's)	1875
16-69	T. G. Wass: Notts. v. Lancs. (Liverpool)	1906
16-83	J. C. White: Somerset v. Worcs. (Bath)	1919
16-103	T. G. Wass: Notts. v. Essex (Nottingham)	1908

FIFTEEN OR MORE WICKETS IN A MATCH

Arkweight, H. A. ..	(1)	18-96	M.C.C. v. Gentlemen of Kent (Canterbury)	1861
Baldwin, H.	(1)	15-142	Hants. v. Sussex (Hove)	1898
Barnes, S. F.	(1)	17-159	England v. South Africa (Johannesburg) ..	1913-14
Blythe, C.	(5)	15-76	Kent v. Hants. (Tonbridge)	1904
		15-99	England v. South Africa (Leeds)	1907
		17-48	Kent v. Northants. (Northampton) ..	1907
		16-102	Kent v. Leics. (Leicester)	1909
		15-45	Kent v. Leics. (Leicester)	1912
Bosanquet, B. J. T. ..	(1)	15-65	Oxford U. v. Sussex (Oxford)	1900
Botten, J. T.	(1)	15-49	N-E. Transvaal v. Griqualand West (Pretoria)	1958-59
Bowes, W. E.	(1)	16-35	Yorks. v. Northants. (Kettering)	1935
Braund, L. C.	(1)	15-71	Somerset v. Yorks. (Sheffield)	1902
Brearley, W.	(1)	17-137	Lancs. v. Somerset (Manchester)	1905
Briggs, J.	(2)	15-28	England v. South Africa (Cape Town) ..	1888-89
		15-57	Londesborough's XI v. Australians (Scarborough)	1890
Burton, G.	(1)	16-114	Middx. v. Yorks. (Sheffield)	1888
Butler, S. E.	(1)	15-95	Oxford U. v. Cambridge U. (Lord's) ..	1871
Callaway, S. T.	(2)	15-175	N.S.W. v. New Zealand XI (Christchurch) ..	1895-96
		15-60	Canterbury v. Hawke's Bay (Napier) ..	1903-04
Cartwright, T. W. ..	(1)	15-89	Warwicks. v. Glamorgan (Swansea) ..	1967
Chatterjee, P.	(1)	15-109	Bengal v. Madhya Pradesh (Calcutta) ..	1955-56
Chester, J.	(1)	15-	M.C.C. v. Cambridge U. (Cambridge) ..	1850
Clarke, W.	(2)	16-	Notts. v. Kent (Nottingham)	1845
		15-98	North v. South (Oval)	1851
Clay, J. C.	(2)	15-86	Glamorgan v. Northants. (Llanelly) ..	1935
		17-212	Glamorgan v. Worcs. (Swansea)	1937
Collins, G. G.	(1)	16-83	Kent v. Notts. (Dover)	1922
Conway, A. J.	(1)	15-87	Worcs. v. Glos. (Moreton-in-the-Marsh) ..	1914
Cooke, F. H.	(1)	15-94	Otago v. Canterbury (Christchurch) ..	1882-83
Cox, G. R.	(1)	17-106	Sussex v. Warwicks. (Horsham)	1926
Davidson, G.	(1)	15-116	Derby v. Essex (Leyton)	1898
Dean, H.	(3)	16-103	Lancs. v. Somerset (Bath)	1910
		15-108	Lancs. v. Kent (Manchester)	1912
		17-91	Lancs. v. Yorks. (Liverpool)	1913
Deas, L. M.	(1)	16-166	Europeans v. Hindus (Bombay)	1905-06
Dennett, G.	(7)	15-96	Glos. v. Middx. (Bristol)	1904
		15-88	Glos. v. Essex (Bristol)	1906
		15-140	Glos. v. Worcs. (Cheltenham)	1906

Fifteen or More Wickets in a Match—*Cont.*

Dennett, G. (*cont.*)		15-21	Glos. v. Northants. (Gloucester)	1907
		15-97	Glos. v. Northants. (Northampton)	1907
		16-146	Glos. v. Hants. (Bristol)	1912
		15-195	Glos. v. Surrey (Bristol)	1913
Dooland, B.	(2)	16-83	Notts. v. Essex (Nottingham)	1954
		15-193	Notts. v. Kent (Gravesend)	1956
Dowson, E. M.	(1)	16-58	Bennett's XI v. Jamaica (Kingston)	1901-02
Drake, A.	(1)	15-51	Yorks. v. Somerset (Weston-super-Mare)	1914
Dwyer, E. B.	(1)	16-100	Sussex v. Middx. (Hove)	1906
Ellis, C. H.	(1)	15-297	Sussex v. Surrey (Brighton)	1863
Emmett, T.	(1)	16-38	Yorks. v. Cambridgeshire (Hunslet)	1869
Farnes, K.	(1)	15-113	Essex v. Glamorgan (Clacton)	1938
Fazal Mahmood	(1)	15-76	Punjab v. Services (Lahore)	1956-57
Fleetwood-Smith, L. O.	(2)	15-226	Victoria v. N.S.W. (Sydney)	1934-35
		15-96	Victoria v. Queensland (Melbourne)	1936-37
Freeman, A. P.	(9)	17-67	Kent v. Sussex (Hove)	1922
		15-224	Kent v. Leics. (Tonbridge)	1928
		16-94	Kent v. Essex (Southend)	1930
		15-142	Kent v. Essex (Gravesend)	1931
		15-144	Kent v. Leics. (Maidstone)	1931
		15-94	Kent v. Somerset (Canterbury)	1931
		17-92	Kent v. Warwicks. (Folkestone)	1932
		16-82	Kent v. Northants. (Tunbridge Wells)	1932
		15-122	Kent v. Middx. (Lord's)	1933
Geary, G.	(1)	16-96	Leics. v. Glamorgan (Pontypridd)	1929
Giffen, G.	(6)	17-201	South Australia v. Victoria (Adelaide)	1885-86
		16-101	Australians v. Derby (Derby)	1886
		16-65	Australians v. Lancs. (Manchester)	1886
		16-166	South Australia v. Victoria (Adelaide)	1891-92
		16-186	South Australia v. N.S.W. (Adelaide)	1894-95
		15-185	South Australia v. Victoria (Adelaide)	1902-03
Gladwin, C.	(1)	16-84	Derby v. Worcs. (Stourbridge).	1952
Glover, G. K.	(1)	15-68	Griqualand West v. Eastern Province (Cape Town)	1893-94
Goddard, T. W.	(7)	16-181	Glos. v. Worcs. (Cheltenham)	1937
		16-99	Glos. v. Worcs. (Bristol)	1939
		17-106	Glos. v. Kent (Bristol)	1939
		15-81	Glos. v. Notts. (Bristol)	1947
		15-134	Glos. v. Leics. (Gloucester)	1947
		15-156	Glos. v. Middx. (Cheltenham)	1947
		15-107	Glos. v. Derby (Bristol)	1949
Grace, E. M.	(1)	15-146	Gents of M.C.C. v. Gents of Kent (Canterbury)	1862
Grace, W. G.	(5)	15-79	Glos. v. Yorks. (Sheffield)	1872
		15-147	M.C.C. v. Kent (Canterbury)	1873
		17-89	Glos. v. Notts. (Cheltenham)	1877
		15-116	Glos. v. Surrey (Cirencester)	1879
		16-60	M.C.C. v. Notts. (Lord's)	1885
Grimmett, C. V.	(1)	16-289	South Australia v. Queensland (Adelaide)	1934-35
Gupte, S. P.	(1)	15-104	Rajasthan v. Vidarbha (Nagpur)	1962-63
Halfyard, D. J.	(1)	15-117	Kent v. Worcs. (Maidstone)	1959
Hammond, W. R.	(1)	15-128	Glos. v. Worcs. (Cheltenham)	1928
Hargreave, S.	(1)	15-76	Warwicks. v. Surrey (Oval)	1903
Harry, F.	(1)	15-70	Lancs. v. Warwicks. (Manchester)	1906
Hearne, J. T.	(4)	15-154	Middx. v. Notts. (Nottingham)	1893
		15-110	M.C.C. v. Oxford U. (Oxford)	1897
		16-114	Middx. v. Lancs. (Manchester)	1898
		15-93	Middx. v. Somerset (Lord's)	1904
Hearne, W.	(1)	15-114	Kent v. Lancs. (Manchester)	1893
Henderson, R.	(1)	15-98	Gents. of England v. Oxford U. (Oxford)	1877
Hinkly, E.	(1)	16-	Kent v. England (Lord's)	1848
Hirst, G. H.	(1)	15-63	Yorks. v. Leics. (Hull)	1907
Hopwood, J. L.	(1)	15-112	Lancs. v. Worcs. (Blackpool)	1934
Howell, W. P.	(2)	15-57	Australians v. Surrey (Oval)	1899
		17-54	Australians v. Western Province (Cape Town)	1902-03
Humphreys, W.	(1)	15-193	Sussex v. Somerset (Taunton)	1893
Illingworth, R.	(1)	15-123	Yorks. v. Glamorgan (Swansea)	1960

Fifteen or More Wickets in a Match—*Cont.*

Bowler	No.	Analysis	Match	Season
Jackson, J.	(2)	15-91	North v. South (Lord's)	1857
		15-73	Notts. v. Surrey (Oval)	1860
Jenkins, R. O.	(1)	15-122	Worcs. v. Sussex (Dudley)	1953
Jupp, V. W. C.	(1)	15-52	Northants. v. Glamorgan (Swansea)	1925
Kennedy, A. S.	(1)	15-116	Hants. v. Somerset (Bath)	1922
Laker, J. C.	(2)	15-97	Surrey v. M.C.C. (Lord's)	1954
		19-90	England v. Australia (Manchester)	1956
Langford, B. A.	(1)	15-54	Somerset v. Lancs. (Weston-super-Mare)	1958
Lillywhite, W.	(2)	16-	Sussex v. Hants. & Surrey (Bramshill)	1826
		15-	England v. Kent (Lord's)	1840
Litteljohn, A. R.	(1)	15-189	Middx. v. Lancs. (Lord's)	1911
Lock, G. A. R.	(2)	16-83	Surrey v. Kent (Blackheath)	1956
		15-182	Surrey v. Kent (Blackheath)	1958
Lockwood, W. H.	(1)	15-184	Surrey v. Glos. (Cheltenham)	1899
Lohmann, G. A.	(2)	15-98	Surrey v. Sussex (Hove)	1889
		15-45	England v. South Africa (Port Elizabeth)	1895-96
McBeath, D. J.	(1)	15-168	Canterbury v. Auckland (Christchurch)	1918-19
McDonald, E. A.	(1)	15-154	Lancs. v. Kent (Manchester)	1928
McDonell, H. C.	(1)	15-138	Cambridge U. v. Surrey (Cambridge)	1904
McIntyre, W.	(1)	15-47	Lancs. v. Derby (Derby)	1877
McKibbin, T. R.	(1)	15-125	N.S.W. v. South Australia (Adelaide)	1896-97
Mailey, A. A.	(1)	15-193	Australians v. Notts. (Nottingham)	1926
Marlar, R. G.	(2)	15-133	Sussex v. Glamorgan (Swansea)	1952
		15-119	Sussex v. Lancs. (Hove)	1955
Marsham, C. D.	(1)	16-93	Gents of England v. Gents of M.C.C. (Lord's)	1855
Matthews, F. C. L.	(1)	17-89	Notts. v. Northants. (Nottingham)	1923
Mead, W.	(2)	17-119	Essex v. Hants. (Southampton)	1895
		15-115	Essex v. Leics. (Leyton)	1903
Meyer, R. J. O.	(1)	16-188	Europeans v. Muslims (Bombay)	1927-28
Moir, A. M.	(1)	15-203	Otago v. Central Districts (New Plymouth)	1953-54
Mold, A.	(4)	15-131	Lancs. v. Somerset (Taunton)	1891
		15-87	Lancs. v. Sussex (Hove)	1894
		16-111	Lancs. v. Kent (Manchester)	1895
		15-85	Lancs. v. Notts. (Nottingham)	1895
Morley, F.	(1)	15-35	Notts. v. Kent (Town Malling)	1878
Mortimore, G.	(1)	15-	Nelson v. Wellington (Nelson)	1862-63
Muncer, B. L.	(2)	15-161	Glamorgan v. Essex (Brentwood)	1948
		15-201	Glamorgan v. Sussex (Swansea)	1948
Mynn, A.	(1)	15-73	Gents of Kent v. Gents of England (Canterbury)	1843
Nash, J.	(1)	15-116	Glamorgan v. Worcs. (Swansea)	1921
Newman, J. A.	(1)	16-88	Hants. v. Somerset (Weston-super-Mare)	1927
Nichols, M. S.	(1)	15-165	Essex v. Glos. (Gloucester)	1938
Nupen, E. P.	(1)	16-136	Transvaal v. Griqualand West (Johannesburg)	1931-32
Parker, C. W. L.	(7)	15-109	Glos. v. Derby (Derby)	1924
		17-56	Glos. v. Essex (Gloucester)	1925
		16-154	Glos. v. Somerset (Bristol)	1927
		15-173	Glos. v. Northants. (Gloucester)	1927
		16-109	Glos. v. Middx. (Cheltenham)	1930
		15-91	Glos. v. Surrey (Cheltenham)	1930
		15-113	Glos. v. Notts. (Bristol)	1931
Parkin, C. H.	(1)	15-95	Lancs. v. Glamorgan (Blackpool)	1923
Parris, F. H.	(1)	15-98	Sussex v. Glos. (Bristol)	1894
Peel, R.	(1)	15-50	Yorks. v. Somerset (Leeds)	1895
Perks, R. T. D.	(1)	15-106	Worcs. v. Essex (Worcester)	1937
Relf, A. E.	(1)	15-77	Sussex v. Leics. (Hove)	1912
Rhodes, W.	(2)	15-56	Yorks. v. Essex (Leyton)	1899
		15-124	England v. Australia (Melbourne)	1903-04
Richardson, T.	(5)	15-95	Surrey v. Essex (Oval)	1894
		15-155	Surrey v. Hants. (Oval)	1895
		15-113	Surrey v. Leics. (Oval)	1896
		15-154	Surrey v. Yorks. (Leeds)	1897
		15-83	Surrey v. Warwicks. (Oval)	1898
Roberts, F. G.	(1)	15-123	Glos. v. Kent (Maidstone)	1897
Robinson, E. P.	(1)	15-78	Somerset v. Sussex (Weston-super-Mare)	1952
Rowan, A. M. B.	(1)	15-68	Transvaal v. Australians (Johannesburg)	1949-50
Smith, S. G.	(1)	16-85	West Indian XI v. Bennett's XI (Port of Spain)	1901-02

Fifteen or More Wickets in a Match—*Cont.*

Smith, T. P. B.	(1)	16-215	Essex v. Middx. (Colchester)	1947
Southerton, J.	(1)	16-52	South v. North (Lord's)	1875
Spofforth, F. R.	(1)	15-36	Australians v. Oxford U. (Oxford)	1886
Statham, J. B.	(2)	15-89	Lancs. v. Warwicks. (Coventry)	1957
		15-108	Lancs. v. Leics. (Leicester)	1964
Tarrant, F. A.	(3)	15-47	Middx. v. Hants. (Lord's)	1913
		16-176	Middx. v. Lancs. (Manchester)	1914
		16-69	England XII v. India XII (Bombay)	1915-16
Tarrant, G.	(1)	15-56	Cambridgeshire v. Kent (Chatham)	1862
Tate, F. W.	(1)	15-68	Sussex v. Middx. (Lord's)	1902
Thompson, G. J.	(1)	15-167	Northants. v. Leics. (Northampton)	1906
Thomson, N. I.	(1)	15-75	Sussex v. Warwicks. (Worthing)	1964
Tinley, R. C.	(1)	15-78	Notts. v. Cambridgeshire (Nottingham)	1862
Titmus, F. J.	(1)	15-95	Middx. v. Somerset (Bath)	1955
Townsend, C. L.	(5)	16-122	Glos. v. Notts. (Nottingham)	1895
		15-184	Glos. v. Yorks. (Cheltenham)	1895
		15-134	Glos. v. Middx. (Lord's)	1898
		15-141	Glos. v. Essex (Clifton)	1898
		15-205	Glos. v. Warwicks. (Cheltenham)	1898
Tribe, G. E.	(2)	15-75	Northants. v. Yorks. (Bradford)	1955
		15-31	Northants. v. Yorks. (Northampton)	1958
Trott, A. E.	(1)	15-187	Middx. v. Sussex (Lord's)	1901
Trumble, H.	(2)	15-199	Victoria v. South Australia (Adelaide)	1888-89
		15-68	Australians v. South of England (Bournemouth)	1902
Turner, C. T. B.	(3)	16-79	N.S.W. v. Shrewsbury's XI (Sydney)	1887-88
		17-50	Australians v. England XI (Hastings)	1888
		15-174	N.S.W. v. Victoria (Sydney)	1890-91
Tyler, E. J.	(2)	15-96	Somerset v. Notts. (Taunton)	1892
		15-95	Somerset v. Sussex (Taunton)	1895
Verity, H.	(5)	17-91	Yorks. v. Essex (Leyton)	1933
		15-104	England v. Australia (Lord's)	1934
		15-129	Yorks. v. Oxford U. (Oxford)	1936
		15-38	Yorks. v. Kent (Sheffield)	1936
		15-100	Yorks. v. Essex (Westcliff)	1936
Vine, J.	(1)	15-161	Sussex v. Notts. (Nottingham)	1901
Vogler, A. E. E.	(1)	16-38	Eastern Province v. Griqualand West (Johannesburg)	1906-07
Walsh, J. E.	(3)	15-100	Leics. v. Sussex (Hove)	1948
		15-164	Leics. v. Notts. (Loughborough)	1949
		16-225	Leics. v. Oxford U. (Oxford)	1953
Wardle, J. H.	(1)	16-112	Yorks. v. Sussex (Hull)	1954
Warren, A. R.	(1)	15-112	Derby v. Notts. (Welbeck)	1904
Wass, T. G.	(2)	16-69	Notts. v. Lancs. (Liverpool)	1906
		16-103	Notts. v. Essex (Nottingham)	1908
Wellard, A. W.	(1)	15-101	Somerset v. Worcs. (Bath)	1947
White, J. C.	(3)	16-83	Somerset v. Worcs. (Bath)	1919
		15-175	Somerset v. Worcs. (Worcester)	1921
		15-96	Somerset v. Glamorgan (Bath)	1932
Wilson, G. A.	(1)	15-142	Worcs. v. Somerset (Taunton)	1905
Wisden, J.	(1)	15-	Sussex v. Kent (Brighton)	1848
Woodcock, A.	(1)	15-136	Leics. v. Notts. (Leicester)	1894
Woods, S. M. J.	(2)	15-88	Cambridge U. v. Thornton's XI (Cambridge)	1890
		15-86	Hawke's XI v. Philadelphians (Philadelphia)	1891-92
Wright, D. V. P.	(3)	16-80	Kent v. Somerset (Bath)	1939
		15-173	Kent v. Sussex (Hastings)	1947
		15-163	Kent v. Leics. (Maidstone)	1949
Young, H.	(1)	15-154	Essex v. Warwicks. (Birmingham)	1899

OUTSTANDING INNINGS ANALYSES

TEN WICKETS

O. *M.* *R.* *W.*		
19.4—16—10—10	H. Verity: Yorks. v. Notts. (Leeds)	1932
16.2— 8—18—10	G. Geary: Leics. v. Glamorgan (Pontypridd)	1929
19 —11—20—10	P. Chatterjee: Bengal v. Assam (Jorhat)	1956-57

Outstanding Innings Analyses—*Cont.*

O. *M.* *R.* *W.*		
12 — 2—26—10	A. E. E. Vogler: Eastern Province v. Griqualand West (Johannesburg)	1906-07
21.3—10—28—10	A. E. Moss: Canterbury v. Wellington (Christchurch)	1889-90
23.2—14—28—10	W. P. Howell: Australians v. Surrey (Oval)	1899
16 — 7—30—10	C. Blythe: Kent v. Northants. (Northampton)	1907

NINE WICKETS

O. *M.* *R.* *W.*		
6.3— 4— 7—9	Ahad Khan: Railways v. Dera Ismail Khan (Lahore)	1964-65
10 — 4—11—9	A. P. Freeman: Kent v. Sussex (Hove)	1922
6.3— 3—12—9	H. Verity: Yorks. v. Kent (Sheffield)	1936
17.1—10—15—9	C. T. B. Turner: Australians v. England XI (Stoke)	1888
14.5— 9—17—9	G. G. Napier: Europeans v. Parsis (Poona)	1909-10
15.5— 6—17—9	P. J. Loader: Surrey v. Warwicks. (Oval)	1958
17.3— 9—17—9	H. L. Jackson: Derby v. Cambridge U. (Cambridge)	1959
15.2— 7—18—9	F. R. Spofforth: Australians v. Oxford U. (Oxford)	1886
13 — 6—18—9	R. K. Oxenham: Australians v. Ceylon (Colombo)	1935-36
25 — —19—9	J. Grundy: Notts. v. Kent (Nottingham)	1864
15.4— 7—19—9	A. M. B. Rowan: Transvaal v. Australians (Johannesburg) ..	1949-50
35.1—25—20—9	W. G. Grace: M.C.C. v. Notts. (Lord's)	1885
19.3— 8—21—9	J. W. Marchant: Wellington v. Hawke's Bay (Wellington) ..	1873-74
15.1— 8—21—9	L. B. Richmond: Notts. v. Hants. (Nottingham)	1922
13.5— 8—21—9	T. W. Goddard: Glos. v. Cambridge U. (Cheltenham)	1929
21.3—10—22—9	R. Peel: Yorks. v. Somerset (Leeds)	1895
10.3— 2—22—9	M. G. Melle: South Africans v. Tasmania (Launceston)	1952-53

EIGHT WICKETS

O. *M.* *R.* *W.*		
14 —12— 2—8	J. C. Laker: England v. Rest (Bradford)	1950
11.1— 7— 4—8	D. Shackleton: Hants. v. Somerset (Weston-super-Mare) ..	1955
16 —11— 5—8	E. Peate: Yorks. v. Surrey (Holbeck)	1883
14 — — 7—8	J. Bickley: England v. Kent & Sussex (Lord's)	1856
9.4 5— 7—8	G. A. Lohmann: England v. South Africa (Port Elizabeth) ..	1895-96
12 — 2— 7—8	C. H. Palmer: Leics. v. Surrey (Leicester)	1955
6.7— 2— 8—8	J. E. D. Sealy: Barbados v. Trinidad (Bridgetown)	1941-42
12 — 7— 8—8	M. G. Melle: Transvaal v. Griqualand West (Johannesburg) ..	1950-51
13.2— — 9—8	G. Wootton: M.C.C. v. Sussex (Lord's)	1863
6 — 1— 9—8	G. Dennett: Glos. v. Northants. (Gloucester)	1907
14.2—10— 9—8	G. E. Tribe: Northants. v. Yorks. (Northampton)	1958
13 — 8—11—8	G. Freeman: Yorks. v. Lancs. (Holbeck)	1868
14.2— 5—11—8	J. Briggs: England v. South Africa (Cape Town)	1888-89
11.4— 6—11—8	B. M. Billimaria: Parsis v. Europeans (Poona)	1896-97
13 — 7—11—8	A. S. Kennedy: Hants v. Glamorgan (Cardiff)	1921
8.2— 2—11—8	W. H. Copson: Derby v. Warwicks. (Derby)	1937
13 — 9—11—8	I. J. Jones: Glamorgan v. Leics. (Leicester)	1965
13.3— —12—8	R. C. Tinley: Notts. v. Cambridgeshire (Nottingham)	1862
20.2—13—12—8	R. Peel: Yorks. v. Notts. (Sheffield)	1888
12 — 8—12—8	R. W. Norden: Transvaal v. Rhodesia (Johannesburg)	1904-05
17 —10—12—8	C. W. L. Parker: Glos. v. Essex (Gloucester)	1925
6.4— 2—12—8	W. H. R. Andrews: Somerset v. Surrey (Oval)	1937
9.4— 3—12—8	G. S. Ramchand: Bombay v. Saurashtra (Bombay)	1959-60
17.1—10—12—8	R. Harman: Surrey v. Notts. (Nottingham)	1964
13 — 6—13—8	J. P. Firth: Wellington v. Hawke's Bay (Wellington)	1883-84
21.3—12—13—8	C. T. B. Turner: Australians v. England XI (Hastings)	1888
9.1— 3—13—8	W. C. Smith: Surrey v. Northants. (Oval)	1910
13.2— 5—13—8	E. Robinson: Yorks. v. Cambridge U. (Cambridge)	1928
8 — 2—13—8	D. P. B. Morkel: South Africans v. Western Australia (Perth) ..	1931-32
12 — 7—13—8	Zafar: Multan v. Quetta (Multan)	1958-59
27.1—17—14—8	A. Shaw: M.C.C. v. Derby (Lord's)	1881
19 —12—14—8	S. Austen: N.S.W. v. Hawke's Bay (Napier)	1893-94
7.5— 1—14—8	H. D. Kanga: Parsis v. Europeans (Poona)	1913-14
7.4— 3—14—8	V. D. Sondhi: Delhi v. Jammu & Kashmir (New Delhi).. ..	1963-64
33.3— —15—8	G. Wootton: M.C.C. v. Surrey (Lord's)	1867
29.3—21—15—8	A. Rylott: M.C.C. v. Kent (Lord's)..	1878

Outstanding Innings Analyses—*Cont.*

O. *M.* *R.* *W.*		
11 — 7—15—8	A. Hearne: Kent v. Glos. (Tonbridge)	1903
17.2—11—15—8	R. Tyldesley: Lancs. v. Northants. (Kettering)	1926
14 — 8—15—8	H. J. Butler: Notts. v. Surrey (Nottingham)	1937
6.4— 2—15—8	S. Ramadhin: West Indians v. Glos. (Cheltenham)	1950

SEVEN WICKETS

O. *M.* *R.* *W.*		
8.3— 6— 3—7	F. R. Spofforth: Australians v. England XI (Birmingham)	1884
9.3— 7— 4—7	W. A. Henderson: N-E. Transvaal v. O.F.S. (Bloemfontein)	1937-38
21.2—18— 6—7	F. Morley: M.C.C. v. Oxford U. (Oxford)	1877
7 — 4— 6—7	A. Waddington: Yorks. v. Sussex (Hull)	1922
14 —12— 6—7	R. Tyldesley: Lancs. v. Northants. (Liverpool)	1924
12.4— 6— 6—7	R. V. Webster: Warwicks. v. Yorks. (Birmingham)	1964
13 — 9— 6—7	R. Illingworth: Yorks. v. Glos. (Harrogate)	1967
24 —20— 7—7	W. Caffyn: Surrey v. Kent (Canterbury)	1862
41.2—38— 7—7	A. Shaw: Notts. v. M.C.C. (Lord's)	1875
10.2— 7— 7—7	F. Morley: Notts. v. Derby (Nottingham)	1879
6.4— 3— 7—7	L. T. Driffield: Cambridge U. v. M.C.C. (Cambridge)	1900
7 — 3— 7—7	J. Bailey: Hants. v. Notts. (Southampton)	1932
13.3— 8— 7—7	G. Geary: Leics. v. Warwicks. (Hinckley)	1936
9.1— 6— 7—7	D. J. Shepherd: Glamorgan v. Hants. (Cardiff)	1966
14 — 9— 8—7	L. Cook: Lancs. v. Derby (Chesterfield)	1920
16 — 9— 8—7	G. R. Cox: Sussex v. Derby (Hove)	1920
10 — 7— 8—7	A. S. Kennedy: Hants. v. Warwicks. (Portsmouth)	1927
11.5— 7— 8—7	James Langridge: Sussex v. Glos. (Cheltenham)	1932
10 — — 9—7	G. Bennett: Kent v. Sussex (Brighton)	1857
9.3— 6— 9—7	T. Emmett: Yorks. v. Sussex (Hove)	1878
22 —15— 9—7	F. Morley: Notts. v. Kent (Town Malling)	1878
19.2—12— 9—7	F. Morley: Notts. v. Surrey (Oval)	1880
6.3— 3— 9—7	F. E. Woolley: Kent v. Surrey (Oval)	1911
7.5— 3— 9—7	C. Blythe: Kent v. Leics. (Leicester)	1912
14 — 7— 9—7	G. G. Macaulay: Yorks. v. Northants. (Kettering)	1933
6 — 1— 9—7	H. Verity: Yorks. v. Sussex (Hove)	1939
12.1— 8— 9—7	J. T. Partridge: Rhodesia v. Border (Bulawayo)	1959-60
16 — —10—7	H. Stubberfield: Sussex v. Kent (Brighton)	1859
20.1—16—10—7	A. Watson: England v. M.C.C. (Lord's)	1877
9 — 7—10—7	A. Mold: Lancs. v. Somerset (Manchester)	1894
8 — 2—10—7	A. J. Hopkins: Australians v. Cambridge U. (Cambridge)	1902
6.2— 1—10—7	A. C. King: Natal v. Griqualand West (Johannesburg)	1906-07
8.2— 4—10—7	J. T. Newstead: Yorks. v. Worcs. (Bradford)	1907
9 — 4—10—7	J. C. White: Somerset v. Glos. (Bristol)	1920
5.3— 2—10—7	P. G. H. Fender: Surrey v. Middx. (Lord's)	1927
20.4—13—10—7	F. M. Sibbles: Lancs. v. Yorks. (Bradford)	1932
17.2—14—10—7	P. J. Robinson: Somerset v. Notts. (Nottingham)	1966

SIX WICKETS

O. *M.* *R.* *W.*		
21.1—20— 1—6	S. Cosstick: Victoria v. Tasmania (Melbourne)	1868-69
4.5— 3— 1—6	V. I. Smith: South Africans v. Derby (Derby)	1947
11 —10— 1—6	Israr Ali: Bahawalpur v. Dacca U. (Bahawalpur)	1957-58
8.4— 7— 2—6	F. E. Field: Warwicks. v. Worcs. (Dudley)	1914
8.1— 6— 3—6	H. F. Boyle: Australians v. M.C.C. (Lord's)	1878
13.3—11— 3—6	A. Penn: Kent v. Sussex (Tunbridge Wells)	1878
10.1— 9— 3—6	R. G. Barlow: Lancs. v. Derby (Derby)	1881
4.4— 3— 3—6	T. G. Wass: Notts. v. M.C.C. (Lord's)	1907
7 — 4— 3—6	G. G. Macaulay: Yorks. v. Derby (Hull)	1921
8 — 5— 3—6	J. A. Cowie: New Zealanders v. Ireland (Dublin)	1937
11 — 9— 3—6	T. L. Goddard: Natal v. Border (East London)	1959-60
9 — 8— 3—6	Rajinder Pal: Delhi v. Jammu & Kashmir (Srinagar)	1960-61
5.3— 3— 4—6	F. R. Spofforth: Australians v. M.C.C. (Lord's)	1878
7.5— 4— 4—6	W. Rhodes: Yorks. v. Notts. (Nottingham)	1901
8 — 5— 4—6	S. T. Callaway: Canterbury v. Wellington (Wellington)	1903-04
9.2— — 5—6	C. Reid: Victoria v. Tasmania (Melbourne)	1870-71
9.2— 3— 5—6	Bennett: Nelson v. Wellington (Nelson)	1885-86
9.1— 6— 5—6	G. S. Boyes: Hants. v. Derby (Portsmouth)	1933

Outstanding Innings Analyses—*Cont.*

O.	*M.*	*R.*	*W.*		
14	11	5	6	J. C. Laker: Surrey v. Notts (Oval)	1955
16	14	5	6	D. J. Shepherd: Glamorgan v. Notts. (Newport)	1961
18.2	13	6	6	W. W. Robinson: Auckland v. Nelson (Nelson)	1873-74
8.4	5	6	6	A. E. Bailey: Somerset v. Warwicks. (Taunton)	1906
8	5	6	6	C. H. Parkin: Lancs. v. Glamorgan (Liverpool)	1924
9.4	7	6	6	J. H. Wardle: Yorks. v. Glos. (Bristol)	1955
4	0	6	6	R. Goel: Southern Punjab v. Northern Punjab (Patiala)	1963-64

FIVE WICKETS

O.	*M.*	*R.*	*W.*		
3	3	0	5	A. D. Pougher: M.C.C. v. Australians (Lord's)	1896
6	6	0	5	G. R. Cox: Sussex v. Somerset (Weston-super-Mare)	1921
5	5	0	5	R. Tyldesley: Lancs. v. Leics. (Manchester)	1924
6.4	6	0	5	P. T. Mills: Glos. v. Somerset (Bristol)	1928
4	3	1	5	F. W. Tate: Sussex v. Kent (Tonbridge)	1888
5.4	5	1	5	J. S. Savage: Lancs. v. Hants. (Blackpool)	1967
15.2	13	2	5	D. Ashby: Canterbury v. Auckland (Auckland)	1877-78
6.1	4	2	5	E. H. Killick: Sussex v. Hants. (Chichester)	1907
5.2	4	2	5	J. C. Clay: Glamorgan v. Somerset (Cardiff)	1922
2.3	1	2	5	E. R. H. Toshack: Australia v. India (Brisbane)	1947-48
5.3	4	2	5	G. A. R. Lock: Surrey v. Worcs. (Oval)	1954
5.1	4	2	5	W. B. Bridge: Warwicks. v. Kent (Blackheath)	1961
4	2	2	5	V. M. Muddiah: Services v. Jammu & Kashmir (New Delhi)	1961-62
2.2	1	3	5	B. D. Hylton-Stewart: Somerset v. Worcs. (Stourbridge)	1912
5	3	3	5	C. F. W. Allcott: New Zealanders v. Somerset (Taunton)	1927
8.2	—	4	5	R. Lang: Cambridge U. v. Oxford U. (Lord's)	1862
9	6	4	5	S. Haigh: Yorks. v. Worcs. (Huddersfield)	1903
4.4	2	4	5	G. A. Rotherham: Warwicks. v. Northants. (Northampton)	1921
7.1	4	4	5	V. Murdin: Northants. v. Worcs. (Northampton)	1921
3	1	4	5	T. W. Goddard: Glos. v. Somerset (Bristol)	1947
8	4	4	5	P. F. Jackson: Worcs. v. Warwicks. (Birmingham)	1950
21.5	18	5	5	J. W. Sharpe: Surrey v. Oxford U. (Oxford)	1889
14	10	5	5	S. Rudder: Barbados v. Trinidad (Bridgetown)	1897-98
4.4	2	5	5	W. Rhodes: Yorks. v. Derby (Bradford)	1910
7	3	5	5	P. A. Wright: Cambridge U. v. Lancs. (Cambridge)	1922
8	5	5	5	Firasat Hussain: United Provinces v. Delhi (Agra)	1934-35
7	4	5	5	C. J. Knott: Hants. v. Sussex (Eastbourne)	1950
15.4	12	5	5	D. Shackleton: Hants. v. Somerset (Weston-super-Mare)	1956
11	7	5	5	S. P. Gupte: Bombay v. Gujerat (Bombay)	1958-59

FOUR WICKETS

O.	*M.*	*R.*	*W.*		
2	2	0	4	Sir F. Bathurst: England v. Kent (Lord's)	1843
3.2	3	0	4	J. R. Napier: Lancs. v. Yorks. (Sheffield)	1888
5	5	0	4	A. Hearne: Kent v. Somerset (Taunton)	1893
0.5	0	0	4	A. F. Borland: Natal v. Griqualand West (Kimberley)	1926-27
2.1	2	0	4	L. C. Eastman: Essex v. Somerset (Weston-super-Mare)	1934
7	7	0	4	L. Amarnath: Railways v. Patiala (Patiala)	1958-59
6	5	1	4	R. C. W. Burn: Brackley's XI v. Barbados (Bridgetown)	1904-05
3.3	2	1	4	A. G. Slater: Derby v. Essex (Leyton)	1913
3	2	1	4	C. A. Sneddon: Auckland v. Hawke's Bay (Auckland)	1920-21
4	3	1	4	J. L. Hopwood: Lancs. v. Glos. (Manchester)	1931
10	9	1	4	R. G. Garlick: Northants. v. Middx. (Northampton)	1950
8.3	6	2	4	D. N. Writer: Parsis v. Europeans (Bombay)	1894-95
3	2	2	4	E. H. Killick: Sussex v. Notts. (Nottingham)	1905
3	2	2	4	H. L. Simms: Europeans v. Muslims (Poona)	1915-16
5	3	2	4	C. V. Grimmett: Australians v. Worcs. (Worcester)	1926
8	6	2	4	H. Larwood: Notts. v. Cambridge U. (Cambridge)	1926
7	5	2	4	H. Chilvers: N.S.W. v. M.C.C. (Sydney)	1936-37
7	5	2	4	L. Amarnath: Southern Punjab v. Sind (Patiala)	1938-39
8.2	—	3	4	S. Dakin: West of England v. M.C.C. (Bath)	1844
8	—	3	4	W. H. Anstead: Surrey v. Kent (Oval)	1870
6.3	4	3	4	J. Young: Derby v. Notts. (Nottingham)	1900
10.2	7	3	4	W. R. Cuttell: Lancs. v. Kent (Manchester)	1904
5	3	3	4	J. A. Newman: Hants. v. Glamorgan (Swansea)	1922

Outstanding Innings Analyses—*Cont.*

O.	*M.*	*R.*	*W.*		
7.3	5	3	4	G. S. Boyes: Hants. v. Somerset (Southampton)	1936
5.4	4	3	4	R. A. Sinfield: Glos. v. Lancs. (Preston)	1936
8	5	3	4	B. L. Muncer: Glamorgan v. Kent (Swansea)	1949
7	5	3	4	C. S. Matthews: Notts. v. Somerset (Frome)	1957
5.5	4	3	4	J. G. Lomax: Somerset v. Cambridge U. (Cambridge)	1959
4	2	3	4	Tahir Ali: Khairpur v. Hyderabad (Hyderabad)	1959-60
7	4	3	4	T. W. Cartwright: Warwicks. v. Surrey (Oval)	1962
5	4	3	4	T. W. Cartwright: Warwicks. v. Notts. (Nuneaton)	1964
4.2	2	3	4	S. E. Leary: Kent v. Oxford U. (Canterbury)	1966
10	6	4	4	H. H. Stephenson: Surrey v. Notts. (Nottingham)	1854
8.3	5	4	4	W. Flowers: Notts. v. Sussex (Hove)	1887
11	9	4	4	J. T. Hearne: M.C.C. v. Australians (Lord's)	1896
3.1	1	4	4	J. H. Vincett: Sussex v. Glos. (Bristol)	1909
4.3	1	4	4	A. Drake: Yorks. v. Somerset (Bath)	1913
8	5	4	4	R. Tyldesley: Lancs. v. Scotland (Manchester)	1925
7	4	4	4	G. A. Wedel: Glos. v. Northants. (Northampton)	1926
11	8	4	4	S. J. Staples: Notts. v. Hants. (Southampton)	1932
8.3	5	4	4	E. A. Bedser: Surrey v. Northants. (Northampton)	1961

A. Drake returned analyses of 4.3—1—4—4 and 6.1—4—3—3 for Yorkshire v. Somerset (Bath) 1913.

T. W. Hayward returned analyses of 0.3—0—0—1 and 0.3—0—0—2 for Surrey v. Leicestershire (Leicester) 1895.

OUTSTANDING MATCH BOWLING ANALYSES

NINETEEN WICKETS

19-90	(9-37 & 10-53)	J. C. Laker: England v. Australia (Manchester)	1956

EIGHTEEN WICKETS

18-96	(9-43 & 9-53)	H. A. Arkwright: M.C.C. v. Gentlemen of Kent (Canterbury) (*This was a twelve-a-side match*)	1861

SEVENTEEN WICKETS

17-48	(10-30 & 7-18)	C. Blythe: Kent v. Northants. (Northampton)	1907
17-50	(8-13 & 9-37)	C. T. B. Turner: Australians v. England XI (Hastings)	1888
17-54	(8-31 & 9-23)	W. P. Howell: Australians v. Western Province (Cape Town)	1902-03
17-56	(9-44 & 8-12)	C. W. L. Parker: Glos. v. Essex (Gloucester)	1925
17-67	(9-11 & 8-56)	A. P. Freeman: Kent v. Sussex (Hove)	1922
17-89	(9-55 & 8-34)	W. G. Grace: Glos. v. Notts. (Cheltenham)	1877
17-89	(8-39 & 9-50)	F. C. L. Matthews: Notts. v. Northants. (Nottingham)	1923
17-91	(9-62 & 8-29)	H. Dean: Lancs. v. Yorks. (Liverpool)	1913
17-91	(8-47 & 9-44)	H. Verity: Yorks. v. Essex (Leyton)	1933
17-92	(8-31 & 9-61)	A. P. Freeman: Kent v. Warwicks. (Folkestone)	1932

SIXTEEN WICKETS

16-35	(8-18 & 8-17)	W. E. Bowes: Yorks. v. Northants. (Kettering)	1935
16-38	(7-15 & 9-23)	T. Emmett: Yorks. v. Cambridgeshire (Hunslet)	1869
16-38	(6-12 & 10-26)	A. E. E. Vogler: Eastern Province v. Griqualand West (Johannesburg)	1906-07
16-52	(9-30 & 7-22)	J. Southerton: South v. North (Lord's)	1875
16-58	(8-21 & 8-37)	E. M. Dowson: Bennett's XI v. Jamaica (Kingston)	1901-02
16-60	(7-40 & 9-20)	W. G. Grace: M.C.C. v. Notts. (Lord's)	1885
16-65	(8-23 & 8-42)	G. Giffen: Australians v. Lancs. (Manchester)	1886
16-69	(8-25 & 8-44)	T. G. Wass: Notts. v. Lancs. (Liverpool)	1906
16-69	(9-35 & 7-34)	F. A. Tarrant: England XII v. Indian XII (Bombay)	1915-16
16-79	(8-39 & 8-40)	C. T. B. Turner: N.S.W. v. Shrewsbury's XI (Sydney)	1887-88
16-80	(8-35 & 8-45)	D. V. P. Wright: Kent v. Somerset (Bath)	1939
16-82	(8-38 & 8-44)	A. P. Freeman: Kent v. Northants. (Tunbridge Wells)	1932
16-83	(8-36 & 8-47)	J. C. White: Somerset v. Worcs. (Bath)	1919
16-83	(6-18 & 10-65)	G. G. Collins: Kent v. Notts. (Dover)	1922
16-83	(8-39 & 8-44)	B. Dooland: Notts. v. Essex (Nottingham)	1954

Outstanding Match Bowling Analyses—*Cont.*

16-83	(6-29 & 10-54)	G. A. R. Lock: Surrey v. Kent (Blackheath)	1956
16-84	(7-43 & 9-41)	C. Gladwin: Derby v. Worcs. (Stourbridge)	1952
16-85	(9-34 & 7-51)	S. G. Smith: West Indian XI v. Bennett's XI (Port of Spain)	1901-02
16-88	(8-65 & 8-23)	J. A. Newman: Hants. v. Somerset (Weston-super-Mare)	1927

FIFTEEN WICKETS

15-21	(8- 9 & 7-12)	G. Dennett: Glos. v. Northants. (Gloucester)	1907
15-28	(7-17 & 8-11)	J. Briggs: England v. South Africa (Cape Town)	1888-89
15-31	(7-22 & 8- 9)	G. E. Tribe: Northants. v. Yorks. (Northampton)	1958
15-35	(7- 9 & 8-26)	F. Morley: Notts. v. Kent (Town Malling)	1878
15-36	(9-18 & 6-18)	F. R. Spofforth: Australians v. Oxford U. (Oxford)	1886
15-38	(6-26 & 9-12)	H. Verity: Yorks. v. Kent (Sheffield)	1936
15-45	(7-38 & 8- 7)	G. A. Lohmann: England v. South Africa (Port Elizabeth)	1895-96
15-45	(7- 9 & 8-36)	C. Blythe: Kent v. Leics. (Leicester)	1912
15-47	(8-31 & 7-16)	W. McIntyre: Lancs v. Derby (Derby)	1877
15-47	(7-27 & 8-20)	F. A. Tarrant: Middx. v. Hants. (Lord's)	1913
15-49	(9-23 & 6-26)	J. T. Botten: N-E. Transvaal v. Griqualand West (Pretoria)	1958-59
15-50	(9-22 & 6-28)	R. Peel: Yorks. v. Somerset (Leeds)	1895
15-51	(5-16 & 10-35)	A. Drake: Yorks. v. Somerset (Weston-super-Mare)	1914
15-52	(7-34 & 8-18)	V. W. C. Jupp: Northants. v. Glamorgan (Swansea)	1925
15-54	(9-26 & 6-28)	B. A. Langford: Somerset v. Lancs. (Weston-super-Mare)	1958
15-56	(7-40 & 8-16)	G. Tarrant: Cambridgeshire v. Kent (Chatham)	1862
15-56	(9-28 & 6-28)	W. Rhodes: Yorks. v. Essex (Leyton)	1899
15-57	(9-31 & 6-26)	J. Briggs: Londesborough's XI v. Australians (Scarborough)	1890
15-57	(10-28 & 5-29)	W. P. Howell: Australians v. Surrey (Oval)	1899
15-60	(8-33 & 7-27)	S. T. Callaway: Canterbury v. Hawke's Bay (Napier)	1903-04

FOURTEEN WICKETS

14-29	(6- 7 & 8-22)	T. Emmett: Yorks. v. Surrey (Sheffield)	1867
14-29	(6-16 & 8-13)	W. C. Smith: Surrey v. Northants. (Oval)	1910
14-29	(8- 4 & 6-25)	D. Shackleton: Hants. v. Somerset (Weston-super-Mare)	1955
14-33	(8-12 & 6-21)	R. Peel: Yorks. v. Notts. (Sheffield)	1888
14-34	(8-15 & 6-19)	A. Rylott: M.C.C. v. Kent (Lord's)	1878
14-37	(7-34 & 7- 3)	F. R. Spofforth: Australians v. England XI (Birmingham)	1884
14-38	(6-18 & 8-20)	W. Mycroft: North v. South (Loughborough)	1875
14-43	(8-21 & 6-22)	S. Haigh: Yorks. v. Hants. (Southampton)	1898
14-43	(7-23 & 7-20)	W. Voce: Notts. v. Northants. (Nottingham)	1929
14-44	(7-31 & 7-13)	R. K. Oxenham: Australians v. Central India & Rajputana (Ajmer)	1935-36
14-45	(6-24 & 8-21)	G. G. Hearne: Kent v. M.C.C. (Lord's)	1879
14-45	(9-17 & 5-28)	G. G. Napier: Europeans v. Parsis (Poona)	1909-10
14-45	(8-23 & 6-22)	W. J. O'Reilly: N.S.W. v. Queensland (Sydney)	1939-40

THIRTEEN WICKETS

13-14	(7- 6 & 6- 8)	F. Morley: M.C.C. v. Oxford U. (Oxford)	1877
13-25	(7-19 & 6- 6)	W. W. Robinson: Auckland v. Nelson (Nelson)	1873-74
13-38	(6-18 & 7-20)	E. Wainwright: Yorks. v. Sussex (Dewsbury)	1894
13-38	(6-27 & 7-11)	T. R. McKibbin: Australians v. Lancs. (Liverpool)	1896
13-29	(7-35 & 6- 4)	J. Briggs: Lancs. v. Derby (Manchester)	1888
13-39	(6-22 & 7-17)	H. R. Bromley-Davenport: Lucas's XI v. British Guiana (Georgetown)	1894-95
13-40	(6-22 & 7-18)	G. Howitt: U.N. England XI v. U.S. England XI (Lord's)	1870
13-40	(6-18 & 7-22)	J. Briggs: Londesborough's XI v. Australians (Scarborough)	1888
13-40	(8-17 & 5-23)	T. G. Wass: Notts. v. Derby (Nottingham)	1901
13-40	(6-27 & 7-13)	S. Haigh: Yorks. v. Warwicks. (Sheffield)	1907
13-40	(5-26 & 8-14)	V. D. Sondhi: Delhi v. Jammu & Kashmir (New Delhi)	1963-64
13-41	(4- 5 & 9-36)	W. Huddleston: Lancs. v. Notts. (Liverpool)	1906
13-42	(6-24 & 7-18)	J. Jackson: North v. South (Tunbridge Wells)	1857
13-43	(6-36 & 7- 7)	G. Geary: Leics. v. Warwicks. (Hinckley)	1936
13-44	(5-16 & 8-28)	H. H. Stephenson: England v. Kent (Lord's)	1858
13-45	(7-33 & 6-12)	F. Morley: Notts. v. Yorks. (Sheffield)	1876
13-45	(7-24 & 6-21)	W. Rhodes: Yorks. v. Somerset (Bath)	1898

Outstanding Match Bowling Analyses—*Cont.*

TWELVE WICKETS

12-18	(6-13 & 6- 5)	Bennett: Nelson v. Wellington (Nelson)	1885-86
12-19	(6-12 & 6- 7)	G. H. Hirst: Yorks. v. Northants. (Northampton)	1908
12-20	(5- 6 & 7-14)	T. Richardson: Surrey v. Leics. (Leicester)	1897
12-23	(8-11 & 4-12)	G. Freeman: Yorks. v. Lancs. (Holbeck)	1868
12-28	(6-19 & 6- 9)	E. Willsher: Kent v. Yorks. (Sheffield)	1865
12-29	(7-12 & 5-17)	G. H. Hirst: Yorks. v. Essex (Leyton)	1901
12-30	(6-11 & 6-19)	T. B. Mitchell: Derby v. Sussex (Chesterfield)	1931
12-33	(4-21 & 8-12)	R. W. Norden: Transvaal v. Rhodesia (Johannesburg)	1904-05
12-33	(3-16 & 9-17)	H. L. Jackson: Derby v. Cambridge U. (Cambridge)	1959
12-34	(7-15 & 5-19)	A. Cotter: Australians v. Worcs. (Worcester)	1905
12-34	(6-20 & 6-14)	G. A. R. Lock: Surrey v. Glamorgan (Oval)	1957
12-35	(6-22 & 6-13)	J. C. Shaw: Notts. v. Kent (Crystal Palace)	1870
12-35	(7- 7 & 5-28)	F. Morley: Notts. v. Derby (Nottingham)	1879
12-35	(8-18 & 4-17)	A. V. Bedser: Surrey v. Warwicks. (Oval)	1953
12-38	(5-16 & 7-22)	L. F. Townsend: M.C.C. v. Rajputan (Ajmer)	1933-34
12-39	(5-12 & 7-27)	Munir Malik: Rawalpindi v. Peshawar (Rawalpindi)	1958-59
12-40	(7-12 & 5-28)	A. Downes: Otago v. Canterbury (Dunedin)	1896-97
12-40	(5-19 & 7-21)	G. G. Macaulay: Yorks. v. Glos. (Gloucester)	1924

ELEVEN WICKETS

11-17	(8-17 & 3- 0)	G. A. R. Lock: M.C.C. v. East Pakistan (Chittagong)	1955-56
11-24	(5- 6 & 6-18)	H. Ironmonger: Australia v. South Africa (Melbourne)	1931-32
11-25	(6- 9 & 5-16)	G. Fowler: Nelson v. Wellington (Nelson)	1887-88
11-27	(8- 9 & 3-18)	G. Wootton: M.C.C. v. Sussex (Lord's)	1863
11-29	(7-12 & 4-17)	F. Martin: M.C.C. v. Sussex (Lord's)	1894
11-30	(8- 5 & 3-25)	E. Peate: Yorks. v. Surrey (Holbeck)	1883
11-30	(4-19 & 7-11)	P. Sitaram: Delhi v. Jammu & Kashmir (Srinagar)	1960-61
11-31	(4-18 & 7-13)	A. E. Trott: Middx. v. Somerset (Lord's)	1899
11-31	(6- 8 & 5-23)	G. G. Macaulay: Yorks. v. Northants. (Northampton)	1922
11-31	(3- 1 & 8-30)	J. A. Newman: Hants. v. Northants. (Northampton)	1926
11-31	(5- 2 & 6-29)	E. R. H. Toshack: Australia v. India (Brisbane)	1947-48
11-31	(5-16 & 6-15)	Iqbal Awan: Bahawalpur v. Khairpur (Bahawalpur)	1964-65
11-32	(6- 7 & 5-25)	J. J. Ferris: M.C.C. v. Notts. (Lord's)	1891
11-34	(7- 9 & 4-25)	G. G. Macaulay: Yorks. v. Northants. (Kettering)	1933
11-34	(7-17 & 4-17)	L. H. Gray: Middx. v. Hants. (Lord's)	1946

TEN WICKETS

10-15	(5- 6 & 5- 9)	F. A. Tarrant: Europeans v. Muslims (Poona)	1915-16
10-20	(6- 4 & 4-16)	F. R. Spofforth: Australians v. M.C.C. (Lord's)	1878
10-21	(3-12 & 7- 9)	T. Emmett: Yorks. v. Sussex (Hove)	1878
10-21	(6-17 & 4- 4)	S. J. Staples: Notts. v. Hants. (Southampton)	1932
10-21	(5-12 & 5- 9)	W. H. Copson: Derby v. Oxford U. (Oxford)	1939
10-22	(6- 8 & 4-14)	A. Shaw: Notts. v. Surrey (Nottingham)	1875
10-23	(6- 8 & 4-15)	W. F. Downes: Otago v. Canterbury (Christchurch)	1866-67
10-23	(5-10 & 5-13)	G. Fowler: Nelson v. Wellington (Nelson)	1883-84
10-24	(4-11 & 6-13)	G. F. Grace: U.S.E.E. v. U.N.E.E. (Northampton)	1872
10-25	(6-12 & 4-13)	G. H. Pope: Derby v. Yorks. (Chesterfield)	1948
10-29	(3-11 & 7-18)	J. T. Newstead: Yorks. v. Leics. (Leicester)	1908
10-30	(5-13 & 5-17)	Lawson: Wellington v. Nelson (Nelson)	1883-84
10-30	(5- 8 & 5-22)	F. Martin: M.C.C. v. Notts. (Lord's)	1894
10-30	(2-22 & 8- 8)	M. G. Melle: Transvaal v. Griqualand West (Johannesburg)	1950-51

MOST INEXPENSIVE ANALYSES

FOUR-BALL OVERS

O. M. R. W.		
25.2—24— 3—1	W. Clark: Middx. v. Notts. (Nottingham)	1882
26 —23— 3—0	J. Beaumont: Surrey v. Oxford U. (Oxford)	1888
29 —25— 5—3	A. Shaw: Shaw's XI v. N.S.W. (Sydney)	1881-82
40 —35— 7—0	A. Shaw: Notts. v. M.C.C. (Lord's)	1882
41.2—36— 7—7	A. Shaw: Notts. v. M.C.C. (Lord's)	1875
48 —40—12—3	A. Shaw: Players v. Gentlemen (Prince's)	1876
53 —43—14—2	E. Lockwood: Yorks. v. Notts. (Sheffield)	1876

Most Inexpensive Analyses—*Cont.*

O. M. R. W.		
60 —47—14—4	James Lillywhite: Sussex v. Kent (Hove)	1879
65.3—45—28—5	W. Attewell: Vernon's XI v. Victoria (Melbourne)	1887-88
81 —65—28—3	W. Attewell: Notts. v. Kent (Maidstone)	1888
89 —62—46—1	W. Attewell: Notts. v. Kent (Nottingham)	1888
98 —69—58—3	E. Peate: Yorks. v. Sussex (Hove)	1884
99 —66—64—3	A. Shaw: North v. South (Nottingham)	1878
114 —72—85—3	A. Watson: Lancs. v. M.C.C. (Lord's)	1884
122.1—81—87—2	J. T. Rawlin: Vernon's XI v. South Australia (Adelaide) ..	1887-88

FIVE-BALL OVERS

O. M. R. W.		
25 —21— 7—4	W. Attewell: Notts. v. Kent (Beckenham)	1889
30.4—22—17—5	J. Briggs: Lancs. v. Oxford U. (Oxford)	1894
45 —32—19—5	W. Attewell: North v. South (Oval)	1889
53 —34—34—4	W. Attewell: Notts. v. Sussex (Nottingham)	1889
64 —35—52—6	W. Attewell: Notts. v. Glos. (Cheltenham)	1895
69 —42—57—3	W. Attewell: Notts. v. Lancs. (Manchester)	1892
76 —43—71—4	W. Attewell: Notts. v. Lancs. (Nottingham)	1889

SIX-BALL OVERS

O. M. R. W.		
32 —27— 5—0	R. G. Nadkarni: India v. England (Madras)	1963-64
35 —29—11—0	W. Rhodes: Yorks. v. Notts. (Nottingham)	1929
44 —32—19—1	W. Rhodes: Yorks. v. Lancs. (Leeds)	1930
47 —29—30—6	C. Cook: Glos. v. Leics. (Bristol)	1956
47.4—31—34—4	R. Kilner: Yorks. v. Leics. (Leicester)	1923
48 —26—44—3	R. A. Sinfield: Glos. v. Warwicks. (Bristol)	1936
53 —28—46—3	R. Kilner: Yorks. v. Lancs. (Manchester)	1927
54 —29—49—4	A. E. Relf: Sussex v. Yorks. (Bradford)	1906
61 —32—51—3	W. Attewell: England v. Australia (Melbourne)	1891-92
63.2—38—57—4	Saeed Ahmed: Western India States v. Bombay (Rajkot) ..	1943-44
76 —47—58—4	V. M. Mankad: India v. England (New Delhi)	1951-52
83 —42—98—5	R. W. McLeod: Victoria v. N.S.W. (Melbourne)	1892-93

EIGHT-BALL OVERS

O. M. R. W.		
26 —17—19—4	L. W. Payn: Natal v. O.F.S. (Bloemfontein)	1946-47
26 —16—28—2	E. S. White: N.S.W. v. Queensland (Sydney)	1935-36
34 —18—29—2	N. B. F. Mann: Eastern Province v. Griqualand West (Port Elizabeth)	1946-47
34 —17—36—4	R. K. Oxenham: Queensland v. Victoria (Melbourne)	1933-34
40.3—16—46—6	H. J. Tayfield: Natal v. Transvaal (Durban)	1946-47
57 —26—55—3	L. Heaney: Transvaal v. Griqualand West (Johannesburg) ..	1947-48
67.6—38—69—6	N. B. F. Mann: Eastern Province v. Transvaal (Johannesburg) ..	1946-47

MOST EXPENSIVE ANALYSES

FIVE-BALL OVERS

O. M. R. W.		
5—0— 50—5	W. G. Grace: South v. North (Hastings)	1893
13—1— 76—0	W. H. Lockwood: Thornton's XI v. Australians (Scarborough) ..	1893
14—0— 94—0	K. S. Ranjitsinhji: Sussex v. Notts. (Nottingham)	1895
19—2—127—2	J. B. Wood: Oxford U. v. M.C.C. (Lord's)	1893
26—5—138—5	E. J. Tyler: Somerset v. Lancs. (Taunton)	1899
30—1—154—1	A. C. S. Glover: Warwicks. v. Yorks. (Birmingham)	1896

SIX-BALL OVERS

O. M. R. W.		
2 —0— 50—0	N. W. Hill: Notts. v. Leics. (Nottingham) .. .. *(Bowled slow full-tosses to give away runs quickly)*	1965
4 —0— 53—0	W. Knightly-Smith: Middx. v. Notts. (Nottingham)	1922
6 —0— 66—0	E. H. Bowley: Rest v. Lord Cowdray's XI (Hastings)	1923

Most Expensive Analyses—*Cont.*

O.	*M.*	*R.*	*W.*		
8.2	0	98	0	T. W. Goddard: Glos. v. Kent (Dover)	1937
11	0	100	2	T. E. S. Francis: Cambridge U. v. Surrey (Oval)	1923
14	0	109	0	E. O. Blamires: Otago v. N.S.W. (Dunedin)	1923-24
14	0	153	3	J. Gunn: Notts. v. Sussex (Hove)	1912
20	0	156	0	E. Price: Essex v. Australians (Southend)	1948
21	1	156	1	V. R. Price: Surrey v. Middx. (Oval)	1919
22	0	188	3	A. Bailey: Somerset v. Kent (Taunton)	1906
34	0	195	2	P. T. Mills: Glos. v. Australians (Bristol)	1921
36	2	208	0	T. P. B. Smith: Essex v. Kent (Brentwood)	1934
40.2	2	227	5	L. C. Braund: Somerset v. Lancs. (Manchester)	1905
46	3	295	3	Anwar: Dera Ismail Khan v. Railways (Lahore)	1964-65

EIGHT-BALL OVERS

O.	*M.*	*R.*	*W.*		
2.7	0	50	0	J. Buchanan: Eastern Province v. Western Province (Cape Town)	1937-38
6	0	71	2	E. D. R. Eagar: Oxford U. v. M.C.C. (Lord's)	1939
8	0	71	4	E. W. Dempster: New Zealanders v. Natal (Pietermaritzburg)	1953-54
8	0	87	5	A. A. Mailey: N.S.W. v. South Australia (Adelaide)	1919-20
9	0	90	1	A. Davis: Tasmania v. M.C.C. (Launceston)	1924-25
12.7	0	149	5	W. E. Merritt: Northants. v. Somerset (Taunton)	1939
20.4	0	174	6	N. L. Williams: Rest v. Australian XI (Sydney)	1926-27
23.2	0	218	5	W. E. Merritt: New Zealanders v. N.S.W. (Sydney)	1927-28
48.7	4	228	5	B. M. Gaskin: British Guiana v. Trinidad (Port of Spain)	1946-47
64	0	362	4	A. A. Mailey: N.S.W. v. Victoria (Melbourne)	1926-27

225 RUNS CONCEDED IN AN INNINGS

O.	*M.*	*R.*	*W.*		
64	0	362	4	A. A. Mailey: N.S.W. v. Victoria (Melbourne)	1926-27
87	12	309	5	G. Giffen: South Australia v. Stoddart's XI (Adelaide)	1894-95
69	7	301	4	B. K. Garudachar: Mysore v. Holkar (Indore)	1945-46
87	11	298	1	L. O. Fleetwood-Smith: Australia v. England (Oval)	1938
46	3	295	3	Anwar: Dera Ismail Khan v. Railways (Lahore)	1964-65
77.1	7	287	8	G. Giffen: South Australia v. N.S.W. (Adelaide)	1899-00
59	2	279	1	Inayat: Dera Ismail Khan v. Railways (Lahore)	1964-65
88	15	275	5	C. S. Nayudu: Holkar v. Bombay (Bombay)	1944-45
80.2	13	266	5	O. C. Scott: West Indies v. England (Kingston)	1929-30
64	4	261	4	C. S. Nayudu: Baroda v. Maharashtra (Poona)	1939-40
54	5	259	0	Khan Mohammad: Pakistan v. West Indies (Kingston)	1957-58
83	17	249	6	J. A. O'Connor: South Australia v. Victoria (Melbourne)	1907-08
85.2	20	247	2	Fazal Mahmood: Pakistan v. West Indies (Kingston)	1957-58
55	3	245	4	A. P. Freeman: M.C.C. v. Victoria (Melbourne)	1928-29
92.3	21	245	4	Ghulam Ahmed: Hyderabad v. Holkar (Indore)	1950-51
52	8	236	3	J. H. Wardle: North v. South (Scarborough)	1947
56	7	232	3	C. J. Eady: Tasmania v. N.S.W. (Sydney)	1898-99
63	10	231	6	C. W. L. Parker: Glos. v. Somerset (Bristol)	1923
38	1	228	2	A. C. Facy: Tasmania v. Victoria (Melbourne)	1922-23
48.7	4	228	5	B. M. Gaskin: British Guiana v. Trinidad (Port of Spain)	1946-47
82	17	228	5	V. M. Mankad: India v. West Indies (Kingston)	1952-53
40.2	2	227	5	L. C. Braund: Somerset v. Lancs. (Manchester)	1905
59	11	226	6	E. B. Shine: Kent v. Surrey (Oval)	1897
49	7	225	2	F. Jarvis: South Australia v. N.S.W. (Sydney)	1900-01

300 RUNS CONCEDED IN A MATCH

Runs			
428	(6-153 & 5-275)	C. S. Nayudu: Holkar v. Bombay (Bombay)	1944-45
394	(4-192 & 6-202)	C. V. Grimmett: South Australia v. N.S.W. (Sydney)	1925-26
374	(5-266 & 4-108)	O. C. Scott: West Indies v. England (Kingston)	1929-30
362	(4-362)	A. A. Mailey: N.S.W. v. Victoria (Melbourne)	1926-27
359	(3-149 & 4-210)	D. G. Chaudhari: Maharashtra v. Bombay (Poona)	1948-49
345	(3-190 & 0-155)	J. D. Scott: South Australia v. N.S.W. (Sydney)	1925-26
331	(6-199 & 2-132)	A. P. Freeman: Kent v. M.C.C. (Folkestone)	1934
326	(6-134 & 5-192)	N. L. Williams: South Australia v. Victoria (Adelaide)	1928-29

300 Runs Conceded in a Match—*Cont.*

Runs			
322	(5-309 & 0- 13)	G. Giffen: South Australia v. Stoddart's XI (Adelaide) ..	1894-95
322	(1-224 & 1- 98)	S. G. Shinde: Baroda v. Bombay (Bombay)	1948-49
321	(3-195 & 1-126)	S. D. Dhanwade: Maharashtra v. Bombay (Poona) ..	1948-49
320	(3-142 & 3-178)	D. G. Phadkar: Bombay v. Maharashtra (Poona)	1948-49
309	(2-122 & 2-187)	Amir Elahi: Prince's XI v. Australian Services (New Delhi)	1945-46
308	(4-129 & 3-179)	A. A. Mailey: Australia v. England (Sydney)	1924-25
306	(2-174 & 2-132)	J. Briggs: Lancs. v. Sussex (Manchester)	1897
304	(2-173 & 0-131)	G. R. Dickinson: Otago v. Wellington (Dunedin)	1923-24
302	(5-160 & 5-142)	A. A. Mailey: Australia v. England (Adelaide) ..	1920-21
301	(4-301)	B. K. Garudachar: Mysore v. Holkar (Indore)	1945-46
300	(6-172 & 4-128)	S. G. Smith: Auckland v. Wellington (Wellington)	1923-24

MOST BALLS BOWLED IN AN INNINGS

Balls	*O.*	*M.*	*R.*	*W.*		
588	98	35	179	2	S. Ramadhin: West Indies v. England (Birmingham) ..	1957
571	95.1	36	155	3	T. R. Veivers: Australia v. England (Manchester) .. (*Including spell of 51 overs*)	1964
555	92.3	21	245	4	Ghulam Ahmed: Hyderabad v. Holkar (Indore)	1950-51
552	92	49	140	3	A. L. Valentine: West Indies v. England (Nottingham)	1950
545	90.5	32	165	2	A. L. Valentine: Jamaica v. British Guiana (Georgetown)	1956-57
542	67.6	38	69	6	N. B. F. Mann: Eastern Province v. Transvaal (Johannesburg)	1946-47
536	67	27	90	1	A. Tayfield: Natal v. Transvaal (Johannesburg)	1948-49
528	88	15	275	5	C. S. Nayudu: Holkar v. Bombay (Bombay)	1944-45
528	66	30	99	4	E. F. Schrieber: Border v. O.F.S. (Bloemfontein) ..	1960-61
528	88	26	208	3	Iqbal Ahwan: Bahawalpur v. Karachi Blues (Karachi) ..	1964-65
522	87	12	309	5	G. Giffen: South Australia v. Stoddart's XI (Adelaide)	1894-95
522	87	11	298	1	L. O. Fleetwood-Smith: Australia v. England (Oval) ..	1938
512	64	0	362	4	A. A. Mailey: N.S.W. v. Victoria (Melbourne)	1926-27
512	85.2	20	247	2	Fazal Mahmood: Pakistan v. West Indies (Kingston) ..	1957-58
510	85	26	178	3	W. J. O'Reilly: Australia v. England (Oval)	1938
510	85	11	209	3	Ghulam Ahmed: Hyderabad v. Bombay (Bombay) ..	1947-48
510	85	16	224	1	S. G. Shinde: Baroda v. Bombay (Bombay)	1948-49
504	84	18	168	4	I. Madray: British Guiana v. Jamaica (Georgetown) ..	1956-57
504	84	19	202	6	Haseeb Ahsan: Pakistan v. India (Madras)	1960-61
501	100.1	31	168	4	A. Shaw: Sussex v. Notts. (Nottingham)	1895
501	83.3	35	150	6	G. Giffen: South Australia v. N.S.W. (Adelaide)	1890-91
498	83	42	98	5	R. W. McLeod: Victoria v. N.S.W. (Melbourne) ..	1892-93
498	83	17	249	6	J. A. O'Connor: South Australia v. Victoria (Melbourne)	1907-08
496	62	15	157	3	L. W. Payn: Natal v. Transvaal (Johannesburg) ..	1948-49
492	123	56	146	5	D. Buchanan: Gents of England v. Cambridge U. (Cambridge)	1880
492	82	17	228	5	V. M. Mankad: India v. West Indies (Kingston) ..	1952-53
490	98	34	151	4	F. Martin: Kent v. Notts. (Nottingham)	1891
489	122.1	81	87	2	J. T. Rawlin: Vernon's XI v. South Australia (Adelaide)	1887-88
488	61	20	152	2	W. Douglas: N-E. Transvaal v. Transvaal (Benoni) ..	1947-48
488	81.2	25	135	5	S. Ramadhin: West Indies v. England (Nottingham) ..	1950
488	61	18	126	5	L. F. Kline: Victoria v. N.S.W. (Sydney)	1956-57
486	81	36	105	5	G. Geary: England v. Australia (Melbourne)	1928-29
486	81	37	172	3	J. H. Wardle: Yorks. v. Derby (Bradford)	1949
482	80.2	13	266	5	O. C. Scott: West Indies v. England (Kingston) ..	1929-30
480	120	81	90	3	W. G. Grace: Glos. v. Notts. (Nottingham)	1885
480	80	22	187	3	W. Huddleston: Lancs. v. Warwick. (Birmingham) ..	1901
480	80	28	138	3	G. S. Boyes: Hants. v. Notts. (Southampton)	1934
480	80	13	178	4	C. K. Nayudu: Holkar v. Baroda (Baroda)	1946-47
480	60	9	167	5	A. M. B. Rowan: South Africa v. England (Port Elizabeth)	1948-49
480	80	21	174	2	Maqsood Ahmed: Karachi Blues v. Karachi Whites (Karachi)	1956-57
480	80	35	113	4	L. R. Gibbs: British Guiana v. Jamaica (Georgetown) ..	1956-57
476	119	40	152	5	J. Southerton: Surrey v. Glos. (Clifton)	1871
474	79	43	106	5	J. C. White: Somerset v. Hants. (Taunton)	1930
474	79	19	184	3	Nasim-ul-Ghani: Karachi Blues v. Karachi Whites (Karachi)	1956-57

Most Balls Bowled in an Innings—*Cont.*

Balls	*O.*	*M.*	*R.*	*W.*		
472	59	24	94	3	H. J. Tayfield: South Africa v. Australia (Durban)	1957-58
470	78.2	21	156	6	G. Giffen: Australia v. England (Melbourne)	1894-95
465	93	33	134	3	J. J. Ferris: Australians v. Players (Lord's)	1890
464	58	14	138	6	J. E. Waddington: Griqualand West v. Transvaal (Kimberley)	1946-47
463	77.1	7	287	8	G. Giffen: South Australia v. N.S.W. (Adelaide)	1899-00
462	77	44	99	3	G. A. R. Lock: M.C.C. v. Pakistan XI (Lahore)	1955-56
462	77	26	139	3	S. F. Rehman: Lahore v. Railways & Quetta (Karachi)	1960-61
460	76.4	35	128	7	S. P. Gupte: India v. New Zealand (Hyderabad)	1955-56
456	114	71	101	5	W. A. Woof: Glos. v. Notts. (Nottingham)	1885
456	114	72	85	3	A. Watson: Lancs. v. M.C.C. (Lord's)	1884
456	76	10	141	1	Maqsood Husain: Hyderabad v. Karachi Blues (Karachi)	1964-65
456	57	6	139	3	J. Waller: N-E. Transvaal v. Transvaal (Benoni)	1947-48
456	57	26	55	3	L. Heaney: Transvaal v. Griqualand West (Johannesburg)	1947-48
456	76	47	58	4	V. M. Mankad: India v. England (New Delhi)	1951-52
456	76	29	136	5	J. H. Wardle: Yorks. v. Worcs. (Worcester)	1953
456	57	25	93	1	A. R. A. Murray: Eastern Province v. Natal (Port Elizabeth)	1955-56
455	75.5	10	186	5	S. G. Shinde: Maharashtra v. Bombay (Bombay)	1943-44
455	75.5	40	94	6	Nasim-ul-Ghani: Karachi v. P.I.A. (Karachi)	1962-63
454	113.2	71	118	4	A. Watson: Lancs. v. Yorks. (Bradford)	1887
453	75.3	22	136	2	J. C. White: England v. Australia (Melbourne)	1928-29
453	113.1	63	126	6	T. W. Garrett: N.S.W. v. Victoria (Melbourne)	1883-84
452	113	66	108	6	W. Flowers: Notts. v. Lancs. (Manchester)	1886
451	75.1	16	190	7	A. Newell: N.S.W. v. South Australia (Adelaide)	1893-94
450	75	25	164	4	G. Giffen: Australia v. England (Sydney)	1894-95
450	90	32	185	6	J. Briggs: Lancs. v. Derby (Manchester)	1896
450	75	16	166	7	C. S. Nayudu: Baroda v. Bombay (Bombay)	1943-44
450	75	16	202	3	V. M. Mankad: India v. West Indies (Bombay)	1948-49

MOST BALLS BOWLED IN A MATCH

Balls	*O.*	*M.*	*R.*	*W.*		
917	152.5	25	428	11	C. S. Nayudu: Holkar v. Bombay (Bombay)	1944-45
848	106	14	394	10	C. V. Grimmett: South Australia v. N.S.W. (Sydney)	1925-26
805	161	71	204	13	J. H. Piton: Transvaal v. Griqualand West (Johannesburg)	1890-91
774	129	51	228	9	S. Ramadhin: West Indies v. England (Birmingham)	1957
766	95.6	23	184	4	H. Verity: England v. South Africa (Durban)	1938-39
749	124.5	37	256	13	J. C. White: England v. Australia (Adelaide)	1928-29
748	92.7	22	255	10	D. D. J. Blackie: Victoria v. South Australia (Adelaide)	1926-27
738	92.2	17	256	1	N. Gordon: South Africa v. England (Durban)	1938-39
736	92	16	267	9	C. V. Grimmett: South Australia v. Victoria (Adelaide)	1924-25
730	91.2	33	190	10	N. B. F. Mann: Eastern Province v. Western Province (Cape Town)	1947-48
728	91	24	203	4	A. B. C. Langton: South Africa v. England (Durban)	1938-39
725	120.5	58	152	11	R. W. McLeod: Victoria v. N.S.W. (Melbourne)	1892-93
720	120	30	299	9	K. K. Tarapore: Bombay v. Maharashtra (Poona)	1948-49
712	89	19	228	11	M. W. Tate: England v. Australia (Sydney)	1924-25
708	118	42	239	8	G. Giffen: Australia v. England (Sydney)	1894-95
696	116	75	127	7	A. L. Valentine: West Indies v. England (Lord's)	1950
695	115.5	50	191	11	G. Giffen: South Australia v. N.S.W. (Adelaide)	1892-93
691	115.1	60	135	6	V. M. Mankad: India v. Pakistan (Peshawar)	1954-55
690	115	70	152	11	S. Ramadhin: West Indies v. England (Lord's)	1950
690	115	46	226	8	G. A. R. Lock: England v. Pakistan (Dacca)	1961-62
688	86	15	258	5	A. P. Freeman: England v. Australia (Sydney)	1924-25
686	85.6	44	123	9	N. B. F. Mann: Eastern Province v. Transvaal (Johannesburg)	1946-47
683	113.5	50	171	6	J. C. White: England v. Australia (Melbourne)	1928-29
682	113.4	19	322	2	S. G. Shinde: Baroda v. Bombay (Bombay)	1948-49
672	84	15	266	7	W. A. Johnston: Australia v. South Africa (Melbourne)	1952-53
668	83.4	27	195	12	H. Ironmonger: Victoria v. South Australia (Adelaide)	1930-31
666	83.2	9	281	8	A. A. Mailey: N.S.W. v. South Australia (Adelaide)	1926-27
664	83	19	191	9	J. E. Waddington: Griqualand West v. N-E. Transvaal (Pretoria)	1955-56
662	110.2	37	184	7	S. Ramadhin: West Indies v. England (Nottingham)	1950

Most Balls Bowled in a Match—*Cont.*

Balls	*O.*	*M.*	*R.*	*W.*		
662	110.2	44	167	7	S. P. Gupte: India v. Pakistan (Lahore)	1954-55
661	165.1	87	202	9	T. W. Garrett: N.S.W. v. Victoria (Melbourne)	1883-84
660	110	55	183	5	A. L. Valentine: West Indies v. England (Nottingham)	1950
659	109.5	29	267	10	V. M. Mankad: Gujerat v. Holkar (Indore)	1950-51
656	109.2	30	225	5	C. V. Grimmett: Australia v. England (Oval)	1930
656	82	19	240	8	F. Ward: Australia v. England (Brisbane)	1936-37
655	109.1	43	192	14	J. J. Ferris: N.S.W. v. South Australia (Adelaide)	1890-91
654	109	41	198	9	H. Trumble: Australia v. England (Adelaide)	1901-02
654	109	37	192	8	C. V. Grimmett: Australia v. South Africa (Melbourne)	1931-32
654	109	17	294	2	C. T. Sarwate: Holkar v. Bombay (Bombay)	1944-45
654	109	62	111	7	V. M. Mankad: India v. England (New Delhi)	1951-52
651	108.3	36	253	8	S. G. Shinde: India v. England (New Delhi)	1951-52
648	108	30	245	9	G. Giffen: South Australia v. Victoria (Adelaide)	1899-00
642	107	35	196	7	K. D. Mackay: Australia v. England (Oval)	1961
640	80	31	135	3	H. J. Tayfield: South Africa v. Australia (Durban)	1957-58
636	106	36	204	11	A. L. Valentine: West Indies v. England (Manchester)	1950
636	79.4	37	142	6	L. R. Gibbs: West Indies v. Australia (Melbourne)	1960-61
633	105.3	52	120	8	C. V. Grimmett: Australia v. England (Nottingham)	1934
632	79	12	207	9	M. W. Tate: England v. Australia (Sydney)	1924-25
632	105.2	13	374	9	O. C. Scott: West Indies v. England (Kingston)	1929-30
630	105	45	165	8	J. W. Sharpe: England v. Australia (Melbourne)	1891-92
630	126	33	306	4	J. Briggs: Lancs. v. Sussex (Manchester)	1897
630	105	41	199	4	J. C. Laker: England v. West Indies (Nottingham)	1957
629	104.5	44	178	9	F. T. Badcock: Otago v. Canterbury (Christchurch)	1923-24
629	78.5	26	166	8	L. Drury: Griqualand West v. N-E. Transvaal (Pretoria)	1955-56
627	78.3	18	241	9	M. W. Tate: England v. Australia (Melbourne)	1924-25
626	78.2	3	326	11	N. L. Williams: South Australia v. Victoria (Adelaide)	1928-29
625	104.1	27	219	6	C. V. Grimmett: Australia v. England (Adelaide)	1928-29
625	78.1	14	178	8	R. Kilner: England v. Australia (Adelaide)	1924-25
624	156	86	184	8	W. G. Grace: Gentlemen v. Players (Oval)	1876
624	78	11	222	5	A. A. Mailey: N.S.W. v. South Australia (Adelaide)	1927-28
624	104	55	132	3	C. S. Marriott: Kent v. Northants. (Dover)	1934
624	104	28	254	6	V. M. Mankad: India v. West Indies (Kingston)	1952-53
623	103.5	37	190	7	A. K. McKinnon: Eastern Province v. Western Province (Cape Town)	1962-63
612	102	16	260	9	E. Jones: South Australia v. Victoria (Adelaide)	1898-99
611	101.5	38	206	14	A. P. Freeman: Kent v. Northants. (Dover)	1934
610	101.4	41	158	10	G. Dennett: Glos. v. Notts. (Nottingham)	1908
608	76	18	173	4	R. L. A. McNamee: N.S.W. v. Queensland (Sydney)	1926-27
607	101.1	26	233	10	A. Newell: N.S.W. v. South Australia (Adelaide)	1893-94
606	101	34	203	6	J. Briggs: Lancs. v. Kent (Manchester)	1900
606	101	41	136	6	G. Geary: England v. Australia (Melbourne)	1928-29
606	75.6	28	161	5	W. J. O'Reilly: Australia v. England (Brisbane)	1936-37
606	101	45	165	6	Fazal Mahmood: Pakistan v. West Indies (Port of Spain)	1957-58
604	75.4	15	244	7	F. Ward: South Australia v. N.S.W. (Adelaide)	1935-36
603	100.3	40	161	6	W. J. O'Reilly: Australia v. England (Adelaide)	1932-33
601	100.1	44	171	13	A. P. Freeman: Kent v. Lancs. (Tonbridge)	1933
600	75	23	161	5	C. F. W. Allcott: Auckland v. Canterbury (Christchurch)	1924-25
600	100	39	180	0	M. W. Tate: England v. Australia (Melbourne)	1928-29
600	100	47	142	9	D. A. Allen: Glos. v. Lancs. (Lydney)	1966

BOWLERS UNCHANGED THROUGH A COMPLETED MATCH

It was fairly usual in the last century, with its relatively small innings totals, for two bowlers to bowl unchanged throughout both completed innings of a match. Since 1900, instances have become increasingly rare and there have been only three post-war instances in English cricket.

SEASON 1852

J. Wisden (10-57) & J. Dean (10-92) . . . . Sussex v. Kent (Brighton)

Bowlers Unchanged Through a Completed Match—*Cont.*

SEASON 1853

W. Hillyer (10-75) & E. Hinkly (10-38) .. .. South v. North (Oval)
W. Hillyer (12-57) & W. Clarke (6-49) .. .. .. M.C.C. v. England (Lord's)
Sir F. Bathurst (11-50) & M. Kempson (9-54) .. .. Gentlemen v. Players (Lord's)
W. Clarke (7-106) & J. Wisden (8-36) .. .. England v. Kent (Canterbury)

SEASON 1854

J. Dean (8-89) &. J. Grundy (11-76) .. .. .. M.C.C. v. Cambridge U. (Cambridge)
J. Grundy (6-39) & T. Nixon (11-46) .. .. M.C.C. v. Surrey (Lord's)

SEASON 1855

J. Wisden (12-92) & J. Dean (6-77) .. .. Sussex v. M.C.C. (Lord's)
T. Sherman (8-71) & John Lillywhite (11-70) .. .. South v. North (Tunbridge Wells)
J. Grundy (10-73) & J. Dean (9-76) .. .. M.C.C. v. Surrey (Lord's)

SEASON 1856

E. Willsher (10-54) & F. Hollands (9-54) .. .. Kent v. M.C.C. (Lord's)
W. Martingell (10-69) & T. Sherman (7-82) .. .. .. Surrey v. Sussex (Oval)
W. Martingell (10-67) & G. Griffith (9-35) .. .. Surrey v. Kent (Tunbridge Wells)

SEASON 1857

W. Caffyn (9-28) & G. Griffith (10-34) .. .. Surrey v. Sussex (Oval)
J. Wisden (11-45) & G. Griffith (8-35) .. .. .. Surrey & Sussex v. England (Brighton)
J. Jackson (13-42) & W. Martingell (7-64) .. .. North v. South (Tunbridge Wells)
W. Caffyn (8-71) & G. Griffith (7-56) .. .. .. Surrey v. North (Sheffield)
John Lillywhite (9-59) & G. Hooker (10-65) .. .. Sussex v. M.C.C. (St Leonard's)

SEASON 1858

C. D. Marsham (7-27) & H. H. Stephenson (13-44) .. .. .. England v. Kent (Lord's)

SEASON 1859

W. Caffyn (12-68) & H. H. Stephenson (5-70) .. .. .. Surrey v. M.C.C. (Oval)
W. Caffyn (11-63) & G. Atkinson (8-46) .. .. U.N.E.E. v. England XI (Lord's)
V. E. Walker (8-89) & G. Wells (9-79) .. .. .. Middx. v. Kent (Canterbury)
J. Jackson (12-74) & J. Grundy (8-96) .. .. North v. South (Canterbury)

SEASON 1860

J. Grundy (9-51) & A. Haygarth (11-56) .. ..M.C.C. v. Sussex (Lord's)
J. Jackson (7-57) & R. C. Tinley (12-93) .. .. North v. Surrey (Oval)
A. B. Rowley (10-48) & J. B. Payne (8-75) .. Gents. of North v. Gents. of South (Manchester)
C. Brampton (12-38) & J. Grundy (8-52) .. .. .. M.C.C. v. Sussex (Lewes)

SEASON 1861

J. Jackson (11-99) & E. Willsher (6-70) .. .. .. Players v. Gentlemen (Lord's)
I. Hodgson (9-88) & G. Atkinson (10-115) .. .. .. Yorks. v. Surrey (Sheffield)
C. Lawrence (10-86) & V. E. Walker (9-104) .. .. .. Middx. v. M.C.C. (Lord's)

SEASON 1862

H. Stubberfield (6-40) & James Lillywhite (14-57) .. .. ..Sussex v. M.C.C. (Lord's)

SEASON 1863

G. Wootton (11-55) & J. Grundy (8-94) .. .. M.C.C. v. Cambridge U. (Cambridge)
G. Wootton (11-27) & J. Grundy (9-50) .. .. .. M.C.C. v. Sussex (Lord's)
J. Jackson (12-43) & J. Grundy (8-48) .. .. Notts. v. Kent (Cranbrook)

SEASON 1864

V. E. Walker (14-103) & T. Hearne (5-94) .. .. .. Middx. v. Sussex (Islington)
E. Willsher (9-55) & G. Tarrant (11-49) .. .. .. Players v. Gentlemen (Lord's)
T. Hearne (7-91) & V. E. Walker (12-85) .. .. .. Middx. v. M.C.C. (Islington)

Bowlers Unchanged Through a Completed Match—*Cont.*

SEASON 1865

W. G. Grace† (13-84) & I. D. Walker (6-86) .. Gentlemen of South v. Players of South (Oval)
G. Bennett (7-58) & E. Willsher (12-28) .. .. .. Kent v. Yorks. (Sheffield)
†Aged 16. His debut in first-class cricket.

SEASON 1866

G. Tarrant (13-77) & F. Reynolds (6-75) .. .. Cambridgeshire v. Yorks. (Bradford)
T. Hearne (12-76) & R. D. Walker (8-73) .. .. .. Middx. v. Notts. (Nottingham)
G. Tarrant (12-84) & Thomas Hayward (8-76) .. Cambridgeshire v. Middx. (Islington)

SEASON 1867

G. Wootton (8-131) & A. Shaw (10-47) .. .. .. M.C.C. v. Oxford U. (Oxford)
James Lillywhite (6-41) & J. Southerton (13-68) .. Sussex v. Kent (Gravesend)
L. Greenwood (11-71) & G. Freeman (8-73) .. .. .. Yorks. v. Surrey (Oval)
L. Greenwood (7-76) & G. Freeman (12-51) .. .. Yorks. v. Lancs. (Blackburn)
G. Tarrant (9-108) & G. Freeman (9-90) .. .. .. North v. Notts. (Nottingham)

SEASON 1868

R. F. Miles (9-45) & E. L. Fellowes (9-29) .. .. .. Oxford U. v. M.C.C. (Oxford)
F. Silcock (7-75) & E. Willsher (12-103) .. .. .. England v. M.C.C. (Lord's)
G. Freeman (12-23) & T. Emmett (8-24) .. .. Yorks. v. Lancs. (Leeds)
G. Freeman (12-61) & T. Emmett (6-58) .. .. .. Yorks. v. Middx. (Sheffield)

SEASON 1869

G. Freeman (13-61) & T. Emmett (5-53) .. .. .. Yorks. v. Surrey (Sheffield)
G. Freeman (4-31) & T. Emmett (16-38) .. .. .. Yorks. v. Cambridgeshire (Leeds)

SEASON 1870

A. Shaw (13-58) & G. Wootton (6-71) .. .. M.C.C. v. Surrey (Oval)
J. C. Shaw (12-35) & G. Howitt (5-63) .. .. .. Notts. v. Kent (Crystal Palace)
G. Freeman (10-43) & T. Emmett (9-92) .. .. Yorks. v. Surrey (Oval)

SEASON 1871

J. Southerton (14-67) & James Lillywhite (6-64) .. .. .. Sussex v. Kent (Brighton
G. Freeman (7-81) & T. Emmett (11-86) .. .. .. Yorks. v. Lancs. (Manchester)
J. Southerton (11-67) & James Lillywhite (8-44) .. .. Sussex v. Kent (Maidstone)
T. Emmett (8-113) & A. Hill (12-57) .. .. Yorks. v. Surrey (Oval)
J. Southerton (14-99) & James Lillywhite (5-84) .. .. .. Sussex v. Surrey (Oval)

SEASON 1872

J. Southerton (13-69) & James Lillywhite (6-35) .. .. South v. North (Liverpool)
W. McIntyre (11-38) & A. Watson (7-72) .. .. .. Lancs. v. Derby. (Derby)
J. Southerton (12-100) & James Lillywhite (6-71) .. .. .. Sussex v. Kent (Hove)
J. Southerton (9-108) & J. Street (11-61) .. .. .. Surrey v. Kent (Maidstone)
J. C. Shaw (4-49) & E. Lockwood (13-82) .. U.N.E.E. v. U.S.E.E. (Bishops Stortford)

SEASON 1873

A. Shaw (7-49) & A. Rylott (9-75) .. .. M.C.C. v. Yorks. (Lord's)
T. Emmett (11-82) & A. Hill (8-47) .. .. Yorks. v. Lancs. (Manchester)
T. Emmett (12-84) & A. Hill (8-55) .. .. Yorks. v. Surrey (Sheffield)
W. McIntyre (11-70) & A. Watson (8-79) .. .. .. Lancs. v. Surrey (Manchester)
W. McIntyre (11-53) & A. Watson (8-48) .. .. Lancs. v. Surrey (Oval)
James Lilywhite (7-101) & R. Fillery (13-123) .. .. .. Sussex v. Surrey (Oval)
James Lillywhite (11-86) & R. Fillery (9-96) .. .. Sussex v. Kent (Lord's)
James Lillywhite (11-99) & R. Fillery (8-110).. .. .. .. Sussex v. Glos. (Hove)
James Lillywhite (8-84) & R. Fillery (10-105).. .. .. Sussex v. Kent (Eastbourne)

SEASON 1874

T. Emmett (9-87) & A. Hill (10-96) .. .. Yorks. v. Notts. (Nottingham)
A. Hill (9-67) & G. Ulyett (10-104) .. .. Yorks. v. U.S.E.E. (Bradford)
A. Hill (10-38) & T. Emmett (8-74) .. .. Yorks. v. Lancs. (Manchester)
James Lillywhite (11-84) & R. Fillery (7-71) .. .. Sussex v. Notts. (Hove)

Bowlers Unchanged Through a Completed Match—*Cont.*

SEASON 1876

W. McIntyre (14-72) & A. Watson (5-63) .. .. .. Lancs. v. Derby. (Manchester)
W. McIntyre (9-96) & A. Watson (10-83) .. .. Lancs. v. Derby. (Derby)

SEASON 1877

W. McIntyre (12-63) & A. Watson (8-63) .. .. .. Lancs. v. Notts. (Manchester)

SEASON 1878

A. Shaw (11-55) & F. Morley (8-72) .. .. .. Notts. v. Australians (Nottingham)
A. Shaw (7-56) & F. Morley (12-70) .. .. Notts. v. Surrey (Nottingham)
A. Shaw (3-69) & F. Morley (14-94) .. .. Notts. v. Yorks. (Nottingham)
W. G. Grace (12-109) & W. R. Gilbert (8-106) .. .. .. Glos. v. Lancs. (Clifton)
A. Shaw (5-49) & F. Morley (15-35) .. .. Notts. v. Kent (Town Malling)
W. Bates (9-34) & T. Emmett (10-21) .. .. Yorks. v. Sussex (Hove)

SEASON 1879

A. Shaw (8-25) & F. Morley (12-35) .. .. Notts. v. Derby. (Nottingham)
A. G. Steel (9-43) & A. H. Evans (10-74) .. .. .. Gentlemen v. Players (Oval)
A. Shaw (5-35) & F. Morley (14-53) .. .. Notts. v. Derby. (Derby)

SEASON 1880

A. Shaw (12-53) & F. Morley (8-62) .. .. M.C.C. v. Oxford U. (Oxford)
A. Shaw (7-54) & F. Morley (11-43) .. ..M.C.C. v. Derby (Lord's)
H. F. Boyle (7-80) & G. E. Palmer (11-89) .. .. Australians v. Players (Crystal Palace)

SEASON 1881

A. Hill (6-85) & E. Peate (14-77) .. .. Yorks. v. Surrey (Huddersfield
E. Peate (8-57) & W. Bates (11-47) .. .. Yorks. v. Notts. (Nottingham)
A. Penn (13-69) & J. Wootton (7-41) .. .. Kent v. Sussex (Maidstone)

SEASON 1882

G. E. Palmer (9-133) & H. F. Boyle (11-107) .. Australians v. Liverpool Club (Liverpool)

SEASON 1883

E. Peate (8-59) & G. P. Harrison (11-76) .. .. .. Yorks. v. Kent (Dewsbury)
R. G. Barlow (6-88) & A. Watson (12-67) .. .. .. Lancs. v. Derby. (Derby)

SEASON 1884

A. Shaw (14-65) & W. Attewell (6-46) .. .. Notts. v. Glos. (Nottingham)
G. Giffen (10-121) & G. E. Palmer (10-72) ..Australians v. Sheffield's XI (Sheffield Park)
F. R. Spofforth (9-61) & G. E. Palmer (11-54) .. ..Australians v. Yorks. (Bradford)
F. R. Spofforth (12-43) & G. E. Palmer (7-72) .. .. Australians v. Middx. (Lord's)

SEASON 1886

F. R. Spofforth (15-36) & T. W. Garrett (5-34) .. Australians v. Oxford U. (Oxford)
E. Peate (12-50) & A. Watson (7-34) .. .. .. North v. Australians (Manchester)

SEASON 1888

J. Briggs (12-45) & R. G. Barlow (6-42) .. .. .. Lancs. v. Glos. (Liverpool)
C. T. B. Turner (11-59) & J. J. Ferris (7-63) .. .. ..Australians v. Middx. (Lord's)
C. T. B. Turner (13-48) & J. J. Ferris (6-48) .. .. Australians v. England XI (Stoke)

SEASON 1889

J. Beaumont (10-49) & G. A. Lohmann (10-49) .. .. .. Surrey v. Kent (Oval)
W. Wright (9-51) & F. Martin (10-65) .. .. Kent v. Yorks. (Maidstone)

Bowlers Unchanged Through a Completed Match—*Cont.*

SEASON 1890

G. A. Lohmann (13-54) & J. W. Sharpe (7-50) .. .. Surrey v. Lancs. (Manchester)
A. Watson (9-13) & J. Briggs (10-41) .. .. Lancs. v. Sussex (Manchester)
F. Martin (11-72) & W. Wright (9-81) .. .. Kent v. Sussex (Town Malling)
A. Watson (6-66) & A. Mold (13-76) .. .. Lancs. v. Yorks. (Huddersfield)

SEASON 1891

G. A. Lohmann (11-40) & J. W. Sharpe (9-31) .. .. Surrey v. Somerset (Oval)
F. Martin (13-48) & W. Wright (6-59) .. .. .. Kent v. Middx. (Lord's)
J. Briggs (8-54) & A. Mold (11-65) .. .. Lancs. v. Sussex (Hove)

SEASON 1892

A. Mold (13-91) & J. Briggs (5-54) .. .. Lancs. v. Kent (Tonbridge)
A. Mold (14-159) & A. Watson (4-67) .. .. Lancs. v. Sussex (Hove)
J. T. Hearne (12-91) & J. T. Rawlin (7-85) .. .. Middx. v. Sussex (Hove)
J. T. Hearne (7-61) & F. Martin (13-51) .. .. .. M.C.C. v. Sussex (Lord's)

SEASON 1893

A. Coningham (9-100) &. R. W. McLeod (10-56) .. Australians v. Liverpool and District (Liverpool)

SEASON 1894

T. Richardson (9-99) & F. Smith (10-71) .. .. Surrey v. Glos. (Oval)
E. Wainwright (13-38) & R. Peel (7-60) .. .. .. Yorks. v. Sussex (Dewsbury)
G. Davidson (9-54) & J. Hulme (10-70) .. .. .. Derby. v. Yorks. (Sheffield)
W. Hearne (13-98) & F. Martin (6-65) .. .. .. Kent v. Surrey (Catford)
S. M. J. Woods (6-124) & F. S. Jackson (12-77) .. .. Gentlemen v. Players (Lord's)
J. T. Hearne (14-66) & A. D. Pougher (5-60) .. .. .. M.C.C. v. Kent (Lord's)

SEASON 1895

J. Briggs (8-78) & A. Mold (9-72) .. .. Lancs. v. Middx. (Lord's)
J. Briggs (12-51) & A. Mold (8-97) .. .. Lancs. v. Leics. (Leicester)
J. Briggs (4-62) & A. Mold (15-85) .. .. Lancs. v. Notts. (Nottingham)
T. Richardson (11-60) & G. A. Lohmann (8-59) .. .. Surrey v. Derby. (Derby)
T. Soar (11-113) & H. Baldwin (8-93) .. .. Hants. v. Derby. (Southampton)

SEASON 1896

J. T. Hearne (12-90) & J. T. Rawlin (7-69) .. .. .. Middx. v. Surrey (Oval)
H. Trumble (6-46) & T. R. McKibbin (13-38) .. .. Australians v. Lancs. (Liverpool)
J. T. Hearne (13-107) & A. D. Pougher (7-103) .. Earl de la Warr's XI v. Australians (Bexhill)

SEASON 1897

T. Richardson (12-20) & T. W. Hayward (7-43) .. .. Surrey v. Leics. (Leicester)
C. H. G. Bland (14-72) & F. W. Tate (6-113) .. Sussex v. Cambridge U. (Cambridge)

SEASON 1899

J. T. Hearne (8-44) & A. E. Trott (11-31) .. .. .. Middx. v. Somerset (Lord's)
E. Jones (10-84) & C. E. McLeod (10-125) .. .. .. Australians v. Middx. (Lord's)

SEASON 1900

W. Rhodes (11-36) & S. Haigh (7-49) .. .. Yorks. v. Worcs. (Bradford)
W. R. Cuttell (8-46) & S. Webb (11-41) .. .. .. Lancs. v. Hants. (Manchester)

SEASON 1901

J. Sharp (11-105) & S. Webb (8-68) .. .. Lancs. v. Kent (Manchester)
G. A. Rowe (6-53) & J. H. Sinclair (13-73) .. .. .. South Africans v. Glos. (Clifton)
C. Blythe (6-85) & J. R. Mason (12-55) .. .. .. Kent v. Somerset (Taunton)
G. H. Hirst (12-29) & W. Rhodes (6-37) .. .. Yorks. v. Essex (Leyton)

Bowlers Unchanged Through a Completed Match—*Cont.*

SEASON 1902

J. Hallows (13-71) & W. R. Cuttell (7-50) .. .. .. Lancs. v. Kent (Tonbridge)
F. W. Tate (8-109) & E. G. Arnold (12-87) .. South of England v. Australians (Bournemouth)

SEASON 1903

S. Haigh (12-52) & W. Rhodes (7-55) .. .. .. Yorks. v. Cambridge U. (Sheffield)
S. Hargreave (15-76) & S. Santall (5-66) .. .. .. Warwicks. v. Surrey (Oval)
G. H. Hirst (10-67) & W. Rhodes (10-81) .. .. Yorks. v. Surrey (Oval)
C. Blythe (12-67) & A. Hearne (7-61) .. .. Kent v. Surrey (Oval)
B. Cranfield (13-102) & L. C. Braund (7-77) .. .. .. Somerset v. Glos. (Gloucester)
F. G. Roberts (11-93) & G. Dennett (9-99) .. .. .. Glos. v. Surrey (Bristol)

SEASON 1904

W. Rhodes (10-39) & S. Haigh (10-49) .. .. Yorks. v. Hants. (Leeds)
J. N. Crawford (10-78) & H. C. McDonell (10-89) .. .. Surrey v. Glos. (Cheltenham)

SEASON 1905

G. J. Thompson (13-105) & H. B. Simpson (6-66) .. .. Northants. v. Leics. (Leicester)

SEASON 1906

W. Mead (10-73) & A. E. E. Vogler (10-90) .. .. M.C.C. v. Leics. (Lord's)
G. Dennett (15-88) & F. G. Roberts (5-111) .. .. .. Glos. v. Essex (Bristol)
G. Dennett (9-109) & P. H. Ford (11-113) .. .. .. Glos. v. Sussex (Cheltenham)
G. G. Napier (7-88) & P. R. May (12-66) .. .. Cambridge U. v. Yorks. (Cambridge)

SEASON 1907

E. G. Arnold (7-66) & J. A. Cuffe (13-76) .. .. .. Worcs. v. Yorks. Bradford)
J. N. Crawford (11-63) & T. Rushby (6-67) .. .. Surrey v. Sussex (Oval)
J. N. Crawford (6-52) & W. C. Smith (11-65) .. .. Surrey v. Derby. (Derby)
H. Dean (7-84) & W. Huddleston (12-82) .. .. .. Lancs. v. Surrey (Manchester)
W. Mead (12-73) & W. Reeves (8-98) .. .. Essex v. Notts. (Leyton)
S. Hargreave (8-82) & S. Santall (11-91) .. .. .. Warwicks. v. Leics. (Coventry)
G. J. Thompson (8-72) & W. East (12-62) .. .. Northants. v. Glos. (Gloucester)
T. G. Wass (9-69) & A. W. Hallam (9-65) .. .. Notts. v. Northants. (Northampton)
T. G. Wass (10-67) & A. W. Hallam (8-84) .. .. .. Notts. v. Derby. (Chesterfield)
G. H. Hirst (11-44) & W. Rhodes (8-71) .. .. .. Yorks. v. Derby. (Glossop)

SEASON 1908

W. S. Lees (8-104) & T. Rushby (9-90) .. .. .. Surrey v. Lancs. (Manchester)
T. G. Wass (16-103) & A. W. Hallam (4-44) .. .. .. Notts. v. Essex (Nottingham)
G. H. Hirst (12-19) & S. Haigh (6-19) .. .. .. Yorks. v. Northants. (Northampton)
F. A. Tarrant (10-46) & A. E. Trott (9-59) .. .. Middx. v. Philadelphians (Lord's)

SEASON 1909

T. G. Wass (10-107) & A. W. Hallam (10-63) .. .. .. Notts. v. Derby. (Nottingham)
W. Huddleston (8-101) & H. Dean (11-102) .. .. .. Lancs. v. Essex (Liverpool)

SEASON 1910

J. T. Hearne (12-70) & F. A. Tarrant (8-59) .. .. .. Middx. v. Glos. (Lord's)
H. Dean (11-67) & W. Huddleston (9-38) .. .. .. Lancs. v. Worcs. (Manchester)
C. Blythe (11-95) & F. E. Woolley (8-91) .. .. .. Kent v. Yorks. (Maidstone)

SEASON 1912

G. J. Thompson (9-55) & S. G. Smith (10-72) .. Northants. v. Essex (Northampton)
C. Blythe (11-56) & F. E. Woolley (9-58) .. .. .. Kent v. Notts. (Canterbury)
C. Blythe (7-81) & D. W. Carr (13-74) .. .. Kent v. Glos. (Dover)
H. Dean (10-66) & W. Huddleston (10-83) .. .. .. Lancs. v. Leics. (Leicester)

Bowlers Unchanged Through a Completed Match—*Cont.*

SEASON 1913

G. J. Thompson (10-104) & S. G. Smith (10-95) .. .. Northants. v. Sussex (Horsham)
T. G. Wass (10-123) & J. Iremonger (10-73) .. .. .. Notts. v. Derby. (Chesterfield)

SEASON 1914

J. W. H. T. Douglas (11-98) & B. Tremlin (9-115) .. .. .. Essex v. Surrey (Oval)
J. W. H. T. Douglas (9-62) & B. Tremlin (10-52) .. .. .. Essex v. Derby. (Derby)
A. Jaques (14-54) & A. S. Kennedy (6-64) .. .. .. Hants. v. Somerset (Bath)
M. W. Booth (5-77) & A. Drake (15-51) .. Yorks. v. Somerset (Weston-super-Mare)
M. W. Booth (12-89) & A. Drake (8-81) .. .. Yorks. v. Glos. (Bristol)

SEASON 1919

E. Robson (8-107) & J. C. White (11-114) .. .. .. Somerset v. Derby. (Derby)
H. L. Collins (12-69) & C. E. Winning (8-63) .. .. A.I.F. v. Somerset (Taunton)

SEASON 1920

A. Waddington (13-48) & E. Robinson (6-34) .. Yorks. v. Northants. (Northampton)

SEASON 1921

A. Waddington (9-61) & E. Robinson (10-70) .. .. Yorks. v. Northants. (Harrogate)
A. S. Kennedy (11-86) & J. A. Newman (9-103) .. .. Hants. v. Sussex (Portsmouth)

SEASON 1922

P. T. Mills (9-43) & C. W. L. Parker (11-50) .. .. Glos. v. Worcs. (Gloucester)
W. E. Astill (10-65) & G. Geary (10-68) .. .. .. Leics. v. Glos. (Bristol)

SEASON 1923

A. S. Kennedy (12-72) & J. A. Newman (7-62) .. Hants. v. Somerset (Portsmouth)

SEASON 1924

C. H. Parkin (10-78) & R. Tyldesley (10-103) .. .. Lancs. v. Warwicks. (Manchester)

SEASON 1925

W. E. Astill (8-35) & G. Geary (11-61) .. .. Leics. v. Glamorgan (Leicester)
M. W. Tate (14-58) & A. F. Wensley (4-52) .. .. .. Sussex v. Glamorgan (Hove)

SEASON 1927

G. G. Macaulay (12-50) & E. Robinson (8-65) .. .. Yorks. v. Worcs. (Leeds)

SEASON 1932

H. Larwood (10-88) & W. Voce (10-35) .. .. .. Notts. v. Leics. (Nottingham)

SEASON 1935

H. A. Smith (11-91) & G. Geary (9-62) .. .. Leics. v. Northants. (Northampton)

SEASON 1952

D. Shackleton (12-67) & V. H. D. Cannings (8-55) .. .. Hants. v. Kent (Southampton)

SEASON 1958

D. Shackleton (7-88) & M. Heath (13-87) .. .. Hants. v. Derby. (Burton upon Trent)

SEASON 1967

B. S. Crump (12-74) & R. R. Bailey (8-95) .. .. Northants v. Glamorgan (Cardiff)

Bowlers Unchanged Through a Completed Match—*Cont.*

INSTANCES IN OVERSEAS MATCHES

Bowlers	Match	Season
F. McDonald (10-31) & J. Mace (8-36)	Otago v. Canterbury (Dunedin)	1863-64
F. R. Spofforth (9-72) & E. Evans (10-52)	N.S.W. v. Victoria (Sydney)	1875-76
F. R. Spofforth (12-105) & G. E. Palmer (7-65)	Australian XI v. Rest (Melbourne)	1880-81
H. F. Boyle (8-46) & G. E. Palmer (9-61)	Victoria v. N.S.W. (Sydney)	1882-83
F. H. Cooke (6-30) & Bennett (12-18)	Nelson v. Wellington (Nelson)	1885-86
D. Dunlop (10-36) & R. Halley (9-52)	Canterbury v. Wellington (Wellington)	1886-87
G. A. Lohmann (9-67) & J. Briggs (11-58)	Shrewsbury's XI v. Australian XI (Sydney)	1887-88
S. T. Callaway (12-58) & W. McGlinchy (8-41)	N.S.W. v. Otago (Dunedin)	1889-90
F. W. Bush (7-70) & H. R. Bromley-Davenport (13-39)	Lucas's XI v. British Guiana (Georgetown)	1894-95
F. W. Bush (14-71) & H. R. Bromley-Davenport (7-35)	Lucas's XI v. Jamaica (Kingston)	1894-95
F. W. Bush (11-91) & H. R. Bromley-Davenport (9-68)	Lucas's XI v. Jamaica (Kingston)	1894-95
G. A. Lohmann (9-88) & G. A. Rowe (10-48)	Western Province v. Griqualand West (Johannesburg)	1896-97
A. H. Fisher (5-31) & A. Downes (12-40)	Otago v. Canterbury (Dunedin)	1896-97
E. Upham (8-72) & K. Tucker (10-89)	Wellington v. Auckland (Auckland)	1899-00
A. Downes (12-108) &. A. H. Fisher (7-55)	Otago v. Wellington (Auckland)	1900-01
J. J. Kotze (11-37) & J. H. Sinclair (8-49)	Transvaal v. Griqualand West (Port Elizabeth)	1902-03
A. H. Metha (9-36) & M. D. Bulsara (8-43)	Parsis v. Europeans (Bombay)	1904-05
A. W. Alloo (10-50) & V. Holderness (10-39)	Otago v. Southland (Invercargill)	1918-19
N. Gordon (9-50) & E. J. Wickham (10-44)	Transvaal v. Eastern Province (Port Elizabeth)	1937-38
Rajinder Pal (9-20) & P. Sitaram (11-30)	Delhi v. Jammu & Kashmir (Srinagar)	1960-61

MOST MAIDEN OVERS IN SUCCESSION

FOUR-BALL OVERS

23	A. Shaw: North v. South (Nottingham)	1876
20	A. Shaw: Notts. v. M.C.C. (Lord's)	1875
20	C. F. Tufnell: Kent v. Notts. (Nottingham)	1878
18	W. Flowers: Notts. v. Sussex (Hove)	1885
15	E. Willsher: South v. North (Canterbury)	1871
15	A. Shaw: M.C.C. v. Yorks. (Scarborough)	1878
14	A. Appleby: Gentlemen v. Players (Lord's)	1870
14	A. Shaw: Players v. Gentlemen (Lord's)	1880

FIVE-BALL OVERS

19	J. W. Trumble: Victoria v. N.S.W. (Melbourne)	1885-86
10	E. Robson: Somerset v. Sussex (Hove)	1897

SIX-BALL OVERS

21	R. G. Nadkarni: India v. England (Madras) (*Spell of* 131 *balls without conceding a run*)	1963-64
17	H. L. Hazell: Somerset v. Glos. (Taunton) (*Spell of* 105 *balls without conceding a run.*)	1949
17	G. A. R. Lock: M.C.C. v. Governor-General's XI (Karachi) (*First* 104 *balls of innings bowled without conceding a run.*)	1955-56
15	W. S. Haig: Otago v. Wellington (Dunedin)	1956-57
14	J. A. Young: Middx. v. Glos. (Bristol)	1949
14	W. E. Alley: Somerset v. Essex (Yeovil)	1960
14	M.E. Scott: Northants. v. Cambridge U. (Cambridge)	1964

EIGHT-BALL OVERS

16	H. J. Tayfield: South Africa v. England (Durban) (137 *balls without conceding a run,* 20000000, *then* 14 *maidens to end innings,* 2 *maidens at start of second innings, and then* 00200100).	1956-57
9	H. J. Tayfield: South Africa v. Australia (Melbourne)	1952-53
9	P. J. Loader: M.C.C. v. Griqualand West (Kimberley)	1956-57

MOST WICKETS IN CONSECUTIVE INNINGS

3 INNINGS

26	C. W. L. Parker (Glos.) ..	1925	(9-44, 8-12, 9-118)
25	A. P. Freeman (Kent)	1932	(8-56, 8-31, 9-61)
25	G. Giffen (Australians) ..	1886	(9-60, 8-56, 8-23)
24	H. Dean (Lancs.)	1913	(7-70, 9-62, 8-29)
24	T. W. Goddard (Glos.) ..	1939	(7-38, 9-38, 8-68)
24	G. A. Lohmann (Hawke's XI)	1895-96	(7-38, 8-7, 9-28)
24	W. Mead (Essex)	1895	(8-67, 9-52, 7-73)
24	C. W. L. Parker (Glos.) ..	1930	(9-44, 8-38, 7-53)
24	G. J. Thompson (Northants.)	1906	(9-64, 7-72, 8-95)
24	J. C. White (Somerset) ..	1921	(7-52, 7-58, 10-76)
24	J. Wisden (Sussex)	1850	(10, 9 and 5)

4 INNINGS

33	G. Giffen (Australians) ..	1886	(9-60, 8-56, 8-23, 8-42)
32	C. W. L. Parker (Glos.) ..	1925	(6-61, 9-44, 8-12, 9-118)
30	A. P. Freeman (Kent)	1932	(5-88, 8-56, 8-31, 9-61)
30	A. P. Freeman (Kent)	1932	(8-56, 8-31, 9-61, 5-143)
30	T. W. Goddard (Glos.) ..	1939	(6-61, 7-38, 9-38, 8-68)
30	C. L. Townsend (Glos.) ..	1895	(8-67, 8-130, 7-54, 7-80)
30	H. Verity (Yorks.)	1933	(7-34, 6-67, 8-47, 9-44)

5 INNINGS

40	G. Giffen (Australians) ..	1886	(7-41, 9-60, 8-56, 8-23, 8-42)
38	C. L. Townsend (Glos.) ..	1898	(8-66, 9-128, 6-77, 8-64, 7-77)
38	A. P. Freeman (Kent) ..	1932	(8-56, 8-31, 9-61, 5-143, 8-44)
37	C. W. L. Parker (Glos.) ..	1925	(5-19, 6-61, 9-44, 8-12, 9-118)
37	H. Verity (Yorks.)	1933	(7-54, 7-34, 6-67, 8-47, 9-44)

6 INNINGS

46	G. Giffen (Australians) ..	1886	(6-71, 7-41, 9-60, 8-56, 8-23, 8-42)
46	A. P. Freeman (Kent)	1932	(8-56, 8-31, 9-61, 5-143, 8-44, 8-38)
44	H. Verity (Yorks.)	1933	(7-29, 7-54, 7-34, 6-67, 8-47, 9-44)
42	C. L. Townsend (Glos.) ..	1895	(8-67, 8-130, 7-54, 7-80, 5-95, 7-122)
41	A. P. Freeman (Kent) ..	1930	(6-97, 8-101, 8-70, 5-40, 8-71, 6-72)

7 INNINGS

51	A. P. Freeman (Kent)	1932	(5-88, 8-56, 8-31, 9-61, 5-143, 8-44, 8-38)
50	H. Verity (Yorks.)	1933	(7-29, 7-54, 7-34, 6-67, 8-47, 9-44, 6-103)
50	C. L. Townsend (Glos.) ..	1898	(8-66, 9-128, 6-77, 8-64, 7-77, 5-51, 7-66)
47	C. L. Townsend (Glos.) ..	1895	(5-43, 8-67, 8-130, 7-54, 7-80, 5-95, 7-122)

EIGHT OR MORE WICKETS BEFORE LUNCH

This bowling feat corresponds to a batsman scoring a century in the pre-lunch period but is far rarer an accomplishment.

The bowler's complete innings analysis is listed as the actual pre-lunch figures are not available in some instances. The innings total appears in parenthesis.

8-48	(80)	E. Barratt: Surrey v. Sussex (Oval)	1883
8-23	(45)	E. Peate: North of England v. Australians (Manchester)	1886
8-12	(24)	R. Peel: Yorks. v. Notts. (Sheffield)	1888
8-13	(35)	G. A. Lohmann: Surrey v. Lancs. (Manchester)	1888
8-29	(59)	G. Bean: Sussex v. M.C.C. (Lord's)	1889
9-41	(90)	A. Mold: Lancs. v. Yorks. (Huddersfield)	1890
8-33	(78)	A. Mold: Lancs. v. Surrey (Manchester)	1896
8-39	(55)	J. Briggs: Lancs. v. Hants. (Manchester)	1897
8-22	(43)	F. W. Stocks: Oxford U. v. Webbe's XI (Oxford)	1899
8-23	(47)	S. Santall: Warwicks. v. Leics. (Birmingham)	1900
8-30	(70)	G. A. Wilson: Worcs. v. Somerset (Taunton)	1905

Eight or More Wickets before Lunch—*Cont.*

9-47	(65)	W. Brearley: Lancs. v. Somerset (Manchester)	1905
8-80	(153)	G. H. Hirst: Yorks. v. Somerset (Sheffield)	1910
9-41	(113)	G. H. Hirst: Yorks. v. Worcs. (Worcester)	1911
8-35	(85)	W. Wells: Northants. v. Yorks. (Sheffield)	1919
8-11	(37)	A. S. Kennedy: Hants. v. Glamorgan (Cardiff)	1921
8-33	(67)	F. C. L. Matthews: Notts. v. Kent (Canterbury)	1924
9-23	(35)	W. R. Hammond: Glos. v. Worcs. (Cheltenham)	1928
8-38	(79)	C. W. L. Parker: Glos. v. Surrey (Cheltenham)	1930
8-44	(85)	H. A. Smith: Leics. v. Northants. (Northampton)	1935
8-18	(62)	W. E. Bowes: Yorks. v. Northants. (Kettering)	1935
8-11	(28)	W. H. Copson: Derby v. Warwicks. (Derby)	1937
8- 2	(27)	J. C. Laker: England v. Rest (Bradford—Test Trial)	1950
9-39	(79)	C. W. Grove: Warwicks. v. Sussex (Birmingham) (*First eight wickets before lunch*).	1952
8-28	(76)	F. S. Trueman: Yorks. v. Kent (Dover)	1954
9-39	(89)	D. J. Halfyard: Kent v. Glamorgan (Neath)	1957
9-57	(153)	K. E. Palmer: Somerset v. Notts. (Nottingham)	1963

DISMISSING EIGHT OR MORE BATSMEN 'BOWLED' IN AN INNINGS

TEN

J. Wisden: North v. South (Lord's)	1850

EIGHT

S. E. Butler (10-38): Oxford U. v. Cambridge U. (Lord's)	1871
James Lillywhite (8-55): Sussex v. M.C.C. (Brighton)	1871
W. Frith (8-18): Canterbury v. Otago (Christchurch)	1880-81
J. Briggs (8-11): England v. South Africa (Cape Town)	1888-89
J. T. Hearne (8-22): Middlesex v. Lancashire (Lord's)	1891
A. Mold (8-49): Lancashire v. Sussex (Hove)	1893
H. Fannin (8-19) Hawke's Bay v. Auckland (Auckland)	1897-98
S. Haigh (8-34): Hawke's XI v. Cape Province (Cape Town)	1898-99
W. P. Howell (10-28): Australians v. Surrey (Oval)	1899
A. Woodcock (9-28): Leicestershire v. M.C.C. (Lord's)	1899
A. E. Trott (8-47): Middlesex v. Gloucestershire (Clifton)	1900
J. J. Kotze (8-18): Transvaal v. Griqualand West (Port Elizabeth)	1902-03
J. B. King (9-62): Philadelphians v. Lancashire (Manchester)	1903
A. E. E. Vogler (8-24): Eastern Province v. O.F.S. (Johannesburg)	1906-07
G. H. Hirst (9-23): Yorkshire v. Lancashire (Leeds)	1910
H. Howell (8-31): Warwickshire v. Northamptonshire (Northampton)	1922
C. W. L. Parker (9-87): Gloucestershire v. Derbyshire (Gloucester)	1922
J. M. Blanckenberg (8-97): South Africans v. Glamorgan (Cardiff)	1924
G. O. Allen (10-40): Middlesex v. Lancashire (Lord's)	1929
A. J. Bell (8-34): Western Province v. Eastern Province (Cape Town)	1929-30
Riaz Akhtar (8-70): Quetta v. Hyderabad (Hyderabad)	1962-63

ELEVEN BOWLERS IN AN INNINGS

Instances of an entire fielding side going on to bowl in the course of an innings, with the fielding team listed first:-

455	Surrey v. Middlesex (Oval)	1866
370	Gentlemen of England v. Cambridge U. (Cambridge)	1881
551	England v. Australia (Oval)	1884
464	Kent v. Sussex (Hove)	1884
698	Sussex v. Surrey (Oval)	1888
445	Natal v. Kimberley (Kimberley)	1889-90
475	Hampshire v. Warwickshire (Southampton)	1897
579	Hampshire v. Surrey (Oval)	1897
310-8	Lancashire v. Leicestershire (Leicester)	1900
609-8d	Sussex v. Leicestershire (Leicester)	1900
463-7	Derbyshire v. Worcestershire (Worcester)	1902

Eleven Bowlers in an Innings—*Cont.*

585-7	Surrey v. Warwickshire (Oval)	1905
627	Nottinghamshire v. Lancashire (Nottingham)	1905
591	Queensland v. New South Wales (Sydney)	1907-08
426-8d	Sussex v. Middlesex (Eastbourne)	1910
495-5d	Warwickshire v. Yorkshire (Huddersfield)	1922
535-6d	Warwickshire v. Middlesex (Birmingham)	1922
257-5	M.C.C. v. Australian XI (Brisbane)	1924-25
355	Gloucestershire v. Warwickshire (Bristol)	1933
385-7	Lancashire v. Somerset (Taunton)	1936
260-7	Glamorgan v. Nottinghamshire (Nottingham)	1951
345-9	Derbyshire v. Leicestershire (Ashby-de-la-Zouch)	1955
200-1	Sussex v. Glamorgan (Hove)	1956
295-3d	Somerset v. Leicestershire (Taunton)	1957
300	Karachi Greens v. Hyderabad (Karachi)	1961-62
378-4	Glamorgan v. Gloucestershire (Bristol)	1965

Twelve players bowled for the Gentlemen v. Cambridge U. (593) at Cambridge in 1880, the match being played twelve-a-side.

ONLY FOUR BOWLERS IN AN INNINGS OF OVER 450 RUNS

Gloucestershire while Warwickshire scored 484-9d (Birmingham)	1899
Lancashire while Yorkshire scored 489 (Leeds)	1921
Gloucestershire while Lancashire scored 469 (Bristol)	1927
Somerset while Leicestershire scored 490 (Frome)	1937
Essex while Lancashire scored 510 (Clacton)	1947
Warwickshire while Middlesex scored 452-5d (Birmingham)	1947
Essex while Somerset scored 488 (Clacton)	1949
New Zealand while England scored 482 (Oval)	1949
Essex while Kent scored 532 (Maidstone)	1950
North-Eastern Transvaal while Transvaal scored 481-6d (Johannesburg)	1952-53

LONGEST DISTANCES FOR A BAIL

The longest recorded distances for a bail to travel after a batsman has been clean bowled are:-

yd.	*in.*		
67	6	by R. D. Burrows in bowling W. Huddleston: Worcestershire v. Lancashire (Manchester)	1911
66		by H. Larwood in bowling G. W. Martin: M.C.C. v. Tasmania (Launceston)	1928-29
64	6	by R. D. Burrows in bowling A. C. MacLaren: Worcestershire v. Lancashire (Manchester)	1901
63	6	by A. Mold in bowling G. A. Lohmann: Lancashire v. Surrey (Oval)	1896

EARLIEST DATES FOR TAKING 100, 200 AND 300 WICKETS

The earliest dates for reaching an aggregate of 100, 200 and 300 wickets are dominated by one man: A. P. "Tich" Freeman, the Kent and England slow bowler. Interspersing well-controlled leg-breaks with googlies and top-spinners he reached 100 wickets in a season 17 times. He is the only bowler to have taken 300 wickets in a season (304, average 18.15 in 1928) and his aggregate exceeded 200 on five other occasions—also a record.

100 WICKETS

June 12 1896	J. T. Hearne
June 12 1931	C. W. L. Parker
June 13 1931	A. P. Freeman
June 14 1930	A. P. Freeman
June 17 1925	M. W. Tate
June 17 1932	A. P. Freeman

200 WICKETS

July 27 1928	A. P. Freeman
August 1 1931	A. P. Freeman
August 6 1930	A. P. Freeman
August 7 1929	A. P. Freeman
August 14 1933	A. P. Freeman

300 WICKETS

September 15 1928 A. P. Freeman

OUTSTANDING BOWLING ON DÉBUT

The feat of taking ten wickets in a match or six in an innings on his first appearance in first-class cricket is a bowler's nearest equivalent to the batsman's century on debut.

TEN WICKETS IN THE MATCH

14-57	James Lillywhite: Sussex v. M.C.C. (Lord's)	1862
14-100	F. Fee: Ireland v. M.C.C. (Dublin)	1956
14-171	F. G. Roberts: Gloucestershire v. Yorkshire (Dewsbury)	1887
14-112	V. R. Price: Oxford U. v. Gentlemen of England (Oxford)	1919
13-84	W. G. Grace: Gentlemen of South v. Players of South (Oval) (*Aged 16*)	1865
12-87	A. H. C. Fargus: Gloucestershire v. Middlesex (Lord's)	1900
12-97	V. M. Muddiah: Services v. Southern Punjab (Patiala)	1949-50
11-43	E. T. A. Fuller: Canterbury v. Otago (Christchurch)	1872-73
11-95	B. Mitchell: Transvaal v. Border (East London)	1925-26
11-100	R. V. Webster: Scotland v. M.C.C. (Greenock)	1961
11-209	L. W. Payn: Natal v. Orange Free State (Bloemfontein)	1936-37
10-44	Javed Akhtar: Rawalpindi-Peshawar v. Services (Rawalpindi)	1960-61
10-73	H. R. A. Kelleher: Surrey v. Worcestershire (Oval)	1955
10-100	T. A. Carlton: Canterbury v. Otago (Christchurch)	1909-10
10-101	S. Webb: Middlesex v. Nottinghamshire (Nottingham)	1897
10-102	J. G. Saunders: Oxford U. v. Lancashire (Oxford)	1966
10-115	J. Hewitson: Lancashire v. Oxford U. (Manchester)	1890
10-136	G. T. S. Stevens: Middlesex v. Hampshire (Lord's)	1919
10-137	A. J. Jessup: Oxford U. v. Free Foresters (Oxford)	1950
10-141	R. Rees: South Australia v. Victoria (Melbourne)	1903-04
10-145	L. O. Fleetwood-Smith: Victoria v. Tasmania (Hobart)	1931-32
10-149	J. I'Anson: Lancashire v. M.C.C. (Lord's)	1896

SIX WICKETS IN ONE INNINGS

(*Excluding bowlers appearing in the above list*)

8-54	V. M. Muddiah: Services v. Southern Punjab (Patiala)	1949-50
8-64	W. B. Gadsden: Natal v. Transvaal (Durban)	1928-29
8-70	G. A. Wilson: Worcestershire v. Yorkshire (Worcester)	1899
8-88	M. H. J. Allen: Northamptonshire v. Nottinghamshire (Nottingham) (*This was his second match, he did not bowl in the first.*)	1956
8-91	F. Barratt: Nottinghamshire v. M.C.C. (Lord's)	1914
7-10	A. C. King: Natal v. Griqualand West (Johannesburg)	1906-07
7-21	K. Walker: Victoria v. Tasmania (Geelong)	1961-62
7-28	C. E. Dench: Nottinghamshire v. M.C.C. (Lord's)	1897
7-32	J. A. Bailey: Essex v. Nottinghamshire (Southend)	1953
7-49	H. Hunt: Somerset v. Derbyshire (Ilkeston)	1935
7-50	L. G. Robinson: Natal v. Griqualand West (Cape Town)	1893-94
7-54	R. F. Delport: Western Province v. Rhodesia (Cape Town)	1950-51
7-58	V. Brewster: Warwickshire v. Oxford U. (Birmingham)	1965
7-70	W. K. Laidlaw: Scotland v. Yorkshire (Harrogate)	1938
7-76	B. Stead: Yorkshire v. Indians (Bradford)	1959
7-77	L. R. Tuckett: Natal v. M.C.C. (Durban)	1909-10
7-91	G. Anderson: Rhodesia v. Transvaal (Johannesburg)	1904-05
7-95	W. H. Ashley: South Africa v. England (Cape Town)	1888-89
7-110	G. N. S. Ridley: Oxford U. v. Gloucestershire (Oxford)	1965
6-19	G. W. Youngson: Scotland v. Ireland (Cork)	1947
6-24	J. S. Rao: Services v. Jammu & Kashmir (New Delhi) (*Including the 'hat-trick'*)	1963-64
6-31	A. Shaw: Nottinghamshire v. Kent (Nottingham)	1864
6-32	S. C. Adams: Northamptonshire v. Dublin U. (Northampton)	1926
6-44	E. A. Barlow: Oxford U. v. Yorkshire (Oxford)	1932
6-46	W. J. Pershke: Oxford U. v. Glamorgan (Oxford)	1938
6-47	J. Iverson: Victoria v. Western Australia (Perth)	1949-50
6-47	B. D. Wells: Gloucestershire v. Sussex (Bristol)	1951
6-52	D. J. Sincock: South Australia v. New South Wales (Adelaide)	1960-61
6-52	R. A. Collinge: Combined Services v. Cambridge U. (Cambridge)	1962

Outstanding Bowling on Début—*Cont.*

6-53	W. Flint: Nottinghamshire v. Middlesex (Lord's)	1919
6-67	Majid Jahangir: Lahore B. v. Khairpur (Lahore)	1961-62
6-70	J. F. Fitzgerald: Cambridge U. v. Essex (Cambridge)	1966
6-111	T. Sutherland: Hampshire v. Warwickshire (Southampton)	1898

K. D. Boyce (Essex) had match figures of 13-108 (9-61 & 4-47) on his first appearance in English first-class cricket v. Cambridge U. (Brentwood) 1966. He had played in one previous first-class match for Barbados at Bridgetown in 1964-65.

J. W. Sharpe (Surrey) had an innings analysis of 5-5 on his debut v. Oxford U. (Oxford) 1889.

R. Roxley (N.S.W.) took the first five wickets to fall in his debut match v. South Australia (Adelaide) 1952-53, finishing with 5-84.

WICKET WITH FIRST BALL IN FIRST-CLASS CRICKET

H. Stubberfield: Sussex v. Surrey (Brighton)	1857
R. G. Barlow: Lancashire v. Yorkshire (Sheffield)	1871
G. McCanlis: Kent v. Surrey (Oval)	1873
J. J. Parfitt: Surrey v. Yorkshire (Oval)	1881
E. C. Streatfeild: Surrey v. Lancashire (Oval)	1890
M. Berkley: Essex v. Yorkshire (Halifax)	1894
L. C. V. Bathurst: Middlesex v. Sussex (Lord's)	1894
T. Lancaster: Lancashire v. Nottinghamshire (Manchester)	1894
H. G. Curgenven: Derbyshire v. Essex (Leyton)	1896
C. Blythe: Kent v. Yorkshire (Tonbridge)	1899
H. J. Hodgkins: Gloucestershire v. Somerset (Bristol)	1900
J. H. Hunt: Middlesex v. Somerset (Lord's)	1902
C. Thorneycroft: Northamptonshire v. Kent (Catford)	1907
L. Cook: Lancashire v. Essex (Manchester)	1907
G. de L. Hough: Kent v. Essex (Leyton)	1919
T. Collins: Nottinghamshire v. Leicestershire (Nottingham)	1921
J. John: Glamorgan v. Somerset (Cardiff)	1922
A. E. Waters: Gloucestershire v. Glamorgan (Cheltenham)	1923
R. H. Sharp: Essex v. Gloucestershire (Leyton)	1925
S. C. Adams: Northamptonshire v. Dublin U. (Northampton)	1926
J. G. O'Gorman: Surrey v. Glamorgan (Oval)	1927
W. H. Copson: Derbyshire v. Surrey (Oval)	1932
F. W. Stocks: Nottinghamshire v. Lancashire (Manchester)	1946
C. Cook: Gloucestershire v. Oxford U. (Oxford)	1946
E. Tilley: Leicestershire v. Derbyshire (Derby)	1946
J. Lee: Leicestershire v. Glamorgan (Cardiff)	1947
R. Hiern: South Australia v. Victoria (Melbourne)	1949-50
G. A. Robertson: Cambridge U. v. Hampshire (Cambridge)	1950
R. Flockton: New South Wales v. Queensland (Brisbane)	1951-52
D. H. Mitchell: Transvaal v. Natal (Durban)	1954-55
F. C. Brailsford: Derbyshire v. Sussex (Derby)	1958
W. G. Davies: Glamorgan v. Surrey (Oval)	1958
N. T. Sawant: Baroda v. Saurashtra (Baroda)	1960-61
M. Hill: New South Wales v. South Australia (Adelaide)	1964-65
B. A. Rothwell: New South Wales v. M.C.C. (Sydney)	1965-66
A. R. Frost: South Australia v. M.C.C. (Adelaide)	1965-66
K. R. Flint: Tasmania v. M.C.C. (Launceston)	1965-66

S. C. Adams, playing for Northamptonshire v. Dublin U. (Northampton) 1926, took two wickets with his first two balls, and three wickets at the cost of a single in his first over.

C. G. Fynn, playing for Hampshire v. Lancashire (Bournemouth) 1930, took two wickets in his first over.

R. R. Phillips, playing for Border v. Eastern Province (Port Elizabeth) 1939-40, performed the 'hat-trick' in his first over in first-class cricket. He had previously played in four matches without bowling.

J. M. Allan (Oxford U.) bowled seven consecutive maidens v. Yorkshire (Oxford) 1953, in his first match, and three more for the wickets of K. R. Miller and I. D. Craig in his second match v. Australians (Oxford), before conceding his first first-class run in his 11th over.

100 WICKETS IN SEASON OF DÉBUT

Only eleven bowlers have taken 100 wickets in the season in which they made their initial appearance in first-class cricket. The age listed is that at the start of the season.

	Age	*Season*	*Overs*	*Mdns.*	*Runs*	*Wkts.*	*Avge.*
G. P. Harrison (Yorkshire)	21	1883	786	328	1326	100	13.26
A. Mold (Lancashire)	23	1889	679	262	1207	102	11.83
C. H. G. Bland (Sussex)	24	1897	1140.2	337	2798	129	21.68
W. Rhodes (Yorkshire)	20	1898	1240	482	2249	154	14.60
F. Barratt (Nottinghamshire)	20	1914	920	192	2507	115	21.80
A. Waddington (Yorkshire)	26	1919	718.1	186	1874	100	18.74
J. M. Gregory† (Australians)	23	1919	830	124	2383	131	18.19
G. W. Brook (Worcestershire)	34	1930	974.4	165	2889	132	21.88
C. Cook (Gloucestershire)	24	1946	1123.1	327	2477	133	18.62
D. B. Close (Yorkshire)	18	1949	1245	324	3150	113	27.87
D. L. Underwood (Kent)	17	1963	941.4	376	2134	101	21.12

† Gregory did not make his début in Australia until 1919-20

100 WICKETS IN FIRST FULL SEASON

The following bowlers took 100 wickets in their first full season having previously played in less than five first-class matches.

	Wkts.	*Avge.*	*Season*	*Previous Matches*
A. G. Steel (Lancashire)	164	9.40	1878	1
N. A. Knox (Surrey)	129	21.44	1905	2
P. Jeeves (Warwickshire)	106	20.88	1913	2
T. J. Durston (Middlesex)	113	21.88	1920	4
A. W. Wellard (Somerset)	131	21.38	1929	2
A. V. Bedser (Surrey)	128	20.13	1946	2
C. Gladwin (Derbyshire)	109	18.36	1946	4
S. Ramadhin (West Indians)	135	14.28	1950	2
A. L. Valentine (West Indians)	123	17.94	1950	2
R. Appleyard (Yorkshire)	200	14.14	1951	3

NO-BALLED FOR THROWING

E. Jones: Australia v. England (Melbourne)	1897-98
C. B. Fry: Sussex v. Nottinghamshire (Nottingham)	1898
C. B. Fry: Sussex v. Oxford U. (Hove)	1898
C. B. Fry: Sussex v. Middlesex (Lord's)	1898
F. J. Hopkins: Warwickshire v. Kent (Tonbridge)	1898
E. R. Bradford: Hampshire v. Leicestershire (Leicester)	1899
E. R. Bradford: Hampshire v. Australians (Southampton)	1899
(*No-balled by both umpires*)	
R. G. Hardstaff: Nottinghamshire v. Australians (Nottingham)	1899
C. B. Fry: Sussex v. Gloucestershire (Hove)	1900
A. Mold: Lancashire v. Nottinghamshire (Nottingham)	1900
E. J. Tyler: Somerset v. Surrey (Taunton)	1900
(*No-balled twice in one over by J. Phillips.*)	
J. J. Marsh: New South Wales v. Victoria (Melbourne)	1900-01
(*No-balled* 19 *times by R. W. Crockett.*)	
A. Mold: Lancashire v. Somerset (Manchester)	1901
(*No-balled* 16 *times in* 10 *overs by J. Phillips.*)	
A. Paish: Gloucestershire v. Nottinghamshire (Bristol)	1903
A. Paish: Gloucestershire v. Yorkshire (Bristol)	1903
(*No-balled by W. A. J. West in consecutive matches, on four occasions in second match.*)	
R. Whitehead: Lancashire v. Nottinghamshire (Manchester)	1908
(*His début match in first-class cricket, he also scored a century*—131*.)	
G. John: West Indian XI v. M.C.C. (Georgetown)	1910-11
R. Halcombe: Western Australia v. Victoria (Melbourne)	1929-30
(*No-balled* 8 *times in succession in the only over he bowled.*)	
E. Gilbert: Queensland v. Victoria (Melbourne)	1931-32
(*No-balled* 8 *times in* 2 *overs.*)	

No-Balled for Throwing—*Cont.*

Mabarak Ali: Trinidad v. Barbados (Bridgetown) 1941-42
(*No-balled* 30 *times in one innings.*)
R. R. Frankish: Western Australia v. Victoria (Melbourne) 1950-51
M. R. Rege: Maharashtra v. M.C.C. (Poona) 1951-52
(*No-balled twice in the only over he bowled.*)
C. N. McCarthy: Cambridge U. v. Worcestershire (Worcester) 1952
G. A. R. Lock: Surrey v. Indians (Oval).. 1952
(*No-balled* 3 *times by W. F. Price, twice in one over.*)
G. A. R. Lock: England v. West Indies (Kingston) 1953-54
G. A. R. Lock: M.C.C. v. Barbados (Bridgetown) 1953-54
(*No-balled by both umpires, once by one and twice in three balls by the other.*)
D. B. Pearson: Worcestershire v. Gloucestershire (Bristol) 1954
K. N. Slater: Western Australia v. Victoria (Melbourne) 1957-58
G. Griffin: Natal v. Transvaal (Durban) 1958-59
G. Griffin: Natal v. Border & Eastern Province (East London) 1958-59
D. B. Pearson: Worcestershire v. Indians (Worcester) 1959
(*No-balled* 5 *times by J. S. Buller.*)
D. B. Pearson: Worcestershire v. Essex (Worcester) 1959
G. A. R. Lock: Surrey v. Glamorgan (Cardiff) 1959
K. J. Aldridge: Worcestershire v. Leicestershire (Kidderminster) 1959
(*No-balled twice by J. S. Buller.*)
J. McLaughlin: Queensland v. New South Wales (Sydney) 1959-60
G. A. R. Lock: Surrey v. Cambridge U. (Cambridge) 1960
K. J. Aldridge: Worcestershire v. Glamorgan (Pontypridd) 1960
H. J. Rhodes: Derbyshire v. South Africans (Derby) 1960
(*No-balled* 6 *times by P. A. Gibb.*)
G. Griffin: South Africans v. M.C.C. (Lord's) 1960
(*No-balled once by F. S. Lee and twice by John Langridge. He was also called for dragging by F. S. Lee each time John Langridge no-balled him for throwing.*)
D. B. Pearson: Worcestershire v. Northamptonshire (Dudley) 1960
(*No-balled twice by T. J. Bartley.*)
G. Griffin: South Africans v. Nottinghamshire (Nottingham) 1960
(*No-balled* 11 *times in the first innings,* 5 *times for throwing and* 6 *times for dragging. He was called* 3 *times for throwing by T. J. Bartley and twice by W. H. Copson. No-balled for throwing* 3 *times in the second innings.*)
E. Bryant: Somerset v. Gloucestershire (Bath) 1960
(*No-balled* 5 *times by H. Yarnold,* 4 *times in one over.*)
G. Griffin: South Africans v. Hampshire (Southampton) 1960
(*No-balled by both umpires once each in first innings and* 4 *times in the second innings,* 3 *times by J. H. Parks and once by H. Elliott.*)
G. Griffin: South Africa v. England (Lord's) 1960
(*No-balled* 11 *times by F. S. Lee in England's only innings.*)
D. W. White: Hampshire v. Sussex (Hove) 1960
(*No-balled* 3 *times by P. A. Gibb, twice in first innings and once in the second.*)
R. T. Simpson: Nottinghamshire v. Derbyshire (Nottingham) 1960
(*No-balled once by H. Yarnold.*)
R. Jairam: Hyderabad v. Madras (Madras) 1960-61
(*No-balled once.*)
B. Quigley: South Australia v. Victoria (Adelaide) 1960-61
(*No-balled twice by C. J. Egar from the bowler's end.*)
B. K. Bose: East Zone v. Pakistan (Jamshedpur) 1960-61
(*No-balled* 3 *times by S. K. Raghunatha Rao.*)
H. J. Rhodes: Derbyshire v. Northamptonshire (Derby) 1961
(*No-balled* 3 *times in one over by P. A. Gibb.*)
P. Bhagwandas: Central Zone v. M.C.C. (Nagpur) 1961-62
(*No-balled twice.*)
C. C. Griffith: Barbados v. Indians (Bridgetown) 1961-62
(*No-balled once.*)
G. Griffen: Rhodesia v. North-Eastern Transvaal (Salisbury) 1962-63
(*No-balled* 7 *times by J. Fletcher.*)
I. W. Meckiff: Victoria v. South Australia (Adelaide) 1962-63
(*No-balled once by J. Kierse.*)
I. W. Meckiff: Victoria v. Queensland (Brisbane) 1962-63
(*No-balled once by W. Priem.*)
K. Gillhouley: Nottinghamshire v. Gloucestershire (Cheltenham) 1963
(*No-balled* 4 *times in succession by J. S. Buller.*)

No-Balled for Throwing—*Cont.*

I. W. Meckiff: Australia v. South Africa (Brisbane) 1963-64
(*No-balled 4 times in his only over by C. J. Egar and subsequently announced his retirement from all classes of cricket.*)
P. Lawrence: Middlesex v. Sussex (Lord's) 1964
(*No-balled twice in one over by R. Aspinall.*)
I. R. Redpath: Australians v. Glamorgan (Cardiff) 1964
(*No-balled once by John Langridge.*)
E. Illingworth: Victoria v. South Australia (Adelaide) 1964-65
(*No-balled twice by C. J. Egar and once by J. J. Ryan.*)
K. N. Slater: Western Australia v. New South Wales (Sydney) 1964-65
(*No-balled once by E. F. Wykes.*)
H. J. Rhodes: Derbyshire v. South Africans (Chesterfield) 1965
(*No-balled twice by J. S. Buller.*)
D. W. White: Hampshire v. Lancashire (Manchester) 1965
(*No-balled once by J. S. Buller. White stumbled in the act of delivery and then flung the ball—apparently in fun—at D. M. Green, the batsman.*)
R. Collymore: British Guiana v. Jamaica (Kingston) 1965-66
(*No-balled 5 times by D. Sang Hue.*)
C. C. Griffith: West Indians v. Lancashire (Manchester) 1966
(*No-balled once by A. E. Fagg*)
P. Roberts: Trinidad v. Jamaica (Kingston) 1966-67
(*No-balled 3 times in one over by D. Sang Hue.*)
D. Archer: Trinidad v. Windward Islands (Port of Spain) 1966-67

PLAYERS' RECORDS—ALL-ROUND CRICKET

THE 'DOUBLE'

In 1873 W. G. Grace became the first player to score 1000 runs and take 100 wickets in a first-class season. Although he repeated this performance in each of the next five seasons, no player emulated him until 1882 when C. T. Studd (Middlesex) achieved the 'double'. Since 1895 however, only two seasons (1951 and 1958) have passed without at least one player performing this feat.

In 1949 D. B. Close of Yorkshire, aged 18, became the youngest player to do the 'double' and the only one to achieve it in his initial season.

Two players, V. W. C. Jupp (Sussex and Northants.), and F. R. Brown (Surrey and Northants.), have completed the 'double' for two counties.

OUTSTANDING 'DOUBLES'

2000 runs and 200 wickets	G. H. Hirst in 1906.
3000 runs and 100 wickets	J. H. Parks in 1937.
2000 runs and 100 wickets	W. G. Grace in 1876.
	C. L. Townsend in 1899.
	G. L. Jessop in 1900.
	G. H. Hirst in 1904 and 1905
	W. Rhodes in 1909 and 1911.
	F. A. Tarrant in 1911.
	J. W. Hearne in 1913, 1914 and 1920.
	F. E. Woolley in 1914, 1921, 1922 and 1923.
	V. W. C. Jupp in 1921.
	L. F. Townsend in 1933.
	E. Davies in 1937.
	James Langridge in 1937.
	T. E. Bailey in 1959.
1000 runs and 200 wickets	A. E. Trott in 1899 and 1900.
	A. S. Kennedy in 1922.
	M. W. Tate in 1923, 1924 and 1925.

The 'Double'—*Cont.*

MOST 'DOUBLES'

16 W. Rhodes.
14 G. H. Hirst.
10 V. W. C. Jupp.
9 W. E. Astill.
8 T. E. Bailey. W. G. Grace, M. S. Nichols, A. E. Relf, F. A. Tarrant, M. W. Tate, F. J. Titmus and F. E. Woolley.

MOST CONSECUTIVE 'DOUBLES'

11 G. H. Hirst (1903-1913)
8 F. A. Tarrant (1907-1914) and M. W. Tate (1922-1929).
7 W. Rhodes, twice (1903-1909 & 1914-1924).
6 W. E. Astill (1921-1926), G. Tribe (1952-1957), and F. E. Woolley (1914-1923).

CRICKETERS ACHIEVING THE 'DOUBLE'

		Season	*Runs*	*H.S.*	*Avge.*	100*s*	*Wkts.*	*Avge.*
Allen, D. A. (Glos.)	(1)	1961	1001	121*	25.02	1	124	19.43
Alley, W. E. (Somerset)	(1)	1962	1915	155	36.82	3	112	20.74
Andrews, W. H. R. (Somerset) ..	(2)	1937	1141	80	20.74	—	143	20.53
		1938	1001	77*	22.24	—	124	21.80
Armstrong, W. W. (Australians) ..	(3)	1905	1902	303*	50.05	4	122	18.20
		1909	1451	110*	43.96	3	113	16.38
		1921	1213	182*	41.82	3	100	14.44
Arnold, E. R. (Worcs.)	(4)	1902	1067	92	26.02	—	113	18.88
		1903	1157	128	30.44	2	143	17.44
		1904	1039	111	25.97	1	114	24.48
		1905	1148	134	37.03	—	115	22.32
Astill, W. E. (Leics.)	(9)	1921	1380	115	27.05	2	153	20.99
		1922	1210	78	23.72	—	144	19.23
		1923	1307	106	27.80	2	114	23.50
		1924	1126	88	25.59	—	103	20.84
		1925	1601	109	32.02	1	105	20.99
		1926	1291	158*	30.02	1	107	24.48
		1928	1127	89	24.50	—	130	22.33
		1929	1004	127	25.10	2	121	20.94
		1930	1022	84	24.92	—	111	22.25
Bailey, J. (Hants)	(1)	1948	1399	88	31.79	—	121	18.13
Bailey, T. E. (Essex)	(8)	1949	1380	93	35.38	—	130	24.20
		1952	1513	155*	36.90	1	103	29.09
		1954	1344	108*	32.78	1	101	21.39
		1957	1322	132	38.88	2	104	17.02
		1959	2011	146	46.76	6	100	24.69
		1960	1639	118	39.02	1	117	20.25
		1961	1240	117*	27.55	1	133	21.01
		1962	1460	124*	35.60	1	125	20.59
Barratt, F. (Notts.)	(1)	1928	1167	139*	29.17	2	114	25.18
Booth, M. W. (Yorks.)	(1)	1913	1228	107*	27.28	1	181	18.46
Bosanquet, B. J. T. (Middx.) ..	(1)	1904	1405	145	36.02	4	132	21.62
Braund, L. C. (Somerset)	(3)	1901	1587	115*	36.06	4	120	30.62
		1902	1423	144	27.53	2	172	19.80
		1903	1425	132	32.38	3	134	21.01
Brockwell, W. (Surrey)	(1)	1899	1542	167	33.52	3	105	25.26
Broderick, V. H. (Northants.) ..	(1)	1948	1066	135	26.65	2	100	22.77
Brown, F. R. (Surrey & Northants.)	(2)	1932	1135	212	32.42	3	120	20.46
		1949	1077	94	24.47	—	111	27.00
Calthorpe, Hon. F. S. G. (Warwicks.)	(1)	1920	1025	102	22.77	1	100	24.26
Cartwright, T. W. (Warwicks.) ..	(1)	1962	1176	210	33.60	1	106	20.05
Close, D. B. (Yorks.)	(2)	1949	1098	88*	27.45	—	113	27.87
		1952	1192	87*	33.11	—	114	24.08
Collins, H. L. (Australians)	(1)	1919	1615	127	38.45	5	106	16.55
Constantine, L. N. (West Indians) ..	(1)	1928	1381	130	34.52	3	107	22.95
Crawford, J. N. (Surrey)	(2)	1906	1174	148	30.10	1	118	20.28
		1907	1158	103	30.47	1	124	16.95
Cuffe, J. A. (Worcs.)	(1)	1911	1054	78	25.70	—	110	23.56
Cuttell, W. R. (Lancs.)	(1)	1898	1003	85*	25.71	—	114	21.21

The 'Double'—*Cont.*

		Season	*Runs*	*H.S.*	*Avge.*	*100s*		*Wkts.*	*Avge.*
Davidson, G. (Derby.)	(1)	1895	1296	80	28.07	—	..	138	16.79
Davies, E. (Glamorgan.)	(2)	1935	1326	155*	28.21	2	..	100	21.07
		1937	2012	140	40.24	3	..	103	23.03
Dooland, B. (Notts.)	(2)	1954	1012	88	28.11	—	..	196	15.48
		1957	1604	115*	28.64	1	..	141	23.21
Douglas, J. W. H. T. (Essex) ..	(5)	1914	1288	146	35.77	2	..	138	19.10
		1919	1178	144	34.64	2	..	136	25.14
		1920	1328	147	32.39	2	..	147	21.38
		1921	1547	210*	37.73	3	..	130	20.32
		1923	1110	147*	29.21	2	..	146	22.35
Drake, A. (Yorks.)	(1)	1913	1056	108	23.46	1	..	116	16.93
Faulkner, G. A. (South Africans) ..	(1)	1912	1075	145*	23.88	2	..	163	15.42
Fender, P. G. H. (Surrey)	(6)	1921	1152	101	21.33	1	..	134	26.58
		1922	1169	185	34.38	2	..	157	21.20
		1923	1427	124*	29.12	2	..	178	19.98
		1925	1042	81*	28.16	—	..	137	21.08
		1926	1043	104	30.67	1	..	112	24.54
		1928	1376	117	37.18	3	..	110	28.17
Flowers, W. (Notts.)	(1)	1883	1144	131	24.86	1	..	113	14.95
Foster, F. R. (Warwicks.)	(2)	1911	1614	200	42.47	3	..	141	20.31
		1914	1460	305*	34.76	1	..	122	18.62
Giffen, G. (Australians)	(3)	1886	1424	119	26.86	1	..	154	17.36
		1893	1133	180	23.12	2	..	118	19.04
		1896	1208	130	25.17	2	..	117	19.29
Gilligan, A. E. R. (Sussex)	(1)	1923	1183	114*	21.12	2	..	163	17.50
Goonesena, G. (Notts.)	(2)	1955	1380	118	28.75	2	..	134	21.05
		1957	1156	211	26.88	1	..	110	23.26
Grace, W. G. (Glos.)	(8)	1873	2139	192*	71.30	7	..	101	12.94
		1874	1664	179	52.00	8	..	140	12.71
		1875	1498	152	32.56	3	..	191	12.92
		1876	2622	344	62.42	7	..	129	19.05
		1877	1474	261	39.83	2	..	179	12.79
		1878	1151	116	28.77	1	..	152	14.50
		1885	1688	221*	43.28	4	..	117	18.79
		1886	1846	170	35.50	4	..	122	19.99
Gregory, J. M. (Australians) ..	(1)	1921	1135	107	36.61	3	..	116	16.58
Gunn, J. (Notts.)	(4)	1903	1665	294	42.69	3	..	118	19.34
		1904	1225	100	30.62	1	..	123	25.27
		1905	1366	178	35.94	3	..	111	25.46
		1906	1395	112	35.76	2	..	112	21.66
Haig, N. E. (Middx.)	(3)	1921	1009	108	22.95	1	..	111	23.10
		1927	1059	104*	22.53	1	..	109	27.45
		1929	1552	130	25.02	2	..	129	24.17
Haigh, S. (Yorks.)	(1)	1904	1055	138	26.37	2	..	121	19.85
Hallows, J. (Lancs.)	(1)	1904	1071	137*	39.66	3	..	108	19.37
Hayward, T. W. (Surrey)	(1)	1897	1368	130	38.00	1	..	114	18.18
Hearne, J. W. (Middx.)	(5)	1911	1627	234*	42.81	4	..	102	22.00
		1913	2036	189	44.26	6	..	124	22.26
		1914	2116	204	60.45	8	..	123	22.69
		1920	2148	215*	55.07	6	..	142	17.83
		1923	1519	232	47.46	5	..	113	20.03
Hirst, G. H. (Yorks.)	(14)	1896	1122	107	28.05	1	..	104	21.61
		1897	1535	134	35.69	1	..	101	23.22
		1901	1950	214	42.39	3	..	183	16.38
		1903	1844	153	47.28	5	..	128	14.94
		1904	2501	157	54.36	9	..	132	21.09
		1905	2266	341	53.95	6	..	110	19.94
		1906	2385	169	45.86	6	..	208	16.50
		1907	1334	91*	28.38	—	..	188	15.20
		1908	1598	128*	38.97	1	..	174	14.05
		1909	1256	140	27.30	1	..	115	20.05
		1910	1840	158	32.85	3	..	164	14.79
		1911	1789	218	33.12	3	..	137	20.40
		1912	1133	109	25.75	1	..	118	17.37
		1913	1540	166*	35.81	3	..	101	20.13
Hopwood, J. L. (Lancs.)	(2)	1934	1672	220	38.00	3	..	111	20.69
		1935	1538	104	33.43	2	..	103	20.55

The 'Double'—*Cont.*

		Season	*Runs*	*H.S.*	*Avge.*	100*s*		*Wkts.*	*Avge.*
Horton, M. J. (Worcs.)	(2)	1955	1296	103	22.73	1	..	103	27.38
		1961	1808	124*	28.25	4	..	101	21.64
Howorth, R. (Worcs.)	(3)	1939	1019	69	21.22	—	..	100	24.34
		1946	1201	114	24.51	2	..	114	19.35
		1947	1510	95	26.03	—	..	164	17.85
Illingworth, R. (Yorks.)	(6)	1957	1213	97	28.20	—	..	106	18.40
		1959	1726	162	46.64	5	..	110	21.46
		1960	1006	86	25.79	—	..	109	17.55
		1961	1153	75	24.53	—	..	128	17.90
		1962	1612	127	34.29	3	..	117	19.45
		1964	1301	135	37.17	2	..	122	17.46
Jackson, F. S. (Yorks.)	(1)	1898	1566	160	41.21	5	..	104	15.67
Jackson, V. E. (Leics.)	(1)	1955	1582	121	29.29	4	..	112	21.71
Jenkins, R. O. (Worcs.)	(2)	1949	1183	91*	28.16	—	..	183	21.19
		1952	1087	85	24.70	—	..	136	25.65
Jessop, G. L. (Glos.)	(2)	1897	1219	140	29.73	4	..	116	17.85
		1900	2210	179	40.18	6	..	104	21.00
Jupp, V. W. C. (Sussex & Northants.)	(10)	1920	1444	151	28.31	3	..	111	18.56
		1921	2169	179	38.73	7	..	121	22.78
		1925	1306	144	27.78	1	..	116	20.68
		1926	1560	197	35.45	2	..	113	19.95
		1927	1519	116	38.94	3	..	121	20.42
		1928	1574	113	34.97	2	..	166	20.15
		1930	1037	142*	28.02	1	..	106	20.96
		1931	1540	128	28.00	2	..	131	24.91
		1932	1712	163	31.70	2	..	130	22.61
		1933	1155	121	28.17	1	..	108	29.46
Kennedy, A. S. (Hants.)	(5)	1921	1305	152*	26.10	2	..	186	21.55
		1922	1129	110*	22.13	1	..	205	16.80
		1923	1327	163*	25.51	2	..	184	19.55
		1928	1437	128	26.61	2	..	105	28.38
		1930	1006	94*	20.53	—	..	120	25.72
Killick, E. H. (Sussex)	(1)	1905	1392	104	26.26	1	..	108	21.93
Kilner, R. (Yorks.)	(4)	1922	1198	124	27.22	2	..	122	14.73
		1923	1404	79	34.24	—	..	158	12.91
		1925	1068	124	30.51	2	..	131	17.92
		1926	1187	150	37.09	1	..	107	22.52
King, J. H. (Leics.)	(1)	1912	1074	104*	22.85	1	..	130	17.63
Knight, B. R. (Essex)	(4)	1962	1689	165	34.46	2	..	100	24.05
		1963	1578	124	28.69	3	..	140	21.72
		1964	1209	97	23.25	—	..	100	27.02
		1965	1172	63	22.98	—	..	125	18.90
Langridge, James (Sussex)	(6)	1930	1386	159*	30.13	2	..	112	20.60
		1931	1007	92*	28.77	—	..	102	18.60
		1932	1192	128	32.21	2	..	115	17.66
		1933	1578	159*	37.57	5	..	158	16.56
		1935	1375	114*	33.53	2	..	102	19.67
		1937	2082	150*	40.82	1	..	101	22.92
Llewellyn, C. B. (Hants.)	(3)	1901	1025	216	31.06	2	..	134	22.53
		1908	1347	154	28.06	3	..	102	25.13
		1910	1232	107	29.33	2	..	152	19.27
Lockwood, W. H. (Surrey)	(2)	1899	1272	131	37.14	3	..	117	19.52
		1900	1367	165	32.54	2	..	125	19.99
Mankad, V. M. (Indians)	(1)	1946	1120	132	28.00	3	..	129	20.76
Martin, S. H. (Worcs.)	(2)	1937	1130	92	21.73	—	..	114	20.25
		1939	1262	102*	25.24	1	..	106	25.00
Mason, J. R. (Kent)	(1)	1901	1561	145	36.30	3	..	118	20.44
Mortimore, J. B. (Glos.)	(3)	1959	1060	76	20.78	—	..	113	18.28
		1963	1425	149	26.88	1	..	102	20.62
		1964	1118	95	19.96	—	..	104	21.44
Muncer, B. L. (Glamorgan) ..	(1)	1952	1097	135	24.37	1	..	105	17.29
Newman, J. A. (Hants.)	(5)	1921	1065	166*	30.42	1	..	177	21.56
		1923	1006	130	22.86	1	..	148	25.35
		1926	1468	134	30.58	1	..	154	24.70
		1927	1448	102*	32.17	2	..	115	23.19
		1928	1474	118	29.48	3	..	112	30.32

The 'Double'—*Cont.*

		Season	*Runs*	*H.S.*	*Avge.*	100*s*		*Wkts.*	*Avge.*
Nichols, M. S. (Essex)	(8)	1929	1301	138	28.91	1	..	104	25.59
		1932	1430	105	31.77	1	..	115	24.92
		1933	1406	135	28.69	3	..	145	20.97
		1935	1249	146	23.56	1	..	157	16.62
		1936	1315	205	29.22	3	..	114	19.42
		1937	1247	120	25.44	2	..	148	18.52
		1938	1452	163	35.41	3	..	171	19.92
		1939	1387	146	35.56	2	..	121	18.87
Palmer, K. E. (Somerset)	(1)	1961	1036	125*	25.90	1	..	114	20.32
Parks, J. H. (Sussex)	(2)	1935	1633	156	33.32	4	..	103	19.57
		1937	3003	168	50.89	11	..	101	25.83
Pearson, F. (Worcs.)	(1)	1923	1052	103*	25.04	1	..	111	22.89
Peel, R. (Yorks.)	(1)	1896	1206	210*	30.15	3	..	128	17.50
Pope, G. H. (Derby.)	(2)	1938	1040	85	29.71	—	..	103	24.13
		1948	1152	207*	38.40	3	..	100	17.24
Pressdee, J. S. (Glamorgan) ..	(2)	1963	1467	88*	33.34	—	..	106	21.62
		1964	1606	133*	37.34	1	..	105	19.39
Relf, A. E. (Sussex)	(8)	1904	1214	154	28.23	2	..	102	26.04
		1905	1386	120	29.48	1	..	111	23.45
		1906	1256	189*	25.63	2	..	106	23.24
		1908	1335	138	28.40	1	..	151	17.53
		1910	1296	87	23.56	—	..	158	19.67
		1911	1691	101*	29.66	1	..	142	21.44
		1912	1312	104	23.85	2	..	133	19.44
		1913	1846	130	31.82	4	..	141	18.09
Rhodes, W. (Yorks.)	(16)	1903	1137	98*	27.07	—	..	193	14.57
		1904	1537	196	35.74	2	..	131	21.59
		1905	1581	201	35.93	2	..	182	16.95
		1906	1721	119	29.16	3	..	128	23.57
		1907	1055	112	22.93	1	..	177	15.57
		1908	1673	146	31.56	3	..	115	16.13
		1909	2094	199	40.26	5	..	141	15.89
		1911	2261	128	38.32	5	..	117	24.07
		1914	1377	113	29.29	2	..	118	18.27
		1919	1237	135	34.36	1	..	164	14.42
		1920	1123	167*	28.07	1	..	161	13.18
		1921	1474	267*	39.83	3	..	141	13.27
		1922	1511	110	39.76	4	..	119	12.19
		1923	1321	126	33.02	2	..	134	11.54
		1924	1126	100	26.18	1	..	109	14.46
		1926	1132	132	34.30	1	..	115	14.86
Robins, R. W. V. (Middx.) ..	(1)	1929	1134	106	26.37	1	..	162	21.53
Root, C. F. (Worcs.)	(1)	1928	1044	107	20.88	1	..	118	29.66
Simms, H. L. (Sussex)	(1)	1912	1099	126	20.73	1	..	107	23.12
Sinfield, R. A. (Glos.)	(2)	1934	1228	83	31.48	—	..	122	23.40
		1937	1001	74*	24.41	—	..	129	22.92
Smailes, T. F. (Yorks.)	(1)	1938	1002	117	25.05	2	..	113	20.84
Smith, R. (Essex)	(3)	1947	1386	86*	28.87	—	..	125	37.26
		1950	1149	80	23.93	—	..	102	34.77
		1952	1044	107*	24.27	1	..	136	28.87
Smith, S. G. (Northants.)	(3)	1909	1091	126	30.30	1	..	115	19.51
		1913	1522	133	37.12	4	..	111	17.25
		1914	1373	177	42.90	1	..	105	16.25
Smith, T. P. B. (Essex)	(1)	1947	1065	163	23.66	1	..	172	27.13
Storey, S. J. (Surrey)	(1)	1966	1013	109*	24.70	1	..	104	18.39
Studd, C. T. (Middx.)	(2)	1882	1249	126*	32.86	4	..	131	16.01
		1883	1193	175*	41.13	2	..	112	17.46
Tarrant, F. A. (Middx.)	(8)	1907	1552	147	32.33	2	..	183	15.70
		1908	1724	157	41.04	5	..	169	16.68
		1909	1643	138	32.86	2	..	125	19.26
		1910	1425	142	36.53	3	..	137	16.18
		1911	2030	207*	46.13	5	..	111	19.23
		1912	1492	140	30.44	2	..	140	14.78
		1913	1630	142	40.75	3	..	136	17.08
		1914	1879	250*	45.82	5	..	138	18.84
Tate, M. W. (Sussex)	(8)	1922	1050	88	19.44	—	..	119	17.42

The 'Double'—*Cont.*

		Season	Runs	H.S.	Avge.	100s		Wkts.	Avge.
Tate, M. W. (*cont.*)		1923	1168	97	22.03	—	..	219	13.97
		1924	1419	164	29.56	2	..	205	13.74
		1925	1290	121	23.45	2	..	228	14.97
		1926	1347	93	32.07	—	..	147	17.51
		1927	1713	146	36.44	3	..	147	20.53
		1928	1469	126	30.60	3	..	165	19.29
		1929	1161	100*	25.80	1	..	156	18.60
Thompson, G. J. (Northants.)	.. (2)	1906	1014	103*	25.35	1	..	136	22.20
		1910	1021	101	23.74	2	..	129	17.86
Titmus, F. J. (Middx.) ..	.. (8)	1955	1235	104	24.70	1	..	191	16.31
		1956	1227	96	28.53	—	..	105	20.84
		1957	1056	70	19.92	—	..	106	19.74
		1959	1273	90	25.75	—	..	104	24.83
		1960	1205	105	27.38	1	..	117	19.83
		1961	1703	120*	37.02	1	..	127	23.11
		1962	1238	74	30.95	—	..	136	20.76
		1967	1093	81	36.43	—	..	106	20.35
Todd, L. J. (Kent)	.. (1)	1936	1320	113	28.08	1	..	103	21.93
Townsend, C. L. (Glos.) ..	.. (2)	1898	1270	159	34.32	5	..	145	20.60
		1899	2440	224*	51.91	9	..	101	29.06
Townsend, L. F. (Derby) ..	.. (3)	1928	1001	98	29.44	—	..	104	23.56
		1932	1497	153*	31.18	1	..	117	18.45
		1933	2268	233	44.47	6	..	100	18.71
Tribe, G. E. (Northants.) ..	.. (7)	1952	1039	78	29.68	—	..	126	25.61
		1953	1260	121	36.00	2	..	108	22.22
		1954	1117	136*	27.92	1	..	149	19.79
		1955	1127	80*	25.04	—	..	176	19.12
		1956	1204	116	32.54	1	..	126	19.02
		1957	1181	101	25.12	1	..	140	18.71
		1959	1082	105*	26.39	1	..	122	23.95
Trott, A. E. (Middx.) ..	.. (2)	1899	1175	164	23.03	2	..	239	17.09
		1900	1357	112	23.87	2	..	211	23.33
Trumble, H. (Australians) ..	.. (1)	1899	1183	100	27.51	1	..	142	18.43
Van Geloven, J. (Leics.) ..	.. (1)	1962	1055	102*	22.93	1	..	100	28.11
Vine, J. (Sussex)	.. (1)	1901	1190	94	28.33	—	..	113	29.72
Wainwright, E. (Yorks.) ..	.. (1)	1897	1612	171	35.82	5	..	101	23.06
Walker, P. M. (Glamorgan)	.. (1)	1961	1347	112*	24.94	1	..	101	24.04
Walsh, J. E. (Leics.)	.. (1)	1952	1106	102	24.04	1	..	122	25.87
Watkins, A. J. (Glamorgan)	.. (2)	1954	1640	170*	34.89	2	..	103	15.82
		1955	1160	111	24.16	2	..	114	20.49
Wellard, A. W. (Somerset) ..	.. (3)	1933	1085	77	27.12	—	..	104	25.57
		1935	1347	112	31.32	1	..	114	20.68
		1937	1049	91*	18.73	—	..	156	23.55
Wensley, A. F. (Sussex) ..	.. (1)	1929	1057	91	21.14	—	..	113	25.22
White, J. C. (Somerset) ..	.. (2)	1929	1179	192	27.41	1	..	168	15.76
		1930	1050	97	26.25	—	..	123	19.51
Wooller, W. (Glamorgan) ..	.. (1)	1954	1059	71	24.06	—	..	107	18.42
Woolley, F. E. (Kent) ..	.. (8)	1910	1101	120	24.46	3	..	136	14.50
		1912	1827	117	41.52	2	..	126	14.30
		1914	2272	160*	45.44	6	..	125	19.45
		1919	1082	164	41.61	3	..	128	17.15
		1920	1924	158	40.93	5	..	185	14.23
		1921	2101	174	42.87	6	..	167	16.14
		1922	2022	188	45.95	5	..	163	18.37
		1923	2091	270	41.00	5	..	101	19.18
Wyatt, R. E. S (Warwicks.)	.. (1)	1926	1485	102	32.28	2	..	102	28.40

. . . . AND SOME NEAR MISSES:

	Season	Runs	Wkts.
Hearne, J. W. (Middx.)	1922	1835	99
Robins, R. W. V. (Middx.)	1937	1076	99
Howorth, R. (Worcs.)	1938	997	108
Brown, F. R. (Northants.)	1952	1118	99
Knight, B. R. (Essex)	1959	995	101

FASTEST 'DOUBLES'

G. H. Hirst completed the 'double' in only 16 matches, on June 28th, 1906. 13 'doubles' have been completed before August:-

June 28	1906	G. H. Hirst (Yorkshire)
July 12	1901	G. H. Hirst (Yorkshire)
July 15	1907	F. A. Tarrant (Middlesex)
July 17	1928	V. W. C. Jupp (Northamptonshire)
July 24	1908	F. A. Tarrant (Middlesex)
July 25	1933	James Langridge (Sussex)
July 25	1963	B. R. Knight (Essex)
July 26	1920	F. E. Woolley (Kent)
July 27	1905	W. Rhodes (Yorkshire)
July 28	1922	F. E. Woolley (Kent)
July 30	1928	M. W. Tate (Sussex)
July 31	1914	J. W. H. T. Douglas (Essex)
July 31	1926	J. A. Newman (Hampshire)

ALL-ROUND CRICKET IN A MATCH

The match 'double' of 100 runs and 10 wickets is an outstanding performance rarely accomplished. Few players manage to achieve such a high level of success with both bat and ball in the same match although many reach an aggregate of 1000 runs and 100 wickets for the season.

The name of the player who is currently being hailed as the greatest all-rounder that the game has ever seen will not be found in the following lists. G. St. A. Sobers has yet to take ten wickets in a match—although he took nine in the second innings against Kent at Canterbury in 1966.

CENTURY and TEN WICKETS IN AN INNINGS

V. E. Walker	(108 & 10-74)	England v. Surrey (Oval)	1859
E. M. Grace	(192*& 10-69)	M.C.C. v. Gentlemen of Kent (Canterbury) ..	1862
	(12-a-side but one man was absent from the Kent team.)		
W. G. Grace	(104 & 10-49)	M.C.C. v. Oxford U. (Oxford)	1886

CENTURY IN EACH INNINGS AND FIVE WICKETS TWICE

G. H. Hirst (111 & 117*, 6-70 & 5-45): Yorks. v. Somerset (Bath) 1906

CENTURY IN EACH INNINGS AND TEN WICKETS

B. J. T. Bosanquet (103 & 100*, 3-75 & 8-53) Middx. v. Sussex (Lord's) 1905

160 RUNS AND 16 WICKETS

G. Giffen (271, 9-96 & 7-70): South Australia v. Victoria (Adelaide) 1891-92

100 RUNS AND 10 WICKETS IN A MATCH

(Including the exceptional examples listed above.)

Allen, G. O. (1)			
38 & 104*,	7-120 & 3-36	M.C.C. v. New Zealanders (Lord's)	1927
Amarnath, L. (1)			
83 & 63,	7-60 & 3-56	Southern Punjab v. United Provinces (New Delhi)	1935-36
Amar Singh (1)			
103 & 55,	6-48 & 4-35	Nawanagar v. Sind (Ahmedabad)	1936-37
Armstrong, W. W. (2)			
126*	5-27 & 5-25	Australians v. New Zealand XI (Christchurch)	1904-05
55 & 50*,	3-20 & 8-50	Australians v. Middx. (Lord's)	1905
Arnold, E. G. (1)			
200*	3-70 & 7-44	Worcs. v. Warwicks. (Birmingham)	1909
Ashton, C. T. (1)			
10 & 98,	7-91 & 3-60	Cambridge U. v. Army (Cambridge)	1923
Bailey, J. (1)			
62 & 88,	6-51 & 5-19	Hants. v. Leics. (Southampton)	1948

All-round Cricket in a Match—*Cont.*

Player / Runs	Wickets	Match	Season
Bailey, T. E. (2)			
59 & 71*,	6-32 & 8-49	Essex v. Hants. (Romford)	1957
60* & 46,	7-40 & 5-61	Essex v. Yorks. (Leeds)	1960
Balaskas, X. C. (2)			
132	5-87 & 6-43	Griqualand West v. Eastern Prov. (Kimberley)	1929-30
101	6-142 & 6-93	Griqualand West v. Western Prov. (Kimberley)	1929-30
Barlow, R. G. (2)			
71 & 39*,	5-27 & 5-92	Lancs. v. Surrey (Manchester)	1883
10* & 101,	4-6 & 6-42	North v. Australians (Nottingham)	1884
Barnett, C. J. (1)			
168	5-63 & 6-40	Glos. v. Lancs. (Manchester)	1938
Bates, W. (1)			
106 & 14,	5-30 & 5-45	Yorks. v. Derby (Leeds)	1886
Bedser, E. A. (1)			
71 & 30,	7-142 & 3-89	Surrey v. Glos. (Oval)	1951
Bettington, R. H. B. (1)			
28 & 95,	4-87 & 6-78	Middx. v. Sussex (Lord's)	1928
Bhatti, Javed (1)			
109	5-29 & 5-59	Bahawalpur v. Multan (Bahawalpur)	1962-63
Bosanquet, B. J. T. (4)			
86 & 82*,	7-61 & 3-119	Leveson-Gower's XI v. Oxford U. (Oxford)	1902
71 & 41*,	6-109 & 4-61	Middx. v. Kent (Tunbridge Wells)	1903
141	5-112 & 5-136	Middx. v. Yorks. (Sheffield)	1904
103 & 100*,	3-75 & 8-53	Middx. v. Sussex (Lord's)	1905
Briggs, J. (3)			
129*	5-25 & 5-16	Lancs. v. Sussex (Manchester)	1890
115	8-113 & 5-96	Lancs. v. Yorks. (Manchester)	1892
112	5-51 & 6-64	Lancs. v. Surrey (Oval)	1893
Brown, L. S. (1)			
63 & 37,	6-89 & 4-54	N-E. Transvaal v. Transvaal (Springs)	1937-38
Browne, C. R. (2)			
102	5-77 & 8-58	British Guiana v. Barbados (Port of Spain)	1925-26
83 & 24*,	5-56 & 6-134	British Guiana v. Trinidad (Georgetown)	1929-30
Buckland, F. M. (1)			
104	4-14 & 6-53	Oxford U. v. Middx. (Lord's)	1877
Bullock, P. W. (1)			
31 & 148,	7-70 & 3-29	Assam v. Orissa (Nowgong)	1951-52
Christian, A. H. (1)			
73 & 57,	7-144 & 4-56	Western Australia v. South Australia (Fremantle)	1908-09
Clark, P. H. (1)			
67 & 52,	4-148 & 8-91	Philadelphians v. Worcs. (Worcester)	1903
Compton, D. C. S. (1)			
137*	6-94 & 6-80	Middx. v. Surrey (Oval)	1947
Constantine, L. N. (1)			
107	7-45 & 6-67	West Indians v. Northants. (Northampton)	1928
Crawford, J. N. (3)			
148	7-85 & 4-63	Surrey v. Glos. (Bristol)	1906
91 & 40,	5-89 & 5-71	South Australia v. N.S.W. (Sydney)	1913-14
110	5-90 & 5-53	Wellington v. Auckland (Auckland)	1917-18
Davidson, A. K. (1)			
44 & 80,	5-135 & 6-87	Australia v. West Indies (Brisbane) (*The only instance of the match double in Test Matches*)	1960-61

All-round Cricket in a Match—*Cont.*

Batting	Bowling	Match	Season
Dexter, E. R. (2)			
113	6-63 & 4-46	Sussex v. Kent (Tunbridge Wells)	1962
27 & 94,	7-38 & 3-58	Sussex v. Surrey (Oval)	1962
Dooland, B. (1)			
115* & 11,	4-54 & 6-48	Notts. v. Sussex (Worthing)	1957
Douglas, J. W. H. T. (2)			
8 & 123*,	7-91 & 7-65	Essex v. Worcs. (Leyton)	1921
210*	9-47 & 2-0	Essex v. Derby (Leyton)	1921
Dowson, E. M. (1)			
71* & 50,	3-47 & 8-68	Cambridge U. v. Surrey (Oval)	1903
Faulkner, G. A. (2)			
42 & 68*,	6-72 & 4-94	Transvaal v. Western Province (Cape Town)	1908-09
54 & 73,	5-32 & 5-106	South Africans v. Queensland (Brisbane) ..	1910-11
Fender, P. G. H. (1)			
104	3-48 & 7-76	Surrey v. Essex (Leyton)	1926
Flowers, W. (3)			
131	4-43 & 6-44	M.C.C. v. Derby (Lord's)	1883
122	6-20 & 8-60	†M.C.C. v. Cambridge U. (Lord's)	1884
107	6-44 & 5-84	Notts. v. Lancs. (Manchester)	1893
Foster, F. R. (1)			
105 & 18,	9-118 & 3-84	Warwicks. v. Yorks. (Birmingham)	1911
Fry, C. B. (1)			
89 & 65,	5-81 & 5-66	Sussex v. Notts. (Nottingham)	1896
Geeson, F. (1)			
104*	6-128 & 6-111	Leics. v. Derby (Glossop)	1901
Giffen, G. (9)			
20 & 82,	9-91 & 8-110	South Australia v. Victoria (Adelaide) ..	1885-86
166	8-65 & 6-60	South Australia v. Victoria (Adelaide) ..	1887-88
135 & 19,	6-82 & 7-77	South Australia v. Victoria (Melbourne) ..	1888-89
237	5-89 & 7-103	South Australia v. Victoria (Melbourne) ..	1890-91
271	9-96 & 7-70	South Australia v. Victoria (Adelaide) ..	1891-92
120	7-122 & 5-28	South Australia v. N.S.W. (Sydney)	1891-92
43 & 181,	9-147 & 2-88	South Australia v. Victoria (Adelaide) ..	1892-93
64 & 58*,	5-175 & 6-49	South Australia v. Stoddart's XI (Adelaide) ..	1894-95
81 & 97*,	7-75 & 8-110	South Australia v. Victoria (Adelaide) ..	1902-03
Grace, E. M. (1)			
192*	5-77 & 10-69	M.C.C. v. Gentlemen of Kent (Canterbury) ..	1862
Grace, W. G. (16)			
134*	6-50 & 4-31	Gentlemen v. Players (Lord's)	1868
81 & 42*,	6-68 & 4-83	W. G. Grace's XI v. Kent (Maidstone) ..	1871
117	7-67 & 5-79	†M.C.C. v. Kent (Canterbury)	1871
114	7-78 & 4-48	South v. North (Oval)	1872
150	8-33 & 7-46	Glos. v. Yorks. (Sheffield)	1872
179	5-76 & 7-82	Glos. v. Sussex (Hove)	1874
23 & 110,	3-61 & 7-58	Gentlemen v. Players (Prince's)	1874
167	4-57 & 7-44	Glos. v. Yorks. (Sheffield)	1874
94 & 121,	6-92 & 4-68	Glos. & Kent v. England (Canterbury) (a) ..	1874
123	5-82 & 6-47	†M.C.C. v. Kent (Canterbury) (a)	1874
127	5-44 & 5-77	Glos. v. Yorks. (Clifton) (a)	1874
7 & 152,	7-64 & 5-61	Gentlemen v. Players (Lord's)	1875
261	5-62 & 6-77	South v. North (Prince's)	1877
89 & 35,	5-64 & 7-92	Glos. v. Middx. (Lord's)	1883
221*	6-45 & 5-75	Glos. v. Middx. (Clifton)	1885
104	2-60 & 10-49	M.C.C. v. Oxford U. (Oxford)	1886
		(a) *Consecutive matches*	
Gregory, R. J. (1)			
171	5-36 & 5-66	Surrey v. Middx. (Lord's)	1930

All-round Cricket in a Match—*Cont.*

Player / Runs	Wickets	Match	Season
Gunn, J. (2)			
95 & 39*,	7-77 & 4-66	Notts. v. Glos. (Gloucester)	1904
148 & 6*,	8-80 & 2-31	Notts. v. Lancs. (Nottingham)	1921
Hartkopf, A. E. V. (1)			
86 & 14*,	5-23 & 8-105	Victoria v. M.C.C. (Melbourne)	1922-23
Hearne, J. W. (6)			
54 & 88,	7-83 & 4-104	Middx. v. Worcs. (Worcester)	1913
106*	7-54 & 7-92	Middx. v. Essex (Leyton)	1914
88 & 37*,	5-78 & 5-91	Middx. v. Essex (Lord's)	1914
79 & 28,	6-74 & 4-73	Middx. v. Notts. (Lord's)	1922
140 & 57*,	6-83 & 6-45	Middx. v. Sussex (Lord's)	1923
14 & 93,	5-38 & 6-36	Middx. v. Glos. (Lord's)	1924
Hill, C. J. (1)			
17 & 91,	7-18 & 5-49	N.S.W. v. Queensland (Sydney)	1932-33
Hirst, G. H. (4)			
86 & 18*,	7-55 & 4-28	Yorks. v. M.C.C. (Lord's)	1901
101 & 4,	4-46 & 7-33	Yorks. v. Kent (Catford)	1906
111 & 117*,	6-70 & 5-45	Yorks. v. Somerset (Bath)	1906
100	9-41 & 2-89	Yorks. v. Worcs. (Worcester)	1911
Hopwood, J. L. (1)			
110 & 45,	1-20 & 9-33	Lancs. v. Leics. (Manchester)	1933
Ikin, J. T. (1)			
67 & 85*,	5-98 & 6-21	Lancs. v. Notts. (Manchester)	1947
Illingworth, R. (1)			
135	7-49 & 7-52	Yorks. v. Kent (Dover)	1964
Jackson, J. (1)			
100	6-23 & 6-20	Notts. v. Kent (Cranbrook)	1863
Jackson, V. E. (1)			
108 & 13,	6-46 & 4-53	Leics. v. Kent (Gillingham)	1954
Jupp, V. W. C. (3)			
102 & 33*,	6-61 & 6-78	Sussex v. Essex (Colchester)	1921
56 & 70,	5-34 & 7-71	Northants. v. Essex (Colchester)	1925
113	7-42 & 5-79	Northants. v. Essex (Leyton)	1928
Langridge, James (1)			
13 & 103,	7-58 & 4-66	Sussex v. Glamorgan (Swansea)	1929
Le Couteur, P. R. (1)			
160	6-20 & 5-46	Oxford U. v. Cambridge U. (Lord's)	1910
Lee, G. M. (1)			
100*	5-65 & 7-78	Derby v. Northants. (Northampton)	1927
Lee, H. W. (1)			
119	5-21 & 6-47	Middx. v. Sussex (Lord's)	1920
Lewis, A. E. (1)			
93 & 20,	6-43 & 4-15	Somerset v. Hants. (Bath)	1911
Llewellyn, C. B. (1)			
153	5-115 & 5-68	Hants. v. Somerset (Taunton)	1901
Lockwood, W. H. (1)			
63 & 37,	6-48 & 6-48	Surrey v. Lancs. (Oval)	1902
McGahey, C. P. (2)			
66 & 91,	6-86 & 6-71	Essex v. Glos. (Clifton)	1901
89 & 14,	7-27 & 3-37	Essex v. Notts. (Leyton)	1906
Mansell, P. N. F. (1)			
94* & 13*,	7-71 & 3-79	Rhodesia v. N-E. Transvaal (Pretoria)	1951-52

All-round Cricket in a Match—*Cont.*

Player / Runs	Bowling	Match	Season
Mason, J. R. (5)			
72 & 46*,	4-23 & 6-34	Kent v. Middx. (Tonbridge)	1900
145	4-26 & 8-29	Kent v. Somerset (Taunton)	1901
126	7-120 & 3-60	Kent v. Somerset (Beckenham)	1904
1 & 100,	6-71 & 4-60	Kent v. Somerset (Taunton)	1904
133	5-102 & 5-120	Kent v. Somerset (Taunton)	1905
Muncer, B. L. (1)			
107*	5-34 & 5-23	Glamorgan v. Derby (Chesterfield)	1951
Murray, A. R. A. (1)			
78 & 44*,	5-77 & 5-54	Eastern Province v. Border (East London) ..	1953-54
Nayudu, C. S. (1)			
127	5-20 & 7-36	Baroda v. Rajputana (Baroda)	1942-43
Neill, R. (1)			
94 & 13,	4-54 & 6-43	Auckland v. Wellington (Wellington) ..	1896-97
Newman, J. A. (1)			
66 & 42*,	8-61 & 6-87	Hants. v. Glos. (Bournemouth)	1926
Nichols, M. S. (3)			
73 & 33,	5-67 & 5-37	Essex v. Sussex (Horsham)	1933
146	4-17 & 7-37	Essex v. Yorks. (Huddersfield)	1935
159	9-37 & 6-126	Essex v. Glos. (Gloucester)	1938
Pougher, A. D. (1)			
5 & 109*,	6-29 & 8-60	Leics. v. Essex (Leyton)	1894
Quaife, W. G. (1)			
104*	5-51 & 7-76	Warwicks. v. Worcs. (Birmingham)	1901
Ram Singh, A. G. (2)			
74 & 70,	5-88 & 6-71	Madras v. Hyderabad (Hyderabad)	1934-35
55 & 91,	5-35 & 5-45	Madras v. Mysore (Madras)	1939-40
Ramchandra (1)			
97* & 5,	7-52 & 3-53	Bengal v. Mysore (Calcutta)	1941-42
Relf, A. E. (2)			
42 & 83,	6-22 & 6-25	Auckland v. Otago (Auckland)	1907-08
103*	8-41 & 7-36	Sussex v. Leics. (Hove)	1912
Rhodes, W. (1)			
183	5-26 & 7-33	Europeans v. Parsis (Bombay)	1921-22
Robinson, E. (1)			
108	7-25 & 4-60	Yorks. v. Hants. (Bradford)	1930
Shukla, A. (1)			
168*	7-43 & 3-87	Uttar Pradesh v. Rajasthan (Udaipur) ..	1961-62
Smith, S. G. (2)			
5 & 136,	2-3 & 8-39	Northants. v. Somerset (Bath)	1912
82 & 20,	6-82 & 4-25	Northants. v. Derby (Northampton)	1913
Smith, T. P. B. (1)			
1 & 101,	2-69 & 8-99	Essex v. Middx. (Chelmsford)	1938
Stoddart, A. E. (1)			
143	7-67 & 3-10	Priestleys' XI v. Jamaica (Kingston)	1896-97
Studd, C. T. (1)			
105*	6-79 & 4-45	Middx. v. Kent (Canterbury)	1883
Tarrant, F. A. (3)			
152 & 11,	7-93 & 5-56	Middx. v. Glos. (Bristol)	1908
14 & 101*,	9-105 & 7-71	Middx. v. Lancs. (Manchester)	1914
68* & 80,	6-82 & 5-67	Europeans v. Hindus (Bombay)	1916-17

All-round Cricket in a Match—*Cont.*

Tate, M. W. (2)

90 & 35,	5-48 & 6-42	Sussex v. Oxford U. (Hove)	1920
101	6-52 & 4-43	Sussex v. Hants. (Portsmouth) *(101 before lunch 1st day)*	1927

Thompson, G. J. (1)

5 & 131*,	6-72 & 4-71	Northants. v. Somerset (Bath)	1913

Townsend, L. F. (2)

106*	6-66 & 5-64	Derby v. Somerset (Weston-super-Mare) ..	1934
44 & 90*,	5-89 & 7-25	Auckland v. Wellington (Auckland)	1934-35

Trott, A. E. (5)

101*	7-74 & 4-66	Lord Hawke's XI v. Transvaal (Johannesburg)	1898-99
64 & 69,	6-57 & 5-56	M.C.C. v. Sussex (Lord's)	1899
123 & 35*,	6-132 & 6-68	Middx. v. Sussex (Lord's)	1899
112	8-54 & 3-84	Middx. v. Essex (Lord's)	1901
68 & 80*,	7-58 & 4-93	Hawke's Bay v. Canterbury (Christchurch) ..	1901-02

Vine, J. (1)

86 & 54,	2-45 & 8-68	Sussex v. Oxford U. (Eastbourne)	1906

Wainwright, E. (1)

10 & 104,	7-66 & 4-57	Yorks. v. Sussex (Sheffield)	1892

Walker, V. E. (1)

20* & 108,	10-74 & 4-17	England v. Surrey (Oval)	1859

Wellard, A. W. (2)

75 & 55,	6-82 & 5-93	Somerset v. Glos. (Taunton)	1929
77 & 60,	7-43 & 3-66	Somerset v. Hants. (Portsmouth)	1933

Woolley, F. E. (6)

77 & 111*,	7-66 & 5-56	Kent v. Glos. (Gloucester)	1914
20 & 139*,	6-52 & 4-80	Kent v. Somerset (Horsham)	1920
174	8-22 & 3-44	Kent v. Glos. (Maidstone)	1921
15 & 109,	7-40 & 3-76	Kent v. Notts. (Nottingham)	1921
156	4-26 & 6-52	Kent v. Warwicks. (Tunbridge Wells) ..	1928
132	6-50 & 4-38	M.C.C. v. Otago (Dunedin)	1929-30

Young, A. (1)

63 & 70,	3-47 & 8-30	Somerset v. Derby (Taunton)	1930

†*These matches were played twelve-a-side, but are regarded as first-class matches.*

CENTURY AND 'HAT-TRICK' IN THE SAME MATCH

W. G. Grace (123): M.C.C. v. Kent (Canterbury) (12-a-side) 1874

G. Griffen (113): Australians v. Lancashire (Manchester) 1884

W. E. Roller (204): Surrey v. Sussex (Oval) 1885

W. B. Burns (102*): Worcestershire v. Gloucestershire (Worcester) 1913

V. W. C. Jupp (102): Sussex v. Essex (Colchester) 1921

R. E. S. Wyatt (124): M.C.C. v. Ceylon (Colombo) 1926-27

L. N. Constantine (107): West Indians v. Northamptonshire (Northampton) .. 1928

E. Davies (139): Glamorgan v. Leicestershire (Leicester) 1937

V. M. Merchant (142): Pereira's XI v. Sir Homi Mehta's XI (Bombay) 1946-47

PLAYERS' RECORDS—FIELDING

Statistics cannot provide a true assessment of the ability of either a fielder or a wicket-keeper; aggregates of catches and stumpings reveal but a part of their value to a team. Fielders in close-to-the-wicket positions are bound to receive more catching chances than out-fielders who rarely qualify for inclusion in these records. Nevertheless, few would dispute that the importance of a Bland in terms of runs saved and batsmen run out is as great as that of an ace slip-catcher or short-leg. Nor could Godfrey Evans's effect on the morale of his bowlers be measured merely by the dismissals he made.

MOST CATCHES IN AN INNINGS

SEVEN

Stewart, M. J.: Surrey v. Northamptonshire (Northampton) 1957
Brown, A. S.: Gloucestershire v. Nottinghamshire (Nottingham) 1966

SIX

Broadbent, R. G.: Worcestershire v. Glamorgan (Stourbridge) 1960
Clay, J. D.: Nottinghamshire v. Derbyshire (Nottingham) 1957
Deas, L. M.: Europeans v. Parsis (Poona) 1898-99
Grieves, K. J.: Lancashire v. Sussex (Manchester) 1951
Griffith, G.: Surrey v. Gentlemen of South (Oval) 1863
Hammond, W. R.: Gloucestershire v. Surrey (Cheltenham) 1928
Hammond, W. R.: Gloucestershire v. Nottinghamshire (Bristol) 1933
Leary, S. E.: Kent v. Cambridge U. (Cambridge) 1958
Robinson, E. P.: Yorkshire v. Leicestershire (Bradford) 1938
Seymour, James: Kent v. South Africans (Canterbury) 1904
Sheppard, J. F.: Queensland v. New South Wales (Brisbane) 1914-15
Smith, M. J. K.: Warwickshire v. Leicestershire (Hinckley) 1962
Tarrant, F. A.: Middlesex v. Essex (Leyton) 1906
Tyldesley, R.: Lancashire v. Hampshire (Liverpool) 1921
Webbe, A. J.: Gentlemen v. Players (Lord's) 1877

FIVE

Abel, R.: Surrey v. Hampshire (Portsmouth) 1898
Ashton, H.: Cambridge U. v. Surrey (Oval) 1922
Astill, W. E.: Leicestershire v. Somerset (Weston-super-Mare) 1920
Atkinson, J.: Tasmania v. Victoria (Melbourne) 1928-29
Bakewell, A. H.: Northamptonshire v. Essex (Leyton) 1928
Barton, M. R.: Oxford U. v. Minor Counties (Oxford) 1937
Bates, W. E.: Glamorgan v. Warwickshire (Birmingham) 1928
Boyle, H. F.: Australians v. Yorkshire (Dewsbury) 1880
Braund, L. C.: Somerset v. Worcestershire (Taunton) 1909
Brown, G.: Hampshire v. Somerset (Bath) 1914
Brown, G.: Hampshire v. Kent (Portsmouth) 1932
Burbidge, F.: Gentlemen v. Players (Oval) 1858
Carr, A. W.: Nottinghamshire v. Leicestershire (Nottingham) 1933
Crapp, J. F.: Gloucestershire v. Lancashire (Manchester) 1949
Daniell, J.: Somerset v. Kent (Taunton) 1901
Ealham, A.: Kent v. Gloucestershire (Folkestone) 1966
(*All off D. L. Underwood's bowling in the same position topographically—long-off to the right-handed batsman*)
East, R. E.: Essex v. Gloucestershire (Ilford) (*All caught and bowled*) 1966
Eyre, C. H.: Cambridge U. v. Weigall's XI (Cambridge) 1904
Fagg, A. E.: Kent v. Hampshire (Southampton) 1952
Fishwick, T. S.: Warwickshire v. South Africans (Birmingham) 1904
Ford, F. G. J.: Cambridge U. v. M.C.C. (Lord's) 1888

Most Catches in an Innings—Five—*Cont.*

Foster, R. F.: Oxford U. v. Webbe's XI (Oxford) 1898
Gillingham, F. H.: Essex v. Surrey (Oval) 1919
Grace, E. M.: Gentlemen of M.C.C. v. Gentlemen of Kent (Canterbury) 1866
Grieves, K. J.: Lancashire v. Glamorgan (Blackpool) 1950
Grieves, K. J.: Lancashire v. Gloucestershire (Bristol) 1954
Gunn, G.: Nottinghamshire v. Surrey (Nottingham) 1909
Haig, N. E.: Middlesex v. Nottinghamshire (Lord's) 1928
Hallam, M. R.: Leicestershire v. Northamptonshire (Leicester) 1964
Hammond, W. R.: M.C.C. West Indies XI v. Leveson-Gower's XI (Scarborough) 1935
Hayes, E. G.: Surrey v. London County (Oval) 1901
Headley, R. G. A.: Worcestershire v. Kent (Dartford) 1964
Headley, R. G. A.: Worcestershire v. Gloucestershire (Cheltenham) 1967
Hughes, G.: Glamorgan v. Essex (Swansea) 1964
Hunt, G.: Somerset v. Hampshire (Weston-super-Mare) 1928
Hutton, L.: Players v. Gentlemen (Lord's) 1952
Ikin, J. T.: M.C.C. v. Auckland (Auckland) 1946-47
Insole, D. J.: Essex v. Lancashire (Blackpool) 1958
Jones, A. O.: Nottinghamshire v. Sussex (Hove) 1907
Lamason, J. R.: Wellington v. Otago (Dunedin) 1937-38
Langridge, John: Sussex v. Somerset (Taunton) 1950
Lee, C.: Derbyshire v. Lancashire (Chesterfield) 1960
Lee, G. M.: Nottinghamshire v. Hampshire (Southampton) 1913
Lock, G. A. R.: Surrey v. Lancashire (Manchester) 1953
Lyon, B. H.: Gloucestershire v. Leicestershire (Cheltenham) 1933
McAlister, P. A.: Victoria v. South Australia (Melbourne) 1901-02
McCool, C. L.: New South Wales v. Rest of Australia (Sydney) 1939-40
Mead, C. P.: Hampshire v. Middlesex (Portsmouth) 1912
Milton, C. A.: Gloucestershire v. Pakistan (Cheltenham) 1954
Morgan, D. C.: Derbyshire v. Glamorgan (Chesterfield) 1960
Nicholls, B. E.: Oxford U. v. Australians (Oxford) 1884
Nichols, M. S.: Essex v. Sussex (Hove) 1926
Nicholson, J. H.: Northamptonshire v. Worcestershire (Dudley) 1928
Nourse, A. D., Jnr.: Natal v. Border (Durban) 1933-34
Oakman, A. S. M.: Sussex v. Glamorgan (Worthing) 1958
Oakman, A. S. M.: Sussex v. Lancashire (Hastings) 1961
Outschoorn, L.: Worcestershire v. Derbyshire (Kidderminster) 1948
Painter, J.: Gloucestershire v. Sussex (Hove) 1891
Paul, A.: Lancashire v. Derbyshire (Derby) 1897
Pierce, T. N.: Barbados v. Trinidad (Bridgetown) 1941-42
Pollock, J. S.: Ireland v. M.C.C. (Dublin) 1956
Pratt, R. L.: Leicestershire v. Derbyshire (Leicester) 1961
Prodger, J. W.: Kent v. Gloucestershire (Cheltenham) 1961
Prodger, J. W.: Kent v. Lancashire (Blackpool) 1964
Quinton, F. W. D.: Hampshire v. Yorkshire (Harrogate) 1896
Rabone, G. O.: New Zealanders v. Oxford U. (Oxford) 1949
Reid, J. R.: New Zealanders v. South Zone (Bangalore) 1955-56
Richardson, V. Y.: Australia v. South Africa (Durban) (*Record for Test Matches*) .. 1935-36
Ryder, J.: Victoria v. M.C.C. (Melbourne) 1922-23
Sellers, A. B.: Yorkshire v. Essex (Leyton) 1933
Smith, M. J. K.: Warwickshire v. Glamorgan (Swansea) 1961
Smith, M. J. K.: M.C.C. v. New South Wales (Sydney) 1965-66
Surridge, W. S.: Surrey v. Lancashire (Oval) 1955
Trumble, H.: Australians v. Cambridge U. (Cambridge) 1890
Trumble, H.: Australians v. Oxford U. (Oxford) 1893
Trumble, H.: Victoria v. South Australia (Melbourne) 1900-01
Tunnicliffe, J.: Yorkshire v. Leicestershire (Leeds) 1897
Tunnicliffe, J.: Yorkshire v. Leicestershire (Leicester) 1900
Tunnicliffe, J.: Yorkshire v. Leicestershire (Scarborough) 1901
Upton, Hon. A.: Gentlemen v. Players (Lord's) 1806
Vigar, F. H.: Essex v. Middlesex (Westcliff) 1946
Vigar, F. H.: Essex v. Northamptonshire (Brentwood) 1946
Vigar, F. H.: Essex v. Surrey (Oval) 1951
Walker, P. M.: Glamorgan v. Leicestershire (Swansea) 1960
Walker, P. M.: Glamorgan v. Derbyshire (Chesterfield) 1961
Walker, P. M.: Glamorgan v. Nottinghamshire (Newport) 1961
Walker, V. E.: Middlesex v. Surrey (Oval) 1865
Watkins, A. J.: M.C.C. v. South Zone (Bangalore) 1951-52
Wensley, A. F.: Sussex v. Warwickshire (Birmingham) 1932

Most Catches in an Innings—Five—*Cont.*

Wensley, A. F.: Sussex v. Surrey (Horsham) 1934
White, C.: Border v. Griqualand West (Queenstown) 1946-47
Williams, N.: Auckland v. Hawke's Bay (Napier) 1894-95
Wood, C. J. B.: Leicestershire v. Warwickshire (Hinckley) 1919
Woolley, F. E.: Kent v. Middlesex (Blackheath) 1926
Woolley, F. E.: Kent v. Hampshire (Canterbury) 1936
Wright, F. W.: Oxford U. v. Surrey (Oval) 1865

MOST CATCHES IN A MATCH

TEN

Hammond, W. R.: Gloucestershire v. Surrey (Cheltenham) (*8 off C.W.L. Parker*) .. 1928

EIGHT

Bakewell, A. H.: Northamptonshire v. Essex (Leyton) 1928
Burns, W. B.: Worcestershire v. Yorkshire (Bradford) 1907
Grieves, K. J.: Lancashire v. Sussex (Manchester) 1951
Hammond, W. R.: Gloucestershire v. Worcestershire (Cheltenham) 1932
Lock, G. A. R.: Surrey v. Warwickshire (Oval) 1957
Milton, C. A.: Gloucestershire v. Sussex (Hove) 1952
Prodger, J. W.: Kent v. Gloucestershire (Cheltenham) 1961

SEVEN

Ashton, H.: Cambridge U. v. Surrey (Oval) 1922
Atkinson, J.: Tasmania v. Victoria (Melbourne) 1928-29
Broadbent, R. G.: Worcestershire v. Glamorgan (Stourbridge) 1960
Brown, A. S.: Gloucestershire v. Nottinghamshire (Nottingham) (*All on third day*) .. 1966
Cooper, G. C.: Sussex v. Nottinghamshire (Hove) (*5 ct. & bowled*) 1961
Crapp, J. F.: Gloucestershire v. Derbyshire (Bristol) 1950
Dean, T. A.: Hampshire v. Essex (Colchester) 1947
Deas, L. M.: Europeans v. Parsis (Poona) 1898-99
De Vigne, S. P.: North-Eastern Transvaal v. Orange Free State (Benoni) 1950-51
Dollery, H. E.: Warwickshire v. Hampshire (Portsmouth) 1953
Fagg, A. E.: Kent v. Hampshire (Southampton) 1952
Felix, N.: Kent v. England (Canterbury) 1847
Ford, A. F. J.: Middlesex v. Gloucestershire (Lord's) 1882
Hughes, G.: Glamorgan v. Essex (Swansea) 1964
Jones, A. O.: Nottinghamshire v. Gloucestershire (Nottingham) 1908
Langridge, John: Sussex v. Somerset (Taunton) 1950
Leary, S. E.: Kent v. Cambridge U. (Cambridge) 1958
Lock, G. A. R.: Surrey v. Lancashire (Manchester) 1953
Mason, J. R.: Kent v. Surrey (Oval) 1905
Milton, C. A.: Gloucestershire v. Lancashire (Cheltenham) 1962
Nicholls, B. E.: Oxford U. v. Australians (Oxford) 1884
Oakman, A. S. M.: Sussex v. Glamorgan (Worthing) 1958
Parker, J. F.: Surrey v. Kent (Blackheath) 1952
Pierce, T. N.: Barbados v. Trinidad (Bridgetown) 1941-42
Poidevin, L. O. S.: Lancashire v. Yorkshire (Manchester) 1906
Pratt, R. L.: Leicestershire v. Derbyshire (Leicester) 1961
Robinson, E. P.: Yorkshire v. Leicestershire (Bradford) 1938
Sellers, A. B.: Yorkshire v. Essex (Leyton) 1933
Stanning, J.: Cambridge U. v. M.C.C. (Cambridge) 1900
Stewart, M. J.: Surrey v. Northamptonshire (Northampton) 1957
Surridge, W. S.: South v. North (Kingston) (*All on second day*) 1952
Tarrant, F. A.: Middlesex v. Essex (Leyton) 1906
Trumble, H.: Victoria v. South Australia (Melbourne) 1900-01
Tunnicliffe, J.: Yorkshire v. Leicestershire (Leeds) 1897
Tunnicliffe, J.: Yorkshire v. Leicestershire (Leicester) 1900
Voce, W.: Nottinghamshire v. Glamorgan (Pontypridd) 1929
Walker, P. M.: Glamorgan v. Northamptonshire (Northampton) 1960
Walker, P. M.: Glamorgan v. Nottinghamshire (Newport) 1961
Wensley, A. F.: Sussex v. Surrey (Horsham) 1934
Woolley, F. E.: Kent v. Warwickshire (Birmingham) 1920

MOST CATCHES IN A SEASON

78	W. R. Hammond	Gloucestershire	1928
77	M. J. Stewart	Surrey	1957
73	P. M. Walker	Glamorgan	1961
71	P. J. Sharpe	Yorkshire	1962
70	J. Tunnicliffe	Yorkshire	1901
70	P. M. Walker	Glamorgan	1960
69	John Langridge	Sussex	1955
65	J. Tunnicliffe	Yorkshire	1895
65	W. R. Hammond	Gloucestershire	1925
65	P. W. Walker	Glamorgan	1959
64	J. Tunnicliffe	Yorkshire	1904
64	K. F. Barrington	Surrey	1957
64	G. A. R. Lock	Surrey	1957
63	K. J. Grieves	Lancashire	1950
63	C. A. Milton	Gloucestershire	1956
63	D. W. Richardson	Worcestershire	1961
61	J. V. Wilson	Yorkshire	1955
61	M. J. Stewart	Surrey	1958
59	John Langridge	Sussex	1933
58	John Langridge	Sussex	1950
58	W. S. Surridge	Surrey	1952
58	M. R. Hallam	Leicestershire	1961
57	A. S. M. Oakman	Sussex	1958
56	W. S. Surridge	Surrey	1955
56	P. J. Sainsbury	Hampshire	1957
56	C. A. Milton	Gloucestershire	1959
55	J. T. Ikin	Lancashire	1946
55	J. V. Wilson	Yorkshire	1951
55	C. A. Milton	Gloucestershire	1952
55	K. F. Barrington	Surrey	1958
55	M. J. K. Smith	Warwickshire	1961

PLAYERS' RECORDS—WICKET-KEEPING

MOST DISMISSALS IN AN INNINGS

EIGHT

	ct. st.		
Grout, A. T. W.	(8-0)	Queensland v. Western Australia (Brisbane)	1959-60

SEVEN

Andrew, K. V.	(7-0)	Northamptonshire v. Lancashire (Manchester)	1962
Brown, J.	(4-3)	Scotland v. Ireland (Dublin)	1957
Farrimond, W. F.	(6-1)	Lancashire v. Kent (Manchester)	1930
Kirsten, N.	(6-1)	Border v. Rhodesia (East London)	1959-60
Long, A.	(7-0)	Surrey v. Sussex (Hove)	1964
Price, W. F.	(7-0)	Middlesex v. Yorkshire (Lord's)	1937
Saggers, R. A.	(7-0)	New South Wales v. Combined XI (Brisbane)	1940-41
Schofield, R. M.	(7-0)	Central Districts v. Wellington (Wellington)	1964-65
Smith, E. J.	(4-3)	Warwickshire v. Derbyshire (Birmingham)	1926
Smith, M. S.	(7-0)	Natal v. Border (East London)	1959-60
Tallon, D.	(3-4)	Queensland v. Victoria (Brisbane)	1938-39
Taylor, R. W.	(7-0)	Derbyshire v. Glamorgan (Derby)	1966
Yarnold, H.	(1-6)	Worcestershire v. Scotland (Dundee)	1951

SIX

Allen, R.	(2-4)	Yorkshire v. Sussex (Hove)	1921
Ames, L. E. G.	(4-2)	Kent v. Sussex (Maidstone)	1929
Ames, L. E. G.	(5-1)	Kent v. Sussex (Folkestone)	1930
Baker, E. A.	(6-0)	Victoria v. New South Wales (Melbourne)	1946-47

Most Dismissals in an Innings—Six—*Cont.*

	ct. st.		
Baker, E. A. ..	(1-5)	Victoria v. New South Wales (Sydney)	1946-47
Bale, E.	(2-4)	Worcestershire v. Australians (Worcester)	1909
Becker, G. C. ..	(6-0)	Western Australia v. Victoria (Melbourne)	1965-66
Bhandarkar, K. V.	(5-1)	Holkar v. Ceylon (Colombo)	1948-49
Binks, J. G. ..	(5-1)	Yorkshire v. Lancashire (Leeds)	1962
Binns, A. P. ..	(3-3)	Jamaica v. British Guiana (Georgetown)	1952-53
Bromham, C. G.	(6-0)	North-Eastern Transvaal v. Western Province (Cape Town)	1939-40
Brooks, E. W. ..	(6-0)	Surrey v. Kent (Blackheath)	1935
Buckingham, J...	(5-1)	Warwickshire v. Sussex (Birmingham)	1939
Butt, H. R. ..	(6-0)	Sussex v. Gloucestershire (Bristol)	1899
Butt, H. R. ..	(6-0)	Sussex v. Hampshire (Hove)	1901
Butt, H. R. ..	(6-0)	Sussex v. Leicestershire (Hove)	1909
Clayton, G. ..	(6-0)	Somerset v. Worcestershire (Kidderminster)	1965
Compton, L. H.	(4-2)	Middlesex v. Essex (Lord's)	1953
Corrall, P. ..	(4-2)	Leicestershire v. Sussex (Hove)	1936
Corrall, P. ..	(3-3)	Leicestershire v. Middlesex (Leicester)	1949
Duckworth, G. ..	(5-1)	Lancashire v. Kent (Dover)	1926
Duckworth, G. ..	(5-1)	Lancashire v. Worcestershire (Worcester)	1936
Elliott, H. ..	(4-2)	Derbyshire v. Worcestershire (Worcester)	1931
Elliott, H. ..	(5-1)	Derbyshire v. Middlesex (Derby)	1932
Elliott, H. ..	(4-2)	Derbyshire v. Lancashire (Manchester)	1935
Endean, W. R. ..	(6-0)	Transvaal v. Rhodesia (Salisbury)	1950-51
Evans, D. L. ..	(6-0)	Glamorgan v. Yorkshire (Swansea)	1967
Foster, T. ..	(6-0)	Derbyshire v. Surrey (Oval)	1883
Gamsy, D. ..	(5-1)	Natal v. Orange Free State (Pietermaritzburg)	1960-61
Garnett, H. G. ..	(6-0)	Lancashire v. Warwickshire (Birmingham)	1914
Gaukrodger, G...	(4-2)	Worcestershire v. Kent (Tunbridge Wells)	1907
Gibb, P. A. ..	(6-0)	Lord Tennyson's XI v. Indian XI (Bombay)	1937-38
Gibson, K. L. ..	(5-1)	Essex v. Derbyshire (Leyton)	1911
Gilligan, F. W. ..	(2-4)	Essex v. Gloucestershire (Cheltenham)	1928
Griffith, M. G. ..	(6-0)	Sussex v. Essex (Clacton)	1964
Griffith, S. C. ..	(6-0)	England v. Australian Services (Manchester)	1945
Grout, A. T. W.	(6-0)	Queensland v. New South Wales (Sydney)	1955-56
Grout, A. T. W.	(6-0)	Australia v. South Africa (Johannesburg)	1957-58
Guillen, S. C. ..	(3-3)	West Indians v. Tasmania (Launceston)	1951-52
Hubble, J. C. ..	(5-1)	Kent v. Gloucestershire (Cheltenham)	1923
Huish, F. H. ..	(1-5)	Kent v. Surrey (Oval)	1911
Hunter, D. ..	(5-1)	Yorkshire v. Surrey (Sheffield)	1891
Hunter, D. ..	(6-0)	Yorkshire v. Middlesex (Leeds)	1909
Hunter, J. ..	(6-0)	Yorkshire v. Gloucestershire (Gloucester)	1887
Inkster, G. B. ..	(4-2)	South Australia v. Victoria (Melbourne)	1926-27
James, K. C. ..	(6-0)	Northamptonshire v. Glamorgan (Swansea)	1937
Jarman, B. N. ..	(5-1)	South Australia v. New South Wales (Adelaide)	1961-62
Jarvis, A. H. ..	(2-4)	Australian XI v. Victoria (Melbourne)	1885-86
Kirby, G. N. G.	(6-0)	Surrey v. Cambridge U. (Guildford)	1949
Knott, A. P. ..	(4-2)	Kent v. Middlesex (Gravesend)	1966
Knott, A. P. ..	(5-1)	Kent v. Northamptonshire (Maidstone)	1966
Knott, A. P. ..	(6-0)	Kent v. Lancashire (Folkestone)	1967
Lambert, W. ..	(3-3)	M.C.C. v. Hampshire (Lord's)	1816
Langley, G. R. ..	(5-1)	South Australia v. Queensland (Brisbane)	1947-48
Levett, W. V. H.	(4-2)	Kent v. Northamptonshire (Northampton)	1934
Levett, W. H. V.	(5-1)	Kent v. Glamorgan (Neath)	1939
Lewis, E. B. ..	(6-0)	Warwickshire v. Cambridge U. (Cambridge)	1956
Lilley, A. A. ..	(4-2)	Warwickshire v. Worcestershire (Birmingham)	1906
Lilley, B. ..	(6-0)	Nottinghamshire v. Somerset (Taunton)	1932
Lindsay, D. ..	(6-0)	South Africa v. Australia (Johannesburg)	1966-67
Long, A... ..	(6-0)	Surrey v. Lancashire (Manchester)	1967
Matthews, M. H.	(4-2)	Oxford U. v. Surrey (Oval)	1937
Meads, E. A. ..	(5-1)	Nottinghamshire v. Derbyshire (Ilkeston)	1948
Meads, E. A. ..	(5-1)	Nottinghamshire v. Kent (Nottingham)	1949
Meyer, B. J. ..	(6-0)	Gloucestershire v. Somerset (Taunton)	1962
Millman, G. ..	(6-0)	Nottinghamshire v. Northamptonshire (Nottingham) ..	1959
Mooney, F. L. H.	(4-2)	New Zealanders v. Worcestershire (Worcester)	1949
Murray, J. T. ..	(6-0)	England v. India (Lord's)	1967
Murrell, H. R. ..	(4-2)	Middlesex v. Gloucestershire (Bristol)	1926
Oates, T. W. ..	(6-0)	Nottinghamshire v. Middlesex (Nottingham)	1906
Oates, T. W. ..	(6-0)	Nottinghamshire v. Leicestershire (Leicester)	1907

Most Dismissals in an Innings—Six—*Cont.*

	ct. st.		
Oldfield, W. A. ..	(3-3)	New South Wales v. West Indians (Sydney)	1930-31
Parks, J. M. ..	(6-0)	Sussex v. Worcestershire (Dudley)	1959
Phillips, H. ..	(3-3)	Sussex v. Surrey (Oval)	1872
Pooley, E. ..	(5-1)	Surrey v. Sussex (Oval) (1st inns)	1868
Pooley, E. ..	(3-3)	Surrey v. Sussex (Oval) (2nd inns)	1868
Pooley, E. ..	(1-5)	Surrey v. Kent (Oval)	1878
Price, W. F. ..	(3-3)	M.C.C. v. Kent (Folkestone)	1934
Price, W. F. ..	(6-0)	Middlesex v. Warwickshire (Lord's)	1938
Russell, T. M. ..	(3-3)	Essex v. Lancashire (Manchester)	1898
Russell, T. M. ..	(2-4)	Essex v. Kent (Canterbury)	1901
Saggers, R. A. ..	(4-2)	New South Wales v. Queensland (Sydney)	1946-47
Scattergood, J. H.	(5-1)	Philadelphians v. Warner's XI (Philadelphia)	1897-98
Shaw, A. A. ..	(3-3)	Sussex v. Cambridge U. (Hove)	1927
Sismey, S. G. ..	(6-0)	New South Wales v. Victoria (Sydney)	1949-50
Smith, H. ..	(3-3)	Gloucestershire v. Sussex (Bristol)	1923
Spooner, R. T. ..	(6-0)	Warwickshire v. Nottinghamshire (Birmingham) ..	1957
Stephenson, H. W.	(5-1)	Somerset v. Glamorgan (Bath)	1962
Strudwick, H. ..	(6-0)	Surrey v. Sussex (Oval)	1914
Swetman, R. ..	(6-0)	Surrey v. Kent (Oval)	1960
Swetman, R. ..	(6-0)	Surrey v. Somerset (Taunton)	1960
Swetman, R. ..	(4-2)	Cavaliers v. Rhodesia (Salisbury)	1962-63
Tallon, D. ..	(1-5)	Queensland v. M.C.C. (Brisbane)	1935-36
Tallon, D. ..	(3-3)	Queensland v. New South Wales (Brisbane)	1938-39
Tallon, D, ..	(5-1)	Queensland v. New South Wales (Sydney) (1st inns) ..	1938-39
Tallon, D. ..	(4-2)	Queensland v. New South Wales (Sydney) (2nd inns)	1938-39
Taylor, B. ..	(6-0)	Essex v. Lancashire (Blackpool)	1958
Taylor, R. W. ..	(6-0)	Derbyshire v. Sussex (Chesterfield)	1963
Timms, B. S. V.	(4-2)	Hampshire v. Leicestershire (Portsmouth)	1964
Trueman, G. ..	(5-1)	New South Wales v. Queensland (Sydney)	1952-53
Turner, M. ..	(3-3)	Gentlemen of England v. Oxford U. (Oxford)	1871
Turner, M. ..	(3-3)	Gentlemen of England v. Cambridge U. (Cambridge) ..	1876
Wade, T. H. ..	(4-2)	Essex v. Lancashire (Clacton)	1947
Walker, C. W. ..	(2-4)	South Australia v. New South Wales (Sydney)	1939-40
Webb, R. T. ..	(3-3)	Sussex v. Nottinghamshire (Hove)	1955
Webb, R. T. ..	(6-0)	Sussex v. Somerset (Hove)	1960
Wilson, A. E. ..	(6-0)	Gloucestershire v. Hampshire (Portsmouth)	1953
Yarnold, H. ..	(3-3)	Worcestershire v. Hampshire (Worcester)	1949

MOST DISMISSALS IN A MATCH

TWELVE

Pooley, E. ..	(8-4)	Surrey v. Sussex (Oval)	1868
Tallon, D. ..	(9-3)	Queensland v. New South Wales (Sydney)	1938-39

ELEVEN

Long, A... ..	(11-0)	Surrey v. Sussex (Hove)	1964

TEN

Corrall, P. ..	(7-3)	Leicestershire v. Sussex (Hove)	1936
Elliott, H. ..	(8-2)	Derbyshire v. Lancashire (Manchester)	1935
Hubble, J. C. ..	(9-1)	Kent v. Gloucestershire (Cheltenham)	1923
Huish, F. H. ..	(1-9)	Kent v. Surrey (Oval)	1911
Jarman, B. N. ..	(7-3)	South Australia v. New South Wales (Adelaide)	1961-62
Johnson, L. A. ..	(10-0)	Northamptonshire v. Sussex (Worthing)	1963
Johnson, L. A. ..	(8-2)	Northamptonshire v. Warwickshire (Birmingham) ..	1965
Oates, T. W. ..	(9-1)	Nottinghamshire v. Middlesex (Nottingham)	1906
Phillips, H. ..	(5-5)	Sussex v. Surrey (Oval)	1872
Pooley, E. ..	(2-8)	Surrey v. Kent (Oval)	1878
Saggers, R. A. ..	(9-1)	New South Wales v. Combined XI (Brisbane)	1940-41
Taylor, R. W. ..	(10-0)	Derbyshire v. Hampshire (Chesterfield)	1963
Wilson, A. E. ..	(10-0)	Gloucestershire v. Hampshire (Portsmouth)	1953

Most Dismissals in a Match—*Cont.*

NINE

	ct. st.		
Ames, L. E. G. ..	(9-0)	Kent v. Oxford U. (Oxford)	1928
Ames, L. E. G. ..	(5-4)	Kent v. Sussex (Maidstone)	1929
Baker, E. A. ..	(2-7)	Victoria v. New South Wales (Sydney)	1946-47
Baker, E. A. ..	(9-0)	Victoria v. New South Wales (Melbourne)	1946-47
Becker, G. C. ..	(8-1)	Western Australia v. Victoria (Melbourne)	1965-66
Broadbridge, W.	(2-7)	Sussex v. Hampshire & Surrey (Bramshill)	1826
Brown, J. ..	(4-5)	Scotland v. Ireland (Dublin)	1957
Clayton, G. ..	(8-1)	Lancashire v. Gloucestershire (Gloucester)	1959
Davidson, H. ..	(6-3)	New South Wales v. South Australia (Sydney)	1928-29
Dolphin, A. ..	(8-1)	Yorkshire v. Derbyshire (Bradford)	1919
Evans, T. G. ..	(8-1)	Kent v. New Zealanders (Canterbury)	1949
Ferrandi, J. H. ..	(7-2)	Western Province v. Transvaal (Johannesburg)	1958-59
Ford, D. A. ..	(4-5)	New South Wales v. Victoria (Sydney)	1963-64
Gamsy, D. ..	(8-1)	Natal v. Transvaal (Johannesburg)	1959-60
Gamsy, D. ..	(7-2)	Natal v. Orange Free State (Pietermaritzburg)	1960-61
Gibson, K. L. ..	(7-2)	Essex v. Derbyshire (Leyton)	1911
Hunter, J. ..	(9-0)	Yorkshire v. Gloucestershire (Gloucester)	1887
Inkster, G. B. ..	(4-5)	South Australia v. Victoria (Melbourne)	1926-27
Jarman, B. N. ..	(9-0)	Australians v. Nottinghamshire (Nottingham)	1964
Joshi, P. G. ..	(6-3)	Maharashtra v. Gujerat (Ahmednagar)	1959-60
Kirsten, N. ..	(7-2)	Border v. Rhodesia (East London)	1959-60
Langley, G. L. ..	(8-1)	Australia v. England (Lord's)	1956
Levett, W. H. V.	(5-4)	Kent v. Nottinghamshire (Maidstone)	1933
Levett, W. H. V.	(7-2)	Kent v. Northamptonshire (Northampton)	1934
Levett, W. H. V.	(5-4)	Kent v. Sussex (Tunbridge Wells)	1935
Lewis, E. B. ..	(8-1)	Warwickshire v. Oxford U. (Birmingham)	1949
Lilley, B. ..	(9-0)	Nottinghamshire v. Somerset (Taunton)	1932
Livsey, W. H. ..	(4-5)	Hampshire v. Warwickshire (Southampton)	1914
Mantri, M. K. ..	(4-5)	Bombay v. Northern India (Lahore)	1941-42
Millman, G. ..	(8-1)	Nottinghamshire v. Warwickshire (Nottingham)	1964
Murray, J. T. ..	(8-1)	Middlesex v. Hampshire (Lord's)	1965
Newton, A. E. ..	(6-3)	Somerset v. Middlesex (Lord's)	1901
Oldfield, W. A...	(4-5)	New South Wales v. West Indians (Sydney)	1930-31
Schofield, R. M.	(9-0)	Central Districts v. Wellington (Wellington)	1964-65
Stephenson, H. W.	(8-1)	Somerset v. Yorkshire (Taunton)	1963
Tallon, D. ..	(4-5)	Queensland v. Victoria (Brisbane)	1938-39
Turner, M. ..	(4-5)	Gentlemen of England v. Oxford U. (Oxford)	1871
Turner, M. ..	(6-3)	Middlesex v. Nottinghamshire (Prince's)	1875
Walker, C. W. ..	(3-6)	South Australia v. New South Wales (Sydney)	1939-40
Wasim Bari ..	(7-2)	Karachi v. Lahore Board (Lahore)	1964-65
Yarnold, H. ..	(5-4)	Worcestershire v. Hampshire (Worcester)	1949

MOST DISMISSALS IN A SEASON

Only seven wicket-keepers have dismissed a hundred batsmen in a season. L. E. G. Ames—who achieved the feat three times—and F. H. Huish were each helped by great Kent slow bowlers; Huish by C. Blythe and Ames by A. P. Freeman. In 1932 Ames stumped almost twice as many batsmen as he caught—a very unusual performance.

		Season	*Total*	*Caught*	*St.*
L. E. G. Ames	Kent	1929	127	79	48
L. E. G. Ames	Kent	1928	121	69	52
H. Yarnold	Worcestershire	1949	110	63	47
J. G. Binks	Yorkshire	1960	108	97	11
G. Duckworth	Lancashire	1928	107	77	30
J. T. Murray	Middlesex	1957	104	82	22
F. H. Huish	Kent	1913	102	70	32
J. T. Murray	Middlesex	1960	102	95	7
R. Booth	Worcestershire	1960	101	85	16
F. H. Huish	Kent	1911	100	62	38
L. E. G. Ames	Kent	1932	100	36	64
R. Booth	Worcestershire	1964	100	91	9

Most catches in a season: 97 J. G. Binks (Yorkshire) 1960
Most stumpings in a season 64 L. E. G. Ames (Kent) 1932

THE WICKET-KEEPERS' 'DOUBLE'

Only two players, L. E. G. Ames and J. T. Murray, have achieved the wicket-keeper's 'double' of 1000 runs and 100 dismissals in a season.

		Season	*Runs*	*H.S.*	*Avge.*	*100s*		*Total*	*Ct.*	*St.*
Ames, L. E. G. (Kent.)	(3)	1928	1919	200	35.53	4	..	121	69	52
		1929	1795	145	35.90	5	..	127	79	48
		1932	2482	180	57.72	9	..	100	36	64
Murray, J. T. (Middx.)	(1)	1957	1025	120	19.71	1	..	104	82	22

LARGEST INNINGS WITHOUT BYES

672-7d	A. P. Wickham: Somerset v. Hants. (Taunton)	1899
659-8d	T. G. Evans: England v. Australia (Sydney)	1946-47
647	L. Alexander: Tasmania v. Victoria (Melbourne)	1951-52
634-4d	Riaz Alam: Hyderabad v. Karachi Blues (Karachi)	1964-65
594-6d	J. H. Board: Glos. v. Hants. (Southampton)	1911
577-4	A. E. Wilson: Glos. v. Glamorgan (Newport)	1939
574-4	W. T. Luckes: Somerset v. Glamorgan (Newport)	1939
570-8d	E. W. Brookes: Surrey v. Essex (Brentwood)	1934
569	S. O. Quin: Victoria v. South Australia (Melbourne)	1935-36
559-9d	W. W. Wade: South Africa v. England (Cape Town)	1938-39
557-7d	H. Smith: Glos v. Surrey (Oval)	1927
555-6d	S. C. Griffith: Sussex v. South Africans (Hove)	1947
553	D. I. Dey: North-Eastern Transvaal v. Australians (Pretoria)	1966-67
551-7	D. Hunter: Yorks v. Surrey (Oval)	1899
551	J. J. Kelly: Australia v. England (Sydney)	1897-98
546	S. C. Griffith: Sussex v. New Zealanders (Hove)	1937
544-5d	Imtiaz Ahmed: Pakistan v. England (Birmingham)	1962
535-8d	N. McCorkell: Hants. v. Leics. (Leicester)	1938
533-5d	R. Swetman: M.C.C. v. Barbados (Bridgetown)	1959-60
533	J. P. Harty: Eastern Province v. Natal (Port Elizabeth)	1962-63
531	D. Lindsay: South Africa v. England (Johannesburg)	1964-65
529-9	J. H. B. Waite: South Africans v. Combined XI (Perth)	1963-64
528	H. B. Taber: N.S.W. v. South Australia (Adelaide)	1965-66
527	H. B. Taber: N.S.W. v. M.C.C. (Sydney)	1965-66
	(*Taber performed this feat twice in consecutive matches and conceded no byes whilst* 1580 *runs were scored against N.S.W.*)	
521-7d	B. Bellamy: Northants. v. Sussex (Hove)	1930
521	W. A. Oldfield: Australia v. England (Brisbane)	1928-29
520-8d	M. Patten: Free Foresters v. Oxford U. (Oxford)	1927
520	J. H. B. Waite: South Africa v. Australia (Melbourne)	1952-53
512	J. D. P. Tanner: Oxford U. v. Lancs. (Oxford) (*On first-class début*)	1947
512	W. T. Luckes: Somerset v. Surrey (Oval)	1936
512	J. M. Brearley: Cambridge U. v. West Indians (Cambridge)	1963
507-6d	E. A. Meads: Notts. v. Kent (Nottingham)	1953
507	S. Katz: Transvaal v. Eastern Province (Johannesburg)	1966-67
504-9d	A. Catt: Western Province v. Australians (Cape Town)	1966-67
501-6d	B. Bellamy: Northants. v. Worcs. (Northampton)	1930
501-8d	A. B. Wheat: Notts. v. Glamorgan (Swansea)	1939
500	J. P. Whiteside: Leics. v. Surrey (Leicester)	1900

In 1965, K. V. Andrew did not concede a bye in the course of 2132 runs being scored against Northamptonshire.

MOST EXTRAS IN AN INNINGS

Inns.	*Ext.*	*B.*	*L.B.*	*W.*	*N.B.*		
529	74	54	16	1	3	British Guiana v. Shepherd's XI (Georgetown)	1909-10
374	73	48	23	2	—	Northants. v. Kent (Northampton)	1955
287	70	24	—	46	—	Cambridge U. v. Oxford U. (Lord's)	1839
539	68	57	6	5	—	Yorks. v. Cambridge U. (Cambridge)	1884
197	66	49	—	17	—	M.C.C. v. Cambridge U. (Cambridge)	1842
200	63	36	—	21	6	Oxford U. v. Cambridge U. (Lord's)	1836
775	63	34	26	—	3	N.S.W. v. Victoria (Sydney)	1881-82
405	62	45	11	3	3	A.I.F. v. Foster's XI (Hereford)	1919
532	62	44	11	7	—	M.C.C. v. Wales (Lord's)	1925
349	61					Governor's XI v. Chief Minister's XI (Bombay)	1962-63

Most Extras in an Innings—*Cont.*

Inns.	*Ext.*	*B.*	*L.B.*	*W.*	*N.B.*		
400	59	46	13	—	—	Army v. Cambridge U. (Cambridge)	1920
423	58	38	18	—	2	M.C.C. v. Notts. (Lord's)	1899
343-9d	58	29	28	1	—	Cambridge U. v. Free Foresters (Cambridge)	1929
380-5	58	41	14	—	3	Wellington v. Auckland (Wellington)	1929-30
387	57	31	16	—	10	New Zealand v. England (Auckland)	1929-30
468-7d	57	27	12	14	4	England v. Australian Services (Lord's)	1945
468	57	39	4	8	6	Yorks. v. Essex (Southend)	1947
266	56	29	5	21	1	Cambridge U. v. Oxford U. (Lord's)	1851
555	56	34	14	8	—	Kent v. Worcs. (Stourbridge)	1909
798	56					Maharashtra v. Northern India (Poona)	1940-41
127	55	45	—	9	1	Cambridge U. v. Oxford U. (Lord's)	1836
409	55	49	4	2	—	Glos. v. Middx. (Lord's)	1888
519	55					Jamaica v. Tennyson's XI (Kingston)	1926-27
188	55	46	2	—	7	Oxford U. v. Harlequins (Oxford)	1927
505-9d	54	32	19	2	1	Somerset v. Middx. (Weston-super-Mare)	1933
703	54					Bengal Cyclone XI v. Bijapur Famine XI (Bombay)	1942-43
204	53	37	—	13	3	M.C.C. v. Oxford U. (Lord's)	1837
388	53	36	12	4	1	Northants v. Leics. (Northampton)	1906
441	53	47	2	—	4	M.C.C. v. West Indian XI (Georgetown)	1912-13
407	53	29	22	—	2	Essex v. Worcs. (Worcester)	1923
305	53	37	5	4	7	Leveson-Gower's XI v. Oxford U. (Eastbourne)	1923
473-6	53	26	10	—	17	Canterbury v. Auckland (Christchurch)	1930-31
359-7d	52	43	8	1	—	Lancs. v. Middx. (Lord's)	1901
370	52					Wellington v. Canterbury (Christchurch)	1922-23
503-9d	52	39	10	3	—	M.C.C. v. Sussex (Lord's)	1905
611	52	41	9	9	1	Sussex v. Essex (Leyton)	1905
592-4d	51	47	3	1	—	Lancs. v. Worcs. (Worcester)	1929
308	51					Baroda v. Maharashtra (Baroda)	1942-43
403	50	37	10	3	—	Eastern Province v. Griqualand West (Johannesburg)	1906-07
246	50	42	5	—	3	Free Foresters v. Oxford U. (Oxford)	1920
480-9d	50	33	11	3	3	Kent v. Hants. (Canterbury)	1923
464-9d	50					Scotland v. Ireland (Greenock)	1926
602-8d	50					Otago v. Canterbury (Dunedin)	1928-29
327	50	37	8	1	4	Australia v. England (Oval)	1934
443-9d	50					Western Province v. Border (Cape Town)	1934-35
903-7d	50	22	19	1	8	England v. Australia (Oval)	1938

INDIVIDUAL CAREER RECORDS

BATTING

All Records are complete to 30th SEPTEMBER, 1967.

Career dates: Dates in italics denote the first half of an overseas season, i.e. *1966* means 1966-67.

"1000s": This column shows the number of a times that a player has scored 1000 runs in a season. J. B. Hobbs's figures of 24 + 2 show that he scored 1000 runs in each of 24 English seasons and also in two more overseas.

30,000 RUNS IN A CAREER

	Career	*Inns.*	*N.O.*	*Runs*	*H.S.*	*Avge.*	*100s*	*1000s*
J. B. Hobbs	1905-1934	1315	106	61237	316*	50.65	197	24+2
F. E. Woolley	1906-1938	1532	85	58969	305*	40.75	145	28
E. Hendren	1907-1938	1300	166	57611	301*	50.81	170	21+4
C. P. Mead	1905-1936	1340	185	55061	280*	47.67	153	27
W. G. Grace†	1865-1908	1493	105	54896	344	39.55	126	28
W. R. Hammond	1920-1951	1004	104	50493	336*	56.10	167	17+5
H. Sutcliffe	1919-1945	1087	123	50135	313	52.00	149	21+3
T. W. Hayward	1893-1914	1138	96	43551	315*	41.79	104	20

Batting-30,000 Runs—*Cont.*

	Career	*Inns.*	*N.O.*	*Runs*	*H.S.*	*Avge.*	*100s*	*1000s*
T. W. Graveney ..	1948-1967	1088	130	43540	258	45.44	115	18+2
A. Sandham ..	1911-*1937*	1000	79	41283	325	44.82	107	18+2
L. Hutton	1934-1960	814	91	40140	364	55.51	129	12+5
W. Rhodes	1898-1930	1528	237	39802	267*	30.83	58	20+1
R. E. S. Wyatt ..	1923-1957	1141	157	39404	232	40.04	85	17+1
D. C. S. Compton ..	1936-1964	839	88	38942	300	51.85	123	14+3
E. Tyldesley.. ..	1909-1936	961	106	38874	256*	45.46	102	18+1
J. T. Tyldesley ..	1895-1923	994	62	37897	295*	40.66	86	19
J. W. Hearne ..	1909-1936	1025	116	37252	285*	40.98	96	19
L. E. G. Ames ..	1926-1951	950	95	37245	295	43.56	102	17
D. Kenyon	1946-1967	1159	59	37002	259	33.63	74	19
W. J. Edrich ..	1934-1958	964	92	36965	267*	42.39	86	15
D. Denton	1894-1920	1163	70	36479	221	33.37	69	21
G. H. Hirst	1891-1929	1215	151	36323	341	34.13	60	19
W. G. Quaife ..	1894-1928	1203	186	36021	255*	35.41	72	24
G. Gunn	1902-1932	1062	82	35234	220	35.95	62	20
John Langridge ..	1928-1955	984	66	34380	250*	37.45	76	17
C. Washbrook ..	1933-1964	906	107	34101	251*	42.67	76	17+3
M. Leyland	1920-1948	932	101	33660	263	40.50	80	17
H. T. W. Hardinge	1902-1933	1021	103	33519	263*	36.51	75	18
M. C. Cowdrey ..	1950-1967	856	93	33346	307	43.70	81	16+6
R. Abel	1881-1904	994	73	32669	357*	35.47	74	14
J. D. Robertson ..	1937-1959	897	46	31914	331*	37.50	67	14+1
J. Hardstaff, Jnr. ..	1930-1955	812	94	31847	266	44.35	83	13+1
James Langridge ..	1924-1953	1058	157	31716	167	35.20	42	20
M. J. K. Smith ..	1951-1967	855	103	31580	204	41.99	55	14+1
C. B. Fry	1892-*1921*	658	43	30886	258*	50.22	94	12
D. Brookes	1934-1959	925	70	30874	257	36.10	71	17
P. Holmes	1913-1935	810	84	30574	315*	42.11	67	14+1
R. T. Simpson ..	*1944*-1963	852	55	30546	259	38.32	64	13+1
K. F. Barrington ..	1953-1967	772	128	30203	256	46.89	74	12+3
L. G. Berry	1924-1951	1048	57	30188	232	30.46	45	18

† The late Roy Webber revised W. G. Grace's figures, eliminating what he considered to be minor matches. The above figures are the generally accepted ones. Webber's revised version reads: 1468 Inns. 103 N.O. 53856 Runs 344 H.S. 39.45 Avge. 124 100s. 28 1000s.

10,000 RUNS IN A CAREER

	Career	Inns.	N.O.	Runs	H.S.	Avge.	100s	1000s
Abel, R.	1881-1904	994	73	32669	357*	35.47	74	14
Alderman, A. E. ..	1928-1948	529	51	12376	175	25.89	12	6
Allen, B. O... ..	1932-1951	512	20	14195	220	28.85	14	6
Alley, W. E. ..	*1945*-1967	633	63	18393	221*	32.26	30	9+1
Ames, L. E. G. ..	1926-1951	950	95	37245	295	43.56	102	17
Armstrong, N. F. ..	1919-1939	637	61	19002	186	32.98	36	13
Armstrong, W. W.	*1898-1921*	407	61	16177	303*	46.75	45	4+2
Arnold, E. G. ..	1899-1913	592	62	15853	215	29.91	24	10
Arnold, J.	1929-1950	710	45	21831	227	32.82	37	14
Ashdown, W. H. ..	1914-1947	812	77	22589	332	30.73	39	11
Astill, W. E. ..	1906-1939	1153	145	22726	164*	22.54	15	11
Atkinson, G. ..	1954-1967	555	36	16487	190	31.76	25	9
Avery, A. V. ..	1935-1954	455	35	14137	224	33.65	25	7
Bailey, T. E. ..	1945-1967	1072	215	28642	205	33.42	28	17
Bakewell, A. H. ..	1928-1936	453	24	14570	257	33.98	31	8
Barber, R. W. ..	1954-1967	602	51	16566	185	30.06	16	7+1
Barber, W.	1926-1947	526	49	16402	255	34.38	29	8
Bardsley, W. ..	*1903-1927*	376	35	17031	264	49.94	53	4+1
Barker, G. ..	1954-1967	687	37	19236	181*	29.59	25	13
Barling, T. H. ..	1927-1948	609	54	19209	269	34.61	34	9
Barlow, R. G. ..	1871-1891	598	63	10762	117	20.11	4	1
Barnes, W.	1875-1894	716	56	15242	160	23.09	21	5
Barnett, C. J. ..	1927-*1953*	821	45	25389	259	32.71	48	12+1
Barrick, D.	1949-1960	490	62	13970	211	32.64	20	7
Barrington, K. F. ..	1953-1967	772	128	30203	256	46.89	74	12+3
Bartlett, H. T. ..	1933-1951	350	34	10098	183	31.95	16	4
Bates, L. A... ..	1913-1935	749	53	19380	211	27.84	21	12
Bates, W.	1877-*1887*	494	20	10214	144*	21.54	10	5

Batting-10,000 Runs—*Cont.*

	Career	*Inns.*	*N.O.*	*Runs*	*H.S.*	*Avge.*	*100s*	*1000s*
Bates, W. E.	1907-1931	685	30	15884	200*	24.25	12	7
Bear, M. J.	1954-1967	529	43	11936	137	24.55	8	4
Bedser, E. A.	1939-1962	692	79	14716	163	24.00	10	6
Benaud, R.	*1948-1963*	359	44	11432	187	36.29	23	—
Bennett, D.	1950-1967	607	123	10574	117*	21.84	4	2
Berry, L. G.	1924-1951	1048	57	30188	232	30.46	45	18
Board, J. H.	1891-*1914*	906	97	15672	214	19.37	9	6
Bolus, J. B.	1956-1967	480	39	14143	202*	32.07	21	7
Booth, B. C.	*1954-1966*	262	34	10824	214*	47.47	26	2+2
Booth, B. J.	1956-1967	410	29	10604	183*	27.83	14	6
Borde, C. G.	*1952*-1967	290	50	10513	177*	43.80	27	1+3
Bosanquet, B. J. T.	1898-1919	381	32	11694	214	33.50	21	6
Bowell, A.	1902-1927	810	43	18510	204	24.13	25	8
Bowley, E. H.	1912-1934	853	46	28163	283	34.89	52	15
Bowley, F. L.	1899-1923	738	25	21121	276	29.62	38	14
Boycott, G.	1962-1967	276	30	11018	246*	44.78	24	5+1
Bradman, D. G.	*1927-1948*	338	43	28067	452*	95.14	117	4+12
Brann, G.	1885-1905	475	43	11201	161	25.92	25	2
Braund, L. C.	1896-1920	752	57	17801	257*	25.61	25	7
Briggs, J.	1879-1900	821	54	14002	186	18.25	10	—
Broadbent, R. G.	1950-1963	520	56	12800	155	27.58	13	7
Brockwell, W.	1886-1903	539	47	13285	225	27.00	22	6
Brookes, D.	1934-1959	925	70	30874	257	36.10	71	17
Brown, F. R.	1930-1959	533	49	13275	212	27.42	22	4
Brown, G.	1908-1933	1012	52	25649	232*	26.71	37	11
Brown, J. T.	1889-1904	633	47	17850	311	30.46	29	10
Brown, S. M.	1937-1955	580	40	15756	232*	29.17	22	9
Brown, W. A.	*1932-1949*	284	15	13840	265*	51.44	39	3+2
Burge, P. J.	*1952-1966*	344	45	14321	283	47.89	37	2+5
Burnup, C. J.	1895-1907	395	25	13614	200	36.79	26	8
Buse, H. T. F.	1929-1953	523	54	10623	132	22.65	7	5
Cadman, S.	1900-1926	690	34	14068	126	21.44	8	2
Calthorpe, Hon. F. S. G.	1911-1935	576	52	12596	209	24.03	13	5
Carpenter, H.	1893-1920	551	26	14939	199	28.45	25	7
Carr, A. W.	1910-1935	710	42	21100	206	31.58	45	11
Carr, D. B.	1945-1967	743	72	19250	170	28.68	24	11
Cartwright, T. W.	1952-1967	524	71	10225	210	22.57	6	3
Chapman, A. P. F.	1920-1939	554	44	16309	260	31.97	27	3+1
Charlesworth, C.	1898-1921	632	27	14289	216	23.61	15	5
Chatterton, W.	1882-1902	507	39	10863	169	23.21	8	3
Clarke, T. H.	1947-*1959*	426	35	11490	191	29.38	12	6
Close, D. B.	1949-1967	854	105	23922	198	31.93	36	14
Coe, S.	1896-1923	775	70	17438	252*	24.73	19	7
Compton, D. C. S.	1936-1964	839	88	38942	300	51.85	123	14+3
Constable, B.	1939-1964	701	82	18849	205*	30.45	27	12
Cooke, T. E.	1922-1937	730	65	20198	278	30.37	32	10
Cooper, E.	1936-1951	444	28	13304	216*	31.98	18	9
Cowdrey, M. C.	1950-1967	856	93	33346	307	43.70	81	16+6
Cox, G.	1931-1960	752	57	22912	234*	32.96	50	13
Cox, G. R.	1895-1928	978	197	14643	167*	18.74	2	1
Crapp, J. F.	1936-1956	754	80	23615	175	35.03	38	14
Crawford, V. F. S.	1896-1910	479	32	11909	172*	26.64	16	5
Croom, A. J.	1922-1939	628	65	17689	211	31.41	24	12
Cutmore, J. A.	1924-1936	595	36	15975	238*	28.58	15	11
Dacre, C. C.	*1914*-1936	437	20	12166	223	29.17	24	7
Daniell, J.	1898-1927	531	54	10468	174*	21.94	9	—
Darling, J.	*1893-1907*	334	25	10637	210	34.42	21	4
Davies, D.	1923-1939	698	62	15458	216	24.30	16	7
Davies, E.	1924-1954	1033	79	26566	287*	27.84	32	16
Dawkes, G. O.	1937-1961	736	105	11411	143	18.08	1	—
Dawson, E. W.	1922-1934	483	17	12662	146	27.17	14	6
Dempster, C. S.	*1921-1947*	305	36	12098	212	44.97	35	5
Denton, D.	1894-1920	1163	70	36479	221	33.37	69	21
Dews, G.	1946-1961	642	53	16803	145	28.52	20	11
Dexter, E. R.	1956-1967	558	47	20707	205	40.52	50	8+2
Dillon, E. W.	1900-1923	414	25	11006	143	28.29	15	3
Dipper, A. E.	1908-1932	865	69	28075	252*	35.27	53	15

Batting-10,000 Runs—*Cont.*

	Career	*Inns.*	*N.O.*	*Runs*	*H.S.*	*Avge.*	*100s*	*1000s*
Dodds, T. C.	*1943*-1960	691	18	19384	157	28.80	17	13
Doggart, G. H. G.	1948-1961	347	28	10054	219*	31.51	20	4
Dollery, H. E.	1933-1955	717	66	24413	212	37.50	50	15
Douglas, J. W. H. T.	1901-1930	1035	156	24530	210*	27.90	26	10
Ducat, A.	1906-1931	669	59	23373	306*	38.31	52	14
Duleepsinhji, K. S.	1924-1932	333	23	15485	333	49.95	50	7
Dyson, A. H.	1926-1948	697	37	17922	208	27.15	24	10
Eager, E. D. R.	1935-1958	599	42	12178	158*	21.86	10	6
Eastman, L. C.	1920-1939	696	50	13438	161	20.80	7	5
Edrich, G. A.	1946-1958	508	60	15600	167*	34.82	26	8
Edrich, J. H.	1956-1967	506	49	20243	310*	44.29	50	9+1
Edrich, W. J.	1934-1958	964	92	36965	267*	42.39	86	15
Elliot, C. S.	1932-1953	468	29	11965	215	27.25	9	6
Emmett, G. M.	1936-1959	865	50	25602	188	31.41	37	13+1
Evans, T. G.	1939-1967	751	50	14878	144	21.22	7	4
Fagg, A. E.	1932-1957	803	46	27291	269*	36.05	58	13
Fane, F. L.	1895-1924	715	42	18527	217	27.52	25	5
Favell, L. E.	*1951-1966*	302	8	10929	190	37.17	23	0+2
Fender, P. G. H.	1910-1936	783	69	19034	185	26.65	21	9
Fishlock, L. B.	1931-1952	699	54	25376	253	39.34	56	12+1
Fletcher, D. G. W.	1946-1961	519	41	14461	194	30.25	22	4
Flowers, W.	1877-1896	683	53	12691	173	20.34	9	2
Foster, H. K.	1894-1925	523	21	17154	216	34.17	29	8
Freeman, J. R.	1905-1928	579	55	14604	286	27.88	26	7
Fry, C. B.	1892-*1921*	658	43	30886	258*	50.22	94	12
Gale, R. A.	1955-1967	436	13	12324	200	29.13	14	6
Gardner, F. C.	1947-1961	597	66	17905	215*	33.71	29	10
Geary, G.	1912-1938	819	138	13498	122	19.82	8	—
Gibb, P. A.	1934-1956	479	33	12520	204	28.07	19	5
Gibbons, H. H.	1927-1946	671	57	21087	212*	34.34	44	12
Giffen, G.	*1877-1903*	421	24	11757	271	29.61	18	4
Gillingham, F. H.	1903-1928	352	24	10050	201	30.64	19	1
Gimblett, H.	1935-1954	673	37	23007	310	36.17	50	12+1
Goddard, T. L.	*1952-1966*	261	16	10192	222	41.60	24	2+1
Grace, W. G.	1865-1908	1493	105	54896	344	39.55	126	28
Graveney, T. W.	1948-1967	1088	130	43540	258	45.44	115	18+2
Gray, J. R.	1948-1966	818	81	22650	213*	30.73	30	13
Gregory, R. J.	1925-1947	646	78	19495	243	34.32	39	9
Gregory, S. E.	*1889-1912*	592	55	15303	201	28.49	25	4
Grieves, K. J.	*1945*-1964	746	79	22454	224	33.66	29	13+1
Gunn, G.	1902-1932	1062	82	35234	220	35.95	62	20
Gunn, G. V.	1928-1950	395	42	10337	184	29.28	11	5
Gunn, J.	1896-1932	847	105	24740	294	33.34	41	11
Gunn, W.	1880-1904	846	71	25457	273	32.84	47	12
Haigh, N. E.	1912-1936	779	49	15208	131	20.83	12	6
Haigh, S.	1895-1913	747	119	11715	159	18.65	4	1
Hall, L.	1873-1894	538	63	10853	160	22.84	11	4
Hallam, M. R.	1950-1967	823	52	22749	210*	29.50	30	13
Hallows, C.	1914-1932	586	66	20926	233*	40.24	55	11
Hamer, A.	1938-1960	515	19	15465	227	31.17	19	10
Hammond, W. R.	1920-1951	1004	104	50493	336*	56.10	167	17+5
Hanif Mohammad	*1951*-1967	285	36	14101	499	56.63	47	2+3
Hardinge, H. T. W.	1902-1933	1021	103	33519	263*	36.51	75	18
Hardstaff, J., Snr.	1902-1926	620	73	17146	213*	31.34	26	7+1
Hardstaff, J., Jnr.	1930-1955	812	94	31847	266	44.35	83	13+1
Harris, C. B.	1928-1951	601	64	18823	239*	35.05	30	11
Harvey, R. N.	*1946-1962*	461	35	21699	231*	50.92	67	3+6
Hassett, A. L.	*1932-1953*	322	32	16890	232	58.24	59	3+2
Hawke, Lord	1881-1911	920	105	16506	166	20.25	13	1
Hayes, E. G.	1896-1926	896	48	27318	276	32.21	48	16
Hayward, T. W.	1893-1914	1138	96	43551	315*	41.79	104	20
Hazare, Vijay	*1934-1966*	357	43	17972	316*	57.23	57	2+5
Headley, R. G. A.	1958-1967	471	45	12281	150*	28.82	16	7
Hearne, A.	1884-1910	825	76	16287	194	21.74	15	4
Hearne, J. W.	1909-1936	1025	116	37252	285*	40.98	96	19
Hedges, B.	1950-1967	744	41	17733	182	25.22	21	9
Hendren, E.	1907-1938	1300	166	57611	301*	50.81	170	21+4

Batting-10,000 Runs—*Cont.*

	Career	*Inns.*	*N.O.*	*Runs*	*H.S.*	*Avge.*	*100s*	*1000s*
Hill, A. J. L. ..	1890-1921	389	26	10141	199	27.93	18	—
Hill, C.	*1892-1925*	417	21	17216	365*	43.47	45	3+2
Hill, N. W.	1953-1967	498	30	13816	201*	29.52	23	8
Hirst, G. H.. ..	1891-1929	1215	151	36323	341	34.13	60	19
Hitchcock, R. E. ..	*1947*-1964	517	71	12442	153*	27.89	13	5
Hobbs, J. B. ..	1905-1934	1315	106	61237	316*	50.65	197	24+2
Holland, F. C. ..	1894-1908	429	29	10384	171	25.96	12	4
Holmes, E. R. T. ..	1924-1955	465	51	13598	236	32.84	24	6
Holmes, P.	1913-1935	810	84	30574	315*	42.11	67	14+1
Hopwood, J. L. ..	1923-1939	575	55	15548	220	29.90	27	8
Hornby, A. N. ..	1867-1899	698	39	15763	188	23.91	15	2
Horner, N. F. ..	1950-1965	656	34	18533	203*	29.79	25	12
Horton, H.	1946-1967	744	84	21669	160*	32.83	32	12
Horton, M. J. ..	1952-1966	686	48	18748	233	29.37	22	11
Howorth, R. ..	1933-1951	611	56	11479	114	20.68	4	4
Hubble, J. C. ..	1904-1929	528	65	10935	189	23.61	5	1
Hymphreys, E. ..	1899-1920	639	45	16603	208	27.95	21	8
Hutchings, K. L. ..	1902-1912	311	12	10054	176	33.62	22	6
Hutton, L.	1934-1960	814	91	40140	364	55.51	129	12+5
Ibadulla, K. ..	*1952*-1967	541	59	13563	171	28.13	20	6
Iddon, J.	1924-1945	712	95	22681	222	36.76	46	13
Ikin, J. T.	1938-1964	554	66	17968	192	36.81	27	10+1
Illingworth, R. ..	1951-1967	701	132	15691	162	27.57	15	7
Imtiaz, Ahmed ..	*1944-1964*	296	31	10005	300*	37.75	22	2+1
Ingleby-Mackenzie, A. C. D.	1951-1966	574	64	12421	132*	24.35	11	5
Insole, D. J. ..	1947-1963	743	72	25237	219*	37.61	54	13
Iremonger, J. ..	1899-1914	534	60	16622	272	35.06	31	9
Jackson, F. S. ..	1890-1907	500	35	15824	160	34.03	31	10
Jackson, G. R. ..	1919-1936	468	22	10288	140	23.06	9	4
Jackson, V. E. ..	*1936*-1958	605	53	15698	170	28.43	21	11
Jardine, D. R. ..	1920-1948	377	61	14823	214*	46.90	35	8+1
Jenkins, R. O. ..	1938-1958	573	120	10073	109	22.23	1	4
Jessop, G. L. ..	1894-1914	855	37	26698	286	32.63	53	14
Johnson, H. L. ..	1949-1966	606	65	14286	154	26.40	16	6
Johnson, P. R. ..	1900-1927	488	24	11931	164	25.71	18	1
Jones, A.	1957-1967	473	32	13062	187*	29.61	14	7
Jones, A. O. ..	1892-1914	774	47	22935	296	31.54	34	9
Jones, W. E. ..	1937-1958	563	64	13535	212*	27.12	11	7
Jupp, H.	1862-1881	677	45	14817	165	23.44	11	6
Jupp, V. W. C. ..	1909-1938	876	84	23278	217	29.39	30	13
Kanhai, R. B. ..	*1954*-1967	271	20	11845	256	47.19	32	3+2
Keeton, W. W. ..	1926-1952	657	43	24276	312*	39.53	54	12
Kennedy, A. S. ..	1907-1936	1025	130	16586	163*	18.53	10	5
Kenyon, D.. ..	1946-1967	1159	59	37002	259	33.63	74	19
Key, K. J.	1882-1909	560	69	12925	281	26.32	13	3
Killick, E. H. ..	1893-1913	770	53	18768	200	26.17	22	11
Kilner, N.	1919-1937	619	42	17522	228	30.36	25	12
Kilner, R.	1911-1927	540	55	14422	206*	29.73	17	10
King, J. H.	1895-1926	988	69	25121	227*	27.33	34	14
Kinneir, S. P. ..	1898-1914	525	47	15641	268*	32.72	26	8
Kippax, A. F. ..	*1918-1935*	254	33	12747	315*	57.69	43	1+2
Knight, A. E. ..	1895-1912	702	40	19357	229*	29.24	34	10
Knight, B. R. ..	1955-1967	524	61	11879	165	25.65	12	5
Langdon, T. ..	1900-1914	519	14	10723	156	21.23	6	3
Langridge, James ..	1924-1953	1058	157	31716	167	35.20	42	20
Langridge, John ..	1928-1955	984	66	34380	250*	37.45	76	17
Lawry, W. M. ..	*1955-1966*	262	23	11809	266	49.41	33	3+2
Leary, S. E.. ..	1951-1967	493	65	13754	158	32.13	17	9
Lee, C.	1952-1964	472	16	12129	150	26.59	8	8
Lee, F. S.	1925-1947	586	38	15310	169	27.93	23	8
Lee, G. M.	1910-1933	622	47	14858	200*	25.84	22	7
Lee, H. W.	1911-1934	716	51	20069	243*	30.17	37	13
Lenham, L. J. ..	1956-1967	491	48	11758	191*	26.54	7	6
Lester, E.	1945-1956	347	28	10912	186	34.20	25	6
Lester, G.	1937-1958	649	54	12857	143	21.60	9	5
Lewis, A. R. ..	1955-1967	421	35	12332	223	31.94	20	7

Batting-10,000 Runs—*Cont.*

	Career	*Inns.*	*N.O.*	*Runs*	*H.S.*	*Avge.*	*100s*	*1000s*
Leyland, M.	1920-1948	932	101	33660	263	40.50	80	17
Lilley, A. A.	1891-1911	639	46	15597	171	26.30	16	3
Lilley, B.	1921-1937	512	79	10496	124	24.24	7	2
Livingston, T. L.	*1941*-1964	384	45	15260	210	45.01	34	7+1
Llewellyn, C. B.	*1894*-1912	461	34	11425	216	26.75	18	6
Lockwood, W. H.	1886-1904	531	44	10673	163	21.91	15	2
Lowson, F. A.	1949-1958	449	37	15321	259*	37.18	31	8+1
Lyon, B. H.	1921-1948	448	20	10694	189	24.98	16	4
Macartney, C. G.	*1905-1935*	360	32	15050	345	45.88	49	3
MacBryan, J. C. W.	1911-1936	362	12	10322	164	29.52	18	4
McCabe, S. J.	*1928-1941*	262	20	11951	240	49.39	29	3
McCool, C. L.	*1939*-1960	413	36	12420	172	32.94	18	5
McCorkell, N.	1932-1951	696	67	16108	203	25.60	17	9
McDonald, C. C.	*1947-1962*	307	26	11375	229	40.48	24	1
McGahey, C. P.	1894-1921	751	65	20723	277	30.20	31	10
McGlew, D. J.	*1947-1966*	299	34	12070	255*	45.54	27	3+1
McIntyre, A. J.	1938-1963	567	79	11145	143*	22.83	7	3
Mackay, K. D.	*1946-1963*	294	46	10823	223	43.64	23	1
MacLaren, A. C.	1890-*1922*	699	52	22022	424	34.03	47	8+1
McLean, R. A.	*1949-1965*	318	20	10969	207	36.80	22	2
Makepeace, H.	1906-1930	778	66	25799	203	36.23	43	13
Manjrekar, V. L.	*1949-1966*	274	35	11952	283	50.00	36	1+1
Mankad, V. M.	*1935-1963*	357	26	11544	231	34.87	26	1
Mann, F. T.	1908-1933	608	47	13154	194	23.44	9	3
Marner, P.	1952-1967	545	55	13835	142*	28.23	14	10
Marshall, R. E.	*1945*-1967	858	39	29750	228*	36.32	60	14
Martin, S. H.	*1925-1949*	457	31	11511	191*	27.02	13	7
Mason, J. R.	1893-1919	557	36	17337	183	33.27	34	8
May, P. B. H.	1948-1963	618	77	27592	285*	51.00	85	11+3
Mead, C. P.	1905-1936	1340	185	55061	280*	47.67	153	27
Melville, A.	*1928-1948*	295	15	10598	189	37.85	25	3
Merchant, V. M.	*1929-1951*	221	44	12876	359*	72.74	43	2+1
Miller, K. R.	*1937*-1959	326	36	14183	281*	48.90	41	2+2
Milton, C. A.	1948-1967	899	108	27300	170	34.51	48	14
Mitchell, A.	1922-1947	593	72	19523	189	37.47	44	10
Mitchell, B.	*1925-1949*	281	30	11395	195	45.39	30	3+1
Morgan, D. C.	1950-1967	813	134	16700	147	24.59	8	7
Morris, A. R.	*1940-1954*	242	15	12489	290	55.01	46	2+4
Mortimore, J. B.	1950-1967	766	71	13194	149	18.98	3	5
Morton, A.	1901-1926	625	56	10933	131	19.21	6	1
Murdoch, W. L.	*1876*-1904	684	48	17070	321	26.83	20	3
Murray, J. T.	1952-1967	627	100	12071	142	22.90	12	5
Mushtaq Ali	*1932-1963*	358	16	12413	233	36.29	30	1
Nayudu, C. K.	*1916-1963*	305	15	10159	200	35.03	21	2
Neale, W. L.	1923-1948	700	79	14752	145*	23.75	14	6
Newham, W.	1881-1905	633	43	14318	210*	24.26	18	4
Newman, J. A.	1906-1930	837	129	15333	166*	21.65	10	6
Nicholls, R. B.	1951-1967	677	37	16537	217	25.83	13	11
Nichols, M. S.	1924-1939	758	85	17843	205	26.51	20	9
Noble, M. A.	*1893-1919*	378	34	14034	284	40.80	37	4+1
Norman, M. E. J. C.	1952-1967	482	29	13626	221*	30.07	21	7
Nourse, A. D., Snr.	*1896-1935*	371	39	14216	304*	42.82	38	3+1
Nourse, A. D., Jnr.	*1931-1952*	269	27	12472	260*	51.53	41	2
Oakes, C.	1935-1954	474	40	10893	160	25.09	14	5
Oakman, A. S. M.	1947-1967	879	76	21257	229*	26.47	22	9
O'Brien, T. C.	1881-1914	452	30	11399	202	27.01	15	2
O'Connor, J.	1921-1939	906	80	28875	248	34.95	72	16
Oldfield, N.	1935-1954	521	51	17811	168	37.89	38	11
Oldroyd, E.	1910-1931	511	58	15929	194	35.16	37	10
O'Neill, N. C.	*1955-1966*	304	34	13805	284	51.12	45	2+6
Ord, J. S.	1933-1953	459	35	11788	187*	27.80	16	6
Outschoorn, L.	1946-1959	595	53	15496	215*	28.59	25	9
Padgett, D. E. V.	1951-1967	639	50	16775	161*	28.48	26	9
Palairet, L. C. H.	1890-1909	488	19	15777	292	33.63	27	7
Palmer, C. H.	1938-1959	588	38	17458	201	31.74	33	8
Parfitt, P. H.	1956-1967	617	76	19858	200*	36.70	44	9+1
Parker, J. F.	1932-1952	523	71	14272	255	31.57	20	9

Batting-10,000 Runs—*Cont.*

	Career	*Inns.*	*N.O.*	*Runs*	*H.S.*	*Avge.*	*100s*	*1000s*
Parkhouse, W. G. A.	1948-1964	791	49	23508	201	31.68	32	15
Parks, H. W.	1926-*1949*	745	98	21725	200*	33.57	42	14
Parks, J. H.	1924-1952	758	63	21369	197	30.74	41	12
Parks, J. M.	1949-1967	943	128	29275	205*	35.92	47	15
Parsons, J. H.	1910-1936	553	51	17909	225	35.67	38	10+1
Pataudi, Nawab of, Jnr.	1957-1967	364	31	11356	203*	34.10	24	4+2
Paynter, E.	1926-*1950*	532	58	20023	322	42.24	45	9+1
Payton, W.	1905-1931	770	126	22132	169	34.36	39	9
Pearce, T. N.	1929-1952	406	54	12060	211*	34.26	22	6
Pearson, F.	1900-1926	811	38	18735	167	24.23	22	8
Peel, R.	1882-1899	689	66	12135	210*	19.46	7	1
Perrin, P. A.	1896-1928	918	91	29709	343*	35.92	66	18
Phebey, A. H.	1946-1964	599	34	14643	157	25.91	13	9
Place, W.	1937-1955	487	49	15609	266*	35.63	36	8
Ponsford, W. H.	*1920-1934*	235	23	13819	437	65.18	47	2+2
Poole, C. J.	1948-1962	637	42	19364	222*	32.54	24	12
Prentice, F. T.	1934-1951	421	24	10997	191	27.70	17	5
Pressdee, J. S.	1949-*1966*	561	86	13805	150*	29.06	13	6
Prideaux, R. M.	1958-1967	498	43	15097	202*	33.18	26	8
Pullar, G.	1954-1967	609	55	19985	175	36.07	39	9+1
Quaife, W. G.	1894-1928	1203	186	36021	255*	35.41	72	24
Ranjitsinhji, K. S.	1893-1920	500	62	24692	285*	56.37	72	11+1
Read, J. M.	1880-1895	599	41	13570	186*	24.31	10	2
Read, W. W.	1873-1897	738	50	21568	338	31.62	37	9
Reid, J. R.	*1947*-1965	414	28	16067	296	41.62	39	2+3
Relf, A. E.	1900-1921	900	69	22176	189*	26.68	26	11
Relf, R. R.	1905-1933	527	18	14441	272*	28.37	24	6
Revill, A. C.	1946-1960	654	53	15917	156*	26.48	16	9
Reynolds, B. L.	1950-1967	657	54	16989	169	28.17	20	10
Rhodes, W.	1898-1930	1528	237	39802	267*	30.83	58	20+1
Richardson, D. W.	1952-1967	660	65	16303	169	27.40	16	9
Richardson, P. E.	1949-1965	794	41	26055	185	34.60	44	11+1
Richardson, V. Y.	*1918-1937*	297	12	10714	231	37.59	27	—
Robertson, J. D.	1937-1959	897	46	31914	331*	37.50	67	14+1
Robins, R. W. V.	1925-1958	566	39	13940	140	26.45	11	4
Robson, E.	1895-1923	761	46	12620	163*	17.65	5	1
Rogers, N. H.	1946-1955	529	28	16056	186	32.04	28	9
Rowan, E. A. B.	*1929-1953*	258	17	11710	306*	48.58	30	2
Roy, P.	*1946-1966*	294	18	11798	202*	42.74	33	1
Russell, A. C.	1908-1930	719	59	27546	273	41.73	71	13
Russell, W. E.	1956-1967	593	50	19187	193	35.33	33	9
Ryder, J.	*1912-1935*	274	37	10494	295	44.28	24	0+1
Sainsbury, P. J.	1954-1967	647	134	13609	163	26.52	5	6
Sandham, A.	1911-*1937*	1000	79	41283	325	44.82	107	18+2
Santall, F. R.	1919-1939	797	86	17730	201*	24.93	21	7
Seymour, James	1900-1926	911	62	27238	218*	32.08	53	16
Sharp, J.	1899-1925	805	75	22715	211	31.11	38	10
Sharpe, P. J.	1956-1967	495	56	13186	203*	30.03	15	7
Shepherd, T. F.	1919-1932	531	61	18715	277*	39.81	42	12
Sheppard, D. S.	1947-*1962*	395	31	15838	239*	43.51	45	6+1
Shipman, A.	1920-1936	661	72	13682	226	23.22	15	8
Shrewsbury, A.	1875-1902	801	88	26306	267	36.89	59	13
Simpson, R. B.	*1952-1966*	377	59	18591	359	58.46	52	2+7
Simpson, R. T.	*1944*-1963	852	55	30546	259	38.32	64	13+1
Sinfield, R. A.	1921-1939	696	86	15674	209*	25.69	16	10
Smith, D.	1927-1952	753	63	21843	225	31.65	32	12
Smith, D. V.	1946-1962	625	66	16960	206*	30.34	19	8
Smith, E. J.	1904-1930	814	55	16997	177	22.42	20	6
Smith, H.	1912-1935	656	56	13413	149	22.35	10	5
Smith, M. J. K.	1951-1967	855	103	31580	204	41.99	55	14+1
Smith, R.	1934-1956	682	88	12042	147	20.27	8	4
Smith, S. G.	*1899-1925*	379	30	10918	256	31.28	14	4
Smith, T. P. B.	1929-1952	692	126	10170	163	17.98	8	1
Sobers, G. St. A.	*1952*-1967	318	45	15998	365*	58.60	50	3+5
Spooner, R. H.	1899-1923	393	16	13681	247	36.28	31	6
Spooner, R. T.	1948-1959	580	72	13874	168*	27.31	12	6
Sprot, E. M.	1898-1914	458	28	12328	147	28.66	13	4

Batting-10,000 Runs—*Cont.*

	Career	*Inns.*	*N.O.*	*Runs*	*H.S.*	*Avge.*	*100s*	*1000s*
Squires, H. S.	1928-1949	658	44	19186	236	31.24	37	11
Staples, A.	1924-1938	512	60	12762	153*	28.23	12	7
Stephenson, H. W.	1948-1964	747	91	13195	147*	20.11	7	5
Stevens, G. T. S.	1919-1933	381	36	10288	182	29.82	12	2
Stewart, M. J.	1954-1967	687	64	21098	227*	33.86	43	12
Stewart, W. J.	1955-1967	433	48	13077	182*	33.96	19	5
Stocks, F. W.	1946-1957	430	45	11397	171	29.60	13	5
Stoddart, A. E.	1885-1900	537	16	16738	221	32.12	26	6
Stone, J.	1900-1923	526	63	10362	174	22.38	6	3
Storer, H.	1920-1936	517	29	13515	232	27.69	18	6
Storer, W.	1887-1905	490	41	12966	216*	28.87	17	7
Subba Row, R.	1951-1964	405	65	14178	300	41.70	30	6
Sugg, F. H.	1883-1899	510	29	11653	220	24.22	15	5
Sutcliffe, B.	*1941-1965*	400	38	17196	385	47.50	44	2+2
Sutcliffe, H.	1919-1945	1087	123	50135	313	52.00	149	21+3
Suttle, K. G.	1949-1967	907	81	26231	204*	31.75	40	15
Tarrant, F. A.	*1898-1936*	535	46	17629	250	36.04	32	9
Tate, M. W.	1912-1937	969	102	21698	203	25.02	23	11+1
Taylor, B.	1949-1967	728	54	15082	135	22.37	6	7
Taylor, H. W.	*1909-1935*	340	27	13105	250*	41.87	30	3
Taylor, K.	1953-1967	485	33	12284	203*	27.17	16	6
Tennyson, Lord	1913-*1937*	759	38	16828	217	23.33	19	7
Thompson, G. J.	1897-1922	606	59	12018	131*	21.97	9	3
Timms, J. E.	1925-1949	847	30	20457	213	25.03	31	11
Titmus, F. J.	1949-1967	828	132	17260	137*	24.79	5	8
Todd, L. J.	1927-1950	727	94	20087	174	31.73	38	10
Tompkin, M.	1938-1956	655	29	19927	186	31.83	31	10
Townsend, A.	1948-1960	553	70	12054	154	24.95	6	5
Townsend, L. F.	1922-1939	786	76	19555	233	27.54	22	9
Tremlett, M. F.	1947-1960	681	49	16038	185	25.37	16	10
Tribe, G. E.	*1945*-1959	454	82	10177	136*	27.35	7	7
Trott, A. E.	*1892*-1911	601	52	10696	164	19.48	8	2
Trumper, V. T.	*1894-1913*	401	21	16939	300*	44.57	42	4+1
Tunnicliffe, J.	1891-1907	806	59	20268	243	27.13	23	12
Turnbull, M. J.	1924-1939	626	37	17543	233	29.78	29	10
Tyldesley, E.	1909-1936	961	106	38874	256*	45.46	102	18+1
Tyldesley, J. T.	1895-1923	994	62	37897	295*	40.66	86	19
Ulyett, G.	1873-1893	912	39	20484	199*	23.46	18	9
Umrigar, P. R.	*1944-1965*	346	41	16023	252*	52.53	49	2+2
Valentine, B. H.	1927-1950	645	38	18306	242	30.15	35	9
Vine, J.	1896-1922	920	79	25171	202	29.94	34	14
Wainwright, E.	1888-1902	603	31	12485	228	21.82	19	3
Walcott, C. L.	*1941-1963*	238	29	11820	314*	56.55	40	2+2
Walker, I. D.	1862-1884	491	39	11098	179	24.55	7	—
Walker, P. M.	1956-1967	569	70	12680	152*	25.41	7	8
Walker, W.	1913-1937	624	60	18259	165*	32.37	31	10
Walters, C. F.	1923-1935	427	32	12145	226	30.74	21	5
Ward, A.	1886-1904	642	51	17783	219	30.08	29	9
Warner, P. F.	1894-1929	875	75	29028	244	36.28	60	14
Washbrook, C.	1933-1964	906	107	34101	251*	42.67	76	17+3
Watkins, A. J.	1939-1963	753	87	20362	170*	30.57	32	13
Watson, F.	1920-1937	688	50	23596	300*	36.98	50	12
Watson, W.	1939-1964	753	109	25670	257	39.86	55	14
Webbe, A. J.	1875-1900	634	58	14236	243*	24.71	14	1
Weekes, E. D.	*1944*-1964	241	24	12010	304*	52.90	36	2+1
Wellard, A. W.	1927-1950	679	45	12515	112	19.73	2	4
Wensley, A. F.	1922-*1939*	590	64	10735	154	20.40	9	3
Wharton, A.	1946-1963	745	69	21796	199	32.24	31	11
White, J. C.	1909-1937	765	102	12202	192	18.40	6	2
Whitehead, H.	1898-1922	680	25	15112	174	23.07	14	4
Whysall, W. W.	1910-1930	601	44	21592	248	38.74	51	10
Wight, P. B.	*1950*-1965	590	53	17773	222*	33.09	28	10
Wilson, A. E.	1932-1955	502	77	10744	188	25.28	7	6
Wilson, J. V.	1946-1963	770	79	21650	230	31.33	30	14
Wilson, R. C.	1952-1967	647	39	19515	159*	32.09	30	13
Wolton, A. V.	1947-1960	478	61	12907	165	30.95	12	7
Wood, C. J. B.	1896-1923	823	54	23879	255	31.05	37	13

Batting-10,000 Runs—*Cont.*

	Career	Inns.	N.O.	Runs	H.S.	Avge.	100s	1000s
Woodfull, W. M. ..	*1921-1934*	245	39	13392	284	65.00	49	3
Woods, S. M. J. ..	1886-1910	690	35	15352	215	23.43	19	4
Wooller, W.	1935-1960	677	77	13586	128	22.64	5	5
Woolley, C. N. ..	1909-1931	658	34	15395	204*	24.67	13	7
Woolley, F. E. ..	1906-1938	1532	85	58969	305*	40.75	145	28
Worrell, F. M. M. ..	*1941*-1964	326	49	15025	308*	54.24	39	2+2
Worthington, T. S...	1924-1947	720	59	19221	238*	29.07	31	10
Wrathall, H. ..	1894-1907	509	20	11023	176	22.54	9	4
Wright, L. G. ..	1883-1909	593	12	15166	195	26.10	20	6
Wyatt, R. E. S. ..	1923-1957	1141	157	39404	232	40.04	85	17+1
Yardley, N. W. D...	1935-1955	658	75	18173	138*	31.17	27	8
Young, A.	1911-1933	537	22	13159	198	25.55	11	5
Young, D. M. ..	1946-1964	842	42	24555	198	30.69	40	13

MOST CENTURIES IN A CAREER

	Career	100s	First	Date of 100th	Last	Inns. for 100 cents.
J. B. Hobbs	1905-1934	197	1905	1923	1934	821
E. Hendren	1907-1938	170	1911	1928	1937	740
W. R. Hammond	1920-1951	167	1923	1935	1947	679
C. P. Mead	1905-1936	153	1906	1927	1936	892
H. Sutcliffe	1919-1945	149	1919	1932	1939	700
F. E. Woolley	1906-1938	145	1906	1929	1938	1031
L. Hutton	1934-1960	129	1934	1951	1955	619
W. G. Grace	1865-1908	126	1866	1895	1904	1113
D. C. S. Compton	1936-1964	123	1936	1952	1964	552
D. G. Bradman..	*1927-1948*	117	1927	1947	1948	295
T. W. Graveney	1948-1967	115	1948	1964	1967	940
A. Sandham	1911-*1937*	107	1913	1935	1937	871
T. W. Hayward	1893-1914	104	1893	1913	1914	1076
L. E. G. Ames	1926-1951	102	1926	1950	1951	915
E. Tyldesley	1909-1936	102	1912	1934	1935	919

J. W. Hearne (1909-1936) 96
C. B. Fry (1892-*1921*) 94
W. J. Edrich (1934-1958) 86
J. T. Tyldesley (1895-1923) 86
P. B. H. May (1948-1963) 85
R. E. S. Wyatt (1923-1957) 85
J. Hardstaff, Jnr. (1930-1955) 83
M. C. Cowdrey (1950-1967) 81
M. Leyland (1920-1948) 80
John Langridge (1928-1955) 76
C. Washbrook (1933-1964) 76
H. T. W. Hardinge (1902-1933) .. 75
R. Abel (1881-1904) 74
K. F. Barrington (1953-1967) 74
D. J. Kenyon (1946-1967) 74
J. O'Connor (1921-1939) 72
W. G. Quaife (1894-1928) 72
K. S. Ranjitsinhji (1893-1920) 72
D. Brookes (1934-1959) 71
A. C. Russell (1908-1930) 71
D. Denton (1894-1920) 69
R. N. Harvey (*1946-1962*) 67
P. Holmes (1913-1935) 67
J. D. Robertson (1937-1959) 67
P. A. Perrin (1896-1928) 66
R. T. Simpson (*1944*-1963) 64
G. Gunn (1902-1932) 62
G. H. Hirst (1891-1929) 60
R. E. Marshall (*1945*-1967) 60
P. F. Warner (1894-1929) 60
A. L. Hassett (*1932-1953*) 59
A. Shrewsbury (1875-1902) 59
A. E. Fagg (1932-1957) 58
W. Rhodes (1898-1930) 58
Vijay Hazare (*1934-1966*) 57
L. B. Fishlock (1931-1952) 56
C. Hallows (1914-1932) 55
M. J. K. Smith (1951-1967) 55
W. Watson (1939-1964) 55
D. J. Insole (1947-1963) 54
W. W. Keeton (1926-1952) 54
W. Bardsley (*1903-1927*) 53
A. E. Dipper (1908-1932) 53
G. L. Jessop (1894-1914) 53
James Seymour (1900-1926) 53
E. H. Bowley (1912-1934) 52
A. Ducat (1906-1931) 52
R. B. Simpson (*1952-1966*) 52
W. W. Whysall (1910-1930) 51
G. Cox (1931-1960) 50
E. R. Dexter (1956-1967) 50
H. E. Dollery (1933-1955) 50
K. S. Duleepsinhji (1924-1932) .. 50
J. H. Edrich (1956-1967) 50
H. Gimblett (1935-1954) 50
G. St. A. Sobers (*1952*-1967) 50
F. Watson (1920-1937) 50

Batting—*Cont.*

1000 RUNS IN AN ENGLISH SEASON MOST TIMES

All dates are inclusive.

28 W. G. Grace (Gloucestershire): 1869-1878, 1883-1890, 1892-1898, 1900-1902.
28 F. E. Woolley (Kent): 1907-1938.
27 C. P. Mead (Hampshire): 1906-1936.
24 W. G. Quaife (Warwickshire): 1896-1906, 1908-1914, 1920-1923, 1925-1926.
24 J. B. Hobbs (Surrey): 1905-1920, 1922-1933.
21 D. Denton (Yorkshire): 1895-1897, 1899-1920.
21 E. Hendren (Middlesex): 1911, 1913, 1919-1937.
21 H. Sutcliffe (Yorkshire): 1919-1939.
20 G. Gunn (Nottinghamshire): 1905, 1908-1911, 1913-1931.
20 T. W. Hayward (Surrey): 1895-1914.
20 James Langridge (Sussex): 1927-1939, 1946-1952.
20 W. Rhodes (Yorkshire): 1903-1926.

BOWLING

2000 WICKETS IN A CAREER

	Career	*Runs*	*Wkts.*	*Avge.*	*100 wkts.*
W. Rhodes	1898-1930	69993	4187	16.71	23
A. P. Freeman	1914-1936	69577	3776	18.42	17
C. W. L. Parker	1903-1935	63821	3278	19.46	16
J. T. Hearne	1888-1923	54342	3061	17.75	15
T. W. Goddard..	1922-1952	59116	2979	19.84	16
W. G. Grace†	1865-1908	51545	2876	17.92	10
A. S. Kennedy	1907-1936	61044	2874	21.24	15
M. W. Tate	1912-1937	50544	2783	18.16	13+1
D. Shackleton	1948-1967	51320	2741	18.72	19
G. H. Hirst	1891-1929	51300	2739	18.72	15
G. A. R. Lock	1946-1967	50730	2678	18.94	14
C. Blythe	1899-1914	42136	2506	16.81	14
W. E. Astill	1906-1939	57784	2431	23.76	9
J. C. White	1909-1937	43759	2356	18.57	14
W. E. Hollies	1932-1957	48656	2323	20.94	14
F. S. Trueman	1949-1967	40628	2235	18.17	12
R. T. D. Perks	1930-1955	53770	2233	24.07	16
J. Briggs	1879-1900	35289	2212	15.95	12
J. B. Statham	1950-1967	35762	2190	16.32	13
G. Dennett	1903-1926	42568	2147	19.82	12
T. Richardson	1892-1905	38794	2105	18.42	10
T. E. Bailey	1945-1967	48170	2082	23.13	9
F. E. Woolley	1906-1938	41066	2068	19.85	8
G. Geary	1912-1938	41339	2063	20.03	11
D. V. P. Wright	1932-1957	49305	2056	23.98	10
J. A. Newman	1906-1930	51211	2032	25.20	9
S. Haigh	1895-1913	32091	2012	15.94	11
A. Shaw..	1864-1897	24179	2001	12.08	9

†*Webber's revised figures are: 50250 runs 2763 wkts (Avge. 18.18) 100 wkts.: 7*

1000 WICKETS IN A CAREER

Allen, D. A.	1953-1967	23311	1006	23.17	1
Arnold, E. G.	1899-1913	24745	1069	23.14	4
Astill, W. E.	1906-1939	57784	2431	23.76	9
Attewell, W.	1881-1900	29745	1932	15.39	10
Bailey, T. E.	1945-1967	48170	2082	23.13	9
Bannister, J. D..	1950-1967	25291	1160	21.80	4
Barratt, F.	1914-1931	27803	1224	22.71	5
Bedser, A. V.	1939-1960	39281	1924	20.41	11
Bestwick, W.	1898-1925	31003	1458	21.33	4
Blythe, C.	1899-1914	42136	2506	16.81	14
Bowes, W. E.	1928-1947	27446	1638	16.75	9
Boyes, G. S.	1921-1939	34610	1472	23.51	3
Braund, L. C.	1896-1920	30388	1113	27.30	4
Briggs, J.	1879-1900	35289	2212	15.95	12
Brown, F. R.	1930-1959	31917	1219	26.18	3

Bowling-1,000 Wickets—*Cont.*

	Career	*Runs*	*Wkts.*	*Avge.*	*100 wkts.*
Buckenham, C. P.	1899-1914	29157	1152	25.31	6
Clark, E. W.	1922-1947	25919	1203	21.54	2
Clay, J. C.	1921-1949	26003	1315	19.77	3
Close, D. B.	1949-1967	26448	1038	25.47	2
Cook, C.	1946-1964	36578	1782	20.52	9
Copson, W. H.	1932-1950	20752	1094	18.96	3
Cornford, J.	1931-1952	26999	1019	26.49	—
Cox, G. R.	1895-1928	42138	1843	22.86	5
Dean, H.	1906-1921	23606	1301	18.14	8
Dennett, G.	1903-1926	42568	2147	19.82	12
Dooland, B.	*1945-1957*	22332	1016	21.98	5
Douglas, J. W. H. T.	1901-1930	44176	1894	23.32	7
Durston, T. J.	1919-1933	23279	1329	22.03	6
Eastman, L. C.	1920-1939	26980	1006	26.81	—
Emmett, T.	1866-1888	21147	1582	13.36	4
Fender, P. G. H.	1910-1936	47457	1894	25.05	7
Field, F. E.	1897-1920	24094	1026	23.48	3
Fielder, A.	1900-1914	26852	1277	21.02	5
Flavell, J. A.	1949-1967	32847	1529	21.48	8
Flowers, W.	1877-1896	18687	1169	15.98	2
Freeman, A. P.	1914-1936	69577	3776	18.42	17
Geary, G.	1912-1938	41339	2063	20.03	11
Giffen, G.	*1877-1903*	21782	1022	21.31	3
Gladwin, C.	1939-1958	30265	1653	18.30	12
Goddard, T. W.	1922-1952	59116	2979	19.84	16
Gover, A. R.	1928-1948	36753	1555	23.63	8
Grace, W. G.	1865-1908	51545	2876	17.99	10
Grimmett, C. V.	*1911-1940*	31740	1424	22.28	3
Grundy, J.	1850-1869	10355	1045	13.05	1
Gunn, J.	1896-1932	30659	1245	24.62	4
Haig, N. E.	1912-1936	30666	1116	27.47	5
Haigh, S.	1895-1913	32091	2012	15.94	11
Hallam, A. W.	1895-1910	19256	1012	19.02	3
Hearne, A.	1884-1910	22925	1144	20.03	—
Hearne, J. T.	1888-1923	54342	3061	17.75	15
Hearne, J. W.	1909-1936	44927	1839	24.43	5
Herman, O. W.	1929-1948	28222	1045	27.00	5
Hilton, M. J.	1946-1961	19536	1006	19.41	4
Hirst, G. H.	1891-1929	51300	2739	18.72	15
Hitch, J. W.	1907-1925	30041	1398	21.48	7
Hollies, W. E.	1932-1957	48656	2323	20.94	14
Howorth, R.	1933-1951	29427	1345	21.87	9
Illingworth, R.	1951-1967	27916	1434	19.46	9
Jackson, H. L.	1947-1963	30101	1733	17.36	10
Jackson, P. F.	1929-1950	30521	1159	26.33	4
Jenkins, R. O.	1938-1958	30925	1309	23.62	5
Jepson, A.	1938-1959	30567	1051	29.08	1
Jupp, V. W. C.	1909-1938	38166	1658	23.01	10
Kennedy, A. S.	1907-1936	61044	2874	21.24	15
King, J. H.	1895-1925	30289	1204	25.15	2
Laker, J. C.	1946-*1964*	35789	1944	18.40	11
Langford, B. A.	1953-1967	26811	1138	23.55	5
Langridge, James	1924-1953	34524	1530	22.56	6
Larwood, H.	1924-1938	24998	1427	17.51	8
Lees, W. S.	1896-1911	29998	1402	21.39	7
Lillywhite, James	1862-1881	17535	1140	15.38	1
Llewellyn, C. B.	*1894*-1912	23715	1013	23.41	3
Loader, P. J.	1951-*1963*	25260	1326	19.04	7
Lock, G. A. R.	1946-1967	50730	2678	18.94	14
Lockwood, W. H.	1886-1904	25245	1376	18.34	7
Lohmann, G. A.	1884-*1897*	25110	1805	13.91	8
Macaulay, G. G.	1920-1935	32440	1837	17.65	10
McDonald, E. A.	*1909*-1935	28966	1395	20.76	7
Martin, F.	1885-1900	22903	1317	17.38	6
Mayer, J. H.	1926-1939	25404	1144	22.20	2
Mead, W.	1892-1913	36387	1916	18.99	10
Mercer, J.	1919-1947	37302	1593	23.41	9

Bowling-1,000 Wickets—*Cont.*

	Career	*Runs*	*Wkts.*	*Avge.*	*100 wkts.*
Mitchell, T. B.	1928-1939	30526	1483	20.58	10
Mold, A.	1889-1901	26012	1673	15.54	9
Morgan, D. C.	1950-1967	29719	1195	24.86	—
Morley, F.	1872-1883	16475	1231	13.38	7
Mortimore, J. B.	1950-1967	30029	1349	22.26	3
Moss, A. E.	1950-1967	26992	1299	20.77	5
Newman, J. A.	1906-1930	51211	2032	25.20	9
Nichols, M. S.	1924-1939	39738	1834	21.66	11
Paine, G. A. E.	1926-1947	23334	1021	22.85	5
Parker, C. W. L.	1903-1935	63821	3278	19.47	16
Parkin, C. H.	1906-1926	18434	1048	17.58	4
Peate, E.	1879-1890	14511	1076	13.48	6
Peel, R.	1882-1899	28446	1754	16.21	8
Perks, R. T. D.	1930-1955	53770	2233	24.07	16
Pollard, R.	1933-1952	25314	1122	22.56	7
Preston, K. C.	1948-1964	30543	1160	26.32	1
Relf, A. E.	1900-1921	39724	1897	20.94	11
Rhodes, W.	1898-1930	69993	4187	16.71	23
Richardson, T.	1892-1905	38794	2105	18.42	10
Richmond, T. L.	1912-1932	24959	1176	21.22	7
Ridgway, F.	1946-1960	25317	1067	23.72	1
Robinson, E. P.	1934-1952	22784	1009	22.58	5
Robson, E.	1895-1923	30334	1147	26.44	—
Root, C. F.	1910-1933	31933	1512	21.11	9
Ryan, F. B.	1919-1931	21314	1008	21.14	5
Santall, S.	1894-1914	29250	1219	23.99	1
Shackleton, D.	1948-1967	51320	2741	18.72	19
Shaw, A.	1864-1897	24179	2001	12.08	9
Shepherd, D. J.	1950-1967	38364	1833	20.92	11
Sims, J. M.	1929-1953	39401	1582	24.90	8
Sinfield, R. A.	1921-1939	28734	1173	24.49	4
Smith, D. R.	1956-1967	24501	1058	23.15	5
Smith, H. A.	1925-1939	27968	1076	25.99	5
Smith, R.	1934-1956	41265	1350	30.56	7
Smith, T. P. B.	1929-1952	45193	1697	26.63	6
Smith, W. C.	1900-1914	18910	1077	17.55	3
Southerton, J.	1854-1879	23268	1626	14.30	10
Spencer, C. T.	1952-1967	32299	1219	26.49	1
Staples, S. J.	1920-1934	30421	1331	22.85	5
Statham, J. B.	1950-1967	35762	2190	16.32	13
Tarrant, F. A.	*1898-1936*	26104	1470	17.75	8
Tate, F. W.	1887-1905	28690	1331	21.55	5
Tate, M. W.	1912-1937	50544	2783	18.16	13+1
Tattersall, R.	1948-1964	24704	1369	18.04	8
Thompson, G. J.	1897-1922	30060	1591	18.89	8
Thomson, N. I.	1952-1965	32785	1596	20.54	12
Titmus, F. J.	1949-1967	42884	1996	21.48	13
Townsend, L. F.	1922-1939	22985	1088	21.12	4
Tribe, G. E.	*1945*-1959	28321	1378	20.55	8
Trott, A. E.	*1892*-1911	35316	1674	21.09	7
Trueman, F. S.	1949-1967	40628	2235	18.17	12
Tyldesley, R.	1919-1935	25980	1509	17.21	10
Verity, H.	1930-1939	29099	1956	14.87	9
Voce, W.	1927-1952	35961	1558	23.08	6
Wainwright, E.	1888-1902	19331	1062	18.20	5
Walsh, J. E.	*1936*-1956	29225	1190	24.55	7
Wardle, J. H.	1946-1958	34910	1842	18.95	10
Wass, T. G.	1896-1920	34091	1666	20.46	10
Watson, A.	1872-1893	18123	1351	13.41	1
Wellard, A. W.	1927-1950	39302	1614	24.35	8
Wensley, A. F.	1922-*1939*	29989	1135	26.42	5
White, J. C.	1909-1937	43759	2356	18.57	14
Willsher, E.	1850-1874	14921	1188	13.07	1
Woods, S. M. J.	1886-1910	21653	1040	20.82	2
Woolley, F. E.	1906-1938	41066	2068	19.85	8
Wright, D. V. P.	1932-1957	49305	2056	23.98	10
Young, J. A.	1933-1956	26795	1361	19.68	8

Bowling—*Cont.*

100 WICKETS IN A SEASON MOST TIMES

23 W. Rhodes (Yorkshire): 1898-1909, 1911, 1914-1924, 1926, 1928-1929.
19 D. Shackleton (Hampshire): 1949-1967.
17 A. P. Freeman (Kent): 1920-1936.
16 C. W. L. Parker (Gloucestershire): 1920-1935.
16 T. W. Goddard (Gloucestershire): 1929-1939, 1946-1950.
16 R. T. D. Perks (Worcestershire): 1934-1939, 1946-1955.
15 J. T. Hearne (Middlesex): 1891-1895, 1897, 1899-1900. 1902-1904, 1906, 1908, 1910-1911.
15 G. H. Hirst (Yorkshire): 1895-1897, 1901, 1903-1913.
15 A. S. Kennedy (Hampshire): 1912, 1914-1925, 1927-1932.
14 C. Blythe (Kent): 1900, 1902-1914.
14 J. C. White (Somerset): 1919-1932.
14 W. E. Hollies (Warwickshire): 1935, 1937-1939, 1946-1952, 1954-1955, 1957.
14 G. A. R. Lock (Surrey & Leicestershire): 1951-1962, 1966-1967.
13 M. W. Tate (Sussex): 1922-1932, 1934-1935 (also in India in 1926-1927).
13 J. B. Statham (Lancashire): 1952-1953, 1955, 1957-1966.
13 F. J. Titmus (Middlesex): 1953-1957, 1959-1965, 1967.
12 J. Briggs (Lancashire): 1887-1897, 1900.
12 G. Dennett (Gloucestershire): 1904-1914, 1921.
12 C. Gladwin (Derbyshire): 1946-1949, 1951-1958.
12 N. I. Thomson (Sussex): 1953-1964.
12 F. S. Trueman (Yorkshire): 1954-1955, 1957-1966.

100 WICKETS IN MOST SEASONS CONSECUTIVELY

19 D. Shackleton (Hampshire): 1949-1967 inclusive.

ALL-ROUND CRICKET

10,000 RUNS AND 1000 WICKETS IN A CAREER

	Career	*Runs*	*Avge.*	*100s*	*Wkts.*	*Avge.*	*'Doubles'*
Arnold, E. G.	1899-1913	15853	29.91	24	1069	23.14	4
Astill, W. E.	1906-1939	22726	22.54	15	2431	23.76	9
Bailey, T. E.	1945-1967	28642	33.42	28	2082	23.13	8
Braund, L. C.	1896-1920	17801	25.61	25	1113	27.30	3
Briggs, J.	1879-1900	14002	18.25	10	2212	15.95	—
Brown, F. R.	1930-1959	13275	27.42	22	1219	26.18	2
Close, D. B.	1949-1967	23923	31.93	36	1038	25.47	2
Cox, G. R.	1895-1928	14643	18.74	2	1843	22.86	—
Douglas, J. W. H. T.	1901-1930	24530	27.90	26	1894	23.32	5
Eastman, L. C.	1920-1939	13438	20.80	7	1006	26.80	—
Fender, P. G. H.	1910-1936	19034	26.65	21	1894	25.05	6
Flowers, W.	1877-1896	12691	20.34	9	1169	15.98	1
Geary, G.	1912-1938	13498	19.82	8	2063	20.03	—
Giffen, G.	*1877-1903*	11757	29.61	18	1022	21.31	3
Grace, W. G. †	1865-1908	54896	39.55	126	2876	17.99	8
Gunn, J.	1896-1932	24740	33.34	41	1245	24.62	4
Haig, N. E.	1912-1936	15208	20.83	12	1116	27.47	3
Haigh, S.	1895-1913	11715	18.65	4	2012	15.94	1
Hearne, A.	1884-1910	16287	21.74	15	1144	20.03	—
Hearne, J. W.	1909-1936	37252	40.98	96	1839	24.43	5
Hirst, G. H.	1891-1929	36323	34.13	60	2739	18.72	14
Howorth, R.	1933-1951	11479	20.68	4	1345	21.87	3
Illingworth, R.	1951-1967	15691	27.57	15	1434	19.39	6
Jenkins, R. O.	1938-1958	10073	22.23	1	1309	23.62	2
Jupp, V. W. C.	1909-1938	23278	29.39	30	1658	23.01	10
Kennedy, A. S.	1907-1936	16586	18.53	10	2874	21.24	5
King, J. H.	1895-1925	25121	27.33	34	1204	25.15	1
Langridge, James	1924-1953	31716	35.20	42	1530	22.56	6
Llewellyn, C. B.	*1894*-1912	11425	26.75	18	1013	23.41	3
Lockwood, W. H.	1886-1904	10673	21.91	15	1376	18.34	2
Morgan, D. C.	1950-1967	16700	24.59	8	1195	24.86	—
Mortimore, J. B.	1950-1967	13194	18.98	3	1349	22.26	3
Newman, J. A.	1906-1930	15333	21.65	10	2032	25.20	5
Nichols, M. S.	1924-1939	17843	26.51	20	1834	21.66	8

All-round Cricket-10,000 Runs and 1,000 Wickets—*Cont.*

	Career	*Runs*	*Avge.*	*100s*	*Wkts.*	*Avge.*	*'Doubles'*
Peel, R.	1882-1899	12135	19.46	7	1754	16.21	1
Relf, A. E.	1900-1921	22176	26.68	26	1897	20.94	8
Rhodes, W.	1898-1930	39802	30.83	58	4187	16.71	16
Robson, E.	1895-1923	12620	17.65	5	1147	26.44	—
Sinfield, R. A.	1921-1939	15674	25.69	16	1173	24.49	2
Smith, R.	1934-1956	12042	20.27	8	1350	30.56	3
Smith, T. P. B.	1929-1952	10170	17.98	8	1697	26.63	1
Tarrant, F. A.	*1898-1936*	17629	36.04	32	1470	17.75	8
Tate, M. W.	1912-1937	21698	25.02	23	2783	18.16	8
Thompson, G. J.	1897-1922	12018	21.97	9	1591	18.89	2
Titmus, F. J.	1949-1967	17260	24.79	5	1996	21.48	8
Townsend, L. F.	1922-1939	19555	27.54	22	1088	21.12	3
Tribe, G. E.	*1945*-1959	10177	27.35	7	1378	20.55	7
Trott, A. E.	*1892*-1911	10696	19.48	8	1674	21.09	2
Wainwright, E.	1888-1902	12485	21.82	19	1062	18.20	1
Wellard, A. W.	1927-1950	12515	19.73	2	1614	24.35	3
Wensley, A. F.	1922-*1939*	10735	20.40	9	1135	26.42	1
White, J. C.	1909-1937	12202	18.40	6	2356	18.57	2
Woods, S. M. J.	1886-1910	15352	23.43	19	1040	20.82	—
Woolley, F. E.	1906-1938	58969	40.75	145	2068	19.85	8
† [Grace, W. G. (By Webber)	1865-1908	53856	39.45	124	2763	18.18	7]

FIELDING AND WICKET-KEEPING

MOST DISMISSALS IN A CAREER

Fielders	*Career*	*Catches*
F. E. Woolley (Kent)	1906-1938	913
W. G. Grace (Gloucestershire)	1865-1908	871
W. R. Hammond (Gloucestershire)	1920-1951	819
G. A. R. Lock (Surrey, Western Australia & Leicestershire)	1946-1967	796
John Langridge (Sussex)	1928-1955	786
E. Hendren (Middlesex)	1907-1938	722
W. Rhodes (Yorkshire)	1898-1930	708
J. Tunnicliffe (Yorkshire)	1891-1907	691
C. A. Milton (Gloucestershire)	1948-1967	676
C. P. Mead (Hampshire)	1905-1936	668
James Seymour (Kent)	1900-1926	622
K. J. Grieves (New South Wales & Lancashire)	*1945*-1964	599
D. B. Close (Yorkshire)	1949-1967	576
A. O. Jones (Nottinghamshire)	1892-1914	575
A. S. M. Oakman (Sussex)	1949-1967	571
P. G. H. Fender (Sussex & Surrey)	1910-1936	558
M. J. Stewart (Surrey)	1954-1967	551
G. H. Hirst (Yorkshire)	1891-1929	550
J. V. Wilson (Yorkshire)	1946-1963	545
D. C. Morgan (Derbyshire)	1950-1967	536
E. G. Hayes (Surrey & Leicestershire)	1896-1926	533
A. S. Kennedy (Hampshire)	1907-1936	523
P. M. Walker (Glamorgan)	1956-1967	523
W. J. Edrich (Middlesex)	1934-1958	522
G. R. Cox (Sussex)	1895-1928	510
L. C. Braund (Surrey & Somerset)	1896-1920	508
D. B. Carr (Derbyshire)	1945-1967	500

Wicket-keepers	*Career*	*Total*	*Ct.*	*St.*
H. Strudwick (Surrey)	1902-1927	1468	1215	253
F. H. Huish (Kent)	1895-1914	1328	952	376
D. Hunter (Yorkshire)	1889-1909	1327	995	372
H. R. Butt (Sussex)	1890-1912	1262	971	291
H. Elliott (Derbyshire)	1920-1947	1195	895	300
J. H. Board (Gloucestershire)	1891-*1914*	1132	797	335
L. E. G. Ames (Kent)	1926-1951	1113	698	415
G. Duckworth (Lancashire)	1923-1947	1090	751	339

Fielding and Wicket-keeping—*Cont.*

Wicket-keepers	*Career*	*Total*	*Ct.*	*St.*
H. W. Stephenson (Somerset)	1948-1964	1080	751	329
J. T. Murray (Middlesex)	1952-1967	1069	909	160
T. G. Evans (Kent)	1939-1967	1059	810	249
R. Booth (Yorkshire & Worcestershire)	1951-1967	1046	877	169
G. O. Dawkes (Leicestershire & Derbyshire) ..	1937-1961	1039	893	146
T. W. Oates (Nottinghamshire)	1897-1925	1005	766	239
W. F. Cornford (Sussex)	1921-1947	1000	656	334
W. F. Price (Middlesex)	1926-1947	964	648	316
B. Taylor (Essex)	1949-1967	964	824	140
J. G. Binks (Yorkshire)	1955-1967	936	785	151
K. V. Andrew (Northants)	1952-1966	903	721	182
J. M. Parks (Sussex)	1949-1967	895	825	70
A. A. Lilley (Warwickshire)	1891-1911	833	679	204
A. Wood (Yorkshire)	1928-1947	848	603	245
W. T. Luckes (Somerset)	1924-1949	820	586	234
E. W. Brookes (Surrey)	1925-1939	819	724	95
E. J. Smith (Warwickshire)	1904-1930	819	676	143
M. Sherwin (Nottinghamshire)	1876-1896	800	579	221
A. J. McIntyre (Surrey)	1938-1960	791	634	157
H. G. Davies (Glamorgan)	1935-1958	788	584	204
B. Lilley (Nottinghamshire)	1921-1937	777	645	132
R. T. Spooner (Warwickshire)	1948-1959	768	589	179

CAREER RECORDS FOR LEADING OVERSEAS PLAYERS

The shorter programme of first-class matches overseas has resulted in only a few overseas batsmen reaching career aggregates of 10,000 runs and, with four notable exceptions, no bowler has taken 1000 wickets.

Players reaching either of these two aggregates are also listed in the appropriate earlier sections. The following tables record the highest aggregates by players from the six major overseas countries.

Overseas players who later migrated to English counties are omitted from these tables unless their 'home' career justifies their inclusion.

BATTING

AUSTRALIA

	Career	*Inns.*	*N.O.*	*Runs*	*H.S.*	*Avge.*	*100s*	*1000s*
D. G. Bradman.. ..	*1927-1948*	338	43	28067	452*	95.14	117	4+12
R. N. Harvey	*1946-1962*	461	35	21699	231*	50.92	67	3+6
R. B. Simpson	*1952-1966*	377	59	18591	359	58.46	52	2+7
C. Hill	*1892-1925*	417	21	17216	365*	43.47	45	3+2
W. L. Murdoch ..	*1876-1904*	684	48	17070	321	26.83	20	3
W. Bardsley	*1903-1927*	376	35	17031	264	49.94	53	4+1
V. T. Trumper.. ..	*1894-1913*	401	21	16939	300*	44.57	42	4+1
A. L. Hassett	*1932-1953*	322	32	16890	232	58.24	59	3+2
W. W. Armstrong ..	*1898-1921*	407	61	16177	303*	46.75	45	4+2
S. E. Gregory	*1889-1912*	592	55	15303	201	28.49	25	4
C. G. Macartney ..	*1905-1935*	360	32	15050	345	45.88	49	3
P. J. Burge	*1952-1966*	344	45	14321	283	47.89	37	2+5
K. R. Miller	*1937*-1959	326	36	14183	281*	48.90	41	2+2
M. A. Noble	*1893-1919*	378	34	14034	284	40.80	37	4+1
W. A. Brown	*1932-1949*	284	15	13840	265*	51.44	39	3+2
W. H. Ponsford.. ..	*1920-1934*	235	23	13819	437	65.18	47	2+2
N. C. O'Neill	*1955-1966*	304	34	13805	284	51.12	45	2+5
W. M. Woodfull ..	*1921-1934*	245	39	13392	284	65.00	49	3
A. F. Kippax	*1918-1935*	254	33	12747	315*	57.69	43	1+2
A. R. Morris	*1940-1954*	242	15	12489	290	55.01	46	2+4
C. L. McCool	*1939*-1960	413	36	12420	172	32.94	18	5
S. J. McCabe	*1928-1941*	262	20	11951	240	49.39	29	3
W. M. Lawry	*1955-1966*	262	23	11809	266	49.41	33	3+2
G. Giffen	*1877-1903*	421	24	11757	271	28.61	18	4
R. Benaud	*1948-1963*	359	44	11432	187	36.29	23	—
C. C. McDonald ..	*1947-1962*	307	26	11375	229	40.48	24	1

Career Records for Leading Overseas Players—*Cont.*

	Career	*Inns.*	*N.O.*	*Runs*	*H.S.*	*Avge.*	*100s*	*1000s*
L. E. Favell	*1951-1966*	302	8	10929	190	37.17	23	0+2
B. C. Booth	*1954-1966*	262	34	10824	214*	47.47	26	2+2
K. D. Mackay	*1946-1963*	294	46	10823	223	43.64	23	1
V. Y. Richardson ..	*1918-1937*	297	12	10714	231	37.59	27	—
J. Darling	*1893-1907*	334	25	10637	210	34.42	21	4
J. Ryder..	*1912-1935*	274	37	10494	295	44.28	24	0+1

SOUTH AFRICA

	Career	*Inns.*	*N.O.*	*Runs*	*H.S.*	*Avge.*	*100s*	*1000s*
A. D. Nourse, Snr. ..	*1896-1935*	371	39	14216	304*	42.82	38	3+1
H. W. Taylor	*1909-1935*	340	27	13105	250*	41.87	30	3
A. D. Nourse, Jnr. ..	*1931-1952*	269	27	12472	260*	51.53	41	2
D. J. McGlew	*1947-1966*	299	34	12070	255*	45.54	27	3+1
E. A. B. Rowan ..	*1929-1953*	258	17	11710	306*	48.58	30	2
C. B. Llewellyn.. ..	*1894*-1912	461	34	11425	216	26.75	18	6
B. Mitchell	*1925-1949*	281	30	11395	195	45.39	30	3+1
R. A. McLean	*1949-1965*	318	20	10969	207	36.80	22	2
A. Melville	*1928-1948*	295	15	10598	189	37.85	25	3
T. L. Goddard	*1952-1966*	261	16	10192	222	41.60	24	2+1
J. H. B. Waite	*1948-1965*	312	33	9698	219	34.76	22	1
K. G. Viljoen	*1926-1948*	209	25	7964	215	43.28	23	2
W. R. Endean	*1945-1963*	230	25	7757	247	37.83	15	1+1
I. J. Siedle	*1922-1936*	204	11	7730	265*	40.05	17	2
E. J. Barlow	*1959*-1967	175	10	7166	212	43.43	16	1+1

WEST INDIES

	Career	*Inns.*	*N.O.*	*Runs*	*H.S.*	*Avge.*	*100s*	*1000s*
G. St. A. Sobers ..	*1952*-1967	318	45	15998	365*	58.60	50	3+5
F. M. M. Worrell ..	*1941*-1964	326	49	15025	308*	54.24	39	2+2
E. D. Weekes	*1944*-1964	241	24	12010	304*	52.90	36	2+1
R. B. Kanhai	*1954*-1967	271	20	11845	256	47.19	32	3+2
C. L. Walcott	*1941-1963*	238	29	11820	314*	56.55	40	2+2
S. G. Smith	*1899-1925*	379	30	10918	256	31.28	14	4
G. A. Headley	*1927*-1954	164	22	9921	344*	69.86	33	2+1
C. C. Hunte	*1950*-1967	222	19	8916	263	43.92	16	1+1
J. B. Stollmeyer ..	*1938-1956*	194	16	7942	324	44.61	14	1+1
B. F. Butcher	*1954-1966*	178	20	7872	209*	49.82	21	2+1
G. E. Gomez	*1937*-1957	182	27	6764	216*	43.63	14	1
S. M. Nurse	*1958*-1967	156	12	6214	213	43.15	19	1
G. Challenor	*1905-1929*	160	9	5822	237*	38.55	15	2
R. J. Christiani.. ..	*1938-1953*	142	16	5103	181	40.50	12	1

NEW ZEALAND

	Career	*Inns.*	*N.O.*	*Runs*	*H.S.*	*Avge.*	*100s*	*1000s*
B. Sutcliffe	*1941-1965*	400	38	17196	385	47.50	44	2+2
J. R. Reid	*1947*-1965	414	28	16067	296	41.62	39	2+3
C. C. Dacre	*1914*-1936	437	20	12166	223	29.17	24	7
C. S. Dempster.. ..	*1921-1947*	305	36	12098	212	44.97	35	5
T. C. Lowry	*1917-1937*	322	20	9421	181	31.19	18	3
M. P. Donnelly.. ..	*1936*-1950	219	26	9210	208*	47.72	23	5
R. C. Blunt	*1917-1931*	204	14	7769	338*	40.88	14	2
W. M. Wallace.. ..	*1933-1960*	190	17	7609	211	43.98	16	2
W. A. Hadlee	*1933-1951*	202	17	7421	198	40.11	17	2
S. N. McGregor ..	*1948-1966*	255	15	6096	114*	25.40	3	—
M. L. Page	*1921-1942*	213	17	5857	206	29.88	9	1
V. J. Scott	*1937-1952*	128	16	5575	204	49.77	16	1
G. T. Dowling	*1958-1966*	172	10	5425	206	33.48	7	—
M. E. Chapple	*1949-1965*	201	16	5344	165	28.88	4	—
J. W. E. Mills	*1925-1937*	161	8	5025	185	32.84	11	2
G. L. Weir	*1928-1946*	172	16	5022	191	32.19	10	1
B. W. Sinclair	*1955-1966*	167	12	5001	138	32.26	6	—

Career Records for Leading Overseas Players—*Cont.*

INDIA

	Career	Inns.	N.O.	Runs	H.S.	Avge.	100s	1000s
Vijay Hazare	*1934-1966*	357	43	17972	316*	57.23	57	2+5
P. R. Umrigar	*1944-1965*	346	41	16023	252*	52.53	49	2+2
V. M. Merchant ..	*1929-1951*	221	44	12876	359*	72.74	43	2+1
Mushtaq Ali	*1932-1963*	358	16	12413	233	36.29	30	1
V. L. Manjrekar ..	*1949-1966*	274	35	11952	283	50.00	36	1+1
P. Roy	*1946-1966*	294	18	11798	202*	42.74	33	1
V. M. Mankad	*1935-1963*	357	26	11544	231	34.87	26	1
Nawab of Pataudi, Jnr.	1957-1967	364	31	11356	203*	34.10	24	4+2
C. G. Borde	*1952*-1967	290	50	10513	177*	43.80	27	1+2
C. K. Nayudu	*1916-1963*	305	15	10159	200	35.03	21	2

PAKISTAN

	Career	Inns.	N.O.	Runs	H.S.	Avge.	100s	1000s
Hanif Mohammad	*1951*-1967	285	36	14101	499	56.63	47	2+3
Imtiaz Ahmed	*1944-1964*	296	31	10005	300*	37.75	22	2+1
Saeed Ahmed	*1954*-1967	227	18	8615	172	41.22	23	1+1

BOWLING

AUSTRALIA

	Career	Runs	Wkts.	Avge.	100s
C. V. Grimmett	*1911-1940*	31740	1424	22.19	3
E. A. McDonald	*1909*-1935	28966	1395	20.76	7
G. Giffen	*1877-1903*	21782	1022	21.31	3
C. T. B. Turner	*1882-1909*	14154	992	14.27	3+1
R. Benaud	*1948-1963*	23193	935	24.80	0+1
H. Trumble	*1887-1903*	17134	929	18.44	4
F. R. Spofforth	*1874*-1897	12646	840	15.05	2
W. W. Armstrong	*1898-1921*	16367	828	19.77	3
J. J. Ferris	*1886-1897*	14249	813	17.52	2
R. R. Lindwall	*1941-1961*	16962	794	21.36	—
A. A. Mailey	*1912-1930*	18775	779	24.10	2
W. J. O'Reilly	*1927-1945*	12850	774	16.60	2
A. K. Davidson	*1949-1962*	14052	672	20.91	—
E. Jones	*1892-1907*	14676	645	22.75	2
M. A. Noble	*1893-1919*	14492	628	23.08	—
I. W. Johnson	*1935-1956*	14419	619	23.29	—
G. E. Palmer	*1878-1896*	10686	614	17.40	3
C. L. McCool	*1939*-1960	16543	602	27.48	—
L. O. Fleetwood-Smith	*1931-1939*	13519	597	22.64	1
W. A. Johnston	*1945-1954*	12934	554	23.34	1
J. V. Saunders	*1899-1913*	12072	553	21.83	1
W. P. Howell	*1894-1905*	11171	521	21.44	1
J. M. Gregroy	1919-*1928*	10579	504	20.99	2
K. R. Miller	*1937*-1959	11080	497	22.29	—
W. J. Whitty	*1907-1925*	11488	491	23.40	1
H. Ironmonger	*1909-1935*	9992	464	21.53	—
G. D. McKenzie	*1959*-1967	14180	457	31.02	—
D. T. Ring	*1938*-1953	12855	451	28.50	—
T. W Garrett	*1876-1896*	8366	445	18.80	2
A. Cotter	*1901-1913*	10739	441	24.35	1
C. G. Macartney	*1905-1935*	8781	419	20.96	—
F. Laver	*1891-1913*	9987	404	24.72	1

SOUTH AFRICA

	Career	Runs	Wkts.	Avge.	100s
C. B. Llewellyn	*1894*-1912	23715	1013	23.41	3
H. J. Tayfield	*1945-1962*	18696	851	21.96	2
J. H. Sinclair	*1892-1911*	10527	491	21.43	—
T. L. Goddard	*1952-1966*	10258	475	21.61	—
A. H. McKinnon	*1952-1966*	9677	459	21.08	—
G. A. Faulkner	*1902*-1924	7852	449	17.42	1
S. J. Pegler	*1908*-1930	8324	425	19.58	2
N. A. T. Adcock	*1952-1962*	6979	405	17.23	1

Career Records for Leading Overseas Players—*Cont.*

	Career	*Runs*	*Wkts.*	*Avge.*	*100s*
A. E. E. Vogler	*1903*-1912	7275	401	18.14	1
R. O. Schwarz	1901-1914	7000	398	17.58	1
J. T. Partridge	*1951-1966*	7808	376	20.75	—
J. E. Waddington	*1934-1958*	9155	375	24.41	—
C. P. Carter	*1897*-1924	6849	366	18.71	—
V. I. Smith	*1945-1959*	8244	365	21.58	—
J. J. Kotze	1901-*1910*	6217	348	17.86	1
G. B. Lawrence	*1955-1966*	6146	342	17.97	—
E. P. Nupen	*1920-1936*	6077	334	18.19	—
P. M. Pollock	*1958*-1967	6783	315	21.53	—
J. T. Botten	*1957-1966*	6057	313	19.35	—
A. D. Nourse, Snr.	*1896-1935*	7125	305	23.36	—
WEST INDIES					
S. G. Smith	*1898-1925*	17277	955	18.09	4
S. Ramadhin	*1949*-1965	15342	758	20.24	2
G. St. A. Sobers	*1952*-1967	16017	584	27.42	—
W. W. Hall	*1955-1966*	12064	479	25.18	—
A. L. Valentine	*1949-1964*	12446	475	26.20	1
L. N. Constantine	*1921*-1945	8738	424	20.60	2
L. R. Gibbs	*1953*-1967	10073	403	24.99	—
F. M. M. Worrell	*1941*-1964	10116	349	28.86	—
C. B. Clarke	*1937*-1960	8694	331	26.26	—
C. R. Brown	1919-*1936*	6557	290	22.61	—
C. C. Griffith	*1959-1966*	5769	290	19.89	1
H. C. Griffith	*1922-1934*	7092	254	27.92	—
D. Atkinson	*1946-1960*	5347	200	26.73	—
NEW ZEALAND					
R. W. Blair	*1951-1964*	9961	537	18.54	—
W. E. Merritt	*1926*-1947	13669	536	25.50	1
J. R. Reid	*1947*-1965	10313	458	22.51	—
F. J. Cameron	*1952-1966*	9658	447	21.60	—
T. B. Burtt	*1943-1954*	9054	408	22.19	1
J. C. Alabaster	*1955-1966*	10248	400	25.62	—
R. C. Motz	*1957-1966*	8743	395	22.13	—
A. M. Moir	*1949-1961*	9040	368	24.56	—
H. B. Cave	*1945-1958*	8664	362	23.93	—
J. A. Cowie	*1932-1949*	7972	359	22.20	1
A. R. MacGibbon	*1947-1961*	9228	352	26.21	—
A. D. Downes	*1888-1913*	4564	311	14.67	—
INDIA					
V. M. Mankad	*1935-1963*	19094	776	24.60	—
C. S. Nayudu	*1931-1960*	16526	619	26.69	—
S. P. Gupte	*1947-1963*	12567	530	23.71	—
Amir Elahi	*1934-1953*	12380	479	25.84	—
D. G. Phadkar	*1942-1959*	10272	465	22.09	—
L. Amar Singh	*1931-1939*	8511	459	18.54	—
L. Amarnath	*1931-1963*	10194	451	22.59	—
R. G. Nadkarni	*1951-1966*	9377	438	21.40	—
R. B. Desai	*1958-1966*	9782	417	23.45	—
Ghulam Ahmed	*1939-1958*	9190	407	22.57	—
PAKISTAN					
Fazal Mahmood	*1943-1963*	8705	459	18.96	—
Mahmood Hussain	*1949-1965*	8004	322	24.85	—
Intikhab Alam	*1957*-1967	8656	317	27.30	—
Shuja-ud-Din	*1946-1965*	6290	283	22.22	—

THE COUNTY CHAMPIONSHIP

PRINCIPAL DATES

1864-86 .. No county championship as such existed, although contemporary references show that a champion county was proclaimed at least from 1864 onwards. There was no generally accepted method of determining the holders of this title. Although the "least matches lost" method existed, it was not consistently applied and evidence exists that the playing quality of a team was equally as important as its results.

1873 .. .. Rules agreed governing playing qualification for counties. Counties considered first-class: Derbyshire, Gloucestershire, Kent, Lancashire, Middlesex, Nottinghamshire, Surrey, Sussex and Yorkshire.

1887 .. .. Introduction of first points system for deciding championship: one point for a win, half for a draw.

1890 .. .. First agreement among the counties themselves concerning the method of deciding the championship.

1891 .. .. Somerset regularly admitted to championship from this date although some contemporary references show the county's inclusion between 1881 and 1885.

1894 .. .. M.C.C. invited to designate the county champions.

1895 .. .. Championship expanded from 9 to 14 counties: Derbyshire (dropped out in 1887) and Hampshire (considered first-class from 1874 to 1878 and—perhaps—from 1880 to 1885) were re-admitted, and Essex, Leicestershire and Warwickshire were admitted.

1899 .. .. Worcestershire were admitted—did not take part in 1919.

1905 .. .. Northamptonshire admitted.

1921 .. .. Glamorgan admitted.

CHAMPION COUNTIES (1864-1967)

1864	Surrey
1865	Nottinghamshire
1866	Middlesex
1867	Yorkshire
1868	Nottinghamshire
1869	Nottinghamshire
	Yorkshire
1870	Yorkshire
1871	Nottinghamshire
1872	Nottinghamshire
1873	Gloucestershire
	Nottinghamshire
1874	Gloucestershire
1875	Nottinghamshire
1876	Gloucestershire
1877	Gloucestershire
1878	Undecided
1879	Nottinghamshire
	Lancashire
1880	Nottinghamshire
1881	Lancashire
1882	Nottinghamshire
	Lancashire
1883	Nottinghamshire
1884	Nottinghamshire
1885	Nottinghamshire
1886	Nottinghamshire
1887	Surrey
1888	Surrey
1889	Nottinghamshire
	Lancashire
	Surrey
1890	Surrey
1891	Surrey
1892	Surrey
1893	Yorkshire
1894	Surrey
1895	Surrey
1896	Yorkshire
1897	Lancashire
1898	Yorkshire
1899	Surrey
1900	Yorkshire
1901	Yorkshire
1902	Yorkshire
1903	Middlesex
1904	Lancashire
1905	Yorkshire
1906	Kent
1907	Nottinghamshire
1908	Yorkshire
1909	Kent
1910	Kent
1911	Warwickshire
1912	Yorkshire
1913	Kent
1914	Surrey
1919	Yorkshire
1920	Middlesex
1921	Middlesex
1922	Yorkshire
1923	Yorkshire
1924	Yorkshire
1925	Yorkshire
1926	Lancashire
1927	Lancashire
1928	Lancashire
1929	Nottinghamshire
1930	Lancashire
1931	Yorkshire
1932	Yorkshire
1933	Yorkshire
1934	Lancashire
1935	Yorkshire
1936	Derbyshire
1937	Yorkshire
1938	Yorkshire
1939	Yorkshire
1946	Yorkshire
1947	Middlesex
1948	Glamorgan
1949	Middlesex
	Yorkshire
1950	Lancashire
	Surrey
1951	Warwickshire
1952	Surrey
1953	Surrey
1954	Surrey
1955	Surrey
1956	Surrey
1957	Surrey
1958	Surrey
1959	Yorkshire
1960	Yorkshire
1961	Hampshire
1962	Yorkshire
1963	Yorkshire
1964	Worcestershire
1965	Worcestershire
1966	Yorkshire
1967	Yorkshire

The County Championship—*Cont.*

MOST OUTRIGHT CHAMPIONSHIP WINS: 30 Yorkshire

EARLIEST DATE FOR WINNING CHAMPIONSHIP: August 12th 1910 Kent.
(Since 1895 expansion)

FINAL POSITIONS SINCE 1895

Season	DERBYSHIRE	ESSEX	GLAMORGAN	GLOUCESTERSHIRE	HAMPSHIRE	KENT	LANCASHIRE	LEICESTERSHIRE	MIDDLESEX	NORTHAMPTONSHIRE	NOTTINGHAMSHIRE	SOMERSET	SURREY	SUSSEX	WARWICKSHIRE	WORCESTERSHIRE	YORKSHIRE
1895	5	9	—	4	10	14	2	12	6	—	12	8	1	11	6	—	3
1896	7	5	—	10	8	9	2	13	3	—	6	11	4	14	12	—	1
1897	14	3	—	5	9	12	1	13	8	—	10	11	2	6	7	—	4
1898	9	5	—	3	12	7	6	13	2	—	8	13	4	9	9	—	1
1899	15	6	—	9	10	8	4	13	2	—	10	13	1	5	7	12	3
1900	13	10	—	7	15	3	2	14	7	—	5	11	7	3	6	12	1
1901	15	10	—	14	7	7	3	12	2	—	9	12	6	4	5	11	1
1902	10	13	—	14	15	7	5	11	12	—	3	7	4	2	6	9	1
1903	12	8	—	13	14	8	4	14	1	—	5	10	11	2	7	6	3
1904	10	14	—	9	15	3	1	7	4	—	5	12	11	6	7	13	2
1905	14	12	—	8	16	6	2	5	11	13	10	15	4	3	7	8	1
1906	16	7	—	9	8	1	4	15	11	11	5	11	3	10	6	14	2
1907	16	7	—	10	12	8	6	11	5	15	1	14	4	13	9	2	2
1908	14	11	—	10	9	2	7	13	4	15	8	16	3	5	12	6	1
1909	15	14	—	16	8	1	2	13	6	7	10	11	5	4	12	8	3
1910	15	11	—	12	6	1	4	10	3	9	5	16	2	7	14	13	8
1911	14	6	—	12	11	2	4	15	3	10	8	16	5	13	1	9	7
1912	12	15	—	11	6	3	4	13	5	2	8	14	7	10	9	16	1
1913	13	15	—	9	10	1	8	14	6	4	5	16	3	7	11	12	2
1914	12	8	—	16	5	3	11	13	2	9	10	15	1	6	7	14	4
1919	9	14	—	8	7	2	5	9	13	12	3	5	4	11	15	—	1
1920	16	9	—	8	11	5	2	13	1	14	7	10	3	6	12	15	4
1921	12	15	17	7	6	4	5	11	1	13	8	10	2	9	16	14	3
1922	11	8	16	13	6	4	5	14	7	15	2	10	3	9	12	17	1
1923	10	13	16	11	7	5	3	14	8	17	2	9	4	6	12	15	1
1924	17	15	13	6	12	5	4	11	2	16	6	8	3	10	9	14	1
1925	14	7	17	10	9	5	3	12	6	11	4	15	2	13	8	16	1
1926	11	9	8	15	7	3	1	13	6	16	4	14	5	10	12	17	2
1927	5	8	15	12	13	4	1	7	9	16	2	14	6	10	11	17	3
1928	10	16	15	5	12	2	1	9	8	13	3	14	6	7	11	17	4
1929	7	12	17	4	11	8	2	9	6	13	1	15	10	4	14	16	2
1930	9	6	11	2	13	5	1	12	16	17	4	13	8	7	15	10	3
1931	7	10	15	2	12	3	6	16	11	17	5	13	8	4	9	14	1
1932	10	14	15	13	8	3	6	12	10	16	4	7	5	2	9	17	1
1933	6	4	16	10	14	3	5	17	12	13	8	11	9	2	7	15	1
1934	3	8	13	7	14	5	1	12	10	17	9	15	11	2	4	16	5
1935	2	9	13	15	16	10	4	6	3	17	5	14	11	7	8	12	1
1936	1	9	16	4	10	8	11	15	2	17	5	7	6	14	13	12	3
1937	3	6	7	4	14	12	9	16	2	17	10	13	8	5	11	15	1
1938	5	6	16	10	14	9	4	15	2	17	12	7	3	8	13	11	1
1939	9	4	13	3	15	5	6	17	2	16	12	14	8	10	11	7	1
1946	15	8	6	5	10	6	3	11	2	16	13	4	11	17	14	8	1
1947	5	11	9	2	16	4	3	14	1	17	11	11	6	9	15	7	7
1948	6	13	1	8	9	15	5	11	3	17	14	12	2	16	7	10	4
1949	15	9	8	7	16	13	11	17	1	6	11	9	5	13	4	3	1
1950	5	17	11	7	12	9	1	16	14	10	15	7	1	13	4	6	3
1951	11	8	5	12	9	16	3	15	7	13	17	14	6	10	1	4	2
1952	4	10	7	9	12	15	3	6	5	8	16	17	1	13	10	14	2
1953	6	12	10	6	14	16	3	3	5	11	8	17	1	2	9	15	12
1954	3	15	4	13	14	11	10	16	7	7	5	17	1	9	6	11	2
1955	8	14	16	12	3	13	9	6	5	7	11	17	1	4	9	15	2

The County Championship-Final Positions—*Cont.*

Season	DERBYSHIRE	ESSEX	GLAMORGAN	GLOUCESTERSHIRE	HAMPSHIRE	KENT	LANCASHIRE	LEICESTERSHIRE	MIDDLESEX	NORTHAMPTONSHIRE	NOTTINGHAMSHIRE	SOMERSET	SURREY	SUSSEX	WARWICKSHIRE	WORCESTERSHIRE	YORKSHIRE
1956	12	11	13	3	6	16	2	17	5	4	8	15	1	9	14	9	7
1957	4	5	9	12	13	14	6	17	7	2	15	8	1	9	11	16	3
1958	5	6	15	14	2	8	7	12	10	4	17	3	1	13	16	9	11
1959	7	9	6	2	8	13	5	16	10	11	17	12	3	15	4	14	1
1960	5	6	11	8	12	10	2	17	3	9	16	14	7	4	15	13	1
1961	7	6	14	5	1	11	13	9	3	16	17	10	15	8	12	4	2
1962	7	9	14	4	10	11	16	17	13	8	15	6	5	12	3	2	1
1963	17	12	2	8	10	13	15	16	6	7	9	3	11	4	4	14	1
1964	12	10	11	17	12	7	14	16	6	3	15	8	4	9	2	1	5
1965	9	15	3	10	12	5	13	14	6	2	17	7	8	16	11	1	4
1966	9	16	14	15	11	4	12	8	12	5	17	3	7	10	6	2	1
1967	6	15	14	17	12	2	11	3	7	9	16	8	4	13	10	5	1

AGGREGATE RECORDS FOR EACH COUNTY

The highest aggregates of runs, centuries, and wickets for each county in a season and in a career are listed. All first-class matches for the county are included, not championship matches alone.

HIGHEST AGGREGATE OF RUNS IN A SEASON

	Season	*Inns.*	*N.O.*	*Runs*	*H.S.*	*Avge.*	*100s*
Derbyshire—D. B. Carr	1959	52	7	2165	156*	48.11	5
Essex—J. O'Connor	1934	47	6	2308	248	56.29	9
Glamorgan—W. G. A. Parkhouse ..	1959	45	3	2071	154	49.30	6
Gloucestershire—W. R. Hammond ..	1933	46	5	2860	264	69.75	11
Hampshire—C. P. Mead	1928	45	9	2854	180	79.27	12
Kent—F. E. Woolley	1928	52	3	2894	198	59.06	10
Lancashire—J. T. Tyldesley	1901	51	4	2633	221	56.02	8
Leicestershire—L. G. Berry	1937	51	4	2446	184*	52.04	7
Middlesex—W. J. Edrich	1947	38	7	2650	267*	85.48	10
Northamptonshire—D. Brookes ..	1952	50	7	2198	204*	51.11	6
Nottinghamshire—W. W. Whysall ..	1929	52	3	2620	244	53.46	7
Somerset—W. E. Alley	1961	58	11	2761	221*	56.82	10
Surrey—T. W. Hayward	1906	53	8	3246	219	72.13	13
Sussex—John Langridge	1949	49	5	2850	234*	64.77	12
Warwickshire—M. J. K. Smith ..	1959	50	10	2417	200*	60.42	6
Worcestershire—H. H. Gibbons ..	1934	57	6	2654	157	52.03	8
Yorkshire—H. Sutcliffe	1932	41	5	2883	313	80.08	12

MOST CENTURIES IN A SEASON

Derbyshire	6	L. F. Townsend in 1933.
Essex	9	J. O'Connor in 1934 and D. J. Insole in 1955.
Glamorgan	7	W. G. A. Parkhouse in 1950.
Gloucestershire	13	W. R. Hammond in 1938.
Hampshire	12	C. P. Mead in 1928.
Kent	10	F. E. Woolley in 1928 and 1934.
Lancashire	11	C. Hallows in 1928.
Leicestershire	7	L. G. Berry in 1937 and W. Watson in 1959.
Middlesex	13	D. C. S. Compton in 1947.
Northamptonshire	8	R. Haywood in 1921.
Nottinghamshire	9	W. W. Whysall in 1928.
Somerset	10	W. E. Alley in 1961.
Surrey	13	T. W. Hayward in 1906 and J. B. Hobbs in 1925.
Sussex	12	John Langridge in 1949.
Warwickshire	8	R. E. S. Wyatt in 1937.
Worcestershire	9	C. F. Walters in 1933.
Yorkshire	12	H. Sutcliffe in 1932.

Aggregate Records for Each County—*Cont.*

HIGHEST AGGREGATE OF WICKETS IN A SEASON

	Season	*Overs*	*Mdns.*	*Runs*	*Wkts.*	*Avge.*
Derbyshire—T. B. Mitchell	1935	866.5	134	3284	168	19.55
Essex—T. P. B. Smith	1947	1606	287	4667	172	27.13
Glamorgan—J. C. Clay	1937	1103.3	229	3052	176	17.34
Gloucestershire—T. W. Goddard	1937	1335	325	3730	222	16.80
	1947	1327.1	323	3636	222	16.37
Hampshire—A. S. Kennedy	1922	1190.3	322	2967	190	15.61
Kent—A. P. Freeman	1933	1829.2	610	3862	262	14.74
Lancashire—E. A. McDonald	1925	1204.4	277	3674	198	18.55
Leicestershire—J. E. Walsh	1948	1124.3	185	3224	170	18.96
Middlesex—F. J. Titmus	1955	1179	443	2312	158	14.63
Northamptonshire—G. E. Tribe	1955	1272	341	3273	175	18.70
Nottinghamshire—B. Dooland	1954	1197.4	393	2708	181	14.96
Somerset—A. W. Wellard	1938	1168.4	233	3152	169	19.24
Surrey—T. Richardson	1895	1444.4	394	3515	250	14.06
Sussex—M. W. Tate	1925	1440	416	2669	198	13.45
Warwickshire—W. E. Hollies	1946	1470	432	2725	180	15.13
Worcestershire—C. F. Root	1925	1440.5	404	3627	207	17.52
Yorkshire—W. Rhodes	1900	1366.4	411	3054	240	12.72

HIGHEST AGGREGATE OF RUNS IN A CAREER

	Career	*Runs*	*H.S.*	*Avge.*	*100s*
Derbyshire—D. Smith	1927-1952	20516	225	31.41	30
Essex—P. A. Perrin	1896-1928	29162	343*	36.18	65
Glamorgan—E. Davies	1924-1954	26104	287*	27.82	31
Gloucestershire—W. R. Hammond	1920-1951	33664	317	57.05	113
Hampshire—C. P. Mead	1905-1936	48892	280*	48.84	138
Kent—F. E. Woolley	1906-1938	48483	270	42.05	112
Lancashire—J. T. Tyldesley	1895-1923	32267	295*	41.68	73
Leicestershire—L. G. Berry	1924-1951	30106	232	30.53	45
Middlesex—E. Hendren	1907-1937	40302	301*	49.81	119
Northamptonshire—D. Brookes	1934-1959	28980	257	36.13	67
Nottinghamshire—G. Gunn	1902-1932	31327	220	36.71	56
Somerset—H. Gimblett	1935-1954	21108	310	37.09	49
Surrey—J. B. Hobbs	1905-1934	43703	316*	49.77	144
Sussex—John Langridge	1928-1955	34152	250*	37.69	76
Warwickshire—W. G. Quaife	1894-1928	34172	255*	35.31	71
Worcestershire—D. Kenyon	1946-1967	34490	259	34.04	70
Yorkshire—H. Sutcliffe	1919-1945	38561	313	50.21	112

MOST CENTURIES IN A CAREER

With a few exceptions the batsman scoring the most runs for a county has also scored the most centuries, the four different records being as follows:

Essex	71	by J. O'Connor	1921-1939
Glamorgan	32	by W. G. A. Parkhouse	1948-1964
Lancashire	91	by E. Tyldesley	1909-1936
Nottinghamshire	62	by J. Hardstaff, Jnr.	1930-1955

HIGHEST AGGREGATE OF WICKETS IN A CAREER

	Career	*Wkts.*	*Avge.*
Derbyshire—H. L. Jackson	1947-1963	1670	17.11
Essex—T. P. B. Smith	1929-1951	1611	26.26
Glamorgan—D. J. Shepherd	1950-1967	1804	20.56
Gloucestershire—C. W. L. Parker	1903-1935	3171	19.43
Hampshire—D. Shackleton	1948-1967	2553	18.35
Kent—A. P. Freeman	1914-1936	3359	14.45
Lancashire—J. B. Statham	1950-1967	1747	15 04
Leicestershire—W. E. Astill	1906-1939	2130	23.19
Middlesex—J. T. Hearne	1888-1923	2133	17.94
Northamptonshire—E. W. Clark	1922-1947	1097	21.31
Nottinghamshire—T. G. Wass	1896-1914	1653	20.40

Highest Aggregate of Wickets in a Career—*Cont.*

	Career	*Wkts.*	*Avge.*
Somerset—J. C. White	1909-1937	2153	18.10
Surrey—T. Richardson	1892-1905	1775	17.91
Sussex—M. W. Tate	1912-1937	2223	16.34
Warwickshire—W. E. Hollies	1932-1957	2201	20.45
Worcestershire—R. T. D. Perks	1930-1955	2143	23.73
Yorkshire—W. Rhodes	1898-1930	3608	16.00

FIRST-CLASS COUNTY CRICKET CLUBS

	DERBYSHIRE	*ESSEX*
Present club formed:	Nov. 4, 1870	Jan. 14, 1876
Colours:	Chocolate, amber and pale blue	Blue, gold and red
Badge:	Rose and crown	Three scimitars above scroll bearing 'Essex'
Champions:	(1) 1936	(0) Third in 1897

	GLAMORGAN	*GLOUCESTERSHIRE*
Present club formed:	July 6, 1888	1871
Colours:	Blue and gold	Blue, gold, brown, sky-blue, green and red
Badge:	Gold daffodil	Coat of Arms of the City and County of Bristol
Champions:	(1) 1948	(3) 1874, 1876, 1877
Joint champions:		(1) 1873

	HAMPSHIRE	*KENT*
Present club formed:	Aug. 12, 1863	Mar. 1, 1859
Substantially reorganised:	July 1879	Dec. 6, 1870
Colours:	Blue, gold and white	Red and white
Badge:	Tudor rose and crown	White horse
Champions:	(1) 1961	(4) 1906, 1909, 1910 and 1913

	LANCASHIRE	*LEICESTERSHIRE*
Present club formed:	Jan. 12, 1864	Mar. 25, 1879
Colours:	Red, green and blue	Scarlet and dark green
Badge:	Red rose	Gold running fox on green background
Champions:	(8) 1881, 1897, 1904, 1926, 1927, 1928, 1930 and 1934	(0) Third in 1953 and in 1967
Joint champions:	(4) 1879, 1882, 1889 and 1950	

	MIDDLESEX	*NORTHAMPTONSHIRE*
Present club formed:	Dec. 15, 1863	1820
Substantially reorganised:		July 31, 1878
Colours:	Blue	Maroon
Badge:	Three Seaxes	Tudor Rose
Champions:	(5) 1866, 1903, 1920, 1921 and 1947	(0) Runners-up in 1912, 1957 and 1965
Joint champions:	(1) 1949	

	NOTTINGHAMSHIRE	*SOMERSET*
Present club formed:	Mar./Apr. 1841	Aug. 18, 1875
Substantially reorganised:	Dec. 11, 1866	
Colours:	Green and gold	Black, white and maroon
Badge:	County Badge of Nottinghamshire	Wessex Wyvern
Champions:	(12) 1865, 1868, 1871, 1872, 1875, 1880, 1883, 1884, 1885, 1886, 1907 and 1929	(0) Third in 1892, 1958, 1963 and 1966
Joint champions:	(5) 1869, 1873, 1879, 1882 and 1889	

First-class County Cricket Clubs—*Cont.*

	SURREY	*SUSSEX*
Present club formed: ..	Aug. 22, 1845	Mar. 1, 1839
Substantially reorganised:		Aug. 1857
Colours:	Chocolate	Dark blue, light blue and gold
Badge:	Prince of Wales' Feathers	County Arms of six Martlets
Champions:	(17) 1864, 1887, 1888, 1890, 1891, 1892, 1894, 1895, 1899, 1914, 1952, 1953, 1954, 1955, 1956, 1957 and 1958	(0) Runners-up in 1902, 1903, 1932, 1933, 1934 and 1953
Joint champions:	(2) 1889 and 1950	

	WARWICKSHIRE	*WORCESTERSHIRE*
Present club formed: ..	Jan. 19, 1884	Mar. 5, 1865
Colours:	Blue, yellow and white	Dark green and black
Badge:	Bear and ragged staff	Shield, *Argent* bearing *Fess* between three *Pears Sable*
Champions:	(2) 1911 and 1951	(2) 1964 and 1965

	YORKSHIRE
Present club formed: ..	Jan. 8, 1863
Substantially reorganised:	Dec. 10, 1891
Colours:	Oxford blue, Cambridge blue and gold
Badge:	White rose
Champions:	(30) 1867, 1870, 1893, 1896, 1898, 1900, 1901, 1902, 1905, 1908, 1912, 1919, 1922, 1923, 1924, 1925, 1931, 1932, 1933, 1935, 1937, 1938, 1939, 1946, 1959, 1960, 1962, 1963, 1966 and 1967
Joint champions:	(2) 1869 and 1949

COUNTY CAPTAINS

Before the abolition of amateur status in first-class cricket after the 1962 season it was unusual for a professional to be officially appointed as county captain. Professionals appointed before 1963 are listed in italics.

DERBYSHIRE

1894-1898	S. H. Evershed
1899-1901	S. H. Hill-Wood
1902-1903	A. E. Lawton
1904-1905	A. E. Lawton and E. M. Ashcroft
1906	A. E. Lawton and L. G. Wright
1907	L. G. Wright
1908	A. E. Lawton and L. G. Wright
1909	A. E. Lawton
1910-1912	J. Chapman
1913-1914	R. R. C. Baggallay
1919-1920	L. Oliver
1921	G. M. Buckston
1922-1930	G. R. Jackson
1931-1936	A. W. Richardson
1937-1939	R. H. R. Buckston
1946	G. F. Hodgkinson
1947-1948	E. J. Gothard
1949	D. A. Skinner
1950	P. Vaulkhard
1951-1954	G. L. Willatt
1955-1962	D. B. Carr
1963-1964	C. Lee
1965-1967	D. C. Morgan

ESSEX

1894	A. P. Lucas
1895-1900	H. G. Owen
1901	H. G. Owen and A. P. Lucas
1902	H. G. Owen
1903	C. J. Kortright
1904-1906	F. L. Fane
1907-1910	C. P. McGahey
1911-1928	J. W. H. T. Douglas
1929-1932	H. M. Morris
1933-1938	T. N. Pearce and D. R. Wilcox
1939	D. R. Wilcox, F. St. G. Unwin and J. W. A. Stephenson
1946-1949	T. N. Pearce
1950	T. N. Pearce and D. J. Insole
1951-1960	D. J. Insole
1961-1966	T. E. Bailey
1967	B. Taylor

GLAMORGAN

1921	N. V. H. Riches
1922-1923	T. A. L. Whittington
1924-1927	J. C. Clay

County Captains—*Cont.*

GLAMORGAN-Cont.

1928 T. Arnott
1929 J. C. Clay and N. V. H. Riches
1930-1939 M. J. Turnbull
1946 J. C. Clay
1947-1960 W. Wooller
1961-1966 O. S. Wheatley
1967 A. R. Lewis

GLOUCESTERSHIRE

1871-1898 W. G. Grace
1899 W. Troup
1900-1912 G. L. Jessop
1913-1914 C. O. H. Sewell
1919-1921 F. G. Robinson
1922-1923 P. F. C. Williams
1924-1926 D. C. Robinson
1927-1928 W. H. Rowlands
1929-1934 B. H. Lyon
1935-1936 D. A. C. Page
1937-1938 B. O. Allen
1939-1946 W. R. Hammond
1947-1950 B. O. Allen
1951-1952 Sir D. Bailey
1953-1954 *J. F. Crapp*
1955-1958 *G. M. Emmett*
1959-1960 *T. W. Graveney*
1961-1962 C. T. M. Pugh
1963-1964 J. K. Graveney
1965-1967 J. B. Mortimore

HAMPSHIRE

1895 R. Bencraft
1896-1899 E. G. Wynyard
1900-1902 C. Robson
1903-1914 E. M. Sprot
1919-1933 Lord (Hon. L. H.) Tennyson
1934-1935 W. G. L. F. Lowndes
1936-1937 R. H. Moore
1938 C. G. A. Paris
1939 G. R. Taylor
1946-1957 E. D. R. Eagar
1958-1965 A. C. D. Ingleby-Mackenzie
1966-1967 R. E. Marshall

KENT

1859-1870 W. S. Norton
1871-1874 No official appointment
1875-1889 Lord Harris
1890-1893 F. Marchant and W. H. Patterson
1894-1897 F. Marchant
1898-1902 J. R. Mason
1903 C. J. Burnup
1904-1908 C. H. B. Marsham
1909-1913 E. W. Dillon
1914-1923 L. H. W. Troughton
1924-1926 W. S. Cornwallis
1927 A. J. Evans
1928-1930 G. B. Legge
1931-1936 A. P. F. Chapman
1937 R. T. Bryan and B. H. Valentine
1938-1939 F. G. H. Chalk
1946-1948 B. H. Valentine
1949-1951 D. G. Clark
1952-1953 W. Murray-Wood
1954-1956 *D. V. P. Wright*
1957-1967 M. C. Cowdrey

LANCASHIRE

1870-1879 E. B. Rowley
1880-1891 A. N. Hornby
1892-1893 A. N. Hornby and S. M. Crosfield
1894-1896 A. C. MacLaren
1897-1898 A. N. Hornby
1899 A. C. MacLaren and G. R. Bardswell
1900-1907 A. C. MacLaren
1908-1914 A. H. Hornby
1919-1922 M. N. Kenyon
1923-1925 J. Sharp
1926-1928 L. Green
1929-1935 P. T. Eckersley
1936-1939 W. H. L. Lister
1946 J. Fallows
1947-1948 K. Cranston
1949-1953 N. D. Howard
1954-1959 *C. Washbrook*
1960-1961 R. W. Barber
1962 J. F. Blackledge
1963-1964 K. J. Grieves
1965-1967 J. B. Statham

LEICESTERSHIRE

1894-1906 C. E. de Trafford
1907-1910 Sir A. Hazlerigg
1911-1913 J. Shields
1914-1920 C. J. B. Wood
1921 A. T. Sharp
1922-1927 G. H. S. Fowke
1928-1929 E. W. Dawson
1930 J. A. de Lisle
1931 E. W. Dawson
1932 Shared between six amateurs
1933 E. W. Dawson
1934 A. G. Hazlerigg
1935 *W. E. Astill*
1936-1938 C. S. Dempster
1939 M. St. J. Packe
1946-1948 *L. G. Berry*
1949 S. J. Symington
1950-1957 C. H. Palmer
1958-1961 *W. Watson*
1962 D. Kirby
1963-1965 M. R. Hallam
1966-1967 G. A. R. Lock

MIDDLESEX

1864-1872 V. E. Walker
1873-1884 I. D. Walker
1885-1897 A. J. Webbe
1898 A. J. Webbe and A. E. Stoddart
1899-1907 G. MacGregor
1908-1920 P. F. Warner
1921-1928 F. T. Mann
1929-1932 N. E. Haig
1933-1934 N. E. Haig and H. J. Enthoven
1935-1938 R. W. V. Robins
1939 I. A. R. Peebles
1946-1947 R. W. V. Robins
1948-1949 F. G. Mann
1950 R. W. V. Robins
1951-1952 W. J. Edrich and *D. C. S. Compton*
1953-1957 W. J. Edrich

County Captains—*Cont.*

1958-1960 J. J. Warr
1961-1962 P. I. Bedford
1963-1964 C. D. Drybrough
1965-1967 F. J. Titmus

NORTHAMPTONSHIRE

1905-1906 T. Horton
1907 E. M. Crosse
1908-1910 T. E. Manning
1911-1912 G. A. T. Vials
1913 G. A. T. Vials and S. G. Smith
1914 S. G. Smith
1919 J. N. Beasley
1920-1921 R. O. Raven
1922 C. H. Tyler
1923-1924 A. H. Bull
1925-1926 J. M. Fitzroy
1927 J. M. Fitzroy and V. W. C. Jupp
1928-1931 V. W. C. Jupp
1932-1935 W. C. Brown
1936-1937 G. B. Cuthbertson
1938-1939 R. P. Nelson
1946 P. E. Murray-Willis
1947-1948 A. W. Childs-Clarke
1949-1953 F. R. Brown
1954-1957 *D. Brookes*
1958-1961 R. Subba Row
1962-1966 *K. V. Andrew*
1967 R. M. Prideaux

NOTTINGHAMSHIRE

1835-1855 *W. Clarke*
1856-1870 *G. Parr*
1871-1880 *R. Daft*
1881-1882 *W. Oscroft*
1883-1886 *A. Shaw*
1887-1888 *M. Sherwin*
1889-1899 J. A. Dixon
1900-1912 A. O. Jones
1913 A. O. Jones and G. O. Gauld
1914 A. O. Jones
1919-1934 A. W. Carr
1935 G. F. H. Heane and S. D. Rhodes
1936-1946 G. F. H. Heane
1947-1950 W. A. Sime
1951-1960 R. T. Simpson
1961 *J. D. Clay*
1962 A. J. Corran
1963-1965 G. Millman
1966-1967 N. W. Hill

SOMERSET

1891-1893 H. T. Hewett
1894-1906 S. M. J. Woods
1907 L. C. H. Palairet
1908-1912 J. Daniell
1913-1914 E. S. M. Poyntz
1919-1926 J. Daniell
1927-1931 J. C. White
1932-1937 R. A. Ingle
1938-1946 E. F. Longrigg
1947 R. J. O. Meyer
1948 N. S. Mitchell-Innes, G. E. S. Woodhouse and J. W. Seamer
1949 G. E. S. Woodhouse
1950-1952 S. S. Rogers
1953-1954 B. G. Brocklehurst
1955 G. G. Tordoff
1956-1959 *M. F. Tremlett*
1960-1964 *H. W. Stephenson*
1965-1967 C. R. M. Atkinson

SURREY

1846-1850 C. H. Hoare
1851-1857 F. P. Miller
1858-1865 F. Burbidge
1866 E. Dowson
1867 W. J. Collyer
1868 C. Calvert
1869-1870 S. H. Akroyd
1871 J. C. Gregory
1872-1875 G. Strachan
1876 A. Chandler
1877-1879 G. Strachan
1880-1893 J. Shuter
1894-1899 K. J. Key
1900-1902 D. L. A. Jephson
1903 L. Walker
1904 No official appointment
1905-1907 Lord Dalmeny
1908-1909 H. D. G. Leveson-Gower
1910 H. D. G. Leveson-Gower and M. C. Bird
1911-1913 M. C. Bird
1914-1919 C. T. A. Wilkinson
1920 C. T. A. Wilkinson and P. G. H. Fender
1921-1931 P. G. H. Fender
1932-1933 D. R. Jardine
1934-1938 E. R. T. Holmes
1939 H. M. Garland-Wells
1946 N. H. Bennett
1947-1948 E. R. T. Holmes
1949-1951 M. R. Barton
1952-1956 W. S. Surridge
1957-1962 P. B. H. May†
1963-1967 M. J. Stewart

† P. B. H. May (ill) did not play in 1960, and A. V. Bedser (Vice-Captain) led the County.

SUSSEX

1839-1846 C. G. Taylor
1847-1862 E. Napper
1863 J. H. Hale
1864 J. H. Hale and C. H. Smith
1865-1873 C. H. Smith
1874 C. H. Smith and J. M. Cotterill
1875 J. M. Cotterill
1876-1878 F. F. J. Greenfield
1879 C. Sharp
1880 R. T. Ellis
1881-1882 F. F. J. Greenfield
1883-1884 H. Whitfield
1885 G. N. Wyatt
1886 F. M. Lucas
1887-1888 C. A. Smith
1889 W. Newham

County Captains—*Cont.*

1890 C. A. Smith
1891-1892 W. Newham
1893-1898 W. L. Murdoch
1899 W. L. Murdoch and K. S. Ranjitsinhji
1900-1903 K. S. Ranjitsinhji
1904-1905 C. B. Fry
1906 C. B. Fry and C. L. A. Smith
1907-1908 C. B. Fry
1909 C. L. A. Smith
1910-1914 H. P. Chaplin
1919-1921 H. L. Wilson
1922-1929 A. E. R. Gilligan
1930 A. H. H. Gilligan
1931-1932 K. S. Duleepsinhji
1933 R. S. G. Scott
1934-1935 A. Melville
1936-1939 A. J. Holmes
1946 S. C. Griffith
1947-1949 H. T. Bartlett
1950-1952 *James Langridge*
1953 D. S. Sheppard
1954 G. H. G. Doggart
1955-1959 R. G. Marlar
1960-1965 E. R. Dexter
1966 Nawab of Pataudi, Jnr.
1967 J. M. Parks

WARWICKSHIRE

1894-1901 H. W. Bainbridge
1902 H. W. Bainbridge and T. S. Fishwick
1903-1906 J. F. Byrne
1907 J. F. Byrne and T. S. Fishwick
1908-1909 A. C. S. Glover
1910 H. J. Goodwin
1911-1914 F. R. Foster
1919 G. W. Stephens
1920-1929 Hon. F. G. S. Calthorpe
1930-1937 R. E. S. Wyatt
1938-1947 P. Cranmer
1948 R. H. Maudsley and *H. E. Dollery*
1949-1955 *H. E. Dollery*
1956 *W. E. Hollies*
1957-1967 M. J. K. Smith

WORCESTERSHIRE

1899-1900 H. K. Foster
1901 R. E. Foster
1902-1910 H. K. Foster
1911-1912 G. H. Simpson-Hayward
1913 H. K. Foster
1914 W. H. Taylor
1920-1921 M. F. S. Jewell
1922 W. H. Taylor
1923-1925 M. K. Foster
1926 M. F. S. Jewell
1927 Hon. C. B. Ponsonby
1928 M. F. S. Jewell
1929 M. F. S. Jewell and Hon. J. B. Coventry
1930 Hon. J. B. Coventry
1931-1935 C. F. Walters
1936-1939 Hon. C. J. Lyttelton
1946 A. P. Singleton
1947-1948 A. F. T. White
1949 R. E. S. Wyatt and A. F. T. White
1950-1951 R. E. S. Wyatt
1952-1954 R. E. Bird
1955 *R. T. D. Perks*
1956-1958 P. E. Richardson
1959-1967 *D. Kenyon*

YORKSHIRE

1863-1870 *R. Iddison*
1871-1875 *J. Rowbotham*
1876-1877 *E. Lockwood*
1878-1882 *T. Emmett*
1883-1910 Lord Hawke
1911 E. J. Radcliffe
1912-1914 Sir A. W. White
1919-1921 D. C. F. Burton
1922-1924 G. Wilson
1925-1927 A. W. Lupton
1928-1929 W. A. Worsley
1930 A. T. Barber
1931-1932 F. E. Greenwood
1933-1947 A. B. Sellers
1948-1955 N. W. D. Yardley
1956-1957 W. H. H. Sutcliffe
1958-1959 J. R. Burnet
1960-1962 *J. V. Wilson*
1963-1967 D. B. Close

COUNTY CAPS AWARDED SINCE 1946

DERBYSHIRE

1946 J. D. Eggar, C. Gladwin, G. F. Hodkinson, P. Vaulkhard
1947 G. O. Dawkes, E. J. Gothard, E. A. Marsh, A. C. Revill
1949 H. L. Jackson, D. A. Skinner
1950 A. Hamer, G. L. Willatt
1951 D. B. Carr, J. Kelly, D. C. Morgan, R. Sale
1954 E. Smith
1956 C. Lee
1958 H. L. Johnson, H. J. Rhodes
1961 R. Berry, I. W. Hall
1962 I. R. Buxton, W. F. Oates, R. W Taylor
1963 A. B. Jackson, G. W. Richardson
1964 M. H. Page
1967 T. J. P. Eyre

ESSEX

1946 H. P. Crabtree, T. C. Dodds, R. F. T. Paterson, F. H. Vigar
1947 T. E. Bailey, L. S. Clark, S. J. Cray
1948 R. Horsfall, F. Rist
1949 D. J. Insole, G. R. Pullinger
1951 P. A. Gibb, K. C. Preston

County Caps Awarded since 1946—*Cont.*

1952 W. T. Greensmith
1954 J. A. Bailey
1955 G. Barker
1956 B. Taylor
1957 L. H. R. Ralph
1958 M. J. Bear
1959 B. R. Knight, L. H. Savill
1960 G. J. Smith
1961 J. Milner
1962 J. C. Laker
1963 K. W. R. Fletcher
1964 R. N. S. Hobbs, P. J. Phelan
1965 B. E. A. Edmeades
1967 K. D. Boyce, R. E. East

GLAMORGAN

1946 W. E. Jones, A. Porter, M. Robinson
1947 B. L. Muncer, A. J. Watkins
1948 P. B. Clift, J. Eaglestone, N. G. Hever, W. G. A. Parkhouse
1951 J. E. McConnon
1952 J. Pleass, D. J. Shepherd
1954 B. Hedges
1955 J. Pressdee
1956 L. N. Devereux
1958 P. M. Walker
1959 D. L. Evans
1960 J. B. Evans, A. R. Lewis
1961 D. Ward, O. S. Wheatley
1962 A. Jones
1963 A. Rees
1965 I. J. Jones, E. Lewis
1967 A. E. Cordle, E. W. Jones

GLOUCESTERSHIRE

1946 C. Cook
1948 T. W. Graveney
1949 Sir D. Bailey, J. K. Graveney, C. A. Milton
1950 D. M. Young
1954 F. P. McHugh, J. B. Mortimore, B. D. Wells
1955 P. Rochford
1957 A. S. Brown, D. Hawkins, R. B. Nicholls, D. R. Smith
1958 B. J. Meyer
1959 D. A. Allen
1961 D. G. A'Court, D. Carpenter, C. T. M. Pugh
1965 S. E. J. Russell, A. R. Windows

HAMPSHIRE

1946 E. D. R. Eagar, A. G. Holt
1947 N. H. Rogers
1948 G. Dawson
1949 V. J. Ransom, D. Shackleton, C. Walker
1950 V. H. D. Cannings
1951 J. R. Gray, L. Harrison
1952 A. W. H. Rayment
1953 D. E. Blake
1954 J. R. Bridger, R. Dare
1955 H. M. Barnard, M. D. Burden, H. Horton, R. E. Marshall, P. J. Sainsbury
1957 M. Heath, A. C. D. Ingleby-Mackenzie
1959 D. O. Baldry
1960 D. W. White
1961 D. A. Livingstone
1963 B. S. V. Timms, A. Wassell
1965 R. M. H. Cottam
1967 B. L. Reed

KENT

1946 T. G. Evans, R. R. Dovey, J. W. Martin, H. A. Pawson
1947 N. W. Harding, P. Hearn, F. Ridgway
1948 E. E. Crush
1949 D. G. Clark, B. R. Edrich, A. W. H. Mallett
1951 M. C. Cowdrey, W. Murray-Wood
1952 R. Mayes, A. H. Phebey, A. C. Shirreff
1953 G. Smith
1954 J. Pettiford, R. C. Wilson
1955 J. M. Allan
1956 D. G. Ufton
1957 D. J. Halfyard, S. E. Leary, J. C. T. Page, J. F. Pretlove
1960 A. L. Dixon
1960 P. E. Richardson
1961 A. Brown, P. H. Jones
1962 A. W. Catt, D. M. Sayer
1963 B. W. Luckhurst
1964 M. H. Denness, D. L. Underwood
1965 A. P. Knott, J. W. Prodger
1966 J. C. Dye
1967 J. N. Graham, J. Shepherd

LANCASHIRE

1946 T. L. Brierley, G. A. Edrich, J. A. Fallows, J. T. Ikin, B. P. King, E. Price, A. Wharton
1947 K. Cranston, R. G. Garlick, B. J. Howard
1948 E. H. Edrich, N. D. Howard
1949 P. Greenwood, K. J. Grieves
1950 A. T. Barlow, R. Berry, M. J. Hilton, J. B. Statham, R. Tattersall
1951 A. Wilson
1952 J. G. Lomax
1953 F. D. Parr
1956 J. Dyson, T. Greenhough, J. Jordan, C. S. Smith
1958 R. W. Barber, P. Marner, G. Pullar
1959 K. Higgs
1960 G. Clayton
1961 J. D. Bond, B. J. Booth, R. Collins
1962 J. R. Blackledge, D. M. Green, C. Hilton
1963 R. Bennett
1964 S. Ramadhin
1965 K. Goodwin, P. Lever, H. Pilling
1966 D. R. Worsley
1967 G. Atkinson, G. K. Knox, J. S. Savage

LEICESTERSHIRE

1946 V. E. Jackson, G. Lester, M. Tompkin, J. E. Walsh
1949 G. Evans, S. J. Symington
1950 C. H. Palmer

County Caps Awarded since 1946—*Cont.*

LEICESTERSHIRE-Cont.

1951 J. Firth, V. S. Munden, G. A. Smithson,
1952 C. T. Spencer
1953 T. J. Goodwin
1954 M. R. Hallam
1955 M. J. K. Smith
1958 B. Boshier, A. C. Revill, J. S. Savage, W. Watson
1959 J. Van Geloven
1960 H. D. Bird
1961 L. R. Gardner, R. Julian, A. Wharton
1962 D. Kirby
1963 C. C. Inman, S. Jayasinghe
1964 B. J. Booth
1965 J. Birkenshaw, J. Cotton, G. A. R. Lock, P. Marner
1966 M. E. J. C. Norman, R. W. Tolchard

MIDDLESEX

1946 J. P. Mann, A. Thompson, J. A. Young
1947 L. H. Compton, A. Fairbairn
1948 P. I. Bedford, J. G. Dewes, E. A. Ingram, H. P. Sharp
1949 J. J. Warr
1951 R. Routledge
1952 D. Bennett, W. Knightly-Smith, A. E. Moss
1953 F. J. Titmus
1955 G. P. S. Delisle
1956 J. T. Murray
1957 R. A. Gale, R. J. Hurst, A. C. Walton
1959 R. W. Hooker, W. E. Russell
1960 P. H. Parfitt
1961 P. I. Bedford, E. A. Clark
1962 C. D. Drybrough
1963 J. S. E. Price, R. A. White
1964 J. M. Brearley
1965 D. A. Bick
1967 M. J. Harris, C. T. Radley, M. J. Smith, M. O. C. Sturt

NORTHAMPTONSHIRE

1946 W. Barron, P. E. Murray-Willis
1947 V. H. Broderick, A. W. Childs-Clarke, C. B. Clarke, K. Fiddling, J. Webster
1948 A. E. Nutter, N. Oldfield
1949 F. R. Brown, R. W. Clarke, R. G. Garlick
1950 T. L. Livingston
1951 F. Jakeman
1952 D. Barrick, G. E. Tribe
1953 E. Davis
1954 K. V. Andrew, S. Starkie, F. H. Tyson
1955 P. Arnold, R. Subba Row
1956 J. S. Manning, B. G. Reynolds
1957 M. J. H. Allen
1960 L. A. Johnson, M. E. J. C. Norman
1961 J. D. F. Larter, A. Lightfoot
1962 B. S. Crump, R. M. Prideaux, P. D. Watts, P. J. Watts
1963 C. Milburn
1964 M. E. Scott
1965 D. S. Steele
1966 H. Sully
1967 Mushtaq Mohammad

NOTTINGHAMSHIRE

1946 E. A. Meads, T. B. Reddick, R. T. Simpson, F. W. Stocks
1947 W. A. Sime, H. Winrow
1949 P. F. Harvey, C. J. Poole
1951 R. J. Giles
1952 J. D. Clay
1953 B. Dooland
1954 E. J. Martin, E. J. Rowe
1955 G. Goonesena, K. Smales
1956 A. K. Walker
1957 G. Millman
1959 N. W. Hill
1960 J. Cotton, J. D. Springall, B. D. Wells
1961 M. Hill
1962 A. J. Corran, I. Davison, H. M. Winfield
1963 J. B. Bolus
1965 C. Forbes, H. I. Moore
1966 M. J. Smedley, R. Swetman, R. A. White
1967 D. L. Murray, M. N. S. Taylor

SOMERSET

1946 F. Castle, G. R. Langdale, J. Lawrence, M. M. Walford
1947 M. Coope, M. F. Tremlett, G. E. S. Woodhouse
1949 E. Hill, S. S. Rogers, H. W. Stephenson
1950 F. L. Angell, E. P. Robinson
1951 J. Redman
1952 G. G. Tordoff
1953 B. G. Brocklehurst, T. A. Hall, C. G. Mitchell, Roy Smith
1954 J. G. Lomax, J. W. McMahon, P. B. Wight, Yawar Saeed
1955 B. Lobb
1956 C. L. McCool, L. Pickles
1957 W. E. Alley, B. A. Langford, D. R. W. Silk
1958 G. Atkinson, K. E. Palmer
1959 K. Biddulph
1960 R. Virgin
1961 C. R. M. Atkinson, A. A. Baig
1962 C. Greetham, B. Roe
1963 F. E. Rumsey
1964 P. J. Eele
1965 G. Clayton
1966 M. Kitchen, P. J. Robinson

SURREY

1946 A. V. Bedser, N. H. Bennett, A. J. McIntyre
1947 E. A. Bedser, D. G. W. Fletcher, J. C. Laker
1948 M. R. Barton, J. W. McMahon, W. S. Surridge
1949 G. J. Whittaker
1950 B. Constable, G. A. R. Lock, P. B. H. May
1952 T. H. Clark
1953 P. J. Loader, R. Subba Row
1955 K. F. Barrington, M. J. Stewart
1958 R. Swetman

County Caps Awarded since 1946—*Cont.*

1959 J. H. Edrich
1960 D. Gibson
1961 A. B. D. Parsons
1962 A. Long, D. A. D. Sydenham, R. A. E. Tindall, M. D. Willett
1964 R. Harman, R. I. Jefferson, S. J. Storey
1966 M. J. Edwards
1967 G. G. Arnold, P. I. Pocock

SUSSEX

1948 P. D. S. Blake
1949 G. H. G. Doggart, J. Oakes, D. S. Sheppard
1950 A. E. James, D. V. Smith, R. T. Webb
1951 A. S. M. Oakman, J. M. Parks
1952 R. G. Marlar, K. G. Suttle
1953 N. I. Thomson
1957 D. L. Bates, L. J. Lenham
1959 E. R. Dexter
1961 R. V. Bell, G. C. Cooper, R. J. Langridge
1963 A. Buss, Nawab of Pataudi, Jnr.
1964 J. A. Snow
1965 T. Gunn
1966 D. J. Foreman
1967 M. A. Buss, A. W. Greig, M. G. Griffith, E. Lewis

WARWICKSHIRE

1946 W. E. Fantham, J. J. Hossell, J. M. A. Marshall, R. H. Maudsley, R. Sale N. A. Shortland, K. A. Taylor
1947 V. H. D. Cannings, C. W. Grove, T. L. Pritchard, J. R. Thompson
1948 M. P. Donnelly, R. T. Spooner, A. Townsend
1949 F. C. Gardner, A. H. Kardar, A. V. Wolton
1951 R. E. Hitchcock, E. B. Lewis, R. T. Weeks
1953 N. F. Horner
1954 J. D. Bannister, K. R. Dollery
1955 R. G. Thompson
1957 K. Ibadulla, M. J. K. Smith, W. J. Stewart
1958 R. G. Carter, T. W. Cartwright
1959 O. S. Wheatley
1961 W. B. Bridge, A. C. Smith
1962 A. Wright
1963 R. W. Barber, E. Legard, R. V. Webster
1964 D. J. Brown, J. A. Jameson
1965 D. L. Amiss
1966 R. N. Abberley

WORCESTERSHIRE

1946 R. E. Bird, A. F. T. White, R. E. S. Wyatt
1947 D. Kenyon, H. Yarnold
1948 L. Outschoorn
1949 M. L. Y. Ainsworth
1950 G. H. Chesterton, G. Dews
1951 R. G. Broadbent
1952 P. E. Richardson
1955 J. A. Flavell, M. J. Horton
1956 R. Booth, D. W. Richardson
1957 R. Berry
1959 K. J. Aldridge, L. J. Coldwell, D. B. Pearson
1960 D. N. F. Slade
1961 N. Gifford, R. G. A. Headley
1962 T. W. Graveney, J. A. Standen
1965 R. G. M. Carter, B. L. D'Oliveira
1966 B. M. Brain, J. A. Ormrod

YORKSHIRE

1946 A. Booth
1947 D. V. Brennan, A. Coxon, G. A. Smithson, J. H. Wardle, W. Watson
1948 R. Aspinall, H. Halliday, E. Lester, J. V. Wilson
1949 D. B. Close, F. A. Lowson
1951 R. Appleyard, F. S. Trueman
1952 W. H. H. Sutcliffe
1955 R. Illingworth
1957 J. G. Binks, W. B. Stott, K. Taylor
1958 J. R. Burnet, D. E. V. Padgett
1959 R. K. Platt
1960 J. B. Bolus, M. J. Cowan, P. J. Sharpe, D. Wilson
1962 M. Ryan
1963 G. Boycott, J. H. Hampshire, A. G. Nicholson
1964 R. A. Hutton

CAPPED BY THREE COUNTIES

R. Berry has the unique distinction of being the only player to have been capped by three counties; Lancashire (1950), Worcestershire (1957) and Derbyshire (1961). A left-arm slow bowler, Berry appeared in two Test Matches against the West Indies in 1950.

THE SHEFFIELD SHIELD

In 1891-92, the Earl of Sheffield toured Australia with a team captained by W. G. Grace and was so enthusiastically received that he donated 150 guineas for the promotion of cricket in Australia. The newly-formed Australian Cricket Council instituted a Shield to be competed for by the leading cricket states (then colonies).

The Sheffield Shield—*Cont.*

Championship cricket in Australia began in the season of 1892-93, although matches between Victoria and New South Wales had been played since the 1850's with South Australia and Tasmania forming teams soon after. With the exception of Tasmania, who have never competed in the championship, these teams alone contested the Sheffield Shield until 1926-27, when Queensland were admitted and from which time all matches were played not to a finish as previously, but on a time basis. Western Australia won the Shield in their first season in the competition (1947-48); admitted on an experimental basis, they played the other states once only and found some weakened by Test calls. Since 1956-57, when Western Australia were admitted to full membership, the Sheffield Shield programme has consisted of 20 matches, each side playing the other on a home and away basis.

HOLDERS

1892-93	Victoria	1915-19	No competition	1946-47	Victoria
1893-94	South Australia	1919-20	New South Wales	1947-48	Western Australia
1894-95	Victoria	1920-21	New South Wales	1948-49	New South Wales
1895-96	New South Wales	1921-22	Victoria	1949-50	New South Wales
1896-97	New South Wales	1922-23	New South Wales	1950-51	Victoria
1897-98	Victoria	1923-24	Victoria	1951-52	New South Wales
1898-99	Victoria	1924-25	Victoria	1952-53	South Australia
1899-00	New South Wales	1925-26	New South Wales	1953-54	New South Wales
1900-01	Victoria	1926-27	South Australia	1954-55	New South Wales
1901-02	New South Wales	1927-28	Victoria	1955-56	New South Wales
1902-03	New South Wales	1928-29	New South Wales	1956-57	New South Wales
1903-04	New South Wales	1929-30	Victoria	1957-58	New South Wales
1904-05	New South Wales	1930-31	Victoria	1958-59	New South Wales
1905-06	New South Wales	1931-32	New South Wales	1959-60	New South Wales
1906-07	New South Wales	1932-33	New South Wales	1960-61	New South Wales
1907-08	Victoria	1933-34	Victoria	1961-62	New South Wales
1908-09	New South Wales	1934-35	Victoria	1962-63	Victoria
1909-10	South Australia	1935-36	South Australia	1963-64	South Australia
1910-11	New South Wales	1936-37	Victoria	1964-65	New South Wales
1911-12	New South Wales	1937-38	New South Wales	1965-66	New South Wales
1912-13	South Australia	1938-39	South Australia	1966-67	Victoria
1913-14	New South Wales	1939-40	New South Wales		
1914-15	Victoria	1940-46	No competition		

RESULTS SUMMARY (1892-1967)

	Début Season	*Played*	*Won*	*Drawn*	*Lost*	*Tie*	*Aban'd*
New South Wales	1892-93	356	191	86	78	1	—
Victoria	1892-93	355	159	91	103	1	1
South Australia	1892-93	352	100	74	178	—	—
Queensland	1926-27	237	43	88	105	—	1
Western Australia	1947-48	122	24	45	53	—	—
		1422	517	384	517	2†	2‡

† Victoria (244 & 197) tied with N.S.W. (281 & 160) at St. Kilda, Melbourne, 1956-57.
‡ Queensland v. Victoria (Brisbane) 1930-31—abandoned without a ball being bowled.

THE CURRIE CUP

This trophy was donated in 1888 by Sir Donald Currie as a Challenge Cup to the team putting up the best performance against the first English team to tour South Africa (1888-89). This honour fell to Kimberley (later renamed Griqualand West) but they lost the first Currie Cup match the following season against their sole challengers, the Transvaal, who thus became the first winners of the competition.

Until 1966-67, the tournament was not normally held when a touring team visited South Africa, occasional friendly inter-provincial matches being played instead.

HOLDERS

1st	1889-90	Transvaal	16th	1921-22	Transvaal, Natal and Western Province (Tied)
2nd	1890-91	Griqualand West	17th	1923-24	Transvaal
3rd	1892-93	Western Province	18th	1925-26	Transvaal
4th	1893-94	Western Province	19th	1926-27	Transvaal
5th	1894-95	Transvaal	20th	1929-30	Transvaal
6th	1896-97	Western Province	21st	1931-32	Western Province
7th	1897-98	Western Province	22nd	1933-34	Natal
8th	1902-03	Transvaal	23rd	1934-35	Transvaal
9th	1903-04	Transvaal	24th	1936-37	Natal
10th	1904-05	Transvaal	25th	1937-38	Transvaal and Natal (Tied)
11th	1906-07	Transvaal	26th	1946-47	Natal
12th	1908-09	Western Province	27th	1947-48	Natal
13th	1910-11	Natal	28th	1950-51	Transvaal
14th	1912-13	Natal			
15th	1920-21	Western Province			

In 1951-52 the teams were divided into two sections:—
Section A: Eastern Province, Natal, Transvaal, Western Province.
Section B: Border, Griqualand West, North-Eastern Transvaal, Orange Free State, Rhodesia.

Season	*Winner of Currie Cup*	*Relegated to B*		*Leader of B Section*
1951-52	Natal	Transvaal		Orange Free State
1952-53	Western Province	Eastern Province		Transvaal
1954-55	Natal	Orange Free State		Eastern Province
1955-56	Western Province	Eastern Province		Rhodesia
1958-59	Transvaal	—	*a.*	Border
1959-60	Natal	Border		{ Eastern Province { Transvaal B
1960-61	Natal	—	*b.*	—
1962-63	Natal	—	*c.*	Transvaal B.
1963-64	Natal	—	*d.*	Rhodesia
1965-66	Natal & Transvaal (Tied)	Western Province		North-Eastern Transvaal *e.*
1966-67	Natal	Rhodesia		North-Eastern Transvaal

Notes: *a.* Although Border were promoted, Western Province who finished last in Section A were not relegated as Transvaal B entered the Cup for 1959-60 and Section A was increased to five teams.

b. The two-section tournament was abandoned—unsuccessfully—in 1960-61 but was resumed for 1962-63 with four teams in Section A.

c. Eastern Province were not relegated as Transvaal B were not eligible for promotion.

d. Rhodesia were promoted but Eastern Province were again reprieved from relegation, Section A being again increased to five teams.

e. North-Eastern Transvaal were not promoted as the Section A teams were limited to four.

RESULTS SUMMARY (1898-1967)

	Début Season	*Played*	*Won*	*Drawn*	*Lost*	*Tie*
Transvaal	1889-90	185	112	39	34	—
Griqualand West	1889-90	164	32	33	99	—
Western Province	1892-93	175	80	39	56	—
Natal	1893-94	171	106	41	24	—
Eastern Province	1893-94	155	41	32	81	1
Border	1897-98	148	46	23	79	—
Orange Free State	1903-04	156	37	32	86	1
Rhodesia	1904-05	89	36	21	32	—
South-West Districts..	1904-05	1	—	—	1	—
North-Eastern Transvaal	1937-38	83	29	18	36	—
Transvaal B	1959-60	32	18	5	9	—
Natal B	1965-66	9	2	5	2	—
		1368	539	288	539	2†

† Orange Free State (100 & 349) tied with Eastern Province (225 & 224-8) at Bloemfontein in 1925-26. Although Eastern Province had 2 second innings wickets in hand this was prior to the 1948 amendment to the tie law. Eastern Province were given first innings points.

WEST INDIAN TOURNAMENTS

Administrators of West Indian domestic cricket have always been hampered by the immense distances separating the various countries. Although most tournaments in the Caribbean have been failures financially, there is always the need to maintain playing interest throughout the region and to develop prospective candidates for Test selection.

Until 1963-64, the countries had either met at one centre and played a knock-out tournament, or two countries had held private two-match series, or two matches had been played at two different venues simultaneously.

INTER-COLONIAL TOURNAMENT

Coming under the first of the categories mentioned above, this was a triangular knock-out tournament between Barbados, British Guiana and Trinidad (distant Jamaica not competing) played on each home ground in turn. Although Barbados beat Trinidad in 1891-92, British Guiana did not compete and the Tournament is not considered to have been inaugurated until the following season. It continued until the last war but was not resumed afterwards.

CHAMPIONS

1st	1892-93	Barbados (Port of Spain)	15th	1923-24	Barbados (Bridgetown)
2nd	1895-96	British Guiana (Georgetown)	16th	1924-25	Trinidad (Port of Spain)
3rd	1897-98	Barbados (Bridgetown)	17th	1925-26	Trinidad (Georgetown)
4th	1899-00	Barbados (Port of Spain)	18th	1926-27	Barbados (Bridgetown)
5th	1901-02	Trinidad (Georgetown)	19th	1928-29	Trinidad (Port of Spain)
6th	1903-04	Trinidad (Bridgetown)	20th	1929-30	British Guiana (Georgetown)
7th	1905-06	Barbados (Port of Spain)	21st	1931-32	Trinidad (Bridgetown)
8th	1907-08	Trinidad (Georgetown)	22nd	1933-34	Trinidad (Port of Spain)
9th	1908-09	Barbados (Bridgetown)	23rd	1934-35	British Guiana (Georgetown)
10th	1909-10	Trinidad (Port of Spain)	24th	1935-36	British Guiana (Bridgetown)
11th	1910-11	Barbados (Georgetown)	25th	1936-37	Trinidad (Port of Spain)
12th	1911-12	Barbados (Bridgetown)	26th	1937-38	British Guiana (Georgetown)
13th	1921-22	No result (Port of Spain)	27th	1938-39	Trinidad (Bridgetown)
14th	1922-23	Barbados (Georgetown)			

1956-57 QUADRANGULAR TOURNAMENT

For the first time all four major countries met in a knock-out tournament held at one venue—Georgetown.

Final: British Guiana beat Barbados on first innings.

1961-62 PENTANGULAR TOURNAMENT

A fifth team, Leeward and Windward Islands, competed in this knock-out tournament held at Georgetown

Final: British Guiana beat Barbados by 4 wickets.

1963-64 REGIONAL TOURNAMENT

For the first time a tournament was staged in more than two centres, the four major countries meeting each other once in a league championship with the six matches being divided equally between Bridgetown, Port of Spain and Georgetown.

Champions: British Guiana

THE 'SHELL' REGIONAL TOURNAMENT

Sponsored by Shell Oil, a regional league championship with five teams competing was first played in the 1965-66 season. The Leeward and Windward Islands separated into two independent teams for the 1966-67 tournament.

CHAMPIONS

1965-66 Barbados
1966-67 Barbados

THE PLUNKET SHIELD

The trophy was presented in 1906-07 by Lord Plunket, then Governor-General of New Zealand, and awarded by the New Zealand Cricket Council to Canterbury. Until 1921, when a championship was organised on a league basis, the Shield had been contested under the challenge match system.

The championship was played between Auckland, Canterbury, Otago and Wellington (apart from the two isolated appearances by Hawke's Bay in 1914-15 and 1920-21) until Central Districts (1950-51) and Northern Districts (1956-57) were admitted.

HOLDERS

		Challenges defeated
Canterbury	1906-07 to December 1907	0
Auckland	December 1907 to February 1911	7
Canterbury	February 1911 to February 1912	2
Auckland	February 1912 to January 1913	1
Canterbury	January 1913 to December 1918	9
Wellington	December 1918 to January 1919	0
Canterbury	January 1919 to January 1920	2
Auckland	January 1920 to January 1921	3
Wellington	January 1921—challenge system ended	0

1921-22	Auckland	1935-36	Wellington	1954-55	Wellington
1922-23	Canterbury	1936-37	Auckland	1955-56	Canterbury
1923-24	Wellington	1937-38	Auckland	1956-57	Wellington
1924-25	Otago	1938-39	Auckland	1957-58	Otago
1925-26	Wellington	1939-40	Auckland	1958-59	Auckland
1926-27	Auckland	1945-46	Canterbury	1959-60	Canterbury
1927-28	Wellington	1946-47	Auckland	1960-61	Wellington
1928-29	Auckland	1947-48	Otago	1961-62	Wellington
1929-30	Wellington	1948-49	Canterbury	1962-63	Northern Districts
1930-31	Canterbury	1949-50	Wellington	1963-64	Auckland
1931-32	Wellington	1950-51	Otago	1964-65	Canterbury
1932-33	Otago	1951-52	Canterbury	1965-66	Wellington
1933-34	Auckland	1952-53	Otago	1966-67	Central Districts
1934-35	Canterbury	1953-54	Central Districts		

RESULTS SUMMARY (1907-67)

	Début Season	*Played*	*Won*	*Drawn*	*Lost*
Auckland	1907-08	171	79	49	43
Canterbury	1907-08	174	72	44	58
Wellington	1907-08	162	70	32	60
Otago	1907-08	159	41	37	81
Hawke's Bay	1914-15	2	—	—	2
Central Districts	1950-51	79	25	30	24
Northern Districts	1956-57	55	9	18	28
		802	296	210	296

THE BOMBAY PENTANGULAR TOURNAMENT

This tournament, held annually at Bombay, was for many seasons the premier championship of Indian Cricket.

Originated in 1892 as the Presidency Match between the Parsis and the Europeans, with a return match being played at Poona from 1895-96, it became the Triangular Tournament when the Hindus entered in 1907, and the Quadrangular when the Muslims, who played with the Hindus initially, formed their own team in 1912. A fifth side, The Rest, entered in 1937 making the tournament Pentangular.

It was abandoned, apparently for political reasons, after the 1945-46 season.

The Bombay Pentangular Tournament—*Cont.*

PRESIDENCY MATCHES

1892-93 Match drawn (Bombay).
1893-94 Match drawn (Bombay)
1894-95 Parsis won by 120 runs (Bombay).
1895-96 Europeans won by 9 wickets (Bombay). Parsis won by an innings & 10 runs (Poona).
1896-97 Europeans won by 10 wickets (Bombay) and 2 wickets (Poona).
1897-98 Match drawn (Bombay), Parsis won by 308 runs (Poona).
1898-99 Europeans won by an innings & 16 runs (Bombay) and an innings & 36 runs (Poona).
1899-00 Match drawn (Bombay). Not played at Poona owing to plague.
1900-01 Parsis won by 135 runs (Bombay). Match drawn (Poona).
1901-02 Parsis won by 8 wickets (Bombay). Europeans won by 192 runs (Poona).
1902-03 Parsis won by 44 runs (Bombay). Europeans won by 4 wickets (Poona).
1903-04 Parsis won by 149 runs (Bombay) and an innings & 6 runs (Poona).
1904-05 Parsis won by 180 runs (Bombay). Abandoned owing to rain (Poona).
1905-06 Parsis won by an innings & 226 runs (Poona). Not played at Bombay.
1906-07 Europeans won by 6 wickets (Poona). Not played at Bombay.

TRIANGULAR TOURNAMENT (*final match results*)

1907-08 Parsis beat Europeans by 143 runs (Bombay).
1908-09 Europeans beat Parsis by 176 runs (Bombay)—Hindus did not compete.
1909-10 Match drawn (Europeans v. Parsis at Bombay).
1910-11 Match drawn (Europeans v. Hindus at Bombay).
1911-12 Parsis beat Europeans by 2 wickets (Bombay).

QUADRANGULAR TOURNAMENT

1912-13 Parsis beat Muslims by an innings & 177 runs (Bombay).
1913-14 Match drawn (Hindus v. Muslims at Bombay).
1914-15 Abandoned without a ball being bowled (Hindus v. Parsis at Bombay).
1915-16 Europeans beat Hindus by 10 wickets (Poona).
1916-17 Match drawn (Europeans v. Parsis at Bombay).
1917-18 Match drawn (Hindus v. Parsis at Bombay).
1918-19 Europeans beat Parsis by 91 runs (Poona).
1919-20 Hindus beat Muslims by an innings & 13 runs (Bombay).
1920-21 Match drawn (Hindus v. Parsis at Bombay).
1921-22 Europeans beat Parsis by an innings & 297 runs (Bombay).
1922-23 Parsis beat Hindus by 121 runs (Poona).
1923-24 Hindus beat Europeans by 9 wickets (Bombay).
1924-25 Muslims beat Hindus by 5 wickets (Bombay).
1925-26 Hindus beat Europeans by 4 wickets (Bombay).
1926-27 Hindus beat Europeans by 11 runs (Poona).
1927-28 Europeans beat Muslims by 4 wickets (Bombay).
1928-29 Parsis beat Europeans by 134 runs (Bombay).
1929-30 Hindus beat Parsis by 5 wickets (Bombay).
1934-35 Muslims beat Hindus by 91 runs (Bombay).
1935-36 Muslims beat Hindus by 221 runs (Bombay).
1936-37 Hindus beat Europeans by 257 runs (Bombay).

PENTANGULAR TOURNAMENT

1937-38 Muslims beat Europeans by an innings & 91 runs (Bombay). Hindus did not compete
1938-39 Muslims beat Hindus by 6 wickets (Bombay).
1939-40 Hindus beat Muslims by 5 wickets (Bombay).
1940-41 Muslims beat Rest by 7 wickets (Bombay). Hindus did not compete.
1941-42 Hindus beat Parsis by 10 wickets (Bombay).
1943-44 Hindus beat Rest by an innings & 61 runs (Bombay).
1944-45 Muslims beat Hindus by 1 wicket (Bombay).
1945-46 Hindus beat Parsis by 310 runs (Bombay).

THE 'RANJI' TROPHY

This championship was instituted in 1934 in memory of the great 'Ranji', K. S. Ranjitsinhji, who had died during the previous year.

To avoid teams having to travel vast distances, the Indian sub-continent was divided into zones, originally four in number but with a fifth (Central) added in 1953-54. A knock-out competition of 4-day matches held within each zone produced zonal champions who met to contest the final stages, again on a knock-out basis, but played to a finish. An open-draw rather than zonal basis was tried unsuccessfully in the 1948-49 season. Since 1957-58 the zonal championship has been decided on a league basis, the five champions still meeting to contest the final stages in a knock-out tournament.

FINALISTS

1934-35 Bombay beat Northern India at Bombay by 208 runs.
1935-36 Bombay beat Madras at Delhi by 190 runs.
1936-37 Nawanagar beat Bengal at Bombay by 256 runs.
1937-38 Hyderabad beat Nawanagar at Bombay by 1 wicket.
1938-39 Bengal beat Southern Punjab at Calcutta by 178 runs.
1939-40 Maharashtra beat United Provinces at Poona by 10 wickets.
1940-41 Maharashtra beat Madras at Madras by 6 wickets.
1941-42 Bombay beat Mysore at Bombay by an innings and 281 runs.
1942-43 Baroda beat Hyderabad at Secunderabad by 307 runs.
1943-44 Western India States beat Bengal at Bombay by an innings and 23 runs.
1944-45 Bombay beat Holkar at Bombay by 374 runs.
1945-46 Holkar beat Baroda at Indore by 56 runs.
1946-47 Baroda beat Holkar at Baroda by an innings and 409 runs.
1947-48 Holkar beat Bombay at Indore by 9 wickets.
1948-49 Bombay beat Baroda at Bombay by 468 runs.
1949-50 Baroda beat Holkar at Baroda by 4 wickets.
1950-51 Holkar beat Gujerat at Indore by 189 runs.
1951-52 Bombay beat Holkar at Bombay by 531 runs.
1952-53 Holkar beat Bengal at Calcutta on first innings (match drawn).
1953-54 Bombay beat Holkar at Indore by 8 wickets.
1954-55 Madras beat Holkar at Indore by 46 runs.
1955-56 Bombay beat Bengal at Calcutta by 8 wickets.
1956-57 Bombay beat Services at New Delhi by an innings and 38 runs.
1957-58 Baroda beat Services at Baroda by an innings and 51 runs.
1958-59 Bombay beat Bengal at Bombay by 420 runs.
1959-60 Bombay beat Mysore at Bombay by an innings and 22 runs.
1960-61 Bombay beat Rajasthan at Udaipur by 7 wickets.
1961-62 Bombay beat Rajasthan at Bombay by an innings and 287 runs.
1962-63 Bombay beat Rajasthan at Jaipur by an innings and 19 runs.
1963-64 Bombay beat Rajasthan at Bombay by 9 wickets.
1964-65 Bombay beat Hyderabad at Hyderabad by an innings and 126 runs.
1965-66 Bombay beat Rajasthan at Jaipur by 8 wickets.
1966-67 Bombay beat Rajasthan at Bombay on first innings (match drawn).

THE 'DULEEP' TROPHY

In 1961-62, a zonal tournament was instituted for the first time and named after another great cricketer, K. S. Duleepsinhji. Run on a knock-out basis, this tournament enables the country's top players to display their ability in the highest company and compete for selection for the Test team.

FINALISTS

1961-62 West Zone beat South Zone at Bombay by 10 wickets.
1962-63 West Zone beat South Zone at Calcutta by an innings and 20 runs.
1963-64 West and South Zones shared the Trophy—match drawn at New Delhi (rain).
1964-65 West Zone beat Central Zone at Bombay by an innings and 89 runs.
1965-66 South Zone beat Central Zone at Madras by an innings and 20 runs.
1966-67 South Zone beat West Zone at Bombay on first innings in a drawn match.

THE 'QUAID-E-AZAM' TROPHY

Inaugurated as Pakistan's national championship in the 1953-54 season, the title "Quaid-E-Azam" means "The Great Leader", an epithet given to the late Mr. Jinnah who played an important part in the creation of Pakistan. Although both the number of competing teams and basis of competition varies from season to season, it is usually organised on similar lines to India's Ranji

The Quaid-e-Azam 'Trophy'—*Cont.*

Trophy with zonal knock-out or league champions competing in a final knock-out stage. The final of the 1964-65 Trophy was not held until the following season and the tournament started in the 1966-67 season has yet to be completed.

FINALISTS

1953-54 Bahawalpur beat Punjab at Karachi by 8 wickets.
1954-55 Karachi beat Services at Karachi by 9 wickets.
1956-57 Punjab beat Karachi Whites at Lahore by 43 runs.
1957-58 Bahawalpur beat Karachi C. at Bahawalpur by 211 runs.
1958-59 Karachi beat Services at Karachi by 279 runs.
1959-60 Karachi beat Lahore at Karachi by 99 runs.
1961-62 Karachi Blues beat Services at Karachi by 4 wickets.
1962-63 Karachi A. beat Karachi B. at Karachi by an innings and 163 runs.
1963-64 Karachi Blues beat Karachi Whites at Karachi by 18 runs.
1964-66 Karachi Blues beat Lahore Greens at Karachi by 105 runs.

THE 'AYUB' ZONAL TROPHY

Introduced while Pakistan's top players were touring India, this competition is run on a knock-out basis with the winners and runners-up of the zonal stage meeting in the semi-final round. In 1962-63, when the Quaid-E-Azam Trophy was also held, the preliminary zonal rounds were not given first-class status. The trophy was donated by and named after Field-Marshal Mohammad Ayub Khan, President of Pakistan, and President of the Board of Control for Cricket in Pakistan.

FINALISTS

1960-61 Railways & Quetta beat Lahore at Karachi on first innings.
1961-62 Karachi beat North Zone at Karachi by 316 runs.
1962-63 Karachi beat P.I.A. at Karachi on first innings.
1964-65 Karachi beat Lahore Board at Lahore by an innings and 91 runs.
1965-66 The final between Lahore Greens and Karachi Blues was postponed first until 1966-67 and then until 1967-68.

UNIVERSITY CRICKET
(Oxford v. Cambridge)

The first match was played at Lord's in 1827 and, the intervention of two World Wars apart, it has been an annual fixture since 1838.

Some players appeared in five of those earliest matches but in the 1860's it was decided that eligibility for the 'Varsity Match' should be limited to a player's first four seasons of residence. Players representing their university against 'the other place' at Lord's are awarded a 'Blue'.

OXFORD UNIVERSITY BLUES

Abell, G. E. B. (Marlborough)—1924-26-27
Ainslie, M. M. (Eton)—1843-44-45 (Captain 1844-45)
Aitken, H. M. (Eton)—1853
Aitken, J. (Eton)—1848-49-50 (Captain 1850)
Alington, H. G. (Rugby)—1859
Allan, J. M. (Edinburgh Academy)—1953-54-55-56
Altham, H. S. (Repton)—1911-12
Arenhold, J. A. (Diocesan College, S.A.)—1954
Arkwright, H. A. (Eton)—1895
Armistead, W. G. (Westminster)—1853-54-56-57
Arnall-Thompson, H. T. (Rugby)—1886
Asher, A. G. G. (Loretto)—1883
Awdry, R. W. (Winchester)—1904
Baig, A. A. (Osmania U.)—1959-60-61-62
Baig, M. A. (Osmania U.)—1962-63-64
Bailey, J. A. (Christ's Hospital)—1956-57-58 (Captain 1958)
Balfour, E. (Westminster)—1852-53-54
Ballance, T. G. L. (Uppingham)—1935-37
Bannon, B. D. (Tonbridge)—1898
Barber, A. T. (Shrewsbury)—1927-28-29 (Captain 1929)
Bardsley, R. V. (Shrewsbury)—1911-12-13
Bardswell, G. R. (Uppingham)—1894-96-97 (Captain 1897)
Barker, A. H. (Charterhouse)—1964-65-67
Barlow, E. A. (Shrewsbury)—1932-33-34
Barnard, F. H. (Charterhouse)—1922-24
Barnes, R. G. (Harrow)—1906-07
Bartholomew, A. C. (Marlborough)—1868

University Cricket—Oxford Blues—*Cont.*

Bartlett, J. N. (Chichester)—1946-51
Barton, M. R. (Winchester)—1936-37
Bassett, H. (Bedford House, Oxford)—1889-90-91
Bastard, E. W. (Sherborne)—1883-84-85
Bateman, E. L. (Repton & Marlborough)—1854-55
Bathurst, F. (Winchester)—1848
Bathurst, L. C. V. (Radley)—1893-94
Bathurst, R. A. (Winchester)—1838-39
Bathurst, S. E. (Winchester)—1836
Bayly, C. H. (Winchester)—1827-29
Beauclerk, C. W. (Charterhouse)—1836
Belcher, T. H. (Magdalen College School)—1870
Bell, G. F. (Repton)—1919
Belle, B. H. (Forest School)—1936
Benn, A. (Harrow)—1935
Bennett, G. (Winchester)—1856
Benson, E. T. (Blundell's)—1928-29
Bere, C. S. (Rugby)—1851
Berkeley, G. F. H. (Wellington)—1890-91-92-93
Bettington, R. H. B. (King's School, Parramatta)—1920-21-22-23 (Captain 1923)
Bickmore, A. F. (Clifton)—1920-21
Bird, J. W. (Winchester)—1827-29
Bird, W. S. (Malvern)—1904-05-06 (Captain 1906)
Birrell, H. B. (St Andrew's, S.A.)—1953-54
Blagg, P. H. (Shrewsbury)—1939
Blaikie, K. G. (Maritzburg)—1924
Blake, P. D. S. (Eton)—1950-51-52 (Captain 1952)
Bligh, E. V. (Eton)—1850
Bloy, N. C. F. (Dover)—1946-47
Boger, A. J. (Winchester)—1891
Bolitho, W. E. T. (Harrow)—1883-85
Bonham-Carter, M. (Winchester)—1902
Boobbyer, B. (Uppingham)—1949-50-51-52
Bosanquet, B. J. T. (Eton)—1898-99-1900
Boswell, W. G. K. (Eton)—1913-14
Bowden-Smith, F. H. (Rugby)—1861
Bowman, R. C. (Fettes)—1957
Bowring, T. (Rugby)—1907-08
Boyle, C. E. (Charterhouse)—1865-66-67
Boyle, C. W. (Clifton)—1873
Bradby, H. C. (Rugby)—1890
Braddell, R. L. (Charterhouse)—1910-11
Bradshaw, W. H. (Malvern)—1930-31
Brain, J. H. (Clifton)—1884-85-86-87 (Captain 1887)
Brain, W. H. (Clifton)—1891-92-93
Brandt, D. R. (Harrow)—1907
Brandt, F. (Cheltenham)—1859-60-61 (Captain 1861)
Branston, G. T. (Charterhouse)—1904-05-06
Brett, P. J. (Winchester)—1929
Briggs, R. (Winchester)—1875-76
Bristowe, O. C. (Eton)—1914
Bromley-Martin, G. E. (Eton)—1897-98
Brooke, R. H. J. (St Edward's, Oxford)—1932
Brooks, R. A. (Quintin)—1967
Brougham, H. (Wellington)—1911
Brownlee, L. D. (Clifton)—1904
Bruce, Hon. C. N. (later Lord Aberdare) (Winchester)—1907-08
Buckland, E. H. (Marlborough)—1884-85-86-87
Buckland, F. M. (Eton)—1875-76-77
Bull, H. E. (Westminster)—1863
Bullock-Hall, W. H. (Rugby)—1857-58-60
Burki, J. (Punjab U.)—1958-59-60
Burn, R. C. W. (Winchester)—1902-03-04-05
Bush, J. E. (Magdalen School, Oxford)—1952
Butler, S. E. (Eton)—1870-71-72-73
Butterworth, R. E. C. (Harrow)—1927
Buxton, R. V. (Eton)—1906

Campbell, D. (Melbourne U.)—1874-75-76
Campbell, I. P. (Canford)—1949-50
Campbell, I. P. F. (Repton)—1911-12-13 (Captain 1913)
Carlisle, K. M. (Harrow)—1903-04-05 (Captain 1905)
Carpenter-Garnier, J. (Harrow)—1858
Carr, D. B. (Repton)—1949-50-51 (Captain 1950)
Carter, E. S. (Durham G.S.)—1866-67
Case, T. (Rugby)—1864-65-67
Case, T. B. (Winchester)—1891-92
Case came into the game by permission of the Cambridge captain in 1891, after the Hon. F. J. N. Thesiger had retired shortly after the start of the match.
Cassan, E. J. P. (Bruton)—1859
Cator, W. (Bromsgrove G.S.)—1860
Cazalet, P. V. F. (Eton)—1927
Cazenove, A. (Private)—1851-52
Chalk, F. G. H. (Uppingham)—1931-32-33-34 (Captain 1934)
Champain, F. H. B. (Cheltenham)—1897-98-99-1900 (Captain 1899)
Cherry, G. C. (Harrow)—1841-42-43
Chesterton, G. H. (Malvern)—1949
Chitty, J. W. (Eton)—1848-49
Clarke, W. G. (Winchester)—1840
Clement, R. (Rugby)—1853
Clube, S. V. M. (St John's, Leatherhead)—1956
Cobb, A. R. (Winchester)—1886
Cochrane, A. H. J. (Repton)—1885-86-88
Coker, J. (Winchester)—1840-42-43-44 (Captain 1842-43)
Colebrooke, E. L. (Charterhouse)—1880
Coleridge, C. E. (Eton)—1849-50
Coleridge, F. J. (Eton)—1847-50
Colley, R. H. (Bridgnorth G.S.)—1853-54-55
Collins, L. P. (Marlborough)—1899
Colman, G. R. R. (Eton)—1913-14
Commerell, W. A. (Harrow)—1843
Cooke, J. (Winchester)—1829
Coote, A. (Eton)—1838-39-40 (Captain 1838)
Corran, A. J. (Gresham's)—1958-59-60
Coutts, I. D. F. (Dulwich)—1952
Cowburn, A. (Winchester)—1841
Cowdrey, M. C. (Tonbridge)—1952-53-54 (Captain 1954)
Coxon, A. J. (Harrow C.G.S.)—1952
Crawfurd, J. W. F. (Merchant Taylors')—1900-01
Crawley, A. M. (Harrow)—1927-28-29-30
Croome, A. C. M. (Wellington)—1888-89
Crutchley, G. E. V. (Harrow)—1912

University Cricket—Oxford Blues—*Cont.*

Cunliffe, F. H. E. (Eton)—1895-96-97-98 (Captain 1898)
Currer, C. S. (Harrow)—1847
Curteis, H. M. (Westminster)—1841-42
Curwen, W. J. H. (Charterhouse)—1906
Cuthbertson, J. L. (Rugby)—1962-63

Darnell, N. (Winchester)—1838-39-40
Darwall-Smith, R. F. H. (Charterhouse)—1935-36-37-38
Daubeny, E. T. (Bromsgrove G.S.)—1861-62
Dauglish, M. J. (Harrow)—1889-90
Davenport, E. (Rugby)—1866
Davidson, W. W. (Brighton)—1947-48
Davies, P. H. (Brighton)—1913-14
Davies, W. H. (Charterhouse)—1846-47-48
Davis, F. J. (Blundell's)—1963
Delisle, G. P. S. (Stonyhurst)—1955-56
De Montmorency, R. H. (Cheltenham & St Paul's)—1899
Denison, H. (Eton)—1829
Denne, T. (Private)—1827
De Saram, F. C. (Royal College, Colombo)—1934-35
Des Vœux, H. D. (Harrow)—1844
Digby, K. E. (Harrow)—1857-58-59
Digby, R. (Harrow)—1867-68-69
Dillon, E. W. (Rugby)—1901-02
Divecha, R. V. (Bombay U.)—1950-51
Dixon, E. J. H. (St Edward's, Oxford)—1937-38-39 (Captain 1939)
Dolphin, J. M. (Marlborough)—1860
Donnelly, M. P. (Canterbury U., New Zealand)—1946-47 (Captain 1947)
Dowding, A. L. (St Peter's, Adelaide)—1952-53 (Captain 1953)
Drybrough, C. D. (Highgate)—1960-61-62 (Captain 1961-62)
Dryden, A. E. (Winchester)—1841-42-43
Duff, A. R. (Radley)—1960-61
Durell, J. D. (Westminster)—1838
Dury, T. S. (Harrow)—1876
Dyer, A. W. (Mill Hill)—1965-66
Dyson, E. M. (Queen Elizabeth G.S., Wakefield)—1958
Dyson, J. H. (Charterhouse)—1936

Eagar, E. D. R. (Cheltenham)—1939
Eagar, M. A. (Rugby)—1956-57-58-59
Easter, R. N. C. (St Edward's, Oxford)—1967
Eccles, A. (Repton)—1897-98-99
Eden, F. M. (Rugby)—1850-51
Eggar, J. D. (Winchester)—1938
Ellis, W. W. (Rugby)—1827
Elviss, R. W. (Leeds G.S.)—1966-67
Evans, A. H. (Rossall & Clifton)—1878-79-80-81 (Captain 1881)
Evans, A. J. (Winchester)—1909-10-11-12 (Captain 1911)
Evans, E. N. (Haileybury)—1932
Evans, F. R. (Cheltenham & Rugby)—1863-64-65
Evans, G. (St Asaph)—1939
Evans, W. H. B. (Malvern)—1902-03-04-05 (Captain 1904)
Evelyn, F. L. (Rugby)—1880
Evetts, W. (Harrow)—1868-69

Fane, F. L. (Charterhouse)—1897-98
Fasken, D. K. (Wellington)—1953-54-55
Fellowes, E. L. (Marlborough)—1865-66-68 (Captain 1868)
Fellows, W. (Westminster)—1854-55-56-57
Fellows-Smith, J. P. (Durban H.S., S.A.)—1953-54-55
Fiennes, W. S. T. W. (Winchester)—1856-57-58
Fillary, E. W. J. (St Lawrence)—1963-64-65
Findlay, W. (Eton)—1901-02-03 (Captain 1903)
Fisher, C. D. (Westminster)—1900
Foord-Kelcey, W. (Chatham House, Ramsgate)—1874-75
Forbes, D. H. (Eton)—1894
Ford, G. J. (King's College, London)—1839-40
Ford, N. M. (Harrow)—1928-29-30
Forster, H. W. (Eton)—1887-88-89
Fortescue, A. T. (Marlborough)—1868-69-70
Foster, G. N. (Malvern)—1905-06-07-08
Foster, H. K. (Malvern)—1894-95-96
Foster, R. E. (Malvern)—1897-98-99-1900 (Captain 1900)
Fowler, G. (Clifton)—1888
Fowler, H. (Clifton)—1877-79-80
Fox, R. W. (Wellington)—1897-98
Francis, C. K. (Rugby)—1870-71-72-73
Franklin, H. W. F. (Christ's Hospital)—1924
Fraser, J. N. (Church of England G.S., Melbourne)—1912-13
Frazer, J. E. (Winchester)—1924
Frederick, J. St. J. (Eton)—1864-67
Fry, C. A. (Repton)—1959-60-61
Fry, C. B. (Repton)—1892-93-94-95 (Captain 1894)
Fuller, G. P. (Winchester)—1854-55

Gamble, N. W. (Southport G.S.)—1967
Game, W. H. (Sherborne)—1873-74-75-76 (Captain 1876)
Garland-Wells, H. M. (St Paul's)—1928-29-30
Garnett, C. A. (Cheltenham & Eton)—1860-62
Garnier, E. S. (Marlborough)—1873
Garnier, T. P. (Winchester)—1861-62-63
Garofall, A. R. (Latymer Upper)—1967
Garth, R. (Eton)—1839-40-41-42 (Captain 1840-41)
Garthwaite, P. F. (Wellington)—1929
Gibbon, J. H. (Harrow)—1869
Gibbs, P. J. K. (Hanley G.S.)—1964-65-66
Gibson, I. (Manchester G.S.)—1955-56-57-58
Gilbert, H. A. (Charterhouse)—1907-08-09
Gillett, H. H. (Winchester)—1857-58
Gilliat, R. M. C. (Charterhouse)—1964-65-66-67 (Captain 1966)
Gilliatt, I. A. W. (Charterhouse)—1925
Gilligan, F. W. (Dulwich)—1919-20 (Captain 1920)
Goldstein, F. S. (Falcon College, Bulawayo)—1966-67
Gordon, J. H. (Winchester)—1906-07
Goring, C. (Winchester)—1836
Green, D. M. (Manchester G.S.)—1959-60-61

University Cricket—Oxford Blues—*Cont.*

Greene, A. D. (Clifton)—1877-78-79-80 (Captain 1880)
Greenstock, J. W. (Malvern)—1925-26-27
Gresson, F. H. (Winchester)—1887-88-89
Grimston, Hon. E. H. (Harrow)—1836
Grimston, Hon. R. (Harrow)—1838
Grover, J. N. (Winchester)—1936-37-38 (Captain 1938)
Groves, M. G. M. (Diocesan College, S.A.)—1964-65-66
Guest, M. R. J. (Rugby)—1964-65-66
Guise, J. L. (Winchester)—1924-25 (Captain 1925)

Hadow, W. H. (Harrow)—1870-71-72
Hale, T. W. (Rugby)—1851-52
Halliday, J. G. (City of Oxford H.S.)—1935
Hamilton, W. D. (Haileybury)—1882
Hanbury, O. R. (Rugby)—1849
Hankey, R. (Harrow)—1853-55 (Captain 1855)
Hare, J. H. M. (Uppingham)—1879
Harris, C. R. (Buckingham R.L.S.)—1964
Harris, Hon. G. R. C. (later Lord Harris) (Eton)—1871-72-74
Harrison, G. C. (Malvern & Clifton)—1880-81
Hart, T. M. (Strathallan)—1931-32
Hartley, J. C. (Marlborough &Tonbridge)—1896-97
Haskett-Smith, A. (Eton)—1879
Hatfeild, C. E. (Eton)—1908
Haygarth, J. W. (Winchester)—1862-63-64
Heath, A. H. (Clifton)—1876-77-78-79
Hedges, L. P. (Tonbridge)—1920-21-22
Henderson, D. (St Edward's, Oxford)—1950
Henley, D. F. (later Henley-Welch) (Harrow)—1947
Henley, F. A. H. (Forest)—1905
Hewetson, E. P. (Shrewsbury)—1923-24-25
Hewett, H. T. (Harrow)—1886
Hildyard, H. C. T. (Eton)—1845-46
Hildyard, L. D'arcy (Private)—1884-85-86
Hill, F. H. (Bradfield)—1867-69-70
Hill, V. T. (Winchester)—1892
Hiller, R. B. (Bec)—1966
Hill-Wood, C. K. (Eton)—1928-29-30
Hill-Wood, D. J. (Eton)—1928
Hine-Haycock, T. R. (Wellington)—1883-84
Hirst, E. T. (Rugby)—1878-79-80
Hobbs, J. A. D. (Liverpool College)—1957
Hodgkinson, G. L. (Harrow)—1857-58-59
Hofmeyr, M. B. (Pretoria, S.A.)—1949-50-51 (Captain 1951)
Holdsworth, R. L. (Repton)—1919-20-21-22
Hollins, A. M. (Eton)—1899
Hollins, F. H. (Eton)—1901
Holmes, E. R. T. (Malvern)—1925-26-27 (Captain 1927)
Hone, B. W. (Adelaide U.)—1931-32-33 (Captain 1933)
Honywood, R. (Eton)—1845-46-47
Hooman, C. V. L. (Charterhouse)—1909-10
Hopkins, H. O. (St. Peter's, Adelaide)—1923
Hore, A. H. (Tonbridge)—1851
Howell, M. (Repton)—1914-19 (Captain 1919)
Hughes, G. E. (Rugby)—1845
Hughes, T. (Rugby)—1842
Hume, E. (Marlborough)—1861-62
Hurst, C. S. (Uppingham)—1907-08-09 (Captain 1909)

Inge, F. G. (Rossall & Charterhouse)—1961-62-63
Inge, W. (Shrewsbury)—1853
Isherwood, F. W. (Rugby)—1872

Jackson, K. L. T. (Rugby)—1934
Jacobson, T. R. (Charterhouse)—1961
Jardine, D. R. (Winchester)—1920-21-23
Jardine, M. R. (Fettes)—1889-90-91-92 (Captain 1891)
Jellicoe, F. G. G. (Haileybury)—1877-79
Jenkins, V. G. J. (Llandovery)—1933
Jones, M. (Harrow)—1849-50
Jones, R. T. (Eton)—1892
Jones, T. B. (Christ College, Brecon & Trinity College, Dublin)—1874
Jones-Bateman, R. L. (Winchester)—1846-48
Jose, A. D. (Adelaide U.)—1950-51
Jowett, D. C. P. R. (Sherborne)—1952-53-54-55
Jowett, R. L. (Bradford G.S.)—1957-58-59

Kamm, A. (Charterhouse)—1954
Kardar, A. H. (Punjab U.)—1947-48-49
Keighley, W. G. (Eton)—1947-48
Kelly, G. W. F. (Stonyhurst)—1901-02
Kemp, C. W. M. (Harrow)—1878
Kemp, M. C. (Harrow)—1881-82-83-84 (Captain 1883-84)
Kenney, E. M. (later Kenney-Herbert) (Rugby)—1866-67-68
Kentish, E. S. M. (Cornwall College, Jamaica)—1956
Ker, R. J. C. R. (Eton)—1842
Key, K. J. (Clifton)—1884-85-86-87
Kimpton, R. C. M. (Melbourne U.)—1935-37-38
Kingsley, P. G. T. (Winchester)—1928-29-30 (Captain 1930)
Knatchbull, H. E. (Winchester)—1827-29
Knight, D. J. (Malvern)—1914-19
Knight, N. S. (Uppingham)—1934
Knight, R. L. (Clifton)—1878
Knott, C. H. (Tonbridge)—1922-23-24 (Captain 1924)
Knott, F. H. (Tonbridge)—1912-13-14 (Captain 1914)
Knox, F. P. (Dulwich)—1899-1900-01 (Captain 1901)

Lagden, R. O. (Marlborough)—1909-10-11-12
Lane, C. G. (Westminster)—1856-58-59-60 (Captain 1859-60)
Lang, T. W. (Edinburgh Academy & Clifton)—1874-75
Law, A. P. (Rugby)—1857
Law, W. (Harrow)—1871-72-73-74 (Captain 1874)
Lear, F. (Winchester)—1843-44

University Cricket—Oxford Blues—*Cont.*

Le Couteur, P. R. (Warrnambool Academy & Melbourne U.)—1909-10-11
Lee, E. C. (Winchester)—1898
Lee, G. B. (Winchester)—1838-39 (Captain 1839)
Legard, A. R. (Winchester)—1932-35
Legge, G. B. (Malvern)—1925-26 (Captain 1926)
Leigh, E. C. (Harrow)—1852-53-54
Leslie, C. F. H. (Rugby)—1881-82-83
Leslie, J. (Harrow)—1843
Leveson-Gower, H. D. G. (Winchester)—1893-94-95-96 (Captain 1896)
Lewis, C. P. (Llandovery & King's, Gloucester)—1876
Lewis, D. J. (Cape Town U.)—1951
Lewis, R. P. (Winchester)—1894-95-96
Lewis, W. H. (Harrow)—1827
Lindsay, W. O. (Harrow)—1931
Linton, H. (Harrow)—1858-59
Linton, S. (Rugby)—1861-62
Lipscombe, W. H. (Marlborough)—1868
Llewelyn, W. D. (Eton)—1890-91
Loch, C. R. F. (Edinburgh Academy & Rugby)—1846-48
Loftus, Lord H. Y. A. (Harrow)—1841
Lomas, J. M. (Charterhouse)—1938-39
Longe, F. D. (Harrow)—1951-52
Lowe, J. C. M. (Uppingham)—1907-08-09
Lowndes, R. (Winchester)—1841
Lowndes, W. G. L. F. (Eton)—1921
Lowth, A. J. (Eton & Winchester)—1938-40-41
Lyon, B. H. (Rugby)—1922-23
Lyon, G. W. F. (Brighton)—1925

McBride, W. N. (Westminster)—1926
McCanlis, M. A. (Cranleigh)—1926-27-28 (Captain 1928)
Macindoe, D. H. (Eton)—1937-38-39-46 (Captain 1946)
McIntosh, R. I. F. (Uppingham)—1927-28
McIver, C. D. (Forest)—1903-04
McKinna, G. H. (Manchester G.S.)—1953
McLachlan, N. (Loretto) — 1879-80-81-82 (Captain 1882)
Maitland, W. F. (Brighton & Harrow)—1864-65-66-67 (Captain 1867)
Majendie, N. L. (Winchester)—1962-63
Mallett, A. W. H. (Dulwich)—1947-48
Manasseh, M. (Epsom)—1964
Marcon, W. (Eton)—1844
Marriott, C. (Winchester)—1871
Marriott, G. S. (Winchester)—1878
Marshall, J. C. (Rugby)—1953
Marsham, A. J. B. (Eton)—1939
Marsham, C. D. B. (Private)—1854-55-56-57-58 (Captain 1857-58)
Marsham, C. H. B. (Eton)—1900-01-02 (Captain 1902)
Marsham, C. J. B. (Private)—1851
Marsham, R. H. B. (Private)—1856
Marsland, G. P. (Rossall)—1954
Martin, E. G. (Eton)—1903-04-05-06
Martin, J. D. (Magdalen College School)—1962-63-65 (Captain 1965)
Martyn, H. (Exeter G.S.)—1899-1900

Mathews, E. (Harrow)—1868-69
Matthews, M. H. (Westminster)—1936-37
Maude, J. (Eton)—1873
Maudsley, R. H. (Malvern)—1946-47
Mayhew, J. F. N. (Eton)—1930
Medlicott, W. S. (Harrow)—1902
Melle, B. G. (S.A. College School & S.A. College, Cape Town)—1913-14
Melville, A. (Michaelhouse, S.A.)—1930-31-32-33 (Captain 1931-32)
Melville, C. D. (Michaelhouse, S.A.)—1957
Metcalfe, S. G. (Leeds G.S.)—1956
Miles, R. F. (Marlborough)—1867-68-69
Mills, B. S. T. (Harrow)—1841-42-43
Minns, R. E. F. (King's, Canterbury)—1962-63
Mitchell, R. A. H. (Eton)—1862-63-64-65 (Captain 1863-64-65)
Mitchell, W. M. (Dulwich)—1951-52
Mitchell-Innes, N. S. (Sedbergh)—1934-35-36-37 (Captain 1936)
Moberley, H. E. (Winchester)—1842-43-44-45
Monro, R. W. (Harrow)—1860
Moore, D. N. (Shrewsbury)—1930
Moore was the appointed captain in 1931, but was unable to play owing to illness.
Mordaunt, G. J. (Wellington)—1893-94-95-96 (Captain 1895)
More, R. E. (Westminster)—1900-01
Morley, J. W. (Marlborough)—1859-60
Morres, E. J. (Winchester)—1850
Moss, R. H. (Radley)—1889
Mountford, P. N. G. (Bromsgrove)—1963
Munn, J. S. (Forest)—1901
Murray-Wood, W. (Mill Hill)—1936
Musters, W. M. (Eton)—1829

Napier, C. W. A. (Harrow)—1838-39
Naumann, F. C. G. (Malvern)—1914-19
Neate, F. W. (St Paul's)—1961-62
Nepean, C. E. B. (Charterhouse)—1873
Nepean, E. A. (Sherborne)—1887-88
Neser, V. H. (S.A. College, Cape Town)—1921
Nethercote, H. O. (Charterhouse & Harrow)—1840-41
Newman, G. C. (Eton)—1926-27
Newton, A. E. (Eton)—1885
Newton-Thompson, J. O. (Diocesan College, S.A.)—1946
Nicholls, B. E. (Winchester)—1884
Nunn, J. A. (Sherborne)—1926-27

O'Brien, T. C. (St Charles' College, Notting Hill)—1884-85
Oldfield, P. C. (Repton)—1932-33
Oliver, F. W. (Westminster)—1856-57
Ottaway, C. J. (Eton)—1870-71-72-73 (Captain 1873)
Owen-Smith, H. G. (Diocesan College, S.A.)—1931-32-33

Page, H. V. (Cheltenham)—1883-84-85-86 (Captain 1885-86)
Palairet, L. C. H. (Repton)—1890-91-92-93 (Captain 1892-93)

University Cricket—Oxford Blues—*Cont.*

Palairet, R. C. N. (Repton)—1893-94
Papillon, J. (Winchester)—1827
Parker, W. W. (Rugby)—1852-53-55
Pataudi, Nawab of, Snr. (Chief's College, Lahore)—1929-30-31
Pataudi, Nawab of, Jnr. (Winchester)—1960-63 (Captain 1963) *Pataudi was also the appointed captain in 1961, but was unable to play owing to injuries received in a car accident.*
Patten, M. (Winchester)—1922-23
Patterson, J. I. (Chatham House, Ramsgate)—1882
Patterson, W. H. (Chatham House & Harrow)—1880-81
Patteson, J. C. (Eton)—1849
Pauncefoot, B. (Rugby) — 1868-69-70-71 (Captain 1869-70)
Pawson, A. C. (Winchester)—1903
Pawson, A. G. (Winchester)—1908-09-10-11 (Captain 1910)
Pawson, H. A. (Winchester)—1947-48 (Captain 1948)
Payne, A. (Private)—1852-54-55-56 (Captain 1856)
Payne, A. F. (Private)—1855
Payne, C. A. L. (Charterhouse)—1906-07
Peake, E. (Marlborough)—1881-82-83
Pearse, G. V. (Maritzburg College, Natal)—1919
Pearson, A. (Loretto & Rugby)—1876-77
Peat, C. U. (Sedbergh)—1913
Peebles, I. A. R. (Glasgow Academy)—1930
Peel, H. R. (Eton)—1851-52
Pelham, S. (Harrow)—1871
Pepys, J. A. (Eton)—1861
Pershke, W. J. (Uppingham)—1938
Pether, S. (Magdalen College School)—1939
Philipson, H. (Eton)—1887-88-89 (Captain 1889)
Phillips, F. A. (Rossall)—1892-94-95
Phillips, J. B. (King's, Canterbury)—1955
Piachaud, J. D. (St Thomas's, Colombo)—1958-59-60-61
Pilkington, C. C. (Eton)—1896
Pilkington, H. C. (Eton)—1899-1900
Pilkington, W. (Midhurst)—1827
Pithey, D. B. (Univ. of Cape Town)—1961-62
Pole, E. (Winchester)—1827
Popham, F. L. (Harrow)—1829
Potter, I. C. (King's, Canterbury)—1961-62
Potts, H. J. (Stand G.S.)—1950
Price, R. (Winchester)—1827-29
Price, V. R. (Bishop's Stortford)—1919-20-21-22 (Captain 1921)
Proud, R. B. (Winchester)—1939
Pulman, W. W. (Marlborough)—1874-75
Pycroft, J. (Bath)—1836

Raikes, D. C. G. (Shrewsbury)—1931
Raikes, G. B. (Shrewsbury)—1894-95
Raikes, T. B. (Winchester)—1922-23-24
Randolph, B. M. (Charterhouse)—1855-56
Randolph, C. (Eton)—1844-45
Randolph, J. (Westminster)—1843
Randolph, L. C. (Westminster)—1845
Ranken, R. B. (Edinburgh Academy)—1860
Raphael, J. E. (Merchant Taylors')—1903-04-05
Rashleigh, J. (Harrow)—1842
Rashleigh fielded substitute for R. Garth in the 1842 match and was allowed to bowl. R. Garth batted.
Rashleigh, W. (Tonbridge)—1886-87-88-89 (Captain 1888)
Rawlinson, G. (Ealing)—1836
Raybould, J. G. (Leeds G.S.)—1959
Reade, H. St J. (Tonbridge)—1861-62 (Captain 1862)
Reid, R. T. (Cheltenham)—1866-67-68
Rice, R. W. (Cardiff)—1893
Richardson, J. V. (Uppingham)—1925
Ricketts, G. W. (Winchester)—1887
Ridding, A. (Winchester)—1846-47-48-49-50 (Captain 1849)
Ridding, C. H. (Winchester)—1845-46-47-48-49
Ridding, W. (Winchester)—1849-50-52-53 (Captain 1852)
Ridding was also appointed captain in 1851, but was unable to play owing to illness.
Ridley, A. W. (Eton)—1872-73-74-75 (Captain 1875)
Ridley, G. N. S. (Milton, Rhodesia)—1965-66-67 (Captain 1967)
Ridsdale, S. O. B. (Tonbridge)—1862
Robertson, G. P. (Rugby)—1866
Robertson, J. C. (Winchester)—1829
Robertson-Glasgow, R. C. (Charterhouse)—1920-21-22-23
Robinson, G. E. (Burton)—1881-82-83
Robinson, H. B. (North Shore, Vancouver, B.C.)—1947-48
Robinson, R. L. (St Peter's, Adelaide & Adelaide U.)—1908-09
Royle, V. P. F. A. (Rossall)—1875-76
Rucker, C. E. S. (Charterhouse)—1914
Rucker, P. W. (Charterhouse)—1919
Rudd, C. R. D. (Eton)—1949
Ruggles-Brise, H. G. (Winchester)—1883
Rumbold, J. S. (St Andrew's, N.Z.)—1946
Russell, H. S. (Harrow)—1839
Ryle, J. C. (Eton)—1836-38

Sabine, P. N. B. (Marlborough)—1963
Sale, R., Snr. (Repton)—1910
Sale, R., Jnr. (Repton)—1939-46
Salter, M. G. (Cheltenham)—1909-10
Samson, O. M. (Cheltenham)—1903
Sandford, E. G. (Rugby)—1859-61
Sankey, P. M. (King's, Canterbury)—1852
Saunders, C. J. (Lancing)—1964
Savory, J. H. (Winchester)—1877-78
Sayer, D. M. (Maidstone G.S.)—1958-59-60
Schwann, H. S. (Clifton)—1890
Scott, Lord George (Eton)—1887-88-89
Scott, J. (Bruce Castle)—1863
Scott, K. B. (Winchester)—1937
Scott, M. D. (Winchester)—1957
Scott, R. S. G. (Winchester)—1931
Seamer, J. W. (Marlborough)—1934-35-36
Seitz, J. A. (Geelong & Melbourne U.)—1909
Shaw, E. A. (Marlborough)—1912-14

University Cricket—Oxford Blues—*Cont.*

Shaw, E. D. (Forest)—1882
Sibthorpe, G. T. W. (Harrow)—1836
Simpson, E. T. B. (Harrow)—1888
Sinclair, E. H. (Winchester)—1924
Singleton, A. P. (Shrewsbury)—1934-35-36-37 (Captain 1937)
Skeet, C. H. L. (St Paul's)—1920
Skene, R. W. (Sedbergh)—1928
Smith, A. C. (King Edward's, Birmingham)—1958-59-60 (Captain 1959-60)
Smith, E. (Clifton)—1890-91
Smith, G. O. (Charterhouse)—1895-96
Smith, M. J. K. (Stamford)—1954-55-56 (Captain 1956)
Smith, V. S. C. (Winchester)—1844-45-46-47 (Captain 1846-47)
Soames, S. (Rugby)—1846-47
Spencer-Smith, O. (Eton)—1866
Spinks, T. (Merchant Taylors')—1840
Stainton, R. G. (Malvern)—1933
Stanning, J. (Winchester)—1939
Stephenson, J. S. (Shrewsbury)—1925-26
Stevens, G. T. S. (U.C.S.)—1920-21-22-23 (Captain 1922)
Stewart, W. A. (Winchester)—1869-70
Stewart-Brown, P. H. (Harrow)—1925-26
Stocks, F. W. (Lancing & Denstone)—1898-99
Sutton, M. A. (Ampleforth)—1946

Taswell, H. J. (Rugby)—1851
Taylor, C. H. (Westminster)—1923-24-25-26
Teape, A. S. (Eton)—1863-64-65
Teesdale, H. (Winchester)—1908
Thesiger, Hon. F. J. N. (Winchester)—1888-90 (Captain 1890)
Thesiger (1st Viscount Chelmsford) retired hurt in the 1891 match, his place being taken by T. B. Case.
Thomas, R. J. A. (Radley)—1965
Thornton, W. A. (Winchester)—1879-80-81-82
Tindall, R. G. (Winchester)—1933-34
Toft, D. P. (Tonbridge)—1966-67
Torre, H. J. (Harrow)—1839-40
Townsend, D. C. H. (Winchester)—1933-34
Townsend, W. H. (Rugby)—1842-43
Townshend, W. (Rossall)—1870-71-72
Traill, W. F. (Merchant Taylors')—1858-59-60
Travers, B. H. (Sydney U., N.S.W.)—1946-48
Trevor, A. H. (Winchester)—1880-81
Tritton, E. W. (Eton)—1864-65-66-67 (Captain 1866)
Trower, C. F. (Winchester)—1838
Tuff, F. N. (Malvern)—1910
Twining, R. H. (Eton)—1910-11-12-13 (Captain 1912)
Tylecote, E. F. S. (Clifton)—1869-70-71-72 (Captain 1871-72)
Tylecote, H. G. (Clifton)—1874-75-76-77

Udal, N. R. (Winchester)—1905-06

Vance, G. (Eton)—1836-38
Van der Byl, P. G. (Diocesan College, S.A.)—1932
Van Ryneveld, C. B. (Diocesan College, S.A.)—1948-49-50 (Captain 1949)
Veitch, H. G. J. (Twyford)—1854-55-56
Vidler, J. L. S. (Repton)—1910-11-12
Von Ernsthausen, A. C. (Uppingham)—1902-03-04
Voules, S. C. (Marlborough)—1863-64-65-66

Waddy, P. S. (King's School, Parramatta, N.S.W.)—1896-97
Waldock, F. A. (Uppingham)—1919-20
Walford, M. M. (Rugby)—1936-38
Walker, D. F. (Uppingham)—1933-34-35 (Captain 1935)
Walker, J. G. (Loretto)—1882-83
Walker, R. D. (Harrow)—1861-62-63-64-65
Wallace, A. (Winchester)—1851
Wallington, E. W. (Sherborne)—1877
Wallroth, C. A. (Harrow)—1872-73-74
Walsh, D. R. (Marlborough)—1967
Walshe, A. P. (Milton, Rhodesia)—1953-55-56
Walter, A. F. (Eton)—1869
Walton, A. C. (Radley)—1955-56-57 (Captain 1957)
Ward, H. P. (Shrewsbury)—1919-21
Ward, Lord (later Earl of Dudley) (Eton)—1841-42
Warner, P. F. (Rugby)—1895-96
Watson, A. G. M. (St Lawrence)—1965-66
Watson, A. K. (Harrow)—1889
Watson, H. D. (Harrow)—1891
Waud, B. W. (Eton)—1857-58-59-60
Webb, H. E. (Winchester)—1948
Webbe, A. J. (Harrow)—1875-76-77-78 (Captain 1877-78)
Webbe, H. R. (Winchester)—1877-78-79 (Captain 1879)
Wellings, E. M. (Cheltenham)—1929-31
Wheatley, G. A. (Uppingham)—1946
Whitby, H. O. (Leamington)—1884-85-86-87
Whitcombe, P. A. (Winchester)—1947-48-49
Whitcombe, P. J. (Worcester R.G.S.)—1951-52
White, H. (Denstone)—1900
Whitehouse, P. M. (Marlborough)—1938
Whiting, A. O. (Charterhouse & Sherborne)—1881-82
Wickham, A. P. (Marlborough)—1878
Wiley, W. G. E. (Diocesan College, S.A.)—1952
Wilkinson, W. A. C. (Eton)—1913
Willes, E. H. L. (Winchester)—1852-53-54 (Captain 1853-54)
Williams, C. C. P. (Westminster)—1953-54-55 (Captain 1955)
Williams, P. (Winchester)—1844-45-46-47
Williams, R. A. (Winchester)—1901-02
Willis, C. F. (Tonbridge)—1847-48-49
Wilson, A. (Rugby)—1848-49-50
Wilson, G. L. (Repton & Brighton)—1890-91
Wilson, R. W. (Warwick)—1957
Wilson, T. S. B. (Bath College)—1892-93
Winn, C. E. (K.C.S., Wimbledon)—1948-49-50-51
Wood, J. B. (Marlborough)—1892-93
Woodcock, R. G. (Worcester R.G.S.)—1957-58

University Cricket—Oxford Blues—*Cont.*

Wordsworth, Charles (Harrow)—1827-29 (Captain 1827-29)
Worsley, D. R. (Bolton)—1961-62-63-64 (Captain 1964)
Worthington, G. (Tonbridge)—1844
Wright, E. C. (Clergy Orphan School, Canterbury)—1897
Wright, E. L. (Winchester)—1905-06-07-08 (Captain 1907-08)
Wright, F. B. (Winchester)—1829
Wright, F. W. (Rossall)—1863-64-65
Wrigley, M. H. (Harrow)—1949
Wyatt, M. T. H. (Private)—1850-51 (Acting Captain 1851)
Wyld, H. J. (Harrow)—1901-02-03
Wynne, J. H. G. (Eton)—1839-40
Wynne-Finch, C. G. (Eton)—1836

Yonge, C. D. (Eton)—1836
Yonge, G. E. (Eton)—1844-45-46-47-48 (Captain 1848)
Young, D. E. (K.C.S., Wimbledon)—1938

Note: R. H. C. Waters (Shrewsbury) was awarded a "Blue" in 1961 but was unable to play in the University match because of injuries received in a car accident.

CAMBRIDGE UNIVERSITY BLUES

Abercrombie, J. (Tonbridge)—1838
Absolom, C. A. (Private)—1866-67-68-69
Acfield, D. L. (Brentwood)—1967
Aers, D. R. (Tonbridge)—1967
Aird, R. (Eton)—1923
Alexander, F. C. M. (Wolmer's College, Jamaica)—1952-53
Allen, A. W. (Eton)—1933-34
Allen, B. O. (Clifton)—1933
Allen, G. O. (Eton)—1922-23
Allom, M. J. C. (Wellington)—1927-28
Allsopp, H. T. (Cheltenham)—1876
Anson, T. A. (Eton)—1839-40-41-42 (Captain 1840-41-42)
Arkwright, H. A. (Harrow)—1858
Arnold, A. C. P. (Malvern)—1914
Ash, E. P. (Rugby)—1865
Ashton, C. T. (Winchester)—1921-22-23 (Captain 1923)
Ashton, G. (Winchester)—1919-20-21 (Captain 1921)
Ashton, H. (Winchester)—1920-21-22 (Captain 1922)
Atkins, G. (Challenor's G.S., Amersham)—1960
Austin, H. M. (Melbourne)—1924

Baggallay, M. E. C. (Eton)—1911
Bagge, T. E. (Eton)—1859-60-61 (Captain 1861)
Bagnall, H. F. (Harrow)—1923
Bailey, T. E. (Dulwich)—1947-48
Baily, E. P. (Harrow)—1872-74
Baily, R. E. H. (Harrow)—1908
Bainbridge, H. W. (Eton)—1884-85-86 (Captain 1886)
Baker, E. C. (Brighton)—1912-14
Balfour, R. D. (Bradfield & Westminster)—1863-64-65-66
Barber, R. W. (Ruthin)—1956-57
Barchard, E. (Winchester)—1846-47-48
Barker, G. (Bury St Edmunds)—1840
Barnett, W. E. (Eton)—1849-50
Bartlett, H. T. (Dulwich)—1934-35-36 (Captain 1936)
Bastard, J. H. (Winchester)—1838-40
Bateman, A. (Brighton)—1859-60-61
Bayford, R. A. (Kensington G.S.)—1857-58-59 (Captain 1859)
Benke, A. F. (Cheltenham)—1962
Bennett, C. T. (Harrow)—1923-25 (Captain 1925)
Benthall, W. H. (Westminster & Marlborough) 1858-59-60
Bernard, J. R. (Clifton)—1958-59-60
Blacker, W. (Harrow)—1873-74-75-76
Blake, J. P. (Aldenham)—1939
Blaker, R. N. (Elizabeth College, Guernsey)—1842-43
Blaker, R. N. R. (Westminster)—1900-01-02
Blayds, E. (Harrow)—1846-47-48-49
Bligh, Hon. Ivo F. W. (later Earl of Darnley) (Eton)—1878-79-80-81 (Captain 1881)
Block, S. A. (Marlborough)—1929
Blofeld, H. C. (Eton)—1959
Blore, E. W. (Eton)—1848-49-50-51 (Captain 1851)
Blundell, E. D. (Waitaki, N.Z.)—1928-29
Bodkin, P. E. (Bradfield)—1946 (Captain 1946)
Boldero, H. K. (Harrow)—1851-52-53
Booth, C. (Rugby)—1862-63-64-65 (Captain 1864)
Booth, H. W. (Eton)—1836 (Captain 1836)
Boudier, G. J. (Eton)—1841-43 (Joint-captain with T. L. French 1843)
Bourne, A. A. (Rugby)—1870
Bray, E. (Westminster)—1871-72
Bray, E. H. (Charterhouse)—1896-97
Brearley, J. M. (City of London)—1961-62-63-64 (Captain 1963-64)
Brereton, C. J. (Marlborough)—1858
Bridgeman, W. C. (Eton)—1887
Brocklebank, J. M. (Eton)—1936
Brodhurst, A. H. (Malvern)—1939
Brodie, J. B. (Union H.S., South Africa)—1960
Brodrick, P. D. (Royal G.S., Newcastle)—1961
Bromley-Davenport, H. R. (Eton)—1892-93
Brooke-Taylor, G. P. (Cheltenham)—1919-20
Broughton, R. J. P. (Harrow)—1836-38-39
Brown, F. R. (Leys)—1930-31
Browne, F. B. R. (Aldro School & Eastbourne)—1922
Brune, C. J. (Godolphin, Hammersmith)—1867-68-69
Brunton, J. du V. (Lancaster G.S.)—1894
Bryan, J. L. (Rugby)—1921

University Cricket—Cambridge Blues—*Cont.*

Buchanan, D. (Rugby)—1850
Buchanan, J. N. (Charterhouse)—1906-07-08-09 (Captain 1909)
Buckston, G. M. (Eton)—1903
Bulwer, J. B. R. (King's, London)—1841
Burghley, Lord (later Marquess of Exeter) (Eton)—1847
Burnett, A. C. (Lancing)—1949
Burnup, C. J. (Malvern)—1896-97-98
Burr, G. F. (Maidstone)—1840
Burrough, J. (King's, Bruton & Shrewsbury)—1895
Bury, L. (Eton)—1877
Bury, T. W. (Winchester)—1855
Bury, W. (Private)—1861-62
Bushby, M. H. (Dulwich)—1952-53-54 (Captain 1954)
Butler, E. M. (Harrow)—1888-89
Butterworth, H. R. W. (Rydal Mount)—1929
Buxton, C. D. (Harrow)—1885-86-87-88 (Captain 1888)

Calthorpe, Hon. F. S. G. (Repton)—1912-13-14-19
Calvert, C. T. (Shrewsbury)—1848
Cameron, J. H. (Taunton)—1935-36-37
Campbell, S. C. (Bury St Edmunds)—1845
Cangley, B. G. M. (Felsted)—1947
Carris, B. D. (Harrow)—1938-39
Carris, H. E. (Mill Hill)—1930
Cawston, E. (Lancing)—1932
Chambers, R. E. J. (Forest)—1966
Chapman, A. P. F. (Oakham & Uppingham)—1920-21-22
Christopher, A. W. M. (Private)—1843
Christopherson, J. C. (Uppingham)—1931
Clement, R. A. (Rugby)—1854
Clissold, S. T. (Eton)—1844-46
Close, P. A. (Haileybury)—1965
Cobbold, P. W. (Eton)—1896
Cobbold, R. H. (Eton)—1927
Cobden, F. C. (Harrow)—1870-71-72
Cockburn-Hood, J. S. E. (Rugby)—1865-67
Cockett, J. A. (Aldenham)—1951
Coghlan, T. B. L. (Rugby)—1960
Colbeck, L. G. (Marlborough)—1905-06
Collins, D. C. (Wellington College, N.Z.)—1910-11
Collins, T. (Bury St Edmunds)—1863
Comber, J. T. H. (Marlborough)—1931-32-33
Conradi, E. R. (Oundle)—1946
Coode, A. T. (Fauconberge School, Beccles)—1898
Cook, G. W. (Dulwich)—1957-58
Cooke, C. R. (Eton & Ipswich)—1858
Cookesley, W. G. (Eton)—1827
Cosh, N. J. (Dulwich)—1966-67
Cotterill, G. E. (Brighton)—1858-59-60
Cottrell, G. A. (Kingston G.S.)—1966-67
Cowie, A. G. (Charterhouse)—1910
Craig, E. J. (Charterhouse)—1961-62-63
Crawley, E. (Harrow)—1887-88-89
Crawley, L. G. (Harrow)—1923-24-25
Croft, P. D. (Gresham's)—1955
Crofts, C. D. (Winchester)—1843
Crookes, D. V. (Michaelhouse, S.A.)—1953
Cumberlege, B. S. (Durham)—1913
Currie, F. L. (Rugby)—1845
Curteis, T. S. (Felsted & Bury St Edmunds)—1864-65

Dale, J. W. (Tonbridge)—1868-69-70
Daniel, A. W. T. (Harrow)—1861-62-63-64
Daniell, J. (Clifton)—1899-1900-01
Daniels, D. M. (Rutlish)—1964-65
Datta, P. B. (Asutosh College, Calcutta)—1947
Davies, G. B. (Rossall)—1913-14
Davies, J. G. W. (Tonbridge)—1933-34
Dawson, E. W. (Eton)—1924-25-26-27 (Captain 1927)
Day, S. H. (Malvern)—1899-1900-01-02 (Captain 1901)
De Gray, T. (later Lord Walsingham) (Eton)—1862-63
De Little, E. R. (Geelong Grammar School)—1889
De Paravicini, P. J. (Eton)—1882-83-84-85
De St Croix W. (Eton)—1839-40-41-42
De Zoete, H. W. (Eton)—1897-98
Deacon, W. S. (Eton)—1848-49-50 (Captain 1850)
Dewes, J. G. (Aldenham)—1948-49-50
Dewing, E. M. (Harrow)—1842-43-44-45 (Captain 1844-45)
Dexter, E. R. (Radley)—1956-57-58 (Captain 1958)
Dickinson, D. C. (Clifton)—1953
Dickinson, P. J. (K.C.S., Wimbledon)—1939
Doggart, A. G. (Bishop's Stortford)—1921-22
Doggart, G. H. G. (Winchester)—1948-49-50 (Captain 1950)
Dolphin, J. (Eton)—1827
Dorman, A. W. (Dulwich)—1886
Douglas, J. (Dulwich)—1892-93-94
Douglas, R. N. (Dulwich)—1890-91-92
Douglas-Hamilton, H. A. (Wellington)—1873-75
Douglas-Pennant, S. (Eton)—1959
Downes, K. D. (Rydal)—1939
Dowson, E. M. (Harrow)—1900-01-02-03 (Captain 1903)
Drake, E. T. (Westminster)—1852-53-54
Driffield, L. T. (Leatherhead)—1902
Druce, N. F. (Marlborough)—1894-95-96-97 (Captain 1897)
Druce, W. G. (Marlborough)—1894-95 (Captain 1895)
Du Cane, A. R. (Harrow)—1854-55
Duleepsinhji, K. S. (Cheltenham)—1925-26-28
Dupuis, G. R. (Eton)—1857
Dyke, E. F. (Eton)—1865
Dykes, T. (Kingston College, Hull)—1844

Ebden, C. H. M. (Eton)—1902-03
Edwards, R. S. (Huntingdon G.S. & Christ's Hospital)—1850
Elgood, B. C. (Bradfield)—1948
Ellis, E. C. (Private)—1829
Enthoven, H. J. (Harrow)—1923-24-25-26 (Captain 1926)
Estcourt, N. S. D. (Plumtree, Southern Rhodesia)—1954

University Cricket—Cambridge Blues—*Cont.*

Evans, R. G. (King Edward's, Bury St Edmunds)—1921
Eyre, C. H. (Harrow)—1904-05-06 (Captain 1906)

Fabian, A. H. (Highgate)—1929-30-31
Fairbairn, G. A. (Church of England G.S., Geelong)—1913-14-19
Falcon, M. (Harrow)—1908-09-10-11 (Captain 1910)
Fargus, A. H. C. (Clifton & Haileybury)—1900-01
Farmer, A. A. (Winchester)—1836
Farnes, K. (R.L.S., Romford)—1931-32-33
Fawcett, E. B. (Brighton)—1859-60
Fenn, S. (Blackheath Proprietary)—1851
Fenn, W. M. (Blackheath Proprietary)—1848 50-51
Fernie, A. E. (Wellingborough)—1897-1900
Fiddian-Green, C. A. (Leys)—1921-22
Field, E. (Clifton)—1894
FitzGerald, R. A. (Harrow)—1854-56
Foley, C. P. (Eton)—1889-90-91
Foley, C. W. (Eton)—1880
Ford, A. F. J. (Repton)—1878-79-80-81
Ford, F. G. J. (Repton)—1887-88-89-90 (Captain 1889)
Ford, W. J. (Repton)—1873
Fowler, T. F. (Uppingham)—1864
Francis, T. E. S. (Tonbridge)—1925
Franklin, W. B. (Repton)—1912
Fraser, T. W. (Jeppe, S.A.)—1937
Freeman-Thomas, F. (later Lord Willingdon) (Eton)—1886-87-88-89
French, T. L. (Winchester)—1842-43-44 (Joint-captain with G. J. Boudier 1843)
Frere, J. (Eton)—1827
Fry, K. R. B. (Cheltenham)—1904
Fryer, C. W. H. (Rugby)—1854
Fryer, F. E. R. (Harrow)—1870-71-72-73 (Captain 1873)
Fuller, E. A. (Rugby)—1852
Fuller, J. M. (Marlborough)—1855-56-57-58 (Captain 1857-58)

Gaddum, F. D. (Uppingham & Rugby)—1882
Gay, L. H. (Marlborough & Brighton)—1892 -93
Gibb, P. A. (St Edward's, Oxford)—1935-36 -37-38
Gibson, C. H. (Eton)—1920-21
Gibson, J. S. (Harrow)—1855
Gillespie, D. W. (Uppingham)—1939
Gilligan, A. E. R. (Dulwich)—1919-20
Gilman, J. (St Paul's)—1902
Godsell, R. T. (Clifton)—1903
Goldie, C. D. (Kensington G.S.)—1846
Goodfellow, A. (Marlborough)—1961-62
Goodwin, H. J. (Marlborough)—1907-08
Goonesena, G. (Royal College, Colombo)—1954-55-56-57 (Captain 1957)
Gordon, Hon. F. A. (later Lord Francis Gordon) (Charterhouse)—1829
Gosling, R. C. (Eton)—1888-89-90
Grace, W. G. Jnr., (Clifton)—1895-96
Grant, G. C. (Trinidad)—1929-30
Grant, R. S. (Trinidad)—1933
Gray, H. (Perse)—1894-95
Grazebrook, H. G. (Winchester)—1829
Green, C. E. (Uppingham)—1865-66-67-68 (Captain 1868)
Green, D. J. (Burton G.S.)—1957-58-59 (Captain 1959)
Greenfield, F. F. J. (Hurstpierpoint)—1874-75 -76 (Captain 1876)
Grierson, H. (Bedford G.S.)—1911
Griffith, M. G. (Marlborough)—1963-64-65
Griffith, S. C. (Dulwich)—1935
Griffiths, W. H. (Charterhouse)—1946-47-48
Grimshaw, J. W. T. (King William's School, Isle of Man)—1934-35
Grimston, Hon. F. S. (Harrow)—1843-44-45
Grout, J. (Private)—1838-39

Hadingham, A. W. G. (St Paul's)—1932
Hale, H. (Hutchin's School, Hobart, Tasmania)—1887-89-90
Hales, J. (Rugby)—1855-56
Hall, P. J. (Geelong)—1949
Hammersley, W. J. (Private)—1847
Hammond, O. (Uppingham)—1855-56-57
Handley, E. H. (Harrow)—1827
Harbinson, W. K. (Marlborough)—1929
Hardy, J. R. (Charterhouse)—1829
Harenc, E. A. F. (Navel College, Portsmouth) —1841
Harper, L. V. (Rossall)—1901-02-03
Harris, J. E. (Sheffield Collegiate)—1859
Harrison, W. P. (Rugby)—1907
Hartopp, E. S. E. (Eton)—1841-42
Harvey, J. R. W. (Marlborough)—1965
Hawke, Hon. M. B. (later Lord Hawke) (Eton) —1882-83-85 (Captain 1885)
Hawkins, H. H. B. (Whitgift)—1898-99
Hays, D. L. (Highgate)—1966
Hayward, W. I. D. (St Peter's, Adelaide)—1950-51-53
Hazlerigg, A. G. (Eton)—1930-31-32 (Captain 1932)
Helm, G. F. (Marlborough)—1862-63
Hemingway, W. M. (Uppingham)—1895-96
Henery, P. J. T. (Harrow)—1882-83
Hewan, G. E. (Marlborough)—1938
Hill, A. J. L. (Marlborough)—1890-91-92-93
Hill-Wood, W. W. (Eton)—1922
Hind, A. E. (Uppingham)—1898-99-1900-01
Hoare, A. M. (Private)—1844
Hoare was appointed captain in 1846, but did not play owing to illness.
Hobson, B. S. (Taunton)—1946
Hodgson, E. F. (Eton)—1836
Holloway, N. J. (Leys)—1910-11-12
Hone, N. T. (Rugby)—1881
Hone-Goldney, G. H. (Eton)—1873
Hope-Grant, F. C. (Harrow)—1863
Hopley, F. J. V. (Harrow)—1904
Hopley, G. W. V. (Harrow)—1912
Horne, E. L. (Shrewsbury)—1855-57-58
Horsman, E. (Rugby)—1827-29
Hotchkin, N. S. (Eton)—1935
Howard-Smith, G. (Eton)—1903

University Cricket—Cambridge Blues—*Cont.*

Howland, C. B. (Dulwich)—1958-59-60 (Captain 1960)
Hughes, G. (Cardiff H. S.)—1965
Hughes, O. (Malvern)—1910
Hughes, T. F. (Private)—1845
Human, J. H. (Repton)—1932-33-34 (Captain 1934)
Human, R. H. C. (Repton)—1930-31
Hume, A. (Eton)—1841-42
Hunt, R. G. (Aldenham)—1937
Hurd, A. (Chigwell)—1958-59-60
Hutton, R. A. (Repton)—1962-63-64

Imlay, A. D. (Clifton)—1907
Ingram, C. P. (Westminster)—1854
Insole, D. J. (Monoux, Walthamstow)—1947-48-49 (Captain 1949)
Ireland, J. F. (Marlborough)—1908-09-10-11 (Captain 1911)
Irvine, L. G. (Taunton)—1926-27

Jackson, F. S. (Harrow)—1890-91-92-93 (Captain 1892-93)
Jagger, S. T. (Malvern)—1925-26
Jahangir Khan, M. (Lahore)—1933-34-35-36
James, R. M. (St John's, Leatherhead)—1956-57-58
Jarvis, L. K. (Harrow)—1877-78-79
Jefferson, R. I. (Winchester)—1961
Jeffery, G. E. (Rugby)—1873-74
Jenner, C. H. (Eton)—1829
Jenner, Herbert (Eton)—1827 (Captain 1827)
Jenner, H. L. (Harrow)—1841
Jenyns, G. F. G. (Private)—1849-50
Jephson, D. L. A. (Manor House, Clapham)—1890-91-92
Jessop, G. L. (Cheltenham G.S.)—1896-97-98-99 (Captain 1899)
Johnson, G. R. (Bury St Edmunds)—1855-56-57 (Captain 1855)
Johnson, P. R. (Eton)—1901
Johnstone, C. P. (Rugby)—1919-20
Jones, A. O. (Bedford Modern)—1893
Jones, R. S. (Chatham House, Ramsgate)—1879-80
Jones-Bateman, J. B. (Winchester)—1848
Judd, A. K. (St Paul's)—1927

Kaye, M. A. C. P. (Harrow)—1938
Keigwin, R. P. (Clifton)—1903-04-05-06
Kelland, P. A. (Repton)—1950
Kemp, G. M. (later Lord Rochdale) (Mill Hill & Shrewsbury)—1885-86-88
Kempson, S. M. E. (Cheltenham)—1851-53
Kempson, W. J. (Rugby)—1855
Kemp-Welch, G. D. (Charterhouse)—1929-30-31 (Captain 1931)
Kenny, C. J. M. (Ampleforth)—1952
Kerslake, R. C. (Kingswood)—1963-64
Khanna, B. C. (Lahore)—1937
Kidd, E. L. (Wellington)—1910-11-12-13 (Captain 1912)
Killick, E. T. (St Paul's)—1928-29-30
King, F. (Dulwich)—1934
King, R. T. (Oakham)—1846-47-48-49 (Captain 1849)
Kingdon, S. N. (Eton)—1827
Kingston, F. W. (Abingdon House, Northampton)—1878
Kirby, D. (St Peter's, York)—1959-60-61 (Captain 1961)
Kirkman, M. C. (Dulwich)—1963
Kirwan, J. H. (Eton)—1839
Knatchbull-Hugessen, C. M. (later Lord Brabourne) (Eton)—1886
Knight, R. D. V. (Dulwich)—1967
Knightley-Smith, W. (Highgate)—1953
Koe, B. D. (Eton)—1838

Lacy, F. E. (Sherborne)—1882
Lacy-Scott, D. G. (Marlborough)—1946
Lagden, R. B. (Marlborough)—1912-13-14
Lancashire, O. P. (Lancing)—1880
Lang, A. H. (Harrow)—1913
Lang, R. (Harrow)—1860-61-62
Langley, J. D. A. (Stowe)—1938
Latham, P. M. (Malvern)—1892-93-94 (Captain 1894)
Latham, T. (Winchester)—1873-74
Lawrence, A. S. (Harrow)—1933
Leake, W. M. (Rugby)—1851-52-53-54
Lee, F. (Rugby)—1860
Lee, J. M. (Blackheath Proprietary & Oundle)—1846-47-48
Leith, J. (Private)—1848
Lewis, A. R. (Neath G.S.)—1960-61-62 (Captain 1962)
Lewis, L. K. (Taunton)—1953
Lockhart, J. H. B. (Sedbergh)—1909-10
Long, F. E. (Eton)—1836
Long, R. P. (Harrow)—1845-46
Longfield, T. C. (Aldenham)—1927-28
Longman, G. H. (Eton)—1872-73-74-75 (Captain 1874-75)
Longman, H. K. (Eton)—1901
Longrigg, E. F. (Rugby)—1927-28
Lowe, R. G. H. (Westminster)—1925-26-27
Lowe, W. W. (Malvern)—1895
Lowry, T. C. (Christ's College, N.Z.)—1923-24 (Captain 1924)
Lucas, A. P. (Uppingham)—1875-76-77-78
Luddington, H. T. (Uppingham)—1876-77
Lumsden, V. R. (Munro College, Jamaica)—1953-54-55
Lyon, M. D. (Rugby)—1921-22
Lyon, W. J. (Highstead, Torquay)—1861
Lyttelton, 4th Lord (Eton)—1838
Lyttelton, Hon. Alfred (Eton)—1876-77-78-79 (Captain 1879)
Lyttelton, Hon. C. F. (Eton)—1908-09
Lyttelton, Hon. C. G. (later Lord Cobham) (Eton)—1861-62-63-64
Lyttelton, Hon. Edward (Eton)—1875-76-77-78 (Captain 1878)
Lyttleton, Hon. G. W. S. (Eton)—1866-67

McAdam, K. P. W. J. (Prince of Wales, Nairobi & Millfield)—1965-66
Macan, G. (Harrow)—1874-75
MacBryan, J. C. W. (Exeter)—1920
McCarthy, C. N. (Pietermaritzburg College, S.A.)—1952

University Cricket—Cambridge Blues—*Cont.*

McCormick, J. (Liverpool College & Bingley) —1854-56 (Captain 1856)
McDonell, H. C. (Winchester)—1903-04-05
MacGregor, G. (Uppingham)—1888-89-90-91 (Captain 1891)
Machin, R. S. (Lancing)—1927
Mackinnon, F. A. (Harrow)—1870
McLachlan, A. A. (St Peter's, Adelaide)—1964-65
McLachlan, I. M. (St Peter's, Adelaide)—1957-58
Macleod, K. G. (Fettes)—1908-09
MacNiven, E. (Eton)—1846
Mainprice, H. (Blundell's)—1906
Makinson, J. (Huddersfield & Owen's College) —1856-57-58
Malalasekera, V. P. (Royal College, Colombo) —1966-67
Mann, E. W. (Harrow)—1903-04-05 (Captain 1905
Mann, F. G. (Eton)—1938-39
Mann, F. T. (Malvern)—1909-10-11
Mann, J. E. F. (Geelong)—1924
Manners-Sutton, Hon. J. H. T. (later Viscount Canterbury) (Eton)—1836
Mansfield, J. W. (Winchester)—1883-84
Maples, W. (Haileybury & Winchester)—1839
Marchant, F. (Rugby & Eton)—1884-85-86-87 (Captain 1887)
Marler, R. G. (Harrow)—1951-52-53 (Captain 1953)
Marriott, C. S. (St Columba's)—1920-21
Marriott, H. H. (Malvern)—1895-96-97-98
Marsh, J. F. (Amersham Hall)—1904
Marshall, H. M. (Westminster)—1861-62-63-64
Marshall, J. H. (King Edward VI School, Birmingham)—1859
Marshall, J. W. (King Edward VI School, Birmingham)—1855-56-57
Martin, M. T. (Rugby)—1862-64
Martineau, L. (Uppingham)—1887
Massey, W. (Harlow)—1838-39
Mathews, K. P. A. (Felsted)—1951
Maule, W. (Tonbridge)—1853
May, P. B. H. (Charterhouse)—1950-51-52
May, P. R. (Private)—1905-06
Meetkerke, A. (Eton)—1840
Mellor, F. H. (Cheltenham)—1877
Melluish, M. E. L. (Rossall)—1954-55-56 (Captain 1956)
Meryweather, W. S. T. M. (Charterhouse)—1829
Meyer, R. J. O. (Haileybury)—1924-25-26
Meyrick-Jones, F. (Marlborough)—1888
Micklethwaite, F. N. (Eton)—1836
Micklethwaite, S. N. (Shrewsbury)—1843
Miller, M. E. (Prince Henry G.S.)—1963
Mills, J. M. (Oundle)—1946-47-48 (Captain 1948)
Mills, W. (Harrow)—1840-41-42-43
Mischler, N. M. (St Paul's)—1946-47
Mitchell, F. (St Peter's, York)—1894-95-96-97 (Captain 1896)
Money, W. B. (Harrow)—1868-69-70-71 (Captain 1870)
Moon, L. J. (Westminster)—1899-1900
Morcom, A. F. (Repton)—1905-06-07
Mordaunt, H. J. (Eton)—1888-89
Morgan, J. T. (Charterhouse)—1928-29-30 (Captain 1930)
Morgan, M. N. (Marlborough)—1954
Morris, R. J. (Blundell's)—1949
Morrison, J. S. F. (Charterhouse)—1912-14-19 (Captain 1919)
Morse, C. (Dedham)—1842-43-44
Morton, P. H. (Rossall)—1878-79-80
Mugliston, F. H. (Rossall)—1907-08
Mulholland, Hon. H. G. H. (Eton)—1911-12-13 (Captain 1913)
Murray, D. L. (Queens Royal College, Trinidad)—1965-66 (Captain 1966)

Napier, G. G. (Marlborough)—1904-05-06-07
Nason, J. W. W. (University School, Hastings) —1909-10
Naumann, J. H. (Malvern)—1913-19
Nelson, R. P. (St George's, Harpenden)—1936
Newton, S. C. (Victoria College, Jersey)—1876
Nicholson, J. (Rugby & Harrow)—1845
Norman, C. L. (Eton)—1852-53
Norman, F. H. (Eton)—1858-59-60 (Captain 1860)
Norris, D. W. W. (Harrow)—1967
Norris, W. A. (Eton)—1851
Northey, A. E. (Harrow)—1859-60
Nunn, F. (Bury St Edmunds)—1859

O'Brien, R. P. (Wellington)—1955-56
Oddie, H. H. (Eton)—1836
Oliver, E. (Repton)—1908-09
Onslow, D. R. (Brighton)—1860-61
Orford, L. A. (Uppingham)—1886-87
Ottey, G. P. (Rugby)—1844-45-46-47

Page, C. C. (Malvern)—1905-06
Palfreman, A. B. (Nottingham H.S.)1966
Palmer, C. (Uppingham)—1907
Parker, G. W. (Crypt, Gloucester)—1934-35 (Captain 1935)
Parker, H. (Maidstone)—1839
Parry, D. M. (Merchant Taylors')—1931
Parsons, A. B. D. (Brighton)—1954-55
Partridge, N. E. (Malvern)—1920
Patterson, W. S. (Uppingham)—1875-76-77 (Captain 1877)
Paull, R. K. (Millfield)—1967
Pawle, J. H. (Harrow)—1936-37
Payne, A. U. (St Edmund's, Canterbury)—1925
Payne, M. W. (Wellington)—1904-05-06-07 (Captain 1907)
Payton, W. E. G. (Nottingham H.S.)—1937
Pearson. A. J. G. (Downside)—1961-62-63
Pelham, A. G. (Eton)—1934
Pelham, Hon. F. G. (later Earl of Chichester) (Eton)—1864-65-66-67(Captain 1866-67)
Pell, O. C. (Rugby)—1844-45-46-47 (Captain 1847)
Penn, E. F. (Eton)—1899-1902
Pepper, J. (Leys)—1946-47-48
Perkins, H. (Bury St Edmunds)—1854

University Cricket—Cambridge Blues—*Cont.*

Perkins, T. T. N. (Leatherhead)—1893-94
Phillips, E. S. (Marlborough)—1904
Pickering, E. H. (Eton)—1827-29 (Captain 1829)
Pickering, W. P. (Eton)—1840-42
Pieris, P. I. (St Thomas's, Colombo)—1957-58
Pigg, H. (Abingdon House, Northampton)—1877
Plowden, H. M. (Harrow)—1860-61-62-63 (Captain 1862-63)
Ponniah, C. E. M. (St Thomas's, Colombo)—1967
Ponsonby, Hon. F. G. B. (Harrow) (later Lord Bessborough)—1836
Pontifex, C. (K.C.S., London)—1851-53 (Captain 1853)
Pope, C. G. (Harrow)—1894
Popplewell, O. B. (Charterhouse)—1949-50-51
Potter, A. (Private)—1849
Powell, A. G. (Charterhouse)—1934
Powys, W. N. (Private)—1871-72-74
Prest, E. B. (Eton)—1850
Prest, H. E. W. (Malvern)—1909-11
Preston, B. (Westminster)—1869
Pretlove, J. F. (Alleyn's)—1954-55-56
Prideaux, R. M. (Tonbridge)—1958-59-60
Pritchard, G. C. (King's, Canterbury)—1964
Pryer, B. J. K. (City of London)—1948
Pyemont, C. P. (Marlborough)—1967

Ramsay, R. C. (Harrow)—1882
Ranjitsinhji, K. S. (Rajkumar College, India)—1893
Ratcliffe, A. (Rydal)—1930-31-32
Raymond-Barker, H. B. (Winchester)—1844
Raynor, G. S. (Winchester)—1872
Reddy, N. S. K. (Doon School, Dehra Dun, India)—1959-60-61
Rees-Davies, W. R. (Eton)—1938
Reynolds, E. M. (Royal Institution, Liverpool)—1853-54
Richardson, H. A. (Tonbridge)—1867-68-69
Richardson, J. M. (Harrow)—1866-67-68
Riddell, V. H. (Clifton)—1926
Riley, W. N. (R.G.S., Worcester)—1912
Rimell, A. G. J. (Charterhouse)—1949-50
Rippingall, S. F. (Rugby)—1845
Roberts, F. B. (Rossall)—1903
Robertson, W. P. (Harrow)—1901
Robbins, R. W. V. (Highgate)—1926-27-28
Robinson, J. J. (Appleby)—1894
Rock, C. W. (Launceston G.S., Tasmania)—1884-85-86
Roe, W. N. (Clergy Orphan School, Canterbury)—1883
Romilly, E. (Bury St Edmunds)—1827
Roopnaraine, R. (Queen's College, Guyana)—1965-66
Rose, M. H. (Pocklington)—1963-64
Rotherham, G. A. (Rugby)—1919
Rought-Rought, D. C. (Private)—1937
Rought-Rought, R. C. (Private)—1930-32
Rowe, F. C. C. (Harrow)—1881
Rowell, W. I. (Marlborough)—1891
Royston, Viscount (Harrow)—1857
Russell, S. G. (Tiffin)—1965-66-67 (Captain 1967)

St John, E. (Private)—1829
Salter, H. W. (Private)—1861-62
Savile, Hon. A. (Eton)—1840
Savile, G. (Eton & Rossall)—1868
Saville, S. H. (Marlborough)—1911-12-13-14 (Captain 1914)
Sayres, E. (Midhurst)—1838-39-40-41
Schultz, S. S. (later Storey) (Uppingham)—1877
Scott, A. T. (Brighton)—1870-71
Seabrook, F. J. (Haileybury)—1926-27-28 (Captain 1928)
Seddon, R. (Bridgnorth G.S.)—1846-47
Sharpe, C. M. (Private)—1875
Shaw, V. K. (Haileybury)—1876
Shelmerdine, G. O. (Cheltenham)—1922
Sheppard, D. S. (Sherborne)—1950-51-52 (Captain 1952)
Sherwell, N. B. (Tonbridge)—1923-24-25
Shine, E. B. (King Edward, Saffron Walden)—1896-97
Shirley, W. R. (Eton)—1924
Shirreff, A. C. (Dulwich)—1939
Shuttleworth, G. M. (Blackburn G.S.)—1946-47-48
Silk, D. R. W. (Christ's Hospital)—1953-54-55 (Captain 1955)
Simonds, H. J. (Eton)—1850
Sims, H. M. (St Peter's, York)—1873-74-75
Singh, S. (Khalsa & Punjab U.)—1955-56
Sinker, N. D. (Winchester)—1966
Sivewright, E. (Eton)—1829
Slack, J. K. E. (U.C.S., London)—1954
Smith, A. F. (Harrow & Wellington)—1875
Smith, C. A. (Charterhouse)—1882-83-84-85
Smith, C. S. (William Hulme's G.S.)—1954-55-56-57
Smith, D. J. (Stockport G.S.)—1955-56
Southwell, H. G. (Harrow)—1852-53
Spencer, R. (Harrow)—1881
Spiro, D. G. (Harrow)—1884
Stacey, F. E. (Eton)—1853
Stanning, J. (Rugby)—1900
Stedman, H. C. P. (Private)—1871
Steel, A. G. (Marlborough)—1878-79-80-81 (Captain 1880)
Steel, D. Q. (Uppingham)—1876-77-78-79
Stevenson, M. H. (Rydal)—1949-50-51-52
Stogdon, J. H. (Harrow)—1897-98-99
Stow, M. H. (Harrow)—1867-68-69 (Captain 1869)
Streatfeild, E. C. (Charterhouse)—1890-91-92-93
Studd, C. T. (Eton)—1880-81-82-83 (Captain 1883)
Studd, G. B. (Eton)—1879-80-81-82 (Captain 1882)
Studd, J. E. K. (Eton)—1881-82-83-84 (Captain 1884)
Studd, P. M. (Harrow)—1937-38-39 (Captain 1939)
Studd, R. A. (Eton)—1895
Subba Row, R. (Whitgift)—1951-52-53
Sutthery, A. M. (Uppingham & Oundle)—1887
Swift, B. T. (St Peter's, Adelaide)—1957
Sykes, W. (Private)—1844

University Cricket—Cambridge Blues—*Cont.*

Tabor, A. S. (Eton)—1872-73-74
Taylor, C. G. (Eton)—1836-38-39 (Captain 1838-39)
Taylor, T. L. (Uppingham)—1898-99-1900 (Captain 1900)
Templeton, C. H. (Winchester)—1827
Thackeray, F. (Eton)—1838-39-40
Thomas, A. (Winchester)—1838
Thompson, J. R. (Tonbridge)—1938-39
Thompson, W. T. (Ruthin)—1836
Thomson, R. H. (Bexhill)—1961-62
Thornewill, E. J. (Harrow)—1856
Thornton, C. I. (Eton)—1869-70-71-72 (Captain 1872)
Thwaites, I. G. (Eastbourne)—1964
Tillard, C. (Repton)—1873-74
Tindall, M. (Harrow)—1935-36-37 (Captain 1937)
Tobin, F. (Rugby)—1870-71-72
Tomblin, A. C. (Uppingham)—1857
Tomlinson, W. J. V. (Felsted)—1923
Topham, H. G. (Repton)—1883-84
Toppin, C. (Sedbergh)—1885-86-87
Tordoff, G. G. (Normanton G.S.)—1952
Townley, T. M. (Eton)—1847-48
Trapnell, B. M. W. (U.C.S., London)—1946
Tremlett, T. D. (Eton)—1854
Trevelyan, W. B. (Edinburgh Academy & Harrow)—1842-43
Tuck, G. H. (Eton)—1863-64-65-66 (Captain 1865)
Tufnell, N. C. (Eton)—1909-10
Turnbull, M. J. (Downside)—1926-28-29 (Captain 1929)
Turner, J. A. (Uppingham)—1883-84-85-86
Turner, J. B. (Blackheath Proprietary)—1841

Urquhart, J. R. (King Edward VI School, Chelmsford)—1948

Valentine, B. H. (Repton)—1929
Vernon, H. (Harrow)—1850-51-52 (Captain 1852)
Vincent, H. G. (Haileybury)—1914

Wait, O. J. (Dulwich)—1949-51
Walker, Ashley (Westminster)—1864-65-66
Walker, F. (Private)—1849-50-51-52
Walker, John (Private)—1847-48-49 (Captain 1848)
Ward, A. R. (Private)—1853
Ward was appointed captain in 1854 but did not play owing to illness.
Ward, E. E. (Bury St Edmunds)—1870-71
Warner, W. S. O. (Torquay)—1867-68
Warr, J. J. (Ealing C.G.S.)—1949-50-51-52 (Captain 1951)
Warren, C. (Oakham)—1866
Watts, H. E. (Downside)—1947
Webb, R. H. (Eton)—1827
Webster, J. (Bradford G.S.)—1939
Webster, W. H. (Highgate)—1932
Weedon, M. J. H. (Harrow)—1962
Weigall, G. J. V. (Wellington)—1891-92
Weighell, W. B. (Bedford G.S.)—1866-68-69
Wells, C. M. (Dulwich)—1891-92-93
Wells, T. U. (Kings, Auckland)—1950
Weston, J. S. (Rugby)—1851-52
Wheatley, O. S. (King Edward's, Birmingham)—1957-58
Wheelhouse, A. (Nottingham H.S.)—1959
White, A. F. T. (Uppingham)—1936
White, A. H. (Geelong)—1924
White, H. S. (Bury St Edmunds & Brighton) —1852
White, R. C. (Hilton, S.A.)—1962-63-64-65 (Captain 1965)
Whitfield, H. (Eton)—1878-79-80-81
Whymper, F. H. (Eton)—1849
Wilcox, D. R. (Dulwich)—1931-32-33 (Captain 1933)
Wild, J. V. (Taunton)—1938
Wilenkin, B. C. G. (Harrow)—1956
Willard, M. J. L. (Judd, Tonbridge)—1959-60-61
Wilkins-Leir, E. J. P. (Marlborough)—1858
Willatt, G. L. (Repton)—1946-47 (Captain 1947)
Wills, T. W. (Rugby)—1856
Wills had been entered at Cambridge and played as Cambridge were one short, but had never actually been in residence.
Wilson, C. E. M. (Uppingham)—1895-96-97-98 (Captain 1898)
Wilson, C. P. (Uppingham & Marlborough) —1880-81
Wilson, E. R. (Rugby)—1899-1900-01-02 (Captain 1902)
Wilson, F. B. (Harrow)—1902-03-04 (Captain 1904)
Wilson, G. (Harrow)—1919
Wilson, T. W. (Repton)—1869
Windows, A. R. (Clifton)—1962-63-64
Wingfield, W. (Rossall)—1855-56-57
Winlaw, R. de W. K. (Winchester)—1932-33-34
Winter, A. H. (Westminster)—1865-66-67
Winter, C. E. (Uppingham)—1902
Winter, G. E. (Winchester)—1898-99
Winthorp, S. (Rugby)—1829
Wood, G. E. C. (Cheltenham)—1914-19-20 (Captain 1920)
Wood, H. (Sheffield Collegiate School)—1879
Woodroffe, K. H. C. (Marlborough)—1913-14
Woods, S. M. J. (Brighton)—1888-89-90-91 (Captain 1890)
Wooller, W. (Rydal)—1935-36
Wright, C. C. G. (Tonbridge)—1907-08
Wright, C. W. (Charterhouse)—1882-83-84-85
Wright, P. A. (Wellingborough)—1922-23-24
Wroth, H. T. (Uppingham)—1845
Wykes, N. G. (Oundle)—1928

Yardley, N. W. D. (St Peter's, York)—1935-36-37-38 (Captain 1938)
Yardley, W. (Rugby)—1869-70-71-72 (Captain 1871)
Young, R. A. (Repton)—1905-06-07-08 (Captain 1908)

University Cricket—*Cont.*

UNIVERSITY MATCH RESULTS

Cambridge has won 50 and Oxford 44 of the 123 official matches played, the remaining 29 being drawn. With the exception of five matches played at Oxford (1829, 1846 & 1848 at Magdalen; 1843 at Bullingdon Green; 1850 at Cowley Marsh) all the fixtures have taken place at Lord's.

1827 Drawn
1829 Oxford—115 runs
1836 Oxford—121 runs
1838 Oxford—98 runs
1839 Cambridge—Innings & 125 runs
1840 Cambridge—63 runs
1841 Cambridge—8 runs
1842 Cambridge—162 runs
1843 Cambridge—54 runs
1844 Drawn
1845 Cambridge—6 wickets
1846 Oxford—3 wickets
1847 Cambridge—138 runs
1848 Oxford—23 runs
1849 Cambridge—3 wickets
1850 Oxford—127 runs
1851 Cambridge—Innings & 4 runs
1852 Oxford—Innings & 77 runs
1853 Oxford—Innings & 19 runs
1854 Oxford—Innings & 8 runs
1855 Oxford—3 wickets
1856 Cambridge—3 wickets
1857 Oxford—81 runs
1858 Oxford—Innings & 38 runs
1859 Cambridge—28 runs
1860 Cambridge—3 wickets
1861 Cambridge—133 runs
1862 Cambridge—8 wickets
1863 Oxford—8 wickets
1864 Oxford—4 wickets
1865 Oxford—114 runs
1866 Oxford—12 runs
1867 Cambridge—5 wickets
1868 Cambridge—168 runs
1869 Cambridge—58 runs
1870 Cambridge—2 runs
1871 Oxford—8 wickets
1872 Cambridge—Innings & 166 runs
1873 Oxford—3 wickets
1874 Oxford—Innings & 92 runs
1875 Oxford—6 runs
1876 Cambridge—9 wickets
1877 Oxford—10 wickets
1878 Cambridge—238 runs
1879 Cambridge—9 wickets
1880 Cambridge—115 runs
1881 Oxford—135 runs
1882 Cambridge—7 wickets
1883 Cambridge—7 wickets
1884 Oxford—7 wickets
1885 Cambridge—7 wickets
1886 Oxford—133 runs
1887 Oxford—7 wickets
1888 Drawn
1889 Cambridge—Innings & 105 runs
1890 Cambridge—7 wickets
1891 Cambridge—2 wickets
1892 Oxford—5 wickets
1893 Cambridge—266 runs
1894 Oxford—8 wickets
1895 Cambridge—134 runs
1896 Oxford—4 wickets
1897 Cambridge—179 runs
1898 Oxford—9 wickets
1899 Drawn
1900 Drawn
1901 Drawn
1902 Cambridge—5 wickets
1903 Oxford—268 runs
1904 Drawn
1905 Cambridge—40 runs
1906 Cambridge—94 runs
1907 Cambridge—5 wickets
1908 Oxford—2 wickets
1909 Drawn
1910 Oxford—Innings & 126 runs
1911 Oxford—74 runs
1912 Cambridge—3 wickets
1913 Cambridge—4 wickets
1914 Oxford—194 runs
1919 Oxford—45 runs
1920 Drawn
1921 Cambridge—Innings & 24 runs
1922 Cambridge—Innings & 100 runs
1923 Oxford—Innings & 227 runs
1924 Cambridge—9 wickets
1925 Drawn
1926 Cambridge—34 runs
1927 Cambridge—116 runs
1928 Drawn
1929 Drawn
1930 Cambridge—205 runs
1931 Oxford—8 wickets
1932 Drawn
1933 Drawn
1934 Drawn
1935 Cambridge—195 runs
1936 Cambridge—8 wickets
1937 Oxford—7 wickets
1938 Drawn
1939 Oxford—45 runs
1946 Oxford—6 wickets
1947 Drawn
1948 Oxford—Innings & 8 runs
1949 Cambridge—7 wickets
1950 Drawn
1951 Oxford—21 runs
1952 Drawn
1953 Cambridge—2 wickets
1954 Drawn
1955 Drawn
1956 Drawn
1957 Cambridge—Innings & 186 runs
1958 Cambridge—99 runs
1959 Oxford—85 runs
1960 Drawn
1961 Drawn
1962 Drawn
1963 Drawn
1964 Drawn
1965 Drawn
1966 Oxford—Innings & 9 runs
1967 Drawn

University Cricket—*Cont.*

UNIVERSITY MATCH CENTURIES

Highest Scores: 238* Nawab of Pataudi, Snr. (Oxford) 1931
211 G. Goonesena (Cambridge) 1957
Most Hundreds: 3 M. J. K. Smith (Oxford) 1954-55-56

Oxford (35)

109	W. H. Game	1876	113	E. R. T. Holmes	1927
117*	F. M. Buckland	1877	106	Nawab of Pataudi, Snr.	1929
107*	W. H. Patterson	1881	238*	Nawab of Pataudi, Snr.	1931
143	K. J. Key	1886	167	B. W. Hone	1932
107	W. Rashleigh	1886	193	D. C. H. Townsend	1934
100	Lord George Scott	1887	108	F. H. G. Chalk	1934
140	M. R. Jardine	1892	121	J. N. Grover	1937
114	V. T. Hill	1892	142	M. P. Donnelly	1946
100*	C. B. Fry	1894	135	H. A. Pawson	1947
121	H. K. Foster	1895	145*	H. E. Webb	1948
132	G. O. Smith	1896	116	M. C. Cowdrey	1953
109	A. Eccles	1898	201	M. J. K. Smith	1954
171	R. E. Foster	1900	104	M. J. K. Smith	1955
100*	C. H. B. Marsham	1901	117	M. J. K. Smith	1956
130	J. E. Raphael	1903	131	Nawab of Pataudi, Jnr.	1960
160	P. R. Le Couteur	1910	100*	M. Manasseh	1964
170	M. Howell	1919	145	D. P. Toft	1967
109	C. H. Taylor	1923			

Cambridge (42)

100	W. Yardley	1870	149	J. T. Morgan	1929
130	W. Yardley	1872	136	E. T. Killick	1930
105*	W. S. Patterson	1876	201	A. Ratcliffe	1931
120	G. B. Studd	1882	157	D. R. Wilcox	1932
102	C. W. Wright	1883	124	A. Ratcliffe	1932
101	H. W. Bainbridge	1885	115	A. W. Allen	1934
103*	E. Crawley	1887	101	N. W. D. Yardley	1937
127	H. J. Mordaunt	1889	122	P. A. Gibb	1938
116	E. C. Streatfeild	1892	100	P. J. Dickinson	1939
115	C. E. M. Wilson	1898	127	D. S. Sheppard	1952
118	E. R. Wilson	1901	116*	D. R. W. Silk	1953
117*	S. H. Day	1902	118	D. R. W. Silk	1954
172*	J. F. Marsh	1904	114	J. F. Pretlove	1955
107	L. G. Colbeck	1905	146	R. P. O'Brien	1956
150	R. A. Young	1906	211	G. Goonesena	1957
118	H. Ashton	1921	111*	G. W. Cook	1957
102*	A. P. F. Chapman	1922	105	E. J. Craig	1961
104	H. J. Enthoven	1924	113	J. M. Brearley	1962
129	H. J. Enthoven	1925	103*	A. R. Lewis	1962
124	A. K. Judd	1927	119	J. M. Brearley	1964
101*	R. W. V. Robins	1928	100	N. J. Cosh	1967

HIGHEST INNINGS TOTALS IN THE UNIVERSITY MATCH

503	Oxford	1900	415-8d	Cambridge	1921
457	Oxford	1947	415	Oxford	1934
453-8d	Oxford	1931	409	Cambridge	1925
432-9d	Cambridge	1936	408-9d	Cambridge	1952
431	Cambridge	1932	403-4d	Cambridge	1922
425	Cambridge	1938	401-3d	Oxford	1954
424-7d	Cambridge	1957	400	Cambridge	1934
422	Oxford	1923			

RECORD WICKET PARTNERSHIPS IN THE UNIVERSITY MATCH

1st	243	K. J. Key & W. Rashleigh	Oxford	1886
2nd	226	W. G. Keighley & H. A. Pawson	Oxford	1947
3rd	183	A. T. Barber & E. R. T. Holmes	Oxford	1927
4th	230	D. C. H. Townsend & F. G. H. Chalk	Oxford	1934
5th	191	J. E. Raphael & E. L. Wright	Oxford	1905

University Cricket—*Cont.*

6th	178	M. R. Jardine & V. T. Hill	Oxford	1892
7th	289	G. Goonesena & G. W. Cook	Cambridge	1957
8th	112	H. E. Webb & A. W. H. Mallet	Oxford	1948
9th	97*	J. F. Marsh & F. J. V. Hopley	Cambridge	1904
10th	90	W. J. H. Curwen & E. G. Martin	Oxford	1906

1,000 RUNS IN A UNIVERSITY SEASON

		Season	*Inns.*	*N.O.*	*Runs*	*H.S.*	*Avge.*	*100s*
D. S. Sheppard	Cambridge	1952	23	3	1581	239*	79.05	7
A. R. Lewis	Cambridge	1962	31	3	1365	148	48.75	3
E. J. Craig	Cambridge	1961	32	4	1342	208*	47.92	5
J. M. Brearley	Cambridge	1964	26	3	1313	169	57.08	4
R. M. Prideaux	Cambridge	1960	34	0	1311	140	38.55	4
Nawab of Pataudi, Snr.	Oxford	1931	16	2	1307	238*	93.35	6
A. R. Lewis	Cambridge	1960	32	2	1307	125	43.56	2
P. B. H. May	Cambridge	1951	24	6	1286	178*	71.44	4
G. H. G. Doggart	Cambridge	1949	24	5	1280	219*	67.36	3
J. G. Dewes	Cambridge	1950	20	4	1262	212	78.87	5
M. P. Donnelly	Oxford	1946	22	2	1256	142	62.80	6
E. R. Dexter	Cambridge	1958	32	2	1256	114	41.86	3
Nawab of Pataudi, Jnr.	Oxford	1961	24	2	1216	144	55.27	4
E. R. Dexter	Cambridge	1957	32	1	1209	185	39.00	2
J. G. Dewes	Cambridge	1949	22	2	1175	204*	58.75	1
J. H. Human	Cambridge	1934	21	3	1160	146*	64.44	5
J. M. Brearley	Cambridge	1961	32	6	1158	145*	44.53	2
A. A. Baig	Oxford	1959	29	4	1148	221*	45.92	3
M. P. Donnelly	Oxford	1947	21	4	1144	154*	67.29	3
A. M. Crawley	Oxford	1928	21	0	1137	167	54.14	5
A. C. Walton	Oxford	1956	29	2	1128	152	41.77	3
M. C. Cowdrey	Oxford	1953	24	2	1124	154	51.09	3
F. C. de Saram	Oxford	1934	23	1	1119	208	50.86	3
E. J. Craig	Cambridge	1962	31	1	1113	157*	37.10	2
G. D. Kemp-Welch	Cambridge	1931	24	1	1111	126	48.30	3
R. C. White	Cambridge	1962	34	1	1103	125	33.42	2
P. A. Gibb	Cambridge	1938	17	1	1075	204	67.18	4
T. C. Lowry	Cambridge	1923	24	2	1077	161	48.95	4
D. S. Sheppard	Cambridge	1950	20	1	1072	227	56.42	4
M. J. K. Smith	Oxford	1954	26	4	1065	201*	48.40	2
M. B. Hofmeyr	Oxford	1950	21	2	1063	162	55.94	4
M. J. Turnbull	Cambridge	1929	24	4	1001	167*	50.05	3
M. J. K. Smith	Oxford	1956	27	2	1001	126	40.04	3

HIGHEST RUN AGGREGATES IN A UNIVERSITY CAREER

		Seasons	*Inns.*	*N.O.*	*Runs*	*H.S.*	*Avge.*	*100s*
J. M. Brearley	Cambridge	1961-1966	120	13	4182	169	39.08	10
D. S. Sheppard	Cambridge	1950-1952	62	5	3545	239*	62.19	14
N. S. Mitchell-Innes	Oxford	1934-1937	78	8	3319	207	47.41	9
E. R. Dexter	Cambridge	1956-1958	92	5	3298	185	37.90	7
J. G. Dewes	Cambridge	1948-1950	62	8	3247	212	60.12	7
A. A. Baig	Oxford	1959-1962	96	6	3182	221*	35.35	6
A. R. Lewis	Cambridge	1960-1962	81	6	3167	148	42.22	6
M. J. K. Smith	Oxford	1954-1956	80	7	3049	201*	41.76	8
Nawab of Pataudi, Jnr.	Oxford	1960-1963	75	6	2932	153	42.49	8
A. M. Crawley	Oxford	1927-1930	63	3	2914	204	48.56	9
E. J. Craig	Cambridge	1961-1963	78	6	2879	208*	39.98	7
P. B. H. May	Cambridge	1950-1952	58	12	2861	227*	62.19	9
M. C. Cowdrey	Oxford	1952-1954	70	5	2848	154	43.81	5
Nawab of Pataudi, Snr.	Oxford	1928-1931	59	5	2744	238*	50.81	9
R. C. White	Cambridge	1962-1965	96	2	2715	151	28.88	3
R. M. Prideaux	Cambridge	1958-1960	92	5	2684	143	30.85	6
G. H. G. Doggart	Cambridge	1948-1950	56	9	2599	219*	55.29	7
E. W. Dawson	Cambridge	1924-1927	87	4	2581	140	31.09	4
D. R. Worsley	Oxford	1961-1964	97	2	2554	139	26.88	2
E. T. Killick	Cambridge	1927-1930	59	3	2534	201	45.25	8
M. B. Hofmeyr	Oxford	1949-1951	65	8	2495	161	43.77	5

University Cricket—*Cont.*

		Seasons	*Inns.*	*N.O.*	*Runs*	*H.S.*	*Avge.*	*100s*
G. T. S. Stevens	Oxford	1920-1923	72	8	2484	182	38.81	2
R. C. M. Kimpton	Oxford	1935-1938	68	7	2412	160	39.54	5
M. P. Donnelly	Oxford	1946-1947	43	6	2400	154*	64.86	9
K. S. Duleepsinhji	Cambridge	1925-1928	57	4	2333	254*	44.02	5
G. Goonesena	Cambridge	1954-1957	87	8	2309	211	29.22	2
C. C. P. Williams	Oxford	1952-1955	75	4	2301	139*	32.40	4
M. A. Eagar	Oxford	1956-1959	93	8	2298	125	27.03	1
J. Burki	Oxford	1958-1960	78	9	2272	144*	32.92	5
H. Ashton	Cambridge	1920-1922	43	8	2258	236	64.51	7
A. C. Walton	Oxford	1955-1957	80	2	2254	152	28.89	3
J. H. Human	Cambridge	1932-1934	48	8	2205	158*	55.12	10
D. B. Carr	Oxford	1948-1951	67	4	2200	170	34.92	5
P. A. Gibb	Cambridge	1935-1938	73	8	2199	204	33.83	5
F. G. H. Chalk	Oxford	1931-1934	77	7	2141	149	30.58	6
N. F. Druce	Cambridge	1894-1897	51	4	2121	227*	45.12	7
N. W. D. Yardley	Cambridge	1935-1938	77	5	2099	116*	29.15	4
R. A. Hutton	Cambridge	1962-1964	82	7	2026	163*	27.01	1
N. J. Enthoven	Cambridge	1923-1926	68	8	2024	129	33.73	2
N. M. Ford	Oxford	1928-1930	62	8	2016	183	37.33	5

MOST WICKETS IN A UNIVERSITY SEASON

		Season	*Overs*	*Mdns.*	*Runs*	*Wkts.*	*Avge.*
O. S. Wheatley	Cambridge	1959	578.1	149	1411	80	17.63
A. G. Steel	Cambridge	1878	456	212	557	75	7.42
I. A. R. Peebles	Oxford	1930	442.2	77	1271	70	18.15
C. M. Sharpe	Cambridge	1875	546.3	168	848	66	12.84
F. R. Brown	Cambridge	1931	499.2	104	1461	66	22.13
C. W. Rock	Cambridge	1886	696.2	326	868	65	13.35
E. M. Dowson	Cambridge	1902	420.3	95	1174	65	18.06
D. M. Sayer	Oxford	1959	509.2	103	1470	64	22.96
D. M. Sayer	Oxford	1958	408.4	129	831	62	13.40
R. H. B. Bettington	Oxford	1923	303.4	60	1010	61	16.55
R. G. Marlar	Cambridge	1953	610.1	172	1619	61	26.54
S. M. J. Woods	Cambridge	1888	500	176	990	60	16.50
F. H. E. Cunliffe	Oxford	1896	471.4	168	984	60	16.40
M. J. C. Allom	Cambridge	1927	465.5	95	1345	60	22.41
G. Goonesena	Cambridge	1955	520.2	140	1290	60	21.50
C. D. Drybrough	Oxford	1961	710.5	247	1667	60	27.78
P. R. le Couteur	Oxford	1910	243.4	39	845	59	14.32
A. Hurd	Cambridge	1960	723.2	214	1883	59	31.91
R. C. Ramsay	Cambridge	1882	534	215	856	58	14.75
A. Hurd	Cambridge	1959	714.2	217	1888	58	32.58
F. S. Jackson	Cambridge	1892	327.2	98	829	57	14.54
H. A. Gilbert	Oxford	1909	350.5	112	756	57	13.26
C. S. Marriott	Cambridge	1921	443.3	128	1064	57	18.66
G. Goonesena	Cambridge	1954	587.3	170	1336	57	23.43
G. G. Napier	Cambridge	1905	338.1	75	973	56	17.37
R. H. B. Bettington	Oxford	1920	292.3	65	847	56	15.12
P. A. Wright	Cambridge	1924	394.2	127	888	56	15.85
R. F. H. Darwall-Smith	Oxford	1937	394.3	77	1102	56	19.67

GENTLEMEN v. PLAYERS

Lord's 1806 to Scarborough 1962

This series of matches between amateurs and professionals ended with the abolition of amateur status in first-class cricket after the 1962 season.

The Lord's match between the Gentlemen and Players was the highlight of the English season before Test Matches became annual events. The M.C.C. selected the teams for the Lord's fixture and an invitation to play was regarded as an honour equal almost to the award of an England cap. Until 1952, when the first professional England captain (L. Hutton) was appointed, captaincy of

Gentlemen v. Players—*Cont.*

the Players was the highest honour open to a professional cricketer. In later years the match at Lord's virtually became a Test trial.

Additional matches were played for many years at Kennington Oval and at the Scarborough Festival and, in 1919, J. B. Hobbs scored a hundred in each of the three fixtures. Other matches under this title were occasionally played at Brighton, Hastings, Prince's, Folkestone, Bournemouth and Blackpool.

CENTURIES

At Lord's

	Gentlemen			Players	
102*	W. Ward	1825	113*	T. Beagley	1821
134*	W. G. Grace	1868	100	J. Saunders	1827
109	W. G. Grace	1870	132	Thomas Hayward	1860
112	W. G. Grace	1872	112*	Thomas Hayward	1863
163	W. G. Grace	1873	122*	Thomas Hearne	1866
152	W. G. Grace	1875	102	R. Daft	1872
169	W. G. Grace	1876	111	A. Shrewsbury	1887
103	A. W. Ridley	1876	130*	W. Barnes	1889
107	A. P. Lucas	1882	103	W. Gunn	1892
100	C. T. Studd	1882	116*	T. W. Hayward	1896
107	E. F. S. Tylecote	1883	125	A. Shrewsbury	1897
118	W. G. Grace	1895	139	W. Gunn	1898
104	C. B. Fry	1899	163	J. T. Brown	1900
102* }	R. E. Foster	1900	111	T. W. Hayward	1900
136 }			140	J. T. Tyldesley	1901
126	C. B. Fry	1901	141	L. C. Braund	1902
232*	C. B. Fry	1903	100	W. H. Lockwood	1902
168*	A. C. MacLaren	1903	139	A. E. Knight	1903
121	K. S. Ranjitsinhji	1904	104 }	J. H. King	1904
114	R. H. Spooner	1906	109* }		
124	D. J. Knight	1919	123*	T. W. Hayward	1905
101	P. G. H. Fender	1921	146*	T. W. Hayward	1907
160	A. P. F. Chapman	1922	154*	J. B. Hobbs	1911
122	G. T. S. Stevens	1923	113	J. B. Hobbs	1919
120	M. D. Lyon	1923	108	C. P. Mead	1921
129	G. T. S. Stevens	1925	140	J. B. Hobbs	1922
108	A. P. F. Chapman	1926	162	A. C. Russell	1922
123	D. R. Jardine	1927	118	J. B. Hobbs	1924
125 }	K. S. Duleepsinhji	1930	113	R. Kilner	1924
103* }			140	J. B. Hobbs	1925
165	Nawab of Pataudi, Snr.	1932	163	J. B. Hobbs	1926
132	K. S. Duleepsinhji	1932	107	H. Sutcliffe	1926
104*	R. E. S. Wyatt	1934	131	E. Tyldesley	1926
175*	H. T. Bartlett	1938	161*	J. B. Hobbs	1932
162*	M. P. Donnelly	1947	110	W. R. Hammond	1932
122	F. R. Brown	1950	120	A. Mitchell	1934
119*	P. B. H. May	1951	105	C. Washbrook	1946
127	C. H. Palmer	1952	101	C. Washbrook	1947
117	R. T. Simpson	1953	132*	L. Hutton	1948
154	C. H. Palmer	1955	123	H. E. Dollery	1950
102*	R. Subba Row	1958	150	D. C. S. Compton	1951
166	M. J. K. Smith	1959	115	M. Tomkin	1955
112	D. S. Sheppard	1962	102	D. V. Smith	1957
109	R. M. Prideaux	1962	101	C. A. Milton	1958
			112	D. B. Close	1959
			100	R. Illingworth	1959

At the Oval

	Gentlemen			Players	
107*	A. Lubbock	1867	119	R. Carpenter	1860
165	I. D. Walker	1868	106	R. Carpenter	1861
215	W. G. Grace	1870	117	H. H. Stephenson	1864
109*	W. B. Money	1870	134	G. Ulyett	1884
117	W. G. Grace	1872	127	A. Shrewsbury	1886
158	W. G. Grace	1873	151*	A. Shrewsbury	1892
144	A. N. Hornby	1877	168*	R. Abel	1894
100	W. G. Grace	1881	100	F. W. Marlow	1895

Gentlemen v. Players—*Cont.*

At the Oval

Gentlemen			Players		
159	W. W. Read	1885	195	R. Abel	1899
112*	C. L. Townsend	1899	134*	T. W. Hayward	1899
123	C. J. Burnup	1900	153*	R. Abel	1900
145	B. J. T. Bosanquet	1904	247	R. Abel	1901
140	W. L. Murdoch	1904	177	T. W. Hayward	1902
128	J. H. Hunt	1904	203	T. W. Hayward	1904
190	R. H. Spooner	1911	104	J. Hardstaff, Snr.	1906
101	C. B. Fry	1912	158	S. P. Kinneir	1911
107	C. L. Jessop	1913	123*	J. W. Hearne	1912
127	Hon. C. N. Bruce	1921	126	J. W. Hearne	1913
112	A. E. R. Gilligan	1924	156	J. B. Hobbs	1914
130	G. O. Allen	1925	120*	J. B. Hobbs	1919
193	D. R. Jardine	1928	127	H. T. W. Hardinge	1921
115	R. E. S. Wyatt	1929	126	T. F. Shepherd	1923
123*	D. R. Jardine	1932	124	A. Sandham	1924
112	Lord Tennyson	1932	103	J. W. Hearne	1925
			125	A. Sandham	1926
			150	E. Hendren	1927
			110	J. B. Hobbs	1931
			120	H. Sutcliffe	1931
			194*	E. Hendren	1932
			125	J. Arnold	1934
			119	H. S. Squires	1934
			106	R. Duckfield	1934

At Prince's

Gentlemen			Players		
104	A. N. Hornby	1873	118	G. Ulyett	1877
110	W. G. Grace	1874			
134	G. F. Grace	1877			

At Brighton

Gentlemen			Players		
217	W. G. Grace	1871			

At Hastings

Gentlemen			Players		
131	W. G. Grace	1894	169	W. Gunn	1891
105	A. O. Jones	1901	117	R. Abel	1892
			108	A. Ward	1897
			124*	G. H. Hirst	1903

At Bournemouth

Gentlemen			Players		
			117	C. P. Mead	1928

At Scarborough

Gentlemen			Players		
174	W. G. Grace	1885	125	G. J. Thompson	1900
134	F. S. Jackson	1900	157*	D. Denton	1906
102	T. L. Taylor	1902	122*	E. G. Hayes	1906
102	C. J. Burnup	1902	105	J. T. Tyldesley	1910
137	E. G. Wynyard	1906	223	C. P. Mead	1911
120	K. L. Hutchings	1908	116	J. B. Hobbs	1919
103	B. J. T. Bosanquet	1911	146	J. W. Hearne	1919
119	G. L. Jessop	1913	138	J. B. Hobbs	1920
101	G. A. Faulkner	1913	105	J. B. Hobbs	1923
101	A. P. F. Chapman	1920	110*	E. Hendren	1923
100	F. T. Mann	1922	266*	J. B. Hobbs	1925
101	A. W. Carr	1925	129	E. Hendren	1925
101*	V. W. C. Jupp	1927	119	J. B. Hobbs	1927
106	M. C. Cowdrey	1951	127	P. Holmes	1927
157	P. B. H. May	1953	116	E. Tyldesley	1927
100	M. C. Cowdrey	1953	144	J. B. Hobbs	1931
133	W. J. Edrich	1953	100	J. Hardstaff, Jnr.	1938

Gentlemen v. Players—*Cont.*

At Scarborough

Gentlemen			Players		
112*	P. B. H. May	1954	241	L. Hutton	1953
133	W. J. Edrich	1955	143*	W. Watson	1953
133	W. J. Edrich	1956	122	J. V. Wilson	1954
104	A. C. D. Ingleby-Mackenzie	1959	124	T. W. Graveney	1956
119	D. R. W. Silk	1960	111	K. F. Barrington	1960
			100	K. F. Barrington	1962

At Folkestone

Gentlemen			Players		
101	Hon. F. S. G. Calthorpe	1927	103	E. Hendren	1927
136	B. W. Hone	1932	138	W. R. Hammond	1927
128	C. P. Johnstone	1933	141*	F. E. Woolley	1928
115	R. C. M. Kimpton	1936	118	A. Sandham	1931
			129	T. S. Worthington	1932
			201	L. E. G. Ames	1933
			117	W. H. Ashdown	1933
			109	G. Geary	1934
			106	W. R. Hammond	1935

HIGHEST INDIVIDUAL INNINGS

266*	J. B. Hobbs (Players)	Scarborough	1925
247	R. Abel (Players)	Oval	1901
241	L. Hutton (Players)	Scarborough	1951
232*	C. B. Fry (Gentlemen)	Lord's	1901
223	C. P. Mead (Players)	Scarborough	1913
217	W. G. Grace (Gentlemen)	Brighton	1873
215	W. G. Grace (Gentlemen)	Oval	1870
203	T. W. Hayward (Players)	Oval	1904
201	L. E. G. Ames (Players)	Folkestone	1933

HIGHEST INNINGS TOTALS

651-7d	Players	Oval	1934
647	Players	Oval	1899
608-8d	Players	Oval	1921
579	Players	Lord's	1926
578	Gentlemen	Oval	1904
561-6d	Players	Folkestone	1927
552-8d	Players	Folkestone	1933

LOWEST INNINGS TOTALS

24	Players	Lord's	1829
31	Gentlemen	Lord's	1848
35	Gentlemen	Lord's	1837
36	Gentlemen	Lord's	1831
37	Players	Lord's	1829
37	Gentlemen	Lord's	1853
39	Gentlemen	Lord's	1840

RECORD WICKET PARTNERSHIPS—GENTLEMEN

1st	203	W. G. Grace & A. J. Webbe at Lord's	1875
2nd	241	W. G. Grace & G. F. Grace at Brighton	1871
3rd	309*	C. B. Fry & A. C. MacLaren at Lord's	1903
4th	205	P. B. H. May & M. C. Cowdrey at Scarborough	1953
5th	172	A. P. F. Chapman & D. R. Jardine at Lord's	1926
6th	164	K. L. Hutchings & F. L. Fane at Scarborough	1908
7th	249	W. L. Murdoch & J. H. Hunt at The Oval	1904
8th	129	T. L. Taylor & E. Smith at Scarborough	1902
9th	193	G. O. Allen & N. E. Haig at The Oval	1925
10th	134	A. E. R. Gilligan & M. Falcon at The Oval	1924

Gentlemen v. Players—*Cont.*

RECORD WICKET PARTNERSHIPS—PLAYERS

1st	263	J. B. Hobbs & H. Sutcliffe at Lord's	1926
2nd	181	J. B. Hobbs & P. Holmes at Scarborough	1927
3rd	298	J. B. Hobbs & E. Hendren at Scarborough	1925
4th	226	E. Hendren & W. R. Hammond at Folkestone	1927
5th	160	J. W. Hearne & F. A. Tarrant at The Oval	1912
6th	204	L. E. G. Ames & W. H. Ashdown at Folkestone	1933
7th	184	D. B. Close & R. Illingworth at Lord's	1959
8th	118	A. E. Knight & S. F. Barnes at Lord's	1903
9th	156	T. W. Hayward & J. T. Hearne at Lord's	1896
10th	140*	G. S. Boyes & A. E. Thomas at Folkestone	1930

BOWLING UNCHANGED THROUGH MATCH

W. Lillywhite (14 wickets) & James Broadbridge (5 wickets) for Gentlemen at Lord's†	1829
W. Lillywhite & James Broadbridge for Players at Lord's	1832
W. Lillywhite (13 wickets) & S. Redgate (5 wickets) for Players at Lord's	1837
J. Wisden (8 wickets) & W. Clarke (12 wickets) for Players at Lord's	1850
Sir F. Bathurst (11-50) & M. Kempson (9-54) for Gentlemen at Lord's	1853
J. Jackson (11-99) & E. Willsher (6-70) for Players at Lord's	1861
G. Tarrant (11-49) & E. Willsher (9-55) for Players at Lord's	1864
A. H. Evans (10-74) & A. G. Steel (9-43) for Gentlemen at The Oval	1879
F. S. Jackson (12-77) & S. M. J. Woods (6-124) for Gentlemen at Lord's	1894

†*Both bowlers were given men*

RESULTS OF MATCHES AT LORD'S

137 matches were played at Lord's between 1806 and 1962. The Players won 68, the Gentlemen won 41 and 28 were drawn. Here are the results after 1919:-

Season	*Result*	*Captain* *Gentlemen*	*Players*
1919	Drawn	P. F. Warner	G. H. Hirst
1920	Players-7 wickets	J. W. H. T. Douglas	W. Rhodes
1921	Players-9 wickets	Hon. L. H. Tennyson	W. Rhodes
1922	Drawn	F. T. Mann	J. B. Hobbs
1923	Drawn	F. T. Mann	J. B. Hobbs
1924	Players-Innings & 231 runs	A. E. R. Gilligan	J. B. Hobbs
1925	Drawn	A. W. Carr	J. B. Hobbs
1926	Drawn	A. W. Carr	J. B. Hobbs
1927	Drawn	A. P. F. Chapman	F. E. Woolley
1928	Players-9 wickets	A. P. F. Chapman	F. E. Woolley
1929	Players-7 wickets	J. C. White	F. E. Woolley
1930	Drawn	A. P. F. Chapman	J. B. Hobbs
1931	Drawn	D. R. Jardine	H. Sutcliffe
1932	Drawn	D. R. Jardine	J. B. Hobbs
1933	Players-10 wickets	D. R. Jardine	H. Sutcliffe
1934	Gentlemen-7 wickets	R. E. S. Wyatt	E. Hendren
1935	Players-9 wickets	R. E. S. Wyatt	W. R. Hammond
1936	Drawn	G. O. Allen	W. R. Hammond
1937	Players-8 wickets	A. B. Sellers	W. R. Hammond
1938	Gentlemen-133 runs	W. R. Hammond	F. E. Woolley
1939	Players-160 runs	W. R. Hammond	E. Paynter
1946	Players- Innings & 140 runs	W. R. Hammond	J. Hardstaff, Jnr.
1947	Drawn	N. W. D. Yardley	L. E. G. Ames
1948	Players-7 wickets	N. W. D. Yardley	L. Hutton
1949	Players-4 wickets	F. G. Mann	D. C. S. Compton
1950	Drawn	F. R. Brown	H. E. Dollery
1951	Players-21 runs	N. D. Howard	D. C. S. Compton
1952	Players-2 runs	F. R. Brown	L. Hutton
1953	Gentlemen-95 runs	F. R. Brown	C. Washbrook
1954	Players-49 runs	D. S. Sheppard	D. C. S. Compton
1955	Players-20 runs	D. J. Insole	A. V. Bedser
1956	Drawn	C. H. Palmer	C. Washbrook

Gentlemen v. Players—*Cont.*

Season	Result	Captain: Gentlemen	Captain: Players
1957	Drawn	P. B. H. May..	D. C. S. Compton
1958	Drawn	D. J. Insole	T. G. Evans
1959	Drawn	P. B. H. May	D. Brookes
1960	Drawn	M. C. Cowdrey	J. B. Statham
1961	Players-172 runs	P. B. H. May	W. Watson
1962	Drawn	E. R. Dexter	F. S. Trueman

APPEARANCES AT LORD'S (1919-1962)

W. R. Hammond and W. J. Edrich each appeared for both the Gentlemen and the Players at Lord's.

GENTLEMEN

Allan, J. M. (1) 1956
Allen, B. O. (1) 1938
Allen, G. O. (6) 1925-29-30-32-34-36
Allom, M. J. C. (2) 1930-32
Ashton, H. (3) 1920-21-22
Bailey, T. E. (10) 1947-49-50-52-53-54-56-59-61-62
Barber, R. W. (4) 1959-60-61-62
Barnett, B. A. (2) 1954-55
Bartlett, H. T. (2) 1938-39
Bartlett, J. N. (1) 1946
Baxter, A. D. (1) 1934
Benson, E. T. (1) 1929
Bettington, R. H. B. (2) 1920-25
Brearley, J. M. (1) 1961
Brennan, D. V. (4) 1950-51-52-53
Brocklebank, J. M. (1) 1939
Brown, F. R. (13) 1931-32-34-35-36-37-38-39-47-49-50-52-53
Bruce, Hon. C. N. (2) 1919-21
Bryan, J. L. (3) 1923-24-25
Calthorpe, Hon. F. S. G. (1) 1925
Carr, A. W. (7) 1919-22-23-24-25-26-29
Carr, D. B. (3) 1950-59-60
Chalk, F. G. H. (1) 1939
Chapman, A. P. F. (9) 1920-21-22-23-26-27-28-30-32
Clay, J. C. (1) 1935
Corran, A. J. (1) 1960
Cowdrey, M. C. (6) 1954-55-56-57-58-60
Craig, E. J. (2) 1961-62
Cranston, K. (2) 1947-48
Crawley, A. M. (3) 1928-29-31
Davies, J. G. W. (1) 1946
Dawson, E. W. (2) 1925-27
Dempster, C. S. (1) 1937
Dewes, J. G. (3) 1948-49-50
Dexter, E. R. (6) 1957-58-59-60-61-62
Divecha, R. V. (1) 1951
Doggart, G. H. G. (2) 1949-50
Donnelly, M. P. (3) 1946-47-48
Douglas, J. W. H. T. (4) 1919-20-21-24
Drybrough, C. D. (1) 1961
Duleepsinhji, K. S. (4) 1925-30-31-32
Edrich, W. J. (6) 1947-48-49-51-53-54
Enthoven, H. J. (2) 1925-26
Evans, A. J. (2) 1919-27
Falcon, M. (1) 1919
Farnes, K. (5) 1933-36-37-38-39
Fellows-Smith, J. P. (1) 1955
Foster, D. G. (1) 1931
Foster, M. K. (1) 1924
Fender, P. G. H. (10) 1920-21-22-23-24-25-26-28-29-33
Fiddian-Green, C. A. (1) 1922
Franklin, W. B. (3) 1926-27-28
Gibb, P. A. (1) 1938
Gilligan, A. E. R. (3) 1922-23-24
Gillingham, F. H. (1) 1919
Goonesena, G. (4) 1954-55-57-58
Griffith, S. C. (5) 1939-46-47-48-49
Haig, N. E. (5) 1921-26-27-28-29
Hammond, W. R. (3) 1938-39-46
Hazlerigg, A. G. (1) 1932
Heane, G. F. H. (2) 1935-39
Holmes, E. R. T. (4) 1927-34-35-36
Howard, N. D. (1) 1951
Howland, C. B. (1) 1959
Human, J. H. (1) 1934
Hurd, A. (2) 1959-60
Ingleby-Mackenzie, A. C. D. (1) 1958
Insole, D. J. (8) 1950-51-52-53-55-56-57-58
Jardine, D. R. (6) 1926-27-28-31-32-33
Jupp, V. W. C. (4) 1920-21-27-28
Kardar, A. H. (1) 1949
Kemp-Welch, G. D. (1) 1931
Killick, E. T. (1) 1929
Kimpton, R. C. M. (1) 1937
Knight, D. J. (2) 1919-20
Knott, C. J. (2) 1946-50
Levett, W. H. V. (4) 1931-32-34-36
Lewis, A. R. (1) 1962
Lewis, E. B. (1) 1957
Louden, G. M. (4) 1919-20-22-23
Lowry, T. C. (1) 1923
Lyon, B. H. (2) 1929-30
Lyon, M. D. (5) 1923-24-26-28-30
MacBryan, J. C. W. (1) 1924
Macindoe, D. H. (1) 1937
Mallett, A. W. H. (2) 1946-47
Mann, F. G. (2) 1948-49
Mann, F. T. (2) 1922-23
Marlar, R. G. (8) 1951-52-53-54-55-56-57-58
Marriott, C. S. (3) 1921-31-33
Maxwell, C. R. (2) 1935-37
May, P. B. H. (7) 1951-52-53-54-57-59-61
McCarthy, C. N. (1) 1952
Melluish, M. E. L. (1) 1956
Melville, A. (3) 1934-35-36
Meyer, R. J. O. (1) 1938
Mitchell-Innes, N. S. (3) 1935-36-37
Moore, R. H. (1) 1938

Gentlemen v. Players—*Cont.*

Oldfield, P. C. (1) 1933
Owen-Smith, H. G. (2) 1933-37
Palmer, C. H. (5) 1948-52-53-55-56
Parsons, J. H. (1) 1930
Pataudi, Nawab of Snr. (3) 1931-32-33
Pawson, H. A. (1) 1947
Pearce, T. N. (2) 1936-48
Peebles, I. A. R. (3) 1930-32-35
Piachaud, J. D. (1) 1961
Pithey, D. B. (1) 1962
Pretlove, J. F. (1) 1955
Prideaux, R. M. (3) 1960-61-62
Read, H. D. (1) 1935
Richardson, P. E. (3) 1956-57-58
Robertson-Glasgow, R. C. (1) 1924
Robins, R. W. V. (4) 1928-29-30-31
Robinson, D. C. (1) 1919
Sayer, D. M. (2) 1959-60
Sellers, A. B. (1) 1937
Sheppard, D. S. (6) 1951-52-53-54-57-62
Sherwell, N. B. (1) 1925
Simpson, R. T. (8) 1947-49-50-51-52-53-54-56
Singleton, A. P. (1) 1946
Smith, A. C. (2) 1960-62
Smith, C. S. (1) 1957
Smith, H. T. O. (1) 1933
Smith, M. J. K. (7) 1955-56-58-59-60-61-62
Stephenson, J. W. A. (3) 1936-38-39
Stevens, G. T. S. (8) 1919-20-22-23-24-25-26-27
Subba Row, R. (3) 1958-59-60
Tennyson, Hon. L. H. (2) 1920-21
Tordoff, G. G. (1) 1955
Trapnell, B. M. W. (1) 1946
Turnbull, M. J. (4) 1933-34-35-36
Valentine, B. H. (3) 1934-39-46
Van Ryneveld, C. B. (1) 1949
Walters, C. F. (2) 1933-34
Warner, P. F. (1) 1919
Warr, J. J. (7) 1950-51-54-55-56-57-58
Wheatley, O. S. (4) 1958-59-61-62
Whitcombe, P. A. (1) 1948
White, J. C. (9) 1921-22-23-24-26-27-28-29-30
Willatt, G. L. (2) 1947-52
Wood, G. E. C. (3) 1920-21-22
Wooller, W. (2) 1948-53
Wyatt, R. E. S. (14) 1926-27-28-29-30-31-32-33-34-35-36-37-38-39
Yardley, N. W. D. (9) 1937-38-46-47-48-49-50-51-54

PLAYERS

Allen, D. A. (1) 1960
Alley, W. E. (1) 1961
Ames, L. E. G. (5) 1931-33-34-37-47
Andrew, K. V. (1) 1962
Appleyard, R. (1) 1954
Arnold, J. (2) 1931-35
Atkinson, G. (1) 1961
Bakewell, A. H. (1) 1931
Barber, W. (1) 1935
Barnett, C. J. (4) 1933-36-37-47
Barrington, K. F. (4) 1955-59-60-61
Barrick, D. (1) 1953
Bedser, A. V. (6) 1948-50-51-52-53-55
Bestwick, W. (1) 1919
Bowes, W. E. (3) 1931-35-39
Bowley, E. H. (1) 1929
Brookes, D. (1) 1959
Brown, G. (2) 1920-21
Butler, H. J. (1) 1947
Cartwright, T. W. (1) 1959
Clark, E. W. (1) 1933
Clark, T. H. (1) 1957
Close, D. B. (3) 1949-59-61
Compton, D. C. S. (13) 1937-38-39-46-47-48-49-51-52-53-54-56-57
Cook, L. (1) 1921
Copson, W. H. (2) 1936-39
Crapp, J. F. (1) 1948
Dollery, H. E. (5) 1939-46-48-50-55
Dolphin, A. (1) 1919
Dooland, B. (2) 1953-54
Ducat, A. (1) 1921
Duckworth, G. (7) 1924-27-28-29-30-32-35
Durston, F. J. (1) 1921
Edrich, J. H. (3) 1959-60-62
Edrich, W. J. (1) 1938
Emmett, G. M. (1) 1953
Evans, T. G. (12) 1946-47-48-49-50-51-52-53-54-56-57-58
Fishlock, L. B. (2) 1936-46
Flavell, J. A. (1) 1961
Fletcher, D. G. W. (2) 1947-52
Freeman, A. P. (5) 1924-28-29-30-32
Gardner, F. C. (1) 1957
Geary, G. (2) 1926-30
Gifford, N. (1) 1962
Gimblett, H. (3) 1936-39-50
Gladwin, C. (1) 1947
Goddard, T. W. (2) 1929-37
Gover, A. R. (1) 1936
Graveney, T. W. (8) 1949-51-53-54-56-57-58-62
Gray, L. H. (1) 1946
Gunn, G. (1) 1919
Hallows, C. (1) 1927
Hammond, W. R. (11) 1927-28-29-30-31-32-33-34-35-36-37
Hardinge, H. T. W. (2) 1921-22
Hardstaff, J. Jnr. (6) 1935-36-37-38-39-46
Harrison, L. (1) 1955
Hearne, J. W. (8) 1919-20-21-22-23-24-25-27
Hendren, E. (13) 1919-20-21-23-24-25-26-27-28-29-30-32-34
Hilton, M. J. (1) 1951
Hirst, G. H. (1) 1919
Hobbs, J. B. (9) 1919-20-22-23-24-25-26-30-32
Hollies, W. E. (4) 1946-49-50-57
Holmes, P. (4) 1925-26-27-28
Horton, H. (1) 1960
Howell, H. (3) 1920-23-24
Hutton, L. (7) 1937-38-39-48-49-51-52
Iddon, J. (1) 1931
Ikin, J. T. (2) 1946-51
Illingworth, R. (1) 1959
Jackson, L. (3) 1949-59-60
Jenkins, R. O. (1) 1949
Kennedy, A. S. (2) 1919-22
Kenyon, D. (3) 1950-54-55

Gentlemen v. Players—*Cont.*

Kilner, R. (4) 1923-24-25-26
Laker, J. C. (3) 1952-56-57
Langridge, James (3) 1933-35-37
Langridge, John (1) 1949
Larwood, H. (3) 1927-30-32
Leyland, M. (7) 1928-29-30-33-34-35-36
Livsey, W. H. (1) 1922
Loader, P. J. (1) 1954
Lock, G. A. R. (4) 1954-55-56-61
Lowson, F. A. (1) 1954
Macaulay, G. G. (2) 1922-25
McCorkell, N. (1) 1936
Marshall, R. E. (1) 1958
Mead, C. P. (6) 1919-20-21-22-23-28
Milton, C. A. (1) 1958
Mitchell, A. (1) 1934
Mitchell, T. B. (2) 1931-34
Moss, A. E. (3) 1953-60-61
Muncer, B. L. (1) 1948
Murray, J. T. (3) 1959-60-61
Nichol, M. (1) 1931
Nichols, M. S. (3) 1933-34-38
Oakman, A. S. M. (1) 1956
O'Connor, J. (1) 1934
Padgett, D. E. V. (1) 1960
Parfitt, P. H. (1) 1962
Parkhouse, W. G. A. (2) 1950-59
Parkin, C. H. (5) 1919-20-21-22-23
Parks, J. H. (1) 1935
Parks, J. M. (3) 1954-55-58
Paynter, E. (4) 1932-37-38-39
Perks, R. T. D. (2) 1931-49
Pollard, R. (2) 1938-46
Pope, G. H. (1) 1939
Price, W. F. (2) 1938-39
Pritchard, T. L. (1) 1948
Pullar, G. (1) 1959
Rhodes, W. (2) 1920-21
Richardson, D. W. (1) 1957
Robertson, J. D. (5) 1947-48-49-51-52
Robinson, E. P. (1) 1946
Root, C. F. (1) 1926
Russell, A. C. (2) 1920-22
Russell, W. E. (2) 1960-61
Shackleton, D. (3) 1950-52-62
Sharpe, P. J. (1) 1962
Sibbles, F. M. (1) 1927
Sims, J. M. (1) 1935
Sinfield, R. A. (1) 1936
Smailes, T. F. (1) 1938
Smith, C. I. J. (2) 1934-37
Smith, D. (1) 1935
Smith, D. V. (3) 1956-57-58
Smith, H. (1) 1923
Smith, T. P. B. (1) 1938
Statham, J. B. (4) 1951-54-58-60
Strudwick, H. (3) 1920-25-26
Stewart, M. J. (2) 1960-62
Sutcliffe, H. (11) 1923-24-25-26-27-29-30-31-32-33-34
Tate, M. W. (9) 1923-24-25-26-27-28-29-30-32
Tattersall, R. (3) 1950-51-53
Thomas, A. E. (1) 1928
Titmus, F. J. (2) 1955-62
Tompkin, M. (1) 1955
Townsend, L. F. (2) 1929-33
Tribe, G. E. (1) 1958
Trueman, F. S. (6) 1956-57-58-59-61-62
Tyldesley, E. (4) 1922-24-26-28
Tyldesley, R. (1) 1925
Tyson, F. H. (3) 1955-56-57
Verity, H. (4) 1931-33-34-36
Voce, W. (1) 1932
Walker, P. M. (1) 1962
Walsh, J. E. (1) 1947
Wardle, J. H. (3) 1948-52-58
Washbrook, C. (6) 1946-47-48-50-53-56
Watkins, A. J. (1) 1952
Watson, F. (1) 1933
Watson, W. (6) 1951-52-53-55-58-61
Wellard, A. W. (1) 1937
Wharton, A. (1) 1956
Woolley, F. E. (14) 1919-20-21-22-23-24-25-26-27-28-29-30-32-38
Wright, D. V. P. (3) 1939-47-50

MATCH RECORDS OF TOURING TEAMS

Tours after 1900 in which no first-class matches were played are excluded from the following touring team playing records which are complete to 30th September, 1967.

The various post-war Commonwealth or Cavaliers touring teams to Southern Africa, the Indian sub-continent, and New Zealand have been included with the records of English teams to those places. These tours were originated in and organised from England and the majority of the non-English players taking part in them had spent a considerable part of their first-class playing careers in Britain. The recent "Rest of The World XI" tours to Britain and Barbados are listed separately.

* Official M.C.C. touring team.
† Played matches in both Australia and New Zealand.
J Played matches in Jamaica only.
P Played matches in Pakistan only.
R Played matches in Rhodesia only.
T Played matches in Transvaal only.

ENGLISH TEAMS IN AUSTRALIA

Season	Captain	First-class matches P.	W.	D.	L.	T.	All-matches P.	W.	D.	L.	T.
1861-62	H. H. Stephenson	—	—	—	—	—	12	6	4	2	—
1863-64†	G. Parr	—	—	—	—	—	12	7	5	0	—
1873-74	W. G. Grace	—	—	—	—	—	15	10	2	3	—
1876-77†	James Lillywhite	3	1	1	1	—	15	5	6	4	—
1878-79	Lord Harris	5	2	0	3	—	13	5	5	3	—
1881-82†	A. Shaw	7	3	2	2	—	18	8	7	3	—
1882-83	Hon. Ivo Bligh	7	4	0	3	—	17	9	5	3	—
1884-85	A. Shrewsbury	8	6	0	2	—	33	16	15	2	—
1886-87	A. Shrewsbury	10	6	2	2	—	29	12	15	2	—
1887-88*a*	G. F. Vernon	8	6	1	1	—	25	10	14	1	—
1887-88†b	A. Shrewsbury	7	5	0	2	—	22	14	6	2	—
1887-88*c*	Combined team	1	1	0	0	—	1	1	0	0	—
1891-92	W. G. Grace	8	6	0	2	—	27	12	13	2	—
1894-95	A. E. Stoddart	12	8	0	4	—	23	9	10	4	—
1897-98	A. E. Stoddart	12	4	3	5	—	22	6	11	5	—
1901-02	A. C. MacLaren	11	5	0	6	—	22	8	8	6	—
1902-03†	P. F. Warner	3	0	1	2	—	3	0	1	2	—
1903-04	P. F. Warner*	14	9	3	2	—	20	10	8	2	—
1907-08	A. O. Jones*	18	7	7	4	—	19	7	8	4	—
1911-12	J. W. H. T. Douglas*	14	11	2	1	—	18	12	5	1	—
1920-21	J. W. H. T. Douglas*	13	5	2	6	—	22	9	7	6	—
1922-23†	A. C. MacLaren*	7	0	4	3	—	8	0	5	3	—
1924-25	A. E. R. Gilligan*	17	7	4	6	—	23	8	9	6	—
1928-29	A. P. F. Chapman*	17	8	8	1	—	24	10	13	1	—
1929-30†	A. H. H. Gilligan*	5	2	1	2	—	5	2	1	2	—
1932-33†	D. R. Jardine*	17	10	5	1	1	22	10	10	1	1
1935-36†	E. R. T. Holmes*	6	3	2	1	—	6	3	2	1	—
1936-37†	G. O. Allen*	17	5	7	5	—	24	7	12	5	—
1946-47†	W. R. Hammond*	17	1	13	3	—	25	4	18	3	—
1950-51†	F. R. Brown*	16	5	7	4	—	25	7	14	4	—
1954-55†	L. Hutton*	17	8	7	2	—	23	13	8	2	—
1958-59†	P. B. H. May*	17	4	9	4	—	20	7	9	4	—
1962-63†	E. R. Dexter*	15	4	8	3	—	27	12	12	3	—
1965-66†	M. J. K. Smith*	15	5	8	2	—	23	13	8	2	—
	TOTAL	344	151	107	85	1	643	272	276	94	1

Two teams toured Australia in 1887-88: *one captained by G. F. Vernon* (*a*) *and the other by A. Shrewsbury* (*b*). *They combined to play one Test Match* (*c*).

ENGLISH TEAMS IN SOUTH AFRICA

Season	Captain	First-class matches P.	W.	D.	L.	T.	All matches P.	W.	D.	L.	T.
1888-89	C. A. Smith	2	2	0	0	—	19	13	2	4	—
1891-92	W. W. Read	1	1	0	0	—	20	13	7	0	—
1895-96	Lord Hawke	4	3	1	0	—	16	7	7	2	—
1898-99	Lord Hawke	5	5	0	0	—	17	15	2	0	—
1905-06	P. F. Warner*	12	7	0	5	—	26	17	4	5	—
1909-10R	H. D. G. Leveson-Gower*	14	7	3	4	—	18	10	4	4	—
1913-14	J. W. H. T. Douglas*	18	9	8	1	—	22	12	9	1	—
1922-23	F. T. Mann*	14	10	3	1	—	22	14	7	1	—
1924-25	Hon. L. H. Tennyson	14	5	7	2	—	21	8	11	2	—
1927-28	R. T. Stanyforth*	16	7	7	2	—	18	7	9	2	—
1930-31	A. P. F. Chapman*	16	5	10	1	—	18	5	12	1	—
1938-39	W. R. Hammond*	17	8	9	0	—	18	9	9	0	—
1948-49	F. G. Mann*	20	9	11	0	—	23	11	12	0	—
1956-57	P. B. H. May*	20	11	6	3	—	22	13	6	3	—
1959-60R	W. S. Surridge (Surrey C.C.C.)	2	0	1	1	—	2	0	1	1	—
1959-60T	D. C. S. Compton (Commonwealth)	3	1	2	0	—	5	2	3	0	—
1960-61	R. Benaud (Commonwealth)	4	4	0	0	—	5	4	1	0	—
1961-62R	E. D. Weekes (Commonwealth)	3	1	1	1	—	3	1	1	1	—
1962-63R	W. Watson (Commonwealth)	2	0	1	1	—	3	0	2	1	—
1962-63	R. Benaud (Commonwealth)	5	1	2	2	—	7	2	2	3	—
1964-65	M. J. K. Smith*	17	10	7	0	—	19	11	8	0	—
1964-65R	D. Kenyon (Worcestershire C.C.C.)	2	1	0	1	—	3	2	0	1	—
	TOTAL	211	107	79	25	—	327	176	119	32	—

ENGLISH TEAMS IN WEST INDIES

Season	Captain	First-class matches P.	W.	D.	L.	T.		All matches P.	W.	D.	L.	T.
1894-95	R. S. Lucas	7	3	2	2	—	..	17	10	3	4	—
1896-97	Lord Hawke	7	3	2	2	—	..	14	9	3	2	—
1896-97	A. Priestley	9	4	0	5	—	..	16	10	1	5	—
1901-02	R. A. Bennett	12	7	0	5	—	..	19	13	1	5	—
1904-05	Lord Brackley	10	6	1	3	—	..	20	11	6	3	—
1910-11	A. F. Somerset*	11	3	3	4	1	..	13	5	3	4	1
1912-13	A. F. Somerset*	9	5	1	3	—	..	9	5	1	3	—
1925-26	Hon. F. S. G. Calthorpe*	12	2	9	1	—	..	13	2	10	1	—
1926-27J	Hon. L. H. Tennyson ..	3	0	3	0	—	..	7	1	6	0	—
1927-28J	Hon. L. H. Tennyson ..	3	0	1	2	—	..	5	1	2	2	—
1928-29J	Sir J. Cahn	3	0	1	2	—	..	5	0	3	2	—
1929-30	Hon. F. S. G. Calthorpe*	12	4	6	2	—	..	13	4	7	2	—
1931-32J	Lord Tennyson	3	0	0	3	—	..	6	1	2	3	—
1934-35	R. E. S. Wyatt*	12	2	8	2	—	..	12	2	8	2	—
1935-36J	P. A. Gibb (Yorkshire C.C.C.) ..	3	1	2	0	—	..	6	1	5	0	—
1938-39J	E. J. H. Dixon (Comb. Us.)	2	0	1	1	—	..	7	2	4	1	—
1947-48	G. O. Allen*	11	0	9	2	—	..	11	0	9	2	—
1953-54	L. Hutton*	10	6	2	2	—	..	17	8	7	2	—
1955-56	M. C. Cowdrey (E. W. Swanton's XI)	4	1	1	2	—	..	6	2	2	2	—
1956-57J	E. D. R. Eagar (Duke of Norfolk's XI)	3	2	1	0	—	..	10	4	6	0	—
1959-60	P. B. H. May*	13	4	8	1	—	..	15	4	10	1	—
1960-61	A. C. D. Ingleby-Mackenzie (E. W. Swanton's XI)	4	2	1	1	—	..	9	5	3	1	—
1963-64J	D. C. S. Compton (Carreras Cavaliers) ..	3	2	1	0	—	..	5	3	2	0	—
1964-65	T. E. Bailey (Carreras Cavaliers) ..	4	0	3	1	—	..	7	1	5	1	—
1965-66J	D. Kenyon (Worcestershire C.C.C.)	1	0	1	0	—	..	5	0	5	0	—
	TOTAL	171	57	67	46	1	..	267	104	114	48	1

ENGLISH TEAMS IN NEW ZEALAND

Season	Captain	First-class matches P.	W.	D.	L.	T.		All matches P.	W.	D.	L.	T.
1863-64†	G. Parr	—	—	—	—	—	..	4	3	1	0	—
1876-77†	James Lillywhite	—	—	—	—	—	..	8	6	2	0	—
1881-82†	A. Shaw	—	—	—	—	—	..	7	5	2	0	—
1887-88†	A. Shrewsbury	—	—	—	—	—	..	3	0	3	0	—
1902-03†	P. F. Warner	7	7	0	0	—	..	18	18	0	0	—
1906-07	E. G. Wynyard*	11	6	3	2	—	..	16	10	4	2	—
1922-23†	A. C. MacLaren* ..	8	6	2	0	—	..	14	11	3	0	—
1929-30†	A. H. H. Gilligan* ..	8	2	6	0	—	..	17	9	8	0	—
1932-33†	D. R. Jardine*	2	0	2	0	—	..	3	0	3	0	—
1935-36†	E. R. T. Holmes* ..	8	2	5	1	—	..	18	5	12	1	—
1936-37†	G. O. Allen*	3	1	2	0	—	..	3	1	2	0	—
1938-39	Sir J. Cahn	1	0	1	0	—	..	10	2	8	0	—
1946-47†	W. R. Hammond* ..	4	2	2	0	—	..	4	2	2	0	—
1950-51†	F. R. Brown*	4	3	1	0	—	..	4	3	1	0	—
1954-55†	L. Hutton*	4	4	0	0	—	..	4	4	0	0	—
1958-59†	P. B. H. May*	5	3	2	0	—	..	5	3	2	0	—
1960-61	D. R. W. Silk*	10	4	5	1	—	..	21	10	10	1	—
1961-62	R. Benaud (Commonwealth)	2	2	0	0	—	..	3	2	1	0	—
1962-63†	E. R. Dexter*	4	4	0	0	—	..	4	4	0	0	—
1965-66†	M. J. K. Smith*	4	0	4	0	—	..	4	0	4	0	—
	TOTAL	85	46	35	4	—	..	170	98	68	4	—

ENGLISH TEAMS IN INDIA, CEYLON AND PAKISTAN

		First-class matches					*All matches*				
Season	*Captain*	*P.*	*W.*	*D.*	*L.*	*T.*	*P.*	*W.*	*D.*	*L.*	*T.*
1926-27	A. E. R. Gilligan*	30	10	20	0	—	34	11	23	0	—
1933-34	D. R. Jardine*	18	10	7	1	—	34	17	16	1	—
1936-37	Sir J. Cahn	1	1	0	0	—	9	3	6	0	—
1937-38	Lord Tennyson	15	4	6	5	—	24	8	11	5	—
1949-50	T. L. Livingston (Commonwealth)	21	10	9	2	—	28	12	14	2	—
1950-51	L. E. G. Ames (Commonwealth)	27	13	14	0	—	29	14	15	0	—
1951-52	N. D. Howard*	23	7	13	3	—	27	10	14	3	—
1953-54	B. A. Barnett (Commonwealth)	21	3	13	5	—	21	3	13	5	—
1955-56P	D. B. Carr*	14	7	5	2	—	16	7	7	2	—
1956-57	W. J. Edrich (C. G. Howard's XI)	2	1	0	1	—	2	1	0	1	—
1961-62	E. R. Dexter*	22	7	13	2	—	24	8	14	2	—
1961-62	R. Benaud (Commonwealth)	3	1	2	0	—	3	1	2	0	—
1962-63	R. Benaud (Commonwealth)	1	1	0	0	—	1	1	0	0	—
1963-64P	P. E. Richardson (Commonwealth)	6	1	5	0	—	6	1	5	0	—
1963-64	M. J. K. Smith*	10	1	9	0	—	10	1	9	0	—
1963-64	A. C. D. Ingleby-Mackenzie (E. W. Swanton's XI)	1	1	0	0	—	1	1	0	0	—
1964-65	P. E. Richardson (Commonwealth)	1	1	0	0	—	2	1	1	0	—
1966-67P	J. M. Brearley*	7	4	3	0	—	8	4	4	0	—
	TOTAL	223	83	119	21	—	279	104	154	21	—

ENGLISH TEAMS IN NORTH AMERICA

		First-class matches					*All matches*				
Season	*Captain*	*P.*	*W.*	*D.*	*L.*	*T.*	*P.*	*W.*	*D.*	*L.*	*T.*
1859-60	G. Parr	—	—	—	—	—	5	5	0	0	—
1868-69	E. Willsher	—	—	—	—	—	6	5	1	0	—
1872-73	R. A. Fitzgerald	—	—	—	—	—	8	7	1	0	—
1878-79	Lord Harris	—	—	—	—	—	1	1	0	0	—
1879-80	R. Daft	—	—	—	—	—	12	9	3	0	—
1881-82	A. Shaw	—	—	—	—	—	5	2	3	0	—
1885-86	E. J. Sanders	2	1	0	1	—	10	8	1	1	—
1886-87	E. J. Sanders	2	2	0	0	—	9	8	1	0	—
1891-92	Lord Hawke	2	1	0	1	—	8	6	1	1	—
1894-95	Lord Hawke	2	2	0	0	—	5	3	2	0	—
1895-96	F. Mitchell	2	1	0	1	—	5	2	1	2	—
1897-98	P. F. Warner	2	1	0	1	—	6	2	3	1	—
1898-99	P. F. Warner	2	2	0	0	—	8	6	2	0	—
1899-00	K. S. Ranjitsinhji	2	2	0	0	—	5	3	2	0	—
1901-02	B. J. T. Bosanquet	2	1	0	1	—	5	3	0	2	—
1902-03	Lord Hawke	—	—	—	—	—	1	1	0	0	—
1903-04	C. J. Burnup (Kent C.C.C.)	2	2	0	0	—	4	4	0	0	—
1905-06	E. W. Mann*	2	1	0	1	—	8	5	2	1	—
1907-08	H. Hesketh-Prichard*	2	0	2	0	—	5	1	4	0	—
1937-38	G. C. Newman*	—	—	—	—	—	19	12	6	1	—
1951-52	R. W. V. Robins*	1	1	0	0	—	22	18	2	2	—
1959-60	D. R. W. Silk*	—	—	—	—	—	24	20	4	0	—
1967	D. R. W. Silk*	—	—	—	—	—	25	21	4	0	—
	TOTAL	25	17	2	6	—	206	152	43	11	—

ENGLISH TEAMS IN SOUTH AMERICA

Season	Captain	First-class matches P.	W.	D.	L.	T.	All matches P.	W.	D.	L.	T.
1911-12	Lord Hawke*	3	2	0	1	—	9	6	2	1	—
1926-27	P. F. Warner*	4	2	1	1	—	10	6	3	1	—
1929-30	Sir J. Cahn	3	1	2	0	—	6	2	3	1	—
1937-38	Sir T. E. W. Brinckman	3	1	1	1	—	11	4	6	1	—
1958-59	G. H. G. Doggart*	—	—	—	—	—	10	9	1	0	—
1964-65	A. C. Smith*	—	—	—	—	—	15	14	1	0	—
	TOTAL	13	6	4	3	—	61	41	16	4	—

ENGLISH TEAM IN EAST AFRICA

Season	Captain	First-class matches P.	W.	D.	L.	T.	All matches P.	W.	D.	L.	T.
1963-64	M. J. K. Smith*	1	1	0	0	—	11	7	4	0	—

AUSTRALIAN TEAMS IN BRITAIN

Season	Captain	First-class matches P.	W.	D.	L.	T.	All matches P.	W.	D.	L.	T.
1878	D. W. Gregory	15	7	4	4	—	37	18	12	7	—
1880	W. L. Murdoch	10	5	3	2	—	37	21	12	4	—
1882	W. L. Murdoch	32	17	11	4	—	38	23	11	4	—
1884	W. L. Murdoch	31	17	7	7	—	32	18	7	7	—
1886	H. J. H. Scott	37	9	21	7	—	39	9	22	8	—
1888	P. S. McDonnell	37	17	7	13	—	40	19	7	14	—
1890	W. L. Murdoch	34	10	8	16	—	38	13	9	16	—
1893	J. M. Blackham	31	14	7	10	—	36	18	8	10	—
1896	G. H. S. Trott	34	19	9	6	—	34	19	9	6	—
1899	J. Darling	35	16	16	3	—	35	16	16	3	—
1902	J. Darling	38	22	14	2	—	39	23	14	2	—
1905	J. Darling	35	15	17	3	—	38	16	19	3	—
1909	M. A. Noble	37	11	22	4	—	39	13	22	4	—
1912	S. E. Gregory	36	9	19	8	—	37	9	20	8	—
1919	H. L. Collins (A.I.F.)	28	12	12	4	—	32	13	15	4	—
1921	W. W. Armstrong	34	21	11	2	—	39	23	14	2	—
1926	H. L. Collins	33	9	23	1	—	40	12	27	1	—
1930	W. M. Woodfull	31	11	18	1	1	33	12	19	1	1
1934	W. M. Woodfull	30	13	16	1	—	34	15	18	1	—
1938	D. G. Bradman	29	15	12	2	—	35	20	13	2	—
1948	D. G. Bradman	31	23	8	0	—	34	25	9	0	—
1953	A. L. Hassett	33	16	16	1	—	35	16	18	1	—
1956	I. W. Johnson	31	9	19	3	—	34	11	20	3	—
1961	R. Benaud	32	13	18	1	—	37	14	21	2	—
1964	R. B. Simpson	30	11	16	3	—	35	14	18	3	—
	TOTAL	784	341	334	108	1	907	410	380	116	1

AUSTRALIAN TEAMS IN SOUTH AFRICA

Season	Captain	First-class matches P.	W.	D.	L.	T.	All matches P.	W.	D.	L.	T.
1902-03	J. Darling	4	3	1	0	—	6	3	3	0	—
1919-20	H. L. Collins (A.I.F.)	8	6	2	0	—	9	7	2	0	—
1921-22	H. L. Collins	6	4	2	0	—	6	4	2	0	—
1935-36	V. Y. Richardson	16	13	3	0	—	16	13	3	0	—
1949-50	A. L. Hassett	21	14	7	0	—	25	18	7	0	—
1957-58	I. D. Craig	20	11	9	0	—	22	11	11	0	—
1966-67	R. B. Simpson	17	7	5	5	—	23	11	7	5	—
	TOTAL	92	58	29	5	—	107	67	35	5	—

AUSTRALIAN TEAMS IN WEST INDIES

Season	Captain	First-class matches P.	W.	D.	L.	T.	All matches P.	W.	D.	L.	T.
1954-55	I. W. Johnson	9	5	4	0	—	12	6	6	0	—
1964-65	R. B. Simpson	11	3	6	2	—	16	4	9	3	—
	TOTAL	20	8	10	2	—	28	10	15	3	—

AUSTRALIAN TEAMS IN NEW ZEALAND

Season	Captain	First-class matches P.	W.	D.	L.	T.	All matches P.	W.	D.	L.	T.
1877-78	D. W. Gregory	—	—	—	—	—	7	5	1	1	—
1880-81	W. L. Murdoch	—	—	—	—	—	10	6	3	1	—
1883-84	J. G. Davis (Tasmania)	4	0	1	3	—	7	2	2	3	—
1886-87	H. J. H. Scott	—	—	—	—	—	5	2	3	0	—
1889-90	J. Davis (N.S.W.)	5	4	1	0	—	7	6	1	0	—
1893-94	J. Davis (N.S.W.)	7	4	2	1	—	8	4	3	1	—
1895-96	L. T. Cobcroft (N.S.W.)	5	3	1	1	—	5	3	1	1	—
1896-97	G. H. S. Trott	—	—	—	—	—	5	3	2	0	—
1896-97	O. Hitchcock (Queensland)	5	3	1	1	—	8	4	3	1	—
1904-05	M. A. Noble	4	3	1	0	—	6	4	2	0	—
1909-10	W. W. Armstrong	6	5	1	0	—	9	7	2	0	—
1913-14	A. Sims	9	6	3	0	—	16	8	8	0	—
1920-21	V. S. Ransford	9	6	3	0	—	14	11	3	0	—
1923-24	C. G. Macartney (N.S.W.)	6	5	1	0	—	12	8	4	0	—
1924-25	E. R. Mayne (Victoria)	6	1	4	1	—	12	4	7	1	—
1927-28	V. Y. Richardson	6	4	2	0	—	13	6	7	0	—
1945-46	W. A. Brown	5	5	0	0	—	5	5	0	0	—
1949-50	W. A. Brown	5	3	2	0	—	14	9	5	0	—
1956-57	I. D. Craig	7	5	2	0	—	12	7	5	0	—
1959-60	I. D. Craig	6	2	4	0	—	9	4	5	0	—
1966-67	L. E. Favell	9	1	6	2	—	10	2	6	2	—
	TOTAL	104	60	35	9	—	194	110	73	11	—

AUSTRALIAN TEAMS IN INDIA AND PAKISTAN

Season	Captain	First-class matches P.	W.	D.	L.	T.	All matches P.	W.	D.	L.	T.
1935-36	J. Ryder (F. A. Tarrant)	17	11	3	3	—	23	11	9	3	—
1945-46	A. L. Hassett (Services)	9	2	5	2	—	10	2	6	2	—
1956-57	I. W. Johnson	4	2	1	1	—	4	2	1	1	—
1959-60	R. Benaud	11	5	5	1	—	11	5	5	1	—
1964-65	R. B. Simpson	4	1	2	1	—	4	1	2	1	—
	TOTAL	45	21	16	8	—	52	21	23	8	—

AUSTRALIAN TEAMS IN NORTH AMERICA

Season	Captain	First-class matches P.	W.	D.	L.	T.	All matches P.	W.	D.	L.	T.
1878-79	D. W. Gregory	1	0	1	0	—	6	4	2	0	—
1882-83	W. L. Murdoch	—	—	—	—	—	2	2	0	0	—
1893-94	J. M. Blackham	2	1	0	1	—	6	4	1	1	—
1896-97	G. H. S. Trott	3	2	0	1	—	6	4	1	1	—
1912-13	S. E. Gregory	2	1	0	1	—	6	4	1	1	—
1913-14	A. Diamond	5	4	1	0	—	48	45	2	1	—
1932-33	V. Y. Richardson	—	—	—	—	—	52	45	6	1	—
	TOTAL	13	8	2	3	—	126	108	13	5	—

SOUTH AFRICAN TEAMS IN BRITAIN

Season	Captain	First-class matches P.	W.	D.	L.	T.	All matches P.	W.	D.	L.	T.
1894	H. H. Castens	—	—	—	—	—	24	12	7	5	—
1901	M. Bisset	15	5	0	9	1	25	13	2	9	1
1904	F. Mitchell	22	10	9	2	1	26	13	9	3	1
1907	P. W. Sherwell	27	17	6	4	—	31	21	6	4	—
1912	F. Mitchell	37	13	16	8	—	37	13	16	8	—
1924	H. W. Taylor	35	8	18	9	—	38	8	21	9	—
1929	H. G. Deane	34	9	18	7	—	37	11	19	7	—
1935	H. F. Wade	31	17	12	2	—	39	22	15	2	—
1947	A. Melville	28	14	9	5	—	33	16	12	5	—
1951	A. D. Nourse, Jnr.	30	5	20	5	—	34	8	21	5	—
1955	J. E. Cheetham	28	15	9	4	—	31	16	11	4	—
1960	D. J. McGlew	30	14	11	5	—	31	15	11	5	—
1961	R. A. McLean (Fezelas)	3	3	0	0	—	21	14	7	0	—
1965	P. L. Van der Merwe	18	5	11	2	—	19	5	11	3	—
1967	W. McAdam (South African Us.)	2	1	1	0	—	21	10	10	1	—
	TOTAL	340	136	140	62	2	447	197	178	70	2

SOUTH AFRICAN TEAMS IN AUSTRALIA

Season	Captain	First-class matches P.	W.	D.	L.	T.	All matches P.	W.	D.	L.	T.
1910-11	P. W. Sherwell	15	6	2	7	—	22	12	3	7	—
1931-32†	H. B. Cameron	16	4	6	6	—	18	6	6	6	—
1952-53†	J. E. Cheetham	16	4	9	3	—	21	7	11	3	—
1963-64†	T. L. Goddard	14	5	6	3	—	28	16	8	4	—
	TOTAL	61	19	23	19	—	89	41	28	20	—

SOUTH AFRICAN TEAMS IN NEW ZEALAND

Season	Captain	First-class matches P.	W.	D.	L.	T.	All matches P.	W.	D.	L.	T.
1931-32†	H. B. Cameron	3	3	0	0	—	3	3	0	0	—
1952-53†	J. E. Cheetham	4	1	3	0	—	5	1	4	0	—
1963-64†	T. L. Goddard	4	1	3	0	—	7	1	6	0	—
	TOTAL	11	5	6	0	—	15	5	10	0	—

WEST INDIAN TEAMS IN BRITAIN

Season	Captain	First-class matches P.	W.	D.	L.	T.	All matches P.	W.	D.	L.	T.
1900	R. S. A. Warner	—	—	—	—	—	17	5	4	8	—
1906	H. B. G. Austin	13	3	2	8	—	19	7	2	10	—
1923	H. B. G. Austin	20	6	7	7	—	26	12	7	7	—
1928	R. K. Nunes	30	5	13	12	—	37	7	18	12	—
1933	G. C. Grant	30	5	16	9	—	43	9	25	9	—
1939	R. S. Grant	25	8	11	6	—	34	10	18	6	—
1950	J. D. C. Goddard	31	17	11	3	—	38	19	16	3	—
1957	J. D. C. Goddard	30	14	13	3	—	34	16	15	3	—
1963	F. M. M. Worrell	30	15	13	2	—	38	19	16	3	—
1964	Sir Frank Worrell	3	1	2	0	—	3	1	2	0	—
1966	G. St. A. Sobers	27	8	15	4	—	34	13	16	5	—
	TOTAL	239	82	103	54	—	323	118	139	66	—

WEST INDIAN TEAMS IN AUSTRALIA

		First-class matches					All matches				
Season	*Captain*	*P.*	*W.*	*D.*	*L.*	*T.*	*P.*	*W.*	*D.*	*L.*	*T.*
1930-31	G. C. Grant	14	4	2	8	—	16	5	3	8	—
1951-52†	J. D. C. Goddard	13	4	1	8	—	15	5	2	8	—
1960-61	F. M. M. Worrell	14	4	4	5	1	22	10	5	5	2
	TOTAL	41	12	7	21	1	53	20	10	21	2

WEST INDIAN TEAMS IN NEW ZEALAND

		First-class matches					All matches				
Season	*Captain*	*P.*	*W.*	*D.*	*L.*	*T.*	*P.*	*W.*	*D.*	*L.*	*T.*
1951-52†	J. D. C. Goddard	4	2	2	0	—	5	3	2	0	—
1955-56	D. Atkinson	8	6	1	1	—	15	11	3	1	—
	TOTAL	12	8	3	1	—	20	14	5	1	—

WEST INDIAN TEAMS IN INDIA AND PAKISTAN

		First-class matches					All matches				
Season	*Captain*	*P.*	*W.*	*D.*	*L.*	*T.*	*P.*	*W.*	*D.*	*L.*	*T.*
1948-49	J. D. C. Goddard	19	6	12	1	—	23	7	15	1	—
1958-59	F. C. M. Alexander	23	13	8	2	—	23	13	8	2	—
1966-67	G. St. A. Sobers	9	4	4	1	—	9	4	4	1	—
	TOTAL	51	23	24	4	—	55	24	27	4	—

NEW ZEALAND TEAMS IN BRITAIN

		First-class matches					All matches				
Season	*Captain*	*P.*	*W.*	*D.*	*L.*	*T.*	*P.*	*W.*	*D.*	*L.*	*T.*
1927	T. C. Lowry	26	7	14	5	—	38	13	20	5	—
1931	T. C. Lowry	32	6	23	3	—	36	7	26	3	—
1937	M. L. Page	32	9	14	9	—	37	13	15	9	—
1949	W. A. Hadlee	32	13	18	1	—	35	14	20	1	—
1958	J. R. Reid	31	7	17	6	1	35	7	21	6	1
1965	J. R. Reid	19	3	10	6	—	21	4	11	6	—
	TOTAL	172	45	96	30	1	202	58	113	30	1

NEW ZEALAND TEAMS IN AUSTRALIA

		First-class matches					All matches				
Season	*Captain*	*P.*	*W.*	*D.*	*L.*	*T.*	*P.*	*W.*	*D.*	*L.*	*T.*
1898-99	L. T. Cobcroft	2	0	0	2	—	4	1	1	2	—
1913-14	D. Reese	4	1	1	2	—	9	5	2	2	—
1925-26	W. R. Patrick	4	0	3	1	—	9	3	5	1	—
1927-28	T. C. Lowry	1	0	0	1	—	1	0	0	1	—
1937-38	M. L. Page	3	0	0	3	—	3	0	0	3	—
1953-54	B. Sutcliffe	3	2	1	0	—	3	2	1	0	—
1961-62	J. R. Reid	3	0	1	2	—	3	0	1	2	—
	TOTAL	20	3	6	11	—	32	11	10	11	—

NEW ZEALAND TEAMS IN SOUTH AFRICA

		First-class matches					All matches				
Season	*Captain*	*P.*	*W.*	*D.*	*L.*	*T.*	*P.*	*W.*	*D.*	*L.*	*T.*
1953-54	G. O. Rabone	16	3	9	4	—	17	3	10	4	—
1961-62	J. R. Reid	18	5	11	2	—	24	7	15	2	—
	TOTAL	34	8	20	6	—	41	10	25	6	—

NEW ZEALAND TEAMS IN INDIA AND PAKISTAN

		First-class matches					*All matches*				
Season	*Captain*	*P.*	*W.*	*D.*	*L.*	*T.*	*P.*	*W.*	*D.*	*L.*	*T.*
1955-56	H. B. Cave	16	3	7	6	—	16	3	7	6	—
1964-65	J. R. Reid	7	0	4	3	—	7	0	4	3	—
	TOTAL	23	3	11	9	—	23	3	11	9	—

INDIAN TEAMS IN BRITAIN

		First-class matches					*All matches*				
Season	*Captain*	*P.*	*W.*	*D.*	*L.*	*T.*	*P.*	*W.*	*D.*	*L.*	*T.*
1911	Maharajah of Patiala	14	2	2	10	—	23	6	2	15	—
1932	Maharajah of Porbandar	26	9	9	8	—	36	13	14	9	—
1936	Maharajah of Vizianagram	28	4	12	12	—	31	5	13	13	—
1946	Nawab of Pataudi, Snr.	29	11	14	4	—	33	13	16	4	—
1952	Vijay Hazare	29	4	20	5	—	34	6	23	5	—
1959	D. K. Gaekwad	33	6	16	11	—	35	7	17	11	—
1967	Nawab of Pataudi, Jnr.	18	2	9	7	—	21	4	10	7	—
	TOTAL	177	38	82	57	—	213	54	95	64	—

INDIAN TEAM IN AUSTRALIA

		First-class matches					*All matches*				
Season	*Captain*	*P.*	*W.*	*D.*	*L.*	*T.*	*P.*	*W.*	*D.*	*L.*	*T.*
1947-48	L. Amarnath	14	2	5	7	—	20	55	8	7	—

INDIAN TEAMS IN WEST INDIES

		First-class matches					*All matches*				
Season	*Captain*	*P.*	*W.*	*D.*	*L.*	*T.*	*P.*	*W.*	*D.*	*L.*	*T.*
1952-53	Vijay Hazare	9	1	7	1	—	10	1	8	1	—
1961-62	N. J. Contractor	9	1	2	6	—	12	2	4	6	—
	TOTAL	18	2	9	7	—	22	3	12	7	—

INDIAN TEAM IN PAKISTAN

		First-class matches					*All matches*				
Season	*Captain*	*P.*	*W.*	*D.*	*L.*	*T.*	*P.*	*W.*	*D.*	*L.*	*T.*
1954-55	V. M. Mankad	14	5	9	0	—	14	5	9	0	—

INDIAN TEAMS IN CEYLON

(Major representative tours only)

		First-class matches					*All matches*				
Season	*Captain*	*P.*	*W.*	*D.*	*L.*	*T.*	*P.*	*W.*	*D.*	*L.*	*T.*
1944-45	V. M. Merchant	1	0	1	0	—	5	2	3	0	—
1956-57	P. R. Umrigar	2	0	2	0	—	3	1	2	0	—
	TOTAL	3	0	3	0	—	8	3	5	0	—

INDIAN TEAM IN EAST AFRICA

		First-class matches					*All matches*				
Season	*Captain*	*P.*	*W.*	*D.*	*L.*	*T.*	*P.*	*W.*	*D.*	*L.*	*T*
1967	Nawab of Pataudi, Jnr.	1	1	0	0	—	7	5	2	0	—

PAKISTANI TEAMS IN BRITAIN

Season	Captain	First-class matches P.	W.	D.	L.	T.	All matches P.	W.	D.	L.	T.
1954	A. H. Kardar	30	9	18	3	—	32	10	19	3	—
1962	Javed Burki	29	4	17	8	—	35	6	21	8	—
1963	Wazir Mohammad (Eaglets)	8	2	4	2	—	20	11	7	2	—
1967	Hanif Mohammad	17	3	11	3	—	22	3	13	6	—
	TOTAL	84	18	50	16	—	109	30	60	19	—

PAKISTANI TEAM IN AUSTRALIA

Season	Captain	First-class matches P.	W.	D.	L.	T.	All matches P.	W.	D.	L.	T.
1964-65†	Hanif Mohammad	4	0	4	0	—	4	0	4	0	—

PAKISTANI TEAM IN WEST INDIES

Season	Captain	First-class matches P.	W.	D.	L.	T.	All matches P.	W.	D.	L.	T.
1957-58	A. H. Kardar	9	1	5	3	—	16	3	10	3	—

PAKISTANI TEAM IN NEW ZEALAND

Season	Captain	First-class matches P.	W.	D.	L.	T.	All matches P.	W.	D.	L.	T.
1964-65†	Hanif Mohammad	10	2	8	0	—	12	4	8	0	—

PAKISTANI TEAMS IN INDIA

Season	Captain	First-class matches P.	W.	D.	L.	T.	All matches P.	W.	D.	L.	T.
1952-53	A. H. Kardar	12	1	9	2	—	12	1	9	2	—
1960-61	Fazal Mahmood	15	0	15	0	—	15	0	15	0	—
	TOTAL	27	1	24	2	—	27	1	24	2	—

PAKISTANI TEAMS IN CEYLON

Season	Captain	First-class matches P.	W.	D.	L.	T.	All matches P.	W.	D.	L.	T.
1948-49	Mohammad Saeed	2	2	0	0	—	4	2	2	0	—
1953-54	A. H. Kardar (Services)	1	1	0	0	—	6	2	4	0	—
1960-61	Shuja-ud-Din (Eaglets)	1	0	1	0	—	4	0	3	1	—
1964	Imtiaz Ahmed (Pakistan A.)	2	0	0	2	—	4	1	0	3	—
	TOTAL	6	3	1	2	—	18	5	9	4	—

PAKISTANI TEAM IN EAST AFRICA

Season	Captain	First-class matches P.	W.	D.	L.	T.	All matches P.	W.	D.	L.	T.
1964	Hanif Mohammad (PIA)	1	1	0	0	—	9	5	3	1	—

PHILADELPHIAN TEAMS IN BRITAIN

Season	Captain	First-class matches P.	W.	D.	L.	T.	All matches P.	W.	D.	L.	T.
1884	R. S. Newhall	—	—	—	—	—	18	8	5	5	—
1889	D. S. Newhall	—	—	—	—	—	12	4	5	3	—
1897	G. S. Patterson	15	2	4	9	—	15	2	4	9	—
1903	J. A. Lester	15	6	3	6	—	20	10	4	6	—
1908	J. B. King	9	3	0	6	—	16	7	3	6	—
	TOTAL	39	11	7	21	—	81	31	21	29	—

CEYLONESE TEAMS IN INDIA

(Major tours only)

Season	Captain	First-class matches P.	W.	D.	L.	T.	All matches P.	W.	D.	L.	T.
1932-33	C. H. Gunasekara	6	2	3	1	—	10	2	7	1	—
1940-41	S. S. Jayawickreme	3	1	1	1	—	5	1	3	1	—
1964-65	M. H. Tissera	8	1	4	3	—	8	1	4	3	—
	TOTAL	17	4	8	5	—	23	4	14	5	—

CEYLONESE TEAMS IN PAKISTAN

Season	Captain	First-class matches P.	W.	D.	L.	T.	All matches P.	W.	D.	L.	T.
1949-50	S. S. Jayawickreme	5	0	2	3	—	6	0	3	3	—
1966-67	M. H. Tissera	5	0	2	3	—	6	0	3	3	—
	TOTAL	10	0	4	6	—	12	0	6	6	—

FIJIAN TEAM IN NEW ZEALAND

Season	Captain	First-class matches P.	W.	D.	L.	T.	All matches P.	W.	D.	L.	T.
1953-54	P. T. Raddock	4	1	0	3	—	17	8	3	6	—

CANADIAN TEAM IN BRITAIN

Season	Captain	First-class matches P.	W.	D.	L.	T.	All matches P.	W.	D.	L.	T.
1954	H. B. Robinson	4	0	2	2	—	15	4	8	3	—

SOUTH AMERICAN TEAM IN BRITAIN

Season	Captain	First-class matches P.	W.	D.	L.	T.	All matches P.	W.	D.	L.	T.
1932	C. H. Gibson	6	2	1	3	—	18	2	11	5	—

REST OF THE WORLD TEAMS IN BRITAIN

Season	Captain	First-class matches P.	W.	D.	L.	T.	All matches P.	W.	D.	L.	T.
1965	J. R. Reid	1	0	1	0	—	2	1	1	0	—
1966	R. B. Simpson	1	0	0	1	—	3	0	0	3	—
1967	G. St. A. Sobers	2	0	2	0	—	4	2	2	0	—
	TOTAL	4	0	3	1	—	9	3	3	3	—

REST OF THE WORLD TEAM IN BARBADOS

Season	Captain	First-class matches P.	W.	D.	L.	T.	All matches P.	W.	D.	L.	T.
1966-67	W. M. Lawry	1	1	0	0	—	2	2	0	0	—

OFFICES, HONOURS AND AWARDS

M.C.C. PRESIDENTS

No records exist giving holders of this office before 1821 but the following list is complete from that year.

The retiring President nominates his successor who, prior to 1951, assumed office at the A.G.M. in May but who now takes over on October 1st, although being nominated in May.

1821	Lord Strathavon
1822	H. T. Lloyd
1823	B. Aislabie
1824	H. T. Lane
1825	C. J. Barnett
1826	Lord Frederick Beauclerk, D. D.
1827	H. R. Kingscote
1828	A. F. Greville
1829	J. Barnard
1830	Hon. G. Ponsonby
1831	W. Deedes
1832	H. Howard
1833	H. Jenner
1834	Hon. A. H. Ashley
1835	Lord Charles Russell
1836	4th Baron Suffield
1837	4th Viscount Grimston
1838	2nd Marquess of Exeter
1839	6th Earl of Chesterfield
1840	1st Earl of Verulam
1841	2nd Earl of Craven
1842	Earl of March
1843	2nd Earl of Dulcie
1844	Sir John Bayley
1845	T. Chamberlayne
1846	4th Earl of Winterton
1847	12th Earl of Strathmore
1848	2nd Earl of Leicester
1849	6th Earl of Darnley
1850	Lord Guernsey
1851	7th Earl of Stamford
1852	Viscount Dupplin
1853	Marquess of Worcester
1854	Earl Vane
1855	Earl of Uxbridge
1856	Viscount Milton
1857	Sir F. H. Hervey-Bathurst
1858	Lord Garlies
1859	9th Earl of Coventry
1860	2nd Earl of Skelmersdale
1861	5th Earl of Spencer
1862	4th Earl of Sefton
1863	5th Baron Suffield
1864	1st Earl of Dudley
1865	1st Earl of Ebury
1866	7th Earl of Sandwich
1867	2nd Earl of Verulam
1868	2nd Baron Methuen
1869	5th Marquess of Lansdowne
1870	J. H. Scourfield
1871	5th Earl of Clarendon
1872	8th Viscount Downe
1873	Viscount Chelsea
1874	Marquess of Hamilton
1875	Sir Charles Legard
1876	2nd Earl of Londesborough
1877	8th Duke of Beaufort
1878	2nd Lord Fitzhardinge
1879	W. Nicholson
1880	Sir William Hart-Dyke
1881	Lord George Hamilton
1882	2nd Lord Belper
1883	Hon. Robert Grimston
1884	5th Earl of Winterton
1885	3rd Baron Wenlock
1886	5th Baron Lyttelton
1887	Hon. Edward Chandos Leigh
1888	6th Duke of Buccleuch
1889	Sir Henry James
1890	22nd Baron Willoughby de Eresby
1891	V. E. Walker
1892	W. E. Denison
1893	6th Earl of Dartmouth
1894	7th Earl of Jersey
1895	4th Baron Harris
1896	14th Earl of Pembroke
1897	3rd Earl of Lichfield
1898	Hon. Alfred Lyttelton
1899	Sir Archibald L. Smith
1900	Hon. Ivo Bligh
1901	4th Earl Howe
1902	A. G. Steel
1903	1st Baron Alverstone
1904	Marquess of Granby
1905	C. E. Green
1906	W. H. Long
1907	1st Baron Loreburn
1908	3rd Earl of Cawdor
1909	10th Earl of Chesterfield
1910	2nd Earl of Londesborough
1911	1st Baron Desborough
1912	9th Duke of Devonshire
1913	Earl of Dalkeith
1914	7th Baron Hawke
1919	1st Lord Forster
1920	4th Earl of Ellesmere
1921	Hon. Sir Stanley (F. S.) Jackson
1922	1st Viscount Chelmsford (F. J. N. Thesiger)
1923	1st Viscount Ullswater
1924	1st Baron Ernle
1925	Admiral of the Fleet Sir John de Robeck
1926	3rd Viscount Hampden
1927	3rd Baron Leconfield
1928	5th Earl of Lucan
1929	Field Marshal Baron Plumer
1930	Sir Kynaston Studd
1931	1st Viscount Bridgeman

M.C.C. Presidents—*Cont.*

1932	Viscount Lewisham	1953	6th Earl of Rosebery
1933	1st Viscount Hailsham	1954	10th Viscount Cobham
1934	2nd Earl of Cromer	1955	Field Marshal Earl Alexander of Tunis
1935	9th Viscount Cobham	1956	Viscount Monckton
1936	6th Baron Somers	1957	16th Duke of Norfolk
1937	Col. Hon. J. J. Astor	1958	Marshal of the R.A.F. Viscount Portal
1938	1st Earl of Baldwin of Bewdley	1959	H. S. Altham
1939	S. Christopherson	1960	Sir Hubert Ashton
1946	General Sir Ronald Adam	1961	Sir William Worsley
1947	Lord Cornwallis	1962	Lord Nugent
1948	Earl of Gowrie	1963	G. O. Allen
1949	H.R.H. Duke of Edinburgh	1964	R. H. Twining
1950	Sir Pelham Warner	1965	Lt. Gen. Sir Oliver Leese
1951	W. Findlay	1966	Sir Alec Douglas-Home
1952	10th Duke of Beaufort	1967	A. E. R. Gilligan

W. Findlay held office from May 1951 until October 1952

M.C.C. SECRETARIES

Secretaries

1822-1842	B. Aislabie
1842-1858	R. Kynaston
1858-1863	A. Baillie
1863-1876	R. A. Fitzgerald
1876-1897	H. Perkins
1898-1926	Sir Francis Lacey
1926-1936	W. Findlay
1936-1952	Col. R. S. Rait-Kerr
1952-1962	R. Aird
1962-	S. C. Griffith

Assistant Secretaries

1878-1907	J. A. Murdoch
1919-1926	W. Findlay
1926-1952	R. Aird
1949-	J. G. Dunbar
1952-1962	S. C. Griffith
1962-	D. B. Carr
1967-	J. A. Bailey

During the 1939-45 war, Sir Pelham Warner acted as secretary, with W. Findlay assisting, while Col. R. S. Rait-Kerr and R. Aird were absent on active service.

M.C.C. HONORARY LIFE MEMBERS

ENGLAND PLAYERS

In July 1949, a Special General Meeting of the M.C.C. decided to offer honorary life membership of the Club to a select number of English professional cricketers who had retired from the game. With the abolition of amateur status in English cricket after the 1962 season, the honour can now be bestowed on any of the retired 'really great' players in recognition of their service to the game and to the M.C.C. in particular.

The following 26 players were the first to receive this honour, being elected on 28 July 1949:-

Barnes, S. F. (Lancs.)
Barnett, C. J. (Glos.)
Bowes, W. E. (Yorks.)
Braund, L. C. (Somerset)
Duckworth, G. (Lancs.)
Freeman, A. P. (Kent)
Geary, G. (Leics.)
Gunn, G., Snr. (Notts.)
Hearne, J. W. (Middx.)
Hendren, E. (Middx.)
Hirst, G. H. (Yorks.)
Hobbs, J. B. (Surrey)
Larwood, H. (Notts.)
Leyland, M. (Yorks.)
Mead, C. P. (Hants.)
Paynter, E. (Lancs.)
Rhodes, W. (Yorks.)
Russell, A. C. (Essex)
Sandham, A. (Surrey)
Smith, E. J. (Warwicks.)
Strudwick, H. (Surrey)
Sutcliffe, H. (Yorks.)
Tate, M. W. (Sussex)
Tyldesley, E. (Lancs.)
Voce, W. (Notts.)
Woolley, F. E. (Kent)

Other England players awarded this honour:-

1951 Ames, L. E. G. (Kent)
1955 Hutton, L. (Yorks.)
1958 Compton. D. C. S. (Middx.), Wright, D. V. P. (Kent)

M.C.C. Honorary Life Members—*Cont.*

1959 Ikin, J. T. (Lancs.)
1960 Evans, T. G. (Kent), Laker, J. C.† (Surrey), Washbrook, C. (Lancs.).
(† *Terminated in July* 1960)
1961 Bedser, A. V. (Surrey)
1967 Edrich, W. J., Laker, J. C. (Surrey) reinstated, May, P. B. H., Watson, W.

OVERSEAS PLAYERS AND ADMINISTRATORS

Australia

1960 Brown, W. A.: Dowling, W. J.: Fingleton, J. H.; Gregory, J. M.; Grimmett, C. V.; Hassett, A. L.; Johnson, I. W.; Johnston, W. A.; Kippax, A. F.; Lindwall, R. R.; McCabe, S. J.; Mailey, A. A.; Miller, K. R.; Morris, A. R.; Oldfield, W. A.; O'Reilly, W. J.; Ponsford, W. H.; Richardson, V. Y.; Ryder, J.; Smith, Sydney; Wall, T. W.; Woodfull, W. M.
1967 Benaud, R.; Davidson, A. K.; McDonald, C. C.; Mackay, K. D.; MacMillan, E. G.

South Africa

1960 Cheetham, J. E.; Chubb, G. W. A.; Coy, A. H.; Frames, A. S.; Howden, J. P. W.; Melville, A.; Mitchell, B.; Nourse, A. D. Jnr.; Nupen, E. P.; Pegler, S. J.; Pitts, S. J.; Taylor, H. W.; Viljoen, K. G.; Vincent, C. L; Wade, H. S.
1967 Endean, W. R.; Rowan, E. A. B.; Van Ryneveld, C. B.

New Zealand

1960 Hadlee, W. A.; Kerr, J. L.; Lowry, T. C.; Phillipps, J. H.; Sims, Sir Arthur; Vivien, H .G; Wallace, W. M.

West Indies

1960 Constantine, L. N.; dos Santos, Sir Errol; Goddard, J. D. C.; Gomez, G. E.; Headley, G. A.; Kidney, J. M.; Stollmeyer, J. B.
1967 Alexander, F. C. M.; Dare, J. St. F.; Lacy, D. P.; Walcott, C. L.; Weekes, E. D.; Worrell, Sir Frank.

India

1960 Amarnath, L.; de Mello, A. S.; Vijay, Hazare; Merchant, V. M.; Mushtaq Ali; Nayudu, C. K.; Maharaj Kumar Sir Vijaya Ananda of Vizianagram.
1967 H. H. Majaraj, Gaekwad of Baroda; Ghulam Ahmed; Mankad, V. M.; Roy, P.; Umrigar, P. R.

Pakistan

1960 Justice Cornelius, Jahangir Khan.
1967 Fazal Mahmood, Imtiaz Ahmed, Mohammad Hussain, Muzafar Husain.

Ceylon

1960 de Saram, F. C., Senanayake, R.

Canada

1960 Gunn, L. J. H.

East Africa

1967 Oates, C. O.

KNIGHTHOODS

The following Knighthoods were awarded for services to cricket; as players, as administrators, or as both. A number of cricketers have been similarly honoured but for their work in spheres other than cricket and they are not included in this list.

Sir Francis (F. E.) Lacey—in 1926, on retirement from the position of Secretary to the M.C.C. which he had held since 1898.

Sir Frederick (F. C.) Toone—on his return from Australia in 1929 with the third M.C.C. team he had managed in Australia. (The three tours were 1920-21, 1924-25, and 1928-29.)

Knighthoods—*Cont.*

Sir Pelham (P. F.) Warner—conferred in the 1937 Coronation Honours List.
Sir Donald (D. G.) Bradman—conferred January 1st, 1949, on his retirement from first-class cricket.
Sir Henry (H. D. G.) Leveson-Gower—conferred on January 1st, 1953, in recognition of 60 years' service to the game.
Sir John (J. B.) Hobbs—conferred in the 1953 Coronation Honours List.
Sir Leonard Hutton—conferred in the 1956 Birthday Honours.
Sir Frank (F.M.M.) Worrell—conferred January 1st, 1964.

BEST BENEFITS

A professional (or contracted) player can usually expect to be awarded a benefit match by his county after about ten years' service. Not all counties can afford to award the gate receipts of a particular match in this way and award instead a 'Testimonial' of either a fixed sum or members' contributions.

A benefit is not subject to income tax, not being included in a player's contracted terms of service—the result of a High Court action in the 1920's by the Inland Revenue authorities against James Seymour (Kent).

BEFORE 1914

£3,703	G. H. Hirst: Yorkshire v. Lancashire	1904
£3,111	J. T. Tyldesley: Lancashire v. Yorkshire	1906
£2,282	J. T. Brown: Yorkshire v. Lancashire	1901
£2,202	W. Rhodes: Yorkshire v. Lancashire	1911
£2,120	W. S. Lees: Surrey v. Yorkshire	1906
£2,071	S. Haigh: Yorkshire v. Lancashire	1909
£2,000	R. Peel: Yorkshire v. Lancashire	1894

1919 *TO* 1939

£4,016	R. Kilner: Yorkshire v. Middlesex	1925
£3,648	M. Leyland: Yorkshire v. Nottinghamshire	1934
£3,059	H. Sutcliffe: Yorkshire v. Surrey	1929
£2,906	C. Hallows: Lancashire v. Surrey	1928
£2,620	P. Holmes: Yorkshire v. Middlesex	1928
£2,620	W. R. Hammond: Gloucestershire v. Hampshire	1934
£2,563	A. Wood: Yorkshire v. Middlesex	1939

SINCE 1946

£14,000	C. Washbrook: Lancashire v. Australians	1948
£13,047	J. B. Statham: Lancashire v. Australians	1961
£12,866	A. V. Bedser: Surrey v. Yorkshire	1953
£12,258	D. C. S. Compton: Middlesex v. Sussex	1949
£11,701	M. J. Hilton & R. Tattersall (Joint Benefit): Lancashire v. Yorkshire	1960
£11,000	J. C. Laker: Surrey v. Yorkshire	1956
£10,702	K. F. Barrington: Surrey v. Yorkshire	1964
£9,750	J. M. Parks: Sussex (no match allotted)	1964
£9,713	L. Hutton: Yorkshire v. Middlesex	1950
£9,331	F. S. Trueman: Yorkshire v. Surrey	1962
£9,100	S. E. Leary: Kent v. Leicestershire	1967
£8,846	J. D. Bannister: Warwickshire v. Worcestershire	1964
£8,600	A. J. McIntyre: Surrey v. Yorkshire	1955
£8,346	W. J. Stewart: Warwickshire v. Worcestershire	1967
£8,154	D. B. Close: Yorkshire v. Surrey	1961
£8,129	J. H. Wardle: Yorkshire v. Surrey	1957
£8,083	W. E. Bowes: Yorkshire v. Middlesex	1947
£8,010	J. T. Murray: Middlesex v. Sussex	1966
£8,000	R. Pollard: Lancashire v. Derbyshire	1949

Sir Donald Bradman received £A 10,000 from his Testimonial match, D. G. Bradman's XI v. A. L. Hassett's XI (1948-49)
W. G. Grace was awarded three Testimonials which raised a total of £8,835.
H. Verity's Memorial Fund amounted to £8,233 in 1945.

CRICKET WRITERS' CLUB 'YOUNG CRICKETER OF THE YEAR' AWARD

Members of the Cricket Writers' Club annually elect by ballot the player whom they consider to have been the best young cricketer of that season. The award was started in 1950, the trophy being presented at the Club's annual dinner.

1950	R. Tattersall (Lancashire)	1959	G. Pullar (Lancashire)
1951	P. B. H. May (Surrey)	1960	D. A. Allen (Gloucestershire)
1952	F. S. Trueman (Yorkshire)	1961	P. H. Parfitt (Middlesex)
1953	M. C. Cowdrey (Kent)	1962	P. J. Sharpe (Yorkshire)
1954	P. J. Loader (Surrey)	1963	G. Boycott (Yorkshire)
1955	K. F. Barrington (Surrey)	1964	J. M. Brearley (Middlesex)
1956	B. Taylor (Essex)	1965	A. P. Knott (Kent)
1957	M. J. Stewart (Surrey)	1966	D. L. Underwood (Kent)
1958	A. C. D. Ingleby-Mackenzie (Hampshire)	1967	A. W. Greig (Sussex)

F.A. CUP WINNERS' MEDALS

First-class cricketers who have gained Football Association Cup winners' medals:-

E. Lubbock (Kent): Wanderers in 1871-72 and Old Etonians in 1878-79
W. S. Kenyon-Slaney (M.C.C.): Wanderers in 1872-73
C. E. B. Nepean (Middlesex): Oxford U. in 1873-74.
F. H. Birley (Lancashire & Surrey): Oxford U. in 1873-74.
C. J. Ottoway (Kent & Middlesex): Oxford U. in 1873-74.
H. W. Renny-Tailyour (Kent): Royal Engineers in 1874-75.
H. Whitfield (Sussex): Old Etonians in 1878-79.
E. G. Wynyard (Hampshire): Old Carthusians in 1880-81.
P. J. Paravicini (Middlesex): Old Etonians in 1881-82.
H. B. Daft (Nottinghamshire): Notts County in 1893-94.
J. Devey (Warwickshire): Aston Villa in 1896-97.
E. Needham (Derbyshire: Shefield United in 1898-99 and 1901-02.
W. George (Warwickshire): Aston Villa in 1904-05.
J. Sharp (Lancashire): Everton in 1905-06.
H. Makepeace (Lancashire): Everton in 1905-06.
A. Ducat (Surrey): Aston Villa in 1919-20.
J. H. A. Hulme (Middlesex): Arsenal in 1929-30 and 1935-36.
E. J. Drake (Hampshire): Arsenal in 1935-36.
H. Carter (Derbyshire): Derby County in 1945-46.
D. C. S. Compton (Middlesex): Arsenal in 1949-50.
L. H. Compton (Middlesex): Arsenal in 1949-50.
J. Dyson (Lancashire): Manchester City in 1955-56.
G. Hurst (Essex): West Ham United in 1963-64.
J. A. Standen (Worcestershire): West Ham United in 1963-64.

G. Hurst is the only first-class cricketer who has won a World Cup winners' medal. As England's centre-forward in the 1966 World Cup Final he scored three goals in the 4-2 defeat of West Germany; the first 'hat-trick' in a final of this competition. A wicket-keeper, Hurst's one appearance in first-class cricket was for Essex against his native Lancashire at Liverpool in 1962.

SPONSORED AWARDS

Sponsorship of awards in sport, and even of sporting events, by commercial organisations developed rapidly in the 1950s. In cricket, the 'County' Cups awarded by 'Brylcreem' became familiar features of the English cricket scene between 1954 and 1962. To promote brighter cricket in 1952 and 1953, the 'News Chronicle' instituted an award for the county scoring most runs per 100 balls received in the Championship. The Lawrence Trophy for the fastest century of the season came to an end in 1939 but was revived in a different form in 1966 and a similar award was given by the 'Daily Mail' in 1950. The 'Wills' (1961) and 'Horlicks' (1966 and 1967) awards consisted of cash prizes for the best individual performances in the season's Test Matches. Best performances for each month of 1967 were rewarded by the 'Gancia' prizes. The following section records full details of the three major awards still in existence by the 1967 season.

THE LAWRENCE TROPHY

In 1934, Sir Walter Lawrence, chairman of a family firm of builders, donated a trophy and a prize of £100 for presentation each year to the batsman scoring the fastest century of the season.

		Score		*Mins.*
1934	F. E. Woolley	104	Kent v. Northamptonshire (Dover)	63
1935	H. Gimblett ..	123	Somerset v. Essex (Frome)	63
			(*His début in first-class cricket*)	
1936	L. E. G. Ames	107	England XI v. Indians (Folkestone)	68
1937	J. Hardstaff, Jnr.	126	Nottinghamshire v. Kent (Canterbury)	51
1938	H. T. Bartlett	157	Sussex v. Australians (Hove)	57
1939	L. E. G. Ames	136*	Kent v. Surrey (Oval)	67

This award was not continued after the war but in 1966 it was revived in a different form by Walter Lawrence & Son Ltd., with the same trophy and a prize of £250 being presented to the England player who scored the fastest Test century of the calendar year. This time the feat was decided not by time but by the fewest deliveries received in reaching the hundredth run.

1966	K. F. Barrington	115	v. Australia (Melbourne)	off 122 balls
1967	B. L. D'Oliveira ..	109	v. India (Leeds)	off 173 balls

THE HORLICKS AWARDS

In 1966, Horlicks Ltd. made awards of £200 for the best batting performance and £200 for the best bowling performance in each Test Match between England and the West Indies. In addition, a prize of £500 was presented to the West Indies team for winning the series. The individual awards were:-

Test	*Batting*	*Bowling*
1st (Old Trafford)	G. St. A. Sobers (161)	L. R. Gibbs (5-37, 5-69)
2nd (Lord's)	G. St. A. Sobers (46, 163*)	K. Higgs (6-91, 2-82)
3rd (Trent Bridge)	S. M. Nurse (93, 53)	W. W. Hall (4-105, 2-52) K. Higgs (4-71, 3-109)
4th (Headingley)	G. St. A. Sobers (174)	G. St. A. Sobers (5-41, 3-39)
5th (Oval)	T. W. Graveney (165) J. T. Murray (112)	J. A. Snow (2-66, 3-40)

Cash prizes were again awarded by Horlicks in 1967 for outstanding performances in the Tests with India and Pakistan. In each match £100 was awarded for the best batting and bowling performances respectively on each side. For the first time an additional award of £50 was made for the best fielding performance.

Sponsored Awards—*Cont.*

England v. India

Test	*Award*	*England*	*India*
1st (Headingley)	Batting	K. F. Barrington (93, 46)	Nawab of Pataudi, Jnr. (64, 148)
	Bowling	R. Illingworth (3-31, 4-100)	No Award
	Fielding		F. M. Engineer
2nd (Lord's)	Batting	T. W. Graveney (151)	B. K. Kunderan (20, 47)
	Bowling	R. Illingworth (1-0, 6-29)	B. S. Chandrasekhar (5-127)
	Fielding	J. T. Murray (6 catches in India's 1st innings—equalling world record)	
3rd (Edgbaston)	Batting	J. T. Murray (77, 4)	A. L. Wadekar (5, 70)
	Bowling	R. Illingworth (2-14, 4-92)	E. A. S. Prasanna (3-51, 4-60)
	Fielding		A. L. Wadekar (5 catches)

England v. Pakistan

Test	*Award*	*England*	Pakistan
1st (Lord's)	Batting	{K. F. Barrington (148, 14) B. L. D'Oliveira (59, 81*)}	Hanif Mohammad (187*)
	Bowling	{R. N. S. Hobbs (1-46, 0-28) K. Higgs (3-81, 0-6)}	{Asif Iqbal (3-76, 1-50) Salim Altaf (3-74, 0-4)}
	Fielding		Pakistan Team
2nd (Trent Bridge)	Batting	K. F. Barrington (109*)	Saeed Ahmed (44, 68)
	Bowling	K. Higgs (4-35, 2-8)	No Award
	Fielding	A. P. Knott (7 catches in début match)	
3rd (Oval)	Batting	{K. F. Barrington (142, 13*) T. W. Graveney (77)}	{£100: Asif Iqbal (26, 146) £50: Mushtaq Mohammad (66, 17)}
	Bowling	K. Higgs (3-61, 5-58)	No Award
	Fielding	D. B. Close	

THE GANCIA AWARDS

In 1967, the House of Gancia, famed for their sparkling wines, became the first Italian business organisation to associate themselves with cricket. Awards of £50 were given to the best batsman and the best bowler of each month, with awards of £200 being presented to the best batsman and best bowler of the season. Details of the 1967 awards:-

	Batting	*Bowling*
May	A. W. Greig (Sussex) ..	J. N. Graham (Kent)
June	D. L. Amiss (Warwickshire)	F. J. Titmus (Middlesex)
July	Majid Jahangir (Pakistan)	D. L. Underwood (Kent)
August	C. A. Milton (Gloucestershire)	I. J. Jones (Glamorgan)

Batsman of the season: Shared by G. Boycott (Yorkshire) and C. A. Milton (Gloucestershire).

Bowler of the season: Shared by K. Higgs (Lancashire and T. W. Cartwright (Warwickshire).

MISCELLANEOUS RECORDS

MOST PLAYERS REACHING CERTAIN AGGREGATES IN A SEASON

Most 3000 run aggregates	5 in 1928
Most 2000 run aggregates	23 in 1959
Most 1000 run aggregates	111 in 1961
Most triple centuries	3 in 1899 and 1934
Most double centuries	34 in 1933
Most centuries	414 in 1928
Most 300 wicket aggregates	1 in 1928
Most 200 wicket aggregates	5 in 1925
Most 100 wicket aggregates	31 in 1961
Most 'doubles'	12 in 1923

YOUNGEST PUBLIC SCHOOLBOYS IN FIRST-CLASS CRICKET

Although several players have appeared in first-class cricket whilst at public school and even as early as their penultimate year, there are seven exceptional instances of boys making their initial appearance with two more summer terms ahead of them:—

H. S. Critchley-Salmonson (Winchester) ..	Somerset	1910
D. J. Knight (Malvern)	Surrey..	1911
E. P. Hewetson (Shrewsbury)	Warwickshire..	1919
H. C. A. Grant (Tonbridge)	Warwickshire	1919
T. G. B. Welch (Malvern)	Northamptonshire	1922
N. S. Mitchell-Innes (Sedbergh)	Somerset	1931
Nawab of Pataudi, Jnr. (Winchester) ..	Sussex	1957

FATHER AND SON IN THE SAME MATCH

PLAYERS

H. H. Bhagwat Sinhji, Maharana of Mewar and his son, Yuvraj Arvind Kumar Singh played for Rajasthan against Vidarbha at Udaipur in the 1961-62 Ranji Trophy.

UMPIRES

M. G. Vijayasarathy and his son, M. V. Nagendra officiated in the Ranji Trophy match between Mysore and Andhra at Bangalore in 1960-61.

Non-First-Class Competition Records

NON-FIRST-CLASS COMPETITION RECORDS

THE GILLETTE CUP COMPETITION

Sponsored by Gillette Industries, this knock-out competition with an overs limitation was first held in 1963 and immediately aroused tremendous spectator support.

A trial mini-competition had been held the previous year between four midlands counties, Northamptonshire beating Leicestershire in the final. The 1963 rules limited each innings to 65 overs with no bowler being allowed more than 15. These limits were reduced to 60 and 13 respectively the following season, the latter being further reduced to 12 in 1966. The five leading minor counties of the previous season have been admitted to the competition since 1964 but not one has succeeded in defeating a first-class opponent.

Each year the competition has culminated in a September Cup Final at Lord's staged, like its Wembley counterpart, in front of a capacity crowd sporting rosettes and banners of allegiance. By strange coincidence, each of the five winning teams has been captained by a player who was either a past, present, or future captain of England.

CUP HOLDERS

		Captain
1963	SUSSEX (168) beat Worcestershire (154) by 14 runs.	E. R. Dexter
1964	SUSSEX (131-2) beat Warwickshire (127) by 8 wickets. ..	E. R. Dexter
1965	YORKSHIRE (317-4) beat Surrey (142) by 175 runs.	D. B. Close
1966	WARWICKSHIRE (159-5) beat Worcestershire (155-8) by 5 wickets.	M. J. K. Smith
1967	KENT (193) beat Somerset (161) by 32 runs.	M. C. Cowdrey
	(*The* 100*th match in the Gillette Cup*)	

GOLD MEDALLISTS

At each match, a former England player adjudicates in the award of a gold medal and cash prize to the MAN OF THE MATCH. R. W. Barber (Warwickshire) is the only player to have won the award four times.

(§ Cup Final)

Alley, W. E.	(3)	Somerset v. Sussex (Taunton)	1966
		Somerset v. Warwickshire (Birmingham)	1967
		Somerset v. Northamptonshire (Northampton) ..	1967
Amiss, D. L.	(1)	Warwickshire v. Somerset (Birmingham)	1966
Arnold, G. G.	(1)	Surrey v. Derbyshire (Oval)	1967
Bailey, H. J.	(1)	Durham v. Nottinghamshire (Chester-le-Street) ..	1967
Bailey, T. E.	(1)	Essex v. Cambridgeshire (Sawston)	1964
Barber, R. W.	(4)	Warwickshire v. Northamptonshire (Northampton)	1964
		Warwickshire v. Cambridgeshire (Birmingham) ..	1965
		Warwickshire v. Gloucestershire (Birmingham) ..	1966
		§Warwickshire v. Worcestershire (Lord's)	1967
Barrington, K. F. ..	(1)	Surrey v. Leicestershire (Leicester)	1966
Bear, M. J.	(1)	Essex v. Derbyshire (Chesterfield)	1966
Bell, T. A.	(1)	Hertfordshire v. Berkshire (Hitchin)	1966
Bennett, D.	(1)	Middlesex v. Gloucestershire (Bristol)	1963
Bolus, J. B.	(1)	Nottinghamshire v. Yorkshire (Middlesbrough) ..	1963
Boycott, G.	(1)	§Yorkshire v. Surrey (Lord's)	1965
Brown, D. J.	(1)	Warwickshire v. Glamorgan (Swansea)	1966
Buss, A.	(1)	Sussex v. Worcestershire (Worcester)	1967
Buxton, I. R.	(1)	Derbyshire v. Essex (Brentwood)	1965
Corran, A. J.	(1)	Nottinghamshire v. Wiltshire (Nottingham) ..	1965

The Gillette Cup Competition—*Cont.*

Cottam, R. M. ..	.. (1)	Hampshire v. Wiltshire (Chippenham)	1964
Cowdrey, M. C.	.. (3)	Kent v. Suffolk (Ipswich)	1966
		Kent v. Essex (Brentwood)	1967
		Kent v. Sussex (Canterbury)	1967
Denness, M. H...	.. (1)	§Kent v. Somerset (Lord's)	1967
Dexter, E. R. ..	.. (2)	Sussex v. Northamptonshire (Northampton)	1963
		Sussex v. Surrey (Hove)	1964
Dixon, A. L. ..	.. (1)	Kent v. Surrey (Oval)	1967
Dyson, J. ..	.. (1)	Lancashire v. Essex (Manchester)	1963
Edrich, J. H. ..	.. (2)	Surrey v. Gloucestershire (Oval)	1964
		Surrey v. Glamorgan (Oval)	1965
Edwards, M. J.	.. (1)	Surrey v. Middlesex (Oval)	1965
Entwistle, R. ..	.. (2)	Lancashire v. Derbyshire (Manchester)	1963
		Lancashire v. Cheshire (Macclesfield)	1966
Fairey, D. H. ..	.. (1)	Cambridgeshire v. Yorkshire (Castleford)	1967
Flavell, J. A. ..	.. (1)	Worcestershire v. Lancashire (Worcester)	1963
Gale, R. A. ..	.. (1)	Middlesex v. Buckinghamshire (Lord's)	1965
Gifford, N. ..	.. (1)	§Worcestershire v. Sussex (Lord's)	1963
Graveney, T. W.	.. (1)	Worcestershire v. Glamorgan (Neath)	1963
Green, D. M. ..	.. (3)	Lancashire v. Kent (Manchester)	1964
		Lancashire v. Middlesex (Lord's)	1966
		Lancashire v. Gloucestershire (Manchester)	1967
Greig, A. W. ..	.. (1)	Sussex v. Hampshire (Hove)	1967
Grieves, K. J. ..	.. (1)	Lancashire v. Glamorgan (Manchester)	1964
Hall, G.. ..	.. (1)	Somerset v. Sussex (Taunton)	1964
Headley, R. G. A.	.. (1)	Worcestershire v. Nottinghamshire (Worcester) ..	1966
Hedges, B. ..	.. (1)	Glamorgan v. Somerset (Cardiff)	1963
Hill, M.. ..	.. (1)	Nottinghamshire v. Somerset (Taunton)	1964
Horton, M. J. ..	.. (2)	Worcestershire v. Essex (Worcester)	1966
		Worcestershire v. Hampshire (Worcester)	1966
Ibadulla, K. ..	.. (2)	Warwickshire v. Lancashire (Birmingham)	1965
		Warwickshire v. Hampshire (Birmingham)	1965
Illingworth, R. ..	.. (1)	Yorkshire v. Warwickshire (Birmingham)	1965
Ingleby-Mackenzie, A. C. D.	(1)	Hampshire v. Kent (Southampton)	1966
Inman, C. C. ..	.. (1)	Leicestershire v. Yorkshire (Leicester)	1965
Jones, I. J. ..	.. (1)	Glamorgan v. Northamptonshire (Northampton) ..	1966
Kitchen, M. ..	.. (1)	Somerset v. Leicestershire (Taunton)	1967
Larter, J. D. F.	.. (1)	Northamptonshire v. Leicestershire (Leicester) ..	1964
Lever, P. ..	.. (1)	Lancashire v. Yorkshire (Manchester)	1967
Livingstone, D. A.	.. (1)	Hampshire v. Lincolnshire (Southampton) ..	1966
Marner, P. T. ..	.. (1)	Lancashire v. Leicestershire (Manchester)	1963
		(*The first 'Man of the Match' Award*)	
Marshall, R. E...	.. (2)	Hampshire v. Surrey (Bournemouth)	1966
		Hampshire v. Lincolnshire (Basingstoke) ..	1967
Milburn, C. ..	.. (2)	Northamptonshire v. Middlesex (Lord's)	1963
		Northamptonshire v. Bedfordshire (Luton) ..	1967
Milton, C. A. ..	.. (1)	Gloucestershire v. Northamptonshire (Bristol) ..	1965
Mordaunt, D. J.	.. (1)	Berkshire v. Somerset (Reading)	1965
Morgan, D. C...	.. (2)	Derbyshire v. Hampshire (Bournemouth)	1963
		Derbyshire v. Northamptonshire (Northampton) ..	1964
Murray, J. T. ..	.. (1)	Middlesex v. Sussex (Lord's)	1966
Mushtaq Mohammad	.. (1)	Northamptonshire v. Nottinghamshire (Northampton)	1967
Nicholls, R. B. ..	.. (1)	Gloucestershire v. Berkshire (Reading)	1966
Palmer, K. E. ..	.. (1)	Somerset v. Lancashire (Manchester)	1967
Palmer, R. ..	.. (2)	Somerset v. Yorkshire (Taunton)	1966
		Somerset v. Lancashire (Taunton)	1966
Parks, J. M. ..	.. (2)	Sussex v. Yorkshire (Hove)	1963
		Sussex v. Durham (Hove)	1964
Pressdee, J. S. ..	.. (1)	Glamorgan v. Essex (Neath)	1964
Prideaux, R. M.	.. (1)	Northamptonshire v. Warwickshire (Northampton)	1963
Reed, B. L. ..	.. (1)	Hampshire v. Glamorgan (Portsmouth)	1967
Richardson, P. E.	.. (1)	Kent v. Sussex (Tunbridge Wells)	1963
Sainsbury, P. J...	.. (2)	Hampshire v. Norfolk (Southampton)	1965
		Hampshire v. Kent (Portsmouth)	1965
Shepherd, D. J...	.. (1)	Glamorgan v. Worcestershire (Newport)	1964
Smith, M. J. K.	.. (2)	Warwickshire v. Hampshire (Birmingham)	1964
		Warwickshire v. Lancashire (Manchester)	1964
Standen, J. A. ..	.. (1)	Worcestershire v. Surrey (Worcester)	1963

The Gillette Cup Competition—*Cont.*

Storey, S. J.	(1)	Surrey v. Middlesex (Oval)	1964
Suttle, K. G.	(2)	Sussex v. Worcestershire (Worcester)	1965
		Sussex v. Middlesex (Hove)	1967
Sydenham, D. A. D. ..	(1)	Surrey v. Cheshire (Hoylake)	1964
Taylor, R. W.	(1)	Derbyshire v. Middlesex (Lord's)	1965
Thomson, N. I... ..	(1)	§Sussex v. Warwickshire (Lord's)	1964
		(*The only medallist later to become an adjudicator for this award*)	
Tindall, R. A. E. ..	(1)	Surrey v. Northamptonshire (Oval)	1965
Titmus, F. J.	(1)	Middlesex v. Yorkshire (Lord's)	1964
Trueman, F. S... ..	(1)	Yorkshire v. Somerset (Taunton)	1965
Virgin, R.	(1)	Somerset v. Nottinghamshire (Taunton)	1965
Wilson, A. R.	(1)	Cambridgeshire v. Oxfordshire (Wisbech)	1967
Young, S. H.	(1)	Durham v. Hertfordshire (Darlington)	1964

PLAYING RECORD OF THE COUNTIES

	Played	*Won*	*Highest Total*	*Centuries*	*Awards*	*Finals*
Derbyshire	7	2	250-9	—	4	—
Essex	7	2	201	—	2	—
Glamorgan	9	4	220-6	1	4	—
Gloucestershire	6	1	327-7	1	2	—
Hampshire	13	8	295-7	1	8	—
Kent	9	5	293-5	2	6	1
Lancashire	14	9	304-9	1	9	—
Leicestershire	5	—	203	1	—	—
Middlesex	10	5	280-8	—	4	—
Northamptonshire	12	7	237-5	—	5	—
Nottinghamshire	7	2	215	2	3	—
Somerset	15	10	251-9	—	9	1
Surrey	13	8	268-6	—	8	1
Sussex	15	12	314-7	3	9	2
Warwickshire	14	10	307-8	4	10	2
Worcestershire	11	6	253-4	1	7	2
Yorkshire	10	6	317-4	1	3	1
Minor Counties	23	3	195	1	7	—
	200	100	327-7	19	100	10

Leicestershire are the only first-class county not to have won a match while Gloucestershire and Nottinghamshire have yet to beat another first-class county.

HIGHEST TOTAL

327-7 off 60 overs: Gloucestershire v. Berkshire (Reading) 1966

LOWEST COMPLETED INNINGS TOTAL

56 of 26.2 overs: Leicestershire v. Northamptonshire (Leicester) 1964

HIGHEST TOTAL BY SIDE BATTING SECOND

270 off 63.3 overs: Yorkshire v. Sussex (Hove) 1963 (Set 293)
252-5 off 56.2 overs: Surrey v. Middlesex (Oval) 1965 (Set 251)

HIGHEST TOTAL BY SIDE BATTING FIRST AND LOSING

250-8 off 60 overs: Middlesex v. Surrey (Oval) 1965

LOWEST TOTAL BY SIDE BATTING FIRST AND WINNING

141 off 54.5 overs: Sussex v. Somerset (Taunton) 1964

EARLIEST FINISH

2.20 p.m. Worcestershire beat Lancashire by 9 wickets (Worcester) 1963

The Gillette Cup Competition—*Cont.*

CENTURIES (19)

Amiss, D. L. (Warwicks.)	113	v. Glamorgan (Swansea)	1966
Barber, R. W. (Warwicks.)	114	v. Northamptonshire (Northampton)	1964
	113	v. Gloucestershire (Birmingham) ..	1966
Bell, T. A. (Herts.)	105	v. Berkshire (Hitchin)	1966
Bolus, J. B. (Notts.)	100*	v. Yorkshire (Middlesbrough) ..	1963
Boycott, G. (Yorks.)	146	v. Surrey (Lord's) .. .. (Final)	1965
		(*Highest score in the Gillette Cup and the only century scored in a final*)	
Cowdrey, M. C. (Kent)	116	v. Suffolk (Ipswich)	1966
Dexter, E. R. (Sussex)	115	v. Northamptonshire (Northampton)	1963
Hallam, M. R. (Leics.)	106	v. Lancashire (Manchester)	1963
Hedges, B. (Glam.)	103*	v. Somerset (Cardiff)	1963
Hill, M. (Notts.)	107	v. Somerset (Taunton)	1964
Horton, M. J. (Worcs.)	114	v. Hampshire (Worcester)	1966
Jameson, J. A. (Warwicks.)	100*	v. Hampshire (Birmingham)	1964
Marner, P. (Lancs.)	121	v. Leicestershire (Manchester) ..	1963
		(*First century of the Competition*)	
Marshall, R. E. (Hants.)	102	v. Lincolnshire (Basingstoke) ..	1967
Nicholls, R. B. (Glos.)	127	v. Berkshire (Reading)	1966
Parks, J. M. (Sussex)	102*	v. Durham (Hove)	1964
Richardson, P. E. (Kent)	127	v. Sussex (Tunbridge Wells)	1963
Suttle, K. G. (Sussex)	104	v. Kent (Tunbridge Wells)	1963

CENTURY BEFORE LUNCH

R. B. Nicholls	101*	(127)	Gloucestershire v. Berkshire (Reading)	1966
R. E. Marshall	102		Hampshire v. Lincolnshire (Basingstoke) ..	1967

BOWLING

SEVEN WICKETS IN AN INNINGS

A. L. Dixon	12-7-15-7	Kent v. Surrey (Oval)	1967
P. J. Sainsbury	13-3-30-7	Hampshire v. Norfolk (Southampton)	1965

FIVE WICKETS IN AN INNINGS

Arnold, G. G.	(1)	5-9	Surrey v. Derbyshire (Oval)	1967
Brown, D. J.	(1)	5-18	Warwickshire v. Glamorgan (Swansea)	1966
Dixon, A. L.	(1)	7-15	Kent v. Surrey (Oval)	1967
Dyson, J.	(1)	5-47	Lancashire v. Essex (Manchester)	1963
Flavell, J. A.	(3)	5-43	Worcestershire v. Glamorgan (Neath)	1963
		6-14	Worcestershire v. Lancashire (Worcester)	1963
		5-40	Worcestershire v. Sussex (Worcester)	1965
Hall, G. ..	(1)	5-34	Somerset v. Sussex (Taunton)	1964
Ibadulla, K.	(2)	5-34	Warwickshire v. Northamptonshire (Northampton)	1964
		6-32	Warwickshire v. Hampshire (Birmingham) ..	1965
Illingworth, R.	(1)	5-29	Yorkshire v. Surrey (Lord's) .. .. (Final)	1965
			(*The only bowler to take 5 wickets in a final*)	
Knight, B. R.	(1)	5-41	Essex v. Derbyshire (Brentwood)	1965
Larter, J. D. F.	(1)	5-24	Northamptonshire v. Leicestershire (Leicester) ..	1964
Palmer, R...	(1)	5-18	Somerset v. Lancashire (Taunton)	1966
Price, J. S. E.	(1)	5-54	Middlesex v. Sussex (Hove)	1967
Roope, G. R. J.	(1)	5-23	Surrey v. Derbyshire (Oval)	1967
Sainsbury, P. J.	(1)	7-30	Hampshire v. Norfolk (Southampton)	1965
Standen, J. A.	(1)	5-14	Worcestershire v. Surrey (Worcester)	1963
Statham, J. B.	(1)	5-28	Lancashire v. Leicestershire (Manchester)	1963
Storey, S. J.	(1)	5-35	Surrey v. Middlesex (Oval)	1964
Trueman, F. S.	(1)	6-15	Yorkshire v. Somerset (Taunton)	1965

HAT-TRICKS

J. D. F. Larter ..	Northamptonshire v. Sussex (Northampton)	1963
D. A. D. Sydenham	Surrey v. Cheshire (Hoylake)	1964

The Gillette Cup Competition—*Cont.*

FOUR WICKETS IN FIVE BALLS

D. A. D. Sydenham Surrey v. Cheshire (Hoylake) 1964

THREE WICKETS IN FOUR BALLS

J. D. Bannister .. Warwickshire v. Somerset (Birmingham) 1966

MOST RUNS CONCEDED BY A BOWLER IN AN INNINGS

89 D. W. White (12-1-89-0) Hants. v. Worcs. (Worcester) 1966

RECORD WICKET PARTNERSHIPS

Wkt.	*Runs*		
1st	134	N. F. Horner & R. W. Barber: Warwicks. v. Northants. (Northampton)	1964
2nd	192	G. Boycott & D. B. Close: Yorkshire v. Surrey (Lord's)	1965
3rd	145	R. G. A. Headley & T. W. Graveney: Worcs. v. Surrey (Worcester)	1963
4th	160	E. R. Dexter & J. M. Parks: Sussex v. Northants. (Northampton) ..	1963
5th	134	J. M. Parks & G. C. Cooper: Sussex v. Durham (Hove)	1964
6th	83	K. F. Barrington & M. J. Edwards: Surrey v. Middlesex (Oval) ..	1965
7th	63	D. C. Morgan & G. W. Richardson: Derby v. Hants. (Bournemouth)	1963
8th	55	B. S. V. Timms & A. T. Castell: Hants. v. Sussex (Hove)	1967
9th	75	B. A. Langford & D. G. Doughty: Somerset v. Glamorgan (Cardiff)	1963
10th	40	G. Cross & J. Cotton: Leics. v. Surrey (Leicester)	1966

SINGLE WICKET TOURNAMENT

Under the sponsorship of Carling's Lager, Single Wicket Cricket, so popular in the early nineteenth century, was revived as a spectator sport at the 1963 Scarborough Festival. The tournament was played on a knock-out basis over two days and was the forerunner of an annual event held at Lord's from 1964. Since 1965, it has been sponsored by Charrington's Breweries, a top prize of £250 being given to the winner.

WINNERS

1963	Scarborough	K. E. Palmer (Somerset)
1964	Lord's	B. R. Knight (Essex & England)
1965	Lord's	Mushtaq Mohammad (Northamptonshire & Pakistan)
1966	Lord's	F. J. Titmus (Middlesex & England)
1967	Lord's	G. St. A. Sobers (Barbados & West Indies)

ROTHMAN'S WORLD CUP TOURNAMENT

In 1966, the second Rest of the World team to have been brought to Britain under the sponsorship of Rothmans of Pall Mall played in a triangular tournament of one-day overs-limitation matches with an England XI and the touring West Indians at Lord's. A similar tournament was held in 1967 with the Pakistanis taking part. Winners of the World Cup and gold medals have been:-

1966 England (Captained by M. C. Cowdrey)
1967 Rest of the World (Captained by G. St. A. Sobers)

Supplement

to

The Kaye Book of Cricket Records

by

Bill Frindall

ISBN 0 7182 0865 X

Printed by C. Tinling & Co. Ltd., London and Prescot.

SUPPLEMENT

TO

THE KAYE BOOK OF CRICKET RECORDS

AUTHOR'S NOTE

This Supplement updates to the end of the 1969 English season and amends where necessary the first edition of The Kaye Book of Cricket Records published in June, 1968. It follows the format and order of the book using the same key symbols and abbreviations.

Items prefaced by the symbol § are amendments to or updatings of items in the original book. Unprefaced items are additions.

In order to minimise the selling price of this Supplement it has been necessary to set it in smaller type than that used in the book. Any future editions of the book will, however, retain the original type-size.

Page xi CONTENTS:
§ line 8: Carrying Bat through Completed Innings Page 78

§ Page 2: KEY TO TEST MATCH GROUNDS—Delete last two items (Melbourne).

RESULTS AND SCORES OF TEST MATCHES

Page 8 *ENGLAND v. AUSTRALIA*

Venue and Result	*England*		*Australia*	
1968 *in England*	1*st inns*	2*nd inns*	1*st inns*	2*nd inns*
Manchester—Australia 159 runs	165	253	357	220
Lord's—Drawn	351-7d	—	78	127-4
Birmingham—Drawn	409	142-3d	222	68-1
Leeds—Drawn	302	230-4	315	312
Oval—England 226 runs...	494	181	324	125

Page 13 *ENGLAND v. WEST INDIES*

Venue and Result	*England*		*West Indies*	
1967-68 *in West Indies*	1*st inns*	2*nd inns*	1*st inns*	2*nd inns*
Port of Spain—Drawn	568	—	363	243-8
Kingston—Drawn	376	68-8	143	391-9d
Bridgetown—Drawn	449	—	349	284-6
Port of Spain—England 7 wkts	414	215-3	526-7d	92-2d
Georgetown—Drawn	371	206-9	414	264
1969 *in England*				
Manchester—England 10 wkts	413	12-0	147	275
Lord's—Drawn	344	295-7	380	295-9d
Leeds—England 30 runs	223	240	161	272

Page 14 *ENGLAND v. NEW ZEALAND*

Venue and Result	*England*		*New Zealand*	
1969 *in England*	1*st inns*	2*nd Inns*	1*st inns*	2*nd inns*
Lord's—England 230 runs	190	340	169	131
Nottingham—Drawn	451-8d	—	294	66-1
Oval—England 8 wkts	242	138-2	150	229

Page 16 *ENGLAND v. PAKISTAN*

Venue and Result	*England*		*Pakistan*	
1968-69 *in Pakistan*	1*st inns*	2*nd inns*	1*st inns*	2*nd inns*
Lahore[2]—Drawn	306	225-9d	209	203-5
Dacca—Drawn	274	33-0	246	195-6d
Karachi—Drawn	502-7	—	—	—

Results and Scores of Test Matches—*Cont.*

Page 18 *AUSTRALIA v. WEST INDIES*

Venue and Result	*Australia*		*West Indies*	
1968-69 *in Australia*	1*st inns*	2*nd inns*	1*st inns*	2*nd inns*
Brisbane[2]—West Indies 125 runs	284	240	296	353
Melbourne—Australia Inns & 30 runs ...	510	—	200	280
Sydney—Australia 10 wkts	547	42-0	264	324
Adelaide—Drawn...	533	339-9	276	616
Sydney—Australia 382 runs	619	394-8d	279	352

Page 19 *AUSTRALIA v. INDIA*

Venue and Result	*Australia*		*India*	
1967-68 *in Australia*	1*st inns*	2*nd inns*	1*st inns*	2*nd inns*
Adelaide—Australia 146 runs	335	369	307	251
Melbourne—Australia Inns & 4 runs ...	529	—	173	352
Brisbane[2]—Australia 39 runs	379	294	279	355
Sydney—Australia 144 runs	317	292	268	197

Page 20 *WEST INDIES v. NEW ZEALAND*

Venue and Result	*West Indies*		*New Zealand*	
1968-69 *in New Zealand*	1*st inns*	2*nd inns*	1*st inns*	2*nd inns*
Auckland—West Indies 5 wkts	276	348-5	323	297-8d
Wellington—New Zealand 6 wkts	297	148	282	166-4
Christchurch—Drawn	417	—	217	367-6

Page 21 *NEW ZEALAND v. INDIA*

Venue and Result	*New Zealand*		*India*	
1967-68 *in New Zealand*	1*st inns*	2*nd inns*	1*st inns*	2*nd inns*
Dunedin—India 5 wkts	350	208	359	200-5
Christchurch—New Zealand 6 wkts	502	88-4	288	301
Wellington—India 8 wkts	186	199	327	61-2
Auckland—India 272 runs	140	101	252	261-5d

Page 23 (**RESULTS SUMMARY**)

§ **RESULTS SUMMARY OF ALL TEST MATCHES, 1876-77 to 1969**

		Tests	*Won by*							*Tied*	*Drawn*
			E	*A*	*SA*	*WI*	*NZ*	*I*	*P*		
England	v. Australia	203	66	80	–	–	–	–	–	–	57
	v. South Africa ...	102	46	–	18	–	–	–	–	–	38
	v. West Indies ...	58	20	–	–	16	–	–	–	–	22
	v. New Zealand ...	40	19	–	–	–	0	–	–	–	21
	v. India	37	18	–	–	–	–	3	–	–	16
	v. Pakistan	18	8	–	–	–	–	–	1	–	9
Australia	v. South Africa ...	49	–	29	7	–	–	–	–	–	13
	v. West Indies ...	30	–	17	–	6	–	–	–	1	6
	v. New Zealand ...	1	–	1	–	–	0	–	–	–	0
	v. India	20	–	13	–	–	–	2	–	–	5
	v. Pakistan	6	–	2	–	–	–	–	1	–	3
South Africa	v. New Zealand ...	17	–	–	9	–	2	–	–	–	6
West Indies	v. New Zealand ...	9	–	–	–	5	2	–	–	–	2
	v. India	23	–	–	–	12	–	0	–	–	11
	v. Pakistan	8	–	–	–	4	–	–	3	–	1
New Zealand	v. India	13	–	–	–	–	1	6	–	–	6
	v. Pakistan	9	–	–	–	–	0	–	4	–	5
India	v. Pakistan	15	–	–	–	–	–	2	1	–	12
		658	177	142	34	43	5	13	10	1	233

Results Summary—*Cont.*

	Tests	*Won*	*Lost*	*Drawn*	*Tied*	*Toss won*
England	458	177	118	163	–	230
Australia	309	142	82	84	1	148
South Africa	168	34	77	57	–	76
West Indies	128	43	42	42	1	71
New Zealand	89	5	44	40	–	49
India	108	13	45	50	–	54
Pakistan	56	10	16	30	–	30

Page 24 *ENGLAND v. AUSTRALIA—IN ENGLAND*

Year	*Tests*	*Nottingham*	*Lord's*	*Manchester*	*Leeds*	*Oval*	*Birmingham*	*Sheffield*
	Pl. E. A. D.	*E. A. D.*	*E. A. D.*	*E. A. D.*	*E. A. D.*	*E. A. D.*	*E. A. D.*	*E. A. D.*
1968 ...	5 1 1 3	– – –	– – 1	– 1 –	– – 1	1 – –	– – 1	– – –
	§96 26 25 45	2 3 6	5 8 9	4 4 12	2 5 7	12 4 8	1 – 3	– 1 –
§ Totals	203 66 80 57							

Page 25 *ENGLAND v. WEST INDIES—IN ENGLAND*

	Tests		*Lord's*	*Manchester*	*Oval*	*Nottingham*	*Birmingham*	*Leeds*
	Pl. E. W. D.		*E.W.D.*	*E.W.D.*	*E.W.D.*	*E.W.D.*	*E.W.D.*	*E.W.D.*
1969 ...	3 2 – 1	... ...	– – 1	1 – –	– – –	– – –	– – –	1 – –
	§ 31 14 9 8		4 1 3	3 2 2	4 2 1	– 2 1	1 – 1	2 2 –

Page 26 *ENGLAND v. WEST INDIES—IN WEST INDIES*

	Tests		*Bridgetown*	*Port of Spain*	*Georgetown*	*Kingston*
	Pl. E. W. D.		*E.W.D.*	*E.W.D.*	*E.W.D.*	*E.W.D.*
1967-68 ...	5 1 – 4	... ...	– – 1	1 – 1	– – 1	– – 1
	§ 27 6 7 14		1 1 4	3 1 4	1 2 3	1 3 3
§ Totals	58 20 16 22					

ENGLAND v. NEW ZEALAND—IN ENGLAND

	Tests		*Lord's*	*Oval*	*Manchester*	*Leeds*	*Birmingham*	*Nottingham*
	Pl. E. N. D.		*E.N.D.*	*E.N.D.*	*E.N.D.*	*E.N.D.*	*E.N.D.*	*E.N.D.*
1969 ...	3 2 – 1	... ...	1 – –	1 – –	– – –	– – –	– – –	– – 1
	§ 21 11 – 10		3 – 3	2 – 3	2 – 2	2 – 1	2 – –	– – 1
§ Totals	40 19 – 21							

Page 27 *ENGLAND v. PAKISTAN—IN PAKISTAN*

	Tests		*Lahore*	*Dacca*	*Karachi*
	Pl. E. P. D.		*E.P.D.*	*E.P.D.*	*E.P.D.*
1968-69 ...	3 – – 3	... ...	– – 1	– – 1	– – 1
	§ 6 1 – 5		1 – 1	– – 2	– – 2
§ Totals	18 8 1 9				

Results Summary—*Cont.*

Page 28 *AUSTRALIA v. WEST INDIES—IN AUSTRALIA*

	Tests						*Adelaide*	*Sydney*	*Brisbane*	*Melbourne*
	Pl.	*A.*	*W.*	*D.*	*T.*		*A.W.D.*	*A.W.D.*	*A.W.D.T.*	*A.W.D.*
1968-69	5	3	1	1	–	... ...	– – 1	2 – –	– 1 – –	1 – –
	§20	13	4	2	1		1 1 2	5 2 –	2 1 – 1	5 – –
§ Totals	30	17	6	6	1					

AUSTRALIA v. INDIA—IN AUSTRALIA

	Tests				*Brisbane*	*Sydney*	*Melbourne*	*Adelaide*
	Pl.	*A.*	*I.*	*D.*	*A.I.D.*	*A.I.D.*	*A.I.D.*	*A.I.D.*
1967-68 ...	4	4	–	–	1 – –	1 – –	1 – –	1 – –
	§9	8	–	1	2 – –	1 – 1	3 – –	2 – –
§ Totals	20	13	2	5				

Page 29 *WEST INDIES v. NEW ZEALAND—IN NEW ZEALAND*

	Tests					*Christ-church*	*Auckland*	*Dunedin*	*Welling-ton*
	Pl.	*W.*	*N.*	*D.*		*W.N.D.*	*W.N.D.*	*W.N.D.*	*W.N.D.*
1967-68 ...	3	1	1	1	... ...	– – 1	1 – –	– – –	– 1 –
	§9	5	2	2		2 – 1	1 1 1	1 – –	1 1 –

Page 30 Add: *NEW ZEALAND v. INDIA—IN NEW ZEALAND*

	Tests					*Dunedin*	*Christ-church*	*Welling-ton*	*Auckland*
	Pl.	*N.*	*I.*	*D.*		*N. I. D.*	*N. I. D.*	*N. I. D.*	*N. I. D.*
1967-68 ...	4	1	3	–	... ...	– 1 –	1 – –	– 1 –	– 1 –
§ Totals	13	1	6	6					

THE GROUNDS

Page 31 **A GUIDE TO THE TEST MATCH GROUNDS**

§ Lines 3 and 7: amend 'seven' to read 'six'.

Page 32

ENGLAND	*No. of Tests*
§ Birmingham	13
§ Leeds	33
§ Lord's, London	56
§ Manchester	44
§ Nottingham	26
§ Oval, London	53

AUSTRALIA	*No. of Tests*
§ Adelaide	29
§ Brisbane	18
§ Melbourne	56
§ Delete [1]East Melbourne (1879 Test only)	
§ Sydney	54

WEST INDIES	
§ Bridgetown	11
§ Georgetown	10
§ Kingston	14
§ Port of Spain	17

NEW ZEALAND	
§ Auckland	14
§ Christchurch	13
§ Dunedin	5
§ Wellington	11

Page 33

PAKISTAN	
§ Dacca	6
§ Karachi	9
§ Lahore	7

RECORD SCORES FOR EACH TEST MATCH CENTRE

§ Dunedin (*Highest*) 359 India v. New Zealand 1967-68

Page 34 **HIGHEST INDIVIDUAL SCORE FOR EACH TEST MATCH CENTRE**

§ Christchurch: 258 S. M. Nurse: West Indies v. New Zealand 1968-69
§ Dunedin: 143 G. T. Dowling: New Zealand v. India 1967-68

TEAM RECORDS

Page 36 **HIGHEST INNINGS TOTALS**

619 Australia v. West Indies (Sydney) 1968-69
616 West Indies v. Australia (Adelaide) 1968-69
568 England v. West Indies (Port of Spain) 1967-68

Page 37 **HIGHEST SECOND INNINGS TOTALS (First innings in brackets)**

616 (276) West Indies v. Australia (Adelaide) 1968-69

Page 38 **HIGHEST FOURTH INNINGS TOTALS**

TO WIN:	348-5	West Indies v. New Zealand ...	Auckland ...	1968-69	
					Set
TO DRAW:	339-9	Australia v. West Indies	Adelaide ...	1968-69	360
					Losing margin
TO LOSE:	355	India v. Australia	Brisbane[2]...	1967-68	39
	352	West Indies v. Australia	Sydney ...	1968-69	382

Page 39 **HIGHEST MATCH AGGREGATES**

Aggregate Scores		*Year*	*Days Played*
1764 for 39 wkts	Australia v. West Indies (Adelaide)	1968-69	5
1644 for 38 wkts	Australia v. West Indies (Sydney)	1968-69	6

Page 40 **LARGEST MARGINS OF VICTORY**

382 runs ... ... Australia v. West Indies (Sydney) 1968-69

Page 42 **HIGHEST SCORES FOR EACH BATTING POSITION**

§ 8 209 (Delete asterisk)
§ 9 160 C. Hill Australia v. England (Adelaide) 1907-08

Page 42 **MOST CENTURIES IN A SERIES (BOTH TEAMS)**

16 Australia (10) v. West Indies (6) 1968-69

MOST CONSECUTIVE DEFEATS

7 India: Leeds 1967 to Sydney 1967-68

Page 44 **MOST CONSECUTIVE MATCHES WITHOUT VICTORY**

§ Delete: 22 New Zealand: Auckland 1962-63 to date.
23 New Zealand: Auckland 1962-63 to Dunedin 1967-68

EACH BATSMAN REACHING DOUBLE FIGURES IN AN INNINGS

1967-68 India (359) v. New Zealand at Dunedin. Lowest score: 12.

PLAYERS' RECORDS—BATTING

Page 45 **2000 RUNS IN TESTS:**

ENGLAND

	M.	*I.*	*Runs*	*A*	*SA*	*WI*	*NZ*	*I*	*P*
						Opponents			
§ M. C. Cowdrey ...	104	171	7228	2186	1021	1751	1034	653	583
§ K. F. Barrington ...	82	131	6806	2111	989	1042	594	1355	715
§ T. W. Graveney ...	79	123	4882	1075	234	1532	293	805	943
§ E. R. Dexter	62	102	4502	1358	585	866	477	467	749
J. H. Edrich	40	63	2711	1090	7	647	726	111	130
G. Boycott	41	70	2609	753	373	919	271	277	16

Player Records—Batting—*Cont.*

AUSTRALIA

	M.	*I.*	*Runs*	*Opponents E*	*SA*	*WI*	*NZ*	*I*	*P*
§ W. M. Lawry	53	95	4478	1909	792	1035	—	653	89
§ R. B. Simpson	52	92	4131	1405	980	844	—	586	316
R. M. Cowper	27	46	2061	686	255	417	—	604	99

Page 46
WEST INDIES

	M.	*I.*	*Runs*	*Opponents E*	*A*	*NZ*	*I*	*P*
§ G. St. A. Sobers ...	76	132	6776	2808	1510	151	1323	984
§ R. B. Kanhai ...	61	108	5056	1887	1336	—	1260	573
B. F. Butcher	44	78	3104	1373	810	216	572	133
S. M. Nurse	29	54	2523	1016	820	558	129	—

INDIA

	M.	*I.*	*Runs*	*Opponents E*	*A*	*WI*	*NZ*	*P*
§ C. G. Borde	54	95	3042	746	482	871	613	330
Nawab of Pataudi, Jnr.	31	56	2203	799	609	257	538	—
M. L. Jaisimha ...	35	64	2013	852	434	233	268	226

PAKISTAN

	M.	*I.*	*Runs*	*Opponents E*	*A*	*WI*	*NZ*	*I*
§ Hanif Mohammad ...	54	95	3858	1039	548	736	565	970
§ Saeed Ahmed	38	72	2833	764	480	707	422	460

Pages 46 and 47 **BEST BATTING AVERAGES**

	Tests	*Inns*	*N.O.*	*Runs*	*H.S.*	*Avge.*	*100s*	*50s*
K. D. Walters (Australia) ...	16	26	3	1706	242	74.17	6	9
§ G. St. A. Sobers (West Indies)	76	132	17	6776	365*	58.92	21	26
§ K. F. Barrington (England) ...	82	131	15	6806	256	58.67	20	35
W. M. Lawry (Australia) ...	53	95	7	4478	201	50.88	13	22

Page 47 **BATSMEN SCORING MOST CENTURIES**

	100s	*H.S.*	*E*	*A*	*Opponents SA*	*WI*	*NZ*	*I*	*P*
§ M. C. Cowdrey (England) ...	22	182	–	5	3	6	2	3	3
§ G. St. A. Sobers (West Indies)	21	365*	9	4	0	–	0	5	3
§ K. F. Barrington (England) ...	20	256	–	5	2	3	3	3	4
W. M. Lawry (Australia) ...	13	201	7	–	1	4	0	1	–
§ R. B. Kanhai (West Indies) ...	12	256	4	4	0	–	0	3	1
T. W. Graveney (England) ...	11	258	–	1	0	5	0	2	3

BATSMEN SCORING 50 FIFTIES

	50s	*A*	*SA*	*Opponents WI*	*NZ*	*I*	*P*
§ M. C. Cowdrey (England) ...	59	16	10	16	9	5	3
§ K. F. Barrington (England) ...	55	18	8	7	4	12	6

Page 48 **HIGHEST AGGREGATES IN A SERIES**

	Season	*M.*	*I.*	*N.O.*	*Runs*	*H.S.*	*Avge.*	*100s*	*50s*
K. D. Walters (A v. WI) ...	1968-69	4	6	0	699	242	116.50	4	2
W. M. Lawry (A v. WI)... ...	1968-69	5	8	0	667	205	83.37	3	2

Page 49 **HIGHEST INDIVIDUAL INNINGS**

258 S. M. Nurse: West Indies v. New Zealand (Christchurch) 1968-69
242 K. D. Walters: Australia v. West Indies (Sydney) 1968-69
239 G. T. Dowling: New Zealand v. India (Christchurch) 1967-68
§ B. F. Butcher's 209 (Nottingham, 1966) was not out: insert asterisk.

Page 50 **Highest Individual Innings**—*Cont.*

205 W. M. Lawry: Australia v. West Indies (Melbourne) 1968-69

A CENTURY ON DÉBUT (*a*) *IN FIRST INNINGS*

Hampshire, J. H. ... 107 England v. West Indies (Lord's) 1969

Note: A. G. Chipperfield scored 99 in his first Test innings (Australia v. England at Nottingham in 1934).

Pages 51 and 52 (*c*) *IN FIRST MATCH AGAINST A SPECIFIC COUNTRY*

Chappell, I. M. ... ... 117 Australia v. West Indies (Brisbane²) ... 1968-69
Lloyd, C. H. ... ... 118 West Indies v. England (Port of Spain) ... 1967-68
Lloyd, C. H. ... ... 129 West Indies v. Australia (Adelaide) ... 1968-69

Page 53 **A CENTURY IN EACH INNINGS OF A MATCH**

242 103 K. D. Walters Australia v. West Indies (Sydney) ... 1968-69
(*The only instance of a batsman scoring a double-century and a century in the same Test Match*)

Page 54 **CENTURY BEFORE LUNCH**—*ON OTHER DAYS*

C. P. Mead ... ... England v. Australia (Oval) 1921

FASTEST CENTURIES

86 min. B. R. Taylor (124): New Zealand v. West Indies (Auckland) ... 1968-69

Page 55 **MOST CONSECUTIVE FIFTIES**

§ J. Ryder's first four fifties were scored in the 1921-22 series.
5 K. D. Walters (Australia): 76, 118, 110, 50, 242, 103 (1968-69).

FASTEST FIFTIES:

§ Delete in toto entry and 4-line note concerning S. A. Durrani.

28 min. J. T. Brown (140): England v. Australia (Melbourne) 1894-95
29 min. S. A. Durani (61*): India v. England (Kanpur) 1963-64
30 min. E. A. V. Williams (72): West Indies v. England (Bridgetown) ... 1947-48
30 min. B. R. Taylor (124): New Zealand v. West Indies (Auckland) ... 1968-69
33 min. C. A. Roach (56): West Indies v. England (Oval) 1933
34 min. C. R. Browne (70*): West Indies v. England (Georgetown) 1929-30

Page 56 **SLOWEST INDIVIDUAL INNINGS**

Runs	*Min.*		
9	120	W. Newham: England v. Australia (Sydney)	1887-88
9	125	T. W. Jarvis: New Zealand v. India (Madras²)	1964-65

MOST CENTURIES IN A SERIES

FOUR:

K. D. Walters ... ... Australia v. West Indies 1968-69

Pages 56 and 57 **YOUNGEST PLAYERS TO SCORE A CENTURY**

Years	*Days*				
20	197	D. G. Bradman	123	Australia v. England (Melbourne)	1928-29
20	240	J. W. Burke	101*	Australia v. England (Adelaide)	1950-51
20	267	G. A. Headley	114	West Indies v. England (Georgetown)	1929-30
20	271	G. A. Headley	112		
20	315	G. A. Headley	223	West Indies v. England (Kingston)	1929-30

§ Delete note about R. G. Pollock in toto and substitute:

G. A. Headley (West Indies) holds the unique record of scoring four Test hundreds before his 21st birthday.

Pages 57–63 **CENTURIES IN TEST CRICKET**

§ *ENGLAND* (*379*)

§ Barrington, K. F.	(20)	143 v. West Indies (Port of Spain)	1967-68
§ Boycott, G. ...	(6)	116 v. West Indies (Georgetown)	1967-68
		128 v. West Indies (Manchester)	1969
		106 v. West Indies (Lord's)	1969
§ Cowdrey, M. C.	(22)	101 v. West Indies (Kingston)	1967-68
		148 v. West Indies (Port of Spain)	1967-68
		104 v. Australia (Birmingham)	1968
		(*In his 100th Test Match*)	
		100 v. Pakistan (Lahore²)	1968-69

Centuries in Test Cricket—*Cont.*

§ D'Oliveira, B. L.	(3)	158	v. Australia (Oval)	1968
		114*	v. Pakistan (Dacca)	1967-68
§ Edrich, J. H. ...	(8)	146	v. West Indies (Bridgetown)	1967-68
		164	v. Australia (Oval)	1968
		115	v. New Zealand (Lord's)	1969
		155	v. New Zealand (Nottingham)	1969
§ Graveney, T. W.	(11)	118	v. West Indies (Port of Spain)	1967-68
		105	v. Pakistan (Karachi)	1968-69
Hampshire, J. H. ...	(1)	107	v. West Indies (Lord's)	1969
Illingworth, R. ...	(1)	113	v. West Indies (Lord's)	1969
§ Milburn, C. ...	(2)	139	v. Pakistan (Karachi)	1969-69
Sharpe, P. J. ...	(1)	111	v. New Zealand (Nottingham)	1969

Pages 63–68
§ *AUSTRALIA* (*269*)

§ Insert after details of C. Bannerman's 165*:

(*The first century in Test Matches*)

Chappell, I. M. ...	(3)	151	v. India (Melbourne)	1967-68
		117	v. West Indies (Brisbane[2])	1968-69
		165	v. West Indies (Melbourne)	1968-69
			(*The 1000th century in Test Matches*)	
§ Cowper, R. M. ...	(5)	108	v. India (Adelaide)	1967-68
		165	v. India (Sydney)	1967-68
§ Lawry, W. M. ...	(13)	100	v. India (Melbourne)	1967-68
		135	v. England (Oval)	1968
		105	v. West Indies (Brisbane[2])	1968-69
		205	v. West Indies (Melbourne)	1968-69
		151	v. West Indies (Sydney)	1968-69

Page 68

Redpath, I. R. ...	(1)	132	v. West Indies (Sydney)	1968-69
§ Simpson, R. B. ...	(8)	103	v. India (Adelaide)	1967-68
		109	v. India (Melbourne)	1967-68
§ Walters, K. D. ...	(6)	118	v. West Indies (Sydney)	1968-69
		110	v. West Indies (Adelaide)	1968-69
		242 } 103 }	v. West Indies (Sydney)	1968-69

Pages 70–72
§ *WEST INDIES* (*138*)

§ Butcher, B. F. ...	(7)	101	v. Australia (Sydney)	1968-69
		118	v. Australia (Adelaide)	1968-69
Carew, M. C. ...	(1)	109	v. New Zealand (Auckland)	1968-69
Davis, C. A. ...	(1)	103	v. England (Lord's)	1969

Page 71

§ Kanhai, R. B. ...	(12)	153	v. England (Port of Spain)	1967-68
		150	v. England (Georgetown)...	1967-68
Lloyd, C. H. ...	(3)	118	v. England (Port of Spain)	1967-68
		113*	v. England (Bridgetown)	1967-68
		129	v. Australia (Brisbane[2])	1968-69
§ Nurse, S. M. ...	(6)	136	v. England (Port of Spain)	1967-68
		137	v. Australia (Sydney)	1968-69
		168	v. New Zealand (Auckland)	1968-69
		258	v. New Zealand (Christchurch) ...	1968-69
§ Sobers, G. St. A.	(21)	113*	v. England (Kingston)	1967-68
		152	v. England (Georgetown)...	1967-68
		110	v. Australia (Adelaide)	1968-69
		113	v. Australia (Sydney)	1968-69

Centuries in Test Cricket

Pages 72–73
§ *NEW ZEALAND (33)*

§ Dowling, G. T.	(3)	143	v. India (Dunedin)	1967-68
		239	v. India (Christchurch)	1967-68
Hastings, B. F. ...	(1)	117*	v. West Indies (Christchurch)	1968-69
§ Taylor, B. R.	(2)	124	v. West Indies (Auckland)	1968-69

Pages 73–74 § *INDIA (76)*

§ Jaisimha, M. L.	(3)	101	v. Australia (Brisbane[2])	1967-68
Wadekar, A. L. ...	(1)	143	v. New Zealand (Wellington)	1967-68

Page 75
§ Line 1: date should read 1961-62 and not 1960-61.

A CENTURY AND A 'DUCK' IN THE SAME MATCH:

ENGLAND

M. C. Cowdrey ...	101 & 0	v. West Indies (Kingston)	1967-68

AUSTRALIA

I. R. Redpath ...	0 & 132	v. West Indies (Sydney)	1968-69

Page 76
WEST INDIES

G. St. A. Sobers	0 & 113*	v. England (Kingston)	1967-68
C. A. Davis ...	103 & 0	v. England (Lord's)	1969

NEW ZEALAND § delete 'Nil'

G. T. Dowling ...	129 & 0	v. India (Bombay)	1964-65
B. F. Hastings ...	0 & 117*	v. West Indies (Christchurch)	1968-69

BATSMEN DISMISSED FOR A 'PAIR'

TWICE Insert after K. D. Mackay: G. D. McKenzie
ONCE *ENGLAND*: D. L. Amiss (1968)
AUSTRALIA: § Delete G. D. McKenzie (1963-64)
A. N. Connolly (1968-69)

Page 77 *WEST INDIES*: W. W. Hall (1967-68)

DISMISSED FOR A 'PAIR' BY THE SAME FIELDING COMBINATION

§ Delete R. Benaud, b Trueman, etc. (instances of being twice bowled for a 'pair' do not qualify for inclusion under this heading).

Page 78

CARRYING BAT THROUGH INNINGS

NEW ZEALAND

G. M. Turner ...	43*(131)	v. England (Lord's)	1969

BATSMEN SCORING OVER 60% OF COMPLETED INNINGS TOTAL:

61.8% (258/417): S. M. Nurse, West Indies v. New Zealand (Christchurch) ... 1968-69

Page 79 **MOST RUNS OFF ONE OVER (SIX-BALL):**

22 (660046) R. C. Motz off D. A. Allen for New Zealand v. England at Dunedin 1965-66

Page 80 **PARTNERSHIP OF OVER 300:**

336 4th W. M. Lawry (151) & K. D. Walters (242): Australia v. West Indies (Sydney) 1968-69

Page 81 **MOST CENTURY PARTNERSHIPS IN ONE INNINGS**

THREE New Zealand (126-1, 103-4, 119-5) v. India (Christchurch) 1967-68

Page 81 **CENTURY PARTNERSHIP FOR SAME WICKET IN EACH INNINGS**

3rd WICKET

118 & 172 R. M. Cowper with A. P. Sheahan (1st Inns) & R. B. Simpson (2nd Inns): Australia v. India (Adelaide) 1967-68

Century Partnerships for Same Wicket in Each Innings—*Cont.*

Page 82

4th WICKET

336 & 209 K. D. Walters with W. M. Lawry (1st Inns) & I. R. Redpath (2nd Inns): Australia v. West Indies (Sydney) 1968-69

SUMMARY OF CENTURY PARTNERSHIPS

§ Substitute the following tables:

For	*Opponents* E	*A*	*SA*	*WI*	*NZ*	*I*	*P*	*Total*
England	—	182	88	62	42	38	19	431
Australia	167	—	59	32	1	22	3	284
South Africa	75	38	—	—	16	—	—	129
West Indies	59	33	—	—	11	33	10	146
New Zealand	13	—	6	4	—	13	4	40
India	27	13	—	19	16	—	8	83
Pakistan	10	3	—	12	5	8	—	38
Total	351	269	153	129	91	114	44	1151

For	*Wicket* 1st	*2nd*	*3rd*	*4th*	*5th*	*6th*	*7th*	*8th*	*9th*	*10th*	*Total*
England ...	84	87	72	66	46	42	18	7	7	2	431
Australia ...	44	60	53	51	33	17	11	10	3	2	284
South Africa ...	27	18	24	22	11	9	11	5	1	1	129
West Indies ...	16	24	27	29	21	19	8	–	2	–	146
New Zealand ...	10	3	8	5	8	1	4	1	–	–	40
India	9	13	19	15	10	10	3	2	1	1	83
Pakistan ...	6	9	8	5	3	3	1	1	1	1	38
Total ...	196	214	211	193	132	101	56	26	15	7	1151

PLAYERS SHARING IN TEN OR MORE CENTURY PARTNERSHIPS

§*ENGLAND* (*26*)

	Total	*1st*	*2nd*	*3rd*	*4th*	*5th*	*6th*	*7th*	*8th*	*9th*	*10th*
§ M. C. Cowdrey	41	5	8	6	13	4	3	1	–	1	–
§ K. F. Barrington ...	35	–	6	10	14	4	1	–	–	–	–
§ T. W. Graveney... ...	26	–	7	6	7	4	1	–	1	–	–

Page 83

G. Boycott	17	5	6	3	3	–	–	–	–	–	–
J. H. Edrich	16	5	4	2	4	1	–	–	–	–	–

§ *AUSTRALIA* (*21*)

	Total	*1st*	*2nd*	*3rd*	*4th*	*5th*	*6th*	*7th*	*8th*	*9th*	*10th*
§ W. M. Lawry	24	12	5	4	2	1	–	–	–	–	–
§ R. B. Simpson	19	10	4	4	–	1	–	–	–	–	–
R. M. Cowper	11	1	3	4	2	–	1	–	–	–	–

Page 84

§ *WEST INDIES* (*11*)

	Total	*1st*	*2nd*	*3rd*	*4th*	*5th*	*6th*	*7th*	*8th*	*9th*	*10th*
§ G. St. A. Sobers ...	35	–	3	4	9	11	7	1	–	–	–
§ R. B. Kanhai	27	2	8	9	5	2	1	–	–	–	–
§ B. F. Butcher	15	–	–	5	5	3	2	–	–	–	–
S. M. Nurse	15	1	2	5	2	4	1	–	–	–	–
§ C. C. Hunte	14	5	5	1	3	–	–	–	–	–	–

§ *NEW ZEALAND* (*3*)

	Total	*1st*	*2nd*	*3rd*	*4th*	*5th*	*6th*	*7th*	*8th*	*9th*	*10th*
G. T. Dowling	10	4	1	2	2	1	–	–	–	–	–

INDIA (*5*)

	Total	*1st*	*2nd*	*3rd*	*4th*	*5th*	*6th*	*7th*	*8th*	*9th*	*10th*
§ C. G. Borde	16	–	–	–	5	6	4	1	–	–	–

CENTURY PARTNERSHIPS (pages 85 to 132)

ENGLAND

1st WICKET

					Opponents					
			Venue	*Series*	*A*	*SA*	*WI*	*NZ*	*I*	*P*
Page 85	J. H. Edrich	G. Boycott	Bridgetown	1967-68	—	—	172	—	—	—
Page 86	G. Boycott	J. H. Edrich	Lord's	1969	—	—	—	125	—	—
	J. H. Edrich	R. M. Prideaux	Leeds	1968	123	—	—	—	—	—
Page 87	G. Boycott	J. H. Edrich	Manchester	1969	—	—	112	—	—	—
			§TOTALS	84	42	18	9	6	7	2

2nd WICKET

					Opponents					
			Venue	*Series*	*A*	*SA*	*WI*	*NZ*	*I*	*P*
	J. H. Edrich	P. J. Sharpe	Nottingham	1969	—	—	—	249	—	—
Page 88	G. Boycott	M. C. Cowdrey	Georgetown	1967-68	—	—	172	—	—	—
	C. Milburn	T. W. Graveney	Karachi	1968-69	—	—	—	—	—	156
Page 89	G. Boycott	C. Milburn	Lord's	1968	132	—	—	—	—	—
	J. H. Edrich	M. C. Cowdrey	Kingston	1967-68	—	—	129	—	—	—
	G. Boycott	M. C. Cowdrey	Port of Spain	1967-68	—	—	118	—	—	—
	J. H. Edrich	M. C. Cowdrey	Birmingham	1968	108	—	—	—	—	—
Page 90			§TOTALS	87	36	17	12	9	8	5

3rd WICKET

					Opponents					
			Venue	*Series*	*A*	*SA*	*WI*	*NZ*	*I*	*P*
Page 91	M. C. Cowdrey	K. F. Barrington	Port of Spain	1967-68	—	—	134	—	—	—
	M. C. Cowdrey	K. F. Barrington	Port of Spain	1967-68	—	—	133	—	—	—
	G. Boycott	T. W. Graveney	Manchester	1969	—	—	128	—	—	—
Page 92	M. C. Cowdrey	K. F. Barrington	Kingston	1967-68	—	—	101	—	—	—
			§TOTALS	72	28	16	13	7	3	5

Century Partnerships England—*Cont.*

4th *WICKET*

			Venue	Series	A	SA	WI	NZ	I	P
Page 93	K. F. Barrington	T. W. Graveney	Port of Spain	1967-68	—	—	188	—	—	—
Page 94	G. Boycott	P. J. Sharpe	Lord's	1969	—	—	126	—	—	—
	J. H. Edrich	T. W. Graveney	Oval	1968	125	—	—	—	—	—
	J. H. Edrich	T. W. Graveney	Bridgetown	1967-68	—	—	109	—	—	—
Page 95			§ TOTALS	66	19	16	10	7	11	3

5th *WICKET*

			Venue	Series	A	SA	WI	NZ	I	P
Page 96	J. H. Edrich	B. L. D'Oliveira	Oval	1968	121	—	—	—	—	—
			§ TOTALS	46	20	9	4	6	5	2

6th *WICKET*

			Venue	Series	A	SA	WI	NZ	I	P
Page 97	J. H. Hampshire	A. P. E. Knott	Lord's	1969	—	—	128	—	—	—
	M. C. Cowdrey	A. P. E. Knott	Georgetown	1967-68	—	—	127	—	—	—
	M. C. Cowdrey	A. P. E. Knott	Port of Spain	1967-68	—	—	113	—	—	—
			§ TOTALS	42	20	10	6	2	2	2

9th *WICKET*

			Venue	Series	A	SA	WI	NZ	I	P
Page 99	G. A. R. Lock	P. I. Pocock	Georgetown	1967-68	—	—	109	—	—	—
			§ TOTALS	7	4	—	1	2	—	—

AUSTRALIA

1st WICKET

			Venue	Series	E	SA	WI	NZ	I	P
Page 100	R. B. Simpson	W. M. Lawry	Melbourne	1967-68	—	—	—	—	191	—
Page 101	W. M. Lawry	I. R. Redpath	Brisbane[2]	1967-68	—	—	—	—	116	—
	W. M. Lawry	R. M. Cowper	Sydney	1967-68	—	—	—	—	111	—
			§ TOTALS	44	25	9	6	—	4	—

2nd WICKET

			Venue	Series	E	SA	WI	NZ	I	P
	W. M. Lawry	I. M. Chappell	Melbourne	1968-69	—	—	298	—	—	—
Page 102	W. M. Lawry	I. M. Chappell	Brisbane[2]	1968-69	—	—	217	—	—	—
Page 103	W. M. Lawry	I. R. Redpath	Oval	1968	129	—	—	—	—	—
	R. M. Cowper	I. M. Chappell	Birmingham	1968	111	—	—	—	—	—
			§ TOTALS	60	34	16	6	1	2	1

3rd WICKET

			Venue	Series	E	SA	WI	NZ	I	P
Page 104	R. B. Simpson	R. M. Cowper	Adelaide	1967-68	—	—	—	—	172	—
	§ Transfer the 126-run partnership and its footnote to page 105.									
	W. M. Lawry	K. D. Walters	Manchester	1968	144	—	—	—	—	—
Page 105	W. M. Lawry	K. D. Walters	Melbourne	1968-69	—	—	123	—	—	—
	A. P. Sheahan	R. M. Cowper	Adelaide	1967-68	—	—	—	—	118	—
			§ TOTALS	53	23	14	8	—	7	1

4th WICKET

			Venue	Series	E	SA	WI	NZ	I	P
	W. M. Lawry	K. D. Walters	Sydney	1968-69	—	—	336	—	—	—
	I. R. Redpath	K. D. Walters	Sydney	1968-69	—	—	210	—	—	—
			§ TOTALS	51	30	10	5	—	6	—

Century Partnerships Australia—*Cont.*

5th WICKET

§ The 198-run partnership was in the 1965-66 series

			Venue	Series	E	SA	WI (Opponents)	NZ	I	P
	A. P. Sheahan	I. M. Chappell	Manchester	1968	152	—	—	—	—	—
Page 108	K. D. Walters	A. P. Sheahan	Sydney	1968-69	—	—	110	—	—	—
			§ TOTALS	33	23	5	4	—	1	—

6th WICKET

			Venue	Series	E	SA	WI (Opponents)	NZ	I	P
Page 109	I. M. Chappell	B. N. Jarman	Melbourne	1967-68	—	—	—	—	134	—
			§ TOTALS	17	10	3	1	—	2	1

WEST INDIES

1st WICKET

			Venue	Series	E	A	NZ (Opponents)	I	P
Page 117	G. S. Camacho	M. C. Carew	Port of Spain	1967-68	119	—	—	—	—
	R. C. Fredericks	G. S. Camacho	Lord's	1969	106	—	—	—	—
	S. M. Nurse	G. S. Camacho	Kingston	1967-68	102	—	—	—	—
	R. C. Fredericks	M. C. Carew	Sydney	1968-69	—	100	—	—	
			§ TOTALS	16	6	3	1	4	2

2nd WICKET

			Venue	Series	E	A	NZ	I	P
	M. C. Carew	S. M. Nurse	Christchurch	1968-69	—	—	231	—	—
	M. C. Carew	S. M. Nurse	Auckland	1968-69	—	—	172	—	—
	M. C. Carew	R. B. Kanhai	Brisbane[2]	1968-69	—	165	—	—	—
Page 118	M. C. Carew	R. B. Kanhai	Adelaide	1968-69	—	132	—	—	—
	R. C. Fredericks	R. B. Kanhai	Sydney	1968-69	—	103	—	—	—
			§ TOTALS	24	11	6	2	2	3

3rd WICKET

			Venue	Series	E	A	NZ	I	P
	S. M. Nurse	R. B. Kanhai	Port of Spain	1967-68	273	—	—	—	—
	S. M. Nurse	B. F. Butcher	Auckland	1968-69	—	—	174	—	—
Page 119	G. S. Camacho	B. F. Butcher	Leeds	1969	108	—	—	—	—
			§ TOTALS	27	13	7	2	4	1

4th WICKET

			Venue	Series	E	A	NZ	I	P
	R. B. Kanhai	G. St. A. Sobers	Georgetown	1967-68	250	—	—	—	—
	§ S. M. Nurse's partner in the 146-run partnership in 1964-65 was C. C. Hunte								
Page 120	R. B. Kanhai	C. H. Lloyd	Port of Spain	1967-68	116	—	—	—	—
	B. F. Butcher	C. H. Lloyd	Bridgetown	1967-68	101	—	—	—	—
			§ TOTALS	29	10	8	2	8	1

5th WICKET

			Venue	Series	E	A	NZ	I	P
	S. M. Nurse	G. St. A. Sobers	Melbourne	1968-69	—	134	—	—	—
Page 121			§ TOTALS	21	9	2	2	6	2

6th WICKET

			Venue	Series	E	A	NZ	I	P
	G. St. A. Sobers	S. M. Nurse	Sydney	1968-69	—	118	—	—	—
	G. St. A. Sobers	D. A. J. Holford	Kingston	1967-68	110	—	—	—	—
			§ TOTALS	19	8	4	1	5	1

(E, A, NZ, I, P are headed *Opponents*.)

Century Partnerships West Indies—*Cont.*

7th WICKET

			Venue	*Series*	*E*	*A*	*NZ*	*I*	*P*
Page 122	C. H. Lloyd	M. C. Carew	Brisbane[2]	1968-69	—	120	—	—	—
			§ TOTALS	8	2	2	1	3	—

9th WICKET

			Venue	*Series*	*E*	*A*	*NZ*	*I*	*P*
	D. A. J. Holford	J. L. Hendriks	Adelaide	1968-69	—	122	—	—	—
			§ TOTALS	2	—	1	—	1	—

NEW ZEALAND

1st WICKET

			Venue	*Series*	*E*	*SA*	*WI*	*I*	*P*
Page 123	G. T. Dowling	B. A. G. Murray	Christchurch	1967-68	—	—	—	126	—
	G. M. Turner	G. T. Dowling	Christchurch	1968-69	—	—	115	—	—
	G. M. Turner	G. T. Dowling	Auckland	1968-69	—	—	112	—	—
			§ TOTALS	10	4	1	2	2	1

2nd WICKET

			Venue	*Series*	*E*	*SA*	*WI*	*I*	*P*
	G. T. Dowling	B. E. Congdon	Dunedin	1967-68	—	—	—	155	—
			§ TOTALS	3	1	—	—	2	—

3rd *WICKET*

			Venue	*Series*	*E*	*SA*	*WI*	*I*	*P*
	B. E. Congdon	B. F. Hastings	Nottingham	1969	150	—	—	—	—
			§ TOTALS	8	2	—	—	5	1

4th WICKET

			Venue	Series	E	SA	WI (Opponents)	I	P
Page 124	G. T. Dowling	M. G. Burgess	Christchurch	1967-68	—	—	—	103	—
			§ TOTALS	5	1	2	—	1	1

5th WICKET

			Venue	Series	E	SA	WI (Opponents)	I	P
	G. T. Dowling	K. Thomson	Christchurch	1967-68	—	—	—	119	—
	B. F. Hastings	V. Pollard	Christchurch	1968-69	—	—	110	—	—
	§ Delete 104-run partnership between Sutcliffe and Pollard								
			§ TOTALS	8	2	2	2	1	1

7th *WICKET*

			Venue	Series	E	SA	WI (Opponents)	I	P
	B. Sutcliffe	V. Pollard	Birmingham	1965	104	—	—	—	—
Page 125			§ TOTALS	4	2	—	—	2	—

INDIA

3rd *WICKET*

			Venue	Series	E	A	WI (Opponents)	NZ	P
Page 127	A. L. Wadekar	R. F. Surti	Melbourne	1967-68	—	116	—	—	—
	A. L. Wadekar	R. F. Surti	Dunedin	1967-68	—	—	—	103	—
			§ TOTALS	19	7	3	4	3	2

Century Partnerships India—*Cont.*

4th WICKET

			Venue	Series	E	A	Opponents WI	NZ	P
Page 128	R. F. Surti	Nawab of Pataudi, Jnr.	Brisbane[2]	1967-68	—	128	—	—	—
	C. G. Borde	R. F. Surti	Adelaide	1967-68	—	121	—	—	—
	R. F. Surti	Nawab of Pataudi, Jnr.	Christchurch	1967-68	—	—	—	103	—
			§ TOTALS	15	1	2	5	5	2

5th WICKET

			Venue	Series	E	A	Opponents WI	NZ	P
	R. F. Surti	C. G. Borde	Auckland	1967-68	—	—	—	126	—
			§ TOTALS	10	4	1	1	3	1

6th WICKET

			Venue	Series	E	A	Opponents WI	NZ	P
Page 129	M. L. Jaisimha	C. G. Borde	Brisbane[2]	1967-68	—	119	—	—	—
			§ TOTALS	10	2	3	3	2	—

PLAYERS' RECORDS—BOWLING

Page 133 **100 WICKETS IN TESTS**

ENGLAND

§ J. B. Statham's average should read 24.84

	Tests	*Wkts.*	*Avge.*	*A*	*SA*	*WI*	*NZ*	*I*	*P*
						Opponents			
§ G. A. R. Lock	49	174	25.58	31	15	39	47	26	16
§ F. J. Titmus	49	146	31.30	40	27	15	28	27	9

AUSTRALIA

	Tests	*Wkts.*	*Avge.*	*E*	*SA*	*WI*	*NZ*	*I*	*P*
						Opponents			
§ G. D. McKenzie ...	49	217	28.58	89	40	47	—	26	15

WEST INDIES

	Tests	*Wkts.*	*Avge.*	*E*	*A*	*NZ*	*I*	*P*
						Opponents		
§ L. R. Gibbs	50	209	27.54	73	61	8	42	25
§ G. St. A. Sobers ...	76	193	34.59	82	51	9	47	4
§ W. W. Hall	48	192	26.38	65	45	1	65	16

Page 134

NEW ZEALAND

§ Delete note in toto.

	Tests	*Wkts.*	*Avge.*	*E*	*WI*	*SA*	*I*	*P*
						Opponents		
R. C. Motz	32	100	31.48	28	17	21	22	12

BEST BOWLING AVERAGES

	Tests	*Balls*	*Mdns.*	*Runs*	*Wkts.*	*Avge.*	*5wI.*	*10wM.*
D. L. Underwood (England) ...	16	3923	294	1128	67	16.83	6	2

§ Delete in toto the penultimate line of this list (K. Higgs).

MOST ECONOMICAL CAREER FIGURES

§ T. L. Goddard conceded 27.54 runs per 100 balls.

§ K. D. Mackay conceded 28.81 runs per 100 balls and should be listed above the entry for J. C. Watkins.

	Runs/100 balls	*Tests*	*Balls*	*Mdns.*	*Runs*	*Wkts.*	*Avge.*
D. L. Underwood (England) ...	28.75	16	3923	294	1128	67	16.83

Page 135 **TEN WICKETS IN A MATCH**

§ *ENGLAND* (72)

			A	*SA*	*WI*	*NZ*	*I*
					Opponents		
1969	D. L. Underwood	Oval	—	—	—	12-101	—
1969	D. L. Underwood	Lord's	—	—	—	11-70	—

Page 136

			A	*SA*	*WI*	*NZ*	*I*
1967-68	J. A. Snow	Georgetown	—	—	10-142	—	—

§ *AUSTRALIA* (42)

			E	*SA*	*WI*	*I*
				Opponents		
1967-68	G. D. McKenzie	Melbourne	—	—	—	10-151
1968-69	G. D. McKenzie	Melbourne	—	—	10-159	—

Page 138 **EIGHT WICKETS IN AN INNINGS**

§ *AUSTRALIA* (5)

			E	*SA*	*WI*	*NZ*	*I*	*P*
					Opponents			
1968-69	G. D. McKenzie	Melbourne	—	—	8-71	—	—	—

NEW ZEALAND

§ Delete the second sentence of the note and substitute the following:

The best innings analysis for New Zealand is 6-38 by G. A. Bartlett against India at Christchurch in 1967-68.

Page 139 **25 WICKETS IN A SERIES**

ENGLAND

	Series	*Venue*	*Tests*	*Wickets & Opponents* *A*	*SA*	*WI*	*NZ*	*I*
J. A. Snow	1967-68	WI	4	—	—	27	—	—

Page 140

AUSTRALIA

	Series	*Venue*	*Tests*	*Wickets and Opponents* *E*	*SA*	*WI*	*I*
G. D. McKenzie	1968-69	A	5	—	—	30	—
J. W. Gleeson	1968-69	A	5	—	—	26	—

Page 141

INDIA

	Series	*Venue*	*Tests*	*Wickets & Opponents* *E*	*A*	*WI*	*NZ*	*P*
E. A. S. Prasanna	1967-68	A	4	—	25	—	—	—

Page 142 **THREE WICKETS IN FOUR BALLS**

D. Shackleton ... ... England v. West Indies (Lord's) 1963

F. J. Titmus ... ... England v. New Zealand (Leeds) 1965
(Four wickets in his 21st over: WOWWOW)

Page 143 **BOWLERS UNCHANGED IN A COMPLETED INNINGS**

§ 6th line of list: J. Briggs took 6-49 at Adelaide in 1891-92

Page 144 Add new item:

BARRED FROM BOWLING IN INNINGS FOR DAMAGING WICKET WITH FOLLOW-THROUGH:

R. C. Motz New Zealand v. India (Christchurch) 1967-68 in 2nd inns—4th day.

PLAYERS' RECORDS—ALL-ROUND CRICKET

1000 RUNS AND 100 WICKETS

ENGLAND: § Tate's initials should read M. W.

	Tests	*Runs*	*Wkts.*	*Tests in which Double was achieved*
§ Titmus, F. J.	49	1311	146	40th
WEST INDIES				
§ Sobers, G. St. A. ...	76	6776	193	48th

Add new item after 100 RUNS AND TEN WICKETS IN A MATCH

100 RUNS AND FIVE WICKETS ON DÉBUT

B. R. Taylor (105 and 5-86) New Zealand v. India (Calcutta) 1964-65

250 RUNS AND 25 WICKETS IN A SERIES

§ 2nd entry: amend the spelling of G. A. Faulkner's name.

PLAYERS' RECORDS—FIELDING

Page 145 **50 CATCHES IN A CAREER**

Catches	*Player*	*For*	*Tests*	*Av./Test*
§ 113	M. C. Cowdrey	E	104	1.08
§ 99	R. B. Simpson	A	52	1.90
§ 96	G. St. A. Sobers	WI	76	1.26
§ 80	T. W. Graveney	E	79	1.01
§ 59	G. A. R. Lock	E	49	1.20
§ 58	K. F. Barrington	E	82	0.70

PLAYERS' RECORDS—WICKET KEEPING

Page 146 **100 DISMISSALS IN A CAREER**

§ 114 (103ct. 11st.) J. M. Parks (E) in 46 Tests.

WICKET-KEEPERS' DOUBLE

§ Parks, J. M. 114 dismissals 1962 runs

NO BYES CONCEDED IN TOTAL OF OVER 500

619	J. L. Hendriks: West Indies v. Australia (Sydney)	1968-69
526-7d	A. P. E. Knott: England v. West Indies (Port of Spain)	1967-68
510	J. L. Hendriks: West Indies v. Australia (Melbourne)	1968-69

Page 147 **HIGHEST NUMBER OF BYES CONCEDED IN AN INNINGS**

38 Conceded by J. M. Parks: England v. West Indies (Kingston) 1967-68

PLAYERS' RECORDS—THE CAPTAINS

RESULTS SUMMARY: § *ENGLAND* (54 captains)

§ A. Shrewsbury won the toss on 3 occasions.

§ W. W. Read did not win the toss in either of his Tests as captain.

Page 148

§ M. J. K. Smith won the toss on 10 occasions.

	Tests as Captain	*Opponents* A	*SA*	*WI*	*NZ*	*I*	*P*	*Results* W	*L*	*D*	*Toss Won*
§ M. C. Cowdrey	27	6	5	10	–	2	4	8	4	15	17
T. W. Graveney	1	1	–	–	–	–	–	–	–	1	–
R. Illingworth	6	–	–	3	3	–	–	4	–	2	3
§ Totals	458	203	102	58	40	37	18	177	118	163	230

§ *AUSTRALIA* (33 captains)

§ T. Hogan should read T. P. Horan.

§ P. S. McDonnell won the toss on 4 occasions.

	Tests as Captain	*Opponents* E	*SA*	*WI*	*NZ*	*I*	*P*	*Results* W	*L*	*D*	*Tied*	*Toss Won*
§ R. B. Simpson ...	29	8	9	5	–	5	2	8	7	14	–	14
W. M. Lawry ...	11	4	–	5	–	2	–	6	2	3	–	2
B. N. Jarman ...	1	1	–	–	–	–	–	–	–	1	–	1
§ Totals ...	309	203	49	30	1	20	6	142	82	84	1	148

WEST INDIES (14 captains)

	Tests as Captain	*Opponents* E	*A*	*NZ*	*I*	*P*	*Results* W	*L*	*D*	*Tied*	*Toss Won*
§ G. St. A. Sobers	29	13	10	3	3	–	9	9	11	–	19
§ Totals	128	58	30	9	23	8	43	42	42	1	71

§ *NEW ZEALAND* (11 captains)

	Tests as Captain	*Opponents* E	*A*	*SA*	*WI*	*I*	*P*	*Results* W	*L*	*D*	*Toss Won*
§ B. W. Sinclair	3	2	–	–	–	1	–	–	1	2	3
G. T. Dowling	9	3	–	–	3	3	–	2	5	2	5
§ Totals	89	40	1	17	9	13	9	5	44	40	49

Page 150 § *INDIA* (15 captains)

	Tests as Captain	*Opponents* E	*A*	*WI*	*NZ*	*P*	*Results* W	*L*	*D*	*Toss Won*
§Nawab of Pataudi, Jnr.	28	8	6	6	8	–	5	13	10	14
C. G. Borde	1	–	1	–	–	–	–	1	–	–
§ Totals	108	37	20	23	13	15	13	45	50	54

Results Summary—*Cont.*

§ *PAKISTAN* (6 captains)

	Tests as Captain	*Opponents* *E*	*A*	*WI*	*NZ*	*I*	*Results* *W*	*L*	*D*	*Toss Won*
Saeed Ahmed	3	3	–	–	–	–	–	–	3	1
§ Totals	56	18	6	8	9	15	10	16	30	30

Page 150 **CAPTAINS WHO INVITED THE OPPOSITION TO BAT**

§ 45 captains have between them invited the opposition to take first innings on 73 occasions. In only 22 instances has this decision resulted in the match being won and on 26 occasions it has brought defeat.

Page 151 § *AUSTRALIA* (9 captains, 16 occasions)

P. S. McDonnell (2) ...	England (Sydney) 1886-87	L	13 runs
	England (Sydney) 1887-88	L	126 runs
§ R. B. Simpson (4) ...	South Africa (Melbourne) 1963-64 ...	W	8 wkts.
W. M. Lawry ...	West Indies (Melbourne) 1968-69 ...	W	Inns and 30

§ *SOUTH AFRICA* (6 captains, 10 occasions)

T. L. Goddard	Australia (Sydney) 1963-64	D	

§ *WEST INDIES* (4 captains, 5 occasions)

G. St. A. Sobers (2) ...	Australia (Sydney) 1968-69	L	382 runs
	New Zealand (Auckland) 1968-69 ...	W	5 wkts.

§ *NEW ZEALAND* (4 captains, 7 occasions)

G. T. Dowling (2) ...	India (Auckland) 1967-68	L	272 runs
	West Indies (Wellington) 1968-69 ...	W	6 wkts.

§ *INDIA* (4 captains, 8 occasions)

§ Nawab of Pataudi, Jnr. (5)	England (Kanpur) 1963-64	D	
	Australia (Brisbane[2]) 1967-68	L	39 runs
	Australia (Sydney) 1967-68	L	144 runs
	New Zealand (Christchurch) 1967-68, ...	L	6 wkts.

Page 152 **MOST CONSECUTIVE MATCHES AS CAPTAIN**

§ West Indies 29 G. St. A. Sobers (Kingston 1964-65 to date)

CAPTAINS' TABLE

	For	*Played*	*Won* (2 pts.)	*Drawn* (1 pt.)	*Lost*	*Points*	*%*
§ M. C. Cowdrey ...	E	27	8	16	3	32	59.25
§ R. B. Simpson ...	A	29	8	14	7	30	51.72
§ G. St. A. Sobers ...	WI	29	9	11	9	29	50.00
Page 153							
§ Nawab of Pataudi, Jnr.	I	28	5	10	13	20	35.71

INDIVIDUAL CAREER RECORDS

Page 153 **BATTING AND FIELDING**

§ Complete Test Match career records for all players appearing in official Tests before the end of the 1969 English season:

ENGLAND (444 Players)

	Tests	*I.*	*N.O.*	*Runs*	*H.S.*	*Avge.*	*100s*	*50s*	*Ct.*	*St.*
§ Amiss, D. L.	5	8	1	125	45	17.85	—	—	4	—
§ Arnold, G. G.	3	3	0	74	59	24.66	—	1	3	—
§ Barber, R. W.	28	45	3	1495	185	35.59	1	9	21	—
§ Barrington, K. F.	82	131	15	6806	256	58.67	20	35	58	—

Batting and Fielding—England—*Cont.*

Page 154

	Tests	I.	N.O.	Runs	H.S.	Avge.	100s	50s	Ct.	St.
§ Boycott, G.	41	70	9	2609	246*	42.77	6	13	9	—
§ Brown, D. J.	26	34	5	342	44*	11.79	—	—	7	—
Cottam, R. M. H.... ...	2	2	1	8	4*	8.00	—	—	2	—
§ Cowdrey, M. C.	104	171	15	7228	182	46.33	22	37	113	—
Denness, M. H.	1	2	1	57	55*	57.00	—	1	3	—
§ Dexter, E. R.	62	102	8	4502	205	47.89	9	27	29	—
§ D'Olivera, B. L.	25	38	6	1390	158	43.43	3	8	19	—

Page 155

	Tests	I.	N.O.	Runs	H.S.	Avge.	100s	50s	Ct.	St.
§ Edrich, J. H.	40	63	4	2711	310*	45.94	8	10	21	—
Fletcher, K. W. R. ...	6	9	1	227	83	28.37	—	1	4	—
§ Graveney, T. W.	79	123	13	4882	258	44.38	11	20	80	—
Hampshire, J. H.	2	4	0	135	107	33.75	1	—	4	—

Page 156

	Tests	I.	N.O.	Runs	H.S.	Avge.	100s	50s	Ct.	St.
§ Higgs, K.	15	19	3	185	63	11.56	—	1	4	—
§ Hobbs, R. N. S.	6	6	3	28	15*	9.33	—	—	6	—
§ Illingworth, R.	36	50	8	801	113	19.07	1	2	28	—
§ Jones, I. J.	15	17	9	38	16	4.75	—	—	4	—
§ Knight, B. R.	29	38	7	812	127	26.19	2	—	14	—
§ Knott, A. P. E.	18	26	4	666	96*	30.27	—	5	52	8

Page 157

	Tests	I.	N.O.	Runs	H.S.	Avge.	100s	50s	Ct.	St.
§ Lock, G. A. R.	49	63	9	742	89	13.74	—	3	59	—
§ Milburn, C.	9	16	2	654	139	46.71	2	2	7	—

Page 158

	Tests	I.	N.O.	Runs	H.S.	Avge.	100s	50s	Ct.	St.
§ Parfitt, P. H.	34	46	5	1765	131*	43.04	7	5	37	—
§ Parks, J. M.	46	68	7	1962	108*	32.16	2	9	103	11
Pocock, P. I.	4	7	0	48	13	6.85	—	—	6	—
Prideaux, R. M.	3	6	1	102	64	20.40	—	1	—	—

Page 159

	Tests	I.	N.O.	Runs	H.S.	Avge.	100s	50s	Ct.	St.
§ Sharpe, P. J.	12	21	4	786	111	46.23	1	4	17	—
§ Snow, J. A.	25	33	11	273	59*	12.40	—	1	9	—
§ Titmus, F. J.	49	68	11	1311	84*	23.00	—	9	35	—

Page 160

	Tests	I.	N.O.	Runs	H.S.	Avge.	100s	50s	Ct.	St.
§ Underwood, D. L. ...	16	19	8	176	45*	16.00	—	—	9	—
§ Amend Ward, A. to read Ward, Albert.										
Ward, Alan	3	3	1	40	21	20.00	—	—	2	—

§ *AUSTRALIA* (247 Players)

Page 161

	Tests	I.	N.O.	Runs	H.S.	Avge.	100s	50s	Ct.	St.
§ Chappell, I. M.	22	38	3	1351	165	38.60	3	7	31	—
§ Connolly, A. N.	19	28	16	83	37	6.91	—	—	12	—
§ Cowper, R. M.	27	46	2	2061	307	46.84	5	10	21	—
Freeman, E. W.	8	13	0	265	76	20.38	—	2	4	—

Page 162

	Tests	I.	N.O.	Runs	H.S.	Avge.	100s	50s	Ct.	St.
Gleeson, J. W.	14	23	6	238	45	14.00	—	—	10	—
§ Hawke, N. J. N.	27	37	15	366	46*	16.63	—	—	9	—
Inverarity, R. J.	3	6	0	113	56	18.83	—	1	3	—
§ Jarman, B. N.	19	30	3	400	78	14.81	—	2	50	4
Joslin, L. R.	1	2	0	9	7	4.50	—	—	—	—

Batting and Fielding—Australia—*Cont.*

	Tests	*I.*	*N.O.*	*Runs*	*H.S.*	*Avge.*	100*s*	50*s*	*Ct.*	*St.*
Page 163										
§ Lawry, W. M.	53	95	7	4478	210	50.88	13	22	20	—
§ McKenzie, G. D.	49	71	9	817	76	13.17	—	2	25	—
Mallett, A. A.	2	4	1	68	43*	22.26	—	—	1	—
§ Mayne, L. R. His correct initials are L. C.										
Page 164										
§ Redpath, I. R.	28	49	4	1623	132	36.06	1	10	39	—
§ Renneberg, D. A. ...	8	13	7	22	9	3.66	—	—	2	—
Sheahan, A. P.	14	25	3	788	88	35.81	—	5	12	—
§ Simpson, R. B.	52	92	7	4131	311	48.60	8	24	99	—
§ Stackpole, K. R.	12	20	1	571	134	30.05	1	3	12	—
§ Taber, H. B.	7	12	2	173	48	17.30	—	—	27	1
§ Walters, K. D.	16	26	3	1706	242	74.17	6	9	4	—

Page 169 §*WEST INDIES* (134 *Players*)

	Tests	*I.*	*N.O.*	*Runs*	*H.S.*	*Avge.*	100*s*	50*s*	*Ct.*	*St.*
§ Butcher, B. F.	44	78	6	3104	209*	43.11	7	16	15	—
Camacho, G. S.	9	18	0	572	87	31.77	—	4	3	—
§ Carew, M. C.	13	25	3	863	109	39.22	1	5	7	—
Davis, C. A.	4	8	0	236	103	29.50	1	—	2	—
Page 170										
Edwards, R. M.	5	8	1	65	22	9.28	—	—	—	—
Findlay, T. M.	2	4	0	51	23	12.75	—	—	9	—
Foster, M. L. C.	1	2	0	7	4	3.50	—	—	—	—
Fredericks, R. C.	10	19	0	525	76	27.63	—	4	11	—
§ Gibbs, L. R.	50	73	22	337	22	6.60	—	—	34	—
§ Griffith, C. C.	28	42	10	530	54	16.56	—	1	16	—
§ Hall, W. W.	48	66	14	818	50*	15.73	—	2	11	—
§ Hendriks, J. L.	20	32	8	447	64	18.62	—	2	42	5
Holder, V. A.	3	6	0	80	35	13.33	—	—	1	—
§ Holford, D. A. J.	15	25	3	488	105*	22.18	1	2	13	—
§ Kanhai, R. B.	61	108	3	5056	256	48.15	12	22	32	—
§ King, L. A....	2	4	0	41	20	10.25	—	—	2	—
§ Lloyd, C. H.	18	33	3	1159	129	38.63	3	5	9	—
§ Murray, D. L.	10	17	3	197	34	14.07	—	—	35	3
Page 171										
§ Nurse, S. M.	29	54	1	2523	258	47.60	6	10	21	—
§ Rodriguez, W. V.	5	7	0	96	50	13.71	—	1	3	—
Shepherd, J. N.	3	5	0	65	32	13.00	—	—	1	—
Shillingford, G. C. ...	2	3	1	11	5*	5.50	—	—	—	—
§ Sobers, G. St. A.	76	132	17	6776	365*	58.92	21	26	96	—
§ Substitutes									25	—

§ *NEW ZEALAND* (121 *Players*)

	Tests	*I.*	*N.O.*	*Runs*	*H.S.*	*Avge.*	100*s*	50*s*	*Ct.*	*St.*
§ Alabaster, J. C.	19	32	6	252	34	9.69	—	—	7	—
Page 172										
§ Bartlett, G. A.	10	18	1	263	40	15.47	—	—	8	—
Burgess, M. G.	8	15	0	358	66	23.86	—	3	6	—
§ Collinge, R. O.	13	18	2	249	54	15.56	—	1	6	—
§ Congdon, B. E.	23	46	2	1284	104	29.18	1	8	14	—
§ Cunis, R. S.	8	14	5	104	20*	11.55	—	—	1	—
§ Dowling, G. T.	29	57	1	1827	239	32.62	3	8	14	—
Hadlee, D. R.	2	3	1	55	35*	27.50	—	—	3	—
Harford, R. I.	3	5	2	7	6	2.33	—	—	11	—
Hastings, B. F.	6	11	2	427	117*	47.44	1	3	3	—
Howarth, H. J.	3	5	3	11	4*	5.50	—	—	1	—

Batting and Fielding—New Zealand—*Cont.*

	Tests	*I.*	*N.O.*	*Runs*	*H.S.*	*Avge.*	100*s*	50*s*	*Ct.*	*St.*
Page 173										
Milburn, B. D.	3	3	2	8	4*	8.00	—	—	6	2
§ Morgan, R. W.	15	28	1	712	97	26.37	—	5	7	—
§ Motz, R. C.	32	56	3	612	60	11.54	—	3	9	—
Murray, B. A. G.	6	12	1	267	74	24.47	—	2	9	—
§ Pollard, V.	23	42	4	755	81*	19.86	—	5	18	—
§ Sinclair, B. W.	21	40	1	1148	138	29.43	3	3	8	—
§ Taylor, B. R.	17	32	5	648	124	24.00	2	2	4	—
Thomson, K.	2	4	1	94	69	31.33	—	1	—	—
Turner, G. M.	5	10	1	309	74	34.33	—	2	7	—
Page 174										
Wadsworth, K. J. ...	3	5	0	52	21	10.40	—	—	8	—
§ Ward, J. T.	8	12	6	75	35*	9.50	—	—	16	1
§ Yuile, B. W.	14	27	3	404	64	16.83	—	1	9	—

§ *INDIA* (117 *Players*)

	Tests	*I.*	*N.O.*	*Runs*	*H.S.*	*Avge.*	100*s*	50*s*	*Ct.*	*St.*
Ali, S. Abid	8	16	0	423	81	26.43	—	2	9	—
§ Bedi, B. S.	11	19	2	120	22	7.05	—	—	4	—
§ Borde, C. G.	54	95	11	3042	177*	36.21	5	18	36	—
§ Chandrasekhar, B. S. ...	16	23	12	72	22	6.54	—	—	5	—
§ Desai, R. B.	28	44	13	418	85	13.48	—	1	9	—
§ Amend spelling of Durani, S. A.										
§ Engineer, F. M.	23	43	1	1285	109	30.59	1	7	36	8
Page 175										
§ Amend spelling of Indrajitsinh, K. S.										
§ Jaisimha, M. L.	35	64	4	2013	129	33.55	3	12	16	—
Kulkarni, U. N.	4	8	5	13	7	4.33	—	—	—	—
§ Nadkarni, R. G.	41	67	12	1414	122*	25.70	1	7	22	—
§ Pataudi, Nawab of, Jnr. ...	31	56	2	2203	203*	40.79	6	11	19	—
§ Prasanna, E. A. S. ...	14	25	4	259	26	12.33	—	—	5	—
Page 176										
§ Sardesai, D. N.	20	37	3	1166	200*	34.29	2	7	4	—
§ Subramanya, V.	9	15	1	263	75	18.78	—	2	9	—
§ Surti, R. F.	23	42	4	1213	99	31.92	—	9	18	—
§ Wadekar, A. L.	13	26	1	863	143	34.52	1	7	21	—
§ Substitutes									34	—

§ *PAKISTAN* (59 *Players*)

	Tests	*I.*	*N.O.*	*Runs*	*H.S.*	*Avge.*	100*s*	50*s*	*Ct.*	*St.*
Aftab Gul	2	2	0	41	29	20.50	—	—	2	—
§ Asif Iqbal	14	23	1	700	146	31.81	1	4	9	—
Asif Masood	2	1	0	11	11	11.00	—	—	1	—
§ Bari, Wasim Delete entry in toto										
Page 177										
§ Hanif Mohammad... ...	54	95	8	3858	337	44.34	12	15	39	—
§ Ilyas, Mohammad Delete entry in toto.										
§ Intikhab Alam	23	38	7	667	61	21.51	—	4	13	—
§ Majid Jahangir	10	15	1	347	80	24.78	—	2	11	—
Mohammad Ilyas ...	10	19	0	441	126	23.21	1	2	6	—
§ Mushtaq Mohammad ...	20	35	4	1135	101	36.61	2	7	5	—
§ Niaz Ahmed	2	3	3	17	16*	—	—	—	1	—
§ Pervez Sajjad	8	10	6	59	18	14.75	—	—	3	—
§ Saeed Ahmed	38	72	4	2833	172	41.66	5	15	10	—
§ Salah-ud-Din	4	6	2	104	34*	26.00	—	—	2	—
Sarfraz Nawaz	1	—	—	—	—	—	—	—	—	—
§ Shafqat Rana	3	3	0	54	30	18.00	—	—	1	—
Wasim Bari...	6	7	1	57	14*	9.50	—	—	8	1

BOWLING

Page 178

ENGLAND

	Tests	Balls	Mdns.	Runs	Wkts.	Avge.	5wI.	10wM.
§ Arnold, G. G.	3	516	27	177	8	22.12	1	—
§ Barber, R. W.	28	3426	111	1806	42	43.00	—	—
§ Barrington, K. F.	82	2715	102	1300	29	44.82	—	—
§ Boycott, G.	41	784	36	339	7	48.42	—	—
§ Brown, D. J.	26	5098	183	2237	79	28.31	2	—
Cottam, R. M. H. ...	2	555	29	180	9	20.00	—	—
§ Cowdrey, M. C.	104	71	0	68	0	—	—	—
Page 179								
§ Dexter, E. R.	62	5317	186	2306	66	34.93	—	—
§ D'Oliveira, B. L.	25	3330	191	1146	25	45.84	—	—
§ Edrich, J. H.	40	30	1	23	0	—	—	—
Fletcher, K. W. R. ...	6	66	3	45	0	—	—	—
§ Graveney, T. W.	79	260	6	167	1	167.00	—	—
§ Higgs, K.	15	4112	193	1473	71	20.74	2	—
§ Hobbs, R. N. S.	6	1147	62	411	12	34.25	—	—
Page 180								
§ Illingworth, R.	36	7603	492	2345	86	27.26	2	—
§ Jones, I. J.	15	3545	98	1769	44	40.20	1	—
§ Knight, B. R.	29	5384	204	2223	70	31.75	—	—
§ Lock, G. A. R.	49	13063	806	4452	174	25.58	9	3
Page 181								
§ Parfitt, P. H.	34	1296	68	564	12	47.00	—	—
§ Parks, J. M.	46	54	1	51	1	51.00	—	—
Pocock, P. I.	4	1080	45	513	12	42.75	1	—
Prideaux, R. M.	3	12	2	0	0	—	—	—
Page 182								
§ Snow, J. A.	25	5977	214	2724	99	27.51	4	1
§ Statham, J. B.	70	16032	592	6262	252	24.84	9	1
§ Titmus, F. J.	49	14163	749	4571	146	31.30	7	—
§ Underwood, D. L. ...	16	3923	294	1128	67	16.83	6	2
Ward, Alan	3	443	15	210	10	21.00	—	—
§ White, D. W. bowled 220 balls								

Page 183

AUSTRALIA

	Tests	Balls	Mdns.	Runs	Wkts.	Avge.	5wI.	10wM.
§ Chappell, I. M.	22	2013	54	930	11	84.54	—	—
§ Connolly, A. N.	19	5025	162	1963	64	30.67	2	—
§ Cowper, R. M.	27	3005	138	1139	36	31.63	—	—
Freeman, E. W.	8	1523	33	774	26	29.76	—	—
Page 184								
Gleeson, J. W.	14	4033	155	1518	47	32.29	2	—
§ Hawke, N. J. N.	27	6974	238	2677	91	29.41	6	1
Inverarity, R. J.	3	6	0	3	0	—	—	—
§ Lawry, W. M.	53	8	1	0	0	—	—	—
Page 185								
§ McKenzie, G. D.	49	14800	439	6203	217	28.58	14	3
Mallett, A. A.	2	510	17	250	6	41.66	—	—
§ Mayne, L. R.—his correct initials are L. C.								
§ Redpath, I. R.	28	50	1	31	0	—	—	—
§ Renneberg, D. A.	8	1598	42	830	23	36.08	2	—
§ Simpson, R. B.	52	5763	225	2352	60	39.20	2	—
§ Stackpole, K. R.	12	1014	36	497	7	71.00	—	—

Bowling—Australia—*Cont.*

Page 186

	Tests	Balls	Mdns.	Runs	Wkts.	Avge.	5wI.	10wM.
§ Walters, K. D.	16	944	19	405	11	36.81	—	—

Page 189
WEST INDIES

	Tests	Balls	Mdns.	Runs	Wkts.	Avge.	5wI.	10wM.
§ Butcher, B. F.	44	256	15	90	5	18.00	1	—
Camacho, G. S.	9	18	1	12	0	—	—	—
§ Carew, M. C.	13	964	41	364	8	45.50	—	—
Davis, C. A.	4	312	8	126	2	63.00	—	—

Page 190

	Tests	Balls	Mdns.	Runs	Wkts.	Avge.	5wI.	10wM.
Edwards, R. M.	5	1311	25	626	18	34.77	1	—
Foster, M. L. C.	1	12	0	7	0	—	—	—
§ Gibbs, L. R.	50	17233	824	5757	209	27.54	13	2
§ Gomez, G. E. bowled 285 maidens.								
§ Griffith, C. C.	28	5631	177	2683	94	28.54	5	—
§ Hall, W. W.	48	10415	312	5066	192	26.38	9	1
Holder, V. A.	3	893	52	335	9	37.22	—	—
§ Holford, D. A. J.	15	2934	81	1331	29	45.89	—	—
§ Kanhai, R. B.	61	50	4	21	0	—	—	—
§ Kentish, E. S. M. bowled 31 maidens and King, F. bowled 140 maidens.								
§ King, L. A....	2	476	19	154	9	17.11	1	—
§ Lloyd, C. H.	18	524	19	202	4	50.50	—	—
§ Nurse, S. M.	29	42	4	7	0	—	—	—
§ Rodriguez, W. V.	5	573	10	374	7	53.42	—	—
Shepherd, J. N.	3	827	44	266	12	22.16	1	—
Shillingford, G. C. ...	2	358	12	160	6	26.66	—	—
§ Sobers, G. St. A.	76	17366	732	6677	193	34.59	6	—

NEW ZEALAND

	Tests	Balls	Mdns.	Runs	Wkts.	Avge.	5wI.	10wM.
§ Alabaster, J. C.	19	3680	166	1697	48	35.35	—	—
§ Bartlett, G. A.	10	1768	63	792	24	33.00	1	—
Burgess, M. G.	8	120	5	58	0	—	—	—
§ Collinge, R. O.	13	2519	102	1144	37	30.91	—	—
§ Congdon, B. E.	23	472	25	225	5	45.00	—	—
§ Cunis, R. S.	8	1791	51	781	20	39.05	—	—

Page 192

	Tests	Balls	Mdns.	Runs	Wkts.	Avge.	5wI.	10wM.
§ Dowling, G. T.	29	36	2	19	1	19.00	—	—
Hadlee, D. R.	2	330	10	179	6	29.83	—	—
Howarth, H. J.	3	996	67	313	8	39.12	—	—
§ Morgan, R. W.	15	783	25	463	3	154.33	—	—
§ Motz, R. C.	32	7034	279	3148	100	31.48	5	—
Murray, B. A. G.	6	6	1	0	1	0.00	—	—
§ Pollard, V.	23	3098	140	1379	24	57.45	—	—
§ Reid, J. R.	58	7719	441	2837	85	33.37	1	—

Page 193

	Tests	Balls	Mdns.	Runs	Wkts.	Avge.	5wI.	10wM.
§ Sinclair, B. W.	21	60	3	32	2	16.00	—	—
§ Taylor, B. R.	17	3153	99	1520	53	28.67	2	—
Thomson, K.	2	21	1	11	1	11.00	—	—
§ Yuile, B. W.	14	2417	139	1043	28	37.25	—	—

Bowling—*Cont.*

INDIA

	Tests	Balls	Mdns.	Runs	Wkts.	Avge.	5wI.	10wM.
Ali, S. Abid	8	962	24	434	14	31.00	1	—
§ Bedi, B. S.	11	2771	138	1058	34	31.11	1	—
§ Borde, C. G.	54	5707	237	2416	52	46.46	1	—
§ Chandrasekhar, B. S. ...	16	4751	221	1942	62	31.32	2	1
§ Desai, R. B.	28	5591	176	2763	74	37.33	2	—

§ Durani, S. A.—correct spelling.

Page 194

	Tests	Balls	Mdns.	Runs	Wkts.	Avge.	5wI.	10wM.
§ Jaisimha, M. L.	35	1899	96	750	9	83.33	—	—
Kulkarni, U. M.	4	448	6	238	5	47.60	—	—
§ Nadkarni, R. G.	41	9175	669	2559	88	29.07	4	1
§ Pataudi, Nawab of, Jnr. ...	31	114	5	80	1	80.00	—	—
§ Prasanna, E. A. S.... ...	14	4595	167	1952	67	29.13	4	—
§ Sardesai, D. N.	20	48	2	33	0	—	—	—
§ Subramanya, V.	9	444	17	201	3	67.00	—	—
§ Surti, R. F.	23	3677	108	1888	40	47.20	1	—

Page 195

	Tests	Balls	Mdns.	Runs	Wkts.	Avge.	5wI.	10wM.
§ Wadekar, A. L.	13	25	0	26	0	—	—	—

PAKISTAN

	Tests	Balls	Mdns.	Runs	Wkts.	Avge.	5wI.	10wM.
§ Asif Iqbal	14	2426	127	910	39	23.33	2	—
Asif Masood	2	444	12	221	6	36.83	—	—
§ Hanif Mohammad... ...	54	194	8	92	1	92.00	—	—

§ Ilyas, Mohammad—delete in toto.

	Tests	Balls	Mdns.	Runs	Wkts.	Avge.	5wI.	10wM.
§ Intikhab Alam	23	4416	149	1923	39	49.30	—	—
§ Mahmood Hussain ...	27	5923	231	2628	68	38.64	2	—
§ Majid Jahangir	10	1242	45	488	12	40.66	—	—
Mohammad Ilyas	10	84	1	63	0	—	—	—
§ Mushtaq Mohammad ...	20	825	35	350	13	26.92	—	—
§ Niaz Ahmed	2	294	14	94	3	31.33	—	—

Page 196

	Tests	Balls	Mdns.	Runs	Wkts.	Avge.	5wI.	10wM.
§ Pervez Sajjad	8	1740	92	581	26	22.34	1	—
§ Saeed Ahmed	38	1842	85	731	21	34.80	—	—
§ Salah-ud-Din	4	546	27	187	7	26.71	—	—
Sarfraz Nawaz	1	204	6	78	0	—	—	—
§ Shafqat Rana	3	18	0	7	0	—	—	—
§ Shuja-ud-Din	19	2301	128	801	20	40.05	—	—

Page 197

SERIES RECORDS
HIGHEST INDIVIDUAL RUN AGGREGATES

ENGLAND v. AUSTRALIA

	Tests	I.	N.O.	Runs	H.S.	Avge.	100s.	50s.
M. C. Cowdrey (E) ...	35	62	4	2186	113	37.68	5	11
K. F. Barrington (E.) ...	23	39	6	2111	256	63.96	5	13

ENGLAND v. WEST INDIES

	Tests	I.	N.O.	Runs	H.S.	Avge.	100s.	50s.
§ G. St. A. Sobers (WI) ...	29	51	7	2808	226	63.81	9	10
M. C. Cowdrey (E) ...	21	36	2	1751	154	51.50	6	10
T. W. Graveney (E) ...	19	31	5	1532	258	58.92	5	5

Highest Individual Run Aggregates—*Cont.*

ENGLAND v. PAKISTAN

	Tests	I.	N.O.	Runs	H.S.	Avge.	100s	50s
§ Hanif Mohammad (P) ...	18	33	2	1039	187*	33.51	3	3
§ T. W. Graveney (E) ...	13	16	0	943	153	58.93	3	5

AUSTRALIA v. WEST INDIES

	Tests	I.	N.O.	Runs	H.S.	Avge.	100s	50s
§ G. St. A. Sobers (WI) ...	19	38	3	1510	168	43.14	4	6
W. M. Lawry (A) ...	10	17	2	1035	210	69.00	4	3

HIGHEST INDIVIDUAL WICKET AGGREGATES

Page 198
ENGLAND v. WEST INDIES

	Tests	Balls	Mdns.	Runs	Wkts.	Avge.	5wI.	10wM.
§ G. St. A. Sobers (WI) ...	29	6938	295	2734	82	33.34	3	—
L. R. Gibbs (WI)	18	6062	348	2001	73	27.41	6	2
§ W. W. Hall (WI) ...	19	4271	139	2121	65	32.63	2	—
C. C. Griffith (WI) ...	15	2913	113	1291	57	22.64	4	—
J. A. Snow (E)	10	2660	84	1361	54	25.20	4	1

Page 199
AUSTRALIA v. WEST INDIES

	Tests	Balls	Mdns.	Runs	Wkts.	Avge.	5wI.	10wM.
L. R. Gibbs (WI)	13	5547	205	1874	61	30.72	4	—
G. St. A. Sobers (WI) ...	19	4895	154	2024	51	39.68	2	—
G. D. McKenzie (A) ...	10	3185	83	1415	47	30.10	2	1
W. W. Hall (WI)	12	2641	38	1395	45	31.00	2	—

Page 201 § (6 lines from foot of page) The name P. A. Gibb has been misspelt.

RECORDS FOR INDIVIDUAL SERIES

Page 203 *ENGLAND v. WEST INDIES*
HIGHEST WICKET AGGREGATE BY A BOWLER IN A SERIES
§ England in West Indies: 27 (av. 18.66) J. A. Snow 1967-68

RECORD WICKET PARTNERSHIPS—ENGLAND
§ 9th 109 G. A. R. Lock (89) & P. I. Pocock (13) at Georgetown 1967-68

RECORD WICKET PARTNERSHIPS—WEST INDIES
§ 9th 63* G. St. A. Sobers (33*) & W. W. Hall (26*) at Port of Spain 1967 68

Page 204 *ENGLAND v. NEW ZEALAND*
BEST INNINGS BOWLING ANALYSIS
§ England in England ... ... 7-32 D. L. Underwood (Lord's) 1969

RECORD WICKET PARTNERSHIPS—NEW ZEALAND
§ 3rd 150 B. E. Congdon (66) & B. F. Hastings (83) at Nottingham 1969

Page 206 *ENGLAND v. PAKISTAN*
LOWEST INNINGS TOTALS
§ England in Pakistan ... ... 274 at Dacca 1968-69

Page 207
HIGHEST WICKET AGGREGATE BY A BOWLER IN A SERIES
§ Pakistan in Pakistan ... ... { 9 (av. 22.88) Antao D'Souza 1961-62
9 (av. 24.88) Saeed Ahmed ... ... 1968-69 }

Page 208 *AUSTRALIA v. WEST INDIES*
HIGHEST INNINGS TOTALS
§ Australia in Australia ... 619 at Sydney 1968-69
§ West Indies in Australia ... 616 at Adelaide 1968-69

Page 209
§*Highest Match Aggregate* ... 1764-39 wkts. at Adelaide 1968-69

HIGHEST INDIVIDUAL INNINGS
§ Australia in Australia ... 242 K. D. Walters (Sydney) 1968-69

Records for Individual Series—Australia v. West Indies—*Cont.*

BEST INNINGS BOWLING ANALYSIS
§ Australia in Australia ... 8-71 G. D. McKenzie (Melbourne) 1968-69

HIGHEST RUN AGGREGATE BY A BATSMAN IN A SERIES
§ Australia in Australia ... 699 (av. 116.50) K. D. Walters 1968-69

HIGHEST WICKET AGGREGATE BY A BOWLER IN A SERIES
§ West Indies in Australia ... 24 (av. 28.79) A. L. Valentine 1951-52
24 (av. 38.45) L. R. Gibbs 1968-69

RECORD WICKET PARTNERSHIPS—AUSTRALIA
§ 2nd 298 W. M. Lawry (205) & I. M. Chappell (165) at Melbourne 1968-69
§ 4th 336 W. M. Lawry (151) & K. D. Walters (242) at Sydney 1968-69
§ 10th 73 J. W. Gleeson (42*) & A. N. Connolly (37) at Sydney 1968-69

RECORD WICKET PARTNERSHIPS—WEST INDIES
§ 2nd 165 M. C. Carew (83) & R. B. Kanhai (94) at Brisbane[2] 1968-69

Page 210
§ 5th 134 S. M. Nurse (74) & G. St. A. Sobers (67) at Melbourne 1968-69
§ 9th 122 D. A. J. Holford (80) & J. L. Hendriks (37*) at Adelaide 1968-69

AUSTRALIA v. INDIA
BEST INNINGS BOWLING ANALYSIS
§ India in Australia ... ... 6-55 S. Abid Ali (Adelaide) 1967-68

HIGHEST WICKET AGGREGATE BY A BOWLER IN A SERIES
§ India in Australia ... ... 25 (av. 27.44) E. A. S. Prasanna 1967-68

RECORD WICKET PARTNERSHIPS—AUSTRALIA
§ 1st 191 R. B. Simpson (109) & W. M. Lawry (100) at Melbourne 1967-68
§ 10th 40 K. D. Walters (94*) & J. W. Gleeson (14) at Sydney 1967-68

RECORD WICKET PARTNERSHIPS—INDIA
§ 4th 128 R. F. Surti (52) & Nawab of Pataudi, Jnr. (74) at Brisbane[2] 1967-68
§ 8th 74 Nawab of Pataudi, Jnr. (75) & R. F. Surti (30) at Melbourne ... 1967-68
§ 9th 54 Nawab of Pataudi, Jnr. (85) & R. B. Desai (14) at Melbourne ... 1967-68

Page 212 *SOUTH AFRICA v. NEW ZEALAND*
RECORD WICKET PARTNERSHIPS—SOUTH AFRICA
§ 6th 83 K. C. Bland (83) & D. Lindsay (37) at Auckland 1963-64

RECORD WICKET PARTNERSHIPS—NEW ZEALAND
§ 2nd 51 W. P. Bradburn (32) & B. W. Sinclair (52) at Dunedin 1963-64

MISCELLANEOUS RECORDS
Page 215 **MOST CONSECUTIVE TEST APPEARANCES**
§ 75 G. St. A. Sobers (West Indies): Port of Spain 1954-55 to date.
§ 61 R. B. Kanhai (West Indies): Birmingham 1957 to Sydney 1968-69.

§ **MOST TEST APPEARANCES**

	Player	*Caps*	*No. of players with* 50 *caps*
England	M. C. Cowdrey	104	18
Australia	R. N. Harvey	79	11
South Africa	J. H. B. Waite	50	1
West Indies	G. St. A. Sobers	76	4
New Zealand	J. R. Reid	58	1
India	P. R. Umrigar	59	3
Pakistan	Hanif Mohammad	54	1
			39

Page 217 **RELATED TEST PLAYERS**

FATHER AND SON

Pataudi, Nawab of, Snr. (England & India) and Jnr. (India)—both captained India.

BROTHERS § Delete this section in toto and substitute the following:

Although there have been many instances of two brothers appearing in Test Matches only a few families have provided three:

THREE Grace: E. M., G. F. and W. G. (England).
[*All three played in the first Test played in England: v. Australia (Oval)* 1880.]
Hearne: A., F. and G. G. (England).
[*F. Hearne also played for South Africa and all three appeared in the* 1891-92 *Test at Cape Town—a match in which their cousin, J. T. Hearne, also played.*]
Mohammad: Hanif, Mushtaq and Wazir (Pakistan).
Tancred: A. B., L. J. and V. M. (South Africa).

TWO PAIRS OF BROTHERS IN ONE TEAM

Pithey, A. J. and D.B., and Pollock, P. M. and R. G., all played against Australia (Melbourne and Sydney) and against New Zealand (Auckland) on South Africa's 1963-64 tour.

BROTHER CAPTAINS

Gilligan, A. E. R. and A. H. H. (England)
Grant, G. C. and R. S. (West Indies)

UMPIRES

§ Amend note to read: Only seven umpires have officiated in more than 25 Test Matches.

Tests	*Umpire*	*Venue of Test*	*First Series*	*Last Series*
33	§ J. S. Buller	England	1956	to date
32	§ C. S. Elliott	England	1957	to date
29	C. J. Egar	Australia	1960-61	to date

Page 218 **ENGLAND TEST SELECTORS**

1968 (*Australia*)—D. J. Insole, A. V. Bedser, P. B. H. May, D. Kenyon.
1969 (*West Indies, New Zealand*)—A. V. Bedser, D. Kenyon, A. C. Smith, W. H. H. Sutcliffe.

Page 219 **COUNTIES PROVIDING ENGLAND PLAYERS**

§ Amend the opening sentence to read: 444 players have represented England in the 458 matches played up to the end of 1969—a total of 5038 caps. * denotes players capped for England whilst appearing for two counties.
§ Substitute 'Eleven' for 'Eight' in the second sentence.

§ *DERBYSHIRE:* 16 *Players* – 56 *Caps*
Ward, Alan ... 3

§ *ESSEX:* 17 *Players* – 198 *Caps*
Fletcher, K. W. R.... 6 § Hobbs, R. N. S. ... 6 § Knight, B. R.* ... 22

§ *GLAMORGAN:* 8 *Players* – 53 *Caps*
§ Jones, I. J. ... 15

§ *HAMPSHIRE:* 13 *Players* – 65 *Caps*
Cottam, R. M. H. 2

Page 220

§ *KENT:* 39 *Players* – 518 *Caps*
§ Cowdrey, M. C. ... 104 § Knott, A. P. E. ... 18 § Underwood, D. L. 16
Denness, M. H. ... 1

§ *LANCASHIRE:* 46 *Players* – 500 *Caps*
§ Higgs, K. ... 15 § Ward, Albert ... 7

Counties Providing England Players—*Cont.*

§ *LEICESTERSHIRE*: 11 *Players* – 55 *Caps*

Illingworth, R.* ...	6	Knight, B. R.* ...	7	Lock, G. A. R.* ...	2

§ *MIDDLESEX:* 44 *Players* – 551 *Caps*

§ Parfitt, P. H. ...	34	§ Titmus, F. J. ...	49

§ *NORTHAMPTONSHIRE:* 12 *Players* – 97 *Caps*

§ Milburn, C. ...	9	Prideaux, R. M. ...	3

§ *SURREY:* 48 *Players* – 742 *Caps*

§ Arnold, G. G. ...	3	§ Edrich, J. H. ...	40	Pocock, P. I. ...	4
§ Barrington, K. F....	82	§ Lock, G. A. R.* ...	47		

§ *SUSSEX:* 33 *Players* – 325 *Caps*

§ Snow, J. A. ...	25

Page 222 (*SUSSEX—cont.*)

§ Dexter, E. R. ...	62	§ Parks, J. M. ...	46

§ *WARWICKSHIRE:* 18 *Players* – 250 *Caps*

§ Amiss, D. L. ...	5	§ Barber, R. W.* ...	19	§ Brown, D. J. ...	26

§ *WORCESTERSHIRE:* 18 *Players* – 161 *Caps*

§ D'Oliveira, B. L.	25	§ Graveney, T. W.*...	31

§ *YORKSHIRE:* 57 *Players* – 790 *Caps*

§ Boycott, G. ...	41	§ Illingworth, R.* ...	30	§ Sharpe, P. J. ...	12
Hampshire, J. H....	2				

Page 223 **COUNTIES PROVIDING ENGLAND'S CAPTAINS**

§ Kent	(52)	§ Cowdrey, M. C. (27)
Leicestershire	(6)	Illingworth, R. (6)
§ Worcestershire	(5)	Graveney, T. W. (1)

FIRST-CLASS CRICKET RECORDS

TEAM RECORDS

Page 226 **HIGHEST INNINGS TOTALS**

824 Lahore Greens v. Bahawalpur (Lahore) 1965-66

Page 230 **INNINGS TOTALS OF 600 AND OVER**

IN AUSTRALIA

§ Western Australia: Delete existing entry and substitute:
615-5d v. Queensland (Brisbane) 1968-69
Australia ... ... 619 v. West Indies (Sydney) 1968-69
§ West Indians ... Delete existing entry and substitute:
616 v. Australia (Adelaide) 1968-69

Page 231 § Penultimate line: venue should read New Delhi.

Page 232 **Innings Totals of 600 and Over**—*Cont.*

IN PAKISTAN

774	Lahore v. Sargodha (Lahore)	1968-69
709	Karachi Blues v. East Pakistan Green (Karachi)	1967-68
680-9d	Karachi v. East Pakistan (Karachi)	1968-69
611	Karachi Blues v. Lahore Greens (Lahore)	1967-68

HIGH SCORING MEMORABILIA

§ Delete the fifth item in toto and substitute:

1925-26 New South Wales scored 554, 705, 642, 593 and 708 in successive innings in the course of their 4-match Sheffield Shield programme.

Page 238 **HIGHEST FOURTH INNINGS TOTALS WITHOUT LOSS**

270-0	(set 346)	Surrey v. Kent (Oval) ... ... *R. Abel (120*) and W. Brockwell (132*) in 170 minutes.*	1900
236-0	(and won)	Orange Free State v. Eastern Province (Port Elizabeth) ... *S. Coen (132*) and J. M. M. Commaille (99*).*	1926-27
226-0	(and won)	Canterbury v. Otago (Christchurch) ... ... *W. A. Hadlee (110*) and J. G. Leggat (110*).*	1948-49
225-0	(and won)	New South Wales v. Queensland (Sydney) ... ... *A. R. Morris (78*) and K. R. Miller (138*) in 120 minutes.*	1950-51
219-0	(set 382)	West Indians v. Nottinghamshire (Nottingham) ... ... *G. Challenor (102*) and P. H. Tarilton (109*) in 150 minutes.*	1923
215-0	(set 337)	Nottinghamshire v. Derbyshire (Worksop) ... ... *W. W. Keeton (100*) and C. B. Harris (107*) in 200 minutes.*	1936
201-0	(and won)	Nottinghamshire v. Essex (Nottingham) ... ... *W. W. Keeton (115*) and C. B. Harris (81*).*	1936

Page 239 **VICTORY AFTER FOLLOWING-ON**

§ Delete third item (1901) in toto.

§ Insert 'at Johannesburg' after '100 runs' in the penultimate item.

1951 Yorkshire (77 & 269-7d) beat Somerset (234 & 62) by 50 runs at Sheffield.

1959 Champion County (Yorkshire (160 & 425) beat The Rest (384-8d & 135) by 66 runs at The Oval.

HIGHEST MATCH AGGREGATES

Runs-Wkts.

1764-39 Australia v. West Indies (Adelaide) 1968-69

Page 240

1644-38 Australia v. West Indies (Sydney) 1968-69

§ *Aggregates of over* 1400 *runs in England:* 1723-31 occurred in 1948.

Page 242 **TIE MATCHES**

Hambledon (140 & 62) v. Kent (111 & 91) at Hambledon 1783

England XI (312-8d & 190-3d) v. England Under-25 XI (320-9d & 182) at Scarborough 1968

Page 245 **TEAMS SCORING FOUR CENTURIES IN AN INNINGS**

Western Australia (594-6d) v. New South Wales (Sydney) 1968-69

D. Chadwick 110, R. J. Inverarity 103, J. T. Irvine 128, R. Edwards 117.*

TEAMS SCORING SEVEN FIFTIES IN AN INNINGS

West Zone (509-8) v. North Zone (Poona) 1967-68

D. N. Sardesai 83, A. L. Wadekar 58, C. G. Borde 52, V. L. Manjrekar 58, R. F. Surti 104, F. M. Engineer 59, R. G. Nadkarni 61.*

Page 246 **SIMILARITY OF DISMISSAL**

FIRST FIVE WICKETS TO FALL IN AN INNINGS

c. J. A. MacLean b P. J. Allan: Queensland v. N.S.W. (Sydney) 1968-69

FIRST FOUR WICKETS TO FALL IN AN INNINGS

c T. M. Findlay: West Indians v. Combined XI (Perth) 1968-69

FIRST THREE WICKETS TO FALL IN AN INNINGS

c R. C. Jordon b J. W. Grant: Victoria v. Queensland (Melbourne) 1968-69

Page 247

SIX BATSMEN IN SUCCESSION IN COURSE OF AN INNINGS

c S. E. Leary: Kent v. Cambridge U. (Cambridge) 1958

FOUR BATSMEN IN SUCCESSION IN THE COURSE OF AN INNINGS

c or st D. Gamsy: Natal v. N-E. Transvaal (Pretoria) 1967-68

c J. M. Parks: Sussex v. Lancs. (Hove) 1969

FIVE DISMISSALS IN ONE INNINGS (OUTSTANDING CASES)

§ last item: Ealham's initials (A. G. E.) have been omitted.

TEN CATCHES BY TEN DIFFERENT FIELDERS IN ONE INNINGS

Leics. v. Northants (Leicester) 1967

J. Birkenshaw was the only player not to take a catch in the first innings of Northants.

Page 248 **UNUSUAL DISMISSALS**

RUN OUT BY THE BOWLER (while backing up before the ball had been bowled)

§ G. Barker (penultimate instance) has no second initial.

I. R. Redpath (9) by C. C. Griffith: Australia v. West Indies (Adelaide) 1968-69

PLAYERS' RECORDS—BATTING

Page 250 **HIGHEST INDIVIDUAL INNINGS**

303* Mushtaq Mohammad: Karachi Blues v. Karachi Us. (Karachi) 1967-68

Page 251 **HIGHEST INDIVIDUAL INNINGS FOR AND AGAINST EACH TEAM**

AUSTRALIA

§ *For* Western Australia ... ... 243 C. Milburn

§ *Against* West Indians ... ... 242 K. D. Walters (Australia)

SOUTH AFRICA

§ *For* Border ... ... 211 W. S. Farrer

§ *Against* Orange Free State ... 279* P. Holmes (M.C.C.)
279* R. A. Gripper (Rhodesia)

§ *For* Rhodesia ... ... 279* R. A. Gripper

WEST INDIES

§ *For* Leeward Islands ... ... 127 L. Sergeant

Page 252

NEW ZEALAND

§ *For* Central Districts ... ... 202* B. E. Congdon

§ *For* West Indians ... ... 258 S. M. Nurse

§ *Against* West Indians ... ... 124 B. R. Taylor (New Zealand)

For Indians ... ... 143 A. L. Wadekar

Against Indians ... ... 239 G. T. Dowling (New Zealand)

HIGHEST MAIDEN CENTURIES

Note: the highest score by a batsman making his début in first-class cricket is 240 by W. F. E. Marx for Transvaal v. Griqualand West at Johannesburg in 1920-21.

Pages 253 to 275 *DOUBLE CENTURIES*

§ Bhandari, P. ... ... (2) 202* Delhi v. Punjab (New Delhi) 1968-69
Bhosle, V. H. ... (1) 208 Bombay v. Rajasthan (Udaipur) 1968-69
§ Boycott, G. ... ... (3) 243 M.C.C. v. Barbados (Bridgetown) 1967-68
§ Chappell, I. M. ... (2) 202* Australians v. Warwickshire (Birmingham) ... 1968
Congdon, B. E. ... (1) 202* Central Districts v. Otago (Nelson) 1968-69
§ De Villiers, D. I. should read De Villiers, D. J.
§ Dexter, E. R. ... (2) 203 Sussex v. Kent (Hastings) 1968
§ Dowling, G. T. ... (2) 239 New Zealand v. India (Christchurch) 1967-68
§ Farrer, W. S. ... ... (2) 211 Border v. Eastern Province (East London) ... 1968-69
Fletcher, K. W. R. ... (1) 228* Essex v. Sussex (Hastings) 1968
§ Flockton, R. scored 264* at Sydney.
Gilliat, R. M. C. ... (1) 223* Hampshire v. Warwickshire (Southampton) ... 1969
Green, D. M. ... (1) 233 Gloucestershire v. Sussex (Hove) 1968
Gripper, R. A. ... (1) 279* Rhodesia v. Orange Free State (Bloemfontein) 1967-68
Groves, B. S. ... ... (1) 237 Natal B v. Orange Free State (Bloemfontein) ... 1967-68
§ Hammond, W. R. scored 237 for Glos. v. Derby (Bristol) in 1938.
§ Kanhai, R. B. ... (4) 253 Warwickshire v. Nottinghamshire (Nottingham) 1968
§ Lawry, W. M. ... (4) 205 Australia v. West Indies (Melbourne) 1968-69
Lloyd, C. H. ... ... (2) 205* West Indians v. South Island (Dunedin) ... 1968-69
201* West Indians v. Glamorgan (Swansea) ... 1969
§ Majid Jahangir ... (2) 200* Punjab U. v. Karachi Whites (Lahore) ... 1967-68
§ Manjrekar, V. L. ... (3) 240* Maharashtra v. Saurashtra (Poona) 1967-68
§ Milburn, C. ... ... (2) 243 Western Australia v. Queensland (Brisbane) ... 1968-69
Murray, B. A. G. ... (1) 213 Wellington v. Otago (Dunedin) 1968-69
§ Mushtaq Mohammad (3) 303* Karachi Blues v. Karachi Us. (Karachi) ... 1967-68
§ Nurse, S. M. ... ... (4) 258 West Indies v. New Zealand (Christchurch) ... 1968-69
§ Pataudi, Nawab of, Jnr. (2) 200 South Zone v. West Zone (Bombay) 1967-68
Richards, B. A. ... (1) 206 Hampshire v. Nottinghamshire (Portsmouth) ... 1968
Salah-ud-Din ... ... (2) 201 Karachi Blues v. East Pakistan Greens (Karachi) 1967-68
256 Karachi v. East Pakistan (Karachi) 1968-69
§ Sardesai, D. N. ... (3) 217 Bombay v. Baroda (Bombay) 1968-69
Shukla, A. ... ... (1) 242* Bihar v. Orissa (Cuttack) 1967-68
§ Simpson, R. B. ... (12) 277 New South Wales v. Queensland (Sydney) ... 1967-68
Viswanath, G. R. ... (1) 230 Mysore v. Andhra (Vijayawada) 1967-68
Walsh, D. R. ... ... (1) 207 Oxford U. v. Warwickshire (Oxford) 1969
§ Walters, K. D. ... (2) 242 Australia v. West Indies (Sydney) 1968-69
§ Wilmot, A. L. ... (2) 207 Eastern Province v. Border (East London) ... 1968-69

Page 275 **CENTURY WITH A RUNNER**

Crutchley, G. E. V. ... 181 Free Foresters v. Cambridge U. (Cambridge)... 1919
Kimpton, R. C. M. ... 102 Oxford U. v. Lancashire (Oxford) 1936
In 70 minutes, with 22 fours and no chances.

CENTURY ON DÉBUT IN FIRST-CLASS CRICKET (pages 275 to 277)

Bacon, F. H. ... 114 Hampshire v. Warwickshire (Birmingham) 1894
§ Barker, G. has no second initial.
Clarke, J. K. ... 112* Rhodesia v. Western Province (Cape Town) ... 1967-68
Ireland, R. N. ... 152* Natal B v. Rhodesia (Salisbury) 1967-68
Lucas, M. ... 107 Queensland v. New South Wales (Brisbane) ... 1968-69
McMullan, J. J. M. 157* Otago v. Southland (Dunedin) 1917-18
Marsh, R. ... 104 Western Australia v. West Indians (Perth) 1968-69
Sahasrabudhe, P. 133 Vidarbha v. Madhya Pradesh (Bersingpur) ... 1968-69
Sergeant, L. ... 127 Leeward Is. v. M.C.C. (St. John's, Antigua) ... 1967-68
Viswanath, G. R. 230 Mysore v. Andhra (Vijayawada) 1967-68

Page 278 **CENTURY IN FIRST MATCH FOR A COUNTY OR UNIVERSITY**

Kanhai, R. B. ... 119 Warwickshire v. Cambridge U. (Cambridge) ... 1968

CENTURY ON DÉBUT IN OTHER COUNTRIES (Pages 278 to 281)

§ Delete two-paragraph introduction in toto.

ENGLISH TEAMS AND PLAYERS

IN WEST INDIES

G. Boycott ... 135 M.C.C. v. President's XI (Bridgetown) 1967-68

IN PAKISTAN

C. Milburn ... 139 England v. Pakistan (Karachi) 1968-69

IN CEYLON

J. H. Edrich ... 177 M.C.C. v. All-Ceylon XI (Colombo) 1968-69

AUSTRALIAN TEAMS AND PLAYERS

IN ENGLAND

E. W. Freeman (116 Australians v. Northamptonshire at Northampton in 1968), scored a century in his first innings in England but had previously played in one match without batting.

WEST INDIAN TEAMS AND PLAYERS

IN ENGLAND

R. C. Fredericks 116 West Indians v. Robins' XI (Eastbourne) 1969

IN NEW ZEALAND

C. H. Lloyd ... 205* West Indians v. South Is. (Dunedin) 1968-69

NEW ZEALAND TEAMS AND PLAYERS

IN INDIA

M. G. Burgess ... 102 Prime Minister's XI v. President's XI (Bombay) ... 1967-68

INDIAN TEAMS AND PLAYERS

IN AUSTRALIA

F. M. Engineer ... 128 Indians v. Western Australia (Perth) 1967-68
M. L. Jaisimha ... 101 India v. Australia (Brisbane) 1967-68

IN NEW ZEALAND

A. L. Wadekar ... 122 Indians v. Central Districts (New Plymouth) ... 1967-68

A CENTURY IN EACH INNINGS OF A MATCH (Pages 281 to 286)

Bolus, J. B. ... (1) 147 101 Nottinghamshire v. Northamptonshire (Nottingham) 1969
Butcher, B. F. ... (1) 115 172 West Indians v. Combined XI (Perth) ... 1968-69
§ Hallam, M. R. scored 210* and 157 against Glamorgan at Leicester, 1959.
Luckhurst, B. W.... (1) 113 100* Kent v. Rest of the World (Canterbury) ... 1968
MushtaqMohammad(1) 128* 123 Robins' XI v. West Indians (Eastbourne) ... 1969
Richards, B. A. ... (1) 130 104* Hampshire v. Northamptonshire (Northampton) 1968
§ Russell, A. C. scored 140 and 111 for England at Durban in 1922-23.
Salah-ud-Din ... (1) 256 102* Karachi v. East Pakistan (Karachi) 1968-69
§ Walcott, C. L. scored 126 and 110 at Port of Spain in 1954-55.
Walters, K. D. ... (1) 242 103 Australia v. West Indies (Sydney) 1968-69

Page 288 *FOUR CENTURIES IN SUCCESSIVE INNINGS*

Note: G. Boycott (Yorks.) hit four centuries in successive innings in County Championship matches in 1968: 100 v. Sussex (Bradford), 132 v. Leics. (Leicester), 180* v. Warwicks. (Middlesbrough), 125 v. Glos. (Bristol). After the match at Leicester, he scored 13 and 6 for M.C.C. v. Australians (Lord's).

THREE CENTURIES IN SUCCESSIVE INNINGS (Pages 288 to 293)

Chappell, I. M. (South Australia) in 1968-69: 188* Combined XI v. West Indians (Perth), 123 v. West Indians (Adelaide), 117 Australia v. West Indies (Brisbane).

Inverarity, R. J. (Western Australia) in 1968-69: 103 v. N.S.W. (Sydney), 108 v. Queensland (Brisbane), 114 v. Victoria (Melbourne).

Page 293 5 *CENTURIES IN* 6 *INNINGS*

Note: I. M. Chappell scored 5 hundreds in 6 innings against the West Indians in 1968-69: 188,* 123, 117, 50, 180 and 165. After his score of 50 he made 10 and 1 in a Sheffield Shield match.

Most Fifties in Consecutive Innings—*Cont.*

Page 294 8 *CONSECUTIVE FIFTIES*
§ Delete in toto the third instance (C. P. Mead).

Other good sequences broken by scores of less than 50
C. P. Mead—162–78–62*–132–222–147–41*–58–80* 1923

TEN CONSECUTIVE FIFTIES ON ONE GROUND
K. F. Barrington at Adelaide: 104–52–52*–63–132* (1962-63) 69–51–63–60–102 (1965-66)
His only innings at Adelaide.

2000 RUNS IN AN ENGLISH SEASON (Pages 295 to 303)

		Season	*Inns.*	*N.O.*	*Runs*	*H.S.*	*Avge.*	*100s*
§ Edrich, J. H. (Surrey)	(5)	1968	50	5	2009	164	44.64	5
		1969	39	7	2238	181	69.93	8
§ Graveney, T. W. had 50 innings in 1952.								
§ Green, D. M. (Lancs. & Glos.) ...	(2)	1968	54	1	2137	233	40.32	4
§ Kenyon, D. had an average of 44.34 in 1953.								
Richards, B. A. (Hants.)	(1)	1968	55	5	2395	206	47.90	5

§ P. J. Sharpe's name has been misspelt.

1000 RUNS IN A SEASON IN AUSTRALIA (Pages 303 and 304)
§ K. F. Barrington scored 1451 in 1962-63 and averaged 85.35.

		Season	*Inns.*	*N.O.*	*Runs*	*H.S.*	*Avge.*	*100s*
Butcher, B. F. (West Indians)	(1)	1968-69	23	1	1191	172	54.13	5
§ Chappell, I. M. (South Australia)	(2)	1968-69	21	3	1476	188*	82.00	6
§ Lawry, W. M. (Victoria) ...	(4)	1968-69	20	2	1140	205	63.33	4
§ Simpson, R. B. (Western Australia and N.S.W.)	(4)	1967-68	20	1	1082	277	56.94	4
§ Sobers, G. St. A. (South Australia and West Indians)	(3)	1968-69	17	2	1011	132	67.40	5
Stackpole, K. R. (Victoria)	(1)	1968-69	22	7	1010	140*	67.33	3
§ Walters, K. D. (N.S.W.) ...	(2)	1968-69	19	0	1078	242	56.73	5

§ Walters, K. D. averaged 70.10 in 1965-66.

1000 RUNS AGAINST A TOURING TEAM IN AUSTRALIA

	Season	*Inns.*	*N.O.*	*Runs*	*H.S.*	*Avge.*	*100s*
Bradman, D. G. v. South Africans	1931-32	8	1	1190	299*	170.00	6
Chappell, I. M. v. West Indians	1968-69	12	1	1062	188*	96.54	5

Page 305 **1000 RUNS IN A SEASON IN SOUTH AFRICA**

	Season	*Inns.*	*N.O.*	*Runs*	*H.S.*	*Avge.*	*100s*
R. G. Pollock (Eastern Province) ...	1968-69	14	2	1043	196	86.91	3
Highest aggregates by home batsmen							
R. G. Pollock (Eastern Province) ...	1968-69	14	2	1043	196	86.91	3
A. Bacher (Transvaal)	1968-69	14	2	904	189	75.33	3
B. A. Richards (Natal)	1968-69	15	2	763	112*	58.69	1

§ D. J. McGlew averaged 50.15 when he scored 953 runs in 1957-58.

OVER 700 RUNS IN THE WEST INDIES (Pages 305 and 306)

	Season	*Inns.*	*N.O.*	*Runs*	*H.S.*	*Avge.*	*100s*
G. Boycott (M.C.C.)	1967-68	16	2	1154	243	82.42	4
M. C. Cowdrey (M.C.C.)	1967-68	15	1	871	148	62.21	4
J. H. Edrich (M.C.C.)	1967-68	17	1	739	146	46.18	1

Page 306 **OVER 600 RUNS IN NEW ZEALAND**

	Season	*Inns.*	*N.O.*	*Runs*	*H.S.*	*Avge.*	*100s*
G. T. Dowling (Canterbury) ...	1967-68	18	1	968	239	56.94	4
B. F. Hastings (Canterbury) ...	1968-69	15	4	872	117*	79.27	4
S. M. Nurse (West Indians)	1968-69	9	0	826	258	91.77	3
G. M. Turner (Otago)	1968-69	16	1	708	167	47.20	2
B. A. G. Murray (Wellington) ...	1967-68	22	0	649	79	29.50	0
G. T. Dowling (Canterbury) ...	1968-69	14	0	629	167	44.92	2
B. E. Congdon (Central Districts) ...	1968-69	15	2	600	202*	46.15	1

Page 307 **1000 RUNS IN A SEASON IN INDIA**

	Season	*Inns*	*N.O.*	*Runs*	*H.S.*	*Avge.*	*100s*
§ A. L. Wadekar (Bombay) ... ...(3)	1968-69	22	2	1006	144	50.30	5

Wadekar also played in two other first-class matches in Southern India in aid of the Koyna Relief Fund. Scores of these matches were omitted from "Indian Cricket 1969" and are, as yet, unavailable.

Page 309 **LEADING HOME BATSMEN OF THE ENGLISH SEASON**

Season		*Inns.*	*N.O.*	*Runs*	*H.S.*	*Avge.*	*100s*
1968	G. Boycott (Yorks.)	30	7	1487	180*	64.65	7
1969	J. H. Edrich (Surrey)	39	7	2238	181	69.93	8

Pages 313 to 315 **CARRYING BAT THROUGH A COMPLETED INNINGS**

(† *One man was absent*)

Akash Lal ... (1) 104* (186) Delhi v. Northern Punjab (Amritsar)... ... 1967-68
§ Barker, G. has no second initial.
§ Barton, W. E. carried his bat through an innings of 150.
Boycott, G. ... (2) 114* (297) Yorkshire v. Leicestershire (Sheffield) ... 1968
53* (119) Yorkshire v. Warwickshire (Bradford) ... 1969
§ Davey, D. C. carried his bat for Natal in 1889-90.
§ Hobbs, J. B. scored 133* against Yorkshire (Oval) in 1931.
Kitchen, M. J. (1) 161* (287) Somerset v. Northamptonshire (Taunton) ... 1968
§ Luckhurst, B. W. (2) 46* (96) Kent v. Hampshire (Bournemouth) ... 1969
§ Miller, L. S. M. is out of alphabetical order.
§ Captain Mitford's initial is P.
Naushad Ali ... (1) 107* (247) East Pakistan v. Railways (Lahore) ... 1967-68
Razaullah ... (1) 25* (67) Khairpur v. Karachi (Karachi) 1968-69
Richards, B. A. (1) 127* (192) †Hampshire v. Northamptonshire (Bournemouth) 1969
§ Thomson, W. K. has been misspelt.
Turner, G. M.... (1) 43* (131) New Zealand v. England (Lord's) 1969
§ Van der Berg, J.H. (2) 47* (177) Eastern Province v. Western Province (Cape Town) 1929-30
§ Wright, W. carried his bat for Nottinghamshire.

Page 325-326 *FAST CENTURIES*

101* in 52 mins. R. G. Pollock (101): International Cavaliers v. Barbados (Scarborough) 1969
103* in 53 mins. R. C. Motz (103*): Canterbury v. Otago (Christchurch) ... 1967-68
§ Delete in toto the instances concerning P. J. Heather (line 8) and W. V. S. Ling (line 11) on page 326. Both hundreds took 65 mins.

FAST INNINGS

34 in 6 mins. R. M. Edwards: Governor-General's XI v. West Indians (Auckland) 1968-69

A CENTURY BEFORE LUNCH (Pages 328 to 333)

On the First Day of a Match

C. A. Perring (122): Griqualand West v. Orange Free State (Kimberley) 1968-69
Majid Jahangir (156): Glamorgan v. Worcestershire (Cardiff) 1969
(*Scored 114* in 150 minutes before lunch.*)
§ G. Barker (1961 instance) has no second initial.

On Other Days

C. P. Mead (182*): England v. Australia (Oval) 1921
(*19* to 128* in 147 minutes on 2nd day*)
§ F. R. Santall. Amend note to read
(*Scored 173* in 116 minutes on third day.*)
D. C. S. Compton (180*): Middlesex v. Essex (Lord's) 1938
(*71* to 180* in 85 minutes on second morning.*)
R. W. Barber (104): Lancashire v. Nottinghamshire (Worksop) 1961
(*In 135 minutes on third day.*)
B. S. Groves (237): Natal B v. Orange Free State (Bloemfontein) 1967-68
(*72* to 237 in 115 minutes on second day.*)

Century Before Lunch—*Cont.*

A. A. Baig (129): Hyderabad v. Kerala (Hyderabad)... 1968-69
(*9* to 121* on second day.*)
M. C. Carew (126*): West Indians v. Oxford & Cambridge Us. (Oxford) ... 1969
(*17* to 126* in 150 minutes on third day.*)
Majid Jahangir (147): Glamorgan v. West Indians (Swansea) 1969
(*In 150 minutes on third day.*)
R. C. Fredericks (129): West Indians v. Hampshire (Southampton) 1969
(*21* to 129* in 150 minutes on third day.*)

MOST RUNS IN PRE-LUNCH SESSION
§ 173 F. R. Santall: delete first half of note, viz. '*Score taken from 28* to 201**'.
165 B. S. Groves (237): Natal B v. Orange Free State (Bloemfontein) 1967-68
(*72* to 237 in 115 minutes on second day.*)

Page 334 *BATSMEN SCORING* 300 *RUNS IN A DAY*
Note: E. Paynter's 322 and R. H. Moore's 316 were scored on the same day: 28th July, 1937.

TEAMS SCORING 600 *RUNS IN A DAY*: add to the South African section at foot of page 334:
628—19 wkts Orange Free State (309) v. Griqualand West (319-9) at Bloemfontein... 1920-21
605—15 wkts Transvaal (339) v. Rest of South Africa (266-5) at Johannesburg ... 1911-12

Page 335 *MOST RUNS OFF ONE OVER*
Six-Ball Overs
36 (666666) G. St. A. Sobers off M. A. Nash: Notts. v. Glamorgan (Swansea) ... 1968
29 (416666) R. R. Collins & B. S. Groves off K. Morris: Natal B v. Orange Free State (Bloemfontein) 1967-68
28 B. N. Jarman off D. A. Allen: Australians v. Pearce's XI (Scarborough) ... 1961
26 (606644) E. F. Parker off F. T. M. Drummer: Rhodesia v. Transvaal (Salisbury) 1968-69
Note: M. J. Procter (Glos.) hit 30 runs off 7 balls from his fellow South African, A. W. Greig (Sussex), at Hove in 1968: 444 off the last three balls of Greig's sixth over and 4464 off the first four balls of his seventh.
Eight-Ball Overs
34 (40446664) R. M. Edwards off M. C. Carew: Governor-General's XI v. West Indians (Auckland) 1968-69

Page 337 *MOST SIXES IN AN INNINGS*
Eight
B. S. Groves (237): Natal B v. Orange Free State (Bloemfontein) 1967-68

HITS FOR SIX OFF CONSECUTIVE BALLS
Six Sixes off Six Balls
G. St. A. Sobers off M. A. Nash: Nottinghamshire v. Glamorgan (Swansea) ... 1968
In same over.
Four Sixes off Four Balls
B. S. Groves off K. Morris: Natal B v. Orange Free State (Bloemfontein) 1967-68
Three Sixes off Three Balls
§ D. Kenyon's name has been misprinted in the 1965 instance.
R. M. Edwards off M. C. Carew: Governor-General's XI v. West Indians (Auckland) 1968-69

MOST BOUNDARIES IN AN INNINGS
§ A. D. Nourse, Snr. hit 53 fours in his 304* in 1919-20.

Page 340 *HIGHEST PROPORTION OF BOUNDARIES IN AN INNINGS*

6s	*4s*		*Inns.*		
4	38	(176)	243	C. Milburn: Western Australia v. Queensland (Brisbane) ...	1968-69

SLOW SCORING
SLOWEST INNINGS
Min.
9 —125 T. W. Jarvis: New Zealand v. India (Madras) 1964-65
§ Vivek Hazare scored 21 in 332 minutes in 1943-44.

Slow Scoring—*Cont.*

Page 341 *AN HOUR BEFORE SCORING FIRST RUN*

§ T. G. Evans spent 95 minutes on nought in the Adelaide Test of 1946-47.

Mins.

82 P. I. Pocock (13): England v. West Indies (Georgetown) 1967-68

70 W. L. Murdock (17): Australia v. England (Sydney) 1882-83

§ Prodger's initials are J. M. (8th item in list).

Page 344 *LONGEST INDIVIDUAL INNINGS*

Mins.

200 —622 Nawab of Pataudi, Jnr.: South Zone v. West Zone (Bombay) 1967-68

Page 345 *BATSMEN MONOPOLISING SCORING*

57* out of 59 C. Inman: Leics. v. Notts. (Nottingham) 1965

Page 346 *BATSMEN MONOPOLISING A PARTNERSHIP*

59*— 4th C. Inman (57) & P. T. Marner (2): Leics. v. Notts. (Nottingham) ... 1965

56 —10th B. J. Meyer (51) & J. Davey (1) (4 ex): Glos. v. Notts. (Nottingham) ... 1968

PLAYERS' RECORDS—PARTNERSHIPS

Page 348 **RECORDS BY WEST INDIAN TEAMS**

§ 5th 335 B. F. Butcher (151) & C. H. Lloyd (201*): West Indians v. Glamorgan (Swansea) 1969

RECORDS BY PAKISTANI BATSMEN

§ 1st should read 277*.

§ 6th 348 Salah-ud-Din (256) & Zaheer Abbas (197): Karachi v. East Pakistan (Karachi) 1968-69

§ 8th 210 Aftab Alam (154) & Wasim Bari (92): Karachi v. Khairpur (Karachi)... 1968-69

§ 9th 190 occurred in 1967.

Page 349 **WICKET PARTNERSHIPS OF OVER 400**

402 4th R. B. Kanhai (253) & Khalid Ibadulla (147*) for Warwickshire... ... 1968

Pages 349 to 368 **HIGHEST PARTNERSHIPS**

FIRST WICKET

328 C. Milburn (243) & D. Chadwick (91): Western Australia v. Queensland (Brisbane) 1968-69

315 D. M. Green (233) & C. A. Milton (122): Glos. v. Sussex (Hove) 1968

281 L. E. Favell (149) & J. E. Causby (137): South Australia v. N.S.W. (Adelaide) 1967-68

268 R. A. Gripper (279*) & J. K. Clarke (130): Rhodesia v. O.F.S. (Bloemfontein) 1967-68

SECOND WICKET

324* M. C. Carew (172*) & R. C. Fredericks (168*): West Indians v. Leics. (Leicester) 1969

298 W. M. Lawry (205) & I. M. Chappell (165): Australia v. West Indies (Melbourne) 1968-69

§ MacBryan and Lyon added 290 (not 286) for Somerset v. Derby (Burton) in 1924.

§ 283 for Natal in 1910-11: Blake's initials are R. H.

281* R. A. Gripper (279*) & R. B. Ullyett (126*): Rhodesia v. O.F.S. (Bloemfontein) 1967-68

271 P. J. Muzzell (174) & W. S. Farrer (143): Border v. O.F.S. (Bloemfontein) ... 1968-69

§ 269 (Page 354, line 1): Murawat Hussain's name is misspelt.

266 B. S. Groves (237) & R. Collins (50): Natal B v. O.F.S. (Bloemfontein) ... 1967-68

THIRD WICKET

§ 319 (page 355): A. Melville's partner was A. D. Nourse, Jnr.

§ 315 (page 355): K. M. Tiwari's name is misspelt.

292 D. N. Sardesai (217) & V. H. Bhosle (103): Bombay v. Baroda (Bombay) ... 1968-69

273 S. M. Nurse (136) & R. B. Kanhai (153): West Indies v. England (Port of Spain) 1967-68

255 C. H. Lloyd (205*) & C. A. Davis (69): West Indians v. South Island (Dunedin) 1968-69

§ Page 357, line 9: G. Barker has no second initial.

FOURTH WICKET

402 R. B. Kanhai (253) & Khalid Ibadulla (147*): Warwicks. v. Notts. (Nottingham) 1968
336 W. M. Lawry (151) & K. D. Walters (242): Australia v. West Indies (Sydney) 1968-69
330 Waqar Ahmed (199) & Shafqat Rana (174): Lahore v. Sargodha (Lahore) ... 1968-69
§ N. C. O'Neill and B. C. Booth added 325 runs (not 323) at Sydney in 1957-58.
262 M. L. Jaisimha (179) & Nawab of Pataudi, Jnr. (127): Hyderabad v. Andhra (Hyderabad) 1967-68
260* I. M. Chappell (188*) & A. P. Sheahan (111*): Combined XI v. West Indians (Perth) 1968-69
258 K. Jayantilal (153) & Wahid Yar Khan (174*): Hyderabad v. Andhra (Guntur) 1968-69
255 H. Pilling (120) & D. Bailey (136): Lancs. v. Kent (Manchester) 1969
254 R. B. Simpson (277) & G. R. Davies (112): N.S.W. v. Queensland (Sydney) ... 1967-68
250 H. P. Ward (122) & R. Nailer (149): Europeans v. Indians (Madras) 1931-32
250 R. B. Kanhai (150) & G. St. A. Sobers (152): West Indies v. England (Georgetown) 1967-68

FIFTH WICKET

335 B. F. Butcher (151) & C. H. Lloyd (201*): West Indians v. Glamorgan (Swansea) 1969
240 Nawab of Pataudi, Jnr. (200) & V. Subramanya (84): South Zone v. West Zone (Bombay) 1967-68
235 M. L. Jaisimha (171) & V. Subramanya (123): South Zone v. West Zone (Bombay) 1966-67

SIXTH WICKET

348 Salah-ud-Din (256) & Zaheer Abbas (197): Karachi v. East Pakistan (Karachi) 1968-69
270 D. R. Walsh (207) & S. A. Westley (93*): Oxford U. v. Warwicks. (Oxford) 1969
244 J. T. Irvine (128) & R. Edwards (117*): Western Australia v. N.S.W. (Sydney) 1968-69
§ 241 N. J. Contractor's partner was J. H. Shodhan.
§ Page 361, last line: delete in toto.

SEVENTH WICKET

246 P. Bhandari (202*) & D. S. Saxena (62): Delhi v. Punjab (New Delhi) ... 1968-69
232 Mushtaq Mohammad (303*) & Wallis Mathias (100): Karachi Blues v. Karachi Us. (Karachi) 1967-68
§ 229 K. J. Schneider's name has been misspelt.
219 B. W. Yuile (146) & B. L. Hampton (107): Central Districts v. Canterbury (Napier) 1967-68
206 B. Dudleston (171*) & J. Birkenshaw (74): Leics. v. Kent (Canterbury) ... 1969

EIGHTH WICKET

210 Aftab Alam (154) & Wasim Bari (92): Karachi v. Khairpur (Karachi) ... 1968-69
192 S. Turner (110*) & R. N. S. Hobbs (100): Essex v. Glamorgan (Ilford) ... 1968
171 I. M. Chappell (123) & K. J. McCarthy (127): South Australia v. West Indians (Adelaide)... 1968-69
§ The 167-run partnership between F. Barratt and A. Staples occurred at Nottingham.
160 M. H. Bowditch (89) & G. S. Hugo (64): Western Province v. Border (Cape Town) 1968-69
158 A. G. E. Ealham (94*) & A. Brown (81): Kent v. Glamorgan (Folkestone) ... 1968

NINTH WICKET

§ W. McIntyre and G. Wootton added 165 and not 167 at Nottingham in 1869.
§ The 167-run partnership between H. Verity and T. F. Smailes occurred at Bath.
166 R. K. Muzzell (139) & G. L. C. Watson (83): Transvaal v. Eastern Province (Johannesburg) 1968-69

TENTH WICKET

130 Salah-ud-Din (97) & Arshad Bashir (41*): Karachi v. Railways (Karachi) ... 1967-68
§ The 113-run partnership between Wallis Mathias and Arshad Bashir occurred in 1965-66.

Page 370 **CENTURY FIRST-WICKET PARTNERSHIP IN EACH INNINGS**

§ Delete in toto line 2 (B. J. Booth and D. J. Constant).

111 127 I. R. Redpath & R. J. Inverarity: Australians v. Derby (Chesterfield) ... 1968

Add to notes: D. J. Constant, playing for Leics. v. Oxford U. (Oxford) 1965, shared in two century opening partnerships—136 with B. J. Booth in the first innings and 101 with S. Greensword in the second.

CENTURY LAST-WICKET PARTNERSHIP IN EACH INNINGS

115 129 L. R. Tuckett with L. G. Fuller (1st Inns.) and F. Caulfield (2nd)—O.F.S. v. Western Province (Bloemfontein) 1925-26

PLAYERS' RECORDS—BOWLING

Page 375 60 *WICKETS IN AN AUSTRALIAN SEASON*

	Season	*Overs*	*Mdns.*	*Runs*	*Wkts.*	*Avge.*
A. N. Connolly (Victoria)	1967-68	398.7	96	1211	60	20.18
G. D. McKenzie (Western Australia) ...	1968-69	458.6	68	1660	60	27.66

50 *WICKETS IN A SOUTH AFRICAN SEASON*

§ Page 376, line 1: R. C. Motz averaged 17.76.

§ line 18: A. E. E. Vogler's name has been misprinted.

	Season	*Overs*	*Mdns.*	*Runs*	*Wkts.*	*Avge.*
G. H. Simpson-Hayward (M.C.C.) ...	1909-10	328.3	50	912	53	17.20

35 *WICKETS IN A WEST INDIAN SEASON*

	Season	*Overs*	*Mdns.*	*Runs*	*Wkts.*	*Avge.*
J. A. Snow (M.C.C.)	1967-68	271.1	64	739	37	19.97

Page 377 45 *WICKETS IN A NEW ZEALAND SEASON*

§ S. Austin conceded 606 runs and averaged 11.65 in 1893-94.

	Season	*Overs*	*Mdns.*	*Runs*	*Wkts.*	*Avge.*
R. C. Motz (Canterbury)...	1967-68	369.2	116	907	47	19.29
R. S. Cunis (Auckland)	1968-69	286.2	53	861	45	18.56

60 *WICKETS IN AN INDIAN SEASON*

§ Page 377, third item: delete in toto.

	Season	*Overs*	*Mdns.*	*Runs*	*Wkts.*	*Avge.*
B. S. Chandrasekhar (Mysore)	1966-67	583.3	141	1624	85	19.10
S. Venkataraghavan (Madras)	1967-68	750.1	223	1761	83	21.21

Page 379 **LEADING HOME BOWLERS OF THE ENGLISH SEASON**

Season		*Overs*	*Mdns.*	*Runs*	*Wkts.*	*Avge.*
1968	D. Wilson (Yorks.)	815.5	335	1521	109	13.95
1969	M. J. Procter (Glos.)	639.3	160	1623	108	15.02

Page 380 **FOUR WICKETS WITH CONSECUTIVE BALLS**

G. Nash ... ... Lancs. v. Somerset (Manchester) 1882

Page 381 *MOST HAT TRICKS IN A CAREER*

4—R. G. Barlow.

§ T. J. Matthews has been misspelt.

BOWLERS WHO HAVE DONE THE HAT-TRICK (Pages 381 to 390)

§ Barlow, R. G. ... (4) Lancs. v. Derby (Manchester)... 1879
Bedi, B. S. ... (1) Delhi v. Punjab (New Delhi) 1968-69
§ Beesly, R. has been misspelt.
§ Birkenshaw, J. ... (2) Leics. v. Cambridge U. (Cambridge) 1968
Britton-Jones, E. (1) Europeans v. Indians (Madras) 1917-18
Buxton, I. R. ... (1) Derby v. Oxford U. 1969
Cartwright, T. W. (1) Warwicks. v. Somerset (Birmingham) 1969
§ Durston's initials should read F. J.
Gaekwad, H. G.... (1) Madhya Pradesh v. Rajasthan (Jabalpur) 1962-63
§ Harman, R. ... (2) Surrey v. Derby (Ilkeston) 1968

Bowlers Who Have Done the Hat-Trick—*Cont.*

§ Higgs, K. ... (2) Lancs. v. Yorks (Leeds) 1968
§ Horsley's initial is J. (not W.).
Julien, B. ... (1) North Trinidad v. South Trinidad (Port of Spain) ... 1968-69
Lankham, W. ... (1) Auckland v. Taranaki (Auckland) 1882-83
Lever, P. ... (1) Lancs. v. Notts. (Manchester) 1969
Majid Jahangir (1) Glamorgan v. Oxford U. (Oxford) 1969
§ C. Olliff's name has been misspelt. § Delete in toto the entry for Rajinder Pal.
Ravinder Pal ... (1) Southern Punjab v. Delhi (Chandigarh) 1965-66
§ A. E. G. Rhodes took his first hat-trick against the Gentlemen of Ireland (page 387, last line).
Rodriguez, W. V. (1) Trinidad v. Windward Is. (Port of Spain) 1968-69
Surti, R. F. ... (1) Queensland v. Western Australia (Perth) 1968-69
Wheatley, O. S.... (1) Glamorgan v. Somerset (Taunton) 1968

Page 393 **ALL TEN WICKETS IN AN INNINGS**

O. M. R.
17.6— 4— 44 I. J. Brayshaw: Western Australia v. Victoria (Perth) 1967-68

NINE OR TEN WICKETS IN AN INNINGS (Pages 393 to 400)

Brayshaw, I. J. ... ... (1) 10-44 Western Australia v. Victoria (Perth) ... 1967-68
§ V. Broderick did not have a second initial.
Cordle, A. E. ... ... (1) 9-49 Glamorgan v. Leics. (Colwyn Bay) ... 1969
Elliott, G. ... ... (1) 9-2 Victoria v. Tasmania (Launceston) ... 1857-58
§ Ranjane's correct initials are V. B. and Wadkar's are R. R.
§ E. Smith took 9-46 for Derby v. Scotland.
§ J. H. Wardle took 9-48 at Hull.
Wheatley, O. S. ... (1) 9-60 Glamorgan v. Sussex (Ebbw Vale) ... 1968

FIFTEEN OR MORE WICKETS IN A MATCH (Pages 401 to 404)

East, R. E. ... ... (1) 15-115 Essex v. Warwicks. (Leyton) 1968
§ T. R. McKibbon's name has been misspelt.
Pervez Sajjad ... ... (1) 15-112 Karachi v. Khairpur (Karachi) 1968-69
Underwood, D. L. ... (1) 15-43 International XI v. President's XI (Colombo) 1967-68

OUTSTANDING INNINGS ANALYSIS (Pages 404 to 408)

NINE WICKETS
O. M. R. W.
19 —17— 2— 9 G. Elliott: Victoria v. Tasmania (Launceston) 1857-58

EIGHT WICKETS
11.3— 6—10— 8 D. L. Underwood: International XI v. President's XI (Colombo) 1967-68
§ C. H. Palmer's analysis should read 14—12—7—8.

SEVEN WICKETS
§ A. Shaw (7—7) bowled 36 maidens.

SIX WICKETS
19 —16— 4— 6 J. Briggs: Lancs. v. Derby (Manchester) 1888
13 —10— 5— 6 F. J. Titmus: Middx. v. Oxford U. (Oxford) 1968
16 —11— 6— 6 W. J. R. Haskell: Wellington v. Otago (Wellington) 1967-68

FIVE WICKETS
10 — 8— 2— 5 D. J. Shepherd: Glamorgan v. Leics. (Ebbw Vale) 1965
10 — 9— 2— 5 J. D. Gray: Warwicks. v. Scotland (Birmingham) (*On début*) ... 1968

FOUR WICKETS
8.1— 7— 1— 4 K. J. Wheatley: Hants. v. Glamorgan (Southampton) 1968
4 — 2— 2— 4 M. Bissex: Glos. v. Sussex (Cheltenham) 1968
7.3— 4— 4— 4 K. S. Vaidyanathan: Madras v. Kerala (Madras) 1965-66
7.5— 4— 4— 4 B. S. Chandrasekhar: Mysore v. Andhra (Anantapur) 1965-66

OUTSTANDING MATCH BOWLING ANALYSES (Pages 408 to 410)

FIFTEEN WICKETS

15-43 (8-10 & 7-33) D. L. Underwood: International XI v. President's XI (Colombo) 1967-68

FOURTEEN WICKETS

§ Delete in toto the first entry (T. Emmett)

TWELVE WICKETS

12-38 (7-19 & 5-19) M. A. Latif: East Pakistan Greens v. Eastern Railways (Dacca) 1967-68

Page 412 **MOST EXPENSIVE ANALYSES** *EIGHT-BALL OVERS*

O. M. R. W.

1— 0—34— 0 M. C. Carew: West Indians v. Governor-General's XI (Auckland) 1968-69

4— 1—62— 0 I. M. Chappell: South Australia v. New Zealanders (Adelaide) ... 1967-68

225 RUNS CONCEDED IN AN INNINGS

O. M. R. W.

49— 2—268— 3 Sher Andaz: Sargodha v. Lahore (Lahore) 1968-69

57— 1—242— 5 Rauf Ansari: East Pakistan Greens v. Karachi Blues (Karachi) ... 1967-68

Page 413 **MOST BALLS BOWLED IN AN INNINGS**

§ C. K. Nayudu bowled 12 maidens, not 13 (page 413, 9 lines from foot).

Balls O. M. R. W.

462 77— 8—204— 5 Humayun Khan: Sargodha v. Lahore (Lahore) ... 1968-69

Page 415 § Heading to read:

BOWLERS UNCHANGED THROUGH BOTH COMPLETED INNINGS OF A MATCH

Page 417 *SEASON 1870*: § delete in toto second item.

Page 422 *INSTANCES IN OVERSEAS MATCHES*

A. E. E. Vogler (14-58) & A. T. Lyons (5-44): Eastern Province v. O.F.S. (Johannesburg) 1906-07

MOST MAIDENS IN SUCCESSION

SIX-BALL OVERS

15 M. C. Carew: West Indies v. England (Port of Spain) 1967-68
(*Conceding one run in first 102 balls which included a runless spell of 90 balls.*)

EIGHT-BALL OVERS

10 R. W. Morgan: Auckland v. Otago (Auckland) 1968-69

Page 424 **EIGHT OR MORE WICKETS BEFORE LUNCH**

8-22 (81) A. G. Nicholson: Yorks v. Kent (Canterbury) 1968

Page 426 **OUTSTANDING BOWLING ON DEBUT**

TEN WICKETS IN THE MATCH

14-59 J. Bevan: South Australia v. Tasmania (Adelaide) 1877-78

SIX WICKETS IN ONE INNINGS

8-37 V. Thambuswamy: Madras v. Andhra (Guntur) 1967-68
7-61 R. C. Merrin: Canterbury XI v. New Zealand Touring Team (Christchurch) 1967-68
7-80 B. Christen: Canada v. M.C.C. (Toronto) 1951
7-86 F. Touzel: Western Province v. Griqualand West (Kimberley) 1968-69
6-114 A. Thomson: Victoria v. New South Wales (Sydney)... 1968-69

Page 427 **WICKET WITH FIRST BALL IN FIRST-CLASS CRICKET**

R. J. Crisp, playing for Rhodesia v. Transvaal (Bulawayo) 1929-30, took wickets with his second and third balls in first-class cricket.

§ Insert "for the wicket of J. V. Wilson" after "maidens" in the first line of the note about J. M. Allan—foot of page 427.

Page 428 **100 WICKETS IN FIRST FULL SEASON**

	Wkts.	Avge.	Season	Previous Matches
W. E. Merritt (New Zealanders)	107	23.64	1927	1

§ Durston's initials should read F. J.

NO-BALLED FOR THROWING (Pages 428 to 430)

D. J. Insole: Essex v. Northamptonshire (Northampton) 1952
B. Fisher: Queensland v. New South Wales (Sydney) 1967-68
(No-balled once by E. F. Wykes)

BANNED FROM BOWLING FOR REMAINDER OF INNINGS—For Damaging Pitch.

M. R. Whitaker ... Cambridge U. v. New Zealanders (Cambridge) 1965
I. J. Jones ... ... M.C.C. v. New South Wales (Sydney) 1965-66
R. C. Motz ... New Zealand v. India (Christchurch) 1967-68

PLAYERS' RECORDS—ALL-ROUND CRICKET

Page 431 *MOST CONSECUTIVE 'DOUBLES'*

6 W. G. Grace (1873-1878) § Tribe's initials are G. E.

CRICKETERS ACHIEVING THE 'DOUBLE' (Pages 431 to 435)

§ V. Broderick has no second initial.
§ G. Davidson averaged 28·17 with the bat and 16·78 with the ball.
§ F. J. Titmus had a batting average of 25·97 in 1959.

MATCH DOUBLES (Pages 436 to 441)

Flanagan, P. J. D. (1)
98 & 17, 8-113 & 2-86 Transvaal B v. Natal B (Johannesburg) ... 1968-69
Liddle, J. R. (1)
31 & 77, 7-97 & 5-115 O.F.S. v. Rhodesia (Bulawayo) 1951-52
Sobers, G. St. A. (1)
17 & 105*, 7-69 & 4-87 Notts. v. Kent (Dover) 1968

PLAYERS' RECORDS—FIELDING

Page 442 *SIX CATCHES IN AN INNINGS*

Bissex, M.: Gloucestershire v. Sussex (Hove) 1968

FIVE CATCHES IN AN INNINGS (Pages 442 to 444)

Kanhai, R. B.: West Indians v. Gloucestershire (Bristol) 1966
Mushtaq Mohammad: Northamptonshire v. Leicestershire (Peterborough) ... 1968
Robinson, P. J.: Somerset v. Lancashire (Weston-super-Mare) 1968
Solkar, E. D.: Bombay v. Rest of India (Bombay) 1968-69
Wilson, D.: Yorkshire v. Surrey (Oval) 1969

Page 444 *EIGHT CATCHES IN A MATCH*

§ Prodger's initials are J. M.

SEVEN CATCHES IN A MATCH

Solkar, E. D.: Bombay v. Rest of India (Bombay) 1968-69

Page 445 **MOST CATCHES IN A SEASON**

§ P. M. Walker held 69 catches in 1960.

PLAYERS' RECORDS—WICKET-KEEPING

Page 445 *SEVEN DISMISSALS IN AN INNINGS*

	ct. st.		
Taber, H. B. ...	(6-1)	New South Wales v. South Australia (Adelaide) ...	1968-69

Page 446 *SIX DISMISSALS IN AN INNINGS*

Jordon, R. C. ...	(6-0)	Victoria v. Queensland (Melbourne)	1968-69
Long, A. ...	(5-1)	Surrey v. Northamptonshire (Oval)	1968

Players Records—Wicket Keeping—*Cont.*

Page 447 *TWELVE DISMISSALS IN A MATCH*

Taber, H. B. ... (9-3) New South Wales v. South Australia (Adelaide)... ... 1968-69

Page 448 *NINE DISMISSALS IN A MATCH*

Gamsy, D. ... (7-2) Natal v. North-Eastern Transvaal (Pretoria) 1967-68
Indrajitsinh, K. S. (5-4) Saurashtra v. Maharashtra (Nasik) 1965-66
Wasim Bari ... (7-2) Karachi Blues v. Hyderabad (Karachi) 1965-66

MOST DISMISSALS IN A SEASON

§ J. G. Binks made 107 dismissals (96ct, 11st) in 1960 and not 108.
§ Most catches in a season: 96 J. G. Binks (Yorkshire) 1960

[*D. A. Allen was bowled by F. S. Trueman and not caught by Binks, as the published scores show, in The Rest's first innings against the County Champions* (*Oval*) *1960. Both official scorebooks confirm this error.*]

Page 449 **LARGEST INNINGS WITHOUT BYES**

619 J. L. Hendriks: West Indies v. Australia (Sydney) 1968-69
526-7d A. P. E. Knott: England v. West Indies (Port of Spain) 1967-68
510 J. L. Hendriks: West Indies v. Australia (Melbourne) 1968-69

INDIVIDUAL CAREER RECORDS—BATTING

§ All records are complete to the end of the 1969 English Season.
(*1945 denotes 1945-46 overseas season. 19+2 1000s=19 times in UK, twice overseas.*)

30,000 RUNS IN A CAREER

	Career	*Inns.*	*N.O.*	*Runs*	*H.S.*	*Avge.*	*100s*	*1000s*
§ T. W. Graveney ...	1948-1969	1178	143	46339	258	44.77	120	19+2
§ M. C. Cowdrey ...	1950-1969	912	98	35567	307	43.69	91	17+6
§ M. J. K. Smith ...	1951-1969	861	104	31880	204	42.11	56	14+1
§ K. F. Barrington ...	1953-1968	831	136	31714	256	45.63	76	12+3
R. E. Marshall ...	*1945*-1969	934	44	31553	228*	35.45	61	15
J. M. Parks ...	1949-1969	1035	140	31372	205*	35.05	48	16
§ L. G. Berry ...	1924-1951	1056	57	30225	232	30.25	45	18

10,000 RUNS IN A CAREER

	Career	*Inns.*	*N.O.*	*Runs*	*H.S.*	*Avge.*	*100s*	*1000s*
§ Alley, W. E. ...	*1945*-1968	682	67	19612	221*	31.88	31	10+1
§ Atkinson, G. ...	1954-1969	608	41	17654	190	31.13	27	9
§ Barber, R. W. ...	1954-1969	651	52	17631	185	29.43	17	7+1
§ Barker, G.	1954-1969	751	40	21011	181*	29.55	28	14
§ Barrington, K. F. ...	1953-1968	831	136	31714	256	45.63	76	12+3
§ Bear, M. J. ...	1954-1968	562	44	12564	137	24.25	9	4
§ Benaud, R. ...	*1948-1967*	365	44	11719	187	36.50	23	—
§ Bennett, D. ...	1950-1968	612	125	10656	117*	21.88	4	2
§ Berry, L. G. ...	1924-1951	1056	57	30225	232	30.25	45	18
§ Bolus, J. B. ...	1956-1969	575	50	17573	202*	33.47	29	9
Bond, J. D. ...	1955-1969	442	58	10238	157	26.66	13	2
§ Booth, B. C. ...	*1954-1968*	283	35	11265	214*	45.42	26	2+2
§ Booth, B. J. ...	1956-1969	503	40	12967	183*	28.00	16	8
Booth, R. ...	1951-1968	667	135	10115	113*	19.01	2	1
§ Borde, C. G. ...	*1952-1968*	331	53	11440	177*	41.15	27	1+3
§ Boycott, G. ...	1962-1969	361	45	14942	246*	47.28	38	7+2
§ Burge, P. J. ...	*1952-1967*	354	47	14640	283	47.68	38	2+5
Butcher, B. F. ...	*1954*-1969	248	28	10940	209*	49.72	29	2+3
§ Carr, D. B. ...	1945-1968	745	72	19257	170	28.61	24	11
§ Cartwright, T. W.	1952-1969	580	75	11180	210	22.13	6	3
§ Close, D. B. ...	1949-1969	915	117	25391	198	31.81	37	14
§ Cowdrey, M. C. ...	1950-1969	912	98	35567	307	43.69	91	17+6
Cowper, R. M. ...	*1959-1968*	213	30	10074	307	55.04	26	1+3
Denness, M. H. ...	1959-1969	387	30	10569	174	29.60	10	7
§ Dexter, E. R. ...	1956-1968	565	48	21093	205	40.79	51	8+2

Batting—10,000 Runs—*Cont.*

	Career	*Inns.*	*N.O.*	*Runs*	*H.S.*	*Avge.*	*100s*	*1000s*
§ Edrich, J. H. ...	1956-1969	620	63	25606	310*	45.97	65	11+1
§ Evans, T. G. ...	1939-1969	753	52	14882	144	21.22	7	4
§ Favell, L. E. ...	*1951-1968*	333	9	11897	190	36.71	25	0+2
Fletcher, K. W. R.	1962-1969	417	49	12113	228*	32.91	15	7
§ Gale, R. A. ...	1955-1968	439	13	12505	200	29.35	15	6
§ Goddard, T. L. ...	*1952-1968*	281	17	10999	222	41.66	26	2+1
§ Graveney, T. W. ...	1948-1969	1178	143	46339	258	44.77	120	19+2
Green, D. M. ...	1959-1969	426	15	11896	233	28.94	12	6
§ Hallam, M. R. ...	1950-1969	904	56	24477	210*	28.86	32	13
Hampshire, J. H. ...	1961-1969	383	36	10238	150	29.50	12	7
§ Hanif Mohammad	*1951*-1969	325	41	15192	499	53.49	48	2+3
§ Headley, R. G. A.	1958-1969	570	51	14937	150*	28.78	17	9
§ Hill, N. W. ...	1953-1968	518	32	14303	201*	29.43	23	8
§ Horton, H. ...	1946-1967	742	83	21651	160*	32.85	32	12
§ Horton, M. J. ...	1952-*1968*	707	49	19497	233	29.63	22	11
§ Ibadulla, K. delete in toto.								
§ Illingworth, R. ...	1951-1969	775	151	17464	162	27.98	18	7
§ Ingleby-Mackenzie's career ended in 1965.								
Inman, C.	*1956*-1969	340	32	10428	178	33.85	14	6
Jaisimha, M. L. ...	*1954-1968*	296	19	10616	259	38.32	25	0+2
§ Jones, A.	1957-1969	572	40	16557	187*	31.12	19	9
§ Kanhai, R. B. ...	*1954*-1969	376	29	16128	256	46.47	43	5+3
Khalid Ibadulla ...	*1952*-1969	626	65	15506	171	27.63	22	6
§ Knight, B. R. ...	1955-1969	602	83	13336	165	25.69	12	5
§ Lawry, W. M. ...	*1955-1968*	351	33	16363	266	51.45	47	2+5
§ Leary, S. E. ...	1951-1969	574	84	15418	158	31.46	18	9
§ Lenham, L. J. ...	1956-1969	534	50	12641	191*	26.11	7	6
§ Lewis, A. R. ...	1955-1969	529	48	15394	223	32.00	24	9
Lightfoot, A. ...	1953-1969	471	59	11163	174*	27.09	12	4
Livingstone, D. A.	1959-1969	458	57	11130	200	27.75	15	5
Lock, G. A. R. ...	1946-*1968*	789	157	10125	89	16.02	—	—
Luckhurst, B. W. ...	1958-1969	388	50	11949	184*	35.35	22	8
§ Macartney, C. G.	*1905-1935*	360	32	15020	345	45.79	49	3
§ Manjrekar, V. L. ...	*1949-1968*	288	38	12717	283	50.86	38	1+1
§ Marner, P. T. ...	1952-1969	639	60	16104	142*	27.81	16	11
§ Marshall, R. E. ...	*1945*-1969	934	44	31553	228*	35.45	61	15
Milburn, C. ...	1960-1969	392	30	12592	243	34.78	23	6+1
§ Milton, C. A. ...	1948-1969	980	115	29669	170	34.29	54	16
§ Morgan, D. C. ...	1950-1969	882	146	18356	147	24.94	9	8
§ Mortimore, J. B. ...	1950-1969	843	83	14195	149	18.67	4	5
§ Murray, J. T. ...	1952-1969	718	111	14101	142	23.23	14	5
Mushtaq Mohammad	*1956*-1969	379	54	14184	303*	43.64	34	5+1
§ Nicholls, R. B. ...	1951-1969	776	45	19039	217	26.04	16	13
§ Norman, M. E. J. C.	1952-1969	568	38	15847	221*	29.90	23	8
§ Oakman, A. S. M.	1947-1968	912	79	21800	229*	26.17	22	9
§ O'Neill, N. C. ...	*1955-1967*	306	34	13859	284	50.95	45	2+6
§ Padgett, D. E. V. ...	1951-1969	729	61	19131	161*	28.63	29	11
§ Parfitt, P. H. ...	1956-1969	714	89	22353	200*	35.76	48	11+1
§ Parks, J. M. ...	1949-1969	1035	140	31372	205*	35.05	48	16
§ Pataudi, Nawab of, Jnr.	1957-*1968*	400	34	12902	203*	35.25	27	4+3
§ Pressdee, J. S. ...	1949-*1968*	577	88	14119	150*	28.87	13	6
§ Prideaux, R. M. ...	1958-1969	621	56	18914	202*	33.47	30	10
§ Pullar, G.	1954-1969	662	62	21301	175	35.50	41	9+1
§ Reynolds, B. L. ...	1950-1969	718	62	18466	169	28.14	21	10
§ Russell, W. E. ...	1956-1969	682	56	21453	193	34.26	34	11
§ Sainsbury, P. J. ...	1954-1969	726	145	15194	163	26.15	5	6
§ Sharpe, P. J. ...	1956-1969	585	68	16035	203*	31.01	20	9
§ Simpson, R. B. ...	*1952-1967*	397	60	19673	359	58.37	56	2+8
§ Smith, M. J. K. ...	1951-1969	861	104	31880	204	42.11	56	14+1

Batting—10,000 Runs—*Cont.*

	Career	*Inns.*	*N.O.*	*Runs*	*H.S.*	*Avge.*	100*s*	1000*s*
§ Sobers, G. St. A. ...	*1952*-1969	423	59	20415	365*	56.08	61	5+6
§ Stewart, M. J. ...	1954-1969	786	82	23679	227*	33.63	45	14
§ Stewart, W. J. ...	1955-1969	489	56	14773	182*	34.11	25	6
§ Suttle, K. G. ...	1949-1969	1009	85	28952	204*	31.33	46	17
§ Taylor, B.	1949-1969	814	59	16385	135	21.70	7	7
§ Taylor, K. ...	1953-1968	524	36	13053	203*	26.74	16	6
§ Titmus, F. J. ...	1949-1969	909	139	18747	137*	24.34	5	8
§ Umrigar, P. R. ...	*1944-1967*	350	41	16155	252*	52.28	49	2+2
Virgin, R. T. ...	1957-1969	449	21	11225	162	26.22	10	7
§ Walker, P. M. ...	1956-1969	664	92	14962	152*	26.15	10	9
§ Wooller, W. ...	1935-1962	679	77	13593	128	22.57	5	5

Note: G. A. R. Lock (England, Surrey, Leics. and Western Australia) is the only player to reach an aggregate of 10,000 runs without scoring a century. His average (16.02) is the lowest for any batsman scoring 10,000 runs.

Page 458 *MOST CENTURIES IN A CAREER*

	Career	100*s*	*First*	100*th*	*Last*	*Inns. for 100 cents.*
§ T. W. Graveney	1948-1969	120	1948	1964	1969	940

§ M. C. Cowdrey (1950-1969) ...	91	§ R. B. Simpson (*1952-1967*) ...	56
§ K. F. Barrington (1953-1968) ...	76	§ M. J. K. Smith (1951-1969) ...	56
§ J. H. Edrich (1956-1969)	65	C. A. Milton (1948-1969)	54
§ R. E. Marshall (*1945*-1969) ...	61	§ E. R. Dexter (1956-1968)	51
§ G. St. A. Sobers (*1952*-1969) ...	61		

INDIVIDUAL CAREER RECORDS—BOWLING

Page 459 *2000 WICKETS IN A CAREER*

	Career	*Runs*	*Wkts.*	*Avge.*	*100 wkts.*
§ D. Shackleton...	1948-1969	53303	2857	18.65	20
§ G. A. R. Lock	1946-*1968*	53022	2782	19.05	14
§ F. S. Trueman	1949-1969	42154	2304	18.29	12
§ J. B. Statham	1950-1968	36995	2260	16.36	13
F. J. Titmus	1949-1969	47203	2183	21.62	14
D. J. Shepherd	1950-1969	42500	2010	21.14	11

Pages 459 to 461 *1000 WICKETS IN A CAREER*

§ Allen, D. A.	1953-1969	26078	1125	23.18	1
§ Bannister, J. D.	1950-1969	26258	1199	21.89	4
Cartwright, T. W.	1952-1969	21318	1108	19.24	7
§ Close, D. B.	1949-1969	27502	1077	25.53	2
Coldwell, L. J.	1955-1969	22791	1076	21.18	2
Higgs, K.	1958-1969	26943	1165	23.12	5
§ Illingworth, R.	1951-1969	30984	1627	19.04	10
Knight, B. R.	1955-1969	26203	1089	24.06	5
§ Langford, B. A.	1953-1969	30065	1250	24.05	5
§ Lock, G. A. R.	1946-*1968*	53022	2782	19.05	14
§ Morgan, D. C.	1950-1969	31302	1248	25.08	—
§ Mortimore, J. B.	1950-1969	33318	1496	22.27	3
§ Moss, A. E.	1950-1968	27035	1301	20.78	5
Rhodes, H. J.	1953-1969	21113	1072	19.69	3
§ Shackleton, D.	1948-1969	53303	2857	18.65	20
§ Shepherd, D. J.	1950-1969	42500	2010	21.14	11
§ Smith, D. R.	1956-1969	27635	1189	23.24	5
Smith, E.	1951-1969	28184	1113	25.32	1
§ Spencer, C. T.	1952-1969	35202	1319	26.68	1
§ Statham, J. B.	1950-1968	36995	2260	16.36	13
§ Titmus, F. J.	1949-1969	47203	2183	21.62	14
§ Trueman, F. S.	1949-1969	42154	2304	18.29	12
§ Wardle, J. H.	1946-*1967*	35027	1846	18.97	10

Bowling—1,000 Wickets—*Cont.*

	Career	*Runs*	*Wkts.*	*Avge.*	100 *wkts.*
Wheatley, O. S.	1956-1969	22856	1098	20.81	5
White, D. W.	1957-1969	25090	1079	23.25	4
Wilson, D.	1957-1969	20392	1002	20.35	5

Page 462 *100 WICKETS IN A SEASON MOST TIMES*
§ 20 D. Shackleton (Hampshire): 1949-1968.
§ 14 F. J. Titmus (Middlesex): 1953-1957, 1959-1965, 1967-1968.

100 WICKETS IN MOST SEASONS CONSECUTIVELY
§ 20 D. Shackleton (Hampshire): 1949-1968 inclusive.

INDIVIDUAL CAREER RECORDS—ALL-ROUND CRICKET

10,000 RUNS AND 1000 WICKETS IN A CAREER

	Career	*Runs*	*Avge.*	100*s*		*Wkts.*	*Avge.*		*'Doubles'*
Cartwright, T. W.	1952-1969	11180	22.13	6	...	1108	19.24	...	1
§ Close, D. B. ...	1949-1969	25391	31.81	37	...	1077	25.53	...	2
§ Illingworth, R. ...	1951-1969	17464	27.98	18	...	1627	19.04	...	6
Knight, B. R. ...	1955-1969	13336	25.69	12	...	1089	24.06	...	4
Lock, G. A. R. ...	1946-*1968*	10125	16.02	–	...	2782	19.05	...	–
§ Morgan, D. C. ...	1950-1969	18356	24.94	9	...	1248	25.08	...	–
§ Mortimore, J. B.	1950-1969	14195	18.67	4	...	1496	22.27	...	3
§ Titmus, F. J. ...	1949-1969	18747	24.34	5	...	2183	21.62	...	8

Page 463 **INDIVIDUAL CAREER RECORDS—FIELDING AND WICKET-KEEPING**

MOST DISMISSALS IN A CAREER—Fielders	*Career*	*Catches*
§ G. A. R. Lock (Surrey, Western Australia & Leicestershire) ...	1946-*1968*	820
§ A. C. Milton (Gloucestershire)	1948-1969	701
§ D. B. Close (Yorkshire)	1949-1969	620
§ K. J. Grieves (New South Wales & Lancashire)	*1945*-1964	610
§ A. S. M. Oakman (Sussex)	1947-1968	594
§ P. M. Walker (Glamorgan)	1956-1969	591
§ M. J. Stewart (Surrey)	1954-1969	585
§ D. C. Morgan (Derbyshire)	1950-1969	573
M. C. Cowdrey (Kent)	1950-1969	527
T. W. Graveney (Gloucestershire & Worcestershire)	1948-1969	527
K. F. Barrington (Surrey)	1953-1968	515
P. J. Sainsbury (Hampshire)	1954-1969	510
§ D. B. Carr (Derbyshire)	1945-1968	501

MOST DISMISSALS IN A CAREER—Wicket-Keepers	*Career*	*Total*	*Ct.*	*St.*
§ J. T. Murray (Middlesex)	1952-1969	1222	1028	194
§ H. Elliott (Derbyshire)	1920-1947	1206	904	302
§ R. Booth (Yorkshire & Worcestershire)	1951-1968	1103	927	176
§ H. W. Stephenson (Somerset)	1948-1964	1081	752	329
§ B. Taylor (Essex)	1949-1969	1077	914	163
§ J. G. Binks (Yorkshire)	1955-1969	1070	894	176
§ T. G. Evans (Kent)	1939-1969	1060	811	249
§ G. O. Dawkes (Leicestershire & Derbyshire) ...	1937-1961	1042	895	147
§ J. M. Parks (Sussex)	1949-1969	1011	934	77
§ K. V. Andrew (Northamptonshire)	1952-1966	905	721	184
§ A. J. McIntyre (Surrey)	1938-1963	797	639	158

CAREER RECORDS FOR LEADING OVERSEAS PLAYERS

Pages 464 to 466 *BATTING*

AUSTRALIA

	Career	*Inns.*	*N.O.*	*Runs*	*H.S.*	*Avge.*	*100s*	*1000s*
§ R. B. Simpson ...	*1952-1967*	397	60	19673	359	58.37	56	2+8
§ W. M. Lawry ...	*1955-1968*	351	33	16363	266	51.45	47	2+5

Career Records for Overseas Players—*Cont.*

	Career	Inns.	N.O.	Runs	H.S.	Avge.	100s	1000s
§ C. G. Macartney ...	*1905-1935*	360	32	15020	345	45.79	49	3
§ P. J. Burge	*1952-1967*	354	47	14640	283	47.68	38	2+5
§ N. C. O'Neill ...	*1955-1967*	306	34	13859	284	50.95	45	2+6
§ L. E. Favell	*1951-1968*	333	9	11897	190	36.71	25	0+2
§ R. Benaud	*1948-1967*	365	44	11719	187	36.50	23	—
§ B. C. Booth	*1954-1968*	283	35	11265	214*	45.42	26	2+2
R. M. Cowper ...	*1959-1968*	213	30	10074	307	55.04	26	1+3
SOUTH AFRICA								
§ T. L. Goddard ...	*1952-1968*	281	17	10999	222	41.66	26	2+1
§ E. J. Barlow	*1959-1968*	202	12	8022	212	42.22	20	1+1
R. G. Pollock ...	*1960*-1969	165	20	7770	209*	53.58	23	1+2
A. J. Pithey	*1950-1968*	213	16	7071	170	35.89	13	—
WEST INDIES								
§ G. St. A. Sobers ...	*1952*-1969	423	59	20415	365*	56.08	61	5+6
§ R. B. Kanhai ...	*1954*-1969	376	29	16128	256	46.47	43	5+3
§ B. F. Butcher	*1954*-1969	248	28	10940	209*	49.72	29	2+3
§ S. M. Nurse	*1958*-1969	210	16	8557	258	44.10	25	1+1
M. C. Carew	*1955*-1969	176	17	5619	172*	35.33	8	1+1
J. S. Solomon ...	*1956-1968*	156	28	5318	201*	41.54	12	—
E. D. St. J. A. McMorris	*1956-1968*	130	14	5028	218	43.34	16	—
NEW ZEALAND								
§ M. P. Donnelly ...	*1936-1960*	221	26	9250	208*	47.43	23	5
§ G. T. Dowling ...	*1958*-1969	236	11	7808	239	34.70	14	—
§ S. N. McGregor ...	*1948-1968*	272	16	6487	114*	25.33	5	—
§ B. W. Sinclair ...	*1955-1968*	194	17	5777	138	32.63	6	—
B. E. Congdon ...	*1960*-1969	198	16	5568	202*	30.59	5	—
INDIA								
§ P. R. Umrigar ...	*1944-1967*	350	41	16155	252*	52.28	49	2+2
§ Nawab of Pataudi, Jnr.	1957-*1968*	400	34	12902	203*	35.25	27	4+3
§ V. L. Manjrekar ...	*1949-1968*	288	38	12717	283	50.86	38	1+1
§ C. G. Borde	*1952-1968*	331	53	11440	177*	41.15	27	1+3
M. L. Jaisimha ...	*1954-1968*	296	19	10636	259	38.39	25	0+2
PAKISTAN								
§ Hanif Mohammad ...	*1951*-1969	325	41	15192	499	53.49	48	2+3
Mushtaq Mohammad	*1956*-1969	379	54	14184	303*	43.64	34	5+1
§ Saeed Ahmed ...	*1954-1968*	266	19	9824	192	39.77	26	1+1

Pages 466 to 468 *BOWLING*

AUSTRALIA

	Career	Runs	Wkts.	Avge.	100s
§ R. Benaud	*1948-1967*	23372	945	24.73	0+1
§ G. D. McKenzie	*1959*-1969	20144	690	29.19	—
A. N. Connolly	*1959*-1969	14304	542	26.39	—

§ W. W. Armstrong's average should read 19.76

§ J. M. Gregory's name has been misprinted.

SOUTH AFRICA

	Career	Runs	Wkts.	Avge.	100s
§ T. L. Goddard	*1952-1968*	10946	503	21.76	—
§ A. H. McKinnon	*1952-1968*	9842	467	21.07	—
§ P. M. Pollock	*1958-1968*	8480	401	21.14	—
§ J. T. Botten	*1957-1968*	7066	361	19.57	—
M. J. Procter	1965-1969	5371	304	17.66	1

Career Records for Overseas Players—*Cont.*

WEST INDIES

	Career	Runs	Wkts.	Avge.	100s
§ G. St. A. Sobers	*1952*-1969	21372	780	27.40	—
§ L. R. Gibbs	*1953*-1969	15482	587	26.37	—
§ W. W. Hall	*1955*-1969	13874	529	26.22	—
§ C. C. Griffith	*1959-1968*	7172	332	21.60	1
G. E. Gomez	*1937-1957*	5052	200	25.26	—

NEW ZEALAND

	Career	Runs	Wkts.	Avge.	100s
§ R. C. Motz	*1957*-1969	11769	518	22.72	—
§ J. C. Alabaster	*1955-1967*	11323	443	25.55	—
B. W. Yuile	*1959*-1969	6794	314	21.63	—

INDIA

	Career	Runs	Wkts.	Avge.	100s
§ R. G. Nadkarni	*1951-1968*	10624	496	21.41	—
§ R. B. Desai	*1958-1968*	11236	470	23.90	—
E. A. S. Prasanna	*1961-1968*	8697	403	21.58	—

PAKISTAN

	Career	Runs	Wkts.	Avge.	100s
§ Intikhab Alam	*1957*-1969	12818	470	27.27	—
Mushtaq Mohammad	*1956*-1969	8375	382	21.92	—
A. H. Kardar	*1943-1965*	8448	344	24.55	—
Pervez Sajjad	*1961*-1969	5547	267	20.77	—

THE COUNTY CHAMPIONSHIP

Page 468 *CHAMPION COUNTIES*

1968 Yorkshire 1969 Glamorgan

Page 469 § *MOST OUTRIGHT CHAMPIONSHIP WINS:* 31 by Yorkshire.

FINAL POSITIONS 1968 and 1969

	D	E	Gm	Gs	H	K	La	Le	M	Nr	Nt	So	Sy	Sx	Wa	Wo	Y
1968	8	14	3	16	5	2	6	9	10	13	4	12	15	17	11	7	1
1969	16	6	1	2	5	10	15	14	11	9	8	17	3	7	4	12	13

Page 471 *HIGHEST AGGREGATE OF WICKETS IN A CAREER*

	Career	Wkts.	Avge.
§ Glamorgan—D. J. Shepherd	1950-1969	1971	20.77
§ Hampshire—D. Shackleton	1948-1969	2669	18.21
§ Lancashire—J. B. Statham	1950-1968	1816	15.12

Pages 472 and 473 *FIRST-CLASS COUNTY CRICKET CLUBS*

§ Glamorgan: Champions (2) 1969 § Yorkshire: Champions (31) 1968

Pages 473 to 476 *COUNTY CAPTAINS*

DERBYSHIRE

§ 1908 A. E. Lawton and R. B. Rickman
§ 1913-1919 R. R. C. Baggallay
§ 1920 J. Chapman
§ 1965-1969 D. C. Morgan

ESSEX

§ 1967-1969 B. Taylor

GLAMORGAN

§ 1967-1969 A. R. Lewis

GLOUCESTERSHIRE

1968 C. A. Milton
1969 A. S. Brown

HAMPSHIRE

§ 1966-1969 R. E. Marshall

KENT

§ 1957-1969 M. C. Cowdrey

LANCASHIRE

1968-1969 J. D. Bond

LEICESTERSHIRE

1968 M. R. Hallam
1969 R. Illingworth

MIDDLESEX

1968 F. J. Titmus and P. H. Parfitt
1969 P. H. Parfitt

NORTHAMPTONSHIRE

§ 1967-1969 R. M. Prideaux

The County Championship—County Captains—*Cont.*

NOTTINGHAMSHIRE
1968-1969 G. St. A. Sobers

SOMERSET
1968 R. C. Kerslake
1969 B. A. Langford

SURREY
§ 1963-1969 M. J. Stewart

SUSSEX
1968 J. M. Parks and M. G. Griffith

SUSSEX—cont.
1969 M. G. Griffith

WARWICKSHIRE
1968-1969 A. C. Smith

WORCESTERSHIRE
1968-1969 T. W. Graveney

YORKSHIRE
§ 1963-1969 D. B. Close

Pages 476 to 479 *COUNTY CAPS AWARDED 1968 and 1969*

DERBYSHIRE
1968 P. J. K. Gibbs, J. F. Harvey, D. H. K. Smith
1969 A. Ward

ESSEX
1968 B. L. Irvine

GLAMORGAN
1968 Majid Jahangir
1969 B. A. Davis, R. C. Davis, M. A. Nash

GLOUCESTERSHIRE
1968 D. M. Green, M. J. Procter
1969 D. R. Shepherd

HAMPSHIRE
1968 B. A. Richards
1969 R. M. C. Gilliat, G. R. Stephenson

KENT
1968 Asif Iqbal
1969 D. Nicholls

LANCASHIRE
1968 F. M. Engineer, D. Lloyd, K. Shuttleworth, B. Wood
1969 C. H. Lloyd, J. Sullivan

LEICESTERSHIRE
1968 B. R. Knight
1969 B. Dudleston, R. Illingworth, G. D. McKenzie

MIDDLESEX
1968 H. C. Latchman
1969 A. N. Connolly, R. S. Herman

NORTHAMPTONSHIRE
1969 H. M. Ackerman

NOTTINGHAMSHIRE
1968 D. J. Halfyard, G. St. A. Sobers
1969 B. Stead

SOMERSET
1968 T. I. Barwell, R. A. Brooks, G. I. Burgess, G. S. Chappell, A. Clarkson, R. C. Kerslake

(*Post-war record—six players in one season*)

1969 R. Palmer

SURREY
1968 W. A. Smith
1969 Intikhab Alam, G. R. J. Roope, D. J. S. Taylor, Younis Ahmed

SUSSEX
1969 P. J. Graves

WARWICKSHIRE
1968 L. R. Gibbs, R. B. Kanhai
1969 W. Blenkiron

WORCESTERSHIRE
1968 G. M. Turner
1969 E. J. O. Hemsley

YORKSHIRE
1969 B. Leadbeater, C. M. Old

MOST CONSECUTIVE CHAMPIONSHIP APPEARANCES

423 K. G. Suttle (Sussex)
412 J. G. Binks (Yorkshire)
399 J. Vine (Sussex)

Page 480 **The SHEFFIELD SHIELD**

Holders ... 1967-68 Western Australia
1968-69 South Australia

§ *RESULTS SUMMARY* (*1892-1969*)

	Début Season	*Played*	*Won*	*Drawn*	*Lost*	*Tied*	*Aban'd*
New South Wales	1892-93	372	194	89	88	1	—
Victoria	1892-93	370	164	97	108	1	1
South Australia	1892-93	368	110	76	182	—	—
Queensland	1926-27	252	48	91	113	—	1
Western Australia	1947-48	138	33	47	58	—	—
		1500	549	400	549	2	2

Page 481 **The CURRIE CUP**

Season	*Winner of Currie Cup*	*Relegated to B*	*Leader of B Section*
1967-68	Natal	N-E. Transvaal	Rhodesia
1968-69	Transvaal	Rhodesia	Western Province

§ *RESULTS SUMMARY* (*1898-1969*)

	Début Season	*Played*	*Won*	*Drawn*	*Lost*	*Tied*
Transvaal	1889-90	197	118	44	35	—
Griqualand West	1889-90	176	33	38	105	—
Western Province	1892-93	187	87	44	56	—
Natal	1893-94	183	110	46	27	—
Eastern Province	1893-94	167	45	37	84	1
Border	1897-98	160	50	28	82	—
Orange Free State	1903-04	168	37	33	97	1
Rhodesia	1904-05	101	40	26	35	—
South-West Districts...	1904-05	1	—	—	1	—
North-Eastern Transvaal	1937-38	95	31	23	41	—
Transvaal B	1959-60	44	22	9	13	—
Natal B	1965-66	21	7	10	4	—
		1500	580	338	580	2

Page 482 **The SHELL SHIELD**

§ Delete second sentence of introduction and amend "five" to read "four" in the first sentence.

Holders 1967-68 No Tournament—M.C.C. Tour
1968-69 Jamaica

Page 483 **The PLUNKET SHIELD**

Holders 1967-68 Central Districts
1968-69 Auckland

§ *RESULTS SUMMARY* (*1907-69*)

	Début Season	*Played*	*Won*	*Drawn*	*Lost*
Auckland	1907-08	181	85	52	44
Canterbury	1907-08	184	77	49	58
Wellington	1907-08	172	72	36	64
Otago	1907-08	169	42	40	87
Hawke's Bay	1914-15	2	—	—	2
Central Districts	1950-51	89	29	35	25
Northern Districts	1956-57	65	9	22	34
		862	314	234	314

BOMBAY PENTANGULAR TOURNAMENT

§ Insert "in a communal form" after "abandoned" (last line of p. 483).

Page 485 **The 'RANJI' TROPHY**
Finalists
1967-68 Bombay beat Madras at Bombay on first innings (match drawn).
1968-69 Bombay beat Bengal at Bombay on first innings (match drawn).

The 'DULEEP' TROPHY
Finalists
1967-68 South Zone beat West Zone at Bombay on first innings (match drawn).
1968-69 West Zone beat South Zone at Hyderabad on first innings (match drawn).

The QUAID-I-AZAM TROPHY
§ Amend spelling of 'Qaid-i-Azam' throughout.

§ Page 486: delete sentence starting "The final . . ." and insert new paragraph:
The 1964-65 and 1966-67 championships were each spread over two seasons.
Finalists
1966-68 Karachi beat Railways at Karachi by 10 wickets.
1968-69 Lahore beat Karachi at Lahore on first innings (match drawn).

Page 486 **The 'AYUB' TROPHY**
Add to introduction: "The fifth competition for this Trophy was spread over three seasons."
Finalists
§ delete in toto entry for 1965-66.
1965-67 Karachi Blues beat Lahore Greens at Lahore by 10 wickets.
1967-68 Karachi Blues beat Rawalpindi at Rawalpindi by 10 wickets.

Pages 486 to 503 **UNIVERSITY CRICKET**

OXFORD UNIVERSITY BLUES
Allerton, J. W. O. (Stowe)—1969
Burton, M. St. J. W. (Umtali H.S., Rhodesia, and Rhodes U.)—1969
§ Easter, J. N. C.—1968 (Amend initials)
§ Gamble, N. W. was educated at Stockport G.S.
§ Garofall, A. R.—1968
§ Goldstein, F. S.—1968-69 (Captain 1968-69)
Heard, H. (Queen Elizabeth's Hospital, Bristol)—1969
Khan, A. J. (Punjab U.)—1968-69
Millener, D. J. (Auckland U.)—1969
Morgan, A. H. (Hastings G.S.)—1969
Niven, R. A. (Berkhamsted)—1968-69
§ Ridley, G. N. S.—1968
Ridley, R. M. (Clifton)—1968-69
§ Walsh, D. R.—1968-69
§ Watson, A. G. M.—1968
Westley, S. A. (Lancaster R.G.S.)—1968-69
Wilson, P. R. B. (Milton, Rhodesia)—1968

CAMBRIDGE UNIVERSITY BLUES
§ Acfield, D. L.—1968
Bhatia, A. N. (Doon, India)—1969
Carling, P. G. (Kingston G.S.)—1968
§ Cosh, N. J.—1968
§ Cottrell, G. A.—1968 (Captain 1968)
Fitzgerald, J. F. (St. Brendan's, Bristol)—1968
Hall, J. E. (Ardingly)—1969
§ Hays, D. L.—1968
Haywood, D. C. (Nottingham H.S.)—1968
Jorden, A. M. (Monmouth)—1968-69 (Captain 1969)
§ Knight, R. D. V.—1968-69
McDowall, J. I. (Rugby)—1969
§ Marlar's name has been misspelt
§ Marshall, J. H. and Marshall, J. W.: amend schools to read King Edward's, Birmingham
Nevin, M. R. S. (Winchester)—1969
§ Norris, D. W. W.—1968
Owen-Thomas, D. R. (K.C.S., Wimbledon)—1969
Pearman, H. (King Alfred's and Aberdeen U.)—1969
§ Ponniah, C. E. M.—1968-69
Ross, N. P. G. (Marlborough)—1969
Short, R. L. (Denstone)—1969

UNIVERSITY MATCH RESULTS
§ First sentence of introduction, p. 500: Cambridge has won 50 and Oxford 44 of the 125 official matches played, the remaining 31 being drawn.
1968 Drawn 1969 Drawn

UNIVERSITY MATCH CENTURIES
§ Oxford (36) 155 F. S. Goldstein (1968)

University Cricket—*Cont.*

HIGHEST RUN AGGREGATES IN A UNIVERSITY CAREER

		Seasons	Inns.	N.O.	Runs	H.S.	Avge.	100s
§ †J. M. Brearley	... Cambridge	1961-1968	127	13	4348	169	38.14	10
† F. S. Goldstein	... Oxford ...	1966-1969	92	1	3082	155	33.86	1

† *Record includes scores for Combined Oxford & Cambridge U. teams against overseas touring teams.*

MATCH RECORDS OF TOURING TEAMS

Pages 510 to 520 Records complete to 30th September, 1969.

[*Key: * Official M.C.C. Touring Team.* P *Played in Pakistan only.* † *Played in Australia and New Zealand*].

ENGLISH TEAMS IN THE WEST INDIES

		First-class matches						All Matches				
Season	*Captain*	*P.*	*W.*	*D.*	*L.*	*T.*		*P.*	*W.*	*D.*	*L.*	*T.*
1967-68	M. C. Cowdrey* ...	12	3	9	0	–	...	16	4	12	0	–
	§ Totals	183	60	76	46	1	...	283	108	126	48	1

ENGLISH TEAMS IN INDIA, CEYLON AND PAKISTAN

		First-class matches						All matches				
Season	*Captain*	*P.*	*W.*	*D.*	*L.*	*T.*		*P.*	*W.*	*D.*	*L.*	*T.*
1967-68	M. J. Stewart (International XI) ...	4	4	0	0	–	...	5	4	1	0	–
1967-68P	R. Benaud (Commonwealth)	8	3	3	2	–	...	8	3	3	2	–
1968-69	M. C. Cowdrey* ...	7	0	7	0	–	...	10	2	7	1	–
	§ Totals	242	90	129	23	–	...	302	113	165	24	–

AUSTRALIAN TEAMS IN BRITAIN

		First-class matches						All matches				
Season	*Captain*	*P.*	*W.*	*D.*	*L.*	*T.*		*P.*	*W.*	*D.*	*L.*	*T.*
1968	W. M. Lawry	25	8	14	3	–	...	29	10	16	3	–
	§ Totals	809	349	348	111	1	...	936	420	396	119	1

WEST INDIAN TEAMS IN BRITAIN

§ 1928 All Matches: P. 38, W 8.
§ 1939 All Matches: P 33, D 17.

		First-class matches						All matches				
Season	*Captain*	*P.*	*W.*	*D.*	*L.*	*T.*		*P.*	*W.*	*D.*	*L.*	*T.*
1969	G. St. A. Sobers ...	19	2	14	3	–	...	23	3	16	4	–
1969	S. M. Nurse (Barbados)...	2	0	1	1	–	...	7	3	1	3	–
	§ Totals	260	84	118	58	–	...	353	125	155	73	–

WEST INDIAN TEAMS IN AUSTRALIA

		First-class matches						All matches				
Season	*Captain*	*P.*	*W.*	*D.*	*L.*	*T.*		*P.*	*W.*	*D.*	*L.*	*T.*
1968-69†	G. St. A. Sobers	15	4	6	5	–	...	23	9	9	5	–
	§ Totals	56	16	13	26	1	...	76	29	19	26	2

WEST INDIAN TEAMS IN NEW ZEALAND

		First-class matches					....	All matches				
Season	*Captain*	*P.*	*W.*	*D.*	*L.*	*T.*		*P.*	*W.*	*D.*	*L.*	*T.*
1968-69†	G. St. A. Sobers ...	6	1	3	2	–	...	7	1	4	2	–
	§ Totals	18	9	6	3	–	...	27	15	9	3	–

NEW ZEALAND TEAMS IN BRITAIN

Season	Captain	First-class matches P.	W.	D.	L.	T.		All matches P.	W.	D.	L.	T.
1969	G. T. Dowling	18	4	11	3	–	...	22	5	13	4	–
	§ Totals	190	49	107	33	1	...	224	63	126	34	1

NEW ZEALAND TEAMS IN AUSTRALIA

Season	Captain	First-class matches P.	W.	D.	L.	T.		All matches P.	W.	D.	L.	T.
1967-68	B. W. Sinclair	4	0	2	2	–	...	7	2	3	2	–
	§ Totals	24	3	8	13	–	...	39	13	13	13	–

INDIAN TEAMS IN AUSTRALIA

§ 1947-48 All matches: W 5.

Season	Captain	First-class matches P.	W.	D.	L.	T.		All matches P.	W.	D.	L.	T.
1967-68†	Nawab of Pataudi, Jnr. ...	9	0	3	6	–	...	15	4	5	6	–
	Totals	23	2	8	13	–	...	35	9	13	13	–

INDIAN TEAM IN NEW ZEALAND

Season	Captain	First-class matches P.	W.	D.	L.	T.		All matches P.	W.	D.	L.	T.
1967-68†	Nawab of Pataudi, Jnr. ...	6	4	1	1	–	...	6	4	1	1	–

REST OF THE WORLD TEAMS IN BRITAIN

Season	Captain	First-class matches P.	W.	D.	L.	T.		All matches P.	W.	D.	L.	T.
1968	Nawab of Pataudi, Jnr. ...	4	1	0	3	–	...	5	2	0	3	–
	§ Totals	8	1	3	4	–	...	14	5	3	6	–

Page 521 to 527 **OFFICES, HONOURS AND AWARDS**

M.C.C. PRESIDENTS

1968 R. Aird

1969 M. J. C. Allom

M.C.C. HONORARY LIFE MEMBERS

ENGLAND PLAYERS

1969 T. E. Bailey (Essex), M. J. K. Smith (Warwicks.)

OVERSEAS PLAYERS AND ADMINISTRATORS

Australia

1969 A. R. Barnes, B. C. Booth, R. N. Harvey, N. C. O'Neill, R. J. Parish, R. B. Simpson, R. Steele, S. Webb

South Africa

1969 D. J. McGlew, R. A. MacLean, H. J. Tayfield.

New Zealand

1969 J. R. Reid, B. Sutcliffe.

West Indies

1969 C. C. Hunte, T. T. Pierce, S. Ramadhin, A. L. Valentine, K. L. Wishart.

India

1969 M. Chinnaswamy, N. J. Contractor, S. P. Gupte, V. L. Manjrekar, D. G. Phadkar, G. S. Ramchand.

Pakistan

1969 Alim-ud-Din, Mahmood Hussain.

BEST BENEFITS

§ J. C. Laker: £11,086

£11,000	A. L. Dixon: Kent v. Gloucestershire	1969

§ K. F. Barrington: £10,711

£10,551	J. H. Edrich: Surrey v. International Cavaliers	1968
£9,592	T. W. Cartwright: Warwickshire v. Worcestershire	1968
£8,390	K. Higgs: Lancashire v. Yorkshire	1968
£8,045	G. A. R. Lock: Surrey v. Yorkshire	1960
£8,005	W. E. Russell: Middlesex v. Sussex	1969

CRICKET WRITERS' CLUB

'YOUNG CRICKETER OF THE YEAR' AWARD

1968 R. M. H. Cottam (Hampshire) 1969 A. Ward (Derbyshire)

SPONSORED AWARDS

THE LAWRENCE TROPHY

		Score		
1968	T. W. Graveney	118	v. West Indies (Port of Spain)	off 174 balls
1969	C. Milburn ...	139	v. Pakistan (Karachi)	off 163 balls

THE HORLICKS AWARDS

1968 England v. Australia: Horlicks Limited awarded £400 per Test, sharing the prize money equally in four separate awards for the best batting and best bowling performances by each team. Series award: £250 "Man of the Series" Award: J. H. Edrich (Surrey and England).

1969 England v. West Indies: Awards totalling £300 per Test (£100 for the best batting performance, £50 for the runner-up, with similar awards for bowling). Series awards:

£200 "Man of the Series" Award: A. P. E. Knott (Kent & England).

£100 award for an outstanding individual performance in the Series: C. H. Lloyd (Guyana & West Indies).

1969 England v. New Zealand: Match awards as for the West Indies Series. Series awards:

£200 "Man of the Series" Award and £100 award for an outstanding individual performance in the series: D. L. Underwood (Kent & England).

NCR 'CENTURY' CRICKET AWARDS—ENGLAND v. AUSTRALIA 1968

The National Cash Register Company offered two awards in 1968 to further the cause of 'brighter cricket':

£250 Fastest Hundred of the Series: B. L. D'Oliveira off 218 balls (Oval).

£250 Highest Over-Rate of the Series: Australia, who averaged 18.68 overs/hour compared with England's 17.69.

MISCELLANEOUS RECORDS

Page 528 **FATHER AND SON IN THE SAME MATCH—PLAYERS**

1853 Wm. Lillywhite and his sons, John and James, played for Sussex v. England at Lord's.

1921 Derbyshire v. Warwickshire (Derby): W. Bestwick and his son, R. Bestwick, bowled together for Derbyshire while W. G. Quaife and his son, B. W. Quaife batted in partnership for Warwickshire.

1922-23 L. S. Constantine and his son, L. N. (later Sir Learie and Baron Constantine), appeared together for Trinidad against Barbados at Georgetown.

1931 Warwickshire v. Nottinghamshire (Birmingham): George Gunn (aged 52) scored 183 and his son, G. V. Gunn, made his maiden hundred (100*).

NON-FIRST-CLASS COMPETITION RECORDS

GILLETE CUP COMPETITION

CUP HOLDERS		*Captain*
1968	WARWICKSHIRE (215-6) beat Sussex (214-7) by 4 wickets ...	A. C. Smith
1969	YORKSHIRE (219-8) beat Derbyshire (150) by 69 runs ...	D. B. Close

Gillette Cup—*Cont.*

GOLD MEDALLISTS

A full list will be given in the next edition of THE KAYE BOOK OF CRICKET RECORDS. The following players have won the Gillete "Man of the Match" Award (a gold medal, a tie and £50) on four occasions:

R. W. Barber (Warwickshire)
D. M. Green (Lancashire and Gloucestershire)
C. Milburn (Northamptonshire)

§ *PLAYING RECORD OF THE COUNTIES*

	Played	*Won*	*Highest Total*	*100s*	*Awards*	*Finals*
Derbyshire	13	6	250-9	—	7	1
Essex	11	4	272-6	—	5	—
Glamorgan	13	6	244-6	1	6	—
Gloucestershire	10	3	327-7	1	4	—
Hampshire	16	9	321-4	3	10	—
Kent	11	5	293-5	2	6	1
Lancashire	16	9	304-9	1	9	—
Leicestershire	9	2	213	1	4	—
Middlesex	16	9	280-8	2	9	—
Northamptonshire	16	9	248	—	7	—
Nottinghamshire	13	6	235-3	2	5	—
Somerset	17	10	251-9	—	9	1
Surrey	16	9	268-6	—	8	1
Sussex	22	17	314-7	4	13	3
Warwickshire	19	14	307-8	4	13	3
Worcestershire	14	7	253-4	1	8	2
Yorkshire	16	11	317-4	1	8	2
Minor Counties	36	6	212-9	1	11	—
	284	142	327-7	24	142	14

§ *LOWEST COMPLETED INNINGS TOTAL*

49 off 35.2 overs: Sussex v. Derby (Chesterfield) 1969

§ *HIGHEST TOTAL BY SIDE BATTING SECOND*

271 off 57.4 overs: Notts. v. Glos. (Nottingham) 1968 (Set 297)

§ *LOWEST TOTAL BY SIDE BATTING FIRST AND WINNING*

98 off 56.2 overs: Worcs. v. Durham (Chester-le-Street) 1968

§ *CENTURIES* (24)

§ R. E. Marshall (Hants)	(2)	140	v. Bedfordshire (Goldington) ...	1968
P. H. Parfitt (Middx.)	... ...	119	v. Nottinghamshire (Nottingham) ...	1969
B. L. Reed (Hants.)	... ...	112	v. Bedfordshire (Goldington) ...	1968
W. E. Russell (Middx.)	... ...	123	v. Surrey (Lord's)	1968
§ K. G. Suttle (Sussex)	(2)	100	v. Northamptonshire (Hove) ...	1968

CENTURY BEFORE LUNCH

R. E. Marshall	107*	(140)	Hampshire v. Bedfordshire (Goldington) ...	1968

FIVE WICKETS IN AN INNINGS

D. L. Bates	(1)	6-30	Sussex v. Glos. (Hove)	1968
T. J. P. Eyre	(1)	6-18	Derby. v. Sussex (Chesterfield)	1969
R. D. Healey	(1)	6-14	Devon v. Herts. (Stevenage)	1969
R. S. Herman	(1)	6-42	Middx. v. Surrey (Lord's)	1968
Majid Jahangir	(1)	5-24	Glamorgan v. Northants. (Northampton) ...	1969
Moore, T. I.	(1)	6-48	Norfolk v. Yorks. (Lakenham)	1969

Gillette Cup—*Cont.*

HAT-TRICKS

R. N. S. Hobbs ... Essex v. Middlesex (Lord's) 1968

FEWEST RUNS CONCEDED BY A BOWLER IN 12 OVERS

4 D. Wilson (12-9-4-1) Yorkshire v. Norfolk (Lakenham) 1969

§ *RECORD WICKET PARTNERSHIPS*

Wkt.	*Runs*		
§ 1st	227	R. E. Marshall & B. L. Reed: Hants. v. Beds. (Goldington) ...	1968
§ 6th	91	P. D. Briggs & G. Hardstaff: Cheshire v. Norfolk (Macclesfield)	1968
§ 7th	86*	T. W. Graveney & G. R. Cass: Worcs. v. Derby. (Derby) ...	1969

THE JOHN PLAYER LEAGUE

Sponsored by John Player and Sons this County League was first played in 1969. In addition to a sponsorship fee divided equally among the first-class counties, the sponsors awarded prize money totalling £10,550. Playing on Sundays and watched by large crowds each first-class county met the other 16 sides once in matches limited to 40 overs per innings. Bowlers were limited to 8 overs each and to run-ups of 15 yards. All records refer to the 1969 season.

CHAMPIONS: 1969 Lancashire
Highest Total: 288-6 Sussex v. Middx. (Hove).
Highest Total by Side Batting Second: 254-7 Leics. v. Sussex (Leicester).
Lowest Total: 56 Middx. v. Worcs. (Kidderminster).
Side Dismissed in Fewest Overs: 16.3 Derby (97) v. Notts. (Chesterfield).
Highest Individual Score: 133* C. T. Radley—Middx. v. Glamorgan (Lord's)
Fastest Fifty: 23 min. K. D. Boyce (50)—Essex v. Lancs. (Chelmsford).
Most Sixes in an Innings: 8 P. T. Marner—Leics. v. Sussex (Leicester).
Most Sixes in a Season: 16 K. D. Boyce (Essex).
Highest Partnership: 170* (2nd) R. T. Virgin (42*) & G. S. Chappell (128*)—Somerset v. Surrey (Brislington)
Most Runs in a Season: 517 (av. 36.92) M. J. Smith (Middx.).
Best Bowling Analysis: 7-15 R. A. Hutton—Yorks. v. Worcs. (Leeds).
Most Economical Analysis: 8—8—0—0—B. A. Langford—Somerset v. Essex (Yeovil).
Most Expensive Analysis: 8—0—73—1—J. Sullivan—Lancs. v. Essex (Chelmsford).
Most Wickets in a Season: 29 R. E. East for Essex.
Most Dismissals in a Season—Wicket-keepers: 21 R. W. Taylor (Derby).
Fielders: 21 R. T. Virgin (Somerset).

Page 534 **SINGLE WICKET TOURNAMENTS**

WINNERS OF THE BASS-CHARRINGTON SINGLE-WICKET TOURNAMENT

1967	Oval	Final rounds abandoned because of rain.
1968	Lord's	K. D. Boyce (Essex) beat J. B. Bolus in the final.